Estate Planning and Taxation

2000 ANNUAL EDITION

Estate Planning and Taxation

2000 ANNUAL EDITION

by **JOHN C. BOST,** J.D., M.S.(Tax)

Professor of Finance
San Diego State University

KENDALL/HUNT PUBLISHING COMPANY
4050 Westmark Drive   Dubuque, Iowa 52002

Formerly entitled *Introduction to Estate Planning*.

DEDICATION

To students of estate planning, past, present and future, for whom this text was created and for whom it continues; to the late Professor Chris J. Prestopino (1943 - 1994) who initiated this textbook; and to my wife, Jennifer, and our two daughters, Heather and Laura, my personal reason for learning about estate planning. John C. Bost

CONTENTS

Income Interests. Overview of Goals of Estate Planning. Important Concepts and Terms Covered in This Chapter.

Retained Life Estate: §2036. Transfers Taking Effect at Death: §2037. Revocable Transfers: §2038. Gift Taxes on Any Transfer within Three Years of Death: §2035(b). Certain Transfers within Three Years of Death: §2035(a). Part-Sale, Part-Gift Transfers: §2043. Two: Estate Tax Deductions. *Marital Deduction: §2056. Charitable Deduction: §2055.* Three: Estate Tax Credits. *Credit/Offset for Gift Taxes Paid or Payable.* The Prior Transfer Credit. *An Extended PTC Example. Credit for Foreign Death Taxes.*

ILLUSTRATIONS

PREFACE

Estate Planning and Taxation is a textbook designed to be used in an academic program. Its concepts are introduced logically rather than encyclopedically; and as the reader's knowledge grows, more advanced principles are covered.

Estate Planning and Taxation is for the professional or student pursuing a career in financial services, taxation, or law in which estate planning and estate and gift taxation is but one of several principal areas of practice. Applicable careers include law, tax accounting, financial planning, insurance sales, paralegal work, banking, trust management, investment brokerage and management, and real estate. Since much of the subject matter is Internal Revenue Code driven, the textbook draws heavily on primary sources of the law, both Code and cases. The textbook is adaptable to law school courses in estate planning and taxation, giving the law student a strongly quantitative slant that is sometimes overlooked in traditional law books, even those dealing with taxes.

The book is divided into three parts. The first two present the basic language and constraints found in estate planning, including the underlying tax and nontax laws that serve as the basis for planning. The third, and largest, part surveys the major estate planning strategies used currently by practitioners. Tax analysis is emphasized. This sequential approach aids learning because estate planning techniques presuppose a familiarity with many fundamental legal concepts, including tax principles.

The organization of *Estate Planning and Taxation* seeks to present a concise, integrated overview, highlighting the essence of concepts without confusing the reader with every technical qualification and reference, a problem which has impaired the readability of many books in the field. For example, the text expects the student to learn only those case names and Code section numbers that have attained the status of common industry jargon (chapter endnotes cite many others). Nonetheless, the book's content is comprehensive. For example, with its quantitative orientation, it demonstrates numerically, wherever possible, the consequences of planning, and of the failure to plan, on family wealth.

Many pedagogical devices are used to aid comprehension. Numerous examples are included in each chapter to clarify concepts. Each chapter contains end-of-chapter questions and problems, many with solutions. Appendixes include a glossary, sample tax returns, tax and valuation tables, as well as those sections of the Internal Revenue Code most relevant to estate planning. A manual containing a test bank is available to instructors who adopt the book.

Estate Planning and Taxation can be used in a two-hour or three-hour quarter or semester introductory college undergraduate course, graduate, or law school course. It can be read in conjunction with a correspondence, certificate-type course offered to the financial services industry; and it can be read independently by anyone seeking a moderately technical overview, including the practitioner in accounting or financial services, the law student, the attorney in general practice, and the very determined lay reader.

ACKNOWLEDGMENTS

For their suggestions and help with the present edition, I wish to thank the following people: Texas Tech University adjunct faculty and attorney Robert E. Barnhill for keeping Chapter 8 up to date; Randy Gardner, CPA, in Lawrence, Kansas for his thoughtful suggests for Chapters 13-18; and San Diego State University graduate students Patricia Schultz and Michael Lengyel for their review of Chapters 1-10. Of course, I take full responsibility for any errors or omissions.

My thanks to the many individuals whose previous contributions continue to be reflected in this textbook: Michael Ahearn, Martin Anderson, Robert Barnhill, Karen Booth, J. Buckhold, Daniel J. Burnside, Paul M. Cheverton, Neil Cohen, Larry Cox, Jeffrey Dennis-Strathmeyer, D. J. Devin, Mark Dorfman, W. W. Dotterweich, Jon Gallo, Keith Fevurly, Mark Greene, Benjamin Henszey, Carole Hill, Joseph W. Janick, Jerry Kasner, Fred Keydel, James K. Leese, H. Russell May, Shekhar Misra, Karen Molloy, Burton Nissing, Gregg Parish, Mary Reese, Phelder St. Germain, Janice Samuells, John Schooling, Jack Stephens, and Richard Wellman.

Of course, special recognition must be given to the founder of this textbook, the late Chris J. Prestopino who died in 1994. He established the model of a textbook rich in examples. It is a tradition that has been carried into each new edition.

Thank you readers of earlier editions for your suggestions. I welcome and encourage comments from students, instructors, and professionals who use this textbook. Through a continuing dialog we can make this book even better in the future.

John C. Bost
email: john.bost@sdsu.edu

ETAX Program Information

On the disk that comes with this textbook you will find ETAX 2000.wb3 for use with QUATTRO PRO (Corel 8) and ETAX 2000.xls for use with EXCEL (Microsoft Excel 97). ETAX 2000 is an estate and gift tax spreadsheet program designed for educational use only. However, it will do all of the basic estate tax, the state death tax credit, and (to a limited degree) the cumulative gift tax calculations. It will not add in the gift taxes paid on gifts made within three years of death, nor will it work with pre-1977 estate or gift tax calculations. Before working with the ETAX program, you should create a backup disk.

Once you bring the file into whichever spreadsheet program (QUATTRO PRO or EXCEL) you use, you will find that you can only input data into certain cells:

- Estates: the **year of death**, the **gross estate**, and **deductions** (you will have to do your own total for marital, charitable, debts and expenses).
- Gifts: the **year of the current gifts**, the **year of prior gifts**, the **current year's gifts** (you must first subtract the annual exclusions) and **prior year's gifts** (the taxable amount, i.e., after subtracting the annual exclusions)
- After entering the data, hit calculate. Your spreadsheet setup should be set for at least five iterations, ten if you want to try to do inter-related calculations such as net gifts. To determine whether you have the iterations set high enough, enter figures high enough to generate a tax at the cells for prior gifts, current gifts, and the gross estate and see whether the resulting tax amounts change after you hit calculate a second time. If they do, notice how many times you must hit calculate before they do not change and set the iterations accordingly.

PART 1

Overview and Conceptual Background

CHAPTER 1

Introduction to Estate Planning

WHAT IS ESTATE PLANNING?

Estate planning is the study of the principles of planning for the use, conservation, and efficient transfer of an individual's wealth. Its concepts are based on the premise that people do not live forever; sooner or later, death will bring about a fundamental shift in the possession and ownership of family wealth. Estate planning seeks to arrange wealth transfers to maximize financial well being both for the client and for the client's survivors. A broader definition of estate planning might include the accumulation of wealth as an estate planning activity. However, this definition broadens the subject's scope by adding investment management— another specialty of considerable scope and one better left for textbooks that focus on investments. Many estate planning practitioners give little or no investment advice. Therefore, the focus of this text is estate planning as *the study of financial planning in anticipation of death,* i.e., the transfer of wealth from one generation to the next.

Planning for future wealth transfers usually requires the preparation of contracts, such as life insurance policies and other documents including wills, trusts, deeds, and powers of attorney. These documents set forth in writing a blueprint for the future management of the individual's financial affairs.

Successful estate planning requires an understanding of many areas of law including the law of property, wills, trusts, future interests, estate administration, intestacy, insurance, income taxation, gift taxation, and estate taxation.

How can knowledge of such an extensive subject benefit you, the reader? As a knowledgeable planner, you can help clients avoid the adverse consequences of inadequate or faulty estate planning. Here are some common situations that arise without proper planning.

EXAMPLE 1 - 1. Joanne died last week, survived by her husband and their two young daughters. Because Joanne did not write a will, the intestate laws of her state require that two-thirds of her $300,000 estate *pass to her daughters*, who will each, upon turning 18, receive the property outright from their guardian-father. The other one-third passes to Joanne's husband. He is shocked that he is not inheriting it all and that as guardian of the daughters' estates he must file annual accountings with the court. In addition to the problem of inefficient distribution, larger estates may owe both state and federal taxes—taxes that could have been minimized by estate planning.

EXAMPLE 1 - 2. Marge and Henry, parents of five-year-old twins, died suddenly without an estate plan. The probate court appointed Marge's sister Julie as *guardian* for the twins. Marge and Henry had been quite critical of how Julie and her husband were raising their own children, but they had not expressed their concerns to anyone else and the court simply followed statutory guidelines in selecting Marge's sister for the job.

EXAMPLE 1 - 3. Maggie was 80 when she died leaving an estate with a net value of $300,000. Six weeks prior to her death, she gave ABC common stock worth $90,000 to her son, Charlie. Maggie's $14,000 basis in the stock became Charlie's basis. Now, if he sells it he will recognize considerable capital gains. Had Maggie kept the stock until her death, giving it to Charlie at that time, he could have sold it at little or no income tax cost, because his basis would have been the stock's value as of her date of death.

EXAMPLE 1 - 4. Shortly before Christine died at the age of 75, her family lawyer drafted a *simple will*, leaving her wealth (estimated to be worth a net value of $1,000,000) to her husband Evan. Since Evan's own estate was worth about the same as Christine's estate, he now realizes that, as owner of all of the family wealth, estate taxes in excess of $500,000 will be due shortly after his death. Most of the tax could have been avoided, if Christine's estate plan had just incorporated the sophisticated estate planning device known as a *bypass trust*.

EXAMPLE 1 - 5. Suppose that, instead of receiving the property by will (as in the preceding example), Evan received it as surviving *joint tenant*. Evan's estate would be faced with the same estate tax problem at his death.

EXAMPLE 1- 6. Leslie is the elderly founder of a highly successful real estate sales company. Unfortunately, she has not done any estate planning and is now very ill. Her children are struggling with several problems, including how to generate sufficient *liquidity* to pay the estate taxes and whether or not to sell the business. Because only a person with a real estate license (which none of the children have) can operate a real estate office, they fear that the business will sell for much less once Leslie dies compared to its value now. Indeed, it could have sold for even more money several years ago when Leslie would have been more active in seeking buyers and working with them on a transition.

EXAMPLE 1 - 7. Elmer, a wealthy man, had a severe stroke three months ago. Unable to communicate, he is hooked up to machines that keep him alive. The doctors say his prognosis is very poor. His family realizes that they should have encouraged Elmer to consult an estate planner years ago while he was still able to express his desires. Documents could have been drafted that would have nominated a person or persons to manage his wealth during his incapacity and would have directed the eventual distribution of his wealth after his death. Other documents would have articulated the appropriate level of medical intervention to apply. Whether the decisions of the doctors and the family concerning his care or the pattern of distribution mandated by the laws of intestate succession really match what he would have wanted will never be known. In addition, if the family cannot reach agreement on medical treatment, a costly court battle could ensue.

EXAMPLE 1 - 8. Several years before he died, at the advice of a friend, Marty executed a revocable living trust leaving all his property to several close friends rather than to the few relatives that had been rather cool to him for years. The trust was completed by filling in the blanks of a form photocopied from the pages of a popular "how to" book. Thinking that the trust took care of his estate, Marty tore up his will (the one that left everything to the same set of friends as specified in the trust). He failed to transfer his assets into the trust and he did not make a new will. A careful reading of the how-to book would have called to his attention the need to fund the trust by transferring assets to the trustee of the trust and the importance of something called a *pour-over will*. Marty did not realize that his self-made estate plan was ineffective in avoiding probate. Worse yet, it did not control who received his estate. Because he did not transfer his property to the trustee of the trust and because he died without a will, Marty's estate will be distributed to his relatives in a manner specified in his state's intestate succession laws.

EXAMPLE 1- 9. At his death, Coldwell owned real estate in six states, including his state of residence. His simple will left his estate to his three children. In addition to the *probate* in his state of domicile, there were five ancillary probates, forcing Coldwell's family to pay court filing fees and hire probate attorneys in all six states. Had Coldwell's estate plan used a *living trust*, these probates (and their associated expenses) would have been avoided.

EXAMPLE 1 - 10. Many years before her death Lola bought Sammy's $30,000 life insurance policy for $5,000. They jointly notified the insurance company to change the beneficiary to Lola and to send all further premium notices to her address, but they did not request a change of ownership. Since Lola had worked in real estate, she insisted that they complete a form called a "Bill of Sale" that she purchased at a stationery store, setting forth the details of the sale, including the identification of policy, and that Sammy sign it before a notary. She recorded this document at the county recorder's office. Eventually Lola had paid sufficient premiums to pay the policy completely. After Lola went into a nursing home, Sammy used a change of beneficiary form supplied by the insurance company to change the beneficiary back to his daughter. After Lola died, her son discovered the Bill of Sale and contacted the insurance company only to learn that Sammy had died two years earlier and they had paid the proceeds to Sammy's daughter. Because the company had never been notified of the change in ownership, they correctly followed Sammy's change of beneficiary designation. His daughter might have been liable but she lived in another state and claimed to have spent almost all of the money. Lola's son concluded that the amount he would have to pay lawyers and the uncertainty of collecting made it unrealistic to pursue his claim. If Lola had just had Sammy sign an irrevocable assignment of the policy to her and sent it to the insurance company, he would have been unable to change the beneficiary designation.

Problems like these occur because people tend to avoid estate planning or attempt "do-it-yourself" solutions that do not work in the manner desired. Lay people have many misconceptions about estate planning because it is a technical subject and the laws vary from state to state. Many people choose to ignore their estate planning needs because estate planning forces them to discuss matters related to their own death. Overcoming inertia often requires the thoughtful, caring encouragement of loved ones and the sensitive approach of the estate planner.

DEVELOPING AN ESTATE PLAN

Developing an estate plan should result in a set of recommendations and related documents that skillfully allow for the best use, conservation, and transfer of the client's wealth. In 1996, the Certified Financial Planner Board of Standards, Inc., (the Board or the CFP Board) identified the following steps in the financial planning process: (1) establishing and defining the client-planner relationship; (2) gathering client data, including goals; (3) analyzing and evaluating the client's financial status (income statement and net-worth balance sheet); (4) developing and presenting financial planning recommendations and/or alternatives; (5) implementing the financial planning recommendations; and (6) monitoring the financial planning recommendations.

Establishing the Client-Planner Relationship

The planner must take the lead in explaining to the client the financial planning process. Some of the issues and concepts will already be familiar to the client, e.g., the purpose of a will, but other matters such as estate taxation or the use of trusts may be quite foreign. The role of the estate planner should be made clear and should be memorialized in an engagement letter that spells out the services to be performed. The cooperation of the client is important to building a successful plan. So the planner must make the client aware of his or her responsibilities, including gathering information, working with the planner to implement the plan, and keeping the planner informed of changes that might require its modification.

Acquiring Client Facts and Goals

To make meaningful recommendations, the planner must acquire sufficient information about the client and the client's family. Essential information must be collected to give the planner a fairly complete picture of the client's family, his or her financial situation, and what the client expects to achieve by implementing an estate plan.

The importance of family. The estate planning opportunities for a wealthy married couple seeking to transfer an estate to the next generation are greater than what is available for a single wealthy parent. Likewise, the estate planning needs of a young couple with minor children will be quite different from a couple whose children are grown. Family members may also be suitable choices for fiduciary positions such as executor, guardian, and trustee. The client needs to make the planner aware of special concerns, e.g., a child with special health needs or a child who is having drug addiction problems. In these situations, special trust planning that provides for long-term asset management may be appropriate .

The client's financial situation and objectives. To understand the client's financial situation, the planner will require several types of statements. First, he or she will need a current *balance sheet*, showing the fair market value of all assets and liabilities. Information on each asset should include the manner in which title is held, date of acquisition, and current adjusted tax basis.

> EXAMPLE 1 - 11. Relying on Marlene's representation that all of her property was in her name alone, an inexperienced planner failed to *examine a copy of the deed*, and prepared a will that left all of her property to her husband. After she died, it was discovered that the most valuable parcel of real estate (acquired by Marlene long before the couple had married) was held in joint tenancy with Marlene's niece. Of course, the niece became the sole owner.

For liabilities, the client should list the lender and the loan terms (maturity, a payment schedule, interest rate, collateral, etc.). In addition to a description of assets and liabilities, the planner will need a *cash flow statement*, describing sources of income and major categories of expenses.

The planner will also need other facts, such as information about the client's expectation of receiving significant gifts or inheritances, and the names of the client's other advisers including accountants, lawyers, investment brokers, life underwriters, real estate agents, physicians, and religious advisors. Further, the planner will need a description of the client's and the spouse's financial objectives, a self-appraisal of their ability to manage their finances, and the location of any estate planning documents, such as wills.

The client's objectives. The planner also needs an understanding of the client's objectives, especially with regard to dispositive preferences (i.e., the plan as to who gets what) for the spouse, the children, and charities; and whether significant transfers are likely to be made during the person's life or whether such are going to take place only at his or her death.

Many planners develop questionnaires and checklists to help them acquire this information as efficiently as possible. A sample questionnaire is included in Appendix 1A at the end of this chapter.

In addition to using the checklist, the planner should routinely examine existing documents, such as the will and evidence of title to property. Too often, checklist information is inaccurate.

Analyzing and Evaluating the Client's Financial Status

After acquiring the necessary facts, the planner will review the facts and prepare a plan incorporating preliminary recommendations and, where appropriate, alternatives. The most common recommendations fall into two areas: financial planning for property transfers and personal planning for the client's incapacity and death.

Developing and Presenting Recommendations and/or Alternatives

Financial planning for property transfers. The major purpose of the plan is to efficiently distribute the client's wealth to the proper persons, in the proper amount, and at the proper time. To do this, the planner must keep in mind the following considerations that relate to more specific estate planning goals:

- deciding whether or not to *avoid probate* as a means of transferring property at the death of the client;
- examining alternatives to reduce and possibly eliminate *transfer taxes* at the death of the client and the client's spouse;
- considering *lifetime transfers*, partly to reduce transfer costs and partly to shift taxable income to a lower tax bracket;
- arranging to provide the needed *liquidity* at the client's disability or death; and
- devising a strategy to unwind the client's *business affairs* in a manner which maintains the greatest income and value for the survivors.

Personal planning for incapacity and death. Personal planning for a client's incapacity tends to focus on arranging for someone to care for the client and the client's property in the event the client becomes incapacitated. It may also include making funeral or cremation arrangements, and assuring that at the time of death, certain religious formalities will be faithfully followed. Personal planning also includes the important task of arranging for someone to care for the client's children if both parents become incapacitated (or die) before the children reach adulthood.

Because this text is primarily devoted to these and other objectives and techniques, further explanation will be provided in subsequent chapters.

Implementing the Plan

After the specifics of a plan are agreed upon, the planner and client should move to implement it. Transfer documents are drafted by an attorney and executed by the client. An insurance agent may be needed to secure the appropriate insurance contracts. If a trust is included in the plan and the client wants a bank trust department named as either initial trustee or as a successor trustee, one of the bank trust officers should be contacted for authorization and advice before the trust document is completed. The trust officer may want the bank's legal department to review the document to make sure that its terms are ones they are willing to carry out. The client should feel comfortable with the bank trust department's personnel, including how they interact with trust beneficiaries and their investment philosophy.

A person "executes" a document by completing it; that is, by taking all of the steps necessary to render it valid. For example, execution of a will normally requires, among other things, that the client sign the will in the presence of witnesses who, by their own signatures, attest to the authenticity of the client's signature.

Monitoring the Financial Planning Recommendations

Depending on the scope of the engagement, part of the estate planning process may include monitoring the estate plan over a long period of time. Because laws change, the client's personal situation and objectives may change. By keeping current, the planner can periodically suggest appropriate revisions to the plan. Events which are likely to require plan revision include marriage, divorce, birth of a child, new legislation, and new court decisions.

For example in 1981, Congress passed the Economic Recovery Tax Act (ERTA) that made many significant changes to the federal transfer taxation laws. One major change involved the taxation of property passing at death to a surviving spouse. Prior to the change, wills and trusts of wealthy individuals were likely to contain a provision that had the effect of passing to the surviving spouse only half of the decedent's estate, because that was the maximum amount that qualified for the marital deduction. However, for transfers that occurred after 1981, the maximum marital deduction increased to cover the person's *entire* estate so long as it was left to the surviving spouse. Concerned that many clients whose estate plans were drafted with the old maximum in mind might not want to leave their entire estate to their spouses, Congress included a transition rule that had the effect of limiting, for most estates, the transfer to the surviving spouse of half of the decedent's estate if the plan used words like, "I leave to my spouse the maximum amount that qualifies for the marital deduction." The transition rule required the phrase be interpreted as though it said, "I leave to my spouse the maximum amount that qualifies for the marital deduction *based upon the law in effect at the time this document was executed*."

The 100% marital deduction became available to those who revised their plans after the law changed, and the estate plans for those people living (dying) in states that passed legislation that said "maximum marital deduction" are to be interpreted to mean the maximum under the new federal law. Thus, most transfer documents had to be revised to take advantage of the more beneficial tax provisions. Many planners contacted their clients to encourage them to update their plans in light of the new law. Chapter 18 has a discussion of the use of disclaimers and other postmortem tax planning techniques to remedy some of the problems that may occur for wealthy clients who die without revising their pre-ERTA estate plans.

THE ESTATE PLANNING TEAM

Generally, estate planning is not conducted by just one professional. The job requires the diverse knowledge and skills of a number of practitioners, including attorneys, accountants, life underwriters, trust officers, and financial planners. These professionals are referred to as the *estate planning team*. Next, we describe the unique contribution each team member makes to the overall planning process.

Attorney

In most states, the only professional who may legally accept payment for rendering legal advice and drafting estate planning documents is an attorney. This makes the attorney an indispensable team member in the estate planning process. If the documents are to correctly express the client's estate plan, their preparation requires an attorney with the ability to make precise legal distinctions. The working years for these documents may be measured in decades, operating long after the client is deceased, and they are likely to be viewed as the final authority concerning the client's estate planning objectives. Thus by putting an estate plan in print, the attorney places his or her professional skill to the test. Eventually, the results (good or bad) will be there for all to see.

Most attorneys accept the responsibility of coordinating the actions of the other members of the estate planning team. This is especially true if the attorney specializes in estate planning and taxation.

The attorney's role might not end at the client's death. He or she may be hired to advise the personal representative of the deceased client's estate. The attorney is likely to aid in the transfer of the client's assets to surviving beneficiaries or in the allocation of assets to various trusts. In addition, the attorney may engage in postmortem tax planning, a job which, as we will see in Chapter 18, entails choosing certain tax options available after the client's death and the preparation of various estate tax returns.

Accountant

By preparing the client's financial statements and yearly tax returns, the accountant is likely to be the professional having the earliest and most frequent contact with the client. Typically, these forms are so financially revealing to accountants that financial planners have described them as the client's "annual financial report."

The accountant is often able to spot specific financial problems requiring attention, especially with regard to the client's business interests. Perhaps the accountant's most important service to the client, insofar as estate planning is concerned, is in encouraging the client to begin the estate planning process. Once the process begins, the accountant may be hired to prepare the client's financial balance sheet, income statement, and cash flow statements. After the client's death, the accountant will probably be called upon to complete the required income tax returns and, if necessary, the estate tax returns.

Life Underwriter

The life underwriter's crucial role is to help the client select appropriate insurance such that it meets the liquidity needs that are bound to arise in the event of the client's disability or death. The efficient use of life insurance requires an understanding of estate planning because proper planning should minimize the transfer costs and assure an adequate level of financial support for the client's surviving beneficiaries.

Given life insurance's natural connection to wealth transfer planning, the life underwriter may be the first professional to recommend estate planning to the client. He or she may therefore be in a position to select the other members of the client's estate planning team.

Trust Officer

A skilled professional executor and trustee, the trust officer performs fiduciary services for clients and estates. A *fiduciary* is a person having a legal duty to act for the benefit of another. The word fiduciary is derived from the Latin word for "trust." A *fiduciary* is any person in a position of trust, loyalty, and confidence, who has the legal duty to act for the benefit of another person, putting that other person's interests above his or her own. Besides trustees, fiduciaries include executors, administrators of estates, guardians, and agents (see Chapter 2 for a further discussion).

If selected to serve as the *executor* of the client's estate, the trust officer manages assets that are transferred through the probate process. Similarly, if selected to serve as *trustee* of a trust created by the client, the trust officer manages assets placed in the trust. Thus, the trust officer can be particularly helpful in the planning stage on the long-term management of assets. It is wise in the planning stages to determine what parameters have been set by various trust departments with regards to the trusts or estates each is willing to handle. Some bank trust departments will not accept a fiduciary position for estates below a certain size, such as those below $500,000. They may also be reluctant to serve as trustee if too much supervision of a beneficiary is expected or if the trust is expected to retain assets that are difficult to manage.

EXAMPLE 1 - 12. Martha's trust named her local bank's trust department to serve as successor trustee of her living trust. After her death, the trust is to provide income during the life of her son, Curtis, and after his death, it is to be distributed to his issue (children, grandchildren, etc.) if any. Otherwise, it will be distributed to Martha's brother William, or William's issue. Because Curtis had a long history of substance abuse, the trust had a clause that required the trustee to withhold distribution of income if Curtis failed to stay free of drugs and alcohol. It also allowed the trustee to distribute *trust corpus* (trust principal) if the trustee thought it would contribute to Curtis' well-being. When Martha died, Curtis was 50, unemployed, and childless. Since the bank's trust officers had not been consulted when the trust was drafted, the bank refused to serve as trustee. It considered the responsibility of deciding when and whether to distribute income and corpus to Curtis to be too great a burden. *** *Query 1. What risk would the bank take if it accepted the job of trustee?*

Financial Planner

The financial planner is the newest member of the estate planning team. The financial planner is the professional skilled in integrating the various parts of a client's financial plan, e.g., making recommendations concerning insurance, investments, retirement planning, income tax planning, and estate planning. He or she may be best suited to serve as the team captain, coordinating the work of the others. The financial planner does not, however, draft the legal documents. As stated earlier, in most states only an attorney is legally permitted to accept payment for doing creating the documents. As the profession matures, it is expected that the financial planner's role will increase.

THE NEED TO ENCOURAGE PLANNING

Many individuals need estate planning but fail to seek it. They simply ignore issues involving their own death, refusing to accept the fact that death can occur quite unexpectedly, and that all of us must die someday. Others are so busy pursuing their careers that they do not make time for planning. Still others lead lives that seem too unsettled to undertake long-range planning. Finally, some fear the family conflicts and expenses that are likely to arise at their death—without considering that good planning is likely to minimize the potential problems, even if not all of the problems can be resolved.

For these reasons, members of the estate planning team should actively encourage individuals to plan their estates. As mentioned earlier, good planning will help dispose of assets fairly, minimize taxes and expenses at death, provide for the care of disabled family members, generate sufficient liquidity, provide for continued income for dependent survivors, and arrange for efficient business succession.

Next, we turn to the organization of this text.

ORGANIZATION OF THE BOOK

This book is divided into three parts. Part 1 (this chapter and the next) introduces the major estate planning concepts used throughout the text. It describes the basic concepts of estate planning and defines many estate planning terms, such as *fee simple, life estate, remainder, probate, trust, irrevocable*, and *insured*.

Part 2 (Chapters 3 through 8) provides the more detailed background knowledge required to understand the techniques of estate planning. It introduces the constraints in planning. In these chapters we cover the principles of transfer taxation (gift and estate) and of property law. These are subjects of great importance to estate planning.

Chapter 3 explores the rudimentary contents of wills and trusts, the two major documents of property transfer. Sample documents, illustrating the simple will, living trust, and testamentary (i.e., the trust-will), are examined to give the reader an early, concrete awareness of the focus of planning.

Chapter 4 explains how property is actually transferred. Included are discussions of supervised probate, probate alternatives in states adopting the Uniform Probate Code, and some examples of summary probate. We cover the role of intestate succession laws as guides for the transfer of property for those who die without a will.

Chapter 5 introduces federal wealth transfer taxation, describing the computation of both the gift tax and the estate tax. It also discusses state death taxes and the computation of the federal state death tax credit.

Continuing the material on wealth transfer taxation, Chapter 6 contains a thorough examination of the federal estate tax, exploring three major areas: components of the gross estate, estate tax deductions, and estate tax credits not covered in Chapter 5.

Chapter 7 covers the federal gift tax and the basis rules.

Chapter 8 is a brief introduction to the federal income taxation of estates, trusts, and their beneficiaries.

Part 3 utilizes the material in Parts 1 and 2 to survey the actual techniques used in planning. It begins with Chapter 9's survey of the principal goals of estate planning. Examples include minimizing the costs of the property transfer process, shifting taxable income to lower bracket taxpayers, and reducing and/or freezing the taxable estate.

Chapter 10 examines the decision whether to have one's estate avoid probate. It considers probate alternatives, including the revocable living trust which seems to be growing in popularity.

Chapters 11 and 12 focus on planning for those transfers at death that can defer, completely eliminate, or reduce a wealthy client's death taxes. The emphasis here is on estate planning for wealthy married couples. We will see that the major transfer strategies incorporate the estate tax marital deduction and the bypass trust. We will also explore techniques used to avoid or lessen the impact of the generation-skipping transfer tax.

Chapters 13 and 14 explore various aspects of planning lifetime transfers. Chapter 13's discussion of gift planning shows that, although gifts can save both income and transfer taxes, the requirement that the person relinquish control over the assets causes many people to choose other forms of property transfers. Chapter 14 describes lifetime transfers where the donor retains some control over the gift property and lifetime transfers where the donor receives some consideration in exchange. The chapter also covers charitable transfers. An Appendix to Chapter 14 summarizes several once popular lifetime transfers, such as the short-term trust, that have lost their appeal due to changes in the tax law. It also describes some dubious estate planning devices.

Chapter 15 assesses common methods of providing the client's estate with adequate liquidity to fund expenses that are associated with dying. Topics include sale of assets before death, life insurance, liquidity planning devices unique to business owners, and valuation discounts.

Chapter 16 explores the principles of planning for closely-held business interests. Their owners have special estate planning problems, including maintaining sufficient income after withdrawing from the business and transferring to their chosen beneficiaries the maximum value attributable to that business. In addition to an extended discussion of these problems, the chapter covers several specific techniques, including sale of the business during the owner's lifetime, the business buyout, family limited partnerships, limited liability companies, and business estate freeze techniques.

Chapter 17 covers miscellaneous techniques that estate planners routinely employ, including providing for minor children, selecting a trustee, planning for nontraditional relationships, and planning for the client's incapacity through the use of durable powers of attorney.

Chapter 18 examines the principles of postmortem tax planning, showing that income tax and estate tax planning occur even after the client's death. Major topics include decisions related to expense deduction elections, disclaimers, and marital deduction planning.

Finally, Chapter 19 presents a hypothetical estate planning case study, with questions for review. The case appeared in one of the early certification examinations of the Certified Financial Planner Board of Standards (the CFP Board). It was then released as an educational aid and is reprinted with the CFP Board's permission. The chapter concludes with the estate planning portion of the CFP licensee's Job Knowledge Requirements (often referred to as the topics list) as determined by the CFP Board's jobs-analysis survey.

QUERIES ANSWERED:

1. The bank's risk is that, if it doesn't monitor Curtis properly and wrongly makes distributions while he is having drug problems, it might be sued by Curtis for allowing his condition to worsen, it might be sued by someone injured by Curtis, or it might be sued by the remaindermen whose remainder interests are diminished. Although the likely success of such suits may be low, and the cost of defending the suits will probably be chargeable to the trust, most trust departments would rather not take on a trust whose terms greatly increase the likelihood of a lawsuit.

QUESTIONS AND PROBLEMS

1. At a dinner party, one of your clients asks you what estate planning entails. Define estate planning for her, and name the areas of the law embraced by it.

2. A man comes into your office to inquire about your services. You find out that he owns a closely-held business and has a wife and two young children. He has not yet done any estate planning. Explain briefly how failure to plan could lead to adverse consequences.

3. Fill in the questionnaire in Appendix 1A with information about yourself. Which items are likely to be the most difficult to complete? Why?

4. Outline the steps required to develop an estate plan.

5. Explain the unique contribution made by each member of the estate planning team.

ANSWERS TO QUESTIONS AND PROBLEMS

1. Estate planning is the study of the principles of planning for the use, conservation, and efficient transfer of an individual's wealth. It embraces the law of property, wills, trusts, future interests, estate administration, intestacy, insurance, income taxation, gift taxation, and death taxation.

2. Examples of how failure to plan could lead to adverse consequences include the following:

    a. Premature death of husband and wife in a common accident resulting in the court appointing an undesirable parental guardian for the children.

    b. Inability to sell the business after the premature death of the owner.

    Please refer to examples 1-1 through 1-10 for common illustrations of the failure to plan.

3. Clients may have difficulty completing the portions of the questionnaire that inquire about how title to property is held, ask for the fair market value of assets, or request information concerning employee benefit plans. Individuals with minor children may find it difficult to choose personal guardians.

4. Steps required in developing an estate plan: The following is taken from the CFP Board of Standard's definition of the financial planning process adopted 9/14/96:

    i. Establishing and defining the client-planner relationship;
    ii. Gathering client data including goals;
    iii. Analyzing and evaluating the client's financial status;
    iv. Developing and presenting financial planning recommendations and/or alternatives;
    v. Implementing the financial planning recommendations; and
    vi. Monitoring the financial planning recommendations.

5. The unique contribution made by each member of the estate planning team includes:

   a. Attorney: drafting legal documents.

   b. Accountant: preparing the client's financial statements and tax returns often gives him or her the greatest and earliest financial contact with the client.

   c. Life Underwriter: providing insurance contracts to meet liquidity needs at the client's death.

   d. Trust Officer: providing fiduciary services as experienced trustee and/or executor.

   e. Financial Planner: potentially capable of creating a complete financial plan, one including recommendations concerning insurance, investments, retirement planning, income tax planning and estate planning.

Sample Client Fact-Finding Questionnaire

Susan R. Goodall
5556 Long Street, Suite 245
Anytown, ST 54321
888/555-3456

DATA SHEET FOR ESTATE PLAN
Married Persons
(With Minor Children)

Please print or type the following information. If you need more space, use the reverse side (include the question number). If you are not certain about an answer, put a question mark. If you have questions, write them down at the end of this data sheet. *It is more important that you return this in a timely fashion than that it be complete.*

1. Husband's (H) full name _____
   Name used on real estate documents _____
   Other or former names _____
   Wife's (W) full name _____
   Name used on real estate documents _____
   Other or former names _____
   Citizenship: Husband _____ Wife _____

2. a. Residents of _____ County.
   b. Address _____
         _____
   c. Home phone # _____ Business # _____

3. Date of Birth: (H) _____ (W) _____
  Place of Birth: (H) _____ (W) _____
  Date of Marriage: _____ Place: _____
  Approximate dates moved to California (H) _____ (W) _____
  Social Security #: (H) _____ (W) _____
  Occupation: (H) _____
          (W) _____

4. FAMILY:
  a. Children of this marriage:

Name	Birth date	Residence (If still living with you, put "Home")
_____	_____	_____
_____	_____	_____
_____	_____	_____

  b. Are there children by prior marriages? Yes/no. If yes, please give full information below:

Name	Birth date	Residence (If still living with you, put "Home")
_____	_____	_____
_____	_____	_____
_____	_____	_____

  c. If there are deceased children who left issue, please give information below:

_____
_____

   d. Living parents (names/addresses):
      (H) _____

      _____

      (W) _____

      _____

   e. Brothers and Sisters (names/addresses):
      (H) _____

      _____

      (W) _____

      _____

   f. Should you or your children adopt a child (or children)should they inherit on the same basis as natural children and/or grandchildren? _____

5. Friends to whom you intend to leave bequests (names/addresses):
   a. _____
   b. _____

6. Estate information (to nearest $10,000)
   a. The <u>net</u> value of our assets is approximately $_____
   b. Our three major assets and their approximate <u>net</u> values are:

   (1) _____ (value $_____)
   (2) _____ (value $_____)
   (3) _____ (value $_____)

7. How is title to your property actually held? Bring title documents with you when you come to see me.

8. Give the following information about your life insurance:

Whose Life? H or W	Company/ Policy No.	Owner H/W/Both	Beneficiary & 1st Alternate	Amount
_____	_____	_____	_____	_____
_____	_____	_____	_____	_____

9. Have you entered into a community property agreement? Yes/no
Have you entered into a prenuptial or postnuptial agreement? Yes/no

10. Distribution. Put your thoughts in general terms at part (b). We will discuss details at the time of interview.

    a. Specific gifts (show gift, i.e., heirlooms, money, etc. and the beneficiaries' names and addresses).
       1. _____
       _____
       2. _____
       _____
       3. _____
       _____
       4. _____
       _____

       For specific gifts, indicate which alternative:
           1st alternative: Property left free and clear _____
           2nd alternative: Property left with encumbrances _____

    b. Residue (1st) _____
       _____
       (2nd) (if people in 1 predecease me) _____
       _____
       (3rd) (if people in 1 & 2 predecease me) _____
       _____

11. Please circle the answer to the following questions. (If yes, give details and, if appropriate, approximate values on the reverse side. If a document is involved, attach a photocopy.)

    a. In any year, have you made gifts to anyone of more than $3,000 prior to 1982 or $10,000 after 1981? (H)Yes/no (W) Yes/no

    b. Do either of you expect to inherit or receive gifts totaling in excess of $100,000 from your parents and/or from others? (H) Yes/no (W) Yes/no

   c. Do you have powers of appointment? (H) Yes/no (W) Yes/no

   d. Do you have Wills already drawn? (H) Yes/no (W) Yes/no

12. If a Trust is contemplated: Proposed Trustee (give the relationship, name, and address if not already listed):
    1st choice: _____
    2nd choice: _____
    3rd choice: _____

13. If there are minor children: Proposed Guardian (relationship/name/address if not already listed):

    1st choice: _____
    2nd choice: _____
    3rd choice: _____

14. Proposed Executor (relationship/name/address if not already listed):

    (H) 1st choice: _____
         2nd choice: _____
         3rd choice: _____

    (W)1st choice: _____
         2nd choice: _____
         3rd choice: _____

15. Are specific burial instructions available to the executor? If yes, explain:
    (H) _____
    (W) _____

16. Do you have a safe deposit box? Yes/no
    a. Where? _____
    b. Who has access? H ____ W ____ Other _____

17. Where shall the original of the will be kept? (check one)
    a. Client's (your) safe deposit box _____
    b. Other place _____ Where? _____

18. How many photocopies of each will do you want, i.e., in addition to the original? H _____ W _____ (Giving a copy to your executor is optional.)

19. Questions to ask your attorney:

    a. _____

    b. _____

    c. _____

    d. _____

    e. _____

    f. _____

    g. _____

    h. _____

CHAPTER 2

Basic Estate Planning Concepts

OVERVIEW

This chapter introduces many basic concepts regularly employed in estate planning. Because they will be referred to throughout the text, the reader is advised to know them well. Some of these concepts are so straightforward that mere use of them in a sentence will make their meaning clear. More involved terms are defined and illustrated. These terms, along with others introduced in later chapters, are included in the Glossary at the end of this book.

CONCEPTS DEALING WITH ESTATES

An *estate* is a quantity of wealth or property. *Property* represents things or objects over which the owner may lawfully exercise the right to use, control, or dispose. More simply, property is anything that can be owned.

Ordinarily, for a person or for a family, an estate represents the total amount of property owned. However, the word *estate* is used in several other contexts in estate planning to mean some other amount. First, in certain situations, estate means the *net* value of property owned, calculated by subtracting the amount of the estate owner's liabilities from the value of all property owned. Second, estate can be limited to the *probate estate*, which constitutes all of the property that passes to others by means of the probate process after the death of the owner. Third, estate may mean the *gross estate* or the *taxable estate*, two concepts used only in connection with taxation at death. As we will see later, the probate estate and the tax-related estate may be very different in size and composition. The net estate and the probate estate are generally less than all property owned; the net estate is less because liabilities are subtracted and the probate estate is less because many things owned, such as those held in joint tenancy and life insurance, pass outside the probate process. The gross estate will equal or exceed the value of all property owned because it includes all things owned and may also include things that are not owned, such as gift taxes paid on gifts made within three years of the donor's death. In Chapter 6 we will cover the concepts of the gross estate and the taxable estate in detail.

CONCEPTS DEALING WITH TRANSFERS OF PROPERTY

One of the primary areas of emphasis in estate planning is on how property is transferred. This section will cover the terminology used in this area.

Transfers of Legal, Beneficial, or Legal and Beneficial Interests

A *transfer* or *assignment* of property refers to any type of passing of property in which the *transferor* gives up an *interest* to the *transferee*. The interest transferred can be purely legal, purely beneficial, or both legal and beneficial. *Legal interest* refers to a situation where title passes. For example, an independent trustee of a trust takes title to all trust assets in order to manage the trust property, but cannot use it in a manner inconsistent with the trust agreement. A mother, who takes title as custodian of a bank account established for her child's benefit under the Uniform Transfers to Minors Act, has legal title but the beneficial interest is owned by the child.

On the other hand, a purely *beneficial interest* occurs when a transferee receives something that carries an economic benefit, but not title. Examples of beneficial interest in property include the temporary or permanent right to possess, consume, pledge, or otherwise benefit from property. If a friend lends you her car while your car is in the shop, you have a beneficial interest in the car without having title. As we shall see, a trust beneficiary's rights are purely beneficial.

Finally, an interest given up by the transferor can be both legal and beneficial, such as where the transferee receives both title and the beneficial interest. An *outright transfer* occurs when one transferee receives both legal and beneficial interests, without restrictions or conditions, as typically happens when one person gives another a birthday present.

Complete versus Incomplete Transfers; Property in General versus a Specific Property Interest

Complete versus incomplete transfers: overview. A transfer of property is said to be *complete* and *irrevocable* when it is no longer rescindable or amendable (i.e., when the transferor has totally relinquished all dominion and control over that property). For example, after purchasing this book, at the expiration of the returns period, you have made a completed transfer of money. On the other hand, a transfer is said to be *incomplete* and *revocable* while it is still rescindable or amendable (i.e., made without total relinquishment of dominion and control over that property).

Property in general versus an interest in property. To fully distinguish between complete and incomplete transfers, one must grasp the difference between property in general and a specific interest in property. *Property in general*, such as 100 shares of ABC stock, means the entire asset, whether physical or intangible, including all rights and interests that go with ownership. In contrast, an *interest in property* means one or more rights to property, such as the right to the first five years of dividends from the 100 shares of ABC stock.

In estate planning, more than one interest in a given item of property may be transferred in a way that highlights the divisibility of the bundle of interests associated with property ownership.

EXAMPLE 2 - 1. Tom transfers 100 shares of stock in trust to Terry. The trust terms give Alan the right to all income for five years, followed by Barbara having the right to receive income for ten years, and finally, after 15 years, the trust is to terminate with the trust assets distributed to Carl. Each person has received an "interest" in the stock. Terry's interest is a legal one (title), Alan and Barbara each have a beneficial one, and Carl's interest is both beneficial and legal. We'll take a more detailed look at trusts later in the chapter.

Complete, incomplete, and partially complete transfers. A transfer of each specific interest in property is either complete or incomplete, while the transfer of more than one interest can be either *totally complete, partially complete, or totally incomplete.*

EXAMPLE 2 - 2. Continuing with the same facts as above, if Tom retained the right to revoke or amend the entire trust, his transfers of property into trust would be incomplete. On the other hand, if Tom retained the right to revoke or amend only Alan's interest, the transfer of Alan's interest would be incomplete, the transfer of Barbara's and Carl's interests would be complete, and Tom's overall transfer of the stock would be said to be partially complete. Finally, if Tom retained no rights whatsoever over the stock, the transfers of interest to Alan, Barbara, and Carl would all be complete.

When we study gift taxes, it will become clear that this issue of whether a transfer is complete or incomplete is important because gift tax law treats completed transfers, even of just a partial interest, as gifts subject to gift taxation.

Sale versus Gift

Most commonly, completed transfers of property interests are undertaken by sale, by gift, or by a combination of both sale and gift. A *sale* is a transfer of property under which each transferor exchanges *consideration* that is regarded as equivalent in value. By contrast, a gift is a transfer of property for which the transferor takes back little or nothing of economic value in exchange. The most common methods of making gift transfers are *outright* and *in trust.*

A bargain sale. A bargain sale occurs when a person (the transferor) transfers property in exchange for property with an economic value to the transferor that the transferor knows is less than the worth of the property he or she is giving up. A bargain sale involves a transfer that is part sale and part gift. The notion of the bargain sale requires us to define a gift somewhat more broadly than in the last paragraph. While the idea of a gift as something given with nothing given in return covers the most common type of gift, it must be recognized that a bargain sale is also a gift, even though property is received in exchange. Federal tax law treats the actual amount of the gift as the difference between the respective values of the consideration exchanged. Thus, a transfer during the life of the transferor will be either a gift or a sale, with a gift defined to include a *bargain sale* (i.e., an exchange of considerations of unequal value, where the parties know and intend them to be unequal).

Inter Vivos Transfer versus Transfer at Death

A transfer of property can be *inter vivos*, meaning that it is made while the transferor is alive, or it can be made at death. Inter vivos is Latin for "among the living." Transfers at death may be made pursuant to a valid document, also called an *instrument*, prepared by the owner before death (e.g., will, trust, title by joint tenancy, or insurance beneficiary designation), or pursuant to state law (intestate succession) in the event that no such document exists.

Fair Market Value of Transfer

The value of a transfer is measured by its fair market value at the time of the transfer. Determining fair market value is the subject of several sections in the text. A generally accepted definition of *fair market value* is "the price at which the property would change hands between a willing buyer and a willing seller, neither being under any compulsion to buy or to sell and both having reasonable knowledge of the relevant facts." The IRS uses this definition in the regulations for valuing gifts and estates.[1]

BENEFICIARIES

A *beneficiary* or *donee* is a person who receives a gift of a beneficial interest in property from a transferor. The transferor is called a *donor*. Although, in the most general sense, donee and beneficiary are synonymous, in certain contexts one or the other term is more commonly used. For example, the recipient of an outright *inter vivos* gift from the donor is usually called a donee. On the other hand, the recipient of a bequest by a will or an interest in a trust is usually called a beneficiary. Occasionally, the term *donee* is used to describe one who has received something without also receiving any beneficial interest, such as where one is given a limited power of appointment, an estate planning tool discussed later.

WILLS, TRUSTS, AND PROBATE

In estate planning, a *decedent* is a person who has died. When a person dies, property owned by the decedent must be transferred. Each state takes special interest in ensuring that all property owned by the decedent is transferred to the proper parties. State law recognizes certain documents prepared by the decedent (wills, trusts, joint tenancy arrangements, life insurance policies, etc.) as legally binding guides for the proper disposition of the decedent's property. A *will* is a written document that expresses a person's desired distribution of his or her property at death. The person making a will is called the *testator*. The will is said to make *testamentary* transfers, however the actual process by which transfer is accomplished is the probate process. At the death of a person, his or her will controls the transfer of property only if there is no guide to the transfer that is recognized as superior. Thus, the will controls property in the decedent's name alone or held with another as a tenant in common, but not property held in trust or in joint tenancy. Property held in trust will be transferred according to the terms of the trust, not according to the terms of the settlor's will, and any attempt to transfer joint tenancy property according to a decedent co-owner's will is bound to fail since the right of survivorship prevails over provisions in a will.

A trust is a fiduciary relationship in which one person (the *trustee*) is the holder of the title to property (the *trust estate* or the *trust corpus*), subject to an equitable obligation to keep or use the property for the benefit of another (the *beneficiary*). The *trust instrument* is the written agreement between the *settlor* (the person creating and funding the trust) and the *trustee* that sets forth for whose benefit the trust is created, how the trust estate is to be managed, its duration, and to whom the corpus must be given when the trust terminates. Trusts are described in greater detail later in the chapter.

Intestate, testate, and partially intestate. If a valid will is found, the decedent is said to have died *testate*. If the document does not dispose of all of the decedent's property, the decedent is said to have died *partially intestate*. If no will is found, the decedent is said to have died *intestate*. However, if all of the decedent's property is disposed of by alternative means (e.g., trusts, joint tenancy), a will may not be necessary, and the absence of a will would not cause any problems as there would be no property subject to its control.

In some cases, the moment that death occurs may have some significance because it might determine the rights of beneficiaries and/or the liabilities of the estate. The Uniform Determination of Death Act, adopted in at least 15 states, addresses this issue by defining death as occurring when the person is brain dead, meaning the absence of brain waves, as well as "cessation of circulatory and respiratory functions."

Probate and the personal representative. *Probate* is the legal process of administering the estate of a decedent. The probate estate consists of all property belonging to the decedent for which there is no other mechanism of transfer. Thus, the probate estate is that property whose disposition is guided by either the decedent's will or by the state laws of intestate succession. Generally, *probate assets* fall into one of three groups: property owned by the decedent as an individual, interests of the decedent held with others as tenants-in-common, and, in some community property states, the decedent's one half interest in community property. Some community property states, such as California, no longer require a probate for property going to the surviving spouse whether that property is the decedent's half of the community property or is the decedent's separate property. *Non-probate assets* include property held in trusts or in joint tenancy, the proceeds of most insurance policies on the life of the decedent (unless payable to the decedent's estate), and most retirement plan assets. Many of these terms will be described later in the chapter.

Essentially, in probate administration, the judge of the probate court determines the validity of the will, if any, and (after a period of administration) authorizes distribution of the probate estate to creditors and beneficiaries. The court appoints a *personal representative* to act as fiduciary to represent and manage the probate estate. If the court appoints the person nominated in the will to be personal representative, that person is called the *executor*. In some states, a female personal representative is called an *executrix*, however the trend is to use the term executor regardless of gender. An *administrator* is a person appointed by the court to represent the estate of a person who died intestate or where the court appoints someone other than the person(s) nominated in the will. The person nominated may have predeceased the testator, may be incapacitated, or perhaps is unfit (e.g., is serving time in prison for bank robbery). If the decedent died testate, but the court appoints someone other than the person nominated in the will, once the will is admitted for probate the personal representative is called an *administrator with will annexed*.

The word "fiduciary" is derived from the Latin word for "trust." A *fiduciary* is a person in a position of trust, loyalty, and confidence, who has the legal duty to act for the benefit of another, putting that other person's interests above his or her own. Besides personal representatives, fiduciaries include trustees, guardians, and agents.

Recipients of probate property. Beneficiaries of a decedent's probate property are called heirs, devisees, or legatees. An *heir* is a person who inherits property from a decedent whether by will, intestate succession, or any other mechanism of transfer such as through a trust or by joint tenancy. *Heir at law* refers to the person (or persons) who have a right to an intestate decedent's property. This is usually accomplished by defining them as included in the issue of the adoptive parent. Degrees of blood relationship, which are important in determining heirs at law, will be covered in Chapter 4. A *devisee* is a beneficiary, under a will, of a gift of real property. A devisee is said to receive a *devise*. A *legatee* is a beneficiary, under a will, of a gift of personal property. A legatee is said to receive a *legacy* or a *bequest*. The trend in modern usage is to use the term bequest for any testamentary gift, whether of real or personal property. The Uniform Probate Code, discussed in the next chapter, uses the term "devise" both as a noun and a verb, to mean a bequest or the act of making a bequest (whether of real or personal property) in connection with transfers by will.

Issue refers to a person's offspring or progeny, including children, grandchildren, great-grandchildren, and the like. A *descendant* is one who is descended from a specific ancestor, e.g., an offspring. Thus, the terms issue and descendants are used interchangeably. Most state succession statutes treat adopted children as though naturally born to their adoptive parents.

Types of bequests. Bequests are categorized as specific, pecuniary, general, residuary, and/or class gifts. A *specific bequest* is a gift of a particular item of property which is capable of being identified and distinguished from all other property in the testator's estate, e.g., "I leave all my household furnishings to Sally Ann," and "I leave my high school ring to my brother Bill." If the property subject to a specific bequest is sold, given away, or lost before the testator's death, under the common law doctrine of *ademption* (from the Latin *ademptio* - a taking away) the bequest fails, meaning that the person does not receive anything to replace the missing property. Although most states follow the common law doctrine, some states' statutes have exceptions that do not result in ademption in certain circumstances, e.g., an asset was acquired by the decedent in a manner that made it clear that it was intended to replace specific devised real or tangible property.[2] A *general bequest* is a gift that can be satisfied out of the general assets of the estate, e.g., the bequest "I leave ten percent of my estate to my brother Henry."

At common law the term *legacy* meant a testamentary gift of money; however, it has come to mean any bequest. *Pecuniary bequest* is the term used to describe a bequest expressed as a specific dollar amount. It is called a pecuniary bequest even though the executor has the option of satisfying it with cash or with assets worth the specified dollar amount. Since the bequest could be paid from any account, or be satisfied by the transfer of any asset not specifically bequeathed, a pecuniary bequest is a type of general bequest. Pecuniary bequests are commonly found in complex estate plans aimed at minimizing death taxes. The bequest is likely to be expressed in terms of a formula, such as "I leave to my spouse the least amount needed to reduce my death taxes to zero." A pecuniary bequest is distinguished from a *fractional share bequest*, which uses fractions (or percentages) in defining the interests of beneficiaries to certain property or to a portion of the estate (e.g., "I leave 65 percent of the residue of my estate to my sister Gladys, and the other 35 percent to my brother Marco.")

What remains of the estate after all of the foregoing bequests are taken into account is called the *residue* of the estate. A *residuary bequest* is a gift of that part of the testator's estate not otherwise disposed of by the will, e.g., "I leave the rest of my estate to Robert Moon." Generally, debts are paid out of the residue and not charged against the specific bequests.

A *class gift* is a gift to a group of individuals that may not be completely defined at the time the gift is made (e.g., "I leave the residue of my estate to my grandchildren living at the time of my death.")

Occasionally, a testator dies leaving insufficient assets to satisfy all bequests and pay all creditors. Under the procedure called *abatement*, bequests are eliminated or reduced so that all debts (and administration expenses) are paid in full, or else the estate is exhausted. In those states that follow the Uniform Probate Code (UPC), shares of the beneficiaries abate in the following order: (1) probate property not disposed of in the will, if there are no residuary bequests, (2) residuary bequests, (3) general bequests, and (4) specific bequests. Some state statutes abate gifts to a spouse, or to issue, only after abatement of gifts to persons not related to the decedent.

EXAMPLE 2 - 3. Lawrence died in a UPC state. Lawrence's will leaves his car to his son, Sam, $20,000 cash to his sister, Vira, and the residue of his estate to his wife, Mary Ellen. Assume that at his death Lawrence owned only the car and $25,000 in cash, and he owed $6,000 in debts. Most states (perhaps all) would require the $6,000 debt be paid, leaving just $19,000 in cash. The UPC abatement would result in Vira getting the $19,000 balance, the car would go to Sam, and Mary Ellen would receive nothing.

Disclaimers

Most people would welcome a large bequest, especially if it came from a distant relative. After all, such gifts may make for financial security. Yet there are times when it makes sense for a beneficiary to refuse a gift or bequest. A *disclaimer* is an unqualified refusal to accept a gift or bequest. Disclaiming may be preferable when it avoids, reduces, or delays transfer taxes. Usually, a person will disclaim property only if it will then pass to a person the disclaimant wants to have it.

To be *tax-effective,* the disclaimer must meet the requirements of both state property law and federal tax law. Under property law, a disclaimant is treated as having *predeceased* the decedent-donor. Consequently, the disclaimed property will pass under one of two possible sets of legal guidelines. Either it will pass to the "alternate taker" in accordance with the terms of the decedent's transfer document (which is usually a will or trust) or, if no such document exists or if the document does not name an alternate taker, the property will pass under laws of intestacy.

> EXAMPLE 2 - 4. Bachelor Barry died recently, and his will left an estate valued at $500,000 to his brother Mike, if living, otherwise to Mike's issue. Mike, age 87, wealthy and in poor health, has three living children. If he immediately disclaims the inheritance, it will pass under the will to his children. The transfer will not be treated as a gift from Mike, but rather as though it passed to them directly from Barry.

> EXAMPLE 2 - 5. Changing the facts in the previous example a bit, assume Barry's will stated that if Mike predeceased Barry, then the bequest would go to Barry's long time friend Charlie. If Mike disclaims, Barry's estate will pass to Charlie rather than to Mike's children. Of course, Mike could assign his interest in the estate to his children, but that would be a gift from him to them.

A disclaimer is considered to be tax-effective if it is done in a manner that complies with requirements set forth in IRC §2518 such that the transfer is not treated as a gift by the disclaimant. When we take up estate and gift taxes, we will cover in detail the requirements for a tax-effective disclaimer, and we will illustrate ways in which disclaimers are used to improve estate plans.

LIFE INSURANCE

A *life insurance* policy is a contract in which the insurance company, in exchange for the payment of premiums, agrees to pay a cash lump-sum amount (called the *face value* or *policy proceeds*) to a person designated in the policy to receive it (the *beneficiary*) upon the death of the subject of the insurance (the *insured*). Usually, the policy names alternate beneficiaries who will receive the proceeds if the named beneficiary dies. One other important party in the life insurance contract is the *owner*, who has title to the policy, and who generally possesses both legal and beneficial interests in the policy. As present beneficial owner, the policy owner has the right to benefit from the policy. Beneficial rights usually include the right to receive policy dividends, the right to designate and to change the beneficiary, and the right to surrender the policy. These rights can have economic value, even before the death of the insured. Whether or not a life insurance policy has economic value prior to the insured's death depends upon the type of policy. If the owner holds title to the policy as the trustee of an irrevocable life insurance trust, then the owner will have legal title but will most likely not have a beneficial interest. Irrevocable life insurance trusts are used to keep life insurance proceeds out of the estate of the insured.

Most *term life insurance* policies have minimal cash value prior to the death of the insured because the premium charged, which increases over time along with the increasing risk of death, simply buys pure protection. If the insured dies during the policy term, the company will pay the face value; otherwise, it will pay nothing. Some multi-year term policies (called *level term*) have a constant premium for a stated period (e.g., five or ten years). This requires a cash build-up during the early years of the period which is used to pay the higher mortality risk in the later years.

In contrast to a term policy, a *cash value* policy accumulates economic value because the insurer charges a constant premium that is considerably higher than mortality costs require during the earlier years. Part of this overpayment accumulates as a *cash surrender value*, which, prior to the death of the insured, can be used by the owner in one of two ways: (1) at any time the owner can surrender the policy and receive this value in cash or, (2) the owner can request a policy loan and borrow up to the amount of this value.

Because life insurance policies can have value prior to the insured's death, and because the insured's death results in the payment of the face amount of the policy in cash to the beneficiaries, life insurance makes a significant contribution to estate planning. It is said to be the only asset that can create an *instant* estate of substantial magnitude for a person of otherwise modest wealth. For a family that includes dependent children, this may be an important means of assuring the financial well-being of the surviving family members if a parent dies. For the wealthy family, life insurance may provide needed cash to pay the death taxes. A discussion of the types of life insurance and more about irrevocable life insurance trusts is found in Chapter 15. To use life insurance properly, the planner must be aware of the impact of taxes, a subject to be introduced briefly next, and explained in detail in Chapters 5 through 8.

TAXATION

In estate planning, the two principal types of taxing authorities are the individual states and the federal government. The four major types of taxes are gift tax, death tax, generation-skipping transfer tax, and income tax.

A *gift tax* is a tax on a lifetime gift; that is, a lifetime transfer of property for less than full consideration.

A *death tax* is essentially a tax levied on certain property owned or transferred by the decedent at death. There are two basic types of death tax statutes, which, depending upon the format, are referred to as either an estate tax or an inheritance tax. An *estate tax* is a tax on the decedent's right to transfer property, while an *inheritance tax* is a tax on the right of a beneficiary to receive property from a decedent. Either way, their net effect is essentially the same: they are both considered death taxes, and the tax is usually paid by the executor out of the decedent's estate before the property is transferred to the heirs. With an inheritance tax, the amount of death tax paid on any given size inheritance is likely to be greater for remote relatives as compared to close relatives, and greatest for non-relatives. For example, amounts going to a surviving spouse might not be taxed at all, and bequests to a child might have a high exemption amount and/or a lower tax rate than property going to a non-relative. The federal death tax is referred to as the federal estate tax. The characteristic of an estate tax is that, for any given net estate (i.e., after the debts and expenses), the tax will be the same regardless of who receives it. For example in the year 2001, the federal tax on a $5 million bequest, after applying a $391,600 federal state death tax credit, would be $1,778,650 whether the estate went to the decedent's children or went entirely to strangers (non-relatives). However, the federal estate tax is not a pure estate tax in that two deductions are based upon the status of the beneficiary. A complete marital deduction is allowed for all property going to a surviving spouse (for a non-USA citizen spouse a special trust might be required, but we'll save that discussion until later), and a complete charitable deduction is allowed for property going to qualified charities. Since these are complete (100%) deductions, subtracted from the gross estate before arriving at the taxable estate, and they are the only two deductions that are based upon the character of the beneficiary, little is lost in our thinking of the federal death tax as an estate tax. At the state level, most states impose an estate tax and others have an inheritance tax. The trend is to impose an estate tax that results in no additional cost to the estate because, although it is paid to the state, the state death tax statute sets the death taxes as being equal to the state's allowable share of the federal state death tax credit. Because of the federal credit for state death taxes, this so-called "*pick-up tax*" reduces the federal death tax by an equivalent amount (i.e., a dollar for dollar credit), thus there is no increase in the over-all taxes. More than half of the states (including California, Florida and Nevada) use the "pick-up tax." The calculation for the "pick-up tax" is explained in Chapter 5. *** *Query 1. Based upon the above discussion, what is the death tax collected by the State of Florida, if one of its citizens dies in 2001 leaving a taxable estate of $5 million?*

A *generation-skipping transfer tax* (GSTT) is a tax on certain property transferred to a "skip person," that is, for the benefit of someone who is more than one generation younger than the donor. Thus, the surviving spouse and the children of a decedent are not skip persons, but grandchildren and great-grandchildren are. Without this tax, wealth could skip several generations and escape one or more levels of transfer tax. For example, without the GSTT, a gift or estate transfer of a $10 million parcel of land to a grandchild would be subject once to a gift tax or death tax, but it would not be taxed twice. It would be taxed twice if it went through the natural succession, i.e., once when the property passes from the client to the child, and again when it passes from the child to the grandchild. Chapter 12 covers the GSTT in more detail. It is enough to say here that the federal generation-skipping transfer tax has a $1 million exemption (indexed for inflation) per transferor, making careful planning in this area necessary only for clients with fairly substantial estates.

An *income tax* is essentially a tax levied on income earned by a taxpayer during a given year. Income tax laws usually distinguish five different taxpayers or entities that must report income by filing income tax returns: individuals, partnerships, corporations, estates, and trusts. Principles of taxation can differ substantially for each. For instance, partnerships generally do not pay income taxes because the partnership is treated as a *pass-through* entity, meaning that its income and deductions are passed through to be reported by the individual partners. Each taxpayer, including partnerships, must submit an annual income tax return that reports certain items including income, deductions, credits, and the tax due (calculated by using tax tables applicable to that entity).   Married individuals may file a *joint income tax return*, in which they report their combined income, deductions, and other information on one return. This textbook will not try to cover income taxes in detail as it is far beyond the scope of this course; however, a good introduction to the income taxation of trusts and estates is found in Chapter 8.

PROPERTY INTERESTS

Estate planning seeks to preserve and efficiently transfer an individual's wealth. Wealth is generally thought of as the property a person owns. This section will describe some of the ways in which property can be owned. Essentially, ownership can be classified in the following ways: the extent of ownership interest in property (e.g., fee simple versus a life estate); the physical characteristic of property (e.g., real versus personal); the type of co-ownership (e.g., joint tenancy versus tenants in common); a legal versus a beneficial interest (e.g., property held in the name of the trustee versus a trust beneficial interest); a present versus a future interest (e.g., an income interest in a trust versus a remainder interest); and a vested versus a contingent interest (e.g., outright ownership of land versus a contingent remainder interest, where the remainderman must outlive the income beneficiary or the trust property reverts back to the trustor's estate).

Classification of Property by Physical Characteristics

Property is classified as real or personal. *Real* property includes ownership interests in land and any improvements, such as buildings, fences, trees, and the like, that are attached to the land. Curiously, an interest for years (a leasehold) in real estate is considered personal property. Accordingly, a good functional definition of *personal property* is all property except interests in land and its improvements.

Property is further divided into tangible and intangible property. Something is tangible if it can be perceived by the senses as having a physical existence. *Tangible personal property* is personal property whose utility comes primarily from its physical characteristics rather than the legal rights conferred upon the owner or possessor of the property. Conversely, *intangible personal property* derives its value from the legal rights it represents. Thus a newspaper is tangible personal property because its value is based on the news printed therein. Initially, one might pay 35 cents to read it. A few days later, the value may drop to almost nothing, being useful only to wrap dead fish or as recycled newspaper. Yet, a very old paper with an article on the front page of historical significance may be worth a lot to collectors of old newspapers. On the other hand, a stock certificate is valuable to the owner of the certificate if the company is a going business, not because of the physical characteristics of the paper it is printed on, but because of the rights it represents, such as the right to vote for the board of directors, the right to dividends when they are declared, and certain liquidation rights. If the company has gone out of business, then the stock certificate has become tangible personal property. The certificate may be worth only the value of the paper it is printed on, or, if it is old or unusual for some reason, it may be of some value as a collector's item.

Intangible personal property includes a *chose in action*, which is a claim for money or property that could be recovered from another in a lawsuit, if such is necessary. A chose in action, pronounced "shows," represents the right to money or property that is owed to the holder of the chose. That right can be transferred, sold, or assigned to another, who can then act on it in his or her own name. The person holding the chose as a result of a transfer is entitled to keep any recovery.

EXAMPLE 2 - 6. Betty borrows $9,000 from Lenny, agreeing to pay it back by December 31 of this year. Lenny signs a piece of paper assigning to his daughter, Christine, his right to collect the debt. Since the debt could be collected by a lawsuit if necessary, it is considered to be a chose in action, and the assignment to Christine gives her the right to collect it.

Basic Interests in Property

The three basic interests in property are fee simple, life estate, and estate for years.

Fee simple. A fee simple interest, often called a *fee* or a *fee simple absolute*, represents the greatest interest that a person can have over *real* property and corresponds to our usual notion of full ownership. Common rights include the right to possess, use, pledge, or transfer the property. If you own a house, even if it is subject to a mortgage, you probably have it in fee.

Life estate. A *life estate* interest in property, like a fee simple, is a powerful form of ownership, but is different in that the interest ceases upon someone's death. Ordinarily, the *measuring life* is that of the owner of the interest. However, it could be any other person.

> EXAMPLE 2 - 7. Doctor Bud assigns his interest in a house to Gladis, his widowed mother, for her to use and enjoy until her death. Mother has received a life estate in the house. Her own life is the measuring life.

A life estate for the life of someone other than the owner of the interest is called an estate *for the life of another*. These are rarely used.

> EXAMPLE 2 - 8. Facts are similar to previous example, except that Gladis' interest will cease upon the death of Bud. Gladis still has a life estate in the house but now Bud's life, rather than her life, is the measuring life. She has an estate for the life of another.

Ordinarily, the owner of a life estate enjoys, for the length of a measuring life, a complete ownership; one that is nearly equivalent to a fee, except that it will end upon the life tenant's death. However, life estates are sometimes created so that the recipient enjoys only a partial present interest in the property.

> EXAMPLE 2 - 9. Aunt Jane, owner of dividend-paying common stock, gives to her niece Barbie the right to receive the dividends for as long as Barbie lives. Barbie has received a life estate in the income of the stock. Under the customary arrangements, Barbie does not have many rights in the stock itself. For example, she does not have the right to possess or sell the stock, or to use it as collateral against a loan. The stock will be held by someone else, either the original owner or, more commonly, a trustee under a trust arrangement.

Trusts are used extensively in estate planning and will be discussed in every chapter of this book. An introduction to trusts follows this discussion of property.

Interest for years. Often, a person transfers possession and/or enjoyment of property to another for a fixed period. This is called an *estate for years*—even if the fixed period is something other than a certain number of years.

EXAMPLE 2 - 10. Professor Jackson rents his cottage to Dr. Johnson, a visiting professor, for the Spring semester. Dr. Johnson has an estate "for years" even though the semester is only four months long.

EXAMPLE 2 - 11. Mary is presently enjoying a life estate, for her life, in the income from certain common stock. Today Mary transfers to Mark her interest for the next two years. If Mary does not survive the full two years, Mark's interest will be cut off upon Mary's death. Mary cannot transfer any greater interest than she actually owns, and Mark's interest is limited to that which Mary can legally give; thus, Mark has an income interest in the stock, ending at the earlier of two years or Mary's death.

A common example of an interest for years is a *leasehold*, which entitles the lessee to possess and use the property (e.g., a house or computer) for a specified time, usually in exchange for a fixed series of payments. Leasehold interests can amount to a valuable part of a lessee's wealth if the fixed payments are below current market rates, and if the lessee is permitted to "sublet" the property.

EXAMPLE 2 - 12. Five years ago, Freda acquired a 15 year leasehold interest in a commercial building, and is obligated to pay $15,000 per year for the entire period. If the rent for comparable buildings is $25,000 per year for the next ten years, and assuming a discount rate of 8%, the value of Freda's leasehold is the present value of $10,000 for ten years, discounted at 8%, or $67,101 [see Table B, annuity factor of 6.7101]. Freda could possibly sell her interest for that amount.

Concurrent Ownership

Property may be owned individually, in which case one person owns and uses it, or it may be owned concurrently, by two or more persons. Where there is *concurrent ownership*, title may be taken as joint tenancy, tenants by the entirety, tenants in common, or as community property.

A common characteristic of all types of concurrent ownership is the *undivided* right to use the entire property, not just a physically identifiable portion. In addition, the co-owners usually each have the right, in the event of a dispute, to have the property physically divided (partitioned), at which time concurrent ownership ends. If the nature of the property is such that it cannot be partitioned, a court may order it sold and the proceeds divided amongst the owners according to their respective shares.

Joint tenancy interests. The defining characteristic of property held in joint tenancy is that, upon death of one co-owner, the decedent's interest automatically passes to the surviving owner(s). The owners are said to hold title in *joint tenancy* or it may be said that they are *joint tenants*. Property law, developed as part of our common law, requires that the interests all be equal, and the owners' respective shares should not be stated as part of the title; thus, "Jim, John, and Jose, as joint tenants," not "Jim, John, and Jose, as joint tenants each owning a one-third share." Because tenants in common can own unequal shares, the share of each is usually expressed in the title; therefore the second statement, with the shares defined as "one-third", might result in a claim by the heirs of a deceased co-owner that tenants in common was actually intended and that the one-third interest belongs to them and not to the surviving co-owners.

Under joint tenancy, ownership passes to the surviving cotenants automatically at a cotenant's death by what is called *operation of law,* meaning that the law recognizes the transfer as immediate upon the cotenant's death without any action required by the survivors. However some authorities, such as banks, will require document revision in order to transact further business. A title company will want proof of the death of a joint tenant before it will issue title insurance should the survivors try to transfer title to someone else.

EXAMPLE 2 - 13. John and Mary own a house as joint tenants. At John's death, Mary automatically becomes the sole owner of the house. However, as a practical matter, she might have to record an affidavit establishing the death of a joint tenant, with a certified death certificate attached, in order to clear the title.

The automatic right of survivorship inherent in joint tenancy prevails over other means of transfers at death, including the will and the trust instrument.

EXAMPLE 2 - 14. Continuing the prior example, if, prior to his death, John had executed a will that left his one half interest in the house to his son, Mary would still receive it by right of survivorship. The joint tenancy designation supersedes the will.

However, in certain jurisdictions, agreements can be executed between joint owners to nullify a joint tenancy designation.

> EXAMPLE 2 - 15. Continuing prior examples, if John and Mary were to execute a written *agreement* stating that it is their intention that the house, presently held in joint tenancy, is in fact to be held by them as community property or as tenants in common (see description below), many jurisdictions will honor the agreement, and the house would not pass to Mary by automatic right of survivorship.

Joint tenancy interests in real estate are created by a written document called a deed. In most states, one cotenant can unilaterally "sever" the joint tenancy without the knowledge or consent of the other tenant(s).

> EXAMPLE 2 - 16. Oscar, Ray, Sam, and Clark own Green Acre Ranch as joint tenants. Without telling the other three, Sam deeds his interest to his friend Ed. Sam has broken the joint tenancy insofar as his interest in concerned. Ed owns a one-fourth interest as a tenant in common with the other three holding title to three-fourths as joint tenants. If Ray then dies, Oscar and Clark will own the three-fourths as joint tenants, and Ed will continue to own one-fourth. If Ed dies, his share will go to his heirs, not to the other co-owners.

Joint tenancies are commonly created among family members, as they are the most likely to appreciate the simplicity of this means of transfer and are least likely to be concerned that the ultimate owner of the property may be determined by who amongst them lives the longest.

Interests by the entirety. An *interest by the entirety* is like a joint tenancy in that it carries with it that key characteristic of joint tenancy, the right of survivorship; however, an interest by the entirety can be created only between husband and wife. Unlike joint tenancy, neither spouse may transfer or encumber the property without the consent of the other. Tenants by the entirety is a common law concept, generally not recognized in the community property states. In addition, a few of the common law states no longer recognize this form of ownership, and will treat an attempt to create it as merely joint tenancy. Where it is recognized, since it is available only to married couples, a divorce will cause a tenants by the entirety title to automatically transmute into a tenants in common form of title.

Tenants in common. Like joint tenancy, *tenants in common* are held by two or more persons, each having an undivided right to possess property. Unlike joint interests, however, interests in common may be owned in unequal percentages, and when one owner dies the remaining owners do not automatically succeed in ownership. Instead, the decedent's interest passes through his or her estate, by will or by the laws of intestate succession. The interest can also be transferred to the trustee of a trust and pass according to the provisions of the trust.

> EXAMPLE 2 - 17. Jack owns a 16 percent real estate interest in common with two other individuals who, combined, own the other 84 percent. Jack's will leaves his entire estate to his wife, Deanna. Upon Jack's death, his will determines who will get his interest, therefore, the 16 percent interest will pass by the probate process to his wife, Deanna, not to the other cotenants.

Interests in common are the title of choice for non-related parties since this form of title, in contrast to joint tenancy interests, creates a means of enjoying common ownership without any of the co-owners losing the right of disposition at death.

Community property interests. In the eight states recognizing it, *community property* is that property acquired by the efforts of either spouse during their marriage while living in a community property state, and such other property which by the agreement of the spouses is converted from separate property into community property. *Separate property* is all other property owned by the spouses (e.g., acquired by only one of the spouses by gift, devise, bequest or inheritance, or by a spouse domiciled in a common law state, or acquired by either spouse prior to their marriage). The traditional community property states are Arizona, California, Idaho, Louisiana, Nevada, New Mexico, Texas, and Washington. In addition, Wisconsin recently adopted a form of community property known as "marital property," based on the Uniform Marital Property Act (UMPA). Most of the community property states follow what is sometimes referred to as the California rule, which is that income from community property is community property, as is anything bought with it, and income from separate property is separate property, as is anything bought with it. Three community property states, Texas, Idaho, and Louisiana, treat income earned from separate property during the marriage as community property, however, even these three states treat the gain on separate property that is sold as separate property, and anything bought with the proceeds of the sale will continue to be separate property.

Community property is owned equally by both spouses. Generally, both spouses must consent to a gift of community property. Community property states allow couples to convert community property to separate property, and vice versa, although some states require a written agreement wherein the spouse whose interest is reduced acknowledges the fact that something has been lost. Separate property is considered entirely owned by the acquiring spouse. In states without community property provisions, of course, all property is separate property. In those states, it would simply be referred to as "the property owned by" Sam, Wanda, or whomever.

> EXAMPLE 2 - 18. Pat and Mary live in New Mexico, a community property state. When they married two years ago, Pat owned a sports car, that Mary now uses. Pat works as a shoe salesman and Mary as a bank teller. Last year Mary's father gave her 100 shares of XYZ stock, which pays a quarterly dividend. Mary used the last dividend check to buy a bicycle. Pat bought a rowboat from money saved from his July paycheck. The stock and bicycle are Mary's separate property. The car is Pat's separate property. All of the other assets, including both salaries, are community property. ***Query 2-2. If Louisiana was their home, what difference would it make insofar as property ownership goes?

Community property laws represent the attempt by certain state governments to impose greater fairness in property ownership by married couples. Under old English common law, the husband owned all property that either husband or wife acquired during their marriage. Even after most states recognized the right of married women to own property, during pre-World War II America, the husband typically earned most of the outside income while the wife performed the non income-producing household chores; therefore, husbands usually acquired title to almost all of the family wealth. At early common law, a wife was entitled to own none of this property until her husband's death, at which time she received a life estate in one-third of her husband's real property. Called a "dower" interest, it has been modified by most common law states; however, it seldom gives the non-working spouse the advantages inherent in the law of community property, which automatically gives both spouses an immediate equal share in all of the property acquired by their efforts during the course of their marriage.

Arizona, California, Idaho, Washington, and Wisconsin have a concept called *quasi-community property*, which is defined as that property, acquired by a resident while domiciled in a non-community property state, which would have been community property had the resident been domiciled in a community property state at the time of acquisition. For example, if a married couple moves to California owning common stock acquired with salary earned during the marriage while they were residents of New York, the stock is quasi-community property. Essentially, quasi-community property is treated as separate property of the acquiring spouse until divorce or death. If the parties divorce, the property is divided in a manner similar to community property. Treatment at death depends on which spouse dies first. If the acquiring spouse dies first, the surviving spouse is entitled to one half of the property. On the other hand, the non-acquiring spouse's rights to the property cease at his or her earlier death.

As different types of co-ownership of property, joint tenancy (JT) and community property (CP) have several major similarities and differences that are summarized in the outline below:

1. Major Similarities:
   a. Both involve ownership by more than one person.
   b. The owners have equal ownership rights and equal rights to use the entire property. Their interests are undivided.
   c. Any owner may demand a division of the property into separate, equal shares.
2. Major Differences:
   a. CP exists only between spouses. JT can exist between any two or more persons.
   b. CP rights arise automatically, by operation of law under state statute, even if title or possession is taken by just one of the spouses. Hence, CP is created immediately upon acquisition of the property. JT rights are usually created by an agreement of the parties (e.g., they ask that stock be issued in their names as joint tenants) and are not governmentally imposed.
   c. JT includes automatic right of succession to ownership (right of survivorship) by surviving joint owners. This right takes priority over any will. In contrast, CP includes no automatic succession to ownership of the decedent's share by the surviving spouse. Therefore, at death, a spouse can transfer his or her share of CP, by will, to someone other than the spouse. However, intestacy will ordinarily result in succession by the surviving spouse under most state laws of intestate succession.

d. Property held in JT will not be subject to the probate process. In contrast, the decedent's share of CP may be subject to probate. Some CP states no longer require a probate, if the property is left to the surviving spouse or if, because of intestacy, the surviving spouse will receive the property by the laws of intestate succession.

It is important to make two observations regarding item 2c: First, some states, such as New York, recognize an agreement between the spouses declaring that specified property is held in joint tenancy "for convenience only;" and second, Arizona, Idaho, Nevada, and Washington have enacted statutes that allow the designation "community property with right of survivorship." This results in the property being treated like joint tenancy in that the decedent spouse's will does not control disposition, and the property transfers to the surviving spouse by operation of law, meaning that there is no need for probate.

Legal versus Beneficial Interests: Introduction to the Trust

Usually, the owner of property has all the rights to possess and enjoy it; however, these interests can be divided such that one party has just the "bare legal title," responsible solely for preserving and managing property for the benefit of another, and the other is entitled to enjoy the property in specified ways. The former holds the *legal interest* while the latter holds a *beneficial interest*, also called an *equitable interest*, in the property. Trusts are the most common legal arrangement to employ this division.

There are three major parties to the trust: trustor, trustee, and beneficiary. The *trustor*, also called *grantor*, *creator*, or *settlor*, is the person who creates the trust, and whose property is used to *fund* the trust. The property held in a trust is called the *principal*, but also the *corpus,* the *res* (Latin for things), or the *trust estate*. The *trustee* is the person, persons, or entity (e.g., bank trust department) who takes legal title to the trust property and manages the trust estate. Usually the trust instrument names an initial trustee and several alternates. The trust *beneficiary* is the person or persons who are named to enjoy beneficial interest in the trust. Placing property in a trust is called *funding* the trust. Funding is accomplished by transferring title of the property into the name of the trustee. Figure 2-1 illustrates the relationship between the parties to the trust.

A trust can be *living* or *inter vivos*, meaning it is funded during the life of the trustor, or it can be *testamentary*, to take effect at the trustor's death with the funding mechanism being the probate process. A testamentary trust is one created by the trustor's will. An example of the provisions of a testamentary trust can be found in Chapter 3, Exhibit 3-3.

> EXAMPLE 2 - 19. On November 23, 1996, trustor Harold Stuart transferred 1,000 shares of ABC stock in trust to Uncle Jay as trustee, with the income payable to Harold's son, Chet, for 11 years, after which the corpus of the trust reverts to Harold. Jay receives only legal title which would probably read, "Jay Stuart, as trustee of the Chet Stuart Trust, dated 11/23/96." Jay is responsible for managing the property during the term of the trust. He can sell the stock and buy other investments in his name, as trustee, but he may not use trust assets for his own benefit, and he is required to distribute all income to Chet, the income beneficiary. Chet has a beneficial interest, that is, an estate for years in the income of the trust.

FIGURE 2 - 1   The Parties to a Trust

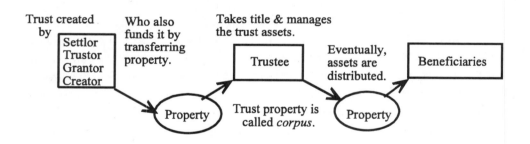

Reasons for creating trusts. Clients may wish to include trusts in their estate plans for five principal reasons: to provide for multiple beneficiaries, to manage their property if they become incapacitated, to protect beneficiaries from themselves and others, to avoid probate, and to avoid or reduce transfer taxes. Since these factors are discussed in detail in numerous sections of the text, the following commentary will be brief.

First, clients may wish to *leave their property to more than one person*, either at the same time or successively, over a period of time, and may need an arrangement that will fairly protect each beneficiaries' individual property rights.

EXAMPLE 2 - 20. After his death, Constantine wants to let his second wife enjoy the use of his property for the rest of her life. After her death, Constantine wants the income from his property to be payable to the children of his first marriage until they reach age 30, at which time he wants them to receive the principal outright. By executing a trust, Constantine can appoint a responsible trustee to manage the property for what may turn out to be a very long time. The trustee can be charged with preserving a proper balance between the differing interests of the beneficiaries.

A transfer into a trust is sometimes called a *split interest* transfer, because it divides rights to the corpus into two or more interests, usually an income interest for a specified period of years or for the beneficiary's life, and a "remainder" interest in the principal. Remainder interests will be described shortly and income versus principal interests will be covered a little later.

Second, clients may create trusts to *manage their property if they become incapacitated.* If, due to injury or old age, a person becomes unable to manage his or her property, who will do so? Upon petition, a court will appoint someone to manage the estate of a disabled person. Depending upon the jurisdiction, the court-appointed caretaker is called a *conservator* (i.e, one charged with "conserving" the disabled person's assets) or a *guardian* (i.e., one is "guarding" the person's interests). Some states use the term guardian for only minors and use the term conservator for adults (the person being cared for is called the *conservatee*). Other states use guardian whether the person cared for is a minor or an adult. In either case, the person caring for the estate must make annual reports to the court and, depending on the circumstances, may have to get court approval for certain expenditures or to sell certain assets.

EXAMPLE 2 - 21. Several years ago, Linda Smith created a *revocable living trust*, changing the title of all her property to read "Linda Smith, trustee of the Linda Smith Revocable Living Trust, dated March 19, 1998." The terms of the trust provide that if Linda becomes incapacitated during her lifetime, her brother Tom will become successor trustee. Linda has taken steps to prevent the need for expensive court procedures to determine who should be appointed guardian or conservator of her property if she becomes incapacitated before death.

Third, clients may wish to create trusts to *protect beneficiaries from themselves and others.*[3] As we shall see in the next chapter, trust documents typically contain provisions restricting use of the property by beneficiaries. For example, trust instruments often provide that the trustee's discretion will determine the amount and timing of distributions to beneficiaries. In addition, they often prohibit any beneficiary from pledging his or her interest in the trust property as collateral for a loan. Many other restrictions can be included.

Fourth, a trust that is funded during the trustor's lifetime allows the property that is placed in the trust to *avoid the probate process*. Trusts funded while the trustor is alive are called *living trusts*. Trusts can also be funded through the probate process, either by means of a *pourover will* (a will that has a previously established trust as its primary beneficiary) or by means of a *testamentary trust* (a will that incorporates a trust within the body of the will). The probate process and means of avoiding probate are discussed in much more detail in Chapter 10.

Fifth, clients may wish to use trusts to *avoid or reduce taxes*. On the inside front cover of the textbook is a table that shows the amount that can be passed tax free (meaning without the payment of gift or estate taxes). Note that for the year 2000 the exclusion amount (i.e., the tax free amount) is $675,000. In general, the exclusion amount has little relevance when property is transferred from one spouse to the other because there is a 100% marital deduction. The exclusion amount is really of concern when property passes to other family members, e.g., to the children. A fair amount of tax planning strategy revolves around using both parents' exclusion amounts while keeping the couple's combined estate intact for as long as either of them is alive. This is accomplished by keeping the estate of the first spouse to die held in trust for the benefit of the surviving spouse, with the children named as the remaindermen. By doing this, the trust estate is not merged with the surviving spouse's estate and both spouses' exclusion amounts are utilized. This text will have a great deal to say about tax planning using trusts after examining the taxation of gifts, estates, trusts, and beneficiaries in Chapters 5 through 7.

Power of Appointment

In arranging property transfers into trust or otherwise, clients can add considerable flexibility to their estate plans by granting a power of appointment. A *power of appointment* is a power to name someone to receive a beneficial interest in property. The grantor of the power is called the *donor*. The person receiving the power is called the *holder* or *donee*. The parties to whom the holder may appoint (i.e., give) property by *exercising* the power are called the *permissible appointees*, and the parties whom the holder actually appoints are called the *appointees*. In addition, the persons who receive the property if the holder permits the power to *lapse* (i.e., does not exercise the power within the permitted period) are called the *takers in default*. In some cases, the holder of a power of appointment can *release* the power by formally relinquishing the right to exercise the power.

Depending upon how it is written, a power of appointment can be exercisable either during the lifetime of the holder or at his or her death, or both during lifetime and at death. If exercisable during lifetime, it is exercisable either sometime during the holder's entire lifetime, or only for a stated period. A *testamentary* power is only exercisable at the holder's death, usually by a provision in the holder's will. The broadest powers allow the holder to exercise both during lifetime and at death.

> EXAMPLE 2 - 22. Assume that Dona grants Harold a power of appointment over her 100 shares of ABC stock, permitting Harold to appoint the stock to Anna, Bobby, or Carol, and designating Terry as the taker in default should Harold fail to appoint the stock within 90 days. Shortly thereafter, Harold appoints Bobby to receive the stock. Dona was the donor, Harold was the holder (of the power), Anna, Bobby, and Carol were the permissible appointees, and Bobby was the actual appointee (of the stock). Terry, the taker in default, didn't get to "take" because the holder did not permit the power to lapse.

Powers of appointment are most often established within the framework of a trust. Figure 2-2 illustrates the relationship between the parties involved in the power of appointment.

FIGURE 2 - 2   The Parties to a Power of Appointment

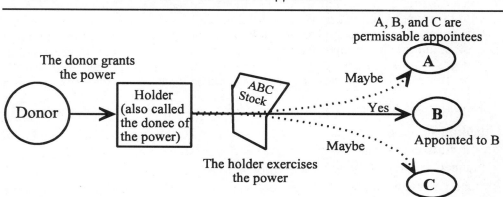

Comparing the relationship between the parties to a power of appointment with the parties to a trust, the donor of the power is usually the trustor. The holder is commonly the trustee but may also be one or more beneficiaries or a trusted friend of the trustor. The permissible appointees are usually the trust's beneficiaries. Trustee powers of appointment may be over trust income, principal, or both income and principal. Trustees may also be granted the power to *distribute income* amongst a group of beneficiaries, which is referred to as "sprinkling the income" of the trust. Where the trustee has this discretion, the trust is referred to as a "sprinkling trust." Almost humorously (we estate planners are always looking for a good laugh), the term "spray" is sometimes used to describe a trust clause that gives the trustee discretion to *distribute principal* in different amounts among permissible beneficiaries. Trust powers of appointment are extremely important estate planning tools, and will be discussed frequently in this book.

In the chapter on estate taxes, we shall see that death taxes play an important role in the use of powers of appointment—so much so that we commonly classify two types of powers using Internal Revenue Code classifications. Under the Code, a power of appointment is either a *general* power of appointment or a *non-general* power of appointment, also called a *limited* or *special* power of appointment. We'll define these terms in greater detail when we start working on estate taxes, noting how the wording of a power can cause property to be included in the holder's estate. The next example shows a common use of a power of appointment.

> EXAMPLE 2 - 23. Charles, a single parent, died recently, and his will placed some of his property in trust for the benefit of his children. A bank is named trustee and is given a non-general power of appointment over the corpus. The bank has, among other things, discretion to distribute corpus to the children in accordance with their needs "for their proper support, health, and education." This year, the trustee has distributed $6,000 to one son and $4,000 to a daughter to pay their college tuition.

Powers of appointment add great flexibility to a client's estate plan by enabling someone to direct trust dispositions after taking into account changes in circumstances that occur long after the trustor's death. This flexibility is enhanced by a widely accepted rule of local property law, under which the property subject to a power of appointment is not considered legally owned by the holder, rather, the holder is simply treated as an agent for the donor. As

Chapter 6 explains, however, federal tax law is not nearly so indulgent. If the power is a general one, it is treated as if the holder owned it.

Present versus Future Interests and Vested versus Contingent Interests

A beneficial interest in property may be classified as a present interest or a future interest, depending upon whether or not the owner has the immediate right to possess or enjoy the property. We shall see later that this distinction is of great importance in connection with the $10,000 annual gift tax exclusion.

An owner of a *present interest* has an immediate right to possess or enjoy the property while an owner of a *future interest* does not, because the latter's right to possess or enjoy the property is delayed, either by a specific period of time or until the happening of a future event. The most common types of future interests are reversions and remainders. A *reversion* is a future interest in property that is retained by the transferor after the transferor transfers to another some interest in the property. The reversion will become a present interest of the transferor, or the transferor's estate, at the termination of all interests that were transferred.

> EXAMPLE 2 - 24.   Jerry transfers property to Eve for her life. It will become Jerry's (or his estate's) present interest at Eve's death. By not designating a remainderman, Jerry has implicitly retained a reversion, also called a reversionary interest.

Technically, a *remainder* is the right to use, possess, and enjoy property after all prior owners' interests end, and all interests must have been created at the same time by a single document. It is a type of future interest held by someone other than the transferor and it will become a present interest when all other interests have ended. The preceding definition of remainder is unnecessarily technical for our purposes, because most remainders in estate planning are quite simple. In estate planning, remainders usually arise in the context of trusts, where the remainderman is entitled to the remaining trust assets at the termination of the trust. In many, if not most, trust situations, the remaindermen are the settlors' children or grandchildren, who will receive the remainder at the death of both settlors (usually a married couple) who are likely to have retained joint life estates in a revocable trust. In some of these estate plans, the trust changes at the death of one spouse into several trusts, including one or more irrevocable trusts.

Where multiple trusts are formed at the death of one spouse, the survivor usually has a life estate in all of the trusts, even any that are irrevocable, and the children wait as remaindermen until the surviving spouse dies.

> EXAMPLE 2 - 25. George irrevocably transfers property to Sally for her life, then to John or his estate. John's future interest in the property is a remainder. It is not a reversion because it does not return to George.

A *vested remainder* is a remainder that is non-forfeitable; it is a remainder whose possession and enjoyment are delayed *only by time*, and are not dependent upon the happening (or not happening) of any future event.

> EXAMPLE 2 - 26. With regard to the transfer by George in the previous example, John's remainder is vested. Nothing prevents him or his estate from receiving possession, except the passage of time. Morbidly but accurately speaking, eventually Sally will die.

A *contingent remainder* is a remainder that is not vested; that is, it is a remainder whose possession and enjoyment are dependent upon the happening of a future event, not on just the passage of time.

> EXAMPLE 2 - 27. Catherine transfers property to Flo for her life, then outright in fee simple to Jason, if alive, otherwise to Chris, if alive, and if not, then it reverts to Catherine. Jason and Chris each have a contingent remainder interest in the property and Catherine has a contingent reversionary interest. If Jason outlives Flo, the property is his; Chris is next in line if Jason doesn't make it; and finally, Catherine, or her estate, will get the property back, if neither Jason nor Chris lives.

Totten Trusts. The *Totten trust* is not really a trust at all, but rather is a bank account that is payable to another upon the death of the account owner. It got its names from a case in which the court decided in favor of the designated other person, over the claim of the decedent's executor. This mechanism of transferring a bank account at the death of the owner is recognized in most, but not all, states. Title is likely to read, "Jane Smith, in trust for Michael Smith," or "Jane Smith, payable upon her death to Michael Smith." In either case, Michael's interest does not vest until Jane dies. Indeed, in spite of the use of the words, "in trust for," there is no trustee and neither Jane nor the financial institution have a fiduciary responsibility to Michael. Jane may withdraw all of the funds or she may change title without Michael ever knowing that the account existed. Once

Jane dies, Michael would be able to claim the account by presenting a certified death certificate.

A few more examples, presented in the context of common transfer devices, should help to clarify the distinctions discussed above.

> EXAMPLE 2 - 28. When Gary died, his will created a trust funded with his entire estate. The terms of the trust give income to his wife, Joan, for her life. At Joan's death, the trust terminates and the property passes outright in fee to Gary's son Max, if still alive, otherwise to the Salvation Army. At Gary's death, Joan received a present interest called a life estate in the income, and Max and the Salvation Army each received a future interest, called a contingent remainder. Max and the Salvation Army share something in common; only one of the interests can ever become a present interest, since an event will occur which will defeat one or the other interest. Max's interest will cease if he predeceases Joan. The Salvation Army's interest will cease if Max survives Joan. Therefore, both have contingent remainder interests because possession is dependent upon the happening of a future event, not on just the mere passage of time.

> EXAMPLE 2 - 29. Sam left property in trust, giving his wife, June, income for life with the remainder going to Sam's son, Kurt, or Kurt's estate. Kurt has a vested remainder in the property. Although initially a future interest, it is certain that it will become a present interest someday; it cannot be defeated. Only the passage of time keeps Kurt's interest from being a present interest. Of course, Kurt may not be alive to enjoy the property, but the beneficiaries of his estate will.

We have seen that the transfer of property in trust results in a division into two interests, with the trustee receiving the legal interest and the beneficiaries receiving the beneficial interests. In addition, transfers into trust typically result in a second type of division of interests when the beneficial interests are split among two or more beneficiaries. Ordinarily, one group of beneficiaries, called the *income beneficiaries,* receive a life estate or estate for years in the trust income, while the other group, called the *remaindermen*, receive the remainder at the termination of the income interests. The many reasons for splitting beneficial interests into a life estate, or into an estate for years and a remainder, will be explained in later chapters. At present, the reader should simply be aware of the interest-splitting nature of the trust. You should recognize that, at the time of the transfer into the trust, the life estate and estate for years are usually, but not always, present vested interests; the remainder is a future interest, either vested or contingent.

Mathematics of Remainders, Reversions and Income Interests

The previous section described the nature of remainders, reversions, life estates, and interests for years. These concepts are important to understanding later chapters, because many common estate planning techniques require their creation.

Up to now, the description of these interests has been qualitative rather than quantitative. Estate planning is inherently "numbers oriented" for two principal reasons. First, estate planning decisions often have a sizable impact on *family wealth*, and clients want to discuss that effect with the planner. Second, property transfer decisions often have *tax consequences* that must be projected and evaluated.

Thus, it is important to understand the quantitative nature of remainders, reversions, life estates, and interests for years. This section demonstrates how they are calculated.

Overview of IRS valuation tables. The calculations can be most easily performed with the help of tables published by the Internal Revenue Service. The Service's complete "Alpha" volume runs 800 pages and costs about $32.00.[4] It includes six different tables and lists tens of thousands of values, most of which are derived from discount rates ranging from 2.2 percent to 26 percent, at two tenths of one percentage point intervals. This conforms precisely with Internal Revenue Code valuation rules, often requiring the use of a current monthly discount rate that is equal to 120 percent of what is called the "applicable federal mid-term rate" (AFMR), which, in turn, is derived from the average market yield on U.S. Treasury obligations with maturities of three to nine years.[5] The rate, often referred to as the §7520 rate, has been rounded to the nearest two tenths of a percentage. Since these rates are published monthly by the Treasury Department, you do not have to figure out the rate. If a rate is given in an example or in problems at the end of the chapters, use that rate to determine the appropriate table to use (do not multiply it by 120%, as that has already been done).

For obvious practical reasons, this text cannot include all pages from the IRS volume but reproduces many of the most useful ones. Appendix A includes part of IRS Tables "S," "B," "K," and "80CNSMT," the four most commonly used tables in estate planning. Appendix Table S and Table B are abridged to list a sampling of present value factors for discount rates of 6, 8, 10, and 12%. Table K gives adjustment factors where payments are made other than annually. Tables

S and B assume an annual payment, with the first payment at the end of the first year. We will be using the actuarial factors in examples and problems as they are especially helpful in the *planning* stage, when estimates are useful in calculating the values of life estates, remainders, and the like. Table 80CNSMT is a one page mortality table, useful for valuing interests that are contingent upon survival.

The following series of examples will illustrate the use of these four tables for the valuation of four basic property interests: remainders, reversions, annuities for life, and annuities for a *term certain*. The discussion makes it clear that the choice of table for a particular problem depends in part upon whether the interest to be valued is predicated on the fact that someone will be paid either all income or a fixed annuity (1) for a fixed number of years, or (2) for life. All examples will assume, unless otherwise stated, that the appropriate rate is 10%, payments are annual, and that the first payment is at the end of the first year.

Valuations predicated on income for term certain: IRS Table B. Each of the first four examples show the value of an income interest that is for a *fixed period of time*, also called a *term certain*.

Valuation of income for term certain. We use IRS Table B to determine the value of a beneficiary's income interest for a term certain. The term is usually given as a certain number of years.

EXAMPLE 2 - 30. Today Dana creates an irrevocable trust, transferring $200,000 in property to the trustee. The trustee is required to distribute annually all income earned from the property to Harry (or his heirs) for a period of ten years. Then, the trust terminates, and all trust principal will be distributed to Stephen (or his heirs). The current value of Harry's ten year annuity for a term certain is calculated as follows: Using Table B (10%), the income interest factor for 10 years is 0.614457. Thus, the current value of Harry's income interest is $122,891 [$200,000 * 0.614457].

Valuation of vested remainder after income for term certain. Similarly, IRS Table B allows us to determine what portion of the property's total value should be allocated to a beneficiary's vested remainder interest that follows someone else's income interest for a definite period of time (i.e., after "term certain").

EXAMPLE 2 - 31. Continuing as in the previous example, the current value of Stephen's vested remainder interest can be calculated starting with the same table. The remainder factor found in Table B (10%) corresponding to 10 years is 0.385543. Thus, the present value of his vested remainder interest is $77,109 [$200,000 * 0.385543].

In the previous two examples, since Harry's and Stephen's interests represent the only two interests in the trust assets, it is logical that the sum of their initial values should total $200,000, the initial value of the trust principal. And for the same reason, it is also logical that the sum of the two table values should add up to one. Consequently, each table value can be determined in a slightly different way. If one value is known, the other can be determined by simply subtracting the known value from 1.0. Thus, the table value for Stephen's interest, 0.385543, could have been calculated by subtracting the table value for Harry's interest, 0.614457 from the number 1.0; or, the remainder value could have been determined by subtracting the value of the income interest from the value of the whole trust ($200,000 - $122,891 = $77,109).

Valuation of reversion. Reversions are calculated in the same way as remainders.

> EXAMPLE 2 - 32.   Revising the terms of the trust in the above ongoing example, assume that at the end of 10 years, the trust will terminate and trust principal will be distributed back to the trustor, Dana (or her heirs). The initial value of Dana's *reversion*, $77,109, is exactly equal to the value of Stephen's remainder, calculated using Table B (10%).

Valuation of remainder (after term certain) contingent upon survival. A remainder after a term certain that is contingent on the remainderman's survival of the term is calculated by multiplying the value of the vested remainder by the probability of the remainderman being alive at the end of the trust. IRS mortality Table 80CNSMT, reprinted in Appendix A, shows the number of people expected to be living at each age based upon statistics for the 1980 census. For example, out of 100,000 people born alive (age 0 = birth), only 94,926 of them are expected to be alive at age 40. Calculating the probability of a person age x surviving to age y involves simply dividing the number of people alive at age y by the number alive at age x. Thus, the probability of a newborn reaching the age of 40 is 0.94926 [94,926 ÷ 100,000].

> EXAMPLE 2 - 33.   Revising the facts again in this ongoing example, assume that Stephen is currently age 40, that his remainder is contingent upon his surviving the ten year period, and that if he fails to survive, the trust principal will pass to someone else. The probability of Stephen surviving to age 50 is calculated, using Table 80CNSMT, by dividing 91,526 (the number alive at age 50) by 94,926 (the

number alive at age 40). This quotient equals 0.964183. Thus, the value of Stephen's *contingent remainder* is $74,347 [0.964183 x $77,109].

Valuation of annuity for term certain. Now, consider a new example in which the annual annuity payment for a term certain is known.

> EXAMPLE 2 - 34. A trust provides for an annual distribution to Brett of $4,000 per year for 15 years, with the first payment to be made exactly one year after the trust is established. The current value of Brett's 15 year annuity interest is calculated in the following manner: Using IRS Table B (10%), the annuity value corresponding to 15 years is 7.6061. Thus, the current value of Brett's annuity interest is $30,424 [$4,000 x 7.6061]. The values in the annuity column are simply the present value factors for an annuity of $1.

All of the calculations in the above examples in some way involve an income interest or an annuity for a fixed number of years. The next section deals with examples involving a different inherent property interest: an income interest or an annuity for life.

Valuations predicated on income interest for life: IRS Table S. Each of the next three examples demonstrates the calculation of the value of an income interest that is for someone's lifetime. For these calculations, we must use IRS Table S for the appropriate interest rate (see Appendix A).

Valuation of life estate. IRS Table S indicates what portion of a property's total value is reflected in the value of a beneficiary's income or annuity interest for life. The regulations do not allow the use of Table S where the person with the measuring life (e.g., the person with a life estate) is terminally ill at the time the interest is being valued. The regulations define terminal illness as "an incurable illness or other deteriorating physical condition...if there is at least a 50 percent probability that the individual will die within 1 year." However, if the person actually lives 18 months or longer, there is a presumption that the person was not terminally ill, unless the contrary is established by clear and convincing evidence.[6] In the examples that follow, unless stated to the contrary, we will assume that the person was not terminally ill, and that Table S could be used to value the interests.

> EXAMPLE 2 - 35. This year Martha creates a trust and funds it with assets that have a value of $100,000. The trust provides Charles, age 50, with a life estate. At Charles's death, distribution of the remainder is to be made to Samuel (or his heirs). The current value of Charles's life estate is calculated as follows: Using IRS Table

S (10%), the "life estate" value corresponding to age 50 is 0.86818. Thus, the current value of Charles's life estate interest is $86,818 [$100,000 x 0.86818].

Valuation of vested remainder after life estate. Similarly, IRS Table S indicates what portion of a trust's total value should be allocated to a beneficiary's vested remainder after the termination of an annuity for life.

> EXAMPLE 2 - 36. Continuing the previous example, the current value of Samuel's remainder interest is determined from the same table. For 10%, the "remainder" value corresponding to age 50 is 0.13182. Thus the current value of Samuel's vested remainder interest is $13,182 [$100,000 x 0.13182].

Similar to the earlier discussion, since Charles's and Samuel's interests represent the only two interests in the trust assets, it is logical that the sum of their current values should total $100,000, the current total value of the trust principal. And again, for the same reason, the sum of the two table values add up to one. Finally, we can determine each of the table values by subtracting the known table value from the number one.

Valuation of reversion after life estate. As with reversions after an income interest or an annuity interest for a term certain, reversions after a life estate are calculated in exactly the same manner as remainders.

Valuation of annuity for life. Now consider a different example in which the annuity payment is fixed as a specific dollar amount.

> EXAMPLE 2 - 37. Muhammad, age 40, is the beneficiary of a testamentary trust which is required to pay him $10,000 per year for life, with the first payment to be made in exactly one year. Again, using IRS Table S (10%), the "annuity" value corresponding to age 40 is 9.2945.[7] Thus, the current value of this life estate is $92,945 [$10,000 x 9.2945]. If the payments were to be made monthly (instead of annually) with the first payment at the end of the first month we would have to use Table K as well. The factor from Table K for a monthly payment (and a 10% rate) is 1.0450, hence the value would be $97,128 [$92,945 * 1.0450].

These IRS tables will be used to value property interests in several sections of the text, covering such estate planning techniques as annual exclusion gifts (Chapter 7), minor's income trusts (Chapter 13), private annuities (Chapter 14), and charitable remainder trusts (Chapter 14).

OVERVIEW OF GOALS IN ESTATE PLANNING

Finally, let's summarize the major goals of estate planning. These goals, outlined below, are described in detail in Chapter 9 as an overview of the specific techniques detailed in Chapters 10 through 18.

A. Nonfinancial Goals
  1. Caring for future dependents.
  2. Accomplishing fair and proper distribution of property.
  3. Attaining privacy in the property transfer process.
  4. Attaining speed in the property transfer process.
  5. Maintaining control over assets.
B. Financial Goals
  1. Non-tax financial goals
     a. Minimizing non-tax estate transfer costs.
     b. Maintaining a satisfactory standard of living.
     c. Ensuring proper disposition by careful drafting.
     d. Preserving business value.
     e. Attaining pre- and postmortem flexibility.
     f. Maximizing benefits for the surviving spouse.
  2. Tax saving goals
     a. Income tax saving goals
        1) Obtaining a stepped-up basis.
        2) Shifting income to a lower bracket taxpayer.
        3) Deferring recognition of income.
     b. Transfer tax saving goals and planning
        1) Reducing the estate tax value.
        2) Freezing the estate tax value.
        3) Leveraging the use of exclusions, exemptions, and credits.
        4) Delaying payment of the transfer tax.
        5) Minimizing the generation-skipping transfer tax.

The next chapter will apply many of the concepts introduced in this chapter to describe the provisions of the major documents utilized in the property transfer process.

IMPORTANT CONCEPTS AND TERMS COVERED IN THIS CHAPTER

Estate
Property
Probate estate
Gross estate
Taxable estate
Transfer
Assignment
Transferor and Transferee
Legal interest
Beneficial interest
Transfer
Outright gift
Complete (transfer)
Irrevocable (transfer)
Incomplete (transfer)
Revocable (transfer)
Interest in property
Partially complete (transfer)
Sale
Consideration
Gift
Bargain sale
Inter vivos
Instrument
Beneficiary
Donee
Donor
Decedent
Will
Testamentary
Executed
Testator
Trust
Intestate
Testate
Partially intestate
Probate
Personal representative
Fiduciary
Executor

Administrator
Heir
Devisee
Legatee
Legacy
Issue
Descendant
Specific bequest
Ademption
General bequest
Pecuniary bequest
Residuary bequest
Residue
Class gift
Abatement
Disclaimer
Life insurance
Insured
Term life insurance
Level term life insurance
Cash surrender value
Cash value life insurance
Unified transfer tax
Gift tax
Death tax
Inheritance tax
Estate tax
Generation-skipping
  transfer tax
Fee simple
Life estate
Measuring life
Interest for years
Leasehold
Real property
Personal property
Tangible personal property
Intangible personal property
Chose in action
Concurrent ownership

Joint interest
Joint tenancy
Interest by the entirety
Tenants in common
Community property
Separate property
Trust
Trustor, grantor, creator
  or settlor
Trust principal or corpus
Trustee
Trust beneficiary
Living trust
Testamentary trust
  or trust-will
Totten trust
Power of appointment
Donor or creator (of a power)
Holder or donee (of a power)
Permissible appointee
Appointee
Exercise (a power)
Release (a power)
Lapse (of a power)
Taker in default
Present interest
Future interest
Reversion
Remainder
Vested remainder
Contingent remainder
Income beneficiary
Remainderman

QUERIES ANSWERED:

1. Since Florida is a "pick-up tax" state, its death taxes equal the federal state death tax credit of $391,600. Thus, for a $5 million dollar taxable estate, the total taxes in Florida would be $2,170,250 [$391,600 + $1,778,650].

2. The bicycle would be community property because, like Texas and Idaho, Louisiana treats income from separate property as community property.

QUESTIONS AND PROBLEMS

1. Describe four different meanings of the concept "estate."

2. (a) Contrast a legal interest from a beneficial interest. (b) Why might a person want to transfer such interests in the same property to different individuals, rather than outright to one person?

3. Kasner "sells" a $10,000 car to his son for $4,000. Technically speaking, is this a sale or a gift? Why?

4. One of your clients shows you the following clipping from a trade journal:

"John Smith, the prominent local celebrity, died on Thursday. His generosity was legendary. Last year, he made a large *outright inter vivos gift* to his alma mater and to another charitable *donee*. In addition, in a lengthy handwritten *will executed* last year, the *decedent* made several large *general bequests* and *specific devises* to the local orphans' fund, including a *transfer* into a *testamentary trust*. Finally, as *holder* of a *power of appointment* over several parcels of land on the outskirts of town, Smith *exercised* the power in favor of several *permissible appointees*, one of whom is a grandson of the *donor*. To the surprise of almost everyone in the family, two *appointees* refused some of the gifts by exercising valid *disclaimers*. And strangely, no *residuary bequest* was included in the will, which means that the *testator* died *intestate* with regard to a considerable portion of his *estate*. Smith nominated as *executor* of his *probate* estate several of his surviving *issue*."

Explain to your client the meaning of each highlighted word.

5. (a) What is probate? (b) What types of assets are subject to probate administration? (c) What types of assets are not subject to probate? (d) Does having a will avoid probate?

6. Contrast the insured, the owner, and the beneficiary of a life insurance policy.

7. At the moment of Lou's death, a life insurance policy was in force in the amount of $250,000, which had a cash surrender value of $60,000. Lou had the power under the policy to change the beneficiary. After Lou's death, his wife, Mary, received a check from the insurance company.

    a. Explain who were the likely parties to this policy:
       1. Insured
       2. Beneficiary
       3. Owner
    b. Did Lou's wife receive $60,000, $190,000, $250,000, or $310,000? Why?
    c. Why will this policy likely help in estate planning for Lou's family?

8. (a) Why is a fee simple interest greater than a life estate or an interest for years? (b) Can you think of any sense in which all three interests can be considered nearly equal?

9. Compare and contrast joint tenancy with tenants in common.

10. Beth tells you that she has a property interest having all of the following characteristics: concurrent ownership with two of her friends, automatic right of succession to ownership, and all three owners are allowed to own unequal percentages. Why must she be mistaken? Explain.

11. Define community property and separate property.

12. Compare community property with joint tenancy.

13. Cindy and Dennis, residents of a community property state, were married in 1995. At that time, they each owned a car and some furnishings. Since then Dennis has been working full-time and Cindy has been working as the mother and homemaker. In 1997, Dennis was given 100 shares of IBM stock. In 1998, Cindy inherited her father's computer. This year, Dennis put one half of a year's salary as down-payment on a house for his family. Making your own assumptions when necessary, identify the community property and the separate property.

14. Continuing the problem immediately above, suppose Dennis paid the down payment on the house with dividend income from the IBM stock, but the house payments were made from Dennis's salary. Is the house community property, separate property, or part community and part separate property?

15. One day your client, Pedro Espinosa, asks you "Why do estate planners recommend trusts?" Briefly answer his question.

16. If you are the holder of a power of appointment, how might you be assisting in the donor's estate plan?

17. Contrast a present interest with a future interest.

18. (a) If Cheryl named Paul today to be the remainder beneficiary of her probate avoiding trust, is Paul's interest most likely a present or future interest? (b) If future, is it most likely to be a vested or contingent one? (c) If contingent, when will it vest, if ever? Explain each answer carefully.

19. Edward transfers $300,000 to an irrevocable trust. The trust terms provide that all income will be payable annually to his son Dale (or to his heirs) for a period of 20 years. At the end of that period, the trust will terminate and all corpus will be distributed to grandson Kevin, age 14 (or to his estate). (a) At a rate of 8%, calculate the current value of Dale's and Kevin's property interests. (b) Recalculate Kevin's remainder interest if it was contingent upon his surviving the income period.

20. Roberta died recently, leaving $500,000 in trust. Roberta's husband Mo, age 65, will receive a life estate in all of the income, payable annually. At his death, all principal will pass outright to Roberta's daughter Sherrie (or her estate). (a) At a rate of 6%, calculate the current value of Mo's and Sherrie's property interests. (b) Also, calculate the values at 12 %. (c) Comment on the influence of a higher discount rate.

21. Thomas Smith, age 30, is beneficiary of a trust which will pay him $3,500 a year for life. At 12%, calculate the current value of this life estate.

ANSWERS TO QUESTIONS AND PROBLEMS

1. Four different meanings of *estate*:

   a. Estate: A quantity of wealth or property.
   b. Net Estate: Property owned reduced by the estate owner's liabilities.
   c. Probate Estate: Property passing through the probate process.
   d. Gross Estate and Taxable Estate: Property subject to death taxation.

2. a. Legal Interest: Ownership of bare legal title. Beneficial interest: Ownership of an economic benefit.

   b. A person might want to transfer legal and beneficial interests to different individuals for any of the following reasons:

      1. To provide for multiple beneficiaries.
      2. To have their property managed for them if they become incapacitated.
      3. To protect beneficiaries from themselves.
      4. To avoid or reduce taxes.

3. Kasner has undertaken a *bargain sale*, which is a hybrid of gift and sale but is commonly classified as a gift. While a sale is a transfer in exchange for full consideration, a gift (and a bargain sale) is a transfer for *less than* full and adequate consideration.

4. Terms from the article:

   ▸ "Outright": subject to no restrictions or conditions; the transferee receives both legal interest and all beneficial interests in the property.
   ▸ "Inter vivos": during the transferor's lifetime.
   ▸ "Gifts": transfers for less than full consideration.
   ▸ "Donee": a person who is receiving or will receive a gift of a beneficial interest in property.
   ▸ "Will": a written document disposing of a person's probate property at death.
   ▸ "Executed": completed, that is, signed in the presence of witnesses. More generally, to execute is to do what is necessary to render the document valid.

- ▶ "Decedent": a person who has died.
- ▶ "General bequests": gifts payable out of the general assets of the estate, but not ones that specify one or more particular items.
- ▶ "Specific devises": gifts of specific real property.
- ▶ "Transfer": the passing of property where the transferor gives up some kind of interest to the transferee.
- ▶ "Testamentary trust": a trust that takes effect at the death of the trustor.
- ▶ "Holder" (of a power of appointment): the person receiving the power.
- ▶ "Power of appointment": a power to name someone to receive a beneficial interest in property.
- ▶ "Exercised": invoked the power by appointing a permissible appointee.
- ▶ "Permissible appointees": the parties whom the holder may appoint by exercising the power.
- ▶ "Donor": a person making a gift.
- ▶ "Appointees": the parties whom the holder actually appoints.
- ▶ "Disclaimer": An unqualified refusal to accept a gift.
- ▶ "Residuary bequest": a gift of that part of the testator's estate not otherwise disposed of by will.
- ▶ "Testator": the person who executed a will.
- ▶ "Intestate": Having died leaving property not disposed of by a valid will.
- ▶ "Estate": the decedent's property owned at death.
- ▶ "Executor": a personal representative who was nominated in the will.
- ▶ "Probate": the court process of administering the estate of a decedent.
- ▶ "Issue": a person's direct descendants.

5. a. Modern usage: the entire court process which oversees the transfer of assets after a person dies. It is intended to protect estate beneficiaries and creditors.

   b. Assets subject to probate administration fall into one of three groups: property owned by the decedent as an individual, interests of the decedent held in common with others, and, in community property states, the decedent's one half interest in community property.

   c. Assets not subject to probate administration are those for which some other mechanism of transfer is legally recognized as controlling. This includes property held in trusts and in joint tenancy, most insurance policies on the life of the decedent (unless payable to his or her estate), and most retirement plan assets.

d. Having a will does not avoid probate. The will acts as a guide for distribution rather than having intestate succession control.

6.   *Insured:* the subject of the insurance; that is, the one whose death triggers payment of the proceeds.
Owner: usually the possessor of both legal and beneficial interests in the policy. Commonly held "incidents" of ownership include the right to dividends, to surrender the policy, to pledge the policy, and to change the beneficiary.
Beneficiary: the person who is named to receive the proceeds.

7. a.   1. *Insured:* Lou, because his death apparently triggered the payment of the policy proceeds.
    2. *Beneficiary:* Lou's wife, who received the proceeds.
    3. *Owner:* Probably Lou-- he had the power to change the beneficiary and, presumably owned the other rights as well.
  b. Lou's wife received $250,000. With most cash value policies, the cash value disappears as an economic benefit at the insured's death.
  c. This policy will likely help in estate planning for Lou's family to help pay for death taxes and other cash obligations arising at Lou's death. Death often triggers *obligations*, and, with the ownership of life insurance, it can also trigger the *liquidity* to cover these obligations.

8. a.   A fee simple interest is greater than a life estate or an estate for years because a fee simple interest does not cease after the passage of time or the happening of a future event.
  b. All three interests can be considered equal in that while the owners enjoy them, they have virtually the same right to use them. Of course, only the fee owner can freely act to destroy or modify the nature of the property.

9. Joint tenancy (JT) and tenancy in common (TIC) contrasted:

Differences:
    a. JT: equal ownership; TIC: can be unequal.
    b. JT: automatic survivorship; TIC: no automatic survivorship.

Similarities:
   a. both held by two or more persons.
   b. both involve an undivided right to possess the property.

10. No valid type of property ownership includes all three characteristics that are described by Beth. Joint tenancies and tenancies by the entirety both require equal percentage ownership. Tenancy in common does not include automatic right of succession to ownership.

11. *Community property* is any property acquired by the efforts of either spouse during the marriage while domiciled in a community property state. It also includes any property which by agreement of the couple they convert from separate into community. Some states require said conversion to be in writing. Excluded is property acquired by gift, devise, bequest or inheritance, and the income from separate property. Texas, Idaho, and Louisiana treat income from separate property as community property.

   Separate property is defined as any property that is not community property, i.e., all property acquired by a person not during marriage, or during marriage in a common law state, and property acquired during a marriage by gift, devise, bequest or inheritance, or often, income earned on property so acquired.

12. Community property vs. joint tenancy interests:

   Major similarities:
   a. Ownership by more than one person.
   b. Owners have equal ownership rights which are undivided, i.e., exercisable over the entire property.
   c. Any owner may demand a division of the property into separate, equal shares.

   Major differences:
   a. CP exists only between spouses. JT can exist between any two or more persons.
   b. CP rights arise automatically (i.e., by operation of law).

    c. JT includes automatic right of succession to ownership by surviving joint owners, a right that takes priority over the will. CP does not, which means that CP can be disposed of by will.

13. Community property: house and salary. Acquired during the marriage, not by gift, inheritance, or the income therefrom.

   Separate property: the cars, the furnishings, IBM stock, computer. Either acquired before the marriage, or during the marriage by gift or inheritance.

14. In most community property states, the house would be part community, part separate, because it was acquired partly with community property and partly with separate property. However, in Texas, Idaho and Louisiana, it would be entirely community property.

15. Estate planners recommend trusts for many reasons, which can be reduced to four major ones: to provide for multiple beneficiaries, to manage the clients' property if they become incapacitated, to protect beneficiaries from their imprudence, and to avoid or reduce taxes. This text will have a lot to say about the use of trusts to meet client goals.

16. By acting as the holder of a power of appointment, you might be assisting in the donor's estate plan in several ways, including making gifting decisions on behalf of the donor (of the power) for possibly a period of many years after the donor's death. Later in the text, students will learn that a power of appointment holder is one type of *surrogate decision maker*.

17. The owner of a present interest has an immediate right to possess or enjoy the property, while the owner of a future interest does not, because possession or enjoyment is delayed, solely in time, or until the happening of a future event.

18. a. Paul would have a future interest, because possession or enjoyment is delayed until Cheryl's death.
   b. Paul's interest is contingent because possession or enjoyment is dependent upon the happening of a future event, rather than merely the passage of time. The event is Cheryl's death occurring without changing the terms of her will and, possibly, Paul surviving Cheryl.

c. Paul's interest will vest at Cheryl's death. Note: If the bequest is "to Paul or his estate," then his or his estate's interest would vest at Cheryl's death, even if Paul predeceases her.

19. a. Dale's interest:

Using IRS Table B (8%), the appropriate factor corresponding to a 20 year income interest is 0.785452. Thus, Dale's interest is worth $235,636 [$300,000 x 0.785452]. This assumes that the first income distribution will be made exactly one year from now.

Kevin's (vested) interest: One method of calculating it: Using the same table, at 8% the appropriate "remainder" corresponding to 20 years is 0.214548. Thus, Kevin's interest is currently worth $64,364 [$300,000 x 0.214548].

Another way: Subtract Dale's table value from 1.0: Thus, 1.0 - 0.785452 = 0.214548. Then perform the same multiplication as in the first method or simply subtract Dale's interest from the value of the trust as a whole: $300,000 - $235,636 = $64,364.

b. Recalculation of Kevin's remainder interest if it were contingent upon his surviving the income period: Kevin's probability of surviving to age 34 is expressed by the fraction 95951/98248, which is the ratio of the number alive at age 34 to the number alive at age 14. Thus, the value of Kevin's contingent remainder interest is $62,860 [$64,364 * (95951/98248)].

20. a. At 6%:

Mo's interest: Using IRS Table S (6%) the appropriate "income interest" corresponding to age 65 is 0.56599. Thus, Mo's interest is currently worth $282,995 [$500,000 x 0.56599]. This assumes that the first income distribution will be made exactly one year from now.

Sherrie's interest: One method of calculating it: Using the same table as above, at 6% the appropriate "remainder" corresponding to age 65 is

0.43401. Thus, Sherrie's interest is currently worth $217,005 [$500,000 x 0.43401].

Another way: Subtract Mo's table value from 1.0: Thus, 1.0 - 0.56599 = 0.43401. Then perform the same multiplication as in the first method. Or stated another way, simply subtract Mo's life estate value from the total value of the trust to arrive at Sherrie's remainder interest: $500,000 - $282,995 = $217,005.

b. At 12%: Mo's interest: $500,000 x 0.75746 = $378,730. Sherrie's interest: $500,000 x 0.24254 = $121,270.

c. As the discount rate increases, the value of the remainder interest drops and the value of the life estate rises because discounting has an over proportionately depressing effect on the more distant cash flows, due to the exponential nature of the mathematical equation for time value of money discounting. Finance oriented types might grasp the reason from this simplified analogy: $1/(1.06)^{20}$ (which equals 0.3118) is considerably less than one half of $1/(1.06)^{10}$ (which equals 0.8900).

21. Using IRS Table S (12%), the appropriate "annuity" corresponding to age 30 is 8.1208. Thus, Thomas Smith's interest is currently worth $28,443 [$3,500 x 8.1208]. This assumes that the next income distribution will be made exactly one year from now.

ENDNOTES

1. IRS Reg. 20.2031-1(b).

2. For the Uniform Probate Code's six exceptions, see UPC §2-606.

3. Somewhat humorously, Edward Schlesinger has described the trust as capable of protecting assets from "inability, disability, creditors, and predators."

4. The Alpha volume, Publication 1457, can be purchased from the U.S. Government Printing Office. These tables are also available in the form of easy-to-use computer software. For example, *Tiger Tables*, available from Lawrence P. Katzenstein at (314) 231-2800, computes all Alpha values plus many other factors, including unitrust remainder factors for from one to ten lives, probabilities of survival, annuity adjustment factors for annuities due, the value of an income beneficiary's interest in a trust with a 5 and 5 power, and commutation tables.

5. See Internal Revenue Code §7520 (see App. A) and §1274(d)(1). Current AFMR rates are released regularly by popular income tax report publishers, such as Prentice Hall and Commerce Clearing House (CCH). CCH reports the monthly changes in the "New Developments" volume of the *Standard Federal Tax Reports*. In that volume, see "New Matters....Cumulative index to 199_ developments," under §7872, under "Applicable Federal Rates Established for (Month), 199_ Rulings" section. CCH also reports these rates in the "Cumulative Index" of its *Federal Estate and Gift Tax Reports*, again under Code §7872. Look for "Applicable Federal Rates..." Monthly news releases are usually issued by the IRS one to two weeks prior to the beginning of the current month and are published in the report of the first week of that month. The AFMR rates also appear under the heading "Credit Markets" in Section C of the *Wall Street Journal* between the 17th and the 22nd of each month.

6. §§1.7520-3(b)(3); 20.7520-3(b)(3)(i); 25.7520-3(b)(3).

7. Students of finance may notice that traditional financial mathematics can *not* derive this number. It is based not only on the time value of money, but also on a life expectancy.

PART 2

Constraints in Planning

CHAPTER 3

Estate Planning Documents

OVERVIEW

Estate planning seeks to facilitate the transfer of the client's wealth as efficiently as possible. Efficiency in estate transfer usually requires the preparation of one or more formal documents that will be accepted by those authorities that ultimately authorize and make the transfers. For example, the proper preparation and execution of a will is essential to the efficient disposal of any probate property. The will must be drafted clearly to ensure that the testator's desires are correctly expressed, and it must be signed and witnessed according to law so that the probate judge will accept it as the guide for the title transfer process.

This chapter, the first of two introducing the principles of property transfer, explores the *documents* commonly used in the process of transferring wealth. Specifically, it examines the creation of four common property transfer mechanisms: joint tenancy, contract, the will, and the trust. The next chapter examines the actual *process* of transfer of property disposed of by these documents, with emphasis on the probate process. Because probate also administers the decedent's intestate property, this chapter also surveys the law of intestate succession.

Generally, property transfers are regulated by state, not federal, law. State laws in this area vary, but there are definite patterns that we can discuss. For instance, more than half of the states have adopted all or a significant part of the Uniform Probate Code (UPC) and, therefore, have many property distribution laws in common. The UPC was introduced in 1966, partly in answer to the criticism that probate procedures in the United States were too costly, too time-consuming, and too complicated. Idaho was the first state to adopt it in 1972. To read Idaho's version of the Uniform Probate Code (UPC) and to see which other states have adopted the uniform probate code, visit the web site maintained by Cornell Law School, URL *http://www.law.cornell.edu/uniform/probate.html.*[1] In presenting the material in this and the next chapter, we will often refer to the laws of those states that have adopted the UPC, especially in three major areas: will execution, intestate succession, and probate administration.

JOINT TENANCY ARRANGEMENTS

The acquisition of title in joint tenancy is ordinarily a simple matter, requiring the completion of one or two preprinted forms. Transfers can be done with or without the aid of an attorney. Deeds to transfer real property into joint tenancy are usually drafted by an attorney, although in some states the job may be done by a real estate agent, by the title company, or by an escrow agent. Similarly, written title in joint ownership of personal property, when it can easily be created, is completed in the office of the professional who helps to acquire it. Examples include title to securities by the investment broker, to a car by the motor vehicle bureau, and to a bank account by the bank.

Later in the text the reader will learn several significant disadvantages to taking title in joint tenancy. Deciding whether joint tenancy is appropriate is not always clear; however, our focus at this point is on how title in joint tenancy is taken, not whether it should be taken.

PROPERTY DISPOSAL BY CONTRACT

A very significant part of a person's estate plan may be transferred pursuant to a contract. Life insurance, pension, and profit sharing plans are common examples of this.

Life Insurance

Wealth derived from life insurance comes in two forms: the policy itself and the policy death proceeds. The policy may be transferred while the insured is alive. After the insured's death, the proceeds are paid by the insurance company to the designated beneficiaries.

During the policy application process, the applicant designates the beneficiary who will receive the proceeds at the insured's death. Once the policy is issued, up until the death of the insured, the policy owner can easily change the beneficiary designation by giving the company written notice using its beneficiary designation form. Very rarely, there is an irrevocable beneficiary designation, i.e., the designation cannot be changed without the consent of the beneficiary or someone besides the owner. Such irrevocable designations may be the result of a divorce settlement or as a condition of a personal loan. Once certain conditions are met, the owner-insured may be free to change beneficiaries, e.g., once the children are grown or the loan is repaid.

Arranging the transfer of title to a life insurance *policy itself* from one owner to another is simple. All that is required is the completion of a short assignment form that can be obtained from the insurance company.

Pension and Profit Sharing Plans

Pension and profit sharing plans are contracts between the employee-client and the employer. Ordinarily, the employer requests that the employee fill out a written form designating the beneficiary, the party who will be entitled to any benefits paid after the employee's death. Thus, the actual process of beneficiary designation for most retirement plans is simple and straightforward.

WILLS AND TRUSTS

In contrast with the above transfer arrangements, the document preparation process for the will and the trust are not simple, for two reasons. First, unlike joint tenancy and written contracts, the will and the trust are capable of disposing of *nearly all* of the client's estate, as well as providing for the care of the client's minor children. Thus, the will and the trust will inevitably be more complicated.

Second, unlike insurance and retirement contracts, which are drafted by the insurer or the employer, the *responsibility for drafting* the will and the trust falls to each individual person.

The following material presents an overview of will and trust construction. Major topics include the legal requirements for a valid will, common will provisions, essential characteristics of trusts, and common provisions of the living trust and the testamentary trust.

THE WILL

Many people die leaving no formal directions as to the disposal of their property, who should manage their estate, or who should care for their minor children. In such cases, the state seeks to make these decisions equitably and sensibly, using statutory rules tailored according to the surviving family situation. However, state law may conflict with the wishes of a decedent, whether unstated or even as recollected by the survivors. Compared to a properly planned estate, intestacy can result in unsuitable property disposition and higher taxes. Individuals can avoid an undesirable outcome by expressing, while still alive, their desires in a legally binding document that serves as a set of directions to be followed by those who survive. The will is the most common formal document for this purpose.

A will is a legally enforceable document that expresses the testator's directions for disposing of his or her probate property at death. In some states, wills can be *oral*, but laws usually greatly restrict the scope of their ability to dispose of wealth, generally limiting the application of oral wills to personal property worth no more than some modest amount, such as $2,000. In addition, the testator, on execution, is often required to be a member of the armed forces or in peril of death. Practically speaking, wills prepared in the estate planning process are written.

Who May Execute a Will

In most states, any individual 18 or older who is of sound mind may dispose of his or her property by will. The implications of this are twofold. First, individuals under the age of 18 cannot transfer property by will unless they are emancipated minors. A minor is emancipated if a court, after a petition and hearing, determines that the child should be free from parental control and given the status of an adult for contractual and other legal matters. In most states, a person under the age of 18 is considered an adult if he or she is married. Thus, in most instances, a deceased minor's property will pass according to the laws of intestate succession, which will usually result in the property passing to the child's parents or if the parents are also deceased, then to siblings. Second, a will can be denied probate if it can be established that the testator, at date of execution of the will, lacked testamentary capacity, was subject to undue influence or fraud, or acted mistakenly. These four concepts are discussed next.

Testamentary capacity. *Testamentary capacity* concerns the testator's mental ability to execute a legally enforceable will. A testator has testamentary capacity if he or she possesses each of the following three attributes:

1. Sufficient mental capacity to understand the *nature of the act* being undertaken (executing a will).
2. Sufficient mental capacity to understand and recollect the general nature of his or her *property*.
3. Sufficient mental capacity to remember and understand his or her relationship to the *persons* who have natural claims on his or her bounty and whose interests are affected by the provisions of the will.

Essentially, in addition to being an adult, testators must know that they are executing a will, they must be aware of what they own, and they must be cognizant of family and friends. On its face, this test seems quite severe; strictly construed, it might prevent many older testators from executing a valid will. However, mere age and physical disability do not negate testamentary capacity. Probate courts have admitted to probate wills executed by individuals who were forgetful, absent-minded, alcoholic, or have behaved peculiarly—even persons declared mentally incompetent, insane, under conservatorship, or who committed suicide shortly after executing a will. Indeed, the threshold is lower than that for contractual capacity, which may be as it should, given that the formation of a contract requires the ability to negotiate with another person, whereas executing a will does not. Nonetheless, failure to meet one or more of these three requirements will result in a finding of insufficient testamentary capacity. Examples of sufficient evidence of incompetence include senility, ongoing hallucinations and irrational beliefs combined, irrational behavior, and totally groundless beliefs about the testator's spouse, children, or siblings. Generally, the outcome hinges on whether or not, at or about the specific time the will was executed, the three-prong test was met. Appellate courts are reluctant to "set aside" a will. They have reversed many of the cases where the jurors found that the testator lacked testamentary capacity, especially those cases where the testator disinherited immediate family members in favor of newly found friends. As a consequence, affirmed findings of testamentary incapacity are very rare.

Anticipating the possibility of a will contest based on lack of testamentary capacity, some attorneys videotape the will execution of a testator who may have questionable capacity, believing that the taping will make capacity more credible. Others believe that videotaping can enhance the success of a contest, reasoning that testators may look terrible on the screen (especially if they are shown lying in a hospital bed), and that the taping constitutes evidence that even the will drafting attorney lacked confidence in the testator's capacity.

Undue influence. A will executed by a testator who was subject to undue influence by someone who stands to benefit, directly or indirectly, may also be denied probate. Undue influence is influence by a confidante that has the effect of overcoming the testator's free will. Examples include improper persuasion and psychological domination, as when "Snake Oil Sam," the smooth-talking newcomer, makes a romantic play for the 92-year-old widow, "encouraging" her to disinherit her children and leave her entire estate to him.

Winning an undue influence case can be difficult. These cases often involve a person with a weak, unsound, or impaired mind. Indeed, the family may not be aware of a new, less favorable will until after the testator is dead. An element of fraud or deceit is a common thread in these cases. Juries tend to side with family members against outsiders whom they see as meddling non-relatives. Thus, a jury is likely to "rewrite" a will in keeping with what the jurors think is fair to the family. But, unless the evidence of undue influence is clearly in the record, this type of verdict is likely to be reversed on appeal.

Fraud. Fraud involves deception through false information. Some courts distinguish two types of fraud based upon the action of the deceiver. Fraud in the inducement is where the testator is persuaded by lies of the wrong-doer to change his or her estate plan. For example, fraud exists if a niece tells her great uncle that she is penniless when, in fact, she is wealthy, or a daughter incorrectly tells her mother that only her sister instigated a conservatorship proceeding, when actually they both did. The other type is called fraud in the execution, where the person is conned into signing a document not knowing that it is a will. An example would be obtaining a person's autograph on a blank sheet of paper, then, with the help of accomplices, placing will language above it and witness signatures below to create what appears to be a genuine will.

Mistake. Very rarely, a will can be successfully contested on the basis of a mistake. Examples include: (*a*) the testator leaves her estate to only one son, mistakenly believing that the other is wealthy; (*b*) the testator mistakenly leaves out an intended clause; or *(c)* the will mistakenly includes an unintended clause.

Ordinarily, a finding of lack of testamentary capacity will invalidate the entire will, while a finding of undue influence, fraud, or mistake might invalidate only those provisions that relate to the specific problem.

Statutory Requirements for Wills

Most states, including those that have adopted the Uniform Probate Code, recognize at least two types of wills, the *witnessed will* and the *holographic will*.

Witnessed will. Although state laws vary, a witnessed or *attested will* must meet the following three requirements:

1. It must be *in writing* (handwritten, typed, etc.).
2. The *testator must sign* the will in the presence of *two witnesses* (three in a few states).
3. The *two witnesses must sign* their names to the will, understanding that the instrument they sign is the testator's will. The main purpose of requiring witnesses is to prevent forgery and coercion of the testator.

Beneficiaries should not be witnesses to a will because that could imperil their right to receive some or all of their bequest. In many states, a bequest to a witness is void, unless the witness is an heir. And in that case, the witness can take no more than his or her intestate share. In some other states, a beneficiary can witness the will, but if someone raises an undue influence challenge, the "interested witness" may take more than the intestate share only if he or she is able to rebut a statutory presumption that the bequest was procured by duress, menace, fraud, or undue influence. Inability to rebut this presumption might not totally invalidate the will, but it will probably invalidate some or all of the bequest to that witness.

Holographic will. If a written will does not meet all of the requirements for a witnessed will, in most states, including those adopting the UPC, it can still be admitted to probate if it meets the requirements for a holographic will. Typical state requirements for a holographic will are:

1. Signature is in the testator's handwriting.
2. All of the "material provisions" of the will are in the testator's handwriting.

In the past, courts often refused to admit to probate holographic documents unless it was clear from reading just the handwritten portions that the document was the decedent's will. In determining what parts of the will must be in the testator's handwriting, some few still follow the old rule, but many states now allow a preprinted will form to be treated as a holographic will so long as both the material provisions and the signature are in the decedent's own handwriting.[2] The material provisions are the dispositive ones (who gets what), the identity of the executor, the nomination of guardians, and the like.

Recently, the Uniform Probate Code added a section that allows a court to accept as testamentary documents instruments that do not meet the formal execution requirements of a witnessed will nor the handwriting requirements of a holographic will, however, the proponent of the imperfectly executed will must establish by "clear and convincing evidence" that the writing being offered was intended by the decedent to be his or her will (or codicil).[3] Clear and convincing evidence is a higher standard of proof than the usual civil case burden known as a preponderance of the evidence.

Contrasting witnessed and holographic wills. There are two major differences between the two sets of formal requirements: first, the witnessed will requires the performance of certain activities by two witnesses. In contrast, the holographic will may, but need not, be witnessed. Second, the holographic will requires that all material provisions of the will be in the testator's handwriting. In contrast, the witnessed will requires that only the testator and the witness's signatures be in the person's own hand, and even this may be unnecessary when a proper authorization is arranged. A testator can execute a will by directing another person to sign for him or her in the presence of the witnesses.[4] Where such is done, it may be the one time where videotaping the signing ceremony should be given serious consideration.

No Contest Clause

In the last few pages, we have described several technical requirements for a valid will including testamentary capacity, absence of undue influence, fraud, mistake, and certain specific execution requirements such as signatures by witnesses and the testator. Anticipating that dissatisfied persons may claim that one or more violations of these requirements has occurred, as a pretext for obtaining more of the estate, testators may insert in their will a "no contest" clause like the one that follows:

> *I have purposely made no provisions herein for any other person or persons, other than as set forth in this will, and if any person contests this will, I revoke any share or interest given such person, and said share or interest shall be disposed of as though said person predeceased me without leaving issue.*

This usually, but not always, discourages will contests for several reasons. First, it will discourage only beneficiaries named in the will, not disinherited persons who stand to lose nothing by contesting. Second, beneficiaries may still wish to contest if they expect to gain considerably more than they will lose. Finally, the UPC states that such clauses are unenforceable if the contestant had probable cause for instituting proceedings.[5] Perhaps most testators would desire this result anyway.

What situations tend to invite will contests? The most common are where the testator chooses to disinherit family members in favor of a friend, a charity, a spouse married shortly before death, or where a testator treats children unequally. If the testator is very old or is ailing physically or mentally, a contest is even more likely.

Will contests are infrequent, and *successful* contests are very uncommon. One study showed that fewer than one percent of wills offered for probate were challenged, and over two-thirds of those challenges were unsuccessful. However, will contests may become more common for several reasons. As the general population continues to age, more elderly people of means will acquire "friends" who offer to assist them in their finances and work their way into the person's estate plan. A high divorce rate has increased the number of children of former marriages, a group that is less likely to get along with the surviving spouse of a later marriage. When any of these situations or factors apply to a particular client, attorneys should take special precautions in drafting and executing the will.

The Simple Will

Wills can be quite lengthy and complex, but this section focuses on a relatively simple will. A *simple will*, as it is generally called, is a will prepared for a family having a small, or even a modest estate, where death taxes are not a significant concern. We will cover estate taxes in Chapter 5 and you will see that the period from 1998 through 2006 is a period of transition. Over those years the amount that can pass tax free (assuming the decedent has not made significant lifetime gifts) will increase from the pre-1998 figure of $600,000 to $1,000,000. The $600,000 was the tax free amount for the period of 1987 through 1997, inclusive.

The simple will usually includes all of the following: nominating an executor and, if there are minor children, a guardian; waiver of the probate bond; and, in most cases, giving the testator's property to the spouse, if alive, otherwise to the children by right of representation.

Exhibit 3-1 presents a simple will that demonstrates the essential nature of this probate property transfer document. The reader is encouraged to study it carefully, so that the analysis that follows is more readily understood.

EXHIBIT 3 - 1 Simple Will

WILL

OF

WILLARD THOMAS SMITH

I, Willard Thomas Smith, a resident of Mytown, Anystate, declare this to be my will. I revoke all prior Wills and Codicils.

First: Family and Guardian I am married to Sue L. Smith, referred to in this will as "my wife." I have three children, all from this marriage, whose names and birthdays are:

Kristi M. Smith	June 27, 1987
Heather L. Smith	April 19, 1989
Todd R. Smith	May 11, 1991

EXHIBIT 3 - 1 Simple Will *continued*

Reference to "my children" or to "my child," shall include children born later and children adopted by me. I have no deceased children.

    If my wife does not survive me, and it is necessary to appoint a guardian, I appoint Curtis J. Quint guardian of the person and estate of each such minor child. If for any reason Curtis J. Quint does not act as guardian, I appoint Maria S. Cruise as guardian of the person and estate of each such minor child.

Second: Executor The executor shall serve as follows:

    A. *Designation* I appoint my wife as my executor. If for any reason she does not so act, I appoint James A. Reliable to be my executor. If for any reason neither my wife nor James A. Reliable acts as executor, I appoint Third National Bank of Mytown to be my executor.

    B. *Bond waiver* No bond, surety, or other security shall be required of my executor.

Third: Disposition of Property I make the following gifts of property:

    A. *Tangible personal property* If my wife survives me by 30 days, I give her all of my interest in our tangible personal property. If my wife does not survive me by 30 days, I give my tangible personal property to my issue, by right of representation, provided they survive me for that period. My executor shall consider their personal preferences in making the division. My executor has my permission to sell any of that property and distribute the proceeds to equalize the shares. My executor shall be discharged for all tangible personal property so given to any minor child if the child, or adult having the child's custody, gives a written receipt to my executor.

    B. *Residue* If my wife survives me by 120 days, I give her the residue of my estate. If my wife does not survive me by 120 days, I give the residue to my issue, by right of representation, provided they survive me for that period. If neither my wife nor any of my descendants survives me by 120 days, I give the residue of my estate according to Mystate's laws of descent and distribution, one half as if I had died with no will on the last day of that 120 day period, and one half as if it were my wife's estate and she had died with no will on that last day.

    C. *Taxes from residue* All death taxes imposed because of my death, as well as interest and penalties on those taxes, whether on property passing under this will or otherwise, shall be paid by my executor from the residue of my estate.

EXHIBIT 3 - 1 Simple Will *continued*

Fourth: Powers of Executor My executor shall have unrestricted powers, without court order, to settle my estate as this will provides. In addition, my executor shall have the following powers:

1. To make interim distributions of principal and income on an interim basis to those entitled to it.
2. To sell, exchange, mortgage, pledge, lease or assign any property belonging to my estate.
3. To continue operation of any business belonging to my estate.
4. To invest and reinvest any surplus money.

I have signed my name to this instrument on March 19, 1999, at Mytown, Anystate.

Willard Thomas Smith
Willard Thomas Smith

Statement of Witnesses The undersigned witnesses declare under penalty of perjury under Anystate law, on March 19, 1999, that we are over twenty-one, that the testator declared to us that this instrument is his will, that he signed this will, and that he requested us to act as witnesses to it. Whereupon he signed in our presence, and we now, in the presence of each other, subscribe our names as witnesses. In doing so, we attest that we believe that the testator is of sound mind and did not act under fraud, duress, or undue influence.

John Meeks	*Jennifer Jarrett*
1341 Park St., Little Town, Anystate	42 Short Rd., Little Town, Anystate

---

Analysis of the simple will. Let's analyze the major provisions of this will, section by section.

Will of Willard Thomas Smith. In this introductory paragraph, the testator "declares" the document to be his will, satisfying the legal requirement that there be evidence of testamentary intent.

A *codicil* is a separate written document that amends or revokes a will. It is executed if the testator wishes to make changes or additions to his or her will. It must meet all of the legal requirements of a will, including subscription by witnesses, although in states that recognize holographic wills, a holographic codicil even to a witnessed will is acceptable if the codicil meets that state's requirements for a holographic will.

One of the more common methods of *revoking* a prior will is by executing a later will that declares such revocation, as is done in the Smith will. Revocation by "cancellation" with a "subsequent instrument," as it is termed, can also be undertaken in any other signed, witnessed statement. A will can also be revoked by a physical act, such as by burning, tearing, canceling, obliterating or destroying it, when such is done by the testator with an intent to revoke.[6]

Revoking all prior wills and codicils eliminates the danger that provisions in prior wills that are inconsistent with the present will may cause confusion. Without a revocation clause, needless litigation might arise over whether or not the provisions in two or more wills are inconsistent. For example, in one state supreme court case, a decedent-testator had written two "last" wills within three weeks. The first simply left "a tract of land" to a friend. The second contained no revocation clause and left "all my effects" to siblings Y and Z. The court permitted a trial to determine whether the first will should be construed along with the second, reasoning that they were not necessarily inconsistent because the testator could have used the word "effects" to mean only personal property.[7] If the testator's intent was to leave everything to Y and Z, inclusion of a revocation clause would have assured this result. If the intent was to preserve the gift of the land to the friend, then that should have been clearly stated in the second will.

First: Family and guardian. Naming all members of the immediate family assists the personal representative in finding relatives and locating assets.

Including *after born children* in the will prevents a child born after the execution of the will from being left to inherit under the laws of intestate succession, a consequence which might conflict with the testator's intent.

A child who is still a minor when both parents are dead will have a *guardian* of the person and of the estate appointed by the probate court. A guardian of the person is responsible for the minor child's care, custody, control, and education, while a guardian of the child's estate is responsible for managing the minor child's property. A testator's nomination carries great weight and is usually followed; however, the probate judge does have the power to appoint someone else if there is good cause for not following the nomination. Nominating an alternate guardian increases the likelihood that the testator's preferences will be followed.

   Second: Executor. Similar to the nomination of a guardian, the nomination of an executor and an alternate executor is helpful to the probate court in its selection process. The court will follow the recommendation of the testator unless there is good cause to do otherwise.

   Unless the bond is waived in the will, the executor is required to post a *fiduciary bond*. A bonding company, for a fee, insures the estate assets against losses caused by the personal representative's breach of fiduciary obligations, whether the breach is the result of negligence or willful misconduct. The will can waive the bond requirement. The testator may consider a bond unnecessary because it results in additional expense to the estate, and/or because the executor is a highly trusted member of the testator's family, such as the surviving spouse, and/or is also one of the major beneficiaries of the estate. Ordinarily, the bond amount will be set by the court to be equal to the total value of the personal probate property plus one year's estimated income from all of the probate property. The idea here is that the personal representative could run off with everything but the real property.

   Third: Disposition of property.   This simple will essentially leaves all property to the testator's spouse, if surviving, otherwise to the children. The interest of the children is sometimes referred to as a "gift-over" to the children. The will distinguishes the tangible personal property from the residue, which consists of all other probate assets. Thus, the spouse must survive by 30 days to take tangible personal property and 120 days to take the residue. If the spouse does not survive the requisite time period, the property passes to the children who do so survive.

   Inclusion of a survival requirement, such as 30 days or 120 days, reduces the likelihood that the death of both spouses in a common accident will result in subjecting some of the family property to two successive probates. This *survival clause*, as it is called, helps in situations not covered by the Uniform Simultaneous Death Act (USDA).

   Enacted by *every* state, the USDA provides that when transfer of title to property depends on the order of deaths, and when no sufficient evidence exists that two people died other than simultaneously, the property of each is disposed of as if each had survived the other. Thus, in the case of a childless married couple, the husband's estate would pass to his blood relatives and the wife's estate would pass to her blood relatives. This statute is of limited value, however, because it does not avoid double probate when the order of deaths can in fact be established. In some states, if it *can* be established that one spouse survived the other, even only by seconds, then the USDA will not apply and, absent a survival clause, there will be a *double probate* of the property owned by the first spouse to die. Perhaps worse, *all* of the property may ultimately pass to that spouse's in-laws, rather than the surviving relatives. Some states, including California, have legislated safeguards against inheritance by in-laws by requiring that the portion of the decedent's estate attributable to the predeceased spouse pass, in some circumstances, to the predeceased spouse's children, parents, or other kin.[8] The Uniform Probate Code requires a beneficiary of an estate to outlive the decedent by *120 hours* or be deemed to have predeceased the decedent. This rule is not applied if it would cause the decedent's property to escheat (revert) to the state.

With regard to *insurance* on the life of a decedent, the USDA states that, in the event of an apparent simultaneous death of the insured and the beneficiary, the policy proceeds are to be distributed as if the insured survived the beneficiary. Thus, the proceeds will be paid to the contingent beneficiary, and if none, then to the owner's probate estate.

Section B of Article Three, covering the "residue," is called the *residuary clause*. Failure to include it in a will can result in *partial intestacy*. In a recent case, the attorney who had drafted the decedent's will admitted that he mistakenly omitted the residuary clause, but that his notes showed that the decedent wanted the residue to go to a specific friend. The court would not allow admission of this evidence, ruling that extrinsic evidence is admissible to explain poorly drafted parts of a will, but cannot be used to put in parts that are missing.[9]

Disposing of estate property by differentiating the tangible personal property from the residue can speed up probate distribution and can often save income taxes. In the chapter on fiduciary income taxes, the concept of distributable net income, or DNI, is discussed. A *specific bequest* of property, such as when the testator specifies a bequest of the tangible personal property, prevents the distribution from being labeled DNI. This generates less taxable income to the distributees (often the spouse and/or children), and correspondingly more taxable income to the estate, which is (hopefully) in a lower rate bracket.

Instead of "tangible personal property," some wills ill-advisedly use the term "personal effects," which really means "tangible personal property, worn or carried about the person or having some intimate relation with the person." Since automobiles and some other property are not considered "personal effects," the broader term *tangible personal property* is preferred. Early distribution of this property also allows the executor to avoid the cost and trouble of storing it.

Distribution by right of representation, or as it is also called *per stirpes*, is a method of allocating a bequest of the decedent's property such that it follows the natural line of descent (e.g., the children of a predeceased child share that child's portion of the estate.)

The laws of intestate succession, also known as "laws of descent and distribution," vary somewhat from state to state. They spell out the priority of succession rights of the decedent's spouse and kin in the event of intestacy. In the event that his wife and all of his descendants fail to survive him by 120 days, the testator has generously chosen to divide his property in halves, with one half going by intestate succession to his relatives and the other half going by intestate succession to his wife's relatives.

Fourth: Powers of executor. Granting explicit powers to the executor can eliminate the need to secure permission of the probate court to undertake certain administrative actions. Ordinarily, testators would like their executors to act without undue delay.

Signature clause and the statement of witnesses. Every state imposes formal requirements regarding the signing of the will by the testator and the role of the witnesses. The paragraph above the witnesses' signatures increases the likelihood of compliance with these formal requirements by explicitly stating them and having the witnesses, by their signatures, acknowledge that such were carried out. The last sentence above the signatures of the witnesses offers some additional evidence of the testator's capacity to execute a will. The Statement of Witnesses is also referred to as the *attestation clause.* When a will is signed and witnessed in the proper manner, such that it is a valid will, it is said to be executed.

Other aspects of the simple will. Simple wills are most commonly drafted by attorneys for clients with modest estates, where death taxes are not a concern. For a married couple, a simple will is usually prepared for each spouse. In most cases, the dispositive clauses are almost identical. Thus, the husband's will leaves all to his wife, if she survives, otherwise to their children. And the wife's will leaves all to her husband, if he survives, otherwise to their children. Such simple wills are commonly called *reciprocal wills*, *mirror wills*, or *mutual wills.*

Occasionally, clients will want *contractual wills*, ones which cannot be revised once one of the parties (usually a spouse) dies. Sometimes these are done in the form of a single will for two people, called a *joint will,* although a joint will need not be contractual. Contractual wills are rare because most clients want the flexibility of being able to change an estate plan after one spouse dies. Joint wills should be avoided unless the clients really want a contractual will, because even if the clients did not intend the joint will to be irrevocable once one of the testators dies, a court may rule that this was the intent because there can be little other reason to create one will for two people.

Wills that are more complex are less likely to be reciprocal in content. Typically, they are prepared by attorneys specializing in estate planning to reflect the inherently different preferences and different financial and tax circumstances of the spouses. This text will highlight many of these differences in later chapters.

Where should the original copy of the will be kept? The client's safe deposit box makes good sense in those states (e.g., California) that do not *seal* boxes at the owner's death. In states where safe deposit boxes are sealed at the owner's death, access to the will is delayed until a state official can join the prospective executor in inventorying the contents of the box so as to ensure that the executor accounts for any jewelry, bearer bonds, and the like that might be there. Some attorneys recommend their own safe. Some people might view this as self-serving, since the executor will have to come to the attorney's office to take charge of the will, thus giving the attorney a good chance of serving as the probate attorney. However, since the testator selected that attorney to draft the estate plan, it would seem reasonable to select that attorney to handle the probate. Some attorneys simply recommend a secure, handy place in the client's home.

Next, we examine the trust, the other major planning document of transfer.

THE TRUST

The principal parties to a trust are the trustor, the trustee, and the beneficiary. As a legal arrangement, a trust is created by the trustor and divides and transfers interests in property between two or more people. Any interests or control over the trust not given to the beneficiaries are either retained by the trustor, granted to the trustee, or held by both.

A trust can take effect during the lifetime of the trustor, or it can take effect at the trustor's death. As we have seen, the former is called a *living* (or *inter vivos*) *trust*, while the latter is called a *testamentary trust*, that is, a trust created in a complex will that is also call a "trust-will." The testamentary trust document is covered later in the chapter.

At any given moment, a trust is either revocable and amendable, in which case the trustor is capable of voiding (canceling) or amending it, or it is irrevocable, that is, not voidable or amendable. A living trust usually contains specific language stating whether it is revocable or irrevocable. A revocable living trust usually, but not always, becomes irrevocable at the death of the trustor(s). Like the contents of most wills, the provisions of a testamentary trust can be amended or revoked before the testator's death by codicil, revocation, or destruction of the testamentary trust. At the testator's death, a testamentary trust takes effect and becomes irrevocable since the only person capable of amending or revoking it, the testator, is, of course, permanently unavailable.

A trust usually contains two different legal types of property; principal and income. The *principal* of a trust is its invested wealth. Its size will fluctuate with changes in the market value, by additions (income or additional property), by charges (expenses or losses), and by distributions from it. In contrast with trust principal, the *income* of a trust is the return in money or property derived from use of the trust principal. Examples of income include cash dividends, rent, and interest. Trust income also has charges against it, most of which reflect expenses incurred in managing the trust property (e.g., insurance premiums and some portion of the trustee's fee). Any trust income not distributed to beneficiaries is said to be *accumulated* in the trust and is generally accounted for as retained income, not principal, unless the trust agreement requires that accumulated income be added to principal.

The accounting distinction between principal and income is particularly important, because most trusts contain provisions that bestow rights to principal and income to different beneficiaries. In the chapter on fiduciary income taxes, we will see that the distinction between principal and income will influence trust income taxation.

The beneficiaries of an irrevocable trust are usually either *income bene-ficiaries* (i.e., those having an interest in the income) or *principal beneficiaries* (for example, a remainderman who stands to receive principal outright when the trust terminates). These two types of beneficiaries may have conflicting or "adverse" interests, because the increased distributions to one will generally decrease the distributions to the other. For example, high yield-low growth stock would tend to benefit the income beneficiaries more than the remaindermen whereas low yield-high growth stock would favor the remaindermen more than the income beneficiaries.

There are other ways of classifying trusts, especially in connection with tax planning. The chapters in Part 3 introduce several tax-saving trusts, including the bypass trust, the Crummey trust, and the QTIP trust. We will precede those topics with chapters that explore the laws of estate, gift, and income taxation. The purpose of focusing on trusts in the present chapter is more basic: to enable the reader to learn the essential structure of the two principal documents creating the trust. The following material describes a living trust and a testamentary trust. Keep in mind these trusts vary greatly, so it is a stretch to call any trust used as an example here "typical".

Living Trust Instrument

A living trust is created by a document of agreement between the trustor (or settlor) and the trustee. Before we examine the actual instrument, let's compare and contrast the characteristics of that document with the will, which is the document most people think of when considering how transfers at death are guided.

Similarities. The will and the living trust instrument are similar in three important ways. First, both serve as the guide to the disposition of one's property at his or her death. Second, both have a fiduciary (the executor or the trustee) who is responsible for managing property for a period of time until the transfers can be completed. Third, both instruments are generally amendable and revocable, at least until the person creating the instrument dies. The will can nearly always be amended by a codicil, or revoked by its destruction or by execution of a later will that explicitly revokes earlier ones. One exception, of course, is the *contractual will*, which becomes irrevocable after the death or incapacity of the first co-testator. The living trust is either revocable or irrevocable. In most states, a trust must state that it is revocable, otherwise it becomes irrevocable upon execution. In the other states, the opposite rule is in effect, such that a trust is revocable unless stated to be irrevocable.

Differences. The will and the living trust instrument are different in three important ways. First, they dispose of a totally different set of property. A living trust instrument disposes of property owned by the trustee, while a will disposes of probate property owned by the decedent at death. Thus, with regard to property transfers, the living trust instrument and the will are mutually exclusive; property owned by the trustee is not probate property, while probate property is owned by the decedent, not the trustee. Of course, the decedent's will can transfer property, by way of the probate process, to the trustee of his or her living trust, or even to the trustee of a trust he or she did not create, such as one created by one's spouse. A will that transfers property to a trustee is called a *pour-over will,* because it scoops up property and "pours" it into an existing trust.

Second, with regard to choosing a fiduciary, a living trust instrument *appoints* a trustee whereas a will *nominates* an executor. Of course, a testamentary trust must nominate both an executor and a trustee. Since the trustor of a living trust is alive when the trustee is appointed, the trustor has control over the appointment. The trust instrument is a legal *contract* between the trustor and the trustee. On the other hand, the probate judge appoints the executor of a will after the testator's death. The judge may appoint someone other than the nominated executor for any number of reasons, including the nominee's inability to serve due to death, disability, or incompetence.

Third, while the formal execution requirements for writing a will are quite strict, the requirements for properly executing a trust instrument are simple to meet. In most cases, the trust document is simply dated and signed by the trustor and the trustee. Witnesses are not required, however some attorneys have the trustor's signature notarized to assure others of its validity, especially those who might have to rely on the document at a time when the trustor is incapacitated or deceased. Although the formalities surrounding the execution of a trust document are simpler than those for a will, the mental capacity necessary is set at a higher standard. The settlor must have contractual capacity. Given the nature of the trust document, this would be, in addition to testamentary capacity, the ability to understand and enter into a bilateral contractual agreement. In most states, one contesting a settlor's (or a testator's) capacity has the burden of proving the lack of capacity by "clear and convincing" evidence. This is a more difficult (i.e., higher) standard than the typical "preponderance" of evidence burden generally placed on the plaintiff in a civil case.

Exhibit 3-2 presents a living trust that is fairly simple since it is not designed to save taxes. Trusts designed to save taxes break into several irrevocable trusts at the trustor's death.

EXHIBIT 3 - 2 Living Trust Instrument

JOHN C. JONES

Revocable Living Trust

Dated March 19, 1999

TRUST AGREEMENT made March 19, 1999, between John C. Jones, as trustor, resident of Common County, Mystate, and John C. Jones, resident of Common County, Mystate, as trustee.

1. Trust property. The trustor has set aside and holds in trust the property described on Schedule One, attached to this instrument. The trustee agrees to hold such property and any later accepted property, in trust, under the terms and conditions provided herein.

2. Successor trustee. If John C. Jones for any reason ceases to act as trustee, his wife, Sarah E. Jones, shall serve as trustee. If Sarah E. Jones is unable or for any reason ceases to act as trustee, then First National Bank of Anytown shall serve as trustee.

3. Power to amend or revoke. The trustor reserves the right at any time to amend or revoke this trust, in whole or in part, by an instrument in writing signed by him and delivered during his lifetime to the trustee.

4. Operation of trust during trustor's lifetime. During the trustor's lifetime, the trustee shall administer and distribute the trust as follows:

a. Trust income. The trustee shall pay the net income to the trustor at convenient intervals but at least quarter-annually.

b. Trust principal. The trustee shall pay to the trustor from time to time such amounts of the principal of this trust as the trustor shall direct in writing or as the trustee deems advisable for the trustor's support and comfort.

5. Operation of trust after trustor's death. Upon the death of the trustor, the trust estate shall be held, administered, and distributed as follows:

a. Wife survives by four months. If the trustor's wife survives trustor by four months, the trustee shall distribute the entire trust estate to the trustee of her revocable trust, dated the same date as this trust, to be held and administered according to its terms. If said trust is no longer in existence, then distribution shall be to trustor's wife, free of trust.

b. Wife does not survive by four months. If the trustor's wife does not survive the trustor by four months and if no then-living child of the trustor is under age twenty-one, then the trustee shall divide the trust into as many equal shares as there are children of the trustor's then living and children of the trustor's then deceased with descendants then living. Each share set aside for a child then deceased with descendants then living shall be further divided into shares for such descendants, by right of representation. The trust estate shall be held, administered, and distributed in the manner described in sub-sections 5(b)(2)(a) and (b), below.

EXHIBIT 3 - 2 Living Trust Instrument *continued*

If neither the trustor's wife nor any of the trustor's descendants survive the trustor by four months, the trustee shall distribute the entire trust estate according to Mystate's laws of descent and distribution, one half as if the trustor had died with no will on the last day of the four-month period and one half as if it were the trustor's wife's estate and she had died with no will on the last day. If the trustor's wife does not survive the trustor by four months and if any then-living child of the trustor is under age twenty-one, then the trust estate shall be held, administered, and distributed as follows:

(1) *Any child under age twenty-one.* So long as any of the trustor's children are living who are under twenty-one, the trustee shall pay to or apply for the benefit of all of the trustor's children as much of the net income and principal as the trustee in the trustee's discretion deems necessary for their proper support, health, and education, after taking into consideration, to the extent that the trustee considers advisable, the value of the trust assets, the relative needs, both present and future, of each of the beneficiaries, and their other income and resources made known to the trustee and reasonably available to meet beneficiary needs. The trustee may make distributions under this provision that benefit one or more beneficiaries to the exclusion of others. Any net income not distributed shall be accumulated and added to principal.

(2) *Youngest child reaches age twenty-one.* When the youngest of the trustor's then-living children reaches the age of twenty-one, the trustee shall divide the trust into as many equal shares as there are children of the trustor's then living and deceased children who left issue. Each share set aside the issue of a deceased child shall be further divided into shares, by right of representation, for such descendants. Each such share shall be distributed, or retained in trust, as hereafter provided.

(a) Each share set aside for a descendant shall be distributed to that descendant free of trust when he or she reaches the age of twenty-one.

(b) Each share set aside for a descendant who had not then reached age twenty-one shall be retained in trust. The trustee shall pay to or for the benefit of that descendant as much of the income and principal of the trust as the trustee, in the trustee's discretion, considers appropriate for that descendant's support, health, and education. When that descendant reaches age twenty-one, the descendant's share shall be distributed to that descendant, free of trust. If that descendant dies before receiving distribution of that descendant's entire share, the undistributed balance of that descendant's share shall be distributed, free of trust, to that descendant's then-living descendants, by right of representation, or if there are none, to the trustor's then-living descendants, by right of representation. The share of a descendant for whom there exists a trust created by this instrument, shall augment that descendant's trust.

6. Restriction against assignment, etc. No interest in the principal or income of this trust shall be anticipated, assigned, encumbered, or subject to any creditor's claim or to legal process before its actual receipt by the beneficiary.

7. Perpetuities saving. Any trust created by this will that has not terminated sooner shall terminate twenty-one years after the death of the last survivor of the class composed of my wife and those of my descendants living at my death.

EXHIBIT 3 - 2 Living Trust Instrument *continued*

8. Powers of trustee. To carry out the purposes of this trust, the trustee is vested with the following powers with respect to the trust estate and any part of it, in addition to those powers now or hereafter conferred by law:

a. To continue to hold any property, including shares of the trustee's own stock, and to operate at the risk of the trust estate any business that the trustee receives or acquires under the trust as long as the trustee deems advisable.

b. To manage, control, grant options on, sell (for cash or on deferred payments), convey, exchange, partition, divide, improve, and repair trust property.

c. To lease trust property for terms within or beyond the term of the trust and for any purpose, including exploration for and removal of gas, oil, and other minerals and to enter into community oil leases, pooling, and unitization agreements.

d. To borrow money and to encumber or hypothecate trust property by mortgage, deed of trust, pledge, or otherwise.

e. To invest and reinvest the trust estate in every kind of property, real, personal, or mixed, and every kind of investment, specifically including, but not by way of limitation, corporate obligations of every kind, stocks (preferred or common), shares of investment trusts, investment companies and mutual funds, and mortgage participations, which persons of prudence, discretion, and intelligence acquire for their own account, and any common trust fund administered by the trustee.

f. In any case in which the trustee is required, pursuant to the provisions of the trust, to divide any trust property into parts or shares for the purpose of distribution, or otherwise, the trustee is authorized, in the trustee's absolute discretion, to make the division and distribution partly in kind and partly in money, and for this purpose to make such sales of the trust property as the trustee may deem necessary on such terms and conditions as the trustee shall see fit.

IN WITNESS THEREOF this instrument has been executed as of the date set forth on the first page of this instrument.

John C. Jones
John C. Jones, Trustor

John C. Jones
John C. Jones, Trustee

[Notarization of the signatures would appear here]

Analysis of the living trust instrument. Let's examine the major provisions of this living trust instrument section by section.

Trust agreement. A trust is, in effect, a contract or agreement between two parties, the trustor and the trustee. Both sides agree to perform certain tasks: among other things, the trustor agrees to deliver property described in Schedule One (not shown) to the trustee, and the trustee agrees to hold, administer, and distribute the trust property in keeping with the terms of the trust.

In this living trust instrument, the trustor names himself to be initial trustee and names alternate successor trustees to take over when he resigns, becomes incapable of performing because of incapacity, or death. In other words, he might want to travel without worrying about managing the trust property or he might become too ill to manage it.

1. Trust property. The instrument specifies that additional assets may be put in trust in the future, even after the trustor's death. For example, a trustor's will can be directed to "pour over" probate property into a trust.

2. Successor trustee. Since the trust instrument states the trustee's name in the opening paragraph, this section need only name successor trustees. It is not unusual to name one or more of the remaindermen, if they are adults, as successors, since the remaindermen have a vested interest in managing and transferring the property efficiently. Sometimes the children are named as successor trustees, with the requirement that they have reached a certain age (e.g., twenty-five), in order to serve. Naming a bank, or other corporate entity, as a successor trustee virtually ensures that an experienced trustee will be available to serve for the duration of the trust. Some corporate fiduciaries will not assume the position of trustee unless the corpus is some minimum value. Where a corporate trustee is being considered, a meeting with the trust officers should be arranged to decrease the likelihood that the position will be refused later.

3. Power to amend or revoke. This trust can be amended or revoked by a written document signed by the trustor and delivered to the trustee. An amendment is similar to a codicil to a will, but without the strict formal execution requirements.

4. Operation of trust during trustor's lifetime. During the trustor's lifetime, the trustee is required to pay to the trustor all income at least quarterly, and any principal as requested. The reader will notice that the wording assumes that the trustor and the trustee are *different parties*. However, as mentioned above, many, perhaps most living trust agreements name the trustor to be trustee. Nevertheless, this paragraph is used in anticipation that, at some point, a successor trustee will take over the management of the trust.

5. *Operation of trust after trustor's death.* This section is substantially longer than the Disposition of Property section in the simple will. It provides for several alternative outcomes depending upon who survives. First, the trust terminates if the trustor's *spouse survives* the trustor by four months, with the result that all trust property will pass to her revocable trust or, if it is no longer in existence, then outright to her.

Second, if the trustor's spouse does not survive by four months and all of the trustor's children are over the age of twenty-one, the trust will terminate and distribute all assets free of trust to the children. However, if one or more of the trustor's living children is *under twenty-one*, the trust continues as one trust. The trustee is instructed to collectively use trust principal and income to provide for all the children's support, education, and other reasonable needs. Thus, the trustee has a limited power of appointment over the entire trust income and principal, with all living descendants named as permissible appointees. Then, when the youngest child reaches twenty-one, the trust is divided into equal shares, one for each child then living, and one for each deceased child for whom there are living descendants. The trust directs distribution to the younger generations by right of representation, also called "traditional *per stirpes*," a concept more fully explained in a later chapter. Each share is then distributed outright to each descendant when he or she reaches age twenty-one. Thus, at the time of the splitting of the corpus, each child and any other descendant beneficiary who is at least age twenty-one will receive his or her share.

Third, if the trustor's spouse fails to survive the trustor by four months and if no living child is under age twenty-one, the trust may or may not terminate, depending upon whether there are underage descendants of deceased children. In any event, however, the trust estate is immediately divided into shares, and each child immediately receives his or her share. The balance of the trust corpus (held for these underage descendants of deceased children) will be administered in a manner (described below) quite similar to the way it is administered for a living child when under the age of twenty-one. As each of these descendants reaches age twenty-one, he or she will receive an outright distribution of his or her share. Accordingly, the trust will terminate when the youngest living descendant of deceased children reaches age twenty-one.

Finally, if the trustor is survived neither by a spouse nor any descendants, the trust terminates and the trust property passes by *intestate succession*, with one half to the trustor's relatives and the other half to the trustor's spouse's relatives. The laws of intestate succession are covered in the next chapter.

The above disposition, using a trustee, has much to recommend it over the will's provisions making outright gifts to the minor children, which requires a court-appointed guardian.

6. Restriction against assignment. This is an example of a *spendthrift clause.* Without it, the laws of many states would allow trust beneficiaries to transfer and encumber their interests in the trust property, and would enable the beneficiaries' creditors to seize trust assets to satisfy their claims. For example, beneficiaries could mortgage their share of trust property, sell a future interest in it, and devise it. A spendthrift clause restricts such transfers. However, it only protects trust property while held by the trustee, not after it has been transferred outright to a beneficiary.

7. Perpetuities saving. This clause is included to prevent a contingent gift from being ruled invalid because it violates a law found in almost all states that requires interests to vest within some reasonable time after the transfer. This law is called the rule against perpetuities. It is discussed in more detail in Appendix 3A, which immediately follows this chapter.

8. Powers of trustee. Since a trustee is likely to manage trust property for a considerably longer period than an executor is likely to manage an estate, the powers granted to the trustee are usually stated in more detail than those granted in a will to an executor. In addition to these powers, both the executor and trustee automatically have other implicit powers derived from statutory law and from case law, unless the document specifically prohibits such powers. For example, trustees have the power to defend against claims brought against the trust property, whether or not that power is specifically granted in the document.

This living trust is uncomplicated primarily because it does not attempt to save estate taxes. If the other spouse survives the trustor spouse by four months, all corpus will pass to the surviving spouse's revocable trust or outright to her. Like the simple will, it is created for families with modest estates, for whom death tax planning is not a significant concern. We will introduce a more complicated tax-saving living trust in the two chapters that deal with estate plans for the wealthy, where estate taxes are a concern.

The third and final document, covered next, combines the disposition characteristics of a will with the many benefits of a delayed trust, one that takes effect after the client's death.

THE TESTAMENTARY TRUST

The testamentary trust, or trust-will, is the third principal document of property disposition commonly prepared by attorneys in the estate planning process. In essence, a testamentary trust is actually one type of *will*; it serves as the guiding document for the distribution of the testator-trustor's probate property at death. In addition, it disposes of some, or all, of the probate property to the trustee of a trust that is newly created according to trust terms that are set forth as part of the will. This trust takes effect after the testator's death at the end of the probate process. The actual creation of the trust, and the funding mechanism, is the order for distribution. The order names (appoints) the trustee, sets forth all of the terms of the trust (generally quoting verbatim from the testamentary trust document), and orders the executor to distribute the estate to the trustee. The trustee uses the order as the governing document when dealing with third parties, such as banks, brokers, and title companies, rather than the original trust-will. Recording a certified copy of the order in those counties where real property is located serves to transfer the property from the estate to the trustee.

As a will, the testamentary trust must conform to all of the legal requirements for the execution of a will. It therefore contains all essential provisions found in any will, such as nomination of a guardian of the person and estate of the testator's minor children, nomination of executors, and a section for the attestation by witnesses. It may also have provisions that make outright gifts of certain property (e.g., the tangible personal property may be given to the spouse or children free of trust).

In addition to containing all of the provisions customarily found in other wills, the testamentary trust, like the living trust, must include *other unique clauses* that relate to the trust itself. Thus, it will include provisions for distributing probate property into the trust, for naming one or more trustees, for stating who will be the trust beneficiaries, for specifying how much income and principal they will receive and when they will receive it, and for describing the trustee's duties and powers in connection with managing the trust property. Of course, all but the first clause just mentioned are also included in a living trust.

It should be noted that being a will, the testamentary trust is not an "agreement" between testator and future trustee. In fact, the potential trustee may not even be aware that he or she will one day be asked to perform this task, and may not even be born when the testamentary trust was signed. Before the court order of distribution, the nominated trustee will have to file with the court a consent to serve as trustee. Exhibit 3-3 presents a relatively uncomplicated testamentary trust.

EXHIBIT 3 - 3 Testamentary Trust (Trust-Will)

WILL OF

WILLARD THOMAS SMITH

I, Willard Thomas Smith, a resident of Mytown, Anystate, declare this to be my will. I revoke all prior Wills and Codicils.

First: Family and Guardian I am married to Sue L. Smith, referred to in this will as "my wife." I have three children, all from this marriage, whose names and birthdays are:

Kristi M. Smith	June 27, 1987
Heather L. Smith	April 19, 1989
Todd R. Smith	May 11, 1991

Reference to "my children" or to "my child," shall include children born later and children adopted by me. I have no deceased children.

If my wife does not survive me, and it is necessary to appoint a guardian, I nominate Curtis J. Quint guardian of the person and estate of each such minor child. If for any reason Curtis J. Quint does not act as guardian, I nominate Maria S. Cruise as guardian of the person and estate.

Second: Selection of Fiduciaries I nominate the following fiduciaries:

A. *Designation of Executor* I nominate my wife as my executor. If for any reason she does not so act, I nominate James A. Reliable to be my executor. If for any reason neither my wife nor James A. Reliable acts as executor, I nominate Third National Bank of Mytown to be my executor.

B. *Designation of trustee* I nominate such of my children as are over the age of twenty-five as co-trustees. If my children are unable to serve as trustees, then I nominate James A. Reliable as the trustee of all trusts provided for under this will. If for any reason neither my children nor James A. Reliable are available to serve as trustee, I nominate Third National Bank of Mytown as trustee.

EXHIBIT 3 - 3 Testamentary Trust (Trust-Will) *continued*

C. *Bond waiver* No bond, surety, or other security shall be required of my executor or of my trustee.

Third: Disposition of Property I make the following provisions for my probate property:

A. *Tangible personal property* If my wife survives me by 30 days, I give her all of my interest in any tangible personal property. If my wife does not survive me by 30 days, I give my tangible personal property in equal shares to those of my children who survive me by 30 days. My executor shall consider their personal preferences in making that division. If my children are still minors, my executor has my permission to sell any of that property and distribute the proceeds to equalize the shares. My executor shall be discharged for all tangible personal property so given to any minor child if the child or adult having the child's custody gives a written receipt to my executor.

B. *Residue* If my wife survives me by four months, I give her the residue of my estate. If my wife does not survive me by four months and all of my living children are then over the age of twenty-one, I give the residue in equal shares: one to each child who survived me by four months, and one share for each deceased child whose issue is then living. If any issue of a deceased child entitled to a share is under age twenty-one, his or her share shall be administered as set forth at subparagraph 2 of this Third Article.

If my wife does not survive me and if any child of mine is under age twenty-one, then the residue of my estate shall not vest in the children as provided above; rather, such property shall be distributed in trust to the trustee named above, to be held, administered, and distributed as follows:

1. *Any child under age twenty-one* So long as a child is under age twenty-one, the trustee shall pay to or apply for the benefit of all of my children, as much of the net income and principal as the trustee in the trustee's discretion deems appropriate for their proper support, health, and education, after taking into consideration, to the extent that the trustee considers it advisable, the value of the trust assets, the relative needs, both present and future, of each of the beneficiaries, and their other income and resources made known to the trustee and reasonably available to meet beneficiary needs. The trustee may make distributions under this provision that benefit one or more beneficiaries to the exclusion of others. Any net income not distributed shall be accumulated and added to principal.

2. *Youngest child reaches age twenty-one* When the youngest child reaches the age of twenty-one, the trustee shall divide the trust into as many equal shares as there are children of mine then living and children of mine then deceased with

---

EXHIBIT 3 - 3 Testamentary Trust (Trust-Will) *continued*

---

descendants then living. Each share set aside for a child of mine then deceased with descendants then living shall be further divided into shares for such descendants, by right of representation. Each such share shall be distributed, or retained in trust, as hereafter provided.

      a.   Each share set aside for a child, or for the descendant of a deceased child who has reached the age of twenty-one, shall be distributed free of trust.

      b.   Each share set aside for a descendant who has not reached age twenty-one shall be retained in trust. The trustee shall pay to, or for the benefit of, that descendant as much of the income and principal of the trust as the trustee, in the trustee's discretion, considers appropriate for that descendant's support, health, and education. When the descendant reaches age twenty-one, that descendant's entire share shall be distributed to that descendant, free of trust. If that descendant dies before receiving distribution of that descendant's entire share, the undistributed balance of that descendant's entire share shall be distributed to that descendant's then-living descendants, by right of representation, or if there are none, to my then-living issue, by right of representation. In the latter event, the share of a descendant for whom there exists a trust created by this instrument shall augment that descendant's trust.

    C. *Taxes from residue* All death taxes imposed because of my death and interest and penalties on those taxes, whether on property passing under this will or otherwise, shall be paid by my executor from the residue of my estate.

    D. *Restriction against assignment, etc.* No interest in the principal or income of this trust shall be anticipated, assigned, encumbered, or subject to any creditor's claim or to legal process before its actual receipt by the beneficiary.

    E. *If all beneficiaries die before full distribution* If neither my wife nor any of my descendants survives me by four months, I give the residue of my estate according to Mystate's laws of descent and distribution, one half as if I had died with no will on the last day of that four-month period, and one half as if it were my wife's estate and she had died with no will on that last day.

    F. *Perpetuities saving* Any trust created by this will that has not terminated sooner, shall terminate twenty-one years after the death of the last survivor of the class composed of my wife and those of my issue living at my death.

Fourth: Powers of Executor My executor shall have unrestricted powers, without court order, to settle my estate as this will provides. In addition, my executor shall have all powers my executor thinks necessary or desirable to administer my estate, including the following:

EXHIBIT 3 - 3 Testamentary Trust (Trust-Will) *continued*

A. To make distributions of principal and income on an interim basis to those entitled to it.

B. To sell, exchange, mortgage, pledge, lease, or assign any property belonging to my estate.

C. To continue operation of any business belonging to my estate.

D. To invest and reinvest any surplus money.

Fifth: Powers of Trustee To carry out the purposes of any trust created under Article Three, and subject to any limitations stated elsewhere in this will, the trustee is vested with the following powers with respect to the trust estate and any part of it, in addition to those powers now or hereafter conferred by law:

A. To continue to hold any property, including shares of the trustee's own stock, and to operate at the risk of the trust estate any business that the trustee receives or acquires under the trust as long as the trustee deems advisable.

B. To manage, control, grant options on, sell (for cash or on deferred payments), convey, exchange, partition, divide, improve, and repair trust property.

C. To lease trust property for terms within or beyond the term of the trust and for any purpose, including exploration for and removal of gas, oil, and other minerals and to enter into community oil leases, pooling, and unitization agreements.

D. To borrow money and to encumber or hypothecate trust property by mortgage, deed of trust, pledge, or otherwise.

E. To invest and reinvest the trust estate in every kind of property, real, personal, or mixed, and every kind of investment, specifically including, but not by way of limitation, corporate obligations of every kind, stocks (preferred or common), shares of investment trusts, investment companies and mutual funds, and mortgage participations, which persons of prudence, discretion, and intelligence acquire for their own account, and any common trust fund administered by the trustee.

F. In any case in which the trustee is required, pursuant to the provisions of the trust, to divide any trust property into parts or shares for the purpose of distribution, or otherwise, the trustee is authorized, in the trustee's absolute discretion, to make the division and distribution in kind, including undivided interests in any property, or partly in kind and partly in money, and for this purpose to make such sales of the trust property as the trustee may deem necessary on such terms and conditions as the trustee shall see fit.

EXHIBIT 3 - 3 Testamentary Trust (Trust-Will) *continued*

I have signed my name to this instrument on March 19, 1999, at Mytown, Anystate.

Willard Thomas Smith

Statement of Witnesses The undersigned witnesses declare under penalty of perjury under Anystate law, on March 19, 1999, that we are over twenty-one, that the testator declared to us that this instrument is his will, that he signed this will, and that he requested us to act as witnesses to it. Whereupon he signed in our presence, and we now, in the presence of each other, subscribe our names as witnesses. In doing so, we attest that we believe that the testator is of sound mind, and did not act under fraud, duress, or undue influence.

John Meeks	*Jennifer Jarrett*
1341 Park St., Little Town, Anystate	42 Short Rd., Little Town, Anystate

---

Notice that, unlike the living trust shown in Exhibit 3-2, this particular testamentary trust creates only a *contingent trust* (i.e., a trust that comes into existence only if a certain event happens, specifically for this trust that both the testator's wife fails to survive him and that one or more beneficiaries is under the age of twenty-one). Not all testamentary trusts are contingent. For example, a testamentary trust could provide that a trust be created that gives the surviving spouse a life estate, followed by a life estate for the children, with the remainder going to the grandchildren.

This chapter has introduced the documents used in the transfer of an estate, with particular emphasis on the simple will, the living trust, and the testamentary trust. The next chapter focuses on the actual process of transfer of the property disposed of by these documents, with particular emphasis on the probate process and its handling of intestate succession. Later chapters will again discuss trusts in connection with saving estate taxes, with special emphasis on what are called bypass trusts and marital deduction trusts.

QUESTIONS AND PROBLEMS

1. (*a*) Name the major documents used in the estate planning process to transfer wealth. (*b*) Do they all require the same effort in their preparation? Why or why not?

2. Describe the five major reasons why a will might not be admitted to probate.

3. Name and describe the two different types of wills recognized by many states.

4. Can a valid will meet the typical statutory requirements for both the witnessed will and the holographic will? Why or why not?

5. (*a*) What is a simple will? (*b*) List its major sections.

6. (*a*) What is a codicil? (*b*) Why is it mentioned in the typical will?

7. (*a*) Why does the will nominate two types of guardians? (*b*) Must the probate judge follow the testator's nominations?

8. Why might it be a mistake to waive (as part of one's will) the requirement of an executor's bond? When does waiving one make the most sense?

9. What is the purpose of a clause directing that all death taxes be paid from the residue?

10. Why does the disposition section in a will contain a survival clause?

11. Describe the contents of the "Statement of Witnesses" section of a will.

12. (*a*) Distinguish between a living trust and a testamentary trust. (*b*) Are all testamentary trusts established in wills?

13. (*a*) Of the three documents highlighted in this chapter, how many are wills? (*b*) How many create trusts?

14. Contrast the living trust in Exhibit 3-2 with the testamentary trust in Exhibit 3-3 in terms of:
    a. When the trust takes effect.
    b. Who is the appointed or nominated trustee.
    c. Whether the trust principal is subject to probate administration at the trustor's death.
    d. Who are the income beneficiaries.
    e. Who are the remaindermen.

15. (a) Describe, in general, how the living trust included in Exhibit 3-2 disposes of income and principal. (b) Which parties stand to receive a contingent future interest? (c) When, if ever, will each future interest become vested?

16. List the sections of a testamentary trust that are common to all witnessed wills and the sections that are found only in testamentary trusts.

17. Finnegan, a widower, died last week. He is survived by the following family members (current ages in parentheses): Two children, Joe (30) and Gary (17). Joe has four children, Jackie (5), John (3), Carol (2), and Bob(1). Finnegan is also survived by three other grandchildren: Floyd (4) and Fred (3), the sons of Finnegan's deceased daughter Kerri, and Kitty (9), the daughter of Finnegan's deceased daughter Shirley. Kerri's and Shirley's husbands, Kurt (29), and Rolf (31), are still alive. Joe has come to your office requesting some information. Assuming that Finnegan's large estate will be distributed in accordance with the testamentary trust contained in Exhibit 3-3, answer the following: (a) *Who* will receive the property (i.e., principal), and (b) assuming no more family members die at a young age, *when* will they receive it?

APPENDIX 3A

The Rule Against Perpetuities

The rule against perpetuities (the Rule) originated in English common law. The statutes of all states except Idaho, Wisconsin, North Dakota, and South Dakota contain some variation of this rule. Charitable trusts are exempt from the Rule, making them potentially infinite in duration.

The Rule acts to prevent a transferor from controlling the disposition of property for an unreasonably long period after making the transfer. The Rule is generally stated as follows:

> *No interest is good unless it must vest, if at all, not later than twenty-one years after some life in being at the creation of the interest.*

Thus, the Rule has the effect of invalidating a future contingent interest which might not vest within twenty-one years after the death of certain people alive (the measuring lives) at the time the document creating the interest became irrevocable.

In estate planning, an interest in property can take effect during the transferor's lifetime, or it can take effect at the transferor's death. A transfer into an irrevocable living trust is an example of the creation of a property interest that will take effect during the transferor's lifetime, whereas a transfer into the typical revocable living trust and a transfer by will are examples of transfers that create interests that do not take effect until the transferor's death.

Thus, to satisfy the requirements of the Rule, the interest must *vest*, if at all, within twenty-one years after the death of someone alive at the moment of transfer into an irrevocable trust, or at the moment of the transferor's death, for interests created by will or by revocable living trust.

The Rule is satisfied if an interest vests (or fails) immediately upon its transfer. Thus, a statement in a will giving a bequest "to John, for his life, then to Mary or her estate," creates vested interests for both John and Mary at the testator's death. Nothing (except, in Mary's case, the passage of time) will prevent them from receiving possession of the property. Of course, if John dies before the testator, his interest (a life estate) will immediately fail. Therefore, the Rule need only be used to determine the validity of contingent future interests; that is, interests that are *not vested* when created.

The requirement that the interest must vest "if at all" means that a contingent future interest will not violate the Rule merely because it failed to vest due to the happening of a contingency that did not work in favor of a named party. Thus, the transfer "to Jane if she survives Margo" gives Jane a contingent future interest that must vest or fail to vest within the permitted time. Failure to vest will not violate the Rule, so long as that failure (or non-failure) must occur within the required period. Thus, Jane will or will not survive Margo, an outcome that will be determined as soon as one of them dies. If one cannot be sure that one or the other of these outcomes will definitely happen during the period, then the interest violates the Rule.

To qualify under the Rule, an interest must vest or fail to vest "not later than twenty-one years after some life in being at the creation of the interest". The "life in being" concept is difficult to explain precisely. For our purposes, however, we can say that the persons permitted to be "lives in being" are usually those mentioned or identified in the transfer document itself. Thus, for the transfer "to Carrie for her life, then to Carrie's living children," Carrie would be the sole measuring life. She is alive at the creation of the children's interest, and the length of her life span will determine the devolution of the property. Taking a second example, the provision that a trust will terminate "twenty-one years after the death of the last survivor of the class composed of my wife and those of my issue living at my death" identifies the measuring lives as all the people in the class. This "perpetuities saving clause," included in the testamentary trust in Exhibit 3-3, is a clause that can further protect an interest from vesting too remotely. It will be discussed further, shortly.

The requirement of vesting within "twenty-one years" after the death of a life in being was originally included to enable the transferor to control the disposition of property for his or her life, for the lives of the children, and for the period of the grandchildren's minority, but no longer. For those individuals, all interests created which are contingent solely upon *parent survival* will usually vest within the required period. The children's interest will vest by the time of the death of the transferor, and the grandchildren's interest will vest within twenty-one years of the death of the last surviving child. Thus, all of their interests will vest within the required period. On the other hand, a great-grandchild's interest will typically (but not always) vest *after* the twenty-one year period, and thus will usually fail.

A violation of the Rule will cause that particular interest to be void. The interest will then revert to the transferor or the transferor's successors.

Let us consider some examples. In each case, assume that the transferor has died, leaving a will containing the disposition clause shown as the initial quote.

EXAMPLE 3A-1. Ted's will stated, "To my wife, Mary, for her life, then to Bill or his estate." Both Mary's and Bill's interests vested immediately when the will took effect (at Ted's death) because at that point, nothing except the passage of time could delay their possession or enjoyment. Therefore, neither interest is contingent, that is, dependent upon the happening of a future event, other than the passage of time. Applying the Rule, their interests "must vest...not later than...." Thus, both interests are valid under the Rule.

EXAMPLE 3A-2. Theresa's will stated, "To my husband, Bert, for his life, then to my son James, if still living, otherwise to Ron or his estate." Bert's vested interest is valid under the Rule for the same reason that Mary's was in the preceding example. Both James and Ron have contingent interests in the property. Thus, we must ask whether they must vest within the specified time. Both James's and Ron's interests will vest, if at all (either one or the other will never vest, depending upon whether or not James survives Bert), within "twenty-one years after some life in being". Bert is "a life in being" at the time of Theresa's death, and both interests will vest or will fail to vest at his death well within the time limit of the Rule. Therefore, both James's and Ron's interests are valid under the Rule.

EXAMPLE 3A-3. Tom's will stated, "To my wife Sarah, for her life, then to my son Greg, for his life, then equally to Greg's living children when the youngest child reaches age 25." Are Greg's children's interests valid under the Rule? Sarah, Greg, and any children alive when the trust became irrevocable at Tom's death are "lives in being" at the creation of the interest. But more children could be born to Greg, and they would not be lives in being at the time the trust became irrevocable, yet they would (by the terms of the trust) each have an interest that could vest, more than twenty-one years after the deaths of Sarah, Greg, and any of the children that were born when the trust became irrevocable. Therefore, all of the grandchildren's interests are void, and Tom or his successors would receive a reversionary interest that follows the death of Greg. Since Tom's only living issue is Greg, violation of the Rule probably means that Greg would have the interests in fee. Note that had the trust called for the interests to vest when Greg's oldest living child reaches age twenty-one, then all the children's interests would vest within a life in being plus twenty-one years, even if none of the children were born when the trust became irrevocable, since all children would be born within Greg's lifetime.

EXAMPLE 3A-4. Continuing with Example 3A-1, assume the following is also included in Ted's will: "...then to my great, great, great-grandchildren..." Assuming that Ted is survived only by children and grandchildren, it is possible that the great, great, great-grandchildren's contingent interest will vest after twenty-one years after the death of all children and grandchildren, who are the only apparent lives in being at Ted's death. Thus, their interests are void.

Here are two general *rules of thumb* when applying the Rule to transfers of interests to surviving issue:

1. Transferors usually can create valid contingent interests for their *grandchildren*, as long as the interests must vest by the time their grandchildren reach age twenty-one. The law tacks on the period of gestation to the twenty-one years; hence a grandchild born after the father's death can have his or interest vest at age twenty-one without violating the Rule.
2. Transferors usually can create valid interests for their *great-grand-children* only if they outlive all of their children.

Today, not all dispositions in violation of the Rule are invalid. Two types of *safeguards* designed to overcome the Rule are available to transferors. First, most states have enacted *statutes* that limit application of the Rule, or even invalidate it entirely. For example, many states have enacted a "wait and see" statute which, in effect, finds an interest void only if the interest turns out *in fact* not to vest within the required period. In addition, some states have a type of wait-and-see statute stating that any interest which actually vests within a certain period of time (e.g., 60 years) after its creation cannot be declared void, even if it violates the Rule. In 1986 the National Conference of Commissioners on Uniform State Laws approved the Uniform Statutory Rule Against Perpetuities, recommending that all states enact it. It includes a wait-and-see period of 90 years after creation.

Another statutory safeguard is the application of the "*cy pres*" rule to enable the courts to correct violations of the Rule, if at all possible, so that the transferor's intentions can be respected. *Cy pres*, French for "as near as possible," is a principle used primarily in the context of charitable bequests, to permit the substitution of one beneficiary for another when the original charitable purpose is impossible, illegal, or impractical to carry out. For example, over a century ago, one testator left property in trust to fight for the cause of abolition. After the 13th Amendment freed the slaves, a court applied *cy pres* to permit the trust to continue by assisting freed slaves.

A second type of safeguard against a perpetuities violation involves the lawyer's insertion in the document of the earlier mentioned *perpetuities saving clause*, similar to the one in the *testamentary trust* in Exhibit 3-3. Such a provision, however, may act to prevent the client from making an otherwise valid transfer, perhaps simply because the attorney chose not to test the interest against the Rule. In fact, none of the above safeguards is as effective as the thoughtful analysis and planning of an expert.

Yet, one must have some sympathy for the lawyers who use the clause. The Rule often requires complex analysis to test a given interest, and it can even puzzle experts. One state supreme court held that, given the complexity of the rule, an attorney who created a will that violated the Rule was not liable because he had used the ordinary skill commonly exercised by lawyers.[10] It is doubtful that a similar case would be decided the same way today.

The purpose of this appendix has been to present an overview of the Rule Against Perpetuities. All members of the estate planning team should have at least a general understanding of the Rule, primarily because it constitutes a constraint on how far into the future one can meddle.

QUESTIONS AND PROBLEMS FOR 3A

1. What is the purpose of the Rule Against Perpetuities?

2. Helen's will leaves one half of her wealth outright to Vinnie and the other half in trust for Johnny, with all income payable annually to Johnny and, at the earlier of Johnny's death or his reaching age twenty-one, corpus to Johnny or his estate. Does this will violate the Rule? Why or why not?

3. Holly's will leaves all of her property in trust, with income to her living children for life, then income to her then-living grandchildren for their lives, and then remainder over to her then living great-grandchildren. Who will get Holly's property?

4. Generally, how do drafters of trust documents avoid violation of the Rule today?

ANSWERS TO QUESTIONS AND PROBLEMS (Chapter, then appendix 3A)

1. a.   The major documents used in the estate planning process to transfer wealth include the will, the trust, joint tenancies, and contractual arrangements, including life insurance and pension and profit sharing plans.

   b.   Not all of them require the same effort in preparation. The will and the trust require more effort in preparation, primarily because they are custom-drafted for each client. The other documents are considerably simpler and do not require an attorney's help. However, as we will see, clients anticipating a potential death tax will do well to seek competent advice.

2. Five major reasons why a will may not be admitted to probate:

   a.   Lack of testamentary capacity; that is, failure to be aware: 1) that they are executing a will; 2) of what they own; 3) of their heirs.
   b.   Undue influence, or over-persuasion.
   c.   Fraud.
   d.   Mistake.
   e.   Format (formality) problems, e.g., one witness where the state of domicile requires two.

3. Two different wills recognized by many states:

   a.   The witnessed will. Typical requirements: 1) must be in writing; 2) testator must sign in the presence of two witnesses.
   b.   The holographic will. Typical requirements: 1) signature in testator's handwriting; 2) all or all of the material provisions in testator's handwriting.

4. In many states, a valid will can theoretically meet the typical requirements for both the witnessed will and the holographic will because the formal requirements are not usually mutually exclusive. Such a will would usually have to be written, with all material provisions written in the testator's hand, and signed in the presence of two witnesses.

5. a. A simple will is one prepared for a family having a modest estate, one for which death tax planning is not a significant concern, and one in which all property is usually devised to the surviving spouse, and, if no surviving spouse, to the children.
   b. Major sections of the simple will include:

      1. Declaration and Revocation;
      2. Family and Guardian;
      3. Executor;
      4. Disposition of Property;
      5. Powers of Executor;
      6. Statement of Witnesses;

6. a. A codicil is a separate written document that amends or revokes a prior will.
   b. It is mentioned in the revocation clause to prevent needless litigation over the construction of two or more wills.

7. a. The will nominates two guardians, one for the person and one for the estate, because each has a different responsibility. In the uncomplicated trust-will, the estate guardian has a smaller role because the trustee manages the client's property to be held in trust for a minor child.
   b. The judge need not follow the testator's nominations if, in his or her judgment, they do not reflect the best interests of the child.

8. Not waiving the bond can protect the estate from breaches of trust by the executor. This may be important when the testator nominates or anticipates that the probate judge may appoint a non-professional, who is not related to the decedent, to be executor.

9. The purpose of the residue tax clause is to relieve non-residuary (and non-probate) beneficiaries from having to pay their share of the death taxes. It may be the fairest provision, particularly when other beneficiaries receive illiquid assets. It also can speed up the probate process.

10. A survival clause avoids the risk of 1) double probate, and 2) unintended disposition to in-laws, etc., when one spouse survives the other a short period.

11. The "statement of witnesses" section of a will includes an attestation by the witnesses, made under penalty of perjury and in the presence of the testator, of the following facts:

• they were over age 21 and competent to witness the will;
• the testator, in their presence, said that the document was his or her will and asked them to act as witnesses, and signed the will;
• they believe the testator was of sound mind and was not acting under duress, fraud, or undue influence.

12. a. A living trust takes effect during the trustor's lifetime, while a testamentary trust takes effect after the testator's death. The latter is funded through the probate process.

   b. Yes, by definition all testamentary trusts are established in wills.

13. a. Two of the documents are wills: Exhibit 3-1 (simple will) and Exhibit 3-3 (trust-will).

   b. Two of the documents create trusts: Exhibit 3-2 (living trust) and Exhibit 3-3 (testamentary trust, a.k.a. trust-will).

14.		**3-2 living trust**	**3-3 testamentary trust**
a.	takes effect?	upon execution & funding	upon probate order
b.	nominated trustees?	John C. Jones (trustor and trustee)	children over the age of 25, if none, then James A. Reliable.
c.	probated?	no, probate avoidance	yes, the funding mechanism is the probate process
d.	income beneficiaries?	initially the trustor, John C. Jones, then children, if wife does not survive the four month survivorship period	none, if wife survives, otherwise the children until they reach the ages set for termination of the trust
e.	remaindermen?	wife, if she survives the four month survivorship period, otherwise the children.	the children, but only if the trust is funded. This happens if wife does not survive the four month survivorship period.

15.		**3-2 living trust**
a.	income beneficiaries	initially the trustor, John C. Jones, then children, if wife does not survive four month survivorship period
b.	principal beneficiaries	initially the trustor, John C. Jones, then his wife (actually, the trustee of her living trust) or their children, if wife does not survive the four month survivorship period. Thus both wife and children are contingent remaindermen.

c. vesting of future interests — The wife's remainder interest vests if she survives four months beyond her husband, the interest of each child will vest only if the wife does not so survive and the child reaches age 21. The children's issue are also contingent remaindermen whose interests vest if a parent (trustor's child) dies before age 21.

16. Sections common to all witnessed wills:

1. Declaration and Revocation,
2. Family and Guardian,
3. Executor,
4. Disposition of Property,
5. Powers of Executor,
6. Statement of Witnesses.

Sections found only in trust wills:

1. Designation of Trustee,
2. Powers of Trustee.

17. Distribution of Finnegan's estate in accordance with the trust-will in Exhibit 3-3:

1. All *tangible personal property* (except vehicles and boats) will transfer immediately outright - equally to Joe and Gary.

2. The *residue* goes into trust, with income to Joe and Gary as the trustee sees fit. In four years, when Gary attains age 21 (or sooner, if Gary dies), the corpus will be divided into shares, which are not necessarily equal, for Joe, Gary, Floyd, Fred, and Kitty. At that time, Joe and Gary's shares will be distributed to them outright. Floyd's, Fred's, and Kitty's shares will be distributed to them when they each reach age 21.

ANSWERS TO QUESTIONS AND PROBLEMS - APPENDIX 3A

1. The purpose of the Rule is to prevent a transferor of property from controlling the disposition of property for an unreasonably long period after making the transfer.

2. Neither disposition violates the Rule. Both interests will vest at Helen's death, which is clearly within 21 years after the death of some life in being.

3. Both Holly and her children are lives in being insofar as this will is concerned. The income interests of the children and the grandchildren vest within the Rule's outer limits but the remainder over to the great grandchildren violates the Rule. The great grandchildren's interests fail because there is a chance that a grandchild will give birth to a great grandchild more than 21 years after Holly's death (the time when lives in being is fixed), hence that grandchild would not be "in being" within the Rule's outer time limit. The remote interests of the great grandchildren are cut off and the grandchildren would end up with remainder interests instead of just income interests.

4. The Rule is frequently avoided today by

   a. statutes, such as the "wait and see" rule, that limit application of the Rule or invalidate it entirely, and
   b. perpetuities saving clauses in trust documents requiring that the trust terminate no later than the outer limits of the Rule.

ENDNOTES

1. According to the Legal Research Institute at Cornell Law School, the following states have adopted all or part of the UPC: Alaska, Arizona, California*, Colorado, District of Colombia, Florida, Hawaii, Idaho, Indiana, Kentucky*, Maine, Maryland, Michigan, Minnesota, Missouri, Montana, Nebraska, New Mexico, New Jersey*, North Dakota, Pennsylvania, South Carolina, South Dakota, and Utah. States marked with an * have adopted the UPC in an incomplete form. (See http://www.law.cornell.edu/uniform/probate.html)

2. See California Probate Code §6111(c) @ http://www.leginfo.ca.gov/calaw.html.

3. See UPC §2-503 (e.g., see South Dakota's Title 29A-2-503 using the URL in footnote 1, supra).

4. UPC §2-504.

5. UPC §2-517.

6. Uniform Probate Code §2-507.

7. *Wolfe's Will,* 185 NC 563, (1923).

8. Cal. Probate Code §6402.5.

9. *Knupp v. District of Columbia,* 578 A. 2d 702 (D.C. Ct. App., 1990).

10. *Lucas v. Hamm,* 56 Cal. 2d 583.

CHAPTER 4

The Transfer of Wealth

OVERVIEW

This chapter considers the actual process or mechanism by which property is transferred, emphasizing transfers taking effect at death. In the preceding chapter, we covered the documents that serve as the guide to the transfers, such as title documents for joint tenancy, property dispositions by contract, the will and the trust instruments, plus the law of intestate succession that serves as a guide where no other legally recognized guide exists.

RATIONALE FOR PROBATE DISTRIBUTION

When a person dies, steps must be taken to transfer ownership of his or her property interests to the proper beneficiaries. Each of the 50 states and the District of Columbia has enacted a probate code that establishes the rules for transferring a decedent's property. These codes serve a dual purpose; they attempt to protect both creditors of the decedent's estate and assure that the appropriate beneficiaries eventually end up with the property after debts and expenses are paid. Where a will exists, the codes seek to assure that the nominated executor is appointed unless there is good cause for appointing someone else. The notice provisions seek to assure that the creditors have a chance to file their claims and that potential beneficiaries, including heirs that have been disinherited, are aware of the proceedings so that the interested parties can raise an issue if the will being offered for probate is not the last will or if there is some irregularity concerning the will being offered. The code sets forth the contents of the petition that starts the probate process and specifies the steps that the administrator must take from start to final distribution. Of course, if there is no will, the probate procedures are still very much the same. The main difference is that the intestate succession laws serve as the guide rather than the will. Will or no will, most of the steps are the same. The notices, the marshaling of assets, the filing of an inventory, reports to the court, filing an accounting, and obtaining an order for distribution all have to be done.

NONPROBATE VERSUS PROBATE ASSETS

In a sense, the probate process stands last in line. Only that property for which there is no other mechanism of transfer is swept into the probate process. As discussed in the last chapter, the other mechanisms include certain title, contract, and trust arrangements. About all that is left, after the non-probate mechanisms are taken into account, is property held in the decedent's name alone, or held with others as tenants in common or with a spouse as community property. Even community property may avoid probate if it is left to the surviving spouse.

Like probate, the non-probate mechanisms for transfer are sanctioned by law. However, they are subject to much less state supervision. With title held as *tenancy by the entirety* or *joint tenancy,* the right of survivorship results in the automatic transfer of ownership to the surviving co-tenants, with the right previously held by the decedent-owner ceasing immediately. This automatic transfer is said to be a transfer by *operation of law*. Although title may pass automatically, as a practical matter additional steps may be necessary to clear title to joint tenancy property; the decedent's name will need to be removed from the actual documents. Fortunately, this is usually processed quickly by the authorities (banks, motor vehicle bureau, etc.) keeping record of the title when a surviving cotenant appears before them with a certified copy of the death certificate. For real estate, to satisfy title companies, the survivors will have to record, in each county where the jointly held land is located, a notarized "affidavit of death of joint tenant" verifying that the person identified in the attached certified death certificate was the co-owner of the parcels identified in the affidavit.

Property that, at the decedent's death, is held in a revocable or irrevocable *living trust* is not held in the decedent's name, but rather the legal title is in the name of the trustee. Since probate administration is concerned with transfer of property held in the decedent's name (individually or concurrently), property held by a trustee is not subject to probate administration. If, in accordance with the underlying trust document, the trustor's death triggers a transfer out of trust to the remainderman, the transfer process is uncomplicated. The trustee simply makes the distribution by deed or assignment, depending on the nature of the assets.

Where the decedent settlor (trustor) was serving as trustee at the time of his or her death, most state laws allow the successor trustee to immediately take over the administration of the estate. Hence no probate administration is required. The successor will have to establish for the benefit of those involved with the transfer process (e.g, brokerage houses, title companies, etc.) that the settlor is dead by producing a certified death certificate and that he or she is the successor trustee, which can usually be established by photo-identification (e.g., the successor trustee's drivers license).

Property owned by the decedent to be transferred at death *into*, rather than out of, a trust will be subject to probate administration. In such instances, the probate process is the funding mechanism for the trust. This will occur for all testamentary trusts because no separate trust exists prior to the death of the testator. Near the conclusion of the probate, the court order for distribution to the trustee has a dual purpose: (1) it serves as the trust funding mechanism, and (2) it serves as the trust document since the terms of the trust, taken from the will, are repeated as part of the order. Where real property is transferred pursuant to a probate order for distribution, whether to the trustee of a testamentary trust or to someone else, no deed is necessary. Rather, the executor records a certified copy of the order in the county where the real property is located. Generally, when a living trust is used, a probate is unnecessary. Nevertheless, the trustor will have created a pourover will, so called because it scoops up assets left out of the trust and "pours" them into it. This "pouring" is done through the probate process, which concludes with an order for distribution to the trustee of the living trust. Of course, with the living trust, the order does not include the language of the trust because it is already in existence as a separate document.

Property disposed of by contract, including *life insurance proceeds* on the life of the decedent and *retirement benefits*, is not subject to probate administration because title to such assets is not held by the decedent. Instead, title is held by the insurance company or the pension fund, respectively, and each has agreed to transfer title directly to the named beneficiary at the death of the decedent; the insurance company or pension fund pays the named beneficiary in accordance with the payout option selected by the decedent or by the beneficiary. Note that the law sanctions the transfer by contract of only certain kinds of assets; mainly those that are closely connected to death (insurance) or are connected to retirement (pensions and the like). If a person attempted to contract with a friend for the transfer of all of his or her property after death, because the law does not sanction a general contract (as opposed to a trust agreement) as a testamentary transfer device, it is unlikely that the friend would get the cooperation of those entities holding the decedent's personal property (e.g., banks, brokerage firms, etc.) or the blessing of title companies for transferring the decedent's real estate. In addition to not avoiding probate, because the contract would not be executed with the formalities required of a will, it probably would not serve as a guide in the probate process either.[1]

In contrast with title held in joint tenancy, title that is held by a decedent either as an *individual*, as a *tenant in common*, or as *community property* does not in itself create a mechanism (or guide) for title transfer. As a result, the states have established the probate process to transfer title, using either the decedent's will or the laws of intestate succession as the guide.

Although it is difficult to gather accurate statistics, it is generally estimated that about half of all adults die without a will. In such circumstances, the state's intestate succession laws will determine proper distribution for all property for which there is no other guide for transfer and the mechanism for the intestate distribution is the probate process. In fact, probating an intestate decedent's estate might be even more important than for a testate decedent, to ensure correct identification of heirs as well as to ensure distribution to them.

Figure 4-1 diagrams the probate and nonprobate interests of a decedent at the moment of death. The left side contains probate assets, including the decedent's

---

FIGURE 4 - 1 A Decedent's Property Interests

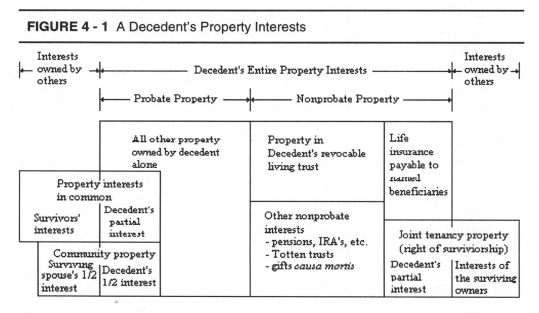

one-half interest in community property, the decedent's interests in probate held in common with others, and the catchall--all other probate property owned individually by the decedent. This would include the value of life insurance *on the life of another* owned by the decedent. Of course, where there is co-ownership, the portion of the interest held *by others,* whether as tenants-in-common, joint tenants, or as community property, is not part of the decedent's probate or nonprobate estate. One should also note that some community property states, such as California, no longer require a probate for property going to a surviving spouse, whether going to her (or him) by virtue of the decedent's will or by intestate succession. Those states may require the surviving spouse to file a simple request for confirmation by the court of the survivor's right to take the property, followed by notice to interested parties, then a hearing, and, finally, a court order granting the confirmation.

The right side contains the nonprobate property including interests in living trusts that are revocable by the decedent, property held in joint tenancy or as tenants by the entirety, life insurance policies on the decedent's life other than those payable to the decedent's estate, and certain other nonprobate interests. Life insurance proceeds payable to the decedent's (probate) estate must, by definition, be a probate asset, since the probate estate will collect the proceeds and hold them pending an order for distribution. Policies issued since World War II are not likely to be paid into the insured's probate estate. In addition to having several layers of alternate beneficiaries, the policy will probably have a provision very similar to intestate succession designating the order of beneficiaries in the event that the named beneficiaries predecease the insured and only as a very last resort have the proceeds payable to the decedent's estate.

The logic of Figure 4-1 suggests a relatively straightforward *procedure* to determine the assets of a decedent that will be subject to probate administration. First, list all of the decedent's property interests held immediately prior to death, including all insurance policies. Then delete from the list all assets for which there is a nonprobate mechanism of transfer, such as property in living trusts, joint tenancy property, and interests payable to a designated beneficiary, such as life insurance, pensions, and finally miscellaneous nonprobate interests such as Totten trusts. What is left should be the decedent's property interests subject to probate administration, mostly property in the decedent's name alone (including insurance on another's life) or held with others as tenants-in-common, and for states that still require probate for community property even when it goes to the surviving spouse, the decedent's half of the community property.

So far, we have seen how the decedent's probate property is determined. The next logical step is to decide who will receive this property. For this, one first looks to the will. If there is no will, the state laws of intestate succession are applied. Details of these succession laws are covered next.

INTESTATE SUCCESSION LAWS

We have seen that a person who dies without a will is said to die intestate and that any probate property will then pass under the state's laws of intestate succession. Further, a person receiving property under these laws is called an heir and is said to inherit the property.

In determining who should inherit, the members of the various state legislatures have used their knowledge of human nature (and a little intuition) to design estate plans for persons dying intestate. Thus, they usually give priority to the decedent's spouse, next to the decedent's issue, and, if there is neither spouse nor issue, then to the decedent's other blood relatives, with priority given to the closest relatives. We will review the Uniform Probate Code's version of intestate succession after we cover degrees of kinship and several common patterns for allocating property amongst a decedent's issue.

Degrees of Consanguinity

Degrees of consanguinity refer to the level of closeness in the blood relationship between a decedent and the decedent's various relatives. As we have said, and as Figure 4-2 depicts, descendants (issue) of the decedent include children, grandchildren, great-grandchildren, and so on. Ascendants (ancestors) include parents, grandparents, great-grandparents, and the like. Descendants and ascendants of a person are said to be in the person's *lineal*, or vertical line. The other relationships shown are *collateral*, meaning that they share with the person a common

FIGURE 4 - 2 Degrees of Consanguinity

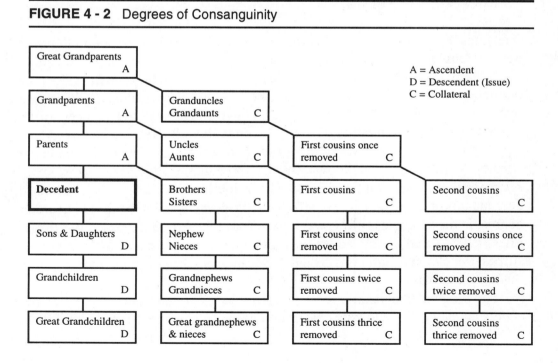

ancestor, but they are neither ascendants nor descendants of the person and thus are not in the person's lineal or vertical line. For example, a nephew of a person is not his or her issue, but shares a common ascendant with the person, namely the person's parent. Since a relative's share of a person's intestate estate is determined by the closeness of the relationship, the decedent is shown at the "center" of Figure 4-2.

The most common method of measuring a relative's degree of consanguinity to the decedent is to count the "steps" along degree lines. For example, the decedent's uncle is three steps from the decedent because we first count two steps upward to the common ancestor and then one step down to the box where the uncle is located. Figure 4-2 can be helpful in determining relative closeness to the decedent of distant surviving relatives, especially in those states that have not adopted the more restrictive succession rules of the Uniform Probate Code. Generally, only persons of the same degree of closeness share an intestate decedent's estate.

Per Stirpes Versus Per Capita

If an intestate decedent's only heirs are one living son and two grandchildren who are the daughters of the decedent's predeceased daughter, how much will each one inherit? Will they each inherit one-third of the estate, or will the son be entitled to a larger proportion because he is a closer descendant? To answer questions like these, we must distinguish between a per capita and a per stirpes distribution. A *per capita* distribution requires that all descendants receive an equal share of the property, or "share and share alike." On the other hand, a *per stirpes* distribution, also known by the more descriptive term *by right of representation,* may result in an unequal distribution, with larger distributions to descendants of a closer degree of affinity to the decedent than to those of a further degree. In the examples below, we will contrast two different types of per stirpes rules, called 'traditional' per stirpes and 'per capita at each generation' per stirpes. Per capita is Latin for "by the head" and per stirpes comes from the Latin for "by the roots."

For a better understanding of the difference between per stirpes and per capita, consider the following description of the family tree illustrated in Figure

4-3. Cross-marks in the diagram indicate descendants who have predeceased the decedent.

FIGURE 4 - 3   Example Illustrating Distribution by Per Stirpes and Per Capita

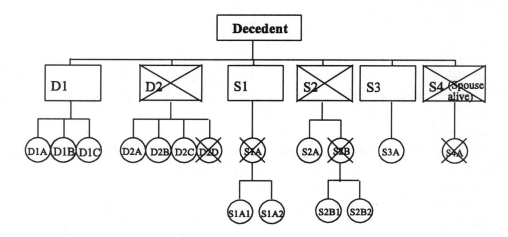

The decedent had the following descendants: Two daughters, D1 and D2, and four sons, S1, S2, S3 and S4. Only D1, S1, and S3 survived the decedent. D1 has three children, D1A, D1B and D1C, all alive. D2 is survived by three children, D2A, D2B, D2C, all alive, but the fourth child, D2D, predeceased the decedent, leaving no issue. S1 had only one child, S1A, who is deceased, but is survived by two children, S1A1 and S1A2. S2 had two children, S2A and S2B. S2A is alive. S2B is deceased, but is survived by two children, S2B1 and S2B2. S2 has no other descendants. S3 and his son S3A both survived the decedent. S4 and his child, S4A, predeceased the decedent. S4 left a spouse but no descendants.

All three rules of distribution, described next, share one basic characteristic: the same people receive a share of the estate. Only the various portions change depending on which rule is applicable. Under all three rules, as one goes down the line of descent, only the surviving members of the *closest generation level* receive a share. In other words, if an ancestor is alive then those in line below do not receive a share.

Thus, in our illustration, only the following nine descendants will receive property under any of the three rules: D1, D2A, D2B, D2C, S1, S2A, S2B1, S2B2, and S3. Why won't the others receive anything? Either because they did not survive the decedent (D2, D2D, S2, S2B, S4, and S4A), or because one of their ancestors (who were descendants of the decedent) survived the decedent (applies to D1A, D1B, D1C, S1A1, S1A2, and S3A).

It also follows that no property will be allocated to any family line if all descendants in that line have predeceased the decedent. For example, S4's blood line (S4A) and S4's spouse, receive nothing.

The three distribution rules differ, however, with regard to *how much* property each descendant will receive. The discussion below will analyze each rule separately.

Per capita. A per capita distribution simply requires that all eligible descendants receive an *equal amount* of the property. Thus, in the example, D1, D2A, D2B, D2C, S1, S2A, S2B1, S2B2, and S3 would each receive a one ninth share.

Per stirpes. A per stirpes distribution would produce a larger distribution to those descendants who are closer to the decedent than to those who are further removed. Historically, two different forms of per stirpes have evolved: traditional per stirpes and per capita at each generation per stirpes. *Traditional per stirpes,* also referred to as by *right of representation,* has been used for hundreds of years. Under it, surviving descendants of predeceased children may take unequally depending upon how many in their family survive. *Per capita at each generation per stirpes*, which treats all members of each generational level equally, has become more common since it replaced traditional per stirpes in the 1990 revision of the Uniform Probate Code.[2]

Determining heirs' interests under either form of per stirpes requires a two step process. First, as in a per capita distribution, the property is divided into shares, one share for each of the decedent's predeceased children having living issue (e.g., D2 and S2 in our example), and one share for each surviving child (e.g., D1, S1 and S3 in our example). How these five shares are distributed for each per stirpes rule under the second step is described next.

Traditional per stirpes. Traditional per stirpes would pass each child's share of property to the closest surviving descendant(s) of the decedent. Thus, in our illustration, each living child, D1, S1 and S3, will receive a one fifth share and their descendants receive nothing. The surviving descendants of a deceased child share equally in their deceased parent's share. Thus, D2's living children, D2A, D2B, and D2C, will share equally in D2's one fifth share. They are said to "represent" their mother. Further, with regard to the one fifth share of the estate that goes to S2's descendants, S2B1 and S2B2 will share equally in what S2B would have received had S2B been alive at decedent's death. Thus, S2A will receive one tenth (one half of the S2 one fifth share) and S2B1 and S2B2, representing their father, each will receive one twentieth.

Summarizing, a traditional per stirpes distribution of the decedent's estate will be divided as follows: D1: 1/5; D2A, D2B, and D2C: 1/15 each (i.e., 1/5 x 1/3); S1: 1/5; S2B1 and S2B2: 1/20 each (i.e., 1/5 x ½ x ½); S2A: 1/10 (i.e., 1/5 x ½); S3: 1/5.

Per capita at each generation per stirpes. Application of per capita at each generation per stirpes would distribute property similar to traditional per stirpes, except that at each generational level the shares of those entitled to receive a portion of the estate (generally because all lineal ancestors between the decedent and the heir are dead) are combined, and then divided equally amongst them. Thus, in the illustration, similar to traditional per stirpes, each living child, D1, S1, and S3 would first receive a one fifth share. Next, unlike traditional per stirpes, because there are an unequal number of eligible children of two of the decedent's children (three from D2 and two from S2), the distribution to the grandchildren and great grandchildren will be different. The two one-fifth shares meant for the grandchildren D2A, D2B, D2C, S2B (for representation purposes) and S2A are combined and distributed equally to D2A, D2B, D2C and S2A, and S2B1 and S2B2 will split equally S2B's share, by representation. Thus each of the four eligible grandchildren will receive two twenty-fifths (i.e., 2/5 x 1/5), and each of the two eligible great grandchildren will receive one half of their parent S2B's two twenty-fifths share, or one twenty-fifth (i.e., ½ x 2/25).

Summarizing, a per capita at each generation distribution of the decedent's estate will be divided as follows: D1: 1/5; D2A, D2B and D2C: 2/25 each; S1: 1/5; S2B1 and S2B2: 1/25 each; S2A: 2/25; S3: 1/5. Notice that each eligible grandchild inherits the *same amount* (2/25s), rather than different amounts (i.e., not 1/15 each to D2A, D2B and D2C, and 1/10 to S2A, as in the case of traditional per stirpes). Whew!

Comparison of the three rules. One advantage of the per capita at each generation form of per stirpes rule is that it gives equal shares to those who are equally related. One advantage of the traditional per stirpes rule is that it passes the same share that the descendants would receive had their ancestors survived, and then died bequeathing the property to the next generation. One advantage of the per capita rule is that it treats everyone equally. This issue is important in planning because clients may strongly prefer one of these types of distributions over the others, and their will or trust document should reflect that preference. Many people would prefer the per capita at each generation per stirpes method if it were explained to them. In contrast, most *attorneys* use estate planning books and estate plan drafting programs that use traditional per stirpes distribution as the default rule. Most state intestate succession laws, including those that have adopted the UPC, also do not use per capita, choosing instead one of the forms of per stirpes distribution.

As mentioned, all three distribution rules are similar in that they dispose of an intestate estate to the same descendants. For each, all descendants who are more remotely related to the decedent will not inherit if an ascendant in a generation closer to the decedent is alive. Preventing inheritance by more remote descendants has the advantage of reducing the number of heirs, thereby making inheritable property more marketable and minimizing the likelihood of inheritance by minors and the need for court-appointed guardians.

Finally, answering the question posed at the beginning of this section, under either per stirpes distribution rule, the son would inherit one half and the granddaughters would each inherit one quarter of the estate. Under per capita distribution, each would inherit one third.

Intestacy in UPC States

We are now ready to look at the rules of intestate succession used by those states which have adopted the Uniform Probate Code. Note that the UPC uses the term descendant rather than issue, reflecting a modern trend to avoid a biological connotation and extend inheritance rights to adopted children.

The Code's principal intestate sections, revised in 1990, are reproduced in Exhibit 4-1. In general, Section 2-101 prefaces the next four sections, which specify actual succession. The intestate share of the surviving spouse is determined by referring to §2-102 for common law states, or to §2-102A for community property states. The intestate share of heirs, other than the surviving spouse, is determined by referring to §2-103. Section 2-104 covers survival situations. Finally, if there are no "takers" under the above sections, §2-105 requires a procedure called "escheat" whereby the property ends up going to the state of domicile. A more specific analysis follows the Code.

EXHIBIT 4 - 1 Intestate Succession under the Uniform Probate Code

---

2-101 Intestate Estate

(a) Any part of a decedent's estate not effectively disposed of by will passes by intestate succession to the decedent's heirs as prescribed in this Code, except as modified by the decedent's will.

(b) A decedent, by will, may expressly exclude or limit the right of an individual or class to succeed to property of the decedent passing by intestate succession. If that individual or a member of that class survives the decedent, the share of the decedent's intestate estate to which that individual or class would have succeeded, passes as if that individual or each member of that class had disclaimed his (or her) intestate share.

2-102 Share of Spouse (Common Law States)

The intestate share of a decedent's surviving spouse is:
(1) the entire intestate estate if:
  (i) no descendant or parent of the decedent survives the decedent; or
  (ii) all of the decedent's surviving descendants are also descendants of the surviving spouse and there is no other descendant of the surviving spouse who survives the decedent;
(2) the first ($200,000), plus three fourths of any balance of the intestate estate, if no descendant of the decedent survives the decedent, but a parent of the decedent survives the decedent;
(3) the first ($150,000), plus one half of any balance of the intestate estate, if all of the decedent's surviving descendants are also descendants of the surviving spouse, and the surviving spouse has one or more surviving descendants who are not descendants of the decedent;
(4) the first ($100,000), plus one half of any balance of the intestate estate, if one or more of the decedent's surviving descendants are not descendants of the surviving spouse.

2-102A Share of the Spouse (Community Property States)

(a) The intestate share of a surviving spouse in separate property is:
  (1) the entire intestate estate if:
    (i) no descendant or parent of the decedent survives the decedent; or
    (ii) all of the decedent's surviving descendants are also descendants of the surviving spouse and there is no other descendant of the surviving spouse who survives the decedent;

EXHIBIT 4 - 1 Intestate Succession under the UPC *(continued)*

---

    (2) the first ($200,000), plus three fourths of any balance of the intestate estate, if no descendant of the decedent survives the decedent, but a parent of the decedent survives the decedent;

    (3) the first ($150,000), plus one half of any balance of the intestate estate, if all of the decedent's surviving descendants are also descendants of the surviving spouse and the surviving spouse has one or more surviving descendants who are not descendants of the decedent;

    (4) the first ($100,000), plus one half of any balance of the intestate estate, if one or more of the decedent's surviving descendants are not descendants of the surviving spouse.

(b) The one half of community property belonging to the decedent passes to the surviving spouse as the intestate share.

2-103 Shares of Heirs Other than Surviving Spouse

Any part of the intestate estate not passing to the decedent's surviving spouse under Section 2-102, or the entire intestate estate if there is no surviving spouse, passes in the following order to the individuals designated below who survive the decedent:

    (1) to the decedent's descendants by representation;

    (2) if there is no surviving descendant, to the decedent's parents equally if both survive, or to the surviving parent;

    (3) if there is no surviving descendant or parent, to the descendant of the decedent's parents or either of them by representation;

    (4) if there is no surviving descendant, parent, or descendant of a parent, but the decedent is survived by one or more grandparents or descendants of grandparents, half of the estate passes to the decedent's paternal grandparents equally if both survive, or to the surviving paternal grandparent, or to the descendants of the paternal grandparents or either of them if both are deceased, the descendants taking by representation; and the other half passes to the decedent's maternal relatives in the same manner; but if there be no surviving grandparent or descendant of a grandparent on either the paternal or the maternal side, the entire estate passes to the decedent's relatives on the other side in the same manner as the half.

EXHIBIT 4 - 1 Intestate Succession under the UPC *(continued)*

2-104 Requirement that Heir Survive Decedent for 120 Hours

An individual who fails to survive the decedent by 120 hours is deemed to have predeceased the decedent for purposes of. intestate succession.

2-105 No Taker

If there is no taker under the provisions of this Article, the intestate estate passes to the state.

Intestate share to surviving spouse. In *common law states*, under §2-102, the surviving spouse is entitled to all of the decedent's intestate estate if the decedent leaves no parent or descendant, or if the decedent does leave descendants, but neither the decedent nor the surviving spouse have other descendants (e.g., child of a former marriage). Alternatively, the spouse takes the first $100,000 to $200,000, plus a fraction of the rest ranging from one half to three-fourths, depending upon whether parents or descendants of the decedent and/or spouse survive. An example of §2-102(3) is where the decedent and surviving spouse leave a child and the surviving spouse has a child from a former marriage. An example of §2-102(4) is where the decedent leaves a child from a former marriage.

Under §2-102A, the surviving spouse's intestate share in *community property states* is identical to that for common law states, except for an additional provision for the distribution of the community property. Thus, that spouse takes the same share of the decedent's separate property as he or she would take in a common law state. In addition, the surviving spouse is entitled to the decedent's entire half of the community property.

Intestate share to others. According to §2-103, other relatives of the decedent are divided into a hierarchical list of classes, corresponding to the degree of blood relationship to the decedent. Thus, to determine which class is entitled to succession of an intestate decedent's property, one would move down the list, stopping at the first class containing at least one living member. Distribution would be made only to members within that class. A summary of this prioritized list follows:

1. Surviving descendants, per stirpes.
2. Parents
3. Descendants of parents, per stirpes.
4. Paternal and maternal grandparents and their descendants, one-half to each side, per stirpes.

UPC §2-106, not quoted above, requires a "per capita at each generation" form of per stirpes whenever descendants inherit by right of representation.

Under §2-104, any heir must survive the decedent by 120 hours to take by intestate succession. This state-imposed survival requirement has the effect of avoiding double probate in some common accident situations.

Finally, under §2-105, if none of the above relatives survive, then the decedent's intestate property passes to the state, under the doctrine of *escheat*. In English feudal law, escheat meant that the feudal lord received a reversion in the property, either because the tenant died without issue or because the tenant committed a felony. In American law, escheat has come to mean a reversion of the decedent's property to the state because no individual is "competent" to inherit. In most states, including California, there will be no escheat unless the decedent is not survived by *any* kin, no matter how remote the relationship. The UPC, on the other hand, limits inheritance to the closer relatives, under the arguable premise that more remote "laughing heirs" would be receiving a windfall not ever intended by the decedent. One wonders whether the typical decedent really would have preferred leaving property to the state or a favorite charity, rather than to some distant relatives. "Heir hunting" firms exist to locate beneficiaries who can't be found by the estate's personal representative. They routinely pull probate court files to see whether a missing heir is mentioned in the proceedings. If so, the firm will try to locate the missing heir and give the person the information necessary to claim the inheritance, but only if the heir agrees to pay a fee. The fee is usually a percentage (e.g., 25 to 33%) of the value of the inherited property.

The examples listed next should help to illustrate these principles. In each case, assume that D is a decedent who died a resident of a common law UPC state, and owned $300,000 in property. Relevant UPC sections are given in brackets.

EXAMPLE 4 - 1. D is survived only by spouse and a cousin. His spouse will inherit all. [§2-102(1)(I)].

EXAMPLE 4 - 2. D is survived by spouse and their five children, one of whom has a daughter. The spouse will inherit all. [§2-102(1)(ii)].

EXAMPLE 4 - 3. Facts similar to Example 4-2, above, except that spouse also has a child of a former marriage. The spouse inherits $150,000 plus one half of the rest, or a total of $225,000. Each of the five children inherits an equal share of the rest, i.e., $15,000. D's granddaughter inherits nothing. [§2-102(3) and §2-103(1)].

EXAMPLE 4 - 4. Facts similar to Example 4-2, above, except that decedent also has a child of a former marriage. The spouse inherits $100,000, plus one half of the rest, or a total of $200,000. Each of the children inherits an equal share of the rest, i.e., $16,667 ($100,000 / 6). D's granddaughter inherits nothing. [§2-102(4) and §2-103(1)].

EXAMPLE 4 - 5. Facts similar to Example 4-2, above, except that spouse survived decedent by only 5 hours. The spouse will not inherit. Each of the five children will inherit one-fifth of the total, i.e., $60,000. D's granddaughter still inherits nothing. [§2-104 and §2-103(1)].

EXAMPLE 4 - 6. D is survived by parents and two children. The children take all. [§2-103(1)].

EXAMPLE 4 - 7. D is survived by spouse, a parent, and a sister. The spouse inherits $275,000 and parents inherit $25,000. The sister receives nothing. [§2-102(2) and §2- 103(2)].

EXAMPLE 4 - 8. D is survived by a sister and two nephews, the sons of D's deceased brother. Based on the required per stirpes distribution, sister inherits $150,000 and each of the nephews takes $75,000. [§2-103(3)].

EXAMPLE 4 - 9. D's closest surviving relative is a second cousin. All property will escheat to the state. [§2-105].

If the decedent had been a resident of a community property state, each of the above dispositions of the decedent's individually owned property would still be correct. In addition, the decedent's half of the community property would pass to the surviving spouse, with the result that the surviving spouse would end up owning all of what had been the couple's community property.

Intestacy in Non-UPC States

The intestate succession laws in non-UPC states vary considerably, but all have a common thread; a spouse takes priority, followed by issue, and, if none, the more remote heirs' interests are determined by degrees of consanguinity. For example, if an intestate decedent is survived by children but no spouse, the children usually take all. If the decedent leaves a spouse and children, the spouse and the children will usually share the property, with the spouse receiving one third to one half of the estate and the children the rest. If the decedent is survived by a spouse but no children, the spouse usually receives all. If, in addition to the spouse, the decedent's parents are still alive, then in some states the spouse gets all, and in others, the spouse shares a portion with the parents. Since state's intestate succession laws do vary, the reader is urged to make an independent investigation of the succession laws in his or her own state. One source is through the Washburn University School of Law's website (*http://www.washlaw.edu/uslaw/statelaw.html*).

Advancements

An *advancement* is a lifetime gift that the donor wants to have treated as an advanced distribution from the donor's estate such that it should be taken into account when the donor dies. Nearly all states have statutes spelling out what is needed to prove that such was the donor's intent, and most states, including those adopting the UPC, require that the donor's intent be in writing or that the donee acknowledge that the gift was understood to be an advancement. Where advancement occurs, the value of the gift at the time of the gift is added to the net value of the decedent's estate before determining intestate shares. The donee's share is then reduced by the value of the gift. If the donee's intestate share is less than the value of the gift, the donee does not have to return the excess, but will not otherwise share in the estate. The other heirs' shares are redetermined excluding the donee and the gift to the donee.

> EXAMPLE 4 - 10. Sherry died intestate, survived by her three children Marie, Dean, and Barbara. Her estate was valued at $120,000. Two years before she died, Sherry gave Marie XYZ stock valued at $30,000. With the gift was a typed letter from Sherry saying that she knew that Marie needed the income from the stock, that she should not have to wait until Sherry died to get it, but that Marie should understand that it would be taken into account when her estate was divided up. Even though the letter would not qualify as a will (it was neither holographic nor witnessed), the gift will be treated as an advancement. The children will inherit the

following amounts: $20,000 to Marie and $50,000 each to Dean and Barbara, and the date of death value of the stock is immaterial. If Sherry's gift had not been an advancement, each of the children would inherit $40,000. In either outcome, Marie will keep the $30,000 gift.

EXAMPLE 4 - 11. Same as before, except Sherry's estate was valued at $45,000, not including the gift to Marie. When the gift is added back, each child's share is $25,000. This is less than what Marie has already received. Therefore she receives nothing, the gift is ignored, and the $45,000 is split equally by Dean and Barbara.

The advancement rules apply only to intestate succession, on the assumption that a testator wishing to reduce a beneficiary's share would do so in the will itself or by codicil. A handwritten statement evidencing an advancement may be treated as a holographic codicil in those states that recognize holographic wills.

LEGAL RIGHTS OF OMITTED AND ADOPTED CHILDREN

After-born, Omitted Child

Occasionally, a parent dies leaving a will that was executed prior to the birth of a child. Will that after-born child receive anything? In most states, including UPC states,[3] an after-born child is entitled to take the share he or she would have received had the decedent died without a will, unless any one of the following is true: (a) the omission was intentional; (b) the will left substantially all of the estate to the other parent; or (c) the testator made some other provision for "after born children."

The child's intestate portion can be the entire estate where the child has no brothers or sisters and the decedent-parent was unmarried, or it might be nothing, as in community property states where the surviving spouse inherits all the community property. In a community property state, the omitted child might have a claim to a share of the decedent's separate property.

An Omitted Child

An omitted child is defined as any living child (or living issue of any deceased child) who was not provided for in his or her deceased parent's will. This may occur because the child was born after the will was executed and the parent's will did not have a clause providing for later born children, or the child may have been alive at the time the will was executed but the parent chose, for whatever

reason, not to mention the child. While some states still permit an omitted child who was born at the time the will was executed to take an intestate share, others, including UPC states, do not. An omitted spouse, an omitted child, and the omitted issue of an omitted deceased child, are referred to as *pretermitted* heirs.

The most common planning strategy to avoid an excessive inheritance by after-born children is to treat them similar to other children by using class gift terminology. For example, by using the terms "descendants" or "issue" in the will or trust to designate the persons who will inherit, rather than specifically naming children, pretermitted child situations are avoided, and thus property left to someone other than the children will be kept from being reduced by an omitted heir's claim.

Adopted Children

With regard to *adopted children*, most states (perhaps all), including those that have incorporated the UPC,[4] treat adopted children, for intestate succession purposes, as though they are the natural children of their *adoptive parents*. So, an adopted child will inherit from the adoptive parents (and their blood relatives), and the adoptive parents (and their blood relatives) will inherit from the adopted child. Conversely, most states give the *natural parents* of a child adopted by another no rights to inherit by intestate succession from their natural child. Similarly, adopted children usually have no succession right to the interests of their natural parents. Called the "fresh start" policy, this rule, breaking inheritance rights between adopted children and their natural parents, reflects public policy belief that implementing a complete substitution of the adoptive family for the natural family is in the child's best interest. Of course any of the parties can change the results by doing an estate plan that does not follow the intestate pattern, hence the natural parent who has established a relationship with her adopted child can leave that child property if she so chooses. If she does not so choose, and fails to mention the child, the child is not considered a pretermitted heir.

> EXAMPLE 4 - 12. Sam and Sue placed their infant child, Gloria, up for adoption. She was adopted by Kevin and Kay. If Sam later dies intestate, in most states Gloria will not inherit any of Sam's property. If Kay then dies intestate, Gloria will inherit equally with Kay's natural children. If Gloria subsequently dies intestate, Kevin and Kay's issue can inherit, but neither Sue, her issue, nor Sam's issue will inherit. Of course, any of these individuals may receive property if they are named in a given decedent's will.

The fresh start rule does not usually apply in the case of a "stepparent adoption," where an adult child is adopted by a stepparent, usually after divorce or after death of a natural parent. An exception is made, allowing inheritance by these adopted children from both their natural parents and their stepparents, reflecting public policy belief that such children will be better off maintaining contact with their biological relatives.

> EXAMPLE 4 - 13. Mike was six years old when his natural parents, Edith and Frank, divorced. Edith subsequently married Archie, who adopted Mike. In most states, Mike will inherit from both Edith and Frank and from Archie, his stepparent.

Omitted heir situations have a peculiar consequence. They result in the limited application of the intestacy laws to a decedent who actually died testate (i.e., with a valid will). Another example of the need for intestacy proceedings when a valid will exists is the situation called *partial intestacy*, in which a will does not dispose of all the decedent's probate property, as when it fails to contain a residuary clause. The latter is more likely to occur when a lay-person does a holographic will than when an attorney drafts the will.

LEGAL RIGHTS OF OMITTED, DIVORCED, AND DISINHERITED SPOUSES

Omitted Spouse

A spouse is most likely to be omitted when the testator married *after* executing a will. The omitted or pretermitted spouse is generally treated in the same manner as an omitted child. In most states, the spouse takes an intestate share unless the omission was intentional or unless provision was made elsewhere for the spouse. And, as in the case of omitted children alive at the execution of the will, an omitted spouse whom the testator married *before* executing the will may or may not take an intestate share, depending upon the applicable state law. In UPC states, that spouse would not take an intestate share.

> EXAMPLE 4 - 14. Prior to Claude and Betty's engagement, Claude prepared his only will. Claude died in a skiing accident on their honeymoon. In most states, since Claude's premarital will *does not provide* for Betty and the omission appears unintentional, the will can be admitted to probate but Betty will receive her intestate share of Claude's property. If, on the other hand, the will *has provided* for Betty,

in some states she will receive just the amount devised to her, which could be more or less than her intestate share. In states that allow a surviving spouse to elect to claim a dower interest in lieu of the amount left by will, Betty could choose to take the dower share instead of what the will has provided for her.

Effect of Divorce

In most states, bequests to a spouse contained in a will executed prior to a divorce are automatically revoked by the *dissolution of marriage*, and, for purposes of the will, the surviving ex-spouse is treated as having predeceased the testator. Thus, in most situations, the property will pass to an alternate beneficiary, probably the decedent's issue, if any.

In contrast to wills, for life insurance policies and retirement contracts, a divorce in itself may not have the effect of invalidating an existing provision designating the ex-spouse as a beneficiary. Nor will a divorce invalidate a bequest to relatives or friends of the ex-spouse.

Protection against Disinheritance of Spouse

Can one spouse totally "disinherit" the other? Most states have laws designed to prevent this. States handle the potential problem of a penniless widow (or widower) by enforcing one or more of the following concepts: community property, dower and curtesy, the spousal right of election, family allowance, and homestead property.

Community property. As we have seen, *community property states* protect spouses by attributing to each spouse ownership of one half of all property acquired by his/her efforts during the marriage while domiciled in a community property state. One would expect spouses to have nearly equal estates if the couple has been married most of their working years and they lived those years in community property states. Of course, a significant inheritance by one of the spouses will result in unequal wealth unless that spouse decides to convert the inherited property into community property. Recently married spouses or spouses that marry late in life, especially after retirement, may own little or no community property. The laws of the community property states do not require the decedent to leave the survivor any of the decedent's half of the community property or any of his or her separate property. Nevertheless, some protection is available under the Retirement Equity Act of 1984, which provides that after a person is married for one year to an employee who is a participant in a retirement plan, the only payment option is a joint annuity unless the nonparticipant spouse consents in writing to some other option.

Dower and curtesy. Originating in English common law, a *dower* represented a surviving wife's life estate interest in a portion of the real property owned by her deceased husband. A *curtesy* represented a surviving husband's life estate in a portion of the real property owned by his deceased wife. These interests have all but disappeared from our legal landscape.

Spousal right of election. All common law states, except Georgia, have enacted legislation replacing dower and curtesy with a spousal right of election, which essentially gives a surviving spouse the right to a choice. Either the spouse can "take under the will," that is, accept the provisions of the deceased spouse's will, if any, or the spouse can "take against the will," that is, elect instead to receive a statutorily specified minimum "elective share." In most states, the "elective share" is equal to that share the spouse would have inherited had the decedent died intestate.

The elective share statutes are not foolproof, however, for at least two reasons. First, a person may be encouraged by his wealthy fiancé (or her wealthy fiancée) to execute a premarital or post-marital agreement *waiving*, or greatly reducing, elective share rights. Such agreements are recognized in most states, provided that they are entered into freely, that they fully disclose both spouses' finances without misrepresentation, and that they clearly spell out those elective rights to be waived. Second, lifetime giving strategies, either outright or in trust, may be successful in circumventing forced share litigation. While the courts in many states have tried to overcome these transfers, success has been spotty.

The elective share provisions of the Uniform Probate Code were revised in 1990 in an attempt to overcome these deficiencies by being more equitable and less arbitrary than elective share statutes predicated solely on intestacy. They allow the surviving spouse a sliding scale elective share. The share is amount equal to a percentage of the "augmented estate." The augmented estate includes the probate estate plus the decedent's interest in property characterized by right of survivorship (joint tenancy, etc.) held with a nonspouse, proceeds on certain life insurance on the decedent's life payable to a nonspouse, and many transfers of property by the decedent during the two year period preceding death if the decedent retained certain interests in the property transferred (such as assets transferred to a revocable trust). The new provisions allow shares ranging from 3 percent, if the spouses were married less than one year, to 50 percent for marriages of 15 years or more, with a minimum share of $50,000. These provisions tend to reduce the significance of the manner in which the decedent held title on the share the pretermitted surviving spouse is allowed to claim.

Family allowance. All states give the probate court legal authority to grant a family allowance, which are funds awarded to support the decedent's spouse and minor children during the period of estate administration. This special award is needed because the court will ordinarily delay property distributions until it can determine that all debts can be paid. In fact, the family allowance takes precedence over claims by taxing authorities and unsecured creditors. Even a disinherited spouse or dependent child might be given a family allowance. The size of the family allowance, which is usually paid in installments, will vary depending on the survivors' needs and the size of the estate.

Homestead and other exempt property. Finally, most states protect surviving family members from being dispossessed of certain property by the decedent's unsecured creditors or by the terms of the decedent's will. The *homestead*, as it is called, usually includes the family home and adjacent property, subject to maximum acreage limitations. Some state statutes may also exempt other property, such as household furnishings, a vehicle, wearing apparel, and the like. Depending on the state, such assets are offered the following protection: exemption from forced sale while the surviving spouse and the decedent's descendants are minors, restriction from inter vivos alienation, testamentary disposition and intestate descent, and exemption from certain taxation. These statutes vary greatly from state to state. The UPC also grants a monetary homestead allowance of $15,000 for the spouse and $15,000 divided among all dependent minor children.[5]

Thus, most states have laws which prevent the death of one spouse from impoverishing the surviving spouse. Surviving children are, however, generally not afforded the same protection. In some other countries, such as France and Switzerland, most of a parent's estate must be left to the spouse and children. It may seem unfair that children in the USA are not similarly protected, since spouses have the ability to protect themselves when they marry but children have no choice when they enter the parent-child relationship. In addition, young children generally cannot support themselves. However, our society's refusal to protect children likely stems from a policy interest in discouraging expensive guardianships on the assumption that the protected spouse will support the minor children. Nonetheless, this is not an ideal solution in a world filled with second and third marriages, where the surviving spouse and the decedent's children may not be related.

Next, we direct our study to the final major subject in this chapter: probate administration process.

PRINCIPLES OF PROBATE ADMINISTRATION

The principles underlying probate administration of an American decedent's estate originated in England, where public officials and the Church of England took control of a decedent's property, or at least supervised those individuals taking control, and then distributed it to the heirs and devisees. The word *probate* stems from the Latin word *to prove*, meaning to certify the validity of a will. When a will is "approved," it is admitted to probate. Today, the term probate is seldom used in the restrictive sense of proving the validity of a will. In modern usage, probate refers to the entire court-related process of the administration of a decedent's estate, including those estates of people who die intestate, and thus have no will to prove.

Probate has been said to have three main *purposes*. First, it *protects creditors* by mandating that valid debts of the decedent be paid. Second, it implements the dispositive wishes of the testator by *supervising the distribution* of estate assets to beneficiaries. And third, probate serves to *transfer clear title* to property; that is, it enables survivors to receive property in a form which is marketable.

Presenting a comprehensive overview of the principles of probate administration in the United States requires generalization since each state has its own set of laws. There are, however, many similarities. Nearly all have at least one set of *formal probate* procedures characterized by the following four attributes:

1. Appointment of the estate's personal representative by the *court.*
2. Presentation of at least two *petitions* and at least two court *hearings*, for which written *notice* has been given to all interested parties. (Interested parties are those who could be affected by the probate process, including

beneficiaries, creditors, and fiduciaries nominated in the will.) Notice to creditors is usually done through newspaper publication.

3. Issuance, by the court, of signed *orders* as a precondition to the performance by the personal representative of certain major steps, such as the sale of real property, payment of attorney's fees, and distribution of probate property.

4. Review and approval, by the court, of one or more financial *accountings* and *reports* on significant matters of concern to the interested parties.

These requirements reflect the strong interest each state has in protecting creditors and beneficiaries.

In addition to providing these elaborate procedures, about half of the states offer the option of *less formal* settlement procedures. These states have adopted all or most of the provisions of the Uniform Probate Code. Flexibility under the UPC enables the estate's interested parties to choose whether to be extensively supervised by the court in the usual manner, to be supervised only with regard to certain specific acts, or to be almost totally unsupervised. While the states that do not allow for less formal administration might still allow for some degree of informality, most of their estates must follow the traditional formal procedures.

This section will examine the traditional approach and the flexible approach to estate administration, partly to show that their underlying philosophies are very different, and partly to give the reader an indication of the current trend in probate reform. Actually, this reform has influenced all states to some degree, including those offering much less flexibility. The traditionalist states are deregulating, but in a more fragmentary manner, as we shall see.

Substantial Formal Supervision: The Non-UPC Model

A somewhat detailed study of the formal probate procedures imposed by a typical non-UPC state, such as California, can give the reader a reasonable grasp of the major requirements of a *formal* probate found in all states, although the details will vary from state to state. In UPC states, the executor has the option of using the formal or informal method unless another interested party objects, in which case the formal process is mandatory. Sections of the California Probate Code are cited parenthetically.

The formal probate process. After a person has died, the executor is expected to start the formal probate process as soon as is reasonably possible.

Petition for probate. The person nominated as executor is required to file a petition for probate within 30 days of gaining knowledge of the testator's will and that he or she has been nominated (§8001). The original will should also be filed with the clerk of the superior court in the county where the decedent resided. California law recognizes a tort cause of action that can be brought against a person for fraudulently destroying, concealing, or "spoiling" a will.

In addition, any person "interested" in the estate may make a similar petition (§8000). Where there is no will, hence no executor, the interested person is likely to be a close relative. Rarely is more than one petition filed. Upon filing the petition, the court clerk must schedule a hearing on the petition within 45 days (§8003). Ordinarily, the person nominated in the will to be executor files the petition, requesting (1) probate of the will, (2) letters testamentary, and (3) authorization to administer under the Independent Administration of Estates Act. Each request will be described briefly.

1. *Probate of the will:* If, after the hearing, the will is "admitted to probate," that will is thereby considered to be the only valid will and, except in the most unusual circumstances, it will serve as the blueprint for distribution.

2. *Letters testamentary* or *letters of administration:* Also known as "letters," this document, usually just one page long, contains the court's formal identification of the person selected by the court as representative of the decedent's estate. A court certified copy of the letters empowers the personal representative to deal with third parties on behalf of the estate. They are called "letters testamentary" if the person selected was nominated in the decedent's will, and "letters of administration" where the selected personal representative was not named in the will. Where there is no will, the personal representative is referred to as simply the administrator. The administrator is called an *administrator with will annexed* if there is a will admitted to probate but either no executor was named in the will (probably a homemade will done without attorney involvement) or neither the named executor, nor the alternate executors, were appointed by the court (perhaps they were unsuitable or unavailable).

3. *Independent Administration of Estates Act:* The California Probate Code allows a somewhat simplified formal probate administration. Essentially, it eliminates the requirement of obtaining court approval for many of the common transactions undertaken by the personal representative. However, some actions

are not exempt and require either express court approval or written notice to all beneficiaries of a proposed course of action, giving them a period of 15 days in which to lodge an objection before the action is taken (§§10,400-10,600).

In addition to making these requests, the petition also makes several representations, including facts about the bond, the heirs, and the beneficiaries. A *probate bond* (also called a *fiduciary bond*) is required unless the will waives it or unless all potential beneficiaries agree to waive it (§8481). The bond protects the estate from a financial loss in the event of wrongful conduct by the personal representative. If the personal representative misappropriates estate property or loses it due to negligence, the bonding company must make the estate whole and then has the right to pursue the personal representative. This right of the bonding company to seek to recover from the personal representative any money it had to pay the estate is call a *right of subrogation*. Ordinarily, the bond amount will be set equal to the total value of the personal probate property plus one year's estimated income from all of the probate property, the idea being that the personal representative cannot run off with the real property (§8482). The bond premium, typically one-half to one percent of the amount of the bond, is charged to the estate. The petition for probate must state either that the will waived the bond, that the beneficiaries all request the waiver of the bond (in which case the waivers should be filed with the petition), or that the requirements for a bond will be met. Where a bond is required, evidence that it has been issued is required before the court will issue letters. As a second representation, the petition for probate is required to identify all beneficiaries named in the will and any heirs at law even though not named as beneficiaries.

Two other forms are ordinarily filed with the court clerk at the time of filing the petition for probate. First, a *Proof of Subscribing Witness* is submitted, in which at least one witness to the will declares that he or she signed the original document, that the decedent appeared to be of sound mind and over age 18 at the time of the signing, and that the witness knows of no evidence that the will was signed under duress, menace, fraud or undue influence. If a witness cannot be found, or if all witnesses have died, proof can be offered by handwriting analysis. To make this task unnecessary, in the spirit of probate simplification, most states now recognize what is called a *self-proved* will, also called a *self executing* will. This is a will containing a formal affidavit as part of the original attestation portion of the will, wherein the witnesses state that all formalities were followed.

This statement will stand unless an interested party challenges the validity of the will. At a minimum, this generally eliminates the need to locate witnesses to attest to the will's validity many years after the execution of the will and, in some states, the affidavit creates a presumption that all formalities were correctly followed, thus putting the burden on any challenger to prove that such was not the case. The "Statement of Witnesses" clauses in the sample wills set forth in Exhibits 3-1 and 3-3 are self-proving.

The second form ordinarily filed along with the probate petition is the *Notice of Petition to Administer Estate* and contains the same information as the announcement notice that must be published (three times prior to the hearing) in a newspaper of general circulation in the city (or county) in which the decedent resided. Exhibit 4-2 shows an example of the information that might be found in a published notice.

The notices, both filed and published, are intended to announce the following to interested parties and to the public:

1. That a petition for probate has been filed.
2. That a hearing will be held.
3. That interested parties may attend the hearing to object to the granting of the petition.
4. That creditors must file claims against the estate within four months after the issuance of letters.
5. That anyone may examine the probate file.
6. That the petitioner is requesting authority to administer the estate under the Independent Administration of Estates Act.

Copies of the filed notice must be mailed to all heirs and potential beneficiaries at least 15 days prior to the date of the hearing (§8110).

The hearing. The initial "hearing" for any particular probate estate may last less than a minute. The judge gives anyone in the courtroom the opportunity to object. Objections are rarely raised. Grounds for objection include the allegation that a more recently executed will exists or that even though the will in question is the only one or the most recent one, it should not be admitted to probate because it was not properly executed due to the testator's lack of capacity, undue influence, fraud, or mistake. If there are objections, the judge will set the matter for further proceedings to settle the dispute, which, if not immediately resolved,

---

EXHIBIT 4-2 Replica of a Newspaper Notice of Petition to Administer Estate

---

NOTICE OF PETITION TO ADMINISTER ESTATE OF
JOHN PAUL JONES, a.k.a. J. P. JONES
CASE NUMBER: P781431

To all heirs, beneficiaries, creditors, contingent creditors, and persons who may otherwise be interested in the will or estate, or both, of JOHN PAUL JONES, a.k.a. J. P. JONES.

A PETITION has been filed by Mary Jones in the Superior Court of Anystate, County of Anycounty.

THE PETITION requests that Mary Jones be appointed as personal representative to administer the estate of the decedent.

THE PETITION requests the decedent's WILL and codicils, if any, be admitted to probate. The will and any codicils are available for examination in the file kept by the court.

A HEARING on the petition will be held on 03-19-99 at 8:30 a.m. in Department 1 located at Superior Court of Anystate, County of Anycounty, 25 County Center Drive, Anycity, Anystate 99999.

IF YOU OBJECT to the granting of the petition, you should appear at the hearing and state your objections or file written objections with the court before the hearing. Your appearance may be in person or by your attorney.

IF YOU ARE A CREDITOR or a contingent creditor of the deceased, you must file your claim with the court and mail a copy to the personal representative appointed by the court within four months from the date of first issuance of letters as provided in Section 9100 of the Anystate Probate Code. The time for filing claims will not expire before four months from the hearing date noticed above.

YOU MAY EXAMINE the file kept by the court. If you are a person interested in the estate, you may file with the court a formal Request for Special Notice of the filing of an inventory and appraisal of estate assets or of any petition or account as provided in Section 1250 of the Anystate Probate Code. A Request for Special Notice form is available from the court clerk.

Attorney for petitioner: Gordon C. Brown, BROWN & BROWN, P.O. Box 0000, Anycity, Anystate, 99999-1111.

PUBLISH: February 19, 22, and 26, 1999.

can turn into a *will contest*. If the petition for probate is granted, the judge signs an *Order for Probate* that first states the court's findings, specifically:

1. All notices have been filed.
2. The decedent died on the specified date.
3. The will in question should be admitted to probate.
4. The petitioner is the appropriate person to serve as the estate's personal representative, either as executor or as administrator with will annexed.

Then, the Order usually requires that:

1. The will is admitted to probate.
2. The named personal representative is appointed.
3. A bond is (or is not) required.
4. The personal representative is (or is not) given authority to administer the estate under the Independent Administration of Estates Act.
5. Letters be issued (upon the posting of the bond, if such is required).

Upon issuance of the Order for Probate, the personal representative secures his or her certified letters from the probate clerk, thus completing the first stage of the formal dealings between the personal representative and the court.

After the hearing. Next, usually in conjunction with the estate's attorney, the personal representative undertakes the marshaling of estate assets and expected claims. Within three months of appointment, the personal representative must file with the probate court a formal document called *Inventory and Appraisement*. This form lists all probate assets showing their fair market value. The personal representative is permitted to determine the value of cash items (e.g., bank deposits, etc.). Other assets must be valued by an appraiser who, depending on state law, may be selected by the court from a list of court approved independent appraisers. Finding a qualified appraiser may also be one of the duties of the personal representative.

The Inventory and Appraisement performs several important functions. First, it lists those assets for which the personal representative is responsible. Second, as a public document available for public inspection at the court house, it describes the contents of the probate estate to all interested parties, including potential heirs, legatees, devisees, and creditors. Third, it provides information to the court to determine, among other things, the proper fiduciary bond amount, the amount of the family allowance, and, if property is sold, the minimum bid that the court will approve. Finally, it may influence the taxing authorities with regard to valuation of assets included on the estate tax returns.

During the *creditors' claim period*, which in most states lasts for four months after the date the letters are issued, each creditor is expected to file with the court or personal representative a document called a *creditor's claim form*. Failure to file within the claim period will bar later collection, unless an exception is allowed (§9100). Exceptions include:

1. Creditors who did not have actual knowledge of the proceedings (§9103).
2. Taxes owed (taxing authorities are not subject to the creditor's period (§9201)).

Availability of a shortened creditor's period is said to be a major advantage of the probate process compared to other mechanisms for the transfer of a decedent's estate, at least for estates that anticipate potential problems with creditors.

During estate administration, the personal representative is responsible for handling the financial affairs of the estate, such as:

1. Paying bills (rent, utilities, property insurance premiums).
2. Accumulating liquid assets so that large bills can eventually be paid (e.g., taxes and legal fees).
3. Protecting estate assets from exposure to loss by insuring and safe- guarding them.

Distribution of estate assets. The net estate will be distributed to the beneficiaries only after all matured debts and taxes, except the federal estate tax, have been paid. However, a partial distribution to beneficiaries may be made upon court approval of a *Petition for Preliminary Distribution*. Ordinarily, this petition is filed only after the end of the creditor's period. Further, the court must be satisfied that the distribution can be made "without loss to creditors or injury to the estate or any interested person." No more than 50 percent of the estate can be distributed in a preliminary distribution (§§11,620-24).

"Final Distribution" is made upon approval of a petition at a hearing, after the court determines that all current debts and taxes have been paid (§11,640). At the same time, the judge normally approves a final estate accounting, attorney's fees, and executor's commissions (§§12,200-252). The accounting may be avoided by waiver of all of the beneficiaries (§933). After distribution and the payment of fees, the executor requests and receives a final discharge (§§12,200-252).

The entire formal probate administration procedure takes from 8 to 24 months, in most cases.

Attorneys' fees for California probate administration work are determined by statute, in the absence of a different agreement by the parties. Statutory probate fees are summarized in Table 4-1.

TABLE 4-1 California Statutory Probate Fees

Probate Estate		Rate	Cumulative: Estate/Fee	
First	$15,000	4.0%	$15,000	$600
Next	$85,000	3.0%	$100,000	$3,150
Next	$900,000	2.0%	$1,000,000	$21,150
Next	$9,000,000	1.0%	$10,000,000	$111,150
Next	$15,000,000	0.5%	$25,000,000	$186,150
Over	$25,000,000	Reasonable amount set by the court		

California Probate Code 10810.

These fees are based on the *gross* probate estate, not net of liabilities, plus gains from the sale of assets, plus income, and less losses from the sale of assets. Gains and losses are based upon the date of death appraised values. California executors are entitled to the same amount (§10800) as shown above for attorneys. California is one of the states that has statutory fees. In most states, probate administration fees must simply be "reasonable" and specific amounts or percentages are not mandated. In other states, probate fees must be "reasonable," but not in excess of a certain percentage (e.g., Iowa sets an upper limit of 2 percent times the value of the probate estate). One attorney in that state has indicated that local courts in Iowa typically and automatically grant the 2 percent ceiling if the executor signs a "waiver of attorney's fee" (routinely done), without making any effort to determine reasonableness This results in a universal 2% rate regardless of time spent.

EXAMPLE 4 - 15. The attorney's fee on a $500,000 California probate estate is $11,150 [4% * $15,000 + 3% * $85,000 + 2% * $400,000]. Additional fees will be allowed for "extraordinary services," such as sale of real property, estate litigation, and preparation of tax returns. The executor's commission will also be $11,150, resulting in a combined charge of 4.46% of the probate estate.

Sometimes attorneys are asked by survivors to act as both estate attorney and executor. Whether they will receive a full double fee will depend upon several factors, including state law and the attitude of the specific probate judge. Some states, including California and New York, have made this 'double dipping' illegal, in the absence of prior court approval. In other states, probate judges frequently reduce the fee in such situations. A possible solution is for persons to negotiate probate fees with the estate planning attorney while they still can, so that the chore does not fall upon the shoulders of grieving survivors. The probate court would probably nullify an agreement that called for fees in excess of the court's own guidelines or in excess of the fees set by statute.

Summarizing the essential components of formal supervision: Formal probate in most non-UPC states requires at least four document filings (petition for probate, a certification establishing that notice of death has been published, an inventory and appraisement, and a petition for authority to make a final distribution), requires at least two formal court hearings (one for the admission of the will to probate and to appoint the personal representative, and another to approve the final accounting and the request for authority to distribute the estate), one newspaper publication of notice, and at least one accounting (unless it is waived by all estate beneficiaries). Many states have acted to simplify probate administration, a major example of which is outlined next.

We now turn to the second major type of state probate supervision, the flexible approach under the Uniform Probate Code. A discussion of one non-UPC state's less comprehensive attempt at simplifying probate procedures can be found in Appendix 4A.

Estate Administration in UPC States: A Study in Flexibility

Except to utilize summary probate procedures for smaller estates and for property passing outright to the surviving spouse, personal representatives in non-UPC states usually must use formal probate. In contrast, probate procedures in a UPC state are much more flexible, allowing interested parties to largely select the degree of supervision they desire. The basic choices are three: complete court-supervised administration; totally unsupervised (informal) administration; or a combination of unsupervised and supervised administration. The UPC also provides a simple summary procedure for estates worth less than $5,000. It is basically similar to that of California's affidavit-of-right procedure, described in Appendix 4A. In most states, modest sized estates can be settled without any administration.

Complete court supervised administration. Some estates in nearly all UPC states will be subject to supervised administration in essentially the same manner as California's formal continuing court supervision model. UPC supervised administration is a bit less regulated, however, because the personal representative is given greater freedom to act independently. Usually, there is no court involvement between the time letters are issued and the time that the personal representative petitions the court for closing of the estate. In contrast, probate administration in non-UPC states, as we have seen, requires court approval of all major transactions. Most personal representatives of estates in UPC jurisdictions choose not to be subject to supervised administration. Occasionally, another interested party will request it because he or she does not fully trust the estate's personal representative and wants to be given notice as to what the personal representative is doing.

Informal and formal administration. In UPC jurisdictions one of two types of procedures are followed: informal or formal administration.

Informal administration procedures usually require no court appearances and very little notice. The application for informal appointment is the simplest way for a personal representative to be appointed. The prospective personal representative files an application with a court registrar, whose role is administrative rather than judicial. Once appointed, the personal representative has the powers needed to perform the job, including the power to deal with creditors and distributees. The personal representative is required to give notice of the appointment to all heirs and devisees by ordinary mail within 30 days of appointment. Within three months, the personal representative must prepare an inventory of the estate and mail it to all parties requesting it. The entire inventory can be valued by the personal representative unless an interested party objects.

Even with informal administration, the personal representative must give formal newspaper notice, similar to the procedure for a formal probate, in order to limit the creditor's claim period to four months from date of first publication. Without published notice to creditors, the limitations period usually runs to three years after the date of the decedent's death.

Six months after appointment, the personal representative can apply to the registrar to close the estate. After another six months, assuming no one has lodged an objection, the personal representative is discharged from all liability except due to fraud or other major offenses. Unless the newspaper notice was given, distributees of estate property will continue to be liable for estate debts until the later of three years after date of the decedent's death or one year after the date of the distribution.

Formal administration procedures under the UPC include the petition for *formal testacy* (proving the will), petition for formal appointment of the personal representative, and petition for formal closing. Each is undertaken in a manner similar to that for supervised administration and requires giving proper notice to interested parties, filing a petition with the court, and appearing at a court hearing.

During informal proceedings, a dissatisfied interested party can petition the court for a formal resolution of a controversy, whereupon the matter will be taken up "in" court. Once the dispute is settled, administration can resume in informal proceedings "out" of court. The UPC's unique method of settling disputes has been described as an "in and out" method.

In addition to the right to petition the court, interested parties have other protective remedies, including the right to request that the personal representative obtain a bond even though it was waived in the will, the right to request a restraining order to keep the personal representative from doing some specific act (such as selling a family heirloom), and the right to demand notice; that is, to receive a copy of any filings or orders in connection with the estate. With the exception of the right to notice, the requests are subject to the court's discretion.

We can now see the relationship between informal and formal proceedings under the UPC. At each significant step in the probate process, the interested parties can elect a different degree of supervision. For example, the probate process may begin with an application for informal supervision of the personal representative. Then a controversy may arise that requires court resolution. Finally, the personal representative may feel compelled to file a formal petition for closing. Only rarely will an interested party petition for completely supervised administration. Generally, it is the desire of all beneficiaries to minimize judicial supervision, because supervision tends to delay distribution.

The movement toward reduced court involvement in estate administration has spread to many non-UPC states, due in part to the influence of the UPC. As illustrated in Appendix 4A, traditional states have moved to reduce court supervision by adopting summary procedures, set-asides, and procedures to reduce the personal representative's court reporting requirements. The overall effect of all state deregulation has been to reduce court congestion considerably.

The next chapter will require a change of focus, from the qualitative to the quantitative. It will be the first of four to introduce the principles of taxation.

QUESTIONS AND PROBLEMS (To find state probate codes, see question 2.)

1. True or false: A decedent's intestate property does not go through the probate administration process. Explain.

2. Describe your state's laws covering inheritance by intestate succession. They are usually found in a chapter of that state's probate or estates and trusts code. The names for these codes vary, for instance: *Decedent's Estates, Guardianships, Protective Proceedings and Trusts* (Arizona); *Estates, Powers & Trusts* (New York); or *Probate Code* (California). (See: *http://www.findlaw.com/11stategov/index.html*)

    If your state is unavailable, describe the UPC rules using South Dakota's *Uniform Probate Code*, Title 29A. Go to *http://www.lexislawpublishing .com/Resources/* and click on "South Dakota Codified Laws."

3. Harry, who is single, has an interest in a house, some furniture, a car, some common stock, and a life insurance policy on his life. The *car* is in joint tenancy with his mother. The *house* is in trust, and the trust instrument says "for Harry's use for life, then to cousin Joe." The life insurance policy names his cousin, Joe, as the beneficiary. Harry owns the *furniture* and the *policy* as an individual. With regard to the *stock*, Harry is an equal tenant in common with Sam. Harry's (valid) will says "I leave my car, my stock, my life

insurance proceeds and my house to Betty." It has no other dispositive provisions.

    a. Assuming that Mother and Joe are Harry's only living relatives and that Betty is a close friend, who will receive what if Harry dies?

    b. What will be included in Harry's probate estate? His non-probate estate? His testate estate? His intestate estate?

    c. Who will be an heir? A legatee? A devisee?

    d. In your state (or under the UPC, if state law is unavailable), will your answers to the above questions change if Harry was also survived by a son? Why or why not?

4. Mary and John are married residents of your state and own the following property: As joint tenants, they own their home and a car. They own 1000 shares of ABC Corporation stock, worth $28,000, as equal tenants in common (assume community property if you are in a community property state). As individuals, Mary owns $350,000 in a money market fund and a life insurance policy on her business partner's life with a current (terminal) value of $22,000. John owns an apartment building. How will this property be distributed, in accordance with your state's laws on intestate succession (if unavailable, use UPC rules), if Mary dies without a will, leaving only the following surviving relatives (unless specified, assume that all surviving children are descendants of both John and Mary):

    a. Only John

    b. John and one child

    c. John and one child, who is the child of Mary and her first husband, Kirk. Does it matter whether the child had been adopted, either by Kirk's second wife or by John, and does it matter when this adoption occurred?

    d. John and three children

    e. John, Mary's mother, and three children

    f. John and Mary's mother

    g. John and Mary's sister

    h. John, Mary's mother, and Mary's fifth cousin

    i. John and Mary's fifth cousin

    j. John dies, then Mary dies survived by Mary's fifth cousin (Note: What happens to the home, the car, and the stock?)

    k.   There are no surviving relatives.

In general (without re-doing the above items), how would it change matters if Mary died with a will containing a residuary clause?

5. Assume that Mary and John own property as stated in the previous problem, that Mary and John are childless, and that Mary's and John's sole surviving relatives are their parents. In a UPC state, who will inherit Mary's money market fund account if John and Mary both die intestate and, alternatively,
   a. John predeceased Mary by one year
   b. John and Mary died in a car accident and the order of deaths cannot be determined
   c. John survived Mary by six hours
   d. John survived Mary by six days

6. Frank and Joan, husband and wife, had two living children, C1 and C2, four years ago when Frank executed his only will. The will leaves half of his property each to C1 and Joan. A year later, C3 was born. Today Frank tells you that he would like to leave all his property (owned as an individual and worth $180,000) to Joan when he dies. Advise Frank, being sure to tell him who would get how much of his property if he died now. Apply your state law or, if unavailable, the UPC.

7. Ten years ago George, who was single, executed his first and only will, leaving everything to his mother. Two years later, George married Karla. Today, George is in your office telling you that he would still like his mother to receive all his property at death. Based on your state law, or the UPC if unavailable, advise George.

8. Who is closer to you, your first cousin or your niece? Why?

9. Imagine that a close friend has died and that you believe she named you executor in her will. Based on the laws of your state, or the UPC, what steps would you need to undertake before and during probate?

10. List the purposes of the form "petition for probate."

11. Find, cut out or photocopy, and bring to class a newspaper published "notice of petition." What is its purpose?

12. Attend a hearing for probate. Give the date of attendance and a brief summary of what you observed.

13. A client of yours shows you an "inventory and appraisement." What are its uses?

14. What is the purpose of the creditor's claim? Who files it?

15. Ordinarily, what must the personal representative accomplish before a judge will permit final distribution under supervised probate?

16. Summarize the minimum legal procedures which are involved in supervised probate in most states.

17. Why is probate in UPC states considered so flexible?

18. Describe the informal probate procedures under the UPC.

19. a. To what extent do you think the laws of intestate succession in your state (or the UPC, if unavailable) are inefficient for parents of minor children?
    b. To what extent does a will leaving everything outright to the surviving parent solve the problem? To what extent do you think such a will fails to solve it?
    c. Can you recommend a better disposition?

20. Denise died recently, having many different ownership interests in property. Determine how much, if any, of each property below will be a probate asset in Denise's estate.
    a. An automobile, held jointly with Jake.
    b. A money fund account, owned by Denise as an individual.
    c. A life insurance policy (L1) on Denise's life, owned by Denise. Herb is beneficiary.

d. A life insurance policy (L2) on Denise's life, owned by her. James, the sole beneficiary, died three years ago.
e. A life insurance policy (L3) on Herb's life, owned by Denise, who is also beneficiary.
f. Common stock, owned by the trustee of a living trust. At the moment of her death, Denise was trustor, trustee, and one of the beneficiaries.
g. Commercial real estate owned in common by Denise (40%) and Herb (60%).
h. Defined benefit pension plan. Denise was participant, and Bob is named surviving beneficiary.
i. Residence, owned by Denise and Herb as community property.

SUMMARY PROBATE PROCEEDINGS IN CALIFORNIA: ONE NON-UPC STATE'S ALTERNATIVES TO FORMAL PROBATE

As we have seen, formal probate typically requires at least four document filings, two formal court hearings, one newspaper publication of notice, and at least one and possibly two accountings. Although these procedures were allegedly designed to protect estate assets and ensure their proper distribution, many are considered unnecessary in rather simple estate situations. Over the years, non-UPC states have also simplified probate procedures for less complicated estates.

This Appendix will summarize the progress of probate simplification in California. Presently, California has two major types of "summary probate," as it is called, neither of which require newspaper notice and both of which require not more than one petition and hearing. The two types, discussed next, are the affidavit of right and the summary distribution to the surviving spouse. As you read this, keep in mind that many UPC states have procedures similar to these.

Affidavit of Right

The affidavit of right is a procedure that permits the settlement of a decedent's affairs more rapidly than formal probate. It is available provided the gross estate (real and personal property) does not exceed $100,000 in value after excluding all property for which there is some other (non-probate) mechanism of transfer. Property in trust, joint tenancy property, life insurance going to named beneficiaries, and Totten trust accounts do not count as part of the $100,000. Also not counted towards the $100,000 limit are motor vehicles and mobile homes, $5,000 in salary, and any property subject to a summary distribution to the surviving spouse (a proceeding described below).This affidavit method of transferring property without any court involvement only applies to a decedent's right to money, tangible personal property, or evidences of a debt, obligation, interest, right, security, or chose in action. The procedure differs slightly if real estate is involved and does require minimal court involvement.

Essentially, for non-real estate assets, an affidavit signed by the "successor of the decedent" is presented to the person or institution holding the property. That party is then required to turn ownership of the property over to the person with the claim. The successor of the decedent is the person with the most legitimate claim to the property. He or she may be an executor named in the decedent's will, the trustee (if there is a pourover will), or in the case of intestacy, a guardian (on behalf of a minor), or one of the heirs claiming on his or her own behalf. Forty days must have lapsed since the decedent's death, and the affidavit must state that no probate has started and that the total property being claimed by this method does not exceed $100,000. It must also state the basis for the person's claim that he or she has the right to the possession of the property. A certified copy of the decedent's death certificate is attached to the affidavit. The recipient of the property is liable for any liens or taxes that are associated with the asset. Of course, if the property is being collected by an executor or trustee, he or she must then make transfers in keeping with the controlling document, i.e., the will or the trust. (13100-13116)

The affidavit of right for *real property* can be used to claim real estate that belonged to the decedent, but only for property up to $20,000 in value. The claimant must wait six months after the decedent's death before presenting an affidavit similar to the one discussed for personal property. This one must be presented first to the superior court, together with a petition requesting certification. The claimant's signature must be notarized. In addition to the death certificate, an inventory of all of the decedent's real property must be included in the petition and an appraisal of the property must be attached. If the testator had a guardian or conservator at the time of his or her death, that person must be given notice of the petition. If the paperwork appears to be in order, the court clerk will issue a certified copy of the affidavit, which the claimant must then record (without all the attachments) in the office of the county recorder for the county where the property is located. The recorded affidavit serves as a quitclaim deed from the decedent to the persons designated in the certified affidavit as the successors of the decedent (13200-13210). Note that this is done without a court hearing.

Summary Distribution to Surviving Spouse

Married spouses in California frequently own separate and community property which, at death, will wind up passing outright to the surviving spouse, either because the spouse was named in the will or by the laws of intestate succession. In two important ways, California probate law has simplified the administration requirements of such property.

Property Held as Community or Quasi-community Property

Similar to the affidavit of right discussed above, the surviving spouse who succeeds to the decedent spouse's community property or quasi-community property, either by will or by intestate succession, can claim it by affidavit. Quasi-community property is that property that would have been community property except for the fact that it was acquired while the couple was living in a non-community property state. There is a forty day waiting period, but the spouse does not have to seek court certification of the affidavit even if real property is involved. If real estate is involved, the affidavit must be notarized so that it can be recorded in the county where the real estate is located. Unlike the affidavit of right discussed above, there is no upper dollar limit. A person other than the surviving spouse can stop the transfer of title by recording, with the county recorder, a notice of the existence of the claim. Generally, the claim is based upon the existence of a will leaving an interest in the property to the person giving notice (13500 - 13545).

Summary Distribution Petition

Second, the surviving spouse can elect what is called summary distribution, which is one that follows a court hearing for the purpose of obtaining written confirmation by the court that such property has in fact passed to him or her. This may be helpful to clear title. At the hearing, if there is no objection, the judge confirms that the property is, in fact, either community or separate property, and that it should, in fact, pass to the surviving spouse. The judge signs an order confirming these findings. A summary distribution petition may be filed regardless of the amount or type of other property owned by the decedent at death. Formal probate may be required for other assets. Further, an affidavit of right and a summary distribution petition may both be used in the same estate for different property, provided that all of the requirements are met. Thus the spouse may claim bank accounts by use of a simple affidavit and the summary court proceeding to confirm his or her rights in real estate or in a business (§§13500 - 13660).

Attorney fees for handling a summary distribution for the surviving spouse are not set by statute. In practice, these fees are substantially less than those for formal probate. One third of the statutory fee is an amount commonly charged and many attorneys will do this for an hourly fee that is substantially less for large estates. Even less is charged for helping with the affidavits needed for a spousal set-aside without a petition for summary distribution.

ANSWERS TO QUESTIONS AND PROBLEMS

1. False. To be intestate is to die leaving probate property that is not disposed of by a valid will. Thus, by definition, intestate property is probate property. Logically, one could argue that intestate property needs probating even more than property disposed of by will, since a legal process is needed to help determine who is to receive the property, as well as to ensure that the intended beneficiaries *will actually receive* it.

2. Under the UPC, as in non-UPC states, succession is determined by degree of affinity. Thus, surviving spouse takes all if there is no surviving issue or parent of the decedent. If there is surviving issue or parent, spouse shares with them. And if there is no surviving spouse, issue, parent, issue of parent, grandparent, or issue of grandparents, then the property escheats to the state.

3.   a. Based on the procedure described in the text, first the <u>nonprobate assets</u> should be considered. Disposal instruments for them supersede the will. Accordingly, the <u>life insurance proceeds</u> will go to Joe, as named beneficiary. The <u>house</u> will pass to Joe, under the terms of the trust. The <u>car</u> will go to Mom, by right of survivorship under joint tenancy. The remaining assets (interest in the common stock, furniture) are <u>probate assets</u>. The <u>stock</u> will pass to Betty, under the will. And finally, the <u>furniture</u> will pass by intestacy to Mom, Harry's closest surviving relative.

   b. In Harry's probate estate: furniture and stock.
   In Harry's nonprobate estate: house, car, and life insurance proceeds.
   In Harry's testate estate: stock.
   In Harry's intestate estate: furniture.

   c. Mother is the only heir. An heir is a beneficiary who would receive property that passes by intestacy.
   Betty is the only legatee. A legatee is a beneficiary, under a will, of a gift of personal property.
   Technically, no one is a devisee; that is, a recipient, by will, of real property.

d. If Harry is also survived by a son, in most states, including those adopting the UPC, *descendants will inherit before parents*. Thus, the son, rather than Mom, will likely inherit the furniture. Also, in some states, the son would receive the stock, under the rule that an omitted child takes an intestate share of the entire probate estate.

4. First, regardless of who besides John survives Mary, John will receive Mary's joint interest in the home and the car, by right of survivorship. In parts j and k, if we assume that John predeceased Mary, then Mary would become sole owner of the home and car, both of which would pass as probate property, by intestate succession in the same manner as all the other property (below).

The following analysis disposes of the $400,000 in probate property, consisting of Mary's individual $350,000 interest in the money fund, her $28,000 tenancy in common/community interest in the 500 shares of stock, and the life insurance policy, worth $22,000. We will assume probate in a pure UPC state:

a. Only John survives: John gets all (§2-102(1)(i)).
b. John and one child survive: Common law and community property states: John gets all. (§2-102(1)(ii).
c. John and one child, who is also the child of Mary's first husband, Kirk:

Common law states: John gets the joint tenancy items (home and car) by operation of law. Note that Mary's intestate estate = $14,000 + $350,000 + $22,000 = $386,000. Only her half of the tenants in common stock is in her estate. According to §2-102(4), John gets the first $100,000 plus 50% of the rest of the intestate estate, i.e., $100,000 + 5% * (14,000 + 350,000 + 22,000 -100,000) = $243,000. Mary's child gets the balance: 14,000 + 350,000 + 22,000 - 243,000 = $143,000. (§2-103(1)).

Community property states: The main difference is that John gets all of the stock (her $14,000 half in addition to the half he already owns), the first $100,000 of the separate property plus 50% of the rest of the intestate estate, i.e., $14,000 + $100,000 + 5\% * (350,000 + 22,000 -100,000) = $250,000. The child's share is the balance: $386,000 - $250,000 = $136,000.

It may matter whether the child had been adopted. If he or she had been adopted as an infant, the *fresh start rule* would probably apply and, in most cases, all inheritance rights between the child and the non-custodial natural parent would be broken. Thus, if Kirk's second wife adopted the child as an infant, the child would probably not inherit from Mary. In this case, the answer to this part would be similar to part "a" and John would inherit all of Mary's estate.

On the other hand, if the child had been adopted as a non-infant (step-parent adoption), then in most states he or she could still inherit from both sets of parents, including Mary (and John).

d. John and three children survive: All states, John gets all. (§2-102(1)(ii)).
e. John, Mary's mother, and three children survive: Same answer as part d, since mother won't share. (§2-102(1)(ii)).
f. John and Mary's mother survive:

Common law states: According to §2-102(2), John gets the first $200,000 plus 75% of the rest of the intestate estate, i.e., $200,000 + 75% * (14,000 + 350,000 + 22,000 -200,000) = $339,500. Mary's mom gets the balance: $386,000 - 339,500 = $46,500. (§2-103(2)).

Community property states: John gets all of the stock ($14,000 represent's Mary's half), and $329,000 of the rest (i.e., $200,000 + 75% * ($372,000 - $200,000)) for a total of $343,000. Mary's mom gets the balance: $386,000 - $343,000 = $43,000 (§2-102A(a)(2) & §2-103(2)).

g. John and Mary's sister survive: John takes all (§2-102(1)(i) & §2-102A(1)(i)).
h. John, Mary's mother, and Mary's fifth cousin survive: Same answer as part f. The fifth cousin receives nothing.
i. John and Mary's fifth cousin survives: Same answer as part a; Mary's fifth cousin takes nothing.

j. Only Mary's fifth cousin survives:

All probate property escheats to the state (§2-105), including the home, the car, and the stock, which Mary presumably received after John's earlier death. Note that the UPC intestate succession only extends upward to the grandparents and downward to their issue; hence the reach only extends out to second cousins and their issue.

k. There are no surviving relatives: All probate property escheats to the state.

If Mary died with a valid will, there would be no intestate property, and all probate property would be disposed of in accordance with the terms of the will.

5. a. John predeceased Mary by one year: Mary's parents will inherit the property (§2-103(2)).
   b. John survived Mary by 10 minutes, but there is no evidence of this: Mary's parents will inherit, as in part a. Section 2-104 does not apply, since John and Mary seem to have died simultaneously.
   c. John survived Mary by six hours: Mary's parents will take the property, as in part b, because §2-104 requires survivorship by at least 120 hours.
   d. John survived Mary by six days: John's estate, and, ultimately, his parents, will take the property. Under §2-104, John met the survival requirement of 120 hours.

6. Under Frank's current will, C2 is an omitted child not protected under the UPC. Therefore, C2 would receive . C3, an after-born child is protected by the UPC and would take an intestate share. However, under §2-102(1)(ii), C3's intestate share would be zero because all children are from their marriage Thus Joan and C1 would split equally the entire $180,000. You should advise Frank to see an attorney to write a new will leaving everything to Joan.

7. If George died today, based on the UPC, unless Karla was otherwise provided for or unless the omission was intentional, Karla would likely take her

intestate share. You should advise George to see a lawyer to write a new will explicitly omitting Karla.

8. Measured by the degrees of consanguinity, your niece, three steps away, is closer to you than your first cousin, who is four steps away.

9.   This question is designed to review the steps in the probate process, whether UPC or non-UPC. Steps for typical formal probate in non-UPC states:

Petition court for probating of will, and file with court a <u>proof of subscribing witness</u> statement and a <u>notice of petition</u> statement.
Purchase a probate bond.
Publish notice in newspaper.
At probate hearing, have issued:
<u>Order for probate</u>
<u>Letters testamentary</u>
Manage the estate.
Develop and file an <u>inventory and appraisement</u>.
File, if desired, a <u>petition for preliminary distribution</u>.
File an estate accounting.
At final hearing, have issued an order for <u>final distribution</u>.
Pay debts and distribute estate assets.

10. The petition for probate requests:

   1. probate of the will;
   2. letters testamentary;
   3. authorization to administer under the Independent Administration of Estates Act, if any.

11. The notice of death clipping should be available from any local newspaper that is recognized by the county in question.

12. The purpose of the hearing for probate is to give anyone in the court the opportunity to object to the petition for probate.

13. Uses of the inventory and appraisement:

    1. delineate the assets for which the personal representative is responsible;
    2. describe the estate to all interested parties;
    3. determine the proper bond amount; and
    4. possibly influence death tax return valuation.

14. Filed by a creditor, the creditor's claim is the method of formally presenting a claim against the estate.

15. Before a judge will permit final distribution under supervised probate, all current debts must be paid.

16. Minimum legal procedures in formal or supervised probate in most states:
    - four document filings (petition for probate, notice of death, inventory and appraisement, and final distribution);
    - two formal court hearings (request for probate and final distribution);
    - one newspaper notice; and
    - one accounting (inventory and appraisement).

17. UPC probate is considered so flexible because of its many options and because the parties can elect different degrees of supervision at each stage of the process.

18. Informal probate administration procedures under the UPC:

    a. application for informal appointment by the personal representative, filed with a court register;
    b. informal preparation of an inventory;
    c. notice to creditors;
    d. payment of debts; and
    e. application for informal closing six months after appointment.

19.   a. Parents of minor children may find the UPC intestacy laws undesirable if a guardian must be appointed because a minor child has inherited property. Happily, this will occur under the UPC only

if one or both of the parents have children of a former marriage. In many non-UPC states, children will inherit even if there are no children of a prior marriage.

b. A will leaving everything outright to the surviving spouse may prevent guardianship proceedings, but its assumption that the surviving spouse will take care of all children may not be correct if the spouse is not the parent of the decedent's children or has children by a prior marriage. Further, the spouse could remarry, diverting assets intended for the children. Finally, the surviving spouse could die before the children reached adulthood, thus creating the need for a guardianship.

c. A better alternative would be providing for a trust for the benefit of the children. Trustees often are subject to less court supervision, and can use discretion in sprinkling trust assets unequally according to the children's needs. Guardians are required to treat each child equally. Finally, trustees are usually granted broad powers and great autonomy in managing trust assets, making a trust more efficient than a guardianship.

20. Generally probate assets include:

   i.   property owned by the decedent as an individual;
   ii. decedent's share of interests held in common with others;
   iii. in some states, the decedent's one half community property interests.

a. Automobile, held jointly with Jake: Non probate asset. Will pass to Jake by automatic survivorship, by operation of law.
b. Money fund account, owned by Denise as an individual: Probate asset.
c. Life insurance policy (L1) on Denise's life, owned by Denise. Herb is beneficiary: Non-probate asset.
d. Life insurance policy (L2) on Denise's life, owned by her. James, the sole beneficiary, died three years ago: Probate asset, since proceeds will be paid to (policy owner) Denise's estate, by default.
e. Life insurance policy (L3) on Herb's life, owned by Denise, who is also beneficiary: Probate asset, policy is owned by Denise as an individual.

    f.   Common stock, owned by trustee of a living trust. Denise is trustor, trustee, and one of the beneficiaries: Non probate asset. Not owned by Denise, as an individual.

    g.   Commercial real estate owned in common by Denise (40%) and Herb (60%): Denise's 40% interest is probate asset.

    h.   Defined benefit pension plan. Denise is participant, and Bob is named surviving beneficiary: Non-probate asset.

    i.   Residence, owned by Denise and Herb as community property: Denise's one half community interest is probate asset.

ENDNOTES

1. But see UPC §2-503, whereby in certain circumstances, a document may be accepted by the probate court as a will even though it does not meet the formal execution requirements.

2. UPC §2-106.

3. UPC §2-302.

4. UPC §2-114(b).

5. UPC §2-402.

ENDNOTES

1. But see UPC §2-503, whereby in certain circumstances, a document may be accepted by the probate court as a will even though it does not meet the formal execution requirements.

2. UPC §2-106.

3. UPC §2-302.

4. UPC §2-114(b).

5. UPC §2-402.

CHAPTER 5

The Federal Unified Transfer Tax

OVERVIEW

This chapter is the first of three covering federal taxation of wealth transfers. Since wealth is transferred during life and at death, we examine the tax imposed on both types of transfers, i.e., on gifts and on estates. Because individuals may be able to save taxes by transferring wealth directly for the benefit of grandchildren, we also consider the generation-skipping transfer tax. It will be introduced at the end of Chapter 7 and covered in more detail in Chapter 12. It is important to understand that these taxes are *excise* taxes, not property taxes. An excise tax is a tax on a transaction. In this case it is levied on the transfer of wealth, with the tax based upon the net value of property transferred. We begin with the basics of gift tax and estate tax law by showing how these two taxes are really part of a unified transfer tax system, even though it is not perfectly unified.

BRIEF HISTORY

Congress created a wealth transfer tax during the Civil War with the enactment of an inheritance tax. It was repealed shortly after the war. In 1916, Congress passed an estate tax with rates ranging between 1 and 10%. As a tax only on transfers at death, it was relatively easy to circumvent through the use of gifts which had the effect of reducing the size of the donor's taxable estate. In 1924,

Congress plugged this loophole by enacting a gift tax. The gift tax was repealed in 1926 and reenacted in 1932, applicable to gifts made after June 5 of that year.

Prior to the gift tax and estate tax being unified in 1977, there were a number of imperfections in the system that could be exploited to reduce the taxes on the transfer of wealth. Because the gift tax *rates* were only 75% of the estate tax rates, giving large gifts reduced taxes for the very wealthy. For any given size taxable estate, the fact that the decedent had made prior taxable gifts did not increase the decedent's estate tax. Estates of decedents who had made taxable gifts still started at the lowest marginal rates and had the same estate tax exemption as estates of persons who had not made taxable gifts. They were said to "take two trips up the rate ladder," since the gift tax and the estate tax are both progressive. Before the 1977 unification of the estate and gift taxes, there was an annual exclusion of $3,000 per donee, a $30,000 lifetime gift exemption for each donor, and a $60,000 estate exemption which was undiminished by the decedent's use of the gift exemption. The annual exclusion (now an "indexed" $10,000 per year) is the amount that is deducted or excluded from taxable gifts. Since it is a per donee deduction, there is no limit to the number of annual exclusions a donor can claim in a calendar year. Furthermore, the exclusion is available even if the donees are not related to the donor.[1] On January 1, 1982, the annual exclusion increased from $3,000 per donee per year to $10,000 per donee per year. Learning to calculate the taxes on pre-1977 transfers is not necessary, although the following examples demonstrate the dramatic change brought about by unification of the two taxes:

EXAMPLE 5 - 1. In 1970, Adele made a gift worth $1,000,000 to her friend Lance. She used her $30,000 lifetime exemption and the $3,000 annual exclusion to bring the taxable gift down to $967,000. Adele paid gift tax of $235,118.

EXAMPLE 5 - 2. When Adele died in 1975, her net estate was left in equal shares to five friends. The gross estate was worth $1,150,000. There were debts and expenses of $150,000 which, combined with the $60,000 estate exemption, resulted in a taxable estate of $940,000. Adele's estate paid estate tax of $303,500. Even though Adele had made the earlier gift to Lance, it did not affect the amount of the estate tax. Notice that for estates there is no per-beneficiary exclusion comparable to the gift tax annual exclusion.

EXAMPLE 5 - 3. Brian also died in 1975 and had an estate identical to Adele's. It too was left to five friends. The gross estate was worth $1,150,000. There were debts and expenses of $150,000, which combined with the $60,000 estate exemption, resulted in a taxable estate of $940,000. Brian's estate paid estate tax of $303,500. The tax on Brian's estate was exactly the same as Adele's, even though Adele had made a huge taxable gift during her lifetime and Brian had not made any taxable gifts.

With the passage of the Tax Reform Act of 1976, a single "unified" rate schedule was adopted, taxing lifetime gifts and transfers at death at the same rate. With the implementation of the "unified" system, the transfer of the estate at death is treated almost as though it were just another gift. Adjusted taxable gifts (i.e., the value of gifts reduced by annual exclusions) serve to boost the donor's taxable estate into its appropriate marginal rates. Furthermore, the donor's post-76 taxable gifts reduce the amount of unified credit available to shelter transfers at death. Before we get into the details of the calculations, compare the tax results in the following examples that repeat the facts of the three prior situations in the current estate tax era. In these examples, unless stated otherwise, we are using the current estate tax rates, the unified credit of $192,800 (appropriate for years between 1987 - 1997, inclusive), and an annual exclusion of $10,000. The annual exclusion was increased from $3,000 to $10,000 for gifts in years after 1981. The $10,000 amount is indexed for inflation starting in 1999.

EXAMPLE 5 - 4. In 1990, Catherine made a gift worth $1,000,000 to her friend Nathan. She used the $10,000 annual exclusion to bring the taxable gift down to $990,000. Catherine paid gift tax of $149,100. Notice that there is no donor lifetime exemption after 1976.

EXAMPLE 5 - 5. When Catherine died in 1995, her net estate was left in equal shares to five friends. The gross estate was worth $1,150,000. There were debts and expenses of $150,000, which resulted in a taxable estate of $1,000,000. Notice, there is no estate exemption for decedents dying after 1976. Because of her earlier gift, $990,000 is added back to Catherine's estate to determine the marginal rate and her unified credit has already been used up against the taxable gift. Catherine's estate paid estate taxes of $434,400. Compare Catherine's estate tax amount to that of Edward's estate in the example that follows.

EXAMPLE 5 - 6. Edward also died in 1995, with an estate identical to Catherine's except that Edward had never made any post-1976 taxable gifts. His estate was also left to five friends. The gross estate was worth $1,150,000. There were debts and expenses of $150,000, which resulted in a taxable estate of $1,000,000. Edward's estate paid estate tax of $153,000. Catharine's estate tax was $434,400, an amount that is $281,400 more than the tax on Edward's estate, because her estate was taxed at higher marginal rates and her unified credit was used up on the 1990 gift to

Nathan. Also notice that Edward's estate tax on his taxable estate of $1,000,000 was $3,900 more than the gift tax on Catherine's $1,000,000 gift. *** *Query 5 - 1. How do you account for the $3,900 difference? What is the transfer tax marginal rate just below $1,000,000?*

EXAMPLE 5 - 7. Suppose Catharine had not made the 1990 gift and that her estate was worth $2,150,000 when she died in 1995. Assume that debts and expenses stayed at $150,000, resulting in a taxable estate of $2,000,000. The estate tax would be $588,000. Compare this to the total paid when there was a gift of $1,000,000 followed by the donor's taxable estate of $1,000,000. There is a $4,500 difference in having it all taxed at death. *** *Query 5 - 2. How do you account for the difference? What is the marginal rate just below $2,000,000?*

In spite of unification, there are advantages to using gifts (large and small) as part of a wealthy person's estate plan. We shall explore later how gifts save transfer taxes by utilizing the annual exclusion, by removing the gift tax from the transfer tax base, and by keeping future appreciation out of the transfer tax base.

UNIFIED TRANSFER TAX FRAMEWORK

The basic model of the present system is to tax wealth transfers cumulatively, while allowing the donors of gifts and estates modest in size to escape transfer taxes through a combination of annual exclusions (for gifts only) and the unified credit (applicable to both gifts and estates). There has been a phase-in of increases to the unified credit and decreases to the top marginal rates. Indeed, the phase-in of increasing unified credits will continue until the year 2006. Before we go into details on the phase-in, peek ahead if you like to Table 5-5 that shows the present marginal rates and Table 5-6 that shows the changing unified credit starting with 1977 (the year he unified credit became law, replacing the old gift and estate tax exemptions). The latter table also shows the "exclusion amount," meaning the amount that passes tax free because it is covered by the available unified credit. Fear not! It is a little complicated at first, but we will take this transfer tax business step-by-step. Most of the examples, used to explore the fundamentals of the transfer tax system, will use years between 1987 and 1997, inclusive, because the rates, the unified credit, and the annual exclusion were all unchanged during that period. We start with simple gifts, ones where the donor made no prior taxable gifts, then move to gifts with the donor having made prior gifts. Next we go to a simple taxable estate, one where the donor made no prior post-76 taxable gifts. Finally, we look at an estate where the decedent had made post-76 taxable gifts.

Appendix D at the end of the text includes a copy of the Federal Gift Tax Return, Form 709, which should help to illustrate the gift tax scheme. The *donor* is responsible for filing the return and paying the tax. The return is due on April 15 of the year following the taxable gifts. An extension to file the donor's income tax return acts as an automatic extension (to the same due date) of the donor's gift tax return. If the donor fails to pay the gift tax due, the donee is secondarily liable for payment (up to the value of the gift) of the tax.

Gift taxes for the first time donor. The steps for calculating the gift tax for a donor who has made no prior taxable gifts are summarized as follows: determine the fair market value (FMV), on the date given, of the property; subtract the annual exclusions (an indexed $10,000 each calendar year for each donee), the marital deduction, and any attached mortgages or liens from the FMV; on this net amount (the taxable gift) use the transfer tax rate table to calculate the tentative tax; and, finally, subtract the unified credit for the year of the gift from the tentative tax to determine the gift tax that must be paid.

TABLE 5 - 1 Federal Gift Tax (Form 709) Basic Model - **No** Prior Gifts

Total current year's gross gifts	$xxx,xxx
Less: Annual exclusion(s) and deductions	(xxx,xxx)
Equals: Total taxable gifts	$xxx,xxx
Calculate: Tentative tax on total taxable gifts	xxx,xxx
Less: unified credit (not to exceed tentative tax)	(xxx,xxx)
Equals: Current gift tax	$xx,xxx

EXAMPLE 5 - 8. In 1989, Deborah made a gift of GnuCo stock worth $430,000 to her sister, Ophelia. Deborah had never made a taxable gift before. The tentative tax on a $420,000 taxable gift (remember the annual exclusion) is $128,600. When $128,600 of Deborah's unified credit was applied (unified credit up to $192,800 was available in 1989), no gift taxes were due.

EXAMPLE 5 - 9. In 1993, Edward made a gift of 1,000 shares of PlehCo stock worth $850,000 to his sister, Gloria. Edward had never made a taxable gift before. The tentative tax on an $840,000 gift is $283,400 which, when reduced by the $192,800 unified credit, resulted in Edward paying gift taxes of $90,600.

EXAMPLE 5 - 10. In 1993, Francis made gifts of 1,000 shares of RenCo stock worth $850,000. His brother, Peter, received 500 shares and his sister, Patricia, received the other 500 shares. The tentative tax on taxable gifts of $830,000 (this time, there are two annual exclusions) is $279,500 and the gift tax, after the $192,800 unified credit, is $86,700.

*** Query 5 - 3. Given the following information, what gift tax did Martha pay? In 1990, Martha gave Quin an apartment building worth $750,000. It was free and clear of debt and liens. Martha was new to making large gifts.

Gift taxes for the experienced donor. Where there have been prior gifts, the steps for calculating the gift tax for new gifts are as follows: the FMV's for all current period (during calendar year) gifts are determined; the annual exclusions and deductions (marital, charitable, and mortgages or liens attached to the property transferred) are subtracted from the current year's FMV (the gross gifts amount) to arrive at current taxable gifts; the current taxable gifts are added to the taxable gifts for prior years to determine the total taxable gifts; then, using the tax rate table, a tentative tax is calculated for both the prior years' cumulative taxable gifts and the total taxable gifts; from the tentative tax on the total taxable gifts, the tentative tax on prior taxable gifts is subtracted to arrive at the tentative tax on current period taxable gifts; the unused unified credit is determined by subtracting the unified credit used for prior years' post-76 taxable gifts from the total unified credit allowable for the current year; and, finally, the unused unified credit (the credit still available) is subtracted from the tentative tax for current gifts to determine the gift tax that must be paid. Note that if the total value of gifts during the year to a particular donee are less than the annual exclusion amount, then those gifts do not need to be reported on the gift tax return (i.e., they will not appear on Form 709). In working problems, students must be careful not to take a full annual exclusion. The best advice is to just ignore those gifts. Of course the preceding advice assumes that the gift is one of a present interest (e.g., an outright gift of property), since there is no annual exclusion available for gifts of a future interest.

TABLE 5 - 2 Federal Gift Tax (Form 709) Overview Model – **With** Prior Gifts

Total current year's gross gifts	\$xxx,xxx
Less: Annual exclusion(s) and deductions	(xx,xxx)
Equals: Current taxable gifts	\$xxx,xxx
Plus: Total prior taxable gifts	xx,xxx
Equals: Total (current and prior) taxable gifts	\$xxx,xxx
Calculate: Tentative tax on total taxable gifts	\$xxx,xxx
Less: Tentative tax on total prior taxable gifts	(xx,xxx)
Leaves: Tentative tax on current taxable gifts	\$xxx,xxx
Less: Unused unified credit (not to exceed tentative tax)	(xx,xxx)
Equals: Current gift tax	\$xxx,xxx

For each example below, refer back to the earlier examples to see how they boost the later transfers into higher marginal rates. Notice that it is the taxable amount (not the gross amount) that does the boosting and that we take into account that the earlier taxable gifts used up some (or all) of the unified credit.

EXAMPLE 5 - 11. In 1991, Deborah gave additional GnuCo stock worth \$730,000 to her friend, Gerry. The gift tax was calculated as follows:

Total current year's gross gifts	\$730,000	
- Annual exclusions	(\$10,000)	
= Current taxable gifts		\$720,000
+ Total prior taxable gifts		\$420,000
= Total taxable gifts		\$1,140,000
Tentative tax on total taxable gifts		\$403,200
- Tentative tax on prior taxable gifts		(\$128,600)
= Tentative tax on current taxable gifts		\$274,600
- Unused unified credit [\$192,800 - \$128,600]		(\$64,200)
Equals: Current gift tax		\$210,400

Notice that it was not necessary to recalculate the tentative tax on the prior taxable gifts since that figure was already available.

EXAMPLE 5 - 12. In 1992, Deborah gave gold bars worth $650,000 to George, her favorite former teacher, and bonds worth $380,000 to her friend, Samantha. The gift tax was calculated as follows:

Total current taxable gifts	$1,030,000	
- Annual exclusions	($20,000)	
= Current taxable gifts		$1,010,000
+ Prior period gifts		$1,140,000
= Total taxable gifts		$2,150,000
Tentative tax on total taxable gifts		$854,300
- Tentative tax on prior taxable gifts		($403,200)
= Tentative tax on current taxable gifts		$451,100
- Unused unified credit [$192,800 - $192,800]		$0
Equals: Current gift tax		$451,100

Again, notice that neither the prior taxable gifts nor the tentative tax on prior taxable gifts had to be calculated, since both figures were already available. The prior taxable gifts were the total gifts from the last taxable period reduced by the allowable annual exclusions. The tentative tax was calculated as one of the steps in determining the gift tax for the earlier period.

*** *Query 5 - 4. On the gifts described next, taking into account Martha's earlier gift, what gift tax did she have to pay? In 1993, Martha gave three more gifts: a new car costing $36,000 to Jake; cash in the amount of $43,000 to Marilyn; and PontoCo common stock worth $88,000 to Eddie.*

Estate taxes for the stingy decedent. Sorry, did not mean stingy; frugal is better. The steps for calculating the estate tax for a decedent who never made any post-76 taxable gifts are summarized as follows: From the decedent's gross estate (generally, all that the person owned at death), subtract the marital deduction and any debts, mortgages, liens, and the expenses of the decedent's estate (i.e., executor's fees, appraiser's fees, and attorney's fees) to arrive at the *taxable estate*. The transfer tax rate table is used to calculate a tentative tax on the taxable estate. Finally, the death taxes that must be paid are determined by subtracting the unified credit from the tentative tax.

TABLE 5 - 3 Federal Estate Tax (Form 706) Basic Model - **No** Prior Gifts

---

Gross estate	$xxx,xxx
Less: Total deductions	(xx,xxx)
Leaves: Taxable estate	$xxx,xxx
Calculate: Tentative estate tax	$xxx,xxx
Less: Unified credit	(xxx,xxx)
Total Death taxes (most states)	($xxx,xxx)
Less: State death tax credit	(xxx,xxx)
Less: Other credits	(xx,xxx)
Equals: federal estate tax	$xxx,xxx

EXAMPLE 5 - 13. When he died in early 1997, Gregg left his entire estate to his three children. The gross estate was valued at $5,840,000. Total debts were $315,000 and expenses of administration were $55,000. He had made no post-1976 taxable gifts. His estate tax is as follows:

Gross Estate	$5,840,000
- Debts & expenses	($370,000)
= Taxable estate = Estate tax base	$5,470,000
Tentative tax on estate tax base	$2,649,300
- Unified credit	($192,800)
= Total Death taxes (for most estates)	$2,456,500

*** *Query 5 - 5. Given the following information, what death tax did Georgine's estate pay? Georgine died in 1996, leaving her $800,000 estate to her children by right of representation. Debts totaled $150,000 and expenses were $50,000. Calculate her estate's death tax.*

*** *Query 5 - 6. Given this information, what death tax did Harold's estate pay? Harold died in 1996, leaving his $980,000 estate to his brother. Debts totaled $65,000 and expenses were $20,000. Calculate his estate's death tax.*

Estate taxes for the generous decedent. Here, we put it all together. The estate taxes for an estate with prior post-76 gifts are calculated taking those gifts into account. These gifts are referred to as *adjusted taxable gifts.* They are adjusted in the sense that the gross value has been reduced by the annual exclusion (gifts that qualified for the marital or charitable deduction are excluded). The sole purpose of the adjusted taxable gifts coming into the estate tax equation is to move the decedent's taxable estate up into the appropriate marginal rates. The rates are appropriate in the sense that we now have a unified transfer tax system and the earlier gifts have already occupied the lower marginal rates. The steps are as follows: Similar to what was done for gifts, start with the gross estate (typically, the FMV of all that the decedent owned at the date of death); subtract debts, expenses, gifts to charities, and other deductions to arrive at the taxable estate; add the adjusted taxable gifts to determine the total estate tax base; use the tax rate table to determine the tentative tax on the total tax base; from the tentative tax, subtract the gift taxes payable on post-76 gifts (for most estates, the gift taxes payable will be the same as the total of the gift taxes paid on the post-76 gifts); subtract the unified credit to arrive at total death taxes (true for those estates that pay only a "pickup" tax, discussed later); and, finally, from the total death taxes subtract the state death tax credit (discussed shortly) to arrive at the federal estate tax.

TABLE 5 - 4 Federal Estate Tax (Form 706) Overview Model - **With** Prior Gifts

Gross estate	$xxx,xxx	
Less: Total deductions	(xxx,xxx)	
Leaves: Taxable estate	xxx,xxx	
Plus: Adjusted taxable gifts (post-76)	xx,xxx	
Equals: Estate tax base	$xxx,xxx	
Calculate: Tentative estate tax		$xxx,xxx
Less: Gift taxes payable on post-76 taxable gifts		(xxx,xxx)
Less: Unified credit		(xxx,xxx)
Less: State death tax credit		(xxx,xxx)
Less: Other credits		(xx,xxx)
Equals: Federal estate tax		$xxx,xxx

Please note, that the gift taxes payable credit is not the tentative tax on those earlier gifts, but rather is the dollar amount after application of the unified credit. Because this credit is designed to compensate for adding the adjusted taxable gifts to the tax base and because it is calculated using the gift taxes payable (i.e., the amount by which the tentative tax exceeded the unified credit) of those prior gifts rather than the tentative tax, we must utilize the full unified credit to arrive at the death taxes.

The state death tax credit does not reduce the total estate taxes. It merely divides the total death taxes between the federal and state governments. Every taxable estate large enough to pay federal estate taxes will use the unified credit and the state death tax credit. The former will apply to every estate to keep the smaller ones (or cumulative transfers, if you will) from being taxed, and the latter is used because every state in the nation collects death taxes that at least equal the federal state death tax credit.

The estate tax return, federal Form 706, is called the United States Estate (and Generation-Skipping Transfer) Tax Return and is reproduced as Appendix C at the back of the book. The return is commonly referred to as the 706. The due date for the 706 is nine months after the date of death. Hence, the 706 for the estate of a wealthy person who died on May 15th is due February 15th of the following year unless that falls on a holiday or a weekend, in which case the return is due on the next business day. We will cover extensions later.

In the example that follows, you need to refer back to the example where Deborah made gifts in 1989, 1991, and 1992 to see how all of those prior gifts affect her estate taxes. You may wish to tag those pages to allow you to flip back and forth as you tackle this problem.

EXAMPLE 5 - 14. Deborah died on March 10, 1997 and left her estate to her four children. Her estate was worth $5,840,000, debts were $315,000, and expenses totaled $55,000. Her estate taxes were due December 10, 1997 (nine months to the day following her death).Taking into account the gifts she made in 1989, 1991, and 1992, her estate tax is as follows:

Gross Estate	$5,840,000
- Debts & expenses	($370,000)
- Marital & charitable deductions	$0
= Taxable estate	$5,470,000
+ Adjusted taxable gifts (post-76)	$2,150,000
= Estate tax base	$7,620,000

Tentative tax on estate tax base	$3,831,800
- Gift tax payable on post-76 taxable gifts	($661,500)
- Unified credit	($192,800)
= Total Death taxes (for most estates)	$2,977,500
- State death tax credit (we're jumping ahead)	($447,200)
- Other credits	$0
= Federal Estate Tax	$2,530,300

Notice that, to calculate the gift tax payable credit, one must add up all the taxes paid, NOT the tentative tax on those prior gifts. The gift taxes paid (payable) were an amount in excess of the available unified credit. Because the entire prior adjusted taxable gifts (post-1976) are included in the tax base, the full unified credit is used in the calculation. *** *Query 5 - 7. Given the following information and taking into account her earlier gifts, what death tax did Martha's estate pay? Martha died in 1996, leaving her $2,550,000 estate to her children. There were debts of $240,000 and expenses of $60,000.*

UNIFIED RATE SCHEDULE

As a result of the Economic Recovery Act of 1981 (ERTA), revised by the Tax Reform Act of 1984 and the Revenue Act of 1987, rates on taxable transfers in excess of $3 million have decreased periodically. Table 5-5 shows the current federal unified transfer tax rate schedule. It is *unified* in the sense that the same rate schedule is used to calculate the tentative tax on taxable gifts and on taxable estates. The phase-in of the decreasing top marginal rates is shown in Table 1 in Appendix A at the end of the book. That table is divided into five parts. The first part shows the rates for *all* transfer years after 1976 for taxable amounts up to $3 million. The next four parts represent transition rates, on amounts over $3 million, that apply for transfers during 1977-81, 1982, 1983, and, finally, those that have been in effect since 1984.

A few examples will demonstrate the application of the unified rates. The facts in these examples are intended to be sufficiently general to apply to both lifetime gifts and transfers at death.

EXAMPLE 5 - 15. The tentative tax on a $600,000 taxable transfer is $192,800. This represents the sum of $155,800 plus $37,000, which is 37% of $100,000, the excess of $600,000 over $500,000. Since the same rate table applies to all years for amounts up to $3 million, $192,800 would be the tentative tax on the amount $600,000 for all years after 1976. Of course, for the years 1987 through 1997 the unified credit was $192,800, hence it covered taxable transfers up to $600,000.

EXAMPLE 5 - 16. The tentative tax on the taxable amount $3,250,000 in any year prior to 1984 is $1,433,300. This represents the sum of $1,290,800 plus $142,500, which is 57% of $250,000, the excess of $3,250,000 over $3,000,000. Because of the decrease in the top marginal rate, the same transfer after 1983 results in taxes of $1,428,300 (i.e., $1,290,800 plus 55% times $250,000).

TABLE 5 - 5 Federal Unified Transfer-Tax Rates - Since 1/1/88

If the Amount is:		Tentative Tax		
Over	But Not Over	Base Amount +	Percent	On Excess Over
$0	$10,000	$0	18%	$0
10,000	20,000	1,800	20%	10,000
20,000	40,000	3,800	22%	20,000
40,000	60,000	8,200	24%	40,000
60,000	80,000	13,000	26%	60,000
80,000	100,000	18,200	28%	80,000
100,000	150,000	23,800	30%	100,000
150,000	250,000	38,800	32%	150,000
250,000	500,000	70,800	34%	250,000
500,000	750,000	155,800	37%	500,000
750,000	1,000,000	248,300	39%	750,000
1,000,000	1,250,000	345,800	41%	1,000,000
1,250,000	1,500,000	448,300	43%	1,250,000
1,500,000	2,000,000	555,800	45%	1,500,000
2,000,000	2,500,000	780,800	49%	2,000,000
2,500,000	3,000,000	1,025,800	53%	2,500,000
3,000,000	10,000,000	1,290,800	55%	3,000,000
* 10,000,000		5,140,800	60%	10,000,000
At the end of the "bubble" the rate drops back to 55%			55%	See Table 5-6.

* For post-1987 transfers above $10,000,000, there is a 5% surcharge that is imposed until the benefit of the unified credit and of lower marginal rates has been taken back.

The Revenue Act of 1987 phased out the tax benefits of the lower rates and the unified credit (described below) for taxable transfers made after December 31, 1987 that exceed $10 million. The net effect is to "recapture" the taxes saved by the lower rates and the unified credit as compared to what would have been paid with a flat 55% rate and no unified credit. This recapture is implemented by imposing an additional 5% tax on taxable transfers above $10 million, with the surcharge ending when the benefits of the lower rates and the unified credit have been recaptured. As the unified credit increases, the 5% surcharge has to be spread over a greater range in order to recapture the taxes saved by the larger unified credit. The range over which the rate jumps from 55% to 60% before dropping back to 55% is referred to as the "bubble." When the unified credit was $192,800 (years 1987 - 1997), the bubble range was from $10,000,000 to $21,040,000 (the surcharge did not go into effect until 1988).[2] When the unified credit reaches $345,800 in the year 2006, the bubble will range from $10,000,000 to $24,100,000. Thus, the effective marginal tax rate for all transfers between 10 million dollars and the end of the bubble will be 60% and, above the bubble, it will drop back to 55%. Table 5 - 6 shows the end of the bubble for each year.

> EXAMPLE 5 - 17. The *tentative tax* on a taxable transfer of $21,040,000 in 1995 is $11,764,800. This amount represents the sum of a) $5,140,800 [the tentative tax on $10,000,000] and b) $6,624,000 [which is 60% of $11,040,000, the excess of $21,040,000 over $10,000,000]. The tentative tax less the unified credit [$11,764,800 - $192,800] results in total taxes of $11,572,000, i.e., exactly 55% of $21,040,000.

Thus, federal unified transfer tax rates are progressive. Marginal rates range from 18% to as high as 60% for amounts in excess of $10 million. The *marginal rate* is the rate levied on the next taxable dollar. The *average rate*, on the other hand, is obtained by dividing the tax by the total taxable amount. For taxable estates above the bubble (e.g., above $21,100,000 after 2005), the marginal and the average rates are both 55%.

UNIFIED CREDIT

In federal estate and gift tax law, a *credit* is a dollar-for-dollar reduction in the *tentative tax*. A *deduction* is a dollar-for-dollar reduction from the gross amount to arrive at the amount taxable. A deduction provides only a fractional reduction in the amount of tax. The fraction is determined by the top marginal tax rates applicable to the particular transfer. The most important transfer tax credit of the five we will study is the unified credit. It will be covered next and the state death tax credit a little later in this chapter. The unified credit is the most important in that it comes into play every time there is a taxable transfer, whether by gift or by way of a decedent's estate. The other credits only apply to the estate tax. We will cover the state death tax in this chapter because it is applicable to all estates that exceed the exclusion amount. The other three credits are the gift tax payable credit (introduced already in this chapter), the prior transfer credit, and the credit for foreign death taxes. These other credits are less likely to be encountered and will be covered at the end of the next chapter.

Prior to 1977 (the first year of the unified credit), a donor was allowed a lifetime exemption (deduction) of $30,000 for gifts in excess of the $3,000 per donee annual exclusions; and an estate exemption (deduction) of $60,000 when the person died. These had the effect of eliminating taxation on modest lifetime gifts and on small estates. These were called the $30,000 gift exemption and the $60,000 estate exemption. Using the gift exemption did not reduce the estate exemption. Thus, an estate with a net value of less than $60,000 was tax free, regardless of the amount of lifetime taxable gifts by the decedent. The Tax Reform Act of 1976 (TRA 76) eliminated the two exemptions and substituted a single *unified credit* applicable to both taxable gifts and taxable estates after 1976. With the new law, the unified credit available at the death of a donor is decreased to the extent that the donor's lifetime gifts used it up.

The unified credit has increased over the years, as shown in Table 5-6.[3] After a decade of increases, the period from 1987 through 1997 saw the unified credit remain steady at $192,800. During that period, the credit sheltered $600,000 in net value transferred from gift and estate taxes. With the Tax Payer Relief Act of 1997, the amount that can pass tax free increases, almost yearly, until it reaches $1,000,000 in the year 2006. What was called the unified credit equivalent, or the credit shelter amount, has been renamed (mis-named some might argue) by the 1997 Act as the *exclusion amount*. This exclusion amount is the taxable amount that can be transferred free of taxes because it generates a tentative tax that is just covered by the unified transfer tax credit.

Table 5-6 shows the unified credit, the exclusion amount, and the "end of the bubble" since 1977. The *exclusion amount* (i.e., the old *unified credit equivalent*, or the *credit shelter* amount) that corresponds to each year's unified credit represents the amount by which the taxable amount can exceed zero and still have the tentative tax be completely sheltered (offset) by the unified credit. The last column shows the end of the 60% marginal rate range (the bubble), i.e., the point at which the marginal rate finally drops back to 55%. As stated earlier, a 5% surcharge only applies to post-1987 taxable transfers above the $10,000,000 level.

TABLE 5-6 Federal Unified Credits, Exclusion Amounts, and the End of the Bubble by Year Since 1977

Year	Unified Credit	Exclusion Amount	End of the Bubble
1977	$30,000	$120,667	
1978	$34,000	$134,000	
1979	$38,000	$147,333	
1980	$42,500	$161,563	
1981	$47,000	$175,625	
1982	$62,800	$225,000	
1983	$79,300	$275,000	*The 5% surcharge*
1984	$96,300	$325,000	*started in 1988.*
1985	$121,800	$400,000	
1986	$155,800	$500,000	
1987 - 1997	$192,800	$600,000	$21,040,000
1998	$202,050	$625,000	$21,225,000
1999	$211,300	$650,000	$21,410,000
2000	$220,550	$675,000	$21,595,000
2001	$220,550	$675,000	$21,595,000
2002	$229,800	$700,000	$21,780,000
2003	$229,800	$700,000	$21,780,000
2004	$287,300	$850,000	$22,930,000
2005	$326,300	$950,000	$23,710,000
2006 & after	$345,800	$1,000,000	$24,100,000

It is unfortunate that Congress put the term *exclusion amount* in the Code to describe that amount which passes tax free. Better terms would have been either the *credit shelter amount* or the *unified credit equivalent*.[4] The 1999 unified credit in the amount of $211,300 shelters $650,000 in taxable transfers from the estate (or the gift) tax, because the tentative tax on that size transfer is exactly $211,300. In 2006, the sheltered amount rises to $1,000,000 because the tentative tax on that amount is $345,800, which matches the unified credit for that year. In doing the calculations, we do not "exclude" the exclusion amount; instead, we determine a tentative tax on the taxable transfer and then apply the appropriate unified credit. Oh well, we will fall in line and refer to this tax free amount as the *exclusion amount*, but please never subtract it when calculating the transfer tax.

EXAMPLE 5 - 18. After the unified credit is subtracted, the *net tax* on the amount $600,000 in 1983 is $113,500, which is the tentative tax of $192,800, reduced by the 1983 unified credit of $79,300.

EXAMPLE 5 - 19. Facts as in the prior example, except the applicable year is any year between 1987 and 1997. After the unified credit is subtracted, the net tax on $600,000 is zero, which is the tentative tax of $192,800, reduced by the applicable unified credit of $192,800. Thus, for those years, the first $600,000 in taxable transfers was totally sheltered by the unified credit.

EXAMPLE 5 - 20. A taxable gift (gross gift less the annual exclusions) of $2,500,000 is made in 2006. The tentative tax is $1,025,800. The unified credit of $345,800 reduces the tentative tax to $680,000. Notice that the exclusion amount did not enter into the calculation of the gift tax in this example, nor in any of the prior examples.

Warning: Do NOT deduct the unified credit shelter amount or as we will now call it, the exclusion amount. You must subtract the unified credit from the tentative tax for all of these transfer tax calculations. The only appropriate use of the term exclusion amount is in giving general advice to clients, such as "in 1999, the tax free exclusion amount is $650,000." However, less confusion would result by just saying, "the amount that can pass tax free is $650,000."

In many situations, the allowable unified credit will be less than the amount in Table 5 - 6. The actual amount of the allowable unified credit is the *lesser of either* the unused unified credit in the year of the transfer *or* the amount of the tentative tax. For example, the allowable unified credit for a $250,000 gift made in 2001 (assuming no prior taxable gifts) is $70,800, i.e., the lesser of $220,550, the unified credit available in 2001, and $70,800, the tentative tax on $250,000.

UNLIMITED MARITAL DEDUCTION

Since 1982, virtually all transfers to a *spouse*, whether made during lifetime or at death, have been tax free; the amount of the transfer is treated as a "marital" deduction from the total gross estate or gross gifts. A brief history of the gift tax and estate tax marital deductions is described next.

The *gift tax marital deduction* was first enacted in 1948 to equalize tax treatment for married taxpayers in common law and community property states.

It allowed a deduction for up to 50% of the value of noncommunity property gifts made to a spouse. TRA 76 changed this limit to 100% of the first $100,000, no deduction for the next $100,000, and 50% for all amounts exceeding $200,000.

The *estate tax marital deduction* was also first enacted in 1948, also to equalize tax treatment across the states. Its amount was limited to one half of the adjusted gross estate. TRA 76 changed this limit to the greater of $250,000 or one half of the adjusted gross estate, subject to further adjustments for any gift tax marital deduction taken and for property held as community property. The *adjusted gross estate* was defined essentially as the decedent's separate property, reduced by deductions for funeral and administration expenses, claims against the estate, and losses during administration.

The *present* 100% "unlimited" gift and estate tax marital deductions became effective in 1982.[5] Starting in 1984, the marital deduction was eliminated for transfers to non-United States spouses unless certain arrangements are made, such as placing the transferred property in special trusts called qualified domestic trusts (QDOT's). We will cover transfers to non-United States spouses in more detail later in the book, but for now we will focus on the basics.

> EXAMPLE 5 - 21. Last year, Wilder gave property worth $10 million to his wife, Simba, a U.S. citizen. Although Wilder's "gross gift" was $10 million, his taxable gift is reduced to zero by the unlimited marital deduction. Thus, there is no tentative tax.

> EXAMPLE 5 - 22. Based on the facts in the prior example, assume instead that Wilder died last year leaving his entire $10 million estate to his wife. His taxable estate and tentative tax are zero, as a result of subtracting the $10 million marital deduction from the $10 million gross estate.

The current unlimited marital deduction will be examined in greater detail in the chapters that follow. Wealth transfer taxes incorporate other significant deductions, but their examination will also be deferred.

UNLIMITED CHARITABLE DEDUCTION

When determining transfer taxes, there is a 100% deduction for gifts or bequests made to qualified charities. Contrast this with income tax law, which limits the amount that can be deducted based upon the type of gift, the nature of the charity (e.g., private foundation versus public charity), and the donor's adjusted gross income. We will reserve for a later discussion the complexities that arise when charitable gifts are made using trust arrangements that benefit both family members and charities.

THE ANNUAL EXCLUSION FOR LIFETIME GIFTS

Any donor can give to any donee gifts that have a value of $10,000, or less, in a given year without reporting the transfer as a gift. The exclusion is called the *annual exclusion*. The $10,000 amount has been indexed for inflation starting for years after 1998, with 1997 being the base year. It will change slowly (every two or three years, if inflation stays low), since the indexed amount is to be rounded down to the next lower multiple of $1,000.[6] The first increase is likely for the year 2000.

> EXAMPLE 5 - 23. In 1999, Warren gave $30,000 cash to his son, Bob, and a boat valued at $15,000 to his fishing buddy, Bill. Assuming no other deductions, and that Warren made no other gifts that year, he would file only one gift tax return, and his current taxable gifts for 1999 would equal $25,000. The first portion of Warren's gift tax return would look as follows:
>
> | | |
> |---|---|
> | Total current year's gross gifts | $45,000 |
> | Less: Annual exclusions and deductions | ($20,000) |
> | Equals: Current taxable gifts | $25,000 |
>
> EXAMPLE 5 - 24. In 1999, Mary gave an apartment building worth $275,000 to her three children as tenants in common. She also gave her brother Frank a used car worth $6,500. She would report gross gifts of $275,000 and taxable gifts, after taking the three annual exclusions, of $245,000. The gift to Frank should not be reported since it is under the annual exclusion amount.

Prior to 1982, the annual exclusion amount was $3,000 and the maximum marital deduction was 50% of the net value of the gift. Starting in 1982, the annual exclusion increased to $10,000 and the marital deduction increased to 100%. To qualify for the annual exclusion, the gift must be one of a present interest, meaning that the donee has immediate access to the gift for use and enjoyment.[7] Thus, a gift to an irrevocable trust giving one person a life estate and another the remainder creates two gifts. The value of the life estate qualifies for the annual exclusion because it is a gift of a present interest, but the remainder does not qualify because it is a future interest.

WEALTH TRANSFERS ARE UNIFIED AND TAXED CUMULATIVELY

In wealth transfer taxation, succeeding transfers are unified, in part because they are taxed cumulatively. Under the *cumulative gift doctrine*, all past and present gifts are accumulated; that is, prior taxable gifts are added to current taxable transfers (whether lifetime gifts or the donor's estate at death) to determine the transfer tax base. There is one purpose, and only one purpose, to having adjusted taxable gifts as part of the estate tax calculation, and that is to boost the decedent's estate into higher marginal rates. These are the appropriate marginal rates when the net estate is viewed as just another in a series of transfers.

As we have seen, TRA 76 created the *unified transfer tax*, combining gift and estate taxation into a single tax structure having one rate schedule. Thus, the transfer at death is treated as just the last in a series of transfers. However, TRA 76 did not achieve complete unification; for instance, the annual exclusion is available only for lifetime gifts. Unification did not produce a tax system that makes planners indifferent as to the timing of transfers; that is, whether one would recommend gifts over holding property until death, or vice versa, depends on the circumstances. For example, lifetime gifts use up less unified credit because of the annual exclusion, but appreciated property transferred at death receives a step-up in basis.

To recapitulate, let us review the points demonstrated in the earlier examples before we go on to cover the state death tax credits.

First, regarding taxable gifts, in calculating the gift tax one includes in the item called "total prior taxable gifts" all taxable gifts made *since 1932*, the year of enactment of the gift tax. On the other hand, as we have said, in calculating the federal estate tax base, one includes in the item called "adjusted taxable gifts" only the taxable gifts made since January 1, 1977, i.e., since unification.

Second, in the *gift tax* model, the "unused unified credit" is the amount of the current unified credit reduced by the unified credit amount already used up to offset tentative gift taxes on gifts in prior years. It is based on the premise that once the amount of the (lifetime) unified credit is used up, each additional dollar of taxable gift is fully taxable. By way of contrast, in the *estate tax* model, the entire unified credit is subtracted from the tentative tax, because the "gift tax payable" credit for prior gift taxes is limited to the amount of gift taxes that would have been paid on the post-1976 gifts using the rates in effect at the date of death. This means that the gift taxes payable credit might be less than what was actually paid. This occurs where there were pre-1977 taxable gifts that pushed the post-1976 taxable gifts into higher marginal rates, or where very large post-1976 gifts were given at a time when the top marginal rates were higher than those in effect when the donor died. For instance, a $7,000,000 (after deducting the annual exclusion amount) gift made in 1981 (when the top marginal rate was 70%) would have resulted in gift tax of $3,903,800. Applying post-1984 rates to the 1981 transfer, the gift tax would be $3,443,800. Since the purpose of using adjusted taxable gifts as part of the estate tax calculation is solely to move the taxable estate into its appropriate (taking into account cumulative transfers) marginal rate, the gift tax payable credit would be $3,443,800, even though $3,903,800 was paid.

Fortunately for most estates, the gift taxes payable credit will equal the gift taxes paid because most decedents did not make taxable gifts both before and after the change in the law (January 1, 1977) that resulted in unification. Even rarer will be estates of decedents who made gifts after December 31, 1976 and before January 1, 1984 that were so large (i.e., above $3,000,000) that the marginal rate for the gift was higher than the rate in effect at the donor's death. Notice that since the taxes were first unified, the tentative tax has remained the same for cumulative transfers up to $3,000,000 and that it has not decreased for transfers over $3,000,000 since the end of 1983. In summary, an estate is required to do a recalculation to determine the credit only if the decedent made taxable gifts above that $3,000,000 level during the period of declining maximum marginal rates (1977-83) or made taxable gifts before 1977 and made at least one post-1976 taxable gift that exceeded the exclusion amount (i.e., taxes were paid on the post-1976 gift). All other estates can simply add up the taxes actually paid on the post-76 gifts to determine the gift taxes paid credit.

Third, the top marginal rates have decreased over the years. They reached their current level in 1984. The unified credit increased every year after its introduction in 1977 until it reached $192,800 in 1987. The unified credit remained steady at $192,800 from 1987 through 1997. The Tax Payer Relief Act of 1997 started it increasing again through the year 2006, at which time it will be $345,800. This will be an exclusion amount of $1,000,000. Hence, a married couple, by doing just a little bit of estate planning, will be able to transfer $2,000,000 to their beneficiaries tax free.

Fourth, gifts are valued as of the day given and estates are valued as of the day of the decedent's death. However, estates are allowed to elect an alternate valuation date of 6 months after the date of death, if certain criteria are met. An estate is allowed to make this *alternative date election* only if doing so will decrease (1) the gross estate and (2) the estate tax. It must also decrease the generation skipping transfer tax, if said tax is applicable. If the election is made, any property still held by the estate for the full six months is valued as of the six month date, rather than as of the date of death; whereas, assets sold, distributed, or otherwise disposed of during the six month period are valued as of the date each was transferred.[8]

THE CREDITS

There are five basic estate tax credits: the unified credit, the credit for state death taxes, the credit for gift tax payable, the credit for tax on prior transfers, and the credit for foreign death taxes. We have already covered the unified credit. The state death tax credit is certain to enter into the calculation of the estate taxes whenever the taxable estate actually exceeds the exclusion amount.

The other three credits just mentioned occur less frequently and are covered briefly at the end of the next chapter. The prior transfer credit is introduced in Chapter 6 and covered again in Chapter 12 as part of advanced planning for very wealthy couples.

Credit for State Death Taxes

Code §2011 allows a credit for *state* inheritance or estate taxes actually paid. The maximum credit is calculated using the State Death Tax Credit Table shown below (and also reproduced in Appendix A).

TABLE 5-7 Federal Credit for State Death Taxes - Based upon federal adjusted taxable estate*

Adjusted Taxable Estate *		Credit is the Total of		
Over	But Not Over	Base Credit +	Percent	On Excess Over
$40,000	$90,000	$0	0.8%	$40,000
$90,000	$140,000	$400	1.6%	$90,000
$140,000	$240,000	$1,200	2.4%	$140,000
$240,000	$440,000	$3,600	3.2%	$240,000
$440,000	$640,000	$10,000	4.0%	$440,000
$640,000	$840,000	$18,000	4.8%	$640,000
$840,000	$1,040,000	$27,600	5.6%	$840,000
$1,040,000	$1,540,000	$38,800	6.4%	$1,040,000
$1,540,000	$2,040,000	$70,800	7.2%	$1,540,000
$2,040,000	$2,540,000	$106,800	8.0%	$2,040,000
$2,540,000	$3,040,000	$146,800	8.8%	$2,540,000
$3,040,000	$3,540,000	$190,800	9.6%	$3,040,000
$3,540,000	$4,040,000	$238,800	10.4%	$3,540,000
$4,040,000	$5,040,000	$290,800	11.2%	$4,040,000
$5,040,000	$6,040,000	$402,800	12.0%	$5,040,000
$6,040,000	$7,040,000	$522,800	12.8%	$6,040,000
$7,040,000	$8,040,000	$650,800	13.6%	$7,040,000
$8,040,000	$9,040,000	$786,800	14.4%	$8,040,000
$9,040,000	$10,040,000	$930,800	15.2%	$9,040,000
$10,040,000		$1,082,800	16.0%	$10,040,000

* The ***adjusted taxable estate*** is the taxable estate less $60,000.

In using Table 5-7, Federal Credit for State Death Taxes, one must first calculate the "adjusted taxable estate," defined as the taxable estate reduced by $60,000. It is important to keep in mind that the taxable estate is the gross estate reduced by all deductions (e.g., debts, marital, etc.), but *before* prior taxable gifts are added into the tax base. Keep in mind that all states, even those with an inheritance tax, collect state death taxes at least equal to the federal state death tax credit. This maximizes their fiscal self-interest. Basically, if the inheritance tax amount is less than the allowable federal state tax credit, the state collects the difference, in addition to the inheritance tax. This tax that picks up the difference is generally called a "soak-up" or "sponge" tax. If the inheritance tax produces a tax greater than the federal state death tax credit, the state collects the greater amount, but the estate's credit on the federal return is still the calculated credit.

> EXAMPLE 5 - 25. Milo died in 1996, leaving his three children a gross estate of $755,000 and total deductions of $46,000. The state inheritance tax required the estate to pay $15,000 based upon the rates for interests transferred to a decedent's children. The federal credit for state death tax for a taxable estate of $649,000 is $18,432. To arrive at this latter figure, first determine the *adjusted* taxable estate, which is the taxable estate less $60,000 (i.e., $755,000 - $46,000 - $60,000), and then apply the rates from the table. The bracket that covers this estate starts at $640,000. The credit at $640,000 is $18,000, and the rate within the bracket is 4.8%. Hence 4.8% of $9,000 (i.e., $649,000 - $640,000) adds another $432, for a total credit of $18,432. Since the state-calculated inheritance tax is only $15,000, the state's "sponge tax" law would require the estate to pay another $3,432.

In the above example, the state collects an extra $3,432 at no extra cost to the estate since it is merely a shift of this amount out of the federal pocket into the state's pocket. If the state collects more than the credit, then it really does cost the estate's beneficiaries.

> EXAMPLE 5 - 26. Suppose in the prior example, the state's inheritance tax caused state death taxes of $20,000. Since the federal state death tax credit would still be $18,432, the extra $1,568 [$20,000 - $18,432] would come out of the beneficiaries' pockets.

For states imposing *only* a pickup tax, no state death tax will be owed by estates with a tax base (taxable estate plus adjusted taxable gifts) less than the exclusion amount. In those states that have an inheritance tax, the state death tax is often *higher* than the federal state death tax credit. Nonetheless, the estate is permitted a credit against the federal tax of only the amount determined as the federal state death tax credit. Thus, except for "pickup tax" states, the state death tax may be only partially covered by the credit.

> EXAMPLE 5 - 27. Kevin lived in a pickup tax state where the death taxes were defined as equal to the federal state death tax credit. When Kevin died in 1999, his gross estate was $1,500,000. He left $300,000 to his church. There were debts and expenses of $200,000. The taxable estate is $1,000,000 and the adjusted taxable estate for calculating the state death tax credit is $940,000 [$1,000,000 - $60,000]. The credit (and the state's death tax) is calculated as follows: At the $840,000

bracket break, the credit is shown as $27,600 plus 5.6% of the amount above that level, or $5,600 [5.6% * ($940,000 - $840,000)], for a total credit of $33,200. Total death taxes (in a pickup tax state) for a taxable estate of $1,000,000, where the death occurs in 1999, is $134,500. Hence, the state will collect $33,200 and the Federal Government will collect $101,300 [$134,500 - $33,200].

EXAMPLE 5 - 28. Nicki was also domiciled in a pickup tax state. When Nicki died in 1999, her gross estate was $1,500,000. She left $300,000 to her mosque. There were debts and expenses of $200,000. Five years before her death, Nicki had made taxable gifts equal to $175,000 to help out her brother and his family. As in the prior example, the taxable estate is $1,000,000 and the adjusted taxable estate for calculating the state death tax credit is $940,000, even though Nicki made significant taxable gifts. Her tax base for calculating the tentative tax is $1,175,000, but this does not affect the state death tax calculation. The total taxes are $206,250, but the state death tax credit is still $33,200, so the federal tax is $173,050.

*** Query 5 -8. Using the information in the last query (following Example 5 - 14), calculate Martha's state death tax assuming her state of domicile was a "pickup" tax state.

FEDERAL GENERATION-SKIPPING TRANSFER TAX

One fundamental policy objective of federal wealth transfer taxation is to tax all individual wealth in excess of a certain amount each time it passes to the next generation. Can the unified estate and gift tax laws completely achieve that goal? They cannot. It is true that they can ensure that property is subject to tax once when it is transferred. But since they both fail to distinguish between transfers made to the next generation and transfers made to more distant generations, they cannot possibly meet that goal.

EXAMPLE 5 - 29. Grandpa died last year leaving most of his large estate to his *granddaughter*. An estate tax will be imposed on this amount now, but not at the death of any of his children.

Only a tax that explicitly addresses the generational relationship between transferor and transferee can consistently tax wealth as it passes to succeeding generations. The generation-skipping transfer tax is designed to meet that objective.

The generation-skipping transfer tax (GSTT) is levied when a transfer is made (by gift or by bequest) to a person two or more generations below the donor. Persons in these lower generations are called *skip persons*. Every donor has a $1 million GSTT exemption, so most donors and most estates are not concerned with this tax. Gifts directly to grandchildren (or any other skip person) that qualify for the annual exclusion are not subject to the GSTT, so they do not use up any of the exemption. There is also a special rule called the predeceased ancestor exception that is applicable only for direct skips. For now think of direct skips as gifts or bequests that go directly to a grandchild or great-grandchild without being held in trust. In general, this rule "moves up" lower generations if a lineal descendant dies before the transfer. However, where transfers to grandchildren exceed the exemption amount (and the predeceased ancestor exception does not apply), the tax is horrendous since it is at the highest transfer tax marginal rate (presently 55%) and is in addition to the gift or estate tax.

IMPERFECT UNIFICATION

Although this chapter introduces the Unified Transfer Tax, there are many ways in which the three taxes (gift, estate, and generation transfer) are not really unified. Indeed, many transfer tax savings techniques take advantage of the fact that our "unified" transfer tax system is less than perfectly unified. To appreciate fully how these strategies work, one should consider how perfect unification might function and how the imperfections inherent in the present system can be exploited to transfer wealth with the least possible transfer tax cost. The following material will first consider what a perfectly unified tax system might be like and contrast it with our present imperfectly unified system. An ongoing example will illustrate the major points.

Perfect unification. With perfect unification of the three transfer taxes, an individual would be *indifferent*, from a total transfer tax planning point of view, as to whether the transfer should be a lifetime gift or a bequest. Under perfect unification, total transfer taxes would be the same whether an individual owned property at death or whether that person gave the property away during life.

To achieve perfect unification of the transfer tax system, all of the following conditions would have to be met:

1. A uniform system of *deductions and credits* for all gift and estate transfers. Otherwise, individuals would prefer to make that transfer which enjoyed the shelter of higher deductions or credits. As it is now, the annual exclusion favors lifetime gifts because there is no similar exclusion at death. Also, transfers to charity during life result in an income tax deduction (while removing the transferred property from the transfer tax base), but a charitable bequest, while it removes the property from the taxable estate, results in no income tax savings.

2. The timing of a gratuitous transfer should not affect the *basis* of the property; either it should remain the same (as is generally the case with gifts) or it should change to its fair market value as of the date of transfer (as is generally the case with transfers at death). As it is now, there are two basic rules, one for gifts and one for estates. If the law changed to just one rule, it would almost have to be for estates to change to the gift tax rule (i.e., a carry-over basis) since it would otherwise be too easy to obtain a step-up in basis if all one had to do was to make a gift of the property. The basis rules are covered in detail in Chapter 7.

3. A tax would be levied on all completed transfers, regardless of the value, and no matter when the transfer was made. All taxes would be levied at the same point in time, namely when the person died. The latter avoids the time value of money problem inherent in making gifts large enough to require the payment of gift taxes and it avoids having the gift taxes paid reduce the tax base.
   a. *All prior gifts* made by the transferor would be added to the transferor's current transfer tax base. No gifts would be excluded, including gifts of very small value (even less than the annual exclusion amount) and gifts made many years ago. The record keeping nightmare that would result will keep this from ever being reality.

b. All prior gifts would be included in the estate tax base at their *date of death value*, not date of gift value. Again, the tracking of the transferred property in order to ascertain its date of death value would be another nightmare that will keep this from becoming part of the law.

c. By not collecting transfer taxes until the donor dies, *gift taxes* would not be removed from the transfer tax base. As it is now, the *time value of money* makes gift taxes more expensive than death taxes; however, if the donor lives three years after making the gift that generated the gift tax, the payment of the tax results in a deduction from the estate tax base. A special rule that requires gift taxes paid on gifts made within three years of the donor's death is discussed in Chapter 6. When gift taxes are taxed as though still part of the donor's estate, it is referred to as "grossing up" the estate.

4. Finally, only *one tax rate schedule* should be applied to all transfers treated cumulatively regardless of whether made during life or at death. Otherwise, individuals would seek to make transfers that would be subject to the lower tax rates. Indeed, if the transfers were not treated cumulatively, a person could take advantage of the lower marginal rates for both the gift tax and the estate tax even if the marginal rates were the same. Since 1977, the estate and gift taxes have been unified but the generation skipping transfer tax has not. Given the GSTT's purpose and the fact that it applies only to transfers to skip persons whereas the other two apply to all transfers (other than to a spouse or charities), it is hard to imagine how it could be unified with the other two.

To see the operation of perfect unification, consider the following numeric example, which incorporates all of the above assumptions. While reading it, please keep in mind that the present tax system does not reflect all of these assumptions; these calculations are shown for illustration purposes only. All transfers will be assumed to be made between 1987 and 1997.

EXAMPLE 5 - 30. Howard, a widower, died owning the following property: land worth one million dollars and one million dollars in cash. Ignoring all deductions and credits except the unified credit, Howard's estate tax is $588,000, calculated as follows:

Gross estate	$2,000,000
Less: Deductions	0
Taxable estate	$2,000,000
Tentative tax	$780,800
Less: Unified credit	(192,800)
Net estate tax	$588,000

Continuing the example, assume that instead of dying owning all of his wealth, Howard *gave* the land to his son four years before his death. At that time, the land was worth $800,000. Under perfect unification, Howard's total combined transfer taxes would still be $588,000. First, Howard would have paid a gift tax of $75,000, calculated as follows:

Current gross gift	$800,000
Less: Exclusions and deductions	0
Taxable gift	$800,000
Tentative tax	$267,800
Less: Unified credit	(192,800)
Gift tax	$75,000

Howard's estate tax and total transfer taxes would be $513,000 and $588,000, respectively, calculated as follows:

Gross estate (includes gift tax paid)	$1,000,000
Less: Deductions	0
Taxable estate	$1,000,000
Plus: Prior gifts (death value)	1,000,000
Estate tax base	$2,000,000
Tentative estate tax	$780,800
Less: Gift tax paid	(75,000)
Less: Unified credit	(192,800)
Net estate tax	$513,000
Total transfer taxes	$588,000

The gross estate of one million dollars is the sum of property owned at death plus the gift tax paid. At death, Howard owned $925,000 in cash, which is the difference between the one million in cash initially owned and the $75,000 gift tax paid. Grossing up then increases the gross estate back to one million dollars. Note that for prior gifts, we would use the date of death value.

Summarizing, under perfect unification, total transfer taxes would be the same whether an individual retained all property until death or whether he or she had made lifetime gifts. In the above example, the gift tax plus estate tax equals $588,000, the same total tax as with no lifetime gifts.

To see how the imperfections affect the unified transfer tax, let's rework the numbers from the last example. First, assuming no lifetime gifts, Howard's net estate tax will be $588,000, as previously shown. However, the lifetime gift alternative under today's imperfect unification has markedly different results.

Howard's gift tax, at the time of the gift, will be $71,100, rather that $75,000, calculated as follows:

Current gross gift	$800,000
Less: annual exclusion	(10,000)
Taxable gift	$790,000
Tentative tax	$263,900
Less: Unified credit	(192,800)
Net gift tax	$71,100

Howard dies owning $928,900 cash (one million dollars less the gift tax paid of $71,100). Because the gift tax is not in the gross estate, Howard's estate tax will be $390,405, rather than $513,000, calculated as follows:

Gross estate	$928,900
Less: Deduction	0
Taxable estate	$928,900
Plus: Adjusted taxable gifts	790,000
Estate tax base	$1,718,900
Tentative tax	$654,305
Less: Gift tax paid	(71,100)
Less: Unified credit	(192,800)
Estate tax	$390,405
Total transfer taxes	$461,505

Howard's total transfer taxes are $461,505, the sum of $71,100 (gift tax) and $390,405 (estate tax). Hence the use of the lifetime gift has saved $126,495 in transfer taxes. Imperfect unification has enabled Howard to *freeze* the tax value of the land at its taxable gift value and to *reduce* his taxable estate by the amount of the annual exclusion and the gift tax paid. Thus, a total of $281,100 escaped transfer taxation. This represents the sum of three amounts: the $10,000 annual exclusion, the $71,100 gift tax paid, and the $200,000 in post-gift appreciation on the land. We can check our result, since the total tax saved will be 45% (the marginal estate tax rate) of $281,100, which equals the tax savings of $126,495.

The effect of not grossing up can be interpreted in a different way: the federal gift tax is calculated on what is called a *tax exclusive basis* (assuming no grossing up), since it is levied on the value of the gift and the gift tax is removed from the donor's wealth when he or she pays it. On the other hand, the estate tax is calculated on a *tax inclusive basis*, since it is levied on the entire estate which includes the amount that will be used to pay the estate tax.

Thus, the present system's failure to completely unify estate and gift taxes can yield substantial transfer tax savings for persons owning medium to larger amounts of wealth. Further discussion of these issues will be deferred to chapters 13 and 14 where we discuss various lifetime transfers.

This chapter has introduced federal wealth transfer taxation, emphasizing the tax calculations. The GSTT, introduced above, is discussed in more detail in Chapter 12. The next two chapters cover the estate tax and the gift tax with regard to other matters that are a little less quantitative in nature.

QUERIES ANSWERED

1. The annual exclusion reduced the gross gift of one million dollars down to $990,000. The marginal rate just below one million dollars is 39%.

2. The estate does not have the benefit of the $10,000 annual exclusion. The marginal rate just below $2 million is 45%.

3. The gift tax on a gross gift of $750,000 (taxable gift of $740,000) is $51,800 [tentative tax of $244,600 minus unified credit of $192,800].

4. The three gifts (all over $10,000) total $167,000. The taxable gift is $137,000. Tentative tax on the total gifts ($877,000) is $297,830, less the tentative tax on prior period gifts ($244,600), resulting in tentative tax on the current taxable gifts of $53,230. Since the unified credit was used against the tentative tax on the 1990 gift, $53,230 is the gift tax due.

5. Georgine's taxable estate is $600,000. The tentative tax is $192,800, which is the same as the unified credit amount, hence zero tax. Notice that we do NOT subtract $600,000, because there is no $600,000 exemption and there is no $600,000 exclusion.

6. Harold's taxable estate is $895,000. The tentative tax of $304,850 minus the $192,800 unified credit gives estate taxes of $112,050.

7. Martha's estate, taking into account her earlier gifts:

Gross Estate	$2,550,000
- Debts & expenses	($300,000)
- Marital & charitable deductions	$0
= Taxable estate	$2,250,000
+ Adjusted taxable gifts (post-76)	$877,000
= Estate tax base	$3,127,000
Tentative tax on estate tax base	$1,360,650
- Gift tax payable, post-76 gifts	($105,030)
- Unified credit	($192,800)
= Total Death taxes	$1,062,820

8. Martha's state death tax (also the amount her estate pays to the state) and the federal amount.

= Total Death taxes		$1,062,820
- State death tax credit	*Use the taxable estate less	*($118,800)
- Other credits	$60,000 before going to	$0
= Federal Estate Tax	the table.	$944,020

QUESTIONS AND PROBLEMS *[For all estate tax problems in this textbook, assume the decedent was domiciled in a pickup tax state.]*

1. Outline the history of federal wealth transfer taxation with emphasis on the changes that took place in 1977, 1982, 1984, and 1998.

2. Why would the imposition of an estate tax at death without an accompanying gift tax be largely ineffective?

3. (*a*) Describe the chronological progression of the amounts of the unified credit. (*b*) What is the term that, because of the Taxpayer Relief Act of 1997, means the largest amount that can be transferred by gift or through a decedent's estate without generating a transfer tax? (*c*) In what sense is this new term a misnomer?

4. Describe the unlimited marital deduction.

5. (a) What is the annual exclusion? (b) Is it available for transfers to non-relatives? (c) When did it increase to $10,000 and what was it immediately before the increase? (d) Explain indexing for inflation as it relates to the annual exclusion.

6. Determine the tentative tax and the amount of gift tax for the following transfers by rock star, Denise:

   a. In 1989, she gave friend, Gilbert, shares of stock worth $350,000 and her friend, Janie, stock worth $140,000.
   b. In 1990, she gave Roger municipal bonds worth $125,000, Max a vacant lot valued at $50,000, and Iris cash in the amount of $35,000.
   c. In 1992, she gave her church stock worth $200,000, her mother, Marlene, a new Cadillac valued at $55,000, and her boyfriend a sailboat worth $180,000.

7. Determine the tentative tax and the amount of gift tax for the following transfers by wealthy mutual fund manager, Martin:

   a. In 1987, he gave his daughter, Caroline, mutual fund shares of stock worth $550,000 and his son, Jon, additional shares worth $380,000.
   b. In 1989, he gave his sister, Dori, tickets for an around-the-world, first class cruise valued at $60,000 plus spending money of $40,000.
   c. In 1991, he gave another $45,000 to Caroline and $95,000 to Jon.

8. Determine the tentative tax and the amount of gift tax for the following transfers by CEO of SoftWearables, Shannon:

   a. In 1993, she gave her husband, Henry, shares in SoftWearables that were worth $850,000 and her daughter, Cheryl, shares in the company worth $130,000. [No split gifts. We will do these in a later chapter.]
   b. In 1995, she gave additional shares to Henry worth $90,000, a car to Cheryl worth $9,000, and to her son, William, and his wife, Ruby, cash in the amount of $100,000 so they could put it as a down payment on a house.

9. When Karla died in 1999, her gross estate was worth $1,980,000. Debts and expenses were $130,000. She left her estate to her four children. Determine: (a) the total death taxes; (b) the state death tax; and (c) the federal estate tax. [Remember, total death taxes is the amount after subtraction of the unified credit.]

10. When Faustino died in 2006, his gross estate was worth $2,150,000. Debts and expenses were $40,000. He left his $500,000 home to his wife, Rosa, a cash bequest of $30,000 to his church, and the rest of his estate to his seven children by a prior marriage. Determine: (a) the total death taxes; (b) the state death tax; and (c) the federal estate tax.

Use the ETAX program to do the problems that follow.

11. When Margaret died in 1996, her gross estate was worth $850,000. Debts and expenses were $210,000. She left her estate to her best friend, Diane. Determine: (a) the total death taxes; (b) the state death tax; and (c) the federal estate tax.

12. When Stephen died in 1996, his gross estate was worth $19,750,000. Debts and expenses were $1,340,000. He left his estate in equal shares to his brother, Mark, and his sister, Leilani. Determine: (a) the total death taxes; (b) the state death tax; and (c) the federal estate tax. [Remember the 5% surcharge.]

13. When rock star Denise (see earlier problem) died intestate in 1997, she left an estate valued at $4,890,300. Debts and expenses were $1,348,900. The entire estate went by intestate succession to her mother. Take the earlier gifts into account as you determine: (a) the total death taxes; (b) the state death tax; and (c) the federal estate tax.

14. When Martin (see earlier problem) died in 1995, his will left $200,000 to his sister, and the residue of his estate to his issue, by right of representation. His estate was valued at $13,840,500 and debts and expenses were $310,740. Take the earlier gifts into account as you determine: (a) the total death taxes; (b) the state death tax; and (c) the federal estate tax.

15. When CEO Shannon (see earlier problem) died in early 1997, her will left half of her net estate (i.e., after debts and expenses but before taking marital or charitable deductions into account) to her husband, $100,000 to her temple, and the rest to her children. She left an estate valued at $14,460,600. Debts and expenses were $2,940,400. Take the earlier gifts into account as you determine: (a) the total death taxes; (b) the state death tax; and (c) the federal estate tax. [Neither the marital share, nor the charitable share, are charged with any of the death taxes.]

16. (a) What is the meaning of perfect unification? (b) In what ways is our present unified transfer tax system imperfect?

Answer to Question: "Why Not Subtract only the *Unused* Unified Credit in Calculating the Federal Estate Tax?"

This Appendix has been written to explain why the full unified credit, rather than just the remaining unused unified credit, is subtracted on the federal estate tax return. Consider a highly abstract example which, for ease of comprehension, makes the following assumptions: the tax rate on all transfers is a flat 50%; the unified credit is $30; there is no annual exclusion; and there are no deductions.

Assume Marie's total wealth consists of $200 in cash. If our basic federal unified transfer tax scheme is working properly and consistently, this wealth should incur a total tax of $70, regardless of whether she makes her transfers during her lifetime or at her death. Proof: Total transfer taxes: 50% * $200 = tentative tax of $100; this amount less the $30 unified credit = $70 in taxes that must be paid.

Now suppose Marie makes post-1976 lifetime gifts of $20 and $90 in two different years (remember, no annual exclusions). Her gift tax returns will show:

	First Gift	Second Gift
Current taxable gifts	$20	$90
Plus total prior taxable gifts	$0	$20
Equals total taxable gifts	$20	$110
Tentative tax on total taxable gifts	$10	$55
Less tentative tax on prior taxable gifts	$0	($10)
Equals tentative tax on current taxable	$10	$45
Less unused unified credit	($10)	($20)
Leaves net gift tax	$0	$25

Next, assume that when Marie dies, her taxable estate is $90, which is the amount of her original net wealth, $200, reduced by the $110 in lifetime gifts. Marie's tax (taking the full unified credit) is $70, as shown below:

Taxable estate	$90
Plus adjusted taxable gifts	$110
Equals estate tax base	$200
Tentative estate tax	$100
Less gift taxes payable credit (1st gift $0 & 2nd $25)	($25)
Less unified credit	($30)
Leaves estate tax	$45

Thus, combined gift and estate tax is $70 [$25 + $45], just as it should be. The average tax rate is 35% (i.e., $70/$200). Had we mistakenly subtracted only the "unused" unified credit on the estate tax return (which, because of the gifts, would have been reduced to $0), we would have calculated estate taxes of $75. Note that the gifts would still be added back to the tax base and we would still claim the gift tax payable credit of $25. We would end up with total taxes of $100 and an average rate of 50%, instead of total taxes of $70 and an average rate of 35%. The upshot would have been the total failure to utilize the unified credit.

The critical reason that the full unified credit is subtracted on the estate tax return is that the tentative estate tax is reduced not by the entire <u>tentative</u> gift tax on lifetime gifts (as we did for the second gift, above), but only by the <u>actual</u> gift tax on lifetime gifts, which is lower than the tentative tax on lifetime gifts by the amount of the unified credit taken during lifetime. Since we have not yet received the benefit of the already used portion of the unified credit, we must take it now by subtracting the full unified credit.

The estate tax return subtracts the gift taxes paid on lifetime gifts from the tentative estate tax only because it reflects a *prepayment of the transfer tax*; not to do so would result in a double tax payment for the gifts. The gift tax return, on the other hand, subtracts the tentative gift tax on prior gifts for a totally different reason. It subtracts it to consistently implement the law's intent to push current gifts into a (potentially) *higher tax bracket*. Since the gift tax return subtracts the full tentative gift tax on prior gifts, it must deduct only the unused unified credit; to subtract the full unified credit on the gift tax return would double count the benefit of the unified credit.

It would have been simpler to understand the unified scheme if the gift tax were calculated like the estate tax by figuring a tentative tax on *all* taxable gifts-- current and prior--and then subtracting from it the entire unified credit, as well as any gift tax paid on prior gifts. Such a scheme would truly make the two transfer taxes appear more similar. Although the gift tax and the estate tax schemes appear to produce inconsistent results, their effect on net cumulative transfers, as we have seen from the above, is the same.

ANSWERS TO QUESTIONS AND PROBLEMS

1. History of federal wealth transfer taxation:

   Civil War: Inheritance tax enacted; repealed shortly thereafter.
   1916   First estate tax.
   1924:   First gift tax; repealed in 1926.
   1932:   Gift tax that paralleled the estate tax enacted.
   1948:   First marital deduction, 50% of the adjusted gross estate (AGE); also first joint income tax returns and first split gift elections.
   1977:   Unified rate schedule in effect. Unified credit replaces the $30,000 lifetime gift exemption and the $60,000 estate tax exemption. Transfers are unified, i.e., cumulative. Gift taxes on gifts within three years are included in the gross estate.
   1982:   The 100% marital deduction and the QTIP election are new. Annual exclusion increased to $10,000 from previous $3,000.
   1984:   The loss of the marital deduction for non-US spouses unless QDOT.
   1986:   Beginning of the new generation skipping transfer tax (old GSTT law retroactively repealed).
   1997:   The unified credit begins increasing 1998 through 2006, when it will cover transfers of $1,000,000. The tax free amount is called the exclusion amount. [The family-owned business interest deduction is added, discussed in Chapter 15.]
   1998   The $10,000 annual exclusion is indexed for inflation [Also indexed are several other key estate planning amounts, e.g., the generation skipping $1,000,000 exemption and $750,000 special use real property reduction. The base year for measuring the inflation is 1997.]

2. The imposition of a transfer tax at death without an accompanying gift tax would be largely ineffective because very elderly or terminally ill persons could circumvent the tax by making lifetime transfers.

3. a. The unified credit increased annually from $30,000 in 1977 to $192,800 in 1987. It stayed at that level through 1997. In 1998, it started increasing again and will increase to $345,800 in 2006.
   b. The new term is the exclusion amount. The exclusion amount for 2006 is $1,000,000 because the tentative tax on that amount is $345,800, which matches the available unified credit for that year.

c. The term *exclusion amount* is a misnomer because it implies that the amount is somehow subtracted or not taxed, but technically it is taxed. However, it is covered by the unified credit, therefore amounts less than the exclusion amount will not result in the payment of any transfer taxes.

4. The unlimited marital deduction allows a deduction for all transfers to a spouse, whether during lifetime or at death. As we'll see later, the property must be included in the transferor's gross estate, it must actually "pass" to the spouse, and the transfer cannot be subject to a terminable interest unless it falls into one of the exceptions described in the chapter.

5. a. The annual exclusion is an amount that can pass gift tax free, without using up any of the donor's unified credit. It only applies to gifts of a present interest. [There is just one exception to the present interest requirement. It applies to certain gifts given to benefit minors that meet the requirements of §2503(c). The exception is discussed later.]
   b. It is available even for gifts to non-relatives, so be nice to everyone.
   c. It went from $3,000 in 1981 to $10,000 in 1982.
   d. Indexing means that the $10,000 will increase from time to time, starting in years after 1998, as inflation decreases the purchasing power of the dollar when compared to the base year of 1997. The increases will be in increments of $1,000, with the rounding always being down to the next lower multiple of $1,000.

6. Gifts by Denise: (a) In 1989 [tt $145,600; gtx $0]; (b) In 1990 [tt current $65,700; gtx $18,500]; (c) In 1992 [tt current $81,850; gtx $81,850].

7. Gifts by Martin: (a) In 1987 [tt $310,700; gtx $117,900]; (b) In 1989 [tt current $35,100; gtx $35,100]; (c) In 1991 [tt current $49,200; gtx $49,200].

8. Gifts by Shannon: (a) In 1993 [tt $29,800; gtx $0]; (b) In 1995 [tt current $25,000; gtx $0]. Watch your annual exclusions.

9. 1999 estate of Karla: (a) the total death taxes [$502,000]; (b) the state death tax [$88,800]; and (c) the federal estate tax [$413,200].

10. 2006 estate of Faustino (a) the total death taxes [$246,000, note deductions total $570,000]; (b) the state death tax [$69,520]; and (c) the federal estate tax [$176,480].

11. 1996 estate of Margaret (a) the total death taxes [$14,800]; (b) the state death taxes [$14,800]; and (c) the federal estate taxes [$0].

12. 1996 estate of Stephen (a) the total death taxes [$9,994,000]; (b) the state death taxes [$2,412,400]; and (c) the federal estate taxes [$7,581,600].

13. 1997 estate of Denise, with earlier gifts (a) the total death taxes [$1,771,170]; (b) the state death taxes [$233,174]; and (c) the federal estate taxes [$1,537,996].

14. 1995 estate of Martin, with earlier gifts (a) the total death taxes [$7,535,656]; (b) the state death taxes [$1,631,562]; and (c) the federal estate taxes [$5,904,094].

15. 1997 estate of Shannon, with earlier gifts (a) the total death taxes [$2,671,055]; (b) the state death taxes [$470,012]; and (c) the federal estate taxes [$2,201,043].

16. a. Perfect unification means a transfer tax system under which individuals would be indifferent, from a total transfer tax planning point of view, between making lifetime or estate gifts.

    b. Our system is imperfect because of:

        1. the non-uniform application of some deductions and credits,
        2. the failure to completely incorporate the cumulative gift doctrine in the area of the inclusion of pre-1977 gifts, the annual exclusion, gift valuation, and grossing up of gift taxes, and
        3. the time value of money.

ENDNOTES

1.   §2503(b)(1)

2.   §2001(c)(2). For noncitizen nonresidents, the additional five percent tax is applied only to the extent necessary to phase out the graduated rates and unified credit actually allowed (generally $13,000) by statute or treaty. §2101(b).

3.   In 1992, H.R.4848, sponsored by Congressmen Waxman and Gephardt, and S.2571, sponsored by Senators Mitchell, Rockefeller, and others (both bills relating to long-term health care), proposed to reduce the tax-free estate to $200,000. The proposal generated so much opposition, it was deleted when the House bill was reintroduced as H.R. 6076.

4.   §2011. The term "exclusion amount" was added by the Tax Payer Relief Act of 1997.

5.   Although there is no marital deduction covering outright gifts to a noncitizen spouse, Congress created a special annual exclusion of $100,000 per year.

6.   §2503(b)(2).

7.   §2503(b)(1).

8.   §2032.

CHAPTER 6

The Federal Estate Tax

OVERVIEW

In general, a federal estate tax return must be filed for any decedent who was a *citizen* or *resident* of the United States if at the time of death the value of the person's gross estate (regardless of where the property is situated[1]) when added to his or her adjusted taxable gifts equals or exceeds the exclusion amount for the year of death.[2] For example, the estate of a citizen who dies in the year 2002, leaving a gross estate of $550,000, and who had made taxable gifts of $300,000, must file a return because the sum exceeds that year's $700,000 exclusion amount. Filing is required even if the entire estate is left to a surviving spouse and the marital deduction reduces the taxable estate to zero; or if the gross estate exceeds the exclusion amount but debts and expenses reduce it below that level.[3]

Once the value of the property transferred at death is determined, that value is added to the adjusted taxable gifts to arrive at the tax base. The unified transfer tax rate is applied to the tax base to determine the tentative tax. Credits are subtracted from the tentative tax to arrive at the estate's tax liability.

A Federal estate tax return must be filed for a decedent *non-citizen, non-resident,* if the person died owning property situated in the United States that was worth more than $60,000.[4] Only the U.S. situs property is taxed,[5] but the estate is entitled to a maximum unified credit of only $13,000.[6] Special rules, beyond the scope of this text, apply for decedents who are citizens of a U.S. territorial possession or are U.S. residents but are also citizens of countries having tax treaties with the U.S.

The executor is responsible for paying the tax.[7] If there is no court appointed executor (or if he or she fails to pay the tax), persons in actual or constructive possession of any of the decedent's property are liable for the tax to the extent of the value of that property.[8] This includes surviving joint tenants[9] and, after the settlor dies, the trustee of his or her revocable living trust.[10]

TABLE 6-1 Federal Estate Tax (Form 706) Comprehensive Outline

Gross estate (§§2031-2045)		$xxx,xxx
Less deductions:		
Debts & expenses (§2053)	xx,xxx	
Losses during administration (§2054)	xx,xxx	
Charitable bequests (§2055)	xx,xxx	
Marital bequests (§§2056-2056A)	xx,xxx	(xxx,xxx)
Leaves: Taxable estate (§2051)		xxx,xxx
Plus: Adjusted taxable gifts (post-76) (§2001)		xx,xxx
Equals: Estate tax base (§2001(b)(1)(A) & (B))		$xxx,xxx
Calculate: Tentative tax (§2001)		$xxx,xxx
Less Credits:		
Gift taxes payable (post-76) (§2001(b)(2))	xx,xxx	
Unified credit (§2010)	xx,xxx	
State death tax credit (§2011)	xx,xxx	
Prior transfer credit (§2013)	xx,xxx	
Other credits (§§2014-2015)	xx,xxx	(xxx,xxx)
Equals: Federal estate tax (§2001)		$xxx,xxx

This chapter is divided into three major parts. Each part will examine a major component of the estate tax return, specifically the gross estate, allowable deductions, and allowable credits. All code sections (e.g., §2033) mentioned in this book refer to the Internal Revenue Code, unless otherwise indicated. Most of these sections are included in Appendix B. Certain section numbers are used in the text because they are used by estate planners as terms meant to convey a concept, e.g., "a §2036 problem" with reference to a trust would mean that the settlor had retained certain interests in it that will cause the trust to be included in the settlor's estate. While studying this chapter, the reader is urged to review Form 706, the U.S. Federal Estate Tax Return (Appendix C). Notice that the first page has the calculation of the estate tax and that the first two lines (the gross estate and allowable deductions) are drawn from the recapitulations found as Part

5 of page 3. As discussion begins to focus on a particular Code section, take the time to read the section, then read it again before you go on to the next topic.

ONE: THE GROSS ESTATE

There is no short definition for the term *gross estate*. Of course, it includes all that one owns in the usual sense of ownership. One should not be surprised that it also includes some property that the decedent did not own at death. Inclusion of property not owned is rare, but occurs where the decedent had sufficient control and beneficial interest in property at death that the control was so similar to ownership that inclusion just seems reasonable, e.g., property held in a revocable trust whereby the trustee holds legal title, but the decedent controlled beneficial interest. In developing the rules, Congress has added Code sections that specify a number of situations where property must be included in a decedent's gross estate even though the decedent lacked title to the property. Indeed, in some circumstances property is included even though the decedent no longer had a beneficial interest in the property, e.g., gift taxes paid on any gift made within three years of death must be included in the gross estate.

Analysis of the components of the gross estate will be divided into four parts. The first part covers interests owned at death (§§2033, 2034, 2039, 2040, 2041, 2042). The second part covers transfers where the transferor retained an interest or control over beneficial enjoyment of the property transferred (§§2036, 2037, and 2038). The third part covers the gift tax paid on any gift made within three years of the donor's death (§2035(b)).[11] Finally, those few types of transfers made within three years of death (§2035(a)) that still require inclusion, even though the decedent-transferor retained neither a beneficial interest nor control of the property.[12] A caution is in order here; the three year inclusion rule applies only to transfers of life insurance policies or to the relinquishments of retained interests within three years of the donor's death. *There is no three year rule for most gifts (e.g., none for cash, land, stock, bonds, jewelry, etc.).*

Basic Interests Owned at Death: §2033

The gross estate includes all property in which the decedent had a beneficial interest.[13] Common examples are fee simple interests such as ownership interests in a house, furniture, personal effects, a business, investments, and in a copyright.

However, the gross estate includes less obvious interests. As a rule, if the decedent had a beneficial interest in property at death, the interest is probably included.

> EXAMPLE 6 - 1. Decedent died on June 18 owning 100 shares of XYZ stock that were worth $10,000. On May 26, a *dividend* of $1.50 per share was declared payable on June 22 to stockholders of record on June 14. Included in the gross estate will be $10,150, representing the value of the stock plus the dividends declared.

> EXAMPLE 6 - 2. The same facts apply as in the prior example, except that the holder-of-record date was June 19. The dividends are not included in the decedent's gross estate because at the date of death the decedent was not legally entitled to them.

> EXAMPLE 6 - 3. Winnie created a life income trust for her brother Charlie, with a vested remainder interest for her nephew Max. When Max died, Charlie was still going strong at age 85 and the trust was worth $1,000,000. Max's gross estate includes the present value of the *vested remainder interest* in the trust. Due to his death, Max will never possess the trust property but his will determines who will eventually have the property. Had he died without a will then his heirs, according to the laws of intestate succession, would eventually receive the property. *** *Query 6 - 1. If the rate for valuing remainder interests was 8% when Max died, what is the included value?*

> EXAMPLE 6 - 4. At her death, decedent owned "tax-free" municipal water district bonds. Although income from such bonds is exempt from Federal income tax, the value of the bonds (plus the accrued interest on them) is included in her gross estate.

> EXAMPLE 6 - 5. A couple lived and worked in a community property state. Stock was purchased using the wife's wages. They had no agreement or special understanding that the stock would be her separate property. When the husband died, the stock was worth $100,000. Even though it was held in the wife's name, it was community property; therefore, one-half of its value ($50,000) must be included in his gross estate.

Section 2033 would also cover the present value of a *joint and survivor annuity*, one which continues to be payable in whole or in part to another after the decedent's death, if the decedent purchased the annuity. Its value would be the present discounted value of the survivor's expected income payments. Code §2039, covered shortly, specifically calls for the inclusion of survivorship annuities in a decedent's gross estate. Overlapping Code sections are not at all unusual. An interest may be included by virtue of a broadly written section such as §2033, and by virtue of a narrowly written, but more detailed, Code section such as §2039.

> EXAMPLE 6 - 6. Movie star Jenny filed a lawsuit against a major studio for breach of contract, seeking four million dollars in damages because, according to her claim, it had failed to cast her in a movie that she understood was hers. The movie was a hit, and she sued for a percentage of the gross profits. After the discovery phase of the trial, it looked as though her claim had merit and the studio started talking seriously about settlement. Unfortunately, Jenny died when her Harley hit a palm tree. The studio is now refusing to settle, so her estate is proceeding to trial. Although the claim is quite speculative, its estimated value is included in her estate.[14]

> EXAMPLE 6 - 7. Jim created an irrevocable trust that gave his daughter Jodi income for her life, after which the corpus would revert to Jim, if living, otherwise to his estate. Jodi was 40 years old, and the trust was worth $100,000 when Jim died. His gross estate includes the value of the vested reversionary interest. *** *Query 6 - 2. If the §7520 rate was 10% when he died, what is the dollar value of the trust corpus included in Jim's estate?*

Finally, consider the consequences of current transfer tax laws on the estates of people who engage in certain illegal activities.

> EXAMPLE 6 - 8. Decedent died when the plane he was piloting crashed. On board was a load of marijuana and a fair amount of "drug money." His gross estate had to include the cash and the street value of the dope because he had "exclusive possession and control" over both when he died. Further, his estate was not entitled to deduct that value of cash and marijuana forfeited under state drug enforcement laws either as a claim against the estate or as a loss during administration. The IRS rationale was that such deductions would "frustrate the sharply defined state and Federal public policy against drug trafficking." Thus, decedent's other assets were used to pay the estate taxes.[15]

As said earlier, Code sections overlap. Some of the overlap is due to an effort by Congress to provide additional detail in its requirements for what property arrangements cause property to be included in the gross estate. Sometimes a seemingly redundant section is there to avoid taxpayer suits that would raise as an issue the question of whether more general language, such as is found in §2033, was really intended to cover some attenuated property interest.

Dower and Curtesy Interests: §2034

A dower interest is a surviving wife's life estate in a portion of the real property owned by her deceased husband, and a curtesy interest represents a surviving husband's life estate in a portion of the real property owned by his deceased wife. The extent of these statutory interests varies from state to state. Some states grant surviving spouses dower and curtesy interests as a percentage of the deceased spouse's real and personal property. As we have seen, one purpose of these laws is to prevent a decedent from entirely disinheriting the surviving spouse. Dower or curtesy interests are included in the gross estate of the first spouse to die.[16]

From an estate tax point of view, dower and curtesy interests and community property interests of the surviving spouse have the same effect. Dower and curtesy interests that can be claimed in fee (e.g., a specific percentage of the estate is set aside in fee for the surviving spouse) are included in the gross estate but are fully deductible as interests passing to the surviving spouse. In those states that still define these interests as life estates for the surviving spouse, the property may still qualify for the marital deduction by use of what is called a qualified terminable interest property election.[17] This special election, called a QTIP election, will be covered in the later chapters. In community property states, the surviving spouse's half-interest in the community property is excluded from the decedent's gross estate because it does not belong to the decedent spouse. These deducted or excluded marital interests are not taxed at the first spouse's death, but are likely to be taxed at the second death.

Survivorship Annuities: §2039

An annuity is a series of two or more periodic payments, usually received by the annuitant monthly, quarterly, or annually. Annuities are commonly used in retirement planning, often in conjunction with pension and insurance contracts. Ordinarily, an employee-"participant," upon retirement, will begin receiving a monthly annuity, possibly for as long as the retiree lives or, perhaps more commonly, for as long as the retiree and the retiree's spouse live. §2039 includes in the decedent's gross estate the date of death value of an annuity "receivable by any beneficiary by reason of surviving the decedent."

From the above description and from earlier examples, it should be clear that a single life annuity for the decedent's life is not part of the decedent's gross estate under §2039, since it ends with the decedent's death. Even if it was considered property owned at death under §2033, the date of death value would be zero.

Inclusion in participant's gross estate. Most survivorship annuities are fully included in the decedent-participant's gross estate. How much is included and how that amount is calculated depends on several factors. If the decedent retired after 1984 or if the pension plan was not a qualified one, the pension is fully included. If it is fully included, the amount included is either the lump sum amount, if the survivor has the right to take a lump sum, or the present value of the future payments, if the survivor must receive periodic payments. Whether one uses Table S or Table B (see the Appendix) depends on whether the payments will continue for the life of the survivor (Table S) or for a fixed number of years (Table B). Prior to 1985, plans that were "qualified" under §401(a) were either partially or fully excluded from the participant's estate. The section is complex, as it details the requirements for plan qualification. The tax advantages of qualified plans are that employer contributions are tax deductible to the employer and are not taxable income to the employee until paid, usually after retirement. In addition, the income earned on contributions is tax-deferred. Generally, non-qualified plans do not receive all of these advantages.

The following summarizes the complex rules for qualified plan annuities:

1. *Fully included annuities.* Regarding any annuity whose payments began after July 17, 1984, or for which prior to that date the decedent had not made an irrevocable election to designate the beneficiaries, the *entire value* of the annuity is included in the gross estate.

2. *Partially excluded annuities.* The estate of retirees who were in pay status (retired and receiving payments) before January 1, 1985, and had made an irrevocable election, after December 31, 1982 and before July 18, 1984, as to the form of benefits that would be paid to the beneficiary, can exclude up to $100,000 of the combined value of survivorship annuities from qualified plans.

3. *Totally excluded annuities.* The estate of retirees that separated from service prior to January 1, 1983, and who had irrevocably elected the form of benefits before that date, can exclude all of the qualified annuity.

The exclusions just described are available only if the proceeds are not payable to the decedent's estate, and if the decedent could not change the form of benefit. Annuities qualifying for this exclusion include the following:

a. Tax-sheltered annuities or tax deferred annuities (TSAs and TDAs, also called 403(b) plans).

b. Individual retirement accounts (IRAs).

c. A portion of the value of the periodic payments under pension plans that have been "qualified" under §401. The amount qualifying for the exclusion is that portion attributable to the employer's contributions.

d. A lump-sum pension payment to a surviving beneficiary, provided the beneficiary elects to forego reduced tax rates produced by "five-year averaging." Five-year averaging is a special method of reducing the beneficiary's tax burden that will no longer be available for tax years starting after 1999.[18]

EXAMPLE 6 - 9. The decedent died this year, after retiring from work in 1985. At death, the decedent had three joint and survivor annuities: one from her former employer's qualified retirement plan, one from a tax-sheltered annuity, and another from an individual retirement account. She had started drawing from all three after her retirement. The value of her gross estate will include the entire value of all three annuities.

EXAMPLE 6 - 10. During his employment, Stan contributed $25,000 to his qualified pension plan and his employer contributed $75,000. The plan provided Stan and his wife with a joint and survivor annuity upon his retirement, which started in 1983. Stan died in 1986, and the value of his spouse's survivorship annuity was $300,000. The amount excluded is the value of the annuity attributable to the employer's contributions up to a maximum of $100,000. The amount attributed to the employer is $225,000 [$300,000*($75,000 / ($25,000+$75,000))]. Thus the amount excluded is $100,000 and $200,000 is included in his gross estate.

EXAMPLE 6 - 11. In the Example immediately above, had Stan retired before 1983 his estate would have excluded $300,000, the entire annuity value. Had he retired after July 17,1984, the entire value would have been included.

In summary, a simple rule applies to decedents who retired after July 17, 1984; the *full* value of all annuities earned through employment or acquired by purchase is included in the decedent's gross estate. For decedents retiring between January 1, 1983 and July 17, 1984, up to $100,000 is excluded. Finally, for those retiring prior to 1983, the *entire* value of all qualifying retirement annuities is excluded.

Inclusion in gross estate of retiree's spouse. When the *participant-retiree's spouse dies first*, inclusion of a portion of the value of the participant's annuity in that nonparticipant spouse's gross estate will depend upon local property law. In community property states, the nonparticipant spouse's community interest in the annuity will be included in his or her own gross estate. That value could be as much as one-half of the total annuity value. On the other hand, in common law states, nothing will usually be included. Regarding property rights to the remaining benefits, case law has held that at the nonparticipant spouse's earlier death, any community interest passes 100% to the participant; the Retirement Equity Act precludes the nonparticipant decedent spouse from making any disposition of it.[19]

Joint Tenancy and Tenancy by the Entirety: §2040

There are two rules for determining the portion of joint tenancy property in the gross estate of a deceased joint owner:

Spousal Rule: *If a married couple are the only joint tenants, when the first spouse dies his or her gross estate must include one-half of the property's fair market value as of the date of death (DOD FMV).*

The Code refers to spousal joint tenancies and tenancies by the entirety as "qualified joint interests." For these, *one-half* of the total value is included *regardless* of the spouses' original contributions. Prior to 1977, the consideration furnished rule also applied to joint tenancies held by husbands and wives. Surviving spouses in several cases have successfully argued that the old rule still applies where the joint tenancy was created pre-1977.[20] By having the property fully included in the first spouse's estate, a full step-up in basis is obtained for income tax purposes. The IRS disagrees with this position. The issue will become less important as we move further away from 1977. Unless stated otherwise, assume all husband and wife joint tenancies were created after 1976.

EXAMPLE 6 - 12. At his death in 1995, Joel and his wife Susan held their home in joint tenancy. Susan paid $100,000 when she bought the house in 1980 using her separate funds. It was worth $400,000 when Joel died. Since the house is a *qualified joint interest*, his gross estate will include $200,000. Susan's new basis is half the old basis plus half the date of death value, i.e., $250,000.

EXAMPLE 6 - 13. In the example immediately above, had Susan died first with Joel the survivor, the results would have been exactly the same.

Consideration Furnished Rule: *Include in the decedent owner's estate only that portion of the DOD FMV of the property attributable to that portion of the consideration (money or money's worth) contributed by the decedent.*

The second rule applicable to all non-qualified joint interests is called the *consideration furnished rule*. With even just one non-spouse as a joint tenant, all interests are non-qualified; e.g., husband, wife, and adult child take title as joint tenants. All three are holders of non-qualified interests. The law starts with the presumption that the decedent co-owner contributed all of the consideration (or was initially the sole owner). To overcome this presumption, the estate has the burden of establishing that the surviving joint tenants contributed to the acquisition of the property. Generally, this is not as difficult as it seems. The IRS is not likely to challenge the contributions where the co-owners would not appear to have had a motive for trying to avoid taxes, nor to make gifts when the joint tenancy was established, and each of the co-owners had sufficient resources to pay his or her own way.

EXAMPLE 6 - 14. In 1955, two brothers, Jake and Ned, prior to either of them marrying, purchased a fishing cabin on a lake, taking title in joint tenancy. Jake died this year. The records as to how much each paid as a down payment have been lost. But Ned can show that he and his brother were both earning about the same amount of money at the time of the purchase and were both about equally wealthy such that one making a gift to the other would not have made much sense. This would probably be sufficient to establish equal consideration.

EXAMPLE 6 - 15. Similar to the prior example, but change it such that Jake was Ned's father and Jake, although wealthy, already owned his own home whereas Ned was just starting out. Even if Ned claims to have paid an equal share of the purchase price, the circumstances do not support the claim and, without better evidence, it would be difficult to overcome the presumption that Jake furnished all of the consideration. Even a canceled check from Ned payable to the seller of the cabin might not be sufficient evidence, since a gift from Jake of the cash followed by Ned's use of the money as his share of the consideration would be treated as if all the funds came from Jake. Ned would need to establish a reasonable explanation for the source of the funds to establish that they came from a source other than a gift from his father.

There is a special rule where a donee (one of the surviving joint tenants) uses funds traceable to a gift from the decedent joint tenant as part of the purchase price. Those funds are treated as being part of the donor-joint tenant's consideration rather than that of the donee. Income from a gift is not traced back to the donor, but capital gain is.

EXAMPLE 6 - 16. Calvin gave his daughter Deirdre 100 shares of XYZ stock worth $50,000. She sold the stock for $70,000 and placed the proceeds of the sale in a bank account in which she already had $30,000. The source of the $30,000 was $10,000 from XYZ dividends and $20,000 from money she saved out of her wages. Calvin and Deirdre purchased a house for $200,000, each putting up half of the purchase price. Deirdre's half share came from her bank account. The house, held in joint tenancy, was worth $300,000 when Calvin died. His estate includes 85% of the DOD FMV, i.e., $255,000. The percentage is calculated by taking Calvin's contribution of $100,000, adding the contribution of Deirdre that is traceable to Calvin's gift to her (another $70,000) and dividing the total ($170,000) by the $200,000 purchase price. Note that the gain is included in the numerator, but not the dividends.

Full inclusion in the decedent-donor's estate is preferred when it results in a step-up in basis without an increase in estate taxes.

EXAMPLE 6 - 17. In 1998, Virginia put her home into joint tenancy with her son Scott. At the time of the transfer, the home was worth $400,000. She filed a gift tax return reporting a $190,000 taxable gift. She died in the year 2000 when the house was worth $500,000. The entire $500,000 is included in her estate, and Scott's basis in the house is $500,000. Her other property was worth $75,000 and her estate paid debts and expenses of $30,000, so her taxable estate was just $545,000 and no taxes were owed. *** *Query 6 - 3. Why did the $190,000 taxable gift not push the estate over the $675,000 mark? See the definition of "adjusted taxable gift" found in §2001(b).*

EXAMPLE 6 - 18. At her death, Rose owned a farm worth $100,000 jointly with her brother Tom. The farm was originally acquired for $50,000, with Rose paying $10,000 and Tom paying $40,000. Assuming the contribution of the survivor can be established, under the consideration-furnished test her estate includes only one fifth of the farm's value, i.e., $20,000, [($10,000/$50,000)*$100,000]. Tom's basis in the farm will be his contribution plus the amount included in Rose's estate, i. e., $60,000 [$40,000 he contributed and $20,000 included in Rose's estate].

EXAMPLE 6 - 19. At her death, Dottie owned $90,000 of ABC common stock jointly with her husband and her son. The survivors know that Dottie actually contributed only $10,000 to the original $50,000 purchase price (and the two of them paid $20,000 each), but they are not sure they can prove it. If they cannot, Dottie's gross estate will include the full $90,000. If they can prove it, her gross estate will include only her proportional share, or $18,000 (i.e., 20%). This is not a qualified joint interest because a non-spouse is also a surviving co-owner.

The consideration furnished rule applies only at the death of a co-owner. There is a gift when different amounts of consideration are used to purchase property and the title is taken in joint tenancy because, by property law rules, all joint tenants' interests must be equal. For gift or sale purposes, the "donee" co-owner has a basis in his or her share that is either carry-over or partly carry-over and partly purchase.

> EXAMPLE 6 - 20. Edith and June purchased a vacation condominium in South Florida for $100,000, taking title as joint tenants. Edith paid $90,000 and June paid $10,000. Edith made a $40,000 gift [$30,000 taxable] to June since June has a 50% interest. June's basis would be $50,000 [$40,000 carried over with the gift and the other $10,000 is her consideration]. If they later sell the property for $150,000, each would recognize a gain of $25,000. If, instead of selling the property when it was worth $150,000, June made a gift of her half to her son, Tommy, she would report a gift of $75,000 [$65,000 taxable gift] and Tommy would have a carry-over basis of $50,000. This transfer would break the joint tenancy, so Tommy and Edith would be tenants in common, each with a 50% share. Regardless of which one died first, Tommy or Edith, 50% of the value would be included in the person's estate.

For purposes of §2040, "joint interests" encompass only two forms of concurrent ownership: joint tenancy and tenancy by the entirety. In contrast to the complex rules just given for these joint interests, when a person dies holding title to property in either tenancy in common or community property, the value that is included in the decedent's gross estate is based upon the decedent's proportionate interest in the property.[21]

Power of Appointment: §2041

Powers of appointment were introduced in an earlier chapter, so this is just a brief review. A power of appointment is a power that allows a person to name someone to receive a beneficial interest in property, even though the person directing the transfer does not own the property. The creator (grantor) of the power is called the donor of the power. The person receiving the power is called the holder or donee. The parties to whom the holder may appoint the property are called the permissible appointees. The parties to whom the holder actually appoints are called the appointees, and the persons who will get the property if no appointment is made are called the takers by default.

For federal estate tax purposes, a power of appointment is either a general power or it is a limited (special) power. A *general* power of appointment is the power of the holder to appoint to the holder, the holder's estate, the holder's creditors, or the creditors of the holder's estate. All other powers are "special" or "limited" powers of appointment, which usually designate as permissible appointees either specific individuals (e.g., the donor gives the holder the power to appoint to the donor's brother Sam or sister Sue) or a class of people (e.g., appoint to any of my issue).

A decedent's gross estate will include the value of any property subject to a *general* power of appointment held by the decedent-holder at death. General powers are included in the gross estate regardless of whether the decedent-holder *exercised* the power at death, or, alternatively, did not exercise it and just permitted the power to *lapse* at death. The key is that at the moment of death, the decedent was the holder of a general power.

> EXAMPLE 6 - 21. At her death, Carol was trustee of an irrevocable trust created by her Uncle Fred. She had the power to invade the corpus of the trust for the benefit of anyone. The trust named Fred's second cousins, Clarence and Sherrie, as remaindermen in the event Carol failed to appoint all of the corpus. In her will, Carol appointed her son David to receive the entire corpus. Carol's gross estate will include the entire value of the trust corpus, since it was subject to a general power which she *exercised* at her death.

> EXAMPLE 6 - 22. The facts are similar to the prior example, except that Carol did not exercise the power at her death. The entire trust corpus is still included in her gross estate even though the power *lapsed* at her death. Note that a proportionate share of the estate taxes would come out of the trust.

> EXAMPLE 6 - 23. The facts are similar to the prior example, except that the power to appoint was on behalf of anyone *except* herself, her creditors, her estate, or the creditors of her estate. This is a "limited" power, not a general power, and thus the property is not included in her gross estate whether she appoints to her son or just lets the power lapse.

Notice that §2041 focuses on decedent *holders* of general powers, not on the donors or the appointees.

Exceptions. There are two major exceptions to the basic rule that being able to appoint to oneself makes the power a general one. Each exception so greatly restricts the circumstances that would allow appointment that Congress quite rightly defined them as not being general powers. Under the first exception, if the decedent's right to exercise a power is limited by an *ascertainable standard*, that is, limited for reasons of "health, education, support or maintenance," it is not a general power. Under the second exception, if the decedent's right to exercise the power requires the *approval* of either the creator of the power or an *adverse party*, it is not a general power. An adverse party is "a person having a substantial interest in the property, subject to the power, which is adverse to exercise of the power in favor of the decedent."[22]

EXAMPLE 6 - 24. During his lifetime, the decedent was the income beneficiary of a trust created by his father. The trust gave him the right to invade corpus for reasons of his "health, education, support, or maintenance." Since the power is limited by an *ascertainable standard*, this right to invade is not a general power, and the trust is not included in the decedent's gross estate even if the decedent was the trustee.

EXAMPLE 6 - 25. Same facts as Example 6-24, except decedent could invade corpus for reasons of his "health, education, support, maintenance, *or happiness.*" The power is not limited by an ascertainable standard; therefore, the invasion right constitutes a general power of appointment, and the entire value of the trust will be included in the decedent's estate even though he never exercised the right to invade.

EXAMPLE 6 - 26. During her lifetime, the decedent was the income beneficiary of a trust established by her grandmother. She could invade corpus for any reason provided she obtained the written approval of her son, the trust's remainderman. Since her son was an *adverse party*, i.e., his remainder interest would be reduced in value if the decedent exercised the power in her own favor, the power is not a general one.

A general power of appointment over property will cause the property to be included in the holder's estate because the power creates rights considered equivalent to ownership. Thus, this estate tax rule makes sense even though under *property law* the holder is not the legal owner of the property regardless of whether the power is general or limited. Given that the holder does not have legal title, even if the property subject to the power is included in the holder's gross estate, it is not included in the holder's probate estate unless the holder transfers it there, an event not likely to happen.

Insurance on Decedent's Life: §2042

Three circumstances that will cause life insurance to be in the insured's gross estate are if: (1) the proceeds are paid to the executor of the decedent's estate, or (2) the decedent at death possessed an incident of ownership in the policy, or (3) the decedent transferred an incident of ownership within three years of death.

Receivable by executor. Very seldom is the executor of the decedent's estate named as a beneficiary or alternate beneficiary. On occasion it happens that at the insured's death no named beneficiaries are living and the proceeds are payable to the estate by default. Modern policies generally have a default clause that directs the company to pay the proceeds to the decedent's heirs if the named primary and alternate beneficiaries predecease the insured. The default clauses read something like intestate succession laws, starting with close family members, moving to more remote relatives if no close family members survive, and to the insured's estate only as a last resort.

Decedent possesses incidents of ownership. Policy ownership gives the owner numerous rights including: to assign, to terminate, to borrow against the cash reserves (if any), to name beneficiaries, and to change beneficiaries. Possession by the decedent of these rights is called *incidents of ownership,* any one of which will result in the proceeds being included in the decedent's estate. The payment of premiums by the insured is not considered an incident of ownership and payment will not by itself cause inclusion. Nonetheless, barring some agreement, the law may create an incident of ownership due to the payment of premiums in community property states. A policy paid for entirely with community property would be half included in the decedent's gross estate regardless of whether it was issued in the insured spouse's name or the non-insured spouse's name. A written agreement specifying that it is the separate property of one of the spouses will negate the community property presumption that normally attaches to property purchased with community funds.

Life insurance transferred within three years of death. If the insured transferred an interest in the policy within three years of his or her death, both §2042 and §2035(a) require inclusion of the proceeds in the insured's gross estate.

EXAMPLE 6 - 27. On June 12, 1999, Marty transferred a $200,000 policy on his life to his son Joseph. Because the policy was a term policy, its value was under $10,000 and Marty did not have to report it as a gift. On January 1, 2001, Marty died in a car accident. Joseph collected the $200,000. Marty's gross estate must include the $200,000 even though he had no incidents of ownership when he died and there were no strings attached to the transfer. The insurance company must issue IRS Form 712 any time insurance is listed on an estate tax return. The form (which must be attached to Marty's 706) will show the date the policy was transferred.

§2042 versus §2033. It is important to distinguish between policies on the decedent's life and policies on the lives of others. Policies on the *decedent's life* are covered by §2042, but what if the decedent owned a policy on someone else's life? The policy is included in the decedent's estate under §2033 as a property interest owned at death. Generally, the value is the cost of replacement rather than the cash surrender value. Cost of replacement is what an insurance company would charge to put the policy in force (with the existing cash surrender value) given the insured's age and health. Where premiums were still being paid on the policy, its value is equal to its interpolated terminal reserve plus that portion of the premium paid that covers the period extending beyond the owner's date of death.

> EXAMPLE 6 - 28. At decedent's death, decedent's wife owned a policy on *his life*, with the proceeds payable to his estate. Decedent's gross estate will include the value of the proceeds under §2042.

> EXAMPLE 6 - 29. Decedent died owning a $60,000 life insurance policy on his mother. The policy had a value of $14,000 at decedent's death. Although §2042 does not apply because decedent is not the insured, the decedent's estate must include the $14,000 value under §2033.

> EXAMPLE 6 - 30. At the moment of his death, decedent owned a $100,000 life insurance policy on his own life. Under §2042 (incidents of ownership), $100,000 will be included in his gross estate. However, if all premiums had been paid for with community property, it is presumed to be community property and only $50,000 would be included. This result could be overcome if the couple had a written agreement stating that the policy was the separate property of one spouse.

After one spouse dies, if the surviving spouse continues to own a policy on his or her own life, the entire proceeds are included in the surviving insured's estate when he or she dies, regardless of whether or not community property funds were the original source of the premiums.[23]

So far, we have studied §§2033, 2034, 2039, 2040, 2041 and 2042, all of which cover interests owned, held, or controlled by the decedent at death such that the interests are included in the decedent's estate. The next section examines a group of Code sections that result in property being included in the gross estate even though the property is no longer owned by the decedent at the time of death. The property is included because the decedent transferred property but kept some interest or control, sometimes just a *little string* attached, such that Congress thought the string justified including the property in the gross estate as if no transfer had taken place.

TRANSFERS WITH RETAINED INTEREST OR CONTROL

If a person transfers property and retains an interest in the property such as the right to control who enjoys it, the retained interest will cause the transferred property to be included in the transferor's estate if the retained interest is still present when the transferor dies.[24] This is true even if the retained interest is one that cannot benefit the transferor economically. The interest will also be included if the transferor releases the retained interest within three years of his or her death.[25] Whether a "string" exists at the time of death or the string is snipped within three years of death, it will be as if the decedent never made the transfer, but instead continued to own the property right to the moment of death. Thus, if one of the retained interest Code sections apply, the property is valued in the gross estate at the death of death fair market value (DOD FMV). It will not be treated for estate tax purposes as an adjusted taxable gift, even though it was a taxable gift when the transfer occurred. The latter sounds bad but it is actually good because it keeps the transfer from being taxed twice. Any gift tax paid on the earlier transfer is allowed as a credit even though the adjusted taxable gift goes to zero in the calculation of the estate tax. The retained interest Code sections are: §2036, Transfers with Retained Life Estate; §2037, Transfers Taking Effect at Death; and §2038, Revocable Transfers.

Characteristics common to all three sections. The three "strings" sections (§§2036, 2037, and 2038) have these characteristics in common:

- ▸ The transfer must have been made by the *decedent*.
- ▸ The transfer was a gift, that is, a transfer "for less than full and adequate consideration in money or money's worth."

▸ The amount included in the gross estate is the value as of the *date of death* (or alternate valuation date), rather than the value at date of transfer.

▸ If the string pertained to only a specific portion of the property transferred, then only that *portion* of the transferred property is included. For example, if the retained control was over only one third of the property, then only one third of its value will be included in the gross estate. However, note that §2036 requires the entire property to be included, even if only the income interest was retained.

▸ A trust is almost always involved.

When the sections overlap, as they often do, the value included in the gross estate is based upon whichever section results in the greatest amount included.

Transfer with Retained Life Estate: §2036

A transfer with retained life estate arises when a decedent has made a transfer, by trust or otherwise, for less than full and adequate consideration and has retained either (1) the possession or enjoyment of (or the right to the *income* from) the property transferred, or (2) the right, either alone or in conjunction with any person, to *designate* who will enjoy or possess the property or its income.

Period of retention. In addition to the above retained control, §2036 applies only if the decedent-transferor retained that control for: (1) life, (2) any period that does not in fact end before the decedent's death, or (3) any period not ascertainable without reference to the decedent's death. In the following §2036 examples, assume that decedent D made a lifetime transfer for less than full consideration.

EXAMPLE 6-31. At a time when D's vacation home was worth $110,000, D said, while handing over a quit-claim deed, "Son, here's title to my vacation home. It's yours now, but I will expect you to let me use it occasionally." When D died, the home was worth $200,000. The date-of-death value of the home will be included in D's gross estate because at the time of D's death, D still retained the *right to enjoy* the property.

EXAMPLE 6-32. D transferred property into an irrevocable trust, retaining the right to the income for his lifetime, with the remainder to go to C. The property's value at date of death is included in D's gross estate because D retained the right to the income for his lifetime. Although the remainder value was treated as a taxable gift when the trust was established, it is not an adjusted taxable gift for estate tax purposes since the entire trust has been included in D's gross estate.

EXAMPLE 6 - 33. D transferred property into an irrevocable trust, with income to remain with D for 20 years. Then the trust would terminate, with the remainder transferred to C. D died 18 years after establishing the trust. The property's value is included in D's gross estate because the *period of retention* did not end before D's death. Again, the adjusted taxable gift would be zero insofar as D's estate and this trust are concerned.

EXAMPLE 6 - 34. The facts as in the prior example, except D lived beyond the 20 year term. D's gross estate would not include the trust property. There would be an adjusted taxable gift equal to the remainder value when the trust was funded. That value would boost the rest of D's taxable estate into higher marginal rates.

EXAMPLE 6 - 35. D transferred property into an irrevocable trust, with income to go to D for up to one month before D's death and the remainder going to C. The fair market value of the property as of D's death is included in D's gross estate because the retained period is *not ascertainable without reference* to D's death.

When is a gift complete? Generally, unless the owner releases dominion and control over the property, there is no gift. With an outright gift, it is easy to determine when this takes place. It is less obvious with gifts in trust where the donor retains some interest. Indeed, the IRS Regulations at §20.2511-2 are less than clear on this matter. We will not cover this completely, but will give you the basics. Bear in mind that a gift may be complete enough to cause a gift (generally, release of title and control), but still result in the property being included in the donor's gross estate due to a retained interest. Obviously, if the donor has the right to revoke a gift, then no gift has really occurred, even if the donee has taken possession of the property. No gift will occur until the right to take back the transfer ends because, until such time, the donor has retained control over who will enjoy the property.

EXAMPLE 6 - 36. Shane created a trust, transferring assets worth $100,000 to the trustee. The trust terms give Richard income for life, so long as the trust remains in existence. Upon Richard's death, the trust terminates, with distribution to Shane's daughter Catherine. The terms of the trust state that it is revocable until the earlier of Richard or Shane's death. The first year the trustee distributed income of $5,000 to Richard. The second year $6,000 was distributed. At the beginning of the third year, when the trust was worth $120,000, Shane died. No gift occurred and, of course, the trust is included in Shane's estate. While Shane was alive, all income was reported on his income tax return and was treated as a gift from him to Richard. Given the amounts and Richard's present interest (as each amount was distributed to him), the annual exclusion would have covered the amounts Richard received before Shane's death. Distributions after Shane's death are from an irrevocable trust. The income is taxable to Richard (the trust would have an income distribution deduction) and is not considered to be gifts. Note: while Shane was alive, the gifts of income are from him, not from the trust. From a transfer tax standpoint, only people make gifts; not trusts, not trustees.

When control is retained by the settlor, no gift is deemed to have occurred. This is true even when the terms of the trust make it clear that the settlor cannot benefit in any way from the retained control. Once the control ceases, either by release, death, or by the terms that established the trust, the transfer occurs. The following examples are based upon Reg. 25.2511-2(c) and (f).

EXAMPLE 6 - 37. Using assets worth $400,000, Abel creates an irrevocable trust for the benefit of Benito and Consuelo with remainder to their children when both are deceased. So long as both are alive, the Trustee is given the power to allocate the income between Benito and Consuelo in such proportions as the trustee thinks is appropriate. When one beneficiary dies, the survivor is to receive all income. Abel serves as the initial trustee. During the first year the trust has income of $30,000, which Abel distributes $25,000 to Benito and $5,000 to Consuelo. No gift occurred when the trust was created, even though it was irrevocable. The income is taxed to Abel, and he has made a gift of $25,000 ($15,000 taxable) to Benito and $5,000 to Consuelo (not taxable because it is completely covered by the annual exclusion).

EXAMPLE 6 - 38. At a time when the trust was worth $500,000, Abel resigned as trustee, giving the successor trustee a letter (with copies to both beneficiaries) that stated his resignation was irrevocable. At that time, Abel has made a $500,000 gift (both gross and taxable). From that moment on, income was no longer taxed to Abel, and distributions were not considered new gifts but merely distributions of income from the irrevocable trust. *** Query 6 - 4. Why is the taxable gift $500,000? What happened to the annual exclusion(s)?

EXAMPLE 6 - 39. Suppose that instead of releasing his retained control by resignation, Abel died while still serving as trustee and that the trust assets were valued at $700,000. The $700,000 would be included in his gross estate and, from that moment onward, the income distributions would be from the trust, not from Abel (nor from his estate).

EXAMPLE 6 - 40. Suppose the terms of the trust created by Abel required him to get Benito's approval for anything other than a 50-50% split of the income, otherwise the income had to be divided equally between Benito and Consuelo. The trust's value is still included because Abel retained the right to designate the recipient "alone or *in conjunction with* any other person."

Because these rules are based upon transfers with interests retained by the donor, we must bear in mind that a transfer of a community property asset is treated as coming one-half from each spouse.

EXAMPLE 6 - 41. The facts are similar to any of the above examples, except that the transfer was of property held prior to the transfer as community property, 50-50 tenancy in common, or spouses as joint tenancy. Only half the value of the property would be included in the transferor's estate, because only half is traceable to a transfer by the decedent.

EXAMPLE 6 - 42. D transferred property into an irrevocable trust, retaining one quarter of the income for himself and distributing the rest to C. After D's death, C is to receive all of the income and after C's death, the remainder will go to R. At D's death, only *one quarter* of the trust's value is included in D's gross estate since that was the extent of D's §2036 retained interest.

EXAMPLE 6 - 43. D transferred property into an irrevocable trust, authorizing the trustee, a bank, in its sole discretion, to distribute trust income to X or Y in such amounts as the bank trust officer thinks appropriate. D retained the power to replace the bank with another corporate trustee. The value of the property is not included in D's gross estate under §2036 because D's right to replace trustees does not amount to the right by D to change or control the enjoyment of the property. However, the property would be included if D kept the right to appoint *herself* as successor trustee.

In the following example, a basic assumption is changed, so that decedent is not the transferor:

EXAMPLE 6 - 44. G transfers property into an irrevocable trust, with income to D for life and remainder to R. The value of the property is not included in D's gross estate under §2036, because D was *not the transferor*. This arrangement is referred to as a bypass trust because the trust assets "bypass" the income beneficiary's estate.

The *reciprocal trusts doctrine*, illustrated in the next example, was established by the courts to apply §2036 to family planning situations which in form avoid the literal terms of that section, but in substance do not. In essence, the transferor has made a transfer of property and at about the same moment received the right to enjoyment of other property arising from a separate but related transaction.

> EXAMPLE 6 - 45. A husband transfers $100,000 in property into irrevocable trust H, with income payable to his wife for her life and the remainder to their children. At about the same time, his wife transfers $100,000 into trust W, with income payable to her husband for his life and the remainder to their children. Under §2036, the corpus of trust H will be included in husband's gross estate and the corpus of trust W will be included in wife's gross estate. These interrelated trusts leave the spouses in essentially the same economic position that they would have been in had they created trusts naming themselves life beneficiaries.[26]

People sometimes engage in transfers designed to appear complete but that involve an implied *understanding* that the transferor has a retained life estate. The IRS has had success in attacking such schemes. Consider the following situation in which a court found §2036 to apply to facts that had been structured to appear as a completed sale.

> EXAMPLE 6 - 46. Mom, age 82 and in poor health, transferred title to her home to her son and his wife in exchange for $270,000, which was the home's fair market value. The terms of this "sale-leaseback" called for a $20,000 down payment and a five year mortgage loan of $250,000. Mom immediately forgave the down payment of $10,000 by each of the spouses. In the next two years, in payment of rent, Mom gave son and his wife $10,000 each, and they promptly returned these amounts in payment of the mortgage. Two days after the sale, Mom executed her last will, which contained a provision forgiving any of the remaining debt at the time of her death. The date of death value of the home was included in her gross estate under §2036. Circumstances strongly suggested an understanding that decedent was permitted to live in the house until death, which she did, and that none of the consideration offered in exchange was ever really going to be paid. Thus, all consideration was disregarded. The following circumstantial factors, all taken together, indicate a strings attached transfer: decedent's age and her health concerns, her forgiveness of the mortgage both during her life and by her will, the fact that the rent payments approximated the interest payments on the note, and the fact that the son was the decedent's only heir and the natural object of her bounty. As a result, Mom was treated as having made a transfer of property for less than full and adequate consideration in which she retained, for a period which did not end before her death, the right to possess or enjoy the property.[27]

Transfers Taking Effect at Death: §2037

A "transfer taking effect at death" will arise when (1) possession or enjoyment of the property through ownership can be obtained only by surviving the decedent and (2) the decedent, at the time of the transfer, retained a reversionary interest, which, at the decedent's death, exceeded 5 percent of the value of the property. Such reversionary interest is defined as the possibility that the property may return to the decedent or may be subject to a power of disposition by him.

> EXAMPLE 6 - 47. D transfers property into a trust, with income to B for B's life, a reversion to D if he survives B, otherwise the remainder to go to R, or R's estate. Assume that D dies at age 70, predeceasing B, who is then 60 years old. On the date of D's death, the value of the trust property was $1 million and the Federal §7520 rate was 8%. Using actuarial tables, it was determined that given D and B's ages, D's contingent reversionary interest (ignoring the fact of his death) was worth more than 5% of the value of the trust. The amount included in D's gross estate is the full value of the trust less the value of B's remaining life estate, i.e., the value of the reversionary interest without discounting it for the contingency that it might not return despite the fact that the property can no longer revert to D. Since B is 60 years old and the rate was 8%, the amount included will be $283,790 [.28379 * $1,000,000; see Table S, 8% rate].

In the preceding example, D had a chance of surviving B at D's death, and based on that a value is calculated for what amounts to a contingent reversion for D. The reader might find this strange given that D, *in fact,* did not outlive B. However, as in certain other valuation situations, this calculation is made without regard to the fact of D's death. Thus, the calculation assumes that at the moment of D's death, both D and B were in normal health for their ages.

Revocable Transfers: §2038

Although §2038's title is "Revocable Transfers," the section covers much more. Transferred property will be included in the decedent-transferor's estate if, at the time of death, the decedent retained the right to change another's enjoyment of the property. The Code refers to this retained right as one to *alter, amend, revoke, or terminate* the enjoyment of the property transferred. Even without any retained economic interest, almost any retained right to change a beneficiary's interest (or even the timing of enjoyment) will cause the full value of the property to be included in the transferor's estate.

> EXAMPLE 6 - 48. D transferred property into a *revocable living trust*, designed mainly to avoid probate at D's death. D retained the power to revoke the trust. D's gross estate includes the value of this property under §2038.

> EXAMPLE 6 - 49. D transferred property into an irrevocable trust that gave B the right to all income. The trust was to last for a term of twenty years, but would terminate earlier in the event of B's death. At such time as the trust terminates, it is to be distributed to B, if living; otherwise, to B's issue. If B leaves no issue, then to C, or C's estate. D retained the right to have the trust terminate earlier than at the end of twenty years if D thought such was in B's best interest. Even though D retained no beneficial interest, the trust property is included in D's gross estate because D retained the power to alter the "enjoyment interests" of others. *** *Query 6 - 5. Why does §2036 also apply?*

Gift *causa mortis*. An interesting concept developed at common law is called a *gift causa mortis*; literally, a gift caused by death. It is applied when a donor, thinking that death is imminent, gives away personal property with the understanding that if the donor dies the property belongs to the donee, but if the donor survives the property must be returned. Obviously, §2038 applies to gifts *causa mortis*.

> EXAMPLE 6 - 50. Elderly Tom, just before entering the hospital, gave Jim his coin collection (worth $150,000) with the understanding that if the heart operation was unsuccessful the collection would be Jim's. Tom died three days after surgery. The collection was included in Tom's estate. Had Tom lived, Jim would have returned the coins and neither the original transfer, nor the return of the coins, would be treated as a gift.

> EXAMPLE 6 - 51. In the preceding example, suppose that Tom gave Jim his coin collection to keep no matter what the outcome of the surgery and that Tom died three days after the surgery. The collection would not be included in Tom's estate. Of course, the adjusted taxable gift value ($140,000) would boost his estate into higher marginal rates and the executor of Tom's estate would be responsible for filing a gift tax return showing the gift.

The law requires that the gift be returned if the donor survives the life-threatening event, even if the donor dies while the donee is still in possession of the property.

EXAMPLE 6 - 52. Athene was fearful that she would not survive major surgery. She gave Mary, her best friend, her collection of Barbie dolls (valued at $50,000), with the understanding that the dolls would be returned if Athene did not die. The surgery was successful and she made a perfect recovery, but was killed in an automobile accident on the way home from the hospital. Now, Mary admits the agreement, but claims the right to keep the dolls because of Athene's death. With the help of the probate court, Athene's executor will rightfully take possession of the dolls.

Gift Taxes on Any Transfer within Three Years of Death: §2035(b)

Since 1977, the Code has included a section (at first §2035(c), but §2035(b) since the TRA '97) that requires inclusion in the gross estate of the gift tax paid by the decedent on *any gift* made within three years of the donor's death. Note, §2035(b) applies only if gift tax was actually paid. Many, indeed most, taxable gifts result in no gift tax because the donor's unified credit usually covers the tentative tax. However, if the gift does result in gift taxes and the donor dies within three years of making the gift, the gift taxes paid become part of the gross estate, subjecting the gift taxes themselves to the estate tax.

Grossing up. This inclusion of the gift tax in the gross estate is referred to as "grossing up" the estate; i.e., the estate is being brought up to the level it would have been had the gift tax not been paid. Keep in mind that the property transferred within three years of death is not brought back into the gross estate, just the gift tax is brought back.

EXAMPLE 6 - 53. In 1998, Mack gave Stacy XYZ stock worth $2,000,000. Mack paid gift taxes in the amount of $574,250. When Mack died in the year 2000, his gross estate (not including the gift taxes) was valued at $6,000,000 and his debts and expenses were $1,000,000. Stacy still owned the XYZ stock, which had risen in value to $2,500,000. Taking the transfer into account: Mack's gross estate is $6,574,250; his taxable estate is $5,574,250; and the adjusted taxable gifts are $1,990,000.

EXAMPLE 6 - 54. Continuing the prior example, had Mack died in 2002 (more than 3 years after making the gift), his gross estate would have been just $6,000,000, the taxable estate $5,000,000, and, of course, the adjusted taxable gifts would still have been $1,990,000. Notice that, regardless of when Mack died, the value of the XYZ stock at Mack's death is irrelevant to the estate tax calculation.

The next three examples (and the table that follows them) compare the estate tax results in three situations: 1) where the decedent did not make large taxable gifts, 2) where the decedent made large taxable gifts far enough in advance of his death to avoid grossing up, and 3) where the gift was so close to the donor's death that grossing up is required.

EXAMPLE 6 - 55. In 1997, X died owning property worth $10 million. X's estate paid death taxes of $4,948,000. X's only child received $5,052,000.

EXAMPLE 6 - 56. In 1990, Y also owned $10 million, but he gave his child $5 million and paid gift tax of $2,192,500. Y died in 1997 (more than three years after making the gift), still owning $2,807,500 [$10 million - ($5 million gift and gift tax paid)]. Y's estate tax base was $7,797,500, and his death tax was $1,544,125. Therefore, Y's child received $6,263,375 [the gift plus the estate property less the death taxes]. Y's child received $1,211,375 more than X's child did [$6,263,375 - $5,052,000]. The $1,211,375 difference is explained partly by the $10,000 gift tax annual exclusion, but mostly by the exclusion from the tax base of the gift taxes.

EXAMPLE 6 - 57. Same facts as before, except Z died within three years of making the gift. The gift tax was included in Z's gross estate, bringing it up to $5,000,000 [$2,807,500 owned + $2,192,500 gift taxes] and resulting in an estate tax base of $9,990,000 [$5,000,000 gross estate + $4,990,000 adjusted taxable gift]. The tentative tax of $5,135,300 was reduced by the credit for gift tax payable and the unified credit to result in death taxes of $2,750,000. Thus Z's child received a total of $5,057,500 [$10 million - ($2,192,500 gift tax + $2,750,000 estate tax)], which exceeds the total $5,052,000 received by X's child by only $5,500, the amount of the tax advantage of the $10,000 annual gift tax exclusion at the marginal rate of 55%.

	X	Y	Z
Gross Gifts	N.A.	$5,000,000	$5,000,000
Less annual exclusions, if any	N.A.	($10,000)	($10,000)
Taxable gifts	N.A.	$4,990,000	$4,990,000
Tentative tax (gifts)	N.A.	$2,385,300	$2,385,300
Less unified credit	N.A.	($192,800)	($192,800)
Gift tax	N.A.	$2,192,500	$2,192,500
Taxable estate	$10,000,000	$2,807,500	$5,000,000
Plus adj. taxable gifts, if any	$0	$4,990,000	$4,990,000
Estate tax base	$10,000,000	$7,797,500	$9,990,000

Tentative tax (estate)	$5,140,800	$3,929,425	$5,135,300
Less gift tax payable credit	$0	($2,192,500)	($2,192,500)
Less unified credit	($192,800)	($192,800)	($192,800)
Estate tax	$4,948,000	$1,544,125	$2,750,000
Total transfer tax (gift+estate)	$4,948,000	$3,736,625	$4,942,500
Net to the children	$5,052,000	$6,263,375	$5,057,500

The fact that gift taxes paid more than three years before death can result in significant tax savings is an important estate planning tool, provided clients are willing to act early enough to avoid the "gross up" rule of §2035(b). Most people, even the very wealthy, are unwilling to generate a gift tax even if it will save substantial transfer taxes.

Tax exclusive versus tax inclusive calculations. A different way of describing the grossing up rule is that the gift tax is generally calculated on a tax exclusive basis, i.e., the amount of the gift tax is not included in the base. The taxes paid are not "taxable gifts" even though they are paid by the donor, nor are they part of the transfer tax base, provided the donor lives for another three years after making the gift that generated the gift taxes. On the other hand, the estate tax is calculated on a tax inclusive basis, i.e., the tax is levied on the "taxable estate" out of which the estate tax is paid and the tax itself is not a deduction. Grossing up converts a tax exclusive gift into a tax inclusive one. As we shall see in our later discussion of the generation-skipping transfer tax, on certain transfers ("direct skips") one computes the tax on a tax exclusive basis, thereby reducing the effective tax rate.

Certain Transfers within Three Years of Death: §2035(a)

Section §2035(a) creates a rule that causes transferred property to be included in the gross estate even though there is no retained interest when the transferor dies. This three year rule is subdivided into these two parts: relinquishment or transfer of certain retained interests and the transfer of life insurance.

A very limited three year rule. A decedent's gross estate includes the value of property relinquished or given away within three years of his or her death, if that property would have been included in the decedent's gross estate under §§2036, 2037, 2038 (the retained interests sections), or §2042 (the life insurance section) had the decedent kept the interest. Do not apply the rule to every transfer made within three years of death as this rule only applies *to two, and only two,* types of transfers; the *severance of a retained* interest (§§2036, 2037, 2038) or the gift of *life insurance* (§2042).

EXAMPLE 6 - 58. D transferred property worth $750,00 into a trust, with income to S or C for S's life, then remainder to B. D retained the right to allocate the income between the two income beneficiaries. The trust terms also stated that the trustee was to allocate income equally between the two income beneficiaries in any year in which D failed to give written directions concerning the allocation. Because of D's retention of control over the property, no gift is deemed to have occurred. When D died, the trust was worth $1,340,000. D died possessing this right to "sprinkle" the trust income; therefore, the entire value of the trust property (as of D's DOD) was included in D's gross estate by virtue of both §2036 and §2038.

EXAMPLE 6 - 59. Same as prior example except that in 1997, when the trust was worth $1,000,000, D relinquished his right to make the income allocation by writing a letter to the trustee stating that he irrevocably released his right to allocate the income. This act caused the gift to be complete. Note that the taxable gift is the full $1,000,000, because neither S nor C have an identifiable present interest. D paid gift taxes of $153,000. From that moment onward, D had no retained interest in the trust. However, §2035(a) applies, and if D dies within three years of the relinquishment, the property (at the DOD value) and the $153,000 in gift taxes are included in D's gross estate with adjusted taxable gifts being zero for estate tax purposes. On the other hand, if D dies more than three years after the relinquishment, neither the property nor the gift taxes are included, and the adjusted taxable gifts would be $1,000,000 for estate tax purposes. Either way, the gift tax payable credit of $153,000 would be available.

EXAMPLE 6 - 60. D established an irrevocable trust managed by an independent trustee. The terms of the trust retained all income for D for a period of 20 years, after which the trust terminated with the remainder interest held by D's adult children. D died 21 years after establishing the trust; thus the trust had terminated the year before. Because D did not "release" a retained interest, the value of the trust assets are not included in D's estate even though D died within three years of the trust's termination. The retained interest had simply expired according to the original terms of the trust.

EXAMPLE 6 - 61. D transferred five bonds to C using the state's *Uniform Gift to Minors Act* to appoint herself custodian. D died before C reached the age of majority; therefore, the bonds are included in D's gross estate. Under the *Uniform Act*, D had the ability to liquidate some (or all) of the bonds and to distribute the proceeds to C or apply them for C's benefit. Thus both §§2036 and 2038 apply.

EXAMPLE 6 - 62. Same as prior example, except that shortly before D's death, C became an adult so D turned the bonds over to C. Even though D died within three years of transferring the bonds, they are not included in D's estate. The transfer was not a "release" of a retained interest, therefore §2035(a) does not apply. D did not release a retained interest. Rather, it ended as a result of C becoming an adult.

Enough trust stuff, time for a life insurance example.

EXAMPLE 6 - 63. In the year 2000, D assigned his ownership interest in a *life insurance* policy on his life to his cousin Vinney. D dies in 2002. The insurance proceeds are included in his gross estate because the transfer occurred within three years of death. Had the transfer not been made, D's gross estate would include the insurance because of §2042. Had he survived more than three years after making the transfer, the value of the insurance on the date of transfer would enter the estate tax calculation as merely an adjusted taxable gift.

Remember that §2001(b) defines adjusted taxable gifts as post-1976 taxable gifts other than ones included in the gross estate of the donor. Hence where §2035(a) applies (or one of the retained interest sections) and the earlier gift is brought back into the gross estate, it will not also be an adjusted taxable gift for estate tax purposes. In other words, where the remainder value of a trust, the release of a retained interest, or the transfer of life insurance was treated as a taxable gift but the property subsequently ends up being included in the gross estate, the adjusted taxable gift value drops to zero for the calculation of the estate tax.

Until recently, the IRS took the position that §2035(a) would apply even if the decedent-insured never owned a life insurance policy if he or she nonetheless either paid the premiums directly or provided the funds with which to pay the premiums. In 1991, to the relief of estate planners, the IRS announced that it would no longer litigate this issue. To avoid the three year rule, planners make every effort to ensure that a wealthy client never possesses any incident of ownership in a newly issued policy. Thus, while the insured will usually have to sign the policy application *as insured*, he or she should never sign *as owner*. If the policy is owned by the trustee of an irrevocable trust, the insured should not be granted any power to change beneficial ownership of the policy or its proceeds.

Finally, the three year rule of §2035(a) does not apply to *premiums* paid by the insured-transferor, even if paid within three years of death. Therefore, such payments do not cause the insurance to be included in the insured's estate. The premiums themselves may be adjusted taxable gifts if they exceed the annual exclusion amount or are transferred in such a manner that no one has a present interest in them, i.e., to an irrevocable life insurance trust which does not contain a Crummey power. There will be more on life insurance trusts later.

Most transfers are not subject to §2035(a)'s three year rule. Thus transfers of stocks, bonds, cash, gold, jewelry, land, and other *garden variety* transfers, even if within three years of the transferor's death, are not brought into the gross estate; they are, and remain, adjusted taxable gifts. Had the gift not been made, the property, if still owned by the decedent at death, would only be included in the gross estate under §2033, not one of those four sections specified in §2035. *Thus, outright gifts of property (other than life insurance) are **not** included in the transferor's gross estate even if made within three years of death.* Accordingly, to understand this material fully, the reader must distinguish a single transaction gift from an indirect (generally through a trust) strings attached transfer, followed by the transferor later relinquishing the retained interest.

EXAMPLE 6 - 64. Leslie gave her son $18,000 in common stock. She died one year later, at which time the stock was worth $200,000. Hey, it was a good investment. *Nothing*, insofar as this gift is concerned, is included in Leslie's gross estate. It is an adjusted taxable gift of $8,000. It is not a §2035(a) gift because it would not have been included under §§2036, 2037, 2038, or 2042 had the gift not been made.

The facts in the example immediately above demonstrate that just because a lifetime gift is not included in the gross estate (at date of death value) does not necessarily mean that it will not be included, at least partly, in the estate tax base since adjusted taxable gifts (gift value reduced by annual exclusions) do boost the taxable estate into higher marginal rates. The distinction between a transferred property being included in the *gross estate* versus its inclusion in *adjusted taxable gifts* is important for valuation reasons. All items in the gross estate are included at their date-of-death (or alternate valuation date) value, while adjusted taxable gifts are included in the tax base (not the gross estate) at date-of-gift value reduced by any available annual exclusion. Also, the state death tax credit is based on the taxable estate (line 3 of the Estate Tax Return), not the tax base (line 5) that results when adjusted taxable gifts are added to the taxable estate.

EXAMPLE 6 - 65. Continuing the prior example, assume that Leslie transferred a life insurance policy on her life instead of transferring stock. At the time of the transfer, the policy's terminal value was $18,000 and its face value was $200,000.

If Leslie died more than three years after the transfer, the gross estate would be unaffected and adjusted taxable gifts would include $8,000 (the $18,000 terminal value reduced by the $10,000 annual exclusion). On the other hand, if Leslie died within three years of the transfer, the gross estate would include the entire $200,000 *face value* and the adjusted taxable gifts would be zero.

Congress singled out life insurance because of its unique characteristic of suddenly, and radically, increasing in value when the insured dies; a feature that strongly motivates taxpayers to avoid subjecting that increase to transfer taxes. In the absence of §2035(a), a deathbed gift of a policy on the life of the donor could cause a quick, relatively large avoidance of estate tax, at little or no gift tax cost. For example, without §2035(a), a deathbed gift of a $1 million term policy might avoid estate tax on the entire face value with no gift tax consequences.

Comparing powers of appointment to retained interests. Consider that almost any retained interest by the settlor (trustor) of a trust results in the inclusion of the trust in the settlor's estate regardless of how innocuous the retained interest was, whereas a power can be very broad and, so long as it is not a general power, the property subject to the power is not in the holder's estate. So, when trying to determine whether a trust that is connected in some way to a decedent should be included in the decedent's estate, it is helpful to use a decision tree:

1. Did the decedent create or fund the trust? If no, go to #5, if yes, go to #2.
2. Did the decedent retain an interest in the trust that either gave the decedent an economic benefit or the ability to control enjoyment? If no, then it is not in the decedent's estate. If yes, go to #3.
3. Did the decedent release the retained interest? If no, it is in the decedent's estate. If yes, go to #4.
4. Was the release within three years of decedent's death? If yes, the property is in the decedent's gross estate at the date of death value. If no, it is not in the gross estate, but it is an adjusted taxable gift.
5. Did someone give the decedent a power to appoint property such that the decedent would be considered the holder of a power? If no, then the trust property is not in the decedent's estate. If yes, go on to #6.
6. Could the decedent at any time have appointed the property to decedent's self, decedent's creditors, decedent's estate, or the creditors of the estate? If yes, it was a general power; go on to #7. If no, it was a limited power, and as such it is not included in the gross estate nor is it an adjusted taxable gift.

*** *Query 6 - 6. Why does a lapsed or exercised limited power not create an adjusted taxable gift?*

7. Was the general power still there when the holder died? If yes, the property subject to the power (whether exercised or lapsed) is included in the holder's estate. If no, go on to #8 if it lapsed during the holder's lifetime, or go to #9 if it was exercised during life.

8. Was the general power greater than the lesser of $5,000 or 5% of the trust (i.e., a 5 & 5 power)? If no, it is not in the gross estate, only because it was not in effect when the holder died. If it did exceed the 5 & 5 limits before it lapsed *and* the holder continued to have an interest in the trust, go back to #1 [the lapsed % that exceeded 5% (or $5,000 if greater) is probably included as a retained interest]. If yes, but the holder had no continuing interest in the trust after the lapse, nothing is included, but the lapsed % that exceeded 5% (or $5,000) is an adjusted taxable gift.

9. When the general power was exercised, was the property given to the decedent or the decedent's creditors, or did the decedent exercise the power in favor of someone else? If exercised in the holder's favor, then there is no taxable gift (but presumably the property increased the holder's estate). If exercised in favor of someone else (i.e., "trustee, please give $25,000 to my friend Betty"), it would be treated as a gift from the holder, and, if over the annual exclusion amount, it would be treated as an adjusted taxable gift.

Use the decision tree above as you work through these examples (assume all trusts are irrevocable unless otherwise stated).

EXAMPLE 6 - 66.   Sandra created an irrevocable trust for her brother Duane. Duane received all income each year, and he could appoint up to 5% of the corpus of the trust to whomever he might choose each year. Duane's children were the remaindermen. When he died, the trust was valued at $1,000,000 and he had never exercised the power. Because this is a general power, even though it lapses unexercised, $50,000 [5%*$1,000,000] is included in his gross estate. Note that the $50,000 remains in the trust (it is not part of Duane's probate estate). The trustee of the trust will have any of Duane's estate taxes attributed to the inclusion of the $50,000 (i.e., the pro rata amount of this trust portion compared to the rest of Duane's taxable estate), unless his estate plan calls for some special allocation of the estate taxes.

EXAMPLE 6 - 67.   David created a trust for Keith. The trustee could distribute as much of the income or trust as the trustee thought would be good for Keith. The trustee never exercised the special power other than to give Keith income from time to time. The trust gave Keith the unrestricted power to appoint up to 25% of the corpus at his death through specific mention of the power in his will. Lillian, or her estate, was the remainderman. Keith died with a will that made no mention of the trust. The trust was worth $1,000,000 when Keith died. Since this is a general power, Keith's estate will include $250,000 [25% * $1,000,000] even though the power was restricted to exercise at death and Keith let it lapse without exercise.

EXAMPLE 6 - 68. Curtis created a trust to benefit Donna for life, with remainder to her children. Roberta was the initial trustee, with Koala National Bank as the successor trustee. The trustee had the power to appoint as much of the trust to Donna as the trustee thought was needed to keep Donna happy. The power was never exercised and the trust was worth $1,000,000 when Donna died. Since Donna was neither a holder nor the settlor, none of the trust is included in her estate. What if Roberta dies before Donna, is any of the trust included in her estate? No, Roberta is a holder, but a holder of a limited power. And Curtis? Nothing is in his estate; he created the trust, but he did not retain any interest.

EXAMPLE 6 - 69. The same facts apply as in the prior example, except Curtis retained the right to appoint himself trustee. The entire trust would be included in his estate, since he retained the power to determine who would enjoy the property even though he could not benefit himself.

EXAMPLE 6 - 70. At a time when the Federal rate for valuing split-interest gifts was 12%, Melinda, aged 65, established an irrevocable trust funded with all her worldly possessions and investments worth $1,000,000. The independent trustee was to pay her income for life with the remainder paid to her friend Dianne. The value of the gift (the remainder) using Table S was $242,540. Since this was a gift of a future interest, there was no annual exclusion. When Melinda died six years later, the trust was worth $1,125,000 and the full amount had to be included in her estate. The adjusted taxable gift for estate tax calculation drops to zero because property that is drawn back into the gross estate is not also counted as an adjusted taxable gift.

EXAMPLE 6 - 71. In 1998, 80 year old Alejandro established an irrevocable trust funded with investments worth $750,000 (just a small portion of his vast wealth). The independent trustee was to pay income to such individuals as Alejandro each year directed In any year Alejandro failed to direct the trustee, the income had to be accumulated. At the end of ten years, the trust was to terminate and the remainder was to be paid to Alejandro's sister Irene or to her issue. Even though the settlor did not retain any economic interest, the retention of control causes this to be an incomplete gift. When Alejandro died five years later, the trust was worth $1,375,000. This is the value included in his gross estate. After ten years, when the trust was worth $1,500,000, it terminated and the property was distributed to Irene. No new gift or transfer taxes occur as a result of this termination.

EXAMPLE 6 - 72. Suppose, in the preceding example, Alejandro died two years after the trust terminated. The results would be quite different. The trust would not be included in his gross estate because he did not have any retained interests when he died. But, with the termination of the trust, his right to direct income ceased and the gift was complete. Alejandro would have paid gift taxes on the gift (the value of the trust at termination less an annual exclusion). What about the fact that the retained interest ceased within three years of his death? Since he did not "release" the retained interest and it merely ended as per the terms of the original trust, §2035(a) does not apply. However, §2035(b) does apply and the gift taxes must be included in his gross estate. Of course, since the trust property itself is not included in the gross estate, an adjusted taxable gift in the amount of $1,490,000 (assuming a termination value of $1,500,000 and an annual exclusion of $10,000) and a gift tax payable credit are part of the estate tax calculation.

For the next four alternative examples, the common facts are as follows: Melanie created an irrevocable trust with assets worth $750,000. The trust required income be paid to Carol or Sean in such amounts as Melanie allocates each year. If she failed to advise the trustee and, after her death, the payments are to be made equally. Once one of the income beneficiaries dies, the income must be paid to the sole survivor; after both income beneficiaries die, the trust terminates and is to be distributed to Ruben or to his estate. Because of Melanie's retained control, no taxable transfer of the corpus occurs until her right to allocate income ends. Until then, she will be taxed on the income and each distribution of income to Carol or Sean must be treated as if it was a gift directly from her.

EXAMPLE 6 - 73. Suppose two years after establishing the trust, Melanie died and the trust was worth $1,180,000. Her estate would include the date of death amount, not because she died within three years of establishing the trust, but because she retained a §2036 interest.

RULES

THE CONNECTION BETWEEN GIFTS & THE DONOR'S ESTATE

These **rules** should help you understand how post-76 gifts relate to the donor's estate:

One: Generally, gifts given are simply "adjusted taxable gifts" to the extent such gifts exceed the annual exclusion. §2001(b)(2).

Two: Gift taxes paid (or payable) are generally allowed as a credit against the tentative tax to offset the fact that the adjusted taxable gifts are used to boost the estate into its appropriate marginal rate. §2001(b)(2).

Three: Gift taxes paid on <u>any</u> gift made within three years of death are added to the gross estate. §2035(b). [This is referred to as "grossing up" the estate.]

Four: Retained interests in transfers (usually transfers in trust) will cause the property transferred to be included in the transferor's estate as though the transfer never took place. §§2036 - 2038.

Five: There are only three exceptions to rule number one:

    a. Transfers of an interest in **life insurance** within three years of death will result in the date of death value being included in the transferor's estate. §2035(a).

    b. The **release** of a **retained** interest within three years of death will result in the date of death value of the trust assets being included in the settlor's estate as though no release occurred. §2035(a).

    c. Where an interest that was given away upon the creation of a joint tenancy is included in a deceased joint tenant's estate because of the "consideration furnished test," it will be included at the date of death value. §2040.

Notes to rules Four & Five: If a transferred property ends up in the gross estate, it will **not** also be an adjusted taxable gift for *estate* tax purposes. If transferred property is in the gross estate, it must be valued as of the date of death **not** the date of the gift. Finally, if gift taxes were paid and the property ends up in the gross estate, the estate is still entitled to a credit against the estate tax for those gift taxes.

EXAMPLE 6 - 74. Suppose that, seven years after establishing the trust, Melanie died. The trust was then worth $1,585,000. The date of death amount is included; again, this is a retained interest and inclusion has nothing to do with a three year rule.

EXAMPLE 6 - 75. Suppose Melanie released her right to decide who gets the income (i.e., she writes a letter to the trustee, irrevocably giving up the right to make any further income allocations) in 1999, when the trust was worth $2,100,000, and died in the year 2001, when the trust was worth $2,250,000. The release was a taxable gift, resulting in her payment of gift taxes in the amount of $608,700 (assuming two annual exclusions of $10,000 each). Because of §2035(a), her gross estate includes the date of death value of the trust, i.e., $2,250,000. Because her gift within three years of death resulted in gift taxes, the $608,700 must also be included. Her adjusted taxable gifts are zero and, of course, a credit of $608,700 for the gift taxes paid is available.

EXAMPLE 6 - 76. Suppose Melanie released her right to allocate income in 1997 when the trust was worth $1,800,000, and died in the year 2001, when the trust was worth $2,250,000. Nothing, insofar as the trust corpus is concerned, is in her gross estate since her death was more than three years after she released her retained interest. When she released the right to allocate income, there was a taxable gift ($1,780,000) that resulted in gift tax of $489,000. Her estate will report $1,780,000 as an adjusted taxable gift and claim a gift tax payable credit of $489,000.

Part-Sale, Part-Gift Transfers: §2043

Many people wrongly believe that a transfer is not a gift if the transferor receives any consideration in exchange. They think that a small token from the donee shelters the transaction from gift taxation. The correct result is that unless the transaction is at arm's length, a gift occurs measured by the *difference* between the respective values of the consideration exchanged.

Where §§2035(a), 2036-2038, or 2041 result in property sold as part of a bargain sale to be included in the seller's gross estate, §2043 provides that the date-of-death value of the property is reduced by a "consideration offset." This means that the estate must include the value at its date of death fair market value, but can subtract the value of the consideration received.

EXAMPLE 6 - 77. D "sold" his son his $20,000 vacation home, reserving the right to use the home from time to time. D was "paid" 200 shares of very speculative stock then worth just $1,000. When D died, the stock was worth $17,000 and the vacation home was worth $30,000. His gross estate will include the date-of-death value of the home [$30,000], less only the $1,000 date of gift value of the consideration received. The post-gift appreciation on both the stock received (because D owns it) and the vacation home (because of the retained interest) are in D's estate. Note that there is no three year rule involved here.

The example immediately above illustrates relatively uncommon estate-planning transfers. Most bargain-sale-type transfers are treated differently because they generally do not include a retained interest or a general power of appointment. Therefore, since the transferred property is not included in the gross estate, the §2043 offset rule does not apply. However, a simple bargain sale will be included in the *estate tax base* as an adjusted taxable gift equal to the original gross gift value, less both the annual exclusion(s) and the consideration received by the donor.

EXAMPLE 6 - 78. In 1999, Jessie "sold" a parcel of land for a mere $200 to her son Charles even though the land was worth $18,000. This sale is not subject to a retained interest or a general power of appointment, therefore §2043 does not apply. Jessie will be treated as having made a gross gift of $17,800 and a taxable gift of $7,800. Eventually, the $7,800 will show up as an adjusted taxable gift that will boost Jessie's estate into higher marginal rates when she dies.

It should be kept in mind that §2043 applies only to transfers included in the gross estate under §§2035(a), 2036-2038, or 2041. Section 2043 does not specifically mention §2042, but §2035(a) does. So, if life insurance is "sold," other than in an arms length transaction within three years of the insured's death, §2043 will apply.

EXAMPLE 6 - 79. Four years before he died, Hissing sold Rita a $100,000 face-value policy on Hissing's life that had a terminal reserve value of $1,800. Rita paid just $500. Since more than three years have passed, his gross estate does not include this policy. However, the transfer-for-value rule will render the proceeds in excess of the purchase price taxable as income to Rita.

EXAMPLE 6 - 80. Based on the facts in the prior example, if Hissing died within three years of the "sale," his estate would be increased by $99,500, based on §2043 (a $500 offset) with reference to §2035(a) that makes reference to §2042.

TWO: ESTATE TAX DEDUCTIONS

Estate tax deductions include funeral expenses, expenses in administering the estate, claims against the estate, debts of the decedent, losses incurred during estate administration,[28] charitable bequests,[29] and the marital deduction.[30] In this section, we will introduce the marital deduction and charitable deduction, both of which are developed in detail in later chapters.

Marital Deduction: §2056

In calculating the taxable estate, the gross estate may be reduced by the value of any qualifying interest in property passing from the decedent to the surviving spouse. Thus, essentially an "unlimited" amount of property passing to the surviving spouse can avoid estate taxation, provided that certain requirements are met.

Requirements for the unlimited marital deduction. Subject to several exceptions, a property transfer to a spouse will qualify for the unlimited marital deduction if it meets the following three requirements:

1. *Included in decedent's gross estate.* The property must be *included* in the decedent's gross estate.
2. *Must "pass" to surviving spouse.* The property must actually *pass* to the surviving spouse.

> EXAMPLE 6 - 81. When Orca died in 2001, she left a $5 million estate. Her will left a pecuniary bequest of $2 million to Walter, her son by a prior marriage, and the residue to her husband Martin. Unfortunately, she used a will form that had the clause "all estate taxes shall be paid from the residue of my estate." Because the tax on the transfer to Walter reduces Martin's interest in the estate, it also reduces the marital deduction which in turn further increases the tax, etc., with the final result that the tax is $1,156,111 and Martin receives just $1,843,889. *** *Query 6 - 7. What is the death tax on $2 million? Would charging her son Walter's share with the estate taxes, but increasing that share such that he still nets $2 million result in an increase in Martin's share given that there would no longer be an interrelated calculation?*

Thus, to qualify for the full marital deduction, most planners will plan for taxes and other expenses to be paid from property *not* qualifying for the marital deduction. Thus in the example above, it might have been better to have Walter's share bear its own taxes. An additional problem of paying estate taxes out of the marital share is the need to make interrelated computations. In order to calculate the amount of the marital deduction, one needs to know the amount of the net tax; however, in order to calculate the net tax, the amount of the marital deduction must be calculated. A solution is determinable, but it requires an interrelated sequence of calculations.

3. *Not a terminable interest.* To qualify for the marital deduction, the interest passing to the surviving spouse cannot be a terminable interest. A *terminable interest*, defined in §2056(b)(1), is one that *might* terminate upon the happening of some event or contingency or upon the failure of some event or contingency. The terminable interest rule was created to ensure that property owned by a married couple is taxed in at least one of the spouses' estates. Without it, property could qualify for the marital deduction in the estate of the first spouse and not even show up in the gross estate of the surviving spouse.

> EXAMPLE 6 - 82. In his will, decedent transfers property into a trust, with income to his wife for her life, then remainder to his child. The value of the life interest to the wife will not qualify for the marital deduction because it will "terminate ... on the occurrence of an event...." The event that causes termination of her interest is her death. In general, unless a special election is made, a *life estate interest* passing to a surviving spouse does not qualify for the marital deduction and is not included in the surviving spouse's estate.

Because of the way the Code defines a terminable interest, a transfer to a surviving spouse will not be considered a terminable one if no other person will possess or enjoy any part of the property after the interest passing to the surviving spouse terminates.

> EXAMPLE 6 - 83. At her death, Mrs. Carrie, an inventor, was receiving annual payments from several companies using one of her patented ideas. Her husband received her entire estate, including the patent rights (good for 20 years when first issued) that still had 14 years left. The value of the patent is included in Mrs. Carrie's estate and it qualifies for a marital deduction because *no other person* will enjoy any part of the property after the patent is finished.

Exceptions to the terminable interest rule. There are several exceptions to the terminable interest rule that will be covered in detail in the chapter that introduces estate plans for wealthy couples. We will just introduce three of the major ones here.

First, the rule will not be violated if decedent-testator conditions a spousal bequest upon surviving no more than *six months* after the decedent's death.[31] Thus, the survival clauses specifying "thirty days" or "four months" are regularly included in the wills and do create terminable interests, but the exception allows them to qualify for the marital deduction provided the spouse lives long enough for the interest to vest. Some states, such as California, have enacted *marital deduction saving* statutes for those wills and trusts that show a clear intention to qualify for the marital deduction but which, due to poor drafting, include a survivorship period in excess of six months. The statutes reduce the survivorship period to six months. Other statutes provide a more generic solution, such as declaring void any provision which would cause the loss of the marital deduction whenever it is clear from the estate plan that the availability of the deduction was intended.[32] Unfortunately, judicial reaction to these statutes has been less than enthusiastically supportive.

Second, a transfer in which the surviving spouse receives a life estate in all of the income, payable at least annually, plus a *general power of appointment*, exercisable during life and/or by will, is allowed to qualify for the marital deduction.[33] This arrangement is used in what is called a *power of appointment trust*, which is one type of marital trust explained in the later chapters on estate planning for wealthy couples.

Third, if the decedent's executor elects to treat certain property as "qualified terminable interest property," or "QTIP," it will qualify for the marital deduction despite the fact that the surviving spouse will not own the property and might have, at most, a limited power over the property.[34] Making the QTIP election requires a trade-off; the property that qualifies for the marital deduction because of the election must be included in the surviving spouse's estate when he/she dies.[35] A further discussion of this important estate planning tool is postponed until we study estate plans for wealthy couples.

Special rules for transfers to non-U.S. citizen spouse. Property passing at death to a *surviving spouse* who is not a U.S. citizen will qualify for the marital deduction if it is placed in a "qualified domestic trust," commonly called a QDOT (or a QDT). Generally, the surviving spouse receives the income for her lifetime. The QDOT assets will be subject to the estate tax (based upon the first spouse to die's estate) when the surviving spouse dies or when corpus is transferred to her free of trust. There is an exception that allows distributions to the surviving spouse for emergencies without the distribution triggering a transfer tax. The marital deduction is also allowed if the surviving spouse becomes a U.S.

citizen within a limited period of time after the first spouse's death.[36] The rationale for requiring the creation of this trust is to ensure collection of the estate tax on the death of a surviving spouse who might otherwise remove the wealth from the United States. The QDOT requirements are covered in greater detail in the chapter on advanced estate planning for wealthy married couples.

Charitable Deduction: §2055

The charitable deduction is evidence of Congressional encouragement of philanthropy. Compared to the various rules limiting the amount of deduction for income taxes, the charitable deduction is quite simple insofar as the transfer tax system is concerned. Outright transfers to qualified charities (most U.S.-based religious organizations, publicly funded educational institutions, organizations for the disabled, for health research, etc.) are 100% deductible for both estate and gift tax purposes. For gifts, the deduction is based on the value of the gift at the moment of transfer. For a bequest, it is the value of the property at the date of death or the alternate valuation date if such is elected.

> EXAMPLE 6 - 84. Anne Scheiber died on January 9, 1995, at the age of 101. She had worked for the IRS. Her salary was just $3,150 per year when she retired in 1943. In 1944, she used her life savings of $5,000 to open an investment account. By living frugally, investing, and reinvesting, her stock and bond investments had grown to over $20 million when she died. Except for $50,000 that went to a niece, the balance of her estate (over $22 million by the time it was distributed) went to Yeshiva University, a small co-ed university in New York City. The bequest specified that it be used for women's scholarships. The estate paid no estate taxes.

> EXAMPLE 6 - 85. David Marine had been a doctor. At the time of his death in 1984, he had accumulated considerable wealth, but very few friends and no close relatives. His executors were given the limited power to appoint his estate to such "persons who have contributed to my well-being or who have been otherwise helpful to me during my lifetime...." The bequest to any one of these persons was limited to no more than 1% of his estate, with a provision that it "may be considerably less." The residue of the estate was left in equal shares to Princeton University and John Hopkins University. The net estate was worth $2,130,081, of which the executors appointed $10,000 to Dr. Marine's housekeeper and another $15,000 to a friend of his. The balance of the estate was divided between the two universities and the executor claimed a $2,105,081 charitable deduction. The IRS successfully challenged the deduction on the grounds that at the time of the doctor's

death, the amount that would eventually go to the universities was unascertainable. The court stated that, although the amount of each bequest was limited to one percent of the corpus, since "the number of such bequests was unlimited and a standard for determining the amount of a bequest was uncertain, the amount of the charitable bequest could not be ascertained at the time of death and the deduction was not available."[37] The tax on $2,130,081 for a death in 1984 was $748,240. ***
Query 6 - 8. What limits, placed on the power of the executors, would have avoided taxes but still maintained significant flexibility?

If a bequest is left to the discretion of the executor (or of a beneficiary), then no estate tax deduction will be allowed even if the person decides to leave a portion of the estate to a charity. Thus, precatory words (i.e., an earnest request) in a decedent's will such as, "I leave $100,000 to Reverend Teagarden with the hope that he will use it for the ministry of the Church," would not result in a charitable deduction.

Transfers made to charities through the use of trusts must meet certain requirements specified in Code §2055. The special requirements for charitable giving through the use of trusts are designed to give reasonable assurance that the charity will actually receive a benefit that is reasonably close to the amount of tax deduction allowed, whether the deduction is an income tax deduction in the case of lifetime gifts or an estate tax deduction for transfers that take place at the death of the donor. Additional material on charitable gifts and the charitable deduction is found in later chapters.

THREE: ESTATE TAX CREDITS

As mentioned in the last chapter, there are five main estate tax credits: the unified credit, credit for state death taxes, credit for gift taxes payable, credit for tax on prior transfers, and the credit for foreign death taxes. Since the unified credit and the state death tax credit were covered in the last chapter, the following material discusses only the other three. Each of these credits represent Congress's attempt to take the sting out of the fact that some transfers may be taxed twice.

Credit/Offset for Gift Taxes Paid or Payable

To help prevent double taxation, the unified transfer tax system allows some level of offset for gift taxes on all gifts included in the decedent's estate tax base. Without this offset, the estate tax would be calculated on all accumulated transfers whether at death or as gifts, unfairly disregarding the fact that a transfer tax had already been paid on some of them. The law allows offsets for two different categories of gift taxes: those paid on pre-1977 gifts, and those paid on post-1976 gifts.

Credit for gift taxes (pre-1977 gifts). The credit for gift tax on pre-1977 gifts shows up on line 17, page 1, of the Federal estate tax return. The amount of the credit is limited to the lesser of the gift tax or the estate tax on the property that is included in the estate.[38] One might wonder why there would be a credit for gift taxes on pre-1977 gifts given that only post-1976 gifts are included as adjusted taxable gifts in calculating the estate tax. Well, it is possible to have a pre-1977 gift pulled back into the donor's gross estate if the gift had a retained interest attached such that §2036, §2037, or §2038 applies; or if the donor-decedent had made a pre-1977 transfer with a retained interest and relinquished the interest within three years of death such that §2035(a) applies.

> EXAMPLE 6 - 86. In 1962, decedent, then age 50, created an irrevocable trust, funding it with $2 million in property. Under the terms of the trust, income was payable to the decedent for life, with remainder to his descendants. Decedent paid a gift tax of $235,118 on the gift of the *remainder* interest. If decedent dies today, his gross estate will include today's value of the entire trust corpus, under §2036. A credit for gift tax paid will be allowed based on the lesser of the gift tax paid in 1962 that is attributable to the gift (pro rata share if more than one gift that year), or the amount of estate tax attributed to having the trust included in his taxable estate (i.e., the pro rata share of the federal estate tax attributable to including the trust in the taxable estate).

Offset for gift taxes payable (post-1976 gifts). By now it should be clear that two categories of post-1976 gifts are included in the decedent's estate tax base. First, as with pre-1977 gifts described in the previous section, post-1976 gifts that fall within the grasp of §2036, §2037, §2038, or §2035(a) are included in the transferor's gross estate. Second, adjusted taxable gifts (post-1976 gifts that are not in the gross estate) are added to the estate tax base. Again, to prevent double taxation, the law allows an offset to the tentative tax for gift taxes paid on these gifts.[39] This offset is calculated by determining the amount that would have been "payable" had the tax rates in effect at the decedent's death been applicable at the time of the gift. Generally, this is simply the total of all gift taxes paid on post-1976 gifts. Since rates for taxable amounts up to $3 million have been the same for all years after 1976, generally, the tax *payable* is different from the actual gift tax *paid* only for very large total taxable gifts, i.e, whose level exceeded this amount. The gift tax paid may be more than the payable amount if the decedent made taxable gifts both pre-1977 and post-1976, since the earlier gifts pushed the later gifts into higher tax brackets but are not included as adjusted taxable gifts for present estate tax calculations. Although the Code does not refer to this offset as a "credit," it has the effect of reducing the tentative tax dollar for dollar to an amount called the "gross estate tax," and it clearly is a credit. This credit is placed on line 9 of page one of Form 706.

THE PRIOR TRANSFER CREDIT

It seems inequitable to tax property twice on those occasions when it passes swiftly through two estates such that the second owner only had a limited opportunity to enjoy the inherited property. Congress obviously agrees. It has given relief in the form of a prior transfer credit (PTC) if the two deaths occur within ten years of each other.[40]

Background on the PTC. As originally enacted, double taxation was avoided by allowing a deduction in the second estate equal to the value of property traceable to the first estate.[41] The relief was available only if the two deaths occurred within five years of one another and the old law required the executor claiming the deduction to trace the property from the first estate into the second. If the inherited property was sold and the proceeds were commingled with other funds out of which both investments and consumables were purchased, it was difficult (sometimes impossible) to trace the property. There was a fair amount of litigation between estates and the IRS over the tracing issue.

The PTC today. Present law allows a tax credit where property is included in the transferor's taxable estate and the transferee dies within ten years of the transferor. The inherited property does not have to be found in the transferee's estate, hence tracing is no longer necessary. Since the credit is intended to reduce the unfairness of taxing property that passes quickly through two estates, a time factor affects the amount of the credit available, decreasing the maximum available by 20% two years after the transferor's death and another 20% for each additional two year period until the credit disappears altogether at the end of ten years. Actually, the credit is available even if the transferee dies two years before the transferor, but the circumstances, involving vested remainder interests, are so rare that they will not be covered. The credit, before applying the time factor, is based upon the amount of additional tax the inclusion of the transferred property generates in each estate. Since this is relief from double taxation, the credit is equal to the lesser of the two amounts.

The above overview greatly simplifies the law. The actual calculation is a three step process. In the explanation that follows, D1 represents the first decedent and D2, the second.

▶ **Credit Limit One**. Compute the portion of the Federal estate tax which bears the same ratio to D1's estate tax as the transferred property bears to D1's taxable estate.

$$CL1 = \frac{adjusted\ value\ of\ transferred\ property}{adjusted\ value\ of\ D1's\ taxable\ estate} * D1's\ federal\ estate\ tax$$

▶ **Credit Limit Two**. Compute the increase in estate tax at D2's death caused by inclusion of the net value of the transferred property. The net value is the value of the transferred property reduced by all death taxes (Federal and state) attributed to it at D1's death. The Federal estate tax is determined with the net value of the property included, then again with it excluded. The difference in the two tax amounts is credit limit two.[42]

Federal tax on D2's taxable estate (including transferred property)	xxxx
Federal tax on D2's reduced estate (reduced by the adjusted value of the transferred property)	(xxxx)
Credit Limit Two	xxx

> ▸ **Time Factor**. The prior transfer credit is the *lesser of* limit one or limit two, times the appropriate time factor percentage based on how many years D2 lived after D1 died.

Years	1 - 2	3 - 4	5 - 6	7 - 8	9 - 10
Percentage	100%	80%	60%	40%	20%

An Extended PTC Example.

As we go through each of the three PTC steps, we will start each with some general comments. For limit one, the numerator is the value of the transferred property, adjusted by deducting liens, mortgages, and the property transferred's proportionate share of Federal and state death taxes. The denominator is D1's taxable estate, adjusted by deducting all death taxes. If the net value of the property (property less liens and mortgages) is used in this step of the calculation, and all death taxes are allocated pro rata, there is no need to make any adjustments for the taxes since the adjusted values (above and below the line) will be in the same ratio as the unadjusted values. If the property in D2's estate is the result of a bequest made "free of estate tax," which probably means the residue of the estate paid the death taxes, the transferred property's value (the numerator) would not be adjusted for taxes but the taxable estate (the denominator) would have to be reduced by all death taxes.

The Federal estate tax is adjusted only if a credit for certain gift taxes had been allowed for D1's estate under §2012 (pre-1977 transfers with a retained interest, such that the property is included in the decedent's estate) or if D1's estate also benefitted from a prior transfer credit. For most PTC computations, no adjustments need to be made to the denominator to adjust the value of D1's taxable estate, other than for death taxes, and (as pointed out earlier) even then an adjustment is not necessary for the numerator or the denominator if the death taxes were proportionately assessed.

EXAMPLE 6 - 87. D1 died January 1, 1994, leaving a taxable estate of $2,500,000. D1's friend, D2, received XYZ stock worth $500,000. The total D1 estate taxes were $833,000. D1's state was a pickup tax state, so it collected an amount equal to the Federal state death tax credit ($138,800), and the balance of $694,200 went to the Federal Treasury. D2 died June 10, 1997, leaving a taxable estate of $1,500,000. D2 had sold the XYZ stock when it was worth $580,000, investing some of the proceeds and spending the rest. In both estates, the death taxes were allocated pro rata. Credit limit one is calculated as follows:

$$CL1 = \frac{\$500,000}{\$2,500,000} * \$694,200 = \$138,840$$

The value of the stock in D2's estate is irrelevant to the PTC calculation. Remember, the assets transferred need not be part of D2's estate, so no tracing of assets is required. The theory is, that if the property had been sold, and the proceeds consumed, the money from the sale allowed D2 to retain other property that is taxed in D2's estate. Notice that the value of D2's estate is not used in calculating credit limit one.

There are three steps to calculating credit limit two. These steps determine that part of the Federal tax that can be attributed to the transferred property that is part of D2's estate. The calculation is done by figuring the Federal estate tax both with the net value of the transferred property included and again with it excluded. The difference is the additional tax attributed to the inclusion. First, calculate D2's Federal estate tax without the PTC. This means, determine the Federal amount that would have been paid on D2's taxable estate, i.e., reduce the tentative tax by the unified credit and the state death tax credit. Second, determine the Federal estate tax on D2's estate with the net value of the transferred property removed. We will call this D2's *reduced* taxable estate. To arrive at the reduced D2 taxable estate, one must subtract the net value of the property transferred from D2's (regular or full) taxable estate. To determine the net value of the transferred property, subtract from the value of the property transferred (as of D1's DOD) its *share* of *all* death taxes (yes, including state death taxes) and any debts, liens, or other obligations which reduced the value of the property when it was transferred from D1 to D2.

Continuing with this example, credit limit two is calculated as follows:

Federal Estate Tax on D2's $1,500,000 taxable estate	$298,600
Less Federal Estate Tax on D2's reduced taxable estate.	
This is the tax on $1,166,600, i.e.,	
$1,500,000 - (5/25 * ($2,500,000 - $833,000))	(178,244)
Credit limit two	$120,356

The figure $298,600 is the Federal estate tax on an estate of $1,500,000 after subtracting the unified credit and the Federal state death tax credit [$555,800 (tentative tax) - $192,800 (unified credit) - $64,400 (state death tax credit)]. The figure (5/25 * ($2,500,000 -(833,000)) in the above example is the value of the property transferred, adjusted for its pro rata share of *all* death taxes. In this hypothetical situation, the decedent's state death taxes are equal to the Federal state death tax credit. Where the state death taxes are greater than the Federal state death tax credit, the actual state death tax paid must be used to make the adjustment. This would not affect limit one (assuming the state death taxes were also allocated pro rata), but it would affect the calculation of limit two since the property transferred must be reduced by all death taxes charged against it. The figure $178,244 is the Federal tax on a taxable estate of $1,166,600, meaning it is the amount that would actually be paid on an estate of that size after taking the unified credit and the state death tax credit [$414,106 (tentative tax) - $192,800 (unified credit) - $43,062 (state death tax credit)].

To finish this example, the time factor adjustment must be made. Since D2 died in the fourth year following D1's death, the allowable credit is 80% of the lesser of the two credit limits. Therefore:

$$80\% \ * \ the \ lesser \ of \left\{ \begin{array}{l} limit \ one\text{: } \$138,840 \\ limit \ two\text{: } \$120,356 \end{array} \right. = \ \$96,285$$

The two year time bracket starts with the actual date of D1's death through midnight of the anniversary two (or four, six, etc.) years later. It is easiest to visualize this (and to be assured of selecting the correct percentage) by drawing a time line, marking off the appropriate two year anniversaries starting with D1's death, and then indicating with a slash the date of D2's death. Indicate on the time line "100%" for the first two years following D1's death, "80%" for the next two years, etc., until you have covered the period that includes D2's death.

The chapter on advanced marital deduction and bypass trust planning goes into detail as to how the PTC is used with marital deduction trusts to reduce taxes, even where no transfer of corpus takes place.

Credit for Foreign Death Taxes

A credit is allowed for most, but not all, foreign death taxes paid on property which is (a) included in the U.S. gross estate, and (b) situated in that foreign country. Similar to the PTC, the amount of credit allowed is the lower of the amount of tax the property generates in the U.S. versus the amount it generates in the foreign country.[43] A detailed explanation of this credit is beyond the scope of this text.

This chapter has examined the principal items found on the estate tax return, including components of the gross estate, estate tax deductions, and estate tax credits. The next chapter examines the components of the gift tax return, covers basis rules as they relate to gifts and estates, and introduces the generation-skipping transfer tax.

QUERIES ANSWERED

1. Using Table S, the remainder factor, using an 8% rate for an 85 year old's life estate, is .66693. Hence, Max's estate would include:

$$.66693 \times \$1,000,000 = \$666,930$$

2. Using Table S, the remainder factor (also used for a reversionary interest), using a 10% rate for a 40 year old's life estate, is .07055. Hence, Jim's estate would include:

$$.07055 \times \$100,000 = \$7,055.$$

3. Because of the consideration-furnished test of §2040, the entire property is included in Virginia's estate, even though half was reported as a gift. The definition of "adjusted taxable gifts," found in §2001(b), excludes any gifts that are included in the gross estate; therefore, the $90,000 taxable gift to her son is removed from the estate tax calculation.

4. Because the trustee will still allocate income between Benito and Consuelo, neither beneficiary has an identifiable present interest. A present interest is a requirement for the annual exclusion.

5. This is another example of an overlap of Code sections. Section 2036(b)(2) requires inclusion where the decedent retains the right to "designate who shall possess or enjoy the property or the income therefrom." By being able to terminate the trust early, D was able to designate who would possess the property; hence, §2036(b)(2) applies as well as §2038.

6. Because the holder of a limited power never made a transfer (but is merely the donee), the exercise or lapse will not cause the holder to be treated as having made a taxable transfer. The exercise or the lapse of a limited power during the holder's lifetime will not create a taxable gift.

7. The death tax on $2,000,000 in the year 2001 is $560,250. Charging Walter's share with the tax, but increasing the share so that he nets $2,000,000, will not increase Martin's share because estate taxes are calculated on a tax inclusive basis. It would take a bequest of $3,156,111 to Walter for him to net $2,000,000. This means that husband Martin would receive $1,843,889, the same as if the taxes were charged to his $3,000,000 share.

8. Instead of limiting the amount that could be given to each appointee to 1%, the limit could have been stated as, "all such appointments cumulatively shall not exceed an amount that will produce a tentative tax equal to the decedent's available unified credit." Or, "cumulatively not to exceed" either some dollar amount, such as $200,000, or some small percentage of the net estate, such as "not to exceed 10% of the adjusted gross estate." Even though these limits do not set an exact amount going to charity, they do produce a minimum amount that must go to charity and the charitable deduction would be based upon that minimum amount. Thus, the first limit (not to exceed the UCE) would result in a charitable deduction of the net estate in excess of the UCE, producing a taxable estate of $600,000 with no tax due.

QUESTIONS AND PROBLEMS

1. Distinguish between the gross estate, taxable estate, and probate estate.

2. When Morton died in 1996, he left his estate to his three children. He left stock worth $560,000, a home worth $345,000, a car worth $9,000, home furnishings worth $23,000, and a bank account with $3,500 in it. The total of his debts and expenses was $45,000. He also had a $200,000 life insurance policy on his life that was paid out to his three children and a vacation cabin worth $150,000 held in joint tenancy with his brother. The brothers had each paid half of the purchase price on the vacation cabin. Calculate : (a) the gross estate, (b) the taxable estate, (c) the probate estate, (d) the total death taxes, (e) the state death tax credit, and (f) the Federal estate tax.

3. (a) What is a dower interest? (b) How is it taxed?

4. When Jack died, his 65 year old wife was entitled to receive a survivor's pension of $1,800 per month for her lifetime from a fully qualified plan (his employer had made all contributions). The §7520 rate used for valuing annuities was 8%. Determine how much is included in his estate if Jack retired in (a) 1986; (b) 1983; or (c) 1980. Use Table K to adjust for the fact that the payments are made monthly.

5. Frank and Kathleen co-owned a home. Frank contributed $25,000 and Kathleen contributed $75,000 of the $100,000 purchase price. When the first co-owner died, the value of the property was $360,000. In each independent case determine: (1) how much is included in the decedent's estate and (2) the survivor's new basis.

   a. They held the property as joint tenants. Frank died first. They were just good friends.
   b. They held the property as joint tenants. Frank died first. They were married.
   c. They held the property as joint tenants. Kathleen died first. They were just good friends.
   d. They held the property as community property. Frank died first.
   e. They held the property as tenants in the entirety. Frank died first.

f. They held the property as tenants in common. Frank died first, leaving his 25% share to Kathleen. (Does it matter for inclusion and basis whether they were married? Does it matter for estate taxes?)

6. (a) What is a general power? (b) What is the significant tax difference between a general power and a limited one? (c) When will a power to appoint to one's self not be a general power?

7. At his death, decedent-trustee was the holder of a power of appointment over property held in a trust created by his rich brother. Determine whether any portion of the trust principal is included in decedent's gross estate given each of the following alternative trustee powers. If a power is exercised in favor of someone other than the holder, state the gift and estate tax consequences that follow.

a. The unrestricted power to appoint property to his surviving descendants by specific mention of the power in his will. Decedent appointed the entire corpus to his grandson.
b. Same as part a, except decedent did not appoint property to anyone at his death.
c. The unrestricted power to appoint property to himself or his descendants. In his will, he appointed property to his grandson.
d. Same as part c, except decedent did not appoint to anyone at his death.
e. The power to appoint property to himself for "health" reasons.
f. The power to appoint property to himself for his "comfort."
g. The power to appoint property to himself, but only with the approval of his son, who was also the remainderman.

For h - i, the following power was included in the trust: the power to appoint to himself or to his children each calendar year and, at his death, if the power was unexercised during that year, the greater of $5,000 or 5 percent of the trust property.

h. In his will, decedent exercised the power, naming his son to receive $50,000 of the $1 million trust corpus.
i. Decedent never exercised this power during his lifetime nor at his death.

For j - m the following 5 & 5 power was involved: The power to appoint to himself or to his children each calendar year up to the greater of $5,000 or 5% of the trust property. At his death the power lapsed, i.e., it could not be exercised through his will or by any other means once he died.

j. Shortly before he died, he exercised the power and had the trustee transfer 5% ($50,000) of the trust to himself.
k. Shortly before he died, he exercised the power and had the trustee transfer 2.5% of the trust ($25,000) to his son and another 2.5% to his daughter.
l. Shortly before he died, he had the trustee transfer 5% to his university to be used for scholarships.
m. Shortly before he died, he exercised the power by having the trustee transfer 3% of the trust to the United Way.

8. Identify two situations where a limited power of appointment might be the right answer to an estate planning problem.

9. True or false? A gift of life insurance within three years of the insured-donor's death is the *ONLY* circumstance where a completed gift (i.e., one with no strings attached) is included in the gross estate of the donor.

10. What do §§2033, 2034, 2039, 2040, 2041, and 2042 have in common?

11. What do Sections 2036, 2037, and 2038 have in common?

12. Under §2036, two very different circumstances will cause a trust to be included in the settlor's estate. (a) Describe the one in which the settlor retains an economic benefit. (b) Describe the one in which the settlor does not retain an economic benefit.

13. Use the language of the IRC to describe the three common retained powers or rights that will cause a trust to be included in the settlor's gross estate under §2038.

14. Explain the impact of §2035(a) by giving specific examples of:

    a. a single transaction lifetime gift where the property transferred is not included in the gross estate.

    b. a single transaction lifetime gift where the property transferred is included in the gross estate.

    c. a relinquishment of a "string" where the trust property is not included in the gross estate.

    d. a relinquishment of a "string" where the trust property is included in the gross estate.

Facts for problems 15 - 18: Gary transferred property worth $60,000 to his sister Pamela. Because of the unified credit, Gary paid no gift taxes when he made the transfer. When Gary died, the property was worth $100,000. For each case, state (insofar as the transfer goes and his estate) what is (a) in his gross estate; and (b) the adjusted taxable gift.

15. Gary transferred stock two years before he died.

16. Gary transferred stock four years before he died.

17. Gary transferred life insurance ($60,000 was its terminal reserve value) two years before he died. Pamela collected the $100,000 proceeds.

18. Gary transferred life insurance ($60,000 was its terminal reserve value) four years before he died. Pamela collected the $100,000 proceeds.

Facts for 19 - 23: Settlor Sam created an irrevocable trust, funding it with $1,000,000 of his own assets. The remaindermen of the trust were Sam's two children. For each independent case that follows, calculate the following: (a) the gross gift; (b) the taxable gift; (c) the amount of the trust included in Sam's gross estate; (d) the adjusted taxable gift; and, (e) the amount of gift tax credit allowed.

19. Sam retained a life estate in the trust. At the time of funding, the Federal rate for split interest gifts (i.e., for valuing remainders, etc.) was 6% and Sam was 60 years old. He died ten years after establishing the trust. The trust was then worth $1,700,000.

20. Sam retained no economic interests in the trust, but the terms of the trust gave him the right to allocate income between his brothers Daniel and James. If he failed to allocate (whether due to inaction or his own prior death), then the trustee was to distribute the income equally, and once one brother died, the surviving brother was to receive all of the income each year. Sam died ten years later, without ever directing the trustee as to how to allocate. Both brothers survived him and the trust was worth $1,700,000.

21. Same facts as the prior example, except in year five, Sam had sent the trustee a letter stating that he forever released his right to make the allocation. The trust was worth $1,350,000 when Sam released his right. Again, when he died in year ten the trust was worth $1,700,000.

22. Same facts as the prior example, except the release occurred in year nine, when the trust was worth $1,600,000. As before, it was worth $1,700,000 in year ten when Sam died.

23. Under what circumstances would the gift taxes paid by Sam be included in his gross estate? Is this a special rule that relates only to transfers into trust?

24. When she died, Roxanna was serving as the trustee of an irrevocable trust that allowed her to distribute corpus or income to her children or the children of her sister Laurie. The trust was worth $700,000 when she died. For each of the following alternatives, determine whether the trust is included in her estate: (a) The trust had been established by the mother of Roxanna and Laurie, many years before. (b) The trust had been established by Laurie, many years before, and at the same time, Roxanna had established and funded a similar trust with Laurie as trustee. (c) Roxanna had established the trust, but kept no economic benefit for herself. (d) Roxanna's rich uncle had established the trust at his death. Initially, Roxanna was also included as a permissible appointee, but she irrevocably released the right to appoint to herself seven years before she died.

25. Identify by number or schedule letter, the two pages of Form 706 where the amount of the total marital deduction must be shown.

26. When Craig died, he left his $14,000,000 estate to his wife, Rebecca. There were debts and expenses of $500,000. Craig and Rebecca were both USA citizens. (a) What is Craig's gross estate? (b) His taxable estate?

27. Florence left her net estate (after debts and expenses) of $1,000,000 to her husband, Juan Carlos. They were both residents of the USA for most of their adult lives. How much U.S.A. estate tax would be paid given each of the following circumstances? (a) Both were citizens of the USA. (b) Florence was a citizen of the USA and Juan Carlos is a citizen of Mexico. (c) Florence was a citizen of Mexico and Juan Carlos is a citizen of the USA. (d) Both were citizens of Mexico.

28. Guy had created a revocable probate-avoidance trust, fully funded before he died. Upon his death, the trust gave 50% of the corpus to the university where he received his bachelor's degree and 50% to United Way. A life insurance policy that he owned paid out $500,000 to a favorite niece. The trust had assets worth $4 million, and debts and expenses totaling $300,000. Determine Guy's (a) probate estate; (b) gross estate; (c) taxable estate; and (d) estate tax.

29. When Ruby died on August 12, 1994, her taxable estate in the amount of $1,400,000 was left to her only son, Thomas. Ruby's estate paid total death taxes of $320,000, of which $58,000 went to the state and $262,000 went to the Federal Government. When Thomas died on February 8, 1996, most of his $1,000,000 taxable estate was comprised of what was left of the estate that he had inherited from his mother. The estate taxes on Thomas's estate, before application of the PTC, would have been $33,200 paid to the state and $119,800 paid to the Federal Government. Calculate the following: (a) limit one; (b) limit two; (c) the PTC; and (d) the Federal and state taxes after applying the PTC.

30. When Vaughan died on May 5, 1993, his taxable estate in the amount of $4,500,000 was left equally to his three children. Vaughan's estate paid total death taxes of $1,923,000, of which $335,600 went to the state and $1,587,400 went to the Federal Government. When Vaughan's oldest child, Stephanie, died on July 4, 1996, her taxable estate of $2,000,000 was left to her two children. The estate taxes on Stephanie's estate before application of the PTC would have been $99,600 paid to the state and $488,400 to the Federal Government. Calculate the following: (a) limit one; (b) limit two; (c) the PTC; and (d) the Federal and state taxes after applying the PTC.

ANSWERS TO QUESTIONS AND PROBLEMS

1. Gross estate is an estate tax concept that includes all that one owned, controlled, and, in some instances, transferred with retained interests. It even includes gift taxes paid on gifts made within three years of death. The taxable estate is the gross estate less debts, expenses, and deductions, such as the marital and charitable deduction. The probate estate consists of that property owned by the decedent for which there is no other mechanism of transfer other than the court process. Generally, it is made up of things owned by the decedent, plus property co-owned as a tenant in common.

2. Morton's estate. (a) GE $1,215,500 [50% of cabin]; (b) the TxE $1,170,500; (c) the probate $940,500; (d) the total DTx $222,905; (e) the S D Tx Cr $43,312; and (f) the Federal Tx $179,593.

3. (a) A dower interest is a surviving wife's statutory interest in her deceased husband's estate. At common law, it is generally a life estate in a portion of the real property. Today, it may be a fee interest in a portion of the estate. (b) The property is included in the decedent's gross estate but generally there is a marital deduction available. If it is just a life estate, it can qualify for the marital deduction through the QTIP election. If it is an interest in fee in a percentage of the estate, that portion going outright to the surviving spouse qualifies for the marital deduction.

4. Annuity. Wife @ 65, $1,800/mo, rate 8%. Retired in (a) 1986 full value: $1,800*12*8.136 = $175,738 (b) 1983: full value, less $100,000 = $75,738; (c) 1980: zero.

5. Frank $25,000 and Kathleen $75,000; at 1st death $360,000. 1) Included and 2) new basis.

   a. Joint tenants. Frank died. Friends. 1) consideration furnished rule, 25%*$360,000 = $90,000; 2) New basis = $90,000 + $75,000 = $165,000.
   b. Joint tenants. Frank died. Married. 1) 50%, $180,000 2) ½ + ½ = $180,000 + $50,000 = $230,000.
   c. Joint tenants. Kathleen died. Friends. 1) $270,000 2) $295,000.

d. Community property. Frank died. 1) 50%, $180,000 2) FMV @ DOD, $360,000.
e. Tenants in the entirety. Frank died. Same as for married joint tenants: 1) $180,000 2) $230,000.
f. Tenants in common. Frank died, his 25% to Kathleen. 1) 25%*$360,000 = $90,000; 2) New basis = $90,000 + $75,000 = $165,000. (Is married important? Not for inclusion, still 25%. For estate taxes? Sure, 100% marital deduction).

6. (a) General power? See Code §2041, i.e., power to appoint to holder, holder's creditors, holder's estate, or creditors of holder's estate. (b) Difference? General power you include and a limited one you do not include. (c) When will a power to appoint to one's self not be a general power? When it is limited by an ascertainable standard (HSEM) i.e., the health, support, education, or maintenance standard, or when the consent of the creator or of an adverse party must be obtained.

7. Note, the trust was created by someone else; therefore, these are all powers, not retained interests.

a. Limited not included, exercise does not matter.
b. Limited not included, exercise does not matter.
c. Can appoint to self, therefore general, all included. That it was exercised will not increase the transfer tax.
d. As in part "c," all included, exercise or no exercise.
e. Limited by an ascertainable standard, the H in HSEM.
f. All included, no ascertainable standard for comfort.
g. Not included, the adverse interest exception.
h. This is a general power if it is there at the time of death, and (exercised or not), it is included. The exercise does not increase the inclusion. It will still be $50,000, i.e., 5%.
i. Same as "h."
j. At the time of death, the power had been exercised for the year, so it was not there. Nothing insofar as the trust is concerned is included. However, the $50,000 might still be in a bank account, unless he gave it away or spent it.

k. Again, nothing to include. But he has made two gifts of $25,000 each; thus, after the annual exclusions there will be an adjusted taxable gift of $30,000.

l. Again, nothing to include. The gift qualifies for the charitable deduction, so not even an adjusted taxable gift to worry about.

m. He still could have exercised a power over 2% of the trust before he died, so 2% times the value of the trust is included.

8. There are many. Here are two: The parents of a mentally disabled child may want to establish a "special needs" trust that grants to a holder of a limited power the discretion to expend trust funds to enrich the child's life, with the expectation that the trust will be there long after the parents are dead. An irrevocable by-pass trust may have terms that allow a surviving spouse to re-allocate the remainder interests of children.

9. True, although students of estate planning keep trying to add others.

10. All cover beneficial interests in property held or controlled by the decedent at death, which are included in the decedent's gross estate.

11. a. Transfer made by decedent...
    b. ...for less than full consideration.
    c. Included in the decedent's gross estate at date of death value; and
    d. amount included is only that portion of the transferred property over which decedent retained control.
    e. Some retained control or interest by decedent.
    f. Usually arising in the context of a trust.

12. (a) A retained life estate. (b) Retained power to decide who (other than the settlor) enjoys the income or the property.

13. The Code refers to the power to revoke, alter, or amend. Three examples:
    - Totten trusts;
    - revocable living trusts;
    - gifts to minors under the Uniform Gifts to Minors Act where the donor serves as custodian.

14. a. Any outright transfer, other than life insurance, avoids inclusion in the gross estate.
    b. Transfer of life insurance on the donor's life within three years of death.
    c. If the string is cut more than three years before the transferor dies, the property will not be included.
    d. If the string is cut within three years of the transferor's death, it is as though the string had not been cut; therefore, the property is included at its date of death value.

15. (a) GE zero; (b) Adj.TxG $50,000. Stock, no three year rule.

16. (a) GE zero; (b) Adj.TxG $50,000.

17. (a) GE $100,000; (b) Adj.TxG zero. Life insurance, special three year rule.

18. (a) GE zero; (b) Adj.TxG $50,000. Life insurance, but beyond the three year reach.

19. (a) GG $366,674 [0.36674 * $1,000,000]; (b) TxG $366,674 [no annual exclusion for future interest gifts]; (c) GE $1,700,000; (d) Adj.TxG zero; (e) GTxCr zero, no taxes paid, tent. x covered by the unified credit.

20. (a) GG zero, retained control; (b) TxG zero; (c) GE $1,700,000; (d) Adj.TxG zero; (e) GTxCr zero.

21. (a) GG $1,350,000; (b) TxG $1,350,000 [no one with an identifiable present interest]; (c) GE zero; (d) Adj.TxG $1,350,000; (e) GTxCr $298,500.

22. (a) GG $1,600,000; (b) TxG $1,600,000 [no annual exclusion except for identifiable present interests]; (c) GE $2,108,000, both §2035(a) and §2035(b) apply; (d) Adj.TxG zero; (e) GTxCr $408,000 [the gift tax on $1,600,000].

23. If Sam died within three years of any gift that triggers the actual payment of gift tax. [A special rule that relates only to transfers into trust?] No, any gift, whether in trust or not and whether life insurance, diamonds, land, stocks or bonds, or whatever can be given, is governed by this rule. If taxes are paid

and death occurs within three years of the gift, the gift taxes are part of the gross estate.

24. (a) Limited power, do not include. (b) Include, the trusts were reciprocal trusts, and Roxanna is considered the settlor with a retained power to control enjoyment. §2036 applies. (c) This would be a retained interest, therefore include even though Roxanna retained no economic benefit. (d) Include, since at one time she held a general power. When she released it, it was as though she was the transferor of the property into the trust. Since she is treated as the transferor, the fact that she controls enjoyment of the income and property causes §2036 to apply, and the trust is included in her estate.

25. The marital deduction amount must be shown on page 3 (line 18 of recapitulation and on page 25 (Schedule M).

26. (a) GE? $14,000,000; (b) TxE? Zero.

27. (a) Zero estate tax, 100% marital deduction. (b)$153,000 estate taxes, no marital deduction. (c) Zero estate tax, 100% marital deduction. (d) $153,000 estate taxes, no marital deduction.

28. (a) No probate estate; (b) GE $4,500,000; (c) TxE $500,000 [$4,500,000 - $300,000 (debts & expenses) - $3,700,000 (charitable, the trust after debts and expenses paid) = $500,000]; and (d) estate tax. None, covered by the unified credit.

29. (a) limit one [$262,000]; (b) limit two [$119,800]; (c) the PTC [$119,800]; and (d) the Federal [zero] and state taxes [$33,200] after applying the PTC.

30. (a) limit one [$529,133]; (b) limit two [$319,014]; (c) the PTC [$255,211 i.e., 80%*$319,014]; and (d) the Federal [$233,189] and state [$99,600] taxes after applying the PTC.

ENDNOTES

1. §2031(a).

2. §6018(a)(1).

3. Reg. §20.2053-7, Deduction for unpaid mortgages.

4. §6018(a)(2).

5. §2103.

6. §2102(c)(1).

7. §2002; *Fleming v. Commissioner*, No. 90-2576, 7th Cir. 1992.

8. §2002, §2203.

9. *Estate of Guide v. Commissioner*, 69 T.C. 811 (1978).

10. LR 8335033.

11. The Taxpayer Relief Act rearranged §2035; old §2035(c) is now §2035(b).

12. Pre- TRA '97 §2035(d)(2) is now §2035(a).

13. §2033.

14. *Davis*, T.C. Memo 1993-155.

15. TAM 9207004.

16. §2034.

17. §2056(b)(7).

18. See §1401(a) of P.L. 104-88).

19. *Ablamis v. Roper*, 937 F2d 1450 (9th Cir. 1991).

20. See *Gallenstein* 975 F. 2d 286 (CA6, 1992) affg. 68 AFTR 2d 91-5721.

21. §2033.

22. §2041(b)(1)(C)(ii).

23. *Estate of Cavenaugh*, 100 TC, CCH ¶12,927 (1993).

24. §§2036, 2037, and 2038.

25. §2035(a)

26. *Estate of Grace*, 395 US 316 (1969).

27. *Maxwell*, 3 F. 3d. 591, affirming 98 T.C. 594 (1992).

28. §2054.

29. §2055.

30. §2056.

31. §2056(b)(3)(A).

32. E.g., CA Probate Code §21,525.

33. §2056(b)(5).

34. §2056(b)(7).

35. §2044.

36. §2056A(a).

37. *Estate of Marine*, 990 F2d 136 (4th Cir. 1993).

38. §2012.

39. §2001(b)(2).

40. §2013.

41. 812(c) of the 1939 Code.

42. Reg. §20-2013-3.

43. §2014.

CHAPTER 7

The Federal Gift Tax and Basis Rules

OVERVIEW

Chapter 5 introduced the gift tax, showing how it is calculated and how it is unified with the estate tax. This chapter examines some more qualitative factors, such as the requirements for a valid gift, types of taxable gifts, how gifts qualify for the annual exclusion, and how certain specific transfers are (or are not) subject to gift tax. While reading the chapter, the reader is urged to review both the overview of the gift tax scheme in Tables 5-1 and 5-2, plus the United States Gift Tax Return, Form 709, included in Appendix D.

FEDERAL GIFT TAX

Estate planners use the word "gift" in different ways. Most people think of gifts as gratuitous lifetime transfers, but estate planners define gifts as completed property transfers in exchange for less than full and adequate consideration. The latter definition is broad enough to include transfers at *death*. Thus, it is correct to say, "...in his will he *gave* the grand piano to his daughter." However, to avoid the necessity of always using the modifier "lifetime," all references to gifts will mean lifetime gifts unless the context clearly indicates otherwise.

Requirements for a Valid Gift: Influence of Local and Federal Law

Whether or not a transfer is treated as a gift is important for two reasons in estate planning. First, it will influence the respective property rights of the parties. Second, it will determine whether a taxable event has occurred. In deciding these issues, two different sets of rules must be examined: local property law and federal gift tax law.

Local property law. To be valid under local property law, a gift must ordinarily meet four requirements.

1. The donor must be capable of transferring property.
2. The donee must be capable of receiving and possessing the property.
3. There must be delivery to, and some form of acceptance by, the donee or the donee's agent.
4. Finally, under local law, a valid gift ordinarily requires donative intent on the part of the donor.

Federal gift tax law. To be subject to taxation under federal gift tax law, a gift must meet all of the above local property law requirements, subject to two major federal modifications.

a. Federal tax regulations explicitly state that *donative intent is not required* for a transfer to be subject to gift tax. Although not required for a gift, the existence of donative intent would be strong evidence that a gift had actually been made.

b. Under the unique language of federal law, the gift tax applies only to a *completed* gift, which arises when "...the donor has so parted with dominion and control as to leave him no power to change its disposition, whether for his own benefit or for the benefit of another..."[1]

Ordinarily, completed gifts are made either outright or in trust. *Outright transfers* made beyond the donor's dominion and control are virtually always complete for gift tax purposes. Transfers in trust, on the other hand, may be complete, incomplete, or partially incomplete. An example of a *complete transfer in trust* is a transfer to an irrevocable trust with no retained interests or controls; the entire transfer is subject to gift taxation. An example of an *incomplete transfer in trust* is a transfer to a typical revocable trust; it is not at all subject to gift taxation because the trustor has retained the power to demand return of the trust property. An example of a *partially incomplete transfer in trust* is one to an irrevocable trust in which the trustor has retained only the right to the income (but not to control it) but not to the remainder; thus there is a complete gift of the remainder interest. Or, the trustor could give away the income interest for a period of time with the corpus reverting to the trustor when the time is up, e.g., another is given the income for ten years after which the trust terminates and the corpus is returned to the trustor or to the trustor's estate. Thus, for transfers in trust in which more than one property interest is created, gift tax law requires that each interest be examined independently to determine whether a completed gift of that interest has been made.

Both federal tax law and local property law influence gift taxation. Summarizing, the relationship between federal law and local law with regards to the requirements for a valid gift may be stated as follows: Local law dictates whether a transfer of *property rights* has in fact been made, irrespective of taxability. On the other hand, federal tax law, in conjunction with local law, specifies whether a gift is subject to taxation. Federal law also spells out rules, discussed later in this chapter, relating to the taxation of specific types of gifts, such as those in connection with powers of appointment, life insurance, joint ownership, and disclaimers.

Who Is Subject to Gift Tax?

The Federal gift tax law applies to all *individual United States citizens or residents* regardless of where the property is located and regardless of whether the transfer is direct or indirect, real or personal, tangible or intangible. The Federal gift tax law also applies to *nonresident aliens* but only with regards to transfers of real property and tangible personal property situated within the United States.[2]

Aspects of Taxable Gifts

Valuation of gift. The value of the gift for tax purposes is its fair market value at the date of the gift. Any consideration received in exchange is subtracted in determining the gross value of the gift.

EXAMPLE 7 - 1. If Sally "sells" a $25,000 automobile for $1 to her son Mark, she has made a gross gift in the amount of $24,999 and must report (after applying a $10,000 annual exclusion) a taxable gift of $14,999.

Measuring the consideration received in exchange. To be recognized, consideration received in exchange must be measurable in money or money's worth. If it is not reducible to money or money's worth, it will be disregarded.

EXAMPLE 7 - 2. Gertrude tells her daughter Alice that her kindness over the past years has been priceless. Gertrude promises Alice that if she continues being so kind she will transfer her $250,000 Dusenberg to her on her next birthday. When Alice's birthday arrives, the card from Gertrude contains the title and keys to the Dusenberg. Even if Alice's sweet attention is worth more than money can buy, it is not considered to be an exchange in money or money's worth. Therefore, Gertrude has made a taxable gift.

The above example illustrates a situation where a gift is subject to gift taxation despite the fact that local law may view the exchange of consideration to be equal, and donative intent, therefore, to be nonexistent.

Fortunately, in the case of property settlements between divorcing spouses, federal law no longer requires a determination of the total value of the consideration exchanged by each spouse. Transfers of property subject to a written divorce or separation agreement are deemed to be made for full and adequate consideration even when it is clear that the "exchange" is not for money or money's worth.[3]

Gifts versus sales. With sales between *related parties,* IRS agents may contend that a gift rather than a sale has been made. However, sales between unrelated parties are presumed not to be gifts.

EXAMPLE 7 - 3. Herb, owner of a retail drugstore, sells his aging delivery pickup truck to Karl, a *stranger,* who read about the truck in the classified section of the newspaper. Karl paid Herb $4,200 and promptly took out a similar ad and sold the truck three days later for $6,700. Herb has made a bad bargain, but not a gift, because the truck was sold in an *arms-length* transaction.

EXAMPLE 7 - 4. Same facts as the prior example, except that Herb, who had already made gifts in excess of $10,000 to his son Jerry, sold him the car for $4,200. Jerry then advertised and sold the car for $6,700. Inasmuch as this was a transaction between relatives, a gift has probably occurred.

Filing and Payment Requirements

When a return must be filed. In general, a gift tax return is due when the donor's income tax return is due (or if the donor is not required to file an income tax return, then when it would have been due had the donor been so required). Usually, this means April 15 of the year following the gift. An extension to file one's income tax return is also an automatic extension to file one's gift tax return. A gift tax return must be filed by any donor who in any calendar year gives:

- more than the annual exclusion amount (i.e., $10,000, indexed) to *any* donee (other than to a spouse or charity), or
- a gift of a *future interest* regardless of how small the value, or
- total gifts exceeding $100,000 to a *non U.S. citizen spouse*, or
- a gift for which both spouses want to elect *gift splitting* even if after the split each gift is less than the annual exclusion amount.

Who files. Only *people* file gift tax returns. For example, if a partnership or a corporation makes a gift, the individual partners or stockholders are considered the donors who must file the return and pay the tax. If the trustee of a revocable living trust makes a gift subject to taxation, it is the grantor who is treated as the donor. If a donor dies before filing a return, the donor's executor must file for the deceased person.

Who pays. The donor is responsible for paying the gift tax;[4] the *donee* is not subject to either gift tax or income tax on the gift.[5] However, there is transferee liability if the donor fails to pay the tax. This means that any donee can be forced to pay the gift tax, up to the value of the gift received, if the donor fails to pay.

Net gift. Some donors, however, might wish to make a *net gift*; that is, to arrange in advance for the *donee* to be responsible for paying the gift tax. The Supreme Court has ruled such a transaction to be part sale, part gift, causing the donor to realize taxable income to the extent that the gift tax paid by the donee exceeds the donor's adjusted basis.[6] However, other advantages may still make the net gift attractive.

> EXAMPLE 7 - 5. In 2003, Vera transferred her horse ranch, valued at $5,000,000, to her daughter Felicity with the understanding that Felicity would pay the gift taxes. The annual exclusion had increased to $11,000. The net gift value was $3,598,710 and Felicity paid gift taxes of $1,390,290.

Deductible Gifts

Two types of gifts are fully deductible, and three are completely excluded from being treated as gifts, with the end result (whether deducted or excluded) that they are not treated as taxable gifts.

Charitable gifts. First, gifts to qualified charities are fully deductible.[7] Owners of "qualified works of art" can loan them to a charity without the loan being treated as a taxable gift, provided the use of the work by the charity is related to its charitable purpose (e.g., an art museum receiving a Van Gogh on loan will put it on display rather than hang it in the director's private study).[8] Generally, gifts to charity also produce an *income tax deduction*, but only up to certain percentages of adjusted gross income. Chapter 14 will discuss strategies for charitable gifts.

Interspousal gifts. Second, under the unlimited marital deduction, gifts to a *U.S. citizen spouse* are fully deductible, provided that they are not terminable interests.[9] However, even terminable interest gifts might qualify for the marital deduction by using a gift qualified terminable interest property (QTIP) election.[10] We will get into an analysis of terminable interests and the estate tax marital deduction in Chapters 11 and 12.

Since 1988, only the first $100,000 per year in gifts to a *non-U.S. citizen spouse* escapes gift taxation.[11] Thus, gifts above $100,000 per year to a non-U.S. citizen spouse use up unified credit and may even generate a gift tax.

Gifts for tuition and medical care. Third and fourth, qualified payments in any amount made directly to an educational institution for tuition, and payments in any amount made directly to a provider of medical care on behalf of any individual are fully excluded from being taxable gifts. Two things to emphasize here: the transfers must be *directly* to the providers, and not to the individuals themselves, and the person benefitting from the payments does *not* have to be related to the donor.[12]

Gifts to political organizations. Fifth, gifts are not taxable if made to a "political organization (within the meaning of section 527(e)(1)) for the use of such organization."[13]

Gift Tax Annual Exclusion and the Present Interest Requirement

During each calendar year, a person may give gifts with a total value of up to $10,000 per donee to as many other people as the person wants to benefit without using up any of the donor's unified credit because such gifts do not count as taxable gifts. The $10,000 is indexed for inflation and is likely to increase by a thousand dollars every three or four years. Note that the donor and donee do not have to be related. The main requirement for obtaining this *annual exclusion*, as it is called, is that the donee have an immediate *present interest* when the donor completes the gift.[14] Present interest gifts are ones where the "enjoyment" of the gift can start immediately, whereas future interest gifts have some condition attached that either might cause some delay or does cause a delay in the donee's possession and enjoyment of the transferred property.

> EXAMPLE 7 - 6. This year, widow Sanderson gave her daughter Polly three corporate bonds each valued at $10,000. Even though Polly may not collect the par value until maturity, and even though the periodic interest income is payable in the future, the gift is of a present interest and qualifies for the annual exclusion. Widow Sanderson did not place any restriction on Polly's *right to enjoy* the bonds. Assuming that she made no other gifts to Polly during the year, the taxable value of the gift is $20,000 [$30,000 - $10,000].

Congress in 1932 chose to deny the annual exclusion for gifts of future interests for three reasons: (1) future interests may be difficult to value; (2) the number of donees of a future interest is often indeterminable at date of gift; and (3) future interests are sometimes created to avoid taxes.

Gifts into trust. Most problems regarding future interest gifts arise in the context of trusts.

> EXAMPLE 7 - 7. Suppose widow Sanderson transferred bonds worth $30,000 to an irrevocable trust, whereby the trustee could give the bonds to Polly whenever the trustee thought it appropriate to do so, but, at the very latest, to transfer them to her on her 25th birthday. The gift, which is reportable for the year the bonds are transferred into the trust, is a $30,000 taxable gift of a future interest. It will not qualify for the annual exclusion because, by the terms of the transfer, the enjoyment can be delayed for a period of time. The result remains the same even if the trustee immediately transfers one of the bonds to Polly.

No annual exclusion means, of course, that absent any deductions, the gift will be entirely taxable, such that part or all of the donor's unified credit will have to be used. Further, at the donor's death, the value of the taxable gift is added to the estate tax base, which may push the donor's estate into a higher marginal rate. Thus, the donor may prefer a disposition that is at least partly sheltered by the annual exclusion.

> EXAMPLE 7 - 8. Altering the facts of the prior example a little bit, assume that instead of being allowed to accumulate the income, the trustee is required to *pay all income* at least annually to Polly, an adult, with the remainder going to Richard at the end of the 10 year term. Upon creation of the trust, two interests arose: a *present interest in the income* for 10 years and a remainder interest. At ten percent, the present value of an income interest for a 10 year period equals .614457 times the value of the stock. The product of 0.614457 * $30,000 is $18,434, which represents the portion of the gift that is considered a present interest qualifying for the annual exclusion up to a maximum for any one donee of $10,000. Hence, the total taxable gift equals $20,000 [$30,000-$10,000]. Note that the amount subtracted from the gross value of the gift is the lesser of the present interest (here $18,434) or the annual exclusion ($10,000 indexed).

> EXAMPLE 7 - 9. Suppose Polly's mother placed bonds worth just $15,000 into the ten year trust; the present interest would be $9,217 [0.614457 * $15,000] and the taxable gift would be $5,873 [$15,000 - $9,217].

2503(c) Trusts. There is just one exception to the rule that there must be a present interest before a gift qualifies for the annual exclusion, and it is found in IRC §2503(c). The annual exclusion is allowed for gifts placed in trust (referred to as a 2503(c) trust) for the benefit of a person who is under the age of 21, even though the beneficiary does not have a present interest. These trusts for youngsters (and others that are more commonly used) are covered in Chapter 13.

The Kiddie Tax

All unearned income of children under age 14 in excess of a statutory amount is taxed at the parents' marginal rate. This special treatment is referred to as the "kiddie tax."[15] The threshold amount was originally $1,000 when the law went into effect in 1987 but, due to indexing, it had climbed to $1,400 in 1998 (see the Table of Indexed Values in Appendix A) and is likely to be $1,450 by the year 2000 or 2001. This is covered in greater detail in Chapter 13.

Gift Splitting

Gift splitting treats a gift of the property owned by one spouse as if it were made one-half by each spouse. It is conceptually similar to federal spousal income splitting on a joint income tax return; indeed, both were first added to the tax code in 1948 as part of a restructuring that attempted to put common law states on a par with the community property states. Also added at that time was the initial marital deduction (equal to 50% of the adjusted gross estate) and the provision that stepped-up both halves of community property even though only one half was included in a decedent spouse's estate.[16]

Under federal gift tax law, a spouse may *split a gift* by making an election, with the consent of the non-donor spouse, on the gift tax return. If the election is made, a gift by the donor spouse of his or her own property is treated as if made one-half by each of them.[17] According to the regulations, the election must cover *all* gifts that were made during the year to third parties by either spouse. The election allows a married person the benefit of two annual exclusions (and two unified credits, if needed) to cover what is really just one gift.

> EXAMPLE 7 - 10. In 1999, Johnna Lynn gives $50,000 of her own money to a nephew. Assuming no other gifts and no gift splitting, her taxable gift, after the annual exclusion, is $40,000. Thus, she must use up a portion of her unified credit. Alternatively, she can *split* this gift with her husband Fred, if he is willing, and each is then considered to have made a gross gift of $25,000. After each donor's annual exclusion, the taxable gift is $25,000 and (assuming no prior taxable gifts) each will use up $4,900 of their unified credit. Johnna Lynn and Fred must both file gift tax returns.

To make the split gift election, the consent of the non-donor spouse is required and two gift tax returns (one by each spouse) must be filed by spouses if, after the split, the values exceed the annual exclusion. Only the donor spouse needs to file a gift tax return if the split brings the gifts below the annual exclusion. There is a place on the donor spouse's tax return for the non-donor to sign, affirming his or her consent to the election.

> EXAMPLE 7 - 11. Billy and Millie are married parents. This year Millie gave $20,000 of her property to their son. Assuming no other gifts, if the couple agree to gift splitting, only Millie will be required to file a gift tax return; Billy's consent will appear on Millie's return

Gift splitting is needed only if the property that is given was owned by just one spouse, since their co-owned property is, by its nature, already "split," making the election unnecessary. This is especially true of community property which is always owned in equal shares (i.e., 50% each) by the spouses.

EXAMPLE 7 - 12. In the prior example, had the $20,000 been community property, jointly held property, or an in-common interest in property (here assume 50%-50%), the gift would be considered as made one-half by each spouse. Since the value of each spouse's half interest is covered by the annual exclusion, neither spouse would need to file a gift tax return.

EXAMPLE 7 - 13. If a couple gave their nephew property, worth $28,000, that had been held in joint tenancy, each spouse will have made a gross gift of $14,000 and a taxable gift of $4,000 (assuming the annual exclusion is still $10,000). Again, there is no need for gift splitting, and each spouse must file a gift tax return because each gift exceeds the annual exclusion.

Somewhat oddly, if a split gift results in the payment of a gift tax and the donor-spouse dies within three years of the gift, the *entire* gift tax paid, not just the one-half, is grossed up in the donor's gross estate.[18]

EXAMPLE 7 - 14. In 1999, from his property, Charles gave cash worth $150,000 to the couple's son and stock worth $150,000 to their daughter. Charles's wife, Susan, gave $9,000 of her property to their son. The effects on reportable gross gifts, annual exclusions, and taxable gifts of the decision whether to split the gifts or not is shown in the table below. If no split gift election is made, Susan will not have to file a Form 709, since her gift is covered by the annual exclusion. If gift splitting is elected, the taxable amount on both returns will be identical.

	Without Gift Splitting		With Gift Splitting	
	Charles' Form 709	Susan's Form 709	Charles' Form 709	Susan's Form 709
		*(not filed)		
Gross Gifts:				
To Son	$150,000	$9,000	$79,500	$79,500
To Daughter	$150,000	$0	$75,000	$75,000
Total per return	$300,000	$9,000	$154,500	$154,500
Total per family	$309,000		$309,000	
Exclusions:				
Gift to Son	$10,000	$9,000	$10,000	$10,000
Gift to Daughter	$10,000	$0	$10,000	$10,000
Total per return	$20,000	$9,000	$20,000	$20,000
Total per family	$29,000		$40,000	
Total per return	$280,000	$0	$134,500	$134,500
Total per family	$280,000		$269,000	

Electing gift splitting reduces the family taxable gifts by $11,000 [$280,000 - $269,000]. The reduction is the result of the additional $11,000 in total family annual exclusions, since with the election Susan is allowed $20,000, rather than just $9,000. Gift splitting can mean lower gift taxes, or, as in this example, it may just result in using up less of the parent's total unified credit.

In summary, gift splitting can lower gift taxes because it permits the use of two full annual exclusions per donee, even though just one gift is given and, for large gifts, both spouses' unified credits are utilized.

Powers of Appointment

General power holders and taxable events. As with the estate tax, only *general powers* are subject to gift tax, and, if there is a gift, it is treated as having come from the *donee-holder*.[19] Of course, when the general power was first created, the donor of the power (if created by gift) or the donor's estate (if created at death by will or trust) may have paid transfer taxes, unless the transfer was not subject to tax because of the annual exclusion, a marital deduction, or the application of the unified credit. For instance, if a donor placed property in an irrevocable trust which gives the income beneficiary a general power over 25% of the trust corpus, it would be the entire property placed in trust that would be the gift, not just the 25% subject to the general power. As was discussed in conjunction with the estate tax, a general power is defined in §2041 as one that the holder can use to benefit the holder, the holder's creditors, the holder's estate, or the creditors of the holder's estate.

Three events during the holder's lifetime can trigger gift tax to the holder of a general power of appointment: exercise by the holder in favor of someone else, release by the holder, or lapse of the holder's right to exercise or release the power. Where the holder exercises the power in his or her own favor, no gift occurs.

EXAMPLE 7 - 15. Carla's estate plan called for the creation of two trusts at her death. Trust A was called the marital trust and gave her husband Ian income for life and a power to appoint the entire corpus to whomever he wished upon his death, with the corpus going to their three children if Ian fails to exercise the general power. The A trust was to be funded with Carla's estate that exceeds the exclusion amount. The other trust was called Trust B and was to be funded with assets equal to the exclusion amount. For this trust, Ian was given a life estate and had a general power to appoint up to 5% of the trust each year to whomever he chooses. At Ian's death, the power lapses and the trust will be distributed to the couple's three children. Because Carla's total net estate was worth only $540,000 when she died in 1999, only Trust B was funded (i.e., the $540,000 estate went into Trust B) and there was no Trust A.

Because Ian has a 5% withdrawal right, there was a marital deduction of $27,000 and the taxable estate was $513,000. Although Trust B is considered to have been taxed, the tentative tax was less than Carla's unified credit so no estate tax was actually paid.

EXAMPLE 7 - 16. In 2000, the trust was worth $560,000 when Ian asked the trustee to distribute corpus worth $25,000 to him. Since this was less than 5% of the value of the trust, the trustee obliged and, since the distribution was to Ian, the holder of the general power, no gift was made.

EXAMPLE 7 - 17. In 2001, the trust was worth $580,000 when Ian asked the trustee to distribute corpus worth $40,000 to Judith. The trustee pointed out that this exceeded his 5% power, so Ian told him to give her the maximum this year and the balance in 2002. The trustee gave Judith $29,000 in 2001 and another $11,000 in January of 2002. Both transfers are treated as gifts directly from Ian. Since the annual exclusion was $11,000 for those two years (due to indexing), only $18,000 of the first gift and none of the second gift was taxable.

EXAMPLE 7 - 18. In 2003, the trust was worth $620,000 when Ian asked the trustee to distribute corpus worth $30,000 to his alma mater, Midwestern State University. The trustee obliged and Ian was able to claim a charitable deduction on his income tax return for the amount of the gift.

EXAMPLE 7 - 19. In 2004, the trust was worth $650,000 when Ian died. He had not exercised his 5% power that year. His estate had to show on schedule H of the estate tax return $32,500 attributable to this general power. If Ian's estate is large enough that estate tax is owed, the trust would have to pay its proportionate share of the estate tax (i.e., $32,500 over the taxable estate times the estate taxes).

In the above examples, we used a general power equal to 5% of the value of the trust for good reason. It is very common to find trusts that give a holder a general power that is limited to exactly that percentage because of a special Code section that we discuss next.

Lapse and 5 & 5 powers. The general rule is that the lapse of a general power is treated as a transfer from the holder to whomever is the taker by default. However, §2041(b)(2) creates an exception that allows the lapse of certain general powers to occur *during the life* of the holder without the lapse being deemed a taxable gift. The exception applies to the lapse during the holder's lifetime of a power, but only to the extent that what could have been transferred (but for the lapse) did not exceed the greater of $5,000 or 5% of the value of the property out of which appointment would have been satisfied. Powers which are drafted to make use of this exception are referred to as "5 & 5" powers, and they permit the holder to appoint property from a trust up to the greater of $5,000 or 5% of the value of the trust corpus. Usually the right is given such that it can be exercised annually and the failure to exercise the right in any year will not increase the dollar amount or the percentage for the next year. In other words, it is a noncumulative, annually lapsing power (or right).

Lapsing powers are often placed in irrevocable trusts created for the benefit of minors in order to obtain the annual exclusion for the parent-donor. The power of the child to withdraw an amount each time the parents add to the trust creates a present interest for the child-donee even though the power to withdraw lapses after a short period of time, as set forth in the trust, and even though there is a strong expectation that the child will not exercise the right to withdraw. This demand right is referred to as a "Crummey demand right" or as a "Crummey power." Trusts for this type of provision are called *Crummey Trusts,* and when established for minor children, they may be called *Minors' Demand Trusts.*

EXAMPLE 7 - 20.   Grantor has set up a minors' demand trust for three grandchildren. Each grandchild can claim up to the lesser of one third of the amount transferred into the trust that year or the annual exclusion amount. If a grandchild does not demand his or her share, the right to claim the gift lapses at the close of the year (with demand rights for gifts made late in the year extended to a minimum of thirty days). If no demand is made during the demand period, the transfer is locked into corpus and, by other trust terms, it stays there until the youngest of the three grandchildren reaches age thirty. If a grandchild dies before termination of the trust, his or her share goes to the other grandchildren who do survive. If initially the trust is funded with less than $15,000 and none of the beneficiaries demand their share, no gift from the beneficiaries is deemed to have been made as a result of the lapses because of the §2041(b)(2) exception. Without this exception, there would be the smallest of gifts, i.e., each beneficiary would be making a contingent future interest gift to the other two. The value of each gift is discounted because it is a future interest gift and discounted further since its value is based upon the very low probability that he or she (each grandchild-donor) might not survive to age thirty. So, although the gift can be valued, it has a very low value because the gift is contingent given that, if the youngest grandchild lives to age thirty, all three of them will take their one-third interest in the trust corpus.

EXAMPLE 7 - 21.   If the initial transfer was $24,000, then each child would be deemed to have made a transfer to the extent his or her share lapsed and exceeded the "5 & 5" limits. Thus, each grandchild would be deemed to have transferred $3,000 to the trust. Since there are two other grandchildren who will be the remaindermen if a grandchild dies, each grandchild will be deemed to have made a gift of a contingent future interest that vests when the youngest child reaches age thirty. The value of the gift from each grandchild can be determined actuarially. For each child, it would be based upon the probability of that grandchild dying before the termination of the trust. Obviously, the gift is very small in value considering the unlikelihood of the event which would cause the gift to vest in the other children (the death of a child before the youngest turns thirty) and the fact that the gift is one of a future interest, since enjoyment upon lapse is postponed until the termination of the trust. Because the gift is one of a future interest, no annual exclusion is available and a gift tax return would have to be filed for each grandchild.

The adverse result of creating lapsing powers of appointment which exceed the "5 & 5" limit is not the gift tax generated, since the gift value is usually extremely small, but rather the retained life estate implications. If a beneficiary has a retained life estate in any property that the beneficiary has previously transferred, whether into trust or otherwise, §2036 causes it to be included in his or her estate at death. The Regulations make it clear that the lapsing of powers which exceed the 5% limit are simply accumulated.[20] There is no attempt to apply sophisticated mathematics to take into account the fact that each subsequent release of a power includes a release of a portion of the trust previously released. The mathematics are kept simple, but this works against the taxpayer (the holder of a power, greater than 5%, who lets the power lapse) in that it causes greater inclusion in the estate of a beneficiary-holder who dies before the trust terminates.

To further clarify, the "5 & 5" exception does not apply to lapses which take place at the death of the holder. Hence, a noncumulative annually lapsing power to annually claim up to 5% of the corpus of a trust each year that was not exercised during the holder's last year of life would cause inclusion in the holder's estate of 5% times the date of death value of the trust (or $5,000 if such was greater).

EXAMPLE 7 - 22. Upon his death in 1994, Benny's father established a trust which gave Benny income for life and a noncumulative, annually lapsing general power of appointment over a portion of the trust. At Benny's death, the trust terminates and the remaining corpus goes to Benny's sister, Rachael, or to her estate. At all times relevant to this example, the value of the trust remained constant at $1,000,000. Benny died in 1998, never having exercised the power. If the power was exercisable over 5% of the trust, then 5% ($50,000) of the trust value would be included in Benny's estate, even though none of the lifetime lapses of the power were deemed to be transfers and even though Benny let the power lapse at his death.

EXAMPLE 7 - 23. If the power had been over 8% of the trust (instead of 5%), then for the years 1994, 1995, 1996, and 1997 each lapse is treated as though 3%

(that which exceeded 5%) was transferred by Benny to the trust with Benny retaining a life estate in the transfers. Section 2036 would cause 12% of the trust to be included in Benny's estate and, since Benny died with an unexercised general power over 8% of the trust, §2041 causes the inclusion of another 8%. Thus, a total of 20% of the value of the trust is included in Benny's estate. *** *Query 7 - 1. How much would be included if Benny had been given a 15% annually lapsing power?*

Ascertainable standard, adverse party exceptions. Similar to estate tax law, a power of appointment to name oneself, one's creditors, one's estate, or the creditors of one's estate is not treated as a general power if the power is subject to an ascertainable standard of health, education, maintenance, or support, or if it is exercisable only in conjunction with either the creator of the power or an adverse party. Ascertainable standard language is commonly used in trust instruments to give flexibility, yet keep the trust out of the holder's estate.

Life Insurance

A taxable gift of life insurance can arise either during the insured's lifetime or at the insured's death.

Assignment. During the insured's *lifetime*, an assignment of ownership rights in the policy may constitute a taxable gift equal to the value of the rights assigned. Ordinarily, the owner assigns all of his or her rights to a policy, and the gift is the value of the policy at that time.

EXAMPLE 7 - 24. Joe assigns his life insurance policy to his son. The policy has a face value of $600,000 and a value for gift tax purposes of $87,000. Joe has made a present interest gross gift of $87,000 and a taxable gift of $77,000.

In contrast to the assignment of ownership interests, the owner's simple act of *naming a beneficiary* does not constitute a taxable gift since no property rights are transferred; the named beneficiary has a "mere expectancy," contingent upon the owner's keeping the policy in force and not changing the beneficiary designation.

The unholy trinity. A taxable gift of life insurance can arise at an insured's *death*. This will occur when the insured, owner, and beneficiary are all different parties. Sometimes this arrangement is referred to as the "unholy trinity."

EXAMPLE 7 - 25. Madeline uses her own separate funds to purchase a $100,000 life insurance policy on her husband Dave's life, naming their son Bret as the beneficiary.

Upon Dave's death, Madeline will have made a $100,000 gift to Bret. A better way to handle this is to transfer the policy to Bret while Dave is still alive.

EXAMPLE 7 - 26. Changing the facts in the preceding example, assume that Dave purchased and owned the policy until his death, paying the premiums entirely with community property funds. At Dave's death, Madeline will have made a $50,000 gift to Bret, reflecting her one-half interest in the proceeds. Madeline may be able to claim half of the proceeds, if she can show that she was unaware of the policy's existence or that she was unaware that her husband had named someone, other than herself, as beneficiary.

In the above example, the other $50,000 is includable in Dave's gross estate under §2042. Can you see why? It is because Dave's community property interest is a 50% ownership in the policy. Estate planners typically avoid this tax trap by having the beneficiary also be the owner any time someone other than the insured owns the policy.

Gifts into Joint Tenancy

Ordinarily, gifts are made when the owner of property transfers his or her entire interest to the donee. Sometimes, however, a donor transfers only a partial interest, as when a donor transfers his or her property into joint tenancy with others.

General rule. The actual moment that a gift occurs when there is a change of title from solely owned into joint tenancy depends upon the nature of the property. In general, ownership and possession of most types of property are considered transferred when documents evidencing a transfer of title are *executed* and *delivered* or *recorded*. Where there are co-owners, the donee need not physically take possession of the document of title but need only acknowledge acceptance of the gift. Thus, a gift usually arises when the donor adds the donee's name to property already owned by the donor or includes the donee's name on the title of newly acquired property. The value of the gift will be the net value of the property interest transferred at the time of the gift.

EXAMPLE 7 - 27. Uncle Charlie buys an automobile for $30,000 cash, *taking title* in joint tenancy with his nephew Brad. Charlie has made a gift of $15,000 to Brad in the year of purchase.

EXAMPLE 7 - 28. Changing the facts in the prior example just a bit, assume that Charlie bought the car two years ago for $48,000, taking title in his own name. This year, when the car is worth $30,000, Charlie instructs the motor vehicle bureau to *change the title* to read: "Charlie Jones and Brad Smith, as joint tenants." This year, Charlie has made a gift to Brad of $15,000.

EXAMPLE 7 - 29. This year, Clive purchased a building for $150,000, taking title in joint tenancy with his five adult sons. This year, Clive has made a gift of $25,000 to each son.

Two exceptions. There are two principal exceptions to the rule that the inclusion of others as co-tenants for less than full consideration results in an immediate gift. First, in the case of a *joint tenancy bank account*, in most states a gift arises upon withdrawal of the funds by the donee, not upon the creation of the jointly held bank account. Second, for a joint tenancy *U.S. government savings bond*, a gift, if any, arises when the bond is redeemed. Thus, if the initial purchaser redeems the entire bond, no gift has occurred. In both instances, no gift has occurred because the original owner/purchaser has retained control over the account or bond since he or she can withdraw all of the funds or cash in the bonds without the aid of the donee joint tenant. Compare that to a transfer of real estate into joint tenancy; once the deed is recorded (or delivered to the donee), the original owner cannot unilaterally recover what he or she has given away, i.e., control of that portion has been lost. This is also true of corporate stocks or bonds. Once the transfer agent has changed title into joint tenancy, the original owner cannot unilaterally change it back into just his or her name without the cooperation of the transferees or a certified death certificate showing them to be deceased.

EXAMPLE 7 - 30. On June 1 of last year, Rochelle deposited $40,000 in a savings account held jointly with her son Conrad. He withdrew $6,800 on February 1 of this year. Rochelle made a gift to Conrad, but not until February 1 of this year. It was covered by the annual exclusion.

EXAMPLE 7 - 31. Lionel purchased a $20,000 EE savings bond years ago, taking title with his son Patrick as joint tenants. At the bond's maturity next month, if Lionel redeems the bond, there will be no gift. If Patrick redeems it, Lionel will have made a gift of $20,000. If they split the proceeds, Lionel's gift to Patrick of $10,000 will be covered by the annual exclusion.

Disclaimers

The prior examples assumed that the donees accepted the gifts as given. Suppose that for some reason the intended donee does not want to accept a substantial gift made under a will, trust instrument, or other document. Obviously, if one accepts a gift or bequest and then transfers the property to another, it will trigger a transfer tax unless the transfer is sheltered by the annual exclusion or a charitable or marital deduction. To avoid creating a taxable transfer, a donee might wish to refuse the gift. Section 2518 allows the donee to "disclaim" a gift in such a way that it will be as though the gift was never made and, in the case of a bequest, as though disclaimant predeceased the decedent-donor. In order to disclaim and have this favorable result, the following requirements must be met:

1. The disclaimer must be "an irrevocable and unqualified refusal...to accept" the interest.
2. The refusal must be in writing.
3. The refusal must be received within nine months after the later of:
    a) the date on which the transfer creating the interest was made, or
    b) the day on which the person disclaiming reaches age 21.
4. The intended donee cannot have accepted any interest in the benefits.
5. And, as a result of the refusal, the interest must pass (without the disclaiming person's direction) to someone else.

With regard to the fourth requirement, acts indicating "acceptance" include using the property, accepting dividends, interest, or rents from the property, and directing others to act with regard to the property. However, acceptance will not be found in cases where the disclaimant merely accepted title to property or merely because title vested immediately in the disclaimant on death of the decedent, as in the case of survivorship under joint tenancy. Benefits received by a person under 21 years of age are disregarded.[21]

Section 2518(b)(4)(A) creates a special privilege for the spouse of a donor or decedent. He/she may disclaim and still retain benefits in the disclaimed property. This is used in estate plans that call for property disclaimed by the surviving spouse to be placed in a trust that gives her (the disclaimant) a life estate and/or the power to withdraw limited by an ascertainable standard.

Meeting all of these requirements is particularly important because failure to meet any one could result in two completed transfers subject to taxation.

EXAMPLE 7 - 32. Gaylord gives his adult son Daniel his vacation bungalow on the lake, completing the necessary transfer of title. After spending a weekend there, Daniel decides that he hates fishing and can't stand the mosquitos, so he transfers title back to Gaylord. Daniel's act is not a valid disclaimer because he *had already accepted* a benefit. Therefore, two gifts occurred; first the one by Gaylord and then the gift by Daniel.

EXAMPLE 7 - 33. During their life, husband and wife owned their home in joint tenancy. Within nine months of husband's death, wife acts to disclaim her survivorship interest. Her disclaimer is not invalid merely because her survivorship interest vested immediately at his death and she continued to live in the house and pay all expenses and related taxes prior to making the disclaimer, provided that while husband was alive the tenancy could be unilaterally partitioned.[22]

EXAMPLE 7 - 34. Mildred died, disposing of her entire $1.8 million estate by will. It read, "to my husband Henry, if living, and, if not, then to our children." Within the nine months following Mildred's death, Henry, before receiving any interest or benefit in the property, presented a written refusal of "so much of Mildred's estate as equals the exclusion amount" to the executor of her estate. Henry has made a valid disclaimer, and he will not be considered to have ever owned that portion of the property. The disclaimed property will now pass by the terms of the will to the children. This will utilize Mildred's unified credit and reduce Henry's taxable estate.

The present law allowing tax effective disclaimers (meaning ones that do not generate additional taxable transfers) is generally seen as a valuable method for correcting inefficient transfers in wills and trust instruments.[23] Chapter 12 will discuss estate plans that utilize disclaimers to add flexibility to estate plans.

Miscellaneous Gift Tax Applications

Reciprocal gifts. Donors who get together on a scheme to use reciprocal gifts in order to gain additional annual exclusions may find their actions subject to IRS scrutiny. The argument will be that substance should prevail over form.

EXAMPLE 7 - 35. Mr. Garbanzo gives $10,000 to his son and $10,000 to Mrs. Ceci's daughter. At the same time, Mrs. Ceci gives $10,000 to her daughter and $10,000 to Mr. Garbanzo's son. The IRS will treat the "mirror images" cross-family transfers as if they were made to each donor's own child. Thus, each parent will be treated as having made a $20,000 gross gift to his own child.[24]

Multiple taxation of transfers. Certain transfers may be subject to both gift tax and estate tax.

EXAMPLE 7 - 36. Pope, age 55, transfers $100,000 in property into an irrevocable trust, retaining a life estate in the income at a time when the §7520 rate is 8%. Pope's son is the remainderman. Pope has made a completed gross gift this year of $22,601, the current value of the remainder (based on Table B (8%), i.e., 0.22601 x $100,000). As a gift of a future interest, it does not qualify for the annual exclusion. At Pope's death, the date of death value of the entire trust corpus is included in his gross estate under §2036(a). The adjusted taxable gift is reduced to zero, and a credit for any gift tax payable is allowed to prevent double taxation. Of course, if Pope's taxable gifts never exceeded the unified credit shelter amount, no gift taxes would have been paid during his lifetime.

Where transferred property comes back into the gross estate because of a string being attached (§§2036 - 2038) or because the transfer falls under one of the §2035(a) exceptions (transfer of life insurance or the severing of a string), the earlier gift will not be considered an adjusted taxable gift for purposes of calculating the donee's estate tax. The last sentence of §2001(b) defines "adjusted taxable gifts" as being post-1976 taxable gifts "other than gifts which are includable in the gross estate of the decedent." The gift tax payable credit (§2001(b)(2)) is still available because the gift taxes would indeed have been paid on such gifts (if the tentative tax exceeded the available unified credit) and the property subject to the prior gift does enter into the estate tax calculation by being included in the gross estate as if no gift had ever taken place.

Basis Rules

The manner in which one acquires property determines the owner's initial basis in the property. Basis is important for two reasons: 1) basis is the starting point for determining depreciation for depreciable property; and, 2) upon sale, it is the difference between the price (net amount realized) and the adjusted basis that determines the amount of gain or loss for income tax purposes.

Gain and loss. The gain or loss realized from the sale of property is calculated by subtracting an asset's *adjusted basis* from the *amount realized*:

$$Gain\ or\ Loss\ =\ Amount\ Realized\ -\ Adjusted\ Basis$$

EXAMPLE 7 - 37. The realized gain on sale of 100 shares of common stock having an adjusted basis of $13,000 and sold for $16,000, net of selling commissions, equals $3,000. Had the stock been sold for $11,000, a loss in the amount of $2,000 would have been realized.

Amount realized is defined as the fair market value of all money or property received, less selling expenses such as commissions.

EXAMPLE 7 - 38. In the prior example, the $16,000 and $11,000 sales proceeds could have been in the form of cash or in kind. Alternatively, the buyer could have canceled an existing debt owed by the seller. Hence, if the buyer actually paid $6,000 cash and assigned to the seller title to his $8,000 automobile and also tore up a $2,000 IOU held on the buyer-debtor, the total amount realized is still $16,000.

Adjusted basis is defined in the Code as the "basis" that is "adjusted." The initial basis for an asset that is *purchased* is its cost. Adjustments to basis include items that reduce basis, such as allowance for depreciation, depletion, and obsolescence. Adjustment items that increase basis include capital expenditures for improvement.

EXAMPLE 7 - 39. In the earlier example, the adjusted basis of $13,000 was probably simply the original purchase price of the stock, net of the trading commission. However, had the asset been a machine used in the taxpayer's business, adjusted basis would likely reflect its current book (depreciated) value, including all capital improvements made subsequent to its acquisition. Hence, the $13,000 adjusted basis for the machine could, for example, be the net result of a $27,000 original purchase price, less $17,000 in accumulated depreciation, plus $3,000 in capital improvements.

Recapture of depreciation, which arises when a depreciable business asset is sold for greater than its adjusted basis, is beyond the scope of this text other than to say that a portion of the gain (the depreciation recaptured) may be taxed as ordinary income rather than at the more favorable capital gains rate.

Intangible assets (stocks, bonds, etc.) and personal use assets (one's home, the family car, etc.) cannot be depreciated. Therefore fewer adjustments to basis are likely with these types of assets, although they do occur.

Holding period. A gain or a loss can be either short-term or long-term, depending upon the length of the holding period. The holding period is how long the asset was held by the seller and, in the case of property acquired by gift, by prior owners too. A gain or a loss is *short-term* if the holding period is not more than one year; it is *long-term* if the property is held more than one year. Inherited property is automatically considered long-term property. If a taxpayer has both long-term and short-term sales during the year, they are reported separately and each type is netted separately to determine whether there is a gain or a loss. The net gain on the sale of appreciated short-term investments is taxed as ordinary income, whereas the net gain on the sale of long-term investments is taxed at the lower capital gains rate. Presently, the maximum capital gains rate for individuals (estates and trusts, too) is 20% (10% for taxpayers in the 15% bracket). An even lower rate of just 18% (8% for individuals in the 15% bracket) applies to sales made after December 31, 2000, for property that at the time of the sale has been held for more than five years.

Realized versus recognized gains and losses. A gain or loss is *realized* when the basic transaction, typically a sale, has occurred. On the other hand, a gain or loss is *recognized* when the taxpayer reports the gain or loss on a tax return. Recognition will commonly occur either because tax law requires recognition in that year or because the taxpayer elects a Code-permitted option to defer the tax to a later time. Common examples of gains or losses that may be recognized in tax years *after* the year of realization include installment sales,[25] tax-deferred exchanges of like-kind property,[26] involuntary conversion[27] (e.g., destruction of a warehouse by fire with insurance proceeds used to purchase a replacement warehouse), and certain capital transactions between corporations and their shareholders. Generally, the rate in effect when the gain is recognized is the rate that is applied, e.g., the capital gain portion of current payments on an installment sale will benefit from the maximum 20% rate even if the sale took place in a year when the maximum rate was 28%.

Property acquired by gift. As described above, the initial basis for property acquired by *purchase* is its cost, which is later adjusted by such items as depreciation and capital improvements, if any. In this section, we will cover the somewhat more complex rules for determining the basis of property acquired by *gift*. In determining whether the donee's gain or loss is short-term or long-term, the length of the donor's *holding period* is added or "tacked on" to the length of the donee's holding period.

Date of gift value equaling or exceeding donor's basis. A simple rule applies for gift property whose date of gift value is equal to or greater than the donor's adjusted basis at the date of gift: the donee's basis will equal the amount of the donor's adjusted basis (herein, we will just use "basis") at the date of the gift. This is called the donee's *carryover basis* (COB for short).

EXAMPLE 7 - 40. Ten years ago, donor purchased common stock for $10,000. Two years ago, donor gave donee the stock when it was worth $11,500. This year, donee sold the stock for $14,500. Since date-of-gift value was greater than donor's basis, donee has realized a gain of $4,500, the difference between the amount realized ($14,500) and donee's COB basis ($10,000).

EXAMPLE 7 - 41. As in the prior example, except that donee sold the stock for $7,000. Since date-of-gift value is greater than donor's basis, donee's basis is still $10,000. Therefore, donee has realized a loss of $3,000, the difference between the amount realized and donee's COB.

Date of gift value less than donor's basis. If a donee receives property with a date-of-gift value that is less than the donor's basis, then for purposes of calculating a *loss* only, donee's basis will be date-of-gift value. For purposes of calculating a gain, though, the COB rule applies, i.e., the donee's basis is the donor's basis at the date of the gift.

EXAMPLE 7 - 42. Donor acquired property several years ago for $6,000. Last year, when it was worth $4,200, donor gave it to donee, who this year sold it for $3,600. Since date-of-gift value is less than donor's old basis, donee's *basis for loss* is the $4,200 date-of-gift value, and hence donee has realized a loss of only $600.

In effect, the donee is not permitted to recognize the portion of the loss resulting from the property's decline in value while owned by the donor.

EXAMPLE 7 - 43. As in the prior example, except that donee sold the property for $7,100. Although date-of-gift value is less than donor's basis, donee's *basis for gain* is the donor's basis at the date of the gift. In this case, donee's basis is $6,000, and donee has therefore realized a gain of $1,100.

Occasionally, gift property having a date-of-gift value less than the donor's basis is sold by the donee for an amount that is less than donor's basis, but more than date-of-gift value. In this case, the donee realizes neither gain nor loss.

EXAMPLE 7 - 44. Several years ago, donor acquired an asset for $2,000 and later gave it to donee when it was worth $1,450. If donee sells the asset for $1,800, no gain or loss will be realized. Since date of gift value ($1,450) is less than donor's basis at the date of the gift ($2,000), for purposes of calculating a *loss*, donee's basis will be date-of-gift value. There is no loss because the amount realized is greater than donee's basis (i.e., $1,800 minus 1,450 is not negative). On the other hand, for purposes of calculating a *gain*, donee's basis will be donor's basis at the date of the gift ($2,000).

Gift tax may increase basis. If the donor pays gift tax on the gift, a portion of that tax is added to the donor's adjusted basis at the date of the gift to determine the donee's new basis. The amount added is that portion of the tax attributable to appreciation. Appreciation is considered to be the difference between the FMV on the date of gift and the property's basis. Hence:

New Basis = Old Basis + ((FMV Gift - Old Basis)/ FMV Gift)) * Gift Tax

EXAMPLE 7 - 45. In 1997, Donor gave stock, purchased for $400,000 twenty years ago, to Donee. The stock was worth $1,010,000 at the time of the gift. Donor paid gift taxes in the amount of $153,000. Donee's new basis equals $492,406, i.e., $400,000 + (($1,010,000 - $400,000) / $1,010,000) * $153,000.

Summary. For most gifts, the donee's basis for calculating a potential gain is just a carryover of the donor's pre-gift basis. There are two special rules: one for a gift of property that has a fair market value less that the donor's basis on the date of the gift and another where the donor has to pay gift taxes. Where the gift value is lower than the donor's basis, donee's basis for calculating a loss is the date-of-gift value and for gain it is the carryover basis, with sales in between resulting in no gain or loss. Where the donor pays gift taxes, the donee gets a partial step-up in basis. The increase is the portion of the gift tax that is attributed to the net appreciation of the gift. "Net appreciation" is the value of the gift less the donor's pre-gift basis. The product of the net appreciation divided by the full value of the gift times the gift taxes is added to the carryover basis to arrive at the donee's new basis.

Inherited property. As a general rule, the basis of property in the hands of a person acquiring the property from a decedent is the fair market value of the property at the date of the decedent's death.[28] This is true whether the person received the property by bequest, devise or intestate succession, or as a surviving joint tenant.

Notice that the change in the basis of property acquired by another's death can be a "step-up" or "step-down" in the basis depending on whether the decedent's pre-death basis was lower or higher than the value at death. However, common usage is to refer to this change at death as a *step-up* in basis. Where special elections apply such as the alternate valuation date election of §2032 or the special use election of §2032A, the value as shown on the estate tax return determines the basis. To simplify our discussion, the "date of death" (DOD) value should be understood to include the alternate valuation or special use valuation, if such are applicable.

If an estate tax return (Form 706) is filed, there is a rebuttable presumption that the Form 706 values are correct.[29] The change in basis occurs whether or not there is a tax, and, indeed, whether or not a return is filed. Thus, when a person dies, even if he or she leaves a very modest estate, the property in the estate will have a change in basis to the date of death value.

Holding period. The holding period for property acquired from a decedent is *long-term*, regardless of the actual holding period. Thus, a decedent could have purchased the asset shortly before death and the devisee could have sold it shortly after death, and any gain or loss will be long-term.

Individually-owned property. Generally, individually-owned property acquired by death is entitled to a full step-up in basis.

> EXAMPLE 7 - 46. Peter held onto land that he had purchased for $500 in 1930 until his death in 1990, when it passed on to his son Frank. Peter's total estate was about $200,000, so there was no need to file an estate tax return. Frank kept the property for six months and then sold it for $75,000. Frank has a realized long term capital gain of $35,000, the gain being the difference between the sale price and the value established at Peter's death. Since it was acquired from a decedent, the holding period for the property is automatically considered long-term.

Co-owned property. If, at death, the decedent was one of several owners sharing title to property, usually only the decedent's share is stepped-up. The factor that determines whether any *surviving* co-owner can also enjoy a step-up in basis for his or her share depends upon how title is held. In general, the surviving co-owner's share does not receive a step-up in basis unless the asset is either owned as community property or for some reason the survivor's share was included in the deceased co-owner's gross estate.

Community property. The new basis is the FMV at the date of death for both halves of the community property even though only one-half is included in the decedent spouse's estate. This is referred to as a full step-up in basis.

Joint tenancy. What is included in the decedent estate and the surviving co-owner's new basis will follow one of two rules which depend on the relationship between the decedent and the surviving co-owners.

Husband and wife rule. Where the only joint tenants (or tenants by the entirety) are husband and wife, then half of the FMV at the date of death is included in the decedent's estate and the surviving spouse's new basis will equal half the total pre-death basis and half the FMV at the date of death.

$$New\ Basis = (DOD\ FMV + Old\ Basis)\ /\ 2$$

Consideration furnished rule. Where the joint tenants include nonspouses, the rule is that the decedent's gross estate includes that portion of the property as the decedent's share of the consideration bears to the total consideration (i.e., the price paid for the property). Decedent's consideration includes any gifts given to other joint tenants and any share acquired by the prior death of a co-owner.

$$Include = (Decedent's\ Consideration\ /\ Total\ Consideration) * FMV\ DOD$$

The new basis for each surviving co-owner's interest is his or her old basis plus an increase by the amount included in the decedent's estate split equally amongst the surviving joint tenants. The examples that follow demonstrate both rules.

EXAMPLE 7 - 47. Ricky and his wife Victoria owned common stock as *joint tenants*. He paid $5,000 and she paid $11,000 of the original $16,000 purchase price. When Ricky died, the stock was worth $22,000. Four months later, Victoria sold the stock for $29,000. The consideration each paid is irrelevant and Victoria's basis is equal to half the old basis plus half the fair market value at Ricky's death; hence, her realized gain is $10,000 [$29,000 - ($16,000 + $22,000)/2].

Consider the very different outcome for *community property*.

EXAMPLE 7 - 48. Same facts as in the prior example, except that at Ricky's death, he and Victoria owned the common stock as *community property*. Once again half would be included in Ricky's estate but Victoria's basis would be the FMV DOD amount of $22,000, and her gain would be only $7,000.

Thus, ordinarily community property states have a decided advantage over common law states with regard to basis adjustments at death. Couples residing in community property states should hold appreciated property as community property. On the other hand, if the property has decreased in value, community property will receive a full *step-down* in basis at the first death and some other form of title might be preferred.

The IRS takes the position that states recognizing the concept "community property with right of survivorship" (e.g., Nevada and Wisconsin) will not have the advantage of a double step-up in basis, but will be treated as husband and wife joint tenants.

> EXAMPLE 7 - 49. Years ago, brothers Steve and Stan purchased stock for $10,000, taking title as joint tenants. Steve paid $6,000 and Stan paid $4,000 towards the purchase. At Steve's death the stock was worth $20,000. Included in Steve's gross estate is 60% of the stock's value because that corresponds to his share of the consideration paid for the stock, even though property law recognized that he owned 50% of the stock immediately before death. Stan's new basis would be $16,000, which is $12,000 (the amount included in Steve's estate) plus Stan's $4,000 basis in his pre-death interest in the property.

> EXAMPLE 7 - 50. Three friends purchased a vacation cabin in 1980. Abe paid $20,000, Betty paid $30,000, and Cathy paid $50,000 of the $100,000 purchase price. In 1985, when the cabin was worth $160,000, Abe died. His estate included 20% of the DOD FMV, i.e. 20% * $160,000 = $32,000. Betty's new basis in her 50% interest in the cabin became $46,000 (½ * $32,000 + her original consideration of $30,000) and Cathy's new basis is $66,000 (½ * $32,000 + her original consideration of $50,000).

> EXAMPLE 7 - 51. Continuing from the last example, in 1990, Cathy died, leaving Betty as the sole surviving joint tenant. The cabin was then worth $224,000. The amount included in Cathy's gross estate is based on her portion ($66,000) of the combined (hers and Betty's) predeath bases of $112,000. Therefore, included in her estate is $132,000 (($66,000 / $112,000) * $224,000), and Betty's new basis would be $178,000 (the $132,000 included in Cathy's estate plus Betty's old basis of $46,000).

It should be noted that a gift from one prospective co-joint tenant to another is treaded as consideration from the donor, not the donee.

> EXAMPLE 7 - 52. Martin gave his son, Andy, $50,000 shortly before they purchased a vacation condo for $150,000. Martin paid $100,000 on the purchase and Andy paid $50,000. When Martin died, the condo was valued at $200,000, all of which had to be included in his estate because Andy's contribution was traceable to Martin's gift.

Tenants in common rule. Tenancy in common is the preferred form of co-ownership for nonrelatives. It does not have the survivorship feature found in joint tenancy, thus the co-owners control the disposition of their respective shares. Unlike joint tenancy, tenants in common can have unequal undivided shares, meaning that you could have one owner owning 20%, another owning 30%, and the third owning 50%. When a tenant in common owner dies, his or her share of the total FMV DOD of the property is included in the decedent's gross estate. The disposition of a deceased tenant in common's interest depends on the decedent's will or, if there is no will, intestate succession laws.

> EXAMPLE 7 - 53. Friends Arthur, Tony, and Maria purchased property as tenants in common. Of the $100,000 purchase price, Arthur paid $50,000 and took a 50% interest, Tony paid $30,000 and took a 30% interest, and Maria paid $20,000 and took a 20% interest. Years later when Tony died, the property was worth $250,000 and his estate included $75,000 since he owned a 30% interest. If Tony left his interest to his widow Nancy, her basis would be $75,000. If he instead left his interest to co-owner Maria, her total basis in the 50% interest she would then own would be $95,000 ($75,000 + her $20,000 contribution).

Note in the preceding example that because the interests were held as tenants in common, property law recognizes unequal shares.

The Rubber Band Rule of §1014(e). Internal Revenue Code §1014(e) provides that where a person gives away "appreciated property" and then inherits the property from the donee within one year of the original gift (i.e., it comes bouncing back as if it had a rubber band attached when it was given), the adjusted basis of the property to the donor will be donee-decedent's adjusted basis immediately before the donee-decedent's death. Appreciated property means property worth more *at the time of the gift* than its basis. Since the donee had a carryover basis, the donor will also get the property back with the basis unchanged.

> EXAMPLE 7 - 54. Walter gives Kerri, his terminally ill wife, title to land that Walter purchased many years ago for $400. The property has a value on the day of the gift of $90,000. Kerri, who dies two months later, devises the land back to Walter, who then sells it for $95,000. Because the property was appreciated at the time Walter gave it to his wife and she died within one year of the gift, Walter realizes a gain of $94,600 on the sale, not just $5,000.

Hence, there is an advantage to gifting low-basis property, in the case of a donor-devisee, if the donee-decedent lives *at least one year* after the date of gift.

This strategy will work even if the original donor is not the spouse of the decedent, but the original gift will use up the donor's unified credit if it is not covered by the annual exclusion. Section 1014(e) does not apply if the donee-decedent leaves the property to someone other than the original donor or the donor's spouse.

Income in respect of a decedent. One major exception to the step-up in basis rule has to do with what is called income in respect of a decedent. This *income in respect of a decedent* (IRD) consists of income (or realized but not yet recognized capital gain) belonging to the decedent that had not been taxed prior to the decedent's death but that would have been subject to income tax had the decedent received it during life. Examples of IRD include the gain portion of an installment sale promissory note where the gain is being recognized only as principle is collected, the vested amount in a qualified retirement plan, IRA accounts (the value in excess of basis, since IRA's can have a basis), dividends declared but not received at the time of death, commissions earned and paid after death, and business accounts receivables. IRD is subject to both estate tax and, when collected, to income tax. It is reported by the actual recipient (executor, trustee, or beneficiary). If estate tax is paid, the recipient of IRD is allowed an income tax deduction for the estate tax that is attributable to the IRD.[30] The deduction is basically the portion of the estate tax attributable to the IRD collected by the recipient.

This chapter has focused on certain qualitative aspects of the federal gift tax. The next chapter will present a brief overview of the federal fiduciary income tax.

QUERIES ANSWERED:

1. A total of 55%, i.e. $550,000 [4 years @ 15% - 5% = 40% and another 15% for the last year].

QUESTIONS AND PROBLEMS

1. List the common law requirements for a valid gift.

2. Addie sells her empty lot, fair market value of $22,000, to a stranger for $19,500. Is there a gift? Why or why not?

3. Would your answer to Question 2 change if the donee was, in fact, Addie's son? One of her employees?

4. (a) If Jones gives Smith 200 shares of a non-dividend-paying stock, is this a gift of a present or a future interest? Why? (b) Why might it matter?

5. Today Lois transfers $10,000 to an irrevocable trust that is required to distribute all income annually to her son, age 55, for his life. Then, remainder to be distributed outright to his issue. Assuming a 10% federal rate, calculate the amount of Lois's taxable gift.

6. In 2001, Brenda gave her daughter Susan XYZ stock worth $700,000. Because she did not want to pay gift taxes, she talked her husband Fred into splitting the gift. Assuming that the annual exclusion has reached $11,000 by 2001, calculate the taxable gift that must be shown on each spouse's gift tax return.

7. In 1995, John gave his daughter some of his separately owned IBM stock worth $300,000. In 1997, John gave his daughter an additional $400,000 in Microsoft stock.
   a. Assuming neither John nor his wife Jenny had ever made any other taxable gifts, calculate the total amount of gift taxes from these gifts, or if no gift tax is due. State how much unified credit each has used, if:
       1. No gift splitting was employed.
       2. John and Jenny split both years' gifts.
   b. Explain the advantages and disadvantages of gift splitting in this situation.

8. Wayne and his wife Sharon own a parcel of land worth $20,000 as equal tenants in common. This year they gave the land to their daughter Christina. Can this gift be split?

9. Assume that one of your wealthier clients is the reluctant holder of a general power of appointment and is not charitably inclined. What action on her part, if any, might minimize total unified transfer taxes?

10. Ralph established a trust in 1985 which gave Linda income for life, remainder to Linda's three children by right of representation. What would be the effect

on Linda's estate at her death of each clause (considered independently) if such is part of the trust: (Explain your answer).

a. The Trustee is given absolute discretion to transfer the principal of the trust to Linda, if doing so would be in her best interest.
b. I give Linda the power to appoint, by direct reference to this power in her Will, the remainder of the trust amongst her children in such portion as she deems appropriate.
c. I give Linda the right to invade the corpus up to a maximum of 3% of the trust in any one year. This right shall be noncumulative.
d. I give Linda the power to invade the corpus of the trust, up to the whole amount, if such be necessary for her health, education, maintenance, or support.

11. Rachel establishes a trust (worth exactly $1,000,000 at all times relevant here) for the benefit of Arthur during his lifetime, with remainder to Sarah upon Arthur's death. Arthur was 50 years old when the trust was established. The terms of the trust give Arthur the right to demand up to the greater of 5% or $5,000 from the trust in any year, but the right is noncumulative. In years 1, 2, 3, 5, and 6, he did not exercise the right. In year 4, he took out the maximum allowed. With appreciation in the remaining assets, the trust quickly returned to $1,000,000, which was its value in the 6th year when Arthur died.

a. In the first year the power lapsed, what was the gift to Sarah?
b. How much of this trust would be included in Arthur's estate?
c. If the demand right had been the greater of 7% or $7,000, what would be the gift to Sarah in the first year? Would a gift tax return have to be filed?
d. If the demand right had been the greater of 7% or $7,000, how much would be included in Arthur's estate?

12. Five years ago, Frank purchased a $280,000 face value life insurance policy on his own life. A year later he assigned (gave) the policy to his son, when it had a terminal value of $110,000. Four months after making this gift, Frank died. Frank's wife had always been beneficiary. Explain all gift and estate tax consequences. (Hint: there are at least three.) Does the marital deduction come into play?

13. A client asks you to explain when the acquisition by gift of joint tenancy property is taxed.

14. Today, Karen and Sal buy 100 shares of ABC Corp. stock for $21,000, writing a check on their joint (or community) checking account and taking title in joint tenancy. Has a gift occurred? Why or why not?

15. Give an example of a way in which a qualified disclaimer can be a valuable estate planning tool.

16. Explain three reasons why gift splitting can be a valuable estate planning tool.

17. This year, Joe gave $1 million cash to his daughter Mary, who gave it to her son Sal, who gave it to his sister Sue. (a) How many gifts subject to taxation have been made? (b) Can §2518 (disclaimers) help? (c) How about §2013 (estate tax credit for tax on prior transfers)?

18. Congratulations! You have just won the state lottery, entitling you to $2 million cash a year for the next 20 years. You direct that your winnings be shared equally with your spouse and your 28-year-old daughter.

    a. Are there any tax consequences?
    b. Could there have been any way to avoid them?

19. Five years ago, Francisco and Dagny executed a "joint and mutual will", which is a single will, revocable only by mutual consent. Essentially, it provided that the first to die leaves his or her property to the survivor, who then leaves everything to the children at his or her death. Francisco died today. (a) Can you think of any possible immediate tax consequences to Dagny? (b) Would your answer be different if Francisco and Dagny wrote two separate wills (instead of a joint one), again leaving everything to each other, and also executed a contract not to change these wills?

20. During the last ten years of her life, Queenie, a widow, undertook each of the following independent transactions. Explain whether or not each constituted a gift subject to taxation.

a. Purchased a life insurance policy on her life, naming her son beneficiary.
b. Transferred title to her personal residence to her daughter and continued to live there, rent-free, for two years, at which time she moved out and formally relinquished all rights to the property.
c. Funded a revocable living trust.
d. Funded an irrevocable living trust, under which her daughter was the sole beneficiary.
e. Purchased some land, taking title in the names of herself and her son as joint tenants. Queenie paid $90,000 of the $100,000 purchase price, and son paid $10,000.
f. Purchased common stock, taking title in the names of herself and her husband as joint tenants.
g. Purchased life insurance on the life of her uncle, naming her daughter beneficiary. Two years later, uncle died and daughter was paid the proceeds.
h. Paid $21,000 in tuition and $8,000 in room, board, and other fees each year for five years for her son's college education.
i. Opened a joint checking account with her daughter, depositing $26,000 of her own funds.

ANSWERS TO THE QUESTIONS AND PROBLEMS

1. Customary local law requirements for a valid gift: (a) A donor capable of transferring property. (b) A donee capable of receiving and possessing the property. (c) Delivery to the donee, and some form of acceptance. (d) Donative intent (not required for a taxable gift).

2. There is probably no gift, since Addie sold the property to a stranger, at arm's length. Probably a bad bargain.

3. If the donee was Addie's son, Addie probably made a gift of $2,500, since intent was probably donative. On the other hand, if the donee was Addie's employee, the difference in values is probably compensation, taxable to Addie's employee.

4. a. This gift of non-dividend paying stock is a gift of a present interest because, on the whole, enjoyment is not postponed. Smith can still presently enjoy the stock in other ways, such as by selling it.

   b. It might matter because gifts of future interests do not qualify for the annual exclusion.

5. This transfer represents a gift of a present interest to son of a life estate in the trust income for son's life, and a gift of a future interest in the remainder to son's issue. The former gift qualifies for the annual exclusion, while the latter does not. The value of the life estate, based on Table S, is $10,000 times .82550, or $8,255. It will qualify for the annual exclusion. The value of the remainder, $10,000 minus $8,255, or $1,745, is a future interest and will not qualify for the annual exclusion. Thus, the total taxable portion of the gift is $1,745.

6. $339,000 [$700,000/2 - $11,000].

7. a. Calculation of gift taxes and the remaining unused unified credits:

| | No Gift Splitting John's 709 | | Gift Splitting Identical returns x 2 | |
	2 yrs ago	last year	2 yrs ago	last year
Current yr gross gifts	$300,000	$400,000	$150,000	$200,000
- Annual exclusions	($10,000)	($10,000)	($10,000)	($10,000)
= Current tx gifts	$290,000	$390,000	$140,000	$190,000
+ Total prior tx gifts	$0	$290,000	$0	$140,000
= Total taxable gifts	$290,000	$680,000	$14,000	$330,000
Ten. tax total gifts	$84,400	$222,400	$35,800	$98,000
- Ten. tax prior gifts	$0	($84,400)	$0	($35,800)
= Ten. tax current	$84,400	$138,000	$35,800	$62,200
- Unused unified	$84,400	$108,400	($35,800)	($62,200)
Equals: Current gift	$0	$29,600	$0	$0

	Total gift taxes	$29,600		$0
	Unused unified			
	John	$0		$94,800
	Jenny	$192,800		$94,800
	Total	$192,800		$189,600

   b. Advantages: 1) Two additional annual exclusions were utilized (assumes Jenny didn't want to use them herself). 2) No gift tax was due by either spouse. 3) Without gift splitting, John used all of his available unified credit, i.e., $192,8000 and paid gift taxes of $29,600. With gift splitting, they each used $98,000 of their respective unified credits.

Disadvantages: 1) Jenny's annual exclusions for both years were used up. Actually, this is not a problem unless she also wanted to make gifts to her daughter. 2) Jenny's unified credit was reduced by $98,000. However, this also should not be considered a significant problem. If Jenny wishes to make large gifts of her own property, she could agree to split them and she would use part of his unused credit.

8. This gift cannot be split because the property is owned by both spouses (in one sense it is already "split").

9. Doing almost anything will subject the property to transfer taxation. Exercising the power in favor of another or releasing the power are taxable transfers to the extent they exceed the annual exclusion. Thus, by releasing or exercising annual exclusion amounts each year, the holder may be able to reduce her future estate size and avoid transfer taxation on future appreciation of the underlying property.

10. a. Assuming the trustee is independent of Linda and did not transfer any of the corpus to her, the trustee is the holder of a limited power. Therefore nothing is included in Linda's estate.
    b. Linda is the holder of a limited power and nothing is included whether or not she exercised the power.
    c. This is a general power and 3% of the trust's value on her death will be included in her estate, assuming she did not exercise the power that last year. If she did exercise it to the full 3%, then none of the trust would be included, but the property taken out would be in her estate unless she gave it away or consumed it.
    d. This is a power limited by an ascertainable standard as such is defined in §2041 and is therefore considered a limited power; therefore, nothing is included.

11. a. No gift taxes are generated because the gift (the lapse of the right to withdraw $50,000) is covered by the 5 & 5 exception.

   b. The 5 & 5 exception does not apply to lapses at death; therefore, $50,000 would be included in Arthur's estate. Note: nothing is actually taken out of the trust due to this inclusion in Arthur's estate; it is included for calculation purposes only. Any estate tax attributed to this inclusion is charged to the trust.

   c. Each year that a lapse occurred (years 1, 2, 3, and 5) due to a year ending without a withdrawal, a gift occurred of the amount not sheltered by the 5 & 5 exception. Thus for each of those years, a gift of a remainder interest in $20,000 must be reported. In the first year, for example, if the federal rate for future interest gifts was 8%, the gift would be: 0.17697 * $20,000 = $3,539 [Table S (8%), 50 yr old, remainder factor].
   Each year that a lapse occurred, a gift tax return would have been required since the amounts over 5% would be deemed gifts of future interests (no annual exclusion), discounted because of Arthur's retained life estate.

   d. For each year a right to withdraw lapsed at the end of a year, it would be as if Arthur had transferred 2% of the corpus into trust and retained a life estate in the property transferred. Lifetime lapses occurred four years (years 1, 2, 3, and 5), thus for these years 8% of the trust is included. In the last year, the entire 7% lapse is included because there is no 5% shelter for lapses at death. So the total of 15% times the value of the trust at his death is included in his estate. Note that the adjusted taxable gifts become zero even though gift tax returns were filed. This is because adjusted taxable gifts do not include gifts that end up being included in the donor's gross estate.

12. *Gift tax*: a. Frank made a taxable gift four years ago of $100,000 (= $110,000 terminal value minus $10,000 taxable gift value). b. Frank's son made a taxable gift to Frank's wife of $270,000 at Frank's death.
   Estate tax: Frank's gross estate will include $280,000 under Section 2035. There will be a marital deduction of $280,000. In addition, grossing up may be necessary.

13. Generally, a gift in joint ownership is taxed when the transfer is made. However, in the case of a joint bank account, a gift arises when the donee

withdraws funds. In the case of U.S. government bonds, a gift arises at redemption.

14. No gift has occurred because there is no transfer of consideration between them. Each owned the same amount before and after the purchase.

15. One example of the use of disclaimers in estate planning is to reduce a donee's future taxable estate.

16. Advantages of gift splitting: 1) It can sometimes subject gifts to a lower marginal rate of tax. 2) It can possibly shelter the entire gift (of between $10,000 and $20,000) by the annual exclusion, where otherwise a portion of the gift might be taxable, thereby using up the unified credit or, worse, incurring a gift tax. 3) It enables the family to use two unified credits, rather than just one, for large gifts.

17. a. Three taxable gifts have been made, unless some of the parties are married.
    b. Section 2518 (disclaimers) cannot help, since the question implies that each person has accepted the money. (c) The Section 2013(a) credit for tax on prior transfers cannot help because it applies only to estate taxes, not gift taxes.

18. a. The IRS could contend that you have made a present interest gift of one third of the commuted value of the annuity each to your spouse and daughter.
    b. The controversy could have been avoided by sharing the purchase of the lottery ticket with them, or giving each of them, prior to winning, a one-third interest on the tickets, possibly by putting their names on it too. However, the IRS has indicated it will probably challenge oral agreements as having been concocted after the lottery was won.

19. a. Dagny may be deemed today to have made a gift to the children of the remainder interest in her property. At Francisco's death, the transfer provisions became irrevocable for Dagny, since at that moment Francisco, who was one of the parties to the agreed upon will, is no longer able to revoke them. Thus, the provisions of the will are now binding on Dagny. In fact, some jurisdictions such as Illinois would consider Dagny's interest

to be simply a life estate, which would deny the marital deduction in Francisco's estate and make Dagny obligated to conserve the property for the benefit of the children.[31] Since Dagny's gift is not one of a present interest, it would not qualify for the annual exclusion. For these reasons, joint and mutual wills are not recommended by estate planners.

b. If Francisco and Dagny executed an enforceable contract not to change these wills, the answer would be essentially the same. The will in part a, in effect, became an irrevocable, enforceable contract at the moment of Francisco's death.

20. a. Not a gift. Queenie's powers to change the beneficiary and permit the policy to lapse means that son received only a (discretionary) contingent future interest, not a completed gift.

b. Probably a gift of at least the remainder subject to tax at time of title transfer. Definitely a gift subject to taxation by the time she relinquished all retained rights.

c. Never a gift subject to taxation, since revocable.

d. A gift subject to taxation. Only present interests, if any, will qualify for the annual exclusion.

e. $40,000 gift to son. It is the difference between the consideration given and the property received ($50,000 - $10,000).

f. A gift to husband, but not subject to taxation. Ordinarily, no form 709 need be filed, and the gift is totally sheltered by the unlimited marital deduction.

g. Assuming that Queenie owned the policy at her uncle's death, there is a gift of the proceeds to her daughter since at the moment of her uncle's death, Queenie could have named herself beneficiary.

h. A gift of $29,000, subject to taxation. However, $21,000 would be excludable if for a qualified tuition payment. The remaining $8,000 should qualify for the annual exclusion.

i. Gift subject to taxation will occur either upon deposit of money or upon daughter's later withdrawal, depending upon the law of Queenie's residence state.

ENDNOTES

1. Reg. §25.2511-2(b).

2. §2501(a)(2), §2511(a).

3. §2516.

4. §2502(c).

5. §102(a).

6. *Diedrich* 457 U.S. 191 (1982).

7. §2522(a).

8. §2503(g).

9. §2523.

10. §2056(b)(7).

11. §2523(i).

12. §2503(e).

13. §2501(a)(5).

14. §2503(b).

15. §63(c)(5), §1(g)(7)(B)(i).

16. The Revenue Act of 1948.

17. §2513.

18. TAM 9128009; §2035(b).

19. §2514(b).

20. Reg. 20.2041-3(d)(5), see also Reg. 20.2041-3(d)(4).

21. Reg. 25.2518-2(3).

22. Reg. §25.2518-2 (d)(1); LR 9135043; LR 9135044; TAM 9208003.

23. Reg. §25.2518-1(b).

24. TAM 88717003.

25. §453.

26. §1031.

27. §1033.

28. §1014(a).

29. Revenue Ruling 54-97, 1954-1 C.B. 113.

30. §691(c)(3).

31. TAM 9023004; *Grimes v. Commissioner* 82-2 USTC (1988).

CHAPTER 8

Fiduciary Income Taxation

OVERVIEW

An estate or trust is a separate legal entity created to transfer property from one party to another. Since both are separate legal entities, each must file a tax return, Form 1041 (the Fiduciary Income Tax return), annually with the Internal Revenue Service (IRS) to report the trust's or estate's taxable events for the year. Fiduciary income taxation is unique because the fiduciary entity can be both a taxable entity and a conduit. As a taxable entity, the estate or trust must pay the required tax due within the prescribed time or be subject to various tax penalties. As a conduit, the entity reports to the beneficiaries how much of the taxable income is included on the beneficiaries' individual income tax returns. All of the entity's taxable events are classified and reported to the IRS by the entity.

The fiduciary is responsible for filing the decedent's final 1040 (the regular Income Tax return) and the 1041's for the trust or estate. If an amount is properly recorded on the final 1040, it is not reported on the first 1041. Death forms a wall between the two tax entities. Once a person dies, his or her tax year ends; therefore, any item collected or paid after death is generally not includible on the deceased's final income tax return. Do not confuse income taxation and transfer taxation. These are two independent tax systems and certain items are taxable for both purposes.

FIDUCIARY ACCOUNTING

Before a fiduciary tax return can be prepared, the income and expenses, for book purposes, must be determined, which mandates an understanding of fiduciary accounting. Further, an understanding of fiduciary accounting is needed to comprehend the tax terminology of Subchapter J (Estates, Trusts, Beneficiaries, and Decedents) of the Internal Revenue Code (IRC). The IRC uses many concepts from fiduciary accounting in determining the taxation of income from a fiduciary entity.

Goals of Fiduciary Accounting

It has long been recognized that fiduciary accounting has a purpose different from financial or tax accounting, and that fiduciary accounting standards are not well defined. Unlike financial accounting, fiduciary accounting must rely on the entity's controlling document (e.g., the will or trust) and state law. A fiduciary entity results from the division of legal and beneficial interests in property. The fiduciary is responsible for managing assets placed under his or her care for the benefit of the beneficiaries. The managerial process places on the fiduciary various duties and obligations. Determining how well the fiduciary carried out his or her duty is one of the primary the goals of fiduciary accounting. Through the preparation of certain reports, the fiduciary can describe to the beneficiaries the results of his or her activities and allows the beneficiaries to judge if the fiduciary has been a good steward. These reports should provide maximum clarity, full disclosure, and a complete description and explanation of all events during the accounting period. Fiduciary accounting uses the cash method for recording transactions.

Allocation Between Corpus and Income

Fiduciary accounting income (FAI) represents the claims of the income beneficiaries against the various inflows and outflows of the entity. Computing the exact amount each beneficiary is entitled to receive is part of the fiduciary's responsibilities. Fiduciary accounting rules provide the mechanism for the accurate allocation of assets between the beneficiaries.

Although most preparers would record inflows as income, this treatment would adversely affect the remaindermen. Further recording all outflows as expense would adversely affect the income beneficiaries. Therefore, a system has been developed to protect the interests of both beneficiaries by allocating the inflows and outflows between income and corpus to compute the correct amounts available to the particular beneficiaries.

The *Uniform Principal and Income Act* (UPIA) was drafted to compute a fair allocation between income and corpus. The UPIA was revised in 1962 and a 1997 revision has been adopted by the National Conference of Commissioners on Uniform State Laws. Until a state makes the UPIA state law, it merely serves as a model of how income and corpus should be computed. Since most states have adopted some version of the UPIA, a review of the Act is helpful in understanding how items should usually be allocated. According to the UPIA, a fiduciary allocates receipts and expenditures using the following steps:

1. The governing document determines how the allocation is to be made;
2. If the document does not provide for the allocation, then state law controls; or
3. If neither allocates the particular item, the fiduciary (executor or trustee) is to use his or her best judgment according to what is reasonable and equitable in view of all beneficiaries' interests in the entity.

The grantor has considerable flexibility in determining how the income from the trust will be determined. When creating the trust, the grantor is allowed to state what items will be attributed to the income beneficiaries and what amounts should remain for the remaindermen. This latitude gives the grantor the ultimate responsibility for determining what property should go to which beneficiary. If the grantor wants every inflow to increase income and every outflow to reduce corpus, then his or her wishes should be followed, since it is the grantor's property that is being allocated. The intent of the grantor is paramount in the allocation of items between income and corpus. Due to the flexibility given the grantor, various items that are income/expense under financial accounting might not be so categorized under fiduciary accounting.

Two additional rules should be remembered while computing fiduciary accounting income:

1. Specific statutes control over general statutes, and
2. Directly related expenditures reduce the related type of receipt.

EXAMPLE 8 - 1.   Under the UPIA, rental income is expressly stated to be income; therefore, the provisions applying to sole proprietorships cannot be used to allocate rental income between beneficiaries. Further, all rental expenses would be deducted from rental income in computing FAI.

What an income beneficiary is entitled to receive from the trust is based on the computation of fiduciary accounting income. The income beneficiary is not allowed to receive any item that is not an income item. If the trust did not receive any income items during the accounting period, the income beneficiary would not receive any distributions. Incorrect allocation results in the wrong beneficiary believing he or she has a claim to a given amount of assets. The fiduciary cannot show favoritism between income beneficiaries and remaindermen or between beneficiaries within the same classification. While the UPIA allows the grantor to give the trustee discretion in determining what amounts are allocated to income and corpus, the trustee's discretion is not as broad as that of the grantor.[1] When discretion is given in the trust document, the trustee must use reasonable discretion in his or her allocations, basing them on the intent of the grantor when construing the entire trust instrument aided by the surrounding circumstances.[2] Terms like "absolute" or "full authority" does not alter the trustee's responsibility to impartially act for the benefit of all beneficiaries.[3]

Effect of Fiduciary Accounting Income on Taxable Income

On the income tax return, the fiduciary is allowed a deduction for income distributions. The amount of this deduction is based on the distributions allowed by the fiduciary entity (the trust or estate) determined under applicable state law. Once the appropriate distribution has been determined, the deductible amount may be limited by federal tax laws. This interrelationship between the Code and state law applies throughout this area of the law, so understanding the state law in this area is very important to determining the correct amount of trust accounting income.

Section 643(b) of the IRC states:

For purposes of this subpart and subparts B, C, and D, the term "income," when not preceded by the words "taxable," "distributable net," "undistributed net," or "gross," means the amount of income of the estate or trust for the taxable year determined under the terms of the governing instrument and applicable local law. Items of gross income constituting extraordinary dividends or taxable stock dividends which the fiduciary, acting in good faith, determines to be allocable to corpus under the terms of the governing instrument and applicable local law shall not be considered income.

Knowing how to compute FAI for the year is vital to preparation of a correct tax return. Furthermore, the taxation of the beneficiaries is based on the amount of distribution to which each is entitled, which in turn is controlled by the trust (or other fiduciary documents) or the state's principal and income laws.

FIDUCIARY INCOME TAXATION

The primary purpose of Subchapter J is to allocate income and deductions between the fiduciary entity and the beneficiaries. Form 1041 is the only tax form designed to serve in a twin capacity. A fiduciary entity can be a taxpaying entity and/or a conduit, flowing various income and expense items out to the beneficiaries. To complicate matters further, proper preparation of Form 1041 requires the preparer to integrate fiduciary accounting income into the computations, so the correct allocation can be determined.

Subchapter J: An Overview of Fiduciary Taxation

Throughout our discussions, always remember that Subchapter J was written not to compute taxable income specifically, but to allocate taxable income to the appropriate party, either the fiduciary entity or the beneficiary.

Section 641 (b)

Section 641 (b) is the key section used to compute the taxable income of the fiduciary entity. Section 641 (b) states:

> *The taxable income of an estate or trust shall be computed in the same manner as in the case of an individual, except as otherwise provided in this part. The tax shall be computed on such taxable income and shall be paid by the fiduciary.*

Since a fiduciary entity is recognized as a separate legal entity, remembering that it is taxed like a person is difficult; however, unlike a partnership or a corporation, a fiduciary entity has been created for managing and eventually transferring property. Due to its unique characteristic, operating a fiduciary entity has more similarities with an individual and his or her handling of property than any other tax entity; therefore, it is logical that the IRC uses the tax rules applicable to individuals in computing the taxable income of a fiduciary entity. If the preparer cannot find a different treatment of any income or expense item in the IRC or regulations, he or she should report the item as one would on a Form 1040.

Tax Accounting Method

A fiduciary entity can use any tax accounting method available to individuals. Selection of accounting method is made on the first Form 1041 filed. Once selected, any change in method is subject to the limitations found in §446. The choice of methods is not limited or determined by the accounting methods used by either the grantor, decedent or the beneficiaries.

Selecting a Fiduciary Income Tax Year

For trusts there is really no choice, they must use a calendar year.[4] Estates do not have the same restriction, so the estate's fiduciary can elect any year that ends on the last day of any month that is not more than 12 months from the date of death.[5] An estate begins on the day after the person dies. Providing the first year does not end more than 12 months after the decedent died, the executor's choice of year end will be acceptable. Beneficiaries must report on their income tax returns income from the fiduciary entity, based not on when the beneficiary received it, but rather as if it was all distributed to the beneficiary on the last day of the *fiduciary entity's tax year*.

> EXAMPLE 8 - 2. Joe died March 23, 1999. The executor elected January 31, 2000, as the end of the estate's first taxable year. In November 1999, the executor made distributions. Any taxable income allocated to the beneficiaries, based on those distributions, is reported by them on their 2000 tax returns.

Regulation §1.641(b)-3 holds that the IRS can terminate the estate for Federal tax purposes and begin taxing the estate as a trust. If the period of administration is unreasonably prolonged,[6] even if a probate court sanctions the continued existence of the estate, the IRS will begin taxing the estate as a trust, if the Service determines that all of the acts generally conducted by an executor have been (or should have been) completed.[7] Taxing the estate as a trust requires the estate to adopt a calendar year-end, forcing it to file a short year return. The provisions of §§446 and 481 (pertaining to adjustments that must be made when a taxpayer changes accounting methods and/or tax year) will be applied to the short year return.

Section 645 was added for decedents dying after August 5, 1997. If both the executor of an estate and the trustee of a Qualified Revocable Trust (QRT) irrevocably elect, the QRT will be taxed as part of the estate for income tax purposes and not as a separate trust. A QRT is a trust or a portion thereof that was treated prior to the decedent's death as a grantor trust under §676. The election applies for the first two taxable years of an estate, if no Form 706 is required to be filed, and for the period ending six months after the final determination of Federal Estate Tax liability, if a Form 706 was filed. Effectively, the trust is merged with the estate and all income and deductions are taxed under the income tax provisions that apply to estates. The election is included with the estate's first income tax return and a copy is attached to the trust's income tax return. The election is effective from the date of death.

The statement attached to the returns must identify itself as the election to include the QRT in the decedent's estate, specify the date of death and recite that the trust had been treated as a revocable grantor trust under §676. It must include the names, addresses and identification numbers of the decedent, the estate and trust. Both the executor (or administrator, if the decedent died intestate) and one trustee must sign and date the statement. Multiple executors and trustees do not have to sign the statement, unless required by local law. If no probate is required, the trustee must sign the statement and note on the statement that no executor or administrator will be appointed. The estate must still obtain a tax identification number, but the trustee will sign every Form 1041 filed for the estate.[8]

An Overview of the Computations

Step one: Determine *adjusted total income*, using the tax rules for individuals, with certain modifications.

Step two: Determine the *income distribution deduction*.

Step three: Subtract the income distribution deduction (this amount is taxed to the beneficiaries) from adjusted total income.

Step four: The amount remaining is subject to tax at the fiduciary level.

The nature of income and of deductions is determined at the fiduciary level. If any income is distributed, it has the same characteristics it would have had if the fiduciary had retained it. Unless the trust document calls for some other allocation, amounts distributed to the beneficiaries consist of a proportional amount of every type of income received by the fiduciary, except capital gains are considered part of corpus and therefore are not generally allocated to beneficiaries unless the governing document requires it, or the entity terminates and all corpus (including, of course, the capital gains for the year) is distributed to the beneficiaries.

Exemptions. While a fiduciary entity is not allowed a standard deduction or a personal exemption, §642(b) allows an exemption depending on the nature of the entity. An estate is allowed a $600 deduction. If a trust must distribute all of its trust accounting income (TAI) currently, it is allowed a $300 deduction. All other trusts are allowed a $100 exemption.

EXAMPLE 8 - 3. Trust Z's governing document requires Trust Z to distribute all of its TAI currently. For the year, Trust Z makes an additional $20,000 corpus distribution. Trust Z is allowed a $300 exemption.

EXAMPLE 8 - 4. Trust X is not required to distribute all of its TAI currently, but the Trustee makes actual distributions exceeding its current year's TAI. Trust X is allowed a $100 exemption only, since the Trust was not required to distribute 100% of its TAI.

Tax rates. Trusts and estates have their own tax rates. Notice that it does not require very much taxable income to make it into the highest tax bracket.

TABLE 8-1 Federal Income Tax Rates: Estates and Trusts - **1999**

Taxable Income		Base amount	+ percent	On excess over
Over	But not over			
$0	$1,750	$0	15.0%	$0
$1,750	$4,050	$263	28.0%	$1,750
$4,050	$6,200	$907	31.0%	$4,050
$6,200	$8,450	$1,573	36.0%	$6,200
$8,450	----	$2,383	39.6%	$8,450

Capital gains. The capital gain and capital loss rules that apply to individuals also apply to estates and trusts.

Filing requirements. Generally, a decedent's estate must file a Form 1041 if: (a) the estate has annual gross income of $600 or more, or (b) the estate has a beneficiary who is a nonresident alien. A trust must file a Form 1041 if: (a) the trust has any taxable income, or (b) the trust has gross income of $600 or more, or (c) the trust has a beneficiary who is a nonresident alien

The return is due by the 15th of the 4th month following the entity's year end and is filed with the Service center for the region in which the fiduciary resides or has its principal place of business. An extension can be obtained by filing Form 8736 for trusts and Form 2758 for estates. Additional time is obtained by filing Form 8800. Fiduciary returns may be filed electronically.

Form 56, Notice Concerning Fiduciary Relationship, should be filed when the trust or estate is created. Form SS-4 must be filed to obtain the fiduciary entity's employer identification number. Although it is called an employer identification number, it is the tax identification number used for income tax reporting, regardless of whether the fiduciary entity has employees.

Taxable Income of a Fiduciary Entity

As we consider some of the different types of income that trusts and estates might receive, we will compare the treatment of these various types of income in the hands of the fiduciary with how it is treated when received by an individual taxpayer.

Interest and dividend income. Individual income tax rules apply to a fiduciary entity in the reporting of interest and dividend. Interest that would have been tax-exempt to an individual, is tax-exempt when received by a trust or estate. The fiduciary is not required to list separately the sources of dividend and interest income. Capital gain distributions received by the fiduciary entity are reported on Schedule D, Form 1041, just as capital gain distributions received by an individual are reported on Schedule D, Form 1040.

Net business and farm income. If an entity operates a sole-proprietorship or a farm, a Schedule C, Form 1040, Schedule C-EZ, Form 1040 or a Schedule F, Form 1040 must be prepared and attached to the Form 1041. The same rules that apply to individuals, when preparing the Schedule C, C-EZ, or F, apply to the entity.

Rents, royalties, partnerships, other estates and trusts, etc. All income from rents, royalties, partnerships, S corporations, other fiduciary entities, and Real Estate Mortgage Investment Conduits are recorded on Schedule E, Form 1040, and the net amount is reported on Form 1041. While preparing Schedule E, all directly related expenses are netted against the gross income from the particular activity. Only the net income is recorded on Form 1041. Interest, dividends, capital gains/losses and ordinary gains or losses from partnerships and other flow-through entities are shown on the appropriate lines on Form

1041 and not on Schedule E. Only estates, grantor trusts, qualified Subchapter S trusts, and Electing Small Business trusts can be S Corporation shareholders.

Net rental and royalty income. In reporting the net income or loss from rent and royalties, the fiduciary must attach Schedule E, Form 1040, to the Form 1041. The amounts shown on Schedule E reflect the total amount of income and expenses directly related to the property but only the entity's share of the depreciation or depletion.

Passive activities. Trusts and estates are subject to the passive activity loss rules and the at-risk rules. In determining the deductible amount of any loss, the at-risk rules are applied first and then the passive activity rules.

A passive activity is a trade or business in which the taxpayer does not materially participate. Based on the Senate Finance Report, the participation of the fiduciary, not the grantor, decedent or beneficiaries, is used to decide if the activity is passive. Currently, no regulations exist establishing a material participation standard for a fiduciary, to help in determining if the activity is active or passive.

> EXAMPLE 8 - 5. Sue was a partner in a computer retail store. The partnership did not have a buy-sell agreement, so when she died, her share of the partnership was transferred to her estate. The executor does not participate in the store's operations. Even if Sue materially participated in the store's operations, her partnership interest will be treated as a passive activity in the hands of the executor and on the Form 1041.

Passive activities - rental real estate offset. A rule limiting the effect of the passive loss limitation rules is the rental real estate offset.[9] If an individual owner of rental real estate actively participates in the management of the rental property, he or she can offset against other income up to $25,000 of net losses. The offset is phased out once his or her modified adjusted gross income exceeds $100,000 and is eliminated once his or her modified adjusted gross income exceeds $150,000.

A trust is not allowed to use the offset. The characterization of property in the hands of the grantor does not carry over to the trust. Even if the trustee or a beneficiary actively participated in the management of the rental real estate, the trust is prevented from using the offset. The character of the loss is determined at the fiduciary level.

An estate is allowed to use the offset for taxable years ending within two years of the decedent's death, providing the *decedent* actively participated in the management of the rental property before his or her death. The offset available to the estate is reduced by how much of the offset is used when preparing the surviving spouse's tax return or the decedent's final 1040.[10]

Concluding remarks about passive activities. For partnership years after December 31, 1997, when a partner dies, the partnership year closes with respect to the deceased partner. Instead of showing the entire distributive share on Form 1041, the deceased partner's share of partnership income, up to the date of death, is reported on the decedent's final 1040. All income after the decedent's death until the end of the partnership's taxable year is shown on the estate's income tax return. The same procedure for allocating S Corporation income can be used to allocate the partnership income between the Final 1040 and the first 1041. Passive losses are not deductible for alternative minimum tax purposes. Net losses from passive activities cannot be transferred to beneficiaries, but are suspended at the entity level, used by the entity to reduce future passive income and become basis adjustments at distribution of the activity. If a passive activity is sold by an entity, any suspended losses could become either a capital loss or a NOL. The rules applicable to allocation of capital losses or a NOL at termination would then govern the loss allocation.

Capital gains and losses. Capital gains and losses are reported on Schedule D, Form 1041. This is one of the few support schedules unique to fiduciary taxation. Parts I and II of Schedule D, Form 1041, are similar to Schedule D, Form 1040. The difference between the two forms is Part III of Schedule D, Form 1041. Part III reflects the allocation of gain or loss between the beneficiaries and the entity. All capital transactions are recorded on Part I and II, Form 1041, with the net gain or loss being reported on Form 1041. The sole purpose of Part III is to record the gain included in distributable net income (DNI).[11]

Sections 1211-1212 (limitations on capital losses and their carryover) and §§1221-1223 (general rules related to capital gains and losses) apply to trusts and estates, just as they do for individuals. Depending on what type of property created the long tem capital gain and the entity's tax rate, the tax rate on long-term capital gains can be 28%, 25%, 20%, 15% or 10%. Individual holding period rules apply when determining if the capital gain or loss is either short or long-term, however one of those rules is that property received from a decedent is automatically long-term.[12] If the entity acquired the asset from a decedent, §1014 is followed to compute the entity's basis, while §1015 is used if the asset was acquired in an inter vivos transfer.

If an entity has a net capital loss, the maximum deduction in a single tax year is $3,000, with no limitation on the length of time the loss is carried forward. Capital losses cannot be allocated to beneficiaries while the entity exists and capital losses never reduce DNI, just as capital gains normally do not increase it. Section 642(h)(1) provides that in the entity's final year, a net capital loss or loss carry forward can be allocated to the beneficiaries using the same rules applicable to allocation of a NOL.

Section 643(e)(3) election. Normally, the entity recognizes no gain or loss when non-cash property is distributed to a beneficiary. Each year, the entity may elect, under §643(e)(3), to treat the distribution as a sale to the beneficiary and recognize any gain or loss on the appropriate schedule, subject to §267 related party rules.[13] If the election is made and the distributed property is a capital asset, the distribution is recorded as a sale of a capital asset, subject to the general capital transaction rules. The election must be made each year, applies to all non- cash distributions for the elected year and once elected cannot be revoked for that year without IRS consent. Unless the distribution meets the requirements of §663(a), i.e, it's a specific or pecuniary bequest, the distribution is included in any DNI allocation, subjecting the beneficiary to taxation.

> EXAMPLE 8 - 6. Dottie's estate distributes 50 shares of stock to Helen, the residuary beneficiary of Dottie's estate. The estate's basis is $100 and the FMV of the stock is $150. If the §643(e)(3) election is made, the estate must recognize a gain of $50 on the "sale" of stock. Since the stock was received from a decedent, the gain will be long-term. The distribution draws out DNI to Helen.

> EXAMPLE 8 - 7. If, by her will, Dottie had left the XYZ stock specifically to Helen, §663(a) would apply and no DNI would be drawn out by the distribution.

Ordinary gain or loss. When reporting ordinary gains or losses, the rules applicable to individuals also apply to fiduciaries. The fiduciary will prepare Form 4797 (Sales of Business Property) and report any ordinary gain or loss from the sale of property, other than capital assets, and from involuntary conversions, other than casualty or theft. If the entity sells a depreciated asset, Form 4797 is completed to compute the ordinary gain and any depreciation recapture. Gains from casualty and theft are also included on this form. Sales of business assets subject to §1231 are reported on this form, whether the property was owned by the entity or by a partnership in which the entity had an interest.

Deductions Allowed in Computing Taxable Income

Generally, the rules for individual taxpayers claiming a deduction carry over to fiduciary income taxes. However, there are some special rules concerning deductions for fiduciary income taxes, such as those that come into play when the fiduciary entity has tax-exempt income.

Interest expense. A fiduciary entity is allowed to deduct interest expense in the same manner as an individual.[14] The fiduciary must classify the interest according to type and then apply any special rules in determining if the interest is deductible. If the interest expense directly relates to a passive activity, trade or business, or other type of income, the interest should be deducted against the specific income type, not as a separate item. Personal interest (i.e., interest on a car loan) is not deductible. The main types of deductible indirect interest are: qualified residence interest and investment interest expenses (unless it is directly related to tax-exempt income).

Deductible interest owed at death can qualify as a deduction in respect of a decedent and becomes deductible by an estate or trust when paid. Interest accruing after the death of the decedent is subject to the double deduction rules under §642(g), which are discussed below. Only interest that the trust or estate is obligated to pay may be deducted.

Expenses related to tax-exempt income. No deduction is allowed for any expense attributable directly or indirectly to tax-exempt income.[15] On Form 1041, only the deductible share of such expenses are recorded. Form 1041 requires an allocation support schedule, showing how the figures were obtained and the gross amount of tax-exempt income. The purpose of allocating the expenses is to reduce the deductible expenses, so that only those related to taxable income are actually deducted.

Any expense directly related to taxable income can be fully deducted. If the fiduciary incurs $5,000 of rental expenses, these can be deducted in full. The problem occurs when the fiduciary incurs expenses associated with trust income as a whole. Most often these indirect expenses are nonbusiness expenses deductible under §212, e.g., trustee and attorney fees. Interest and taxes should be fully deductible, since they are deductible under specific IRC sections. The IRS and the courts paint a broad stroke when defining what is an indirect expense. The fiduciary must be prepared to defend his or her position if he or she excludes a particular indirect expense from reduction. If the trust or estate makes a distribution to a charity, the charitable contribution deduction must also be reduced, since the charity is deemed to receive part of the tax-exempt income.

Indirect expenses of the entity must be reduced by a proportionate share of the tax-exempt income. The fiduciary is allowed to use any reasonable method, based on the facts and circumstances.[16] However, two methods are provided for in the regulations. Under both methods, the net income or the gross income method, the fiduciary computes a ratio to figure out how much of the indirect expenses are not deductible.

With the *net income method*, the fiduciary computes the amount of gross FAI and then subtracts the expenses directly related to each particular income item. Then for each specific type of income, a ratio is computed, with the numerator being the net amount of that specific type of income and the denominator being the total net FAI.

With the *gross income method*, the fiduciary uses gross FAI as his or her denominator and gross income from the activity as his or her numerator. The only difference between the net income method and the gross income method is that with the gross income method directly related expenses are not subtracted before the allocation is made. Normally, direct expenses have a larger impact on taxable income; therefore, use of the gross income method will increase deductible expenses, since a smaller amount of the indirect expenses is being allocated to tax-exempt income.

Unless capital gains are included in FAI or in DNI, none of the expenses are allocated to capital gains, since expenses cannot be allocated against income that is excluded from DNI. If the amount of expenses directly attributable to tax-exempt income exceeds the total amount of tax-exempt income, the excess cannot be allocated to taxable income.[17]

EXAMPLE 8 - 8. Trust Z has rental income of $15,000, dividends of $10,000 and tax-exempt income of $5,000. The Trust had rental expenses of $4,000 and accounting fees of $2,000. Using both methods, accounting fees would be allocated as follows:

Fiduciary accounting income:

	Gross	Net
Rental income	$15,000	$11,000
Dividends	$10,000	$10,000
Tax-exempt income	$5,000	$5,000
Trust accounting income	$30,000	$26,000

Allocation of accounting fees: Net income method

($11,000/$26,000)	X	$2,000	=	$846
($10,000/$26,000)	X	$2,000	=	769
($5,000/$26,000)	X	$2,000	=	385
		Total		$2,000

Allocation of accounting fees: Gross income method

($15,000/$30,000)	X	$2,000	=	$1,000
($10,000/$30,000)	X	$2,000	=	667
($5,000/$30,000)	X	$2,000	=	333
		Total		$2,000

Under the gross income method, only $333 of accounting fees would not be deducted, whereas the net income method results in $385 not being deducted.

Depreciation. If a fiduciary entity owns qualified property, it is allowed to deduct depreciation, depletion and amortization (after this called depreciation), using the same rules applicable to individuals. Estates and trusts are not allowed a §179 deduction. The fiduciary selects the appropriate depreciation method, prepares Form 4562 and attaches it to Form 1041 to show the total amount of deductible depreciation. While the deductible amount is computed at the fiduciary level, the fiduciary entity **may not** be eligible to take any depreciation deduction. Depreciation must be apportioned between the entity and its beneficiaries under special rules. Deductible depreciation allocated to the entity from a partnership, trust, or estate is allocated under the same rules. The asset's basis is computed using the rules in §1014, for testamentary transfers, or §1015, for inter vivos transfers.

If the entity is entitled to take all or part of the deduction, depreciation directly related to a particular activity is reported on the specific support schedule (Schedules C, E or F), while all other depreciation is reported on Line 15a, Form 1041. If the entity is **not** entitled to a depreciation deduction, **no** deduction is recorded on Form 1041 nor on any support schedule. Tax depreciation not reported on Form 1041 is allocated to the income beneficiaries is reflected on their Schedule K-1, Lines 4 b, c, d or Lines 5 b, c, d.

Depreciation Apportionment rules. Apportionment of depreciation is covered in §642(e), which states:

> *An estate or trust shall be allowed the deduction for depreciation and depletion only to the extent not allowable to beneficiaries under §§167(d) and 611(b).*

Section 167(d) applies to depreciation, while §611(b) pertains to depletion. The general rule for allocating depreciation between the entity and its beneficiaries is:

1. To the extent there is a reserve for depreciation for FAI purposes, allocate the tax depreciation to the entity, and
2. If tax depreciation exceeds accounting depreciation or if there is no depreciation reserve for accounting purposes, allocate the tax depreciation between the entity and the beneficiaries based on the allocation of FAI between the parties.[18]

The key to apportioning the tax depreciation between the entity and its beneficiaries is determined by how depreciation is handled for FAI purposes. Whether a reserve exists for FAI purposes is based on the terms of the document and state law. Generally, a reserve exists when FAI is reduced by some amount of depreciation. The fiduciary may reduce FAI for depreciation when the entity operates a sole proprietorship or general partnership and when the document requires a depreciation deduction or the fiduciary makes an improvement that would be depreciated under generally accepted accounting principles (GAAP). Depending on the state, income from rental property and natural resources may be reduced by depreciation. To the extent FAI is reduced by depreciation, the tax depreciation is allocated to the entity.

EXAMPLE 8 - 9. Trust X owns a drug store, which is operated as a sole proprietorship. GAAP depreciation equals $10,000 and net income from the store is $50,000. If tax depreciation is equal to or less than $10,000, all of the tax depreciation will be reported on Schedule C, Form 1041. If tax depreciation is $15,000, the extra $5,000 is allocated under the set of rules discussed next.

When tax depreciation exceeds the reserve or there is no reserve for FAI purposes, tax depreciation follows FAI. Any beneficiary who receives FAI receives the "excess" tax depreciation, also. For accounting purposes, a charity is treated as any other beneficiary, so if the charity receives FAI, the charity would receive its share of tax depreciation, too. If no reserve exists and the entity is required to distribute all the FAI, the beneficiaries would be entitled to the entire depreciation deduction, and no depreciation deduction would taken on Form 1041.

> EXAMPLE 8 - 10. Trust Y has rental property. Under state law, no depreciation is allowed and the document is silent concerning a reserve. Since FAI is not reduced by depreciation, the allocation of tax depreciation follows the allocation of FAI. For tax purposes, rental depreciation is $20,000. FAI is $50,000. By the terms of the trust, FAI was allocated as follows: Allan - 50%; Bea - 25%; Charity - 10% and Trust Y - 15%. The tax depreciation would be allocated as follows: Allan - $10,000; Bea - $5,000; Charity - $2,000 and Trust Y - $3,000. Trust Y would file Form 4562 (Depreciation and Amortization) to report the $20,000 of depreciation and it would include $3,000 on Schedule E, Form 1041. The depreciation allocated to Allan and Bea would be recorded on their Schedules K-1, Line 5b and the trustee would inform the Charity of the $2,000 depreciation allocation. Charities do not receive a Schedule K-1, since Schedule K-1 is reserved for beneficiaries who receive distributable net income.

> EXAMPLE 8 - 11.   Trust Z owns rental property. For FAI, depreciation of $10,000 is deducted. Tax depreciation is $25,000. By the terms of the trust, FAI is allocated as follows: Art - 60%; Beth - 30% and Trust Z - 10%. The first $10,000 of tax depreciation must be allocated to Trust Z. Of the remaining $15,000, Art receives $9,000, Beth $4,500 and Trust Z $1,500. On Schedule E, Form 1041, Trust Z would report depreciation of $11,500 and on Art's Schedule K-1, Line 5b $9,000 would be reported while on Beth's Schedule K-1, Line 5b $4,500 would be recorded.

The existence or absence of a reserve for FAI does not alter the amount of deductible depreciation for tax purposes. All an accounting reserve does is determine who gets the deduction. If the depreciation is directly allocable to the beneficiaries, the depreciation is ignored for DNI purposes and has no impact on its computation or allocation. To the extent depreciation is deductible on Form 1041, depreciation reduces adjusted total income, which reduces the DNI allocated to the beneficiaries. Any tax adjustment for depreciation for alternative minimum tax purposes is allocated under the same rules.

An exception for depletion. Under fiduciary accounting rules, 27½% of income from natural resources, other than timber, must be allocated to corpus. Several courts have labeled this allocation as a set aside to fund a depletion reserve to protect the corpus.[19] As a reserve, the tax depletion is first allocated to the reserve. Since the amount allocated under fiduciary accounting (27½%) is greater than the allowable tax percentage depletion (15%), all the tax depletion should be allocated to the entity. Timber has no fixed percentage, but does require an allocation of inflows to corpus.

> EXAMPLE 8 - 12. Trust Y owns oil royalty property. In 2001, Trust Y had $10,000 of royalty income and $1,500 of tax depletion. Although the trust required all FAI to be distributed, the entire $1,500 of tax depletion would be reported on Schedule E, since the $1,500 (tax depletion) is less than the $2,750 of royalty income (accounting reserve) allocated to corpus. The beneficiary would receive a distribution of $7,250 with no depletion allocation. Trust Y would report the entire $10,000 less the $1,500 depletion, but of the net $8,500, $7,250 would be taxable to the beneficiaries, leaving $1,250 taxable to Trust Y.

Taxes. A trust or estate can deduct any taxes allowed under §164. These taxes normally include: state, local and foreign income taxes and property taxes. Sales tax is not deducted, but is added to the cost-basis of the item purchased. If the taxes are attributable to a specific type of income, they should be deducted in arriving at the net income from that income type. If any generation-skipping transfer tax (GSTT) is paid on income distributions, the entity may deduct these taxes, providing they were not deducted in determining the GSTT.[20] Other Federal income, excise, and custom taxes are not deductible.

Double deductions. Section 642(g) provides that estate expenses under §§2053 or 2054 can be deducted on Form 1041. This is allowed only if the expenses were not deducted on Form 706 and a statement waiving the right to deduct the expenses on Form 706 should be filed with Form 1041. This election is not an "all or nothing" election. The fiduciary has the discretion to deduct all, part, or none of the expenses on Form 1041 or on Form 706. These expenses do not include deductions in respect of a decedent, which can be deducted on both returns. Deductions in respect of a decedent are expenses that accrued prior to the decedent's death such that they are deductible as debts on the estate tax return (Form 706) and, when paid, are deductible as expenses on the fiduciary income tax return (Form 1041). Property taxes that became a lien before the decedent's death, and were paid by the executor, are an example of a deduction in respect of a decedent. Since the top income tax rate is 39.6%, an additional computation must be made to decide where the greater tax savings can be achieved. Due to the unified credit, the first dollar of taxable estate will be taxed at 37%. The marginal estate tax rate above $3,000,000 is 55% and within the surcharge "bubble" it is 60%. As was discussed in Chapter 5, the surcharge bubble refers to the extra 5% tax that is applied to estates between $10,000,000 and the point at which the surcharge "recaptures" the taxes saved by the lower rates and the unified credit as compared to what would have been paid if there was a flat 55% rate and no unified credit.

Although §2053 expenses can be deducted on either the estate or income tax return, do not forget that certain §2053 expenses reduce the marital and charitable deductions, so an election to take these expenses on the income tax return could cause a taxable estate to result. Estate transmission expenses are deemed paid from the gross estate reducing assets that can be distributed to the surviving spouse. Deducting these expenses on the income tax return prevents a reduction of the gross estate and with a smaller marital deduction, a taxable estate arises.

Charitable deduction. Section 642(c) details the rules covering a permitted charitable contribution deduction and computation of the allowed deduction is recorded on Schedule A, Form 1041 and carried over to Line 13, Form 1041. Section 642(c) states:

> "...there shall be allowed as a deduction in computing its taxable income...any amount of the gross income, without limitation, which pursuant to the terms of the governing instrument is, during the taxable year, paid for a purpose specified in §170(c)...."

Before a deduction is allowed, certain requirements must be met. These requirements are:

1. The will or trust document must authorize the contribution,
2. The amount of deduction is limited by gross income, and

3. Only those amounts actually paid during the year or during the following year may be deducted.[21]

For purposes of the deduction, gross income includes any amount earned on the trust's or estate's assets, any IRD, and any current year capital gains paid, permanently set aside, or credited to the charity. All other amounts paid from corpus or tax-exempt income are not deductible. Specific and pecuniary bequests and non-cash contributions are customarily paid out of corpus, so no deduction is allowed. The amount the charity actually receives is determined by FAI and the document, so the actual distribution may be less than gross income. Only amounts actually paid can be deducted, even if gross income is higher. Of the amount distributed to the charity, it consists of every type of FAI received by the entity, subject to the special allocation rules. If the entity has tax-exempt income or depreciation, then these items must be allocated to the charity, just like to any other beneficiary.

The entity must actually distribute the property to the charity before a deduction is allowed. A special election can be made to treat distributions made during the following year as made in the current year, so the entity is allowed a current year deduction. If the fiduciary so elects, any payment made after the close of the current taxable year (year one), and before the close of the second taxable year (year two), may be treated as paid in year one for tax purposes. The election is irrevocable and must be made in the timely filed tax return for year two (including extensions). Failure to make the actual distribution before the due date of the year one tax return will require the fiduciary to forego the deduction and file an amended return for year one once the distribution is made during year two. This election is unique for charitable contributions and is separate from the 65-day rule.[22]

EXAMPLE 8 - 13. Trust X is allowed to distribute 10% of TAI to the local cancer society. The Trustee cannot compute the available deduction until after the close of the current year (2000). The Trustee can elect to treat any distribution made at any time during 2001 as made in 2000, so he can get a charitable deduction for 2000.

Estates and pre-October 9, 1969 irrevocable trusts are allowed a deduction for amounts permanently set-aside for future payment to a charity. While funds do not have to be placed in a separate account, some bookkeeping entry must be made to show the set-aside. For an amount to be considered permanently set-aside, there must exist no more than a remote possibility that another beneficiary could receive the funds.

> EXAMPLE 8 - 14. Estate Y requires the Executor to accumulate 50% of each year's capital gains for future distribution to Big Brothers. In 2000, Estate Y had capital gains of $10,000, so Estate Y can take a charitable deduction of $5,000 in 2000, even though the $5,000 might not be distributed for several years.

No deduction is allowed unless the document allows the entity to make a charitable contribution. Where the document does not provide for a charitable contribution, any payment made by the fiduciary is nondeductible and could subject the fiduciary to a surcharge. If a beneficiary authorizes the fiduciary to make the beneficiary's payment to a charity, the beneficiary will be allocated the income and take any charitable deduction on his or her individual Form 1040. The law is uncertain on whether a fiduciary entity can deduct charitable contributions made by a partnership or S corporation and passed through to the entity. Unless the document specially grants the fiduciary the authority to make charitable contributions, there appears to be no authority for allowing a deduction.

Administration expenses. Administration expenses unique to the operation of a fiduciary entity are deductible to the extent:

1. They are reasonable in amount;
2. incurred in the ordinary and necessary administration of the entity;
3. not allocable to the production or collection of tax-exempt income; and
4. have not been deducted for federal estate tax purposes.[23]

Administrative expenses that would fit this definition are:

1. fiduciary fees and commissions;
2. attorney fees;
3. accounting fees including fees for the preparation of any tax returns and for both court and informal accounting;
4. miscellaneous administrative expenses including court costs, fiduciary bonds, appraisals, advertising, investment advisory fees etc.; and
5. non-business casualty and theft losses.

Administrative expenses directly related to the production of income are not deductible on an estate tax return (i.e., the 706). Since income earned after death is not included in the gross estate, expenses related to the income are not deductible for estate tax purposes.

Net operating loss (NOL). In fiduciary accounting, losses from business operations are added to corpus, resulting in no loss carry back or carry forward. Further, a loss from operations does not reduce the FAI available for distribution to the beneficiaries.

> EXAMPLE 8 - 15. Trust X operates a drug store as a sole proprietorship. In 2000, the store had a net loss of $5,000. The FAI for 2000 would not be reduced by any of the $5,000 loss. If the drug store has net income in 2001 of $3,000, the entire $3,000 would be allocated to FAI, and FAI would not be reduced by any part of the prior year's loss.

For tax purposes an NOL creates a different tax situation. Estates and trusts are allowed a net operating loss deduction under §172.[24] The entity's NOL is computed following individual income tax rules, except for two main changes. A NOL cannot be increased by the charitable contribution deduction or the income distribution deduction. If a trust or estate has a NOL, the NOL must be carried back two years, unless waived, and carried forward twenty years. Except in the entity's final year, a NOL can only be used by the trust or estate. If a NOL exists in the termination year, the NOL is allocated to the corpus beneficiaries, who may use it on their personal returns and only carry forward any unused portion. The beneficiaries do not get a new twenty year carry forward period. In computing and determining the tax treatment of a NOL, only the rules under §§172, 642(d) and 642(h)(1) apply. Any other rules applicable to losses do not apply.

Personal expenses. Fiduciary entities may not deduct personal expenses. Personal expenses are expenses not associated with the management, conservation or maintenance of property, e.g., interest on the decedent's credit card debt paid by the executor. If a house is used as the personal residence of a beneficiary, the expenses related to the house, like utilities, repairs and yard maintenance, are not deductible. Qualified residence interest and property taxes would remain deductible. A beneficiary's temporary use of a house, before the sale or disposition of the house, should not disallow the deductions, since the expenses are of an investment nature and not personal.

Section 67(a) subjects trusts and estates to the limitation on deductibility of miscellaneous itemized deductions. Only to the extent these deductions exceed 2% of adjusted gross income are they deductible. The expenses must be reduced by tax-exempt income before applying the 2% floor. Section 67(b) lists various expenses that are not subject to the limitation and include the charitable deduction, interest expense, taxes, and deductions in respect of a decedent. Examples of expenses subject to the limitation are: safe deposit box rental, collection fees, and appraisal fees.

Section 67(e)(1) makes a special exception for fiduciary entities. Deductions, which are incurred concerning the administration of an estate or trust, which would not have been incurred if the property were not held in the trust or estate, are not subject to the 2% floor. Most administrative expenses should qualify for the exception; however, the IRS and the Tax Court have applied a harsh definition as to which expenses can be excluded. In the 1993 case, *O'Neill, Jr. v. Commissioner*,[25] the Sixth Circuit overruled the Tax Court and held that investment advisory expenses are not subject to the 2% floor. In the *O'Neill* case, nonprofessional trustees incurred substantial advisory fees in the management of a $4.5 million trust. Since state law placed a fiduciary duty on the trustees to manage the trust corpus properly, the trustees argued that the advisory expenses were unique to the trust's administration. The IRS and the Tax Court found that investment advisory fees were not unique to the administration of a fiduciary entity, since individuals incurred investment advisory fees, also. Only those expenses not payable by individuals could be unique to a fiduciary entity and subject to the exception. The Sixth Circuit disagreed. The Court accepted the trustees' arguments and found that advisory fees incurred by nonprofessional trustees are unique to the administration of a trust. The IRS has indicated it will not follow *O'Neill* outside the Sixth Circuit.[26]

Adjusted gross income (AGI) of a fiduciary entity is computed in the same manner as it is for an individual. Section 67(e) allows the fiduciary to deduct all administrative expenses, the income distribution deduction, and the entity's exemption in arriving at AGI. The instructions to Form 1041 contain an algebraic formula to compute AGI if DNI is less than the income distributed. If the amount distributed is less than DNI, the instructions recommend using the income distributed to compute AGI; however, the distribution deduction must be reduced by any amount attributed to tax-exempt income.

Funeral and medical expenses. Funeral and medical expenses deserve special attention because funeral expenses can only be deducted on the estate tax return and medical expenses can never be deducted on Form 1041. Medical expenses paid within one year of death can be deducted on the decedent's final return or on the estate tax return. An election is filed with the decedent's final return electing to take the medical deductions against income. If the medical expenses are deducted on the decedent's final 1040, they are subject to the 7.5% adjusted gross income limitation.

THE EFFECT OF TRANSFERS AND DISTRIBUTIONS

In this section, we consider the income tax implications of making asset transfers to and from estates, trust, and beneficiaries. Generally, non-cash distributions (in-kind distributions) are subject to the same rules as cash distributions. The beneficiaries must include in income distributions of property if DNI is allocated to the distribution. This results in the beneficiaries having to pay tax, though they might not have the cash. Further, the type of income that comprises DNI determines the taxability of the distribution, not the type of property received as a distribution.

General Rule for Property Transfers

If the transfer of property is not considered a sale by the fiduciary entity (§643(e)(3) election or pecuniary bequest), the basis of the property in the hands of the beneficiary is the entity's adjusted basis in the property immediately before distribution.[27] The beneficiary can tack the entity's holding period to his holding period. The entity can only consider the lesser of the property's basis or its FMV when computing the income distribution deduction. This can result in the beneficiary having a basis greater than her taxable income.

Transfers Subject to §663(a)

If the transfer qualified under Section 663(a)(1), the beneficiary does not have any taxable income and the entity has no distribution deduction, since this type of distribution does not qualify for the distribution deduction. The beneficiary's basis is the entity's basis, if the beneficiary sells the property at a gain, or the FMV of the property at distribution, if the property is sold at a loss.[28] The entity's holding period is tacked onto the beneficiary's holding period.

Transfers Subject to a §643(e)(3) Election

If the entity elects to treat the distribution as a sale under §643(e)(3), the beneficiary's basis equals the entity's basis immediately before distribution, adjusted for any gain or loss recognized. Since the entity's basis is used to determine the beneficiary's basis, the beneficiary can probably tack on the entity's holding period. The entity can consider the FMV of the property when computing the income distribution deduction.

> EXAMPLE 8 - 16. Trust X has DNI of $50,000. Trust X distributes stock valued at $50,000 to June. The trust's adjusted basis in the stock is $10,000. Effect of no election: (1) No gain on transfer; (2) DNI is reduced by $10,000, so trust pays tax on $40,000; and (3) June has income of $10,000 and her basis is $10,000. If the election is made: (a) Trust has gain of $40,000; (b) DNI is reduced to zero; the gain does not increase DNI and the distribution deduction is increased to $50,000; and (c) June has income of $50,000 and her basis is $50,000.

Transfers to Satisfy a Pecuniary Bequest

A capital gain or loss is recognized when a trust or estate transfers property to satisfy a pecuniary gift, bequest, or claim, which is defined as a required distribution of a specific sum of money or specific property. The gain or loss is determined by the difference between the FMV of the property on the date of transfer and the entity's basis in the property. The entity is considered to have distributed cash and the beneficiary turned around and bought the property.[29] If the distribution does not meet the requirements of §663(a), the gain might be included in any DNI allocation, subjecting the beneficiary to taxation. If the distribution does meet the requirements of §663(a) or the gain cannot be included in DNI, the entity must pay taxes on the gain without any distribution deduction. The beneficiary's basis is the FMV of the property at the time of distribution and he must begin a new holding period. The distribution deduction equals the FMV of the property, providing sufficient DNI exists.

> EXAMPLE 8 - 17. Norm's will requires a $10,000 distribution to Keith. Instead of distributing cash, the Executor distributes stock valued at $10,000. The estate's basis in the stock is $7,000. The estate must report a $3,000 long-term gain on its Form 1041, but can include the full $10,000 when computing the income distribution deduction. Keith's basis in the stock is $10,000 and he must hold the stock for 12 months before being eligible for long-term gain treatment on sale. The estate must pay taxes on the gain, since it cannot be included in DNI.

> EXAMPLE 8 - 18. Norm's estate has estate accounting income (EAI) of $15,000. The Executor decides to distribute a car valued at $15,000, instead of cash, to Ann. Since EAI is not a pecuniary bequest, no sale occurs, unless §643(e)(3) is elected. If the car's basis is $9,000, Ann's basis is $9,000 and she can tack the estate's holding period to her's on any future sale. When computing the income distribution deduction, the Executor must use $9,000.

Transfers of Passive Activities

There are some fairly specific rules concerning transfers of passive activity investments between the grantor/decedent and the fiduciary entity and between the fiduciary entity and the beneficiaries. These rules are in addition to the rules that apply to in-kind property distributions.

Lifetime transfers from a grantor to a trust. If a grantor has any suspended losses when he or she transfers the investment to a trust, the losses are added to the basis. While the grantor is treated as disposing of the asset, according to the passive activity rules, he or she cannot recognize any of the suspended losses on his or her personal return.[30]

> EXAMPLE 8 - 19. Harry owns a partnership interest in an office building. His basis in the partnership is $100,000; however, he has $20,000 in suspended losses. The trust's basis in the partnership will be $120,000, and Harry cannot use the

suspended losses in the future to reduce his passive income. The trust cannot use the $20,000 in suspended losses to include its depreciation deduction.

Transfers from a decedent to an estate. The death of a person is treated as a distribution of his or her entire interest in the asset, so on the decedent's final return, the suspended losses can be used to reduce other income, subject to one limitation. The recipient's basis of property received at death is its fair market value (FMV) at date of death.[31] When suspended losses exceed the increase in basis, the excess suspended loss (the suspended loss less the increase in basis) can be deducted on the decedent's final return only.[32]

> EXAMPLE 8 - 20. Mary died on November 12, 2001. Her basis in a partnership was $20,000. The FMV of the partnership interest was $50,000. Mary had $100,000 of suspended losses. On Mary's final return, $70,000 of the losses may be deducted. ($50,000 - $20,000 = $30,000; $100,000 - $30,000 = $70,000)

> EXAMPLE 8 - 21. Martin died on December 31, 2000. His basis in a partnership was ($200,000). The FMV of the partnership interest was $30,000. His suspended losses totaled $150,000. None of the suspended losses will be recognized on Martin's final Form 1040 and the estate's basis will be $30,000. Since the increase in basis, $230,000, exceeded the total suspended losses, neither Martin nor the estate can deduct the losses.

Transfers from trust/estate to a beneficiary. Transfers of passive activities to a beneficiary are treated in the same manner as transfers from a grantor to a trust. Any suspended losses incurred by the entity are added to the basis and the entity is prevented from using the losses in the future.[33] If the distribution of a passive activity by an executor is considered a sale under Reg. §1.1014-4 (e.g., a distribution of property rather than cash to satisfy a pecuniary bequest), the estate can use the suspended losses on Form 1041. The related party rules of §267 prevent a trustee from utilizing the suspended losses by making a similar "sale" distribution.[34]

INCOME DISTRIBUTION DEDUCTION AND THE TAXATION OF BENEFICIARIES

As said earlier in the chapter, the main focus of Subchapter J is to allocate taxable income between the fiduciary entity and the beneficiaries. The trust or estate receives a deduction based on the taxable income distributed to the beneficiaries during the year. The deductible amount is computed on Schedule B, Form 1041 and recorded on Line 18, Form 1041. Since a fiduciary entity can distribute income and corpus, depending on the terms of the fiduciary document, an amount called distributable net income (DNI) must be calculated. Section 643(a) defines DNI. DNI limits the amount of taxable income allocated to the beneficiaries. Any amount distributed greater than DNI will be considered either undistributed net income (UNI) or corpus.

Key Definitions

Simple trust. The IRC establishes two types of trusts for calculating the income distribution deduction. Sections 651-652 are used to compute the distribution deduction for simple trusts and §§661-663 are used to compute the deduction for complex trusts. The terms "simple" and "complex" are not found in the Code, but are used throughout the regulations. The definition of a trust can change from year-to-year; however, in its final year, a trust will always be complex.

Section 651 defines a simple trust as a trust that:

1. is required to distribute all of its trust accounting income (TAI) currently;
2. no amount from the trust can be used for charitable purposes; and
3. there are no distributions in excess of TAI for the year.

The trust document determines if the first two requirements are met. The word income in §651(a)(1) refers to trust accounting income.[35] If the document requires the trustee to distribute all the current year's TAI, the beneficiaries are deemed to have received the TAI for taxation purposes, whether it is actually distributed or not. If the document does not require all the TAI to be distributed currently, the trust cannot be classified as a simple trust, even if the trust actually distributes all of its TAI for the year.

A simple trust is limited in the type of distributions it can make. If the trust could have made a distribution that would qualify for a charitable deduction, the trust cannot be classified as a simple trust, even if no charitable distributions are actually made.[36] Further, if the trust makes distributions greater than TAI, it cannot be a simple trust. Although corpus distributions are allowed under the trust document, the trust will be a simple trust, unless distributions greater than current year's TAI are actually made. In years the trust does not make any corpus distributions, it will be a simple trust, and in years it makes a corpus distribution it will be a complex trust.

A simple trust is allowed a deduction for the TAI distributed limited by DNI.[37] The amount of the deduction must be reduced by any amount not included in gross income less any applicable expenses. This requires the fiduciary to reduce the available deductions by any amount of tax-exempt income, net of related expenses, included in TAI.

Complex trusts. If a trust does not meet the definition of a simple trust, it is a complex trust. The income distribution deduction for complex trusts and all estates is determined under §§661-663. A trust, which can accumulate income, can make charitable contributions or makes a corpus distribution will be a complex trust. Since a trust must distribute all remaining corpus in its final year, a trust will always be a complex trust in its final year. The main difference between the computation of the income distribution deduction for simple and complex trusts is the use of a tier system for complex trusts. The tier system results in a greater amount of DNI being allocated to beneficiaries who receive required TAI distributions.

Distributable net income (DNI). DNI is the statutory limit for the income distribution deduction. DNI determines the maximum distribution deduction. If actual distributions exceed DNI, the entity gets no deduction for the excess; however, if distributions are less than DNI, only the amount actually distributed can be deducted.[38] Section 643(a) defines DNI as the entity's net taxable income modified as follows:

1. No deduction for the income distribution;
2. No deduction for the personal exemption;
3. Net undistributed capital gains allocated to corpus are subtracted;
4. Net capital losses are added back;
5. Net tax-exempt income is added back; and
6. For simple trusts only, subtract any undistributed extraordinary dividends or taxable stock dividends that the fiduciary allocated to corpus in good faith.

DNI is reduced by all tax deductible expenses. Whether these expenses are deducted from income or corpus for accounting purposes is ignored. DNI is a tax computation; therefore, accounting allocations of expenses is disregarded, unless the Code specifically requires the allocation to be considered. This treatment of corpus expenses allows income beneficiaries to benefit, from a tax standpoint, from corpus expenses paid during the year, since DNI limits the taxable income allocated to the income beneficiaries, thereby, reducing how much income they must pay taxes on.

To visualize the allocation of FAI and DNI, think about Neapolitan ice cream. Unlike swirl ice cream, each flavor of Neapolitan is separate from the other flavors. If a person wanted only vanilla ice cream, he or she could remove vanilla from the "block of ice cream" leaving the other flavors. Gross accounting income, net accounting income and DNI form our "blocks of ice cream." Each block is composed of various "flavors" of income. When the fiduciary "scoops" the beneficiaries their share of FAI or DNI, each beneficiary receives some of every flavor. Exactly how much of each flavor a beneficiary receives is determined by the total composition of the block. If 50% of the total block is rental income, the beneficiary's "scoop" is 50% rent. Although there are many similarities in the configuration of each block, each block is different. In most situations, the FAI and DNI blocks contain the same flavors/income, but the percentage of flavors that comprise each block changes, based on the different rules used to build the blocks.[39] The construction of these "blocks of income" is the crux of computing the beneficiaries' allocation.

The composition of DNI is unique for each year. If DNI is not fully allocated to the beneficiaries during the particular year, the remaining block of DNI ice cream is stored in the freezer for distribution in later years. When distributions in a future year exceed that year's DNI, the fiduciary will look in the freezer for any prior year's DNI. When prior year's DNI, otherwise known as undistributed net income (UNI), is found in the freezer, the fiduciary must distribute the old DNI ice cream, based on the current year's accumulation distribution. If there remains either current year DNI or prior years' DNI, the beneficiary will be subject to some form of taxation for the particular year. Once all of the ice cream has been totally distributed, no further taxation can occur for the beneficiaries. By following the ice cream, the fiduciary will know if the beneficiaries are subject to taxation.

EXAMPLE 8 - 22. In 1999, Trust X had DNI of $20,000. The composition of DNI was: 50% rent, 25% dividends, 15% taxable interest and 10% exempt interest. Distributions for the year were $15,000, so $15,000 of DNI was allocated to the beneficiaries and $5,000 remained with Trust X. Since $500 of the retained DNI was exempt ($5,000 * 10%), Trust X had taxable income of $4,400 ($4,500 - 100) and taxes of $1,051.50. UNI for 1999 was $3,448.50 ($4,500 - 1,051.50). If 2000 distributions exceed 2000 DNI, all or part of the 1999 UNI will be distributed in 2000. Of the $15,000 distributed to the beneficiaries, $10,000 was allocated to Harry and the rest to Terri. Of Harry's DNI, $5,000 was rent, $2,500 was dividends, $1,500 was taxable interest and $1,000 was exempt. Of Terri's DNI, $2,500 was rent, $1,250 was dividends, $750 was taxable interest and $500 was exempt. Once the composition of DNI is calculated, it remains the same for all beneficiaries and the entity.

Computation of DNI and the Income Distribution Deduction

Since the purpose of DNI is to compute the income distribution deduction, the best place to begin in calculating DNI is with the entity's adjusted total income (Line 17, Form 1041). Adjusted total income (ATI) is the total amount of taxable income for the year that must be taxed to someone, either the entity or the beneficiaries. If ATI is negative, the entity has a net capital loss, a NOL and/or excess deductions. Then, DNI will be zero, since DNI can *never* be negative. ATI is modified by two adjustments: one for tax-exempt interest and one for capital transactions.

Tax-exempt interest. Net tax-exempt interest is gross exempt interest less any expenses not deductible due to the exempt interest limitation. When calculating the deductible expenses for ATI, direct and indirect expenses related to tax-exempt income are not deductible. These nondeductible expenses reduce gross exempt interest and the net amount is added to ATI when computing DNI. DNI is net income, so the final amount is a composite of each type of income net of expenses.

The income distribution deduction is the amount of taxable income allocated to the beneficiaries. If the entity has any net tax-exempt income, it must be removed from both DNI and the distributions before calculating the income distribution deduction. Once the net exempt income is removed, the lesser of DNI or the distributions becomes the income distribution deduction.

EXAMPLE 8 - 23. Trust Z has DNI of $30,000 of which $2,500 is exempt interest. Distributions for the year are $45,000. DNI and the distributions must be reduced by $2,500, since the entire amount of exempt interest is distributed. The income distribution deduction is $27,500, which is the lesser of deductible DNI ($27,500) and deductible distributions ($42,500). If distributions were $21,000, exempt interest of $1,750 (($21,000/$30,000) * $2,500) would be removed from distributions, since the entire amount of exempt interest is not distributed. Here, the income distribution deduction would be $19,250, since deductible distributions ($19,250) would be less than deductible DNI ($27,500).

Capital transactions. Capital transactions rarely affect DNI. Only capital gains can be added to DNI and this occurs infrequently. DNI is determined as if no capital transactions occurred during the year, so the net effect of all capital transactions is initially removed from ATI. Only net gains are added back to ATI. Capital gains are included in DNI when:

1. Capital gains are included in fiduciary accounting income;
2. The entity's final tax year;
3. The entity is required to distribute a specific amount each year and an insufficient amount of accounting income exists to meet the required distribution;
4. The fiduciary is required to distribute the proceeds from the sale of a specific asset; and
5. The fiduciary establishes a practice of using the capital gains to determine the entity's distributions and actually distributes the capital gains.

These specific incidents are narrowly interpreted, so capital gains are not included in DNI very often. Once the net tax-exempt interest and the adjustment for capital transactions are made to ATI, the result is DNI for purposes of computing the income distribution deduction.

Allocation of DNI. The DNI allocated to the beneficiaries determines the income distribution deduction. DNI is allocated to beneficiaries who receive a distribution from the entity. The type of distribution, income or corpus, is irrelevant. If the entity made a distribution, DNI is allocated to it. Not all distributions are considered when allocating DNI to the beneficiaries. The following distributions are ignored when allocating DNI and computing the income distribution deduction:

1. Charitable distributions;
2. Distributions under §663(a) (explained below); and
3. Distributions in the current year that were considered when computing the income distribution deduction in a previous year.

Required FAI distributions are considered made whether a check was written or not. All other distributions must have been made before they can be considered. If an in-kind distribution was made, instead of cash, the lesser of the entity's basis or the fair market value (FMV) of the property is used to figure out the distributed amount. The distributed value can be increased if the transfer of property was considered a sale by making either a §643(e)(3) election or transferring property to satisfy a pecuniary bequest.

Section 663(a). Section 663(a) allows certain distributions to be free of any DNI allocation. The terms of the governing document establish if the gift or bequest meets the requirements. Unless the money or identity of the property are ascertainable under the document, the distribution will be included when allocating DNI for the income distribution deduction. To meet the test for a specific sum of money, the amount to be distributed must be fixed by the document and ascertainable at the date of death or inception of the trust. The amount cannot be subject to the fiduciary's discretion, a fraction of the taxable estate or determinable after subtracting administrative expenses. Most formula bequests do not meet the test, since the amount of the bequest is not determinable at death.[40] Specific property must be fixed as to kind and amount in the document. Certain pecuniary bequests meet the requirements of §663(a), while others do not.

The 65 day rule. The trustee or executor can elect to treat all or part of the distributions made within 65 days after the end of the trust's or estate's year as made in the current year.[41] The election is filed with the current year's tax return and prevents the amounts actually paid from being deducted in the year actually paid. Only amounts necessary to remove any remaining current year's DNI can be distributed under the 65 day rule. Effective for tax years beginning after August 5, 1997, estates can make a 65 day election. [42]

Taxation of Beneficiaries

According to Regulation §1.652(b)-3, the character of the income and deductions:

... shall have the same character in the hands of the beneficiary as in the hands of the estate or trust. For this purpose, the amounts shall be treated as consisting of the same proportion of each class of items entering into the computation of DNI as the total of each class bears to the total DNI of the estate or trust unless the terms of the governing instrument specifically allocate different classes of income to different beneficiaries.

The composition of DNI determines the type of income distributed and taxed to the beneficiaries. If 80% of DNI is taxable income and 20% is tax-exempt interest, then 80% of the DNI allocated to the beneficiaries will be taxable income. The other 20% will be tax-exempt interest. Remember the Neapolitan ice cream analogy discussed earlier. For tax purposes, the "scoops" (distributions) received by the beneficiary are based on the composition of DNI. Anytime a "scoop" is made; the beneficiary partakes in each flavor. The fiduciary is not allowed to "pick and choose" which flavor a beneficiary gets, unless the document provides for a special allocation. Special allocations are discussed later.

Schedule K-1. The fiduciary records on Schedule K-1 the amounts taxable to the beneficiaries. The K-1 is shown on a net basis. Any amounts recorded on the Schedule are net of any expenses, so the beneficiaries report the net effect of any allocation only. Only net income can be allocated to the beneficiaries, except in the final year, when losses can be allocated to the corpus beneficiaries. Negative numbers are not shown on the Schedule K-1, except in the final year.

In determining the amounts reported on the K-1, the fiduciary must first compute the composition of DNI. This is done by allocating the entity's expenses against its income. Only income included in DNI can be reduced by the entity's expenses. The allocation of expenses follows a prescribed pecking order, and can result in DNI consisting of only one type of income, although the entity might have had four different classes of income originally. These rules apply to both simple and complex trusts and estates.

Allocation expenses against income. The order of allocating expenses against income is as follows:

1. All deductions directly attributable to a particular class of income are deducted from that income, e.g., all rental expenses reduce rental income.

2. All deductions not directly attributable to a specific type of income may be allocated to any type of income, as long as some deductions are allocated to tax-exempt income.[43] This rule provides some flexibility to the fiduciary. Depending on the needs of the beneficiaries, the fiduciary can allocate the indirect deductions against any type of income included in DNI. If the beneficiaries need a larger amount of portfolio income, to deduct some personal investment interest expense, for example, the fiduciary can allocate a larger amount of indirect costs to passive income, provided the fiduciary does not create a passive loss. If the reverse is true and the beneficiaries need passive income, none of the expenses have to be allocated to passive activities, but can be allocated solely to portfolio income.

3. Passive losses can only be deducted to the extent of passive income. Net passive losses cannot be allocated against any other type of income and are retained (suspended) by the entity. If directly related tax-exempt expenses exceed tax-exempt income, excess expenses cannot be deducted against any other type of income.

4. Any excess deductions (directly related expenses exceed the specific income), excluding passive losses and tax-exempt expenses, can be allocated against any type of income, just like indirect expenses discussed above. The income must be included in DNI before expenses can be allocated against it.

Unless a specific allocation in the fiduciary document prescribes otherwise, a charity-beneficiary is deemed to receive some of each type of income included in DNI.[44] This rule prevents an improper shifting of taxable income to the charity. Use of the gross income method, discussed above under "Expenses related to tax-exempt income," normally results in more taxable income being allocated to the charity reducing the taxable income allocable to the beneficiaries.

Special allocations. Sometimes the fiduciary document provides for a specific allocation of income to certain beneficiaries. These specific allocations can take many forms.

EXAMPLE 8 - 24. Trust X is to distribute all the income from an apartment house to Sam. This is a specific allocation allowed under the Regulations; therefore, Sam is taxed on any taxable income attributable to the apartment house. Sam's distribution is solely dependent on that specific type of income.

EXAMPLE 8 - 25. Trust X is to distribute $10,000 to Kathy, to be paid from tax-exempt income to the extent possible and the rest from taxable income. This would not be recognized as a specific allocation, so Kathy is allocated some of each type of income included in DNI, even if the fiduciary actually pays the $10,000 entirely from tax-exempt income. Kathy's distribution is fixed whatever the amount of tax-exempt income earned by the entity, so the only effect of the allocation is an attempt to apportion more of the tax-exempt income to her, which is not allowed under the Code.

EXAMPLE 8 - 26. Trust X is to distribute one-half of the tax-exempt interest to Anita. This is an allowable specific allocation, since Anita's distribution is determined solely by the amount of tax-exempt interest earned by the trust.

For a specific allocation, such as the one in the prior example, to be effective in allocating the entity's DNI, the document must not give the trustee any discretion in how the allocation is made. The special allocation rule applies to charitable distributions also. In drafting, if the grantor wants a certain beneficiary to receive a specific type of income, he or she can include a provision in the fiduciary document requiring the fiduciary to allocate that type of income to the beneficiary; however, he or she must make sure to draft the provision to comply with the requirements of the Code. The fiduciary cannot make a special allocation on his or her own.

Specific allocations will be given effect in the allocation of DNI from a fiduciary entity, providing they have an economic impact independent of the income tax consequences.[45]

Excess deductions. In years when interest, taxes, and administrative expenses exceed income, the entity has excess deductions. Since these expenses cannot be included in a NOL under §172 and cannot be allocated to the beneficiaries, the entity has wasted excess deductions, because they are lost forever. Only in the final tax year can the entity allocate these excess deductions to the corpus beneficiaries following the same rules used for allocating a NOL or net capital loss. The beneficiaries may take the allocated deductions as miscellaneous itemized deductions on their personal returns. If the beneficiary does not itemize, or if the 2% AGI floor is too great, the beneficiary cannot carry back or carry forward any unused amount.

Tiers, Tiers, Too Many Tiers

Tiers are only applicable to complex trusts and to estates, and are used to allocate DNI among the beneficiaries. Section 662(a) defines the tiers. A complex trust or estate may or may not have tiers; the fiduciary must look to the governing instrument. A simple trust does not have tiers, since only one type of distribution exists, and DNI is allocated totally to that distribution.

First tier distributions. Section 662(a)(1) defines the first tier distributions as:

> *...the amount of income for the taxable year required to be distributed currently to such beneficiary, whether distributed or not.*

If the governing instrument requires a certain amount of FAI to be distributed currently, the beneficiaries must pay taxes on that amount, limited by DNI. Section 662 applies if any part of the FAI is subject to a required distribution. The beneficiaries must pay taxes on the income, even if a distribution is not actually made.

DNI is recalculated if the entity has charitable *and* first tier distributions. DNI is computed as if no charitable contribution was made and is allocated to the beneficiaries to the extent they received first tier distributions. DNI for first tier distributions is called "modified DNI." Modified DNI applies to first tier distributions only and exists only when the trust has a charitable contribution and first tier distributions. Beneficiaries of first tier distributions have a potentially larger tax liability, since they lose some or all of the benefit resulting from the charitable contribution deduction.

EXAMPLE 8 - 27. Trust A had the following income for the year:

Taxable interest	$20,000
Tax-exempt interest	$10,000
Total income	$30,000

Trust A is required to distribute $24,000 of its current income to Alberta. The rest of the income can be distributed to Beth or the Red Cross or accumulated, and the trustee can make corpus distributions to Beth or to the Red Cross. The trustee made the following distributions:

Beth	$10,000
Red Cross	$18,000

DNI is computed as follows:

Taxable interest	$20,000	
Charitable deduction	(12,000)	[$6,000 exempt]
Tax-exempt interest	4,000	[$10,000-$6000]
DNI	$12,000	

Modified DNI is computed as follows:

Taxable interest	$20,000
Tax-exempt interest	10,000
Modified DNI	$30,000

Alberta is allocated $24,000 of modified DNI, which would consist of $16,000 taxable and $8,000 tax-exempt. Beth would not have any taxable income, since DNI would be zero ($12,000 - $24,000).

The effect of modified DNI, as reported on Form 1041:

Taxable interest	$20,000	
Charitable deduction	(12,000)	[$6,000 exempt]
Income distribution	(8,000)	[$4,000 exempt]
Taxable income	$ 0	
Taxable to Alberta	$16,000	[$8,000 exempt]
Taxable to Beth	$ 0	

Second tier distributions. Section 662(a)(2) defines second tier distributions as follows:

All other amounts properly paid, credited, or required to be distributed to such beneficiary for the taxable year.

The main difference between first and second tier distributions is the provision that first tier distributions must come from current income, while second tier distributions can come from current income, accumulated income or corpus. If none of the distributions *must* be paid from current income, all distributions will be considered a second tier. *Any* income that must be paid is included in the beneficiary's income, to the extent of DNI, even if not actually paid. All other amounts must actually be paid to the beneficiaries before included in their income. Examples of second tier distributions under Regulation §1.662(a)-3(b) are:

1. Distributions made to a beneficiary in the discretion of the fiduciary.
2. Distributions required by the terms of the governing instrument upon the happening of a specified event.

EXAMPLE 8 - 28. Trust Y requires one-half of the trust corpus be distributed to Yolanda on her thirtieth birthday. When Yolanda turns 30 and receives the distribution, the distribution will be classified as a tier two distribution.

The amount of second tier distributions taxable to the beneficiaries is determined by DNI less any amounts allocated to first tier distributions. If more than one beneficiary receives distributions, each beneficiary must include his or her proportionate share in gross income. A beneficiary's proportionate share is an amount that bears the same ratio to DNI, less any first tier distributions, as the beneficiary's distribution bears to the total second tier distributions.

EXAMPLE 8 - 29. Trust Z has TAI and DNI of $30,000. The trust is required to distribute $15,000 of current income to Adams. The fiduciary has discretion to distribute the remaining income to either Bea, Charles or Dan or accumulate it. The fiduciary also can invade corpus for all four beneficiaries. Trust Z distributes $5,000 each to Bea, Charles and Dan and distributes an additional $5,000 to Adams. DNI would be allocated to each beneficiary as follows:

	Distribution	DNI
Adams	$20,000	$18,750
Bea	5,000	3,750
Charles	5,000	3,750
Dan	5,000	3,750
Totals	$35,000	$30,000

Adams is allocated a greater part of DNI, since he is received a first tier distribution of $15,000. The other $15,000 distribution was second tier, and the extra $5,000 would either be a distribution from corpus or from accumulated income.

No modifications of DNI are made in determining the taxation of second tier distributions. While the charitable contribution deduction is ignored in determining the DNI allocated to first tier distributions, no similar adjustment is made in allocating DNI to second tier distributions. As was shown in the example above, the adjustment for the charitable deduction made to first tier distributions results in a larger portion of DNI being allocated to first tier distributions; thereby, reducing the benefit of the charitable deduction to first tier distributions and reducing the DNI allocated to second tier distributions. Although income is allocated to a charitable contribution before any other expense, the larger the first tier distributions, the less benefit the beneficiaries, as a group, will receive from the charitable gift. To prevent this impact, as much of the distributions as possible should be allocated to the second tier. Since the governing document determines if a distribution will be first or second tier, careful drafting is needed to achieve the desired result.

Income in Respect of a Decedent

Section 691 details the tax treatment of income in respect of a decedent (IRD). Treasury Regulation §1.691(a)-1(b) defines IRD in these terms:

> In general, the term "income in respect of a decedent" refers to those amounts to which a decedent was entitled as gross income but which were not properly includible in computing his taxable income for the taxable year ending with the date of his death or for a previous taxable year under the method of accounting employed by the decedent.

IRD is income to which the decedent was entitled, but due to his or her death was not includible in his or her taxable income. An example of an IRD is salary earned but not paid to a cash basis taxpayer. Although the taxpayer had earned the salary, since it was not paid until after his or her death, it could not be included on his or her final income tax return. Since the income was never subject to income tax, upon the receipt of the income, someone must pay income taxes on it. Section 691 provides the rules concerning the taxation of this type of income. No step-up in basis exists for IRD at death.

IRD must be included in the income of the party that receives the IRD in the year of receipt. Therefore, if an estate receives the IRD, it must include it in income; however, if the beneficiary receives the IRD directly, the beneficiary is taxed on it. Whoever collects the IRD is entitled to any deductions associated with the IRD. The character of IRD is the same as if the decedent had received the property before death.

The unique characteristic about IRD is its dual taxation. IRD is included in the gross estate of the decedent, so it is subject to estate taxes. Further, IRD is subject to income tax on receipt. The recipient of an IRD is entitled to an income tax deduction attributable to the estate taxes paid on the net value of the IRD. This reduces the effect of dual taxation. Examples of IRD:

1. If the decedent completed all events sufficient to close a sale but did not collect the proceeds before death, on collection the proceeds will be IRD.

2. If the decedent had a contingent claim to sales proceeds, the completion of the agreement after death will result in IRD.[46]

3. The forgiveness of debt at death on an installment note is IRD. If the decedent had any unrecognized gain from the sale, the forgiveness of debt would trigger the recognition of the entire unreported gain and the gain would be IRD to the estate.[47]

4. Distributions from a qualified plan or an IRA made after death are IRD. Any distribution representing a nondeductible contribution is not taxed, since the decedent paid taxes on this amount before death.

Certain expenses are deductible for both estate and income tax purposes if they are related to IRD and have accrued prior to the decedent's death. The types of expenses are limited to:

1. Business expenses - §162
2. Interest deductions - §163
3. Deduction for taxes -
4. Expenses to produce income -
5. Depletion deduction - §611
6. Foreign tax credit - §27

Medical expenses, alimony, capital losses, net operating losses and charitable contributions are expressly excluded and cannot be deducted for income tax purposes by the recipient of IRD.

Estate Tax Deduction

IRD is included on both the estate tax and income tax returns. To offset some of this double taxation, the *recipient* of IRD is entitled to an income tax *deduction* for that portion of the estate taxes attributed to including IRD in the gross estate.[48] Further, an income tax deduction is allowed for generation skipping transfer taxes ascribed to IRD items included in a taxable termination or direct skips caused by the transferor's death.[49] The deduction must be allocated among the recipients of IRD, based on their proportionate share of the gross IRD received.

The deduction is allowed each year IRD is included in income. To compute the deduction, all items treated as IRD in the gross estate are aggregated. The total is reduced by all DRD to arrive at a net value. The value of IRD is the lesser of the amount included in the gross estate or the amount included in income. Once the net value is determined, estate taxes are recomputed by excluding the net value from the gross estate. The difference between the original estate tax and the recomputed estate tax is the IRD deduction. The deduction is allocated among the various IRD items. All deductions and credits must be adjusted to reflect the elimination of the net IRD values. If a specific bequest of IRD is made to a surviving spouse or a charity, the deduction is eliminated.

EXAMPLE 8 - 30. The Estate is the beneficiary of Decedent's IRA. At the Decedent's death, the IRA was valued at $2,000,000 and the Decedent's taxable estate was $5,000,000. With the IRA, Decedent's FET was $2,390,800, and without the IRA, Decedent's FET would have been $1,290,800. As the IRA is distributed to the Estate, the Estate can reduce any income taxes payable by the $1,100,000 of FET paid on the IRA.

EXAMPLE 8 - 31. The Decedent was entitled to salary of $5,000, dividends of $3,750 and rental income of $1,250 at his death. Decedent owed real estate taxes of $2,500 on the rental property. S2 (decedent's spouse) inherited the stock portfolio, his daughter, Jane, was entitled to the real estate, and the Estate received the salary. S_2 inherited ½ of the Decedent's estate and the Estate's marginal rate is 55%. The marginal rate is applied to the net IRD of $7,500 ($10,000 less $2,500) less the net IRD deemed allocated to the marital deduction ($3,750). The $2062.50 deduction ($7,500 - $3,750 * 55%) is allocated as follows:

	IRD Received	Percentage	Deduction
Estate	$5,000	50.0%	$1,031
S2	$3,750	37.5%	$773
Jane	$1,250	12.5%	$258
Total	$10,000	100.0%	$2,063

Throwback Rules

Prior to TRA '97, any trust that did not distribute all of its current year's DNI had to contend with what were called the *throwback rules*.[50] TRA '97 changed the law such that these rules are no longer a problem for most domestic trusts, but they still apply to foreign trusts, some domestic trusts that were once foreign trusts, and to certain trusts that were created before March 1, 1984, if they are considered multiple trusts under Code Section 643(f).[51] Under the throwback rules, if all of the current year's DNI ice cream is not scooped, the trust pays taxes on the remaining amount and stores the difference in the freezer. The stored taxable income (DNI) turns into what is called undistributed net income (UNI). Congress enacted these laws in 1969 to prevent a perceived abuse. People were saving taxes by having the trust pay taxes on the trust's taxable income and then distributing it in a later year, free of any additional taxes. For those trusts that still must contend with these rules, if the trust has any leftover DNI, it must keep a record of the retained amount and "distribute it" when later years' distributions exceed that particular year's DNI. Once distributed, the beneficiary must recompute his or her prior years' taxes, as if the amount was distributed in the year originally earned. To simplify this computation, the beneficiary uses an averaging approach and only has to recompute taxes for three years.

Fortunately, Congress finally realized that, with the compressed tax rate brackets, these throwback rules cause an excessive amount of paperwork, but rarely resulted in the collection of additional taxes. With the change in the law, most domestic trusts are exempt from these throwback rules, starting with tax years beginning after August 5, 1997.

CONCLUSION

Some main points to remember:

1. Trusts and estates are taxed like individuals, with a few modifications.
2. The primary purpose of Subchapter J is to allocate income and expenses between the fiduciary entity and the beneficiaries.
3. Knowing the fiduciary document, state law, and fiduciary accounting is important to the successful completion of a fiduciary tax return.
4. There are two primary parts to preparing a fiduciary income tax return:
   a. Computing adjusted total income; and
   b. Allocating the income and deductions between the entity and the beneficiaries, which requires determining DNI and the income distribution deduction.

QUESTIONS AND PROBLEMS

1. What is the purpose of fiduciary accounting?

2. Explain the general rules for allocating between income and corpus.

3. The document is silent on how to allocate rental income and expenses. Under state law, rental receipts are allocated to income, but state law provides that net business income is allocated to corpus. The deceased owned several rental properties, which were reported by the deceased on his income tax return as a business activity. How should the executor account for the rental properties on the estate's books?

4. How does fiduciary accounting impact fiduciary income taxation?

5. Explain the purpose of Subchapter J.

6. Explain the main rule concerning the computation of fiduciary taxable income.

7. Explain the general rule concerning the deductibility of depreciation for fiduciary entities.

8. Which of the following statements are **true**?

   1. Trusts must use a calendar year end.
   2. Estates must use a calendar year end.
   3. The fiduciary must file a special notice to elect its tax accounting method.
   4. The fiduciary's tax return is due on the 15th day of the 4th month following its year end.
   5. Fiduciary returns can be filed electronically.

a.	1, 2 and 4 only	d.	2, 3 and 5 only
b.	1, 4 and 5 only	e.	1, 3 and 5 only
c.	2, 3 and 4 only		

9. Which of the following does NOT apply to the taxation of capital transactions?

    a. The maximum net capital loss deduction for any year is $3,000.
    b. Net capital losses do not decrease DNI.
    c. Transferring assets to satisfy a pecuniary bequest is considered a sale.
    d. Capital gains are included in DNI, normally.

10. Explain how the deceased's suspended passive activity losses are handled.

11. What are the three methods available for computing the allocation of indirect expenses to tax-exempt income?

12. Which of the following statements are **false**?

    1. Trusts cannot take the rental real estate offset.
    2. Income in respect of a decedent receives a "stepped-up" basis.
    3. The character of IRD is the same as if the decedent had received the property.
    4. Medical expenses can be deducted on both the fiduciary income tax and estate tax returns.
    5. Net operating losses are deductions in respect of a decedent.

        a. 2, 4 and 5 only   d. 1, 3 and 4 only
        b. 1, 3 and 5 only   e. 2 only
        c. 2, 3 and 4 only

13. What are the three requirements of §642(c) concerning the deductibility of charitable contributions?

14. State the rule that determines if a trust gets a $100 or $300 exemption.

15. State the three requirements for a trust to be classified as a simple trust.

16. Which of the following statements are **true**?

    1. DNI can never be negative.
    2. DNI can include tax-exempt income.

3. The executor can elect the 65 day rule for estate distributions.
4. DNI is allocated to specific bequests.
5. Charities never receive DNI.

     a. 1, 3 and 5 only   d. 1, 4 and 5 only

     b. 2, 3 and 4 only   e. All are true.

     c. 1, 2, 3, and 5 only

17. Describe the "sweet" composition of FAI and DNI.

18. How is DNI allocated?

19. Explain how DNI is taxed to the beneficiaries.

20. What are the rules concerning allocating expenses between the various types of income?

ANSWERS TO THE QUESTIONS AND PROBLEMS

1. Fiduciary accounting allocates the annual inflows and outflows between income and corpus. Income beneficiaries are entitled to the fiduciary accounting income while the remaindermen are entitled to the remaining corpus once the entity ends. Fiduciary accounting apportions the various receipts and distributions between income and corpus, so the fiduciary will know the correct amount to distribute to the appropriate beneficiaries.

2. According to the UPIA, a fiduciary allocates receipts and expenditures using the following steps:

   1. First, the creating document determines how the allocation is to be made;
   2. Second, if the document does not provide for the allocation, then state law controls; or
   3. If neither allocates the particular item, the trustee is to use her best judgment according to what is reasonable and equitable in view of all beneficiaries' interests in the entity.

3. The fact that the decedent recorded the use as a business activity is ignored when determining the proper accounting method for fiduciary purposes. Specific statutes control over general statutes. Since a specific statute exists for rental receipts, all rental receipts and directly related expenses are allocated to accounting income.

4. §643(b) holds that the unmodified word "income" means fiduciary accounting income. Throughout the IRC, the word "income" is used frequently; therefore, knowing how to compute FAI for the year is vital, so a correct tax return can be prepared. Furthermore, the taxation of the beneficiaries is based on the amount of their distributions, which is controlled by the fiduciary documents and accounting.

5. Subchapter J was written not to compute taxable income specifically, but to allocate taxable income to the appropriate party, either the fiduciary entity or the beneficiary.

6. Section 641 (b) provides that the taxable income of an estate or trust shall be computed in *the same manner as in the case of an individual*, except as otherwise provided in this part. Due to its unique characteristic, operating a fiduciary entity has more similarities with an individual and his handling of property than any other tax entity; therefore, it is logical that the IRC uses the tax rules applicable to individuals in computing the taxable income of a fiduciary entity. If the preparer cannot find a different treatment of any income or expense item in the IRC or regulations, she should report the item as she would on a Form 1040.

7. The amount of depreciation is computed following the same rules that apply to individuals, except no §179 deduction is allowed. To the extent there is a reserve for depreciation for accounting purposes, the entity takes the tax deduction for computation of its taxable income. If any tax depreciation remains, it is allocated between the entity and its beneficiaries according to the allocation of accounting income.

8. B - 1, 4 and 5 only. §645 requires trusts to use a calendar year end. Estate can elect a fiscal year end. No special election must be filed to elect an accounting method, because one is elected when the first return is filed. Trusts and estates have the same filing deadline as individuals. Also, fiduciary entities can file electronically, like individuals.

9. D - capital gains are rarely included in DNI. Except in the final year or when the fiduciary establishes a practice of distributing the capital gains, capital gains do not increase DNI.

10. The death of a person is treated as a distribution of his entire interest in the asset, so on the decedent's final return, the suspended losses can be used to reduce other income, subject to one limitation. The recipient's basis of property received at death is its fair market value (FMV) at date of death. When the suspended losses exceed the increase in basis, the loss can be deducted on the decedent's final return.

11. The three methods for allocating indirect expenses to exempt income are: the gross accounting income method, the net accounting income method and any defensible, reasonable method.

12. A - 2, 4 and 5 only. Trusts cannot take the rental real estate offset. Estates can for the first two years, providing the decedent actively participated and the surviving spouse does not take the entire offset. IRD does not receive a stepped-up basis, which causes its dual taxation. IRD retains its character in the hands of the estate or its beneficiaries. Medical expenses cannot be claimed on Form 1041. Net operating losses expire with the deceased and cannot be deducted by either the estate or its beneficiaries.

13. Before a deduction is allowed, certain requirements must be met. These requirements are:

    1. The will or trust document must authorize the contribution,
    2. The amount of deduction is limited by gross income, and
    3. Only those amounts actually paid during the year or during the following year may be deducted.

14. Section 642(b) allows an $300 exemption if the trust must distribute all of its TAI currently. All other trusts are allowed a $100 exemption.

15. Section 651 defines a simple trust as a trust that:

    1. Is required to distribute all of its TAI currently;
    2. No amount from the trust can be used for charitable purposes; and
    3. There are no distributions in excess of TAI for the year.

16. C - 1, 2 , 3, and 5 only. DNI can never be negative. If it is, the entity has a net capital loss, a net operating loss or excess deductions, which are not negative DNI. While DNI can include tax-exempt income, the income distribution deduction dose not include adjusted tax-exempt income. The §663(b) 65 day rule is available for estates (added by TRA '97) as well as for complex trusts. §663(a) prevents DNI from being allocated to specific bequests. Only non-charity beneficiaries receive DNI.

17. The "sweet" composition of FAI and DNI is similar to Neapolitan ice cream. Unlike swirl ice cream, each flavor of Neapolitan is separate for the other flavors. If a person wanted only vanilla ice cream, he could remove vanilla from the "block of ice cream" leaving the other flavors.

Gross accounting income, net accounting income and DNI form our "blocks of ice cream." Each block is composed of various "flavors" of income. When the fiduciary "scoops" the beneficiaries their share of FAI or DNI, each beneficiary receives some of every flavor. Exactly how much of each flavor a beneficiary receives is determined by the total composition of the block. If 50% of the total block is rental income, the beneficiary's "scoop" is 50% rent. Although there are many similarities in the configuration of each block, each block is different. In most situations, the FAI and DNI blocks contain the same flavors/income, but the percentage of flavors that comprise each block changes, based on the different rules used to build the blocks. The construction of these "blocks of income" is the crux of computing the beneficiaries' allocation.

18. DNI is allocated based on its composition and the current year's distributions. The composition of DNI is unique for each year. If DNI is not fully allocated to the beneficiaries during the particular year, the remaining block of DNI ice cream is stored in the freezer for distribution in later years. When distributions in a future year exceed that year's DNI, the fiduciary will look in the freezer for any prior year's DNI. When prior year's DNI, otherwise known as undistributed net income (UNI), is found in the freezer, the fiduciary must distribute the old DNI ice cream, based on the current year's accumulation distribution. If there remains either current year DNI or prior years' DNI, the beneficiary will be subject to some form of taxation for the particular year. Once all of the ice cream has been totally distributed, no further taxation can occur for the beneficiaries.

19. Sections 652 and 662 state the character of the income and deductions shall have the same character in the hands of the beneficiary as in the hands of the estate or trust. The amounts shall be treated as consisting of the same proportion of each class of items entering into the computation of DNI as the total of each class bears to the total DNI of the estate or trust unless the terms of the governing instrument specifically allocate different classes of income to different beneficiaries. The composition of DNI determines the type of income distributed and taxed to the beneficiaries. If 80% of DNI is taxable income and 20% is tax-exempt interest, then 80% of the DNI allocated to the beneficiaries is taxable income and 20% will be tax-exempt interest. Remember the Neapolitan ice cream analogy

discussed earlier. For tax purposes, the "scoops" (distributions) received by the beneficiary are based on the composition of DNI. Anytime a "scoop" is made; the beneficiary partakes in each flavor. The fiduciary is not allowed to "pick and choose" which flavor a beneficiary gets, unless the document provides for a special allocation.

20. Expenses are allocated against income in the following order:

1. All deductions directly attributable to a particular class of income are deducted from that income.
2. All deductions not directly attributable to a specific type of income may be allocated to any type of income, as long as some deductions are allocated to tax-exempt income. This rule provides some flexibility to the fiduciary. Depending on the needs of the beneficiaries, the fiduciary can allocate the indirect deductions against any type of income included in DNI. If the beneficiaries need a larger amount of portfolio income, to deduct some personal investment interest expense, for example, the fiduciary can allocate a larger amount of indirect costs to passive income, provided the fiduciary does not create a passive loss. If the reverse is true and the beneficiaries need passive income, expenses can be allocated solely to portfolio income and none to the passive activities.
3. Passive losses can only be deducted to the extent of passive income. Net passive losses cannot be allocated against any other type of income and are retained (suspended) by the entity. If directly related tax-exempt expenses exceed tax-exempt income, excess expenses cannot be deducted against any other type of income.
4. Any excess deductions (directly related expenses exceed the specific income), excluding passive losses and tax-exempt expenses, can be allocated against any type of income, just like indirect expenses discussed above. The income must be included in DNI before expenses can be allocated against it.

ENDNOTES

1. The court may interfere with the trustee's discretionary power in the event of fraud, misconduct or a clear abuse of discretion. *Beaty v. Bales*, 677 S.W.2d 750 (Tex App - San Antonio 1984). However, absolute or uncontrolled discretion may not be given to a trustee in Texas.

2. *Thorman v. Carr*, 408 S.W.2d 259 (Civ. App. 1966) ref. n.r.e.

3. Id. The presence or absence of such words as "absolute," "full" or "uncontrollable" in describing discretionary powers is of no significance.

4. IRC §645.

5. Congress is considering limiting the estate's year end to October, November or December.

6. Reg §1.641(b)-3(a)

7. *Earl A. Brown, Jr.*, 890 F2d 1329 (5th Cir, 1989).

8. Rev Proc 98-13, 1998-4 IRB 21

9. IRC §469(i)

10. IRC §469(i)(4)(B)

11. Rules covering allocation of capital gains to DNI will be discussed later in the Chapter.

12. IRC §1223(11).

13. Currently, estates are not subject to the related party rules. Congress has proposed to subject §643(e)(3) transfers of estates to the related party rules under §267.

14. IRC §163

15. IRC §265

16. Rev. Rul. 63-27, 1963-1 CB 57

17. Reg.§1.652(b)-3(d)

18. Reg. §1.167(h)-1(b)

19. See *Interfirst Bank of Fort Worth, N.A. v King*, 722 S.W.2d 18, (App. 12 Dist 1986) and *Hay v US*, 263 F.Supp. 813 (D.C. 1967)

20. IRC §164(a)

21. IRC §642(c)

22. IRC §642(c)(1) and Reg. §1.642(c)-1

23. Reg. §1.212-1(i)

24. IRC §642(d)

25. 994 F2d 302 (CA-6, 1993).

26. 1994-38 IRB 4

27. §643(e)(1)

28. IRC §§1014, 1015

29. Rev Rul 67-74, 1967-1 CB 194 and Regs. §1.651(a)-2(b)

30. IRC §469(j)(6)

31. IRC §1014

32. IRC §469(g)(2)

33. IRC §469(j)(12)

34. See endnote 12, *supra*

35. IRC §643(b)

36. Reg. §1.651(a)-4

37. IRC §§651(a) and (b)

38. IRC §§651(b) and 661(a)

39. For accounting purposes, 50% of the block might be rent, while for DNI purposes, only 25% of the block would be rent.

40. Rev. Rul. 60-87, 1960-1 CB 286; Reg.§1.663(a)-1(b)

41. IRC §663 (b)

42. TRA'97 (Pub. L. 105-34, Section 1306(a)) amending §663(b)

43. Reg. §1.652(b)-3.

44. Reg. §1.662(b)-2

45. Reg §1.652(b)-2

46. Let. Rul. 9023012

47. IRC §691(a)(5)(A)(iii); Let. Rul. 9108027; *Estate of Frane*, 998 F2d 567 (CA-8, 1993)

48. IRC §691(c)

49. IRC §691(c)

50. IRC §§665-668

51. See §665(c)

PART 3

The Techniques of Planning

CHAPTER 9

The Goals of Estate Planning

OVERVIEW AND CAUTION

This chapter is an introduction to the most commonly encountered estate planning goals and the planning techniques that seek to accomplish them. The goals are categorized as financial and non-financial. Some techniques accomplish more than one goal, although some goals may be in conflict with other goals.

In reading this chapter, it would be well to keep in mind that individuals invariably have one very fundamental goal in common, which may be far more important than saving taxes or attaining any other specific goal. The primary goal is *happiness and peace of mind*, and specific estate planning strategies may conflict with this primary goal. For example, large gifts may reduce transfer taxes, but they may also jeopardize happiness by imperiling the donor's sense of financial security. The planner should be especially attuned to the individual's emotional and psychological preferences and not persist in recommending techniques that are in conflict with them. Planning strategies are not ends in themselves; they are a means to an end; specifically, the individual's greater happiness.

NONFINANCIAL GOALS

Some specific objectives in estate planning cannot be measured in dollars and cents. These nonfinancial goals, often called "personal planning," include caring for one's dependents, attaining privacy and speed in the property transfer process, and appropriately managing assets.

Caring for Dependents

One main objective is to provide care for family members affected by a person's disability or death. For example, *disability* may trigger the need for someone to step-in to care not only for the disabled person, for his or her property, and perhaps most importantly for his or her minor children. Advanced planning makes it more likely that the actual wishes of the person will be carried out. Various methods to accomplish these tasks are examined in Chapter 17.

Accomplishing Fair and Proper Distribution of Property

Good estate planning seeks to dispose of a person's property to the appropriate parties in the proper amounts at the right time. Many factors will influence the choice of the best succession and distribution techniques, and every ensuing chapter will discuss them.

Attaining Privacy in the Property Transfer Process

Other things being equal, most people prefer that their wealth be transferred as privately as possible. They realize that their intended beneficiaries will experience less stress by avoiding public scrutiny. We have seen in Chapter 4 that the methods of property transfer are characterized by different degrees of privacy, with the probate process considerably more public than the process of transferring property by trust. Of course, if privacy were the only criterion, no one would prefer the probate alternative. Probate does, however, offer some advantages, and each person should weigh the advantages for his or her own estate against the disadvantages and decide accordingly. The decision whether or not to avoid probate is the main focus of Chapter 10.

Attaining Speed in the Property Transfer Process

Similar to privacy, speed in property transfer is desired by most people and is often less attainable with the probate alternative. On the other hand, joint tenancy may be the quickest way to transfer property at the death of a co-owner, but it is also very inflexible. Living trusts are expensive to establish, but allow the most flexible and long range estate planning. These various trade-offs are discussed in Chapter 10.

Maintaining Control Over Assets

As we shall see in later chapters, many lifetime estate planning strategies require that a person relinquish beneficial interests in property by making actual transfers. Few people relish this; they would rather hold on to their property for as long as possible. But estate planning goals, such as reducing estate taxes, might motivate some to make lifetime transfers.

Further, different lifetime transfer strategies require different degrees of transfer. Usually, the more complete the transfer, the more likely other goals can be accomplished. As you read about the various estate planning techniques, for each one consider the degree of transfer involved and ask yourself whether most wealthy individuals would be willing to undertake it or whether the particular strategy is likely to have very limited appeal.

FINANCIAL GOALS

We will divide our discussion of financial goals into non-tax related financial goals and tax related financial goals.

Non-tax Financial Goals

Financial goals that are not tax-related include acquiring adequate liquidity, minimizing non-tax estate transfer costs, maintaining a satisfactory standard of living, ensuring proper disposition by careful drafting, preserving business value, and attaining pre- and postmortem flexibility.

Acquiring adequate liquidity. The death of a person may trigger the need for liquidity to pay taxes, administration expenses, claims, and for the needs of a surviving family. Many, if not most, wealthy people lack sufficient liquidity to immediately take care of all of these things. This is especially true if much of the person's wealth was tied-up in real estate or a closely held business. Chapter 15 is devoted entirely to liquidity planning and will describe the major methods of increasing liquidity, including the sale of assets, acquiring life insurance, using valuation discounts, and making tax-delaying or tax-reducing elections that are available only to the estates of deceased business owners.

Minimizing non-tax estate transfer costs. Non-tax estate transfer costs include attorney and trustee fees, executor commissions, court costs, and several other probate fees such as the bond premium. Chapter 10 will examine these costs while exploring the decision to avoid probate.

Maintaining a satisfactory standard of living. We shall see that many tax objectives can be achieved with lifetime transfers. The planner should ensure, however, that clients will retain sufficient assets and income to maintain a satisfactory standard of living. This may require foregoing certain tax-saving transfers, such as outright gifts, in favor of retaining property. Or it may call for making other less complete or less costly transfers, such as an installment sale, which, in turn, can generate valuable consideration. These alternatives will be explored in detail in Chapters 13 and 14, covering lifetime transfers.

Ensuring proper disposition by careful drafting. In the planning process, most people assume that no matter what happens, their intended beneficiaries will in fact receive their accumulated wealth. People trust their attorney to draft transfer documents properly. However, drafting skill varies greatly, and poor drafting can frustrate an individual's dispositive preferences in many ways. The examples below are merely illustrative.

EXAMPLE 9 - 1. Martha's simple will does not include a survival clause, creating the risk that her property will be inherited by her *in-laws* rather than by her parents.

EXAMPLE 9 - 2. Unaware of QTIP trust planning, an attorney drafts a simple will for Francis which leaves all of his property outright to his second wife, running the risk that she may neglect to adequately provide for her *stepchildren* (Francis's children from his prior marriage), who are living with Francis's first wife.

EXAMPLE 9 - 3. A trust-will is drafted for a client, in which estate property will be held in trust until the youngest of the client's grandchildren reaches age 25. The disposition may be ruled invalid for violation of the *rule against perpetuities*.

EXAMPLE 9 - 4. Donald's attorney drafts a tax-saving testamentary trust into which nearly all of Donald's estate is intended to pass. However, because much of Donald's property is still held in *joint tenancy* with his wife, that property will not pass to the trust at his death but will go outright to his wife by automatic right of survivorship. At that point, the only way for her to move the property into the trust will be by making a taxable gift. And, a §2036 problem can arise if the gift is made into a trust *for her benefit*.

In each of these situations, more careful planning and drafting could have eliminated the risk of these unintended dispositions without significantly altering the person's objectives. Careful planning and drafting is an essential prerequisite to the achievement of dispositive goals.

Preserving business value. The death of a business-owner can precipitate a serious and very rapid decline in the value of that business. In Chapter 16, we see that certain *arrangements* by an owner will minimize (or even avoid) the decline in value, thereby greatly increasing the likelihood that the pre-death value of the business, rather than evaporating, passes to the owner's heirs.

Attaining pre- and postmortem flexibility. Flexibility in estate planning means that as circumstances change, the client or the individual's surrogates can intelligently alter arrangements to accomplish desired goals. While the client is still alive and mentally competent, flexibility can fairly easily be maintained by the client periodically reviewing the estate plan and revising it when necessary. After the client either loses mental capacity or dies, flexibility, although not entirely impossible, is more difficult to sustain. Yet, as we shall see next, considerable flexibility can be maintained if the client anticipates the problem by providing in advance for *surrogate decision makers*.

The critical need for flexibility by naming surrogate decision makers emerges often in the context of providing for young children (even young adults) in the event that both parents die prematurely. For example, without planning, the parents' property is usually required by law to be held by a legal guardian and transferred outright to the children when they reach legal adulthood at age 18. But most parents would prefer to delay outright distribution until the children are older and more mature. Such can be accomplished by designating responsible parties (whether as trustees, agents, or holders of limited powers) to act on their behalf. Flexibility through the use of surrogate decision makers may take the form of powers of appointment (usually found in trusts, see Chapters 11 and 12), durable powers of attorney (usually a separate document designating an agent to carry out certain acts, see Chapter 17), and disclaimers (usually written by the disclaimant in response to a proffered gift or bequest, see Chapters 7, 12, and 18).

Maximizing benefits for the surviving spouse. Most wealthy couples want to be assured that the surviving spouse will live comfortably and at the same time minimize transfer taxes. Poor planning may result in an inefficient transfer, accomplishing one goal at the expense of another, when both could have been obtained.

> EXAMPLE 9 - 5. Cliffton *writes his own will*, even though he is quite wealthy. Although he is married to Pamela, his will leaves a substantial portion of his property outright to their middle-aged children, even if Pamela survives him, because all he wants is to be certain that his unified credit is utilized. Cliffton's estate plan succeeds in utilizing his unified credit and in having the property that is left to the children bypass Pamela's estate, but in so doing, he has unnecessarily denied her the use of the property.

Chapters 11 and 12 discuss tax reducing plans that provide for the surviving spouse's welfare without sacrificing other important objectives.

> EXAMPLE 9 - 6. Continuing the prior example, Cliffton could achieve his goals by leaving the property in *trust* for the benefit of Pamela and the children. Without causing any increase in transfer tax, the trust could give Pamela the following rights: (1) the right to the income from the property for her life; (2) the power to invade the trust corpus for reasons of health, education, support, or maintenance; and/or (3) the power to determine whether the property should continue to be held in trust after her death or be immediately distributed at that time.

Tax Related Financial Goals

Income taxes and transfer taxes represent the largest cause of estate shrinkage to medium and larger sized estates. Most of the specific planning strategies covered in this text will seek to reduce these taxes.

Income tax savings goals. Planning strategies designed to save income taxes generally seek to step-up basis, shift income to lower bracket taxpayers, and to defer the recognition of income.

Obtaining a stepped-up basis. Achieving a step-up in basis is especially important to a transferee who wants to sell an appreciated asset. However, much of estate planning favors lifetime *gifts*, where the transferee receives not a stepped-up, but a carryover basis. On the other hand, a step-up is the usual rule for inherited property. Thus, other things being equal, planners recommend deferring the transfer of appreciated assets until the owner's death. Of course, basis is just one of many considerations involved in making lifetime transfers, a subject that will be more thoroughly explored in Chapters 13 and 14.

Shifting income to a lower bracket taxpayer. Wealthy people are usually in the highest income tax brackets, whereas the income of other family members, such as parents and children, may be in the lower tax brackets. As we have seen, under our progressive income tax rate structure, marginal and average rates of tax generally increase with increasing taxable income.

Congressional tax reform directed a three-pronged attack on popular methods of shifting income to a lower-bracket family member. First, it adopted the *"kiddie tax,"* described in Chapter 13, that virtually eliminates any benefit of shifting income to children who are under the age of 13. Second, Congress has made income shifting relatively less attractive by lowering the maximum marginal rate to its present 39.6% level; still high compared to the 15% bracket, but paling in comparison to earlier maximum rates that were as high as 91%. And third, although *completed* transfers (gifts) can still shift some income, two major lifetime *incomplete* transfer devices that were once very much in vogue, the short-term trust and the spousal remainder trust described in Appendix 14A, are no longer available due to revisions to the *grantor trust rules*.

Many of the examples in the remainder of this book will assume a 50% "combined" marginal income tax rate for wealthier individuals, based on the premise that state and local taxes are commonly in the low double-digit range. Thus, for each additional dollar of taxable income, a high income taxpayer will incur 50 cents in tax. Likewise, every deduction of a dollar will save 50 cents in tax.

Of course, taxpayers in the highest tax bracket are most likely to be interested in making income shifting transfers. In 1999, a married couple with joint taxable income in excess of $283,150 will have reached the top federal marginal rate of 39.6%. A single individual taxpayer hits the top rate at a lower level. It makes sense that the greatest tax savings occur when the additional income collected by the transferee is either not taxed or is taxed at the 15% marginal rate. Thus, the most likely persons to benefit from income shifting include minor children over age 13, young adults in college, and, perhaps, the donor's parents. This is especially true where the wealthy person is presently making after-tax gifts to the lower tax bracket donee.

Figure 9-1 illustrates the progression of maximum marginal federal income tax rates since 1952.

FIGURE 9-1 Maximum Marginal Federal Income Tax Rates, 1952-Present

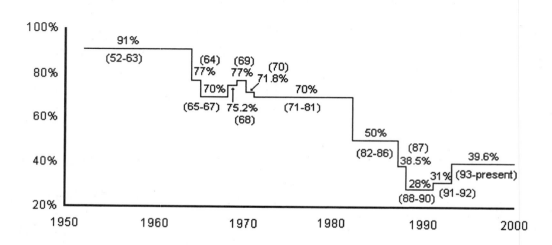

Can all income potentially receivable by one person be taxed to another? The answer is no, because tax law distinguishes two types of income: personal service income and other income. Under the *assignment of income doctrine*, earnings from services performed will always be taxable to the person performing those services. However, income from investment property can be taxed to another if the property is satisfactorily transferred for his/her benefit before the income is realized. Hence, accrued interest or dividends declared prior to the date of the gift are taxed to the donor even if paid to the donee.

Usually income is shifted by a complete transfer (i.e., an outright gift) of the income generating property, but with some techniques the transfer is partially incomplete such as the custodial gift and the irrevocable trust discussed in

Chapter 13. We shall also see in Chapter 18 that income shifting to save income taxes can be accomplished by the timing of distributions from decedent's estates to the beneficiaries. And there are some opportunities to use multiple taxpaying entities rather than just one, such as electing to treat a trust held for the children of deceased parents as separate trusts for each child rather than just one trust. Since the income tax rates are progressive, taxes are saved by having multiple taxpayers. This is referred to as taking multiple "trips up the rate ladder."

Tax reform since 1986 has dramatically reduced the benefits of shifting income to trusts and estates. In addition to radically lowering the maximum marginal tax rate for individuals, Congress greatly reduced the tax bracket amounts for trusts and estates that are subject to the lower rates. Thus, incremental income taxed to estates and trusts hits the top of the rate ladder at a much lower income level than is true for income taxed to individuals. A trust is in the top tax bracket (currently 39.6%) by the time it reaches taxable income of $9,000 (see Table 8-1).

Deferring recognition of income. Careful planning can defer tax on the gain from the sale to later years. Examples of transfers that defer taxable gain are the installment sale and the private annuity, covered in Chapter 14. And in Chapter 18, we will see that an estate can defer income by carefully choosing its fiscal year end. Deferral of the tax enables the taxpayer to use the money to earn income until the taxes finally have to be paid.

Transfer tax savings goals. Techniques designed to reduce transfer taxes generally do so by accomplishing one or more of the following: *reduce* (maybe to zero) the amount deemed to be taxable; *freeze* the estate tax base; and *leverage* the use of exclusions, exemptions, or the unified credit. To some extent, all three techniques make use of imperfections in the unified transfer tax system that were discussed at the end of Chapter 5.

Reducing the estate tax base. Certain planning arrangements reduce the estate tax base, subjecting less of the person's wealth to transfer taxation. Each dollar of value that is removed from the transferor's tax base and still makes it to the intended beneficiary represents money saved at the transferor's highest transfer tax marginal rate (i.e., anywhere from 37% to 60% depending on the ultimate value of the cumulative transfers).

EXAMPLE 9 - 7. A month before she died, Sharon, a widow whose net estate was worth just under three million dollars, gave each of her children, their wives, and their adult children checks in the amount of $10,000. There were ten donees in all.

Due to the annual exclusion, none of the gifts were taxable and her estate tax base was reduced by $100,000. The transfers lowered her estate tax by $53,000, given that the marginal rate just below three million dollars is 53%.

Other reduction techniques examined in later chapters include gifts into trust (Chapter 13), judicious use of the unlimited marital deduction (Chapters 11 and 12), bypass planning (Chapters 11 and 12), election of the alternate valuation date (Chapters 15 and 18), the family-owned business exclusion, special-use valuation (for farm or other closely held businesses that rely on real estate property), valuation discounts for gifts of family limited partnership interests, fractional interest discounts, and conservation easements (all discussed in Chapter 15).

Freezing the estate tax base. In contrast with techniques that can reduce the estate tax base, certain property arrangements are designed mainly to *limit the future increase* in the estate tax base by freezing a portion of the person's wealth at its *current value*. Thus, all future appreciation in this portion is excluded from transfer taxation.

EXAMPLE 9 - 8. In 1999, Nicky, a single parent, sells one of his vacation homes to his son Donny for $128,000. Nicky received $15,000 as a down payment and a secured installment note in the amount of $113,000 that requires interest-only payments (at 7.5%) for ten years followed by interest and principal payments amortized over another 15 years. If Nicky dies in the next ten years, his estate includes the note valued at approximately $113,000 (actual value depends upon how well it is secured and prevailing interest rates), whatever is left of the $15,000 down payment (or the investments therefrom), and the interest payments. Hopefully, the value of the vacation home at the time of Nicky's death is considerably more than it was when he sold it to Donny.

Transfers are often a blend of reducing and freezing a portion of the tax base, rather than being exclusively one or the other.

EXAMPLE 9 - 9. Assume that Nicky, from the last example, made a *gift* of the vacation home rather than selling it to Donny. He would file a gift tax return and report a taxable gift of $118,000. Assuming no prior taxable gifts, no gift tax is due because of the shelter of the unified credit. If Nicky dies ten years later when the value of the vacation home is $200,000 (or, for that matter, any amount), Nicky's estate tax base will include just the taxable gift value of $118,000. With regard to that particular asset, Nicky's estate tax base has been partially reduced (the $10,000 annual exclusion portion) and partially frozen (the taxable gift portion).

Leveraging the use of exclusions, exemptions, and the unified credit. In business, leveraging means to structuring a transaction in a certain way such that the end result is magnified or enhanced. Thus, one can *borrow* to magnify profit potential of an investment. Of course, doing so may also magnify the loss.

> EXAMPLE 9 - 10. Brenda has $50,000 that she would like to invest in XYZ stock. When the shares are selling at $50/share, she uses a margin account with her brokerage firm to purchase 2,000 shares at a cost of $100,000. Her shares are collateral for the matching loan by the brokerage firm. If the value increases to $60/share, her shares will have increased in value by $20,000 compared to an increase of $10,000 had she not borrowed. Of course, if the shares had decreased to $40,000/share, her decrease would have also been $20,000.

Much of estate planning leveraging seeks to magnify the end results of transactions and does so with less of a downside risk compared to the borrowing example. Many of these transactions, if successful, greatly reduce the estate tax and, if not successful, leave the transferor no worse off than had he or she simply not made the transfer (other than whatever costs are associated with making the transfer). As with freezing, many of these transactions are a blend of reduction, freezing, and leveraging with the characterization being based upon what is expected to produce the greatest reduction in transfer taxes.

> EXAMPLE 9 - 11. Wendy gave a life insurance policy on her life to her son Matthew. Although it had a face value of $500,000, it was valued at only $30,000 for gift tax purposes. When Wendy died six years later, Matthew collected the $500,000 proceeds and Wendy's estate reported a $20,000 adjusted taxable gift. Had Wendy died within three years of the transfer, then §2035(a) would have applied and the $500,000 would be included in her estate (the adjusted taxable gift would be reduced to zero). Thus, if successful, the transfer greatly leverages the transfer of wealth at a very small transfer tax cost. If it is not successful, the result is basically what would have occurred had no transfer taken place.

The use of life insurance and life insurance trusts in estate planning is covered extensively in Chapter 15. Other examples of techniques that use leveraging are the benefits of the grantor retained income trust (GRIT), the qualified personal residence trust (QPRT), and the private annuity (all of which are covered in Chapter 14), and the corporate recapitalization (discussed in Chapter 16). Each of these may also have an element of estate freezing.

Delaying payment of the transfer tax. In certain situations, transfer taxes can be deferred, even though a completed transfer has taken place.

> EXAMPLE 9 - 12. Danny is contemplating several transfers of property from his large estate. His wife, Barbara, has an equally large estate, and can live very comfortably off her own wealth. If Danny gives his wealth to Barbara at his death, there will be no immediate estate tax on that property, since the transfer will be totally sheltered by the unlimited estate tax marital deduction. But the estate tax will only be deferred, not eliminated. The property will probably be taxed at Barbara's later death. In fact, the gift to her will probably increase the overall estate tax on that property (compared to the amount of tax that their combined estates would pay if he left the property outright or in trust to the children), since the transfer to Barbara (*a*) foregoes the use of the unified credit at Danny's death; and (*b*) will increase the size of Barbara's gross estate, possibly pushing it into a higher marginal rate. Thus, Danny faces the alternative of either deferring a potentially larger tax or, more immediately, incurring a (smaller) estate tax on his wealth.

Chapters 11 and 12 discuss the interrelationship between the marital deduction and the unified credit. Other transfer tax deferral devices covered in later chapters include the application of §6166, dealing with the payment of the estate tax in future installments for a decedent-owner of a closely held business; §6163, which allows the deferral of that portion of the tax attributed to a vested remainder interest; §6161, pertaining to the deferral of the tax for good cause (all covered in Chapter 15), and the simple practice of delaying property transfers (Chapter 13).

This chapter has introduced the specific techniques of estate planning by presenting the main goals underlying them. The next chapter begins our detailed study of these techniques with an examination of the decision to avoid probate.

QUESTIONS AND PROBLEMS

1. Consider that goals sometimes conflict. (a) What is probably the typical client's principal goal in estate planning? (b) Give your own example of how a more specific goal described in this chapter can conflict with it.

2. List and briefly describe a person's nonfinancial estate planning goals.

3. List and briefly describe a person's non-tax financial estate planning goals.

4. Describe the advantage of selecting a surrogate decision maker in the estate planning process.

5. For the years in question, Mom and Dad are in the combined 50% marginal income tax bracket and the standard deduction for a minor claimed as a dependent is $700. How much income tax can the family save this year if they can shift $20,000 in taxable income to the following alternate taxpayers whom, we will assume, have no current gross income? Both children (12-year-old daughter and 16-year-old son) are claimed as dependents. Also, for each taxpayer, state the maximum potential total income not taxable at all, and taxable at 15%.

   a. Shift to their daughter.
   b. Shift to their son.
   c. Shift to an irrevocable trust that distributes all the income annually to their daughter. (See Table 8-1 in chapter 8 for trust income tax rates.)
   d. Shift to an irrevocable trust that accumulates all income annually for the benefit of their son.
   e. Shift to an irrevocable trust that accumulates $1,700 and distributes the balance annually to their son.

6. List and briefly describe a person's income tax savings goals.

7. List and briefly describe a person's transfer tax savings goals.

ANSWERS TO QUESTIONS AND PROBLEMS

1. (a) The client's principal goal is happiness and peace of mind. Estate planning deals principally with property transfer decisions, many of which may be fundamentally unsettling for individuals. (b) Answers will vary but an example might be making a large lifetime gift to a young adult child.

2. Nonfinancial estate planning goals:

   a. Caring for future dependents, including the client and the client's minor children.
   b. Attaining privacy in the property transfer process.
   c. Attaining speed in the property transfer process.
   d. Maintaining control over assets.

3. Non-tax financial estate planning goals:

   a. Minimizing non-tax estate transfer costs.
   b. Maintaining a satisfactory standard of living.
   c. Ensuring proper disposition.
   d. Preserving business value.
   e. Attaining pre- and postmortem flexibility.
   f. Maximizing benefits for the surviving spouse.

4. The advantage of selecting a surrogate decision maker is flexibility in planning after the client becomes incapacitated or dies.

5. Without income shifting, the parent's tax would be: $20,000 * 50\% = \$10,000$

   a. Shift income to daughter: kiddie tax applies.

      The first $700 of unearned income to the daughter would be tax free. The next $700 would be taxed at daughter's 15% rate. Based on the kiddie tax, the remaining $18,600 would be taxed at the parent's 50% rate.

Tax = $700* 15% + $18,600 * 50% = $105 + $9,300 = $9,405
Total tax savings = $10,000 - $9,405 = $595
Maximum not taxable at all and taxable at 15%: $700 at 0% and $700 at 15%.

b. Son would be taxed on all but $700 of the income.

Tax = 15% * $19,300 = $2,895
Total tax savings = $10,000 - $2,895 = $7,105
Maximum not taxable at all and taxable at 15%: $700 at 0% and $19,300 at 15%.

c. Same answer as part "a," based on the combined effect of the conduit principle and the kiddie tax.

d. Trust would be taxed on all but $100 (its personal exemption) of the income. Tax = $2,360 + 39.6% * ($19,900 - $8,350) = $2,360 + $4,574 = $6,934; total tax savings = $10,000 - $6,934 = $3,066
Maximum not taxable at all and taxable at 15%: $100 at 0% and $1,700 at 15%.

e. Trust would be taxed on $1,700. Trust tax = $1,700 * 15% = $255
Son would be taxed on $17,500 of the $18,200 distribution. Son's tax = $17,500 * 15% = $2,625.
Tax savings = $10,000 - ($255 + $2,625) = $7,120
Maximum total combined trust and individual income that is not taxed at all and is taxable at 15% is: $800 ($100 for the trust and $700 for Son) and $19,200, respectively.

6. Income tax savings goals:

a. Obtaining a stepped-up basis.
b. Shifting income to a lower bracket taxpayer.
c. Deferring recognition of income.

7. Transfer tax savings goals:

    a.   Reducing the taxable estate.
    b.   Freezing the taxable estate.
    c.   Delaying payment of the transfer tax.
    d.   Leveraging the use of exclusions, exemptions, and the unified credit.
    e.   Minimizing the generation-skipping transfer tax.

CHAPTER 10

The Decision to Avoid Probate

OVERVIEW

As we have seen, the term probate has come to mean the entire court process by which the state supervises the orderly distribution of a decedent's probate property. Since probate has significant drawbacks, most people prefer to have their estates use one of its two major alternatives, joint tenancy or the living trust. These are referred to as *will substitutes* because they supersede any provisions in the deceased person's will. This chapter surveys the advantages and disadvantages of all three mechanisms of transfer. To some degree the choice is subjective; what is best depends on the individual's personal assessment of the pros and cons of each choice in the light of his or her personal circumstances. We will conclude the chapter with a summary of circumstances that might cause a person to favor one mechanism of transfer over one of the other two mechanisms.

Another type of asset specific alternative to probate is the *pay-on-death* account that is recognized in many states. These may be a bank or savings account (sometimes referred to as Totten trusts) controlled by the depositor so long as he or she is living but with a provision that the account is payable to another if it is still open when the depositor dies. Most states allow pay-on-death accounts to be used with checking and savings accounts, money market accounts, and certificates of deposit.

A growing number of states have adopted the Uniform TOD Securities Registration Act which allows individual securities (e.g., stocks and bonds) and brokerage accounts to be held in a manner that causes the security (or the brokerage account) to be transferred to a named beneficiary upon the owner's death. The TOD in the title of the Act refers to "transfer on death," and these are called "TOD accounts" or "TOD securities."[1] Although Totten trust accounts and TOD accounts avoid probate, they are, of course, included in the owner's gross estate.[2]

Several other alternatives to probate are not discussed in detail at this time. Some contracts, such as life insurance and retirement plans, avoid probate but they have limited general application for two reasons. First, the decision whether or not to utilize these contracts is usually independent of the decision whether or not to avoid probate. For example, life insurance is purchased for reasons other than avoiding probate--such as the need for cash at someone's death; acquiring it is not influenced by the method chosen to transfer property. Second, these limited alternatives to probate are "asset specific," that is, they cannot be used as a general guide for the rest of the person's property. For example, a Totten trust only avoids probate for a particular bank account held "in trust" for someone other than the account's owner. In contrast, a will and a living trust can serve as the guides for transferring virtually any asset. Joint tenancy also applies only to specific assets held in that form of title but almost any property can be held in this form. In this chapter, we'll use the term joint tenancy generically to include tenancy by the entirety keeping in mind that the latter is available only to married couples.

We begin our comparative study of probate and its two major alternatives by examining the pros and cons of probate.

THE BENEFITS AND DRAWBACKS OF PROBATE

Below, we describe probate's major benefits and drawbacks. For a more thorough understanding of the probate process, the reader is urged to first review the discussion of probate found in Chapter 4.

The Benefits of Probate

The major benefits of probate include fairness promoted by court supervision, orderly administration of assets, greater protection from creditors, and some limited income tax savings.

Court supervision promotes fairness. Formal probate requires substantial court supervision, a process that, at its best, promotes fairness. Through the use of petitions, accountings, hearings, and court orders, probate seeks to ensure that asset distribution is fair. No other estate transfer procedure is so controlled by public authorities.

The public-forum nature of probate encourages review and evaluation by numerous observers. Judges and official clerks are called on to approve major estate activities. In addition, other interested private parties such as beneficiaries and creditors have an opportunity to object to perceived inequities in estate administration. For example, they can object to many court rulings, including admission of a certain will to probate, appointment of a certain personal representative, payment of a certain creditor, and distribution of estate assets to a certain individual. They can raise these objections in the probate court itself; the parties need not seek a remedy elsewhere, and they can often do it without hiring a lawyer. In contrast, objections to disposition by joint tenancy or through a living trust require a different, procedurally more complicated, legal action.

Critic's response. Critics of probate contend that the additional degree of equity fostered by probate administration is, at best, minimal. They argue that judges and other public officials too often give only superficial review of proposed actions and rubber-stamp their approval of the conduct of executors. Supporters of probate respond to this criticism saying that judges implicitly and successfully rely on the interested parties, who are formally notified of the proceedings, to speak up in court if they feel they are being treated unfairly. Critics contend, however, that the average interested person would not be aware of the occurrence of many types of subtle wrong doing.

The claim that probate encourages fairness is also subject to challenge because of the recent trend in the direction of reduced supervision. In Chapter 4, we learned that many states permit "informal" or "summary" probate procedures that can greatly reduce court surveillance. Also, we saw that UPC states permit the estate's personal representation to select the degree of supervision he or she desires. If "informal probate" is chosen, the estate will receive almost no direct supervision by the court. Thus, in many states, the risk of misadministration in probate is similar to that for trusts because of the opportunity to avoid the public forum. Of course, in UPC states the ability of beneficiaries to request greater formal supervision of the executor at any time during the probate process reduces the risk of mismanagement.

In conclusion, through supervision probate promotes fairness, the strength of this generalization has been weakened by the degree to which the courts only superficially oversee administrative activities, and by the recent movement of the states to reduce the degree of mandatory court supervision.

Orderly administration of assets. Probate offers an orderly administration of estate assets. Supervision by the court and by other public officials ensures further that property transfers and title clearance will be done correctly.

Greater protection from creditors. As we saw in Chapter 4, probate procedures typically require creditors to formally file their claims against probate assets within a certain period of time, such as four months from date of issuance of letters testamentary. Failure to timely file a creditor's claim can forever bar collection from those assets. Nonprobate assets, on the other hand, may only be protected by the state's general limitations period, which can be several years. Thus, asset disposition by probate can offer distributees greater protection from creditors much sooner than other means of transfer, however, as we will discuss in a moment, there is a movement amongst the states to shorten the creditors' claim period for non-probate methods of transfer.

Actual notice: the Tulsa decision. In 1998, the U.S. Supreme court ruled in *Tulsa Professional Collection Services v. Estate of Pope* that creditors who are "known or reasonably ascertainable" to the personal representative must be given "actual" notice of the limited creditors' claim period, rather than be given just "constructive" notice by publication.[3] Notice by mail is considered acceptable actual notice.

The following is a partial listing of creditors who are usually known or can be reasonably ascertained by the personal representative:

- Hospital where decedent died, all treating physicians, ambulance company and paramedics,
- Landlord or mortgage company,
- Pool-service, gardener, maid, newspaper delivery service,
- Installment payment creditor,

- Creditors who have already sent decedent unpaid bills,
- Credit card issuers,
- Creditors that show-up as "interest deductions" on the decedent's last few years' income tax returns,
- Ongoing creditors determined from decedent's correspondence and canceled checks,
- Persons given a guarantee by the decedent as the owner of a closely held business.

Under *Tulsa*, actual notice need not be given to potential creditors whose claims are a matter of "conjecture," i.e., deduced by surmise or guesswork. An example of a conjectural claim would be that any of a deceased doctor's former patients might eventually assert a malpractice claim against the doctor's estate. The executor does not have to notify all former patients to "submit their claims or lose their right to sue." Indeed, that would likely cause needless problems. The creditors' claim period does not affect the rights of secured creditors to the extent that the debt is covered by collateral.

Individuals who anticipate that there may be hidden, or unknown claims, that are difficult to identify may decide that the shorter limitations period is a significant advantage for their estates. For example, professionals such as, doctors, lawyers, architects, engineers and accountants are potentially vulnerable to malpractice claims which, if instituted after their death, stand a greater chance of succeeding, partly because the defense's best witness, the decedent, is not available to testify. The shorter probate creditors' claim period decreases this threat.

If there is insurance to cover a claim, the claim is not barred by the short probate creditors' period. The estate may be named as a party to the suit, but the real party in interest is the insurance company that will have to pay the claim. Generally, unless the injured party files a creditor's claim within the regular creditor's claim period, state probate statutes limit the recovery to the amount of insurance coverage. Most malpractice insurance is issued on a "claims made" basis, meaning that the insurance covers only errors that occur while the policy is in force and only if a claim is submitted while it is in force. However, when a professional retires, he or she can purchase what is called "tail coverage" that continues to cover latter claims for errors made during the period covered by the insurance. There are several reasons why a person might miss the creditors' claim period, yet have a valid claim but for the tortfeasor's death. First, where there is *delayed discovery*, most statute of limitations do not begin to run until the wrong doing is discovered or should have been discovered, e.g., negligence by a doctor may not be discovered until long after an operation. Second, where there is *delayed injury or damage*, the limitations period does not begin to run until the injury or damage actually occurs. For instance, an error in will drafting might prevent an estate from claiming a marital or charitable deduction, the error would not cause any damage until the testator's death, which might be years after the will was drafted.

Many people, especially those not likely to be the target of litigation, will find the benefit of the shorter creditors' period to be of little value. In view of the fact that probate makes the decedent's assets known to anyone interested enough to "pull the file," many people prefer the more private methods of asset distribution.

In UPC states, decedents' estates can have the same claims protection without supervised probate. For example, informal UPC probate offers the four-month creditors' period because its provisions allow for the filing of a legal notice to creditors. As mentioned in Chapter 4, if the notice is not issued, the UPC imposes a three-year creditors' limitations period, starting at date of death. Certain other forms of summary probate in non-UPC states treat the claims period differently. For example, in California, the four month probate claim period is not available under summary distribution to the surviving spouse (described in Appendix 4A), but a more general Civil Code section requires that limit claims against any decedent be asserted within one year after the person's death.[4]

Income tax savings. As we saw in Chapter 8, the probate estate is considered a separate tax entity during its existence, taxable at its own rates. Hence, some modest income shifting with an additional taxpaying entity is possible. For example, during estate administration, undistributed income (FAI) earned on estate property will be taxed to the estate rather than to the beneficiaries. This can reduce total income taxes if the estate is in a lower tax bracket than its beneficiaries. However, as mentioned in Chapter 9, the advantage has been somewhat undercut by tax reform since 1986, which has generally lowered and compressed the income tax rate brackets for trusts and estates.[5] Income tax planning for estates is described briefly in Chapter 18.

The Drawbacks of Probate

Probate has several distinct disadvantages, including complexity, cost, lack of privacy, delay, and danger of unintended disposition.

Complexity. As we saw in Chapter 4, formal probate is a complex process, requiring petitions, accountings, hearings, and other complicated legal procedures. Most laypersons hire a lawyer to meet these requirements. Critics argue that supervised probate is usually an unnecessary, clumsy process offering considerable make-work for the legal profession, especially paralegals and legal secretaries. Others respond that in the many states that allow informal probate procedures, the probate process transfers a decedent's property almost as easily as does a living trust.

Cost. The cost of probate can be high. Usually, the probate administration expenses range between 2 and 10% of the probate estate's gross value. The percentage will likely decrease as the size of the estate increases (especially for those subject to informal UPC administration) because certain tasks must be performed regardless of the size of the estate.

The *personal representative's commission* usually constitutes the largest probate expense. Of course, a beneficiary of the estate, who serves as personal representative, might waive the commission. The statutes of most states either provide for "reasonable" compensation of the personal representative or a statutory commission based on a percentage of the estate's total value. In general, personal representatives' commissions for formal probate range between 2 and 5% of the gross value.

The next largest probate administration expense is usually the *attorney's fee*. Most states' statutes do not set attorneys' fees, leaving it to the judge for each case to decide and approve a *reasonable* fee, whereas other states have a statutory fee set as a percentage of the estate's total value. Where commissions and fees are set as a percentage of an estate's total value, the percentage generally decreases as the size of the estate increases, e.g., it might be 4% of the first $100,000 and 2% of the value above $100,000. In general, attorneys' fees usually range between 2 and 5% of the gross value of the probate estate. Other administration expenses unique to probate include fiduciary bond fees, appraisers' fees, and court costs, including filing fees.

Probate administration costs will be higher for estates containing real property located in other states. Under what is called *ancillary administration*, that property is probated in the state in which it is located. This usually required hiring an attorney who practices in the other state to handle the ancillary administration.

Other factors that will affect the level of probate administration costs include the nature of the estate property (e.g., closely held business interests, expensive artwork, etc., versus marketable securities), the complexity of the estate distribution plan, and whether a will contest occurs.

Contrary to popular belief, probate does *not* increase estate taxes. Indeed, since probate costs are deductible, probate may actually reduce estate taxes, but increasing costs in order to decrease estate tax is not wise planning since a dollar deduction produces less than a dollar saved in taxes. As previously discussed in Chapters 4 and 6, the probate estate and the gross estate are different concepts.

Lack of privacy. Probate is a public process; all probate proceedings are subject to public scrutiny. For example, any person can inspect a decedent's probate file, which will eventually include the decedent's will, the estate inventory and appraisal, any creditor's claims, and the order for final distribution. Those particularly interested in inspecting a file would include survivors who are fighting and members of the press seeking a story about a newsworthy decedent. Commonly cited examples of celebrities receiving considerable publicity which could have been avoided by using trusts include the estates of Amanda Blake, Greta Garbo, Natalie Wood, John Wayne, Darryl Zanuck, and the controversy surrounding the conservatorship for Groucho Marx.

The probate files of most decedents are not seen by anyone other than court officials. Interested parties, such as the decedent's relatives and the executor can have the attorney for the estate send them copies of every document that is filed, and many probate attorneys do this as a matter of practice without any request that they do so, thus the most interested parties have no reason to review the court's file unless one harbors suspicion that not everything is being sent.

In some situations, a person may actually prefer the lack of privacy inherent in probate. For example, the public aspects of probate might discourage or uncover fraudulent dealings undertaken by unscrupulous survivors.

Delay. Even for smaller estates, probate administration takes considerable time, ranging from nine months to several years before final distribution is made. In any particular case, the delay can be quite unpredictable. Delay can be especially hard on grieving survivors, partly because it can increase or prolong tension and conflict among them. As a specific example of delay in probate, payment of proceeds of life insurance on the decedent's life to the decedent's testamentary trust will be delayed until the trust takes effect, which usually can be no sooner than the expiration of the creditor's period, several months after date of death. Thus, complete, immediate liquidity cannot be provided to the decedent's survivors. However, preliminary distributions of significant amounts can usually be made earlier if the executor can make a good faith representation that doing so will not jeopardize creditors.

Danger of unintended disposition. The nature of probate may in some cases increase the risk of an undesired *will contest*, one which may be settled with a distribution of assets in a manner that conflicts with testator intent. For example, a person named only in a prior will might contest the decedent's last will on a technicality. The person might, for example, claim that the decedent failed at the time of execution to verbally request that the witnesses sign the will. In contrast with probate, other nonprobate documents of transfer are more difficult to contest, partly because execution requirements are less stringent; thus a mistake in execution formality that would invalidate the transfer is less likely to occur. However, recent changes in the UPC make a successful challenge on a mere technicality more difficult. Section 2-503. *Writings Intended as Wills, etc.* reads as follows:

> *Although a document or writing added upon a document was not executed in compliance with Section 2-502, the document or writing is treated as if it had been executed in compliance with that section if the proponent of the document or writing establishes by clear and convincing evidence that the decedent intended the document or writing to constitute (i) the decedent's will, (ii) a partial or complete revocation of the will, (iii) an addition to or an alteration of the will, or (iv) a partial or complete revival of his [or her] formerly revoked will or of a formerly revoked portion of the will.*

With a better understanding of the pros and cons of probate, let us now consider the two principal alternatives to probate. We first turn to the simpler alternative, disposition by joint tenancy.

THE JOINT TENANCY ALTERNATIVE

Disposition by right of survivorship under title held in joint tenancy is one major alternative to probate. It, too, has several advantages and disadvantages.

Advantages of Joint Tenancy

Joint tenancy has a number of distinct advantages: low administrative cost; convenience, speed and privacy; clear, undisputed disposition; the ability to avoid creditors' claims; and income shifting.

Low administrative cost. Joint tenancy is inexpensive, both to create and to terminate. Both actions typically involve simply adding or deleting names on a certificate of ownership. Financial institutions, and others holding record of titles, will aid the survivors in making the change. The removal of the deceased cotenant's name from title usually requires the presentation of a death certificate and the completion of a short, preprinted form signed by one or more of the surviving joint tenants. In order to clear title to real estate, one of the surviving joint tenants may have to sign a declaration under penalty of perjury, identifying the decedent described in an attached death certificate as being one of the owners whose name appears on the title of certain real estate. The notarized declaration and the certified copy of the death certificate are then recorded in the county where the real estate is located.

Convenience, speed, and privacy. The simplicity inherent in creating and terminating joint tenancies makes them a convenient, easily understood, and speedy dispositive device. Any existing will or trust is disregarded as irrelevant to the automatic survivorship inherent in joint tenancy. Unlike probate property, which is a matter of public record, joint tenancy property will pass to the surviving cotenants in relative privacy. Compared to the ease of "pulling a file" at the probate court, it is more difficult for the public to obtain information about jointly held stock, bank accounts, and the like, although real estate, including that held in joint tenancy, is usually recorded in the county recorder's office.

Clear, undisputed disposition. Suits contesting joint tenancies are rare, partly because the legal formality requirements for taking title in joint tenancy are clear and minimal. There is little to challenge. In addition, the method of holding title in joint tenancy is usually clearly indicated. For example, some states require the words, "joint tenancy with right of survivorship and not as tenants in common," a title description that further minimizes confusion. In contrast, interested parties are more able to challenge the validity of a will, in part because its execution requirements and dispositive provisions are far more complex.

Circumstance may open the way to a successful challenge. In some cases, courts have held that the decedent created a joint tenancy *for convenience only*, and did not intend to leave his or her interest to the surviving cotenants. For example, an elderly person may create a joint tenancy solely to seek assistance in property management. A younger person may have been named as a cotenant simply to help write checks on the elder person's checking account.

Ability to reduce creditors' claims. Property held in joint tenancy is not subject to the claims of a *deceased cotenant's* unsecured creditors, because death results in an instantaneous and automatic transfer of ownership to the surviving cotenants. However, a creditor may be able to recover under the theory that the deceased cotenant made a transfer considered to be "fraudulent" as to creditors, however, such claim would require evidence that the decedent created the joint tenancy at a time when he or she was insolvent, or that the transfer was done with the intent to defraud creditors or to hinder the collection of a debt. Obviously, joint tenancy property is subject to claims resulting from debts incurred by the *surviving cotenants*, whether or not incurred jointly with the decedent.

> EXAMPLE 10 - 1. Three years ago, Starfield financed the purchase of a car, which was used as collateral against the loan. Starfield died this year owning, among other things, the car (a probate asset), and some securities held in joint tenancy with his sister. If the bank loan goes into default, the bank will be able to recover the car. If proceeds from the sale of the car are not sufficient to pay off the loan, the bank may be able to reach other assets in Starfield's probate estate, but it would not be able to seize the securities that now belong to the sister.

Income shifting. By placing property in joint tenancy with other family members, a high income individual may be able to shift income to lower-bracket taxpayers. The donee's ownership interest is usually immediately transferred to them and, consequently, income generated by the transferred share belongs to them, too. There are some exceptions, depending on state law, bank accounts may not be considered as transferred (even though title is changed to joint tenancy) until money is withdrawn by the donee and EE savings bonds might not be considered as transferred until the owners submit them for payment and split the proceeds.

Disadvantages of Joint Tenancy

The disadvantages of joint tenancy: inflexible, uncontrolled and inefficient disposition; surrender of ownership and control; incomplete probate avoidance; between spouses, if one spouse dies, a lower basis when compared to community property; and the risk of higher transfer taxes.

Inflexible, uncontrolled, and inefficient disposition. Joint tenancy is an inflexible, uncontrolled, and inefficient dispositive device. Disposition is clear but rigid: The surviving cotenants take outright, pro-rata, the deceased cotenant's interest, and the last surviving cotenant winds up with an individual, fee simple interest in the property; thus, obviously, right of survivorship cannot control disposition of property when the last cotenant dies.

Danger of uncontrolled, undesired disposition. Joint tenancies can result in uncontrolled and undesired dispositions in three major ways.

First, by taking title in joint tenancy, one risks distribution of the property to *unintended beneficiaries*, either as a result of chance, or by the intent of surviving cotenant. For example, consider a joint tenancy between a childless couple. If both were to die in fairly rapid succession, such as in a common accident, all of the property would end up with heirs or beneficiaries of which ever of them lived the longest, even if survival was just a matter of a few days.

If instead of dying, one of them survived, he or she would have the right to direct disposition of all of what once belonged to both of them, to anyone by will, trust, or other document. This risk can be avoided with a will or a trust, documents that can control asset disposition after the survivor's death by using a survival clause and other provisions, such as giving the survivor only a life estate with the remainder going to someone else. Such long range planning does not apply to assets held in joint tenancy. By taking title in joint tenancy, spouses leave ultimate disposition to chance, empowering the survivor to disregard the other's dispositive wishes.

EXAMPLE 10 - 2. Cheryl remarries after the death of her first husband, and wishing to have her estate avoid probate, names her new husband Donny as co-joint tenant of her residence. Although Cheryl's will leaves all of her property to her children, Donny will become the sole owner of the house if he survives Cheryl.

Second, disposition by joint tenancy, when not coordinated with other planning, can result in an unintended *disproportionate distribution* of the person's estate.

> EXAMPLE 10 - 3. Coco owned a bank account with a $1,000 balance and other property worth over $400,000. Her will left her entire estate to her children, and directed that all taxes and debts be paid out of the probate estate. About one year before her death, she put her sister's name on the bank account as a joint tenant, making it easier for her sister to help her pay bills. Shortly before her death, Coco sold stock worth $100,000, depositing the proceeds into the joint bank account. Assuming that debts and expenses amounted to $50,000 at her death, Coco's children will receive property worth about $250,000 (i.e., $400,000 - $100,000 - $50,000), and her sister will receive $101,000. Although Coco may have intended to leave her sister a small sum, placing the proceeds of the stock in the joint account has resulted in her receiving more than 25% of Coco's net wealth.

Third, joint ownership *prevents* an individual from making other, less direct but *more desirable types* of transfers at death, such as giving someone a temporary interest, e.g., an income interest to one person and a remainder interest to another person or to a charity. Most long range planning objectives can not be accomplished if property is held in joint tenancy.

Danger of inefficient disposition. Even if joint tenancies are expected to dispose of a person's assets to the right parties in the right amounts, they may do so inefficiently, generating delay and asset shrinkage. Three inefficiencies will be explored.

First, the property passing to the surviving cotenant will not be subject to those *protective provisions* often included in trusts regarding responsible asset management. As a consequence, asset depletion may harm a surviving cotenant who lacks experience in the care and management of property.

> EXAMPLE 10 - 4. In Example 10 - 2 above, if Cheryl had named her oldest child to be cotenant, disposition to Cheryl's husband could have been avoided, but that child would become the sole owner of all property, to the exclusion of the other children. If that lucky but generous child later splits the property with the siblings, he or she will have made gifts subject to taxation. These two problems could have been avoided by naming all children as cotenants, but Cheryl may not have wished to make an immediate gift of her property to all of the children.

Second, creating joint tenancies may expose those assets to the *claims of the creditors of the other cotenant* even though the initial owner was merely seeking an inexpensive way to avoid probate and did not really intend the cotenant to have an interest. For example, if a parent adds her adult child as a cotenant on her home and the child causes an automobile accident, a judgment against the child could force the partition and sale of the home.

Third, joint tenancies can result in *probate administration* and, possibly, intestacy. Joint tenancy does not avoid probate administration at the death of the last surviving cotenant, nor does it in the case of the simultaneous death of the cotenants.

> EXAMPLE 10 - 5. Russ and his wife Patti were advised to avoid probate by creating joint tenancies. After Russ died, Patti survived only a few years, never realizing that at her death all of their property would be subject to probate administration. When she died, Patti's estate had to be probated.

> EXAMPLE 10 - 6. Based on the facts in the prior example, above, if Russ and Patti instead died in a common accident, where there was no sufficient evidence as to who survived the other, under the Uniform Simultaneous Death Act, each cotenant is presumed to survive the other, resulting in each cotenant's half interest in the property being subject to probate administration.

The living trust, discussed in the next major section, does not have this drawback; it is designed to avoid probate administration at the death of both spouses.

Surrender of ownership and control. As discussed in Chapter 7, creating an interest in joint tenancy will usually constitute an immediate, completed *gift* by the person or persons who contributed more than their share of the purchase price, said gift being made to any cotenant who has contributed less than his or her proportional share. Property law requires that each joint tenant owns an equal share of the property. Each owner has the right to convert his or her share of the property into a tenancy-in-common interest, capable of being sold or devised to non-cotenant. This might not be a problem for joint tenancies between people who contribute equal shares of property, nor for happily married spouses. Between others, however, the probate avoidance of joint tenancy may not be worth the owner's immediate surrender of significant property interests.

Creating an immediate vested present interest in the donee-cotenant can give rise to other problems. The donee may be unable to later disclaim the gift to save transfer taxes. If the donee becomes incompetent, a guardianship may have to be appointed. The donor may need the donee's permission to sell the asset. Finally, the asset may be subject to the claims of the donee's creditors.

In contrast with joint tenancy, other documents of transfer, such as the will and the trust instrument, can *delay* the making of an outright transfer of ownership until the person's death. Instead of creating present interests, they provide for *future interests*, ones that are *contingent* upon future events, such as the owner not revoking the interests. Most individuals do not wish to make outright gifts, even if doing so will allow their estate to avoid probate.

The basis problem. As we have seen earlier, the rule for basis adjustment for appreciated joint tenancy property at the death of one spouse results in a "one-half" step-up. A step-up in basis for the entire value of the property may be achieved by one of the techniques described next.

Gift-death-devise strategy. First, the property could be *given to a donee* who is expected to die before the donor with the expectation that, at the donee's death, the entire property will be devised back to the donor and it will receive a full step-up in basis. This strategy will be certain to work satisfactorily only in situations where the donee can be trusted to actually devise the property to the donor, such as where the parties are happily married. It will also succeed only if the donee's death occurs at least one year after the initial gift because, under IRC §1014(e), failure of the donee to survive at least a year after the gift was given will cause the transfer at death of the property back to the donor to be treated for the purpose of its basis adjustment as if neither transfer ever occurred.

Community property ownership. The second way in which avoiding joint tenancy can open up an opportunity for a step-up in basis for the entire value of property involves the ownership of community property between spouses. As we saw in Chapter 7, unlike joint tenancy property, both halves of community property receive a step-up in basis at the death of the first spouse. Thus, married couples in *community property* states (even those of modest wealth) may be especially interested in avoiding joint tenancy arrangements, choosing instead to dispose of community property by will or trust instrument. Some community property states do not require a probate to pass property to a surviving spouse.[6]

When step-up not necessary. For some individuals, however, a basis step-up may not be important. For example, their property may not have appreciated substantially, indeed, if it has depreciated, then the strategies mentioned above would actually result in a full step-down in basis. Basis is not important if the survivor is not expected to sell the property. Or if any gain from sale of the property is sheltered by certain provisions of the Internal Revenue Code, e.g., sheltering gain up to $250,000 ($500,000 for a married couple) on the sale a principal residence[7] and deferring the gain on a like-kind exchange.[8]

Possible higher estate tax. Joint tenancies can increase estate tax for two reasons: because of the somewhat harsh provisions of §2040 for non-spouses and because of their effect on the size of the surviving cotenant's gross estate.

§2040 consequences. When we first studied §2040, we learned that the *entire value* of property held in joint tenancy by a decedent is includable in the decedent's gross estate, except in two situations. First, if the joint tenancy was held solely with the surviving spouse, exactly one half is included. Second, if the joint tenancy was held by the decedent and at least one person who is not the decedent's spouse, the decedent's gross estate will include the entire value of the property, reduced only by an amount attributable to that portion of the consideration shown to have been furnished by the survivors. Thus, a higher than necessary estate tax can result if a joint tenancy has a nonspouse cotenant and if the surviving cotenant is unable to prove his or her contribution.

This inability to prove contributions may be a blessing in disguise. If the deceased joint tenant's taxable estate is less than the exclusion amount, there will be no transfer tax and yet the surviving joint tenants will have a new basis equal to the date of death fair market value.

> EXAMPLE 10 - 7. Clarissa and her brother, Scott, purchased a condo on the Florida coast for $100,000. They took title in joint tenancy. The condo was worth $300,000 when Scott died. Scott's other worldly possessions were worth approximately $180,000. Because Clarissa and Scott failed to keep adequate records concerning the purchase of the condo, it was deemed to be 100% in Scott's gross estate. As a consequence, Clarissa's basis in the condo is $300,000. Scott's estate paid no estate tax because the net value was less than the exclusion amount.

Larger survivor's gross estate. Joint tenancies may result in a higher than necessary estate tax for the estates of the *surviving cotenants* because their estates will be "loaded up" with the predeceased cotenant's property. We shall see in Chapter 11 that in the case of wealthy couples, total estate tax can be reduced by rejecting a "100% marital deduction" plan (the automatic result for husband and wife joint tenancies). Taxes are saved by passing less property outright to the surviving spouse. These estate tax savings usually rely on trusts that create a life estate for the survivor but keep the trust out of the survivor's gross estate. This kind of estate planning may also save taxes for couples in nontraditional relationships.

Possible gift taxation. Creation of joint tenancies between non-spouses can result in a taxable gift if unequal contributions are made and if the value of the gift exceeds the annual exclusion. In contrast, disposition by will or by the typical living trust instrument produces no immediate gift during the person's lifetime because, as we have said, the documents generally do not create vested interests.

Finally, the person may not be able to avoid joint tenancy with regard to certain property. For example, some bank lenders may require that spouses hold title in their home in joint tenancy rather that in trust as a condition to granting a loan secured by the property. As living trusts become more popular as estate planning devices, and lending institutions become more familiar with them, this requirement by lenders is less likely to occur, although the spouses may still be asked to either personally guarantee the loan and to give their written assurance that there is nothing in the trust document that would prevent them from using the property as collateral.

In view of the many significant drawbacks to joint tenancy, especially for individuals with medium or large estates, planners generally recommend the other major alternative to probate, the living trust, discussed next.

THE LIVING TRUST ALTERNATIVE

The most popular alternative to probate for wealthy people is the funded living trust. While the trustor is alive, the living trust is usually revocable, which means that its terms are amendable and, if later desired, its assets can be taken out of trust by the trustor. Most trustors name themselves trustee of their living trust during their lifetime.

At the trustor's death, the revocable trust becomes irrevocable and either terminates, with the corpus distributed to the remaindermen, or it continues in existence until a later date. A typical revocable living trust created by a husband and wife has all assets placed in one trust, which is revocable by them during their lifetimes. At the first spouse's death, different things can happen depending on the plan. A commonly used estate plan for smaller estates has the decedent's share of the trust property continue in a revocable trust such that the trust corpus simply belongs entirely to the surviving spouse. Then, at his or her later death, the trust again without probate, is either terminated with distribution to the children or it is continued for a period of time for their benefit. Other distribution arrangements, particularly those designed to reduce estate tax, are discussed in Chapter 11.

Taxation of a living trust depends on whether or not it is revocable. A *revocable* living trust usually has no additional transfer or income tax consequences during the trustor's lifetime. A transfer to it does not constitute a taxable gift since the transfer is not complete. And under the grantor trust rules, all income earned by a revocable trust is taxable to the grantor, that is, the trustor. In contrast, an *irrevocable* living trust is usually a separate income-taxpaying entity; all transfers into it usually constitute completed gifts, and, except when either the grantor trust rules or the kiddie tax apply, all undistributed fiduciary accounting income (FAI) is taxed to the trust, while all distributed FAI is usually taxed to the beneficiaries.

Funded irrevocable living trusts also avoid probate. Not as commonly used as the revocable living trust because they involve gifting, they will be discussed at length in Chapters 13 and 15, in the context of gift giving and life insurance planning.

Advantages of the Living Trust

The living trust has several distinct advantages over other transfer devices. They include greater organization, greater assurance of probate avoidance, lower total costs, greater privacy and speed, opportunity to observe a chosen fiduciary, ability to use the trust as an alternative to a conservatorship, and possible reduced litigation.

Greater organization. Establishing a living trust requires the person to organize his or her property during lifetime, thereby enhancing efficient personal financial planning.

Greater assurance of complete probate avoidance. Compared with joint tenancies, the living trust offers greater certainty that probate will be avoided at the death of the surviving partner.

EXAMPLE 10 - 8. Kim and Chris wish to provide for asset disposition in a manner similar to that directed in a simple will, but also wish to avoid probate on all property. Their planner makes it clear to them that joint tenancies will not achieve the latter goal because the surviving cotenant will wind up owning the property, making it eventually subject to probate. Instead, they execute a living trust instrument, funding the trust with all of their property. The trust will continue to exist for both their lifetimes. At the survivor's death, the assets will pass from the trusts to their designated beneficiaries, free from probate.

The above example was intentionally unclear about both the individuals' sex and marital status. In this context, neither is material; unmarried individuals, including members of the same sex, may legally take title in joint tenancy and may legally co-execute a single trust instrument.

Lower total cost than probate. Compared to will preparation and probate, the combined cost of preparation and administration of the living trust is usually significantly less. The following material discusses both preparation costs and total cost.

Preparation costs. The cost of having a living trust prepared is usually higher than the cost of preparing a will for at least two reasons. First, the trust instrument is usually a more complicated document. Its provisions must arrange for the immediate receipt of property, for the management of that property, and for the proper distribution of the property and the trust income for a period that might span several generations. Second, with the living trust, the attorney must still draft a will. As previously discussed, the establishment of the living trust does not totally eliminate the need for a will. Because people sometimes fail to completely fund their trusts, some will die owning property in their own name, rather than in the name of the trustee. Planners provide for disposition of this probate property with what is called a *pourover will*, specifying that any of the testator's assets not in the trust shall be distributed or "poured over" into the trust at the trustor's death. Because it disposes of all property outright to only one party (the trustee), the pourover will is usually very brief, adding little to the preparation cost of avoiding probate with the living trust. Thus, some probate administration costs may be incurred on assets passing under the pourover will.

Total cost. While the specific cost of preparing the living trust may be higher, the total cost of the living trust alternative is usually lower due to the relatively high cost of formal probate *administration* at death. In contrast with formal probate, administration of a living trust at the trustor's death involves minimal legal work and usually no court appearances. The pourover will might not be probated, depending upon the size of the probate estate and the scope of the state's informal or summary administration rules. However, some *other postmortem legal duties* that are required under the probate alternative may also have to be performed under the trust alternative. They include:

- Marshaling and safeguarding assets
- Preparing an inventory of the assets
- Obtaining appraisals
- Preparing and filing estate tax returns
- Preparing and filing income tax returns
- Paying creditors
- Instituting litigation to protect assets
- Changing title to assets
- Distributing assets to beneficiaries
- Obtaining receipts from beneficiaries

While the costs of these actions usually do not add up to anywhere near the total cost of formal probate administration, they are not insignificant. The efficiency of *informal* probate administration in *UPC states* can make probate an attractive alternative to the living trust, measured by the criterion of cost.

Other factors that affect the relative costs of probate versus the living trust include whether someone other than the grantor or a family member will serve as trustee or executor, the ability to deduct these costs as an income tax miscellaneous itemized deduction, and the schedule of local court fees and costs.

Greater privacy. A trust instrument is usually very private, not subject to public inspection. Although property transfers into and out of a living trust may require *examination of the trust instrument* by financial and other institutions, the document usually need not be made publicly accessible. County recorders may require a filing of the trust in the public records, but usually only brief sections of the document need be submitted. In fact, many attorneys in the estate planning process draft a separate short (one or two pages) document called a "trust abstract," a "memorandum of trust," or a "confirmation of trust." This short document is made available to persons or institutions dealing with the trustee, in lieu of the full trust instrument. At a minimum, the abstract will contain sections describing the identity of trustee and successor trustee, and the trustee powers relevant to investing and to transferring assets. It should be formally executed by the trustor and trustee, and their signatures should be notarized. In this way critical parts of the trust, including dispositive provisions, may be kept secret.

However some states, such as New York which impose an inheritance tax on trust property, may require the public *filing of an inventory*, which will reveal the nature and value of the trust's assets and the names of its beneficiaries. In addition, in the litigation process, a determined contestant may gain access to the contents of a living trust through litigation.

As mentioned earlier, privacy may be especially desired by particularly wealthy or prominent individuals. They may wish to avoid any additional publicity and any inspection by disinherited or contentious survivors, who may be seeking the opportunity to wage a court challenge to a decedent's estate plan.

Speed. Property can usually be transferred out of a trust somewhat more sooner than out of a probate estate because the transfer process is not subject to supervision and approval by the court. However, failure to perform certain postmortem legal duties (detailed above) can subject the trustee to significant personal liability and can trigger costly and unnecessary litigation for the beneficiaries. Thus, for example, in those states where creditors' claims can be made against trust assets, the trustee will want to delay distribution. And for larger trusts owing a sizable estate tax, the trustee may delay major distributions of trust assets until an estate tax "closing letter" from the IRS is received. Generally, if there are no audit problems, the closing letter comes about ten months after the estate tax return is filed.

Speed of disposition of real property located in a *different state* is more rapid if the property is held in a living trust rather than disposed of by will because ancillary administration is avoided. However, some states require reporting procedures for trusts that are quite similar to the probate administration process.

Opportunity to test the future. By placing assets into a revocable living trust, the trustor has the opportunity to test the future by making the estate plan largely operational during lifetime. By naming another party trustee, the trustor can observe firsthand how well the assets are being managed and can make needed adjustments in management provisions before death. In addition, the trustee can be given the opportunity to become *familiar* with the trust assets during the trustor's lifetime, thus increasing the likelihood of a smooth transition period after the trustor's death.

Alternative to guardianship or conservatorship. A person who becomes physically or mentally incapable of managing assets will need someone to provide that management. Just as a guardianship may have to be established to manage a minor's estate, a guardianship or conservatorship may be necessary to manage the estate of an incapacitated adult. Like probate administration, guardianships and conservatorships are supervised by the court, which usually requires periodic accountings and formal court approval for many acts of asset management.

Used in lieu of a guardianship or conservatorship, the living trust is a good vehicle to avoid the expense, delay and publicity of probate-type administration before the trustor's death. The typical living trust begins with the trustor acting as trustee. Subsequently, a successor trustee takes over when the trustor relinquishes the role, becomes incapacitated, or dies. Thus, the living trust instrument has an additional benefit that is simply not available with a will; it provides for the management of property at the trustor's incapacity. Some commentators consider this *the major advantage* of the living trust, especially for older people, making the will alternative seriously deficient by comparison.

Another less expensive alternative to the guardianship or conservatorship is the durable power of attorney for financial matters, discussed in Chapter 17, but it does not avoid probate nor does it provide much guidance for the long term management of assets.

Possible reduced litigation. As we have seen, the probate process can offer a relatively convenient opportunity for a dissatisfied survivor to initiate a will contest. Such disputes over disposition of a person's property may be minimized with a living trust for two reasons. First, the trustor as the initial beneficiary is able to live with the trust, receiving and making distributions and transferring property to it. These acts may constitute evidence of a well thought-out estate plan. In contrast, a will ordinarily is simply a document, one not perceived to have much impact on the testator's day-to-day life, thus, contesting parties may be more successful in showing that the testator's will does not reflect his or her actual intent.

Second, disputes over a person's estate plan may be minimized with a living trust to the extent that the actual litigation may be more difficult to accomplish. However, commentators are in disagreement over how difficult it is to challenge the provisions of a living trust. Some maintain that the living trust is more difficult to contest since it requires the initiation of a lawsuit. In addition, transfers from a trust generally do not require notice to anyone. In contrast, probating the will, as we have seen, does involve notice to interested parties, an act which may in itself trigger a contest. Other commentators argue that a trust can be contested on substantially the same grounds as those that are used to contest a will. Common grounds, it will be recalled, include fraud, undue influence, lack of capacity and improper execution. Indeed, creating a trust may require a higher mental capacity than is required to create a valid will. Courts generally require that the trustor have contractual capacity at the time the trust is created. Since contracting requires negotiation between two parties, it is thought to require sharper mental faculties than required to execute a will. Whether that is really true is questionable, given that little negotiation really takes place in the creation of most trusts.

Other advantages of living trusts. Living trusts are normally simpler to revise than wills. While a *codicil* to a will requires certain execution formalities (described in Chapter 3), an *amendment* to a living trust needs no formalities or witnesses, and may be in the trustor's handwriting. However, if the trustee is someone other than the trustor, he or she should at least be notified of the revision, and most attorneys also have the trustee sign and notarize the amendment.

Use of a living trust eliminates any gap in asset management when the trustor dies. While the trustee (or successor trustee) of a living trust is empowered to carry on immediately, no one is authorized to act with regard to probate property until the court appoints a personal representative, at least several days after the testator's death. Of course, most assets do not require immediate attention.

Property held in a revocable living trust will receive a step-up in basis because it is treated, from an income tax point of view, as owned by the grantor and, therefore, it is included in the decedent's gross estate.

Disadvantages of the Living Trust

The living trust has several disadvantages, including the burden of funding, possibly greater legal uncertainty, and some minor tax factors.

Funding burden. Establishment of a joint tenancy is a one-step process. The very act of creation of the joint interest creates the appropriate title. On the other hand, the establishment of a living trust to avoid probate is a two-step process. First, the trust document is executed by the trustor and the trustee, somewhat like a two party contract. Second, the trust is *funded*; that is, legal title to the property is transferred from the trustor to the trustee. Some trustors never do the latter because they are unaware that the additional step of funding is necessary. Others are aware of it but simply never get around to doing it. Most find it downright inconvenient, because it requires trips to the bank and to other places where title is officially kept. And people who actively trade their property, such as those involved in frequent real estate deals and securities transactions, may especially dislike the greater complexity inherent in continually keeping property in their name as trustee. However, opening a brokerage account under the trustee's name greatly simplifies the task of keeping track of the trust's investment assets.

Failure to fund the trust will usually result in the trustor's property passing through probate, hopefully guided into the trust by a pourover will.[9] Most attorneys avoid this undesired outcome by overseeing the initial funding of the living trust themselves, rather than leaving the responsibility to the client. This may increase somewhat the legal cost of setting up the living trust.

Planners may be able to help their clients who have created living trusts by enlisting the aid of the client's accountant to monitor the funding of the trust. The accountant is asked to pay particular attention to the client's tax related forms, such as 1099s and K1s, issued by banks, partnerships, S corporations, and other asset account holders, to make sure that the trustee is shown as owner of the property.

Longer creditor's period. As described earlier, probate generally offers a shorter creditors' claim period than is available for the living trust. The latter is usually subject to the claims for the regular statute of limitations period, the length of which depends upon the nature of the claim. These periods are likely to be from one to three years long. However, this disadvantage may be disappearing. Some states have enacted an overall creditors' claim period of just one year that starts from the death of person. There may be exceptions to the one year limitation for decedent's estates that are subject to some other more specific limitation on creditors' claims, e.g., if there is a probate proceeding, then the shorter provision for probate estates would apply. The one year statute of limitations applies regardless of the manner in which the decedent held his or her property, and regardless of whether the regular statute of limitations for a particular claim would have ended earlier or later than the one year period had the person lived.[10]

There is also a trend in state law towards allowing living trusts to take advantage of a shortened creditors' claim period (e.g., four months) provided the trustee follows certain notice to creditors procedures that are quite similar to those required in probate proceedings. The law is likely to require the trustee seeking to take advantage of the shortened claim period to publish a notice to creditors in a newspaper of general circulation, to make a reasonable search for creditors, and to give any creditors located actual notice of the method of perfecting their claims.[11]

Tax factors. There are a few minor tax disadvantages to the living trust.

- Compared to the $600 available to an estate, a trust, after the grantor's death, has a smaller personal income tax *exemption*: either $100 or $300.
- As mentioned earlier, real property held in trust and located in states other than an individual's residence state is usually considered by a person's residence state to be intangible personal property. Most states impose a death tax on such *trust owned property*, which might otherwise escape taxation if it were disposed of by will, since "real property" located outside a state is not ordinarily subject to its tax. Of course no additional tax would be incurred if both states impose only a "pickup" type death tax.

In the past, the IRS maintained that any transfer (gift) directly from a revocable probate avoidance trust to a person selected by the settlor was included in the settlor's estate, if the settlor died within three years of the transfer. The argument was that §2038 applied to the trust and, therefore, any gift type transfer at the request of the settlor (or done by a settlor-trustee) was a release of the settlor's retained interest, hence the three year rule of §2035(d)(2) applied. That section is now §2035(a) under the 1997 Tax Act's renumbering of §2035. This argument was made even though the transfer would not have been included in the settlor's estate had the settlor personally made the transfer. The Taxpayer Relief Act of 1997 added §2035(e), which removes the problem by specifying that such transfers are to be treated as though made by the settlor.

Miscellaneous disadvantages. There are several other disadvantages to the living trust, all of which can be considered relatively minor for most people.

Financing problems. In some states, if the trustor wishes to refinance property after it has been placed in trust, the lenders might require that the trustee transfer title back to the trustor until the refinancing is completed, after which it can again be transferred back to the trustee. As lenders have become more familiar with trusts fewer are requiring these extra steps, although the trustor is usually required to co-sign the loan documents in his or her individual capacity and give written assurance that the trustee has authority to encumber the property.

Divorce. In a few states, divorce may result in an improper distribution of assets from a living trust. As mentioned in Chapter 4, in most states a dissolution of marriage automatically revokes a disposition to an ex-spouse contained in a *will* executed prior to the divorce. In contrast, some state statutes do not have similar provisions applicable to living trusts. However, in states adopting Uniform Probate Code §2-804(b), divorce or annulment revokes *any* revocable disposition of property to an ex-spouse or to a relative of an ex-spouse. That section also severs any survivorship interests of the former spouses in property held by them at the time of the divorce, transforming property that they held as joint tenants, tenants by the entirety, and as community property with the right of survivorship into tenancies in common. It also cancels the nomination of an ex-spouse (or the ex-spouse's relatives) for any fiduciary position; and it cancels the conferring of any general or limited powers to appoint property.

Other disadvantages. Living trusts may have disadvantages in certain special situations, two of which will be mentioned briefly without additional explanation. First, beneficiaries of a living trust may lose a defense against liability for *environmental clean-up* of real property held in the trust. In contrast, that defense is available to persons *acquiring* the property "by inheritance or bequest."[12] Second, use of a living trust may reduce allowable *Medicaid benefits* for the beneficiary-spouse of a decedent who establishes a discretionary living trust. The problem will not arise for testamentary trusts.[13]

Living trusts require careful analysis, planning and preparation. Clearly, the decision whether or not to create a revocable living trust requires the planner's critical evaluation of many challenging issues, and drafting a living trust requires the knowledge of an experienced estate planning attorney. The tasks of evaluation and careful drafting require a skill level far above those of most practicing generalist, let alone someone lacking even rudimentary training in the issues. Nonetheless, recently, casual salespersons, sometimes traveling door-to-door, have been approaching the elderly in large numbers, offering to prepare living trusts. Tactics alleged by opponents include using high pressure sales pitches, imposing high prices, making misrepresentations and mistakes about the relative costs and advantages of living trusts, carelessly failing to ensure that property is transferred to the trust, producing an ineffective document, and making false claims of endorsement by legitimate nonprofit organizations or using "sound-alike" names that make them appear to be protective associations for the elderly. Some states have taken legal action against these operations, but these unprofessional practices will continue as long as there are greedy people willing to prey on vulnerable elderly persons.

QUANTITATIVE MODEL FOR COMPARISON OF COSTS OF PROBATE VERSUS LIVING TRUST

This section applies the principles of finance to develop a model for comparing the costs of probate with the costs of the living trust. The technique used will incorporate the *time value of money* concept known as present value.

> EXAMPLE 10 - 9. Patty is evaluating the decision whether to avoid probate of her assets, worth $1 million, by setting up a revocable living trust. Her life expectancy is 10 years. With regard to costs, she has made the following estimates:
>
> Under the probate alternative: drafting her will, $600; probate administration, $25,000; and other costs at death, including accountant's fees, $1,000.
>
> Under the trust alternative: drafting the trust and the pourover will, $1,600; annual record-keeping until death,[14] $300 per year; nonprobate administration cost at death, $2,500; costs in higher income taxes due to inability to use a probate estate as a separate taxpayer, $1,100; and other costs at death, including accountant's fees, $1,000.
>
> In calculating the total cost for each alternative, Patty could simply add up the expenses, with the result that the probate alternative at $26,000 would appear to be more than twice the $11,000 trust cost. Simply adding up the costs, however, does not take into account the time value of money.

To correctly compare amounts incurred at different points in time, we must make adjustments to reflect the fact that money not spent today can be invested profitably until the time that it must be spent. We can do this by calculating the sum of the *present values of the costs for each alternative*. The present value of an expense is the amount that would have to be invested today to accumulate the funds necessary to pay that expense when it comes due.

To better understand the present value concept, consider an intuitively simple illustration. At an assumed annual rate of investment of 10%, one would need to invest $100 today to accumulate the amount $110 payable in one year. In other words, at 10%, the present value of $110 payable in one year is $100. Present values of any amount can be derived from present value tables such as Table B for a term of years and Table S for amounts payable for life or at the end of a person's life. Table B (10%) depicts the present values of a single $1 amount to be paid in the future, assuming an investment rate of 10%. Thus, the present value of $1 in one year at 10% is $0.909091, or a bit less than 91 cents. Since we have been calculating the present value of the amount $110, not $1, our answer must be the product of $110 and 0.909091, or $100.

How can we calculate the present value of the amount $300 payable each year for the next 10 years, with the first payment due in one year? Described in other words, we must calculate the total amount to be invested today which will enable us to fund this annuity, that is, to fund this entire progression of equal payments. To do this, we calculate the present value of the annuity. Table B in Appendix A shows the present values of a $1 annuity for specified periods, assuming certain investment rates.

> EXAMPLE 10 - 10. With regard to Patty's actual figures, at 10%, the present value of $1 to be paid in 10 years is $0.386. We will use this lump-sum discount factor in the calculations that follow. The "annuity factor," as it is called, corresponding to 10 years and 10% is 6.145. Since we wish to determine the present value of an annuity of $300, not $1, the answer must be the product of $300 and 6.145, or $1,844.

We are now ready to calculate Patty's total costs for the two alternatives in a manner which adjusts for the time value of money. The figures are shown in Table 10-1 and Table 10-2.

TABLE 10-1 Present Value of Costs of Probate

Items	Years	Amounts	Discount Factor	Present Value
Drafting	Now	$600	1.000000	$600
Administration	10	$25,000	0.385543	$9,639
Other costs	10	$1,000	0.385543	$386
		Total present value of probate costs		$10,625

TABLE 10-2 Present Value of Costs of Living Trust

Items	Years	Amounts	Discount Factor	Present Value
Drafting	Now	$1,600	1.000000	$1,600
Administration	10	$2,500	0.385543	$964
Record keeping	1-10	$300	6.144600	$1,864
Higher estate tax	10	$1,100	0.385543	$424
Other costs	10	$1,000	0.385543	$386
Total present value of living trust costs				$5,238

Thus the sum of the present values of the costs are $10,625 for probate and $5,238 for the trust. These represent the total amounts that Patty would have to invest today, at 10%, to properly accumulate and pay all of the individual forecasted costs when they are due.

The analysis could be refined slightly to include the tax deductibility of these expenses. For example, as we shall see in Chapter 18, administration costs may be deducted on the estate tax return. Thus, if T represents the marginal estate tax rate, the after-tax cost of an estate tax deductible expense is the product of that expense times the expression one minus T.

The estimates in the above example have been made for illustration purposes only and should not be used as a general indicator of costs. Actual costs will vary considerably, depending on specific factors, such as the laws of the decedent's particular residence state and the cost of professional services in the decedent's locale. However, to generalize, the present value cost of formal probate is usually higher than the present value cost of the living trust by at least 20%.

WHICH ALTERNATIVE IS BEST?

Obviously, the decision whether or not to avoid probate is not always a simple one. It requires that each person examine and subjectively weigh the advantages and disadvantages of each, in the context of the laws and procedures of his or her state of domicile. It should be clear that there is no answer that is correct for all situations. In fact, some individuals owning larger estates may be advised to execute a will to probate certain assets and to transfer the remaining assets by living trust in order to obtain the unique benefits of both arrangements. What follows is a description various circumstances that might influence individuals to favor one or the other of the alternatives.

Probate preferred: Individuals who will lean toward the probate alternative include:

1. *Professionals*, such as self-employed engineers and accountants, who stand to gain additional security from the short creditors' claim period.
2. Those who have *large, complicated estates,* or who expect family *disharmony* after their death, may benefit from the extra protection potentially available through court supervision.
3. Residents of *UPC states* where the cost advantage to avoiding informal probate is minimal.
4. Young, healthy individuals who expect to be acquiring numerous assets and would find onerous the constant *funding* requirement of the living trust.

Joint tenancy preferred: Since joint tenancy has some very significant disadvantages, however the ease of transfer may make it appealing, especially for owners with relatively modest estates. Individuals are inclined to prefer it only if one, or perhaps all, of the following circumstances apply:

1. The person wants the property to pass *outright* to the surviving joint tenants. This implies that there is no need for trusts, to save income or transfer taxes, to avoid guardianships, to delay distributions to younger survivors, or to provide for multiple beneficiaries over time by creating life estate and remainder interests.
2. A complete *step-up* in income tax basis at a person's death is *not needed*, or is available because the older (dying) joint tenant contributed all of the consideration to acquire the property.
3. The creation of the joint tenancy interest does *not* result in the immediate payment of *gift taxes*.

Living trust preferred: Individuals who will tend to prefer a living trust typically include those who want to avoid probate but do not like joint tenancy because of its significant disadvantages. For example:

1. Those with *larger estates* who wish to avoid the estate tax by using sophisticated trust arrangements, e.g., a bypass trust (discussed in the next chapter).
2. Those who place high priority on *privacy and speed* in the property transfer process.
3. Individuals for whom the *total cost* of the living trust is expected to be considerably lower than the cost of probate; reasons include the following:
   a. Probate administration expenses are expected to be high, perhaps because the person is a resident of a non-UPC state, or because an independent executor must be named.
   b. Nonprobate administration fees are low, perhaps because a family member is willing to serve as trustee.
4. Individuals who do *not* anticipate a trust *funding burden* associated with numerous acquisitions of property.
5. Finally, individuals who wish to avoid the publicity and cost of court appointed *guardians or conservators* in the event they become incapacitated.

QUESTIONS AND PROBLEMS

1. Discuss the validity of the claim that probate promotes fairness.

2. (a) Why isn't probate private? (b) Is the living trust always private?

3. (a) How has the advantage of probate's limited creditors' claim period been undermined recently? (b) Will any individuals still prefer probate to minimize creditor problems?

4. (a) Who might wish to contest a will by claiming the execution was invalid? (b) Why might it be easier to do than to challenge a living trust?

5. Summarize the advantages and disadvantages of using joint tenancies to avoid probate.

6. (a) Why should the living trust cost less than the formal probate alternative? (b) Are all cost components lower?

7. Wesley has just received his lawyer's bill for developing a plan that avoids probate with a living trust. Included is a charge for drafting a will. Did the law firm make a billing mistake?

8. Today Dennis executed a living trust, with his sister as the only remainder beneficiary. Upon driving home from the lawyer's office, Dennis is killed in an auto accident. All of his property is still held in joint tenancy and tenancy in common form with his brother, Elmer. Is there a problem? Why or why not?

9. A person is considering whether to have a will done or to create and fund a living trust. Assume that the person's life expectancy is 15 years and the investment rate of return is 10%. Given the estimated costs that follow, compare the cost factors for each alternative. (a) For the probate alternative: drafting the will, $300; formal probate administration, $40,000; other costs at death, including accountants' and appraiser's fees, $2,300. (b) For the trust alternative: drafting costs, $2,200; record-keeping until death, $250 per year;

nonprobate administration costs at death, $3,100; costs in higher income taxes due to the inability to use a probate estate as a separate taxpayer, $1,000 (assume a one year probate); other costs at death, including accountants' fees, $3,600.

10. Now evaluate the cost of *informal* probate versus the living trust. Assume all facts given in the problem immediately above, except that informal probate administration will cost $20,000.

11. (a) What people are likely to prefer that their estate be transferred through the probate process? (b) To avoid probate by using joint tenancies? (c) To avoid probate by using a living trust?

12. For each of the following individuals, explain which of the three major types of asset disposition would probably best suit them.

    a. A 19 year old single college student owning only personal effects totaling $6,000.
    b. A former stockbroker who spent two years in prison for securities fraud.
    c. Michael Jackson, the entertainer.
    d. A plumber and his wife who own only a house, two cars and some other personal property. They have two middle aged, financially responsible children.

13. For each of the individuals listed in the question immediately above, invent an additional hypothetical fact or circumstance that would move you to recommend a method of asset disposition *different* from your original choice.

ANSWERS TO QUESTIONS AND PROBLEMS

1. Supporters of probate claim that court supervision in a public setting promotes fairness. Critics claim that judges and other officials offer only rubber stamp approval of administration acts, and that the trend of probate reform towards reduced supervision minimizes the credibility of this contention.

2. a.   Probate isn't private because:

   1. All probate documents are available for inspection by the public.
   2. Probate proceedings are public.

   b.   By and large, the living trust is truly private, except in cases where the trust (or portions of it) must be filed with the county recorder, or shown to a financial institution, or where an inventory of trust assets must be filed for inheritance tax purposes.

3. a.   The advantage of probate's limited creditor's period has been undermined recently by the U.S. Supreme Court's decision in *Tulsa*, holding that creditors "known or reasonably ascertainable" to the personal representative must be given "actual" notice of the limited creditor's period, rather than just "constructive" notice, by publication. Actual notice need not be given to potential creditors whose claims are a matter of "conjecture," i.e., deduced by surmise or guesswork. An example of a conjectural claim would be a malpractice claim against a professional that has not yet resulted in a demand. The *Tulsa* decision has generated great uncertainty among probate lawyers, who fear that dilatory creditors may flood the courts arguing that they were known or reasonably ascertainable. The upshot is that the creditors limitations period now offers far less certainty that all claims will be barred.

   b.   Individuals who anticipate more claims after their death may still find the shorter limitations period a significant advantage. For example, professionals such as lawyers and accountants are potentially vulnerable to malpractice claims which, if instituted after their death, stand a greater chance of succeeding, partly because the defense's best witness, the decedent, is not available to testify. The shorter creditors' period can sometimes minimize this undesired outcome.

4. a. Disinherited and contentious survivors and others who may stand to gain may wish to contest the execution of a will.

   b. Some commentators contend that since a will contest is initiated in probate court, it is a simpler process than contesting a trust, which requires separate legal action. Others say that a trust can be contested on substantially the same grounds that are used to contest a will. Common grounds include fraud, undue influence, lack of capacity and improper execution.

5. Advantage of Joint tenancies to avoid probate

   a. Low administrative cost
   b. Convenience and speed
   c. Clear, undisputed disposition
   d. Reduced creditor's claims
   e. The possibility of income shifting.

   Disadvantage of joint tenancies:

   a. Inflexible disposition
   b. Incomplete probate avoidance (at death of surviving cotenant).
   c. Loss of ownership and control
   d. Loss of step-up in basis in part of the property
   e. Possible higher estate tax
   f. Possible gift tax.

6. a. The living trust should cost less than the formal probate alternative because of the typically large executor commissions and attorney fees in probate administration.

   b. Not all costs of a living trust are lower. The cost of *drafting* a trust might be higher, however, because:

1. The trust is usually a more complex document than the will.
2. A pourover will must be drafted.

7. No, the lawyer did not make a billing mistake. The higher cost reflects the need to draft a pourover will, as well as a trust.

8. There is a problem. The trust will not control disposition over any of the assets. Elmer will receive Dennis's property interests, because joint tenancy disposition normally supersedes disposition by trust. Regarding the tenancy in common interests, which will go through probate, if the attorney included a pourover will, Dennis's sister will receive them. Without a pourover will, the laws of intestate succession will determine who inherits those interests. Conclusion: living trusts must be funded to be effective.

9.

PRESENT VALUE COST OF FORMAL PROBATE

	Year	Amount	Factor	Present value
Drafting	now	$300	1.000	$300
Administration	15	$40,000	0.239	$9,560
Other costs	15	$2,300	0.239	$550
		Total Present Value of Formal Probate		$10,410

PRESENT VALUE COST OF LIVING TRUST

	Year	Amount	Factor	Present value
Drafting	now	$2,200	1.000	$2,200
Record keeping	1-15	$250	7.6061	$1,902
Administration	15	$3,100	0.239	$741
Higher tax	15	$1,000	0.239	$239
Other costs	15	$3,600	0.239	$8,604
		Total Present Value of Living Trust		$13,686

10.   PRESENT VALUE COST OF INFORMAL PROBATE

	Year	Amount	Factor	Present value
Drafting	now	$300	1.000	$300
Administration	15	$20,000	0.239	$4,780
Other costs	15	$3,600	0.239	$860
Total Present Value of Informal Probate				$5,940

11. a. Individuals most likely to prefer probate include:

1. Professionals, such as self-employed lawyers, engineers, and accountants, who stand to gain additional security from the short creditors' limitations period.
2. Those who have large, complicated estates or who expect family disharmony after death, may benefit from the extra protection potentially available through greater court supervision.
3. Wealthier residents of UPC states where the cost advantage to avoiding probate is minimal.
4. Young, healthy individuals who expect to be acquiring numerous assets and would find onerous the constant funding requirement of the living trust.

b. Individuals most likely to avoid probate by using joint tenancies:

1. The person who wants the property to pass outright to the surviving joint tenants. This implies that there is no need for trusts after death, to save taxes or to provide for multiple beneficiaries.
2. Those who anticipate that a complete step-up in income tax basis at their death is not needed, or not available by other means. This may include situations where property has not appreciated substantially, or where the survivors do not plan to sell the property, or where they expect any gain from sale of the property to be sheltered by provisions of the Internal Revenue Code.
3. Those living in states where the creation of the joint tenancy interest does not result in an immediate gift.

c. Individuals most likely to avoid probate with the living trust:

1. Those with larger estates who wish to avoid the estate tax consequences of joint tenancy.
2. Those who want greater privacy and speed in the property transfer process.
3. Individuals for whom the total cost of the living trust is expected to be considerably lower than the cost of probate. Reasons include the following:
    i. Probate administration expenses are expected to be high, perhaps because the person is a resident of a non-UPC state, or because an independent executor must be named.
    ii. As trustee, the person will not need to pay for record-keeping.
    iii. Nonprobate administration fees are low, perhaps because a friend will serve as successor trustee.
4. Individuals who do not anticipate a trust funding burden associated with numerous acquisitions of property.
5. Individuals who wish to avoid the publicity and cost of court appointed guardians or conservators if and when they become incapacitated.

12. a. 19 year old college single student owning only personal effects totaling $6,000: Probate with a will. In virtually all states, formal administration would not be necessary because of the minimal size of the estate.
    b. Former stockbroker who spent two years in prison for securities fraud: Probate, to avoid the longer creditor's limitations period. (Former clients and others may wish to institute civil claims.)
    c. Michael Jackson, the entertainer: A revocable living trust, to retain privacy.
    d. Plumber and wife: Probably joint tenancy, because it is inexpensive, and, because of the family's modest wealth, joint tenancy will not have the tax disadvantages normally inherent in that form of asset distribution.

13. a. College student: Receives large inheritance or wins lottery-- living trust.
    b. Stockbroker: leaves prison for a totally new career and survives 30 years and wants the privacy of a living trust.

c. Michael Jackson: Has contentious relatives and wishes the probate court to oversee distribution of his estate.
d. Plumber: house is worth $700,000 and wife wants to sell it at husband's death. Lives in a community property state so can enjoy full step-up in basis with a will or a living trust.

ENDNOTES

1.   To obtain a copy of the Uniform TOD Securities Registration ACT see The National Conference of Commissioners on Uniform State Laws' official Website (maintained by the University of Pennsylvania Law School) at the following URL: *http://www.law.upenn.edu/bll/ulc/*

2.   IRC §§2036 - 2038.

3.   *Tulsa Professional Collection Services v. Estate of Pope* 485 US 478, 108 S.Ct. 1340 (1988).

4.   See California Code of Civil Procedure §366.2 at California's Website: *http://www.leginfo.ca.gov/calaw.html*

5.   See Figure 9-1.

6.   See the discussion, at the end of Chapter 4, of California's nonprobate procedure for setting aside property to a surviving spouse.

7.   IRC §121.

8.   IRC §1031.

9.   *Heggstad v. Heggstad*, 20 Cal. Rptr. 2d 433 (1993).

10.   See California Code of Civil Procedure §366.2 at California's Website: *http://www.leginfo.ca.gov/calaw.html*

11.   See California Probate Code §§19000-19100 at California's Website: *http://www.leginfo.ca.gov/calaw.html*

12.   42USC §9601(35)(A)(iii).

13.   42USC §1396a(k).

14.   Fees incurred for the production of income, such as trustee fees of a living trust, income tax preparation fees and record keeping fees, are miscellaneous itemized deductions, subject to the 2% deduction floor.

CHAPTER 11

Common Estate Plans: Using Bypass and Marital Deduction Trusts

OVERVIEW

This chapter will demonstrate how bypass planning and the marital deduction are used by wealthy couples to reduce estate taxes. More advanced application of these techniques, including use of the prior transfer credit, special estate plans, and trusts that obtain the marital deduction for non-U.S. spouses are the subject of Chapter 12.

Once the unified credit reached $192,800 in 1987, anyone could transfer an estate of up to $600,000 completely free of estate taxes. When the unified credit finally reaches $345,800 in 2006, estates of $1,000,000 will pass tax free, and married couples with combined estates as high as $2,000,000 will be able to pass them to their heirs free of estate taxes just by doing a little bit of estate planning.[1]

> EXAMPLE 11 - 1. In 1999, an elderly couple together own property with a net worth about equal to the exclusion amount, i.e., about $650,000. Without any estate planning, other than simple wills, it is likely that their children will eventually receive their estate free of tax, regardless of how ownership of the property was originally divided between the spouses, and no matter which spouse dies first. This is true because the exclusion amount will be increasing over the next several years, so it is likely that their combined estates will remain tax free. If the value exceeds the exclusion amount, then tax savings could be accomplished with a little more planning. This might include gifts to reduce their estate and/or the use of multiple trusts so as to utilize both spouse's unified credits.

Minimizing estate taxes is a concern mainly for families whose taxable estates are expected to exceed the exclusion amount at the second spouse's death. With lifetime gifts within the annual exclusion amount and various estate tax deductions (such as administration expenses and debts), gross estates over the exclusion amount will be transferred tax free if the gifts and deductions reduce it to the exclusion amount or less. Thus, our focus is on those married couples whose estate *tax base* significantly exceeds the exclusion amount.

EXAMPLE 11 - 2. At the time of her death in 2000, Ellen's gross estate was $750,000; debts were $120,000; administration expenses were $50,000. Lifetime taxable gifts totaled $70,000 (i.e., gifts less any annual exclusion). Her taxable estate was $580,000 and the estate tax base is $650,000. Thus, there would be no estate tax because the estate tax base does not exceed $675,000, the exclusion amount.

EXAMPLE 11 - 3. Joshua died in 1988, leaving his half of their community property to his wife, Mary. Neither owned significant separate property and the community property was worth $650,000 at that time. Because of good investment advice from an estate planner (I think he said put it in the market), Mary's estate was worth $1,250,000 when she died in 1998. Her estate passes to her two grown children, but not until after $246,250 in estate tax is paid. Had Joshua's half of the community property been placed in a bypass trust that benefitted Mary for her lifetime and then passed on to the children, no taxes would have been owed.

ABBREVIATIONS, SIMPLIFICATIONS, AND ASSUMPTIONS

The term "transfer" refers to lifetime gifts and transfers at death. The calculations in examples assume that the "pick up" tax is the only state death tax. The pick up tax is a state estate tax that is exactly equal to the federal credit for state death taxes. Unless stated otherwise, we will assume that any lifetime gifts were less than the annual exclusion amount. To simplify discussion, figures for estates will be net values (i.e., all deductions, except the marital deduction, have already been taken). For some extended examples, we will assume transfers took place between 1987 and 1997, a period when the rates and exclusion amount were stable. For short or single transaction examples, various years will be used.

In the discussions that follow, we will generally refer to the "first spouse to die" and the "second spouse to die" as S1 and S2, respectively. As a practical matter, wives outlive their husbands by an average of almost 10 years, hence it is not unusual in estate planning discussions to refer to S1 as the husband and S2 as the wife. From a tax standpoint, the crucial factor is not whether the husband or the wife dies first, but what property each owns when S1 dies and the structure of their estate plan. For example, the order of death might have very significant implications if one spouse is working and the other is not, or if there is a great disparity in their incomes or in their individual net wealth.

Starting in 1984, the marital deduction was eliminated for property going to any non-US citizen spouse unless complex requirements are met to assure the property transferred stays in the U.S., where it is likely to be taxed as it passes to the next generation. Because there is a different marital deduction structure for non-citizen spouses, our examples are for U.S. citizens until we specifically address planning for the non-citizen spouse in the next chapter.

THE MARITAL DEDUCTION: THEN AND NOW

It is helpful to understand the history of the marital deduction before getting into an extended discussion of the basic estate plans.

Subject to certain requirements which we will discuss later, today's gift and estate tax law allows a 100% marital deduction for transfers between spouses. The law allows one spouse to transfer any amount of property to the other spouse without gift or estate taxes.

As hard as it is to believe, there was no marital deduction until several years after World War II. Then, for almost 30 years, the marital deduction for property passing from one spouse to the other was limited to 50% of the net value of S1's estate. Only since 1982 has the 100% marital deduction been part of the law.

The first marital deduction applied to estates of decedents dying after April 2, 1948. It set the maximum marital deduction at 50% of S1's adjusted gross estate (AGE), i.e., S1's gross estate less the deductions allowed for expenses, indebtedness, taxes, and losses[2]. Of course the maximum marital deduction was achieved only if at least half the estate was left to S2, since the marital deduction claimed could not exceed the value of the property passing from S1 to S2.

The purpose of the marital deduction was to eliminate disparate treatment originating from differences in the two systems of state property laws. Some states, for example California and Texas, are community property states that trace their property law to early Roman law. In a community property state each spouse owns half of all property acquired by the labor of either spouse while married and domiciled in a community property state. Other states, like Kansas and New York, are common law states that trace their property law to early English law. In common law states the husband generally held title to all property acquired during the marriage. Husbands tend to die before their wives, thus, before the change in 1948, for any given amount of combined wealth, a family in a common law state was likely to pay a higher estate tax when the first spouse died than would have been paid had the family resided in a community property state.

Years	Maximum Marital Deduction
1917 - 1947	▸ no marital deduction allowed
1948 - 1976	▸ 50% of AGE, except no marital deduction for community property.
1977-1981	▸ Greater of $\quad$ 50% of AGE $\quad$ or $\quad$ $250,000
1982 to present	▸ 100% of amount S1 ----> S2 with no limit.

During the early period from 1948 through 1981, the marital deduction was designed such that if the husband died first the resulting taxable estate would probably be the same regardless of the couple's domicile. No marital deduction was allowed for S1's half interest in community property since allowing a marital deduction for community property would have resulted in a "quartering" of the estate, which would have perpetuated the inequality between the two property law systems.

EXAMPLE 11 - 4. Guilliano died in 1960, while residing in Kentucky. He left his estate to his wife Cheryl. During the entire marriage they lived in Kentucky and acquired property with a net worth of $1,000,000. Because Kentucky is a common law state, 100% of the property was included in Guilliano's gross estate. The marital deduction removed half, leaving $500,000. The $60,000 death tax exemption reduced the taxable estate to $440,000. If Guilliano had lived and died in Texas, a community property state, the $1,000,000 would have been community property. Only his half would have been included in his estate. There would have been no marital deduction, and after the exemption, the taxable estate would have been $440,000, the same result as in Kentucky.

Of course, there were still inequalities. For instance, if a person died domiciled in a common law stated and owned very little property, it was unlikely that there would be an estate tax even if the surviving spouse was already wealthy. In a community property state, if the wealth was acquired while the couple was married, then half of the property would be included in the estate of the first spouse to die, and since no marital deduction was allowed for community property, it would be subject to tax. Under current law, with the 100% marital deduction, it makes little sense to continue to allow a full step-up for community property. Indeed, in the near future, Congress might decide to change that by allowing only a half step-up for community property, much like the treatment presently given to spousal joint tenancies.

A Blip in the Law

From 1977 through 1981, the law allowed a marital deduction equal to the greater of 50% or $250,000 of the adjusted taxable estate. For large estates, those with AGE's in excess of $500,000, the maximum was 50% of AGE (just as it would have been pre-1977) but, for estates under $500,000 the $250,000 was obviously the greater amount. Thus, for estates between $250,000 and $500,000 the marital deduction became proportionally large; with smaller estates and for estates equal to, or below $250,000, it became a 100% marital deduction.

To keep community property states on a par with common law states, Congress allowed a marital deduction for small estates that included community property to assure that the estate received at least the $250,000 minimum marital deduction. The formula for calculating the alternative marital deduction started with $250,000, which was reduced by half of the decedent's separate property (because the separate property was allowed a 50% marital deduction), then it was further reduced by the community property included in the decedent's estate (since the half belonging to the survivor already escaped taxation). The resulting number was the maximum alternative marital deduction for an estate with community property.

EXAMPLE 11 - 5. Mac died in 1977. He left his half of the couple's $400,000 community property estate to his wife Tina. His adjusted gross estate was $200,000. Subtracting the $200,000 community property included in his gross estate from the $250,000 results in a $50,000 alternative marital deduction. Subtracting the alternative marital deduction from $200,000 results in a taxable estate of $150,000. If the couple had lived in a common law state, the result would have been the same, assuming that the entire $400,000 estate belonged to Mac. It would have been reduced by the full $250,000 minimum marital deduction to result in a taxable estate of $150,000.

EXAMPLE 11 - 6. June died in 1980. Her estate was left to her husband Brian. She owned separate property worth $60,000 and held $300,000 as community property with Brian. Her gross estate would be $210,000 less a marital deduction of $100,000, leaving a taxable estate of $110,000. The marital deduction was calculated by subtracting half of her separate property ($30,000) and half of the community property ($150,000) from $250,000. The result ($70,000) when added to the marital deduction ($30,000, which is 50% of her $60,000 separate property) produces the total available marital deduction. The $110,000 figure is the same as would have been taxed if June had owned $360,000 (her separate property plus all of the community property) and received a $250,000 marital deduction.

Learning to compute this alternative marital deduction is no longer a useful skill. Your time would be better spent working in the garden or teaching your dog to shake hands.

THE TERMINABLE INTEREST RULE

When the marital deduction first became part of the law, any transfer to a surviving spouse of what is called a *terminable interest* failed to qualify for the marital deduction.[3] A transfer is a terminable interest if the interest transferred to S2 ends at, or before, S2's death or upon the happening of some event, i.e., S2's remarriage. The reason for this limitation on the marital deduction is that to do otherwise might allow most estates, even those of the wealthy, to completely escape taxation. This would occur because the marital deduction would reduce or eliminate tax at S1's death on property that would later skip S2's estate (and, therefore, would escape the estate tax) when S2 died because S2 did not own the property. The most commonly encountered terminable interest is a trust created by S1 that, at his death, reserves a life estate for S2 with the remainder to the couple's children. S2's interest is a terminable interest because, her only interest in the property will terminate at her death and the "enjoyment" of the property will pass to the children.

For purposes of the marital deduction, a *terminable interest*[4] is defined as a property interest with these three characteristics:

- It is subject to some future absolute or *contingent* termination of S2's interest;
- the possibility of termination was created by S1 and, if it occurs, there will be a shift in the interest; and
- some other person or entity (other than S2 or her estate) will enjoy (i.e., possess or own) the property.

The Elements of the Terminable Interest Rule

The question is not whether a termination must occur, but whether, viewed as of the moment of S1's death, a termination *might* occur. Thus, the second and third requirements of the rule exclude situations where the terminable nature was not created by S1, including those unique property interests that simply end by their very nature. Thus, a bequest conditioned on the surviving spouse living for nine months beyond S1's death is a terminal interest, even if she does survive. An ownership interest for a period of years granted to S1 by a third party could be left to S2 for the remainder of the term, and it would not be a terminal interest. Like wise, a lease or a patent will terminate but the interest of S1 does not shift to someone else.

> EXAMPLE 6-7. Mark's will stated: "I leave the residue of my estate to my wife, Gloria, provided she survives to the close of probate, and if she does not so survive then it shall be divided amongst my issue by right of representation." His one million dollar estate was transferred by probate to Gloria within a mere five months of his death. Nevertheless, the bequest does not qualify for the marital deduction since Gloria *might* have died before the close of the probate, in which case her interest would have terminated. He created the terminable character of the interest. The interest might have gone to Mark's issue, who then would have enjoyed the property. Because it meets all three elements of the rule, it is a terminable interest and no marital deduction is allowed for the property even though Gloria received the property, and even though it will be in her estate unless she consumes it or gives it away.

EXAMPLE 11 - 7. When Lori died, she left her patent for turning base metals into gold to her husband Earl. The patent still had eleven years before it expired. Even though a patent by its very nature must terminate, the interest does not shift to someone else. Furthermore, it is not considered a terminable interest because even though Lori invented the process and obtained the patent, she did not create the termination. Therefore, the value of the patent qualifies for the marital deduction.

EXAMPLE 11 - 8. Selina owned a strip mall. She did not own the land, but was the lessee under what was originally a 99 year land-lease. At the time of her death the land-lease still had 63 years remaining. Even though the mall was built on leased land, Salina's interest was very valuable. (It is not uncommon to find commercial property on leased land. At the end of the lease, the land, together with any structures, reverts to the lessor.) When she died, she left her entire estate to her husband, Duane. Since Selina never owned any more than a leasehold, the shift in interest back to the lessor at the end of the lease is not one that she created. Thus, the value of her interest in the leasehold qualifies for the marital deduction. If, however, she had left the mall to Duane for ten years, and then to her son for the balance of the lease, it would have been a terminable interest and not even the value of the lease for the period that Duane would have it qualifies for the deduction.

Why Have a Terminable Interest Rule?

Consider what would happen if the law allowed a marital deduction for a terminable interest, such as a life estate for a surviving spouse, without requiring inclusion of the terminable interest property in S2's estate. The value of the property would be split into two parts, the life estate and the remainder interest. There is no denying that a life estate can be a valuable interest and that the interest can be valued using actuarial methods.

When the interest is created at S1's death, a marital deduction based upon a life estate might swallow up most of the value of the transfer, leaving very little (i.e., just the remainder interest) subject to the transfer tax. The tentative tax on this might be covered by S1's unified credit. Since the beneficiary of a life estate is not treated as a transferor when the life estate terminates at the beneficiary's death, none of the property subject to the life estate would be included in S2's estate.

EXAMPLE 11 - 9. Suppose the law did allow a marital deduction based upon the value of a life estate (remember, it never has and it probably never will) and that S1 died in 2002, leaving S2 a life estate in a trust worth $3,000,000. If S2 was 60 years old and the Federal rate for split interests was 10%, the value of S2's life estate is 0.77326 x $3,000,000 = $2,319,780 (the value of the remainder is $680,220). The tentative tax on a $680,220 transfer is $222,481, which is covered by S1's $229,800 unified credit, hence, no tax would be due at S1's death. Then when S2 passes away in 2006 and the trust property, then worth $4,000,000, is transferred to S1's children, there is nothing to include in her estate. Thus, assets worth $4,000,000 would pass tax free to the next generation. Wake up, it is just a dream.

TERMINABLE INTEREST RULE EXCEPTIONS

Why have exceptions to the terminable interest rule? The law creates a number of exceptions to the terminable interest rule, each of which allows the marital deduction even though the interest is technically a terminable interest. Congress certainly did not want a loophole that would allow large estates to avoid estate taxes, however, there are policy and/or practical reasons for each of the exceptions. Additionally, all of the exceptions are ones in which the property qualifying for the marital deduction is ultimately included in S2's estate, unless S2 consumes it or gives it away. If S2 gives it away in large chunks (greater than the annual exclusion), her gifts may use up her unified credit.

Six months or common disaster rule:§2056(b)(3). Almost from the start of the marital deduction and its related terminable interest rule, Congress created an exception to the rule for "six months or common disaster" survivorship clauses, so long as S2 survived long enough to satisfy the contingency and receive the property. Typically, these clauses make a bequest contingent upon the beneficiary actually out living the decedent by six months or some period shorter than six months. The law also allows the marital deduction for a marital bequest conditioned upon S2 surviving a common accident. A "common disaster" clause might state, "if my wife and I are injured in the same accident, and I die, I leave her my estate provided she eventually recovers from said accident." Even though recovery might take longer than six months, this bequest would qualify for the marital deduction so long as recovery did occur. Therefore, a survivorship clause, as part of the decedent's will or living trust, can be part of the estate plan, and a marital deduction will be allowed provided the survivor actually survives to receive the property.[5]

A survivorship clause may be specific, relating just to certain bequests, or it may cover all beneficiaries, e.g., *"For purposes of this Will, a beneficiary shall not be deemed to have survived me if that beneficiary dies within six months of my death."*

The clause avoids a double probate in situations where the beneficiary does not live long enough to really utilize the bequest. It also allows the testator to determine the alternate beneficiary of the bequest, rather than allowing it to be governed by the disposition of the beneficiary's estate. Without a survivorship clause the property goes into the beneficiary's estate even if the beneficiary lives just a moment longer than the testator.

Whether a bequest is a terminable interest is determined as of the death of S1; it does not depend upon whether the interest in fact terminates. Therefore, without the §2056(b)(3) exception, no marital deduction would be allowed for estates that actually passed to the surviving spouse if the bequest was subject to a survivorship clause.

Qualified Terminable Interest Property (QTIP): §2056(b)(7)

There are valid estate planning reasons for creating terminable interests whereby a surviving spouse is given income from a decedent spouse's estate for life, and yet the surviving spouse is given little or no control over the ultimate disposition of the property. With the population living longer, and with the high rate of divorce, marriages with one or both spouses having children by prior marriages are quite common. It is natural that a person with considerable wealth entering into a second (or third) marriage would want to take care of the new spouse, yet also desire to assure that his or her wealth does not go to the new spouse's family after both are deceased.

Prior to 1982, the maximum marital deduction for a large estate was equal to 50% of the estate's net value. To qualify for the marital deduction, the surviving spouse had to receive the property, or at least be given a general power of appointment over it. To obtain the maximum marital deduction, at least half of S1's estate had to be transferred to the surviving spouse. Thus, S1 was forced to choose between obtaining the maximum marital deduction and losing control over who would ultimately own the property, or retaining control and giving up the marital deduction. Fortunately, the QTIP election is now part of the law. It allows the marital deduction without forcing S1 to give up control as to whom will eventually receive the property.

Under the prior law (i.e., before we had the 100% marital deduction), leaving more than half of S1's estate to S2 did not increase the marital deduction for large estates, therefore, the most common plan left S2 only so much of S1's estate as qualified for the marital deduction. This could be either outright or in a trust that gave S2 a life estate and a general power to appoint the corpus.[6] The rest of S1's estate was transferred to a bypass trust, usually (but not in all cases) one giving the income from that trust to the surviving spouse for her life, with the remainder going to S1's family after her death. This arrangement did not sacrifice estate tax dollars on the first death and avoided having the corpus of the bypass trust included in S2's estate.

Without a new exception to the terminable interest rule, the change allowing a 100% marital deduction for transfers after 1981 would have created a dilemma for every couple who had kept their wealth separate because they had children by prior marriages. They would have been forced to choose between providing for the surviving spouse or assuring that their estates passed to their own children. The planner would have been forced to either transfer control of everything in excess of the exclusion amount to the surviving spouse or else pay an estate tax on the first death.

Fortunately, an option known as the QTIP election was added to the law.[7] This election allows the executor of S1's estate to obtain a marital deduction for what is called "Qualified Terminable Interest Property," referred to by the acronym QTIP. To qualify for this election, the terminable interest property must meet these requirements:

- The surviving spouse must receive all income from the property for life.
- The right to the income cannot be contingent.
- During the surviving spouse's life, the property cannot be appointed to anyone other than to the surviving spouse.[8]

The executor must make an election to claim the marital deduction for the QTIP property when S1's estate tax return is filed. The law allows the executor to make the QTIP election on less than 100% of the terminable interest property. This is done by electing to QTIP a fraction of the property. Thus, if the terminable interest property is in the form of a trust with a life estate for the surviving spouse, remainder to their children, and the trust is funded with property exceeding the applicable exclusion amount, the executor might elect to

QTIP only that portion of the trust which exceeds the value of the exclusion amount.

There is no free lunch. That fraction of the QTIP property which receives a marital deduction at S1's death must be included in S2's estate at the time of S2's death.[9] Hence, the choice in making a QTIP election is how much of the terminable interest property to tax at S1's death versus how much to tax at S2's death.

> EXAMPLE 11 - 10. Fernando died in 1988 leaving his entire estate, $1,127,452, less debts & expenses of $197,420, in an irrevocable trust for his wife, Arcela. She was given a life estate and a limited power to appoint corpus at her death amongst their three children. Arcela had a modest estate of her own. Since the executor of Fernando's estate wanted to postpone all taxes until after Arcela's death, he QTIP'ed that portion that exceeded the exclusion amount estate, i.e., that fraction above the exclusion amount. Since the net value of the trust was $930,032, the QTIP fraction is:
>
> $$\frac{\$930,032 - \$600,000}{\$930,032}$$

When this fraction is multiplied by the net value of the trust, the marital deduction is $330,032, resulting in a taxable estate of exactly $600,000.

The QTIP fraction serves a dual role; it determines how much of the QTIP property qualifies for the marital deduction on the first death and, just as importantly, it determines how much of that property (valued at the second death) must be included in S2's estate.

> EXAMPLE 11 - 11. When Arcela died in 2006, the trust Fernando had established for her had grown from its initial net worth to $2,854,372, with debts of $420,870, for a net value of $2,433,502. Arcela had her own property worth $780,450 and her estate had debts and expenses that totaled $110,400, for a net value of $670,050. She too left her estate to their children. In determining her taxable estate her executor would have to add to what she owned the portion of the trust that had previously been QTIP'ed:
>
> $$\frac{330,032}{930,032} * \$2,433,502 = \$863,555$$

Adding this amount to $670,050 results in a taxable estate of $1,533,605.

*** *Query 1. What would the QTIP fraction have been if the net value of the trust at Fernando's death had been $1,789,373? What dollar value of the trust would be included in Arcela's estate given that change?*

The QTIP fraction equation given above utilizes S1's exclusion amount and defers all taxes to the second death. The exclusion amount in the formula must be adjusted to take into account any use of the unified credit elsewhere, either because S1 made taxable gifts during life or left part of the estate to someone other than the surviving spouse. Such transfers use up unified credit (unless to a charity). Hence, the exclusion amount in the numerator should equal the exclusion amount that remains available.

EXAMPLE 11-12. Suppose Fernando also owned a $250,000 life insurance policy that named his daughter by a prior marriage as the beneficiary. Now his gross estate would be $1,377,452. The net value after debts and expenses would be $1,180,032 [$250,000 life insurance plus the $930,032 in the trust]. The life insurance would utilize $250,000 of the exclusion amount, hence, the QTIP fraction in the above example would be ($930,032 - $350,000) divided by $930,032. The portion of the QTIP property elected for the marital deduction would be equal to $580,032. Thus, after the marital deduction, the taxable estate would again be $600,000, comprised of the $250,000 life insurance policy and the $350,000 portion of the QTIP property that was not covered by the marital deduction. [$1,377,452 - $197,420 -$580,032 = $600,000]

Of course, 100% of the QTIP property in the above example could have qualified for the marital deduction, but electing to QTIP 100% of the trust would have reduced S1's taxable estate below the exclusion amount, thus wasting part of S1's unified credit and needlessly increasing the amount of the property which would eventually be included in S2's estate.

There are times when it is advantageous to generate a tax on the first estate by using a QTIP fraction which is less than that necessary to defer all taxes. For instance, if S1 left QTIP property worth $5,000,000 in trust for S2, and S2 has no estate of her own, it might be advantageous to QTIP half of the $5,000,000 trust. By doing so, the QTIP half will qualify for the marital deduction leaving a taxable estate of $2,500,000. Upon S2's death, half of the trust will be included in her estate. The tax on two estates worth $2,500,000 each is considerably less than the tax on two estates where one is equal to the exclusion amount (i.e. between $600,000 and $1,000,000) and the other is equal to five million dollars less the exclusion amount (i.e. between $4,400,000 and $4,000,000). Two shorter trips up the rate ladder are cheaper than one long one. Furthermore, as will be discussed in the next chapter, generating a tax in both estates sometimes allows the second estate to utilize a prior transfer credit, further reducing the total estate taxes.[10]

Although most of our examples, and most real life QTIP trusts, concern decedent's estates, the QTIP election is also available for lifetime transfers of terminal interest gifts.[11] It could be utilized by a wealthy spouse who wants to bring the value of his or her spouse's estate up to at least the exclusion amount. The use of the QTIP trust allows the wealthier spouse to keep the property in his or her family, whereas an outright gift surrenders control of the property. Of course, to utilize the less wealthy spouse's unified credit, the wealthy spouse must be willing to part with some property even if the other spouse (the donee spouse) dies first.

EXAMPLE 11-13. Eighty year old Ellen had a net worth of $4,500,000 when, after ten years of widowhood, she married Frank, a kindly gentleman of modest means. Ellen wanted to take care of Frank, should she die before him. She was also willing to have a significant portion of her estate go immediately to her children if Frank died before her. Therefore, in 1999, she established a lifetime QTIP trust. The trust was funded with stocks and bonds worth $1,000,000. The terms of the trust give Frank a life estate, and, if Frank died first, her children would receive only so much of the corpus as equals the exclusion amount available for Frank's estate (taking into account his own property and any taxable gifts he might have made), the balance of the trust would revert back to Ellen; if she was not alive at that time the trust would go to her children. She filed a gift tax return and elected to QTIP all of the trust.

EXAMPLE 11-14. When Frank died in 2003, the QTIP trust had a net worth of $1,380,000 and his own property had a net worth of $75,000, for a total of $1,455,000. Frank's family received his property, and Ellen received $755,000 from the trust, which was just enough to bring Frank's taxable estate down to the exclusion amount (i.e., down to $700,000). The balance of the trust (i.e., $625,000) went to her children. Thus, the tentative tax on Frank's estate equaled $229,800, which in turn was completely covered by his unified credit. If Ellen had been dying at the time of Frank's death, she could have reduced overall taxes by disclaiming her reversionary interest (the $755,000), which would have kept it out of her estate, allowing it to be taxed at the lower marginal rates of Frank's estate rather than at the top marginal rates of her estate. With a disclaimer, all of the trust property would have gone to her children.

General Power of Appointment Exception:§2056(b)(5)

A power to appoint property is the right to tell the owner of the property to transfer it to someone else. Powers of appointment were discussed in greater detail in Chapter 6. As a reminder, the Code defines a general power as "a power which is exercisable in favor of the decedent, his estate, his creditors, or the creditors of his estate. . . ."

> EXAMPLE 11-15. Fred creates an irrevocable trust for Jerry's benefit. The terms of the trust provide Jerry with all the income from the trust and give her the right, when she reaches age twenty-five (25), to have the trustee terminate the trust and transfer all assets to anyone that Jerry designates (including herself). From the moment Jerry reaches age twenty-five (25), she has a general power of appointment.

The holder of a general power must include in his or her estate the value of property which could have been transferred by the exercise of a general power of appointment, regardless of whether it is ever exercised. It is enough that it merely could have been exercised. Limited powers do not result in inclusion of the property in the estate of the holder, provided the holder of the power did not create the power. Where the holder also created the power, the Internal Revenue Code treats it as a retained interest rather than as a power to appoint.

A marital deduction is allowed for property passing in trust from S1 to S2, provided S2 is given income for life in the property and has a general power of appointment over the property exercisable during life and/or at death.[12] Since S2 is a holder of a general power, the property will be included in S2's estate, or if she appoints it during life to someone else, it will be a gift from her to that person. Thus, although the transfer into a general power of appointment trust may technically be a transfer of a terminable interest, it is allowed to qualify for the marital deduction because (unless consumed) it will eventually be either given away by S2 or in S2's estate. Since Congress is allowing a marital deduction based upon S2 receiving a life estate, the trust must either require the trustee to make the trust assets productive, or state law (and most states have such laws) must give S2 the power to require the trustee to make them productive. If the trust document gives the trustee absolute investment power, especially if it includes a statement allowing investment in unproductive assets, the marital deduction may not be available even though S2 is given a life estate.[13]

EXAMPLE 11-16. Upon her death, Geraldine creates a trust for her husband Bob. It is funded with assets having a net value of $950,714. Bob is given a life estate in the trust and the power, exercisable only by specific mention of the power in his will, to appoint the corpus to whomever he chooses. If he fails to exercise the power, the property is to be distributed by right of representation to their issue. The trust will qualify for the marital deduction because of §2056(b)(5). Therefore, although it is in Geraldine's gross estate, it is not in her taxable estate. But when Bob dies, because the power is a general one, the entire trust will be included in his gross estate whether or not he exercises the power.

EXAMPLE 11-17. Upon his death in 2002, Gerry's estate plan creates a trust to benefit his wife Betty. It is funded with property worth $2,000,000. The terms of the trust give Betty a life estate and the power to appoint the corpus to any of their five children when she dies. If she does not appoint the corpus, it will be distributed by right of representation at her death. Because Betty only has a limited power to appoint, §2056(b)(5) does not apply, and there is no automatic marital deduction. Assuming no QTIP (discussed later) election is made, the trust will be taxed at Gerry's death (resulting in death taxes of $551,000), but no additional taxes will be owed when the trust terminates at Betty's death. The latter is true no matter how much the trust has grown, and no matter how much Betty exercises her limited power to change the remainder interests of the children.

Pensions for the Benefit of S2: §2056(b)(7)(C)

In the case of an annuity included in S1's estate that is payable to S2 alone during S2's life, the QTIP election is automatic unless the executor of S1's estate affirmatively elects to have the annuity taxed in S1's estate. Electing to have it taxed will avoid having any value that remains at S2's death taxed as part of S2's estate, whereas allowing the automatic QTIP results in that value being included in S2's estate.

Charitable Remainder Trusts with a Life Estate for S2:§2056 (b)(8)

Property transferred to a qualified charitable remainder trust,[14] which has the surviving spouse as its only non-charitable beneficiary, qualifies for the marital deduction, even though it is a terminable interest. This is a special rule and no QTIP election is necessary. It is not included in S2's estate, although it would make no difference if it were included since it would then qualify for a charitable deduction. If the executor is in doubt as to whether the trust is a "qualified charitable" remainder trust, he or she should make a protective QTIP election, i.e., list it as part of the QTIP property on Schedule M of the 706. It will then be in S2's estate, but it will qualify for a charitable deduction.

THE BASIC ESTATE PLANNING PATTERNS

Planning to minimize the estate tax with the marital deduction and the bypass arrangement generally involves some variation of one of three basic planning options. They are the *100% marital deduction*, the *AB Trust*, and the *ABC Trust*. These options do not depict precise will or trust arrangements, instead they trace the overall flow of property after S1's death. Our concern is with the timing of estate tax payments, the amount of those taxes, and which spouse (S1 or S2) controls who will eventually receive the property. First, we will take up the simplest plan, where S1 transfers all his estate to S2. Next, we will cover the bypass trust because it is common to almost all multiple trust plans. Lastly, we will take a look at the basic multiple trust plans, before going back to the QTIP election and how it is used in conjunction with the ABC Trust plan.

PLANNING OPTION 1: SIMPLE 100 PERCENT MARITAL DEDUCTION

Often, the unlimited marital deduction provides a simple and practical estate planning strategy. It entirely shelters all property S1 transfers to S2 from gift tax and estate tax. In the simple 100% marital deduction strategy, S1 leaves all property to the surviving spouse. The transfer is protected from transfer tax by the 100% marital deduction. Outright transfers by S1 to S2 that qualify for the 100% marital deduction include: gifts, transfers by will, transfers by right of survivorship when title is held solely by the spouses in joint tenancy or tenancy by the entirety, and insurance on S1's life payable to S2. Transfers in trust for the benefit of S2 qualify too if they meet certain criteria.

EXAMPLE 11-18. Tom and Gerri each have estates of $400,000. At her death in 2000, Gerri leaves her entire estate to Tom by a simple will. There is no estate tax because the estate is sheltered by the 100% marital deduction. At Tom's death in

2004, he leaves the combined estate then worth $825,000 to their child. There is no estate tax because of his available exclusion amount.

Advantages of the 100 Percent Marital Deduction

The main attraction of the simple 100% marital deduction strategy is its simplicity. It is very easy to understand and inexpensive to establish. More elaborate estate planning may not be necessary for clients whose combined estates are less than one exclusion amount. Some clients may not be concerned about whether taxes will be due after the second death, e.g., where the couple leaves no issue or where they plan to leave a large enough portion of their estate to charities such that at the second death the taxable estate will be less than the exclusion amount.

Of course, these simple plans give S2 total dispositive control over all of the couple's property. This may be an advantage or a disadvantage, depending on the circumstances. S2 will receive full ownership of the property, a fee simple interest. S2 can use it, consume it, gift it, or sell it. If she still owns it at her death, she can leave it to whomever she chooses, in such manner as she chooses.

Not all marital deduction plans confer full dispositive control to S2. S1 may retain dispositive control by placing the property in a trust known as a qualified terminable interest property (QTIP) trust. These are most commonly found in multiple trust plans known as ABC trust plans. (Patience, we will get to this soon.) However, a QTIP trust can be used alone where S1 wants dispositive control but sees no need for multiple trusts.

Disadvantages of the 100 Percent Marital Deduction

The 100% marital deduction that transfers all control to S2 has several significant drawbacks for large estates.

Higher total estate tax. The first drawback for wealthier couples is a higher total estate tax due to two factors. First, each spouse has the protection of the unified credit, but when S1 gives his entire estate to S2 protected by the marital deduction, his unified credit is unused. Unless S2 consumes or gives away S1's property using the annual exclusion or charitable gifts, it will become part of S2's transfer tax base, subject to either gift tax or estate tax to the extent that the combined value exceeds S2's exclusion amount. Second, because the two estates are combined and subject to estate tax as one estate, there is only one "run up the rate ladder." Up to a point, marginal rates increase with the size of the estate. The larger the estate, the higher the rate of tax on the top dollar. Even if there were no unified credit, two one million dollar estates would pay less tax than one two million dollar estate.

> EXAMPLE 11-19. H and W own a family estate of two million dollars, with each owning one-half. They have simple wills leaving property to one another, or to the children if the other is deceased. At S1's death there will be no estate tax because the entire one million dollars passes to S2, sheltered by the marital deduction. If S2 dies in the year 2001, having neither transferred nor consumed the property, a two million dollar taxable estate will result in estate taxes of $551,000.

The simple 100% marital deduction planning is said to have the effect of "over qualifying" or "overusing" the marital deduction, resulting in a "loading up" of the taxable estate of S2, and subjecting a greater amount of the couple's wealth to tax at the second death than would occur with a more complex plan. In summary, two negative results can occur as a result of pouring the first estate into the second; the unified credit of S1 is wasted, and a portion of the combined estate may be subjected to higher marginal rates than would have been encountered with a more complex estate plan.

May not avoid probate. If a couple uses simple wills to carry out their 100% marital deduction planning, or if they hold everything in joint tenancy, there will be a probate, at least at the second death. Some states do not require a probate for property left from one spouse to the other. Of course, the use of living trusts as part of the estate plan overcomes this problem.

Not available for non-citizen spouses. The marital deduction only applies to property left to citizen spouses. The property of U.S. citizens is subject to estate taxation anywhere in the world. However, the property of non-citizens is only subject to estate tax if it is located in the U.S. Because a non-citizen spouse could take the property and leave the country (preventing estate taxation at S2's death), the marital deduction does not apply to property left to non-citizen spouses unless special trusts (with U.S. trustees) are used. This will be discussed in the next chapter.

BYPASS PLANNING

The common theme of most bypass planning is the division of S1's estate into a bypass portion and a marital deduction portion. The bypass portion is transferred to someone other than S2 in a way that bypasses S2's estate. It is important to note that the bypass portion is considered to be "taxed" at the first death even if the use of S1's unified credit results in no tax being due. The marital deduction portion is transferred to S2 in a way that qualifies it for the marital deduction. Bypass planning thus avoids the two major problems with simple marital deduction planning. It makes use of S1's unified credit, and it potentially provides two runs up the rate ladder, depending on the details of the bypass plan chosen.

There are many variations on the bypass planning theme including the way the bypass property is transferred (whether outright or in trust), the number of trusts used and their characteristics, the proportion of S1's property in the bypass portion, and whether it will equal the exclusion amount (so no tax will actually be paid) or exceed it (and cause some tax at the first death). Usually, the bypass portion is eventually transferred to the couple's children, but there are many other possibilities. Remember, it is called bypass planning because it bypasses S2's estate (or some other income beneficiary's estate) for tax purposes. It is taxed in S1's estate whether taxes are paid or not, e.g., the tentative tax may be fully absorbed by the decedent's unified credit.

Simple outright bypass. The simplest form of bypass is the outright bypass where the exclusion amount is left directly to someone other than S2.

> EXAMPLE 11-20. Herbert had an estate worth $1,500,000 when he died in 2003. To his daughter, Denise, he left property worth $700,000 protected from tax by his unified credit, and to his wife, Wilma, he left property worth $800,000 protected from tax by the marital deduction. When Wilma died in 2005, she left to Denise an estate valued at $900,000 protected by her exclusion amount. There was no estate tax paid at either death. If Herbert had left the entire $1,500,000 estate to Wilma, it would have been protected at his death by the marital deduction, but at Wilma's death, it would have exceeded her available exclusion amount. Assuming even modest growth, an estate of $1,600,000 would produce a tax of $274,500

Bypass share: Outright or in trust? The couple might have strong reservations about the bypass plan if, at S1's death, it caused an immediate, outright transfer to the children. The children may be too young to be responsible for the property. S2 may need either the income from the property, or the property itself, for support. S2 might prefer to retain control over the management of those assets ultimately intended for the children. These are common and legitimate objections to the use of an immediate, outright transfer to the children to effect a bypass. Fortunately, the bypass can be arranged, and these objections overcome, by means of transfers into trusts.

Recall that by limiting the powers given to the beneficiary of a life estate, the trust is excluded from the holder's gross estate. The beneficiary can have the right to take the income and a power of appointment that does not rise to the level of a general power of appointment, such as the right to take principal measured by the "ascertainable standard."

Generally, bypass property is taxed at the time it is initially transferred for the benefit of the income beneficiary, but not again when the income beneficiary dies. The amount transferred in this fashion might be equal to the exclusion amount, i.e., just enough to create a tentative tax equal to the unified credit. Thus, although technically the transfer is taxed, the donor, or in the case of a bequest, the decedent's estate, does not have to pay any transfer tax.

For most of our discussion we will assume that the income beneficiary in question is S2, and that the bypass property is a bypass trust established by S1. We make this assumption because it is the most frequently encountered bypass arrangement, but there are other possibilities. The bypass plan works because the transfer of an amount sufficient to use S1's unified credit to someone other than S2 can be arranged to conform to both spouses' overall estate planning objectives.

In a typical bypass trust, the children of the marriage are the ultimate beneficiaries, or remaindermen. Neither spouse is likely to object to the children as the remaindermen of the bypass trust created at S1's death, since in all likelihood, both spouses expect their combined estates to eventually go to their children. S2 usually has the income from the bypass property as well as access to the principal for purposes of health, education, support or maintenance, without the property being included in her estate.

MULTIPLE TRUSTS IN ESTATE PLANNING: BASIC PATTERNS

Each of the three plans (including the 100% marital deduction plan discussed earlier) can be set up with a will or a trust instrument. Due to the costs and lack of privacy associated with probate, most wealthy couples that spend the time, energy, and money to have one of these more complex estate plans written, choose the living trust over the testamentary trust (although either will accomplish the tax savings discussed in this chapter). For the most part, we will assume a living trust for these multi-trust plans.

The documents that implement the process usually separate it into three phases. The first phase can be described as the family trust phase. There is usually only one trust in this phase. The couple's property is transferred to the trustee while the trustors are alive, hence it is called a "living" trust or an "inter vivos" trust. Most married couples serve as the initial trustees of their family trust, and they reserve the power to revoke or amend it.

The second phase starts with the death of one of the spouses, S1. The family trust is divided into multiple trusts after the first spouse dies. The multiple trusts are funded from the family trust at that time. It is not known which spouse will be the first to die at the time the plan is drafted, hence the distribution of assets into the various trusts is based on the order of the two deaths. Generally, in these complex estate plans, Trust A receives all of S2's property. Sometimes, some of S1's property goes into Trust A too, depending upon the size of S1's estate and the type of estate plan. Trust B will be funded from S1's estate. Whether Trust B receives all of S1's estate, or only part of it, will again depend upon the size of S1's estate and the type of estate plan. If there is a Trust C, it too will be funded from S1's estate. The funding of these trusts is fixed by the plan and the trustee generally has very little flexibility to change the plan. After S1's death, Trusts B and C become irrevocable. S2 can control the distribution of assets only according to the terms of those trusts, e.g., she may or may not be given a limited power to appoint corpus when she dies or she may have a power to withdraw limited to an ascertainable standard. Usually, these plans allow S2 to amend (or even revoke) Trust A, since corpus is principally from S2's property.

The third phase commences with S2's death. If the plan has been properly carried out, the different trusts will already be funded. The executor, filing the estate tax return, must determine which trusts (or portions thereof) are included in S2's estate. After paying the estate tax, the trustee distributes the remaining trust property outright to the children if they have reached the specified age specified in the trust document, commonly 25, 30, or 35. On the other hand, if the children are much younger, then the two trusts (AB plan) or three trusts (ABC plan) are likely to be merged into a single "pot" trust until the children reach the age specified in the trust, at which time the trust is subdivided into equal shares for the children. The subdivision (creating separate trusts) is usually specified as when either the youngest reaches a certain age (i.e., twenty-one) or when the oldest reaches some age, although the trust can set a specific date after which division should be made, such as, "as soon after January 1, 2010 as the division can be accomplished."

Sometimes a testamentary trust arrangement is used for these complex estate plans, although it is less common than using the living trust. The testamentary trust is a lengthy will that incorporates a trust. With the testamentary trust, there is a probate after the testator dies. At the conclusion of the probate, the trust is funded by a court order, which incorporates into the order the trust language from the will. The order directs the distribution of the probate property to the trustee, who is charged with managing the trust estate in keeping with the terms of the trust. There may be several trusts depending upon the specific estate plan. Once the probate is completed and the trust or trusts are funded, the process is just like plans that start with an inter vivos family trust.

When you work with these complex estate plans, at the first death start by determining the property (and its value) included in S1's estate to arrive at S1's gross estate (net estate before the marital deduction if the values given are net values). At the same time, you will have determined the value of S2's estate as it is at S1's death. The next step is to review their estate plan to determine how the property is to be allocated to each of the trusts. At the second death, the trusts are already funded, therefore, after determining the net value of each trust, the task is merely to determine what portion of each trust is included in S2's estate. The portion included may depend upon the trust's characteristics (e.g., because of S2's general power to appoint the corpus of Trust A, it is always included) or it may depend upon what was done at S1's death (e.g., whether a QTIP election was, or was not, made on a terminable interest trust).

Definitions. In the discussions that follow, we will be using the shorthand terms "AB Trust" and "ABC Trust." Attorneys who draft trust documents and estate planners may choose different titles for the component trusts, although the terms AB Trust or ABC Trust are frequently used as short hand designations, and will effectively convey the general pattern to those familiar with estate planning. The naming of trusts seems to be as variable as the naming of neighborhood cats. The same cat may have a different name in each house he visits. The following names are frequently used for these trusts, but there are many others possibilities:

- Trust A may be called the Survivor's Trust, the Marital Trust, or the General Power of Appointment Trust.
- Trust B may be called the Bypass Trust, the Exclusion Trust, the Credit Shelter Trust, or the Nonmarital Trust.
- Trust C may be called the QTIP Trust, the QTIP Marital Trust, or even Trust Q.

Depending on the plan and how Trusts B and C are defined, either may be called the Residuary Trust. Thus, if in an ABC Trust plan Trust B is defined in terms of the amount necessary to utilize the available unified credit and the residue of S1's estate flows into Trust C, the latter may be called the Residuary Trust. On the other hand, if Trust C is defined as the minimum amount that, when qualified for the marital deduction, will reduce S1's taxable estate to the exclusion amount, with the balance flowing into Trust B, then it is Trust B that may be called the Residuary Trust.

PLANNING OPTION 2: THE AB TRUST

The modern AB Trust plan is based on using the marital deduction and both spouses' unified credits. We say "modern" because the unlimited marital deduction has only been available to estates of decedents dying after 1981. The "B" Trust is the bypass component. The "A" Trust is the surviving spouse's trust. The two components are structured and funded so as to leave the maximum amount possible to the surviving spouse while still utilizing both spouses' unified credits. Payment of transfer taxes is deferred until S2's death. For large estates, which ever spouse lives longest, thus becoming S2, will ultimately control who receives the bulk of the couple's estate. Only Trust B, the exclusion amount trust, has the remainder interest fixed by S1 at S1's death. *This plan makes sense for wealthy couples whose children are solely from their present marriage since the plan may give S2 ultimate control over the greater portion of the couple's combined estate.*

EXAMPLE 11-21. The combined value of Hal and Wanda's property at S1's death in 2002, is $5,000,000. It does not matter whether Hal or Wanda dies first because the trusts are set up so that Trust A becomes S2's trust and Trust B, the trust that initially holds the exclusion amount, receives assets with a net value of $700,000. The balance of the estate, in the amount of $4,300,000, would go into Trust A. Trust B would have the remaindermen irrevocably designated (probably the couple's children), while Trust A would be subject to the control of S2. There is no requirement that the couple's children ultimately receive the property from Trust A. If S2 remarries, or for any reason, decides they are not deserving, she can change the remaindermen for that trust. Because, it is not part of S2's estate, Trust B will not be taxed again at S2's death even if it then exceeds the exclusion amount.

The Character of Trust A

Trust A receives all of S2's property, plus all of S1's property that exceeds S1's available exclusion amount. S1's unified credit is applied against taxable transfers up to the exclusion amount. These taxable transfers include property going into Trust B, property going to people other than S2, and lifetime taxable gifts made by S1. To obtain the marital deduction at S1's death for property transferred from S1's estate into Trust A, the trust must have two characteristics: (1) S2 must receive all the income for life, paid at least annually; and (2) S2 must be given a general power of appointment exercisable during life and/or at her death. Of course, if S2 has a general power to appoint exercisable during her entire lifetime, she also has income for life even if the trust is silent in that regard.

The Character of Trust B

The funding for Trust B is usually defined in terms of S1's available exclusion amount. It usually receives exactly enough of S1's estate to cause a tentative tax equal to S1's "available" unified credit. What is available starts with the exclusion amount for the year S1 died and is reduced by the value of property passing to someone other than S2 and any post-1997 taxable gifts. Methods for achieving the right amount of funding are described at the end of this chapter under the heading "Allocating Assets to the Trusts." For most estates, the initial value of Trust B will be the exclusion amount since this will cause a tentative tax equal to the unified credit available in the year of S1's death. The tentative tax is then canceled out by unified credit.

Since the purpose of this trust is to utilize S1's unified credit and avoid inclusion in S2's estate, any characteristics that would cause inclusion (such as giving S2 a general power of appointment over trust corpus) must be avoided. The marital deduction is not sought for Trust B, so while it is common to give S2 all income for life, such is not required. The terms could call for sprinkling the income amongst S2 and the children, or it could even allow the trustee to accumulate income or distribute corpus to persons other than S2. Most AB plans give S2 all of the income from Trust B, probably for psychological reasons since it is not necessary for tax reasons. A general power to appoint would cause inclusion in S2's estate, so it is to be avoided. However, S2 may be given a power to invade the corpus limited by ascertainable standards or S2 may be given a special power to allocate the remainder. A special power, in those plans using one, is likely to be limited to the couple's children and/or specific charities, adding flexibility to the plan within limits, without causing the trust property to be included in S2's estate.

AB Trust Plan's Benefits

The AB Trust plan provides the opportunity for S2 to manage the assets from both estates, enjoy all of the income, and have access to all of the principal, even though that in Trust B can be reached only if necessary (i.e., by applying the ascertainable standard). In the event both spouses die while their children are young, the plan allows disbursement to the children to be delayed until they are old enough to manage the property. An AB Trust can provide flexibility so that S2 can change the distribution plan in response to changed circumstances, it makes use of the marital deduction to delay taxation until the second death, and it uses S1's unified credit. The following example compares the estate taxes using the unlimited marital deduction with the result of using an AB Trust plan.

> EXAMPLE 11-22. S1 dies in the year 2004 (when the exclusion amount is $850,000) and S2 dies in the year 2007 (when the exclusion amount is $1,000,000). All of the estate, with a net value of $4,000,000, belongs to S1 and poor S2 owns nothing. In an AB Trust plan, even though S2 has no assets, the plan calls for S2's property to go into trust A since, before either spouse dies, no one can be certain

which spouse will be S1 and which S2, or whether a spouse with little or no property might acquire a substantial estate before S1's death.

	100% Marital Deduction		AB Trust	
	S1 dies 2004	S2 dies 2007	S1 dies 2004	S2 dies 2007
GE	$4,000,000	$4,000,000	$4,000,000	$3,150,000
	$4,000,000)	$0	($3,150,000)	$0
TE	$0	$4,000,000	$850,000	$3,150,000
		$1,840,800	$287,300	$1,373,300
		($345,800)	($287,300)	($345,800)
	$0	$1,495,000	$0	$1,027,500

A tax savings of $467,500 results. This is partly due to $850,000 being "taxed" at S1's death even though no tax is owed. The reason that the tax savings is more than the $287,300 unified credit is that the $850,000 held in Trust B would have otherwise been taxed in S2's estate at S2's highest marginal rates, i.e., those between $3,150,000 and $4,000,000. Avoiding those higher marginal rates results in an additional $180,200 saved. Of course, if Trust B grew in value between the two deaths, even more would be sheltered since a credit shelter trust (or any other bypass trust) is not taxed at S2's death, regardless of its value at that time.

EXAMPLE 11-23. This example is similar to the last example except both spouses have community property and separate property. To allow easier comparison between the examples, the total net value will stay at $4,000,000, and the plans and timing of the two deaths will remain the same. S1 has separate property worth $1,350,000, S2 has separate property worth $1,700,000, and they own community property worth $950,000.

	100% Marital Deduction		AB Trust	
	S1 dies 2004	S2 dies 2007	S1 dies 2004	S2 dies 2007
GE	$1,825,000	$4,000,000	$1,825,000	$3,150,000
MD	($1,825,000)	0	($975,000)	0
TE	0	$4,000,000	$850,000	$3,150,000
TT	0	$1,840,800	$345,800	$1,373,300
UC	0	($345,800)	($345,800)	($345,800)
ET	0	$1,495,000	0	$1,027,500

Notice the gross estate at S1's death is the same for both plans. S1's estate consisted of separate property plus one-half of the community property, i.e., $1,350,000 + 50\% * 950,000 = \$1,825,000$. Of course, our assumption, made for the sake of simplicity, that the values remain the same between S1's death and S2's death is unrealistic. The use of S1's unified credit is not being postponed until S2's death, since Trust B is actually taxed at S1's death but the tentative tax is completely covered by the S1's unified credit. Trust B is not taxed at S2's death because it entirely bypasses S2's estate.

If either spouse is uncomfortable with the control given to S2 by the AB Trust plan, they should consider the ABC Trust plan which reduces the amount of property over which S2 exercises ultimate control, yet still allows estate taxes to be postponed until the second death.

PLANNING OPTION 3: THE ABC TRUST

The ABC Trust plan is like the AB Trust plan except that S1's net estate in excess of the exclusion amount goes into Trust C instead of passing to Trust A. The terms of Trust C qualify it for the marital deduction through the QTIP election, thus, making it possible to defer all estate taxes until the second death. The real advantage of this plan when compared to the AB Trust is that S1's estate in excess of the exclusion amount goes into Trust C which cannot be changed by S2. Since Trusts B and C are irrevocable, S1 can rest in peace. knowing that the remaindermen for these two trusts are fixed. S2 may be given the power, limited by an ascertainable standard relating to health, education, support, or maintenance, to invade the corpus of Trusts B and C. This invasion right can even be limited such that it only becomes available to S2 when Trust A has less than a certain value remaining, e.g., only if Trust A is worth less than the exclusion amount. S1 can also give S2 a limited power of appointment, exercisable only by will, over Trusts B and C. Remember, neither a limited power to appoint, nor a power to invade limited by an ascertainable standard, will cause inclusion of the property in the holder's estate. Even though S2 is given these powers, it is S1 who defines their limits.

The Character of Trust A

This Trust A is likely to have the same characteristics as Trust A in the AB Trust plan. Trust A receives property equal in value to all of S2's separate property and S2's one-half interest in community property. S2 is given a general power to appoint the corpus of this trust or to revoke it. Unless property actually passes from S1's estate into Trust A, there is no marital deduction for property in this trust because it will hold property that already belongs to S2. It is not unusual for S1's plan to leave some property, such as all the tangible personal property, to S2's Trust A. The transfer of such property into Trust A would automatically qualify for the marital deduction. Of course, there is also an automatic marital deduction for property (such as cars and the household bank account) held in joint tenancy by the couple.

The Character of Trust B

Trust B will have the same characteristics as Trust B in the AB Trust plan, including being defined in terms of S1's available exclusion amount. Thus, in most instances the value of the trust will initially be the S1's available exclusion amount. As the exclusion amount increases such that it shelters higher and amounts (e.g., $700,000 in 2002, $1,000,000 in 2006), the "available exclusion amount" language allows the estate plan to make the most of the increased bypass opportunity. Again, the trust can be a sprinkling trust without harming the planning objectives but, more commonly, S2 is given all income for life. As will be discussed in the next chapter, giving S2 income for life (also referred to as a life estate) in this trust may, under certain circumstances, allow a larger prior transfer tax credit. This is a bypass trust in that it will be taxed at S1's death and escape tax (regardless of its growth) at S2's death.

The Character of Trust C

Trust C must meet all the Code QTIP requirements[15] to ensure the marital deduction is available should S1's executor decide that it is in the estate's best interest to claim a marital deduction. The requirements are that S2 must receive income for life and no one can hold a power to appoint the trust property to anyone other than S2 during her lifetime. This trust usually receives that portion of S1's estate that exceeds the exclusion amount. When a QTIP election is made for Trust C, the executor of S1's estate is claiming a marital deduction and, in effect, making a pact with the IRS that the property will eventually be subject to transfer tax triggered by S2 making a gift of her interest in the trust or by her death.[16] If the QTIP election is not made, Trust C will be taxed at S1's death and will not be taxed again when S2 dies, even though S2 enjoys a life estate. Thus, Trust C is a marital deduction trust if the election is made, and a bypass trust if it is not.

Typically, S2 enjoys a life estate (a requirement for the QTIP) in the trust property. She has the use of any tangible property that is part of this trust (such as the home and its contents) and must receive the income from investment property, placing it in her own personal accounts or in her Trust A accounts.

If the QTIP election is not made, S2 must withdraw the income from the trust. Leaving it in Trust C would be treated as a gift from her into the trust over which she has a retained life estate, creating a §2036 retained life estate problem. Of course this is only a problem if the QTIP election is not made since, if it is made over the whole trust, the trust will be included in S2's estate anyway.[17]

The QTIP election is made on Schedule M of S1's U.S. Federal Estate Tax Return, Form 706. Once the election is made (or not made) on a return and the time for filing the estate tax return has passed, the executor cannot change the decision. Fortunately, the QTIP election can be made even on a late filed return.

Trust C cannot be a sprinkling trust since S2 must receive all income from the trust for life. The income must be distributed at least annually, and S2 must have the right to require the Trustee to change unproductive assets (ones that produce little or no income) into reasonably productive income producing assets. Even if some required terms are not in the trust, state law often remedies the deficiency. Most states have statutes which require trusts that appear (in the context of the overall estate plan) as though they were intended to qualify for the QTIP election to distribute income at least annually, and give the surviving spouse the right to require the trustee to make unproductive assets productive. These statutes satisfy the QTIP requirements even if the trust instrument is silent on the timing of income distributions, or if at the time of S1's death, a significant portion of the trust estate is made up of unproductive assets (such as undeveloped land) and the trust terms say nothing about the Trustee being obligated to make them productive. Note, as long as S2 has the right to require unproductive assets be made productive, the trustee need not make the assets more productive for the QTIP election to be made. Of course, if S2 makes the request and a significant portion of the corpus is comprised of very low yield assets, the trustee must comply with the request and seek a higher return.

S2 can be given a power to invade corpus, limited by an ascertainable standard. She can also have a limited power to appoint corpus so long as it is exercisable only at her death. The limited power to appoint is usually limited to allocation amongst the couple's children and, perhaps, specific charities.

The trust instrument can also add flexibility by giving S2 a 5 & 5 power; however, S1 would be giving up some certainty as to who will ultimately receive the corpus. If one of the reasons for choosing the ABC plan was to assure that S1's property would go to S1's children by a prior marriage, a 5 & 5 power might not be desirable since each exercise by S2 takes property out of the trust.

The Appropriate QTIP Election

When a QTIP election is available after S1's death, the executor must determine how much of the QTIP property to QTIP, i.e., the optimal portion of S1's estate to have taxable at S1's death. Subtracting that optimal amount from S1's total estate gives the marital deduction desired. The marital deduction is obtained by making a QTIP election of part (or all) of the QTIP property. If the document allows a division of the QTIP trust into two or more trusts, one of which the executor (the trustee) elects to completely QTIP and the other for which no election is made (let's call them Trust CQ and Trust CNQ, respectively), some additional planning opportunities exist. With the division, the trustee can "spend down" Trust CQ if S2 needs to utilize corpus. Since a QTIP'ed trust is in S2's estate, reducing a Trust CQ is better than reducing a single partially QTIP'ed Trust C since, in the later case, any reduction to the trust would reduce pro rata both the QTIP and the non-QTIP portion of the trust. However, if the document is silent as to the trustee's power to create separate trusts, the Regulations require that the QTIP election be for a specific portion (i.e., on a fractional basis) of the full value of the trust. A fraction is created with the QTIP marital deduction amount as the numerator and entire value of the QTIP property as the denominator. This is the fraction of the QTIP property that is protected by the marital deduction at S1's death. This fraction also determines how much of the QTIP property will be taxed at S2's death. To determine the taxable part at S2's death, the value of the QTIP property at S2's death is multiplied by the QTIP fraction. Before applying this to specific estate plans let us break this process down into six steps.

Step by Step: Determining and Using the QTIP Fraction

Step 1. Determine the desired taxable estate for S1: Usually, the executor wants to postpone all taxes to the second death, but still use S1's unified credit. This means using the marital deduction to bring the taxable estate to the exclusion amount, e.g, $675,000 in the year 2000. However, if generating some taxes at the first death saves taxes in the long run, it might be advantageous to bring the taxable estate to some higher value.

Step 2. Determine the QTIP marital deduction (QTIP MD) amount necessary to arrive at the desired taxable estate: Total S1's Estate − S1's Desired Taxable Estate = MD amount. If the marital deduction is only by way of a QTIP election, this will also be the QTIP MD amount. If some property passes to S2 immediately by joint tenancy, or by being transferred from S1's estate into a trust that S2 controls (Trust A), such will qualify for an automatic marital deduction (automatic MD). The automatic MD must be subtracted from the MD amount to arrive at the needed QTIP MD.

Step 3. Determine the value of the QTIP property: This is the property, almost always a trust, that meets the QTIP code requirements (§2056(b)(7)) and to which the QTIP election will apply to give us the QTIP MD. Which trust is the QTIP trust depends upon the particular estate plan, e.g., with the ABC plan it is the value of Trust C, usually S1's estate less the exclusion amount (the exclusion amount having been transferred into Trust B). Generically, we will refer to it as the QTIP Trust.

Step 4. The fraction: Create a fraction with the QTIP MD (Step 2) over the QTIP Trust (Step 3) to arrive at the QTIP fraction.

$$\frac{QTIP\ MD}{QTIP\ Trust} = QTIP\ Fraction$$

Step 5. S1's taxable estate: S1's taxable estate is S1's total estate less any automatic MD and less the product of the QTIP fraction and the QTIP Trust. Check your calculation, the result should match the desired taxable estate (Step 1).

$$S1\ Taxable\ Est. = Total\ Est. - automatic\ MD - (\frac{QTIP\ MD}{QTIP\ Trust} * QTIP\ Trust)$$

Step 6. S2's taxable estate: At S2's death, to determine S2's total estate, the QTIP Trust (*as it is then valued*) is multiplied by the QTIP fraction to determine the amount of the QTIP Trust included in S2's estate. This in turn is added to the rest of S2's estate (generally, Trust A).

$$S2's\ Taxable\ Est. = Trust\ A + (\frac{QTIP\ MD}{QTIP\ Trust[S1'sDOD]} * QTIP\ Trust[S2'sDOD])$$

If the trust document allows the trustee to divide Trust C into Trust CQ (to be QTIP'ed) and Trust CNQ (which is not QTIP'ed), there are a few changes to the steps. One would still go through steps 1 - 2 as before, then at step 3, Trust CQ would be allocated the QTIP marital deduction amount and Trust CNQ the balance of S1's property. The fractions at step 5 would be 100% (1/1) for Trust CQ and zero for Trust CNQ. Finally, step 6 would have S2's estate equal to all of S2's property, plus all of Trust CQ. Since Trusts B and CNQ are fully included in S1's taxable estate, they are both bypass trusts and, as such, they are not included in S2's estate.

Extended Example

The extended example set that follows is designed to increase your understanding of the QTIP election. Using a modern ABC plan, the example compares the result of death taxes for a 100% QTIP election, to what happens where there is no QTIP election. Later, we will explore what happens when S1's executor makes a partial QTIP election where the trustee does not have authority to divide Trust C into separate trusts. For examples in this chapter, we will ignore the prior transfer credit, as it will be covered in connection with multiple trust plans in the next chapter. We will assume that Trust C meets all of the QTIP requirements. *** *Query 2. Why not include the modern AB Trust plan as part of this QTIP example?* The assumption is also made that S2 does not remarry, therefore, there is no marital deduction for S2's estate. To simplify these examples, all figures are given net of debts and expenses, and the values of the trusts increase modestly each year during the ten years between the two deaths. The assumption that the two deaths occur ten years apart avoids having to tackle the prior transfer credit as part of the example.

Step by Step: Applied to the ABC Trust Plan

Step 1. Determine the desired taxable estate for S1, e.g., equal to the exclusion amount so as to postpone all taxes, or have S1 and S2's estates equal as of S1's death, or some dollar amount as determined by the executor to be optimal in reducing overall taxes for the two estates.

Step 2. Total Estate – Desired Taxable Estate = QTIP MD amount.

Step 3. Trust C is the QTIP Trust, defined as being S1's estate in excess of the exclusion amount (Trust B):

$$S1\text{'s Total Estate} - \text{Trust B} = \text{Trust C}$$

Step 4. Create a fraction with the QTIP MD amount (Step 2) over the QTIP Trust (Step 3) to arrive at the QTIP fraction:

$$\frac{QTIP\ MD}{Trust\ C} = QTIP\ Fraction$$

Step 5. S1's taxable estate is S1's total estate less the product of the QTIP Trust and the QTIP fraction. The result should match the desired taxable estate (Step 1).

$$S1 \; Taxable \; estate = Total \; estate - (\frac{QTIP \; MD}{Trust \; C} * Trust \; C)$$

Step 6. At S2's death, the amount *then* in Trust C is multiplied by the QTIP fraction in order to determine the amount of Trust C that must be included in S2's estate. Add that amount to the rest of S2's estate (e.g., Trust A) to determine S2's total estate.

$$S2's \; Taxable \; Est. = Trust A + (\frac{QTIP \; MD}{Trust \; C \; [@ \; S1's DOD]} * Trust \; C \; [@S2's DOD])$$

Facts for this Extended Set: Henry (S1) and Wilma (S2) lived, and died, in a community property state. Their estate plan was an ABC Trust plan as described above. When Henry died in 1997, they owned property valued as follows:

S1's separate property	$1,500,000
Their community property	$1,800,000
S2's separate property	$2,000,000
Total	$5,300,000

Note: If Henry and Wilma lived in a common law state, the outcome would be exactly the same if we simply divide the community property equally between them:

S1's separate property	$2,400,000
S2's separate property	$2,900,000
Total	$5,300,000

In fact, the property laws for common law and community property states result in ownership rights for each spouse that largely depend on how the spouses acquired their property.

After Henry's death the trusts were funded with assets having a net value as shown here:

Trust A	$2,900,000
Trust B	$600,000
Trust C	$1,800,000
Total	$5,300,000

The values for these three trusts as of Wilma's death in 2007 will be given in Step 6.

PART ONE: The executor of Henry's estate elects to postpone all taxes until Wilma's death but desires to utilize Henry's unified credit. Given that he died in 1997 means the optimal taxable estate is equal to the exclusion amount, i.e., $600,000.

Step 1. The desired taxable estate for S1 = $600,000.

Step 2. $2,400,000 - $600,000 = $1,800,000

Step 3. The QTIP property: S1's Total Estate – Trust B = Trust C.

$$\$2,400,000 - \$600,000 = \$1,800,000$$

Step 4. Create a fraction with the QTIP marital deduction amount from Step 2 divided by the Trust C amount from Step 3 to arrive at the QTIP fraction.

$$\frac{\$1,800,000}{\$1,800,000} = 100\%$$

Step 5. S1's taxable estate is S1's total estate less the product of Trust C and the QTIP fraction:

$$S1\ Taxable\ Estate = \$2,400,000 - ((\frac{\$1,800,000}{\$1,800,000}) * \$1,800,000)$$
$$= \$600,000$$

Step 6. At S2's death in the year 2007, the amount *then* in Trust C is multiplied by the QTIP fraction to determine the amount of Trust C that must be included in S2's estate. Add that amount to Trust A to determine S2's total estate. Assume that in the ten years the values for the three trusts increased to the following:

Trust A		$4,700,000
Trust B		$975,000
Trust C		$3,100,000
	Total	$8,775,000

Note: The entire amount of Trust C (as it is at S2's death) is included in S2's estate. In this case, since *all* of Trust C was QTIP'ed, S2's estate is:

$$\$4,700,000 \text{ [Trust A]} + \$3,100,000 \text{ [Trust C]} = \$7,800,000$$

Trust A was not part of Henry's taxable estate because it contained only Wilma's property. Trusts B and C combined equal Henry's gross estate because all of Henry's property is allocated to these two trusts. Regardless of whether a QTIP election is made, the value of Trust B will be taxed as part of Henry's estate, although with a 100% QTIP of Trust C there will be no tax due, since the unified credit will match the tentative tax generated by Trust B. While Trust C's value is always part of the *gross* estate, it need not be taxed if the QTIP election is made to cover the entire trust, because it then is protected by the marital deduction and will be taxed in S2's estate.

When Wilma dies, there are several reasons why Trust A is included in her estate. She holds a general power over it, which would cause inclusion of any property transferred to it by Henry; and she transferred her own property to it, retaining the right to revoke the transfer. Trust B is excluded from Wilma's estate because it is a bypass trust. Wilma did not fund Trust B, therefore, she could not have a retained interest in it; nor did she hold a general power of appointment over it. Trust C is included in her estate only because of the QTIP election after Henry's death. This was a trade-off: it allowed Trust C to escape tax when Henry died, so it had to be included in her estate when Wilma died.

Notice that the QTIP election, or the failure to elect, does not change the amount of property going into each trust. Of course, if no QTIP election is made, then taxes must be paid from Trusts B and C at S1's death, since the value is in excess of the exclusion amount.

PART TWO: Change the facts, suppose the executor of Henry's estate decided that it was best NOT to postpone any taxes on Henry's share of the property, and therefore, elected NOT to make a QTIP election. This means the desired taxable estate equals all of Henry's property, i.e., $2,400,000. Even though it's obvious that the amounts going into Trusts B and C (all of Henry's estate) will be the amount taxed at his death, and Wilma's property (all of Trust A) will be the only property taxed at her death, the steps are set forth here to make it apparent that we are following the same format, an important lesson before we start working on partial QTIP elections.

Step 1. The Desired Taxable Estate for S1 = $2,400,000.

Step 2. Total Estate – Desired Taxable Estate = QTIP Election amount.

$$\$2,400,000 - \$2,400,000 = \$0$$

Step 3. Trust C is the QTIP property.

$$S1's\ Total\ Estate - Trust\ B = Trust\ C = \$1,800,000$$

Step 4. Create a fraction with the QTIP MD from Step 2 over Trust C (Step 3) to determine the QTIP fraction.

$$\frac{\$0}{\$1,800,000} = zero$$

Step 5. $$S1's\ Taxable\ estate = Total\ estate - (\frac{QTIP\ MD}{Trust\ C} * Trust\ C)$$

$$S1\ Taxable\ Estate = \$2,400,000 - ((\frac{\$0}{\$1,800,000}) * \$1,800,000)$$
$$= \$2,400,000$$

Step 6. In this case, since none of Trust C was QTIP'ed, S2's estate is just $4,700,000 [The value of Trust A only].

In all of these plans Trust A is included in S2's estate because it holds S2's property and, as to any property that flows into Trust A from S1's estate, S2 holds a general power of appointment over this trust. Where S1's executor forgoes the QTIP election, Trust C is taxed at S1's death and then escapes tax at S2's death. Trust B is not included in S2's estate because it is a bypass trust, already taxed in S1's taxable estate, but bypassing the estate of S2. When possible, Trust B is funded with property expected to appreciate because it escapes tax at S2's death, even if its value greatly exceeds the exclusion amount.

OPTIMAL ALLOCATION: THE PARTIAL QTIP ELECTION

Trust C has the chameleon character of being like a marital deduction trust if the QTIP election is made, or a bypass trust if the QTIP election is not made. However, the law allows still more flexibility by allowing partial QTIP elections. This allows a portion of the QTIP trust (Trust C in the ABC plan) to qualify for the marital deduction at S1's death. When the executor of S1's estate makes such an election, a portion of the QTIP trust, the QTIP fraction portion, acts like a marital trust and the rest of the trust acts like a bypass trust. The QTIP election portion of Trust C escapes taxes at S1's death because of the marital deduction, but that same fraction of the QTIP trust, valued at S2's death, is included in S2's estate when S2 dies. The non-QTIP election portion is taxed at S1's death but not at S2's death.

A partial QTIP may be desirable to lower the overall estate taxes by taking advantage of lower marginal rates in both estates and by utilizing the prior transfer credit (discussed in conjunction with the marital deduction in the next chapter). Generally, executors choose to postpone all taxes until S2's death, even though the absolute amount of total taxes paid will almost always be greater when this is done. Given the time value of money, postponing taxes makes sense rather than paying taxes at the first death. Besides, if taxes are paid at the first death, they are paid out of property intended to produce income for the surviving spouse; whereas, postponing the taxes takes them out of the property going to the children (or others, if there are no children).

The picture changes dramatically if it is known at the time S1's estate tax return is being prepared that S2 is quite certain to die soon. In that case, paying taxes for both estates, rather than just at S2's death, will not only utilize both estates' lower marginal rates, but S2's estate will be able to use a prior transfer credit which substantially reduces taxes on the second death.

Where S2's death is likely to occur within two years of S1's death, the optimal allocation between the two taxable estates depends upon such factors as the age of S2 at the time of S1's death, the Federal rate for valuing split interests, and the size of the combined estates. Generally, the lower the Federal rate, the older the surviving spouse, and the larger the estate, the higher the percentage that should be allocated to S1's taxable estate and the lower to S2's. For instance, if the §7520 rate is 8%, S2 is 68 years old, dies within two years of S1, and the combined estate value is $10 million at the time of S1's death, the tax bill is lowest if $7,500,000 is taxed in S1's estate and only $2,500,000 is taxed in S2's estate. However, if all taxes are deferred until the second death, whether through a QTIP or regular marital deduction, with only the exclusion amount being sheltered at S1's death, the estate taxes would be about $1,000,000 more than they would be with the optimal allocation.

Several competing factors must be considered when deciding the appropriate QTIP fraction. One consideration is the time value of money. If the deaths are not expected to occur close together, taxes paid a long time in the future are less burdensome than taxes paid today. However, if the property appreciates substantially between the deaths, the total tax bill will be higher. If property is appreciating very rapidly, sometimes it makes sense to get the tax paid sooner on a smaller amount. Another consideration is the prior transfer credit which substantially reduces taxes at the second death, but only if the deaths are close together in time. One must also consider the relative size of the two estates. A QTIP election can only shift the taxable estate in S2's direction, so optimization by QTIP election works only when S1's estate is larger than S2's, and only if it is large enough to equal the optimal S1 taxable estate.

Where the second death is likely to occur within a few years after the first death, and the estates have a combined value in excess of two exclusion amounts, the optimal allocation usually has S1's taxable estate slightly larger than that of S2, thus when the two estates are about equal in size, or when S2 has the larger estate, there should be no QTIP election because doing so would only further increase S2's taxable estate.

Since deductions other than the marital deduction are generally beyond the executor's control,[18] the focus in the examples to follow is on the marital deduction, which can be increased or decreased depending upon the QTIP fraction. For simplicity, we will continue to ignore the other deductions.

Partial QTIP Election Examples

While it seems more complex, the process for calculating estates with a partial QTIP election is the same process discussed earlier for the "all or nothing" QTIP elections. Where it was "all," the QTIP fraction was equal to one[19] and where it was "nothing," it was equal to zero.[20]

EXAMPLE 11-24. Sam has an estate of $2 million and his wife Susan has an estate of $700,000. His executor elects to have $1,100,000 taxed at Sam's death in 1997. The value of the three trusts at Sam's death would be: Trust A, $700,000; Trust B, $600,000; and Trust C, $1,400,000.

Step 1. Sam's desired taxable estate is $1,100,000.

Step 2. Sam's Total Estate – Desired Taxable Estate = QTIP MD

$2,000,000 - $1,100,000 = $900,000.

Step 3. Trust C is the QTIP property: $1,400,000.

Step 4. $\dfrac{QTIP\ MD}{Trust\ C} = \dfrac{\$900,000}{\$1,400,000} = QTIP\ Fraction$

Step 5. $Sam's\ Taxable\ estate = Sam's\ Total\ Estate - (\dfrac{QTIP\ MD}{Trust\ C} * Trust\ C)$

$\$2,000,000 - (\dfrac{\$900,000}{\$1,400,000} * \$1,400,000) = \$1,100,000$

Step 6. At Susan's death, Trust A has grown to $875,000; Trust B has grown to $750,000; and Trust C to $1,800,000. The portion of Trust C included in her estate:

$\dfrac{\$900,000}{\$1,400,000} * \$1,800,000 = \$1,157,143$

Thus, $1,157,143 of Trust C is included in Susan's estate. Which, when added to Trust A gives a total estate of $2,032,143 [$875,000 + $1,157,143]. Notice that Trust B is not taxed at Susan's death, even though it exceeded the exclusion amount when she died.

Equalizing Estates

Most combined estates (i.e., S1 plus S2 at S1's death) valued up to about twelve million dollars will save almost as much tax by simply equalizing the two taxable estates as is saved with the optimal allocation, when these two alternatives are compared to the 100% QTIP option. The example that follows assumes that the executor seeks to have both taxable estates equal as of S1's death. Equalizing the estates uses the six step process that we have used previously. If S1's estate is larger than S2's, the two are averaged and the average is the desired taxable estate for Step 1.

EXAMPLE 11-25. Using the facts from the prior Sam and Susan example, suppose Susan is in extremely poor health at Sam's death and, therefore, the executor chooses to equalize the estates.

Step 1. Sam's desired taxable estate:

$$Average: \quad \$2,000,000 + \$700,000 = \frac{\$2,700,000}{2} = \$1,350,000$$

Step 2. Sam's Total Estate – Desired Taxable Estate = QTIP MD:

$$\$2,000,000 - \$1,350,000 = \$650,000.$$

Step 3. Trust C = $1,400,000.

Step 4. $\quad \dfrac{QTIP\ MD}{Trust\ C} = \dfrac{\$650,000}{\$1,400,000} = QTIP\ Fraction$

Step 5. $\quad Sam's\ Taxable\ estate = Sam's\ Total\ estate - (\dfrac{QTIP\ MD}{Trust\ C} * Trust\ C)$

$$\$1,350,000 = \$2,000,000 - (\frac{\$650,000}{\$1,400,000} * \$1,400,000)$$

Step 6.   Suppose at Susan's death Trust A has grown to $875,000, but because taxes were paid out of Trust B and C, they had grown to just $610,000 and $1,425,000, respectively. The portion of Trust C that would be included in her estate would be:

$$\frac{\$650,000}{\$1,400,000} * \$1,425,000 = \$661,607$$

Susan's estate would be $1,536,607 [Trust A $875,000 + $661,607 from Trust C].

There is a shortcut to equalize the estates that reaches the same result. S2's estate is subtracted from S1's estate and half the difference is the amount of the QTIP election (Step 2). Here is the short cut, using Sam and Susan's estate from the above example:

$$\frac{Sam's\ estate\ -\ Susan's\ estate}{2} = QTIP\ MD$$

$$\frac{\$2,000,000\ -\ \$700,000}{2} = \$650,000$$

Notice that this is the same result as Step 2. *** *Query 3. The QTIP election in the above example was calculated to equalize the estates, why then are they not equal?*

Allocating Assets to the Trusts

Estate planning involves planning for an uncertain future. The planner and client must guess how much and what kind of property will be in the estate. They must also guess whether the intended beneficiaries will be alive, and what their circumstances will be at the time the estate is distributed. Because of this uncertainty, planning documents are drafted to deal with uncertainty. Two drafting techniques for structuring disposition clauses in wills or trusts are pecuniary bequests and fractional share bequests.

A *pecuniary bequest* passes property to various shares such that the value of the assets adds up to the dollar value needed to satisfy the pecuniary bequest. For example, the clause funding Trust B might read: *"assets equal in dollar value to the amount which will generate a tentative tax exactly equal to S1's available unified credit, and all assets above that amount are given to the trustee of Trust A."*

Or, the marital bequest going to Trust A of an AB trust plan (or Trust C, in an ABC trust plan) could be defined in dollars: *"assets equal in dollar amount to the marital deduction necessary to reduce S1's taxable estate such that it generates a tentative tax exactly equal to S1's available unified credit are allocated to Trust A, all other assets are allocated to Trust B."*

Using a *fractional share bequest,* both bypass and marital shares will receive a fractional interest in each and every asset in the estate: *"Trust C shall consist of the smallest fractional share of S1's estate that, when added to all other interests in property that pass from S1 to S2, and qualify for the marital deduction, will eliminate, or reduce to the maximum possible extent, any estate tax. The balance of S1's estate shall be allocated to Trust B."*

The factors involved in deciding which type of provision to use are beyond the scope of this text.

QUERIES ANSWERED

1. The QTIP fraction and the marital deduction that result in a $600,000 taxable estate when applied to the trust at Fernando's death are as follows:

$$\frac{\$1,789,373 - \$600,000}{\$1,789,373} * \$1,789,737 = \$1,189,373$$

If the trust was worth $2,334,220 at Arcela's death, the amount included in her estate would be:

$$\frac{\$1,189,373}{\$1,789,373} * \$2,334,220 = \$1,551,526$$

2. Trust B in the modern AB trust is equal to the available exclusion amount, and everything above the exclusion amount is transferred to Trust A; hence, S1's estate receives a marital deduction equal to the value of that property. With this plan there is no terminable interest property to QTIP.

3. Sam and Susan's taxable estates are not equal because Trusts A and C changed in value between the two deaths. Trust B has no effect on the estate value at the second death because it is a bypass trust.

QUESTIONS AND PROBLEMS - Use the ETAX program to do the problems that require calculation of estate or gift taxes.

1. What is the largest estate size that an *individual* can transfer, estate tax free, with a *simple will* to (a) a spouse; (b) any other individuals? Explain, and state any assumptions made.

2. (a) What is the largest net estate that a *husband and wife* can transfer, estate tax free, with *simple wills* to their children? (b) Does it make any difference how much is owned by each spouse? Explain.

3. (a) What is the largest net estate that a *husband and wife* can transfer to their children, estate tax free, with *an exclusion amount* bypass plan? (b) Does it make any difference how much is owned by each spouse? Explain.

4. One spouse has considerable wealth and the other very modest wealth.
   a. Why is an exclusion amount bypass plan a "hit or miss" arrangement?
   b. What is the minimum amount of property that each spouse must own to assure a bypass plan will work?
   c. What change could the couple make that would remove the "hit and miss" aspect of the plan?
   d. Regarding the change in part c, how much should be involved?
   e. What factors help determine whether a bypass should entail an outright transfer or a transfer into trust? Is estate tax savings a factor? Why or why not?

5. For the 100% marital deduction describe (a) the major advantages and (b) the major disadvantages.

6. Assuming a wealthy couple has a simple 100% marital deduction plan, explain how each of the following defer or reduce the estate tax for S2: (a) remarriage; (b) consumption; or (c) gifts. (d) Explain the drawbacks to each of these estate planning devices.

7. Draw a time-line showing the changes in the marital deduction. Be sure to include the start of the QTIP marital deduction and the elimination of the marital deduction for non-citizens who do not use trusts.

8. Briefly state the reason for the terminable interest rule. Then explain why Congress allows each of the following exceptions to the rule:
   a. The six months survivorship clause.
   b. The transfer to a general power of appointment trust.
   c. The transfer to a QTIP trust, with a QTIP election.
   d. The pension to the surviving spouse automatic QTIP election.
   e. The life estate for S2, with remainder to a charity.

9. Explain why each of the following bequests to a surviving spouse would or would not qualify for a marital deduction:
   a. A bequest of a sum, not to exceed $100,000, that she could use to purchase a residence, provided she relinquish her dower (life estate) rights to decedent's home. She did relinquish the right within two months of S1's death, and the executor immediately paid $100,000 towards her purchase of a $160,000 home.
   b. Decedent's will gave S2 the right to elect either a life estate in S1's home or to take $100,000 outright. She chose the $100,000.
   c. Decedent's living trust left his entire estate in trust for S2. She had a power to appoint the trust to anyone, even to her estate at her death. The remainder went to their children if she did not exercise the power to appoint. The trustee could accumulate income if such was not needed for S2's reasonable support and maintenance. The trust had a corpus valued at $950,000. Decedent's pourover will left his property, in trust, to the trustee of his living trust. They also held $300,000 in a joint bank account; the source of this money was money inherited from the decedent's parents. Consider both the trust, specifically §2056(b)(5), and

the bank account, §2040. With the latter, what effect does the pourover will have?

d. When he died in 2002 Decedent left his entire $1,000,000 estate to his only son, with a provision that if his son died it would go to his son's issue by right of representation. Because of a pre-nuptial agreement, S2 could not claim a dower interest. The son, who had no issue, disclaimed so much of the estate as exceeded the exclusion amount estate, by writing a letter to S1's executor stating, "My father should not have disinherited my mother. I hereby refuse to accept any of my father's estate that is in excess of the exclusion amount and I assign that excess to my mother." The probate court accepted this as a valid assignment of the son's interest in the probate property that exceeded $700,000 in value and, at the conclusion of the probate, ordered the excess ($300,000) distributed to S2. Review §2518 to determine whether this qualifies as a tax effective disclaimer and, therefore, qualifies for the marital deduction. Would your answer change if the son had issue at the time of his father's death and when he wrote the letter to the executor?

10. Explain why each of the following would or would not qualify for the QTIP election.

a. An estate plan executed before 1982 created at S1's death, in 1997, a trust holding S1's entire estate worth a net of $2,500,000. The trust required that all income be distributed at least annually to S2, and after S2's death the property was to be distributed to the couple's issue by right of representation. The independent trustee was given the power to distribute corpus to S2, if the trustee thought the income was insufficient for her happiness.

b. The same facts as in (a) except the trustee could also distribute funds to pay medical bills or educational expenses of the couple's children.

c. The couple's estate plan was an ABC Trust plan. Decedent's estate had a net worth of $4,000,000 consisting mainly of undeveloped land. Terms of the trust, that also applied to Trust C, said that the trustee would not be liable for failing to diversify investments, nor for continuing to hold property that was in trust at the time of the settlor's death, nor for failing to make such property productive. In giving an answer, you should consider both how this "absolution from liability" clause might be interpreted and state marital deduction-savings statutes that might help state law. A weaseling answer would be good.

d. The couple had an ABC Trust plan. S1's estate was worth $2,000,000 and S2's estate was worth about the same. Although Trust C had a provision giving S2 income for life, it also said, that in the event S2 became mentally incompetent, the trustee could directly pay S2's bills for living expenses and accumulate any moneys not needed. The executor of S1's estate QTIP'ed all of Trust C. S2 died eleven months after S1's death. S1's executor has filed an amended 706, that states the QTIP was claimed in error because Trust C could not qualify for the QTIP election. The executor attached a check for the estate tax. Was the executor right? What benefits are sought by the executor?

11. In multi-trust estate plans, why is Trust A often called the survivor's trust?

12. In a multi-trust plan, when and why is Trust B likely to be called the credit shelter trust? Under what circumstances are taxes likely to be paid from it? Why is it unlikely that taxes will be paid from it at S2's death, even if it exceeds the exclusion amount?

13. In an ABC Trust plan, Trust B funding is likely to be defined as "an amount that uses up the available unified credit" rather than in specific dollar terms. Use the changes made by the TRA of '97 and the possibility of taxable gifts to explain why it is defined in this manner.

14. H and W own a family estate worth $3 million, with H owning $2,700,000 and W owning $300,000. Assuming there is no estate growth between the two deaths (both pre-1998), and that no prior transfer credit is available, use the ETAX program to complete the following table showing the amount and timing of estate tax payments for each of the following alternatives Also determine the amount that passes to their children. On the left side we assume H dies first and on the right side that W dies first. Assume that, if taxes are paid at the first death, they are paid out of Trust B. (a) a 100% marital deduction; (b) an AB Trust; (c) an ABC Trust, where the executor postpones all tax by making 100% QTIP election for Trust C; and (d) an ABC Trust

where the executor equalized the estate by use of a partial QTIP election. Start by showing the value of each trust for the two multi-trust plans:

H dies first - AB Trust plan: Trust A _____ Trust B _____
ABC Trust plan: Trust A _____ Trust B _____ Trust C _____

W dies first - AB Trust plan: Trust A _____ Trust B _____
ABC Trust plan: Trust A _____ Trust B _____ Trust C _____

$3 M, less ET = net	H dies first		W dies first	
	H's ET	W's ET	W's ET	H's ET
100%MD	_____	_____	_____	_____
	net to children = _____		net to children = _____	
AB Trust	_____	_____	_____	_____
	net to children = _____		net to children = _____	
ABC 100%	_____	_____	_____	_____
	net to children = _____		net to children = _____	
ABC equal	_____	_____	_____	_____
	net to children = _____		net to children = _____	

15. (a) Re-work Question 14, assuming that between the first and second deaths all property doubles in value. (b) What conclusions can be drawn?

$6 M, less ET = net	H dies first		W dies first	
	H's ET	W's ET	W's ET	H's ET
100%MD	net to children = _____	_____	net to children = _____	_____
AB Trust	net to children = _____	_____	net to children = _____	_____
ABC 100%	net to children = _____	_____	net to children = _____	_____
ABC equal	net to children = _____	_____	net to children = _____	_____

FACTS FOR 16 - 20: S1 and S2 lived in a common law state. S1 owned property having a net value of $2,325,780 and S2 owned property having a net value of $1,451,700. Assume debts and expenses are zero, and that no prior transfer credit is available because the two deaths are more than 10 years apart. First determine S1's estate before the marital deduction, and the values for trusts A and B for the AB Trust, and trusts A, B, and C for the ABC plan. Those numbers will not change regardless of what S1's executor does insofar as the QTIP election. For the second part of each problem you will need to know the value of the Trusts when S2 died: For the AB Trust plan, when S2 died Trust A was worth $5,525,638 and Trust B was worth $1,086,000. For the ABC Trust plan, when S2 died Trust A was worth $2,524,506, Trust B was worth $1,086,000, and Trust C was worth $2,778,506.

16.1   The couple had an AB Trust estate plan. Determine: (a) S1's gross estate and taxable estate; (b) the values of Trust A and Trust B.

16.2   Determine S2's taxable estate.

17.1   The couple had an ABC Trust estate plan. S1's executor elected to postpone all taxes until S2 died, but fully utilize S1's unified credit. Determine: (a) S1's gross estate; (b) the values of Trust A, Trust B, and Trust C; (c) the QTIP fraction; and (d) how the fraction is applied to arrive at the taxable estate.

17.2   Determine S2's taxable estate.

18.1   The couple had an ABC Trust estate plan. S1's executor elected to pay all taxes at S1's death, so no QTIP election was made. Determine: (a) the QTIP fraction and (b) show how it is applied to arrive at the desired taxable estate. [The value of S1's gross estate and values of Trust A, Trust B, and Trust C at S1's death will be the same as previously determined, since they are not dependent upon whether or not a QTIP election is made.]

18.2   Determine S2's taxable estate.

19.1   The couple had an ABC Trust estate plan. S1's executor elected to make a QTIP election that would equalize the two estates, at least as of S1's death. Determine: (a) the QTIP fraction and (b) show how it is applied to arrive at the desired taxable estate.

19.2   Determine S2's taxable estate.

20.1   The couple had an ABC Trust estate plan. S1's executor elected to make a QTIP election such that S1's taxable estate would equal $1,456,000. Determine: (a) the QTIP fraction and (b) show how it is applied to arrive at the desired taxable estate.

20.2   Determine S2's taxable estate.

FACTS FOR 21 - 25: S1 and S2 lived in a community property state. S1 owned property having a net value of $1,897,560, S2 owned property having a net value of $466,048, and they owned community property worth $893,200. Assume debts and expenses are zero and that no prior transfer credit is available because the two deaths are more than 10 years apart. Again, you must start by determining S1's estate before the marital deduction, and the values for trusts A and B for the AB Trust, and trusts A, B, and C for the ABC plan. Those numbers will not change regardless of what S1's executor does insofar as the QTIP election. For the second part of each problem you will need to know the value of the Trusts when S2 died: For the AB Trust plan: When S2 died Trust A was worth $4,620,189 and Trust B was worth $1,086,000. For the ABC Trust plan: When S2 died Trust A was worth $1,587,095, Trust B was worth $1,086,000, and Trust C was worth $2,808,098.

21.1   The couple had an AB Trust estate plan. Determine: (a) S1's gross estate and taxable estate; (b) the values of Trust A and Trust B.

21.2   Determine S2's taxable estate.

22.1   The couple had an ABC Trust estate plan. S1's executor elected to postpone all taxes until S2 died, but fully utilize S1's unified credit. Determine: (a) S1's gross estate; (b) the values of Trust A, Trust B, and Trust C; (c) the QTIP fraction; and (d) how the fraction is applied to arrive at the taxable estate.

22.2   Determine S2's taxable estate.

23.1   The couple had an ABC Trust estate plan. S1's executor elected to pay all taxes at S1's death, so no QTIP election was made. Determine: (a) the QTIP fraction; and (b) show how it is applied to arrive at the desired taxable estate. [The value of S1's gross estate and values of Trust A, Trust B, and Trust C at S1's death will be the same as previously determined, since they are not dependent upon whether or not a QTIP election is made.]

23.2   Determine S2's taxable estate.

24.1   The couple had an ABC Trust estate plan. S1's executor elected to make a QTIP election that would equalize the two estates, at least as of S1's death. Determine: (a) the QTIP fraction; and (b) show how it is applied to arrive at the desired taxable estate.

24.2 Determine S2's taxable estate.

25.1 The couple had an ABC Trust estate plan. S1's executor elected to make a QTIP election such that S1's taxable estate would equal $1,900,000. Determine: (a) the QTIP fraction; and (b) show how the fraction is applied to arrive at the desired taxable estate.

25.2 Determine S2's taxable estate.

ANSWERS TO THE QUESTIONS AND PROBLEMS:

1. Estate size: (a) a spouse - no limit if S2 is a US citizen, otherwise, only the exclusion amount, e.g., $850,000 if S1 died in 2004. Note, the decedent still has the use of a unified credit even if S2 is not a citizen; (b) Others? Explain. The exclusion amount for the year of death, e.g., $1,000,000 for deaths in 2006 or later. This is reduced by any exclusion amount used up during life due to post-76 taxable gifts. There is no limit, if the giving is to a charity.

2. (a) Just the exclusion amount e.g., $700,000 if the second death is in 2002 or 2003. Only the last-to-die's unified credit means anything. (b) No, the last to die has it all anyway.

3. (a) The exclusion amount times two, since both unified credit's will be used, e.g., $2,000,000 if both deaths occur after 2005. (b) Yes, each must have an estate at least equal to the exclusion amount to have both fully utilize their respective unified credit's.

4. Spouses with unequal wealth.
   a. If the poor spouse dies first, less than a full exclusion amount will be sheltered.
   b. The exclusion amount.
   c. Transfer some of the rich spouse's property to the less wealthy spouse.

d. Enough so that the less wealthy spouse has an estate at least equal to the exclusion amount.

e. Outright transfers are most likely where there are children by a prior marriage, and S1 has sufficient wealth to both take care of S2 (a QTIP trust) and still leave some significant portion of the estate to his children. The children by the first marriage do not have to wait until S2 dies to inherit part of the estate (i.e., at least the exclusion amount). If children are only from this marriage or if S2 will need the income from S1's entire estate, an AB or ABC arrangement is more likely, since S2 can have all the income for life. With the ABC, S1 can assure that his or her property will eventually go to S1's family. Estate tax is not a major consideration as to which bypass plan to use, however, for very large estates, the ABC when coupled with the prior transfer credit is preferred over the outright bypass or the AB trust. We take up this combination in the next chapter.

5. (a) Simple. See the chapter discussion for details. (b) Loss of utilization of S1's unified credit & the exclusion amount that goes into S2's estate is taxed at the highest marginal rates insofar as her estate goes.

6. (a) Remarriage: another marital deduction, including possibly using a lifetime QTIP gift, if the new spouse is old & poor. (b) Consumption: spend it and it is not there for the taxman. (c) Gifts: using annual exclusion and/or unified credit of the survivor gets some portion of the estate transferred tax free (annual exclusion amounts) and any future appreciation avoids tax. (d) Explain the drawbacks to each of these estate planning devices. It's obvious, but still worth thinking about. Remarriage: S2 might disinherit the children of the first marriage, or at least make them wait until the new spouse dies before they come into their inheritance. Consumption: Well unless it is spent on the kids, they hate to see too much of that wealth disappear. Generally, no one likes to see his or her wealth decrease. Gifts: parallel comments as to consumption.

7. Show the big changes as starting in 1977 (unification, same rates, etc.), 1982 (100% marital deduction, QTIP, & $10,000 annual exclusion), and 1984 (QDOT).

8. No marital deduction is allowed unless S2's interest is vested. (a) The six months survivorship clause. If S2 makes it, the property is in S2's estate. If S2 does not make it, then no MD. (b) The transfer to a general power of appointment trust. The GPA causes the trust to be included in S2's estate. (c) The transfer to a QTIP trust, with a QTIP election. If no election is made, no MD. If it is made, then the QTIP portion is taxed at S2's death. (d) The pension to the surviving spouse automatic QTIP election. The surviving spouse collects the pension for his or her life, and the PV of the remaining payments are included in S2's estate when S2 dies. (e) The life estate for S2, with remainder to a charity exception. The only beneficiaries are S2 and the charity.

9. Explain why certain bequests do or do not qualify for a marital deduction:

(a) No marital deduction for two reasons: (1) whether she would get the money was uncertain; and (2) the amount was uncertain (Est. of Edmonds, 72 TC 970). Notice that had she claimed her dower rights, those would have qualified for a QTIP election since they were a vested life estate in QTIP property.

(b) The $100,000 does qualify. S2 has alternate bequests, vested at S1's death, wherein she makes the choice. This should qualify even if the other alternative was one that did not qualify, so long as the one she chose did qualify. Est. of Tompkins, 68 TC 912

(c) The property in trust will not qualify since §2056(b)(5) requires income for life for S2 and the trustee's power to accumulate spoils this. The title to the joint bank account controls regardless of the pourover will, therefore, $150,000 is included in S1's estate and is removed from his taxable estate by a marital deduction of $150,000.

(d) The property "assigned" is transferred to S2 just as if it had been left to her or had passed to her by intestate succession, therefore, it qualifies for the marital deduction. Notice that the last part of §2518 allows even an "assignment" to qualify so long as the assignee is the person that would have received the property as a result of the disclaimer without the assignment language. That last statement tells us that had the son had issue, his issue would have received the property as a result of a disclaimer absent the assignment language, therefore, had he had issue, this would have been treated as a gift from the son, and would not have qualified for the marital deduction. Indeed, the son would have to file a gift tax return.

10. Explain why certain bequests do or do not qualify for the QTIP election.

(a) Even pre-QTIP law trusts can qualify for the QTIP election, provided they meet the QTIP requirements; This one does. Note that the power to distribute to S2 is alright; the trust just cannot allow distributions to anyone other than S2 during S2's life-time.

(b) It will not qualify as it is written, for the reasons given for the last question. Perhaps the children will make a tax effective disclaimer (see §2518) of this potential benefit, in which case it would qualify.

(c) If the language is interpreted to mean that the trustees need not invest in productive property even if S2 so requests, then by being allowed to retain unproductive property deprives S2 of an income interest, therefore, a QTIP election is not available. If the language merely protects the trustee from liability in the event the value of the property goes down (or fails to keep up with other reasonable investments), even though prudence would have suggested diversification, the QTIP should be available. Many states have laws that give the surviving spouse the right to compel the trustee to make the property productive in the absence of language to the contrary in the trust document. Those states that have such laws generally compel interpretation of vague language, such as discussed here, in such a way as to obtain the marital deduction if it is clear from the overall estate plan that such was the intent of the estate plan. Since this language is applied to Trust C, a trust intended to qualify for the marital deduction, the clause would be given the interpretation that S2 could compel the trustee to make the property productive, e.g., develop it or sell it and re-invest in income earning investments.

(d) Probably so. S2 did not have a vested life estate since, under some circumstances, the trustee had authority to accumulate income. The executor seeks to undo the QTIP and pay some taxes on S1's death (in light of S2's death so soon), thereby using the lower rates of S1's estate and setting S2's estate up for the benefit of a prior transfer credit.

11. It generally is funded with S2's property, and even if some of the corpus has as its source property from S1, S2 has a GPA over the trust.

12. In the two multi-trust plans studied in this chapter, it (Trust B) is defined in terms of S1's available unified credit. For those plans that use the exclusion amount to define the value for funding this trust, credit shelter is a good descriptive name for the trust. However, we will see in the next chapter that some plans define trust B such that it does not equal the exclusion amount. If Trust C is not 100% QTIP'ed, Trust B may have to pay its share of the estate tax. If it is a exclusion amount trust, no tax is paid out of it at the second death because it is not part of S2's estate (i.e., none of her property went into it so no retained interests, there is no general power of appointment over it, and it would not have been QTIP'ed).

13. Because, even with plans that have Trust B as a credit shelter trust, it might be more or less than the exclusion amount that existed when the estate plan was drafted. The TRA '97 has greatly increase the exclusion amount. By using language that funds the trust based upon available unified credit, the documents do not have to be changed whenever Congress increases the unified credit. If the settlor has made taxable gifts post-76, some of the unified credit will have been used up. Likewise, if some of S1's estate is left to someone other than to S2 or to a charity, that bequest will use up unified credit, thus reducing Trust B.

14. Taxes, with various plans, varying the who (H or W) dies first.
    a. 100%MD: H $0, $1,098,000, $1,902,000; W the same.
    b. AB: H $0, $784,000, $2,216,000; W $0, $939,000, $2,061,000.
    c. ABC(100%): H $0, $784,000, $2,216,000; W $0, $939,000, $2,061,000.
    d. ABC =: $363,000, $363,000, $2,274,000; W $0, $939,000, $2,061,000.

15. a. Rework Question 14, between the 1st and 2nd deaths property doubles.
       1. 100%MD: H $0, $2,748,000, $3,252,000; W the same.
       2. AB: H $0, $2,088,000, $3,912,000; W $0, $2,418,000, $3582000.
       3. ABC(100%): H $0, $2,088,000, $3,912,000; W $0, $2,418,000, $3,582,000.
       4. ABC equal: H $363,000, $1,098,000, $4,539,000; W $0, $2,418,000 $3,582,000.
    b. Conclusion: not making the QTIP election often lowers overall taxes, but it ignores timing of the payments and the fact that waiting until both

spouses are dead means that neither S1 or S2 really pay the taxes. Finally, if S1 is insurable, rather than paying the taxes at S1's death, use some of the money "saved" by postponing the payment to buy life insurance on S2's life, holding it in an irrevocable life insurance trust.

16.1   AB Trust estate plan: (a) S1's gross estate [$2,325,780] and taxable estate [$600,000]; (b) Trust A[$3,177,480] and Trust B[$600,000].

16.2   S2's taxable estate:[$5,525,638; just Trust A].

17.1   ABC Trust estate plan. (postpone taxes): (a) S1's gross estate [$2,325,780]; (b) Trust A [$1,451,700], Trust B [$600,000], Trust C [$1,725,780]; (c) QTIP fraction [$1,725,780/$1,725,780 = 1]; and (d) taxable estate: $2,325,780 - ($1,725,780/$1,725,780) * $1,725,780 = $600,000

17.2   S2's taxable estate: $2,524,506 + (1) * $2,778,506 = $5,303,012 [Tr A + QTIP fraction * Tr C]

18.1   ABC Trust estate plan (pay all taxes): (a) QTIP fraction [0/$1,725,780 = 0]; and (b) taxable estate: $2,325,780 - (0) * $1,725,780 = $2,325,780

18.2   S2's taxable estate: $2,524,506 + (0) * $2,778,506 = $2,524,506

19.1   (a) QTIP fraction [$437,040/$1,725,780] and (b) taxable estate: $2,325,780 - ($437,040/$1,725,780) * $1,725,780 = $1,888,740

19.2   S2's taxable estate: $2,524,506 + ($437,040/$1,725,780) * ($2,778,506) = $3,228,141

20.1   (a) [(Step 2) $2,325,780 - $1,456,000 = $869,780. Step 3 is the value of Trust C, therefore Step 4: QTIP fraction $869,780/$1,725,780] and (b) taxable estate (Step 5): $2,325,780 - ($869,780/$1,725,780) * $1,725,780 = $1,456,000

20.2   Determine S2's taxable estate (Step 6): $2,524,506 + ($869,780/$1,725,780) * ($2,778,506) = $3,924,852

21.1   (a) S1's gross estate [$2,344,160] and taxable estate [$600,000]; (b) the values of Trust A [$2,656,808] and Trust B [$600,000].

21.2   Determine S2's taxable estate. Just Trust A: [$4,620,189]

22.1 (a) S1's gross estate [$2,344,160]; (b) the values of Trust A [$912,648], Trust B [$600,000], and Trust C [$1,744,160]; (c) the QTIP fraction [$1,744,160 /$1,744,160 = 1]; and (d) the taxable estate: $2,344,160 - (1) * $1,744,160 = $600,000

22.2 Determine S2's taxable estate: $1,587,095 + (1) * $2,808,098 = $4,395,192 [Tr A + QTIP fraction * Tr C]

23.1 (a) the QTIP fraction [0/$1,744,160 = 0]; and (b) taxable estate: $2,344,160 - 0 * $1,744,160 = $2,344,160

23.2 Determine S2's taxable estate. Trust A only [$1,587,095].

24.1 (a) the QTIP fraction [$715,756/$1,744,160]; and (b) taxable estate: $2,344,160 - ($715,756/$1,744,160) * $1,744,160 = $1,628,404

24.2 Determine S2's taxable estate: $1,587,095 + ($715,756/$1,744,160) * $2,808,098 = $2,739,462

25.1 (a) the QTIP fraction; and (b) taxable estate: $2,344,160 - ($444,160/$1,744,160) * $1,744,160 = $1,900,000.

25.2 Determine S2's taxable estate: $1,587,095 + ($444,160/$1,744,160) * $2,808,098 = $2,302,193.

ENDNOTES

1. IRC §2010.

2. §§2053 and 2054.

3. IRC §812(e)(1)(B) of the 1939 Code.

4. IRC§2056(b)(1).

5. IRC §2056(b)(3).

6. IRC §2056(b)(5).

7. IRC §2056(b)(7).

8. IRC §2056(b)(7)(B).

9. IRC §2044.

10. IRC §2013 and Reg. §20.2013 - 4, Example (2).

11. IRC §2056(b)(5).

12. IRC §2056(b)(5).

13. Reg. §20.2056(b)-5(f)(5)

14. IRC §664.

15. IRC §2036(b)(7).

16. IRC §2044.

17. IRC §2044.

18. Deciding whether to claim deductions as estate tax or income tax deductions may be within the executor's control.

19. $\dfrac{Trust\ C}{Trust\ C} = 1$

20. $\dfrac{0}{Trust\ C} = 0$

CHAPTER 12

Advanced Bypass and Marital Deduction Planning

OVERVIEW

This chapter continues the discussion of marital deduction and bypass planning, starting with variations on the basic trust plans described in the last chapter, followed by a review of a couple older plans seen now only in estate planning museums. The calculation of the prior transfer tax credit is explained, as is its rather surprising application to bypass trusts. The chapter concludes with an examination of the generation-skipping transfer tax; and its impact on marital deduction and bypass planning.

VARIATIONS ON A THEME

There are variations on the AB Trust and the ABC Trust plans that may better suit certain families, yet utilize both unified credits and, like the ABC plan, keep the option at the first death of paying estate taxes or deferring them to the second death.

THE AsuperB TRUST PLAN

The AsuperB Trust plan has Trust A defined as all of S2's property and Trust B defined as all of S1's property. It is simpler than the ABC plan as there is one less trust, and given the absence of any reference to a separate exclusion amount trust, it may be more readily understood by clients. The AB Trust plan takes an automatic marital deduction for the property in excess of the exclusion amount because that excess is transferred from S1's estate into Trust A; however, the AsuperB plan allows the executor of S1's estate to decide (via QTIP) whether to pay taxes at the first death or to postpone them until the second death.

Trust B must have all the QTIP attributes that allow a QTIP election if it is desired, i.e., mainly income for life for S2 and no power to appoint to anyone other than S2 during S2's lifetime. Of course utilization of S1's unified credit is important so, even if one wished to pay no taxes, the executor would use that QTIP fraction for Trust B that would reduce S1's taxable estate to the available exclusion amount. Once again, the six step process is used, starting with determining the optimal taxable estate at S1's death.

> EXAMPLE 12-1. When S1 died in the year 2002, the couple's AsuperB Trust plan gave S2 a life estate in Trust B, plus a power to withdraw corpus that was limited to an ascertainable standard. At S2's death, Trust B property is distributed to S1's children by a prior marriage. Trust A is revocable by S2 and her children by a prior marriage are the remaindermen. Their combined net worth was $3,877,250; of which S1's property, worth $2,843,760, was allocated to Trust superB; and S2's property, worth $1,033,490, was allocated to Trust A. To postpone all taxes until S2's death, the executor of S1's estate wants to QTIP Trust B to bring S1's taxable estate to $700,000.

Step 1. The desired taxable estate for S1 = $700,000.

Step 2. Determine the QTIP MD: Total Estate – Desired Taxable Estate = QTIP MD.

$$\$2,843,760 - \$700,000 = \$2,143,760$$

Step 3. For the AsuperB plan there is no separate exclusion amount trust, therefore Trust B is the QTIP property, i.e., S1's Estate = Trust B (the superB) = the QTIP property = $2,843,760.

Step 4. Create a fraction with the QTIP MD (Step 2) over the QTIP property (Trust superB) to arrive at the QTIP fraction.

$$\frac{QTIP\ MD}{Trust\ B} = QTIP\ Fraction$$

$$\frac{\$2,143,760}{\$2,843,760} = QTIP\ Fraction$$

Step 5. S1's taxable estate is S1's total estate less the product of the QTIP property and the QTIP fraction.

$$S1's\ Taxable\ estate = Total\ estate - (\frac{QTIP\ MD}{Trust\ B} * Trust\ B)$$

Therefore, S1's TxE = $2,843,760 - $2,143,760 = $700,000.

Step 6. Assume that S2 dies in 2010, and that Trust A is then worth $1,137,642 and Trust B is then worth $3,117,970. At S2's death, the total estate is equal to all of Trust A plus the QTIP fraction multiplied by the amount *then* in Trust B.

$$S2's\ Taxable\ estate = Trust\ A + (\frac{QTIP\ MD}{Trust\ B} * Trust\ B)$$

S2's taxable estate is:

$$S2's\ TxE = \$1,137,642 + \frac{\$2,143,760}{\$2,843,760} * \$3,117,970$$

$$= \$3,488,117$$

Of course, S1's executor can make a partial QTIP that equalizes the estates if that produces a better result than either making a partial QTIP to defer all taxes or making no QTIP election (resulting in a tax on all of Trust B). If S1's executor was very certain that S2 was going to die shortly after S1 (or if S2 had already died when S1's executor was preparing the estate tax return) the QTIP might be made to equalize the two estates.

EXAMPLE 12-2: Using the same values from the previous example, equal estates at S1's death would be:

Step 1.

$$\frac{S1's\ E + S2's\ E}{2} = \frac{\$2,843,760 + \$1,033,490}{2} = \$1,938,625$$

Step 2. Determine the QTIP MD: Total Estate – Desired Taxable Estate = QTIP MD amount = $2,843,760 - $1,938,625 = $905,135

Step 3. Trust B is the QTIP property, i.e., S1's Estate = Trust B (the superB) = the QTIP property = $2,843,760.

Step 4. Create a fraction with the QTIP MD (Step 2) over the QTIP property (Trust superB) to arrive at the QTIP fraction.

$$\frac{\$905,135}{\$2,843,760} = QTIP\ Fraction$$

Step 5. S1's taxable estate is S1's total estate less the product of Trust B and the QTIP fraction.

$$S1's\ Taxable\ estate = \$2,843,760 - (\frac{\$905,135}{\$2,843,760} * \$2,843,760)$$

$$=\$2,843,760 - \$905,135$$

$$= \$1,938,625$$

Step 6. S2's estate includes all of Trust A, plus the QTIP fraction times Trust B (valued at S2's death):

$$S2's\,TxE. = \$1,137,642 + \frac{\$905,135}{\$2,843,760} * \$3,117,970 = \$2,130,055$$

There are several reasons a couple might prefer the AsuperB plan over the AB plan. *S1 may not want to have property in excess of the exclusion amount pass into S2's control, as must happen with the AB plan, yet their total estate might be just approaching, or be just slightly greater than, the exclusion amount. For a couple in that situation, an ABC plan, with the complicating factor of the third trust, might be over planning.* For instance, if S1 died with an ABC estate plan in 2003, leaving a net estate worth $725,000, Trust B would be funded with assets worth $700,000 and Trust C with assets worth a mere $25,000; both trusts would have to file state and federal income tax returns each year, and the trustees would have to maintain separate accounts for each trust. With the AsuperB plan, Trust B would be funded with assets worth $725,000 and there would be no Trust C. If the executor chose to postpone estate taxes, the QTIP fraction would be $25,000/$725,000. For an elderly couple whose combined estate is over one exclusion amount but less than two exclusion amounts, given that there is a high probability that S1's estate will be under the exclusion amount, the simpler but equally effective AsuperB plan might be preferred to the ABC plan. If, at S1's death, the superB Trust is slightly, or even greatly, above the exclusion amount a partial QTIP can be used to defer taxes.

Even for large estates there is at least one advantage in the AsuperB as compared to the ABC Trust, but it comes with a trade-off. The funding provisions of most ABC plans define either the B Trust or the C Trust as a pecuniary bequest, e.g., "After the death of the first Settlor, the trustee shall allocate to Trust B property equal in value to that amount which will be needed to increase the taxable estate to the largest amount that will not result in a federal estate tax being imposed on the deceased Settlor's estate after allowing for available unified credit." The "equal in amount" language translates into dollar terms, e.g. $850,000 if the first death occurs in 2004, therefore it is a pecuniary bequest. Where, as usually happens, it takes months, and occasionally years, for the trustee to allocate the assets in the family trust (or for the probate estate to obtain an order for distribution) to the separate trusts, the values are likely to be very different from those at the date of death. Where a pecuniary bequest is funded with assets that have appreciated in value, the difference between the basis (the date of death value or alternative date value) and the fair market value on the date of funding is a capital gain to the family trust (or to the probate estate) making the transfer. Since the gain occurs when the family trust (or probate estate) is terminating, the gain is passed on to the pecuniary trust which must then pay taxes on the gain. Of course, the trust would then have a basis in those assets equal to their fair market value at the time of funding. If property used to fund the trust has decreased in value between S1's death and funding, no loss is recognized because the family trust and the pecuniary trust (B or C) are considered related parties. The superB Trust avoids this problem of gain recognition because it is not defined in pecuniary terms but rather in terms of "all of S1's property."

Many plans using multiple trusts give all tangible personal property (cars, furniture, etc.) to S2 or to the trustee of S2's Trust A. Since such property is not investment property, it might be best to allow S2 to control those assets without any need to account for them to the remaindermen.

THE AB WITH DISCLAIMER INTO C TRUST PLAN

A wealthy couple with a long and trusting marriage, with no children by prior marriages, might prefer that the first to die transfer his or her entire estate to the survivor; trusting the survivor to eventually take care of the children and the grandchildren. Nevertheless, they would most likely want to at least use the shelter of a bypass trust to utilize S1's exclusion amount, thus the AB Trust plan would seem ideal, but it has drawbacks. Because the marital deduction is automatic for property transferred from S1's estate into Trust A, the AB plan does not allow sophisticated postmortem planning, such as the equalization of estates or some other apportionment between the two taxable estates, whereas, the AB with disclaimer into C Trust plan (ABdC) does allow the post mortem manipulation of relative size of the two taxable estates. This plan begins by defining Trust B as the exclusion amount trust, with S1's estate in excess of the exclusion amount left to the trustee of Trust A (who also holds S2's property). So far this sounds just like the modern AB Trust plan, however this one adds a provision that any of S1's property in excess of the exclusion amount that is disclaimed by S2 will be transferred to Trust C, a QTIP trust.

A disclaimer is tax effective (or "qualified") if it is done in a manner that the disclaimant (S2) is not treated as having made a taxable gift. In general, to be tax effective, the person making the disclaimer must act within nine months of the interest's creation, he or she cannot "direct" to whom the property goes, nor can he or she receive any benefit from the property disclaimed. There is an exception to the "no benefit" rule, §2518(b)(4)(A) allows an interest disclaimed that passes "to the spouse of the decedent, ..." to qualify as a tax effective disclaimer. Thus, the surviving spouse (S2) can receive income from the disclaimer trust (Trust C), can be given a 5 & 5 power (used for herself only), or can be the holder of a power to withdraw, limited by an ascertainable standard, without any of these "benefits" causing the disclaimer to result in a taxable gift. Furthermore, none of the benefits will cause the disclaimer trust to be included in S2's estate. However, a 5 & 5 power will cause the inclusion in S2's estate of that small portion of the trust that could have withdrawn just before her death had she exercised the power.

Since the disclaimant cannot direct where the disclaimed property goes, *this Trust C*, unlike the one in the ABC plan, must *not* give S2 even a limited power to appoint the property. Remember, for the typical ABC Trust, flexibility is enhanced by giving S2 a limited power to appoint Trust C corpus at her death.

The disclaimer is most likely to be used where, due to S2's poor health or extreme old age, S2 is not likely to live for very long after S1's death. Since the decision to disclaim is not made until after S1's death, the assessment of S2's health is not to be made until that time. However, §2518 requires that the decision of whether or not to disclaim must be made within nine months immediately following S1's death.

> EXAMPLE 12-3. When S1 died in 2003, the couple had an ABdC Trust. It gave S2 a life estate in Trust B, plus a power to withdraw corpus limited to an ascertainable standard, and she was given a limited power to appoint Trust B corpus amongst their children. In the absence of exercise of the power the remainder would be distributed to their issue by right of representation. Trust A was revocable by S2, and, to the extent she did not appoint it, the remainder would also go to their issue by right of representation. Their combined net worth was $5,831,010; with S1's property worth $4,360,790 and S2's property worth $1,470,220. No disclaimer was made. Trust B received $700,000 from S1's estate; and the rest, plus all of S2's property, was added to Trust A, giving it a value of $5,131,010. Since the property in excess of the exclusion amount went to Trust A, the estate automatically received a $3,660,790 marital deduction, thereby reducing S1's taxable estate to $700,000.

> EXAMPLE 12-4. Suppose, instead of just S1 dying in 2003, S1 and S2 were in a fatal car accident which caused S2 to die just a couple of days after S1. The executor of S2's estate disclaimed all of S1's estate in excess of the exclusion amount with the result that it went into Trust C instead of into Trust A. The three trusts are valued as follows: Trust A $1,470,220; Trust B $700,000; and Trust C $3,660,790. S1's executor could then QTIP 100% of Trust C to postpone all taxes until after S2's death, but doing so would create very unequal estates. This would be foolish, given that the tax on S2's estate would be due just a few days after the tax on S1's estate. Therefore, the executor of S1's estate should QTIP Trust C so as to equalize the two estates. (You should be able to identify the 6 step process even though some steps are combined.)

$$\frac{S1's\ E + S2's\ E}{2} = \frac{\$4,360,790 + \$1,470,220}{2} = \$2,915,505$$

The QTIP election necessary to reduce S1's estate from $4,360,790 to $2,915,505 is:

$$QTIP\ MD = \frac{\$1,445,285}{\$3,660,790} * \$3,660,790 = \$1,445,285$$

Therefore, taxable estates of S1 and S2 are:

$$S1\,'sE \;=\; \$4{,}360{,}790 \;-\; \$1{,}445{,}285 \;=\; 2{,}915{,}505\;\; and$$

$$S2\,'sE \;=\; \$1{,}470{,}220 \;+\; \frac{\$1{,}445{,}285}{\$3{,}660{,}790} \;*\; 3{,}660{,}790 \;=\; \$2{,}915{,}505$$

With the ABdC plan the equalization (or some other allocation between the two estates) can be accomplished by S2 (or S2's executor) making a partial disclaimer sufficient to equalize the two estates; and S1's executor forgoing the QTIP election.

EXAMPLE 12-5. S2's executor in the preceding example could simply disclaim that portion of S1's estate that would result in the two estates being equal in value as of S1's death. This requires a disclaimer by S2 (or rather by the executor of S2's estate, since S2 died soon after S1) of all of S1's estate that *exceeds* $1,445,285 (what is disclaimed will not go to S2, what is not disclaimed will). Trust A is then worth $2,915,505 [$1,470,220 + $1,445,285)], Trust B is worth $700,000, and Trust C is worth $2,215,505 [$3,660,790 - $1,445,285]. S1's estate equals the combined value of trusts B and C [$2,915,505]; and S2's estate equals the value of Trust A, also $2,915,505.

It may be easier to determine the appropriate disclaimer amount (without a QTIP) to equalize the two estates (assuming S1's estate is greater than S2's estate) if one simply divides the combined estates into two equal shares, places one share in Trust A, and spreads the balance between Trust B (receiving the exclusion amount) and Trust C the rest (the amount disclaimed). If equalization is desired, and S1's estate is smaller than S2's estate, S2 should disclaim all of S1's estate because failure to do so will simply increase S2's estate, resulting in an even greater inequality.

EXAMPLE 12-6. Using the facts in the prior example, let's calculate the disclaimer by the divide and allocate method. The combined value is $5,831,010, which when divided by two gives a desired taxable estate of $2,915,505. This, then, is the value of Trust A. The sum of Trusts B (valued at $700,000) and C (the balance at $2,215,505) equal S1's total taxable estate, which, of course, is equal to the desired taxable estate of $2,915,505. Since Trust C is "filled" by the disclaimer, the amount to be disclaimed is $2,215,505. It is simple algebra: Desired taxable estate = Trust B + Trust C. Therefore, Trust C = Desired taxable estate - Trust B. Since Trust B is equal to the exclusion amount, it is easy to solve for Trust C, which will equal the amount that must be disclaimed.

A tax effective disclaimer must be delivered to S1's executor within nine months after S1's death, therefore, if S2's state of health is uncertain as that dead-line approaches, S2 can make a disclaimer, and the decision as to whether Trust C should be QTIP'ed can be delayed a further six months by obtaining an extension to file the estate tax return, together with an extension to pay the tax. S2's poor health, and the need for additional time to assess the wisdom of making the QTIP election, is sufficient justification for the six month extension. Six months is the longest allowed extension for filing the estate tax return if the executor is within the country.[1] Although it is possible to make a QTIP election on a late filed return, the penalties for late filing (if one decides to generate a tax at S1's death) might out-weigh any benefits derived by splitting the tax between the two estates.

Choosing between the ABC plan and the ABdC plan is like choosing between varieties of apples rather than between apples and oranges. The main difference being that, with the ABdC plan, S2 decides whether to take control of S1's estate that exceeds the exclusion amount, whereas S2 has no such option with the ABC plan. Although a limited power may be part of the ABC plan for both Trusts B and C, it can only be used with Trust B in the ABdC plan. Also, the ABdC Trust is a much more complicated plan to explain to clients. In those situations where a tax should be generated at the first death, it may be more difficult to carry out with the disclaimer plan if S2 is in poor health, whereas, with the ABC plan, it is S1's executor who makes the QTIP election.

For large estates using the ABC plan, where taxes might be saved by making a partial QTIP election but, because of the time-value of money, the executor is leaning towards deferring the taxes until the second death, the executor is always well advised to obtain the six-month extension to allow the longest possible time to evaluate S2's heath before making (or foregoing) the QTIP election. With the ABdC, the disclaimer must be made within nine months of S1's death or it is not tax effective, so it is not possible to get an extra six months to "wait-and-see."

True, with an ABdC plan, S2 can always make a disclaimer that would accomplish the optimal split between the two taxable estates, and the executor of S1's estate could then wait until the six month extension period is almost up to file the return, making or not making the QTIP election at that time (depending upon S2's health), but that is a much more complicated way to create an ABC plan. Besides, as stated earlier, the ABdC plan must have a more restrictive Trust C, i.e., S2 must be denied a limited power of appointment. Furthermore, S2 might be too ill to make a disclaimer, a circumstance that might indicate that generating a tax in S1's estate would be wise. A court is likely to rule that the right to disclaim is personal to S2, so long as she is alive and might not allow a conservator to make a disclaimer on her behalf, whereas the decision to make a QTIP election rests with S1's executor. Even if S2 is nominated as executor of S1's estate, but is too ill to serve, the alternate executor would be in a position to make the appropriate election QTIP election with the regular ABC Trust plan.

A durable power of attorney, discussed later in this book, could be written for S2 with enough specificity to allow the holder of the power to make a disclaimer if S2 is too ill to do it herself. Unless there is specific language authorizing the agent to make a disclaimer, it might not withstand a challenge by the IRS that it was revocable by S2, if she were to regain her health. Of course, if S2 dies before the nine months are up, S2's executor can make the disclaimer, assuming he or she can be appointed by a court in time. Given that S2 is dead, the probate court is not likely to object to a disclaimer that is made to save death taxes, especially if the remaindermen of all trusts are the same people.

NONCITIZEN SURVIVING SPOUSES: THE QDOT TRUST

Generally, all property passing outright to a surviving spouse qualifies for the marital deduction, however, with the Technical and Miscellaneous Revenue Act of 1988 (TAMRA), Congress removed benefit of the marital deduction for property transferred, after November 10, 1988, to a non-U.S. citizen spouse.[2] There are several ways that the marital deduction can be salvaged. One, if S2 becomes a U.S. citizen before the estate tax return is filed and provided that she has remained a resident of the U.S. at all times following S1's death, property passing to her will qualify for the marital deduction.[3] Two, S1's property can be placed in a "qualified domestic trust"[4] (QDOT) that gives some assurance that the property will eventually be taxed in the U.S. The intent of the law is to ensure the eventual collection of estate tax on marital deduction property given to a spouse who may have less secure ties with the U.S. than are thought to exist for most citizens.

The requirements for a QDOT to qualify for the marital deduction are set forth in IRC §2056A. At least one of the trustees of a QDOT must be a U.S. citizen or domestic corporation. The Secretary of the Treasury is given authority to write regulations to assure the collection of the tax on distributions from these trusts. Those regulations require that the trustee keep sufficient assets within the U.S. to assure payment of the tax or that the trustee have a minimum net worth to assure the payment.[5] The third requirement is that S1's executor must elect to have the marital deduction apply to the trust. Note, the election can be made even on a late filed return, so long as it is not more than one year late.[6]

Estate tax is imposed (once S1's unified credit is exhausted) on any corpus distributed prior to the spouse's death, and on the value of the corpus remaining at the spouse's death (or sooner, if the trust ceases to qualify as a QDOT). However, distribution of income, and distribution of principal on account of "hardship," are exempt from the tax.[7] The tax is the amount that would have been imposed, after all credits, had the property subject to the tax been included in S1's taxable estate.

The trust need not have been created by the decedent prior to death; either the executor or the surviving spouse may create the QDOT prior to the due date of S1's estate tax return (including extensions). For a QDOT created after S1's death, the surviving spouse must irrevocably assign property that she would have otherwise received from S1 to the trust before the due date of the return.[8]

The surviving noncitizen spouse's choice of whether or not to transfer S1's property into a QDOT trust may be based on the decision to defer or to equalize their estates. If S2 creates and funds a QDOT trust, S1's estate will get a marital deduction for the property, but the property will be subject to estate tax at S2's death (or earlier, if trust property is transferred to S2 during her lifetime). Alternatively, if S2 accepts the property without transferring it to a QDOT, the property will be subject to S1 estate taxation immediately, but may avoid estate tax later to the extent S2 can convert the property into "non-U.S. situs" assets. Some noncitizen S2s may prefer to pay the tax up-front, then take the property, and disappear. The exclusion amount still shelters some of (or all) S1's estate, even if the estate is left to a non-U.S. citizen spouse. Furthermore, property that would have qualified for a marital deduction but for the fact that S2 was not a citizen will qualify for a prior transfer credit (PTC) if her estate is taxed in the U.S. at her death. This credit is calculated without being diminished by the usual PTC time factor (i.e., the decrease in the PTC by 20% every two years following S1's death does not apply here).[9]

ESTATE PLANS SELDOM SEEN

Next, we cover several estate plans that you are not likely to see in your practice but they are of interest because they will come up from time to time at continuing education seminars or in discussions with colleagues. The Estate Trust was never popular because of its limitations; the Traditional AB Trust was very popular until 1982, when the 100% marital deduction and the QTIP election made it obsolete. The QTIP election and the lowering of the top marginal rates made the inflexible Estate Equalization Trust less desirable than ABC Trusts, since the latter can accomplish the same tax savings but gives S1 greater control over who will be the remaindermen and gives S1's executor more options.

ESTATE TRUST

An unusual type of marital trust called the Estate Trust is almost never used. Its unique feature is that during S2's lifetime the terms of the trust allow the trustee discretion as to how much income to distribute to S2, but at S2's death all accumulated income and corpus must be distributed to S2's probate estate. Consequently, trust income can be accumulated and taxed at trust rates, but given the compressed nature of those rates, there is little reason to use this trust in an attempt to save income taxes. The reason this plan qualifies for the marital deduction is that it is not considered a terminable interest since the interest of S2 does not shift to someone else (see the definition of a terminable interest found at §2056(b)(1)). Given the greater flexibility of the QTIP trust, which allows the marital deduction while letting S1 control the remainder interest, it is difficult to imagine a reason to use one of these trusts.

THE TRADITIONAL AB TRUST

The Traditional AB Trust (TAB) is the name now given to those estate plans drafted between 1948-1981 that were designed to use the maximum marital deduction then available. For large estates, the maximum marital deduction was 50% of the adjusted gross estate (AGE). That amount was "given" to S2 by way of a marital deduction trust (Trust A), and that portion of S1's estate that could not escape taxation at S1's death was left to a bypass trust (Trust B), thus avoiding S2's estate. The tax savings for these plans came not at the first death but at the second death. The idea was to transfer into Trust A, in addition to S2's property, so much of S1's estate as exactly equaled the maximum marital deduction available to S1's estate, and to pass the rest of S1's estate (the taxed portion) into Trust B. Smaller estates (those under $500,000) could use the alternate minimum marital deduction of $250,000 for decedents dying between 1977 and 1981, inclusive, but for larger estates, even during that time-frame, the 50% AGE was the controlling factor. Because the pre-1982 marital deduction was limited to 50% of AGE, the property going into Trust B would have been taxed even if it passed directly to S2, therefore, placing it in Trust B did not increase the estate tax at S1's death, but doing so did allow it to avoid S2's estate when S2 died.

As with the more modern plans, Trust A generally held all of S2's property; in addition it received from S1's estate the maximum marital deduction amount. In common law states this would be equal to 50% of S1's net estate. In community property states, because the marital deduction was not allowed for the community property, the marital deduction was 50% of S1's separate property.

The names given the two trusts are similar to the names now used for the modern AB Trust plan. Trust A might have been called the Survivor's Trust, the Marital Deduction Trust, or General Power of Appointment Trust. S2 had to receive all income for life and hold a general power of appointment over it.[10] The names and characteristics of Trust B were similar to those for the Trust B of the modern AB trust except instead of being equal to the exclusion amount, the trust was funded with all that property which would not qualify for the marital deduction, hence, 50% of S1's separate property and S1's half of the community property. The trust was likely to be called Trust B or the Bypass Trust. Like the credit shelter trust of the modern AB plan, it could be a sprinkling trust benefitting the children as well as S2, but it was much more common that all income was given to S2. A sprinkling trust with S2 as both the trustee and as one of the potential beneficiaries has all the trust income taxed to S2 anyway. This defeats one of the primary reasons for having a sprinkling provision in a trust, namely the ability to lower over-all income taxes within a group of beneficiaries by distributing more income to the lower tax bracket members. It was very common to give S2 invasion rights limited to an ascertainable standard. Also common were B Trusts in which S2 had limited powers to appoint amongst the children, and, less commonly, S2 was given a 5 & 5 power.

EXAMPLE 12-7. Compare two pre-1982 estate plans. The first one is a simple will plan, one where S1 leaves everything to S2 and, upon S2's death, everything goes to their children. The second one is a TAB in which, after S1's death, S1's taxable estate goes into a bypass trust (Trust B) and the maximum marital deduction amount, plus all of S2's property goes into Trust A, a general power of appointment trust. Upon S2's death, Trusts A and B terminate and go to their children. When S1 died in 1965, S1 owned separate property worth $1,800,000 and S2 owned separate property $200,000; in addition they had community property worth $300,000. S2 died in 1976 and between deaths the assets doubled in value. (Pre-1977 tax rates are used.)

With plan one, all of S1's estate (less the estate tax) was transferred to S2. With plan two, Trust A was funded with property worth $1,250,000 [the ½ of S1's separate property that qualifies for the marital deduction, plus S2's separate property and S2's half of the community property] and Trust B with property worth $1,050,000 out of S1's estate [½ S1's separate property, plus S1's half of the community property]. All estates claimed the $60,000 estate tax exemption that was available at the time.

| | S1 100%> S2 | | TAB Trust | |
	S1 d1965	S2 d1976	S1 d1965	S2 d1976
GE	$1,950,000	$3,956,000	$1,950,000	$2,500,000
MD	(900,000)	0	(900,000)	0
EstEx	(60,000)	(60,000)	(60,000)	(60,000)
TxE	$990,000	$3,896,000	$990,000	$2,440,000
Tax	$322,000	$1,776,800	$322,000	$968,800

The entire estate tax savings of $808,040 [$1,776,800 - $968,800] occurred at the second death; the bypass trust kept Trust B property from being taxed again in S2's estate. The value of Trust B [$1,050,000 - $322,000 = $728,000] doubled; therefore, $1,456,000 avoided the second tax. The tax saved is equal to 55.5% of the latter figure, corresponding roughly to the pre-1977 average marginal rate between $2,500,000 and $4,000,000.

Notice that, with a TAB, the marital deduction for Trust A is in terms of a dollar amount (not as a QTIP fraction) because part of S1's separate property is transferred from S1's estate into Trust A, the trust over which S2 has a general power of appointment; therefore, the marital deduction is automatic, unlike the QTIP trust for which an election must be made in order to claim a marital deduction. Furthermore, at S2's death, all of Trust A is included in S2's estate, not just a fraction of it. Some plans written prior to 1981 still exist, and as demonstrated in the above example, Trust B may exceed the exclusion amount at S1's death. Even though it makes little sense today to have S1's separate property split equally between Trusts A and B, neither the executor, the surviving spouse, nor the trustee can rewrite the decedent's estate plan. However, the tax laws allow the executor of S1's estate to obtain a marital deduction on Trust B by making the QTIP election, provided S2 has the requisite income interest in the trust. Fortunately, most of the old TAB plans give S2 a life estate in Trust B. As discussed before, the QTIP'ed portion is expressed as that fraction of Trust B necessary to bring S1's taxable estate down to the desired taxable estate (e.g., down to the exclusion amount). It is that same fraction that determines the amount of Trust B that is later included in S2's estate, therefore, the election must be expressed as a fraction rather than as a dollar amount. *** *Query 1. What would be the QTIP fraction for the above example had S1 died in 2001 instead of 1965, and the executor wanted to postpone all tax?*

THE ESTATE EQUALIZATION AB TRUST

The funding of the two trusts created at S1's death required the executor of S1's estate to have S2's property valued too. Trust B was funded such that it exactly equaled half of the combined values. These plans enjoyed some popularity for very large estates when the maximum marginal rate was 77% for estates over $10 million. With the QTIP trust and the possibility of using a partial QTIP election there is much greater flexibility in allocation between the two estates, and if S2 is healthy at the time S1's estate tax return is prepared it is likely that Trust C will be fully QTIP'ed, therefore there is no need to have S2's property valued, whereas with the old Estate Equalization AB Trusts, all assets had to be valued to determine the funding amount for Trust B. With an ABC plan, an AsuperB plan, or an ABdC plan, S2's property needs to be appraised at S1's death only if the executor of S1's estate desires to use the QTIP election to equalize (or optimize) the two taxable estates.

General Comments on Estate Planning Using Trusts

From an estate planning standpoint, almost anything that can be described in words, with or without examples, that one can get a trustee to agree to carry-out, can be accomplished through the use of trusts, so long as it is legal and not against public policy. Any of the plans discussed here can be accomplished by a testamentary trust just as well as through a living trust with the exception of avoiding probate at the first death. With a testamentary trust the funding process at the first death is the probate court's order for distribution.

State death tax. For the most part, we have ignored the influence of state death taxes. Generally, their effect is relatively small compared to the impact of the federal tax, and in most states are of no consequence due to the federal credit for state death taxes. As explained earlier, a slight majority of the states, plus the District of Columbia, impose only a pickup tax, that is, an amount exactly equal to the federal credit for state death taxes. Consequently, in these states, no additional taxes are paid as a result of the state death tax. The remaining states impose a death tax that may be larger than the pickup amount, but usually is not unless the estate is going to non-family members.

Revocable living trust versus the testamentary trust. The main advantage to the living trust is that it avoids probate of the settlor's assets to the extent they are held in trust at the time of the settlor's death. The testamentary trust is funded through the probate process and does have the advantage that in most states the probate process considerably shortens the period during which creditors can assert their claims.

One living family trust or separate trusts for each spouse. A one trust document plan for both spouses, called a *joint spousal grantor trust*, will work as long as the assets of each spouse are carefully identified and distinguished. It does not have the gift tax danger and dispositive restrictions of the joint and mutual will, which generally is irrevocable as to all probate assets at the first spouse's death. In contrast, the most usual pattern in the joint trust is for the surviving spouse's assets, plus any assets from S1's estate that are added to Trust A, to remain subject to S2's control.

If commingling of spousal assets (individually owned property) is a significant risk, each spouse could execute his or her *own* living trust document. Another reason for two trusts is that a poorly drafted joint spousal grantor trust document could give rise to estate or gift tax consequences for wealthier clients, particularly when the spouses fund the trust with different amounts of individually owned property. For example, the spouse contributing the greater amount may be deemed to have made a taxable gift of a terminable interest in a portion of the trust to the other spouse, if the terms of the trust do not qualify the transfer for the marital deduction. The latter is not likely to occur with a well drafted joint trust because they are usually revocable so long as both spouse's are alive, and the portions that are irrevocable after the first death are designed to either use the unified credit or to qualify for the marital deduction.

Debts and expenses. Of course, any estate will have deductible debts and expenses, which will alter the calculations. Expenses in administering a decedent's probate estate typically range between 5 and 10% of the total estate. Ordinarily, estate planners handle debts and expenses in the following manner: Regarding *debts*, in performing the calculations, planners use net worth as the value of the estate property; regarding *expenses*, planners either estimate the expenses or simply ignore them because they are not likely to have a significant influence on the choice of estate plans. Given the complexity of multiple trust plans, most planners want to keep the calculations used as examples as simple as possible without misleading the client. Perhaps making a gift of a copy of this book is a good idea.

THE PTC AND BYPASS TRUSTS

Illogical though it might be, the prior transfer credit (PTC) is available for D2's interest in a life estate created by D1 (as in Chapter 6, when this PTC topic was introduced, we will refer to the first to die as D1 and the second to die as D2).[11] What is deemed to have been transferred from D1 to D2 is the value of the life estate, measured as of the date of D1's death. Valuation is based upon the life table factors published by the Treasury, even though, due to the PTC time factor, this credit would seldom be available to anyone who lived out the life expectancy stated in the table. In the example that follows, D1 is D and B (the income beneficiary) is D2.

EXAMPLE 12-8. On March 4, 1992, when D died, her net estate, worth $2,359,985 went into a Trust, with income for life to B (age 60) with a remainder to R (age 40). D's estate paid death taxes of $764,393, of which $127,599 was paid to D's state and the balance, $636,794 was paid to the Federal Government. B died on August 10, 1994, leaving an estate with a net value of $1,850,775 to three nephews. The trust established by D was distributed to R a few months after B's death. Although the trust's value was then in excess of $4 million, no additional taxes were paid because the trust was not included in B's estate.

PTC Step 1. The value of the property *transferred* to B before adjustment for taxes is the value of B's life estate. The federal rate for valuing split interest gifts for the month of March, 1992, was 8%, therefore, the life estate factor for a 60 year old income beneficiary was .71621, and the value of the property deemed to be "transferred" is $1,690,245. Limit one is:

$$LT1 = \frac{\$1,690,245}{\$2,359,985} * \$636,794 = \$456,078$$

Of course, the fraction reduces to the life estate factor since we used the factor in the first place to arrive at the value of the life estate. Therefore, limit one in this case can be calculated by multiplying the factor times the federal tax, as follows:

$$LT1 = .71261 * \$636,794 = \$456,078.$$

PTC Step 2. The tax on B's $1,850,775 taxable estate without a PTC is $520,849, of which $88,856 is state death tax and $431,993 is the federal estate tax. To determine the second limit, the federal tax on the reduced estate must be calculated and subtracted from the federal tax on B's taxable estate. The reduced estate is $1,850,775 less the amount deemed transferred and subtracted from the federal tax on B's taxable estate net of its share of the total death taxes:

Federal Estate Tax on B's $1,850,775 taxable estate.	$431,993
Less Federal Estate Tax B's reduced estate of $707,996	
i.e., $1,850,775 - .71621 * ($2,359,985 - $764,393)	(21,575)
Credit limit two	$410,418

Remember, the amounts shown as federal estate tax, $431,993 for the full estate and $21,575 for the reduced estate, are the actual federal estate taxes (after the unified credit and the state death tax credit) on taxable estates of $1,850,775 and $707,996, respectively. To arrive at the *reduced taxable estate*, B's taxable estate is reduced by the net value of what was deemed to have been transferred to B. What was deemed transferred is the value of B's life estate in the B and C trusts, after all the estate taxes generated at S1's death have been removed from them, i.e., 0.71621*($2,359,985 - $764,393). Note that $764,393 is the total tax at D's death, not just the federal tax.

PTC Step 3. Since B died more than two years, but less than four years, after D, the time factor is 80% and the actual PTC is:

$$80\% \ * \ \text{the lesser of} \begin{cases} \textit{limit one}: \$456,078 \\ \textit{limit two}: \$410,418 \end{cases} = \ \$328,334$$

Therefore, B's estate pays taxes as follows:

Death taxes before PTC & State D Tx Cr	$520,849
less State Death Tax Credit	(88,856)
less Prior Transfer Credit	(328,334)
Federal Estate Tax	$103,659

Total taxes = $88,856 + $103,659 = $192,515

The state death tax credit is not changed by the presence of a PTC. In the above hypothetical, the PTC eliminates over three-quarters of the second tax even though none of the corpus of the trust was actually transferred into B's estate.

If the remainderman dies after the income beneficiary, but still within ten years of the settlor (D1), there will also be a PTC for the remainderman's estate based on the remainder value at D1's death of the remainderman's interest. If the remainder is vested, and remainderman dies before the income beneficiary, the remainderman-decedent's interest in the remainder must be valued for inclusion in the remainderman's estate. This value is based upon the beneficiary's age (B's age), the value of the trust, and the federal split-interest gift rate (§7520 rate) at that time. R in the above example would become D2 for purpose of computing the PTC for his estate. Obviously, the income beneficiary will be older than he or she was when the trust was established, therefore the remainder factor (from Table S) is likely to be higher, however this depends upon the federal §7520 rate at R's death. Thus, the amount included in R's estate insofar as the trust is concerned would be the remainder factor (based B's age) times the trust's value as of R's death.

These changes are taken into account when calculating the value of the remainder in R's (D2) gross estate, but in calculating the value of what was transferred for determining the PTC limits, one must continue to use the value of the remainder as of D1's death. Remember, any change in value, insofar as the *property transferred* is concerned, is irrelevant to the PTC calculation. What is deemed to have transferred, is based on the values at D1's death, and that is the value used in calculating R's reduced estate. To the extent the value of a trust (or a vested remainder in a trust) is actually part of D2's estate, any change will change the value of D2's taxable estate.

THE PTC AND THE QTIP ELECTION

The PTC has its greatest estate planning potential when utilized in conjunction with the ABC, AsuperB, or ABdC estate plans, because the partial QTIP election gives S1's executor some control in the allocation of the couple's total estate between the two taxable estates. For large estates, if the surviving spouse is diagnosed as terminally ill before S1's estate tax return is filed, it may be better to make either no QTIP election or only a partial QTIP election, so that some taxes are generated in the first estate, which in turn will generate a PTC for the second estate. The optimal QTIP election is one where the QTIP fraction used is one that will best utilize lower marginal tax rates for both estates and the PTC for S2's estate in such a way that the greatest amount possible passes to the children. This is demonstrated in the example set that follows. Keep in mind that the maximum extension to file is six months, therefore, the maximum period after S1's death to assess S2's health is 15 months.

FACTS FOR THE EXAMPLE SET: At the time of S1's death on October 11, 1993, S1 and S2 had community property worth $843,760, S1 owned separate property worth $4,450,920, and S2 owned separate property worth $975,688. Their estate plan was a modern ABC Trust plan, with S2 having a life estate in Trusts B and C. S1 died at age 75, survived by 65 year old S2. The federal rate for valuing split interest gifts for October of 1993 was 6%. The net value going into each trust after S1's death was: Trust A $1,397,568; Trust B $600,000; and Trust C $4,272,800. When S1 died, S2 was in

.extremely poor health, but had a greater than 50% probability of living at least a year.

EXAMPLE 12-9. S1's executor was very diligent at assembling the information and valuations necessary to file the estate tax return by its due date of July 11, 1994. He elected to QTIP all of Trust C so as not to pay any tax. Unfortunately, S2 died December 27, 1994. The assets in the three trusts had increased in value by 10%. As a result, the three trusts at S2's death were worth: Trust A $1,537,325; Trust B $660,000; and Trust C $4,700,080; for a total value of $6,897,405. S2's taxable estate was the combined value of Trusts A and C, so, although this strategy resulted in zero taxes at S1's death, S2's executor paid $2,878,573 at S2's death. The net amount going to the children was the total of the three trusts, less the tax:

$$\$6,897,405 - \$2,878,573 = \$4,018,832$$

EXAMPLE 12-10. In this alternative version, S1's executor was very cautious. Although she had also diligently assembled the information and valuations necessary to file the estate tax return by its due date of July 11, 1994, she obtained an extension to file and to pay until January 11, 1995; intending to re-assess S2's health as that latter date approached. S2's death on December 27, 1994 made re-assessment unnecessary.

The assets in the three trusts had increased in value by 10%. S1's executor chose the optimal QTIP election, even though it meant Trusts B and C would have to paid their pro rata share of the S1 estate taxes about a year earlier than if they were postponed until S2's return was due, and some interest would have to be paid for the six month extension period. The interest amount for both the federal and state death taxes would also be deductible on S1's return (the interest deduction is an interrelated calculation). Since she had obtained an extension to file and to pay, no penalties had to be paid.

To work through to the amounts paid at each death we will follow the six step QTIP calculations (combining some of the steps in the interest of brevity). At Step 5, we will calculate S1's taxes. To simplify, interest is not taken here as a deduction although in a real situation it would be. Step 6 is followed by the three step PTC calculation for S2's estate to determine S2's taxes. From the value of the three trusts at S2's death, we will subtract the amount of taxes for both estates, and also subtract the estimated interest on S1's late paid taxes to come up with the net amount going to the children. Finally, we compare the net amount going to the children with this alternative to the net amount with the 100% QTIP alternative.

Step 1. By trial and error the executor determined that the best result (the largest after tax transfer to the children) was accomplished when S1's taxable estate equaled $3,811,009.

Step 2. The marital deduction necessary to achieve the desired taxable estate:

$$\$4{,}872{,}800 - \$3{,}811{,}009 = MD = \$1{,}061{,}791$$

Step 3. Trust C is the QTIP property, therefore the QTIP fraction is:

$$\$1{,}061{,}791/\$4{,}272{,}800$$

Steps 4 & 5. S1's taxable estate equals S1's estate less the marital deduction that results from the QTIP election. Therefore, S1's taxable estate equals:

$$\$4{,}872{,}800 - \$1{,}061{,}791 = \$3{,}811{,}009$$

This results in federal taxes of $1,283,310 and state death taxes of $260,745, for a total of $1,544,055.

Step 6. S2's estate equals Trust A plus the QTIP fraction times Trust C's value at S2's death. Therefore, S2's taxable estate equals:

$$S2'sE = \$1{,}537{,}325 + (\frac{\$1{,}061{,}791}{\$4{,}272{,}800}) * \$4{,}700{,}080 = \$2{,}705{,}295$$

Having determined S2's taxable estate, we turn our attention to calculating the PTC and the estate taxes that will have to be paid.

PTC Step 1. Limit one: Since the federal rate for October of 1993 was 6% and S2 was 65 years old, the factor for computing her life estate value was .56599.

$$.56599 * \$1{,}283{,}310 = \$726{,}314$$

PTC Step 2. Limit two: The total taxes on an estate of $2,705,295 before taking the PTC is $941,806, of which $156,066 is the state death tax and $785,740 is the federal death tax.

Federal Estate Tax on $2,705,295	$785,740
Less Tax on S2's reduced Taxable Estate of $821,258,	
i.e.,$2,705,295 - .56599 * ($4,872,800 - $1,544,055)	(59,470)
Credit limit two	$726,270

Again, a reminder that the federal tax amounts used to arrive at limit two, are the tax on S2's taxable estate and on S2's reduced taxable estate, calculated by taking *both* the *unified credit* and the *state death tax credit* into account.

PTC Step 3. Since S2 died within two years of S1's death, the time factor is 100% and the actual PTC is:

$$100\% \; * \; \textit{the lesser of} \left\{ \begin{array}{l} \textit{limit one: } \$726,341 \\ \textit{limit two: } \$726,270 \end{array} \right. = \; \$726,270$$

Therefore, S2's estate pays taxes as follows:

Death taxes before PTC & State D Tx Cr	$941,806
less State Death Tax Credit	(156,066)
less Prior Transfer Credit	(726,270)
Federal Estate Tax	$59,470

The total death tax for both estates using the optimal QTIP election is $1,759,591 [$1,544,055 + $156,066 + $59,470] compared to $2,878,573 when the 100% QTIP election is made. The difference in tax is $1,118,976 of which $726,470 is attributable to the PTC and the balance is due to the utilization of lower marginal rates in the first estate rather than "loading up" the second estate by making a 100% Trust C QTIP election. S1's estate would have to pay approximately $70,000 in interest (about 4.5% because it was for just six months) on the late paid taxes. Compare the value going to the children using the optimal QTIP election with what was previously calculated. In both cases we are assuming the total value of the three trusts at S2's death to be the same since S1's taxes were not paid until after S2 died. Therefore, the value of the trusts (at S2's death) less the taxes and the interest (estimated to be $70,000) would be as follows:

$$\$6,897,405 - \$1,759,591 - \$70,000 = \$5,067,814$$

The optimal QTIP results in $1,048,982 [$5,067,814 - $4,018,832] more to the children than with the 100% QTIP election.

This potential savings that comes from using the PTC with multiple trust plans is obviously just as important as the utilization of both unified credits. It results from the phantom transfer from S1's estate to S2, (the fact that an estate is allowed a PTC based upon the hypothetical value of S2's life estate) even though, due to S2's death, very little is actually transferred. Of course it is limited in usefulness to those times when the two deaths are close enough in time to utilize the PTC.

The optimal QTIP fraction depends on the following factors:

- the federal rate for valuing split interests such as life estates;
- the age of S2;
- the combined value of the couple's estates; and finally,
- whether S1's estate equals (or exceeds) the amount necessary to make the optimal mix.

Given the multiple factors (age, rate, values) and the fact that only a portion of S1's estate is deemed to have been transferred, the optimal QTIP fraction tends to be one that taxes more of the combined total in S1's estate. However, for combined estates between $1,200,000 and $6,000,000, if the second death is very likely to occur within two years of the first, the optimal result will generally require a QTIP election that brings S2's estate almost equal to that of S1. With very large estates, the optimal QTIP fraction is likely to be one that causes S1's taxable estate to be considerably larger than S2's. For instance, with combined estates over $20,000,000, the optimal allocation between the two estates is likely to require a taxable estate for S1 that is significantly larger than that of S2. For these large estates, as much as 75% to 80% of the combined values should be taxed at S1's death, with only 20% to 25% at S2's death, if the goal is to pass the greatest amount possible to the children or other heirs. The exact ratio can be determined by trial and error - or by using a computer program. Even for very large estates, a QTIP election that equalizes the two estates generally produces results fairly close to those achieved by the optimal QTIP election; and certainly very superior to the 100% QTIP alternative. *** *Query 2. Using the facts from the above example set, what is the QTIP fraction that equalizes the two estates as of S1's death? Remember, the fraction is applied only to Trust C.*

THE GENERATION SKIPPING TRANSFER TAX

Up to now, we have focused our tax planning discussion on how gifts and trusts are used to reduce transfer taxes for the nuclear family, i.e., S1, S2, and their children. Similar planning works for transfers to more remote family members. For example, a childless couple could develop a bypass plan for nephews and nieces. A bypass trust plan works well for any survivors who belong to the same, or to the next generation, but complexity arises when a bypass trust (or an outright transfer) skips the estates of the transferor's children and goes to grandchildren or great-grandchildren. The Generation-Skipping Transfer Tax (GSTT) is designed to capture additional taxes, such that the total transfer tax approximates that which would have been collected had the property been taxed at each generation. It is imposed on direct skips, taxable terminations, and taxable distributions to, or for the benefit of, a skip person. A skip person is a beneficiary who is at least two generations younger than the transferor. For this discussion, think in terms of grandparent, parent, and grandchild, with the grandchild being the skip person vis-a-vis the grandparent. Keep in mind that this GSTT is not appreciably "unified" with gift and estate taxes; it is a separate tax having its own unique rules. The tax is reported on Form 706 (for transfers at death) and Form 709 (for gifts), these tax returns are located in Appendices C and D, respectively.

Purpose of the GSTT

The purpose of the GSTT is to assure that large estates are subjected to a transfer tax as they pass from one generational level to the next. Prior to the mid-1980's, a common method for the very wealthy to pass their estates through many generations with a minimum of transfer tax was to create trusts that would benefit first the children for their lives, then the grandchildren for their lives, and then the great-grandchildren for as long as the rule against perpetuities would allow. Transfer tax (either the estate tax or the gift tax) would be levied only when the trust was initially funded. Because the income beneficiaries had no powers to appoint corpus, nor any other interest in the trust that would cause it to be included in their estates, no new taxes were levied as the interests shifted from one generation to the next. These were the ultimate bypass trusts designed to last a hundred years or more.

The first generation-skipping transfer tax was enacted in 1976. Although planners found it very complicated, they quickly learned that the tax was easy to circumvent. As a result, in 1986, Congress acknowledged its error by repealing it retroactively, and at the same time, enacting a more comprehensive version as described below. Trusts that were irrevocable prior to September 25, 1985 are "grandfathered in," that is, they are not subject to the generation-skipping transfer tax.

Overview of the Current GSTT

The solution devised by Congress is to tax transfers that skip a generation even if they are subject to the regular gift or estate tax. The tax levied on a generation skipping transfer (GST) is called the Generation Skipping Transfer Tax (GSTT). A GST is a transfer to a "skip person," defined as a person two or more generations below the transferor or a trust whose beneficiaries are all skip persons.[12] The basic rule, simple enough to state but complicated in the application, is as follows:

$$\text{GSTT} = \text{the Taxable Amount x the Applicable Rate}^{13}$$

Think of the taxable amount as the value of the gift or estate that is given to a skip person or to skip persons. Complications set in because the taxable amount depends upon whether the transfer is a direct skip, a taxable termination, or a taxable distribution. The *applicable rate* is the maximum federal estate tax rate multiplied by the inclusion ratio. The *inclusion ratio* is determined by the amount of the one million dollar per donor GST exemption that the donor can allocate to GST transfers. We will start by covering the calculation of the tax for each of the three types of skips. To keep this as simple as possible, the initial examples will assume that the donor does not allocation any of his or her GST exemption to the transfer. Later we will consider the allocation of the exemption and look at examples where it is a factor.

Calculating the GSTT

The taxable amount depends upon whether the transfer is a direct skip, a taxable termination, or a taxable distribution. Keep in mind that the goal is to approximate the transfer tax that would be levied if the property passed through each generational level. Generally, unless the governing instrument (e.g., a will or a trust) by specific reference to the GSTT provides otherwise, the GSTT must be charged to the property transferred.

Direct skips. A direct skip is a transfer to a skip person where that transfer is subject to an estate or gift tax.[14] These are likely to be outright gifts or bequests from grandparents to grandchildren. For all direct skips, other than a direct skip *from* a trust, the liability for paying the GSTT is placed upon

ادف

the transferor.[15] The taxable amount, in the case of a direct skip, is the value of the property received by the transferee.[16] This means that in the case of a bequest, the taxable amount is the bequest net of its share of debts, expenses, etc., and death taxes (both federal and state). Where the direct skip property is included in the transferor's estate that makes alternate valuation or special use valuation election, the value of the property for purpose of the GSTT is the same as used for the estate.[17] Where a taxable termination is the result of the death of an individual, the trustee can reduce the taxable amount by making an alternate valuation election §2032.[18] For gifts of a present interest, the annual exclusion also reduces the taxable amount for GST purposes.

> EXAMPLE 12 - 11. In 2001, Barry made a gift of Bucky Company common stock, worth $750,000, to his granddaughter Julie. He had applied his million dollar exemption to a 1997 million dollar taxable gift to other grandchildren, and the annual exclusion was applied to a gift made earlier in the year to Julie. Because of those earlier gifts, the gift of Bucky Company stock required Barry to pay gift taxes of $294,750 and GSTT of $412,500 [$750,000 x 0.55].

Things get a little more complicated with direct skips from a decedent. The GSTT is paid by the estate (the transferor) and the GSTT should not itself be subjected to the GSTT, therefore multiplying the net estate by 55% will produce a tax that is too high. The result for an estate should be the same as if the transfer was a direct skip gift. Let's look at the last example, after the regular gift tax had been paid, Barry (the donor) parted with assets worth $1,162,500 to make a gift to Julie of $750,000. The $1,162,500 is the gift of $750,000 plus the GSTT of $412,500. In order to leave a skip person $750,000 by way of a bequest (instead of a gift) requires a net estate (after estate taxes, but before the GSTT) of $1,162,500. The GSTT of $412,500 divided by $1,162,500 equals 0.3548387, which is the GSTT rate for direct skips from a decedent.

> EXAMPLE 12 - 12. During her life, Tisha had used up her one million dollar exemption on gifts to grandchildren. Her net estate, after payment of the federal estate tax and the state death tax was $1,162,500. She left her entire estate to Frank, her favorite grandson. The estate must pay $412,500 in GSTT [0.3548387 x $1,162,500] and Frank will actually receive just $750,000.

The steps that a decedent's estate must take to calculate the GSTT for a direct skip are found in Part 2 of Schedule R of the U.S. Estate Tax Return (Form 706). Notice that, after subtracting debts, regular death taxes, and the exemption, the net amount left is divided by 2.818182 to determine the GSTT (see line 8 of Schedule R). How does this number relate to the 0.3548387 rate given above? Dividing "1" by 0.3548387 equals 2.818182, therefore the result will be the same whether one divides the net transfer (net after regular tax) by 2.818182 or whether one multiplies it by 0.3548387.

Taxable terminations. A taxable termination means that a shift in interest from one generation to the next has occurred as a result of the death of a person, the release of an interest, the passage of time, or for some other reason. The trustee is liable for the GSTT in the case of a taxable termination and in the case of a direct skip from a trust. The taxable amount is the value of the property with respect to which the taxable termination has occurred, reduced by any expenses or indebtedness that would be deductible under §2053. As mentioned earlier, the §2032 alternate valuation election is available (assuming it will reduce the GSTT) if the taxable termination is the result of the death of an interested party. Such would be the case if the settlor established a trust, giving his children income for life, then income for the life of grandchildren, and finally distribution to the grandchildren. Once the last of the settlor's children died and the income interest in the trust shifted to grandchildren, there would be a taxable termination. If the value of the trust had decreased in the six months following the death of the last of the settlor's children to die, the trustee could elected the alternate valuation date in order to reduce the GSTT.

Just because a GST trust terminates, does not mean that a taxable termination has occurred. Whether it is also a taxable termination depends on whether the termination resulted in a shift from one generation to another. Furthermore, as shown in the examples that follow, a taxable termination may occur without the trust itself terminating. Once the interests of all members of a generational level terminate and a tax is levied, the younger generations are considered to have moved up a generation such that individuals at the new top generation level are no longer skip persons. This "move-up" avoids having the GSTT apply again when transfers are made to members of this generation, since it was already imposed when the property interest shifted to the generation.[19]

EXAMPLE 12 - 13. When grandpa Xuyen died in 1990 his estate plan created a trust which gave income for life to his son Ha, remainder to Ha's issue by right of representation, except that if any of Ha's children were under age 35, the assets were to remain in trust until the youngest reached age 35. Because the executor allocated the one million dollar exemption to direct skips, none of the exemption was allocated to the trust. When Ha died in 1995, the trust was worth $2,000,000 and Ha's youngest child, Yi Yun, was 32 years old. Because the death of Ha causes the interest to shift to a younger generation, a taxable termination occurs even though the trust itself does not terminate. The tax payable by the trustee is $1,100,000, leaving just $900,000 in the trust.

EXAMPLE 12 - 14. Continuing the prior example: In 1998, shortly after Yi Yun's 35th birthday, the trust corpus, valued at $1,090,000, was distributed to him and his brother Sui-on. Since this is not a shift in generations (Yi Yun and Sui-on are now in the oldest generation and not considered skip persons), there is no new GSTT (nor any other transfer tax) resulting from the trust's actual termination. Had Yi Yun died after his father, but before his 35 birthday, with the result that his interest went to his children, there would be a GSTT on his share. On the other hand, if he died before his 35th birthday, but left no issue with the result that Sui-on received his share, there would be no additional GSTT because the two brothers are in the same generation.

Taxable distributions. The Code gives a functional definition for a *taxable distribution*: "the term 'taxable distribution' means any distribution from a trust to a skip person (other than a taxable termination or a direct skip)."[20] This covers situations where a trust has beneficiaries in two or more generations, and the trustee can, and does, distribute to one of the beneficiaries in one of the lower generations. The transferee (i.e., distributee-beneficiary) is liable for the GSTT. The taxable amount is the value of the property received by the transferee, reduced by any expenses or indebtedness that would be deductible under §2053.

EXAMPLE 12 - 15. Using the facts from the prior two examples, if while Ha (the son of the trustor) is still alive, the trustee, using powers given to her by the terms of the trust, makes a $500,000 distribution to grandson Yi Yun, it would be a taxable distribution. The GSTT in the amount of $275,000 is charged to Yi Yun with the result that he only gets $225,000.

Because the GSTT liability is placed upon the transferee, if the trustee pays the GSTT, it is treated as a taxable distribution. The amount that must be "distributed" to achieve a desired net distribution can be solved algebraically.

Let the gross distribution be Dg and the net distribution be Dn, then solve for Dg as follows:

Dg - GSTT = Dn; and since GSTT = 0.55 x Dg,

Dg - 0.55 x Dg = Dn. Therefore, (1- 0.55) x Dg = Dn; and finally,

Dg = Dn/0.45.

EXAMPLE 12 - 16. Suppose in the prior example, the trustee was willing to pay the tax so that Yi Yun would receive $500,000. This will require the trustee parting with $1,111,111 whether the trustee pays the GSTT of $611,111[0.55 x $1,111,111] and distributes $500,000 to Yi Yun or the trustee distributes $1,111,111 and lets Yi Yun pay the tax on it.

EXAMPLE 12 - 17. Suppose the trustee distributed trust corpus worth $500,000 to Siu-on (Yi Yun's brother) after Ha's death (i.e., after the taxable termination had occurred), but before the trust had terminated. This distribution is not a taxable distribution for GSTT purposes, because by that time the two brothers were in the oldest generation of living beneficiaries having an interest in the trust, hence they were no longer skip persons.

Applicable Rate

The applicable rate is made up of two components: the maximum federal estate tax rate and the inclusion ratio. Remember, the GSTT is equal to the taxable amount (a reference to the transferred property) times the applicable rate (a tax rate modified to take into account the allocation of the one million dollar exemption).

Maximum federal estate tax rate. The term maximum federal estate tax rate is the maximum imposed by §2001 which presently is 55%.[21] Notice it does not include the 5% surcharge that tosses estates in the "bubble" above $10,000,000 into a 60% marginal rate. The purpose of the surcharge (discussed in Chapter 5) is to "take back" the benefits of the unified credit and the lower marginal rates and, as a surcharge, it is not deemed to increase the maximum federal rate above 55%.

The inclusion ratio. Think of this as that portion of the transfer that is *not saved* from the dreaded GSTT by the one million dollar exemption. The GST exemption is indexed for inflation for transfers occurring after 1998.

Increases will be rounded down to the next lowest multiple of $10,000. The base year for measuring the change is 1997.[22] As of 1999, the GST exemption had increased to $1,010,000. It will probably continue to increase by $10,000 every couple of years. The inclusion ratio is defined as the value one minus the "applicable fraction,"[23] or

$$1 - \frac{GSTT\ exemption\ allocated}{Net\ FMV\ of\ property\ tranferred}$$

The "net FMV value of the property transferred" means net of debt, expenses, liens, death taxes (federal and state) charged to the property, as well as any charitable deduction. Generally, the allocation of the exemption is an elective one made by the donor in the case of gifts and by the executor in the case of estates. It is not unusual to make allocations within a multiple trust estate plan such that all of the GST trusts have inclusion ratios of either zero or one. We will get into this allocation of the exemption to various trusts in the section on efficient utilization of the exemption.

EXAMPLE 12 - 18. When Ruben died $3,000,000 of his estate (net of regular death taxes) was left to his grandchildren. The executor allocated the entire one million dollar exemption to this bequest, resulting in an applicable fraction of one-third ($1,000,000/$3,000,000) and an inclusion ratio of two-thirds (1 - 1/3). The GSTT would be $3,000,000 x 0.55 x .6666667, which is $1,100,000.

EXAMPLE 12 - 19. When Josephine died she left her $3,000,000 estate (this was net of regular death taxes) in trust for her son Albert, with remainder to his issue. Since this was her entire net estate, the exemption was allocated to this trust. While Albert was still alive, the trustee made a distribution out of corpus in the amount of $360,000 to Albert's daughter, Martha. This, of course, was a taxable distribution. Given the inclusion ratio, the applicable rate would be 0.55 x .6666667. Therefore, the tax on the distribution would be: $360,000 x 0.55 x .6666667 = $132,000.

EXAMPLE 12 - 20. When Albert died the trust was worth $4,500,000. His death caused a taxable termination. The applicable rate is as before: 0.55 x .6666667. The GSTT is: $4,500,000 x 0.55 x .6666667 = $1,650,000.

Timing the Exemption Allocation

As indicated earlier in this discussion, the allocation of the exemption is not automatic. Generally, at the death of a transferor, one should allocate in a manner that is most likely to reduce the GSTT, taking into account the present value of money. Because most taxpayers would prefer to postpone taxes of whatever variety, the Code has as a default position the automatic allocation of the exemption to lifetime direct skips unless the donor elects not to have the automatic allocation apply.[24]

Discretionary allocations. Given a choice the person making the decision would like to accomplish two or three things, some of which may be in opposition or which may require the use of a functioning crystal ball. Consider the following examples:

> EXAMPLE 12 - 21. Eunice never trusted her two boys to wisely handle investments. The oldest, Jimmy, she had given up on, but for the youngest boy, Billie, she wanted to provide a good living, while making sure he could not squander the estate that she had put together. She loved her grandchildren, who have turned out to be fine adults. She left her estate in equal shares, one share immediately to Jimmy's children by right of representation and the other in trust for Billie for his lifetime, the remainder, free of trust, to Billie's children by right of representation. The plan specifically gave her executor authority to allocate the exemption as the executor deemed appropriate. Her estate, after payment of all federal estate and state death taxes, had a net value of $1,500,000. Her executor could allocate $750,000 of the exemption to the direct skip and $250,000 to the trust, or vice-versa, or equally between the two transfers, or in any other proportion. If it is fully allocated to the trust, the trust will have a zero inclusion ratio such that, even if it is worth more than one million dollars when it terminates, no GSTT will be due. However, doing so will cause an immediate GSTT for the portion of the direct skip not covered by the exemption. Allocating $750,000 to the direct skip will post-pone all GSTT until the trust ends, but the trust will have an inclusion ratio of two-thirds.

Forced delay of allocations. In the case of inter vivos gifts, if the property would be included in the donor's estate due to a retained interest (§§2036 - 2038), the allocation cannot be made until the close of the *estate tax inclusion period* (ETIP). The ETIP is the point at which the retained interest either ends (released or ends by the terms of the transfer) or the donor dies.

EXAMPLE 12 - 22. Stacie funds a ten-year qualified personal residence trust (QPRT) with her $550,000 home. The remaindermen are her three grandchildren. At the end of the ten-year term the house is worth $750,000. At that time the ETIP ends and she can allocate $750,000 of the exemption to the transfer.

EXAMPLE 12 - 23. Suppose, in the prior example, that Stacie died in year seven when the home was worth $625,000. At that time the ETIP would end, and her executor could allocate $625,000 of the exemption to the transfer. In both cases, Stacie would have preferred to have made the allocation at the beginning of the trust, when the initial transfer was made so as to use only $550,000 of her exemption.

Special Rules Pertaining to Generations & the GSTT

There are a number of special rules related to GSTT, some of which we will cover here, others which we will just warn you that they exist, but that are beyond the scope of this text.

Generation assignment. Where transferees are related to the transferor the assignments are fairly straight forward. The Code requires that one start with the transferor's grandparents and count down generations to the transferee and compare the number to the number of generations between the grandparent and the transferor, if the difference is greater than one, the transferee is a skip person.

EXAMPLE 12 - 24. Jack wishes to leave half of his multi-million dollar estate to his brother's daughter Alice and the other half to Alice's two children, Martin and Paula. Are any or all of these skip persons? Jack's grandfather is two generations above him. From the grandfather to Alice is three generations. Three minus two equals one, so Alice is not a skip person. It is four generations from the grandfather to Martin and Paula. Four minus two equals two, therefore, both Martin and Paula are skip persons.

Predeceased parent exception. A special rule (called the *predeceased parent exception)* allows a direct skip person to "move up" a generation if his or her parent is a lineal descendent of the transferor (or the transferor's spouse) and the parent dies before the transfer occurs (i.e, the date of the gift or the date the transferor dies).[25] It does not apply to skip persons not related to the transferor, nor to collateral heirs (e.g., nieces and nephews), with one exception, if the transferor has not lineal descendants, a transfer to a collateral relative whose parent is deceased qualifies for the predeceased parent exception.[26] The move up exception also applies if the parent (of the person who would otherwise be a skip person) dies within 90 days of the transferor, provided the parent is treated as having predeceased the transferor, either because of a survivorship clause in the transferor's estate planning documents (i.e., the grandparent's will or trust) or because of applicable state law has a statutory survivorship period.[27] This is a good reason to consider including a general 90 day survivorship clause in estate planning documents.

> EXAMPLE 12 - 25. Sarah's will left her multimillion dollar estate to her issue by right of representation. All three children survived her, but one child, named Richard, died 75 days after her. Richard left two children who were entitled to inherit his entire estate. Sarah's will had a 60 day survivorship clause. Since Richard lived beyond the 60 days, he was entitled to a one third share of Sarah's estate. Richard's executor disclaimed Richard's share so that it could pass directly to his children. This share is subject to the GSTT because insofar as Sarah's will (and her state of domicile) is concerned he did not predecease her. Had her will included a 90 day survivorship clause (or an even a longer one) Richard would have been considered to have predeceased Sarah and there would be no GSTT.

A disclaimer will not work insofar as the predeceased parent exception is concerned, i.e., it will not move the disclaimant's children up a generation. Thus in the above example, even though the disclaimer worked for other purposes (e.g., avoiding Richard's gross estate for regular estate tax and avoiding his probate estate), for GSTT purposes the disclaimer will not cause Richard to be treated as though he had predeceased Sarah. In the typical estate plan for wealthy couples that use multiple trusts, it is very likely that the contingent remaindermen are skip persons. This may cause a GSTT problem.

Common facts for the *alternative* examples that immediately follow: S1 and S2 had four children all of whom had children of their own. The estate plan included a bypass trust, carved out of S1's estate. The trust gave S2 a life estate, with the remainder to the couple's issue, by right of representation. When S1 died, the trust was worth $4,000,000. When S2 died, the trust was worth $6,000,000.

> EXAMPLE 12-26. All four children survived their mother (S2) and took equal shares of the trust estate. The GSTT did not apply because the children of the transferor are not skip persons.

EXAMPLE 12-27. All four children outlived their father (S1), but one of them died before S2, leaving two adult children (grandchildren of S1 and S2). When S2 died the three living children each received a one-fourth share, and the two grandchildren a one-eight share. The portion of the trust going to the grandchildren is subjected to the GSTT even though their parent is deceased. The predeceased parent exception applies only to direct skips, so the grandchildren do not move up even though their parent died before the parent's interest in the trust vested.

Marital relationships. A transfer to one who is related to the transferor's spouse is in the generation level determined as if the transfer was from the spouse rather than from the transferor. The counting up (and down) from the spouse to her (or his) grandparent is just for the purpose of determining whether a donee is a skip person. For all other purposes the transfer is treated as coming from the transferor, unless the couple elect to "split the gift"[28] in which case both spouses are treated as being donors.

A spouse or ex-spouse of a transferor is treated as in the same generation as the transferor, regardless of age difference. This "same-generation-treatment" will continue even if a marriage ends due to the transferor's death or ends by divorce, which some people say is a little like death. Likewise, anyone married to a lineal descendant of the transferor's grandparents (or a lineal descendant of the transferor's spouse's grandparents) is in the same generation as that person's spouse (i.e., the lineal descendent) even if the marriage ends.

EXAMPLE 12 - 28. Jennifer wishes to leave a portion of her estate to the widow of her uncle's grandson. Would this be a generation skipping transfer? The widow of the grandson is in the same generation as was the grandson. The parent of the grandson is at the same generation level (count up and count back down) as Jennifer. Therefore, the grandson was (and his widow is) just one generation below Jennifer and no generation skipping transfer will occur.

Transferees who are not lineal descendants. If the lineal descendent rules and the spouse rules do not apply, then assignment to generations is based upon the difference in age between the transferor and the transferee. A person older than, or not less than 12.5 years younger than, the transferor is considered to be in the same generation as the transferor. A person 12.5 to 37.5 years younger is in the next generation below, and similar rules apply to assign individuals to still younger generations based upon 25 year increments. Obviously, a person 40 years younger is a skip person and a person 30 years younger is not.

Planning Considerations: Efficient Utilization of the Exemption.

Generally, one would like the exemption to reduce GSTT sooner, rather than later, to cover completely a GST trust which is likely to grow, and to limit its allocation to trusts that will actually go to skip persons.

These are facts for the extended set of examples that follow: Andre and Mary have three children, Tom, Carol, and Whitney. Their ABC Trust plan allows Trust C to be divided into as many as three trusts after the first spouse's death. The division will depend on how much is QTIP'ed and the best allocation of the GSTT exemption. There is a provision for a Trust C_E to hold such property as is to be GSTT exempt (in addition to Trust B), a Trust C_Q to hold the QTIP'ed non-exempt portion, and Trust C_{NQ} to hold that portion not QTIP'ed. The terms of the trust provide that after the surviving spouse's death (S2), any distribution to a skip person should be satisfied first from GSTT exempt property, next to the extent possible from property included in S2's estate, and last from other trust property; with the distributions from all trusts adjusted to allow overall distribution to Andre and Mary's issue by right of representation. It also provides that if Trust C_E is QTIP'ed, estate tax charged to the QTIP property at S2's death is to be first charged to Trust C_Q before any is charged to Trust C_E.

When Andre died in 1994, his property was worth $3,000,000 and Mary's property was worth $800,000. Trust A was funded with all of Mary's property (i.e., $800,000), Trust B with assets worth $600,000, and Trust C, before division, with the $2,400,000 balance.

EXAMPLE 12 - 29. The executor of Andre's estate decided to postpone all taxes until Mary's death, therefore, a QTIP election was made covering all $2,400,000 allocated to Trust C. To fully utilize Andre's one million dollar exemption, a $400,000 reverse QTIP election was made. Thus the Trustee divided Trust C into Trust C_E holding assets worth $400,00 and Trust C_Q holding assets worth $2,000,000. Both C trusts were QTIP'ed (i.e., an election was made to qualify both for the marital deduction) and Trust C_E was reverse QTIP'ed. The executor allocated Andre's exemption to Trust B and to Trust C_E.

EXAMPLE 12 - 30. How would things change if the executor decided to equalize the two estates by a QTIP election covering just part of the Trust C property? Again Trust A would have Mary's property and Trust B would be funded with $600,000. However, to equalize the two estates as of Andre's death, the non-QTIP (NQ) portion of Trust C plus Trust B must equal the value of the combined estates divided by two. Since both the combined value of the estates and Trust B's value are known, one simply solves for NQ, i.e., NQ = ($800,000 + $3,000,000)/2 - 600,000 = $1,300,000. Now what? The trustee divides this amount between Trust C_E (which this time will not be QTIP'ed) and Trust C_{NQ} (which also will not be QTIP'ed), and the balance goes into Trust C_Q which will be QTIP'ed. Trust C_E receives $400,000, which together with Trust B, is allocated the exemption. Trust C_{NQ} receives $900,000 [$1,300,000 - $400,000] and the balance of Trust C is allocated to Trust C_Q. Thus Trust C_Q (and the marital deduction) will be $1,100,000 [$2,400,000 - $1,300,000]. Recap: Andre's estate: $3,000,000 - $1,100,000 = $1,900,000. And, Mary's estate as of Andre's death: $800,000 + $1,100,000 = $1,900,000.

Where does all this take us? Why so many different trusts? First, the combination of the Trust B and the Trust C_Q assure that S1's full exemption will be utilized even if all of the Trust C property is QTIP'ed. Remember, a QTIP tosses the QTIP'ed property into S2's gross estate, where for GSTT (and estate tax, too) it is treated as a transfer from S2. The reverse QTIP allows QTIP'ed property to be treated as if it came from S1, but only for the purpose of using up S1's GSTT exemption. It does not affect the QTIP marital deduction. Then why have a separate Trust C_E if no QTIP election is made, after all the Trust C property will be taxed only in S1's estate and the exemption (to the extent not allocated to Trust B) can be allocated to it? When the plan was designed all Andre and Mary's children were alive. If the children outlived their parents no GST would occur. However, since the remaindermen's interests in Trusts B and C do not vest until after S2's death, a GST may occur as to property in those trusts even if all three children are alive when S1 dies. A GST may occur if any children die, leaving issue, before S2 dies. The predeceased parent rule applies only to direct skips, and since S2's interest in these trusts intervenes, a grandchild would not move up a generation even if his or her parent dies before the grandchild's interest vests. By creating trusts with zero inclusion ratios (Trust B and Trust C_E) and requiring that distributions to skip persons be made first from those trusts, with all trusts used to adjust distributions to accomplish a "by right of representation" distribution, the GSTT will be kept to a minimum. By having

Trust C_Q charged with the taxes at S2's death rather than taking them out of Trust C_E also serves the purpose of reducing the GSTT impact.

> EXAMPLE 12 - 31. Consider what happens at Mary's death, assuming that the executor at Andre's death QTIP'ed to postpone all taxes, and between the two deaths Tom died, leaving two adult children. At the time of Mary's death the four trusts had the following net values:

	FMV		Tax		Net to Distribute
Trust A	$1,100,000	-	$194,000	=	$906,000
Trust B	$700,000	-	$0	=	$700,000
Trust C_E	$500,000	-	$0	=	$500,000
Trust C_Q	$2,300,000	-	$1,399,000	=	$901,000
Totals	$4,600,000	-	$1,593,000		$3,007,000

> S2's taxable estate is equal to the combined values of Trust A and both Trust C's. The tax on an estate of $3,900,000 is $1,593,000. Trust A is charged with the amount of estate tax it would have paid had it alone been taxed, and since the estate tax on a taxable estate of $1,100,000 is $194,000, said amount is charged to Trust A. The balance of the estate tax, in the amount of $1,399,000 [$1,593,000- $194,000], is charged to Trust C_Q. Since the two living children receive one-third of the after tax value of the trusts, each "share" is $1,002,333. Tom's two children will divide a $1,002,333 share. Because they are skip persons, their share comes first from Trusts B and C_E. These two trusts have sufficient assets to satisfy their share and, because of the trusts have a zero inclusion ratio, the bequest to them is completely sheltered from GSTT. Indeed, since the rest of the estate is treated as coming from Mary (S2) no distributions would be hit with a GSTT even if all three of the children had died before Mary.

> EXAMPLE 12 - 32. Next consider what happens at Mary's death assuming that it occurs more than ten years after Andre's death (no PTC to worry about) and that Trust C had been QTIP'ed to equalize estates. Again, between the two deaths Tom died leaving two adult children. At the time of Mary's death, the five trusts had the following net values:

	FMV		Tax allocated		Net to Distribute
Trust A	$1,100,000	-	$194,000	=	$906,000
Trust B	$700,000	-	$0	=	$700,000
Trust C_E	$500,000	-	$0	=	$500,000
Trust C_{NQ}	$900,000	-	$0	=	$900,000
Trust C_Q	$1,400,000	-	$639,000	=	$761,000
Totals	$4,600,000		$833,000		$3,767,000

S2's taxable estate is equal to the combined values of Trust A and Trust C_Q, i.e., $2,500,000. The tax on $2,500,000 is $833,000. Trust A is charged with taxes of $194,000 and the balance of $639,000 [$833,000- $194,000] is charged to Trust C_Q. Since one-third of the after-tax value of the trusts is $1,002,000, with the grandchildren's share coming completely from Trusts B and C_E completely sheltered from GSTT.

EXAMPLE 12 - 33. Finally, consider what would have happened if the facts were as described in the prior example, except that Carol had also died leaving one child. Now two-thirds of the estate is left to skip persons (insofar as Andre is concerned). The Trusts and the allocation of the regular death estate taxes remains the same. The grandchildren's total after-tax share (before GSTT) is worth $2,004,000; of which $1,200,000 is drawn from Trusts B and C_E. The balance of $804,000 can be drawn from trusts taxed in Mary's estate. Mary is the transferor of the $804,000. Since Tom and Carol pre-deceased Mary, the predeceased parent rule moves the grandchildren up a generation vis-a-vis Mary, and no GSTT is due. Only distributions from Trust C_{NQ} are neither sheltered by the exemption nor treated as transfers from Mary. However, all distributions from Trust C_{NQ} will be to children, thus no GSTT. Hence, only if all three children predeceased Mary would there be a GSTT and the taxable amount would be the amount in Trust C_{NQ}.

Credit for Certain State Taxes

If a generation-skipping transfer (other than a direct skip) occurs at the same time as, and as a result of, the death of an individual, there is allowed a credit against the federal GSTT equal to the lesser of the state GSTT or 5% of the federal GSTT.[29] Most states have simply adopted a state GSTT "pickup" tax equal to 5% of the federal GSTT for such indirect skips.

Certain Transfers Excluded from the GSTT

The annual exclusion applies to GST present interest inter vivos gifts. Those inter vivos gifts that would not be treated as taxable gifts because of §2503(e) (payments directly to educational institutions or to medical providers) are also excluded from the definition of a GST.[30]

Grandfathering in Some Grand Old Trusts

Some generation-skipping trusts that were around when the GSTT laws went into effect are exempt from the GSTT. To be grandfathered, a trust had to be irrevocable as of September 25, 1985; or the skip must be caused by a will, a testamentary trust, or a trust in existence on October 21, 1986 that became irrevocable as a result of the testator or trustor's death before January 1, 1987. A grandfathered trust will lose its exempt status if the trustee accepts additions of property, or if modifications are made to it, after the dates just mentioned.

The Need for GSTT Planning

It should be evident by now that planning for the one million dollar lifetime GSTT exemption requires careful thought and attentive drafting of complex will or trust clauses, and can add considerably to the expense of estate planning. It also forces the planner to openly discuss with the client an unpleasant fact: the eventual death of the client's children.

No GSTT planning necessary for some clients. Which wealthier clients most probably *do not need* GSTT planning? First, clients with estates not expected to exceed one million dollars when combined with taxable gifts need not ever worry about a GSTT. They may, however, wish to do some trust planning to skip a generation by transferring some property for the benefit of their grandchildren, confident that GSTT law will automatically allocate the one million dollar exemption at their death, so that all trusts created will have an inclusion ratio of zero.

Second, those who do not wish to directly include grandchildren in their plan may not need GSTT planning. For example, clients preferring a 100%

marital deduction plan, as in a simple will, probably want their property to pass entirely to the surviving spouse and the children, all of whom are nonskip persons. Even clients anticipating a bypass may have no wish to provide for grandchildren. Of course, with either plan the property may wind up passing under the instrument to grandchildren (i.e., "descendants" or "issue") if a child predeceases a grandchild. However, the property involved may be sheltered from the GSTT under the *predeceased parent exception*, with the help of some careful drafting, to ensure that a direct skip will in fact occur or that the interest is covered by the one million dollar exemption.

Third, in some situations, GSTT trust planning will suggest that person leave the estate *outright to the children*, perhaps with just the hope and a prayer that the children will preserve the property for ultimate disposition to the grandchildren. Having a large estate divided amongst the transferor's children may actually result in a greater amount finally landing in the hands of the grandchildren. This may occur due to two factors: (1) the use of each child's unified credit can reduce the overall estate tax, but they would not be effective against the GSTT if the property stayed in a bypass trust; and (2) effective marginal estate tax rate just above the exclusion amount is lower than the 55% GSTT tax rate.

Clients needing GSTT planning. Which wealthier clients are most likely to need careful GSTT planning? Any of the following:

▶ "dynastic"-oriented clients wishing to perpetuate their wealth,
▶ clients with wealthy children,
▶ clients who believe that their children cannot handle large amounts of money maturely, and
▶ clients who wish to give to their grandchildren things that their children cannot or will not give.

Summary. There are several methods of at least partially circumventing the GSTT, particularly through the use of the one million dollar GSTT exemption. In general, only family estates exceeding $2 million in total value at the first spouse's death are prevented from arranging totally GSTT-free generation-skipping transfers.

Generation-skipping planning is modestly popular to clients today. However, interest in generation-skipping estate planning should grow in the years to come, if only because clients will be living longer and will be more likely to know their great grandchildren. A recent U.S. Census Bureau report concluded that by 2040, the nation could have more people over 65 than under 21, and that the *four-generation family* will become common.

QUERIES ANSWERED

1. Since Trust B is valued at $1,050,000 and the desired taxable estate in 2001 to postpone taxes until S2's death is $675,000, S1's estate needs an additional marital deduction of $375,000. Therefore,

$$QTIP\ fraction\ =\ \frac{\$375,000}{\$1,050,000}$$

2. The numerator of the fraction is the amount necessary to bring S1's estate equal to S2's, and the denominator is the value of Trust C. Total value of their combined estates divided by two [$6,270,368 ÷ 2 = $3,135,184] gives the desired taxable estate at S1's death. Subtract that amount from S1's estate to arrive at the needed marital deduction [$4,872,800 - $3,135,184 = $1,737,616]. Therefore, the QTIP fraction is $1,737,616/$4,272,800 which, since the value of Trust C is the same as the denominator of the fraction, results in a taxable estate for S1 of: $4,872,800 - $1,737,616 = $3,135,184.

QUESTIONS AND PROBLEMS

FACTS FOR 1 - 9: S1 and S2 lived in a common law state. S1 owned property having a net value of $4,487,287 and S2 owned property having a net value of $1,321,980. Assume debts and expenses are zero, and that no prior transfer credit is available because the two deaths are more than 10 years apart. The numbers for the AsuperB at S1's death will not change regardless of what S1's executor does insofar as making the QTIP election, but the A and the dC trusts in the ABdC plan depend upon whether or not S2 disclaims, and if she does, then to what extent she disclaims. The second part of each problem asks you to determine S2's taxable estate. For that calculation you will be given the value of the trusts as of S2's death; of course, these are made up numbers that factor in some growth between the first and second death.

1.1 The couple had an AsuperB Trust estate plan. S1's executor elected to postpone all taxes until S2 died, but fully utilize S1's unified credit. Determine: (a) S1's gross estate; (b) the values of Trust A and Trust B; (c) the QTIP fraction; and (d) how the fraction is applied to arrive at the taxable estate.

1.2 Determine S2's taxable estate given that Trust A was then worth $2,298,923 and Trust B $7,045,041.

2.1 The couple had an AsuperB Trust estate plan. S1's executor elected to pay all taxes at S1's death. Determine: (a) the QTIP fraction; (b) show how it is applied to arrive at the desired taxable estate.

2.2 Determine S2's taxable estate given that Trust A was then worth $2,298,923 and Trust B $4,555,008.

3.1 The couple had an AsuperB Trust estate plan. S1's executor elected to make a QTIP election that would equalize the two estates, at least as of S1's death. Determine: (a) the QTIP fraction; (b) show how it is applied to arrive at the desired taxable estate.

3.2 Determine S2's taxable estate given that Trust A was then worth $2,298,923 and Trust B $5,400,535.

4.1 The couple had an AsuperB Trust estate plan. S1's executor elected to make a QTIP election such that S1's taxable estate would equal $2,330,000. Determine: (a) the QTIP fraction; (b) show how it is applied to arrive at the desired taxable estate.

4.2 Determine S2's taxable estate given that Trust A was then worth $2,298,923 and Trust B $5,868,012.

5.1 The couple had an ABdC Trust estate plan. The widow chose not to disclaim any property. Determine: (a) S1's gross estate; (b) the values of Trust A, Trust B, and Trust C; and (c) S1's taxable estate.

5.2 Determine S2's taxable estate given that Trust A was then worth $6,641,322 and Trust B $875,400.

6.1 The couple had an ABdC Trust estate plan. S2 and the executor for S1's estate worked together. S2 disclaimed all property that would otherwise have flowed into Trust A; S1's executor elected to pay all taxes at S1's death. Determine: (a) S1's gross estate; (b) the values of Trust A, Trust B, and Trust C [remember that Trust C is equal to the value of the property disclaimed]; (c) S1's taxable estate.

6.2 Determine S2's taxable estate given that Trust A was then worth $2,298,923, Trust B $597,883, and Trust C $3,873,571.

7.1 The couple had an ABdC Trust estate plan. S2 and the executor for S1's estate worked together, S2 disclaimed all property that would otherwise have flowed into Trust A; S1's executor elected to make a QTIP election that would equalize the two estates, at least as of S1's death. Determine: (a) the values of Trust A, Trust B, and Trust C; (b) the QTIP fraction and (c) show how it is applied to arrive at the desired taxable estate.

7.2 Determine S2's taxable estate given that Trust A was then worth $2,298,923, Trust B $799,842, and Trust C $5,182,024.

8.1 The couple had an ABdC Trust estate plan. S2 and the executor for S1's estate worked together. S2 disclaimed just enough property to equalize the estates, at least as of S1's death; S1's executor made no QTIP election. Determine: (a) the values of Trust A, Trust B, and Trust C; (b) show how this disclaimer works to bring about the desired taxable estate.

8.2 Determine S2's taxable estate given that Trust A was then worth $5,051,157, Trust B $667,134, and Trust C $2,562,798.

9.1 The couple had an ABdC Trust estate plan. S2 and the executor for S1's estate worked together, S2 disclaimed just enough property to bring S1's taxable estate to $1,500,000; S1's executor made no QTIP election. Determine: (a) the values of Trust A, Trust B, and Trust C; (b) show how this disclaimer works to bring about the desired taxable estate.

9.2 Determine S2's taxable estate given that Trust A was then worth $7,493,815, Trust B $790,897, and Trust C $1,186,346.

FACTS FOR 10 - 18: S1 and S2 lived in a community property state. S1 owned property having a net value of $2,220,480 and S2 owned property having a net value of $800,660, and they owned community property worth

$1,596,400. Assume debts and expenses are zero and that no prior transfer credit is available because the two deaths are more than 10 years apart.

10.1 The couple had an AsuperB Trust estate plan. S1's executor elected to postpone all taxes until S2 died, but fully utilize S1's unified credit. Determine: (a) S1's gross estate; (b) the values of Trust A and Trust B; (c) the QTIP fraction; and (d) how the fraction is applied to arrive at the taxable estate.
10.2 Determine S2's taxable estate given that Trust A was then worth $2,845,970 and Trust B $$5,373,250.

11.1 The couple had an AsuperB Trust estate plan. S1's executor elected to pay all taxes at S1's death. Determine: (a) the QTIP fraction; (b) show how it is applied to arrive at the desired taxable estate.
11.2 Determine S2's taxable estate given that Trust A was then worth $2,845,970 and Trust B $3,400,523.

12.1 The couple had an AsuperB Trust estate plan. S1's executor elected to make a QTIP election that would equalize the two estates, at least as of S1's death. Determine: (a) the QTIP fraction; (b) show how it is applied to arrive at the desired taxable estate.
12.2 Determine S2's taxable estate given that Trust A was then worth $2,845,970 and Trust B $4,057,301.

13.1 The couple had an AsuperB Trust estate plan. S1's executor elected to make a QTIP election such that S1's taxable estate would equal $1,500,000. Determine: (a) the QTIP fraction; (b) show how it is applied to arrive at the desired taxable estate.
13.2 Determine S2's taxable estate given that Trust A was then worth $2,845,970 and Trust B $4,727,110.

14.1 The couple had an ABdC Trust estate plan. The widow chose not to disclaim any property. Determine: (a) S1's gross estate; (b) the values of Trust A, Trust B, and Trust C; and (c) S1's taxable estate.
14.2 Determine S2's taxable estate given that Trust A was then worth $7,151,221 and Trust B $1,068,000.

15.1 The couple had an ABdC Trust estate plan. S2 and the executor for S1's estate worked together, S2 disclaimed all property that would otherwise have flowed into Trust A; S1's executor elected to pay all taxes at S1's death. Determine: (a) S1's gross estate; (b) the values of Trust A, Trust B, and Trust C [remember that Trust C is equal to the value of the property disclaimed]; (c) S1's taxable estate.

15.2 Determine S2's taxable estate given that Trust A was then worth $2,845,970, Trust B $675,896, and Trust C $2,724,627.

16.1 The couple had an ABdC Trust estate plan. S2 and the executor for S1's estate worked together. S2 disclaimed all property that would otherwise have flowed into Trust A; S1's executor elected to make a QTIP election that would equalize the two estates, at least as of S1's death. Determine: (a) the values of Trust A, Trust B, and Trust C; (b) the QTIP fraction and (c)show how it is applied to arrive at the desired taxable estate.

16.2 Determine S2's taxable estate given that Trust A was then worth $2,845,970, Trust B $806,439, and Trust C $3,250,862.

17.1 The couple had an ABdC Trust estate plan. S2 and the executor for S1's estate worked together. S2 disclaimed just enough property to equalize the estates, at least as of S1's death; S1's executor made no QTIP election. Determine: (a) the values of Trust A, Trust B, and Trust C; (b) show how this disclaimer works to bring about the desired taxable estate.

17.2 Determine S2's taxable estate given that Trust A was then worth $4,109,611, Trust B $726,013, and Trust C $2,067,648.

18.1 The couple had an ABdC Trust estate plan. S2 and the executor for S1's estate worked together. S2 disclaimed just enough property to bring S1's taxable estate to $1,500,000; S1's executor made no QTIP election. Determine: (a) the values of Trust A, Trust B, and Trust C; (b) show how this disclaimer works to bring about the desired taxable estate.

18.2 Determine S2's taxable estate given that Trust A was then worth $5,549,221, Trust B $809,544, and Trust C $1,214,316.

FACTS FOR 19: S1 died May 7, 1994, survived by S2 who was then 70 years old. The federal rate for valuing split interests (life estates, etc.) was 8%. They had an ABC plan that named their children as remaindermen of all trusts. At S1's death their holdings had the following net value:

S1's separate	$3,450,090
S2's separate	$1,970,400
Total value	$5,420,490

S1's executor QTIP'ed Trust C to equalize the two estates and paid estate taxes of $944,430; of which $787,928 was federal tax and $156,502 was state.

S2 died August 23, 1995 and the trusts had the following values:

Trust A	$2,246,256
Trust B	$496,761
Trust C	$2,359,691

S2's taxable estate was $2,858,800. The estate would have had to pay state taxes of $169,574 and federal taxes of $853,590 without the PTC credit.

19.1 Determine, as of S1's death: (a) the value of Trust A, Trust B, and Trust C; (b) the QTIP fraction necessary to equalize the two estates; and (c) S1's taxable estate.

19.2 Given the information on the values for the three trusts at S2's death, show how one arrives at S2's taxable estate.

19.3 Determine: Limit one.

19.4 Determine: Limit two.

19.5 Determine: (a) the PTC after adjusting for time; (b) the state death tax; and (c) the federal estate tax.

19.6 Had S1's executor postponed all taxes to the second death, the value of the three trusts, given the same percentage growth, would have been as follows: Trust A $2,246,256; Trust B$684,000; and Trust C $3,249,103. This would have resulted in state death tax of $450,243 and federal tax of $2,020,204. (a) How much more total tax would have been paid? (b) What is the net value going to the children in each case. [In both cases, subtract the death taxes at S2's death from the value of the trusts at that time, since any taxes at S1's death had already been paid (and removed) from the trusts.] (c) Why is the difference in tax not equal to the difference in the amount going to the children?

FACTS FOR 20: S1 died on September 15, 1994, survived by S2 who was then 80 years old. The federal rate for valuing split interests (also called the §7520 rate) was 6%. They had an ABC plan that named their children as remaindermen of all trusts. At S1's death their holdings had the following net value:

S1's separate	$2,549,000
community property	$864,500
S2's separate	$1,284,600
Total value	$4,698,100

S1's executor QTIP'ed Trust C to equalize the two estates and paid estate taxes of $759,035, of which $632,311 was federal tax and $126,724 was state.

S2 died December 10, 1997 and the trusts had grown about 11%, having the values as follows:

Trust A	$1,905,704
Trust B	$496,435
Trust C	$1,970,225

S2's taxable estate was $2428780, the estate would have had to pay state taxes of $133102 and federal taxes of $665000 without the PTC credit.

20.1 Determine, as of S1's death: (a) the value of Trust A, Trust B, and Trust C; (b) the QTIP fraction necessary to equalize the two estates; and (c) S1's taxable estate.
20.2 Given the information on the values for the three trusts at S2's death, show how one arrives at S2's taxable estate.
20.3 Determine: Limit one.
20.4 Determine: Limit two.
20.5 Determine: (a) the PTC after adjusting for time; (b) the state death tax; and (c) the federal estate tax.
20.6 Had S1's executor postponed all taxes to the second death, the value of the three trusts, given the same percentage growth, would have been as follows: Trust A $1,905,704; Trust B $666,000; and Trust C

$2,643,188. This would have resulted in state death tax of $341,076 and federal tax of $1,608,814. (a) How much more total tax would have been paid? (b) What is the net value going to the children in each case. (c) Why is the difference in tax not equal to the difference in the amount going to the children?

FACTS FOR 21: S1 died April 15, 1992, survived by S2 who was then 60 years old. The federal rate for valuing split interests was 12%. They had an AsuperB plan with their children named as the remaindermen. At S1's death their holdings had the following net value:

S1's separate	$3,900,700
S2's separate	$480,640
Total value	$4,381,340

S1's executor QTIP'ed Trust B so as to equalize both estates, at least as of S1's death, and paid estate taxes of $681,428; of which $567,375 was federal and $114,054 was state.

S2 died November 18, 1993. The trusts had grown by about 9% [the tax at S1's death was paid from trust B], therefore the trusts had the following values:

Trust A	$523,898
Trust B	$3,509,006

Since S2's taxable estate was $2,062,213, the estate would have had to pay state taxes of $104,079 and federal taxes of $514,707 without PTC credit.

21.1 Determine as of S1's death: (a) the value of Trust A and Trust B; (b) the QTIP fraction necessary to equalize the two estates at S1's death.

21.2 Given the information on the values for the two trusts at S2's death, show how one arrives at S2's taxable estate.

21.3 Determine: Limit one.

21.4 Determine: Limit two.

21.5 Determine: (a) the PTC after adjusting for time; (b) the state death tax; and (c) the federal estate tax.

FACTS FOR 22: S1 died May 5, 1996, survived by S2, who was then 75 years old. The federal rate was 10%. They had an AsuperB plan. At S1's death their holdings had the following net value:

S1's separate	$3,798,400
community property	$945,050
S2's separate	$1,304,500
Total value	$6,047,950

S1's executor QTIP'ed Trust B such that S1's taxable estate was $3,425,282 and paid estate taxes of $1,331,905; of which $1,109,878 was federal and $222,027 was state.

S2 died October 10, 1996. The trusts had grown by about 5% [S1's estate taxes were paid from Trust B], therefore the trusts had the following values:

Trust A	$1,865,876
Trust B	$3,085,971

S2's taxable estate was $2,476,899. The estate would have had to pay state taxes of $136,952 and federal taxes of $684,728 without the PTC credit.

22.1 Determine as of S1's death: (a) the value of Trust A and Trust B; (b) the QTIP fraction necessary to have a taxable estate equal the desired S1 taxable estate.

22.2 Given the information on the values for the two trusts at S2's death, show how one arrives at S2's taxable estate.

22.3 Determine: Limit one.

22.4 Determine: Limit two.

22.5 Determine: (a) the PTC after adjusting for time; (b) the state death tax; and (c) the federal estate tax.

23. The Drexlers own a total of $2 million in assets, with one-half owned by each spouse. Their simple wills pass property from S1 to S2, then at S2's death all property passes outright to their *grandchildren* (rather than to their children). They believe that their property will not be subjected to the GSTT because they each have a one million dollar GSTT exemption. Explain what would happen with their present arrangement and how they could effectively avoid the GSTT.

24.   A bypass trust provides for income to the trustor's wife for her life, then remainder outright to his daughter, if she survives her mother; otherwise, to the daughter's *issue*.
    a. Could there be a potential GSTT problem?
    b. Is the size of the trust a factor?
    c. Can you suggest a solution to the problem?

25.   Burdick, a widower, wanted his grandchildren, Diana and Chris, to ultimately receive the bulk of his estate. So, at his death he created two irrevocable trusts, which, after payment of estate taxes, each had a net worth of one million dollars. Burdick's daughter, Heather, will receive all income from each trust for her lifetime, after which the trusts will terminate, and be distributed to the grandchildren. Diana's trust contains only fixed income securities and Heather's trust only common stock. The corpus of Diana's trust remained unchanged, while the corpus of Heather's trust tripled between Burdick's death and Heather's death.

    a. Calculate the GSTT due at Heather's death for Diana's trust, for Heather's trust, and for both trusts combined. Assume, alternatively, that at his death, the executor for Burdick's estate allocated the one million dollar GSTT exemption in the following manner:
        1. Entirely to Diana's trust.
        2. One-half to Diana's trust and one-half to Heather's trust.
        3. Entirely to Heather's trust.
    b. What conclusions can be drawn?

26.   a. How does the reverse QTIP election work?
    b. Is it needed to obtain a marital deduction?

27.   Which clients do not need to worry too much about GSTT planning and which ones do need to worry about it?

28.   Explain the GSTT exemption.

ANSWERS TO THE QUESTIONS AND PROBLEMS:

FOR 1 - 9: common law state. S1 $4,487,287 & S2 $1,321,980.

1.1 AsuperB Postpone: (a) S1's GE [$4,487,287]; (b) Tr A [$1,321,980] and Tr B [$4,487,287]; (c) the QTIP [$3,887,287/$4,487,287]; and (d) applied to arrive at the TxE [fraction times Tr B = MD, GE - MD = TxE = $600,000].

1.2 S2's TxE [Tr A + QTIP x Tr B = $8,401,964],Tr A $2,298,923 and Tr B $7,045,041.

2.1 AsuperB Trust. pay taxes: (a) the QTIP [no QTIP or 0% or 0/Tr B]; (b) TxE [Tr B only,$4,487,287].

2.2 S2's TxE [Tr A only, $2,298,923];Tr A $2,298,923, Tr B $4,555,008.

3.1 AsuperB. QTIP to equalize: (a) the QTIP [$1,582,654/$4,487,287]; (b) TxE [(Tr A + Tr B)/2 = $2,904,634].

3.2 S2's TxE [Tr A + QTIP x Tr B = $4,203,677]; Tr A $2,298,923 and Tr B $5,400,535.

4.1 AsuperB. QTIP so S1's TxE equals $2,330,000. (a) the QTIP [GE - desired taxable estate = MD (numerator); MD/Tr B = QTIP fraction, i.e., $2,157,287/$4,487,287]; (b) arrive at the desired TxE [S1's GE - (QTIP x Tr B), i.e., $2,330,000].

4.2 S2's TxE [Tr A + QTIP x Tr B = $5,120,001]; Tr A $2,298,923 and Tr B $5,868,012.

5.1 ABdC. no disclaimer (a) S1's GE [$4,487,287]; (b)Tr A [$5,209,267], Tr B [$600,000], and Tr C [zero]; and (c) S1's TxE [$600,000].

5.2 S2's TxE [$6,641,322]; Tr A $6,641,322 and Tr B $875,400.

6.1 ABdC. S2 disclaimed all property, S1's exe. paid all taxes. (a) S1's GE [$4,487,287]; (b) Tr A [$1,321,980],Tr B [$600,000],Tr C [$3,887,287]; (c) S1's TxE [$4,487,287].

6.2 S2's TxE [$2,298,923], Tr A $2,298,923, Tr B $597,883, Tr C $3,873,571.

7.1 ABdC. S2 disclaimed all property, QTIP to equalize: (a)Tr A [$1,321,980], Tr B [$600,000], Tr C [$3,887,287]; (b) the QTIP [$1,582,654/$3,887,287]; (c) TxE [$2,904,634].

7.2 S2's TxE [$2,298,923 + $2,109,788 = $4,408,711; notice that Trust B exceeds The exclusion amount but is not taxed @ S2's death] Tr A $2,298,923, Tr B $799,842, Tr C $5,182,024.

8.1 ABdC. S2 disclaimed just enough to equalize, no QTIP: (a)Tr A [$2,904,634], Tr B [$600,000], Tr C [$2,304,634]; (b) show works to TxE [$4,487,287 - $1,582,654 = $2,904,634; notice that Tr A = Tr B + Tr C].

8.2 S2's TxE [$5,051,157]. Tr A $5,051,157, Tr B $667,134, Tr C $2,562,798.

9.1 ABdC. Disclaimed to bring S1's TxE to $1,500,000: (a) Tr A [S2's estate + (S1's estate > $1,5000,000) = $4,309,267], Tr B [$600,000],Tr C [$900,000]; (b) show works to TxE [S1's estate > $1,5000,000 = MD = $2987287; TxE = S1's estate - MD = $1,500,000].

9.2 S2's TxE [Tr A only; $7,493,815] Tr A $7,493,815, Tr B $790,897, Tr C $1,186,346.

FOR 10 - 18: community property state. S1 $2,220,480; S2 $800,660; community $1,596,400.

10.1 AsuperB. Postpone: (a) S1's GE [$3,018,680]; (b) Tr A [S2 + ½ * cp = $1,598,860] & Tr B [S1 + ½ * cp = $3,018,680]; (c) the QTIP [MD/Tr B = $2,418,680/$3,018,680]; and (d) applied to arrive at the TxE [fraction times Tr B = MD; and GE - MD = TxE = $600,000].

10.2 S2's TxE [7151220]; Tr A $2,845,970 and Tr B $5,373,250.

11.1 AsuperB. Pay all taxes: (a) the QTIP [zero]; (b) applied to arrive at TxE [No marital deduction, therefore TxE = Tr B = $3,018,680].

11.2 S2's TxE [Tr A = $2,845,970]; Tr A $2,845,970 and Tr B $3,400,523.

12.1 AsuperB. QTIP to equalize: (a) the QTIP [$709,910/$3,018,680]; (b) applied to arrive at the desired TxE [GE - MD = $2,308,770].

12.2   S2's TxE [$3,800,135] Tr A $2,845,970 and Tr B $4,057,301.

13.1   AsuperB. QTIP S1's TxE equals $1,500,000. (a) the QTIP [(Tr B-$1,500,000)/Tr B]; (b) applied to arrive at the desired TxE *Notice that S1's GE goes into Tr B; the MD is that QTIP fraction times Tr B that produces a number that when subtracted from Tr B results in the desired taxable estate.* [TxE = Tr B - (Tr B*(Tr B - $1,500,000)/Tr B)) = $1,500,000.]

13.2   S2's TxE [$5,224,151]; Tr A $2,845,970 and Tr B $4,727,110.

14.1   ABdC. No disclaimer. (a) S1's GE [$3,018,680]; (b)Tr A [$4,017,540], Tr B [$600,000], and Tr C [zero]; and (c) S1's TxE [$600,000].

14.2   S2's TxE [$7,151,221]; Tr A $7,151,221 and Tr B $1,068,000.

15.1   ABdC. Disclaimed all & pay all taxes at S1's death. (a) S1's GE [$3,018,680]; (b) Tr A [$1,598,860], Tr B [$600,000], and Tr C [$2,418,680]; (c) S1's TxE [$3,018,680].

15.2   S2's TxE [$2,845,970] Tr A $2,845,970, Tr B $675,896, &Tr C $2,724,627.

16.1   ABdC. Disclaimed all & elected QTIP to equalize (a)Tr A [$1,598,860], Tr B [$600,000], and Tr C [$2,418,680]; (b) the QTIP [$709,910/$2,418,680]; and (c) to arrive at the desired TxE [$3,018,680 - $709,910 = $2,308,770].

16.2   S2's TxE [$3,800,135]; Tr A $2,845,970, Tr B $806,439, and Tr C $3,250,862.

17.1   ABdC. Disclaimed to equalize (a) Tr A [$2,308,770], Tr B [$600,000], and Tr C [$1,708,770]; (b) disclaimer works to bring about the desired TxE

17.2   S2's TxE [$4,109,611]; Tr A $4,109,611, Tr B $726,013, and Tr C $2,067,648.

18.1   ABdC. Disclaimed to bring S1's TxE to $1,500,000 (a) Tr A [$3,117,540], Tr B [$600,000], and Tr C [$900,000]; (b) disclaimer brings about the desired TxE [GE - MD = TxE = $1,500,000].

18.2 S2's TxE [$5,549,221]; Tr A $5,549,221, Tr B $809,544, and Tr C $1,214,316.

19.1 (a) Tr A [$1,970,400], Tr B [$600,000], and Tr C [$2,850,090]; (b) the QTIP to equalize [$739,845/$2,850,090]; (c) S1's TxE [$2,710,245].
19.2 S2's TxE [$2,858,800].
19.3 Limit one. [$455,044; factor .57752 x $787,928].
19.4 Limit two. [$587,296; S2's "reduced taxable estate" = $1,411,731 and the federal tax on it is $266,294].
19.5 (a) the PTC [$455,044; death within 2 years, therefore, 100% of the lower of the two limits]; (b) the St D Tx [$169,574; notice that it is as given, it did not change]; and (c) the FET[$853,590 - $455,044 = $398,545].
19.6 Compares postponing to above: Tr A $2,246,256, Tr B$684,000, and Tr C $3,249,103 and St D Tx $450,243 and FET $2,020,204. (a) tax difference? [equalized: postpone; ($944,430 + $169,574 + $398,545) - ($450,243 + $2,020,204) = $957,898]; (b) different net to the children [$5,102,708 - $568,119 = $4,534,589 versus $6,179,359 - $2,470,447 = $3,708,912; $4,534,589 - $3,708,912 = $825,677]; (c) Why is the difference in tax not equal to the difference in net to the children? *Some of what is lost by not using the PTC and the lower marginal rates (equalizing estates) is made up by the fact that postponing allows the amount that would have otherwise been paid at S1's death to grow between the two deaths.*

20.1 (a) Tr A [$1,716,850], Tr B [$600,000], and Tr C [$2,381,250]; (b) the QTIP to equalize [$632,200/$2,381,250]; and (c) S1's TxE [$2,349,050].
20.2 S2's TxE [$2,428,780].
20.3 Limit one. [$215,940; .34151 x $632,311].
20.4 Limit two. [$301,388].
20.5 (a) the PTC [80% x $215,940 = $172,752]; (b) the St D Tx [$133,102]; and (c) the FET.[$492,248].
20.6 Compares postponing to above: Tr A $1,905,704, Tr B $666,000, and Tr C $2,643,188 = $5,124,892. St D Tx of $341,076 and FET of $1,608,814. (a) tax difference? [equal: postpone; $1,384,385 -

$1,949,890 = $565,505; for equal estates, do not forget to add in tax at S1's death]; (b) different net to the children? [$4,372,364 - ($1,331,020 + $492,248) = $3,747,014 versus $5,124,892 - $1,949,890 = $3,265,002, therefore: $3,747,014 - $3,265,002 = $482,012]; (c) Why is the difference in tax not equal to the difference in net to the children? [See answer at 19.6.]

21.1   (a) Tr A [$480,640] and Tr B [$3,900,700]; (b) the QTIP to equalize. [$1,710,030/$3,900,700].

21.2   S2's TxE [Tr A + Tr C x ($1,710,030/$3,900,700) = $2,062,213].

21.3   Limit one. [.81376 x $567,375 = $461,707].

21.4   Limit two. [reduced S2 estate = zero, therefore zero tax & difference = $514,405].

21.5   (a) the PTC [lesser limit @ 100% (less than two years), i.e., $461,707]; (b) the St D Tx [$104,079, as given]; and (c) the FET.[$514,405 - $461,707 = $52,698].

22.1   (a) Tr A [$1,304,500 + ½ x $945,050 = $1,777,025] and Tr B [$3,798,400 + ½ x $945,050 = $4,270,925]; (b) QTIP to TxE equal desired S1 TxE [desired estate = $3,425,282 (given); (Tr B x $845,643/$4,270,925) = MD of $845,643; S1's E - MD = $4,270,925 - $845,643 = $3,425,282].

22.2   S2's TxE [Tr A + QF x Tr B = $1,865,876 + ($845,643/$4,270,925) x $3,085,971 = $2,476,899].

22.3   Limit one. [.56144 x $1,109,878 = $623,130].

22.4   Limit two. [Reduced S2 estate = $826,815; Fed tax on reduced estate = $61,371 & the difference = limit two = $623,358].

22.5   (a) the PTC [less than two years, 100% of the lower of the two limits = $623,130]; (b) the St D Tx [$136,952]; and (c) the FET.[$61,599].

23.   If S2 is survived by his or her grandchildren's parents, the Drexlers' property will not pass totally GSTT-free, under a simple will. At S2's death, S2's one million dollar exemption will be allocated to the entire $2 million transfer to the grandchildren. The result will be an inclusion ratio of 0.5 [$1 million/$2 million] and a GSTT on one-half of the property. In addition, asset values could appreciate before S2's death.

24. a. GSTT problem? There could be a potential GSTT problem if daughter fails to survive her mother. In that event, a transfer out of trust to the daughter's issue (e.g., a grandchild of the trustor) could be a taxable distribution subject to the GSTT. The predeceased parent direct skip exception rule would not apply. As a taxable distribution, it is not a direct skip.

  b. Size of the trust can be a factor because of the one million dollar GST exemption, which can exempt part or all of the distribution.

  c. The commonly used solution is to allocate a portion of the one million dollar exemption to the bypass trust assets.

25. a. Calculation of GSTT for different GSTT allocation arrangements. The GSTT will be incurred at Heather's death, because there will then be taxable distributions to the grandchildren. General rules:

Inclusion ratio = 1 minus (Amount of GSTT exemption allocated to transfer/Total value of property transferred)

GSTT = Taxable amount x .55 x Inclusion ratio.

  1. Entirely to Diana's trust.

GSTT on Diana's trust:
Inclusion ratio = 1 minus ($1 million/$1 million) = 0
  GSTT = $1 million x .55 x 0 = $0

GSTT on Heather's trust:
  Inclusion ratio = 1 minus ($0/$1 million) = 1.0
  GSTT = $3 million x .55 x 1.0 = $1,650,000

GSTT on Both trusts combined:
GSTT = $0 + $1,655,000 = $1,655,000

  2. One-half to Diana's Tr And one-half to Heather's trust.

Inclusion ratio for each trust = 1 - ($500,000/$1 million) = .5

GSTT on Diana's trust:
GSTT = $1 million x .55 x .5 = $275,000

GSTT on Heather's trust:
GSTT = $3 million x .55 x .5 = $825,000

GSTT on Both trusts combined:
GSTT = $275,000 + $825,000 = $1,100,000.

3. Entirely to Heather's trust.

GSTT on Diana's trust:
Inclusion ratio = 1 minus ($0/$1 million) = 1
GSTT = $1 million x .55 x 1 = $550,000

GSTT on Heather's trust:
Inclusion ratio = 1 minus ($1 million/$1 million) = 0
GSTT = $3 million x .55 x 0 = $0

GSTT on both trusts combined:
GSTT = $550,000 + $0 = $550,000

b. What conclusions can be drawn? Allocating the GSTT exemption entirely to Heather's trust, the trust containing the appreciating assets, saved the most GSTT. In general, one should allocate the exemption:
   1. so that each trust has an inclusion ratio of either exactly one or exactly 0, but not in between; and
   2. to the trust whose assets are most likely to appreciate by a greater amount.

26.a. Reverse QTIP? The property in the reverse QTIP trust is treated as if it came from S1 for GSTT purposes, therefore S1 is able to use the entire one million dollar GST exemption.
   b. No, the QTIP election obtains the marital deduction but creates the problem that the QTIP trust is then treated as if it came from S2. The reverse QTIP allows dual treatment, both the marital deduction and

treatment as if in S2's estate for regular estate taxes, and treatment as if it was only from S1 for GSTT purposes.

27. Clients whose estates are not expected to exceed one million dollars, and those who do not wish to directly include grandchildren in their plan, do not need to worry too much about the GSTT. For example, clients preferring a 100% marital deduction plan, as in a simple will, probably want their property to pass entirely to the surviving spouse and then to the children. Even clients anticipating a bypass may have no wish to provide for grandchildren. Of course, with either plan the property may wind up passing under the instrument to grandchildren (i.e., "issue") if a child predeceases a grandchild. However, the property involved can usually be sheltered from the GSTT under the predeceased parent direct skip rule, with the help of some careful drafting, to ensure that a direct skip will in fact occur.

Clients who should do some GSTT planning include: "dynastic" oriented clients wishing to perpetuate themselves through multi-generation trusts; clients with very wealthy children; clients who believe that their children cannot handle large amounts of money maturely; and clients who wish to give to their grandchildren significant amounts of wealth.

28. Explain the GSTT exemption. It is a one million dollar per donor exemption from the GSTT tax. It is allocated automatically to direct skips and can be allocated systematically to generation skipping trusts.

ENDNOTES

1. §6081

2. §2056(d)

3. §2056(d)(4)

4. §2056(d)(2)(A)

5. Reg. §26.2056A-2(d)

6. Reg.§20.2056A-3(a)

7. Reg. §20.2056A-2(d).

8. §2056(d)(2)(B)

9. §2056(d)(3)

10. §2056(b)(5)

11. The reader may wish to review the basic prior transfer credit material presented in Chapter 6 before tackling this material.

12. §2613(a).

13. §2602.

14. §2612(c)(1).

15. §2603(a)(3).

16. §2623.

17. §2624(b)

18. §2624(c)

19. §2612(a)(1)

20. §2612(b).

21. §2641(b).

22. §2631(c)(1).

23. §2642(a)

24. §2632(b)(1) - (b)(3).

25. §2651(e)(1)

26. §2651(e)(2)

27. Reg. §26.2612-1(a)(2)(i)

28. §2513.

29. §2604.

30. §2611(b)(1).

CHAPTER 13

Lifetime Transfers I: Overview and Survey of Gift Planning

OVERVIEW

The last two chapters focused on property transfers at death. This chapter will introduce lifetime transfers of property, examining the techniques utilized in *giving gifts*, the most popular type of intra-family lifetime transfer. The techniques of planning for other lifetime transfers, including incomplete transfers, intra-family sales, and charitable gifts will be described in Chapter 14.

Lifetime transfers take many forms and are made for many reasons. They are made to individuals and to charities. They are made outright or to a fiduciary, such as a trustee or custodian. They can take the form of a completed transfer, such as a sale or a gift; or they can remain incomplete, as in the case of a transfer with a retained interest. They include transfers of total interests in property or just partial interests.

While you read this chapter and the next, you will want to keep in mind two important principles. First, different types of transfers are designed to accomplish different types of goals. Second, the less complete the transfer, the less likely the transfer will achieve desired *tax* goals. This latter point cannot be over emphasized because donors often prefer to retain some control over the transferred property. By definition, every lifetime transfer requires the relinquishment of some control. Gifts mean loss of access, control, and flexibility; individuals who are reluctant to give this up are likely to feel uncomfortable with a gift giving program as part of their estate plan no matter what the magnitude of the financial rewards might be. Planners should be sensitive to this issue.

To minimize loss of access, control, and flexibility, some individuals may contemplate gifts to family members who secretly agree to always make the assets available to the donor. This arrangement is a retained interest which, if it came to light after the donor died, would cause the property to be included in the donor's estate. There are other problems with this arrangement: First, the donees may have a "change in attitude," later disposing of the gift asset or refusing to share it or return it. Second, the gift assets are subject to the claims of the donee's creditors.

We begin our discussion of lifetime transfers with an examination of completed lifetime gifts, hereafter simply called *gifts*. For present purposes, we shall define a gift as any transfer that gives rise to potential gift taxation. As explained in Chapter 7, a gift is *complete* for tax purposes when there is surrender of dominion and control and delivery of an interest in property by a donor capable of transferring that property to an accepting donee capable of receiving and possessing it.

Essentially, a gift may be made outright, or it may be made to another party, usually a fiduciary, for the benefit of the donee. An *outright* gift results in the receipt by the donee of a fee simple interest in the gift property, yielding to the donee all of the rights that accompany that interest. Thus, an outright gift extends to the donee the greatest flexibility of ownership and control.

However, the donor may not wish to bestow that degree of flexibility. For example, a donor may wish to make a sizable gift to help his or her child finance *future* college expenses, but may be reluctant to make an outright gift. The usual alternative to an outright gift is a transfer to a *fiduciary*, who is responsible for managing the property and distributing its income and principal in accordance with the legal conditions either contained in the underlying document or established by local law. Significant gifts for a minor are especially likely to be in the name of a fiduciary, such as a custodian, trustee, or guardian. Gifts to adult donees are usually outright but are sometimes made in trust.

The next two sections will describe the major non-tax and tax considerations in making substantial gifts. The discussions will assume an outright gift unless some other type of gift (e.g., one in trust) is specifically mentioned.

NON-TAX MOTIVES FOR MAKING GIFTS

Consider the many non-tax motivations that encourage people to make gifts, such as the desire by parents or grandparents to provide for an expensive education, to help children finance a home or an automobile, to help establish or expand a business, to encourage a child to work in the parent's business, to help a child who has experienced a significant loss or who is unemployed, to care for elderly parents, and the simple desire to witness a donee's enjoyment of the benefits that a gift can bring. Individuals will be most willing to make gifts for the *tax* advantages to be described next when they are also motivated by one or more of these *non-tax* objectives.

TAX CONSIDERATIONS IN MAKING GIFTS

One should consider the death tax and income tax advantages and disadvantages of making gifts.

Tax Advantages of Gifting

Gifts are commonly made to save federal, state, and local death taxes, GSTT, and federal, state, and local income taxes. In the examples that follow, look for two common tax threads. First, many gifts can be made at no gift tax cost. Second, even if a gift tax is incurred, gifts may still be desirable because they have the potential of reducing total transfer taxes and income taxes.

Death tax and GSTT advantages. Death tax and GSTT advantages include the ability to reduce or freeze the taxable estate in three ways: using the shelter of the annual exclusion and the unified credit, avoid grossing up the gift taxes, and excluding postgift appreciation. Each will be discussed next.

Shelter of annual exclusion and unified credit. Most people about to embark upon a program of gifting will be able to transfer a significant portion of their estate, free of gift tax, death tax, and GSTT. The gift tax and GSTT annual exclusions enable a donor to gift, free of tax, $10,000 (indexed for years after 1998) per donee per year. Couples can split gifts to double the amount to $20,000 per donee per year.

EXAMPLE 13 - 1. Mom wishes to gift maximum equal amounts of her own property to her three children and three grandchildren. Each of the six donees can receive $10,000 each year, gift tax and GSTT free, adding up to a current aggregate annual tax-free gift total of $60,000.

In the above example, because total gross gifts to any one donee during a given calendar year will amount to no more than the annual exclusion, the donor need not even file a gift tax return.

EXAMPLE 13 - 2. Altering the facts in Example 13-1 a bit, assume that Dad also wishes to make similar annual exclusion gifts of *his own* property interests. Each of the six donees can now receive $20,000 each year for a current annual gift total of $120,000. Neither parent needs to file a gift tax return.

EXAMPLE 13 - 3. In the $120,000 total gift example immediately above, if greater than $60,000 of the gift property belonged to one of the two donors, they would have to *split* the gifts by filing gift tax returns for each year. However, the tax outcome would be unchanged; of the total of $120,000 in gifts per year, no gift tax or GSTT would be due because taxable gifts would still equal zero.

Generalizing from these examples, the total number of annual exclusions available over time equals the number of donors times the number of donees times the number of years of gifting. Thus, in the above examples, if the donors engaged in gifting each year for the next eight years, they could make 96 annual exclusion gifts totaling at least $960,000 [i.e., (2 x 6 x 8) x $10,000]. As indexing results in higher annual exclusions, even more can be given without using up any unified credit.

Actually, a donor can give a much larger amount, gift tax (and GSTT) free, if the donor is willing to use up some unified credit (and, if applicable, the GST exemption). Thus, a couple with five suitable donees could give away, tax free, over three million dollars in the next 10 years. Of course, the couple would use up their unified credits, making any additional the lifetime or death-time taxable transfers subject to tax at the marginal rate of 41%. Regarding *GSTT*, a couple can gift, GSTT free, a total of $2 million (two $1 million lifetime GST exemptions). Gifts under the annual exclusion amount do not use up any of the donor's GST exemption. For the examples that immediately follow, we will us an annual exclusion amount of $10,000, even though by the year 2007 it is likely to be $12,000 or $13,000.

EXAMPLE 13 - 4. Prior to the year 2007, Corey, a bachelor, had already made total lifetime taxable gifts of that used up his exclusion amount. In the year 2007, he made a single gift of bonds worth $20,000. His gift tax is $4,100, determined as follows:

Gross Gift	$20,000
Less annual exclusion	($10,000)
Current taxable gift	$10,000
Plus prior taxable gifts	$1,000,000
Total Taxable gifts	$1,010,000
Tentative tax on total	$349,900
Less tentative tax on pre-1990 taxable gifts	($345,800)
Tentative tax on current gifts	$4,100
Less unused unified credit	$0
Gift tax payable	$4,100

Since the annual exclusion applies only to lifetime transfers, a somewhat different tax result would occur if the most recent transfer was made at death.

EXAMPLE 13 - 5. Assume the same basic facts as in Example 13-5, except that Corey died in the year 2007, still owning the bonds worth $20,000, and therefore transfers them at death. The estate tax due will be $8,200, calculated as follows:

Taxable estate	$20,000
Adjusted taxable gifts	$1,000,000
Estate tax base	$1,020,000
Tentative tax	$354,000
Less unified credit	$345,800
Estate tax	$8,200

The $4,100 difference in the tax for the two prior examples is due to the absence of a per donee exclusion in calculating the estate tax.

Summarizing, making annual exclusion gifts, gifts sheltered by the unified credit, and gifts sheltered by the GST exemption enable individuals to substantially reduce their gross estate without having to pay gift taxes or GST tax.

No grossing up. The second death tax and GSTT advantage of gifting is the ability to exclude from the gross estate the amount of any *gift tax* paid on gifts given more than three years before death. Unlike the estate tax, the gift tax is calculated on a tax-exclusive basis. Review the examples in the grossing up section of Chapter 6 that illustrate the estate tax advantage of paying a gift tax.

Postgift appreciation. The third death tax and GSTT advantage of gifting is the ability to exclude postgift appreciation of the gifted property from future estate tax and GSTT. Gifts accomplish this tax saving in two different ways. First, gifting will usually *freeze* estate tax values by limiting the estate tax value of the transferred asset to its adjusted gift value. Second, gifting can *leverage* the use of exclusions, exemptions, and the unified credit by transferring assets whose present low value is totally sheltered by these tax breaks, thereby excluding from estate tax and GSTT the entire value of the asset, including all future appreciation. The following example illustrates the usefulness of freezing and leveraging techniques.

> EXAMPLE 13 - 6. Eighty-two year old Jeanne's estate consists of $2 million in municipal bonds and $1 million in common stock. More than able to live well on the bond income, Jeanne gifts all of the stock to an irrevocable trust paying the income to her three children for their lives with the remainder going to her grandchildren. Jeanne allocates her $1 million GST exemption to this transfer. In this simple but effective estate freeze, Jeanne has virtually ensured that she will die with an estate tax base at about $3 million (assets owned at death plus adjusted taxable gifts), no matter how much the value of the stocks rise. And Jeanne has leveraged the use of her $1 million GST exemption. For example, if the stock is eventually worth $4 million when it passes to the grandchildren, each $1 in current GST exemption will have sheltered $4 from GSTT.

Comprehensive example. By way of a complete review of these three major tax advantages of making lifetime gifts, consider the following comprehensive example. Assume that all transfers occur between 2006 and 2016, the unified credit remains at $345,800 and that the annual exclusion remains at $10,000 (even though we know it will probably be around $14,000 by then). While the numbers focus solely on estate tax savings, please keep in mind that substantial GSTT savings would also occur if the gifts were to a skip person.

> EXAMPLE 13 - 7. In the year 2006, Burt, a widower who has made no prior taxable gifts, has a net estate of $5 million. He predicts that the property will double in value to $10 million in 10 years (his expected life span). While a planner would likely advise a number of gifts to take advantage of multiple annual exclusions over the years, for simplicity, we will assume that Burt agrees to make just one really big gift this year: $2,000,000 to his only child.

Suppose Burt makes the gift: Burt will pay a gift tax calculated as follows:

Gross Gift	$2,000,000
Less annual exclusion	($10,000)
Taxable gift	$1,990,000
Tentative tax	$776,300
Less unified credit	($345,800)
Gift tax payable	$430,500

Burt dies in the year 2016 with an estate valued at $5,139,000 He started with $5,000,000, but gave away $2,000,000 and paid gift taxes of $430,500. What remained was worth $2,569,500, which doubled over the decade. Burt's estate tax is calculated as follows:

Taxable estate	$5,139,000
Adjusted taxable gifts	$1,990,000
Estate tax base	$7,129,000
Tentative tax	$3,561,750
Less gift tax payable credit	($430,500)
Less unified credit	($345,800)
Estate tax	$2,785,450

Burt's child will receive a total of $6,353,550, which is the sum of the value of Burt's estate reduced by the estate tax (i.e., a net value of $2,353,550), plus $4 million, the date of death value of the gift property.

Burt does not make the gift: Alternatively, if Burt does not make the gift, the estate tax is calculated as follows:

Taxable estate	$10,000,000
Adjusted taxable gifts	$0
Estate tax base	$10,000,000
Tentative tax	$5,140,800
Less unified credit	($345,800)
Estate tax	$4,795,000

Burt's child will receive a total of $5,205,000, which is the estate of $10 million less the estate tax. This is $1,148,550 [$6,353,550 - $5,205,000] less than achieved by making the $2,000,000 gift.

Let's analyze the increased wealth to the next generation that results from making this large gift. As a result of Burt's gift, his son will receives $1,148550 more than he would have had without the gift. Since the changes occur at the top marginal rates, which for Burt's estate is 55% we should be able to track the source of the difference. Note that, because the gift tax was paid early, it did not have a chance to double, so that decrease what went to Burt's son. Here is a summary of elements (three positive and one negative) that cause the difference:

▸ appreciation on $2 million avoided tax @ 55%	$1,100,000
▸ the gift tax ($430,500, doubled) avoided tax @ 55%	$473,550
▸ annual exclusion avoided tax @ 55%	$5,500
▸ less the appreciation on the gift tax	($430,500)
Net increase to Burt's son	$1,148,550

This example assumed that Burt made only one lifetime gift to just one person, thereby reaping the benefit of only one annual exclusion. Substantially more transfer tax would be saved if Burt made many smaller gifts to several persons *each year* until his death, utilizing the shelter of multiple annual exclusions.

Must gifts be made more than three years before death to keep the assets out of the gross estate? No, donors can make deathbed gifts to take advantage of the annual exclusion. Only gifts of life insurance or the relinquishments of a §2036, §2037, or §2038 retained interest is subject to the three year rule.[1] The use of financial durable powers of attorney that allow an agent to make gifts on behalf of an incapacitated person are discussed in Chapter 17. The IRS has ruled that the document creating a durable power must expressly authorize the agent to make gifts, otherwise any gifts are considered to be revocable transfers and, therefore, incomplete.[2]

In conclusion, a program of gifting can result in substantial estate tax and GSTT savings and the ultimate transfer of a larger amount of wealth to succeeding generations. The gifts can be tax sheltered by the annual exclusion as well as by the exclusion of both the gift tax and postgift appreciation from the donor's taxable estate.

Income tax advantages. The making of gifts also offers some income tax advantages, including the shifting of income.

Shifting income. As we saw in earlier chapters, gifts can result in some income shifting. In general, because the donee (or trust, for gifts into an irrevocable trust) becomes the owner of gifted property, any income earned on that property will be taxed to the donee (or trustee or trust beneficiary), who is usually subject to a lower marginal income tax rate. Further, the reduced taxable income to the donor might put her or him in a lower tax bracket. As explained in more detail at the end of this chapter, outright gifts to children under age 14 will not save much income tax due to what is called the *kiddie tax*.

Where the kiddie tax does not apply, shifting income can save significant taxes for the family as a whole. For a single tax payer, the 15% bracket goes up to $25,750 in 1999 taxable income. In contrast, a *trust's* 15% bracket ends at taxable income of less than $2,000, reflecting Congress's strong interest in discouraging the use of trusts to shift income. Rather than making annual gifts to a relative to help with living expenses, it might be wise to transfer income producing assets, especially if the property is likely to return to the donor when the donee died.

> EXAMPLE 13 - 8. Each year, Aaron and his wife Sue made gifts of approximately $20,000 to Aaron's mother, Cynthia, to supplement her meager social security income. Since they were in a combined state and federal income tax bracket of 46%, they decided to transfer $300,000 in assets to Cynthia, with the understanding that she at her death she would leave the property to them. If the property produces $20,000 in taxable income, the income tax saved by the extended family is $6,200 ($20,000 * (43%-15%)) per year. Of course the transfer was a taxable gift, but Aaron and Sue might "regain" the unified credit used up by disclaiming the inheritance, and letting the property pass on to their own children. Cynthia's estate is not large enough to generate an estate tax, much less a GSTT.

Obtaining a step-up in basis. In Chapter 7, the reader learned that the income tax basis of any property owned by a decedent at death will be stepped-up to date of death value. This step-up is particularly valuable for people wishing to sell rapidly appreciating property. Unfortunately, the property owner must *die* to accomplish the step-up. Astute readers may wonder whether gifting may be able to accelerate the timing of this step-up. For example, could A, owner of a low basis asset and in excellent health, gift the asset to B, who is dying, to achieve an earlier basis step-up in the asset, which A will later sell after having received the asset back by way of B's will or trust? As we'll see in two examples later in the chapter, the answer is yes, as long as B doesn't die within one year of the gift date.

Tax Disadvantages of Gifting

There are several tax dangers and disadvantages in making lifetime gifts, including prepaying the transfer tax, adverse §2035 consequences, the danger that the gift is later ruled incomplete, and loss of step-up in basis.

Prepaying the transfer tax. A *large gift* can result in a gift tax liability that must be paid by April 15 of the following year, thereby reducing the donor's available funds for investment. Nonetheless, prepayment of the transfer tax is justifiable if it has the effect of substantially reducing the donor's estate tax. This will happen if the gift property appreciates greatly before the donor's death or if it appreciates modestly and the donor can avoid grossing up by surviving at least three years after making the gift. On the other hand, gifting property and prepaying the transfer tax may be a costly mistake if the property *declines* in value and/or the donor *dies within three years* of making the gift. Then, no transfer taxes will have been saved, the donor lost the use of the gift tax money, and the donee may have a lower carry over basis in the property. Thus, to assess the likelihood of financial success resulting from a large gift, the planner should consider factors such as the life expectancy of the donor, the expected appreciation potential of the property, the different basis rules, and the utility of the property to the donor and donee.

Even if a large gift is totally sheltered by the unified credit, it will have the effect of reducing the amount that can be transferred at death free of tax since it will be included in the estate tax base as an adjusted taxable gift. Before recommending large gifts or a gift-giving plan, the planner must also determine whether the gifts will also be subject to state gift tax since there is no federal credit for state gift taxes paid, whereas, there is a federal state death tax credit.[3]

An additional adverse §2035 consequence: unsheltered postgift appreciation. We mentioned in the preceding discussion that if a gift is made within three years of death, §2035(b) requires the gift tax paid to be included in the donor's gross estate under the "gross-up" rule. In addition to this adverse consequence, recall the discussion in Chapter 6 that the entire *date-of-death value* of the gift property is included in the donor's gross estate if the retained interest rules of §§2036, 2037, 2038 apply, or if an incident of ownership in life insurance was retained, §2042, at the date of death. Section 2035(a) causes inclusion if the decedent transferred (released) a retained interest or an incident of ownership in life insurance within three years of death.

In summary, §2035(a) and §2035(b) can have the effect of taking back all three major advantages of gifting. These two sections require grossing up of gift taxes and, in the case of life insurance and transfers in which retained controls are relinquished within three years before death, including all postgift appreciation in the taxable estate. Remember that if a transfer is pulled back into the gross estate, the benefit of the annual exclusion is also lost. In essence, insofar as death taxes are concerned, it is as though the gift never took place.

Gift later ruled incomplete. If it is later determined that a gift was not complete, the date-of-death value of the property will be included in the donor's gross estate in spite of the fact that the donor, in all good faith, paid a gift tax at the time of the gift. The estate will receive a credit for the gift tax paid, but from a transfer tax perspective the gift will be considered as not having been made.

EXAMPLE 13 - 9. Carmen transferred title to her house to her sons, but continued to live in the house rent free. Her sons had there own homes. It should not be to difficult to establish that there was an understanding that she retained the right to live there. This would cause the value of the house to be included in her estate.[4]

EXAMPLE 13 - 10. Dan created an irrevocable trust, giving the trustee discretion to determine how much income to distribute each year to Dan's children. Dan also reversed the right to replace the trustee. Because the terms of the trust were silent as to whether Dan could replace the trustee with himself, it is likely that he has a retained interest.[5]

EXAMPLE 13 - 11. On her deathbed, decedent made a gift by writing a check on her bank account. She died before the check was cashed. Because she had the power to revoke by stopping payment, the gift was considered to be incomplete and the money was included in her gross estate.[6]

Loss of step-up in basis. A major tax disadvantage of making lifetime gifts is the loss in the step-up in basis that would have been received on appreciated property had it been retained by the donor until death. This is a drawback for a donee who wishes to sell the appreciated property. On the other hand, if the donee has no plans to sell the property during his or her lifetime or intends to trade the asset in a tax-deferred exchange, the disadvantage is not as significant since there will be a step-up in basis at the donee's death.

EXAMPLE 13 - 12. Granny has always wanted to do something nice for her loving, adult grandson. She gives him some real property that she and her deceased husband acquired in the 1920's. When Granny dies, the gift property will not receive a step-up in basis, and grandson may own an asset with a sizable unrealized gain to be recognized if he sells it. However, this potential taxable gain will vanish if grandson dies still owning the property.

Other disadvantages. Two other *tax disadvantages* to consider are noted briefly.

Net gifts. First, a particular income tax disadvantage applies to net gifts, discussed in Chapter 7, whereby the donee agrees to pay the gift tax thus reducing the value of the gift, which in turn reduces the gift tax. A net gift can result in a taxable gain to the donor if the gift tax paid by the donee exceeds the donor's basis in the property.

Valuation disputes with IRS. Second, a significant valuation problem can arise with gifting. The IRS will sometimes successfully challenge the value of a gift in both gift tax and estate tax audits, even many years after the gift was made because of the lack of an effective statute of limitations.

Estate and gift tax statute of limitations. The statute of limitations for both estate tax returns and for gift tax returns is three years. If the return is timely filed, the three years starts from the due date of the return, if it is filed late, then it is three years from the time it is filed.[7] There are exceptions to the three year rule. For instance, if the return under reports the value of the gross estate or the total gifts by more than 25%, the statute of limitations is increased to six years after the return is filed, and there is no time limit if the return is not filed or if one is filed with the intent to commit fraud or to willfully evade taxes.[8]

TYPES OF ASSETS TO GIVE

In giving, the donor usually has a wide selection of assets from which to choose. From an estate planning perspective, some assets make better gifts than others. The following constitutes a basic set of guidelines for selecting gift property. As the examples will illustrate, the choice of the best asset will usually depend on the specific family situation.

Basis Considerations

An asset's basis will influence its potential gift appeal.

Gifting high-basis assets to reduce taxable gain. Other things being equal, a high-basis asset makes a better gift than a low-basis asset, if the donee is likely to sell the asset soon after receiving it. As we have seen, the general rule is that the donee retains the donor's basis. A sale by the donee at a price above this basis results in a taxable gain. Obviously, the higher the basis, the lower the taxable gain.

> EXAMPLE 13 - 13. Donor wishes to give donee $100,000 in marketable securities. Donor owns stock A, now worth $100,000, which she purchased two years ago for $95,000; and stock B, also worth $100,000, which was acquired 15 years ago for $20,000. The donee plans to sell the stock he receives when it reaches $110,000 in value. The donee will realize a gain of only $15,000 on the sale of stock A but a gain of $90,000 on the sale of stock B. Needless to say, the donee would prefer to receive stock A.

Although a high-basis asset usually makes a good gift from an income tax point of view, it will make an unattractive gift if its basis is higher than its date-of-gift value. Property in which the owner has an *unrealized loss* is not a good asset to give because the donee, upon selling it, will not be able to recognize that loss. A better strategy would be for the donor to sell the property, realize the loss, and then give the cash to the donee.

Gifting low-basis assets for other reasons. In some circumstances, giving low-basis assets makes sense. For example, if for liquidity or other reasons a donor *plans to sell* a retained asset at the time of giving another asset, he or she should consider gifting a lower-basis asset and selling the higher-basis asset in order to personally incur a lower tax outlay. This strategy is especially productive if the donee is in a lower tax bracket or has no immediate plans to sell the property received as a gift. Gain realized upon later sale by the donee will at least be deferred and may be totally eliminated, if the donee dies before the asset is sold. Keep in mind the rubber band rule, discussed in Chapter 7, whereby appreciated property that returns to the donor as a result of the donee's death has a carry-over basis, i.e., the adjusted basis to the surviving donor is the same as the donee-decedent's adjusted basis immediately before he or she died.

Assets having sentimental or utilitarian value are more likely to be kept by a donee. If a gift is going to be kept by the donee, basis considerations are irrelevant.

Postgift Appreciation

General considerations. If estate tax reduction is a major goal, the generous donor should consider gifting *growth assets*, i.e., assets expected to appreciate substantially, rather than assets whose value is likely to remain stable or fall. Some assets have greater appreciation potential than others. Assets such as life insurance and equity interests in either a closely held business or in real estate (in a good location) are likely growth prospects, while assets such as patent and royalty rights, which have values that usually decline over time, often do not make good gift assets. Cash and cash equivalents are also less desirable, because their values do not rise. In general, from a transfer-tax point of view, assets having a combined low gift tax value and potentially high estate tax value make the best gifts.

Opportunity shifting. An excellent example of a gift of highly appreciating assets is called opportunity shifting. It involves the transfer of an asset before its value is objectively ascertainable. For example, business people may recognize the potential of a profitable commercial enterprise before it blossoms sufficiently into a verifiably valuable opportunity. By transferring ownership during its early stages, a value shift can occur without transfer-tax cost and before the income the venture generates is considered attributable to the donor.

> EXAMPLE 13-14. Dad, owner of a successful computer component firm, has just established a new corporation to pursue the viability of a recently developed engineering idea. The new firm is capitalized at $50,000, and Dad gives an adult daughter 20% of the stock and places another 20% in an irrevocable trust for the benefit of his minor son.

This example demonstrates the creation of *additional taxpaying entities*, the new corporation and the trust, as well as the *splitting* income and wealth among more family members before the value of the enterprise has manifested itself. Similar techniques can be arranged for almost any asset that is expected to appreciate in value. Good hunches by savvy people are the major sources of intra-family opportunity shifting.

Administration Problems

Assets that are likely to create problems in estate administration may make good gift assets. For example, *art works*, especially those currently worth less than the annual gift tax exclusion, may not need to be valued if transferred by lifetime gift. They could create valuation disputes, a potentially higher estate tax, and additional costs of valuation if transferred at death. A business included in the decedent's estate may cause a conflict between the executor (charged with safeguarding assets) and the heirs, especially if some heirs are running the business and others are not.

Other Asset Choice Considerations

Transfer income earning assets to shift income. Where income shifting is a planning goal, high income earning assets make better gifts. As we have seen, income tax law in general requires an actual transfer of the "tree" (asset) in order to transfer the "fruit" (income) of that tree.

Avoid gifting assets with tax benefits to donor. The high-income donor should ordinarily consider gifting assets that do not have *built-in tax benefits* such as income exclusions, deductions, or credits which would be of less value to a lower bracket donee. The person should consider retaining assets such as tax shelters, municipal bonds, and income-producing real property in his or her own portfolio. However, when a tax-shelter property reaches the "crossover point" and begins to throw off "phantom income" to the investor, it may be a good time to gift the property, thereby shifting the income to a lower bracket.

Gift nonbusiness assets to qualify for §303, §2032A and §6166. Giving nonbusiness property may offer death and income tax advantages by reducing the decedent's taxable estate and by increasing the portion of the estate that is considered business, so that specific provisions of the Internal Revenue Code that are favorable to business owners apply. These provisions allow the following tax saving opportunities:

▶ **§303** - This section allows the estate to pay death taxes, funeral bills, and administrative expenses, with cash from a closely held corporation provided the corporation stock is valued at 35% or more of the decedent's adjusted gross estate (AGE). The corporation can buy back stock from the decedent's estate with the transaction being treated as a capital transaction instead of a dividend distribution. Since the stock held by the estate will have received a step-up in basis due to the owner's death, there should be very little, if any, capital gain.[9]

▸ **§2032A** - This section allows the real estate used in a closely held business to be reduced by up to $750,000 based upon its special use valuation. The decedent's special use real estate must equal or exceed 25% of the decedent's AGE and the real estate combined with the rest of the special use business must equal or exceed 50% of the AGE.[10]

▸ **§2057** - The family owner business interest deduction discussed in Chapter 15 is available only if the business represents 50% or more of the decedent's AGE.[11]

▸ **§6166** - This section allows payout over 14 years (with a favorable late payment interest charge on the deferred tax) provided the business is equal to or greater than 35% of AGE.[12]

For individuals with business interests that don't meet the percentage requirements, gifts of nonbusiness assets will increase the business percentage. However, IRC§2035(c)(1) requires that the percentage requirements for §303 and §2032A be met with any transfers within 3 years added back into the gross estate. §2035(c)(2) requires that for §6166 business meet the 35% threshold with and without gifts made within three years of decedent's death. Note that this "adding back" is done to determine whether the estate still meets the percentage thresholds, it does NOT mean that the gifts are actually added into the gross estate for tax purposes.

EXAMPLE 13 - 15. Farmer Brown had the following assets immediately before and after he gave away his XYZ stock to his three children:

items	FMV @ DOG	2032A %	FMV @ DOG	2032A %
stock	$750,000			
farmland	$700,000	32.6%	$700,000	50.0%
farm equipment	$150,000	39.5%	$150,000	60.7%
other property	$550,000		$550,000	
total	$2,150,000		$1,400,000	

To qualify for §2032A, the business land must equal 25% or more of AGE, and the land and other business property (tractors, etc.) must equal 50% or more of AGE. The gift accomplishes this, provided the thresholds are still met when he dies.

EXAMPLE 13 - 16. Farmer Brown dies about three years after making the gift of stock. The stock has increased in value to $800,000 and the other items (still owned by him when he died) have the values shown in the table:

items	FMV @ DOD	2032A %	FMV @ DOD	2032A %
stock	$800,000			
farmland	$740,000	32.0%	$740,000	48.8%
farm equipment	$125,000	37.4%	$125,000	57.1%
other property	$650,000		$650,000	
total	$2,315,000		$1,515,000	

If his death was just short of three years, the land percentage is met (i.e, 32% > 25%), but the total special use business percentage is not met (i.e., 37.4% < 50%). Thus, special use is not available. If his death is just beyond the three year reach of §2035(c)(1), then the gift is not added back to determine §2032A, and the two §2032A percentage limits are exceeded (i.e., 48.8% > 25% and 57.1% > 50%).

Notice that the 35% threshold for §6166 (drawn-out payment schedule) is met both with and without the gift. Therefore the §6166 election is available regardless of whether the death was just under or just over three years after the gift. One final comment: even if farmer Brown died within three years of the gift, the stock's appreciation is NOT being taxed, nor is the annual exclusion lost. The gift of the stock is still an adjusted taxable gift of $720,000 (three kids, three annual exclusions). It is not part of the gross estate. It is brought back merely to test whether the elections (§§ 303, 2032A, and 6166) are available.

Miscellaneous tax factors. Some assets should not be gifted if they may generate adverse tax consequences. For example, consider an asset for which the donor had taken the *investment tax credit*, which was repealed by TRA 86. If the donor gifts the asset before the end of its useful life, he or she will be required to "recapture" part of the credit, that is, repay part of the taxes saved from the credit.

In at least one situation, gifts to children can generate a tax benefit otherwise unavailable to the parents.

EXAMPLE 13 - 17. Because of their high income, the Piatts are not qualified to contribute before-tax dollars to an *Individual Retirement Account* (IRA). Their adult son, John, is qualified, but he cannot afford to make the contributions. John enters into an informal agreement with his parents, who will give him $1,500 a year, to help contribute $2,000 to his own IRA. This annual arrangement is to continue indefinitely, so long as John adds $500 and does not make any premature withdrawals. Each year, John will save hundreds of dollars in income tax by taking the IRA deduction. The Piatts have the satisfaction of knowing that they have increased the financial security of his later years.

As a result of the kiddie tax, generous parents may wish to transfer to their young children property that *does not generate taxable income*, at least not until the children reach age 14. Possible assets include U.S. government EE bonds, municipal bonds, interests in land, a closely held business, and growth stocks. In many situations, the parent can then determine the timing of the tax "hit" by choosing which year to liquidate the assets and, consequently, which year to realize the likely gain. It should be mentioned that the popular U.S. Government EE savings bonds are not transferable. An outright gift of them is considered a redemption. However, there is no restriction on an owner adding co-owners.

GIFTS TO THE SPOUSE: TECHNIQUES AND CONSIDERATIONS

Inter-spousal Gifts to Save Death Taxes

In the last two chapters, we examined in some detail several marital deduction techniques designed to minimize, or at least postpone, the estate tax for a married couple. We will now see that when one spouse is substantially wealthier than the other and there is a significant chance that the less wealthy spouse will die first, death taxes can sometimes be saved by means of bypass planning coupled with a program of inter-spousal gifts. However, this strategy will not work if the basic testamentary scheme involves the simple 100% marital deduction, as the following example shows. For this example, and for the next several examples, we will keep the values constant. However, keep in mind, a bypass trust is not taxed at the second death even if its value is then in excess of the exclusion amount.

> EXAMPLE 13 - 18. Husband has a $2 million estate and wife owns nothing. Their estate plan leaves everything to the survivor, who then leaves everything to their children. Without a change in their estate plan, restructuring the distribution of wealth between them by means of completed gifts will result in no estate tax saving. In each case, the first death occurs in 2000 with an exclusion amount of $675,000 and the second in 2001 when it had increased to $700,000. The first spouse to die,

whether husband or wife, will leave an estate subject to no estate tax, either because there is no gross estate (wife dies first) or because the entire gross estate is sheltered by the 100% marital deduction (husband dies first or gifts were made to balance the estates). Thus, either spouse, as S2, will wind up owning the entire $2 million at death no matter how much each spouse owned prior to their deaths, and inter-spousal gifts will not change the total estate tax. See Figure 13 - 1.

FIGURE 13-1 No Inter-spousal Gifts, 100% MD Plan (Example 13-18)

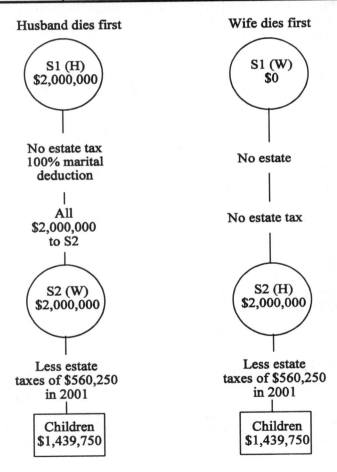

Husband dies first	Wife dies first
S1 (H) $2,000,000	S1 (W) $0
No estate tax 100% marital deduction	No estate
All $2,000,000 to S2	No estate tax
S2 (W) $2,000,000	S2 (H) $2,000,000
Less estate taxes of $560,250 in 2001	Less estate taxes of $560,250 in 2001
Children $1,439,750	Children $1,439,750

The same result as shown in Figure 13 - 1 will occur if the couple held everything in joint tenancy. The right of survivorship results in all property eventually being owned by whichever spouse lives the longest.

However, if the spouses use a bypass trust, estate tax may be saved by means of lifetime inter-spousal gifts, as the following two examples demonstrate. First we'll see the effect if no gift is made, and then we'll calculate the estate tax savings from an inter-spousal gift.

EXAMPLE 13 - 19. Let's assume that the couple in Example 13-18 creates a *credit shelter bypass*, but the husband makes *no lifetime gifts*. The family wealth will pass in the following manner: S1 will incur no estate tax no matter which spouse dies first, either because that spouse owns no property or because of the combined

FIGURE 13-2 No Inter-spousal Gifts, AB Trust plan (Example 13-19)

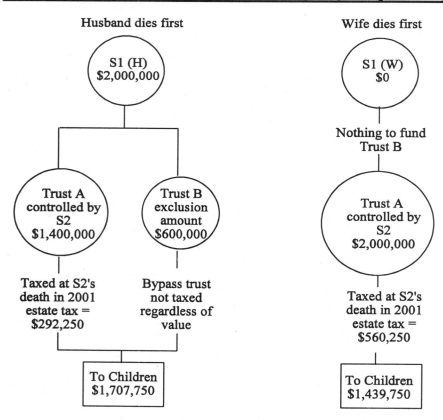

shelter of the marital deduction and the unified credit. If husband dies first, wife will receive $1.4 million and $600,000 will pass to the bypass share. Upon wife's death in 2001, her estate will incur an estate tax of $292,250 leaving a net combined amount to the children of $1,707,750, which is the sum of $1,707,750 from her, plus 600,000 from the bypass trust. Alternatively, *if wife dies first*, husband's $2 million estate at his later death will incur an estate tax of $560,250, leaving a total of only $1,439,750 to pass to the children. No bypass would be created if wife died first since wife had no assets to put into a bypass trust. See Figure 13-2.

Now consider the effect of an *inter-spousal gift* upon this credit shelter bypass plan.

FIGURE 13-3 A Million Dollar Gift AB Trust plan (Example 13-20)

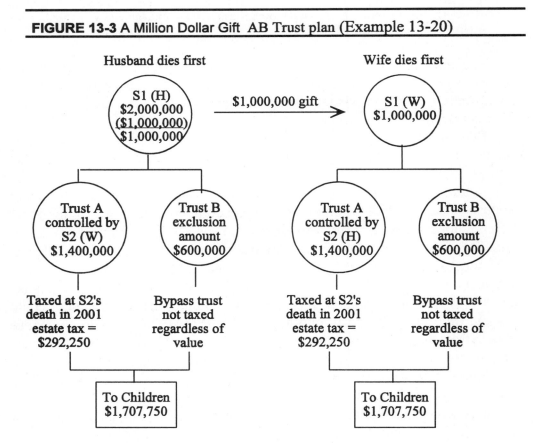

EXAMPLE 13 - 20. Assume that the husband in Example 13-19 *gives* a trust controlled by his wife one half of his wealth. The effects on estate tax under a credit shelter bypass plan are as follows. Since the gift was made between spouses no gift tax will be due. The gift will not even be listed on husband's estate tax return as an adjusted taxable gift because the transfer tax scheme subtracts the marital deduction amount in arriving at adjusted taxable gifts. If the husband dies first, the results will be the same as in the 'no-gifts' Example 13-19: there will be no estate tax upon husband's death, and an estate tax of $292,250 upon wife's later death. However, if *wife dies first*, a markedly different result will occur as compared to when she had no estate. Wife's estate will still incur no estate tax, but on husband's later death there will be an estate tax of $292,250 an amount that is $268,000 less than the result in Example 13-18 in which no gift was made. Thus, the children will be able to receive a total of $1,707,750, rather than $1,439,750. Husband's gift of one half of his wealth to wife will, if wife predeceases husband, generate a transfer tax saving of $268,000. See Figure 13-3.

The inter-spousal gift saved estate tax because it enabled the less wealthy S1 to devise property into the bypass, thereby reducing S2's gross estate and estate tax. Similarly, other inter-spousal gifts can generate large tax savings for other types of bypass arrangements.

Drawbacks. In spite of the large potential estate tax saving, the wealthier spouse may have some reservations about making a sizable gift to his or her spouse.

Relinquishment of control. First, for the transfer to be complete, the donor spouse must be willing to surrender complete dominion and control to his or her spouse. In this age of high rates of marital dissolution, planners should be mindful of the possibility of future marital strife and its effect on the overall plan. The donor might regret that the gift was ever made. Further, even if the spouses are happily married, the wealthier spouse may still be reluctant to relinquish control over so much wealth. As a possible solution, the donor spouse could instead transfer the property into a living QTIP trust that prevents the donee spouse from exercising dispositive control over the corpus. However, if the donee spouse does in fact die first, §2036 may require later inclusion of the corpus in the donor's (S2's) gross estate to the extent that the latter retained any benefit or control (such as a life estate in the income).

FET saving unlikely. Second, demographic statistics indicate two salient facts: many more wives survive their husbands than vice versa and husbands in noncommunity property states are likely to be wealthier than their wives. Thus, in the most common situations, where the wealthier spouse (husband) dies first, a prior lifetime gift to the less affluent spouse (wife) will have saved no estate tax, as Example 13-18 demonstrated. Thus, estate-leveling inter-spousal gifts designed to maximize estate tax saving through bypass plans will accomplish this goal in only a minority of family situations.

In conclusion, completed inter-spousal gifts, when added to an estate bypass plan, can occasionally result in estate tax savings. The strategy will work in situations where the less wealthy spouse is expected to die first and where the spouses are happily married, elderly, and reasonably confident in each other's ability to faithfully handle such an undertaking.

Inter-spousal Gifts to Save Income Taxes

Ordinarily, there is no *lifetime* income tax advantage to inter-spousal gifts. As we have seen, the joint income tax return, filed by the overwhelming majority of spouses, has the effect of combining spousal income and produces one tax, no matter which spouse earned the income. However, a completed gift from one spouse to the other can save income taxes if the donee spouse dies first, and the donor later sells it at a gain. The tax-saving results from the opportunity to experience a step-up in basis before sale and was illustrated earlier in this chapter. Of course one must avoid §1014(e)'s rubber band rule: if one gives appreciated property and the donee bequeaths it back within one year, there is no step-up in basis.

EXAMPLE 13 - 21. Bob gave his wife stock that he had bought for $6,000. It was worth $50,000 when he gave it to her. She died seven months later, leaving the stock, then worth $55,000, to Bob. He was unable to obtain a step-up in basis due to the restriction in Code Section 1014(e). However, had wife *lived longer than one year*, Bob's basis would have been $55,000 (assuming that as the date of death value), because of the resulting step-up in basis.

EXAMPLE 13 - 22. In the prior example, had Bob's wife bequeathed the property to her *bypass trust* for the benefit of husband, §1014(e) would not apply because the property would pass to a different party (the trustee) and not back to the donor-spouse. Thus, a step-up would have been available even if the donee spouse had not lived one year after the gift had been made.

Couples using gift giving strategies, such as those in the example illustrated in Figure 13-3, will save estate tax and income tax. In community property states, of course, since the surviving spouse receives a step-up in basis at S1's death for all community property owned, this gifting strategy need only be considered for separate property.

Next, we turn to considerations in making gifts to minor children.

GIFTS TO MINORS: TECHNIQUES AND CONSIDERATIONS

Gifts to minor children are somewhat unique, not in their tax-saving potential so much as in the manner by which their transfer is usually arranged. As mentioned earlier in this chapter, gifts to minors are usually not made outright but are made instead through a *fiduciary* in the form of a guardianship, a custodianship, or a trust.

Outright gifts transfer the greatest amount of control to the donee, invite the least amount of challenge from the IRS, and are the least complicated to make. But an outright gift to a person, whether a minor or an adult, will only work satisfactorily when the donee has sufficient maturity to rationally possess, conserve, and enjoy the gift property. In other circumstances, the transfer should be made to a *fiduciary*. Many states have statutes that require gifts, above some set value, given to a minor be held for the minor by a fiduciary. The transfer to a fiduciary should be arranged to achieve the same tax advantages (use of the annual exclusion and shifting of income) as are available with an outright gift. It should protect the donee from the risks of his or her own immaturity and comply with any restrictions that state law places on the ownership and use of property by minors.

Before examining types of fiduciary gifts that meet these objectives, recall that if income from a gift is used to discharge the *obligation of support* of the donor-parent, that income will be taxable to the parent.[13]

EXAMPLE 13 - 23. Dad gives 14-year-old Junior $500 so that Junior can purchase lunches during his freshman year in high school. Junior deposits the money in his own savings account, subsequently withdrawing interest as well as principal to buy the lunches. The interest income will be taxable to Dad as income used in discharge of a support obligation.

This rule applies even if the source of the income is not from the parents, e.g., income from a trust.

Thus, in order to enjoy the full tax advantages of a completed gift to a minor, income from the gift must not be used to discharge support obligations. Ordinarily, parents are not obligated to support their adult children, so the issue does not usually apply to adult donees. However, there are exceptions. In about some states including Illinois and New Jersey, judges in divorce cases have imposed the duty of support for *higher education* for adult children. However, several factors limit the application of this exception. In 1992, Pennsylvania's Supreme Court ruled that divorcing parents will no longer be so obligated, reasoning that children become adults at age 18 and that the state's legislature had not explicitly addressed the issue. No court has required parents in an *intact family* to pay for an adult child's higher education.[14]

Gifts Under Guardianship

Individuals may make completed gifts to themselves or others as guardians for the benefit of minor children.

Drawbacks. Gifts under guardianships have some significant drawbacks. First, to be legally valid, the transfer must be made with local (probate) court supervision, which usually requires the expense of time and money in securing court approval, a bond, an annual accounting, and other legal necessities. State laws vary on specific requirements. Further, property held in a guardianship is difficult to manage efficiently because many actions, including the purchase and sale of property, require court approval. Court supervision does afford the ward greater potential protection from misuse of the property by the adult fiduciary, but protection is rarely a major consideration. Finally, another disadvantage of guardianships is that the guardian must turn the property over to the ward at majority (age 18), an age donors usually consider too immature to receive a fee simple interest in most gift property.

Custodial Gifts

Uniform Gifts To Minors Act. The Uniform Gifts to Minors Act (UGMA), adopted in one form or other in all states, allows a relatively simple method of making fiduciary gifts to minors of certain property. No court supervision is required. The gift property is transferred in the name of someone, acting "as custodian for (minor's name) under the (state name) Uniform Gift to Minors Act." This type of titling serves to "incorporate by reference" all of the provisions of that Act, including broad investment powers under the "prudent person" standard, and the ability of the custodian to spend property on behalf of the minor without a court order. Further, a bond need not be given; and, unless the donor or donee request them, accountings are not necessary. Thus, custodial gifts have many advantages over guardianships.

Permissible gift property under UGMA includes securities, cash, life insurance, and annuities, but there is legislative movement by several states to greatly expand this list. In most UGMA states, real property cannot be held in custodial form.

Uniform Transfers To Minors Act. In 1983 the National Conference on Uniform Laws adopted the Uniform Transfers to Minors Act (UTMA) designed to replace the UGMA. Major changes include the following:

1. It allows *any property interests* to be transferred, including real estate, partnership interests, patents, royalty interests, and intellectual property.
2. It allows custodial gifts *at death* by permitting a fiduciary (executor or trustee) to establish a custodianship if authorized in a governing will or trust.
3. It authorizes transfers to a custodian from persons *other than* the transferor who are obligated to the minor (examples of situations include a personal injury recovery, life insurance proceeds payable to a minor beneficiary, and a joint bank account of which the minor is a surviving cotenant).
4. It allows a transferor to revocably nominate a custodian to receive property *in the future*.

The following states have adopted UTMA without significant alterations: Arkansas, California, Colorado, Connecticut, Florida, Hawaii, Idaho, Illinois, Missouri, Montana, Nevada, New Hampshire, North Carolina, North Dakota, Oregon, Rhode Island and West Virginia.

Evaluation of custodial gifts. A custodial gift can save the time and expense involved in establishing a trust. They are considered completed gifts that qualify for the annual exclusion. Although custodianships are like trusts in many ways, they are more restrictive for the following reasons:

- A custodial gift may be *created for only one person*; a trust can provide for multiple beneficiaries, with unequal distributions among them.
- A custodianship is *not a separate legal entity*; all income is taxable to the minor. In contrast, an irrevocable trust is a separate taxpayer, enabling one additional "run up the rate ladder."
- Because the law gives the custodian the power to distribute income or principal to the minor, if the *donor serves as the custodian* and predeceases the minor, §2036/§2038 bring the custodial property into the custodian's gross estate. In contrast, some irrevocable trusts can avoid this estate tax problem by denying the trustee this power.
- Donees usually must receive custodial property outright *by age 21*; trust beneficiaries' distributions of principal may be delayed to a later age.
- Finally, a custodianship *does not have spendthrift provisions.*

UTMA provides that custodial property may not be used to satisfy any obligation of support for the minor, such as an obligation stemming from a divorce decree. Thus, custodial gifts if properly structured can achieve essentially all of the tax advantages of completed outright transfers.

Gifts to Irrevocable Minors' Trusts

Although both gifts under guardianships and custodial gifts are usually an improvement over substantial outright gifts to minors, there are serious drawbacks, some of which have been mentioned above. They usually terminate at or shortly after the donee's age of majority, at which time the donee enjoys fee simple ownership of the property. They may be restrictive, either in the red tape involved to create and continue them (gifts under guardianships) or in the type of property that usually may be given (custodial gifts) under the laws of many states. They are also inflexible in that the controlling state law usually is not or cannot be modified by private document. Thus, the donor under a guardianship arrangement usually cannot provide, by private document, that court supervision will not be required. The presence of these and other drawbacks lead many donors to use irrevocable trusts for gifts to minors.

In structuring gifts in trust for the benefit of minors, planners usually seek to obtain all of the tax benefits available to outright gifts. The four major tax objectives are:

1. Using the annual gift tax exclusion to avoid gift taxes and the use of the unified credit,
2. Excluding the gift from the donor's gross estate,
3. Excluding all postgift appreciation in the value of the gift property from the donor's estate tax base, and
4. Shifting the taxable income earned on the gift property to the trust or to the donee.

The irrevocable trust may also have the non-tax advantage of insulating the gift property from the parents' creditors and, in some cases, from the child's creditors.

Drafting an irrevocable trust takes great care because the nature of such transfers seems to invite scrutiny by the IRS. For example, the donor may wish to act as trustee and to restrict the minor child's enjoyment of the trust principal and income for some period of time. These requirements reflect the donor's desire to retain a considerable degree of control over the gift property. The problem is that a very fine line exists between harmless controls and controls that are deemed to be retained interests by the donor. Earlier in this chapter, we saw some outright gift situations in which the transferor was penalized by income and estate tax provisions for retaining too much control. To this list, we must add certain ill-designed transfers into trusts for the benefit of minors. The following discusses particular tax hurdles facing the planners of irrevocable minors' trusts and several methods for dealing with these problems. The discussion will include qualifying transfers into minors' trusts for the annual exclusion, a word of estate tax caution, the mention of an income tax concern, and finally a GSTT caveat.

Qualifying for the annual exclusion. As mentioned in Chapter 7, to qualify for the gift tax annual exclusion, the donee must be given a *present interest*, that is, an unrestricted right to the immediate use, possession, or enjoyment of property or the income from property. The reader might ask how a gift into trust for the benefit of a minor can qualify for the annual exclusion when, in fact, the minor is not typically given the unrestricted right to the immediate use of either the principal *or* the income. The answer lies in an exception carved out by the Internal Revenue Code, and two planning devices sanctioned by the courts, even if not loved by the IRS. The three alternatives are called the 2503(c) Trust, the Crummey Trust, and the Mandatory Income Trust. The text of §2503 is included in Appendix B.

2503(c) Trust: Under §2503(c), a gift in trust is not considered a gift of a future interest (even though it really is one) if three conditions are met.

First, the trust must provide that the property and income may be expended by or for the benefit of the donee before the donee attains age 21.[15] This requirement creates the same potential retained interest problem (§2036-§2038) for grantors wishing to be trustees as it does for custodial gifts. Second, any portion of the property not so expended must pass to the donee at age 21. Third, if the donee dies before age 21, the property must either be payable to the donee's estate or the donee must hold a general power of appointment over the property. This is met even if the general power is exercisable only through the donee's will; and the trust contains a clause making siblings the takers by default. In most states, a minor is not legally competent to execute a will. Thus, in the event of the death of the minor, the trust property would most likely go to his or her siblings.

The 2503(c) exception was created to allow parents to make gifts that take advantage of the annual exclusion without giving their young children actual control of the property given. The §2503(c) trustee need not distribute the corpus when the beneficiary reaches age 21, as long as the beneficiary can request complete distribution at age 21 and the beneficiary is so informed.[16]

The Crummey Trusts and lapsing withdrawal powers. Crummey is the name of a taxpayer who succeeded in federal court in getting an annual exclusion by establishing a trust containing withdrawal rights for the benefit of minor children.[17] The typical *Crummey Trust* clause provides that the child has the right to withdraw, for a brief period (30 to 90 days) as set in the trust document, after each transfer of property into the trust, the *lesser* of the amount of the available annual exclusion or the value of the gift property transferred. Since the child has the right to withdraw that amount, the gift is considered a gift of a present interest satisfying the §2503(b) present interest requirement and the donor receives an annual exclusion for the gift. To be effective, the child must be given actual notice of the withdrawal right.

Use of a Crummey power can result in undesired gift tax and income tax consequences. For example, a beneficiary's failure to exercise a Crummey power in a given year may mean that the beneficiary has made a *taxable gift* by permitting a general power of appointment to lapse.[18] The gift tax value would be the amount that the value permitted to lapse exceeded the greater of $5,000 or 5% of the aggregate value of the property from which the exercise of the power could be satisfied. For example, suppose $120,000 was contributed as an initial gift in trust, with a child of the trustors having a $20,000 demand right that lapses 90 days after each addition. When the demand right lapses unexercised, the amount that $20,000 exceeds the greater of $5,000 or 5% of $120,000 (i.e., $14,000) is treated as a future interest gift to the remaindermen. As a gift of a future interest, it will not qualify for the annual exclusion. The taxable gift value will be very small since only the amount that goes to someone other than the person who let the withdrawal right lapse is considered a gift; and even that must be discounted since it is a future interest. Furthermore, if the person who let the withdrawal right lapse eventually receives the corpus of the trust, the gift will not be an adjusted taxable gift since the transfer (a contingent remainder) has reverted to the beneficiary.[19] The latter situation is the usual case, since the beneficiary with the withdrawal right is usually also the remainderman, especially for minors' trusts. Given the extremely small gift tax value and the likelihood that the transfer would not enter into the estate tax calculation most planners ignore this tax consequence. Some avoid the problem by limiting the annual withdrawal right to the 5 and 5 limits, i.e., the greater of *$5,000* (rather than the $10,000 annual exclusion amount) or 5%, or by giving the beneficiary a general testamentary power of appointment over the trust principal.

Mandatory Income Trust (MIT). A trust that requires mandatory distribution of income annually to the minor, either outright or to the minor's custodial account, as the way of entitling the donor to the annual exclusion is called a *mandatory income trust*. The gift is considered as comprising two parts, the income interest and the remainder or reversion interest. Tax law considers the former to be a present interest qualifying for the annual exclusion and the latter to be a future interest that does not so qualify. The alternative fractions making up the gift are derived from Tables S or B, depending upon the nature of the income interest.

EXAMPLE 13 - 24. Gerry transferred $100,000 into an irrevocable trust established for his friend, Betty, giving her income for life with the corpus to revert to Gerry, or to his issue, after Betty's death. Betty just turned 85 years old and the rate for valuing split interest gifts was 8%. Therefore, the factor would be 0.33307. This means that $33,307 represents the value of the income interest qualifying for the annual exclusion. Since the present value exceeds $10,000 the full annual exclusion is allowed. *** Query - 1. At what age would the annual exclusion drop below $10,000 for the gift to Betty?

Because §2503(b) requires the donee to have a present interest in order for a gift to qualify for the annual exclusion, and because this trust makes use of the present interest value of the income stream to satisfy that requirement, it is called a §2503(b) Trust by some estate planners. This is an unfortunate choice of terms since many other trusts qualify for the annual exclusion by creating a present interest, e.g., Crummey trusts, wherein the demand right satisfies that requirement. We will use MIT instead of §2503(b), but be aware that the latter is still in common use.

Comparison of the three minors' trusts. MITs and §2503(c) Trusts have become less attractive since the Crummey decision. Prior to Crummey, planners had to choose between an arrangement requiring annual distribution of all trust *income* to the minor [satisfying §2503(b)] or one effectively requiring distribution of the entire trust *corpus* at age 21 [satisfying §2503(c)]. Although some planners favored the MIT for larger gifts, the choice was not enthusiastically made, partly because the value of the income interest qualifying for the annual exclusion had to be discounted. The Crummey provision solved this dilemma by enabling the donor to give the child the *right to demand* a modest amount from the trust annually, without handing income or principal over to the child at age 21. Usually the child is made to realize that there is much to lose by exercising the demand right. For example, the child might lose a greater inheritance in the future, or the parent might simply refuse to make any more gifts into the trust. However, the IRS takes the position that the child's power of withdrawal cannot be illusory, as it would be if there was an "understanding" or "agreement" not to exercise it.[20]

Income taxation has recently become a more important factor in choosing a minor's trust. The short tax rate "ladder" for trusts encourages people to seek to avoid trust taxation of income. A newly created Crummey-type trust may be able to avoid taxation at the trust level by giving the Crummey power holder a general power of appointment over trust income, as it is earned, causing it to be taxed to the holder even if the income is not withdrawn.

EXAMPLE 13 - 25. Eight years ago, Knute created irrevocable Crummey-type trusts for his two sons, then ages 6 and 7. Each trust now contains assets valued at approximately $140,000, generating about $9,000 in accumulated income which is taxable to the trust, some at its marginal rate of 39.6%.

A recent court decision made Crummey powers even more attractive by sanctioning annual exclusions for the trustor's *grandchildren* who were given a 15- day $10,000 demand right. The significance was that the grandchildren were only contingent beneficiaries of the trust principal because they stood to receive principal distributions *only* if their parents predeceased the termination of the trust. In *Cristofani*, the IRS unsuccessfully argued that it was so unlikely that the grandchildren would receive the principal, there was "no imaginable reason" why the grandchildren would not exercise their withdrawal rights unless there was, in fact, a prior *understanding* that they would not do so. Hence, they really had no present interests in the transfers. The court rejected this implied agreement argument, ruling that the test of a Crummey power is the legal right of the beneficiary to demand the property, not the likelihood of actually receiving the property. The IRS intends to continue litigating the court's broad interpretation of *Crummey* in situations similar to *Cristofani*, but only in cases arising outside the Federal 9th Circuit.[21] While this case supports the use of Crummey-type gifts to contingent beneficiaries, commentators are increasingly concerned that Congress may restrict or eliminate the Crummey withdrawal power as a means of creating a present interest. If Congress chooses to do so, it might grandfather (allow the annual exclusion) for existing irrevocable trusts, or perhaps eliminate it even for them unless there is an assurance that the beneficiary will eventually receive the property or at least, as in the §2503(c) Trust, that it will be taxable in the beneficiary's estate if he or she does not get to enjoy it.

EXAMPLE 13 - 26. Christopher resides in the 9th Circuit. He creates an irrevocable trust to last for ten years. The trust provides for distribution of the remainder to his two children, if surviving. A predeceased child's share shall go to his or her issue. One child has three children and the other has two, for a total of five grandchildren. All seven beneficiaries are given Crummey demand powers. Beginning this year, Christopher can fund the trust annually with $70,000 in property, entirely sheltered by seven annual exclusions even though the trust corpus will most likely go just to the two children.

Estate tax caution. In designing the irrevocable trust, the estate planner must be mindful of the dangers of letting the donor retain controls that would cause the property to be includible in the donor's gross estate. For example, as mentioned earlier in the chapter, naming the grantor trustee of a §2503(c) trust will cause estate tax inclusion of the trust assets at the grantor's death unless the trust has already terminated. The underlying Code provisions have been covered in Chapter 6, specifically: §2036, transfers with retained life estate, and §2038, revocable or amendable transfers. The reader is urged to review them at this point.

GSTT caveat. As implied above, Crummey trusts often provide for transfer to the beneficiaries' *issue or descendants* if the beneficiary fails to survive. As a taxable termination or taxable distribution, such transfers will *not* be sheltered from the GSTT as an annual exclusion gifts because such gifts are not direct skips. Planners recommend avoiding this GSTT consequence either by having the donor allocate a portion of the $1 million exemption to transfers to the Crummy trust, or by setting up a separate trust for each skip person, with each trust conforming to certain requirements under §2642(c)(2).

Income tax concerns and the kiddie tax. The donor of a gift in trust for a minor child usually wishes to avoid being taxed on the income received by the trust, preferring instead to let the trust be taxed to the extent the income is accumulated, or to let the child be taxed to the extent that the income is paid to the child. However, the trust must be designed so as not to conflict with the numerous grantor trust rules. For example, reservation by the donor of the right to make withdrawals from the trust will cause the income to be taxed to the donor. This will not apply if the grantor retains a reversion that can only occur on the death of a beneficiary (before age 21) who is a lineal descendant of the grantor and holds all present interests in any portion of the trust.[22]

As briefly mentioned earlier in the text, starting in 1987, all unearned income of children under age 14 in excess of a statutory amount is taxed at the child's parents' marginal rate. This special treatment is referred to as the "kiddie tax" and is applied if either parent is alive at the end of the tax year. This special treatment end the tax year in which the child turn 14. The threshold amount was originally $1,000 but, due to indexing, it has climbed to $1,400 in 1998 (see the

Table of Indexed Values in Appendix A) Of that amount, half (i.e., $700 in 1998 or 1999) is a standard deduction for a taxpayer claimed as a dependent by another (e.g., a child claimed as a dependent by her parents) and the next $700 is taxed at the child's base rate of 15%.[23] No adjustment is made until the Consumer Price Index (CPI) moves the base value up at least $50 (indeed, the change is always rounded down to the next lower 50 dollars). The base amount remained at $1,400 for 1999,[24] but is expected to increase to $1,450 by 2000 or 2001.

A separate return can be filed for the child using IRS Form 8615 or, for convenience, the parent's return may include the income of a child under 14 if the child has only dividend and interest income totaling no more than $7,000 (started as an indexed $5,000). "Piggyback" reporting on the parent's return (by attaching Form 8814) has some drawbacks. The child cannot take advantage of certain other deductions, such as charitable donations and the additional standard deduction for being blind. Also, using the parents' return increases their adjusted gross income, which raises the threshold amount used to determine cutbacks in itemized deductions and personal exemptions.

The source of the child's unearned income is immaterial; excess unearned income is taxed at the parent's rate even though they were not the original source of the property producing that income.

EXAMPLE 7 - 27. In 1999, Dale and Josette's joint taxable income in the current year is $60,000, putting them in the 28% marginal rate bracket. Their 12-year-old daughter Lara has $3,500 in unearned income, including $1,550 in dividends from stock received as a gift from Dale's parents, and $1,950 in interest from a bank savings account, the deposits of which originated from earned income (compensation) to Lara when she was a newspaper delivery girl. Dale and Josette elect to report Lara's income on a separate return. Of the first $1,400 of unearned income, $700 will be tax-free, and $700 will be taxed at 15%. The amount $2,100 (i.e., $3,500 - $1,400) will be taxed at the parents' marginal rate of 28%. Lara's total tax will be $693.

EXAMPLE 7 - 28. Based on the facts of the example immediately above, if Dale and Josette report Lara's income on their own return, Lara's total tax will be $775. The first $500 will be tax-free, and $500 will be taxed at 15%, the remainder (i.e., $2,500) will be taxed at 28%, for a total tax of $775. Therefore, reporting Lara's income on the parents' return increases the tax by $82.

This tax moves the federal government a step closer toward taxing the family as a single economic unit.

EXAMPLE 7 - 29. Continuing the prior examples, if Lara turns age 14 the following year during which time she has exactly the same income, her total tax will drop to $420, since the first $700 will still be taxed at zero, but the balance of $2,800 will be taxed at her own 15% rate. This is a savings of $273 when compared to the kiddie tax result.

As these examples suggest, parents who anticipate paying their children's college expenses may wish to transfer assets to the children to reduce the income tax bite. In addition, income tax laws may help them to acquire certain investments to finance college expenses without transferring assets and at no tax cost. They should consider qualified U.S. Saving Bonds, Hope Scholarship Credits, Lifetime Learning Credits, Educational IRA's, and qualified state tuition programs. Most of these tax benefits have phase-out provisions that decrease or remove the benefit for high income individuals. For instance, interest on certain U.S. Savings Bonds (e.g., series EE) purchased and owned by one or both parents themselves (or by the student, if at least 24 years old) after 1989 and redeemed to pay tuition and fees will not be subject to income tax. However, this interest exclusion is subject to phase-out based on the taxpayer's "modified adjusted gross income" in the year the bonds are cashed. The phase-out brackets are indexed for inflation. In 1999, the phase-out for single and head of household taxpayers starts at $53,100 and is complete at $68,100, and for joint return filers it starts at $79,650 and ends at $109,650. For this particular purpose the Code defines *modified adjusted gross income* as adjusted gross income without regard to §911, §931 or §933 (foreign income exclusions), and after application of §86 (taxable social security income), §219 (retirement contribution deductions), and §469 (limit on deductibility of passive losses).

This chapter has introduced the planning for lifetime transfers, devoting considerable detail to gifts. Chapter 14 will explore another group of lifetime transfers: ones different from gifts discussed in this chapter in that they are either incomplete, or, if complete, they involve transfers to charity.

QUERY ANSWERED

1. Using the abbreviated table you can calculate that she would have to be between 105 (factor of .14110 * $100,000 = $14,110) and 109 where the value drops to $3,704. With the full table you would find that Betty would have had a present interest of $8,319 at age 108. The factor for a person that old is .08319, which times $100,000 gives $8,319 as her present interest, if she were that old when the trust was established. The annual exclusion would be limited to that amount and Gerry's taxable gift would then be $91,681 instead of $90,000.

QUESTIONS AND PROBLEMS

1. Good planning requires that the prospective donor feel comfortable with a proposed lifetime transfer. How can lifetime transfers be a source of discomfort?

2. One of your friends explains to you that she'd like to make a lifetime transfer to her child, perhaps in the form of a gift. However, she is not clear on how gifts differ from other lifetime transfers. Inform her.

3. Now that your friend is aware of the unique nature of a gift, explain to her the difference between an outright and a non-outright gift.

4. What is the approximate minimum net worth that (a) a single person and (b) married couple should own (or expect to own) before considering gifting amounts of $10,000 or more in order to save estate tax? Why?

5. Carrie, a rich elderly widow, expects to live 10 years. She would like to begin a program of lifetime gifting to her four children.
   a. What equal amount can Carrie give to each child, per year, without paying any gift tax, while fully using up her unified credit? In addition, calculate the combined value of all gifts 1) each year, and 2) over ten years. Assume no prior taxable gifts.
   b. How would your answers to part "a" change if Carrie created a trust naming her four children primary beneficiaries and her eight grandchildren contingent beneficiaries?
   c. Why might Carrie be willing to use up her unified credit?

6. In terms of estate tax savings, is a gift of $20,000 by an unmarried donor to one donee in one year necessarily twice as valuable as a gift of only $10,000? Why or why not? Discuss in terms of estate reduction and estate freezing.

7. Why is the ability to avoid grossing up a tax advantage to gifting?

8. Two years ago, Zack gave his daughter, Luna, a one acre plot of desert land in Nevada, then worth $9,000. Subsequently, oil was found, making the plot worth $900,000. Assuming no prior taxable gifts,
   a. Given these facts, what value is included in Zack's estate tax base if he dies today? Explain.
   b. How much would be included if, instead, Zack made the gift four years ago and died today? Explain.
   c. How much would be included if, instead, Zack made the gift in 1981 and dies today? Explain.

9. Describe the attributes of those individuals who would be most willing to make sizable gifts.

10. Summarize the major tax disadvantages to gifting.

11. "Higher-basis assets make better gifts." From an income tax point of view, is this statement true, false, or uncertain?

12. Discuss any significant reasons why each of the following assets have particularly attractive or unattractive gift potential.
    a. Stock: donor's basis, $60,000; fair market value, $20,000.
    b. Stock: donor's basis, $20,000; fair market value, $800,000. Does age of the donor matter at all?
    c. Life insurance on the donor's life.
    d. Rights to a patent.
    e. Undeveloped land.
    f. A junk bond.
    g. A corporate dividend check that the donor endorses over to the donee.

13. a. Under what circumstances can an interspousal gift save estate tax?
    b. Under what circumstances can an interspousal gift save income tax?

14. Contrast the advantages and disadvantages of the alternative methods of making gifts to minors.

15. Explain the public policy reason for dispensing with the present interest requirement for trusts that satisfy §2503(c).

16. Paradiso, a client, asks you to review the recommendation of one of your competitors. That planner proposed transferring $10,000 per year for life into an irrevocable trust, whose terms provide that all income will be accumulated until Paradiso's son Max (age 4) reaches age 35. At that time, all accumulated income will be distributed to Max, who will thereafter receive all income currently until Paradiso's death, at which time, the trust will terminate and all principal will be distributed outright to Max.
    a. Will the periodic transfers be free of gift tax? Why or why not?
    b. Will this arrangement reduce Paradiso's future estate tax or freeze any part of his estate? Why or why not?
    c. If your answer to part a is no, suggest three alternative provisions in the trust that will change the result.
    d. Which of the three provisions in part c probably most reduces the maximum life of the trust?

e. Which of the three provisions in part c will probably be most appealing to Paradiso, who is quite reluctant to allow distribution of either income or principal until Max reaches age 35?

f. How much income shifting per year, if any, will your answer in part "e" accomplish?

17. A friend of yours needs some planning advice. She wants to start a college fund for her 8-year-old daughter. Her goal is to accumulate approximately $50,000 in 10 years, at which time equal monthly payments can be made to daughter over a period of the following 4 years.

a. If neither income shifting nor estate tax reduction are important, is a program of gifting really necessary? Why or why not?

b. If your friend wishes to shift income to her daughter (who for simplicity, we'll assume, has no taxable income of her own), recommend strategies for each of the following alternative sets of assumptions: (1) The friend wishes to accumulate a fund that can revert back to her if her daughter later decides not to attend college. (The answer to this part will not be found in this book. Hint: EE bonds) (2) The friend would like an arrangement under which she can continue funding after her daughter's graduation.

c. In part "b" above, recommend suitable investments to purchase. (Hint: is the daughter a "kiddie"?)

18. Under simple assumptions, what is the largest family estate size that a husband and wife can own and transfer, estate tax and gift tax free, assuming all of the following: a credit shelter bypass plan; that S1 is expected to live six years and S2 fifteen years; and both spouses wish to make annual exclusion gifts each year to each of their four children?

ANSWERS TO THE QUESTIONS AND PROBLEMS

1. Lifetime transfers can be a source of discomfort if the person really doesn't want to relinquish the degree of control or beneficial interest in the property required to meet an estate planning goal.

2. A completed gift, as distinguished from other lifetime transfers (sales and incomplete gifts), has the following attributes:
   a. It has potential gift tax consequences.
   b. It can shift income.
   c. It results in the donor's total loss of beneficial control and enjoyment in the property.

3. An outright gift ordinarily results in the receipt by the donee of a complete interest (i.e., both legal and beneficial) in the gift property. A non-outright gift is usually made to a fiduciary, which means that any particular beneficiary receives only a beneficial interest. Usually, a beneficial interest is not in fee simple. For example, it may be a future interest, such as a remainder. Or it may be a present interest for a limited time, such as a life estate. As implied above, under most non-outright transfers, beneficiaries have no management rights to the property.

4. (a) The exclusion amount (e.g., $700,000 in 2003); (b) double the exclusion amount. Gifting to save estate tax by individuals having less wealth is unnecessary, since (as shown in Chapters 5, 11, and 12) property transfers at death sheltered by the unified credit can reduce estate tax to zero without the necessity of lifetime gifting.

5. a. Total gifts over 10 years = $400,000 (i.e., 4 children x $10,000 annual exclusion x 10 years) + $1,000,000 exemption equivalent of the unified credit = $1.4 million total gifts for all years. Total gifts per year = $1.4 million divided by 10 = $140,000. Therefore, equal amount of gifts per child per year = $140,000 divided by 4 = $35,000.

Combined value of all gifts: 1) Each year: $140,000 (i.e., 4 x $35,000). 2) Over ten years: the value is $1,400,000 (i.e., 10 x $140,000).

b. Based on the *Cristofani* case, if Carrie gave all twelve beneficiaries Crummey withdrawal powers, she could gift a total of $220,000 to the trust each year, or a total of $2,200,000 over ten years. She could give $1,000,000/10 = $100,000 per year sheltered by the unified credit, and $10,000 x 12 = $120,000 per year sheltered by the annual exclusion. By giving additional Crummey powers, Carrie will be able to gift an additional $800,000 free of gift tax.

c. Carrie might be willing to use up her unified credit to be able to effect a small estate freeze, i.e., to exclude future asset appreciation of the gifted property from her estate tax base. Only $25,000, the *taxable gift* value of each $35,000 gift will be included at her death, rather than the entire date of death value of the $25,000 portion that would otherwise not be gifted.

6. No, a gift of $20,000 by an unmarried donor to one donee in one year is not necessarily twice as valuable, estate tax-wise, as a gift of only $10,000. The first $10,000 can truly *reduce* the estate tax base by causing the gross estate to be lower by that amount. The second $10,000 will not reduce the estate tax base any additional amount. While the gross estate will be an additional $10,000 lower, adjusted taxable gifts will be $10,000 higher, resulting in no further change in the estate tax base. Although the second $10,000 amount does not reduce the estate tax base, it does *freeze* it at that $10,000 gift tax value. Both $10,000 gifts will keep all future appreciation in the value of the gift property out of the donor's estate tax base. Of course, this benefit is inherent in the notion of a freeze, but the two concepts are somewhat different.

7. Avoiding grossing up makes the gross estate lower by the amount of the gift tax paid, thereby saving estate tax.

8. a. & b. Regardless of when Zack died, nothing related to the gift would be includible in his estate tax base if the gift was made after 1981. It is not includible in the gross estate, since §2035 includes only one kind of outright gift: life insurance. The gift is not includible in adjusted taxable gifts because

the taxable amount is zero, i.e., $9,000 value of gross gift minus $9,000 annual exclusion.

c. On the other hand, if Zack made the gift before 1982, the amount of the adjusted taxable gift, $9,000 - $3,000 = $6,000, is includible in adjusted taxable gifts, and consequently, the estate tax base. However, as in parts "a" and "b," nothing is includible in Zack's gross estate.

9. Attributes of individuals most willing to make sizeable gifts: Wealthy, older, generous, having rapidly appreciating assets.

10. Major tax disadvantages to gifting:

   a. Time value of money is a drawback to prepaying the gift tax.
   b. Possible adverse §2035 consequences with certain transfers.
   c. The gift may later be ruled incomplete.
   d. Loss of step-up in basis.

11. Uncertain. A higher basis will make a better gift only if all of the three assumptions below can be made:

   a. The basis doesn't exceed the current value of the gift. Otherwise, the donor should prefer to realize the loss him/herself. If the donor doesn't realize the loss, no one else can either.
   b. The donee is likely to sell the gift asset before his/her death.
   c. The donor, for other reasons, is not left in the position of having to sell another asset with a lower basis.

12. In each case, we consider only the significant conceptual points:
   a. Stock with $60,000 basis and $20,000 fair market value: This is an asset with a basis that is *too* high. Not a good gift asset - better for donor to sell and deduct the loss.
   b. Stock with $20,000 basis and $800,000 fair market value: This asset has already appreciated greatly. From a basis point of view, not a good gift asset because of the carryover basis rule. However, if the donee is not likely to sell the asset before death, perhaps because he/she is very old,

then basis considerations may not be important. Also, there will be gift tax consequences. Finally, the above assumes that the asset is not expected to appreciate greatly in the future. If it is, then it may still have attractive gift potential.

   c. Life insurance on the donor's life: An excellent gift asset, assuming donor is expected to live at least three years. It has a relatively low gift tax value and a high estate tax value. Basis considerations are not usually significant, unless the donee plans to surrender or sell the policy.

   d. Patent rights: From a transfer tax point of view, not often a good gift because a patent usually depreciates over time. Thus, patents often have a higher gift tax value and a lower estate tax value.

   e. Undeveloped land: Assuming substantial post-gift appreciation, undeveloped land is a good gift asset if it reduces estate tax.

   f. A junk bond: No appreciation potential, but it may be able to shift some income (junk bonds ordinarily pay relatively large coupon interest amounts).

   g. Cash dividend check, issued by a corporation, that is endorsed over to the donee: Cannot shift the dividend income because the stock itself wasn't transferred. Similar to a gift of cash.

13. a. An inter-spousal gift can save estate tax when the wealthier spouse transfers enough property to the poorer spouse, who dies first, so that the bypass share can be fully funded.

   b. An inter-spousal gift can save income tax when a relatively low basis asset is transferred to the spouse dying first, who then retransfers it at death to the donor spouse. The donee spouse must live at least one year after the gift is made.

14. Gift under guardianship:
   a. Is costly.
   b. Requires court supervision.
   c. Is difficult to manage efficiently.
   d. Provides greater protection from abuses by guardian.
   e. Must be turned over to donee at age of majority (age 18).

Custodial gifts:
a. Are simply arranged.
b. Are often limited to certain types of property.
c. Must be turned over to donee, usually by age 21.
d. Have adverse estate tax consequences if donor is custodian.

Gifts to an irrevocable trust:
a. Are more complex to set up.
b. Have much greater flexibility, especially regarding distribution of income and principal to the beneficiary.
c. Have potential adverse estate tax, gift, and income tax consequences if not structured correctly.

15. The public policy reason for the exception under Section 2503(c) is to avoid encouraging sizable present interest gifts to minors.

16. a. The periodic transfers will not be free of gift tax because they are transfers of future interests, since all income is accumulated and presumably the trust does not presently meet the requirements of either §2503(b), §2503(c) or Crummey. Of course, no gift tax will be owed until Paradiso's entire unified credit is used up.
    b. This arrangement will not reduce Paradiso's estate because his gifts will not qualify for the annual exclusion. But it will *freeze* a portion of his estate by eliminating from the estate tax base the future appreciation in the trust assets.
    c. The three alternative provisions are the following:
       1. MIT provision: each year, all income distributed to Max.
       2. §2503(c) provision: principal distributed outright to Max when he turns 21, trustee can use property for Max, etc.
       3. Crummey provision: annual withdrawal right of lesser of annual exclusion amount or amount actually transferred.
    d. The §2503(c) provision probably most reduces the trust's life. Under its rules, when Max turns age 21, he must be able, at minimum, to request complete distribution.
    e. The Crummey provision would probably be most appealing to Paradiso, since it would not require distribution of either income or principal until

Max reaches age 35. Of course, Max would have the withdrawal right for a brief period each year, but most donors are successful in totally discouraging beneficiaries from exercising that right.

f. The Crummey trust can usually accomplish only a very modest degree of income shifting. In addition to the $100 personal exemption, only $1,700 in taxable income (in 1998) to a trust is taxed at the 15% rate. The excess will be taxed to the trust at 28%. If Paradiso is in the 28% bracket, this means an annual savings of only $249 [$1,700 * (28% - 15%) + 28% * $100].

17. a. If neither income shifting nor estate reduction are important, the friend need not make any gifts; she could simply accumulate a fund in her own name. Gifting to establish the fund would serve no purpose.

b. To shift income, the friend will need to make gifts of income generating property.

   1. By purchasing U.S. Government EE bonds in joint name with her daughter, the friend might be able to "have her cake and eat it." No taxable gift occurs until redemption. Reporting of income can be deferred until redemption. If daughter attends college, daughter can redeem and pay the income tax. If daughter chooses not to be a student, Mom may be able to redeem and pay the tax.

      An additional alternative for tuition financing by middle income individuals would be to have the person purchase EE bonds in her own name and later sign them over to the college directly in payment of tuition. Under recent tax legislation (§135) the bonds, if cashed in 2000, would be entirely exempt from federal income tax for families with modified AGI of less than $76,250. There is a gradual phase-out of this exception above this AGI, with total phase-out at $106,250.

   2. Two possible alternatives to enable the arrangement to continue after graduation are the Crummey trust and the §2503(b) trust. Most planners prefer Crummey, partly because the entire gift amount qualifies for the annual exclusion and partly because income need not be payable or paid in any given year.

c. (Yes, the daughter will be a "kiddie" until the tax year she reaches age 14). To avoid the kiddie tax, investments chosen should not throw off taxable income until that time. The person should consider EE bonds, municipal bonds, zero or low dividend paying growth stocks, etc.

18. From Chapter 11, we saw that without gifting, a married couple can pass $2 million under a credit shelter bypass plan, since each spouse can shelter $1,000,000 with his or her unified credit. With gifting, each spouse can shelter an additional amount equal to the product of his or her life expectancy times 4 (# children) times $10,000. Thus S1 can shelter an additional 6 * 4 * $10,000 = $240,000, and S2 can shelter an additional 15 * 4 * $10,000 = $600,000. As a consequence, the largest family estate size that this couple can totally shelter from estate tax and gift tax is $2,840,000 (i.e., $2,000,000 + $240,000 + $600,000).

ENDNOTES

1. See Chapter 6, under §2035 materials, for detailed explanations.

2. TAM 9231003.

3. §2011.

4. §2036

5. §2036

6. §2038

7. IRC §6501(a).

8. Exceptions to the three year rule, generally, see §6501(c), and the 25% under reporting, see §6501(e).

9. §303.

10. §2032A.

11. §2057.

12. §6166.

13. IRC §677(b).

14. Wall Street Journal, November 19, 1992, p. B1.

15. Controls over the expenditures can disallow the annual exclusion. *Illinois National Bank of Springfield v. U.S.* 756 F.Supp. 1117 (1991).

16. LR 8507017

17. *Crummey v. Commissioner*, 397 F.2d 82 (9Cir. 1968).

18. §2514(e).

19. §2001(b)

20. Rev. Rul. 81-7, 1981-1 CB 474.

21. *Estate of Maria Cristofani* 97 TC 74 (1991).

22. §673(b).

23. §63(c)(5), §1(g)(7)(B)(i).

24. Rev. Proc. 98-61.

CHAPTER 14

Lifetime Transfers II: Other Intra-family Transfers; Charitable Transfers

OVERVIEW

Gift planning, the subject of the previous chapter, is often rejected by individuals for two reasons. First, by their very nature, gifts generally mean nothing in return. They reduce wealth making the donor feel less financially secure, a feeling people would rather not experience. Second, making a gift means less control over the property, a difficult step for many potential donors.

This second chapter on lifetime transfers explores two types of intra-family arrangements. In the first type, such as the installment sale or the private annuity, the transferor receives *consideration*. In the second type, such as the grantor retained interest trust, the transferor retains an interest in the transferred property. The chapter will also cover the popular types of lifetime charitable transfers, including outright charitable transfers and split interest charitable transfers, such as the annuity trust, the unitrust, and the pooled income fund. With charitable trusts, the transferor may be able to increase income and receive an income tax deduction.

INTRA-FAMILY TRANSFERS FOR CONSIDERATION

In this section, we'll study lifetime transfers that are different from the others in two important ways. First, they differ from gifts because they *generate consideration* to the transferor. Second, they differ from the second type of lifetime intra-family transfer to be covered later in this chapter in that like gifts, they are *complete*, that is, they entail the total transfer of (one or) all interests in the asset.

Intra-family Loan

Lending money or other property to family members is a simple method of transferring assets in exchange for consideration. Often, the financial benefits of an intra-family loan are worth the financial and emotional risks.

Financial benefits of intra-family loans. Loans work best when borrowing rates and investing rates of return are far apart. In 1999, when short-term borrowing rates were 9% or higher and one-year certificates of deposit earned about 3.5%, a short-term loan of $10,000 at 6% could save the borrower at least $300 per year and generate additional annual pretax income to the lender of about $250. Long-term loans could save far less per year because rate differentials were not nearly as pronounced, but over a thirty year period, the accumulated amounts are still significant. Additional advantages of intra-family home mortgages are the ability to avoid or reduce the up-front points and application fees charged by commercial lenders, and the long loan processing time. Also, parents (or other relatives) may make loans to children with credit histories that would not satisfy commercial lenders. Another strategy is to have children wishing to make gifts to supplement their parents' income, borrow from the parents and pay an above-market rate of interest (or at least more than what their parents are earning on their certificates of deposit).

Financial risks of intra-family loans. In addition to the risk of unexpected taxation (to be described shortly), intra-family loans entail other financial risks. A child may not be a good credit risk, making the loan payments difficult to collect resulting in family friction. If the loan is secured, the lien must be properly filed to ensure the lien's priority over other creditors.

Nonfinancial risk of intra-family loans. The risks of an intra-family loan can also be partly emotional. Some parent-lenders later discover that their children have taken the immature attitude that since mom and dad have a lot of money they need not be repaid. Family loans can also engender jealousies and antagonisms between relatives and in-laws.

Taxation of non-gift intra-family loans. Taxation of intra-family loans that contain no gift element is relatively straightforward.

Income taxation. Interest paid by the borrower is, of course, taxable income to the lender. Interest is not tax deductible to the borrower unless the loan is secured by a principal or secondary residence, incurred in connection with a trade or business, or related to an investment.[1] If the loan is in default, the lender will not be able to deduct the loss unless a businesslike effort is made to collect it.

Gift taxation. No gift will result if the borrower's note reflects an arms-length transaction. Thus, there must be provision for repayment and the interest rate charged must be reasonable.

The lender may elect to *forgive* loan payments under the shelter of the annual exclusion. However, if the IRS can establish that a prior agreement had been made to forgive all payments, it will contend that the entire loan constituted an immediate gift. To avoid this result, a lender might accept each payment, and later gift a somewhat different amount back to the borrower.

Estate taxation. The value of the note is included in the lender-decedent's gross estate at death.[2]

Taxation of gift-type intra-family loans. The income and gift tax effects discussed above assume a true loan, one that does not have a gift element. In other words, the borrower exchanges full consideration in the form of a note which when issued has a present value equal to the amount borrowed.

Other intra-family loans entail additional tax risks. Individuals may wish to charge no interest, or an interest rate that is below market rates. Tax law treats these "below market" loans between family members as "gift loans," possibly subjecting the lender to income and gift taxation.

Income taxation. In subjecting these loans to income tax, the law[3] assumes a fiction. The forgone interest is treated as if the borrower really paid it, and then the lender gave the money back to the borrower. Thus, the lender is expected to report as income the imputed interest payments. Whether or not a loan is "below market"depends on whether the lender charged a rate at least equal to the applicable federal rate (AFR), as described in §1274(d) and published by the U.S. Treasury each month.

There are two exceptions to the imputed interest rules. First, they do not apply to loans up to $10,000 used to purchase non-income producing property, such as an automobile. Second, they do not apply to loans up to $100,000 if the borrower's net investment income is less than $1,000. This might work well for investment-poor students needing large amounts to fund educational expenses, such as for law school or medical school, or for a child needing the money for a down payment on a house. If net investment income exceeds the $1,000 limit, the imputed interest is limited to the actual amount of that income.

Gift taxation. If the loan rate is below market, the lender will also be treated as having made a gift. If the loan is a term loan, one with a specified maturity, the value of the gift is the difference between the amount loaned and the discounted present value of the note. If the loan is a demand loan, one with no specified maturity date and the lender has the right at any time to demand full repayment, the lender will be treated as having made an annual gift of the imputed interest for the portion of the year the loan was outstanding, less the amount of interest actually received. A more detailed discussion of the tax effects of below market "interest free" loans is contained in Appendix 14A that immediately follows this chapter.

Properly structured, intra-family loans can be beneficial to both lender and borrower, provided that both understand the terms, which should be reduced to writing.

Ordinary Sale

A person can sell property at its fair market value to another family member. Under certain circumstances, an ordinary sale is beneficial to both family members. The owner of property may truly wish to sell at a fair price, but would prefer to keep the asset in the family; the buyer will be spared the effort and expense of looking for similar property, and commissions that might have been incurred are avoided. As a true sale, there may be income tax consequences to the seller. Careful records should be kept, since intra-family sales might receive greater IRS scrutiny than a sale between unrelated parties, especially if the transaction is sizable. The buyer, of course, has the burden of acquiring the cash or other acceptable property needed for the purchase. The seller is not allowed to deduct any loss incurred on the sale, due to the Code's prohibition against loss recognition on sales between related parties.[4]

Bargain Sale

If a person has mixed transfer motives, on the one hand wishing to gift a particular asset to a family member and on the other hand not willing to completely forgo all consideration in return, a bargain sale may be appropriate. As described in Chapter 2, under a bargain sale, the owner sells the asset for an amount less than what would be regarded full and adequate consideration. The difference between the consideration received by the seller-donor and the value of the asset transferred is a gift to the buyer-donee for tax purposes. Regarding income tax, the seller would recognize a gain to the extent the consideration received exceeds his or her basis. The buyer-donee's basis is the greater of the donor's carry-over basis or the amount paid.[5]

> EXAMPLE 14 - 1. Mom owns property with a basis of $90,000 and a current value of $240,000, which she sells to her son for $110,000. Mom's taxable gain is $20,000, the difference between $110,000 and her $90,000 basis. Son's new basis is $110,000, his purchase price. Mom has also made a gift of $130,000, the difference between the FMV of the property and the consideration paid to her.

A taxable bargain sale may not be the best outcome, however, if a true tax-free gift was intended. Occasionally, an intended gift is treated as a bargain sale.

> EXAMPLE 14 - 2. La Croix borrows money from a bank to purchase a building. After claiming depreciation on the property for a number of years, he "gives" the property to his daughter, who assumes the debt. The transaction will be treated as a bargain sale, if his adjusted basis is less than the outstanding debt. La Croix will be considered to have received consideration in the amount of the debt assumed.[6]

As a compromise between a gift and a sale, the bargain sale can be arranged to reflect the person's degree of generosity.

Installment Sale

Instead of selling the asset to a family member for immediate cash, the owner could sell it in exchange for an installment note. In other words, the buyer agrees to make periodic payments of principal and interest, based on a fair market rate of interest. This is referred to as seller financing; and the seller is said to *take back paper*, a reference to the seller receiving a note instead of cash. An installment sale can defer income tax on some or all capital gain while keeping post-sale appreciation out of the seller's gross estate.

Income taxation. Under the income tax installment sales rules, the seller may spread recognition of the gain over the collection period.[7] Although it is presumed that the seller will use the installment method to recognize gain, the seller can make an election to recognize the entire gain in the year of sale which might make good sense if the seller has offsetting capital losses for the year. If the installment method is used, the gain is recognized in proportion to the amount of each payment of principal. A percentage of each principal payment, measured by the gross profit (gain) divided by the amount of principal payments to be made, is included as capital gain. There are restrictions on deferral of gain on an installment sale of certain trade or business inventory.[8] Losses are never reported on an installment basis.

> EXAMPLE 14 - 3. Mom, a widow, sells her rental house to her daughter for $80,000, payable with a down payment of $10,000. Interest is payable monthly, and principal will be payable in five equal annual $14,000 payments. Mom's current adjusted basis in the house is $20,000. Her gross profit is $60,000, and each year she will recognize a capital gain of 75% or $60,000/$80,000 of the principal amount received. Thus, in the year of sale, her reportable gain is $7,500 of the $10,000 received. In each of the succeeding five years, she will report a gain of $10,500 (i.e., 75% * $14,000).

Any *interest* received on the balance due is also taxable income. Interest paid is fully deductible by the buyer if it is considered business interest, investment interest which is offset by net investment income, interest on a debt secured by a primary or secondary residence, or some other type of qualified interest.

At least two different events will trigger to the seller an *immediate recognition* of part or all of the remaining gain. If the seller sells or "otherwise disposes" of the installment note, or if the seller cancels the note, then he or she will have to report currently the remaining gain from the original transaction. Gain recognition is also triggered if the buyer of the property is a related party who resells the property within two years of the purchase.[9]

The buyer of the property, as in any valid sale, will enjoy a step-up in basis in the property to the amount of the purchase price. However, with regard to the seller's note, the transfer of the note at the death of the seller *will not generate a stepped-up basis* in the note because the unrecognized gain is considered income in respect of a decedent.[10] The legatee-heir will continue to report installment gain in the same manner as the seller.

Gift taxation. If the installment transaction is a bona fide sale for full and adequate consideration, there are *no gift tax* consequences to the lender. Lack of full consideration occurs when the interest rate specified in the note is considered inadequate.

> EXAMPLE 14 - 4. Continuing with the above example, assume the installment note specifies an interest rate of 10%, which is equal to the current applicable federal rate (AFR). Since the rules for installment sales under §7520(a)(2) require a minimum rate of *120%* of the current AFR to avoid the inference of a gift, the present value of the sum of all principal and interest payments, discounted at 12%, will be less than $80,000, the current value of the house. Thus, Mom will be treated as having made a gift of the difference. For a small loan, the annual exclusion will cover the gift.

A parent may wish to *forgive* one or more of the purchaser's future payments. In the usual case, only the amount forgiven constitutes a taxable gift in the year forgiven and it qualifies for the annual exclusion.

> EXAMPLE 14 - 5. Continuing the above series of examples, if daughter wants to use the money to buy a car so Mom forgives a $14,000 annual payment, Mom has made a gift of that amount. After the annual exclusion, Mom's taxable gift is $4,000. If Mom is married and her husband agrees to split the gift, the taxable gift would be zero. However, from an income tax stand point, Mom will be treated as though she received the payment and then returned it to daughter.

The IRS quite correctly maintains that if the seller, at the time of the sale, had an understanding with the buyer that the seller would *not* collect on the note, then the *entire value* of the property is a taxable gift. However, an IRS challenge has rarely prevailed where the note has been correctly drafted and properly secured.

Estate taxation. Ordinarily, when the holder of an installment note dies, only the present value of the installment note is included in his or her gross estate.

> EXAMPLE 14 - 6. Continuing the prior example, if Mom dies just before the fourth payment is due, her gross estate will include the discounted value of the note. Of course, Mom's gross estate will also include any proceeds from receipt of earlier payments from daughter, to the extent retained by Mom, or any assets she purchased

with those proceeds. However, her gross estate will not include the value of the installment asset sold.

If the seller made a partial gift and took back paper secured by the property transferred, and dies before the note is paid off, the date-of-death value of the property sold would be included in the seller's gross estate less only the actual consideration paid.[11] This arrangement would be considered a transfer for less than full and adequate money, or money's worth, with a retained income interest.

Since family transactions are often scrutinized more carefully by the IRS, the owner should be strongly advised to determine the value of the asset by qualified appraisal and to use an adequate rate of interest.

Self-canceling provision. The seller may seek to avoid inclusion of the value of the note in his or her gross estate by incorporating a self-canceling provision, specifying that no further payments will be made after his or her death. Since the initial value of a *self-canceling installment note* (called a "SCIN") is less than one whose payments cannot be prematurely canceled, the buyer will have to give additional consideration, usually in the form of a higher principal amount or a higher interest rate.[12] And, of course, the older the individual, the greater the additional consideration. Otherwise, the IRS could assert the existence of a gift element in the transaction, again creating the risk of §2036(a) application.

> EXAMPLE 14 - 7. Marty, age 53, sells property currently worth $100,000 in exchange for a 20 year self-canceling installment note. The likelihood of Marty dying before reaching age 73 is .3129964 [1 minus (61673/89771)], see Table 80CNSMT. To reflect this additional consideration, Marty sets the face amount of the note at $131,300.

Case law has ruled that the value of the canceled notes under a SCIN is not includable in the note holder's gross estate.[13] However, cancellation of payments will trigger recognition of the entire remaining gain on the decedent-note holder's *estate income tax* return.[14] While the gain will be income in respect of a decedent, no income tax deduction for its proportionate share of the estate tax is available because the note is not included in the decedent's gross estate. Because the tax on this gain is recognized by the estate, it is not a debt at the time of death and therefore is not deductible from the gross estate. Planners may still wish to recommend the SCIN to wealthier individuals whose potential estate tax rate exceeds their marginal income tax rate.

The SCIN represents aggressive planning and should be used only when the individual is willing to be subject to potentially greater income tax exposure.

The appeal of installment sales. Tax deferral, through installment sales, is attractive because it spreads the gain over a number of years. However, there are restrictions on installment reporting for certain sales. The sale of publicly traded property (e.g., stocks and bonds) does not qualify for installment reporting. Also, a portion of a sale might not qualify (under the so-called "proportional disallowance rule") if the sales price exceeds $150,000. Thus, the installment sale is available mainly for the occasional sale of real estate or tangible personal property.

Intra-family sales, whether of the ordinary, bargain, or installment variety, are significant value-shifting devices. The sale can freeze a portion of the person's estate, since post-sale appreciation will inure to the new owner, whose gross estate is probably far smaller than the seller's and who will probably live considerably longer.

Private Annuity

Overview. A private annuity usually involves the sale of an asset by the owner in exchange for the unsecured promise of a life annuity by another family member. It is similar to a commercial annuity which is purchased from an insurance company or other financial institution.

> EXAMPLE 14 - 8. Schwab, age 65 and in poor health, agrees to transfer a $100,000 asset ($20,000 basis) to his son, under a private annuity arrangement when the federal rate for valuing annuities is 10%. Based on Table S (10%), Schwab will receive $14,042 a year for life ($14,042 = $100,000/7.1213).

The private annuity generates periodic income for the annuitant and can completely exclude the transferred property from his or her gross estate.

Taxation of a private annuity. The tax aspects of the private annuity are as fairly simple for the gift and estate tax, but quite complex when it comes to income tax.

Gift taxation. Generally, there is *no taxable gift* as long as the value of the property transferred equals the discounted present value of the annuity promised. So long as, when the private annuity was established, the annuitant had a greater than 50% probability of living more than one year (or actually did live 18 months or more), the IRS generally accepts the use of the Alpha Tables (Treasury's actuarial tables) for valuing the private annuity.[15] If a gift element is present, there is the risk that it will be deemed a transfer for less than money's worth with a retained interest resulting in the date of death value of the asset being included in the annuitant's estate.[16]

Income taxation. *No gain* is immediately recognizable upon creation of a private annuity because the amount realized (i.e., the value of the unsecured promise to pay an annuity for someone's life) is not considered immediately ascertainable. Thus, as with the installment sale, gain is reported as the annuity payments are *received*. But unlike the installment sale, taxability of the payments is governed by the annuity rules of §72. A portion of each payment is treated as a tax-free return of the annuitant's basis, also called the *investment in the contract*. The excluded fraction, called the *exclusion ratio*, is calculated by dividing the investment in the contract by the *expected return*, which is the total of all amounts the annuitant expects to receive under the annuity contract. In the typical case, the expected return equals the total of all expected payments over the annuitant's life expectancy obtained from the mortality table found in IRS Reg. §1.72-9.

> EXAMPLE 14 - 9. Based on the last example, Schwab's tax-free portion of the payment is $1,000, which is the product of an annual payment, $14,042, and the exclusion ratio, of .07121. This ratio is calculated by dividing the investment in the contract, $20,000, by the expected return, $280,848, which is the product of $14,042 and 20, Schwab's life expectancy, derived from the regulations. Schwab will be required to report as gain $4,000, or one twentieth of his $80,000 total gain in each of the first twenty years. Thus, for the first twenty years, of the entire $14,042 payment, Schwab will report $4,000 as taxable gain and $9,042 as ordinary income. The remaining $1,000 will be an income tax-free return of capital. If Schwab outlives his 20 year life expectancy all subsequent payments constitute ordinary income. If he dies within 20 years, gain reporting stops and he will receive a loss deduction on his final income tax return for the unrecovered basis.

Estate taxation. When the annuitant dies, *none* of the transferred property is included in his or her estate tax base inasmuch as there was no retained interest in the property transferred. The original exchange, if done properly, is considered a sale of the property for its full worth. As with any life estate based upon the life of its owner, the lifetime annuity terminates becoming valueless at the death of the annuitant.

EXAMPLE 14 - 10. Continuing the example above, if Schwab lives for two years, his son will have paid less than $30,000 for an asset worth $100,000. In connection with this transaction, Schwab's gross estate will include nothing more than the portion of the two payments that Schwab received, and still retained at death.

However, as with the installment sale, if the original transaction were to be ruled a *gift* because the value of the annuity promised the annuitant is less than the value of the property transferred, the annuitant's gross estate will include the *entire* date-of-death value of that property as a §2036(a) transfer with a retained life estate, reduce only by the payments actually received. Such effect would wipe away the major tax appeal of the transaction, a danger that can be minimized by securing a qualified professional appraisal. For some additional protection, some experts suggest incorporating as a provision in the annuity contract a "valuation readjustment" or "savings" clause. The clause would require the purchaser to pay additional consideration if the IRS determines that property was undervalued. The IRS has attacked these clauses, arguing that (1), as completed gifts, the transactions cannot be altered, and (2) they are contrary to public policy since the revaluation is triggered only if the parties get caught.

Analysis of private annuities. The advantages and disadvantages of the private annuity are described next.

Two advantages. First, from an estate tax point of view, the private annuity is even better than the installment sale: It can result in *complete* exclusion of the asset value from the annuitant's estate tax base. Second, as illustrated in the most recent example, the total amount eventually paid by the obligor can be expected to be *relatively small* in situations where non-terminal annuitants have shorter than average life expectancies.

Disadvantages. The private annuity has three significant drawbacks. First, while the seller in an installment sale can, and usually does, require security, the annuitant under a private annuity cannot use the transferred property as security because doing so will result in it being included in the annuitant's gross estate.[17] Thus, private annuity arrangements are always unsecured, which may cause the annuitant some concern. Lack of security will increase the risk of not being repaid, a result that could be unsettling, especially to an annuitant who is more or less depending on the payments for support. Second, while interest paid by the purchaser under an installment sale may be tax deductible, *no part* of the annuity payment under a private annuity is deductible.[18] Third, if the annuitant lives a very long life, the obligor has made a *bad bargain*.

EXAMPLE 14 - 11. Continuing the example above, if, instead of dying, Schwab regains his health and lives 20 years, his son will have paid more than $280,000 for the $100,000 asset. Schwab's gross estate may have to include this amount (which is nearly three times the value of the asset transferred), plus its resulting income, if he doesn't consume or gift these receipts during his lifetime.

Since the private annuity can accomplish significant estate freezing without gift tax consequences, it can be a very attractive transaction if the parties are willing to assume the inherent risks. As we have seen, it works best when the person wants to save estate tax, is not expected to live more than a few years, has a significant cash flow need, and trusts the other party (the obligor) to make the payments as promised. These characteristics do not apply to most people, not even to most wealthy people.

INCOMPLETE INTRA-FAMILY TRANSFERS

This section briefly covers three currently used incomplete intra-family transfers, the intentionally defective irrevocable trust, gift-leaseback, and the grantor retained interest trust.

Intentionally Defective Irrevocable Trust

When a person wishes to make gifts to significantly reduce estate tax, has little interest in shifting income, and wishes to retain some control over the transferred assets, the planner may wish to consider recommending an intentionally defective irrevocable trust (IDIT). Taking advantage of the differences in tax rules between §2036 - 2038 (estate tax) and §671-677 (grantor trust income tax rules) with regard to retained powers, transfers to an IDIT are made complete for federal estate and gift tax but incomplete for income tax. Thus, the trust corpus is not included in the grantor's gross estate, similar to the treatment of any other completed gift; but, because the trust provides for grantor retained powers uniquely proscribed by the grantor trust rules, all trust income is taxable to the grantor. This result offers an additional opportunity to save estate tax since income tax paid by the grantor rather than by the trust beneficiary has the effect of additionally reducing the amount of assets held by the grantor at death, at no gift tax cost.

EXAMPLE 14 - 12. In 2000, Maxwell transfers $685,000 to an IDIT for the benefit of his adult son, Kirk. Since Maxwell has made no prior taxable gifts, he can totally shelter the current gift from gift taxation with the annual exclusion and unified credit. Required to distribute all income to Kirk annually, the trustee distributes $50,000 income in the first year. Maxwell is obligated to pay an additional $17,500 income tax, based on his 35% combined marginal rate. This year Maxwell has effectively transferred an additional $17,500 for the benefit of his son, free of gift tax.

Powers that the grantor may wish to retain over an IDIT include acting as trustee and having the grantor's spouse as one of the trust beneficiaries. As trustee, the grantor can have the following powers: to invest, to allocate receipts between income and principal, to vote shares of stock held in the trust, and to distribute income or principal to trust beneficiaries for such reasons as "sickness," "emergency," or "disability." Naming the spouse one of the beneficiaries enables the grantor to retain indirect access to the trust. Of course, any distributions to the spouse could increase his or her estate, which may run contrary to the estate tax goals of the trust.

The IRS may argue that payment of income taxes by the grantor constitutes a gift. At least one commentator believes the IRS will not succeed, provided the trust instrument is worded carefully.

The advantages of the IDIT over a simple gift include retained control and greater potential estate tax avoidance at little or no additional gift tax cost.

Gift-Leaseback

When a business-owning parent wishes to establish a program of gifting but is held back for lack of available assets, he or she might find the answer in a gift-leaseback arrangement. As its name suggests, the parent gives a business asset outright or in trust to a lower-bracket family member and leases the asset back for use in the business. The parent is able to continue using the asset, can take a deduction for the lease payment, and can still enjoy all the other advantages inherent in gifting.

The ability to *deduct* the lease payments under a gift-leaseback depend in part on the location of the person's business and in part on how carefully the arrangement is structured. In some circuits, the Federal appellate courts have disallowed the deduction, while other circuits have allowed it as a legitimate business expense. Even in circuits that allow the deduction, the transaction must be properly structured. Some requirements for success include having a legitimate business purpose, charging a reasonable lease payment, having a written and enforceable lease, and, if the gift is in trust, naming an independent trustee who is not subservient to the donor.

The Anti-Freeze Rules: §2701-§2704

Advent of §2036(c) and Chapter 14. Prior to 1987 estate planners had devised a nifty way to transfer business interests using corporate shares or partnership interests. To greatly simplify, using the corporate freeze as an example, the wealthy business owning parents would recapitalize the corporation, issuing preferred shares (that they would keep) that had a value as close as possible to the underlying value of the business (it then follows that the value of the common shares must be near zero), and they would give to their children the common shares. Since the value of the preferred shares do not fluctuate very much (they are interest rate sensitive, i.e., if market rates go up the value of the preferred tend to go down), the future grow in the value of the underlying business was reflected entirely in the value of the common stock.

> EXAMPLE 14 - 13. In 1980, wealthy Warschauer owned a gold mining company worth about $1,000,000. He foresaw that the value was likely to increase dramatically, especially since his son David had started working for him and had devised new methods of extracting gold out of what had been considered "spent" ore. Warschauer recapitalized his company, turning in his old common shares and taking for himself 10,000 voting preferred shares, each with a $100 par value, and 1,000 new common shares. The preferred shares were to pay a $7 dividend per $100 par value. Since the preferred shares were worth almost $1,000,000, the common shares were worth very little. Warschauer gave the common shares to his son. Ten years later when the company was worth $3,000,000, the preferred shares were still worth about a million dollars, but the common shares owned by David were worth about two million. Growth in the value of the business was achieved in part by the fact that the board of directors never declared any dividends for the preferred or the common shares.

> EXAMPLE 14 - 14. In 1982, 50 year old Myron transferred $1,000,000 into an irrevocable trust. He retained the income interest for 15 years, giving his three

children the remainder at the end of the term. If Myron died during the term, the trust corpus reverted back to his estate. At the time the trust was funded, the federal rate for valuing remainders was 10%. Hence, the remainder value was $178,507. [0.239392 * $1,000,000 * (68,248/91,526)] The remainder factor is from Table B and the discount for the possibility that Myron might die is based upon the number of people alive at age 50 that will probably make it to age 70 as shown in Table 80CNSMT. The exclusion amount in 1982 was $225,000, which more than covered the gift. The trustee invested in growth stock that paid virtually no dividends (Myron did not need, nor did he want, any additional income) and, of course, there was a prolonged bull market such that when the trust terminated in 1997 the corpus was worth over $4,500,000.

What the IRS found to be abusive was that the value of what was retained (the income interest) was based upon the assumption that income would actually be paid to the person who created the transfer (the parents holding the preferred stock or the settlor of the trust), whereas in practice the wealthy were using these transfer devices as ways to move wealth to the younger generation at minimum transfer tax cost. The IRS was not very successful in court with its arguments that either there was a transfer with a retained interest (which would cause the transferred property to be included in the transferor's estate) or that the income interest was greatly overvalued. The loses were immensely frustrating to the IRS, which appealed to Congress to draft legislation to stop these abuses. In an attempt to restrict these estate "freezing" techniques, in 1987, Congress enacted §2036(c), which took an *estate tax approach*. Using very general language, §2036(c) required the inclusion in the decedent's gross estate of the *entire* date of death value of virtually all property in which the transferor retained significant income interests. Incredibly confusing and, perhaps overly broad, §2036(c) created such taxpayer opposition that it was repealed retroactively in 1990, and replaced by the special valuation rules of §2701-04. These are often called the "Chapter 14 rules" after their location in the Internal Revenue Code.

In adopting Chapter 14, Congress abandoned the estate tax approach, and instead focused on a *gift tax* approach, which means subjecting certain transfers to gift taxation when the initial transfer is made, rather than later taxing the property at the transferor's death. In essence, Chapter 14 rules require that certain transfers of property incorporating retained income interests must be valued in their entirety, reduced only by the value of "qualified" retained income interests. Thus, any retained interests that do not qualify under the Code are disregarded, with the result that the entire value of the transferred property is subject to immediate gift taxation. Thus, for gift tax purposes, Chapter 14 treats the nonqualified retained interests as if they had, in fact, not been retained.

§2702: Transfers of interests in trusts. While §2701 deals specifically with transfers of corporate or partnership interests to family members (covered in Chapter 16), §2702 addresses transfers to family members through the use of *trusts*. The sections are similar in that both treat nonqualifying retained interests as having a value of zero. They both use the subtraction method of valuation to determine the tax value of the gift, meaning that if what was retained is valued at zero, then the entire value (whether it is a business interest or property placed in a trust) is shifted to the gift. In general terms, under §2702, applicable to transfers in trust, the special valuation rules apply when:

> ...*a transfer is made in trust for the benefit of a member of the transferor's family and an interest is retained by the transferor or an applicable family member.*

What follows are the key terms that need to be defined or described in order to understand this area of the law.

"Member of transferor's family." A member of the transferor's family, more inclusive than under §2701, includes the transferor's ancestors, descendants, spouse and siblings, ancestors and descendants of the transferor's spouse, and spouses of the transferor's ancestors, descendants and siblings.[19]

"Applicable family member." An applicable family member includes the same members included under §2701.[20] These are the transferor's spouse, ancestors of the transferor or the transferor's spouse, and any spouse of such ancestor.[21]

Exceptions to §2702. §2702 does not apply (*a*) to retained interests in a personal residence in which the term holder resides, and *b*) possibly for certain tangible property, such as undeveloped real estate or art. In addition, the zero valuation rule under §2702 does not apply to two types of qualified retained income interests, called a "qualified annuity interest" and a "qualified unitrust interest." Among other requirements, the income must be payable at least annually, and must be stated as a fixed dollar amount (annuity interest) or a fixed percentage of the fair market value of the trust property, determined annually (unitrust interest).

EXAMPLE 14 - 15. In the earlier example, had Myron made his transfer this year, and had his fifteen year income interest been structured to qualify as either an annuity interest or a unitrust interest, the full value of that interest could be deducted from the value of the transfer in calculating the value of Myron's immediate taxable gift resulting in a taxable gift of far less value. However, if the trust simply called for Myron to retain "all income" for the fifteen years, the income interest would be valued at zero and the entire one million dollar value of the trust would be treated as a taxable gift.

We shall see that the trusts incorporating these techniques have come to be called grantor retained trusts, or GRIT's, for short.

Grantor Retained Interest Trust

With a grantor retained interest trust, the person transfers property into an irrevocable trust, retaining the right to income for a period of years, after which the trust ends and the trust property is transferred to the remaindermen who are usually relatives of the grantor. The acronym "GRIT" is used in this text to refer to all varieties of grantor retained interest trusts, including common law GRIT's, GRAT's, GRUT's, and others that fall under §2702. Who will eventually receive the corpus, and whether the corpus is included in the settlor's gross estate, usually depends on the type of GRIT created and how long the settlor lives. With all GRIT's, if the person *does not survive* the income period, §2036(a) will apply and the GRIT will have served no useful purpose. The date of death value of the trust will be included in the grantor's gross estate and the adjusted taxable gift (insofar as the GRIT is concerned) is zero. In fact, some GRITs (i.e., all those except GRATS and GRUTS--see below) provide that the corpus will revert to the settlor's estate, if he or she does not survive. This is accomplished by granting the settlor a contingent testamentary power of appointment over the trust corpus. Reversion is made contingent upon the settlor not surviving the period. Putting the contingent reversion in the terms of the trust reduces the remainder value. Since the remainder value is the taxable gift, making it smaller reduces the unified credit used. If the settlor *does survive* the income period, the result is the same for all GRITs: the settlor's entire beneficial interest in the trust ceases, the corpus vests in the remaindermen (usually the settlor's children), and the gift value will be an adjusted taxable gift when the settlor dies.

   Tax consequences. A properly structured GRIT has *gift tax*, *estate tax* and *income tax* consequences worth knowing about.

Gift taxation. At the creation of the GRIT, the value of the gift equals the entire value of the property transferred into the trust reduced by the value of the retained interests. Whether the value of a retained interest is deemed to equal zero or some larger amount depends upon the characteristics of the GRIT and the provisions of §2702. If §2702 applies (e.g., the remaindermen are the settlor's children), all *retained* interests are valued at zero (called the *zero valuation rule*) unless the retained interest is a *qualified retained interest*, an interest in a personal residence trust, or an interest in a tangible personal property trust. From an estate planning stand point, one wants the retained interest to be valued at greater than zero (the higher the better), thereby reducing the gift tax valuation. It is said that §2702 uses the "subtraction method" to arrive at the value of the gift. One starts with the value of the property transferred into trust and subtracts the allowable value of the retained interest. Hence, if the retained interest is given zero value (because it doesn't meet §2702's requirements), the taxable gift value will be the total value of the property transferred into the trust.

Since the gift portion of a GRIT is one of a future (remainder) interest, it does not qualify for the annual exclusion. As a result, any resulting taxable gift must use unified credit, if available and will require payment of gift tax once all the donor's unified credit is used up. Assuming §2702 applies, the basic rules for assuring that the retained interest will be valued at greater than zero (i.e., its actuarially determined value), are set out below:

1. There must be a qualified retained interest that assures that the grantor will definitely receive fixed annual payments.

   These payments can be fixed in dollar amount (the trust will be called a GRAT, a grantor retained annuity trust). The trust can require annual payment increases, but in valuing the retained interest one is allowed to factor in the increases only to the extent that they do not exceed 120% of each prior year's payment.[22] A GRAT may state the initial payments in absolute dollar amounts (e.g., "$1,500 per month") or as a percentage of the initial amount placed in the trust (e.g., "6% times the initial value of the trust, payments to be made quarterly").

   The payments can also be fixed as a percentage of the trust's value determined annually (the trust will be called a GRUT, a grantor retained unitrust). As with the GRAT, the GRUT can provide for increasing percentages each year, but the retained interest will be valued only to the extent that the increase in the fixed percentage does not exceed 120% of the prior year's percentage.[23]

2. The zero valuation rules do not apply to Personal Residence Trusts and Qualified Personal Residence Trusts. These are valued under §7520, meaning that they are treated as common law GRITS. More on this later.

3. The retained interest in a "Tangible Property" GRIT will be valued at the FMV of the term interest, but the settlor has the burden of establishing the price at which the term interest could be "sold."

Income taxation. As a grantor trust, all trust income is taxable to the trustor until the end of the stated period, if he or she lives that long.[24]

Estate taxation. If the settlor *survives* the income period, none of the corpus will be includable in the gross estate. However, the taxable gift value will be included in the estate tax base as an adjusted taxable gift.

If the settlor *dies before* the expiration of the income period, as mentioned above, the date-of-death value of the corpus will be included in the settlor's gross estate as a transfer with retained income or enjoyment which did not in fact end before the transferor's death.[25] Thus, the premature death of the settlor does not reduce estate tax. Fortunately, this type of estate planning has very little downside risk; if the settlor had not set up the GRIT, the property would have been in the person's gross estate at date of death values anyway. Therefore, if the person outlives the term overall transfer taxes are greatly reduced, but dying during the term has as its only downside the cost of establishing the trust (mainly attorney's fees) and the cost of maintaining it (mainly accountant's fees). Remember, if the corpus comes back into the gross estate, the earlier gift disappears as an adjusted taxable gift for estate tax purposes.[26]

GST taxation. The ability to leverage the one million GST exemption to a GRIT transfer is limited by statutory law. Under §2642(f),[27] the GST exemption cannot be allocated to most GRITs until the close of the "estate tax inclusion period" (called ETIP), which occurs when the property would no longer be includable in the settlor's gross estate in the event the settlor died. In most GRIT situations, this would be the *end of the specified income period*, at which point §2036(a) no longer applies. The value of the property against which the allocation may be made will equal the value that is included in the settlor's gross estate or the GRIT's value at the end of the term. An allocation of the GST exemption for most non-GRIT transfers is made *at the time the GSTT trust becomes irrevocable. This principle has the effect of attaining* maximum leverage for appreciating assets. In the case of a GRIT, the exemption allocation is delayed until the end of the income period or the death of the grantor, whichever comes first. This means that more of the person's GST exemption will be used up for two reasons: First, the allocation will have to be made to the *entire value* of the property, rather than just the present value of the remainder. Second, in the case of assets *appreciating* during the income period of the GRIT, the allocation amount will be higher. However, even though the advantage of leveraging the exemption under a GRIT is restrained, it is not eliminated since any appreciation *after the term* [i.e., after the retained interest period] is sheltered from future GSTT. Thus, allocating the GST exemption to a GRIT will not result in as much leveraging as with an ordinary lifetime gift. However, it generally will yield more leveraging than with a transfer at death because the leveraging period may also include a period during the settlor's lifetime.

GRIT Planning.

The following material explains how GRITs were structured before tax reform and then describes planning opportunities currently available.

The "common law" GRIT. Prior to the passage of §2702, relatively uncomplicated GRITs were quite successful in freezing the value of appreciating property at little or no gift tax cost. The following example portrays what is now called a "common law GRIT." The following series of examples uses *current* IRS valuation tables (see Table B (10%) in Appendix A), so that the reader can validate first hand the calculations.

> EXAMPLE 14 - 16. In 1985, Haney, when he was 58 years old, created a GRIT, funding it with $500,000 in common stock. The trust terms retain for Haney all income from the trust, payable at least annually, for the lesser of 10 years or for Haney's life. If Haney dies before the end of the 10-year period, the trust will terminate and the corpus will revert to his estate. If Haney survives the 10-year period, the trust will terminate and the corpus will then be distributed outright to Haney's son. When the trust was established, Haney made a *taxable gift* of the remainder interest in the stock, which, at 10%, is valued at $161,996 [= $500,000 x .385543 x (72082/85776). As a future interest, the remainder does not qualify for

the annual exclusion. Haney owed no gift tax, he simply used up some of his unified credit.

EXAMPLE 14 - 17. Continuing the above example, if Haney died four years after establishing the trust, the date of death value of the corpus would be included in his gross estate and Haney would have gained no estate tax advantage. The only disadvantage was the fees paid to establish and maintain the trust for the four years.

EXAMPLE 14 - 18. If Haney *died twelve years later* when the corpus was worth $1 million, his gross estate would include nothing in connection with this property, although the adjusted taxable gift would be $161,996. By surviving the income period, Haney succeeded in freezing the transfer tax value of this stock at $161,996, the original gift tax value of the remainder interest. This amount is less than the value of the stock when transferred to Haney's son, and probably far less than its value when Haney died. Described in other terms, Haney leveraged the exclusion amount many times over.

Review of §2702. In general, §2702 applies when there is a transfer of an interest in a trust to, or for, the benefit of a member of the transferor's family, where the transferor (or an "applicable family member") has retained an interest in the trust. §2702 GRITs that fall under the zero valuation rule must treat the entire value of the transfer as a taxable gift unless the Code allows otherwise, e.g., the interest is a qualified one.

EXAMPLE 14 - 19. If Haney, from the example above, had created his GRIT today, the entire value of the transfer, $500,000, would be treated as a taxable gift. §2702 applies because the trust was for the benefit of a member of the transferor's family. The zero valuation rule applies because the arrangement does not fall under one of the qualified retained interest exceptions. Thus, under the subtraction method of valuation, the gift tax value equals $500,000, the total value of the transfer, reduced by zero, the allowable value of the retained interest.

Careful GRIT planning will include one of two strategies: Either planners will structure a common law GRIT to avoid §2702 entirely; or they will create a GRIT that avoids the zero valuation rule. A GRIT transfer to a non-family member (described next) is an example of the former strategy. Examples of the other approach will be explained shortly.

GRIT transfers to non-family members. Section 2702 only applies if (1) the transferor (i.e., the grantor or settlor) or an "applicable family member" retains an interest, and (2) an interest is transferred to a "member of the transferor's family." Applicable family members are the transferor's spouse, an ancestor of the transferor or of the transferor's spouse, and the spouse of any ancestor.[28] Members of the transferor's family are: the transferor's spouse; any ancestor or lineal descendant of the transferor or the transferor's spouse; any sibling of the transferor and; any spouse of the transferor's ancestors, lineal descendants, or siblings.[29] Think of the applicable family members as the older generation who are likely to set-up one of these trusts. The older generation will retain an interest for a term of years, then the trust will terminate, and the corpus will go to the younger generation (the members of the transferor's family). Most likely, a parent (or parents) will establish a GRIT to eventually benefit children or grandchildren. Notice that, by these definitions, even though brothers and sisters are members of the transferor's family, nephews and nieces are not. Nor is a best friend or a "significant other" considered a member of the transferor's family. In other words, the common law GRIT is alive and well, if the remainderman is not a member of the transferor's family as defined in the Code.

> EXAMPLE 14 - 20. In the prior example, had the beneficiary of the transferred interest been Haney's *nephew* rather than his son, the entire actuarial value of the retained income interest could be subtracted in arriving at the gift tax value. It would be a common law GRIT.

Examples of common non-applicable family member situations (i.e., we can still use the common law GRIT that does not "fix" the amount of income) are trusts with unmarried partners and/or close friends as remaindermen. It should be clear now that we call the GRIT in the above example a common law GRIT, because it does not fall under the restrictive requirements of §2702. For it, we can use the remainder column of the appropriate Table B to determine the value of the gift. For trusts that must comply with §2702, the income interest must be fixed in some manner (merely retaining "all income" for the income beneficiary is not good enough).

The five types of §2702 GRITs described in the next few pages avoid the harsh zero valuation rule (for the retained interests) by satisfying one or more of the requirements found in the Code. They are the GRAT, GRUT, tangible personal property GRIT, and two types of personal residence GRITs.

GRAT and GRUT. The zero valuation rule of §2702 does not apply to "qualified" retained income interests, i.e., one of the two types of income interests that meet §2702(b)'s detailed technical requirements. Trusts must have either a *qualified annuity interest* or a *qualified unitrust interest*, and the trusts prepared with these interests in mind are called the *grantor retained annuity trust* (GRAT), and the *grantor retained unitrust,* (GRUT). Among other requirements, the payment must be made at least annually. For a GRAT, the payment must be stated as a *fixed dollar amount*, sometimes stated as a percentage of the initial value of the trust corpus. For a GRUT, the annual payment is a *fixed percentage* of the fair market value of the trust property *determined each year*. The GRATs and GRUTs that are subject to the §2702 rules (i.e., the remaindermen are members of the transferor's family) can have a contingent reversion. However, because it is not a qualified retained interest (it is not certain to happen), it will be subject to the zero valuation rule, hence it will not decrease the remainder value the way it does when included as part of a common law GRIT or a QPRT.

> EXAMPLE 14 - 21. Jake creates a GRAT, transferring $200,000 in trust and retaining the right to an annual payment equal to 6% of the initial corpus. Thus, Jake will receive $12,000 each year.

> EXAMPLE 14 - 22. Pam creates a GRUT, transferring $200,000 in trust and retaining the right to six percent of the fair market value of the trust property, determined annually. The first year she will receive $12,000. If the trust is worth $210,000 on the valuation date of the second year, she will receive $12,600 for that year. On the other hand, if the value of the trust drops to $190,000, the payment decreases to $11,400. The annual valuation day is likely to be set in the trust agreement as January 1 of each year, since most reporting and planning is done on a calendar year basis.

Individuals choosing who would prefer to minimize their receipt of unneeded income that may someday augment their gross estate will probably prefer a GRAT, under which income payments are based on the *initial* value of the corpus. This is especially true if the corpus will be funded with assets expected to appreciate over the retained income period. Those who would prefer to have income increase over the years would probably prefer a GRUT on the assumption that values will increase, thus resulting in increase income payments.

The detailed rules for GRATs and GRUTs are very similar to the rules for charitable remainder trusts (called CRATs and CRUTs), described later in this chapter.

"Zeroing out" a GRAT or a GRUT. If the payments to the settlor are high enough, the value of the retained interest could equal the value of the property transferred into trust. This is referred to as *"zeroing out"* a GRAT. That is, the remainder interest is valued at zero.

EXAMPLE 14 - 23. If the §7520 rate is 6% when Mark creates a 15 year GRAT with assets valued at $1 million, he could zero it out if he retained an annuity of $103,963 per year.

Note that with a zeroed-out GRAT, not only is there is no gift tax, the grantor does not use up any unified credit. Thus, the GRIT can result in a large estate tax base *reduction*, as well as a freeze, at no transfer tax cost. Although these were much the rage at estate planning seminars in the early 1990s, including excitement about one and two year term zeroed out GRATs (yes, the retained income amounts were huge), the IRS has taken the position that a GRAT cannot be successfully zeroed out. It claims that, for any GRAT whose annuity amount will exhaust the corpus precisely at the termination of the trust, the value of the retained interest cannot equal the initial corpus because of the possibility that the grantor may die prior to the expiration of the trust term.[30] The IRS has taken the position that an intended zeroed out GRAT may not be adequately funded to make all the payments if: 1) the annual payment is set at a level that would exhaust the corpus before the end of the income period; or 2) the exercise of a trustee power to invest in highly speculative assets would substantially increase the chance of a loss.[31] For our examples, we will assume a less aggressive position. by using GRITs that last more than just a couple of years and that leave some reasonable value allocated to the remainder interest.

Tangible personal property transfers. The zero valuation rule of §2702 does not apply to tangible personal property where: (*a*) the failure by a term interest holder to exercise his or her rights would not have a substantial effect on the value of the remainder interest, and (*b*) the property is of a type for which no depreciation deduction would be allowable. In such case, the value of the retained interest is set equal to the amount the interest could be sold for to an unrelated third party. One possible type of property is artwork, such as a painting.

EXAMPLE 14 - 24. Drew, age 65, gives his daughter a remainder interest in a painting, worth $1 million, and retains a 13- year term certain interest. The gift tax value is the million dollars reduced by the amount Drew can show that an unrelated third party would pay for the right to possess the painting for 13 years.

In view of the fact that the IRS requires evidence of "actual sales or rentals that are comparable" to sustain the value of the term interest, few individuals will be able to successfully employ this strategy.

Personal residence trust. Finally, the zero valuation rule of §2702 does not apply to a GRIT whose sole asset is a personal residence of the term interest holder. The details and restrictions are quite complex, probably discouraging all but the most ambitious planners and their clients.

> EXAMPLE 14 - 25. Marcus, on his 60th birthday, creates a 10-year GRIT, structuring it to contain only his $200,000 personal residence. The result is the same as that described for a common law GRIT. Thus, if the §7520 rate is 8%, we would use the remainder factor of 0.463193 from Table B (8%) to arrive at a remainder value of $92,639. Assuming that the terms of the trust create a contingent reversion should Marcus not live the 10-year term, the probability that he will die reduces the gift value to $75,513 [i.e., (68248/83726) * $92,639]. See Table 80CNSMT.

Qualified personal residence trust. More planners will recommend a personal residence GRIT as a result of recent regulations which have outlined the conditions required for a 'safe-harbor' residence trust called a qualified personal residence trust (QPRT).[32] Among the rules, the QPRT can hold an interest in only one residence. It can receive additions of cash to pay six months of mortgage payments, but any excess cash must be distributed to the term holder. The trustee may sell the residence, hold the proceeds, and buy another residence within two years from the sale. If the residence ceases to be a personal residence of the term holder, the trust corpus must be held for the balance of the term interest and must meet all of the requirements for functioning exclusively as a qualified annuity interest trust, similar to a GRAT.

Calculating the gift for a QPRT. The remainder value is the gift. Its value, when the settlor has a contingent reversion, is calculated as follows:

$$\text{Remainder value} = R_t*(\#Y/\#X) * \text{FMV of the property}$$

Where: Rt stands for the term of years remainder factor for the given interest rate of "t";[33] #X is the number of persons alive at starting age for the settlor; and #Y is the number alive at ending age for settlor.[34]

EXAMPLE 14 - 26. The 7520 rate is 8.0% and the settlor is 75 at start of a 10-year QPRT. The house being used to fund the trust is worth $500,000. $R_t = .463193$; #X for age 75 (1980 census) = 56799; and #Y for age 85 (1980 census) = 27960.

Therefore, the remainder value for this QPRT is:

$$.463193 * (27960/56799) * \$500,000 = \$114,006$$

Remember, that if the settlor dies during the term of the trust, its fair market value will be included in the settlor's estate. However, the adjusted taxable gift value drops back to zero because §2001(b) defines adjusted taxable gifts as being those post-1976 taxable gifts except for those "gifts that are includable in the QPRTs, like other qualified GRITs, carry very little downside risk, other than the attorneys' fees in establishing them and the accountants' fees in maintaining them.

Must a settlor who survives the term of the QPRT vacate the residence? No, because he or she can rent it from the remainderman. However, the agreement must be arms length, with lease payments equal to fair rental value, in order to avoid the risk of §2036(a) application.[35] At one time, planners thought that the settlor could purchase the home from the trustee just as the term of the trust came to an end, but regulations proposed by the Treasury prohibit purchase by the settlor, the settlor's spouse, or an entity controlled by either of them.[36] Clearly, some people will not appreciate this aspect of the QPRT. Others, however, will welcome the ability to transfer property to their children at a greatly reduced transfer tax cost.

PLANNING FOR CHARITABLE TRANSFERS

We now shift gears and examine transfers designed to assist charitable institutions while also providing significant benefits to donors.

Introduction to Charitable Giving

Transfers to charity, whether lifetime or at death, are supported by several provisions of the Internal Revenue Code that allows generous deductions on a contributor's income tax, gift tax, and estate tax returns. While charitable transfers can be made during lifetime or at death, lifetime transfers are the primary focus of this section, partly for consistency with the chapter theme, partly because lifetime charitable transfers often are more complex and need greater elaboration, and partly because they have a significant income tax advantage over charitable transfers at death. Lifetime gifts to charity are of essentially two types: outright gifts or split-interest gifts.

At the outset, it should be noted that significant charitable gifts may result in a significant net decrease in a person's wealth. Thus, the person will usually need to possess a charitable motive to feel comfortable about making charitable transfers. The material presented below describes some ways to minimize the decline in family wealth resulting from a charitable donations.

Tax Consequences of Charitable Transfers

Income tax consequences. To qualify for an itemized charitable income tax deduction, the donee charity must meet the requirements under the Code.[37] In addition, the Code contains complex limitations on the amount of charitable contributions deductible from income by individuals in any given tax year. As shown next, there are limitations on both the total amount deductible for all charitable gifts and on the specific amount deductible for any particular gift.

Limitations on total amount deductible. In general, total deductible charitable contributions may not exceed 50% of a taxpayer's "contribution base" (CB), the name for an amount that is approximately equal to adjusted gross income.[38] However, there are some major exceptions with regard to this 50% limitation. Taxpayers are limited to 30% of the CB for contributions to private foundations. In addition, deductible limits for both public charities and private foundations are reduced to 30% and 20%, respectively, for contributions of most kinds of "capital gain property" (see below).[39] Contributions in excess of these limits may be carried over for five years.[40] To further complicate matters, since 1991, charitable deductions are part of the itemized deductions which for high income taxpayers are subject to a 3% overall floor.

EXAMPLE 14 - 27. Fanny Superstar, a prominent singer, just donated her $15 million Malibu estate to charity. This year she earned $20 million in income. She can deduct $5.4 million, which is $6 million (30% * $20 million) reduced by the 3% floor(3% * 20 million). She can carry over the remaining $9 million ($15 million -

$6 million) to later years. Assuming that her income remains about the same for the next three years and that her combined marginal tax rate is 50%, Fanny should save approximately $2.7 million in each of the first and second years, and $1.2 million in the third year, for a total income tax savings of about $6.6 million.

Amount deductible for a particular gift. The amount deductible from adjusted gross income for any particular charitable gift is usually its *fair market value*, subject to the total annual limitations outlined above. However, there are two important *exceptions for noncash gifts*. First, if sale of the property would have resulted in ordinary income or in short-term capital gain, the asset is called "ordinary income property," and the donor is limited to deducting the *adjusted basis* of the property, with a 50% CB limit.

Second, if the property would have resulted in a long-term capital gain had it been sold instead of donated, the asset is called "capital gain property," and one of three alternative tax consequences will occur. If the property is tangible personalty given to a public charity which *uses it* in its activities, then the *fair market value* is deductible (with a 30% CB limit). If, on the other hand, the charity is a private foundation, or if it is a public charity which *cannot* use the donated property in its activities, then the amount deductible is limited to the donor's *basis*, with a CB limit of 50% for donations to public charities and a 30% limit for donations to private charities. An example of a "related use" is placing a donated painting on a wall of the donee art museum or the donee university. An example of an unrelated use would be the storage of the painting in the institution's basement or the immediate sale of the painting. Finally, if the donation to a public charity qualifies for a deduction based on its fair market value, but with a 30% CB limitation, the taxpayer can elect to use the property's basis as the deduction and raise the CB limit to 50%.[41]

EXAMPLE 14 - 28. Charles, a real estate developer earning $380,000 in adjusted gross income this year, has four assets (each currently worth $100,000), one of which he is considering donating to a public charity. Besides *cash*, Charles has a parcel of *real estate* which his business purchased three years ago and which currently has an adjusted basis of $20,000. Charles also has two blocks of *common stock*, each of which cost $20,000. Stock A was purchased three years ago, and Stock B was acquired last month. The following describes (ignoring the 3% floor) the amount deductible if Charles contributes, alternatively, each asset to the charity which, for the moment we shall assume, can properly use any of the assets in its activities.

1. Cash: $100,000 deduction.
2. Business real estate: $20,000 deduction.
3. Stock A: $100,000 deduction. This stock could be the stock of Charles's real estate development corporation. The charity could be given the right to redeem the stock for cash.
4. Stock B: $20,000 deduction.

The charitable deduction for business real estate is limited to the developer's basis because the property represents his business inventory. A better alternative might be to sell the inventory and donate the after-tax cash proceeds. Assuming a 50% combined marginal tax rate, Charles could donate $60,000 cash ($100,000-($100,000-$20,000) * 50%), yielding a tax saving of $30,000 ($60,000 *50%). In contrast, donating the property would save only $10,000 in tax (50% * $20,000). Of course, the charity would be receiving only $60,000 (cash) rather than $100,000 (real estate).

Any charitable contributions of $250 or more must be substantiated contemporaneously in writing by the donee charity. The writing should state the amount of cash donated, a description (but not necessarily the value) of the property, and a good faith estimate of the value of any property it provided in consideration for the donation.[42] In addition, a donor of property exceeding $5,000 in value is required to obtain a "qualified appraisal" and supply additional information detailing the transaction.

This summary of the annual limitations has been a short overview. Individuals wishing to make contributions of this relative size should consult a tax adviser specializing in this area.

Outright Gifts to Charity

Several planning strategies evolve from the tax rules just discussed.

Income tax consequences. In many cases, contributing *capital gain property* to a public charity is more advantageous than contributing cash.

EXAMPLE 14 - 29. Jeff, who is in the 35% combined (i.e., state and federal) ordinary income tax bracket and a 22% combined capital gains tax bracket, wishes to contribute $5,000 to his favorite public charity. Jeff could give an original oil painting, acquired for $1,000 and now worth $5,000, or he could sell the painting and donate the cash proceeds. If Jeff contributes the painting, his after-tax cost will be $3,250 which is the $5,000 value of the painting, less the $1,750 tax savings from the deduction. Alternatively, if Jeff sells the painting and still donates the full $5,000, his after-tax cost will be $4,130, which is the $5,000 donated cash, plus the $880 tax on the gain ($4,000 * 22%), minus the $1,750 tax saving from the deduction.

Owners of nonmarketable property that they wish to sell may consider making a *bargain sale* of the property to charity. The income tax consequences of a bargain sale to charity are not the same as a bargain sale to a private individual. With the related party bargain sale, no loss can be recognized and a gain is recognized only if the bargain price exceeds the seller-donor's basis. But for a bargain sale to a charity, the transaction is treated as though it is two transactions in one: a sale and a gift. The old basis is allocated to each part in direct proportion to the part's value when compared to the whole. Thus, where B represents the old basis, B_g represents basis allocated to the gift portion and B_s represents the basis allocated to the sale portion, G stands for the value of the gift, which is the difference between the amount paid (S for sale) by the charity and the fair market value (FMV) of the property transferred to the charity at a bargain price.

$$B_g = (G/FMV)*B$$
$$B_s = (S/FMV)*B$$
$$Gain = S - B_s.$$

EXAMPLE 14 - 30. This year, Margaret transferred her vacant city lot to her church. She inherited the lot from her mother. It was valued in her mother's estate at $100,000, which of course established Margaret's basis. At the time of transfer, the lot was worth $500,000. Since Margaret is cash poor and wants to purchase a $500,000 life insurance policy, so her son won't be too disappointed about her transferring the lot. The church has agreed to pay Margaret $150,000 for the lot. Margaret's gain:

Gain = $150,000 - ($150,000/$500,000)*$100,000 = $120,000

Of course Margaret will have a charitable deduction of $350,000, the difference between the FMV and the amount paid to Margaret. If Margaret has modest income, she and the church might wish to structure this as an installment sale whereby the church pays the price in five $30,000 annual installments. Margaret's excess income tax charitable deduction can be carried forward, and the installment reporting will avoid bunching up the capital gain in the first year.

As in a private sale, an outright gift of *mortgaged property* to charity is treated as a bargain sale, resulting in taxable gain to the donor. However, the bargain sale may be a simpler way to sell difficult to market assets, such as an interest in a closely held business.

Gift tax consequences. Similar to the unlimited marital deduction, an unlimited gift tax deduction is allowed for the present value of gifts to qualifying charities.[43] The rules covering the charitable deduction no longer require that a gift tax return be filed, even if the gifts exceed the annual exclusion amount.

Estate tax consequences. Similar to lifetime inter-spousal gifts, *lifetime* gifts to charity are not included in the donor's estate tax base. They are not includable in the gross estate because they are not owned by the decedent at death, nor are they adjusted taxable gift.

Outright bequests to charity are totally deductible from the gross estate.[44] Thus, a multimillionaire could give all (or all but the exclusion amount) of his or her entire estate to charity and ensure total avoidance of the estate tax. Of course, he or she could also accomplish this goal by making a series of lifetime charitable transfers. In fact, lifetime charitable transfers are preferable to donations at death, as the next example illustrates.

> EXAMPLE 14 - 31. Sampson wishes to make an outright gift of $100,000 to his church which has been a source of continuous spiritual support to him and his family for many years. Sampson's estate planner recommends a lifetime transfer over a similar transfer at death, reasoning as follows: If Sampson donates the property at his death, his gross estate will be reduced by the amount of the gift, but he will enjoy no income tax benefit.[45] Alternatively, if Sampson makes the gift during his lifetime (even a deathbed gift), not only will his gross estate and estate tax base be lower by the date-of-death value of the gift property, but Sampson will also be able to save income taxes by deducting some or all of the value of the gift from his income.

Other tax planning for outright gifts to charity. Several other strategies include inter-spousal transfers, redemption bailout of corporate stock, gifts of life insurance, and the gift annuity.

Inter-spousal transfers. If a person insists on making a testamentary bequest to charity, the planner might urge the person to consider making an outright gift to the surviving spouse, who could then donate the property to charity. While the estate tax consequences are the same, the income tax results will improve, since S2 will be able to enjoy a charitable income tax deduction.

Of course, S2, as fee simple recipient of the property, could decide not to make the donation. Placing the property in a QTIP trust, with the charity named as the remainderman, will ensure receipt by the charity, but not until after S2's death, thus there is no income tax advantage.

Redemption bailout of corporate stock. A person owning stock in a closely held corporation may wish to gift some stock to a charity which will later tender the stock for redemption by the corporation. Advantages include saving income tax, "bailing out" corporate earnings and profits without incurring dividend income, helping younger family shareholders concentrate their ownership, and enabling the charity to receive cash. This arrangement should be undertaken with great caution, however, and may be challenged if the IRS believes it can prove the existence of an "understanding" between donor and charity that the charity would surrender the shares for redemption. In that case, the donor would be forced to incur a taxable gain.

Charitable gifts of life insurance. Lifetime gifts to charity of life insurance policies are popular. The insured can transfer an existing policy to charity, or the person can purchase a new policy naming the charity as beneficiary and assigning to the charity all ownership rights in the policy. The insured may agree to continue to pay the premiums. The person should be able to take income tax and gift tax charitable deductions for the policy's terminal value at the date of the gift (or adjusted basis, if less, in the case of income tax) and take additional income tax deductions as premiums are paid.

Gifts of Split Interests

Despite the added income tax advantage of lifetime charitable gifts, even individuals with strong charitable motives are often reluctant to make outright, present interest gifts to charity because they are not willing to *relinquish total control* of an asset. For example, they may be relying on an asset as a source of income or enjoyment, or they may have been planning to pass the asset on to the children. Reluctant individuals may be more willing, however, to make what could be called a compromise charitable gift, that is, a split-interest gift in which only part of an interest in property is given to charity. The person will often be able to accomplish *three objectives:* retain a much-desired portion of the interest, transfer the less-needed part, and still enjoy substantial income tax and death tax savings.

A split interest arrangement divides the asset into two separate property interests, the income interest and the remainder interest. The owner has the ability either to retain the right to the income from the asset, and presently gift the remainder interest to charity, or to gift the income interest to charity and designate a private party to take the remainder.

Arrangements for donating remainder interests to charity. Three devices recognized by tax law are commonly used by individuals to retain an income interest in an asset and gift the remainder interest to charity. Two of them, broadly called *charitable remainder trusts*, are the annuity trust and the unitrust. The third is called the *pooled income fund*. For each, the charity receives an irrevocable (vested) remainder interest in the asset. These 'strings-attached' arrangements will cause the date of death value of the property to be included in the donor's gross estate.[46] Fortunately, an equivalent charitable deduction will reduce the taxable amount to zero.[47]

Charitable remainder annuity trust. Under the charitable remainder annuity trust (CRAT), the person receives a fixed annuity income of at least 5% of the *original value* of the assets transferred into trust, payable at least annually, usually for life. The value of the deductible interest is calculated from IRS valuation Table S.

> EXAMPLE 14 - 32. Carrie, age 75, creates a CRAT, funding the trust with $100,000 cash. The trust provides for a 5% annual payment to Carrie for her life. At an assumed rate of 10%, the value of Carrie's retained income interest, derived from Table S, is $28,072, the product of the table value (5.6144) and $5,000, the annual trust income. Therefore, Carrie's deductible remainder interest is $71,928, the difference between the total value of the property and the value of the retained income interest.

Charitable remainder unitrust. The charitable remainder unitrust (CRUT) is much like the CRAT, except that the annual income depends on a fixed percentage of the *current fair market value* of the assets in the trust, re-determined annually. Thus, the amount of the annual income paid to the person will vary (hopefully upward) from year to year.[48]

The CRUT can provide for the income to be the *lesser* of the unitrust amount or the amount actually earned on the trust property, with any deficiencies payable in later years when earnings are higher. Thus, the owner of a rapidly appreciating, low-dividend-paying corporation can contribute stock to a CRUT and enjoy a large stream of income years later, after retirement, when the stock starts paying dividends. This "net income with make-up" unitrust (NIMCRUT) represents risky planning; the IRS has challenged these arrangements.

Calculation of the amount of the deductible remainder interest for a CRUT is complex and will not be derived in the examples that follow.

> EXAMPLE 14 - 33. Bob and Jeanne Ferrell, both age 65, wish to establish a CRUT to supplement their income and to benefit their favorite charity. They fund the trust with $100,000 of rental real estate having a tax basis of $20,000. The rental property is appreciating at an average annual rate of 8%, but has paid them only 2% a year in income ($2,000 this year). The trust provides that they will be paid an annual amount equal to 6% of the value of the trust corpus, determined annually.
>
> It will cost the Ferrells $4,000 in legal fees to establish the trust. If the trust corpus can grow by three percent annually (i.e., 10% overall return, less 6% to the Ferrells, less one percent trustee fee), the Ferrells will receive the following pre-tax amounts during the first five years: $6,000, $6,180, $6,365, $6,556, and $6,753. Assuming that the surviving spouse dies in 20 years, the last annual income payout in that year will be $10,521. Based on the IRS valuation tables, at 10%, the Ferrells will be able to deduct a charitable remainder interest of approximately $36,000, which at their 50% combined tax rate will immediately save them $18,000 in income tax. The Ferrells have, of course, relinquished the right to transfer the remainder interest, which is projected to be $209,743 ($100,000 stock growing at 10% - 6% - 1% = 3% annually for 20 years, reduced by 55% estate tax at S2's death).
>
> This arrangement has significantly supplemented the Ferrell's income. However, the plan has modestly improved their wealth position. At 10%, the net present value of this strategy, compared with doing nothing, is $9,853. Present value of benefits: tax savings from charitable deduction: $18,000; twenty years of new increasing after-tax income: $45,135. Present value of costs: preparation fees: $4,000; loss of the 2% rental income: $18,105; and the after tax value of forfeited remainder: $31,177.

> EXAMPLE 14 - 34. In the example immediately above, if the Ferrells like every-thing about the proposed CRUT except having to forfeit their disposition of the remainder interest, they may consider adopting what has been called a "wealth replacement plan." That requires funding an *irrevocable life insurance trust* with a second-to-die insurance policy in the amount of approximately $210,000, naming their children as trust beneficiaries.

The facts in the two examples above make many favorable assumptions, and probably represents the 'best case' scenario. At the other extreme, consider the following:

EXAMPLE 14 - 35. It is five years later, and the Ferrells have had some terrible luck. First, because of their poor health, Bob and Jeanne were able to acquire life insurance on their lives only at a *very high premium*. Second, market investment rates of return have declined significantly, generating far less income to the Ferrells than the amounts projected by the planner. In fact, the income generated has been far below the required trust distributions, and each year the Ferrells have had to report the amount of these deficiencies as a *taxable capital gain*. Third, lower market rates have caused the quarterly life insurance premiums to rise, and have delayed substantially how soon the "vanishing" premiums will actually end, which means the Ferrells can expect to pay far more in total for the policy than the planner's computer-forecasted "illustrations" initially projected. Fourth, due to sizable investments in junk bonds and unprofitable real estate, the life insurance company is in danger of *insolvency*, with its remaining assets being seized by the state Department of Insurance. Fifth, the Ferrells were unable to deduct the entire $36,000 in the first tax year, due to the *AGI limitations*. The nondeductible portion had to be carried over to the next tax year. Sixth, because the rental real property was subject to a mortgage, the transfer of it constituted a bargain sale, resulting in a *taxable capital gain* to the Ferrells,[49] and creating the risk of disqualification of the trust as a charitable remainder trust.[50] Seventh, the trust invested in a spaghetti factory, a trade or business considered not substantially related to the performance of its exempt purpose, causing the trust to *lose its tax exempt status* and making all undistributed trust income taxable.[51] Eighth, the land under the spaghetti factory was found contaminated with toxic waste, making the Ferrells potentially liable under federal law for clean-up costs. Finally, Bob and Jeanne have always been quite confused about this *complex* arrangement. For example, they are not able to fully understand why two trusts had to be created. They are now seeking another attorney to determine if they can recover damages from their once enthusiastic financial advisors.

Of course the above hypothetical depicts a "worst case" scenario, with certain trust assets encumbered, contaminated, and producing unrelated business income. Ordinarily, trustees will want to avoid acquiring such difficult assets.

At their best, charitable remainder trusts offer to an individual the advantages of higher cash flow during lifetime, lower investment risk and greater portfolio diversification. At their worst, they can be a confusing financial burden. Recent case law involves many planners battling with the IRS or attempting to reform their client's defective charitable trusts. In one recent case, a $25 million estate lost an $18 million deduction because its charitable trust was not in the form of an annuity trust, a unitrust, or a pooled income fund.[52] Although the IRS Regulations are exceedingly complex, requiring the drafting of long and technical documents, the Treasury has issued safe harbor sample documents which may be suitable for most people's needs. However, this is an area where very experienced counsel is needed.

Disillusioned clients will become more prevalent if financial planners continue to aggressively promote these trusts primarily as a means of increasing retirement income and avoiding capital gains tax. Advertisements appear in newspapers with the main pitch being "stop paying unnecessary taxes" with little or no mention that a sizable charitable contribution is required.

If you have clients interested in using charitable trusts as part of their estate plan, you should consider associating with an expert who is experienced in these complex matters. The charities themselves often have lists of estate planners who are conversant with charitable trusts.

Pooled income fund. Instead of a separate trust created by the donor or the donor's advisers, a pooled income fund is an investment fund created and maintained by the *target charity* which "pools" property from many similar contributors. Thus, the donor is spared the expense of planning and drafting a trust, an arrangement which would be considered 'overkill' when the charitable donation is relatively small (e.g., $10,000 to $100,000).

Many pooled income funds limit donations to cash and cash equivalents. The pooled income fund ordinarily provides that the charity will pay to the grantor an income for life and, if desired, for the life of the grantor's spouse, based on the rate of return actually earned by the fund as a whole. At their death, the property passes to the charity. Valuation of the charitable deduction is calculated using Treasury tables available from the IRS.

Comparison of the three techniques. All three techniques have the advantages of providing an income for life, reducing estate tax, and obtaining a relatively immediate income tax deduction. The CRAT may appeal to individuals who desire the certainty of a fixed income, even in a declining market. The CRUT may be preferred by those willing to risk fluctuating income for the opportunity to realize higher income payments. Thus the CRUT can offer a hedge against inflation. Assets in a CRUT do require an annual valuation, a possible extra trust cost. The pooled income fund may be preferred by those who would like to avoid having to establish and maintain a trust. Pooled income funds, however, are not permitted to invest in tax-exempt securities.[53] Also not all qualifying charities have created pooled income funds. Most colleges, however, use them to encourage charitable contributions by well-heeled alumni.

Arrangement for donating income interests to charity: The charitable lead trust. Instead of contributing a remainder interest, a person can donate an asset's income interest for a period of years to charity, with the remainder interest then passing to a private party (either reverting to the grantor or spouse, or passing to another person, such as a child or grandchild). The person or the person's estate will receive an income tax deduction for the value of the income interest, based on Treasury valuation tables. However, to get the charitable deduction, unless the trust is established at the grantor's death, the trust must be set up as a grantor trust, making the income taxable to the grantor.[54] Thus, charitable lead trusts are often designed to take effect after the person's death.

In a manner similar to a zeroed-out GRAT, a charitable lead trust may be structured to generate a charitable deduction equal to almost 100% of the current value of property transferred by way of the trust. If done successfully, the value of the remainder interest (probably given to the settlor's children) will approximate zero, resulting in very little use of the settlor's unified credit. Further, nothing (or very little) is included in the individual's taxable estate. Either the person will not own the property at death (because it was a lifetime charitable gift), or, if this is done as part of a testamentary plan, the estate will be entitled to a charitable deduction that offsets most of the value of the property going into the charitable lead trust. The goal is for the property to not only benefit the charity for a period of years, but to grow in value such that the remaindermen eventually receive a sizable distribution at the end of the term, all without incurring transfer taxes on the donated property. As the examples below show, success of the charitable lead trust depends on the actual rate of future asset appreciation.

> EXAMPLE 14 - 36. Reed creates a lifetime charitable lead trust, funding it with $100,000 in stock of his closely held corporation. The trust is obligated to pay a "guaranteed annuity" of $11,750, or 11.75% of the initial value of the corpus annually to the charity for a period of 20 years. Then, the trust will terminate and the remaining corpus, if any, will be distributed outright to Reed's surviving children and grandchildren. Assuming a 10% discount rate, the IRS Table annuity factor is 8.5136. The value of the charity's 20 year income interest is $100,034.80, the product of $11,750 and 8.5136. Reed's deduction is limited to $100,000, the value of the property. Since the value of the present income interest is higher than the value of the property, the value of the remainder interest is zero, which means that Reed has made no taxable gift.

EXAMPLE 14 - 37. Continuing the example immediately above, assume 20 years have passed. The closely held stock in the trust has performed so far in excess of 10% that its annual income has been more than ample to pay the annuity. As a result, the trust corpus and accumulated income is now worth $800,000. This amount will pass outright to Reed's descendants completely transfer-tax free.

EXAMPLE 14 - 38. Altering the projected outcome in the example above, assume again that 20 years have passed, but the closely held stock has earned only a 10% annual average rate of return, forcing the trustee to use trust corpus to satisfy in part the $11,750 annual distribution requirement. The corpus is now worth nothing (just as the IRS tables anticipated) and Reed's descendants, as remaindermen, will receive no trust distribution.

The outcomes in the preceding examples represent the two extremes of very good and very bad fortune. For most individuals, the likely result will be somewhere in between. The gift tax value of the remainder will not likely be zero, which means the grantor will have to partially use up his or her unified credit on a future interest gift that does not qualify for the annual exclusion. In addition, at eventual distribution date, the corpus will have appreciated somewhat, but not greatly.

Charitable lead annuity trusts are more attractive when interest rates are relatively low. A low (discount) rate results in a higher valuation of the deductible charitable interest donation, and a lower valuation of the taxable remainder interest gift.

EXAMPLE 14 - 39. Charlie established a charitable lead trust for a 20 year term with assets worth $1,000,000. The trust must pay the charity $70,000 per year. If the §7520 rate is 6% the "lead" interest for the charity is worth $802,893 [$70,000 * 11.4699], but if the rate is 12% the lead interest is just $522,858 [$70,000 * 7.4694]. Thus, the lower the rate, the better the charitable deduction for Charlie.

The charitable lead trust works best for wealthy, estate tax-avoiding individuals who can afford to forego substantial income for a period of time, and own a significant amount of highly appreciating assets that generate sufficient income to meet the required payout to the charity.

CONCLUSION

This chapter has focused on various non-gift, lifetime intra-family transfers and charitable gifts that really work. The techniques not only reduce taxes, but they also help other members of the person's family and/or they help charities by providing funds that allow them to carry out their charitable purposes. It is often a win-win situation. Some of the techniques allow both families and charities to increase their wealth.

This is not the case with matters taken up in Appendix 14A that follows immediately after this chapter. It examines various defective incomplete transfers. The first five were once popular, but have been rendered ineffective due to changing tax laws. The sixth has always been defective. They are: the interest-free loan, short-term trust, spousal remainder trust, sale of a remainder interest, joint purchase, and family estate trust. You are urged to read this appendix, partly to gain a historical perspective, partly because some clients will still be involved in prior-consummated transfers of this kind, and partly to be aware of formerly popular devices about which clients will inquire for some time to come.

QUESTIONS AND PROBLEMS

1. Why are many planning-minded persons disinclined to make gifts?

2. How can a bargain sale add flexibility to gift planning?

3. (a) Describe the installment sale. (b) What tax advantage does it have over the ordinary sale?

4. Summarize the major advantages and disadvantages of the private annuity.

5. Crucible, a wealthy 60-year-old, asks you for advice on lifetime transfers. His daughter is interested in acquiring his antique car, which is worth $40,000 and has a basis of $10,000. In each of the following alternatives, calculate Crucible's taxable gain for each future year.
   a. Ordinary sale.
   b. Installment sale, over 10 years (no down payment), with equal annual payments on principal, plus interest at a rate of 10% on the outstanding balance. (Query - will there be any other taxable income?)

6. The Platos are a husband and wife in their 70s, with an adult daughter age 45. They wish to make a lifetime transfer of a considerable amount of wealth to her, and you recommend four alternatives for consideration: A large outright gift; an installment sale; a private annuity; and a grantor retained annuity trust.
   a. Which transfer would probably involve the greatest present value of expected total costs to daughter? Why?
   b. Which one will probably save the most estate tax? Why?
   c. Which is probably the safest in terms of IRS challenge? Why?
   d. In which have the Platos retained the greatest interest? Why?
   e. Name several other factors that will influence which transfer, if any, the Platos will ultimately select.

7. Under what circumstances will a gift-leaseback work well?

8. Discuss the income-shifting and estate tax-reducing ability of the grantor retained interest trust.

9. Explain the reason for the advantage of each of the following *charitable* transfers.
   a. Gift of appreciated property rather than cash derived from the sale of the property.
   b. Lifetime gift rather than gift at death.
   c. Gift of a split interest rather than a whole interest.

10. Stover is 70 years old and is currently in the 35% combined state and federal marginal income tax bracket. He wishes to gift to charity his block of ABC Corp. stock, currently worth $20,000. His adjusted basis in the stock is $2,000.
   a. Calculate Stover's "after (income) tax cost" if he bequeaths the stock to the charity and dies shortly thereafter.
   b. Perform the same calculation as in part a, above, assuming that Stover sells the stock and gives the entire $20,000 cash to charity during his lifetime.
   c. Calculate Stover's after-tax cost, assuming instead that he makes a lifetime gift of the stock to charity.
   d. What should Stover plan to do?

11. Compare the advantages of the CRAT, the CRUT, and the pooled income fund.

12. Use the table that follows to compare the advantages of various lifetime transfers. In each box, place the number that you think describes how well that transfer accomplishes each goal using the following rating system: 3 = excellent; 2 = good; 1 = fair; 0 = poor. Use a range if the outcome is uncertain and be prepared to explain why you choose a number or a range.

TABLE 14-1 Comparative Advantages of Lifetime Transfers

Types of Transfers	Goals									
	Ability to Retain		Ability to Avoid		Step up in Basis	Shift income	Estate Tax Base		Avoid Probate	Low risk of IRS attack
	Control	Income	Income Tax	Gift tax			Reduce	Freeze		
Annual exclusion gifts										
Large outright gifts										
Ordinary sale										
Bargain Sale										
Installment sale										
Private annuity										
Gift-lease back										
Grantor retained interest trust (GRIT)										
Irrevocable Life Insurance Trust										

ANSWERS TO THE QUESTIONS AND PROBLEMS

1. Planning-minded persons are often unwilling to make outright gifts because they don't want to relinquish: 1) dominion and control over assets; and 2) income earned from the assets.

2. A bargain sale can add flexibility to gift planning because it can be structured to reflect the degree of generosity that the person feels. The sale can require any amount of consideration in payment for the transferred asset.

3. a. Under an installment sale, the seller transfers an asset in exchange for a note which obligates the buyer to make periodic payments of income and principal.
   b. Compared to the ordinary sale, it has the tax advantage of spreading recognition of the seller's taxable gain over the collection period.

4. Advantages of the private annuity:
   a. Hopefully, there is no gift tax on the transfer.
   b. Hopefully, the asset is not included in the annuitant's estate tax base. Thus, it can reduce or freeze the gross estate.

   Disadvantages of the private annuity:
   a. The contract cannot be secured.
   b. No part of the annuity payment is deductible by the obligor.
   c. If the annuitant lives a very long life, the obligor will have made a bad bargain.
   d. There is a §2036 danger, if the value of the property transferred is greater than the value of the annuity received.

5. a. Ordinary sale: Gain = $40,000 - $10,000 = $30,000. Entire tax is due in year of sale.
   b. Installment sale: Gross profit = $30,000. Seventy-five percent of each principal payment is taxable in the year received (= $30,000 gross profit ÷ $40,000 selling price). Thus, each year, taxable capital gain is .75*$4,000 = $3,000. Any interest received, of course, is taxable, too.

6. a. A gift and a GRAT require no payments by the daughter. On the other hand, both the *installment* sale and the *private annuity* obligate the daughter to pay the entire present actuarial value of the asset transferred. Which of the two would in fact cost more will depend on how long the individuals lived. For example, if the donors lived an unusually long life, the private annuity would cost more, because the payments will have to be made for the annuitants' entire life.

   b. The *private annuity* will probably save the most estate tax. At the annuitants' death, nothing in connection with the transaction (except any annuity payments not spent) will be includable in the annuitants' estate tax base. The large outright gift and the GRAT (unless it is zeroed out) will probably require inclusion of an adjusted taxable gift in the estate tax base which could increase estate tax by raising the tax bracket. The value of the note under an installment sale would be includable in the grantor's gross estate.

   c. The *large outright gift* is probably safest, assuming that the valuation is acceptable to the IRS. It is the least aggressive and least controversial strategy. The installment sale, quite established in the law, is almost as safe. On the other hand, the IRS challenges private annuities and GRATs frequently.

   d. The Platos will retain the greatest interest with the GRAT, since they will retain an estate for years in the asset, and, likely, a reversion right if they die within the income period. They would retain no interest in the large outright gift, and only an income interest in the installment sale and the private annuity.

   e. Other factors include:
      The person's health
      Desire to retain control
      Daughter's financial status
      The person's need for income
      Appreciation potential of the asset
      Income tax bracket of daughter
      Daughter's maturity
      Adjusted basis of the asset

7. A gift-leaseback will work well for a business-owning individual who wishes to shift income to a lower bracket family member and has business assets that can be transferred.

8. Income shifting: As a grantor trust, the GRIT cannot shift income during the period when the grantor retains the right to income.

   FET reduction: By transferring appreciating assets directly to a younger generation family member, the GRIT can avoid estate tax in both spouses' estates. Of course, any taxable gift will be included in the grantor's taxable estate.

9. a. A gift of appreciated property will eliminate the need to recognize the unrealized gain on the property, thereby reducing the net, after tax-cost of the charitable expense.
   b. A lifetime gift will reduce income tax (charitable deduction) and exclude the gift from the gross estate. A gift at death will only reduce the taxable estate but not reduce income tax.
   c. Gift of a split interest can enable the donor to retain a highly desired portion of the property, such as a life estate in the income.

10. a. Gift of stock at death: After (income) tax cost = $20,000, since no income tax deduction will be available.
    b. Sale of stock and lifetime gift of cash proceeds: Stover will pay income tax of $6,300 (=.35*18,000). If he gives the entire gross proceeds of $20,000, his charitable deduction will generate a tax savings of $7,000 (=.35*$20,000). Thus, Stover's after-tax cost will be $19,300 (=$20,000 + $6,300 - $7,000).
    c. Lifetime gift of stock: Stover's charitable deduction will generate a tax saving of $7,000 (=$20,000*.35). Thus, his after-tax cost will be $13,000 (=$20,000 - $7,000).
    d. All things the same, Stover should seriously consider making a lifetime gift of the stock, to minimize the after-tax cost of the contribution.

11. All of the techniques offer individuals an opportunity for a large current charitable deduction, coupled with a (potentially high) income stream for the rest of their lives.

> CRAT: Offers the certainty of a fixed income for life.
> CRUT: Offers possibly higher income payments in future years, because income is based on a fixed percentage of current value.
> Pooled Income Fund: Offers opportunity for a split interest charitable gift without the need to set up and maintain a private trust.

12. Numbers are somewhat subjective and may depend upon the particular fact situation and/or assumptions made. Good for class discussion or several students should compare their answers.

Defective Incomplete Transfers

OVERVIEW

This appendix will describe six defective transfer devices that are presently not recommended by planners. The first five have been virtually legislated out of existence by Congress between 1984 and 1990. And the sixth has always been riddled with tax defects, making it inherently defective.

The evolution of income tax law in the last few years has resulted in depriving taxpayers of the major tax benefits earlier available through the use of the *interest free loan*, the *short-term trust*, the *spousal remainder trust*, the *sale of a remainder interest*, and the *joint purchase*. The interest-free loan was first to go with the passage of TRA 84. The next two were killed by TRA 86. The last two were rendered ineffective by Case law and by the Revenue Reconciliation Act of 1990. They were all vulnerable to attack because, unlike the transfers covered in Chapter 13 and 14, each was able to accomplish, in a very large way, at least two of the following: shift large amounts of income; enable the transferor to retain a substantial interest in or control over the property; or freeze large estate tax values at little or no gift tax cost.

The *family estate trust* has never worked, since its operation clearly violates major holdings of case law and provisions of the Internal Revenue Code.

This appendix has been written for three reasons. First, it will give the reader a better historical perspective on lifetime transfers. Second, these strategies may have been employed by some individuals in the past, and may still be in use. The reader should be aware of their operation since questions will be raised about their efficacy. Finally, the planner can expect even clients to be curious about these formerly popular devices, for years to come.

INTEREST-FREE LOAN

Until 1984, the interest-free loan (IFL) was considered an attractive device to shift income to a lower-tax-bracket family member. However, the Tax Reform Act of 1984 all but destroyed its appeal. The following material presents an overview of the major tax and non-tax considerations in making IFLs and describes the few areas in which IFLs still might be put to use.

An arm's-length loan, in which the lender charges a fair market rate of interest, does not achieve many estate planning objectives. It does not shift income significantly, although it may provide for the borrower an otherwise unavailable loan opportunity. An interest-free loan of cash, on the other hand, may be able to shift taxable income from the lender to the borrower. Since the borrower is free to use the loaned property to generate income without incurring a financing charge, the loan may put the borrower in a higher standard of living. Further, the income generated may be taxed at a significantly lower rate. Unfortunately, other tax consequences often render IFLs largely unattractive.[55] As the following material suggests, tax controversy has highlighted their brief history.

Gift Tax Consequences

In 1984, the U.S. Supreme Court settled a longstanding conflict between taxpayers and the IRS by ruling that an IFL constitutes a taxable gift of the reasonable value of the use of the money loaned.[56] In calculating the taxable gift value, the taxpayer is required to use a federal rate of interest, which is published monthly by the IRS and set approximately equal to the rate that is paid by the U.S. Treasury on securities of similar maturity.

IFLs can be made for a fixed term, or they can have a demand provision. If the loan is made for a *fixed term*, the gift is considered as having been made as of the loan inception, with the gift amount equal to the difference between the amount loaned and the discounted present value of the note.

> EXAMPLE 14 - 40. Dad and Mom lend $100,000 cash, interest-free, to Mary who has just graduated from dental school and wishes to start a practice. Mary signs a 10-year note, with no principal payable until maturity. Assuming that the current federal long-term rate is 10%, the present discounted value of the note is approximately $38,500, and Mom and Dad are deemed to have made a gift of approximately $61,500, the difference between the amount transferred and the value received.

If, on the other hand, an interest-free loan incorporates a *demand loan*, with the loan callable by the lender at any time, then at the end of each year the lender will have made a gift of one year's imputed interest.

> EXAMPLE 14 - 41. Assume the facts in Example 14- 35, except that the note is a demand loan with no maturity. If the loan is still outstanding at the end of their first taxable year, Mom and Dad will have made a gift of one year's interest, imputed to be $10,000, calculated on the basis of the assumed 10% short-term federal rate. For every year that the loan remains outstanding, a similar gift computation will have to be made.

Thus, in order to minimize the gift tax, an IFL must have no maturity. And, to prevent the entire transfer from being treated as an outright gift, the loan must have a demand provision.

If an interest-free demand loan becomes unenforceable, a more significant taxable event will have occurred.

> EXAMPLE 14 - 42. Assume the facts in Example 14-36. Four years go by, and the state's statute of limitations runs out preventing any collection on the original note. In that year, a taxable gift of the entire loan principal is triggered.

Thus, IFLs must be redrafted periodically to prevent this unfortunate tax consequence.

Despite the court decision subjecting interest-free loans to gift taxation, most lenders will not owe any gift tax because of the combined shelter of the annual exclusion and the unified credit. Thus, the parents in the above examples will incur no gift tax liability, unless they have already made taxable gifts large enough to have fully used up their unified credits. In general, the gift tax issue should not discourage many from the use of interest-free loans as a method of shifting income to a lower tax bracket. However, the income tax issues, discussed next, usually will.

Income Tax Consequences

The IRS has argued, in a business context, that the interest forgone by a corporate lender constitutes taxable income to an employee-executive borrower. To date, the IRS has had little success in the courts, and unless it can influence Congress to act, imputed interest income on an interest-free loan will not likely be taxed to the *borrower*.

In 1984, Congress did act, however, to tax the *lender* on the amount of the interest forgone under an IFL.[57] This forgone interest is treated as if it had been received by the lender and paid by the borrower. Thus, the lender is deemed to have received taxable interest, which is includable in gross income. Similarly, the borrower is deemed to have paid interest, which ordinarily is not tax deductible unless it is considered business interest, investment interest which is offset by investment income, or interest on a debt secured by a primary or secondary residence. In short, there is usually greater taxable income without the corresponding deduction.

> EXAMPLE 14-43. Dad, in the 31% income tax bracket, makes a $20,000 interest-free demand loan to his son, who is in the 15% bracket and is able to invest the proceeds in a bank time deposit yielding an annual return of 8%. Assuming an applicable federal rate of 10%, the tax consequences in the first full year are as follows:
>
> *Gift tax treatment*: At the end of each year, Dad will be deemed to have made a gross gift of $1,600, the amount of the forgone interest. Because of the annual exclusion, there will be no taxable gift.
>
> *Income tax treatment in the absence of the 1984 Act*: Each year, son would earn $1,600 taxable income on the deposit, paying a tax of $240. Instead, had Dad invested the loan money, he would have paid a tax of $496. Thus, in the absence of the 1984 act, under TRA 86 tax rates the family would have saved $256 in income tax.

Income tax treatment under the 1984 Act: If son does not itemize, he will still pay a tax of $240, and in addition, Dad will pay a tax of $496 on the $1,600 of imputed interest, for a total of $736. On the other hand, if son itemizes, the $1,600 imputed interest payment is an investment interest expense which he can deduct. In this case, the son's tax would effectively be zero, the Dad's tax would still be $496, so the family as a whole would not have any tax savings from the loan.

The 1984 Act incorporated four exceptions, which may provide the basis for a very modest degree of income shifting. First, where the proceeds of an IFL between individuals are invested by the borrower to yield less than $1,000 income in any given year, forgone interest will not be imputed. Thus, at an assumed 8% investment return, a person could lend $12,500 interest free, without being subject to income taxation.

The second exception to the 1984 Act applies to a loan balance of $10,000 or less to any individual, which is not subject to imputed interest unless it is used to purchase income-producing assets.

Third, the amount of the imputed interest is limited to the borrower's net investment income for the year in cases where the aggregate amount of outstanding loans between two individuals does not exceed $100,000, provided that one of the principal purposes of the loan is not federal tax avoidance.

The fourth exception to the 1984 Act applies to loans to employees and to corporate shareholders, who are permitted to borrow up to $10,000 without imputing forgone interest, provided that one of the principal purposes of the loan is not federal tax avoidance.

Interest-free demand loans should be made in the form of cash, rather than other property. A transfer of noncash in exchange for a note might be treated as a taxable *sale* to the extent of the consideration received.

Estate Tax Consequences

At the lender's death, the gross estate will include the current value of the note. The market value of a *demand note* will equal the face amount of the note, since the decedent, just prior to death, could have demanded full repayment.[58] On the other hand, the market value of a *term note* will usually be different from the face amount and is calculated by using a market rate of interest to discount the value of the future payments. In executing either kind of note, the lender has not really been able to reduce his or her gross estate significantly. The interest-free loan was never designed to reduce death taxes.

In conclusion, because of its serious tax consequences and the compression of income tax rates, the IFL will no longer be used much.

SHORT-TERM TRUST

Prior to March 2, 1986, the short-term trust was a very popular device to shift income to a lower-bracket taxpayer. Also called the Clifford trust, after the taxpayer who lost a court case in a situation where the he had tried to shift income using a trust of short duration. Congress then stepped in and set the standards for trusts that would be acceptable for shifting income.[59] The Code required that the trust be irrevocable for at least 10 years or for the life of a beneficiary, after which the trust corpus would revert to the settlor.

Gift Tax Consequences

If the income had to be paid to the income beneficiary for the term of the trust, then it was considered to be a present interest and, as such, it qualified for the annual exclusion. The reversionary interest was what was being kept by the settlor, hence it was not a gift (even though it is a future interest).

Income Tax Consequences

Grandfathered trusts. Income earned on the property placed in a 10-year short-term trust on or before March 1, 1986, will not be taxable to the transferor-grantor, except when the kiddie tax applies. Instead, the income will be taxed to the trust or to the beneficiary, depending on whether it is accumulated or distributed. And the accumulated income later distributed to the beneficiary could be subject to some additional tax, under the throwback rules, unless the beneficiary is under age 21.

The failure to avoid the grantor trust provisions of the Internal Revenue Code will cause income received by the trust to be taxable to the grantor. Thus, the short-term trust had to be carefully drafted to avoid running afoul of the grantor trust rules. For example, the trust had to be irrevocable for at least 10 years from the date the trust was *funded* with the property, not from the date the document was executed.

> EXAMPLE 14 - 44. In 1983, Omid created an irrevocable trust for the benefit of his 17 year old daughter Hazel. The trust terms required the trustee to pay Hazel all of the income from the trust for ten years, after which the corpus would revert to Omid. It was funded with stocks and bonds worth $100,000. Because it complied with the short term trust laws, Hazel reported the income each year until the trust terminated. Actually, the trust would have first reported it, taken a distribution deduction for the income distributed to Hazel, and sent her a "K-1" that told her how much she had to report on her income tax returns. Assuming an 8% rate for valuing the income interest, Table B shows 0.536807 as the appropriate factor for a ten year income interest. Therefore, the gift to Hazel was valued at $53,680.70. It was a present interest, so the taxable gift that Omid reported was $43,680.70

Nongrandfathered trusts. TRA 86 destroyed the income tax benefit of the short-term trust by deleting the 10-year exception under Internal Revenue Code (IRC) Section 673. Thus, for any transfers into trust after March 1, 1986, the grantor is treated as the owner of any portion of a trust in which the grantor has any *reversionary interest which exceeds 5%* of the value of such portion. Thus, the typical new short-term trust will be treated as a grantor trust.

How long must a short-term trust created after March 1, 1986, last so that the present value of the remainder interest does not exceed 5% of the corpus? IRS tables indicate that the reversion cannot occur for at least 32 years! Although several commentators are suggesting that there may be situations where this period is acceptable, in most cases, grantors will not wish to make an irrevocable transfer of property for such a long time. Most individuals will no longer wish to shift income with the short-term trust. Thus, the short-term trust is no longer able to save income tax by shifting income.

Estate Tax Consequences to the Grantor

Several estate tax consequences may occur when the grantor dies. First, if creation of the trust resulted in a "taxable gift," that is, the transfer of an amount in excess of the annual exclusion and other deductions, then that taxable value will be added to the estate tax base, as an "adjusted taxable gift." Of course, a credit will be applied for any gift tax paid, but the taxation of adjusted taxable gifts along with the rest of a decedent's estate may subject the gift to a higher marginal rate of taxation than that incurred when the gift tax was calculated.

A second estate tax consequence at the grantor's death will be the addition to the gross estate of the actuarial value of the decedent-grantor's interest in the trust property. Determination of that amount will depend on when the decedent dies, as explained next.

If the grantor of a short-term trust dies *before the trust reverts*, the value of the gross estate will include the value of the grantor's reversionary interest at death. Derived from the U.S. Treasury estate tax valuation table found in Treasury Regulations 20.2031-7, the value depends on the assumed rate of interest and the number of years remaining to reversion. For example, assuming a 10% discount rate, if a grantor dies exactly five years prior to reversion, the gross estate will include 62.0921 percent of the decedent's share of the trust property.

If the grantor of a short-term trust dies *after reversion*, the value of the gross estate will include the date of death market value of the property that had reverted, if still owned, or the value of any other assets acquired with the property. However, since the property is back in the transferor's estate, it will not also be an adjusted taxable gift for estate tax purposes.

As an income tax planning device, the short-term trust was often used for two common types of beneficiaries: children and elderly parents. These are people for whom many individuals would like to offer assistance and who are often in lower income tax brackets. Due to tax reform, these short-term trust are no longer useful.

SPOUSAL REMAINDER TRUST

A popular income-shifting device prior to TRA 86 was the spousal remainder trust (SRT). As in the case of the short-term trust, the grantor, typically a high-income-tax-bracket parent, transferred income-earning property to an irrevocable trust, which for a specified period paid all income to a low-income-tax-bracket family member, typically a young adult child, and remainder to the grantor's spouse. Properly arranged, the value of the income interest, which is valued in a manner similar to the short-term trust, would qualify for the annual gift tax exclusion. However, unlike the short-term trust, whose property reverted to the grantor, the SRT corpus then passed to the grantor's spouse. Although the value of the remainder interest will not qualify for the annual exclusion, it will not be subject to gift tax, due to the unlimited gift tax marital deduction.

> EXAMPLE 14 - 45. In 1985, Dad created an SRT, funding it with $30,000 in bonds. Income is required to be paid annually to his daughter, a college freshman, for the next four years. At the end of the fourth year, the corpus will pass outright to Mom. Based on the valuation tables, the value of a gift of an income interest for a four-year term certain represents 31.6987 percent of the total value of the property transferred. Although Dad has made a gross gift to his daughter of $9,510, there will be no taxable gift, since the gift of the income interest is sheltered entirely by the annual exclusion and the gift of the remainder interest is sheltered entirely by the marital deduction.

Prior to TRA 86, the SRT had several advantages over the short-term trust. First, because the corpus does not revert to the grantor, the trust was not required, under the grantor trust rules, to remain in existence for at least 10 years. Thus, the trust could terminate at any time, and if it terminated sooner than 10 years, the relative value of the transferred income interest would be less than that for the short-term trust. This meant that a greater amount of property could be transferred to the SRT free of gift tax. Further, earlier termination might have encouraged grantors to make successive annual gift tax-free transfers into the trust, unimpeded by the requirement of waiting 10 years after the date of the most recent transfer to terminate the trust.

The SRT often facilitated the couple's estate tax planning objectives. It helped to equalize the spouses' estates in order to minimize the combined estate tax, and remainder interests were transferred to the less wealthy spouse by means of the SRT.

Compared with the short-term trust, the SRT had one potentially major disadvantage: at the termination of the trust, the property passed to the grantor's spouse, rather than the grantor. The SRT worked best in a harmonious family setting. Any SRT having an agreement in which the remainderman spouse agreed to immediately retransfer the remainder interest to the grantor was attacked by the IRS, which claimed that the grantor in fact retained a reversion, thereby destroying all income and transfer-tax benefits.

TRA 86 destroyed the usefulness of the spousal remainder trust by amending Section 672 to treat any power or interest held by a spouse (who lives with the grantor) as if that interest was held by the grantor. Therefore, the traditional spousal remainder trust, funded after March 1, 1986, will be treated as if it will revert to the grantor, making it a *grantor trust* and thereby preventing the shifting of income to the lower-bracket-income beneficiary. Thus, there is no longer any reason to choose this once appealing transfer strategy.

SALE OF A REMAINDER INTEREST AND JOINT PURCHASE

The ordinary sale, bargain sale, installment sale, and private annuity may all be unacceptable to some individuals who, during their lifetimes, do not want to surrender the present enjoyment of property. All of these sales techniques involve the immediate transfer of the right to possession and enjoyment. Prior to 1986, another type of sale, however, the *sale of a remainder interest*, did not have this drawback. Although it was coming under increasing attack from the IRS, it was an attractive alternative. Like the other devices, it was able to freeze estate tax values, generate cash flow, and assist family members. Unlike the others, it also permitted the individual to retain the right to possession and enjoyment of the property "sold" until death.

> EXAMPLE 14 - 46. In 1982, a 60-year-old parent had some valuable jewelry and a physician-son who agreed to purchase the remainder interest in the gems. Assuming 10%, the son paid 22.674% of the current value of the jewelry for the right to receive it outright at the person's death. The person was able to own and enjoy the jewelry for life. And the estate tax value of the asset was still effectively frozen, since the person's gross estate would include only the amount of the sale proceeds that has been retained at death. Of course, the son would not receive possession of the jewelry until the person's death, but he probably would have received it no sooner anyway.

With an installment sale, the seller could occasionally forgive a payment, which constituted a taxable gift that qualified for the annual exclusion. Use of the installment sale also postponed recognition of the seller's gain. In determining gain or loss with the sale of a remainder interest, the income tax basis in the remainder interest is apportioned between the remainder interest and the retained life estate. Thus, in our example, the son's tax basis became 22.674% of the former basis.

Exclusion of the remainder interest from the seller's gross estate was not guaranteed, however, as the IRS may have contended that the only way to escape the trap of §2036 is for the purchaser to have paid the full value of the property, not just the value of the remainder interest. Of course, this would have made the transaction even less attractive to the buyer than an ordinary sale.

The passage of §2036(c) in the Revenue Act of 1987 (and a subsequent court decision) increased the likelihood of inclusion, due to the emphasis of that section on estate freezing transfers.[60] But the risk of §2036 could have been greatly minimized if, instead of making a transfer of property, the individual and another family member joined in purchasing property from a *third party*, with the individual purchasing a life interest and the family member (usually a member of the younger generation) acquiring the remainder interest. As a result, this "joint purchase" or "split purchase" rapidly replaced the sale of a remainder interest as a preferred method of transferring wealth after 1986.

Finally, the passage of §2702 in 1990 entirely killed both the sale of a remainder interest and the joint purchase. In either case, the individual will be treated as having made a gift to the extent that the value of the underlying property exceeds the price paid by the other purchaser.

THE FAMILY ESTATE TRUST: A TRAP FOR THE UNWARY

The reader should be cautioned against recommending the so-called estate planning device, the family estate trust. Also called a constitutional trust or an equity trust, the family estate trust is an arrangement fraught with tax danger. Many variations have been created, but they all have the following characteristics:

1. The same person acts in four different capacities: grantor, trustee, trust employee, and beneficiary.
2. The grantor transfers assets into the trust in exchange for "certificate units." The trustee leases the employee's services to others (typically including the individual's current employer), who pay a salary directly to the trustee.
3. The certificate units entitle the grantor to share in the trust's income.
4. Upon the grantor's death, the trust assets pass to others, not to the grantor's estate.

The family estate trust has been touted as a great tax saver. It is said to be able to reduce income tax by shifting income to a lower bracket (the trust and other family members) and to reduce the individual's death taxes by shifting assets before death to other beneficiaries. In fact, just the opposite is true. The IRS has been aggressively and successfully challenging family estate trusts in the courts, which have regularly upheld the following tax consequences:

1. Under the *assignment-of-income doctrine*, wages assigned to the trust are still taxable to the wage earner, not to the trust.
2. Personal living expenses are not deductible.
3. Fees to set up the trust are not deductible.
4. The date-of-death value of the property owned by the trust is subject to inclusion in the *gross estate* of the trustor as an incomplete transfer.

5. At least two tax *penalties* may be imposed. First, a negligence penalty of 20% of the additional tax due is usually assessed. Second, tax preparers will be charged penalties of hundreds of dollars for each return found to exhibit negligent or willful attempts to understate the tax liability.

In view of the tax exposure, individuals should steer clear of the family estate trust.

ENDNOTES

1. §163.

2. §2033.

3. §7872(a)(1).

4. §267.

5. Reg. 1.1015-4(a)(1)

6. *Juden*, 89-1 USTC 9142; 63 ¶ AFTR 2d 89-595 (ECA-8, 1989)

7. §453

8. §453(b)(2) & §453(l)

9. §453(e)(1).

10. Income in respect of a decedent (IRD) is discussed in Chapter 7.

11. §2043.

12. For an example of a successful SCIN involving a $12 million note, see *Wilson*, TCM 1992-480.

13. *Estate of Moss,* 74 TC 1239 (1980).

14. *Frane v. Commr*, 998 F. 2d 567 (CCA-8, 1993) in part reversing *Estate of Frane,* 98 TC 26 (1992); §691(a)(5).

15. Reg. §25.7520-3(b)(3)

16. §2036(a).

17. IRC Section 2036. See also *Bell Estate v. Commr,* 60 TC 469 (1973).

18. §453(b)(1); *Rye v. United States,* 92-1 USTC ¶50,186.

19. §2702(e).

20. §2702(a)(1).

21. §2701(e)(2).

22. Reg. §25.2702-3(b)(1)

23. Reg. §25.2702-3(c)(1)

24. §677(a)

25. §2036(a)

26. §2001(b)

27. §2642.

28. §2701(e)(2); Reg. §25.2701-1(d)(2)

29. §2701(e) and §2704(c)(2); Reg. §25.2702-2(a)(1)

30. LR 9239015.

31. Regs. §25.2702-3(e), Exs. 1 & 5; LR 9248016, relying on RR 77-454.

32. §25.2702-5

33. Table B, term of years remainder values.

34. 80CNSMT, 1980 census survival values.

35. LR 9249014.

36. Prop. Reg. §25.2702-5(c)(9)

37. §170(c).

38. §170(b)(1)(F).

39. §170(b)

40. See §§170(b)(1)(B), 170(b)(1)(C), 170(b)(1)(D), & 170(d)(1)(A)

41. §170(b)(1)(C)

42. §170(f)(8).

43. §2522(a).

44. §2055(a).

45. *U.S. Trust Co. v. U.S.*, 803 F. 2d 1363 (CCA-5, 1986).

46. §2036(a).

47. §2055.

48. Valuation of unitrust interests are calculated based on §7520 applicable federal rates released monthly by the IRS, along with unitrust valuation factors derived from the Treasury department's *Actuarial Values-- Beta Volume* (IRS Pub. 1458), available from the U.S. Government Printing Office ((202) 783-3238).

49. Reg. §1.1011-2(a)(3); LR 7908016.

50. In LR 9015049, the IRS disqualified a proposed unitrust funded with mortgaged property.

51. §681(a). The rules on unrelated business taxable income are found in §511, et. seq.

52. *E. La Meres Estate*, TC CCH 12,880.

53. §642(c)(5)(C).

54. Attaining grantor trust status without subjecting the corpus to estate taxation under §2036-2038 can be a challenge, see LR 9224029 and LR 9247024.

55. Actually, any loan made at a rate of interest below an acceptable market rate will be subject to taxation. However, we will continue to use the term *IFL* to refer to all below-market loans.

56. *Dickman v. Commissioner*, 104 S. Ct. 1086 (USSC, yr).

57. §7872.

58. If the executor is not a family member, he or she (or it, in the case of a bank) may choose to call the note due and payable after the death of the lender in order to properly manage the estate.

59. Clifford lost the case, however. *Helvering v. Clifford*, 309 U.S. 331 (USSC, 1940). After the Clifford decision, Congress added the 10-year requirement to the Code, under Section 673, et. seq.

60. One court held that consideration for purposes of §2036 must equal the entire value of the property. *Gradow* 897 F.2d 516 (et, 1990).

CHAPTER 15

Liquidity Planning

OVERVIEW

This chapter will explore the role of liquidity in estate planning. It will summarize the liquidity needs at death, examine the sources of liquidity available to the estate before and after death, and describe the planning techniques commonly undertaken. Planning devices covered include the sale of assets before death, life insurance, valuation discounts and control premiums, and several strategies unique to business owners, including sale of the business and information on several Internal Revenue Code sections intended to provide tax relief for those estates that include significant business interests.

SUMMARY OF CASH NEEDS AT DEATH

Types of cash needs. Death may trigger a need for liquidity. Money is needed to pay for a variety of obligations, such as expenses directly related to the person's death, funds for a readjustment period, and costs for the care of dependents.

With regard to directly related expenses, there may be *taxes*, including federal and state death taxes, and expenses of estate (probate and/or trust) administration, including payments to lawyers, executors, accountants, appraisers, and trustees. There may be *debts and claims* against the decedent's estate, including last illness and funeral expenses. There may be immediate cash needs for the maintenance and welfare of the surviving family. And there may be cash bequests and other transfers that must be made to the decedent's heirs and beneficiaries.

Funds may be needed during the readjustment period as the surviving family members struggle to rearrange their lives.

Perhaps the greatest need is for money to support surviving dependents. How much is needed depends upon who (and how) many are dependent. For children, there is a need for food, shelter, and education that may continue for many years. For a disabled dependant, the time frame may be measured by the person's life expectancy. For some families, there may be the need for funds to continue running the family business.

Cash needs for larger estates. Cash needs can be influenced by estate size and family situation. In general, cash needs arise with increasing estate size. For very large estates, the estate tax may create the greatest cash need. Most very wealthy couples choose an estate plan that incorporates both a marital deduction and an exclusion amount trust. These combine at the first death to result in no estate tax. However, this merely delays the cash need until the second death, when taxes can no longer be postponed.

Cash needs for smaller estates. In contrast with the estates of wealthy individuals, young families with modest estates will often have relatively large cash needs at the death of either spouse. These people do not have the economic advantages of the wealthy, so although transfer taxes are not a problem, there is the immediate need to replace the income or services that had been provided by the deceased spouse. As the children get older, the total present value of the cash needs tends to decline.

Next, we turn our attention to the major sources of estate liquidity.

SALE OF ASSETS DURING LIFETIME

We will begin our discussion of the sources of estate liquidity with one of the simplest liquidity-generating devices. During lifetime, a person might sell particular assets to raise money. Relatively high basis assets are preferable, of course, because they result in little or no taxable gain. In fact, assets that have a built-in loss make the best assets for sale, because the loss can be used to offset other taxable gains or to reduce taxable income. Death eliminates this potential tax benefit by stepping down the basis to date-of-death value, and a gift of the asset results in the donor being stuck with basis for determining a loss that is equal to the lower of the fair market value on the date of the gift or the donor's carry-over basis.

Relatively low basis assets, on the other hand, are less attractive assets for sale because of the resulting tax on the gain. This tax is eliminated if the owner keeps the asset until death. However, one might offset the gain with losses, whether incurred during the current taxable year or carried over from previous years. A sale may be practical in situations where other factors justify paying a tax whose maximum marginal rate on long-term (i.e., held more than one year) capital gains is 20% (or just 10% for taxpayers in the 15% tax bracket). After the year 2000, property held more than five years will be subject to a maximum rate of 18% (9% for 15% tax bracket taxpayers). In addition, a sale might be justified for an interest in a closely held business if the sale during the owner's life is likely to command a substantially higher price than if sold after the owner's death.

LIFE INSURANCE

Next, we turn our attention to perhaps the most commonly used estate liquidity source, life insurance.

Introduction

Let's first review the basic terminology. In its simplest form, a life insurance policy is a contract: owned by the person called the *owner*; that pays an amount called the *face value*; to the person called the *beneficiary*; upon the death of the person called the *insured*. Life insurance has several uses, but in estate planning, its major purpose is to provide funds to cover cash needs arising at a person's death.

We will cover three major topics in this section. First, we will survey the various types of insurance policies commonly used.[1] Next, we will review the major concepts in the income, gift, and estate taxation of insurance. Finally, we will examine the insurance planning techniques frequently used to provide needed liquidity.

Types of Insurance

It seems as though there are an endless variety of insurance policies sold in the United States today. There are policies called level term, decreasing term, mortgage payment insurance, whole life, variable life, etc. However, most are variations of one of two basic life insurance products; either term insurance or cash value insurance.

Term insurance. The simplest form of insurance is a one-year policy whose *increasing periodic premium* is based on the likelihood of death in that year. If the insured dies, the beneficiary is paid the face value. If the insured does not die, the company owes nothing and the contract terminates. This is the essence of term insurance: whether or not the company is financially obligated to pay depends solely on whether or not the insured dies during the contract period.

Most term insurance is *renewable*; that is, the company is obligated to sell another year's insurance at a previously agreed-upon price, at the option of the policy owner. Evidence of insurability, such as a physical exam, cannot now be required. Most term policies are renewable to some maximum age set by the company, e.g., age 70 or 75. The premium, or cost of annually renewable term insurance policies, rises annually with increasing age, reflecting the increased likelihood of death. Other term insurance policies have premiums that remain constant for 5, 10, or 20 years, and then rise to a new plateau for another similar period. These are called "five year level term" or "ten year level term" depending upon the period during which the premiums stay the same. With most term insurance contracts, the premiums are guaranteed for one, five, or ten years. Thereafter, premiums can be raised but not above some stated maximum. Regardless of how often the premium rises, all term insurance is characterized by periodic increases in the premiums and by the fact that the company will not offer the insurance coverage beyond some maximum age.

Cash value insurance. In contrast to term insurance, cash value insurance is characterized by a constant ("level") periodic premium. It is also characterized by certainty: when a cash value insurance contract ends, either because the insured dies or because the policy owner no longer wants coverage, the company will ordinarily be obligated to pay a significant amount of money. If the insured dies, the company will pay the face value, of course, as it does on its term insurance policies. If, on the other hand, the owner *surrenders* a cash value policy before the insured's death, the company will be obligated to pay an amount called the *cash surrender value*.

Cash value insurance originated as a solution to a problem perceived to be inherent in term insurance. Many years ago, when term insurance was just about the only policy sold, agents found that policy owners frequently terminated their insurance as it became more and more expensive with the advancing age of the insured. To retain policyholders, companies started offering cash value insurance, charging a constant premium. Evidence shows that such policies are not as likely to be canceled by policyholders, despite advancing age. Essentially, the earlier years' premiums are more than the company actuarially needs to fund death and other claims, and the later years' premiums are less than the company needs. The extra premium in the early years enables the company to accumulate a type of actuarial reserve. Typically, the policyholder may borrow, pledge, or in the event of surrender prior to the insured's death, receive the cash value outright.

All else being equal, cash value policy premiums usually are three to five times the initial premium charged for an annually renewable term policy for a given policyholder. Of course, over time, the annual term policy premiums will exceed the annual premiums on the cash value policy. For cash value policies, the guaranteed cash surrender values are listed, year by year, in the policy itself.

EXAMPLE 15 - 1. Audrey, an insurance salesperson, offers Gerard, age 45, a choice of two policies, each having a face value of $100,000. First, she describes a cash value *whole life* policy, sold by the ABC Co., which has a level annual premium of $2,700. Its cash surrender value at the end of the fifth policy year will be $7,500. At the end of the 20th policy year, the cash value will be $43,500. Audrey then describes an annually renewable term policy that is guaranteed renewable to age 75. The policy, sold by the XYZ Co, has premiums for the first five years of $500, $550, $610, $680, and $750. If Gerard keeps the policy long enough, the premiums will be over $4,500 per year by the time he reaches age 70.

Whole life policy. All cash value policies have a maturity date, that is, a date at which, if the insured reaches it alive, the face value will be paid. A whole life cash value policy, as its name implies, has a maturity date that extends beyond the "whole life" of most insureds, typically the insured's 95th or 100th birthday.

EXAMPLE 15 - 2. In Example 15-1 above, if Gerard purchases the whole life policy and keeps it in force, ABC will send him a check for $100,000 if he lives to be 100. Of course, if he does not live to be 100, the company will send his beneficiaries the $100,000.

Universal life Policy. During periods of high interest rates, traditional cash value policies, such as whole life, tend to lose their allure because the guaranteed cash value growth rate is typically set quite low in comparison to the returns available on other short-term, interest-sensitive investments. Naturally, people considering insurance tend to be more attracted to term insurance, with the idea that the money saved from the much lower initial premiums will be invested elsewhere to earn higher yields. In response, the insurance industry developed a product called universal life insurance, which is essentially a form of cash value insurance that offers the policyholder greater flexibility and, sometimes, greater investment yield. It offers greater *flexibility* because the policyholder is permitted to vary the amount of the face value and the premium payments from time to time to meet changing financial conditions. Variable universal life can offer greater investment *yield* because the policy owner selects from an array of portfolios (similar to a mutual fund family) managed by the insurance company for the investment of his or her excess premiums. The portfolios of non-variable universal life typically hold debt instruments of shorter duration than do portfolios of whole life policies. As such, in periods of high interest rates these universal life portfolios also offer greater investment yields than do whole life portfolios. With either variable or non-variable universal life, then, the insurance company (and the policyholder) hope that the underlying portfolios will outperform the typical whole life guaranteed rate. If successful, some of the additional value is used to pay for additional insurance coverage, additional cash value, and/or reduced premiums. The typical universal life policy offers a guaranteed rate of appreciation of some low amount, commonly 4%, with the provision that a higher rate will be earned if the investments are more profitable.

Universal life insurance has been criticized as being too complex compared to whole life and term insurance and because its flexibility makes it virtually impossible to make cost comparisons when considering its purchase.

Split-dollar cash value insurance arrangements. More a unique method of paying cash value insurance premiums than a different type of insurance, a split-dollar arrangement is most commonly found as a nonqualified employee fringe benefit. In the typical plan, the employer pays to the insurer a portion of the premium equal to the lesser of the total premium or the increase in the cash value. The employee pays the balance of the premium. When the insured dies or when the policy is surrendered, the employer ordinarily receives an amount equal to the premiums it paid. The remainder is paid to the policy owner (if surrendered) or the beneficiary (if the insured dies). Split-dollar insurance enables the employee to purchase cash value insurance less expensively than if purchased alone.

Taxation of Life Insurance

This section will survey the major concepts in the federal income, gift, and estate taxation of insurance. Many of these topics were covered in greater detail in Part 2 of the text, and the reader is referred there for elaboration and clarification.

Income taxation. Two major income tax aspects of life insurance are the taxation of the cash value accumulation and the taxation of the policy proceeds. To qualify for the two favored tax treatments described next, an insurance policy must meet the requirements under §7702, enacted to discourage the popularity of certain universal life and endowment type policies containing an unusually large investment element relative to the size of the death protection component.

Income taxation of cash value accumulation. Increases in cash value buildup are not ordinarily subject to income taxation while the policy is in force.[2] When a cash value policy is surrendered, any excess of the cash surrender value (amount realized) over the total premiums paid (adjusted basis) is included in the owner's gross income. Usually this excess, if any, is quite small and not a significant tax burden.

Generally, loans from the cash build up in a policy are not taxable unless the amount withdrawn exceeds the amount paid into the policy. However, if the policy is a "modified endowment contract," loans may be taxable. As defined in IRC §7702(A), a modified endowment contract is a life insurance policy entered into after June 20, 1988, that fails the "seven pay test." Failure occurs any time the cumulative premiums paid into the policy in the first seven years exceed the total of net level premiums which would have been sufficient to provide a paid-up policy, based upon the initial death benefit, after seven annual payments.

Congress set out to plug a loophole whereby insurance companies were selling single premium life insurance policies (with very little life insurance protection) as tax-free investment vehicles rather than as life insurance. With a modified endowment contract, withdrawals and distributions, even as loans, are treated as taxable income to the extent of any cash value accumulation. The portion of a withdrawal or distribution which is included in the policy owner's gross income (i.e., the lesser of the amount withdrawn or the accumulated cash build-up in excess of premiums paid at the time of withdrawal) is subject to an additional ten percent income tax unless the owner is over 59 ½, disabled, or receiving the payment as part of a series of equal annuity payments for life.

Income taxation of policy proceeds. Section 101 generally excludes from gross income all proceeds received from a life insurance policy paid by reason of the insured's death. The Code has carved out an exception to the proceeds exclusion rule for policies that have been transferred for valuable consideration. The amount included in the transferee-owner's gross income in the year when the insured dies equals the policy proceeds, reduced by the amount of the initial consideration (i.e., the price paid to acquire the policy) and the premiums paid after acquisition. This *transfer for value rule*, as it is called, does not apply to policy transfers to the following parties:

- The insured (or to a grantor trust[3] of the insured);
- a partner of the insured;
- a partnership in which the insured is a partner;
- a corporation in which the insured is a shareholder or officer; or
- a transferee whose basis will be determined by reference to the transferor's basis (i.e., the donee of a gift of the policy).[4]

EXAMPLE 15 - 3. For over 15 years, Terry was the owner of a $10,000 face value insurance policy on his life. Last year, he *gave* the policy to his beneficiary-son, Ralph, who began to pay the premiums. Terry died last month. No portion of the proceeds will be includable in Ralph's gross income because Ralph did not buy the policy.

EXAMPLE 15 - 4. If, in the prior example, we assume instead that Terry *sold* the policy to Ralph for $100, and that the premiums paid by Ralph totaled $400, Ralph's gross income will include $9,500.

EXAMPLE 15 - 5. Ulysses and Zeno are *business partners*. For years, each owned an insurance policy on his own life. Now, their attorney is drafting a "cross-purchase business buyout" contract, and the partners have agreed to exchange policies, with some cash also included as part of the transaction. Thus, Ulysses will become owner and beneficiary of the policy on the life of Zeno, and Zeno will become owner and beneficiary of the policy on the life of Ulysses. Upon the death of either partner, no part of the proceeds will be includable in the other's gross income.

The above example illustrates the use of existing insurance policies to fund a business buyout agreement.

Viatical settlements and accelerated death benefits. The Health Insurance Portability and Accountability Act, signed into law in August of 1996, allows people diagnosed with a terminal illness to "cash in" their life insurance early without having to pay income tax on the proceeds. These funds are available either directly from the insurance company, provided the policy has an accelerated death benefit (ADB) provision, or from an outside company that offers what is called a viatical settlement. The ADB is either part of the original insurance contract or is added later as a rider. The insurance company agrees to pay the proceeds at a discount from the face value of the policy. The fewer number of months the insured is expected to live, the less the discount and the greater the proceeds.

A viatical settlement is an agreement between a company representing a group of investors and an individual with a projected life expectancy of less than 48 months due to a terminal illness. The insured who enters into one of these contracts is called the viator and the company is called a viatical company.

Under the 1996 Act, in order for the ADB or the viatical settlement to be income tax free, a physician must certify that the insured has an illness or physical condition that can reasonably be expected to result in death within 24 months from the date of certification. Most ADB clauses set a maximum life expectancy that is considerably shorter (e.g., just 12 months or even as short as six months). Viatical companies generally seek contracts where death is expected to occur within 24 months. They may enter contracts where the life expectancy is considerably longer, but the favorable income tax benefits for the viator are not be available.

EXAMPLE 15 - 6. Karol has an advanced case of AIDS that has failed to respond favorably to any of the recent treatments. She decides that she would like to take her three children to visit their grandparents in Amsterdam. Her funds are extremely limited, so she contacts a viatical company to see if there is an interest in her $300,000 term policy. At the company's request, her doctor furnishes a complete medical report and signs a certificate that gives his opinion that Karol's life expectancy is between 12 and 18 months. The company agrees to pay $200,000 immediately, with an additional sum payable to her children. The additional amount is $50,000 if she dies in the first month after the settlement, reduced by two thousand dollars for each additional month, or portion of a month, that she lives beyond the first month.

The insured may use the ADB or viatical proceeds in any way he or she desires. Given the substantial discounts, most people will not utilize an ADB clause or enter into a viatical settlement if there are other reasonable sources of funds. Hence, it is likely that the funds will be used to pay for medical treatment or special nursing care where no other reasonable source of payment is available, but the law does not require that the money be so used. Indeed, the insured could use the funds for one last glorious trip to a place he or she always wanted to visit.

The law also has similar favorable treatment for persons who are "chronically ill" and can benefit from an ADB payment or a viatical settlement. The proceeds are tax free only if used for "costs incurred by the payee...for qualified long-term care services" where such care is not covered by insurance or otherwise subject to reimbursement.

Gift taxation. There are two common situations where insurance is subject to gift taxation. First, a taxable gift may arise when the owner *assigns* the ownership to another person without receiving consideration in return. Ordinarily, the gift of an insurance policy will qualify for the annual exclusion, unless it is made to an irrevocable trust. Even then, if a beneficiary of the trust is given a Crummey demand power, the annual exclusion is available. Second, a taxable gift of the policy proceeds may arise when the insured dies. If the insured, owner, and beneficiary are all different parties, the proceeds are considered a gift from the policy owner to the beneficiary. The effect of this rule, as we shall see shortly, is to compel planners to recommend that the same (non-insured) party be both owner and beneficiary.

Estate taxation. Life insurance is most commonly included in a decedent's federal estate tax base under Code §§2001, 2033, 2035(a), or 2042. Since this material was covered in detail in Chapter 6, each section will be reviewed only briefly here.

Under §2001, the decedent's *adjusted taxable gifts* will include the date-of-gift value less the available annual exclusions for *any* life insurance policy for which the decedent made a completed transfer after 1976 but more than three years before death.

Under §2033 (property owned at death), the value of a life insurance policy on the *life of someone other than the decedent* will be included in the decedent's gross estate to the extent of the decedent's date of death ownership interest in the policy.

Under §2035(a), the proceeds of a life insurance policy on the *life of the decedent* will be included in the decedent's gross estate if within three years of death the decedent made a completed transfer of any incidents of ownership in the policy.

Under §2042, proceeds on the *life of the decedent* are includable in the decedent's gross estate if, at the insured's death, either the proceeds were receivable by the decedent's executor or the decedent possessed any incidents of ownership in the policy.

With these tax rules in mind, let us turn to the techniques of insurance planning.

Life Insurance Planning

The fundamental goal in using life insurance in liquidity planning is to provide for cash needs while minimizing income, gift, and estate taxation, as well as other costs. To do this efficiently, we need to carefully choose the most appropriate insured, owner, and beneficiary for each life insurance policy purchased to meet an estate's cash needs.

Selecting the insured. Proper family planning would provide for insurance on the life of each spouse whose death is expected to trigger a cash need. For *smaller estates*, this could occur at the death of either or both spouses, depending on certain factors, such as the size of each spouse's economic contribution to the family.

For *larger estates*, we have seen that effective planning (with the use of the marital deduction trust and the credit shelter bypass trust) usually eliminates the need to pay estate tax at the death of the first spouse (S1), but it creates a relatively large need at the surviving spouse's death (S2). Thus, ordinarily, little or no insurance is required on S1's life to pay estate tax. The real insurance need will be on S2's life. However, some insurance may be needed at S1's death to meet nontax needs, such as to cover certain last expenses, readjustment needs, and cash requirements during the dependency period. This will be particularly important for parents with substantial earned income who are supporting younger children.

Insurance arrangements for the second death. Since most couples do not know for certain whether the husband or the wife will be the surviving spouse, both may need to be insured. Several commonly used purchase arrangements are discussed next.

1. *Full coverage for both spouses.* One simple but costly plan is to insure both spouses for the full amount of protection needed at the surviving spouse's death. Because of needless extra cost, this plan is seldom recommended.

2. *Minimal coverage for both spouses.* An alternative method of insuring the spouses is to purchase immediately a small amount of insurance on both spouses

which, upon the death of either, can be used to purchase a "fully paid up" larger policy on the life of the survivor. This eliminates the cash flow drain on the surviving spouse's assets that would otherwise be used to pay the premium.

3. *Second-to-die insurance.* A third method of insuring both spouses for cash needs at the survivor's death is to purchase what is called *second-to-die insurance*, also called *survivorship life insurance*. Both spouses are insured in one policy, but the contract requires payment only when the second death occurs. This alternative saves premium dollars in two ways: First, only one policy is purchased. Second, the contingency insured against is more remote in time than that insured against under a single-life policy, consequently, the premiums are lower than a similar policy on either spouse's life. Even though one spouse may be uninsurable, a second-to-die policy should still be available since the medical underwriting standards are eased as long as one spouse is healthy.

4. *Full coverage for wife only.* Another alternative is to insure only the wife, assuming she has the longer life expectancy. If she survives her husband, the contract becomes, de facto, a second-death policy. If she predeceases him, the proceeds can be invested to pay the estate tax at his later death. The cost of insuring only the wife is likely to be more expensive than a second-to-die policy.

Selecting the owner and beneficiary. The amount of planning effort needed to choose who will be owner and beneficiary usually depends on the size of the family estate. In the case of a married couple, selecting the owner and beneficiary for a *smaller estate* is rather simple since no transfer taxes are expected so long as the net value of the combined estates (with the insurance included) is less than the exclusion amount. Each spouse may own policies on his or her own life with the proceeds payable to the other. The contingent beneficiary could be the couple's children, if sufficiently mature, or could be the trustee of the couple's probate-avoidance living trust.

On the other hand, when transfer tax costs are a concern, more thought must be given to these matters. We consider next the effect of naming various parties as owners and beneficiaries.

Spouse as owner and beneficiary. Naming one or the other spouse as owner or beneficiary will not minimize transfer costs. It will usually subject the proceeds to a transfer tax, probate administration, or both, depending on which spouse dies first. Consider the somewhat complicated tax and probate consequences for each of the possible outcomes.

First, if the *insured spouse dies first and is the owner,* the proceeds will be includable in his or her gross estate under §2042. If the proceeds qualify for the marital deduction, thereby avoiding taxation at the first death, they will be included in the *gross estate* at the second death, barring consumption, gifting, or remarriage. If the *insured spouse dies second and is the owner*, then the proceeds will be included in his or her *gross estate* with no marital deduction available.

Second, if the *insured spouse dies first and the noninsured spouse is the owner and beneficiary*, then the proceeds will be included in the *gross estate* at the second death, barring gifting, remarriage or consumption. From the discussion of gift taxation of insurance earlier in the chapter, it should be clear that if the noninsured spouse is named *owner* and someone else is the beneficiary, then, when the proceeds are paid, the owner-spouse will have made a *taxable gift* to the beneficiary. Thus, even the noninsured spouse should not be named either owner or beneficiary if the surviving spouse's estate is likely to exceed the exclusion amount.

Conclusions. In planning for wealthy couples, two important conclusions can be drawn from the above. First, naming *either spouse* as owner or beneficiary of a policy on the life of a spouse will subject the proceeds to transfer taxation at least at the second death. Thus, to minimize transfer taxes, neither spouse should be designated owner or beneficiary of an insurance policy on the life of the other. Second, since a taxable gift will occur whenever the insured, owner, and beneficiary are all different parties, *whoever is selected should be named both owner and beneficiary*, to avoid gift tax consequences.

Child as owner and beneficiary. Instead of a spouse, one of the couple's children could be named owner and beneficiary. The child could be *requested* to use the proceeds to provide liquidity to the estate upon the death of the insured. This alternative will work best when the child is sufficiently *mature* to handle the responsibility. Nonetheless, there will always be a risk that the child may permit the policy to lapse. Or the child, having received the policy proceeds upon the death of the insured parent, may be *unwilling* to provide the funding needed by the estate. Once the child receives the proceeds, any gratuitous transfer of the funds to the estate will be treated as a *taxable gift* unless the child is the sole beneficiary of the estate. To avoid making a gift, the child could purchase estate assets or lend money to the estate.

Irrevocable trust as owner and beneficiary. Generally, the irrevocable life insurance trust (ILIT) is the solution with the fewest drawbacks.

Organization and structure of an ILIT. The person to be insured creates the ILIT and selects an independent trustee. The trustee then obtains insurance on the trustor's life, naming the trustee as the owner and beneficiary of the policy. Obviously the trust must be irrevocable or §2038 would draw the trust (i.e., the insurance proceeds) into the trustor's estate. The trustor must not be named a trust *beneficiary*, because of possible §2036(a) problems; and since the uninsured spouse is usually one of the beneficiaries of an ILIT, he or she should not be a trustor. This will require greater care in preparation in community property states.

Upon the death of the insured, the trustee is authorized to lend the proceeds to the insured's estate and to purchase assets from the estate. If the insured is S1, then the trust corpus usually continues to provide benefits to S2 in the form of a bypass trust, similar to the ones discussed in Chapter 11. At the death of S2, the trust is again authorized to lend cash to the S2 estate and to purchase estate assets. The trust could then be terminated, with corpus payable to the children. Alternatively, the trust could be continued, distributing income to the children until either they reach a specified age or, in the case of a generation-skipping trust qualifying for the one million dollar lifetime exemption, until the grandchildren reach a specified age.

An ILIT may be used as a source to pay estate taxes, in which case it is important to choose a policy that the insured knows will be there when it is needed. Since term insurance becomes increasingly expensive as the insured gets older and may not even be available beyond a certain age (i.e., most insurance companies do not write term policies for people over the age of 75), term insurance is a poor choice for an ILIT established for this purpose.

For a single individual, a whole life policy makes sense. If another type of cash value insurance, such as universal life, is considered, one must make sure that there is a guaranteed proceeds amount sufficient to pay the taxes regardless of how long the insured lives.

A married couple has two choices. If the sole purpose is to create a fund to pay estate taxes at the second death, then a second-to-die policy is the least expensive for any given level of coverage. With a sophisticated estate plan incorporating bypass and marital trusts, the taxes are most likely to be postponed until the second death. But what about those rare situations where S2 is dying at the time of S1's death and the executor wants to generate a tax at S1's death? Will use of a second-to-die policy cause hardship or force the executor to postpone the taxes to the second death even though it means more overall estate taxes? The answer is no. These situations anticipate the death of the second spouse shortly after the first death. Section 6161 allows executors to postpone payment of the estate tax for reasonable cause. Thus the executor of S1's estate would not be forced to sell assets but would file the return, report the estate tax owed, and request a one year extension with an explanation as to why cash is presently unavailable.

A second-to-die policy is not advisable if the primary purpose is to provide income to the surviving spouse. The income earners (one or both) should be separately insured taking into account the amount of insurance needed to replace the insured's earning capacity. For any given family wealth level (until we reach the very wealthy), a young couple with dependent children will need greater amounts of insurance than an older couple with grown children. Therefore, term insurance is appropriate since it allows them the most insurance for their premium dollars. If the couple can afford additional insurance and is concerned about covering estate taxes in the event both die young, then they should consider another ILIT to purchase a second-to-die policy.

Who should pay the premiums on the trust-owned policy? One alternative is to fund the trust with sufficient income-earning assets to enable the trust to pay them. Unfortunately, the grantor trust rules will make that income taxable to the grantor (trustor) rather than the trust.[5] A preferred alternative has the trustor making annual gifts to the trust in amounts sufficient to pay the premiums. The insured-spouse in community property states should make the periodic gifts from his or her separate property to keep the proceeds out of the estate of the noninsured spouse, who is beneficiary of the trust. By having a Crummey demand right held by the insured's children, these gifts qualify for the annual exclusion.

Impressive ILIT achievements. For a *married couple* with an estate that exceeds the exclusion amount, only the ILIT achieves all of the following goals:

1. Excludes the insurance proceeds from *income taxation* and from the *taxable estates* of both spouses and, perhaps, the children.
2. Excludes the insurance proceeds from the *probate estates* of both spouses.
3. Enjoys the shelter of the gift tax *annual exclusion* for transfers to the trust of both the policy and the funds needed to pay policy premiums.
4. Ensures that a *responsible party* will in fact provide the needed post-death liquidity.
5. Makes the *proceeds available* to the surviving spouse for health or certain other reasons.

A *single person* can also effectively use an ILIT to achieve similar tax and nontax goals.

Income tax, estate tax, and GSTT issues. Regarding the first goal, an ILIT will not ordinarily fall within the grasp of §2036 (retained life estate). However, because they are not direct skips, annual exclusion transfers into the trust will not insulate the corpus from GSTT. Thus, planners may elect to allocate some of the one million dollar GST exemption to such transfers, anticipating that the premature death of a child may give rise to a taxable distribution or a taxable termination.

Excluding the insurance proceeds from the gross estate of a decedent has the additional benefit of avoiding transferee liability for payment of the estate tax. In one case, the decedent died possessing incidents of ownership in a $50,000 life insurance policy. The IRS was unable to collect $62,378 in estate tax from the decedent's assets which were then owned by his nonresident alien widow, living in Venezuela. However, the insurance beneficiary, a U.S. citizen, was held liable for $50,000 of the taxes.[6]

If an existing policy is transferred to the trust, the trustor-insured must live *three years* after the policy is transferred to ensure that §2035's three year rule for life insurance transfers does not apply. Whenever possible, the policy should be purchased by the trustee to avoid the three-year rule. If the insured transfers an existing policy, the annual exclusion will not be available unless the trust gives the beneficiaries a Crummey invasion power.

The trust can include a *contingent marital deduction clause*, so that if the three-year rule causes the proceeds to be included in the insured's gross estate, then the trust is required to pay the widow income for life payable at least annually. This clause would allow a QTIP election and the resulting marital deduction would avoid estate taxes. Of course, a QTIP election will cause the trust to be included in S2's estate. On the other hand, if the insured lives longer than three years, the ILIT avoids both estates, the contingent income clause that would have mandated income payments solely to S2 becomes meaningless, and the trust can be a sprinkling trust that distributes income to the children as well as to S2.

If each spouse is an insured, then two trusts will have to be established, with each trust owning one policy. These trusts must be drafted very carefully to avoid §2036(a) problems.

If the trust is *required* to use insurance proceeds to pay the decedent's estate debts, including taxes, the proceeds will be includable in the decedent's gross estate under §2042. The trustee should instead be simply *advised* that it may *lend* the proceeds to the estate or *purchase* estate assets to achieve funding.

Although GSTT rules prevent annual exclusion gifts to a single trust for the benefit of both nonskip and skip persons from also being sheltered from the GSTT, planners achieve complete shelter from GSTT in one of two ways. Either they create one trust and use the trustor's $1 million GST exemption to shelter these gifts, or they create two trusts, one for the benefit of only nonskip persons (e.g. spouse and children) and the other for the benefit of only skip persons (grandchildren, etc.).[7]

Avoiding probate. Regarding the second goal for the ILIT, the policy proceeds avoid probate at both spouses' deaths because neither spouse owns the policy or the proceeds.

Shelter of annual exclusion. Most ILIT's are drafted with clauses that give Crummey demand rights to the children and even to the grandchildren. These clauses are inserted to create the necessary present interest so that the annual exclusion is available to cover the funds supplied by the insured to the trustee so that the trustee can pay the premiums. Because the holders of the powers must be given a reasonable time in which to exercise their demand rights, the trustee must receive the funds far enough in advance of the premium due date to give the holders notice and have the demand period expire before the payment must be made. The demand period (typically 30 or 60 days) must be stated in the ILIT as part of the Crummey provision.

Selection of trustee as responsible party. An insured spouse who is also trustor should not be named trustee since this could constitute an incident of ownership in the policy. The other spouse could be named trustee without this adverse result.

Most corporate trustees are reluctant to become trustees of an insurance trust prior to the insured's death, if the trust is otherwise unfunded. Even if it is funded, the advent of higher-risk, higher-return life insurance policies, and growing insurance company insolvency problems have made more and more trustees, particularly corporate trustees, increasingly concerned about possible *liability* if expected policy death benefits are not entirely paid or if the policy turns out to be relatively uncompetitive. In addition, an ILIT may not be profitable for a corporate trustee even after the proceeds are received, particularly if they must be allocated in one of two all too common ways: proceeds immediately distributed to trust beneficiaries, or used to acquire closely held business stock, an asset considered difficult to manage.

To overcome the liability concerns and encourage a fiduciary to act as trustee of a life insurance trust, the trust may include language that exculpates the trustee from liability in connection with holding the life insurance policy. The trust must make it clear that the trustee is released from liability for investing only in life insurance since the failure to diversify investments violates the prudent investor rule. The trust can indemnify the trustee, i.e., reimburse the trustee for any expenses, including attorney's fees, that might arise from a challenge by the remainderman. Exculpatory clauses are enforced by the courts, but are strictly construed against the trustee. They offer no protection from acts of "bad faith," "reckless indifference," "gross negligence," or "willful misconduct."

Finally, the planner can arrange for a non-corporate fiduciary, such as a family friend, to act as initial trustee, with the corporate fiduciary succeeding as trustee only after the insured(s) have died and the proceeds have been paid. Of course, the family friend should also have the benefit of the exculpatory clauses just discussed.

Life insurance is an important liquidity source because it supplies cash exactly when it is needed: at the death of the individual. With careful planning, it can also avoid all transfer taxes.

FLOWER BONDS

This topic should come under the heading: "Sometimes Congress Does the Darnedest Things." In the 1950's and early 1960's, the federal government issued Treasury bonds that could be used at their par value, plus accrued interest, to pay the federal estate tax, provided the bonds were part of the decedent's estate. Since the bond yields, while reasonable when issued, were quite low (3% to 5%) compared to other safe investments in the 1970's and 1980's, they began selling at deep discounts. This created some estate planning opportunities for persons with terminal illnesses to purchase bonds at as little as 85% of par shortly before death. The decedent's executor could use them to pay the estate tax, achieving an increase in value in a short time span. Because the worth of the bonds jumped from their discounted value to their par value when the owner died, the bonds were called *flower bonds*. Of course, to the extent the bonds could be used to pay estate taxes, their value in the estate was the par value. Thus, some of that 15% increase in value was lost to increased estate taxes.

Discounts decreased as the bonds in circulation reached maturity. The last ones came due November 15, 1998, which means the estate planning opportunities are gone.

LIQUIDITY PLANNING DEVICES UNIQUE TO BUSINESS OWNERS

When the owner of a closely held business dies, severe liquidity problems can arise. Not infrequently, the largest portion of the estate consists of the interest in the business that, almost by definition, is very illiquid. The need to pay the estate tax nine months after date of death may cause surviving family members to feel compelled to sell the business. Some advanced planning by the business owner and some special Code sections should help the heirs get through the transition crisis.

Sale of the Business

Consideration should be given to the pre-death *sale* of the business to one or more individuals, or to a *merger* with a publicly held firm, as a means of converting a relatively illiquid asset to a liquid one. A pre-death sale will ordinarily trigger a capital gains tax. An owner who for that reason chooses not to sell or merge before death should consider executing a funded *buyout agreement* with the other owners. The buyout contract, discussed later in the text, obligates the other owner(s) to pay the decedent's estate a predetermined amount in exchange for the decedent's interest in the firm. Since the sale will occur after death, the resulting step-up in basis of the decedent's interest eliminates or substantially reduces any capital gains tax.

Congress has placed in the Internal Revenue Code a number of relief provisions for estates that include substantial business interests. It is common in the estate planning field to identify the techniques by their Code section numbers.

Estate Tax Deferral: §6166, §6161 and §6163

Installment payment of the estate tax: §6166. Congress added §6166 to the Code, applicable to estates of decedents dying after 1976, to lessen the liquidity crisis that often accompanies the death of a successful business owner. If the estate is eligible and the executor makes the election, the estate tax attributed to a closely held business interest can be paid over a fourteen year period. The portion deferred is the ratio of the net value of the business over the value of the adjusted gross estate. The first four annual installments are interest only payments. They start on the one year anniversary of the original due date. Starting in the fifth year, the estate pays the estate tax in 10 installments, each one equal to one-tenth of the deferred tax, plus the interest accrued since the last annual payment. Although the estate must pay interest on the deferred tax, interest on a portion of the deferred tax is at a much lower rate than the regular rate for underpaid (i.e., late or deferred) tax payments.

Three conditions must be met for qualification under §6166. First, the value of the decedent's interest in the business must be at least *35%* of the value of the *adjusted gross estate* (AGE). The AGE is the gross estate reduced by debts, expenses, losses, and certain taxes (i.e., accrued income taxes and property taxes, but not the death taxes themselves).[8] Second, the decedent's interest must have been in a *closely held business*, which is defined as: (1) a sole proprietorship; or (2) a partnership in which at least 20% of the capital interest is included in the decedent's gross estate or that has 15 or fewer partners; or (3) a corporation in which at least 20% of the voting stock is included in the decedent's gross estate or that has 15 or fewer shareholders. Third, to qualify, the sole proprietorship, partnership, or corporation must have been actually carrying on a *trade or business* at the time of the decedent's death.

EXAMPLE 15 - 7. Jack died in the year 2000, owning stock in a closely held corporation. His shares had a value of $1,000,000. Jack's gross estate was worth $3 million. There were debts and expenses that totaled $500,000. The federal estate tax was $666,450 (after the state death tax credit). Since the closely held business interest was 40% of AGE, the estate qualifies for §6166 extended payments. The amount of the tax that may be deferred is $266,580 [40% * $666,450].

In the past, the executor had the option of deducting the interest paid on the §6166 extended tax payments either on the estate tax return (Form 706) or on the estate income tax return (Form 1041).[9] This deduction has been eliminated for estates of decedents dying after 1997, but continues to be available for estates that are already on an extended payment plan.[10] Deducting interest on the estate tax return continues to be available for interest on estate taxes paid late, regardless of whether the executor obtained an extension to pay based upon reasonable cause (i.e., §6161) or negligently paid them late without obtaining an extension. The interest that must be paid on late or deferred estate taxes should be deducted on the estate tax return because it saves more tax than claiming it for income tax purposes, since the estate tax rate is higher than the income tax rate. For §6166 interest, the executor claims the deduction using Form 843 (Refund Claim) since the deduction can only be taken after the interest is paid.[11] Estates often wait until after the seventh or eighth principal payment (out of the ten scheduled for the §6166 extension) to claim the deduction because it reduces the estate tax to the extent that the last couple of payments are eliminated. A complex interrelated calculation is required because the interest paid reduces the estate tax, which in turn reduces the interest owed, which in turn increases the estate tax, etc.[12]

Late payment interest on a portion of the deferred estate tax is charged at a mere 2% rate. The Taxpayer Relief Act of '97 reduced the rate (previously 4%) for eligible estates of persons who die after December 31, 1997. The 2% *portion*, as it is now called, is the amount of deferred tax that equals the tentative tax generated on the quantity $1,000,000 plus the exclusion amount, less the unified credit. Thus, in 1998 the 2% portion would be the tentative tax on $1,625,000 less the unified credit, i.e., $612,050 - $202,050 = $410,000. The $1,000,000 amount is indexed for inflation starting in 1999, using 1997 as the base year. The balance of the deferred tax also has a reduced interest rate. It is equal to 45% of the regular "underpayment" interest rate imposed by IRC §6601(a). Estates that are still paying on pre-1998 §6166 payment plans can elect to take advantage of the new lower interest rates, but only if the estate's representative waives the right to claim a deduction for any remaining interest payments. This waiver is likely to be advantageous for estates with deaths after 1994. For estates of decedents with earlier deaths, more dollars will probably be saved by claiming the interest deduction than will be saved by utilizing the lower interest rates.

EXAMPLE 15 - 8. Hitch died in 1999, leaving his children an estate that included a closely held business. The estate qualified under IRC §6166 to extend $1,500,000 of its federal estate tax. Because of indexing, the $1,000,000 amount had increased to $1,080,000. The tentative tax on $1,730,000 (i.e., exclusion amount for 1999 + $1,080,000) is $659,300. Subtracting the unified credit for 1999 (i.e., $211,300) gives us $448,000 as the 2% portion. If, during the first year's deferral period, the regular underpayment rate is 8%, the balance of the deferred taxes would be charged interest at a 3.6% rate (45% * 8%). Hence, the first interest payment (due one year after the regular due date of the estate tax return) would be: $46,832 [2% * $448,000 + 3.6% * $1,052,000]. Assuming the regular late payment interest rate remained at 8%, the payment due on the fifth year anniversary would be $196,832 (10% of the deferred taxes plus a year of interest).

Estate tax deferral under §6166 reduces the estate's immediate cash needs. Since this is a relief provision designed to reduce the likelihood of a forced sale, it should be no surprise that the sale, redemption, or other disposition of all, or a significant portion of, the business, or the unauthorized failure to make timely interest or principal payments, causes the deferred taxes to be immediately due. However, §6161, discussed next, can be used to defer an installment, provided a timely request is made.

Extension to pay tax for reasonable cause: §6161. Upon a showing of "reasonable cause" by the estate, the IRS has discretion under §6161 to grant a one year extension to pay the estate tax. This section is available to any estate, not just those that hold a business interest. Extensions can be repeated for a total extended period of 10 years. Warning: a request for an extension must be made before the due date of the return, and subsequent requests must be made before the current annual extension has expired. Failure to timely file the request will result in a denial of the request, regardless of how meritorious the reason was for asking for the extension. Examples of situations satisfying this requirement include:

- The estate has illiquid assets or has liquid assets that are not yet available to the executor.
- A large part of the estate is in the form of assets which consist of rights to receive payments in the future (royalties, accounts receivable, etc.).
- The estate includes a claim to substantial assets that cannot be collected without litigation.
- The estate does not have sufficient funds to pay taxes and provide for a family allowance and claims.
- The estate cannot borrow except at rates that would constitute a hardship.

Ordinarily, reasonable cause will not be found merely because liquid assets (listed securities) must be sold at what the executor considers distressed prices. Of course even with an extension to pay, there will be interest charged (at the late payment rate). The good news is that the interest is deductible on the estate tax return. Generally, claiming the interest is done by way of a claim for refund after the tax and the interest are paid.

Estates may use a §6161 extension or the §6166 installment plan to pay the *generation-skipping transfer tax*, but in the case of §6166, only if the tax results from a direct skip.[13]

Deferral of estate tax for a reversion or a remainder interest: §6163. Section 6163 allows estate tax deferral for that portion of the tax attributed to having a reversionary or remainder interest included in a decedent's gross estate. The tax can be postponed until six months after the termination of the "precedent" interest, i.e., the interest immediately preceding the reversion or remainder. The termination might occur many years after the decedent's death.

> EXAMPLE 15 - 9. When he died, Jake created an irrevocable trust out of a portion of his estate. The trust pays all income to Jake's disabled son, Billy, for his lifetime. Then, the remainder is payable to Jake's daughter, Diane, or to her estate. Diane died in the year 2000. At that time, the trust was worth $400,000, Billy was 80 years old, and the federal rate was 8%. The present value of her remainder interest in the trust was $234,528 [$400,000 * 0.58632]. Her taxable estate, including the vested remainder, was $2,000,000. The total federal tax on her estate was $460,650, hence her estate was able to defer $54,018 [$460,650 * ($234,528/$2,000,000)] until six months after Billy dies. There will be interest to pay on the deferred tax (at the regular underpayment rate), but it can be claimed as a deduction, thereby reducing the tax.

Stock Redemption: §303

The Internal Revenue Code provides another method to lessen the impact of taxes on the estates of decedents whose businesses are incorporated. The general rule is that when a closely held corporation buys back the shares of its stockholders, the proceeds must be treated as dividend income unless the transaction falls within one of the special redemption Code sections. Section 303 is one of those special sections in that it allows a closely held corporation to redeem some of a decedent's shares with the transaction treated as a sale of the stock rather than the receipt of a dividend. Given that the owner's death will have stepped-up the *adjusted basis* of the stock, very little, if any, gain is likely.

EXAMPLE 15 - 10. Polly's estate included 1,000 shares of stock in a closely held corporation. Each share was value at $150 per share for estate tax purposes. Immediately before her death, each share had an adjusted basis of just $10. Eight months after her death, to help the estate pay some of its expenses, the board of directors of the corporation agreed to redeem 300 shares from the estate at a price of $160 per share. Business was good, and the $160 was a realistic share price at the time of the purchase. If the entire redemption qualifies under §303, the estate will have a taxable long-term gain of $3,000 (reflecting a $10 gain on each share purchased). If the redemption does not qualify for capital gain treatment, the estate will be deemed to have received a dividend of $48,000 (300 shares at $160 per share), all of which will be treated as ordinary income.

There are three major requirements to qualify under §303. First, as with the §6166 deferral, the value of the decedent's interest in the stock must be at least 35% of the adjusted gross estate. Second, the *amount paid* by the corporation in redemption of the shares *may not exceed* the sum of federal and state death taxes, generation-skipping transfer taxes, and funeral and administration expenses. Notice that the limit for capital gain treatment does not include the decedent's debts, although they are used in calculating the adjusted gross estate. Third, the shareholder (usually the estate) must be obligated to pay the taxes and/or the expenses.[14]

If more is paid, the excess will be treated as a dividend payment by the corporation. If the excess distributions exceed the amount of the corporation's earnings and profits, the excess is considered a nontaxable return of capital. However, if the firm distributes appreciated property instead of cash, the distribution will probably be considered a sale by the corporation, with the corporation forced to recognize a taxable gain.

Lifetime planning may assure that §6166 and §303 are available to an estate that might not otherwise meet the 35% test. The owner can increase his or her interest in the firm, or reduce the size of his or her nonbusiness estate by making *gifts*, thereby reducing the adjusted gross estate and increasing the portion represented by the business. These strategies require advance planning. Section as §2035 requires that any gifts made within three years of death be included in the gross estate, not for tax purposes but merely to determine whether the percentage requirements of §6166 and §303 are met. Obviously, bringing non-business gifts into the gross estate enlarges the denominator, making qualification less likely.

EXAMPLE 15 - 11. Gabe's estate included his closely held corporation. His gross estate was valued at $5,000,000. Debts and expenses were $1,000,000 and the value of his shares were $1,500,000. The estate meets the 35% requirements of both §303 and §6166 since the shares represent 37.5% of the AGE.

EXAMPLE 15 - 12. Same as the prior example, except Gabe gave his daughter real estate worth $250,000 two years before he died. At his death, the property was worth $300,000. Inclusion of this property in the gross estate for purposes of determining the percentage brings the AGE to $4,300,000 and drops the percentage to 34.8%. For calculating the estate tax, the gift is simply a $240,000 adjusted taxable gift. The date of death value was used only to determine whether the estate qualified for the benefits of §303 and §6166.

Special Use Valuation: §2032A

Another relief provision available to the business owner's estate, called *special use valuation*, is provided by §2032A. This Code section permits qualifying estates to value at least a portion of the real property in the estate at its "qualified use" value, i.e., its value as a farm or other trade or business rather than at its highest and best use.

Suppose a person has owned her farm for many years and her children want to continue to work the farm for the foreseeable future. The farm was originally located outside the city limits, but urban growth is beginning to surround the area. The farm's FMV is considerably greater than the capitalized value of the farm income. Valuation at its highest and best use might force the survivors to sell the land to pay the large estate tax. On the other hand, valuation at its use as a farm might enable the survivors to carry on the business.

Requirements. The five major requirements and conditions under §2032A are briefly described below.

1. The property must have been held for "qualified use" and actively managed by the decedent or the decedent's family for *five out of the eight years* prior to the decedent's death.
2. The net value of the real and personal property devoted to the qualifying use must equal at least *50%* of the value of the adjusted value of the gross

estate.[15] The adjusted value of the gross estate is the gross estate reduced by mortgages and liens (not unsecured debts or expenses).

3. The net value of the real property portion must constitute at least *25%* of the adjusted value of the gross estate.[16]

4. The qualifying property must pass to qualifying heirs. The heirs must sign a recapture agreement that acknowledges that a lien will be placed on the property and that the taxes saved will be recaptured by the government if the heirs do not continue the *qualified use* for at least *10 years* after the decedent's death. A qualified heir is a member of the decedent's family who acquired the property from the decedent.[17] A qualified use is one in conjunction with farming or other trade or business. As a general rule, active participation is required. The mere leasing of the farmland to others will not qualify.[18]

5. The executor must make the election on the estate tax return and attach the recapture agreement. The return must show how the special use value was determined. The rules and a §2032A checklist immediately follow Schedule A in the estate tax return.

If the election is made, the maximum amount by which the value of the special use *real estate* can be reduced is $750,000.[19] The $750,000 amount is indexed for inflation for years after 1998, with 1997 being the base year. Assuming 60% as the maximum marginal estate tax rate, the maximum that can be saved by this election is $450,000 on a $750,000 special use reduction in the value of the real estate. While this is not an insignificant amount, if there is a very large disparity between the "highest and best use" and "qualified use" values, the tax savings may be too small, and the remaining burden too great, for the heirs to avoid selling the business.

Since the election applies only to real property and has some onerous requirements, it is not used very frequently. Business owners dying after 1997 may be able to use §2057 which requires that the business interest, not necessarily including real estate, meet a 50% of AGE threshold. If §2032A or §2057 is available, the estate will also qualify for §6166 deferral since its threshold is only 35% of AGE.

Recapture. If the qualified heir discontinues the special use or sells his or her interest (other than to another qualified heir) within 10 years, the taxes saved are recaptured. For example, if the qualified heir allows others to lease the property for cash, it will result in a cessation of the qualified use and the recapture of the taxes saved.[20] However, there is an exception for the surviving spouse that allows him or her to rent the property to other family members without causing recapture.[21] Once an event occurs that triggers the recapture, the heirs (remember they had to sign a recapture agreement when the §2032A election was made) have just six months to file Form 706-A, *United States Additional Estate Tax Return*, and pay the additional tax. If the special use is discontinued, then the amount recaptured is the amount of tax saved. If the property is sold, the recaptured amount is the lesser of the taxes saved or the difference in the proceeds from the sale and the special use valuation. The application of these recapture rules to partial sales is beyond the scope of this text. Two examples will help clarify recapture in general.

EXAMPLE 15 - 13. When Gerard died in 2000, his estate included a persimmon farm that qualified for special use valuation. The real estate had a fair market value of $2,000,000 and a special use valuation of $1,000,000. The $750,000 reduction in the value of the real estate reduced the federal estate taxes by $352,500. Three years after her father's death, Julie (the sole heir) decided to turn the farm into a dude ranch. The cessation of use caused the $352,500 to be recaptured. It had to be paid six months after the change was made.

EXAMPLE 15 - 14. Suppose, instead of changing the use, Julie sold the farm. The amount of recapture would depend upon the price. Since the special use value shown on the return was $1,250,000, a price up to $1,602,500 [the scheduled value plus the taxes saved] would recapture the difference between $1,250,000 and the sales price. A sale above $1,602,500 would recapture all of the taxes saved. Hence, a sale for $1,500,000 would result in a recapture of just $250,000, whereas a sale for $2,200,000 would result in the recapture of the entire $352,500.

When recapture occurs, the heir does not have to pay interest on the recaptured taxes. However, the heir can elect to pay the interest (going back to the original due date of nine months after the date of death) and in exchange take a step-up in the basis of the special use property to what it would have been had special use not been elected.[22] Obviously, one must run the numbers comparing the capital gains taxes saved to the cost of paying the interest. In general, the closer in time the sale is to the original due date of the return, the lesser the interest and the greater the likelihood that the benefit of the increase in basis will exceed the interest expense. Unlike the general rule that allows estates to deduct on the estate tax return any interest paid due to the late payment of estate taxes, if one makes this election no deduction is allowed for the interest on the recaptured taxes.

If the qualified heir dies before the ten year recapture period has ended, the recapture threat also dies (i.e., the heir's estate could sell the property immediately without causing a recapture). Likewise, the sale to another qualified family member avoids recapture, but the buyer must also agree to the recapture provisions for the remainder of the ten year period. The recapture rules for changes in ownership or changes in use are complex and beyond the scope of this text.

Family-owned Business Interest Deduction: §2057

Another relief provision was added to the estate tax law, effective for estates of owners of family businesses who die after December 31, 1997. If the business interest is a qualified one, the executor can elect to exclude from the taxable estate up to $675,000 of the business' value. The actual amount depends upon the value of the business interest and the extent to which the executor wishes to claim the deduction. Many of the rules are similar to those for §2032A, e.g., the business must represent a significant portion of the adjusted value of the gross estate and the interest must go to qualified heirs. Since this, like §2032A, is a deduction, the tax dollars are saved at the estate's highest marginal rates.

When initially enacted in 1997, the family-owned business deduction was an exclusion equal to the difference between $1,300,000 and an exclusion amount based on the unified credit.[23] This meant that, as the exclusion based on the unified credit increased from $625,000 in 1998 to $1,000,000 in 2006, there would be a corresponding decrease in the family-owned business exclusion from $675,000 to $300,000. The 1998 Tax Act[24] changed this to allow a maximum deduction of $675,000 regardless of year. The deduction is coordinated with the exclusion based on the unified credit because the combined amounts cannot exceed $1,300,000. Thus, when the exclusion amount that is based on the unified credit reaches $1,000,000, an estate that qualified for the full $675,000 deduction might decide to claim a deduction of $675,000 and an exclusion amount (in the form of a unified credit) of $625,000. Alternatively, the estate could claim a deduction of $300,000 and have an exclusion amount of $1,000,000 (again in the form of the unified credit) or some other in-between combination, so long as the total is $1,300,000. Since the deduction saves taxes at the highest marginal rate and the exclusion amount equates to the unified credit, the greatest tax savings occur if the estate maximizes the deduction and reduces the exclusion amount. Less than the maximum deduction might be claimed if the estate was going to owe zero tax because of marital or charitable deductions.

> EXAMPLE 15 - 15. Mercedes Aroeste died in 2006, leaving her estate to her two children. Included was a business with a net value of $2,000,000 and other assets with a value of $1,000,000. The children were sure that they would continue to operate the business for at least 10 years. Thus, they were not worried about tax recapture, and they wanted to reduce the taxes as much as possible. The tax would be $738,000 [taxable estate of $2,325,000 after the $675,000 deduction, a tentative tax of $940,050 and a unified credit of $202,050 instead of $345,800.]

> EXAMPLE 15 - 16. Same facts as in the prior example except, for whatever reason, the children wanted to minimize the deduction (i.e., $300,000) and maximize the exclusion amount ($1,000,000). The tax would be $786,000 [taxable estate of $2,700,000, a tentative tax of $1,131,800 and a unified credit of 345,800.]

Requirements. The following five requirements must be met:

1. The decedent (or a member of the decedent's family) must have been a citizen or resident of the U.S. at the time of death.
2. The decedent (or a member of the decedent's family) must have materially participated in the business for five out of the eight years preceding the decedent's death.
3. The interest must be a "qualified" family-owned business.
4. The net value of the business interest that passes to "qualified heirs" must equal at least 50% of the decedent's AGE. Here, unlike §2032A, unsecured debts (claims against the estate) as well as mortgages and liens are deducted to arrive at AGE.
5. The executor must make the election on the estate tax return and file a tax recapture agreement signed by all qualified heirs.

Qualified family-owned business. The term "qualified family-owned business" means an interest in a trade or business located in the U.S. that is either a sole proprietorship or a family controlled entity (i.e., a partnership, a corporation, an LLC, etc.). A family controlled entity is one in which ownership by the decedent and members of the decedent's family fits into one of the following three patterns:

1. They owned at least 50% of the entity.
2. They owned at least 30% of the entity, and their interest when combined with the interests of one other family equals or exceeds 70% of the total ownership.
3. They owned at least 30%, and their interest when combined with the interests of two other families equals or exceeds 90% of the total ownership.

EXAMPLE 15 - 17. When entrepreneur Bob Hitchens died in 2000, his estate included an interest in Hookles, Inc., a commercial fishing company that owned several vessels. Bob, working with some friends, started the business 20 years ago. His interest was valued at $1,500,000 for estate tax purposes. The rest of his assets were valued at $1,300,000. There were debts that totaled $300,000. Bob's only son, Bob Hitchens, Jr., is the sole heir and plans to continue working in the family fishing business. The ownership interests are as follows:

Owner	Relationships	Percentage owned
Bob Hitchens	decedent	15%
Barbara Owens	decedent's sister	25%
Barry Taller	Fred's father	20%
Fred Taller	Barry's son	10%
Sandra Fisher	not related to the others	30%

Bob's interest qualifies for the family-owned business exclusion. Bob had worked in the business for more than 5 out of the 8 years preceding his death. The 50% of adjusted value of the gross estate test is met because his interest represents 60% of the adjusted value of the gross estate. Bob Jr. is the qualified heir. The decedent's interest combined with his sister's interest exceeds 30%. When added to the Tallers' interests, the total is 70%, which is just the minimum percentage required when two families dominate a business. The maximum deduction is $675,000, which results in a taxable estate of $1,825,000 instead of $2,500,000.

EXAMPLE 15 - 18. Suppose Sandra Fisher (from the prior example) died in 2005, and her interest, representing over 50% of adjusted value of her gross estate, was left to her daughter. Prior to Sandra's death, Barbara Owens had sold her interest to another family friend such that the ownership interests were as follows:

Owner	Relationships	Percentage owned
Sandra Fisher	decedent	30%
Bob Hitchens, Jr.	not related to others	15%
Maxine Waters	not related to others	25%
Barry Taller	Fred's father	20%
Fred Taller	Barry's son	10%

Although Sandra's interest meets all of the other requirements, it fails to meet any of the family control combinations: by itself it is 30%, not 50%; the highest combination for two families (Fisher and the Tallers) is 60%, not the required 70%; and the highest three-family combination (Fisher, the Tallers, and Waters) is 85%, not the required 90%.

Some advanced planning may have allowed Sandra's estate to utilize §2057. If she had purchased a portion of Barbara Owens' interest sufficient to bring her interest to 40%, the total would have reached the 70% requirement when combined with the Tallers' interests. Another possibility would have been to spin off her interest as a separate entity. Indeed, the control percentages would be met if Sandra's interest and any other family's interest were spun off as a separate entity, e.g., her interest and the interest of Bob Hitchens, Jr., spun off together, would result in interests of 66 2/3% and 33 1/3%, respectively.

Non-U.S. citizen qualified heirs. If the qualified heir is not a U.S. citizen, the deduction is available only if the interest will be held in a qualified trust or if the heir either reaches an agreement with the IRS on posting a bond or placing a tax lien on the property. The qualified trust is similar to the QDOT needed in order to obtain the marital deduction for property left to non-U.S. citizen spouses (see the QDOT discussion in Chapter 12).

Special rules related to gifts. In meeting the 50% of the adjusted gross estate requirement, the estate can add back gifts of the business interest that were made to qualified heirs, provided the heirs hold such property at the time of the decedent's death. The amount is also added to the adjusted value of the gross estate (i.e., it is added to both the numerator and the denominator). The gifts are added back at their full value without reduction for the annual exclusion. Indeed, even gifts that were less than the annual exclusion amount are added back for the sole purpose of determining whether the estate meets the 50% threshold (they are not part of the taxable estate nor of adjusted taxable gifts).

Gifts of non-business property (other than de minimus gifts) to the decedent's spouse within ten years of death and to other persons within three years (other than gifts to family members under the annual exclusion amount) are added to the adjusted value of the gross estate, thus making it more difficult to meet the 50% threshold. This was done to keep owners from making death bed transfers of non-business assets in order to meet the 50% requirement.

EXAMPLE 15 - 19. When Candace Scott died in 2001, her gross estate was worth $4,000,000, including her shares in a closely held business. The shares were valued at $1,700,000 and were left to her daughter, a qualified heir who intends to continue working in the business. There were debts and expenses of $200,000. Six years before her death, Candace had given her daughter, Laura, shares in the family business. Those shares were valued for gift tax purposes at $730,000. Each year, for the last four years, she made gifts of the family stock to a minor's demand trust established for her only grandson. Each gift was worth $10,000, but a Crummey power held by the grandson kept her from having to use any unified credit. Two years before her death, Candace gave her daughter, Laura, stocks in publicly traded companies. The stocks were valued at $240,000 for gift tax purposes, and Candace paid gift taxes of $115,000. The rest of the shares in the family business were owned by Candace's brother, Brian Kaye.

The shares in the family business just barely qualify for the §2057 deduction. The numerator equals $2,470,000: $1,700,000 from the shares owned at death, $730,000 from the gift to Laura, and $40,000 from the transfer to the grandson's trust. The denominator (the adjusted value of the gross estate) equals $4,925,000: the gross estate of $4,000,000, plus the two gifts that are included in the numerator (even ones less than the annual exclusion amount) and the non-business interest gift to Larry because it was made within three years (this is a special rule for determining the 50% test; the gifts are not included in the gross estate for calculating the estate tax), and the gift tax of $115,000 because it was paid on a gift made within three years of death (i.e., a §2035(b) gross up). The ratio is 50.2%. If the gifts to the grandchild's trust did not exist, and all else remained the same, the ratio would be 49.7% and the business interest would not qualify.

Recapture. Similar to §2032A, there are recapture of tax rules for §2057. Recapture will be triggered if the qualified heir ceases to materially participate in the business for three years out of any eight year period within the ten years following the decedent's death. The participation requirement can be satisfied by a member of the qualified heir's family. The recapture amount is the adjusted tax difference times the applicable percentage. The adjusted tax difference is the portion of the qualified business interest that ceases to be qualified compared to all that qualified (and, although the Code is not specific, presumably only the qualified interest to the extent it was claimed as a deduction) times the difference in what would have been paid had there been no election and what was paid using the election. The applicable percentage decreases over the ten-year recapture period. The maximum recapture is as follows:

If the event causing recapture occurs in the following year of the applicable material participation:	applicable percentage (i.e., the % of tax recaptured):
1 through 6	100%
7	80%
8	60%
9	40%
10	20%

EXAMPLE 15 - 20. Using Mercedes Aroeste's estate (see the first §2057 example), had the heir sold the business in the eighth year, the recapture would be the difference in the tax on a $3,000,000 taxable estate in 2006 and the $738,000 paid, times 60% (applicable percentage): 60% * ($945,000 - $738,000) = $124,200.

Note that there is interest on this additional tax at the "underpayment rate" established under section 6621 for the period beginning on the original due date of the return and ending when the tax is paid. Just as with §2032A recapture, the code refers to this as an additional tax rather than the deferral of the original tax. Consequently, the interest is not deductible.

EXAMPLE 15 - 21. Had the Mercedes Aroeste's estate elected to minimize the deduction and maximize the exclusion (see the second §2057 example), the estate would have paid more tax, but the recapture would be less: 60% * ($945,000 - $786,000) = $95,400.

Combining §2057 with §2032A. Perhaps the biggest boon will be for estates that also qualify for §2032A. With the addition of §2057, many of these closely held businesses will see sufficient estate tax reductions so that they will not be forced to sell the business to pay the taxes.

EXAMPLE 15 - 22. When old McDonald died in 1999, his farm was much sought after by developers. However, his children wanted to continue to farm the land. The land was worth $3,000,000 developed, but only $1,000,000 as farmland. The ducks, pigs, cows, tractors, and other equipment were worth $500,000. His other assets were worth $2,000,000. There was a $300,000 mortgage on the farm and there were personal loans of $140,000. Estate expenses totaled $260,000. His estate qualified for both the §2032A valuation and the §2057 deduction.

The adjusted value of his gross estate was $5,200,000 [gross estate of $5,500,000 ($3,000,000 + $500,000 + $2,000,000) less the $300,000 mortgage]. The §2032A 50% requirement was met because the farm's total net value was 61.5% of the adjusted value of the gross estate, i.e., $3,200,000/ $5,200,000 [($3,000,000 + 500,000 - $300,000)/$5,200,000]. The 25% land percentage was met because the land was 51.9% of the adjusted value of the gross estate, i.e., $2,700,000/$5,200,000 [($3,000,000-$300,000)/$5,200,000)]. The land, special use valued, was included in the estate at $2,250,000 (assuming inflation does not kick the deduction above $750,000 for 1999).

The adjusted gross estate for §2057 purposes was $4,840,000 (here the unsecured debts are also deducted) and the business percentage was 50.4% [($3,000,000 - $750,000 + $200,000)/$4,840,000]. Since McDonald owned all of the farm and it was going to his children who plan to continue to work it as a farm, all other §2057 conditions are met. The executor claims the maximum family-owned business deduction in the amount of $675,000.

Using both Code sections brought the taxable estate down from $4,800,000 to $3,375,000 (i.e., $4,800,000 - $750,000 - $675,000). However, the unified credit that must be used (because of the §2057 election) was $202,050 rather than $211,300. Nevertheless, the estate taxes dropped from $2,069,500 to $1,295,000. This was a savings of $774,500. Because the business was valued at over 35% of AGE, §6166 is also available to allow payment of a portion of the estate taxes over a fourteen year period (see the discussion of §6166 above).

The main difference between the two sections is that §2032A has a real estate requirement (i.e., minimum real estate value of 25%) and §2057 has the family control requirement that can be met in one of several different ways. Thus, a business that owns valuable boats, trucks, and construction equipment might qualify for §2057 even though §2032A is not available due to the lack of real estate. If a decedent had a 25% interest in a farm that he and a friend had run as a partnership and all of the other §2032A requirements were met, the section would be available to reduce the decedent's real estate interest in the farm by as much as $750,000 (indexed). Section 2057 would not be available because the decedent's interest, being less than 30%, does not meet any of the family control requirements. Finally, where the business interest was very close in value to 50% on the net value of the decedent's estate, because of unsecured debts (claims against the estate), an estate might qualify under §2057 but not qualify under §2032A. If one is trying to couple §2032A and §2057, it is unclear whether in trying to meet the 50% requirement of §2057 the business would first have to reduce the value by the §2032A exclusion amount (i.e., the $750,000 exclusion for real estate) or whether one could use the fair market value. In the above example, the estate qualified even with the exclusion. Given that both are relief provisions, there is a good argument that availability of each is independent and that the percentage threshold is calculated using the fair market value. There is also a slight difference in the calculation of the numerator that makes it a little harder to qualify for §2032A than for §2057 in that the former does not allow a deduction (in arriving at the numerator) for claims against the estate whereas the latter does.

> EXAMPLE 15 - 23. Farmer Leroy's gross estate is valued at $5,100,000 at the time of his death in 1999. His farmland is worth $2,000,000 and the equipment, etc., is worth $500,000. His only debt (this is a hypothetical) is a valid claim for $200,000 that arose out of a slander suit. His estate does not qualify for §2032A, but it does qualify for §2057. The respective percentages and fractions are: 49% ($2,500,000/$5,100,000) for §2032A and 51% ($2,500,000/ $4,900,000) for §2057.

Qualified Conservation Easement: §2031(c)

If a person dies owning land that is appropriate for a conservation easement, the Taxpayer Relief Act of 1997 added a new provision that allows some tax relief.

The complicated rules will just be summarized here. Basically, the executor can donate (this had better be done with the blessing of the heirs) a conservation easement to certain organizations and exclude a portion of the value of the land, up to certain dollar limits, from the gross estate. The election is made by the executor on the estate tax return. This election is available even if the decedent's estate plan made no provision for a conservation easement.

A *conservation easement* is one that protects: the natural habitat of fish, wildlife, or plants; a historical site (land and/or structures); or open space for public benefit, i.e., a scenic or recreational benefit. The easement must be donated to a charitable organization or to a governmental agency. The land has to meet one of the following location requirements: (1) in or within 25 miles of a metropolitan area; (2) in or within 25 miles of a national park or wilderness area; (3) in or within 10 miles of an Urban National Forest. The decedent or a member of the decedent's family must have owned the property for three years prior to the decedent's death.

If the executor makes the election, donates the easement, and fulfills all of the other requirements of the section, then the estate can deduct the lesser of: (A) the applicable percentage of the value of the land subject to the easement, reduced by any charitable deduction that results from said donation, or (B) the easement exclusion limitation. The *applicable percentage* is 40% times the value of the land reduced by 2 percentage points for each percentage point (or fraction thereof) by which the value of the qualified conservation easement is less than 30% of the value of the land (determined without regard to the value of the easement). The easement exclusion limitation starts at $100,000 for estates of decedents dying in 1998 and increases $100,000 each year until it reaches $500,000 for the year 2002 and beyond.

EXAMPLE 15 - 24. When she died in 1999, Alice Le Mond's estate included acreage near a national park. Without a conservation easement, it was worth $450,000 for estate tax purposes. An easement for riding and hiking was negotiated with the Park Service. Appraisers determined that the value of the easement to the park was $160,000. Since this is greater than 30% of the value of the land, there is no percentage reduction. The estate can deduct the lesser of 40% [$180,000] times the value of the land or the exclusion limit for 1999 [$200,000]. If the easement was valued at $117,000 (i.e., 26% of the value of the land) the deduction would be 32% [i.e., 40% - 2 * (30% - 26%)] times the value of the land, resulting in an exclusion of $144,000 [i.e., 32% * $500,000]. Had she died in 1998, the limit would have been $100,000.

There is a recapture provision that takes effect if the easement agreement has not been implemented within the earlier of two years after the decedent's death or the sale of the land by the estate or the heirs.

VALUATION DISCOUNTS AND CONTROL PREMIUMS

Over the years, the courts have offered taxpayers the ability to generate liquidity by significantly discounting the transfer tax value of closely held business interests, real property, and securities subject to special market circumstances. The most common discounts are the minority discount, lack of marketability discount, and fractional interest discount.

Minority Interest Discount for Business Interests

A *minority interest* is an interest in a business that, in terms of voting, is not a controlling interest. The owner, acting alone, lacks the power to affect changes in policy, structure, or strategy.

> EXAMPLE 15 - 25. Jack owns 50.1% of a corporation worth $1 million, and Jill owns 49.9%. Jill owns a minority interest. Alone, Jill cannot run or control the business, set compensation levels, sell or encumber business assets, elect herself an officer, or control corporate policy. Jill would most certainly have difficulty selling her interest to a third party for $499,000.

Ownership of a partnership interest may also qualify for a minority interest discount. The Uniform Partnership Act codifies the common law rule that each partner has just one vote, regardless of his or her capital (investment). The partnership agreement can change this by providing greater voting control to certain partners.

For transfer tax valuation, minority discounts of between 15 and 50% are obtainable for such interests. Factors influencing the size of the discount include the overall quality of management, composition of other share holdings, size of the business, history of profitability, existence of business opportunities not currently being exploited by management, and degree of the company's financial leverage.[25]

In some situations, minority interest discounts are not available. The IRS contends that a gross estate including two separate minority interests in the same property which add up to a majority interest should be denied the benefits of minority interest discounts.[26]

> EXAMPLE 15 - 26. Dad's estate plan will leave his 40% business interest at his death to a marital trust. At Mom's later death, her gross estate will include Dad's interest in the marital trust, as well as her own 40% business interest. The IRS is likely to challenge a minority discount for either interest.

Planners should be able to circumvent this problem by either having S1 dispose of his or her interest to the bypass trust, which is not taxed to S2, rather than to the marital trust, or having one or both spouses make a lifetime transfer of the interest (by gift, installment sale, etc.).

Minority interest discounts are not available to stock subject to a §2032A special use valuation election.

A donor holding a majority stock position who gifts some of the shares can reduce both the retained shares and the gifted shares to a minority position.

Valuation discounts and imperfect unification. Earlier we discussed the fact that the federal "unified" transfer tax system is not perfectly unified. Imperfections include the allowance of an annual exclusion for lifetime gifts, failure to include post-gift appreciation in the estate tax base, and the ability to avoid grossing-up gift taxes on gifts made more than three years before death. To these we add the ability to obtain valuation discounts for certain lifetime gifts that would not be available to transfers at death.

> EXAMPLE 15 - 27. Fiore owns 100% of the stock in a closely held corporation worth $300,000. This year, he gave each of his three children one third of the stock. Taking a 25% minority interest discount on each transfer, Fiore will report on Form 709 three gross gifts of $75,000 (= $100,000 - .25 x $100,000), totaling $225,000. Thus, in addition to saving taxes by taking three annual exclusions, Fiore has reduced his future gross estate by an extra $75,000 (= 3 x ($100,000 - $75,000)). Had Fiore kept the stock and bequeathed it to the three children, these minority discounts would not have been available.

Revenue rulings have stated that a minority interest will not be disallowed solely because a transferred interest, if combined with interests held by family members, would be part of a controlling interest.[27] Valuation discounts for such gifts are allowed because the gift tax is computed on a *per gift* basis. Estates cannot claim discounts for transfers of whole assets that are broken into fractional interests as part of the distribution, since the asset is valued at its fair market value as of the moment of the owner's death. Thus, valuation discounts create a fourth instance of imperfect unification.

Control premium. Case law recognizes that a fractional interest in property can actually be worth *more* than its proportional share.[28] For example, the value of a 51% interest in a particular closely held firm has been ruled to be worth greater than 51% of that firm's underlying value. A higher value reflects a premium for holding a controlling interest. In one case, the decedent owned about 52% of the voting stock in a corporation, giving him, among other things, the power to elect all directors. The court approved a 38% control premium, raising the value of the decedent's interest from $372,152 to $514,000.[29]

The control premium is essentially the "flip side" of the minority discount. While including property subject to a control premium in the gross estate will ordinarily increase estate tax, careful planning can actually reduce estate tax, to the extent that the majority interest is bequeathed to the surviving spouse.

EXAMPLE 15 - 28. Anderson was the sole owner of a $1 million closely held corporation. At his death, he bequeathed 51% of the stock to his surviving widow and 49% to his son. In connection with this business interest, Anderson's gross estate includes $1 million. Based on a control premium of 10%, the marital deduction is $561,000 (110% * 51% * $1 million). The control premium has reduced Anderson's taxable estate by $51,000.

In community property states, control premiums cannot apply to stock held as community property since neither spouse has majority control.

Lack of Marketability Discount for Business Interests

Due to lack of an established market, restricted stock, stock in a closely held business, and partnership interests are invariably more difficult to sell than business stock that is publicly traded. Thus, discounts for lack of marketability ranging from 15% to as high as 50% are obtainable. These discounts apply to both minority and majority interests.

Factors influencing the size of the discount include: the extent of the resale restrictions; SEC restraints on marketability; the dollar value of the stock; the firm's growth expectations; and the size of the company's total assets and equity.

Use of minority interest and lack of marketability discounts can leverage the benefit of the gift tax annual exclusion.

> EXAMPLE 15 - 29. Crabb's closely held business was recently appraised at $1 million. He gave his daughter a two percent interest in the business. After applying a 40% minority interest discount and a 25% lack of marketability discount, the value of Crabb's reportable gross gifts was $9,000 [2% * $1,000,000 * 60% * 75%]. Although this is under the annual exclusion amount, Crabb's accountant had him file a gift tax return that fully disclosed the discounts and how the value was determined so as to start the statute of limitations running. If no return is filed or if the return does not adequately explain the method of arriving at the value, the IRS could challenge the valuation many years later.

Some courts have allowed taxpayers both a minority discount and a lack of marketability discount, while others have collapsed the two into one discount. Whether collapsed or not, a combined discount of 30% to 40% is generally considered safe, whereas discounts of more than 50% are seen as too aggressive. Determining and documenting the appropriate valuation discounts has become a highly paid specialty within the appraisal community.

Fractional Interest Discount for Real Property

Undivided interests in real property can generate a fractional interest discount because such interests are neither easily partitioned nor readily marketable.

> EXAMPLE 15 - 30. Jones died owning a 58% interest in common in commercial real property that was appraised for $2,000,000. His estate was allowed a 25% fractional interest discount that resulted in his estate listing a value of $870,000 on the estate tax return [58% * $2,000,000 * 75%].[30]

The fractional interest discount for real property, strongly opposed by the IRS, is analogous to the minority interest and lack of marketability discounts for stock. The IRS has taken the position that the only discount allowed should be the cost of a partition action.[31] It should be noted, however, that the problem of control premiums in real estate does not arise because all owners must agree on significant property decisions.

Other Valuation Discounts

Worth mentioning briefly are three other valuation discounts:

- Securities, even publicly traded ones, that are subject to special *securities law restrictions* can be discounted. Restrictions include lack of registration and the need to sell the stock by private placement.
- Large quantities of a stock listed on an exchange can receive a *blockage discount* if their sale all at one time could have a depressing effect on the market price. However, if the block represents a controlling interest in the corporation, possibly triggering an even higher price, a *premium* may be attached to its value. Blockage discounts may be available for other property, such as a large number of paintings left in the estate of a prominent artist.[32]
- A discount may be allowed for a business that lost a *key person* (e.g., the decedent) who was responsible for its goodwill.

Valuation discounts can generate significant transfer tax savings. For estates, there is the slight negative trade-off of a lower income tax basis as a result of the lowered value for estate tax purposes. This negative trade-off does not apply to gifts since the basis is a carryover from the donor's basis.

FAMILY LIMITED PARTNERSHIPS

Family limited partnerships (FLPs) have been used by families in agricultural areas for decades as a means of getting children involved in running the ranch or farm. Only recently have they become a popular planning tool for any family run business. FLPs offer many attractive estate planning advantages over most other business forms and transfer devices. However, due to the costs of establishing them and the appraisal costs associated with making multiple transfers of the limited partnership interests, they usually are not recommended unless the parents owning the business have a net worth in excess of two or three million dollars. For those that qualify, a FLP has numerous advantages: (1) the parents can give away wealth and still retain control; (2) transfers can be made at substantial discounts compared to the value of underlying assets, thus saving unified credit and gift taxes; (3) restrictions can be placed on transfers by children; and (4) there is some protection from creditors.

Family partnerships are sanctioned by the IRC with certain requirements set forth in §704(e). Among other things, the income and tax benefits must be distributed or allocated according to each owner's percentage in the partnership. The general partners may be paid for their personal services to the partnership. Also, capital must be "a material income-producing factor," meaning that a family partnership cannot be used to redistribute income generated from the personal services of one or more of the general partners.

Establishing a family limited partnership. To establish a family limited partnership, one must follow the requirements of the state's limited partnership act. This will probably require publication of the names of the general partner and the limited partners. The Uniform Limited Partnership Act requires that there be at least one general partner and one limited partner. With a FLP, it is common for one or both parents to serve as the general partners. They may start by owning all but a very small portion of the limited partnership units. Over time, the parents transfer by gift a significant portion of the limited partnership units to the children. Given the wealth of the parents, it is unlikely that this transfer can be accomplished utilizing gifts covered by annual exclusions alone. Thus, to make this work usually requires the parents using up both of their unified credits, and perhaps even paying some gift tax.

Under unusual circumstances, such as the death or bankruptcy of the general partner, most limited partnership agreements give the limited partners the right to elect a new general partner. As with most real estate limited partnerships, a limited partner cannot take assets from the partnership or otherwise force liquidation of the partnership before its term is up. The term is likely to be set at 50 years. However, these agreements usually provide that after both general partners are deceased, the limited partners can vote to liquidate the partnership. Whether this would take a super majority of the limited partnership interests depends upon the terms of the agreement.

FLP costs. The major costs are attorney's fees to establish the partnership, probably between $3,000 to $7,000 depending on the nature of the business assets, and appraisal fees to establish both the underlying value and the appropriate discounts, probably in the range of $10,000 to $25,000. In addition, when partnership shares are transferred as gifts, an appraisal will again have to be performed. The high cost of appraisals is one reason that the parents should consider large initial gifts right after the partnership is established. However, subsequent appraisal fees by the same appraisal firm should be considerably lower than the first ones, since the company will be familiar with the business. There will also be annual accounting fees for preparation of the partnership returns and the K-1s that must be distributed to all partners. There may also be annual state fees for the right to do business as a limited partnership within the state.

Discounts. The two types of valuation discounts discussed earlier in the chapter play a significant role in making the use of an FLP attractive. Limited partnership units are transferred at a huge discount because the units have limited marketability and because the owners of the limited partnership units have extremely limited control.

> EXAMPLE 15 - 31. In the year 2001, the Jackson family created a family limited partnership with Jack and Lilly Jackson as general partners. The net value of their combined estates was $18,000,000, which includes their ranch valued at $6,000,000. The limited partnership interests represented 95% of the total value of the ranch. The other 5% was allocated to the general partnership interest. The limited partnership portion was divided into 95 limited partnership units. Immediately after formation of the limited partnership, 20 units were transferred to each of the three children.
>
> The lack of marketability discount was determined to be 30% and the minority interest discount was 25%. The following was reported by each parent as the taxable gift to each child: ($6,000,000 * 70% * 75% * 20% * 50%) - $10,000 = $305,000 [FMV ranch x (1 - 30%) * (1 - 25%) * 20% interest * 50% because split between two parents, - annual exclusion = taxable gift.] Each parent reports three such gifts (for a total taxable gift of $915,000) and pays gift taxes of $92,100.
>
> The total gift tax for both parents is $184,200. The Jacksons have moved 60% [$3,600,000 at FMV] of the ranch to their children. Because of the size of their combined estate, assuming the plan calls for postponing all estate taxes until the second death, the estate of the last parent to die will be in the 60% marginal rate bracket. If that death occurs in the year 2006 or later (avoids grossing up the gift taxes and the exclusion amount is fully phased in), the discounted transfers and the reduction of the estate by the gift taxes paid will have saved total transfer taxes of $1,224,420. Compare the two scenarios, assuming values remain the same, estate tax is postponed to the second death, and that both deaths occur after 2005.

Tax on $17,000,000 [S1's bypass holds $1,000,000] $8,995,000

Tax on $13,980,800 * $7,586,380
  Plus gift taxes on the two gifts $ 184,200
  Total transfer taxes $7,770,580

Taxes saved: $8,995,000 - $7,770,580 = $1,224,420

Any post-gift appreciation escapes estate taxes and the estate may be able to claim discounts for the limited partnership interest that it holds. Only S2's estate owes taxes, but, the adjusted gifts of $915,000 and the gift taxes paid credit of $92,100 must be taken into account.

Appraisals. Despite numerous attempts by the IRS to disallow discounts for intrafamily transfers, it lost numerous court cases and finally conceded the existence of the discounts provided the taxpayer can back them up by creditable professional appraisals using relevant market data for the discounts. These discount appraisals are in addition to the appraisal of the underlying assets owned by the partnership.

Ability to control gifted assets. In addition to the discounts, the most attractive feature of the FLP is the ability of the donor to retain control over the assets. While key rights of a limited partner must be recognized, the general partner maintains all the managerial control over the partnership assets, determining when and whether to make income distributions to all the partners or to reinvest the income into additional assets. For most wealthy individuals, the biggest roadblocks to making substantial gifts are the donor's reluctance to lose control of his or her business or other important valuable assets and concern about how well the donee-children will use the gifts. The control offered to the parent-general partner makes this an acceptable vehicle to give assets now, especially when one can utilize the tax benefits of valuation discounts and low values on appreciating assets.

Getting the children involved. Once the children have a vested interest in the business, they may take a greater interest in how it works. Annual reports

---

* The taxable estate at S2's death: $18,000,000 - $3,600,000 (the units transferred) - $184,200 (gift tax paid) - $325,000 (the bypass trust created at S1's death utilizes the increase in the exclusion amount that occurred between the time the gifts were made and the S1' death).

must be given to all partners and formal partnership meetings with all the family partners present are a good time to discuss the family investments and why they performed well or poorly. To avoid having the children liable as general partners, they cannot be involved in the actual management of the business and they must not appear to outsiders to be general partners.

Using the children's lower tax brackets. One benefit of a family limited partnership is that it is possible to shift income into the lower tax brackets of the children. This applies to the percentage interest the child actually owns in the partnership. When a parent is in the 39.6% federal income tax bracket and the child is in the 15% tax bracket, this can make a significant difference.

Protection against failed marriages of children. One nice protection is that the assets can be held as the separate property of each of the children. While the income distributed is usually commingled with the child's other assets, the partnership interest is usually clearly identified as the child's separate property. In community property states, only the community property is divided in a divorce proceeding. While everything is presumed to be community property unless it can be traced to a gift, an inheritance, or to property owned prior to the marriage, it should be easy to establish that the units were acquired as gifts and therefore stay in the family. Of course, a child who is not worried about divorce can change them into joint tenancy or into community property by written agreement with his or her spouse.

Loss of step-up in basis on gifted assets. One disadvantage of gifting assets is that the donees (the children) lose the ability to get a step-up in basis at the death of the parent of the part of the partnership that was given to the children. When the assets have a very low tax basis, this reduces the tax benefits of the family limited partnership. Of course, if the children do not intend to sell the business, then the low basis is a price worth paying to avoid the transfer tax costs.

Limited asset protection. Often highlighted are the FLP's asset protection capabilities. It is true that limited partnership units given several years before the parents have financial difficulty should not be subject to levy by the parents' creditors. Most states have some form of fraudulent transfers act that allows creditors to attach property transferred by debtors for inadequate consideration when the transfer takes place in the face of mounting financial pressure. However, if sufficient time has passed, the parent is generally the only one liable to his or her personal creditors and, as general partner, the only one liable to the creditors of the partnership.

In the past, creditors of limited partners collected from the limited partners by using a court-issued *charging order* that allows creditors to collect the money distributed to a partner. Unfortunately for the creditor, the partnership income tax liability of the partner whose interest was seized was also passed on to the creditor. All limited partners must be treated the same insofar as distributions are concerned, and those distributions are controlled by the general partner. The idea in using the FLP as an asset protection device has been to starve out a creditor by not making distributions even though FLP profits force the limited partners and any creditor with a charging order to recognize taxable income. In theory, the tax liabilities should put the creditor in a mood to greatly discount the debt in order to avoid additional tax liability. Some state court decisions have held that if a charging order does not result in timely payment of the debt, the creditor can foreclose on the debtor's partnership interest, forcing the liquidation of enough of the underlying assets to pay the creditor provided the foreclosure does not unreasonably interfere with the partnership business. If other courts adopt this approach, then a charging order can delay the creditors of a child-limited partner but would eventually allow them to be fully paid by means of foreclosure if the income distributions are withheld. The partnership agreement should give the family a first right of refusal for any attempted sale by the limited partners.

If asset protection is crucial to family members involved in a business enterprise, they should consider the newest business organization to gain widespread acceptance, the limited liability company.

THE LIMITED LIABILITY COMPANY

The limited liability company (LLC), like the limited partnership, is strictly a creation of the various state legislatures. Unlike the partnership, it does not have common law roots, but every state (and the District of Columbia) has adopted an LLC statute since Wyoming led the way in 1977. Why the sudden popularity? When done correctly, an LLC offers business owners the chance to have the limited liability of a corporation with the tax pass-through advantages of a partnership. Each owner-investor is called a *member* and his or her ownership share is called a *membership interest*.

Creating a Limited Liability Company. Owners must comply with the state statute, and they must consider the IRS rules concerning taxation of business entities. On January 1, 1997, Treasury regulations became effective that made the old rules of trying to avoid looking like a corporation obsolete. Most business entities can select for themselves whether to be classified for tax purposes as a corporation, a partnership, or disregarded as a separate entity by checking the appropriate boxes on federal Form 8832. The new regulations[33] (called the *check-the-box regulations*) make it much easier for owners to choose the tax status of their businesses. A business entity with two or more owners can elect to be taxed as either a corporation or a partnership. A business owned by just one person (or a married couple filing jointly) can elect to be taxed as a corporation or be disregarded as a separate tax entity (i.e., be taxed as a sole proprietorship) regardless of the actual business organization. Hence, in a state that allows a single owner LLC, the owner could choose to be taxed as a corporation or as a sole proprietor. An LLC owned by two or more people can choose between being taxed as a partnership or as a corporation. The default classification (one need not file the form) is partnership treatment for eligible domestic entities with two or more owners and sole proprietorship (disregarded as a separate entity) for businesses with just one owner (or a married couple). [34]

Advantages compared to corporations. Both the LLC and the corporate form give the owners the protection of limited liability. An owner is liable only for torts in which he or she is actually involved. If one drives the company car on business and causes an accident in which others are injured, only the business and the owner-driver are liable. The other co-owners are not liable. Furthermore, none of the co-owners are liable for contracts entered into in the company's name. Of course, for either of these business forms the owners may be asked to personally guarantee certain contracts, such as leases and loans, which will create personal liability. However, absent some personal guarantee by the owners, contractual liability attaches solely to the business entity and not to the owners.

LLCs have a single level of taxation at the membership level. Of course, S corporations also have this characteristic, but LLCs do not have the restrictions on stock ownership that S corporations have. Trusts, foreign individuals, and other corporations can be members. Although LLCs are most likely to be closely held, there is no restriction on the number of owners, whereas federal law limits to 75 the number of S corporation shareholders. S corporations are limited to one class of stock, whereas LLCs can have membership interests with different rights to income allocation, capital preferences, and voting.[35]

Advantages compared to partnerships. Both LLCs and partnerships share the advantage of single-level taxation, but partnerships have the disadvantage of all partners being fully liable for all contracts taken in the partnership name and any torts that arise out of the partnership business whether committed by a partner or by a partnership employee. Both allow withdrawal of assets, subject to the partnership or LLC agreement, without such withdrawals being deemed income. Of course, withdrawals do affect the owners' capital accounts. Some states require LLCs to pay some minimal annual fee (generally less than $1,000) whereas general partnerships are usually exempt from such fees.

Advantages compared to limited partnerships. The advantages and disadvantages are similar to those stated for the general partnership, except limited partners enjoy limited liability. Unlike LLCs, the limited partnership must have at least one person, the general partner, exposed to unlimited personal liability. Furthermore, limited partners must not be involved in the day to day management of the partnership, or they will lose their limited liability insofar as third parties rely on their appearance as general partners in extending credit to the partnership.

Repeal of the *General Utilities* Doctrine. Prior to the 1986 Tax Reform Act, a corporation distributing assets as part of a liquidation of the corporation was able to avoid tax at both the corporate and shareholder level.[36] The 1986 Tax Reform Act changed the rule such that a corporation distributing appreciated property, whether or not the distribution is pursuant to a liquidation, must recognize the capital gain.[37] Thus, many existing corporations holding significant amounts of appreciated assets, whether the corporation is a C type (taxed as a separate entity) or S type (taxed as if a partnership), may find it too costly from a tax standpoint to convert to LLC status. Partnerships and LLCs do not recognize gain on their dissolution, nor will an owner be taxed on the liquidation unless he or she receives cash in excess of his or her basis.

OTHER LIQUIDITY SOURCES

Additional sources for estate liquidity deserve a brief mention.

Employee Retirement Benefits

An employee may have accumulated substantial retirement benefits. If these benefits are payable after the employee's death (i.e., if there is a survivorship annuity and/or a vested amount), the estate or the employee's spouse can use these funds to defray some of the cost related to the employee's death. However, such benefits are generally income in respect of a decedent (i.e., the money would have been subject to income tax had the decedent received it) and it will be taxable income when paid to the beneficiary.

Postmortem Liquidity Planning Techniques

There are a host of strategies that can be undertaken after death over which an individual has little or no control during lifetime. Postmortem devices, such as disclaimers and the alternate valuation date election, are examined in Chapter 18, which surveys postmortem tax planning.

This chapter has examined planning for liquidity. Chapter 16 will present the principles of planning for the closely held business.

QUESTIONS AND PROBLEMS

1. How will the following factors influence liquidity needs at death?
   a. Size of the family estate.
   b. Whether the decedent is S1 or S2.
   c. Age of the family members.

2. "High-basis assets make desirable assets for a predeath sale designed to generate liquidity." True, false or uncertain? Explain.

3. (a)What traits distinguish cash value insurance from term insurance? (b) Universal life insurance from other types of cash value insurance?

4. Is life insurance ever subject to income taxation? Explain.

5. Explain the two primary ways in which life insurance can be subject to gift taxation.

6. Life insurance can be subject to estate taxation under §§2001, 2033, 2042, and 2035(a). Briefly explain the application of each.

7. Who, if anyone, should be the *insured* of a policy designed to provide liquidity to a family estate of $250,000, assuming the following alternative facts?
   a. Spouses in their 30s; husband working; wife at home with two young children.
   b. Spouses in their 30s; both working; no children.
   c. Spouses in their 50s; both working; children are self-supporting adults living elsewhere.
   d. Single adult; no children.
   e. Single parent of one six-year old child.
   f. Retired couple; self-supporting adult children living elsewhere.

8. Re-answer part a, d, and f of Question 7, assuming instead a $4 million family estate owned by spouses who wish to set up a credit shelter bypass plan. In each case, would it matter how liquid the family wealth was?

9. What factors influence the selection of the owner and primary and contingent beneficiaries of an insurance policy on the life of a spouse in a small family estate situation?

10. (a) Describe the characteristics of the irrevocable life insurance trust. (b) What are its advantages?

11. A rich client of yours is about to acquire a $500,000 life insurance policy on his life, naming his wife owner and beneficiary. They each have a net worth of $1 million. Advise him.

12. Would any of your answers to Question 11 change if the net family estate was worth about $800,000? Why or why not?

13. Five years ago, Mary assigned ownership of an insurance policy on the life of her husband, Bud, to the trustee of Bud's living trust. The trustee is beneficiary, and terms of the trust provide that at Bud's death Mary is entitled to a life estate in the trust income. If Mary survives Bud, could there be an estate tax problem?

14. April, age 40, is a recently divorced single mother of two young children. She is not on friendly terms with her ex-husband who, in her opinion, is a "selfish spendthrift." April owns few assets and asks your estate planning advice to help achieve her goal of financial security for her children.

15. How are the arrangements based on §§6166, 303, 2032A, and 2057 each designed to provide estate liquidity?

16. At his death, Silva owned a successful farm near an expanding metropolitan area. As a farm, the land was worth $350,000, but a real estate developer is now willing to pay Silva's estate $1,200,000 for it. The rest of his estate has a net value of $400,000. What is Silva's total gross estate if (a) the executor does not elect §2032A, and (b) an election is made?

17. At the time of his death in 1999, Nicolas Emery's estate included a small private lake that he and his family ran as a private resort where families enjoyed boating and fishing. Capitalization of the earnings of the present

enterprise gives a value of $800,000 for the land. The boats, several utility vehicles, fishing equipment, portable concession stands, picnic tables, etc., are valued at $200,000. His home and other investments (not related to the business) were worth $1,600,000. Nicolas owed miscellaneous debts of $150,000 and estate expenses were $25,000. Developers would like to buy the property from the estate, put in a hotel and golf course at one end, and subdivide the rest as exclusive residential sites. The beneficiaries of his estate are §2032A qualified heirs and wish to continue the present business use. (a) What is the minimum fair market value that would have to be assigned to the land and lake for Nicolas's estate to qualify for special use? (b) Suppose the FMV was established to be $1,500,000, what would be the special use value (i.e., what value would be shown on the estate tax return)? (c) Use the ETAX program to determine the estate tax savings.

18. Using the facts from the prior problem, except that, instead of a FMV of $1,500,000 for the land and lake, it was determined to be worth $2,400,000. (a) What is the §2032A value? (Assume no inflation change for the §2032A amount). (b) Explain how Nicolas's estate also qualifies for §2057. (c) What is the maximum §2057 deduction? (d) Use your ETAX program to compute the estate tax with and without the benefit of the two elections.

19. (a) How have check-the-box regulations made it easier for closely held businesses to select the appropriate organization with less worry about tax implications? (b) For a business with just a few owners, why is the LLC likely to be favored over the corporate form? Can all of the advantages of the LLC be obtained by making a Subchapter S election? (c) What is likely to keep the owners of an S corporation from liquidating it and reforming as an LLC?

20. Minnie and Mark, both age 68, are married parents of two adult children, Betty and Bryan. They own a $500,000 interest in a closely held business and $100,00 in other assets. Betty pretty much runs the business and would like to continue to do so after her parents are gone. Bryan has no interest in owning or running the business. If Minnie and Mark wish to leave all their property equally to their children after their own deaths, is there a distribution problem? Can life insurance help solve it?

ANSWERS TO THE QUESTIONS AND PROBLEMS

1 a. Generally speaking, cash needs will rise with increasing estate size, due to the estate tax.

   b. In most cases, the death of S1 will result in no estate tax, due to the shelter of the marital deduction and the unified credit. On the other hand, the death of S2 can result in a significant estate tax for families with medium to large estates.

   c. The younger the minor children, the greater the typical amount of liquidity needed to fund the economic loss provided by that deceased spouse for the remainder of the children's period of dependence. Also, the older the person, the less time there is to accumulate liquidity.

2. True. The sales of the assets will result in little or no taxable gain, or they will produce a loss which in the usual case will be deductible only by the owner.

3. a. The traits that distinguish cash value insurance from term insurance are: (1) The pattern of the *premiums* over time (cash value: constant premiums; term: increasing premiums). (2) Whether or not the proceeds are *certain* to be paid (cash value: certain; term: uncertain).

   b. The traits that distinguish universal life (UL) insurance from other types of cash value insurance are: (1) degree of flexibility - UL policies permit the policyholder to vary the face value and premium payments; and (2) investment yield - UL policies offer a variable yield, based on shorter-term investment rates.

4. Life insurance can be subject to income taxation in the following ways:

   a. Income taxation of cash value accumulation: Not taxable during accumulation period. When surrendered for cash value, the excess of the cash value over total premiums paid is taxable income.

   b. Income taxation of policy proceeds: Generally excluded unless the policy was transferred for valuable consideration.

5. Gift taxation of life insurance can arise either when a policy is assigned, or at the insured's death, whenever the insured, owner, and beneficiary are all different parties.

6. Estate taxation can arise under Code §§2033, 2042, 2001, 2035, as described in detail in Chapter 6. The following is a summary.

Under §2001, the decedent's *adjusted taxable gifts* will include the date-of-gift taxable terminal value of *any* life insurance policy for which the decedent made a completed transfer more than three years before death.

Under §2033 (property owned at death), the terminal value of a life insurance policy on the *life of someone other than the decedent* will be includable in the decedent's gross estate to the extent of the decedent's date of death ownership interest in the policy.

Under §2042, proceeds on the *life of the decedent* will be includable in the decedent's gross estate if, at the insured's death, either the proceeds were receivable by the decedent's executor or the decedent possessed any incidents of ownership in the policy. Interestingly, the entire proceeds under split dollar arrangements are includable even though part of the proceeds is payable to a third party, such as the employer.

Under §2035, the proceeds of a life insurance policy on the *life of the decedent* will be includable in the decedent's gross estate if, within three years of death, the decedent made a completed transfer of incidents of ownership in the policy.

7. The major question in deciding whom to insure is whose death will result in financial loss that should be replaced.

   a. *Spouses in their 30's; husband working; wife at home with two young children:* Both spouses may need insurance: for the husband to replace his lost income; for the wife to finance day care services, etc., while the widower is working.

   b. *Spouses in their 30s; both working; no children:* Often, neither spouse needs coverage, because the (modest) loss from the death of either is assumable. However, this depends on their relative current standard of living and desired standard of living when the first one dies. Spouses who live modestly and save a lot may not need life insurance if the survivor can live on one salary and the expected investment income. On the other hand, spouses who save little and live expensively (costly home, cars, lifestyle, etc.) and want the surviving spouse to continue enjoying this lifestyle will probably need a considerable amount of insurance on the lives of both spouses.

c. *Spouses in their 50's; both working; children are self-supporting adults living elsewhere:* Essentially same answer as part b, except less insurance usually necessary because the surviving spouse's expected life span is lower and expected investment income is often greater.

d. *Single adult; no children:* No insurance usually necessary.

e. *Single parent of one six-year old child:* Considerable insurance would ordinarily be needed for the parent to provide funds needed to raise the child.

f. *Retired couple; self-supporting adult children living elsewhere:* Answer depends on surviving spouse's other expected sources of income. To the extent that retirement benefits will continue and investment income will be high, less insurance is needed.

8. With a larger estate size, death taxes might be an estate expense. In each case, the individuals may wish to pay the taxes out of liquid estate property, making insurance unnecessary. If there are insufficient liquid assets, then insurance may be needed.

a. Possibly a *joint life policy* on the death of the second spouse. See text for discussion of other alternatives, which include insuring *both spouses* for the full amount, insuring *both spouses* for only a small amount that can be used to purchase a fully paid up policy on the life of the survivor, and insuring the *wife only.*

d. No insurance usually necessary. Most couples probably let the relatively unrelated estate beneficiaries worry about paying the estate tax on what could be a $4 million windfall (less the taxes, of course).

f. Same as part a. It might matter how liquid the family wealth was. As mentioned above, liquid assets could be used to pay part or all of the estate tax, thus reducing the need for insurance.

9. In the small family estate, convenience and other non-tax factors would influence the decisions as to who should be the owner and primary and contingent beneficiaries. The insured's spouse could be named owner and primary beneficiary to avoid probate in the insured's estate. The contingent beneficiary could be a child or a trustee of a trust for the benefit of the child.

10. a. Characteristics of the irrevocable life insurance trust: (1) It is created by the insured. (2) Trustee is owner and beneficiary of the policy. (3) Trust terminates at or after S2's death.

    b. Advantages: (1) There is no transfer taxation of proceeds at either spouse's death. (2) It is not included in either spouse's probate estate. (3) It qualifies gifts of the policy and the policy premiums for the annual exclusion. (4) It qualifies for the gift tax annual exclusion for gifts to the trust. (5) It ensures that a responsible party will provide the needed liquidity. (6) Proceeds are available to S2 subject to an ascertainable standard.

11. Naming the insured's spouse to be owner or beneficiary will usually either cause the proceeds to be subject to estate or gift tax at that spouse's death, and/or to be included in that spouse's probate estate. The preferred plan is an irrevocable life insurance trust for the reasons discussed in the answer to the previous question. Even in the case of a single person, the trust is preferred because it avoids estate taxation and probate. It also insures that a responsible party is managing the policy and eventually the proceeds.

12. The answers to the above question would very likely change. Given the increasing exclusion amount, a family estate size of $800,000 owned by two spouses with an ABC estate plan would allow most, or perhaps all, of the insurance owned by the spouses to avoid estate tax without resorting to an ILIT.

13. As indicated in the chapter, Mary may be considered to have made a Section 2036(a) transfer with a retained life estate which would include the entire policy proceeds in her gross estate.

14. To establish an asset base to provide income to her children in the event of her premature death, April should establish an irrevocable life insurance trust, a device that can function reasonably free from the control of her ex-husband. The trustee would be the policy beneficiary, directed to provide for the children's needs. The trustee ought to be instructed to pay funds, whenever possible, directly to the provider.

15.   §6166: By deferring tax payments over 14 annual payments, some of the deferred tax will benefit from a mere 2% late payment rate.

§303: By reducing income tax on stock redemptions used to pay death taxes and administrative expenses. The buy-back is treated as a capital exchange and the stock receives a new basis due to the owner's death.

§2032A: By reducing the taxable estate. The real estate devoted to special use may be lowered by as much as $750,000 (indexed) to its special use value.

§2057: By reducing the taxable estate. The family-owned business deduction may lower the taxable estate by as much as $675,000 (however the maximum unified credit would then be $202,050, i.e., producing an exclusion amount of $625,000).

16. a. If the property does not qualify for special use valuation, the land will probably be valued at $1,200,000, its highest and best use value, making the gross estate equal to $1,600,000.

    b. If the property does qualify for special use valuation, the land will be valued at $450,000 (which is the $1,200,000 highest and best use value, reduced by $750,000, the maximum amount allowed by law), making the gross estate equal $850,000.

17. (a) Answer: $1,400,000. The minium value could be determined by trial and error or by using algebra. Let the value of the business land be X. We know that to qualify, X plus the other business property must equal 50% of the adjusted value of the gross estate. Thus we must solve for X in the following equation: $(X + \$200,000) = (X + \$1,600,000 + \$200,000)/2$; simplified: $X = \$1,600,000 + \$200,000 - \$400,000 = \$1,400,000$. (b) Since the FMV is $1,500,000 and special use is $800,000, the maximum reduction in the value of the real estate is $700,000 (not $750,000). (c) Without the election, the

taxable estate would be $3,125,000 [$1,500,000 + $200,000 + $1,600,000 - $150,000 - $25,000] and the tax would be $1,148,250. With the election, the taxable estate is $2,425,000 and the tax is $777,750. The difference is $370,500.

18. (a) $2,400,000 - $750,000 = $1,650,000. The difference between FMV and special use is greater than $750,000, therefore the maximum reduction in the value of the real estate is $750,000. (b) The business, even specially valued, is greater than 50% of adjusted value of the gross estate: ($1,650,000 + $200,000)/($1,650,000 + $200,000 + $1,600,000) = 53.6%. (c) The maximum deduction is $675,000. However, for years after 1998, using the maximum deduction will result in a corresponding reduction in the exclusion amount (i.e., a reduction in the unified credit). (d) Without the two reductions, the taxable estate is $4,025,000 and the tax is $1,643,250 (using 1999 unified credit of $211,300). With the two exclusions the taxable estate is $2,600,000 [$4,025,000 - $750,000 - $675,000] and the unified credit is $202,050. The tax is $876,750 and the difference is $766,500.

19. (a) The regulations allow the owners to choose to be taxed as a partnership or corporation, if two or more owners, or as a corporation or sole proprietorship if just one owner (or a married couple) regardless of the actual structure. Since closely held businesses usually prefer to have a pass through entity in order to avoid having tax at the entity level and again at the owner level, the check the box regulations have made it very easy for new businesses to avoid the corporate tax. (b) Even though the check the box regulations allow a corporation to be taxed as a partnership, the recognition of capital gains tax on the distribution of appreciated assets from a corporation (§311) will cause many to favor the LLC. A Subchapter S corporation is taxed as a partnership for the most part. However it also has the §311 problem and, compared to the LLC, it is much more restricted as to capital structure (only one class of stock) and as to who may own shares (75 limit, generally only individuals can own it, no non-resident aliens allowed). (c) The Code §311 requirement that gain be recognized upon distribution of appreciated assets.

20. The problem is that an equal distribution of the $600,000 estate will mean leaving to Bryan at least a $200,000 interest in the business, an asset he does not want. A survivorship (second death) life insurance policy in the amount of $400,000 could result in Betty receiving the entire $500,000 business and Bryan receiving $400,000 in cash proceeds and the remaining $100,000 in other assets. Thus, life insurance can simplify distribution of "lumpy" estate assets to survivors with widely different lifestyles and preferences.

ENDNOTES

1. In this chapter, the word *insurance* will be used as shorthand to mean life insurance.

2. *Theodore H. Cohen*, 39 TC 1055 (1963), acq. 1964-1 CB 4.

3. *Swanson*, 33 TCM 296, (1974), aff'd. 518 F2d 59 (8th Cir., 1975); Rev. Rul. 85-13 1985-1 CB 184.

4. §101(*a*)(2).

5. §677(a)(3).

6. *Baptiste*, TCM 1992-198; §6324(a)(2).

7. IRS §2642(c)(2).

8. §6166(b)(6); §2053(d)

9. §163(h)(2)(E).

10. §2503(d) added by the Taxpayer Relief Act of 1997.

11. Rev. Rul. 80-250 1980-2 CB 278.

12. Cecil Cammack, Jr., at Cammack Computations Co., 1-800-594-5826, will do these computations at a very reasonable price.

13. LR 9314050.

14. §303(b)(3).

15. §2032A(b)(1)(A).

16. §2032A(b)(1)(B).

17. §2032A(e)(1).

18. §2032A(b)(2).

19. §2032A(a)(2).

20. *J. Fisher*, TC CCH 12,923 (1993).

21. §2032A(b)(5)(A).

22. §1016(c)

23. Initially §2033A, renumbered as §2057 by the 1998 Tax Act.

24. IRS Restructuring and Reform Act of 1998 (Pub L 105-206, 112 Stat 685).

25. *John and Viola Moore v. Commissioner*, 62 TCM 1128 (1991) (35% discount on gift of partnership interest); *Estate of Winkler v. Commissioner*, 62 TCM 1514 (1991) (20% discount on nonvoting stock); *Estate of Catherine Campbell v. Commissioner*, 62 TCM 1514 (1991) (56% discount); *Estate of Lenheim v. Commissioner*, 60 TCM 356 (1990); *Nancy Moonyham v. Commissioner*, TC Memo 1991-178.

26. TAM 9140002.

27. Rev. Rul. 93-12, 1993-7 IRB 13.

28. *Estate of Chenowith v. Commissioner* 88 TC 1577 (1987).

29. *Estate of Salsbury v. Commissioner* 34 TC Memo (CCH) 1441 (1975).

30. *Smythe v. U.S.* 86-1 U.S. Tax Cases (CCH).

31. See TAM 9336002.

32. *G.O'Keeffe Estate* TC ¶12,886(M) (50% blockage discount allowed).

33. §301.7701-1 through §301.7701-4. See *US v. Kintner*, 216 F. 2d 418 (9th Cir. 1954), for the case that lead to the old regulations based upon corporate characteristics.

34. §301.77013(b)(1).

35. §1361(b)(1) sets forth the restrictions for S corporations.

36. *General Utilities & Operating Co.*, 296 U.S. 200, 56 S.Ct. 185 (1935)

37. §311

CHAPTER 16

Planning for Closely Held Business Interests

OVERVIEW

A closely held business is a firm privately owned by one or a few individuals who actively participate in its management. Unique estate planning problems can arise for owners of a closely held business. Typically, the firm generates the major source of its owner's *income* and represents the single largest part of his or her *family wealth*. Too often, however, the firm can sustain or increase that level of income and value only if the owners continue to be actively involved in its management. For example, a closely held corporation is rarely in a position to start paying a dividend after the owner dies if it was not paying them before.

This income and value can be jeopardized by two events, each of which is certain to occur. First, each owner's *involvement* with the firm is destined to end, and the enterprise will lose his or her economic contribution. Second, the ownership interest in the business must eventually be *transferred*, subjecting it to transfer costs, including taxes.

Estate planning seeks to minimize the adverse impact of these significant events by attempting to achieve four basic objectives:

1. To generate sufficient *income* for the owner and the owner's family after the owner's active involvement in the business ends.

2. To transfer to the owner's chosen beneficiaries the maximum *value* attributable to that business.
3. To minimize the *costs* of transferring the business interest to the owner's chosen beneficiaries.
4. To provide sufficient *liquidity* to pay the transfer costs.

This chapter will focus on how closely held business interests accomplish these goals. Shares in publicly traded corporations require far less attention from estate planners. Their owners can easily accomplish these objectives for two reasons. First, withdrawal of any one owner will have a far less depressing effect on business value and income, making continuity more assured. Publicly traded firms usually employ far more personnel, making business success much less dependent on the efforts of any one individual. In contrast, studies indicate that only 30-35% of successful closely held family businesses survive in the second generation, and only 10-20% survive in the third generation. In many cases, this is due to unresolved family conflicts. Second, the goal of liquidity is invariably easier to achieve for owners of publicly held firms because the owner's survivors receive marketable securities.

However, liquidity problems can arise for wealthier individuals owning publicly traded stock that is either a large block or "restricted" under federal securities law. Large block holdings (i.e., tens of thousands of shares) may give rise to the problem of *blockage*, which is the temporarily depressing effect on the market price that results from selling a large block all at once. While federal tax law will allow some valuation discount for blockage effects, overall liquidity is nonetheless reduced. *Restricted stock* is usually acquired either from an affiliate of the issuing company or in a private, unregistered transaction. Federal securities law prohibits restricted stock from being sold without either registering it under the Securities Act of 1933 or meeting an exemption from registration. The most common methods of disposing of such stock are by a secondary offering, a private placement, or by "Rule 144 sales," none of which are simple transactions. Although blockage and restricted stock can lead to significant liquidity problems, their consequences will be felt by only a handful of estates. Their impact on overall liquidity is not nearly as great as the depressing effect of death or withdrawal of an owner on the value of a closely held business interest.

Thus, owners of closely held businesses have relatively unique problems. This chapter will survey the major principles and techniques of estate planning devoted to assisting them. The chapter will first present an overview of general planning in this area, then examine in greater detail the business buyout agreement, and finally, the special valuation rules from Chapter 14 of the Internal Revenue Code as they relate to corporate recapitalizations and partnership capital freezes.

VALUING THE BUSINESS

The subject of the *value* of a closely held business can arise in several contexts. How is business valuation determined? Often, as we have seen, correct valuation is necessary for tax purposes, and the Treasury and the courts have written much on the subject. The following briefly outlines the major influences on business value by summarizing the eight general factors invariably requiring careful consideration. These items are taken from Revenue Ruling 59-60,[1] the Treasury's classic exposition on valuation of the shares of closely held stock.

1. Nature and history of the business.
2. Economic outlook and conditions of the economy and industry.
3. Book value of the stock and financial condition of the company.
4. Company earning capacity.
5. Company dividend-paying capacity.
6. Extent of company goodwill and other intangibles.
7. Recent sales of the company's stock and the size of the block to be valued.
8. Market price of publicly traded stock in the same industry.

The extent of use of each factor depends upon the underlying facts concerning the specific business interest.

PLANNING IN GENERAL FOR CLOSELY HELD BUSINESS INTERESTS

All estate planning for closely held business interests is premised on the fact that the owner cannot carry on forever. As mentioned, we are certain of the occurrence of two future events: that the owner's active *involvement* in the management of the firm will terminate, and that the *ownership* interest will be transferred. These events have major economic implications for the four objectives mentioned earlier.

Withdrawal from the Firm: Minimizing Decline in Income and Value

Owners have the ability to choose when to terminate their active management of the firm. Some elect to remain active until disability or death. The rest withdraw sooner, for any number of reasons, including the desire to adopt a new lifestyle, to consume more of the wealth that time and hard work have created, and to step aside to provide a business opportunity for a son or daughter. No matter when the owner plans to withdraw, if the departure is expected to reduce the value and income derived from the business, the owner can take several steps to minimize the decline.

Delegate responsibility. First, the owner can plan early to "share the entrepreneurial spirit" by passing on knowledge of the business and by delegating greater responsibility to those who one day may be able to replace his or her contribution. To provide an *incentive* to assume this responsibility, the business can contribute to certain tax-favored fringe benefit plans, including medical insurance contracts, group-term life insurance, and retirement plans. In general, contributions to these plans are income tax deductible by the firm and are either tax free or tax deferred to the employee.

Execute contracts for future income. Second, the owner can use current business value to raise his or her own future *income* by executing certain *contracts*, such as a nonqualified deferred compensation plan, disability income insurance, and a qualified retirement plan. Nonqualified deferred compensation is a custom-tailored agreement under which the employer agrees to pay the employee in the future for services rendered presently. Tax law ordinarily permits the income tax to be similarly deferred. The professional athlete, a person with a brief but often lucrative career, is a frequent party to the deferred compensation contract.

Freeze the estate. Third, the firm may be able to undertake a corporate recapitalization or create a partnership capital freeze. These are intricate transfer devices which, in addition to sustaining value and income, can *reduce transfer taxes*. Each can offer additional employment incentives to family members, and each may be able to freeze the value of the owner's interest in the business while continuing to provide him or her with rights to substantial income and voting power in the business affairs. However, as we shall see later, recent tax legislation has severely restricted their potential value, and the owner should be advised to seek expert tax counsel when exploring these techniques.

Maintain a list of instructions. Fourth, the owner can place in a safe deposit box a list of business instructions for the surviving family. The list could include recommendations as to whether to sell the firm or continue running it, the name of the chosen successor, a list of business advisors, and the location of key company documents. These arrangements can reduce stress and risk of failure, particularly after the sudden death of the owner.

Execute a buyout contract. Finally, if an abrupt departure by the owner is likely to result in a significant decrease in the value (and in the income) of the business, the owner might consider selling the business or negotiating a contract for its future sale. By staying on as a consultant during a transition phase, the decrease in value may be avoided. Selling a business will be explored later in the chapter.

In summary, by planning early, the owner can usually take one or more significant steps to forestall a large decline in the future income from, and the value of, interests that will pass to his or her chosen beneficiaries.

Transferring the Business Interest

As well as minimizing the decline in business value resulting from withdrawal from the firm, the owner will want to choose *when* and *to whom* to transfer the business interest. Planning for the transfer will depend in large part on whether the person wishes to transfer the equity interest itself to a family member, or whether he or she intends to sell it to an unrelated party and later transfer the sale proceeds to the chosen beneficiaries. The next two sections will probe these alternatives.

Transfer of an equity interest to a family member. Some owners will want to make a transfer of some or all of the business to a particular family member who is willing and able to take over its management. Many transfer devices are available. The most common ones are discussed next.

Lifetime strategies. As mentioned earlier, to encourage the family member to adopt a long-term commitment and to prevent deterioration in business value and income, the owner should consider starting a program to prepare a family member for eventual ownership and control. In addition to delegating increasing amounts of responsibility, the owner can offer incentives, such as *gifts* of ownership interests in the business, possibly in the form of stock or stock options. The transfers can be outright, or they can be in trust, with the owner and family member acting as co-trustees. Transfers using trusts can promote a more orderly transition by enabling the owner to monitor and develop the family member's interest, abilities, and commitment.

Instead of making a completed gift, the owner may wish to arrange a gift-leaseback, installment sale, sale-leaseback, or private annuity. In fact, an installment sale can be a simple, inexpensive, and relatively tax-safe estate freezing alternative to the corporate recapitalization or the partnership capital freeze. The latter two are discussed later in the chapter. In general, most aspects of gifts and other transfers of business interests can be analyzed in a manner similar to lifetime transfers of business interests that are not closely held. The reader is referred to Chapters 13 and 14 for greater detail.

Transfer at death strategies. Instead of making a lifetime gift of the business interest to a family member, the owner, to retain complete control, may prefer to pass it on at death. This approach makes it possible to use techniques that are not available for lifetime gifts, such as: the use of §303 stock redemptions, if the business is incorporated; the §2032A special use valuation; and the business exclusion of §2033A; and finally, the extended payment plan of §6166. Furthermore, the estate taxes may be funded through the use of an irrevocable life insurance trust, a funding source that is not likely to be available for gift taxes. These benefits were discussed in the last chapter. In addition, business interests that have appreciated in value receive a step-up in basis if they are part of the decedent's estate, but have a carry-over basis if transferred as gifts.

However, there are several drawbacks to waiting until after the owner dies to transfer a closely held business.

Liquidity problems. First, estate liquidity problems may arise if a non-spouse survivor winds up owning a relatively illiquid asset having a substantial taxable value. For a discussion of several methods of handling liquidity problems, review the material on liquidity planning in Chapter 15.

> EXAMPLE 16 - 1. Keith, a widower, died two years ago, the very successful owner of a business whose going concern value was $6 million. The estate tax attributable to this value was $3,300,000 (= .55 x $6 million). Due to lack of succession planning, Keith's children were forced to sell the business last month to a competitor for the firm's $3 million liquidation value, with the unfortunate result that the IRS became a larger "beneficiary" than the children.

Unprepared survivors. Second, transfers at death of closely held business interests to unprepared survivors who subsequently decide to carry on the business can generate severe problems. The combined tasks of dealing with grief and assuming new business duties can cause panic, guilt, exhaustion, family squabbles, and finally, failure. Adverse parties such as customers, employees and creditors may be tempted to take advantage of the new owner's naivete. While careful planning can reduce this risk, it cannot entirely eliminate it, particularly if the successors are not very experienced in business. Realistically, only a minority of owners will actually plan for this outcome. A 1988 Laventhal & Horwath poll of family business owners found that only 45% had selected successors, and only one in three had developed a strategic plan.[2]

Uncertainty and friction. Third, transfers at death of closely held business interests to beneficiaries not involved in the business but who do not intend to sell may be ill-advised if the beneficiaries have no desire to manage the firm. By its nature, the closely held business requires active cooperation among its owners, cooperation which usually requires constant interaction. Unaware of the firm's precise manner of operation, uninvolved owners can precipitate uncertainty and friction among the manager-owners and other employees, especially if they disagree with how the business is being run.

Hard for survivors to sell. Fourth, transferring business interests at death can create problems for surviving transferees who do wish to sell out. In structuring the terms of the sale, survivors will not be able to take advantage of the owner's knowledge and experience. The business may no longer be as productive, a fact that could substantially lower the bid price. The bidders may not be willing to pay the surviving beneficiaries a fair value for the deceased owner's interest, particularly if it is a minority interest. The survivors may have little bargaining power in view of their probable (and perhaps apparent) need for cash. Furthermore, the uniqueness of the business usually limits the prospective buyers. It is not like selling a home or the shares of a publicly traded corporation.

Legal and tax complexities. Fifth, legal and tax complexities may arise. If a shareholder's interest in S corporation stock is to be distributed at death to a trust, such as a bypass or a marital trust, that trust must be designed to qualify as a "Qualified Subchapter S Trust" in order not to jeopardize the corporation's Subchapter S status. Essentially, an S corporation is a corporation that is treated by federal income tax law as if it were a partnership; income is taxed to the individual shareholders rather than to the corporation. Requirements to qualify as a "Qualified Subchapter S Trust" include naming only one income beneficiary.[3]

Valuation disputes with IRS. Finally, *disputes with the IRS* over the estate tax valuation of a closely held business are common and often result in litigation or settlement at higher than expected values. The Code imposes an estate tax penalty of 20% of the tax underpayment for *valuation understatements* at less than 50% of the correct value. The penalty applies only if the additional tax owed exceeds $5,000.[4] A pre-death sale can ensure that the owner will be available to intelligently confront the IRS.

For these and many other practical reasons, the owner would normally be well-advised not to delay until death the gifting of a business interest to other family members.

Sale to an unrelated party. Instead of transferring an ownership interest to the surviving beneficiaries, the owner could arrange the sale of the business interest to an unrelated party. Potential buyers include the key employees of the business, other individuals, and other firms, including competitors. In addition to eliminating potential friction, the beneficiaries are likely to receive other assets (cash or publicly traded stock) that produce income with little effort or skill on their part. The following material explores several aspects of the sale option, including timing and tax effects.

Timing. The business could be sold before or after the owner withdraws from active management. *While the owner is still active*, the entire firm could be sold outright, or some of its assets could be sold and then leased back to the firm. An arrangement could be made to sell the firm when the owner withdraws at retirement, disability, or death. Actual timing of the sale will often depend largely on the personal, non-economic preferences of the owner. The material below discusses the economic and tax factors influencing that decision.

In general, the greater the expected decline in the value of the firm resulting from the owner's withdrawal, the greater the economic motive to sell it while it is still being actively run by the person. Value will fall most for single-owners, especially those offering professional services, such as physicians, accountants, and attorneys. Often, the primary business assets of these firms are the personal customer relationships which, in many cases, are not transferable. Other closely held businesses, such as product-oriented firms and service firms with more than one owner, may be more able to retain their value after departure of the owner.

Sale of the business interest prior to the owner's withdrawal will often bring a *higher price* since potential buyers can currently observe that the business is operating successfully under the direction of an active owner. Further, the person's astute awareness of the firm's identity and its earnings potential will provide additional bargaining power during the negotiations. And if the sale is completed while the person is alive, the agreement may include an obligation of the new owner to retain the seller as an "adviser" or "consultant," as a way of increasing the seller's future income. Finally, sale of a closely held business prior to the owner's death can minimize unsettling disputes with the IRS over the firm's actual estate tax fair market value.

Alternatively, the business interest could be sold at or after *the owner's withdrawal* from the firm. If the sale is structured in advance to take effect at the person's disability or death, it is called a *business buyout agreement*, an arrangement to be discussed shortly.

Taxable gain. Selling the business for cash prior to the owner's death will give rise to the *immediate recognition* of a taxable gain, unless the transaction is an installment sale or other tax deferred exchange. On the other hand, transferring the interest at death can eliminate most or all of the taxable gain because of the *step-up* in basis that the interest will receive at death. However, at a probable tax rate of 20%, the tax impact of a pre-death sale for cash may turn out to be a reasonable price to pay to achieve substantial estate liquidity, especially in view of the high costs of alternate liquidity sources, such as insurance on the life of an elderly person.

Form of the transaction. Sale of the business can take one of several forms. It can be for *immediate cash*: to one or a few individuals; to many individuals; as in a public offering; or to a corporation. It can be in the form of an installment sale with any of these parties, with the seller's recognition of the taxable gain spread over the collection period. The sale can be for *stock*, in a tax-deferred exchange with a publicly held firm. Or the capital gains tax may be eliminated entirely by a step-up in basis if the transfer is after the owner's death.

A common planning device employed to sell a closely held business to one or a few individuals is the *business buyout agreement*, also called a buy-sell agreement, in which the firm, one or more owners, employees, or other parties contract in writing with the owner in advance to purchase his or her interest in the business, usually at the owner's death or disability. The buyout agreement offers many advantages, including future liquidity, a guaranteed market, and possibly greater certainty as to the selling price. Often, the purchase is funded with life and disability insurance.

Consideration should be given to incorporating an unincorporated business for several reasons. Incorporating will generate divisible shares of ownership which may be easier to transfer or liquidate when the need arises. Incorporating will also enhance continuity, since a corporation has an indefinite existence that might help the business survive the principal shareholder's departure. One disadvantage of forming a typical C corporation is that almost any distribution of corporate property to the shareholders will be taxed to them as dividend income, which is subject to double taxation, once at the corporate level and again at the shareholder level. Two exceptions to this double taxation problem are the IRC §303 redemption to pay death taxes (covered in Chapter 15) and a complete redemption of the deceased shareholder's stock.

The Need for Early Planning

When should planning for closely held business interests begin? For many reasons, planning should begin early, when the person is still active and in good health. First, the business owner can more clearly express specific estate planning *objectives* at this point, and his or her knowledge and expertise can provide professional planners with greater help in reaching these objectives. Second, the person will be able to take advantage of planning concepts that are available only to *healthy* individuals, including relatively inexpensive life and disability insurance. Third, if the business will eventually have to be sold, *careful planning* can eliminate the need for a sudden forced sale at the owner's incapacity or death, both times when the business, having lost the owner's services, is clearly less valuable.

With these general principles in mind, let's examine the specific legal arrangements to which we have been referring.

BUSINESS BUYOUT AGREEMENT

Earlier we learned that placing upon one's survivors the burden of selling the business after the owner's death can create problems. These problems can be eliminated or minimized by the owner's careful preparation of a business buyout agreement. Executed by the owner and one or more prospective purchasers, the buyout agreement obligates the other parties to purchase the interest of the owner upon the occurrence of specific future events, such as at the onset of his or her permanent disability or upon his or her death.

Types of Agreements: Cross-purchase, Entity-redemption, or Mixed

The three most common types of buyout agreements are distinguished by the identity of the contracting parties. The first type, called the *cross-purchase* agreement, provides that the owners, usually all of them, purchase the interest of a particular owner. In many contracts, the owners undertake a reciprocal cross-purchase agreement, in which each owner agrees to purchase a pro rata share of the interest of any owner that dies. The second type, called the *entity* or *redemption* agreement, has the business itself purchase the interest of one or more owners. The third type, called the *mixed* agreement, usually gives the business an option to purchase an owner's interest and gives the other owners the option or obligation to purchase the balance. As a hybrid of the other two, the mixed agreement has the characteristics of both cross-purchase and entity-redemption. It is often considered the most flexible arrangement.

Taxation of Buyout Agreements

As we shall see, the most critical issues in taxation of buyout agreements arise in the estate tax area.

Gift taxation. Generally, the execution of a buyout agreement does not result in a taxable gift. However, an agreement having a contract price below fair market value will if it gives a purchaser an unqualified present purchase right.

Income taxation. Income tax effects of buyout agreements will depend on the type of the agreement.

Cross-purchase agreement. The *selling owner*, usually the estate of a decedent-business owner, will be selling a capital asset subject to capital gain treatment. However, in view of the *step-up* in basis at decedent's death, the only gain recognized will be on any appreciation that occurred after the date of death. The *buyer's* new basis will be the purchase price of the business interest acquired.

Entity-redemption agreement. The *acquiring business's* new basis will be its purchase price, which is not a tax deductible expense. If the business has been paying premiums on life insurance to fund the arrangement (see below) it will not be allowed a tax deduction for those premiums. They must be paid with after-tax dollars.[5] Further, any cash value buildup on a policy and any receipt of proceeds, while not included as ordinary income, may be subject to the alternative minimum tax.[6]

The *selling party*, again usually the decedent-owner's estate, will be taxed on the sale proceeds as a dividend, to the extent of the corporation's earnings and profits. Dividend treatment can be avoided if the sale can qualify for favorable redemption treatment under §302 or §303. Both sections permit the redeeming party to treat the sale as a disposition of a capital asset rather than the receipt of a dividend. This means that there is generally little or no taxable gain due to the step-up in basis at death. Without this favorable treatment, the entire receipt would be taxable at ordinary income rates.

Mixed agreement. Tax aspects for contracting parties under a mixed agreement follows the patterns mentioned above.

> EXAMPLE 16 - 2. Stan and Oliver, equal owners of a corporation, are trying to decide whether to arrange a cross-purchase or an entity-redemption buyout plan. The adjusted basis of each of their stock in the business is $20,000. They project that the business will be worth $200,000 when the first owner dies. Thus, under

either arrangement, the purchase price is expected to be $100,000, and the total value of the surviving owner's stock will equal $200,000, the total value of the business. However, the survivor's basis will be different, depending on which arrangement is selected. If a cross-purchase plan is chosen, the surviving shareholder's basis in his stock will increase to $120,000, which is $20,000, the basis of the pre-owned stock, plus $100,000, the purchase price of the decedent's stock. Alternatively, if an entity-redemption arrangement is chosen, the basis of the surviving shareholder's stock will remain $20,000, because he will not have purchased any additional shares.

Estate taxation. The deceased owner's gross estate will invariably include some value attributable to the decedent's ownership interest held at the moment of death. Ordinarily, the estate executor will prefer avoiding a dispute with the IRS over this value. One method of avoidance has been to establish a selling price in the buyout agreement that will, by law, *fix the value* for estate tax purposes. Only half-jokingly, one commentator has said that in the absence of a price "set" by a buyout agreement, the "value" of the business can be said to be the amount agreed upon by "a willing IRS agent and a willing executor, neither of whom has ever owned a business."

Agreements prior to §2703. Prior to October 9, 1990, the effective date of §2703, fixing the value of the business for estate tax purposes was far simpler because case law was quite generous in allowing fixed values that may have been substantially below fair market value. Three valuation methods are commonly included in buyout contracts: First, a *specific dollar amount* is specified, with a provision made for periodic review so the owners can revise the amount as conditions change. Without provision for a review, if, the value of the business subsequently increased, the purchasing owners would receive a windfall at the expense of the selling owner. Unfortunately, experience has shown that inertia reduces the likelihood of periodic reviews.

Second, the selling price can be determined by *appraisal*, the agreement specifying that a qualifying appraiser will determine the value of the business at the time of sale. The appraisal method has the advantage of ensuring that a current value is used.

Third, business buyout agreements can use a *formula* method of valuing business interests. Preferably, the appropriate formula is determined by an expert appraiser. Its terms ordinarily call for valuation to be a specified percentage of book value or a multiple of current earnings. A formula is more flexible and often more accurate than a specific amount since the derived selling price will vary with economic conditions. However, because a formula is more arbitrary than an appraisal, it may later turn out not to reflect current economic conditions.

Impact of §2703. Currently, to fix the estate tax value of the business equal to the buyout agreement amount, agreements (executed after October 8, 1990) must meet specific statutory requirements under §2703(b)[7] and its final regulations:

1. The agreement must be a *bona fide* business arrangement.
2. The agreement *cannot be a device* to transfer property to members of the decedent's family for less than full and adequate consideration in money or money's worth.
3. The terms of the agreement must be *comparable* to similar arrangements entered into by persons in an arm's length transaction.

Some comments on these requirements. The thrust of these requirements is to ensure a value reasonably close to the value of the business interest at the moment of the transfer. Thus, an agreement under which the surviving owner, a son, is obligated to purchase the parent's $1 million business interest (current value) for a fixed $300,000 (historical contract value) would be currently labeled a "disguised bequest," and not meet requirements 1 and 2. On the other hand, prices set between unrelated owners are not usually subject to intense scrutiny by the IRS if the transaction otherwise appears to be made at arm's length. IRS regulations provide that a buyout agreement will meet all three requirements if more than 50% of the value of the property subject to the agreement is owned by persons who are not "natural objects of the transferor's bounty."[8]

Planners feel that the comparability requirement of item 3 will create considerable uncertainty and additional expense for difficult appraisals, in particular because typical buyout agreements are not public documents. However, for businesses in some industries, agreements may be able to specify a formula, such as a multiple of sales or earnings, if that formula is known to be the predominant valuation method for the industry.

Even though valuation discounts may be available, the estate could wind up paying more estate tax than it should if valuation is not set for estate tax purposes. Planners must consider the §2703 valuation rules carefully. Including a "savings" clause that increases the selling price in the event of an audit to the estate tax value as finally determined may not work. Such clauses, seen as mere attempts to pass property at less than its true value, have been challenged by the IRS as against public policy [9]

EXAMPLE 16 - 3. Dad's will provided leaving the exclusion amount to a bypass trust and the residue of his estate to a marital trust for Mom. Dad executed a business buyout agreement with his son, who was obligated to buy Dad's 1,000 shares of closely held business stock for $1 million. When Dad died in 2002, he owned the stock and $1,500,000 in other property. Son paid Dad's estate $1,000,000 for the stock and Dad's executor distributed $700,000 to the bypass trust and $1.8 million to the marital trust. After an IRS audit, Dad's executor agreed that the stock's fair market value was $2 million. Thus, Dad's gross estate totaled $3,500,000 not $2,500,000 as had been shown on the estate tax return. Only the $1.8 million that went into the marital trust qualified for the martial deduction, thus the taxable estate was actually $1,700,000, resulting in estate taxes of $416,000. The additional $1 million is considered as having been left to the son and, in the absence of a clause allocating taxes to the credit shelter trust, he would have to pay 10/17ths of the tax and the other 7/17ths would be charged to the bypass trust. The tax could have been avoided had the buyout agreement provided for a realistic selling price. Consider the two alternatives.

	Alternative Values Given the Stock		
	Sales Agreement $1 million		Realistically Valued $2 million
Gross Estate	$3,500,000	*1*	$3,500,000
Less Marital Deduction	$1,800,000	*2*	$2,800,000 *3*
Taxable Estate	$1,700,000		$700,000
Tentative Tax	$645,800		$229,800
Less Unified Credit	($229,800)		($229,800)
Estate Tax	$416,000		$0

notes

1 $3,500,000 = stock @ $2 million & other property @ $1,500,000

2 marital deduction = $1,800,000 - exclusion amount into Trust B

3 marital deduction = $2,800,000 - exclusion amount into Trust B

Funding

A business buyout agreement can require that the survivors pay a cash lump sum at the triggering event, or it can require payment of cash in periodic installments. The choice sometimes depends upon the nature of the triggering event.

Cash lump-sum payment. Buyout agreements that require payment of a cash lump sum equal to the entire contracted price are most likely to be funded with life insurance and/or lump-sum disability insurance.

Life insurance. The principles of the acquisition of life insurance to fund a business buyout agreement will be influenced by the type of buyout chosen. Under an *entity* agreement, the firm purchases and acts as beneficiary of a policy on the life of each business owner. Each policy is in the amount that is necessary to buy out that owner's interest. In a (reciprocal type) *cross-purchase agreement*, each contracting party purchases and acts as beneficiary of a policy on the life of each of the other contracting owners.

> EXAMPLE 16 - 4. Sol and Harry are equal shareholders of a corporation that has a net worth of $300,000. The men have executed an *entity* buyout arrangement. The corporation will own and be the beneficiary of two $150,000 face value policies, one on Sol's life and one on Harry's life. The men plan to review and update this amount periodically as the value of the business changes.

> EXAMPLE 16 - 5. Facts essentially similar to those in the prior example, except that a *reciprocal cross-purchase* plan is adopted. Sol will own and be beneficiary of a $150,000 policy on Harry's life, and Harry will own and be beneficiary of a $150,000 policy on Sol's life.

A reciprocal cross-purchase arrangement funded with life insurance becomes *unwieldy* when the agreement includes numerous owners, because each contracting party will have to purchase a policy on the life of each other contracting owner. For example, although only 2 policies would have to be purchased for a firm with two contracting owners, 6 policies would have to be purchased for three owners, and 12 policies for four owners. In general, the number of policies purchased under a cross-purchase plan would be $n(n - 1)$, where n equals the number of contracting owners. Under an entity plan, the business itself would simply purchase one policy on the life of each contracting owner. Thus, only n policies would have to be purchased.

The number of policies needed under a cross-purchase arrangement can be reduced somewhat by using one of two specialized life insurance contracts. First, two contracting parties may be able to purchase a *first to die* joint lives policy which pays the proceeds to the survivor upon the first death of the two insured parties. The premium cost should be less than the total cost for two separate policies because only one payout will be made. Second, some companies offer a policy covering more than two insured owners for different amounts based on their respective ownership interests.

An entity agreement funded with life insurance might trigger a corporate *alternative minimum tax* because the "book income" of the corporation will include the insurance proceeds whereas its taxable income will not. For any buyout agreement, insurance premiums are not deductible from income, even if paid by the firm.[10] Thus, all premiums are paid with after-tax dollars.

With a cross-purchase agreement between owners who are not close in age (or who have unequal interests), a larger premium will likely be paid by the younger owner (or the owner with the smaller interest). The greater burden falls on this owner, who is probably less affluent, because he or she will either be insuring an older person or will need a policy with a higher death benefit in order to buy out the larger share.

Using the firm's assets. A second method of funding a lump-sum payment under an entity arrangement is with the firm's own *cash or noncash assets*. This can make life insurance unnecessary, but too often the business will not own sufficient distributable assets, particularly the amount of cash that may be needed to pay estate debts.

Lump-sum disability insurance. Finally, in an attempt to accommodate buyout agreements, more and more insurance companies are offering disability policies promising to pay a lump sum at the onset of disability, rather than the usual income stream.

Certain triggering events not conducive to lump-sum agreements. Other, usually uninsurable events triggering the buyout could be retirement, divorce, insolvency of an owner, criminal activity, and loss of a professional license. However, since none of these other events can be reasonably expected to generate a sizable cash flow, a full-cash buyout under such circumstances may be financially difficult.

Installment payments. In lieu of choosing a lump-sum payment, the parties can agree to an *installment sale* of the business interest. The installment sale can make the purchase of life insurance unnecessary and can be a source of periodic income to the seller and the seller's family. However, installment payments carry the risk that the purchasers will be unable to make the payments, a situation that can lead to disaster if the family again winds up owning a business that is now failing. Further, a decedent owner's family may dislike receiving deferred payments if the estate has the need for immediate liquidity to pay a large estate tax or other outlay incurred at death. Finally, an installment note creates a potentially stressful creditor-debtor relationship between the decedent's surviving family and the successor business owners.

In conclusion, the advantages of the business buyout agreement include business continuity, liquidity, a guaranteed market, and possibly greater certainty over the selling price. The preceding overview material merely highlights the general principles of this complex subject. A business buyout agreement should not be executed without the help of expert legal advice.

FREEZING THE VALUE OF THE BUSINESS INTEREST

Overview

The United States has many very successful owners of closely held businesses. Some have amassed a degree of wealth that they themselves consider to be more than adequate to provide for their income and capital needs for the rest of their lives. Nevertheless, few of them look forward to relinquishing control of their business interests, even though they realize that someday their wealth must be transferred. When the time comes, most want the transfer tax to be as low as possible.

Prior to 1987, highly successful entrepreneurs had several relatively safe, although complicated, methods of freezing the transfer tax value of their businesses without giving up control. The two most common methods were the corporate recapitalization and the partnership capital freeze. Through a reorganization of the firm's capital structure, the owner could retain voting control of the firm, continue to receive the about same amount of income from the firm, freeze the value of their own interest for transfer tax purposes, while assuring that any future appreciation in the value of the business would benefit other (usually younger) family members.

By adding Chapter 14 (§2701-§2704) to the Internal Revenue Code in 1990,[11] the Federal government has substantially restricted the prospects for freezing the value of a business interest while still retaining control of it. The material that follows first discusses the use of business estate freezing during its heyday and then reviews the present law.

Corporate Recapitalization

Recapitalization under prior law. Prior to Congress's "anti-freeze" legislation, a corporate recapitalization (these were often called "recaps") might be structured as follows: Prior to the recap, the owner had a controlling interest in a company through the ownership of most or all of the common stock. A recapitalization involved turning the common stock back to the corporation in exchange for a combination of common stock and voting preferred shares. The preferred was given a dividend rate high enough that it was worth almost as much as the underlying value of the firm. The person would then transfer the common stock to younger generation family members. The common shares could rightfully be deemed to have very little value, given the high value placed on the preferred shares. The retained voting preferred shares assured the transferor that he or she would always be able to out-vote the common stock shareholders on any issue. Obviously, any future growth in value of the business inures to the common stock, given that preferred shares generally have a fixed upper limit to their income production and a fixed value in the event the company is liquidated. In the following three examples, assume the date to be prior to the first anti-freeze legislation of late 1987.

> EXAMPLE 16 - 6. Alfred owns all 1,000 shares of the common stock of a highly successful computer software corporation called AlfSoft, Inc. Each share is valued at $2,000. The company will have $260,000 in net income this year, however, within the next six months, the company expects to be releasing a revolutionary new software package that might triple the company's sales and double its net worth. Alfred is divorced and has two children, Kyle and Maude. Kyle, age 37, has worked for the firm for ten years and shows great promise to take over when Alfred departs. Maude, age 34, a tenured biology professor, has never been interested in working for the company. At his death, Alfred wishes to leave his entire estate in approximately equal shares to the children.

A recapitalization of the firm is undertaken. In exchange for Alfred's 1,000 shares of common stock, the corporation issues three classes of new stock:

1. 20,000 shares of nonvoting noncumulative *preferred stock*, with a par value of $100, are retained by Alfred. These are valued at close to $2 million.
2. 480 shares of nonvoting common stock, 230 shares to Kyle, 230 shares to Maude, and 20 shares to Alfred. These shares have almost no value.
3. 20 shares of voting common stock, to Alfred.

Both types of common stock will share, pro rata, in any income available after payment of preferred dividends and in any increase in the firm's value. Alfred's estate plan is changed to leave his preferred shares equally to his two children, the 20 shares nonvoting common to Maude, and the 20 shares voting common to Kyle.

Assume that when Alfred dies (about ten years after the recap), the business is worth $6 million. Assuming the preferred stock's value remains at $2 million, the total value of the common shares will be $4 million, or $8,000 per share. Included in his gross estate is the value of the preferred stock ($2 million), plus the value of the 40 shares of common stock ($320,000). Thus, nearly all of Alfred's interest in the firm remained frozen at its value as of date of recapitalization, and nearly the entire post-recapitalization appreciation inured tax free to the interests held by Kyle and Maude.

EXAMPLE 16 - 7. In the prior example, instead of passing the voting common shares at his death, Alfred could make periodic gifts of them to Kyle in amounts not exceeding the annual gift tax exclusion. In this way, Alfred would have both given additional incentive to Kyle to remain with the firm and, at the same time, reduced even further the value of the business interest taxable in his estate at his death.

The ideal recap was designed to have the following tax-related benefits:

1. No taxation to the corporation arising from the recap.
2. No taxable income to the owner upon receipt of the new shares.
3. Little or no taxable gift by the owner.
4. At death, the amount included in the owner's taxable estate attributable to the firm would approximately equal the value of the owner's interest in the business at the date of the recap.

Even prior to the passage of anti-freeze legislation in 1987, the IRS took the position that the value of the common shares transferred could not possibly equal zero because the value of the preferred shares could not be made to equal the total value of the firm. Consequently, it argued, some positive value would have remained in the common stock, value which was therefore transferred as a taxable gift to the other family members.

Former impact of §2036(c). Enacted in 1987, and repealed retroactively by the 1990 Act, §2036(c) virtually eliminated the use of the estate freezing recapitalizations after December of 1987. We can skip the details, basically, when owners retained income producing assets that had fairly limited growth potential (i.e., preferred stock) and gave away assets with great growth potential (i.e., common stock), the transaction was treated as though there was a retained interest in the gift, hence when the owner-transferor died his or her gross estate had to include the date of death value of the entire business, including the assets that had been given away.

Current impact of §2701. Section 2701 takes a very different approach to limiting the use of business estate freezes. While the thrust of §2036(c) was to impose an *estate tax* at the transferor's later death, §2701 is directed at imposing a *gift tax*, at the time of the transfer. Thus, instead of including the date of death value of the business in the transferor's gross estate, it seeks to subject the transfer to gift taxation.

Because §2701 tends to diminish the value of retained interests, the value of the gift under the new law is likely to be large. Remember, the lower the value of the retained interest, the higher the value of the taxable gift, and vice versa. Unless the retained interest has a right to a "qualified payment" it will be valued at zero. Where the dividends are made cumulative and payable on a periodic basis they are considered "qualified payments" whose value can be subtracted from the total value of the business in determining the value of the gift of the common stock.

Even with preferred stock that features cumulative dividends, another transfer tax might arise after the recapitalization. If the business fails to make the qualified payments, the new law imposes an additional transfer tax at death, or sooner if the retained interest is transferred during lifetime, based upon the value of the cumulative unpaid payments.

Now let's examine those Chapter 14 sections that relate to the transfer of family business interests, keeping in mind that this is just a brief survey of a very technical area.

§2701: Transfers of corporate or partnership interests. In essence, under §2701, the value of a gift of an interest in a corporation or partnership to a family member will not be reduced by any interests retained by the donor unless certain specific conditions are met.

Stated in the broadest terms, the §2701 valuation rules apply to any post-October 8, 1990 transfer by an individual of certain junior equity interests in a corporation or partnership to a member of the transferor's family, if the transferor or an applicable family member retains an applicable retained interest in the corporation or partnership immediately after the transfer. Since this area of the law has many technical terms having very specific meaning, the major terms will be briefly defined before we attempt to understand the transfer tax implications of these special valuation rules.

"Transfer." A transfer of a business interest can be direct or indirect. Examples of an indirect transfer include a contribution to capital, a redemption and a recapitalization or other change in capital structure.[12]

"Junior equity interest." A junior equity interest includes common stock, or, in the case of a partnership, any interest in which the rights to income and capital are junior to the rights of all other equity interests, e.g., common stock compared to preferred stock.

"Member of the transferor's family." Family members of the transferor include the transferor's spouse, descendants of the transferor and the transferor's spouse, and any spouse of such descendants.[13] These are the people likely to receive the common stock from the transferor.

"Applicable family member." An applicable family member of the transferor includes the transferor's spouse, *ancestors* of the transferor or the transferor's spouse, and any spouse of such ancestor.[14] These are the people likely to be trying to shift wealth to the younger generation family members.

"Applicable retained interest." An applicable retained interest is any interest (except publicly traded stock) having either (*a*) a *distribution right*, but only if the transferor and applicable family members hold control (50% or more) of the business immediately before the transfer, or (*b*) a liquidation, put, call or conversion right, irrespective of the degree of control held by the parties.[15]

EXAMPLE 16-8. If undertaken today, the AlfSoft, Inc., corporate recapitalization described earlier would fall within the valuation rules of §2701. Alfred, transferred a junior equity interest (common stock) in a corporation to members of his family (his son and daughter), and retained an applicable retained interest (preferred stock) with respect to a business over which Alfred had control immediately before the transfer.

Section 2701 does not apply when the transferred interest is of the same class as the retained interest, or if market quotations are "readily available" for the retained interest, or if the retained interest is proportionally the same as the transferred interest.[16]

> EXAMPLE 16 - 9. Up to now, Rocky has been the sole owner of RR Corporation, which has issued only one class of stock. Today, Rocky gives 10% of his common stock to his daughter, retaining the remaining 90%. Section 2701 does not apply, and the traditional rules would be used to value the transferred shares.

Effect of valuation treatment under §2701. When §2701 applies, three specific valuation rules must be observed:

1. The junior equity must be assigned a value of at least ten percent of the value of the business.[17] This is the "minimum value" rule.
2. The transferred interest must be valued by the "subtraction method."
3. The retained rights other than "qualified payments" must be assigned a value of zero.[18] This is the so-called "zero valuation rule." However, the transferor can elect to have certain nonqualified payment rights treated as "qualified."

Regarding the second rule, a simplified application of the subtraction method would start with the value of the entity, subtract the value of all family held senior equity interests (with nonqualifying retained interests valued at zero), to arrive at the gift amount that must be allocated pro rata to the transferred interests.[19]

> EXAMPLE 16 - 10. Based on the AlfSoft, Inc., recapitalization in the preceding examples, the value of Alfred's gift equals $2 million, which is the value of entity reduced by zero, the value of Alfred's retained interest because it is nonqualifying. Since Alfred's son receives all transferred interests, the entire $2 million is allocated to those interests. Thus, Alfred has made a $2 million gross gift to his son.

Regarding the third rule, retained rights to *qualified payments* do not fall within the zero valuation rule. A qualified payment is defined as "any dividend payable on a periodic basis under any cumulative preferred stock (or a comparable payment under any partnership interest) to the extent that such dividend (or comparable payment) is determined at a fixed rate." The Section goes on to state that, "a payment shall be treated as fixed as to rate if such payment is determined at a rate which bears a fixed relationship to a specified market interest rate." [20] In addition, on the gift tax return the donor (e.g., the transferor giving away the common stock) can elect to treat a non-qualified payment right as though it was a qualified one, with the result that the retained interest would have a value greater than zero.

> EXAMPLE 16 - 11. Had Alfred, in the above examples, retained a right to *cumulative* preferred stock with a set dividend rate (e.g., 8% of par), the payment right would be treated as a *qualified payment* such that the value of the retained preferred stock could be subtracted from the value of the business in determining the value of Alfred's gift. Even for noncumulative preferred stock, Alfred could elect to have it treated as if it had a qualified payment right. Either way, if the value of the qualifying preferred stock was $1,500,000, Alfred would have made a gross gift of $500,000. If, on the other hand, the preferred stock was worth $1,950,000, Alfred's gift would be given a value of $200,000, because of the rule that the "junior equity" interests must be assigned a minimum value of 10% of the value of the entire business.

If the qualified payments are not made when due, then their value (increased as though the payment had been made on time and reinvested) will at some point be treated as though it is a taxable gift by the transferor or as though the value is part of the transferor's gross estate. The increase in value for payments not timely made is the amount that would have been earned had the payments been timely made, and then invested at the interest rate originally used to determine the value of the retained interest. The forgoing treatment of missed payments is also true where the transferor elected to treat nonqualifying payments as qualifying, and the business then fails to make the payments. Recognizing that there are good business reasons for not declaring dividends, Congress (through the Code) allows a grace period of four years. If a payment is made within 4-years of its due date, it will be treated as having been timely made.

If the transferor dies still owning an applicable retained interest (e.g., the preferred shares) for which there are cumulated unpaid dividends, his or her gross estate will be increased by the amount that should have been paid, with the amount further increased as though it had been reinvested since its payment due date at the yield rate originally used to value the retained interest. If the transferor gives away the retained interest (e.g., the preferred stock) while there are cumulated unpaid dividends, then the unpaid amount (increased as though invested) is treated as a gift. In addition, if payments are received more than four years after they are due, the taxpayer (holder of the shares) can elect to threat the hypothetical increase in value (the increase that would have been there had the payment been timely received and invested) as a gift made during the year.

EXAMPLE 16 - 12. Richard holds all the outstanding stock of RichGold Company, Inc. He exchanges his shares in a recapitalization for 20,000 shares of 10-percent cumulative voting preferred stock, each with a $100 par paying 8%, and 1,000 shares of no-par voting common stock. He then transfers the common stock to his daughter Maureen. Section 2701 applies to the transfer and the gift is calculated using the subtraction method. The preferred shares should pay dividends of $152,000 each year. After not paying any dividends for three years, the corporation's board of directors declared a dividend payment on the preferred shares and Richard received a payment of $152,000. The payment, because it came within the four year grace period, is treated as if it was timely made.

EXAMPLE 16 - 13. Continuing with the prior example, assume that the second $152,000 payment is made exactly five years late and that Richard decides to treat as a gift the hypothetical increase in value that investing the dividends would have produced. The amount of the gift is the *additional* amount that Richard would now have, if the $152,000 had been invested at 8% compounded annually for the five years, i.e., $152,000 * (1.08)^5 - \$152,000 = \$71,338$.

EXAMPLE 16 - 14. Suppose Richard dies in 2005 and the dividends for the prior three years are the only ones past due. Since his death is a taxable event, each payment that is past due must be included in Richard's gross estate (i.e., 3 * $152,000), plus the income that would have been generated on each payment invested on the due date. Thus, there would be three years of hypothetical income for the earliest missed payment, two years on the next, and one year for the last. Had the three payments been received on time and reinvested so as to earn 8%, Richard's estate would have had an additional $545,205 (i.e., 3 * \$152,000 + (\$152,000 * (1.08)^6 - \$152,000))$. This amount must be added to his gross estate.

Note that a corporation is not legally required to pay dividends even if it has the money to do so. Any unpaid dividends are "past due" only in an Internal Revenue Code sense. The general rule is that only the board of directors can declare a dividend.

EXAMPLE 16 - 15. Same facts as in the prior example, except in stead of dying, Richard gave all of the preferred shares to Maureen when dividends for the prior three years were past due, the result would be the same, except the value of the missed dividends (i.e., 3 * $152,000), and their related hypothetical investment return (i.e., $89,205), would be added to the value of Richard's taxable gifts for the year.

To avoid double taxation of the retained interest, the Code allows a deduction from the donor's taxable gifts (if the taxable event is a gift) or the donor's adjusted taxable gifts (if the taxable event is the donor's death). The deduction is the lesser of the amount by which the value of the initial transfer was increased due to the application of the §2701 subtraction method and the amount "duplicated" in the tax base at the subsequent transfer.

> EXAMPLE 16 - 16. Martha owned 10,000 shares of $100 par value noncumulative preferred stock (bearing an annual dividend of $10 per share) of Ahtram Company, Inc., and 500 shares of its common stock. The underlying value of the Company was $1,500,000 and the preferred and common had values of $1,000,000 and $500,000, respectively. On March 10, 1999, she transfers all of the common shares to her son Ethan. Since §2701 applies to the transaction and Martha does not make an election to treat the retained shares as having "qualified rights," the subtraction method results in a transfer valued at $1,500,000. Notice that the increase is $1,000,000 since the common stock is valued at $500,000.

> EXAMPLE 16 - 17. On May 2, 2001, Martha dies still owning the preferred stock. An appraisal determines that the value is $950,000. Given that this is less than the $1,000,000 increase in value of the initial transfer, her adjusted taxable gifts are reduced by $950,000 to reflect this duplicated amount. If, on the other hand, the stock is valued in her estate at $1,050,000, then earlier increase in the taxable gifts is the lesser amount, and the decrease to her adjusted taxable gifts is $1,000,000.

§2703: Valuation of property subject to rights and restrictions. Section 2703 requires that the value of any property subject to rights and restrictions on that property held by anyone shall be valued for transfer tax purposes without regard to the reduced valuation effect of those rights or restrictions.

> EXAMPLE 16 - 18. Shortly before his death this year, Hansen, sole shareholder of the common stock of his $1 million closely held corporation, executed a contract with his daughter, who is obligated to purchase all of Hansen's stock at Hansen's death for $400,000. Under §2703, Hansen's gross estate will include the stock at a value of $1 million; the reduction in actual value attributable to the obligation to sell the stock must be disregarded.

More specifically, the rights and restrictions that must be disregarded under §2703 include:

1. Any option, agreement, or other right to acquire or use the property at a price less than the property's fair market value (determined without regard to such option, agreement, or right), or
2. any restriction on the right to sell or use the property.[21]

Section 2703 does not apply to any agreement, option, right, or restriction, which meets all of the following requirements:

1. It is a bona fide business arrangement.
2. It is not a device to transfer the property to members of the decedent's family for less than full and adequate consideration in money or money's worth.
3. Its terms are comparable to similar arrangements entered into by persons in an arm's length transaction.[22]

> EXAMPLE 16 - 19. Shortly before his death this year, Trafalgar, sole owner of the common stock of his $1 million closely held corporation, executed a contract with a non-relative business associate, who is obligated to purchase all of Trafalgar's stock at Trafalgar's death for $960,000. The valuation rules under §2703 are not likely to prevent the inclusion of Trafalgar's stock in his gross estate at a value of $960,000.

Section 2704: Taxation of lapse of voting and liquidation rights and restrictions in a corporation or partnership. Section 2704 is of relatively limited application, and is just briefly summarized here. It addresses the influence on federal transfer taxation of the lapse of a voting or liquidation right in a corporation or partnership.

In general, if there has been a lapse and the person holding the right before the lapse and the members of that person's family hold control of the entity both before and after the lapse, then the lapse is treated as gift or a transfer at death, as the case may be, subject to tax. The value of the transfer subject to taxation is equal to the excess of the value of all interests held by that person before the lapse (determined as if the rights were nonlapsing) over the value of such interests immediately after the lapse.

Clearly, properly applying the Chapter 14 valuation rules to individual situations requires considerable expertise and careful thought, and should be undertaken only with the help of a tax expert. However, all planners should have a general understanding of this commonly discussed topic.

When may recaps work? Estate freezing recaps of the type created prior to §2036(c) may still work for some *family members*, such as nieces and nephews, and between unrelated parties, since §2701 does not apply to recaps benefitting such transferees. The definition of "applicable family members" includes only the transferor's spouse, descendants, descendants of the spouse, and all spouses of the above.[23]

In lieu of a recap, which is clearly a complex transaction, the owner might consider a simple outright gift of the business. Gifting is simple, and control can be retained by transferring nonvoting stock.

Finally, there are available other types of business freeze techniques not affected by the antifreeze rules because no form of lifetime gifting is involved. They are discussed briefly next.

Testamentary freeze. This involves a bequest of common stock to younger generation beneficiaries and preferred stock to the spouse.

Postmortem recapitalization freeze. A recapitalization after the owner's death, in which the marital trust receives the preferred stock and the bypass trust receives the common stock.

Postmortem funding freeze. The marital trust receives assets not likely to appreciate and the bypass trust receives appreciating assets.

Generation-skipping freeze. The children receive, by gift or bequest, the preferred stock and the grandchildren receive the common stock.

Notwithstanding these possible opportunities, the current limitations and restrictions are numerous, and commentators have been guarded about the extent to which corporate recapitalizations will be used in the future.

Partnership Capital Freeze

It may be possible to reorganize an unincorporated firm to achieve the same results as the estate-freezing recap. Conceptually similar to the recap, under the partnership capital freeze, two classes of partnership interests are created, one for the older, wealthier, family members and one for the younger family members. The interests of the older family members is given rights that limit the upside value, thus assuring that future appreciation in the business will accrue to the shares of the younger generation. As with the corporate recap, the partnership capital freeze deals in a complex, rapidly changing area of tax law, subject to the provisions of §2701 and also to frequent IRS attack. Again, planning should be approached carefully, with the help of competent counsel.

This chapter has presented an overview of the objectives and techniques of estate planning for closely held business interests. The next chapter will examine miscellaneous planning techniques not covered in earlier chapters.

QUESTIONS AND PROBLEMS

1. What could you say to a person who owns a closely held business if, although he seems to respect your advice, he stubbornly refuses to consider estate planning?

2. What unique estate planning problems are common to owners of closely held businesses?

3. Identify the objectives of estate planning for owners of closely held business interests.

4. One of your friends is worried about the possible future decline in the value of his firm upon his departure. Recommend ideas that can help minimize that decline.

5. (a) Describe the inter-vivos methods of transferring business interests to family members. (b) When are such transfers ill-advised?

6. (a) You are trying to encourage one of your friends to consider selling her business to a third party while she is still alive. Describe the benefits of this strategy. (b) Is planning for a sale after death always unwise? Why or why not?

7. Horne requests your advice. He has a simple will, but has done no other planning. His major asset is a closely held business. Neither his wife nor his children have any interest in continuing the business after his death. Horne does not wish to retire. Recommend a significant planning strategy for his consideration.

8. Describe the alternative methods for payment that can be arranged when a business is sold.

9. When should planning for closely held business interests begin? Why?

10. (a) Describe the essential characteristics of the typical business buyout agreement. (b) What are its advantages?

11. What is the tax advantage of including a method for determining the selling price in a properly drafted business buyout agreement?

12. (a) Describe the three methods by which a business buyout agreement can be funded. (b) Why might types of funding influence the choice of whether a cross-purchase or an entity plan is adopted?

13. Why might income taxation influence the choice of whether a cross-purchase or an entity plan is adopted?

14. McQueen is the sole surviving shareholder of the M-C Corporation. Forty years ago, he and Cross acquired the business. Just prior to Cross's death two years ago, each had a $46,000 basis in their stock. McQueen purchased Cross's shares from the Cross estate for $180,000, pursuant to a buyout agreement. Presently, McQueen is thinking of selling the firm. Because McQueen's estate will eventually go to his wife, estate taxes are not part of his concern. Analyze the overall economic desirability of each of the following alternatives, stating first the advantages and then the disadvantages. Assume a combined marginal tax rate of 50% for ordinary income and 25% for capital gains. Be sure to consider all of the objectives of planning for closely held business interests, in addition to income taxation matters.
   a. McQueen presently sells his shares for $600,000 cash.
   b. McQueen presently exchanges his shares for 6,000 shares of the publicly traded XYZ Corporation, which is currently trading at $100 per share.
   c. McQueen continues to own the shares until death, which is actuarially expected to occur in five years. The shares, worth $600,000 at death, will be bequeathed to his wife, who we believe may be able to sell them for $400,000 cash.
   d. McQueen continues to own the shares until death (date of death value is still $600,000), at which time the KR Corporation, a competitor of M-C, purchases the shares from McQueen's estate for $700,000 cash, pursuant to a buyout agreement, executed presently.

ANSWERS TO THE QUESTIONS AND PROBLEMS

1. You could describe to your stubborn friend the problems he and his family may face if he were to involuntarily withdraw from management tomorrow, either as a result of disability or death. Problems include inability to generate sufficient future income, incurring significant unnecessary loss in the value of the business, facing excessive transfer costs, and failing to provide sufficient liquidity to pay these costs. For more detail, see the material in the early part of the chapter.

2. Unique estate planning problems common to owners of closely held businesses:
   a. The business typically represents the single largest part of the owner's wealth and generates the major source of his or her income.
   b. Too often, that value and income can only be sustained by the owner's active involvement in management.
   c. Therefore, this value or income can be jeopardized by the owner's withdrawal from the firm and the subsequent transfer of the business interest.

3. Objectives of estate planning for owners of closely held businesses: (a) income continuation; (b) transfer of maximum business value; (c) minimum transfer cost; and (d) adequate liquidity.

4. Common methods for minimizing the decline in value of the firm upon owner departure:
   a. Delegate greater responsibility; provide incentives.
   b. Use current business value to raise future income.
   c. Negotiate a contract for present or future sale.

5. a. Types of inter-vivos business transfers to a family member: completed gifts, installment sale, sale-leaseback, and private annuity.
   b. The owner may insist on retaining complete control over the business or the other family members may be ill-prepared to run the business.

6. a. Benefits of sale to a third party while person is still alive:
    1. Eliminate potential friction between survivors and other owners and managers.
    2. Survivors receive more liquid assets.
    3. A higher selling price.
   b. Planning for a post-death sale may not be unwise if a buyout agreement is executed since it enhances the potential proceeds from the business transferable to the owner's survivors.

7. Horne should consider negotiating a buyout agreement with co-owners, executives, or competitors, to avoid the prospect of his survivors having to run the business. This strategy will also avoid the post-death sale of the business at a substantially reduced price.

8. Alternative methods for payment when a business is sold include:
   a. Sale for present cash, publicly or privately.
   b. Sale for future cash, under an installment sale.
   c. Sale for stock, under a tax-deferred exchange with a publicly traded firm.

9. To incorporate the owner's expertise into the plan, to take advantage of planning concepts available only to healthy individuals, and to avoid a sudden, forced sale, planning should begin when the owner is active and in good health.

10. a. Under a typical business buyout agreement, each party is obligated to purchase the interest of each other party at that party's earlier disability or death.
    b. Advantages include: (1) liquidity; (2) a guaranteed market; and (3) greater certainty over the selling price

11. The tax advantage of including a method for determining the selling price in a buyout agreement is that the price will set the value of the business that is included in the decedent-owner's gross estate.

12. a.   The business buyout agreement can be funded with life insurance, by an installment sale, or, under an entity agreement, with the firm's liquid assets.

   b.   Funding with life insurance can rule out a cross-purchase plan because of the numerous policies which must be acquired if the contract has three or more parties.

13. Income taxation can influence the choice of the plan because the cross-purchase plan can generate a step-up in basis of the acquiring owner's stock.

14. It should be mentioned at the outset that either estate tax is not a major issue, or it is an issue but conclusions based on estate tax projections are quite speculative.

   a.   Immediate sale for $600,000 cash -
      Advantages: (1) immediate liquidity; (2) complete withdrawal can be psychologically beneficial; (3) elimination of worry for survivors; (4) sell now, when the firm is (perhaps) peaking in value.
      Disadvantage: Income taxation on capital gain:
         Gain = $600,000 - ($180,000 + $46,000) = $374,000
         Tax = $374,000 * 25% = $93,500
         Net Proceeds = $506,500

   b.   Stock for stock: exchange:
      Advantages: (1) immediate liquidity; and (2) no income taxation, either now or at death .
      Disadvantage: Individual's ownership is not diversified.

   c.   Sale by surviving spouse for $400,000:
      Advantage: Step-up in basis at death
      Disadvantages:
      1.   Sells for $200,000 less than stepped-up basis. However, the after-tax loss could be somewhat less. Assuming the entire loss is immediately deductible against other capital gains, the after-tax loss would be $200,000 times (1 - 25%) = $150,000. Conversely, the taxes saved = $200,000 x 25% = $50,000. Net proceeds = $450,000.

However, without offsetting gains this loss may be deductible only up to $3,000 per year, until her death (after that: no deduction). The above calculations ignore this important time value of money consideration.

Assuming that Mrs. McQueen has a 20 year life expectancy and that she will be deducting only $3,000 per year for life, the present value of the annual $3,000 deduction at an assumed 8% §7520 rate is $29,454. The present value of the tax savings from the annual deductions will be $14,727 [50% * $29,454], if the deductions reduce ordinary income each year, and only $7,364 [.25% * $29,454], if it offsets capital gains. Net result: net present value of the proceeds is between $407,364 and $414,727, which is a lot less than the $450,000 based on the assumption of an immediate deduction of the entire loss.

1. Risk that business is not sold or is sold for less. Probably the worst alternative of all.

Note: Mrs. McQueen may wish to list the gross estate value of the business on McQueen's estate tax return at $600,000, not $400,000, so as to achieve a larger basis step-up, inasmuch as the estate tax will still be zero. Conversely, the IRS may argue for a $400,000 value. Mrs. McQueen could succeed if she could show that the business interest dropped $200,000 after McQueen died.

d. Sale to competitor at death for $700,000 pursuant to a buyout agreement:
Advantages: (1) step-up in basis at death; (2) $100,000 greater proceeds; and (3) liquidity. There will be no tax, assuming that the estate tax value of the business is fixed at $700,000.

Disadvantage: If buyout agreement is not revised regularly, there is the risk that the contract price will be below the date of death fair market value.

ENDNOTES

1. 1959-1 C.B. 237.

2. *Wall Street Journal*, May 7, 1990, p. B1.

3. §1361(d)(3).

4. §6662(a) and (g).

5. §264(a)(1).

6. §56(g)(4)(B).

7. §2703.

8. Reg. §25.2703-1(b)(3).

9. In *Commissioner vs. Procter* 142 F.2d 824 (4th Cir. 1944).

10. §264(a)(1).

11. Revenue Act of 1987.

12. §2701(e)(5).

13. §2701(e)(1).

14. §2701(e)(2).

15. §2701(b).

16. §2701(a)(2).

17. §2701(a)(4).

18. §2701(a)(3)(A).

19. Reg. §25.2701-3(b).

20. §2701(a)(3)(A).

21. §2703(a).

22. §2703(b).

23. §2701(e)(1).

CHAPTER 17

Miscellaneous Lifetime Planning

OVERVIEW

In the past seven chapters, we have covered six major estate planning topics: avoiding probate, wise use of the marital deduction, bypass planning, lifetime transfers, liquidity planning, and planning for closely held business interests. This chapter will cover other miscellaneous aspects of lifetime planning. First, it will explore a number of more narrow topics, many of which are interrelated only because they influence the preparation of a person's will or trust instrument. Examples include provisions for the care of minor children, selection of the executor and trustee, survival clauses, and the allocation of death taxes. Next, the chapter will examine estate planning for people in nontraditional relationships. The final section focuses on documents and strategies used in planning for the person's own incapacity, includes a discussion of two types of durable powers of attorney and the living will.

WILL AND TRUST PLANNING

Wills and trusts are the major documents used in estate planning. The material below describes several planning matters that are usually covered when wills and trusts are drafted. In reading this material, you may wish to refer back to the will and trust documents in Exhibits 3-1, 3-2, and 3-3.

Planning for the Care of Family Members: An Introduction

The chance of disability and of premature death should compel one to plan for the care of dependant family members. A serious disability may require the selection of others to care for the *individual* and for the individual's property. The death of a parent of a minor child might require the selection of one or more persons to care for the *child*. Prior planning enables the selection process to reflect the wishes of the person most closely concerned with the outcome. Planning for the care of minor children is discussed in the next section. Planning for the seriously disabled person's care is surveyed at the end of the chapter. We begin, however, with a discussion of factors common to both.

Planning for the care of both the orphaned child and the incapacitated individual have three factors in common. First, by not making arrangements in advance, individuals force their local *court* to assume greater responsibility in arranging for this care. Without help from the individual, the court, in its attempt to act in the dependent's best interest, must rely on *secondhand information* obtained from other family members and from friends. To best ensure that the court's decisions reflect his or her wishes, the person should plan to express those wishes in writing before it is too late.

Second, for both minors and incapacitated adults, the law distinguishes two types of care: care of the person and care of the property. An individual legally responsible for the care of the *person* is charged with providing for the everyday physical and psychological needs. An individual legally responsible for the care of the *property* of a minor or incapacitated person is charged with safeguarding, investing, and spending that person's wealth.

Third, because care of the person and care of the property entail such dissimilar responsibilities, *different parties* may be nominated and appointed to perform each task.

Planning for the Care of Minor Children

The material below explores the arrangements that are undertaken to provide care for minor children in the event both parents die prematurely.

The parental guardian. In the typical household, the married parents of a child are the *natural* and *legal guardians* of their children. Thus, upon the death of one parent, the surviving parent will continue as sole guardian. Only in the most unusual situations will the courts deny this right. On the other hand, when a minor child survives the death of *both* parents, the state must select a successor guardian. The selection process typically culminates in an order by a judge of the probate court after a noticed hearing. The court will usually appoint the person nominated in the parent's will, unless the nominee is unwilling, unable, or unsuitable to perform. If the will contains no nomination, or if there is no will, the court must examine the family situation more carefully, relying on other information, including a list of willing friends and relatives, as well as the expressed preferences of the child, if sufficiently mature to have and express an opinion. Since the court's main criterion is the best interests of the child, it seeks to appoint that person who is best capable of providing the minor with such basics as food, clothing, shelter, medical care, and schooling, as well as providing psychological well-being, love, and attention.

Since the court's eventual selection of a guardian may not reflect the deceased parent's unexpressed wishes, and to avoid guardianship "warfare," the parent should clearly assert that preference by nominating a personal guardian in the will. Considering the stakes, it may be the most important estate planning action taken by young parents.

The ideal parental guardian. Who should be nominate? An ideal parental guardian possesses the following qualities:

1. The *integrity, maturity, physical stamina*, and *experience* expected of a parent.
2. A strong *concern* for the minor's welfare.
3. The ability to provide a *stable personal environment* conducive to raising a child in a manner consistent with the parent's particular moral, religious, social, and financial situation.

Of course, these attributes are ideals. Often, it is difficulty finding more than one or two capable and willing nominees, none of whom might be ideal. But however imperfect, a nomination greatly reduces the risk of an undesired appointment. Nominating more than one parental guardian allows for an successor guardian who will serve in the event that the first choice is unwilling or unable to serve, or once appointed is unable to continue to serve.

Once the choice is made, the parent should be encouraged to periodically review the nomination in light of both the minor's changing needs and the nominee's changing personal and financial situation.

Three fiduciary choices for financial matters. Anticipating the possibility that they both may die before their children are grown, parents will usually want to provide for adequate financial care for their orphaned minor children. They will ordinarily want to transfer all or most of their probate and nonprobate property for the benefit of the children. Common nonprobate sources of property for the children include life insurance proceeds, survivorship under joint tenancy arrangements, trust property, and gifts from others.

While most states allow a minor to receive outright a modest amount of property, larger amounts are required to be turned over to a *fiduciary* legally responsible for their care and custody. What acceptable fiduciary arrangements are available? While the law recognizes parental guardianships as the only legal arrangement for the minor's *personal* care, it recognizes several arrangements for the minor's *financial* care. The parents may choose a financial guardianship, a trust, or a custodianship under one or the other Uniform Acts. Each is surveyed briefly.

Financial guardianship. A financial guardian, also called an estate guardian, is typically appointed by the court in a manner similar to the procedures used for appointment of a parental guardian. Usually required to file a formal accounting with the court every one or two years, the financial guardian must obtain written permission from the court to undertake transactions that are out of the ordinary, such as the sale of real property. Reflecting the general trend in probate reform, some states have enacted streamlined guardianship proceedings to minimize court involvement.

In general, the *criteria* for selecting a financial guardian are radically different from those used in selecting a parental guardian. As we have mentioned, while the primary consideration in selecting the parental guardian is parental ability, the primary focus in selecting the financial guardian is *skill in financial management*. Since skill in financial management is also the primary criterion used to select a trustee, we shall defer further discussion of its attributes to the sections on selecting the executor and the trustee.

Trust for the minor. Instead of a financial guardian, a trustee can be chosen to manage the property left for the benefit of a minor child. Whether a living trust or a testamentary trust, the trust may be part of the parents' overall estate plan, with the children named as remaindermen.

The trust has advantages over the financial guardianship. First, it is a *private* arrangement, not usually subject to court supervision. While a guardianship requires the filing of a bond, periodic accountings, and court approval for asset transfers, a trust can avoid these costly and time-consuming activities. However, some states require ongoing probate court supervision of testamentary trusts after the trustor's death, but the trend has been to eliminate this requirement.

Second, the trust offers great *flexibility*; the parents can tailor it to their personal wishes. For example, while guardianship property usually must be surrendered outright to the minor upon reaching age 18, the age of majority, trust property can be retained in trust until the age specified in the trust. Further, while a separate guardianship must usually be established for each minor, a single trust can have multiple beneficiaries, as in the case of the family pot trust, described later in the chapter. And the trustee can be given discretion to distribute different amounts of trust assets to different beneficiaries at different times. For example, the trustee can be given the power to distribute principal to an income beneficiary, to accumulate income and add it to principal, or to "spray" or "sprinkle" income among the beneficiaries. Finally, the trust is more flexible because it can include a spendthrift provision, a protective clause to be described later. Financial guardianships are not established with such refinements.

A third advantage of the trust over the financial guardianship rests on the fact that the *statutory and case law* of trusts is much more well defined. Thus, a trustee will often feel less uncertain than a guardian about the potential adverse consequences of a particular fiduciary act or decision.

A financial guardianship usually arises by default when parents die without having an estate plan in place. Guardianships are rarely preferred over trusts because they tend to be more expensive and, for the fiduciary, more cumbersome.

Custodianship under the Uniform Acts. Finally, the parents may wish to leave property to a custodian for the benefit of a minor child under the Uniform Gifts to Minors Act or the Uniform Transfers to Minors Act in the manner described in Chapter 13. Like trusts, custodianships offer greater privacy than financial guardianships, since they are not subject to court supervision. However, like guardianships, custodianships are quite inflexible because they are usually controlled by statute. For example, in most states property held by the custodian must be turned over to the minor upon reaching age 21. Also, most states limit the kinds of property that can be transferred under the Uniform Gifts to Minor's Act, which is the only one of the two acts that has been adopted in many states.

Selection of Executor and Executor's Powers

As we have said, the executor is responsible for representing and managing a decedent's probate estate. Specific tasks of this multifaceted job include marshaling and valuing the decedent's assets, filing tax returns, paying taxes and debts, distributing assets, and accounting for the entire process. It also involves dealing with grieving family members, distributing personal effects, and resolving family conflicts, all of which can be emotionally taxing. Finally, the executor must keep assets invested, sell them to pay taxes, and possibly manage or liquidate the decedent's business. While most of these jobs can be performed by the estate attorney's office, total estate expenses may be higher due to a larger attorney fee and the executor is still primarily responsible to the court for completing these acts.

Selection. Who should be nominated for the job of executor? An ideal nominee possesses the following qualities:

1. *Longevity*, that is, the likelihood of being able to serve after the death of the testator, perhaps many years hence.
2. *Skill in managing* legal and financial affairs.
3. *Familiarity* with the testator's estate and the testator's wishes.
4. Strong *integrity* coupled with *loyalty* to the testator.
5. *Impartiality* and absence of conflicts of interest.

An ideal financial guardian will also possess these qualities. Let us use these criteria to evaluate the candidates who are most likely available to serve.

Family member or a friend. Nominating a family member or a friend to be executor might reduce administration costs paid to people who are not beneficiaries. Family members and friends usually possess a strong degree of familiarity and loyalty. However, they often have only modest legal and financial skills, which may compel them to pay for professional advice. While they can normally delegate some of their work to the estate attorney, they cannot delegate their legal responsibility, since the executor cannot avoid personal liability for certain types of mistakes that might occur in administration. Nonetheless, in small estates most mistakes are not costly, and, in general, nominating as executor the spouse, an adult child, or a good friend makes sense. Naming the spouse is probably the most popular choice.

Corporate executor. The testator may prefer to select a corporate executor such as a bank trust department. Reasons include inability to find and select a responsible family member or friend, conflict among family members, or a complex estate. Banks usually do a satisfactory job in managing estate assets. However, because they are usually unfamiliar with the decedent's family, they might not offer as much of a personal touch in the administration process. For example, they may have difficulty deciding who should be given minor personal effects which the decedent did not specifically devise. Finally, many banks will not agree to be executor if the estate is too small, if they dislike certain provisions of the will, or if they are not also nominated trustee under the estate plan's trust arrangements.

Attorney. Should an attorney, such as the testator's attorney, be considered for nomination as executor? Probate attorneys usually do a good job in managing assets during the probate period, because they commonly possess a substantial degree of expertise acquired over the years by doing the work delegated by their many executor-clients. Nomination of the testator's attorney, however, may increase the risk of a *will contest*. Dissatisfied with the will provisions, an aspiring beneficiary might allege that the nomination is further evidence that the testator was subject to "undue influence" and intimidation, and might petition that the will not be admitted to probate. However, keep in mind that successful will contests are rare.

In addition, nominating an attorney might not reduce administration costs, since many attorney-executors hire other attorneys to represent the estate. Finally, and perhaps most significant, acting as an executor can create potential *conflicts of interest* for the attorney in the areas of drafting, confidentiality, and the duty to deal impartially with beneficiaries. For example, an attorney who anticipates becoming a fiduciary may be tempted to insert in the client's will a self-serving exculpation (hold harmless) clause for all simple negligence acts. In fact, these ethical issues may compel an attorney to refuse the nomination. Some states have made it illegal for the drafting attorney to name him or herself as executor or trustee unless the attorney is related to the testator or settlor by blood or marriage. The prohibition can be overcome by having the settlor meet with an independent attorney who, after the meeting, signs a paper certifying that the attorney has conducted an independent review of the situation and has advised the settlor of the significance of nominating the first attorney to a fiduciary position.[1]

Other considerations. The testator should also nominate an *alternate* executor to serve in case the primary nominee is unwilling or unable to serve. Many people nominate a bank as the alternate because they are confident that a corporate executor will always be available to serve. Regardless of the choice of executor, the testator should always consult with the nominees to get their consent, and should periodically review the choice in light of changing circumstances.

Executor's powers. What powers should be explicitly granted to an executor? Most simple wills either do not delineate the powers of the executor or list just a few powers. The will in Exhibit 3-1 explicitly grants to the executor the powers to distribute principal and income; to sell, lease, mortgage, pledge, assign, invest, and reinvest estate property; and to operate a business.

When a will "is silent" regarding a specific proposed action of the executor, we look for authority first to the provisions of the state's estates and trusts or probate code *statutes*, which usually delineate many executor's powers. If nothing pertinent is found, the executor may feel obliged to request permission from the *court*. For example, in the absence of explicit permission in the will, executors in many states must seek formal written permission to sell real property. Thus, specifying powers explicitly in the will can offer the executor greater *flexibility* by minimizing unnecessary delays in probate. And enumerating powers in the will can reveal more to the survivors about the testator's *wishes*, especially with regard to the degree of court supervision originally envisioned by the testator.

Allocation of Death Taxes

Which beneficiaries should bear the burden of death taxes? All of them, or only some? If only some, which ones? If all, should the taxes be shared equally or in proportion to the amount bequeathed? A number of important considerations in determining how to allocate death taxes are examined next.

Federal law. In the absence of a provision in the will, both federal and state law determine which beneficiaries will share the cost of death taxes. Federal law controls the burden on a few types of assets. The Internal Revenue Code provides that the pro rata share of estate tax on life insurance,[2] property subject to a general power of appointment,[3] QTIP property[4] (usually at the second death), and property included in the gross estate because of a retained interest[5] is payable out of those assets.

State law. Under state law, with regard to all assets owned by the decedent, the old common law rule provided that death taxes were paid from the residuary probate estate. However, most states have changed this rule by enacting a type of *equitable apportionment statute* which spreads the tax burden more or less proportionately among all of the beneficiaries receiving the taxed assets. Thus, even recipients of nonprobate assets, such as property held by the decedent in joint ownership, would owe a portion of the tax. Of course, *charitable recipients* and most *spouses* would not ordinarily incur a tax burden, since their distributions are deducted before one arrives at the taxable estate.

Tax clause in will. The testator can override these federal and state directives by expressly including a tax clause in the will.

Residuary tax clause. Some attorneys do this by routinely drafting wills containing a tax clause embracing the old common law rule: all taxes will be paid out of the residuary estate. Payment of taxes from the residue can speed up the probate process by making it unnecessary to obtain reimbursement from non-residuary and nonprobate beneficiaries. In addition, recipients of specific non-residuary bequests of illiquid assets are not forced to search for the required cash. And paying the taxes out of the residue may be especially helpful if the will specifically bequeaths certain assets over which the testator does not wish the *tax burden* to fall. For example, if the testator leaves only one relatively illiquid asset, such as a piano, to a particular beneficiary, should that person have to pay any transfer taxes attributable to it? Most people would probably say no unless that beneficiary is known to have considerable wealth, or at least access to a reasonable amount of discretionary liquid assets.

Problems with the residuary tax clause. There are at least three situations where a residuary tax clause will conflict with the testator's wishes. First, the testator may specifically bequeath an asset such as a closely held business that comprises a very *large portion* of the entire estate. If the tax clause allocates the entire tax burden to the residue, the effect may be to radically reduce the reduce or eliminate it entirely.

> EXAMPLE 17 - 1. Livingston's estate consists of a closely held business currently worth $800,000 and other assets also worth $800,000. He has two children: A, who works in the business, and B, who does not. Livingston would like to leave the business to A and other property of the same value to B. The attorney drafts a will bequeathing the business to A and the residue to B, and includes a conventional "boiler plate" residuary tax clause. At Livingston's death, B's after-tax share will be reduced to about $400,000, or one-half of the amount passing to A.

Second, many testators view their *residuary legatees* as the primary "objects of their bounty" and want them to receive as much wealth as possible. An apportionment tax clause would more closely meet this objective.

A third consideration is the effect of the tax allocation upon a bypass plan that provides for determination of the amount of the *marital deduction by formula*. To minimize estate tax, such plans invariably incorporate an allocation clause placing the burden of the tax on property that is subject to the estate tax. Which clause is chosen, of course, depends on whether the marital share comes from a specific bequest (residuary tax clause preferred) or from the residue (apportionment clause preferred).

Whatever the provisions of state law, the testator should consider including a tax clause in the will for greater certainty. Determining the best tax clause is a difficult job, particularly when there are several beneficiaries. An undesired provision can mean unnecessary delay or a pattern of property distribution radically different from that envisioned by the testator. Yet rarely will the courts override the provisions of a will or the applicable statute to prevent an undesired result. Consequently, the testator should consider the alternatives carefully.

Survival Clauses

The phrase "If A survives me, I give her. . ." is a survival clause and is commonly included in wills and trusts instruments, mainly to avoid the consequences of a lapse.

Effect of a lapse. A lapse occurs when a beneficiary named in a will fails to survive the testator. Each state's probate code contains sections which determine, in the absence of a provision in the will, to whom a lapsed testamentary bequest will pass. A very common type of *antilapse statute*, as it is called, provides that bequests to one of the testator's *predeceased blood relatives* will instead pass to that relative's *surviving issue*. The UPC limits the antilapse to predeceased grandparents and descendants of grandparents.[6]

> EXAMPLE 17 - 2. Rudolph died. His will left his car to his *brother*, Randall, and the residue of his estate to his friend James. Randall predeceased Rudolph. Due to the state's antilapse statute, the bequest of the car will pass to Randall's only son, Jeremy.

Antilapse statutes expressly apply only to wills, not living trust instruments or property held in joint tenancy. However, some courts have applied their antilapse statutes to living trust instruments by analogy. On the other hand, the interests of predeceased co-joint tenants are always cut off by their death; thus, the surviving co-tenants will share a greater percentage of the property.

If the state has *no antilapse statute*, or if the particular statute does not apply, perhaps because the lapsed bequest was to a beneficiary not related to the deceased, or in a UPC state to a remote relative, then a lapsed specific bequest will ordinarily pass to the *residuary beneficiary*.

> EXAMPLE 17 - 3. In Example 17-2, if the car was left to Rudolph's predeceased *friend* Josef instead of Randall, the car will pass to James, the residuary beneficiary, because the state's antilapse statute applies only to relatives.

These last two results are unfortunate if the testator actually wished, in the event the named beneficiary predeceased the testator, to leave the property to certain of the named beneficiary's survivors who are not blood relatives. An example might be a son- or daughter-in-law, such as the dearly loved ex-spouse of the testator's child who is raising the testator's grandchild.

> EXAMPLE 17 - 4. Grandpa, a widower, died recently, and in his will he left his entire estate to his son. Because the son predeceased Grandpa the property will pass to son's children, based on the state's antilapse statute. Nothing will pass directly to Mary, who is son's ex-spouse and will be raising the children alone. This result could easily have been avoided if Grandpa's will had explicitly named Mary to receive a portion of his property in the event that his son predeceased him.

If a *residuary gift lapses* in the absence of a specific antilapse statute provision, the property will pass by *intestate succession*.

EXAMPLE 17 - 5. In Example 17-3, if James had also predeceased Rudolph, the residuary bequest will lapse, and the estate will pass in accordance with that state's intestacy laws.

Avoiding a lapse with a survival clause. A lapse can usually be avoided with a *survival clause* designating an alternate taker.

EXAMPLE 17 - 6. Continuing the series of examples above, if Rudolph's will instead left the car to Isaac "in the event that Randall fails to survive me," and Isaac survives Rudolph, then Isaac, the alternate taker, will receive the car.

Survival period. A survival clause may require survival for some *period* beyond the testator's death. An example would be the phrase, "...if she survives me *by 30 days...*" Extending the survivorship requirement reduces the likelihood that bequeathed property will be subject to two successive probates in situations when the beneficiary dies shortly after the decedent.

EXAMPLE 17- 7. In Example 17-2, if Randall survived Rudolph by only one month, the car will still pass to Randall and also be subject to administration in his estate. If instead Rudolph's will bequeathed the car to Randall "if he survives me by six months, otherwise to Isaac," then Isaac will receive the car, which will be subject to administration only in Rudolph's estate.

Estate tax and survival periods. Bypass planning also influences the decision whether or not to use a survival period. One rule of thumb used is to insert a survival period requirement in the wills or trusts of both spouses unless their estates are substantially unequal in amount. In that case, use it only in the document of the less wealthy spouse. The basic rationale is twofold: first, to take advantage of both unified credits when ever it is practical to do so, and second, to avoid unnecessarily loading up a wealthy S2's taxable estate.

In a common accident, there may be an estate tax reason for providing that the *beneficiary* will always be presumed to have survived the testator. For example, to achieve *estate equalization* (see Chapter 11) in a common accident situation, disposition of property can be based on a stated assumption that the wealthier spouse (W) predeceased the less wealthy spouse (L). In that event, W's estate will receive a marital deduction, reducing the taxable estate, while L's gross estate will increase by the amount of the bequest. To prevent property from passing to L's named beneficiaries, W's bequest can be structured to qualify as a QTIP transfer.

> EXAMPLE 17-8 While alive, both William, owner of $1 million in property, and his wife Mary, owner of $200,000 in property, executed simple wills leaving all their property to the other spouse, if he/she survived by four months, otherwise to the children of each of their prior marriages. William died in early 2001 and Mary survived him by just 36 days. Thus, all of William's $1 million estate, reduced by an estate tax of $125,250, passed outright to his children, and all of Mary's $200,000 estate (no estate tax) passed outright to her children. The entire estate tax could have been avoided had William's will been different in two ways: first, if there had been no required survival period; and second, if the will passed $675,000 to a credit shelter bypass trust and $325,000 to a QTIP trust, with his children as the remaindermen of both trusts.

Selecting length of survival period. How long should the survival period be? Making it at least several months in duration will provide for the multiple death event which, relatively speaking, probably occurs most frequently: death of the decedent and the intended beneficiary in a common accident. However, specifying too long a survival period can delay distribution of estate assets since the executor will be required to wait that long to determine whether or not the named beneficiary in fact survived that period. Further, as mentioned in Chapter 6, a marital bequest will not qualify for the marital deduction if it is contingent on the spouse's surviving the decedent by any period greater than six months.

Many planners use a survival period of about one month for tangible personal property and between four and six months for other property. The shorter period for tangible personal property reflects the usual testator's desire to permit the surviving beneficiary to be able to use such property almost immediately, if even for only a short while, and to avoid storage and other additional costs.

Selection of Trustee and Trustee's Powers

Below we consider the factors involved in selecting a suitable trustee, and in determining which trustee powers to include in the trust instrument. It should become clear that the factors are quite similar to those mentioned earlier, in the section dealing with the selection of an executor.

Selection. We saw that a good executor (and financial guardian) is characterized by longevity, skill in managing, familiarity, integrity, loyalty, and impartiality. In general, these traits also apply to selecting a trustee, except that in the case of a trustee, greater weight is accorded to skill in ongoing financial management. Since the trustee's job is often long term, the trustee's ability to manage and invest property over a long period becomes a major factor. As in the case of the executor, potential nominees include family members, friends, the family attorney, and a corporate fiduciary.

Family member, friend. Selecting a family member or friend to be trustee can minimize costs, maximize administrative speed, and may ensure a personal relationship with the survivors.

Disadvantage of family member as trustee. Selecting a family member to be trustee can also result in mismanagement, since few family members have much experience in maintaining, investing, and accounting for an investment portfolio, all critical responsibilities of the trustee. Thus, family members may feel compelled to hire professionals for advice. In addition, family conflicts can arise. For example, nominating the person's children from a former marriage to be trustees of a QTIP trust can create a difficult situation for the person's second and surviving spouse.

Selecting a trust beneficiary to be trustee can also cause problems of proper distribution. For example, in one case, the trustee, who was also a remainder beneficiary, was ordered by the court to make additional distributions to the decedent-trustor's disabled son, under a trust which allowed such distributions.[7] In this situation, a conflict of interest resulted in a breach of fiduciary obligation that nearly frustrated the deceased trustor's dispositive intent to provide care for his disabled son.

Attorney. Selecting an attorney to be trustee can create the same minor risk of a will contest as in nominating an attorney to be executor. In addition, since management of the trust may be a long-term assignment, the client should determine whether the attorney has the time and expertise required to perform effectively. Finally, anticipating trusteeship, the attorney may be tempted to include unconventional *self-serving clauses* in the trust instrument, similar to the problems described earlier in the selection of the attorney as executor.[8]

Corporate trustee. Selecting a corporate trustee, such as a bank trust department or a trust company, increases the likelihood that an impartial satisfactory job will be performed. Most corporate trustees try to match the investment strategy for the trust assets to the needs of the beneficiaries, balancing both the income beneficiary's needs with the interests of the remaindermen. The trust instrument can give some guidance as to the settlor's view of appropriate asset allocation. Most trust departments try to build long-term personal relationships with the beneficiaries.

Cotrustees. A common choice is the cotrusteeship of family member and corporate trustee. It can combine the advantages of each: personal knowledge of the family situation and competent asset management. Also, naming the surviving spouse to be a cotrustee can be psychologically uplifting to that spouse.

Ordinarily, cotrusteeships do not save management fees, since the corporate trustee will probably charge its customary fee. There may be some situations where corporate trustees will turn down cotrustee arrangements, particularly when they anticipate that the other trustee may be difficult to accommodate. When cotrustees disagree, they may have to seek a resolution in court, unless the trust instrument authorizes a less formal method, such as giving the corporate trustee the final say.

Nominating an alternate trustee. As in nominating an executor, the settlor should always nominate a successor trustee and should consult with the proposed trustees to ensure that the job will be accepted. Many bank trust departments set minimum asset amounts, which creates the possibility that they may refuse to manage small trusts. Minimum amounts can range between $100,000 and $500,000, depending upon the bank and the ease with which the portfolio's assets can be managed.

Trustee's powers: three common options. The settlor has at least three commonly used options in deciding what trustee powers to confer in a trust document.

No explicit powers. First, the settlor can specify no powers, relying entirely on implied powers, and on that state's statutory and case-law framework, which explicitly confers some powers to trustees. Many states have adopted the Uniform Trustees Powers Act, which codifies numerous trustee powers. This approach is often used for settlors having relatively small estates and no assets requiring difficult administration.

Some explicit powers. The second approach is to rely on the state's laws in general and explicitly grant in the trust instrument other desirable powers not found in the statute. Such an approach may facilitate asset administration. This is the approach used in Exhibit 3-2, the living trust, and in Exhibit 3-3, the trust-will.

Many, many explicit powers. A third approach is not to rely at all on state law and instead draft a document that exhaustively includes all powers that the trustee should be permitted to have. The resulting independent tailor-made document eliminates certain risks, such as future legislative and judicial revision of the law, and the uncertain consequence of a change in the settlor's resident state. On the negative side, a custom-drafted form is a more complex document, more expensive to draft, more difficult to read, and perhaps more prone to internal inconsistency.

Timing Trust Distributions

Age. All estate planning trusts specify a time when the corpus will be distributed outright to the beneficiaries. Determining in advance the best time can be difficult for a parent with minor children, because the parent may not be able to accurately predict their rates of maturation. A parent may prefer to delay distribution of corpus to a later age, such as age 30 or 40, while others prefer staggered ages, e.g., one third of the trust be distributed at age 21, half the balance at age 25, and the remainder at age 30. Other parents, seeking an alternative to mandatory distribution, simply give the beneficiary a power of withdrawal over the property once the beneficiary reaches some specified age. Thus, their trustee would continue to manage the property indefinitely if the beneficiary became unable or unwilling to make a withdrawal request.

Some individuals prefer to leave the bulk of their wealth to charity. They may fear the potentially devastating impact the anticipation of inherited wealth can have on immature children. Some children of wealthy families are prone to a malady, one commentator has called "affluenza," whose symptoms include a lack of connection between work and reward, inadequate self discipline, a distorted view of money, lack of motivation, guilt, and low self-esteem. For this, and a variety of other reasons, some people choose not to leave their children any inheritance.[9]

Single versus multiple trusts. For parents with more than one child, a separate trust can be established for each child, or a single trust can include all children. How much each child will receive may depend on how many trusts are created.

Multiple trusts. Creating multiple trusts, i.e., a *separate trust* for each child, adds flexibility but increases administration costs. In addition, separate trusts may be considered unfair to the younger children for the following reason. If the parent lives, expenses in raising all children will ordinarily come from family property in general and not from separate shares reserved for each child. Thus, expenses to raise even the youngest child will come from what could be called the family "pot" of wealth. On the other hand, if the parent dies leaving orphaned minor children, and if a separate trust is immediately created for each child, the pot will likely be split before all expenses in raising the children have been incurred. Thus, each child's remaining expenses will be financed out of his or her own separate share, rather than from the pot. Consequently, the younger children will receive a relatively smaller final distribution upon reaching adulthood because living expenses over a longer period of time will have been charged only to their shares. A single trust can solve this problem.

Single pot trust. The name given by some attorneys to a type of single trust created for more than one child, one that retains the "pot" characteristic, is the pot trust or family pot trust. Under its usual terms, the trust remains undivided until the *youngest child reaches age 21*, the age at which parental obligations are commonly perceived to terminate. At that time, the assets are divided into *equal separate shares*, one for each child. The assets are distributed outright, or they are held for distribution at some older age.

The choice of the age at which the assets in a pot trust are divided into separate shares or separate trusts involves a *trade-off* between inequality and delay. The younger that age, the more *unequal* will be the total cumulative amounts distributed to the children, but the *sooner* will the older children be certain of the size of their shares. Conversely, the older the age at which the assets are divided into separate shares, the less the inequality, but the later the share amounts will be determined.

EXAMPLE 17 - 8. Mrs. Hunsaker, a widow, is pondering the type of distribution clause for her trust. She has two children, Colleen, age 20, and Nancy, age 15. Colleen is a senior in college and is engaged to be married, and Nancy, still in high school, is headed for college. One alternative would be to split the trust into two equal shares immediately upon her death, with outright distribution to each child at age 21. Another alternative would be to delay dividing the assets into equal shares until Nancy reaches age 21, at which time both children would receive equal shares outright. If Mrs. Hunsaker dies just after the trust is executed, with the first alternative, Colleen will receive her distribution in less than one year and none of it will have been used to finance Nancy's living expenses. With the second alternative, Colleen will have to wait until age 26 to receive her distribution, and the entire corpus will have been available to meet Nancy's living expenses, including most of her college education.

Delaying division of the trust assets probably better reflects the financial condition that would have resulted had the parent not died: One pot of wealth would have been the source for both children's needs. For this reason, most attorneys recommend delaying the division. However, some attorneys recommend dividing the corpus of a pot trust into separate shares sooner, when the *oldest child reaches age 18*, rather than age 21, reasoning that parents would probably prefer that each child bear subsequent (perhaps very unequal) costs (e.g., college, graduate school) only out of his or her own share. This, of course, reflects a very different philosophy of family financial planning. The planner should determine which best suits the preferences of each client rather than using boiler plate changes.

Restrictions against Assignment

As mentioned in Chapter 3, the settlor may wish to include a *spendthrift clause*, insulating the trust from the claims of the beneficiaries' creditors and restricting beneficiaries from transferring their interests in trust income or principal prior to their receipt. Spendthrift clauses are legally recognized in the majority of American jurisdictions, even if the beneficiary is not a "spendthrift." They can help a financially prudent beneficiary (e.g., a professional) by protecting trust assets from most creditors. However, such clauses are not foolproof. Although they may deny a creditor the right to demand that the *trustee* directly hand a distribution over to it, they do not prevent the creditor from exercising the usual legal remedies (i.e., action in court) against a beneficiary *after* the beneficiary receives a distribution. In addition, all states will enforce a promise made by the beneficiary prior to a distribution that the beneficiary will hand it over to the creditor once it is received. Thus, while a spendthrift clause can discourage excessive spending, it cannot completely prevent the beneficiary from "spending" trust property prior to receiving it, as long as there are potential creditors around who are willing to risk having to seek payment from the beneficiary.

Several states, including California, have recently enacted exceptions to the general rule, that spendthrift trust assets are not subject to the claims of beneficiaries creditors. Common exceptions apply, including:

- ► revocable trusts, if the trustor is a beneficiary.
- ► cases involving spousal and child support judgments.
- ► situations where the creditor is a government agency.

In addition, California has established a procedure similar to wage garnishment for judgment creditors of up to 25% of amounts distributable in excess of support needs. Spendthrift clauses work best in discretionary trusts, ones in which the beneficiary has no legally enforceable right to income or principal.

Special Needs Trust. One interesting application of the spendthrift concept is a discretionary spendthrift trust used for the benefit of a *developmentally disabled child* after the parent's death. Called a *special needs trust*, it may not work in some states where courts have ruled it in violation of public policy. It seeks to insulate trust assets from governmental claims, and, at the same time, keep the child eligible for public benefits, including Supplemental Security Income (SSI), Medicaid, and Social Security Disability Insurance (SSDI). The special needs trust provides for the health, safety, and welfare of the beneficiary in ways not provided by any public agency, that no part of the corpus may be used to replace public benefits. In the event that the trust renders the beneficiary ineligible for public benefits, the trustee is authorized (but not required) to terminate the trust and distribute the corpus to a "precatory trustee," who is requested (but not required) to provide for the disabled person's basic living needs. The word *precatory* originated from the word 'pray,' i.e., meaning to request some favor from another person. Precatory language is used in a will or trust when the writer wants to recommend a course of action but not impose an enforceable obligation on anyone.

Foreign trust. Individuals owning substantial liquid assets and wishing to more completely protect them from *their own creditors* may consider creating a foreign "protection of assets" trust. Certain jurisdictions including the Bahamas, Bermuda, and the Cayman Islands offer great protection from pre- and post-judgment remedies of future creditors. Drawbacks include setup costs in excess of $25,000, considerable reporting requirements, and ethical issues. However, at its best, such a trust will trigger no additional taxes.

Trust Taxation: A Summary

Now that the text has covered the major types of trusts used in estate planning, it might help to summarize and compare the gift, estate and income taxation of these trusts. See Table 17-1. In interpreting the comments, keep in mind that some of these trusts come into being under the terms of other trusts, sometimes as a result of the settlor's death. Thus, the nature of a trust may change over time. For example, the bypass and marital trusts usually come into existence soon after one spouse dies. Thus, the comments for the living trust above apply to tax effects during the settlor's lifetime or at his or her death, while the comments for the bypass and marital trusts refer to tax effects at, or after, the settlor's death.

Table 17-1 Summary of Trust Taxation

Trust Type	Taxable Gift?	In Gross Estate?	Income Taxed to Grantor?
Revocable Living Trust	No, not a completed gift.	Yes, in grantor's gross estate, (§2038) but may qualify for marital or charitable deduction.	Yes, it is a grantor trust (§676).
Bypass Trust	No, starts @ grantor's death.	S1: yes S2: generally not, but QTIP & superB can also be bypass trusts	No, taxed to the trust or to the beneficiaries.
Marital Trusts (QTIP, GPA, & Estate Trust)	Generally not created until grantor's death. Can create QTIP during life & obtain marital deduction.	S1: QTIP, not if election is made, other two automatic marital deduction S2: QTIP - it depends, other two yes	No, but generally taxable to S2 (QTIP & GPA required, Estate Trust if distributed).
Minor's Trusts (§2503(c), MIT, or Crummey)	Only to extent not sheltered by annual exclusion.	Not unless grantor retained control over enjoyment (§§2036 or 2038), over annual exclusion would be an adjusted taxable gift.	No, taxable to trust or beneficiaries (so long as not used for support).
Intentionally Defective Irrevocable Trust	Only to extent not sheltered by annual exclusion.	No, but if originally a gift, then it may be an adjusted taxable gift.	Yes, by design. Taxes paid also reduce grantor's taxable estate.
Irrevocable Life Insurance Trust	Only to extent not sheltered by annual exclusion.	No, but if originally a gift, then it may be an adjusted taxable gift.	Generally not. Usually not funded with income producing assets.
Grantor Retained Income Trust	Yes, remainder value if retained interest is qualified, otherwise, whole trust.	Yes, if dies before term ends. Otherwise no, but if originally a gift, then it may be an adjusted taxable gift.	Yes, to the extent of income interest. Trust may also pay taxes.
Charitable Remainder Trust	Remainder is a completed gift, but not taxable (§2055)	Yes, in the gross estate, but it qualifies for charitable deduction	Yes, to extent of income interest. Trust doesn't pay taxes

PLANNING FOR NONTRADITIONAL RELATIONSHIPS

From time to time, planners will be asked for advice by *unmarried* clients involved in nontraditional, long term-relationships with members of the same or opposite sex. These relationships present some unique planning challenges and can lead to a set of surprisingly different planning strategies. Two characteristics not applicable to married couples explain most of the differences. First, being unmarried, the partners *will not be entitled* to the advantages offered by law to married couples. Second, since unmarried partners usually do not have children in common, they usually have *totally different sets of surviving kin*. Thus, while they may have a strong desire to leave most or all property for the benefit of the partner *for life*, they will not want the partner to be able to control disposition of their property at or after the partner's death. Underlying strategies based on these characteristics are discussed next.

Greater Need to Avoid Intestacy

Unmarried partners are not included as heirs in intestate succession statutes, making written estate planning documents even more important. Intestacy will have the undesired effect of *disinheriting* the surviving partner, who is hardly ever a blood relative.

Less Shelter from Estate Tax May Dictate Larger Bypass

In theory, the largest combined estate size that unmarried partners can transfer to survivors, estate tax free, with a credit shelter bypass is two times the exclusion amount, e.g., $2,000,000 after the year 2006, just as for married couples. However, *in fact*, the true maximum is usually less, to the extent that one of the partners owns less than the exclusion amount. While the exclusion amount will be sheltered at the first death by the unified credit, any excess amount cannot be sheltered by the marital deduction. Thus, estate planning cannot "zero out" the estate tax for any first partner to die (P1) owning greater than the exclusion amount. Since P1 will incur an estate tax whether the excess is left to the surviving partner (P2) or to a bypass trust, P1 may prefer to leave the *entire* estate to the bypass trust, in order to minimize P2's estate tax, and to ensure that the property will ultimately pass to P1's surviving kin.

As a partial solution, the partners may agree to arrange separate wills leaving everything to one another, and agreeing that at P2's death, property originating from P1 will pass to P1's surviving kin. However, short of executing a joint and mutual will, P1 has no way to prevent P2 from revising the instrument later on. Thus, the surest plan requires use of bypass trusts to minimize P2's estate tax and ensure that each will have selected his or her own remaindermen as the ultimate beneficiaries of their respective estates.

Greater Need for Life Insurance at First Death

Since a taxable estate exceeding the exclusion amount will owe an estate tax, liquidity planning will often require life insurance on P1 as well as P2. The proceeds can still be kept out of both partners' gross estates with irrevocable life insurance trusts.

Lifetime Giving More Important

Inability to save as much estate tax on transfers at death may prompt unmarried partners to engage in greater gift planning. Although unmarried partners will not be able to utilize the gift tax marital deduction, they can still take advantage of one annual exclusion per donee per year. Thus, they can still undertake an ongoing program of lifetime giving to reduce their estate tax base. Careful planning should *avoid outright gifts* to the partner, however, to enable the donor, as a potential P1, to retain final dispositive control. Instead, the planner should encourage gifting *in trust*, with provisions granting a life estate in the income to the partner and the remainder to the trustor's surviving relatives. As future interests, however, the remainder interest portion of such gifts in trust will not qualify for the annual exclusion and will either use up the settlor's unified credit or result in an actual gift tax.

Joint Tenancies in Community Property States May Be More Attractive

Finally, in community property states, joint tenancies as a means of disposing of property of unmarried decedents may be more attractive, relative to the will and the trust. Only married couples can own community property. Lacking the income tax advantage of a full step-up in basis, a uniquely community property characteristic, unmarried couples, especially those with smaller estates, may choose joint tenancies as a simple form of co-ownership. From a tax basis point of view, joint tenancies will be no worse than any other form of ownership of property. Furthermore, if the first partner to die is the one who owned the property before it was transferred into joint tenancy, this form of ownership also provides a full step-up in basis since the entire value would be included in his or her estate. However, from a control point of view, joint tenancies may still not be desirable. It does not keep dispositive control in the hands of the original owner, whereas a trust would do so.

We turn next to the second major topic of the chapter: planning for one's own incapacity.

PLANNING FOR INCAPACITY

More and more, disability is preceding death as people live longer and longer. To cite just two examples of demographic data, consider a 1992 U.S. Census Bureau report that the number of Americans 65 and older grew by 22% in the 1980's, more than twice the growth rate for the nation as a whole. It also found that two thirds of Americans 75 and older consider themselves "healthy".

A person's disability may create the need for care by a surrogate decision maker. Since the person will usually have specific preferences regarding care, planning for incapacity while the person is physically and mentally fit increases the likelihood of more satisfying final years.

As in the case of minors, the law recognizes two types of care for incapacitated adults: care for the person's property and personal care for the person. The final two sections of this chapter deal with planning for each.

Property Management for an Incapacitated Person

Four techniques are available to care for the property of an incapacitated person: the guardianship or conservatorship, revocable living trust, durable power of attorney for property, and the special needs trust. Only the last two will be described in detail.

Guardianship or conservatorship of an estate. Similar to the guardianship of the estate of a minor, all states provide a court-supervised arrangement to manage the property of an incapacitated individual. Called a *guardianship* or a *conservatorship*, depending on the state, establishment of either normally requires a court hearing, and the appointment of a guardian who is ordinarily subject to continuing court supervision. The guardian or conservator is required to give periodic accountings to the court and is typically required to obtain court permission before engaging in most property transactions. Most guardians and conservators have little or no discretionary authority. However, some states are reducing court involvement in guardianships and conservatorships in much the same way they are reducing court involvement for probate proceedings.[10]

For reasons similar to those for avoiding probate, many people will plan to avoid the necessity of having a property guardian or conservator. Some individuals, however, may prefer the protection offered from their closer court supervision. People owning larger estates, or those who cannot recommend a friend or relative to manage property, might prefer a court-administered alternative. Most people will prefer one or both of the arrangements described next.

Revocable living trust. In planning for incapacity, a person could create a revocable living trust, funding it with family assets, and serving as its initial trustee. The trust instrument could provide for a successor trustee when the person became unable to manage the trust's financial affairs. The successor trustee could be the spouse, an adult child, another relative, a trusted friend, or a corporate trustee. In comparison with a guardianship or conservatorship, a living trust offers the advantages of privacy, flexibility, and freedom from court appearances and accountings. On the other hand, since the trust is a private, unsupervised arrangement, there exists greater potential for *undiscovered fraud and mismanagement* by the successor trustee.

One additional disadvantage of the trust arrangement to handle incapacity is the possible requirement of a *formal legal determination* of the settlor-trustee's *incapacity* before a successor trustee can take over the job. Embarrassing litigation can develop between the settlor and a family member who is attempting to establish that the settlor-trustee is incompetent. However, this conflict can also arise if a guardianship or conservatorship is being established. The trust can contain a clause providing for a *private* determination of incapacity, in a manner similar to that provided by the springing durable power of attorney for property, discussed next.

Durable power of attorney for property. Creation of a trust can be relatively expensive. Persons owning smaller estates may prefer to execute a simpler document, known as a durable power of attorney for property. Popularized by the Uniform Probate Code, the durable power of attorney for property has been recognized by the statutes of every state. The durable power of attorney for property is different from the durable power of attorney for health care, described in the next section. Since state laws vary, the reader is strongly urged to examine the law of his or her particular state.

A power of attorney is a written document executed by one person, called the *principal*, authorizing another person, called the *attorney-in-fact* or the *agent*, to perform designated acts on behalf of the principal. A durable power of attorney for property (DPOA) creates an agency relationship that allows the agent to perform acts to protect the principal's property interests, even if the principal becomes incapacitated.

Durable versus nondurable powers of attorney. General powers of attorney can be either durable or nondurable. A nondurable power of attorney is not a practical alternative for caring for the property of elderly individuals because the power becomes legally invalid at the onset of the principal's incapacity, just when the agency is needed most. In one situation, an attorney-in-fact under a nondurable power of attorney gifted property after the principal became mentally incompetent and the IRS ruled that the gift was voidable under local law (by a court-appointed guardian or by the principal had he regained mental capacity), and therefore the gift was included in the principal's gross estate under §2038.[11]

The *durable* power of attorney was developed to overcome this deficiency. Thus, a DPOA is durable because it survives the principal's incapacity. Exhibit 17-1 illustrates the common provisions of a DPOA. The italicized sentence makes it "durable." ·

EXHIBIT 17-1 Durable Power of Attorney (for property)[12]

DURABLE POWER OF ATTORNEY

JOHN JONES, PRINCIPAL

TO WHOM IT MAY CONCERN:

I, John Jones, a resident of Anytown, Anystate, in the county of Anycounty, do hereby constitute and appoint Aaron Agent, a resident of Anytown, Anystate, to be my attorney-in-fact, with full power to name and stead and on my behalf and with full power to substitute at any time or times for the purposes described below one or more attorneys and to revoke the appointment of my attorney so substituted and to do the following:

1. To manage my affairs; handle my investments; arrange for the investment, reinvestment, and disposition of funds; exercise all rights with respect to my investments; accept remittances of income and disburse the same, including authority to open bank accounts in my name and to endorse checks for deposit therein or in any bank where I may at any time have money on deposit and sign checks covering withdrawals therefrom.
2. To endorse and deliver certificates for transfer of bonds or other securities to be sold for my account and receive the proceeds from such sale.
3. To sign, execute, acknowledge, and deliver on my behalf any deed of transfer or conveyance covering personal property or real estate wherever situated (including transfers or conveyances to any trust established by me), any discharge or release of mortgage held by me on real estate or any other instrument in writing.
4. To negotiate and execute leases of any property, real or personal, which I may own, for terms that may extend beyond the duration of this power and to provide for the proper care and maintenance of such property and pay expenses incurred in connection therewith.
5. To subdivide, partition, improve, alter, repair, adjust boundaries of, manage, maintain, and otherwise deal with any real estate held as trust property, including power to demolish any building in whole or in part and to erect buildings.
6. To enter into a lease or arrangement for exploration and removal of minerals or other natural resources or to enter into a pooling or unitization agreement.
7. To hold securities in bearer form or in the name of a nominee or nominees and to hold real estate in the name of a nominee or nominees.
8. To continue or participate in the operation of any business or other enterprise.
9. To borrow money from time to time in my name and to give notes or other obligations therefore, and to deposit as collateral, pledge as security for the

---

EXHIBIT 17-1 Durable Power of Attorney *continued*

---

payment thereof, or mortgage any or all my securities or other property of whatever nature.

10. To have access to any and all safe deposit boxes of which I am now or may become possessed, and to remove therefrom any securities, papers, or other articles.

11. To make all tax returns and pay all taxes required by law, including federal and state returns, and to file all claims for abatement, refund, or other papers relating thereto.

12. To demand, collect, sue for, receive, and receipt for any money, debts, or property of any kind, now or hereafter payable, due or deliverable to me; to pay or contest claims against me; to settle claims by compromise, arbitration, or otherwise; and to release claims.

13. To employ as investment counsel, custodians, brokers, accountants, appraisers, attorneys-at-law, or other agents such persons, firms, or organizations, including my said attorney and any firm of which my said attorney may be a member or employee, as deemed necessary or desirable, and to pay such persons, firms, or organizations such compensation as is deemed reasonable and to determine whether or not to act upon the advice of any such agent without liability for acting or failing to act thereon.

14. To expend and distribute income or principal of my estate for the support, education, care, or benefit of me and my dependents.

15. To make gifts to any one or more of my spouse and my descendants (if any) of whatever degree (including my said attorney who is a spouse or descendant of mine) in amounts not exceeding $10,000 annually with respect to any one of them and gifts to charity in amounts not exceeding 20% of my federal adjusted gross income in any one year.

16. To renounce and disclaim any interest otherwise passing to me by testate or intestate succession or by inter vivos transfer.

17. To exercise my rights to elect options and change beneficiaries under insurance and annuity policies and to surrender the policies for their cash value.

In general I give to my said attorney full power to act in the management and disposition of all my estate, affairs and property of every kind and wherever situated in such manner and with such authority as I myself might exercise if personally present.

EXHIBIT 17-1 Durable Power of Attorney *continued*

This power of attorney shall be binding on me and my heirs, executors, and administrators and shall remain in force up to the time of the receipt of my attorney of a written revocation signed by me.

This power of attorney shall not be affected by my subsequent disability or incapacity.

IN WITNESS THEREOF, I have set forth signature on March 19, 1999.

_____ *John Jones* _____

STATE OF ANYSTATE

COUNTY OF ANYCOUNTY

On <u>March 19, 1999</u>, the above named <u>John Jones</u> appeared and acknowledged the foregoing instrument to be his/ free act and deed.

_____ Mary D. Notary _____
Notary Public

My commission expires: January 1, 2001

This particular example of a DPOA form can be criticized for being simply a *unilateral authorizing instrument*, which means that the named attorney-in-fact would not be liable for failure to act. Some commentators recommend instead creating a *bilateral contract* between principal and attorney-in-fact, particularly if the latter is not the principal's spouse, to eliminate this problem. This may require a signature by the attorney in fact.

Non-springing versus springing DPOAs. There are two common types of DPOAs. The first type becomes effective as soon as it is executed. The second type, called a "springing" DPOA, becomes effective *at* the principal's incapacity. It will contain the following clause, in addition to those found in Exhibit 17-1:

In the event that I have been determined to be incapacitated to provide informed consent for medical treatment and surgical and diagnostic procedures, I wish to designate as my surrogate for health care decisions:[followed by the identification of the agent].

Some attorneys recommend that a physician or a "trusted committee" of three of the client's trusted friends and relatives should be empowered to determine when the power of attorney becomes effective.

To be valid, of course, any DPOA must be *executed* prior to the principal's incapacity. To ensure competent execution, many advisers recommend the preparation of a DPOA for an older client at the time the will is being prepared.

Advantages of the DPOA. The DPOA has several advantages over the other devices designed to manage an incapacitated person's property. Compared to a guardianship or conservatorship, the DPOA is less expensive to create and to administer. The non-springing type can avoid the necessity of a court-held incompetency proceeding, an event that can be painful and embarrassing to all parties, especially the proposed conservatee. Compared with the living trust, the DPOA is also less expensive to create and administer. Some individuals who refuse to set up a trust may be willing to execute a DPOA, because of its relative simplicity. Yet a trust can continue long after the settlor's death, whereas a DPOA, being based on agency law, must terminate when the principal dies. It may be durable but it is not that durable.

The trust and the DPOA need not be considered alternatives. Greater flexibility may result if a DPOA authorizes the attorney-in-fact to add newly acquired property (by gift, inheritance, etc.) to the principal's partially funded living trust, or to fund an existing unfunded revocable living trust (a "standby trust") with the principal's assets, at the onset of incapacity. Upon funding, the assets could be managed by a skilled trustee. Thereafter, the attorney-in-fact may be permitted to perform other duties that were not given to the trustee, including establishing and funding other trusts, making gifts and disclaimers, and appearing at tax audits.

Regarding the power of the attorney-in-fact to make gifts, one court has ruled that failure to explicitly include that power in the document will totally frustrate gift planning. In that case, the attorney-in-fact did make gifts before the principal's death. Relying on Virginia's narrow construction of powers-of-attorney law, the appellate court treated the gift as revocable at the time of the principal's death, resulting in inclusion of gifted assets in the gross estate under §2036(a) and §2038.[13] However, in a more recent Virginia case, the Tax Court allowed gifts by an attorney-in-fact because Virginia law authorizes attorneys-in-fact to make gifts "in accordance with the principal's personal history of making or joining in lifetime gifts."[14]

Drawbacks of the DPOA. The DPOA has a potential drawback for the attorney in-fact. If the attorney-in fact dies first, the IRS might claim that principal's property must be included in the *attorney-in-fact's* gross estate on the theory that the attorney-in-fact held a general power of appointment over the property. The fact that the agent has a fiduciary duty to use the power only for the best interest of the principal should be enough to prevent a claim of inclusion from being successful. Completely eliminating this danger may require prohibiting entirely the ability of the attorney-in-fact to make gifts to him or herself, or limiting such gifts to an ascertainable standard, or to the greater of $5,000 or 5% of the value of the property.

A non-tax drawback to the DPOA concerns its *acceptance*. Certain financial institutions may be unwilling to honor the DPOA if they cannot satisfy themselves that it is currently valid. The power, they reason, may already have been revoked by the principal or the principal may be dead. Due to their uncertainty about the validity of custom-drafted DPOAs, they may insist on the use of their own form. The industry's increasing use of the DPOA should substantially lessen these concerns. The attorney can minimize acceptance problems with careful and specific custom drafting of enumerated powers, and by having the principal periodically re-execute the DPOA to prevent it from appearing outdated. Nevertheless, some institutions refuse to accept a DPOA, and some banks and the IRS will, but might require the use of their own forms.

Other helpful techniques to maximize acceptability include a provision in the document that empowers the attorney-in-fact to bring legal action against a recalcitrant third party and indemnifies the third party when it acts in reliance on the document and the agent's instructions. However, pursuing legal action can be expensive and time consuming. Finally, the person, while still competent, can show the document to banks, insurance companies, health care providers, etc., to find out whether it will be accepted, and to stop dealing with those institutions that refuse. New York has a statute making it unlawful to refuse to recognize the New York statutory form DPOA and indemnifying banks that honor them. California's statute permits the filing of an action to compel the honoring of a statutory durable power and specifies that a refusal is unreasonable if the sole reason for the refusal is that it is not on the third party's (e.g., a bank's) own form.[15]

The second non-tax drawback of the DPOA is that it can be *misused*. Lawyers will attest to situations where attorneys-in-fact have used a disabled client's property in a manner clearly contrary to the principal's best interest. Although such behavior is actionable, it is rarely challenged. Because the DPOA delegates very fundamental property rights, a person considering signing one should first think long and hard about the possible consequences.

Special needs trust and other asset "spend-down" planning. A different kind of living trust may be capable of preserving assets owned by persons anticipating possible long-term disability.

The medical profession has been tremendously successful in prolonging the life of the seriously ill, often at great economic cost. Such patients often need *custodial care* for help with feeding, bathing, dressing, and transportation. Later, they may need *skilled nursing care* provided in a licensed facility, and costing $3,000 per month or more. Their condition may finally require a lengthy period of *hospitalization*, costing far more. Private and public insurance can help pay these costs, but often not entirely. Long-term care insurance has recently become available, but policies usually are expensive and contain significant restrictions and exclusions, so few people are willing to buy it. Federal Medicare insurance for patients over 65 will pay for up to 150 days of hospitalization, with sizable deductibles after the first 50 days. Medicare pays for little or no post-hospitalization nursing facility care. These limitations in private and public insurance raise the possibility that a person will totally deplete the wealth acquired over a lifetime, thereby preventing any significant amount going to the children.

To prevent this, some people are turning to attorneys who specialize in *elder law*. Many recommend "spending down" assets through the use of gifts and trusts. This action seeks to accomplish two goals. First, it strives to insulate the person's assets from the claims of health care providers and government agencies. Second, it attempts to impoverish the person sufficiently to qualify for certain types of federal and state assistance, including Supplemental Security Income, In-Home Supportive Services, In-Home Medical Care Services, and perhaps most importantly, Medicaid. Each state, in exchange for matching federal Medicaid grants, imposes federally influenced limits on both 1) assets (roughly $3,000 for spouses living together, and $70,000 if one spouse is in a nursing home, not counting the residence), and 2) income (income limit depends upon the actual cost of medical and custodial care).

Three common spending-down strategies will be compared. First, the individual may wish to make *outright gifts* of property to children. However, outright gifts have the major drawback covered in earlier chapters: the donor loses total control over the property. Second, the person could purchase a single premium annuity. Although distributions from the annuity do count for purposes of the income test, the overall value of the annuity does not count under the assets test. Finally, and perhaps most effective, the person could make substantial gifts to an irrevocable *special needs trust*, also called a *discretionary support trust*. Under this trust, the settlor retains the following powers and interests:

- While competent, the power to act as trustee.
- While *not* competent, or while completely disabled and subject to catastrophic health care costs, the right to invade principal on the basis of health, education, maintenance or support.
- The power to appoint an unlimited amount of trust property to family members other than the trustor.
- The power to change beneficiaries so as to reallocate the estate among the children, if desired.

In addition, a group of other persons, including children, advisors, and siblings (the more the better) are given a power to authorize the trustee to revest any trust property in the trustor. Any one of these persons may individually exercise this power.

The special needs trust is a bypass trust, hence it is not included in the beneficiary's gross estate, and its assets are not counted for purposes of eligibility under Medicaid. The trustee may also own a long-term health care insurance policy to further exclude payments from the income test. If the residence is in this grantor trust, it will qualify for the §121 exclusion of $250,000/500,000 of gain. In addition, all trust assets will obtain a basis step-up at the trustor's death. Under Medicaid rules, the person would be ineligible for public assistance for up to thirty six months (sixty months, in the case of certain transfers, including those to revocable trusts) after the date of the transfers into trust.[16] In addition, states may recover property after the beneficiary's death from the probate estate as well as other former assets of the beneficiary, including those conveyed to a survivor, heir, or assign through joint tenancy, tenancy in common, survivorship, life estate, and living trusts. Property in the estate of the surviving spouse is exempt.

Although the law prohibits nursing homes from charging patients greater than the amount paid under government assistance, the person's trust assets can be used to improve care by acquiring for the patient services not funded by public assistance. These could include an extra private nurse, physiotherapists, additional medication, or a paid companion who reads to the patient or takes the patient on special outings. However, even with these extras, wealthier people are probably not be interested in spending down or in establishing a special needs trust. Most will want a higher quality of care and may not like being regarded as a "welfare case."

Helping a client who owns a sizable estate to impoverish him or her self so as to qualify for public assistance funds is a controversial subject and raises ethical issues. Many planners will not recommend it, because they see it as taking unfair advantage of an imperfect system designed for truly needy people. It also encourages children to treat Medicaid as if it were "their personal inheritance insurance." Others find no moral dilemma, and consider it no different from tax planning, such as recommending a credit shelter bypass trust to minimize estate tax. Perhaps all planners would agree that clients should be encouraged to consider, at a minimum, other basic protective planning steps, such as purchasing an effective long-term care insurance policy or saving for their future care.

Personal Care for the Incapacitated Person

Similar to the procedure for selecting the guardian of a minor child, the procedure for selecting the person who will care for an incapacitated adult is usually undertaken in the county probate court after a noticed hearing. Some states call this fiduciary a *guardian* or *committee*, while others use the name *conservator*. States define guardian, conservator, and committee differently. In some states, such as California, a conservator is a person appointed by the court to manage the personal care, and the property of, an adult unable to provide for their own personal needs and/or unable to manage their financial resources, while a guardian is appointed to perform such services for a minor. In other states, such as New York, a conservator deals primarily with an "impaired" person's property, while a committee cares for both the person and the property of an "incompetent" person. The UPC parallels the New York terminology and, in addition, permits a guardian to be appointed to oversee the person and the property of an "incapacitated" person. In any case, the court chooses the party only after careful, formal consideration.

Selecting a personal care provider. Who should the person nominate to provide personal care in the event of his or her incapacity? Ordinarily, the person has few choices.

Spouse, family members. The spouse is usually the best first choice. Next come other family members, especially adult children. However, the children may lead busy lives and may not be capable nor willing to do all the work required. This problem is even more likely to arise for a person in an advanced stage of incapacity, such as the onset of incontinence. Prior to this degree of impairment, the individual may simply need home delivery of meals, housekeeping services, or adult day care, all of which are commercially available. While these services are not inexpensive, some programs are government subsidized. Services can be arranged for a fee by a "private geriatric care manager," who is often a social worker or nurse. Helpful sources of information include: County and local departments for the aging, for referrals on services for elders; the National Association of Area Agencies on Aging (800-677-1116), which has an "elder care locator"; the National Association of Professional Geriatric Care Managers (602-881-8808); the National Academy of Elder Law Attorneys (602-881-4005); and the Children of Aging Parents, which offers a clearing house of information including contacts for support groups for adult children.

Nursing home. As a person gets older, it may be wise to visit residential health care facilities for the elderly. Such facilities vary widely in cost, extent of services offered, and the degree of incapacity permitted. At one end of the spectrum is the traditional nursing home, which offers complete care, but is quite expensive. Some critics feel entering a nursing home is tantamount to "a life sentence to mental and physical imprisonment," where patients lose nearly all of their independence in a dehumanizing environment.

Assisted living. Other less structured facilities offer a new and increasingly popular style of housing called assisted living for elderly people without serious medical problems. Private apartments are provided, as well as meals, laundry, housekeeping, social activities, transportation, and regular visits by nurses. Such facilities usually cost considerably less than nursing homes and offer the greatest degree of independence possible.[17]

Life care facility. Finally, one other type of organization called a life-care facility offers at a hefty price the right to occupy, for life, an apartment in a large residential health-care facility, which also provides, on the premises, all meals and around-the-clock nursing, medical, and hospital services.

Some figures from the U.S. Census Bureau regarding the elderly living in commercial facilities like the three described above plus long-term care rooms in hospital wards, and soldiers', fraternal or religious homes for the aged, may be helpful. In 1990, 1.8 million people lived in commercial facilities for the elderly. Not surprisingly, women outnumbering men almost three to one. Residents 85 and older constituted 42% of those residents, up from 34% in 1980. Overall, only 5.1% of the nation's elderly reside in these facilities, but the figure was 24.5% of those 85 and older. Only one in seven had a spouse still alive.

Delegation of health care decisions. Until recently, people have not had the ability to delegate the power to make *medical* decisions. Today, almost all states recognize an individual's ability either to delegate important medical decisions or at least to state in writing what those decisions should be.

Cruzan case. The need to state medical choices clearly and in writing is dramatically illustrated by the 1990 U.S. Supreme Court decision, *Cruzan v. Missouri*.[18] A victim of an automobile accident seven years earlier, 32 year old Nancy Cruzan remained in a persistent vegetative state, with functioning respiratory and circulatory systems, but little else. She could not swallow food, and she was unable to recognize her relatives. After it became clear that there was no reasonable hope of any improvement in her condition, her family sought to let her die by withdrawing her feeding tube. The state of Missouri would not allow it, despite the fact that a year before the accident, Nancy had told a friend that "if sick or injured she would not wish to continue her life unless she could live at least halfway normally." On appeal, the U.S. Supreme Court affirmed, approving the Missouri requirement that the family would have to show "clear and convincing evidence" of Nancy's wishes to remove life sustaining equipment, something the jury determined that the Cruzans did not establish.

After the Supreme Court decision and just after the Cruzans requested a new hearing in the local court claiming new evidence that Nancy would not wish to live, the state attorney general withdrew as a party to the case, which meant that there was no longer anyone to oppose removal of Nancy's feeding tube. Nancy died at age 33 on December 26, 1990, twelve days after the tube was removed.

Based on the Supreme Court's ruling, it would appear that standards of proof such as Missouri's "clear and convincing evidence" may be difficult to meet without a written statement by the incapacitated person. Estate planning has two common written documents for this purpose: the durable power of attorney for health care and the living will.

Durable power of attorney for health care. Like the durable power of attorney for property (DPOA), the durable power of attorney for health care (DPOAHC) appoints a person as attorney-in-fact to make decisions on behalf of the principal. However, the documents are different in three important respects.

Types of decisions. First, the DPOAHC concerns *medical*, not property decisions. Examples of medical decisions listed in this type of "advance directive" include the power to secure the placement in or removal from a medical facility, to withhold future medical treatment, to use or not use medication, to perform or not perform surgery, and the power to use or not use artificial life-sustaining methods, such as respiration, nourishment, and hydration. As one might expect, this last power is quite controversial, and some legal commentators have defended it ardently. Reflecting an increasingly popular dissatisfaction with the zealous use of artificial life-sustaining methods, some have argued that rapid advances in medical technology, combined with the implicit premise of medicine to "do everything" for patients, violate patients' rights. These advances in medicine may actually condemn the very sick to an existence void of relationship in antiseptic hospital-like settings, an existence that many feel is worse than death.

Designating a surrogate with the power to terminate life support can be helpful in situations where the physician in charge refuses to act. One study has shown that physicians are reluctant to terminate life support in cases where the patient would take a relatively long time to die, where the life support became necessary because of medical errors, and in cases where the patient has already been on life support for a relatively long period of time.[19]

Springing power. Second, the DPOAHC differs from the DPOA in that the DPOAHC is always a springing power, while the DPOA can be non-springing. Thus, the DPOAHC becomes effective only upon the principal's incapacity, that is, upon his or her inability to make health care decisions. The DPOAHC does not apply just to situations where the principal is terminally ill, but to all situations where the principal is unable to give "informed consent" with respect to a particular medical decision.

Separate documents. Third, while it is possible to include the legal content of a DPOAHC within a DPOA document they are usually drafted as separate documents. They involve very different situations, different evolving law, and possibly different attorneys-in-fact. In addition, many attorneys prefer to use a preprinted state medical association form for health care because of its widespread acceptance by the medical profession. In contrast, a custom-drafted form can generate decision-making delays when a hospital requires its own lawyers to carefully evaluate it. Appendix 17A shows an example of a statutory form of DPOAHC from a state that also permits custom instruments.

Acceptance of the document. The DPOAHC is statutorily recognized in almost every state. State law varies in terms of both the scope of the authority of the attorney in fact to act on behalf of the principal and the protection afforded to health care providers who act on those instructions. Some states such as California have statutes permitting health care providers to *assume* that a DPOAHC is valid in the absence of knowledge to the contrary. Offering some support, the American Medical Association has ruled that it is appropriate for doctors to withdraw life-supporting, artificial feeding systems from hopelessly comatose patients.

Drawback. One drawback of the DPOAHC concerns the fact that it is so powerful. It can place reluctant family members in the difficult position of having to make critical life or death decisions, ones they may regrettably relive in their minds over and over, long after the crisis has ended. Nevertheless, the durable power of attorney for health care has become one of the most popular estate planning devices.

Living will. The DPOAHC has become widely accepted in the United States. Before then, most states only recognized some variation of the living will, which typically addresses just one of the two features of the DPOAHC. Typically the living will detail those health care interventions that the person does or does not wish to be subjected to in situations when he or she is no longer capable of making those decisions, but did not designate an agent to make medical decisions for the person signing the document.

Appendix 17B illustrates one example of a living will. The reader will notice that this particular one, reflecting the modern trend towards designating an agent for health care decisions, enables the signer to name another person, called a "proxy," to "act on my behalf" regarding these wishes. Living wills are recognized in the statutes of most states. Many attorneys in states where living wills are not yet officially recognized, nevertheless urge their clients to execute them, with the expectation that the courts will accept them if and when tested.

Disadvantages of living wills. When compared to the DPOAHC, living wills have at least five limitations. First, a traditional living will does not appoint a surrogate decision maker, which restricts its flexibility considerably, especially in view of the rapid advances in medical technology. Second, living wills are typically very brief, covering only a few possible outcomes, mostly in the area of life-sustaining treatment. No living will, no matter how detailed, can spell out all of the possible treatment decisions that may be needed. Third, most living will statutes apply only to terminal patients, not those who are just incurably ill, such as a person in a persistent vegetative state. Many states require that death be "imminent." Fourth, the language of living wills is usually quite vague, failing to define important terms, leaving the physician and the family to disagree over proper care. Finally, a number of states living will statutes provide that a physician is obligated to comply with the directives in a living will concerning withdrawal or withholding of life-sustaining procedures. In the event the physician chooses not to comply, he or she must transfer the patient to another physician.

With regard to the second and fourth limitations, more and more attorneys are drafting quite specific living wills (and DPOAHCs, for that matter). For example, the client may be asked to enter preferences in writing in a matrix-table depicting alternative medical scenarios and procedures. The *rows* of the matrix might list ten to fifteen medical *procedures*, such as invasive diagnostic tests; CPR; pain medication; artificial nutrition and hydration; mechanical breathing, and the like. The *columns* of the matrix might list alternative physical *scenarios*, such as coma or persistent vegetative state with no chance of regaining awareness; irreversible brain damage or disease; irreversible brain damage or disease combined with terminal illness; coma with small chance of recovery and greater chance of surviving with brain damage, etc. Then, for each cell in the matrix-table, the client would insert one of several letters signifying a desired action, such as U = uncertain; N = do not want procedure; T = yes, try procedure but have it stopped if no clear improvement is shown; and Y = yes, try procedure for as long as possible. The danger in documenting this detail is that the person may thoughtlessly and hastily fill in the blanks on a written instrument that may wind up being the only hard evidence available, thereby ruling out the possibility of an alternative choice which may reflect the careful contemplation of the person's sincere loved ones.

Miscellaneous factors. In some states, planners recommend that clients execute both a living will and a DPOAHC, particularly in states where DPOAHCs are not written to include the main characteristic of the living will. Finally, in their attempt at coordination, more and more states are adopting integrated statutes that deal with both types of advance directive.

Several states, including Virginia, recognize a variation on the living will called the *directive to physicians*, giving instructions with regard to the use of life-sustaining treatment. The directive to physicians has been largely rendered obsolete in most other states by the common acceptance of the DPOAHC.

Whatever documents are used, they should be updated periodically, for three reasons. First, state law may require it. Second, the person's wishes may have changed. And third, the planner should make sure the documents remain consistent with the rapidly changing law in this area.

This chapter has described miscellaneous lifetime estate planning techniques not covered earlier. Chapter 18 will examine tax planning techniques which can be employed on behalf of the person after the person's death.

QUESTIONS AND PROBLEMS

1. (*a*) Describe the attributes of an effective parental guardian, executor, and trustee. (*b*) Why are they different?

2. One of your friends asks you to describe the legal alternatives available to provide for her young son's financial care. Be sure to mention the advantages and disadvantages of each.

3. What factors will influence which beneficiaries a testator should choose to bear the burden of death taxes?

4. (*a*) What is a survival clause? (*b*) How does it overcome the consequences of a lapse?

5. Describe the family pot trust and the trade-off involved in determining the age of distribution to young adult beneficiaries.

6. Cassie's will simply says, "I leave all my securities to John, and everything else to Mary." If John predeceases Cassie, analyze the possible recipients of the securities, using the alternative assumptions made in the text about the contents of the will and the influence of state law. Apply the law of your state, if possible.

7. You are the creditor of a deadbeat who is a beneficiary under a trust containing a spendthrift clause similar to the one in Exhibit 3-2. What ability, if any, do you have at getting at the trust assets?

8. Kris and Pat, companions for many years, do not plan to ever marry. Neither have children. Kris owns property worth $1,500,000 and Pat owns property worth $300,000. Given that Kris dies in 2001 and Pat dies in 2011 (just over 10 years apart), show how the total estate tax owed depends upon their estate plan by working through each of the choices that follow. For each, the property value between the two deaths remains constant, being reduced only by the taxes paid at Kris's death.

A.   Simple wills, naming each other as contingent beneficiaries, leaving all property to the partner, if surviving.

B.   An AB Trust arrangement with the excess over the exclusion amount going outright to Pat (or Trust A, revocable by Pat) and Kris's estate taxes are charged solely to the B Trust.

C.   An AB Trust arrangement with the excess over the exclusion amount going outright to Pat (or Trust A, revocable by Pat) and Kris's estate taxes are shared proportionately between the share going to Trust B and the share going to Pat.

D.   An AsuperB arrangement whereby all of Kris's *property* is placed in Trust B (with Pat's property in Trust A) and it is charged with the taxes.

E.   In general, what difference would it make if Pat survived Kris by less than 10 years?

F.   How well can each of the plans listed above achieve both partner's desire to leave their property to their own relatives after the surviving partner dies?

G.   Would lifetime gifting reduce their total estate tax? Might it be inconsistent with their goals?

9. What legal alternatives does a person have in property planning for his or her own incapacity? Describe the advantages and disadvantages of each.

10. Your 86-year-old mentally competent client wishes to plan for her incapacity but refuses to immediately transfer her assets to anyone. Is planning impossible, or does this refusal merely create a particular problem?

11. Your friend says, "I just signed four estate planning documents at my estate planning attorney's office." Name and briefly describe the likely four.

12. An attorney jokingly tells a client: "Today you'll be signing two documents, one for wealth and one for health. One gives someone the power to steal from you, while the other gives someone the power to kill you." (a) What two documents is she talking about? (b) Is there any truth to her cynicism?

13. Explain several reasons why you might urge a person to consider additional estate planning after each of the following events?

a. marriage
b. birth or adoption of a child
c. divorce
d. remarriage
e. death, separation or divorce of any child
f. family estate amount becomes medium sized
g. retirement
h. death of spouse
i. death of a parent
j. changes in tax laws
k. a change in the value of the person's business
l. a change in the person's state of domicile

14. In view of your answers to the question immediately above, what do you think of mail-order type estate plans, or other marketing approaches for plans that render it difficult to revise the plans periodically?

ANSWERS TO THE QUESTIONS AND PROBLEMS

1. a. Attributes of a good parental guardian, executor, and trustee.

   Parental Guardian: (1) Integrity, maturity, physical stamina and experience needed to be a permanent parent; (2) strong concern for the minor's welfare, and (3) a stable personal situation.

   Executor: (1) Longevity; (2) skill in managing legal and financial affairs; (3) familiarity with the testator's estate and wishes; (4) integrity and loyalty.

   Trustee: Same as those for executor, except greater weight on skill in financial management.

   b. The attributes are different because of the differing responsibilities. Parental skills are most important for a personal guardian. On the other hand, property management skills are most important for an executor and trustee, with even greater significance for the trustee, because of the possible time span of the job.

2. Legal alternatives available for a minor's financial care include guardianship, trust, and custodianship.

   a. Guardianship: Advantage: Substantial court supervision
      Guardianship: Disadvantages: (1) Expensive; (2) inflexible; (3) public (4) limited duration.

   b. Trust: Advantages: (1) Private; (2) flexible; and, 3)potentially less expensive
      Trust: Disadvantage: Not court supervised

   c. Custodianship: Advantages: (1) Inexpensive and (2) private.
      Custodianship: Disadvantages: (1) Inflexible; (2) not court supervised; (3) limited duration; and (4) property limitations.

3. Factors in deciding who should bear the burden of death taxes include:

   a. How liquid is the bequest?
   b. How wealthy is the beneficiary?
   c. How much access to liquid assets does the beneficiary have?
   d. Is a large specific bequest being made?

4. a. A survival clause requires that the named beneficiary survive the testator to take a bequest. If not, the bequest is made to an alternate taker.
   b. A survival clause overcomes the consequences of lapsation by allowing the testator, rather than state law, to determine who is to be the alternate taker.

5. The family pot trust is a single trust originally for the benefit of two or more beneficiaries, at least one of whom is a minor. Corpus is typically not divided into separate shares for the beneficiaries until the youngest reaches a certain age, such as 21. Selecting that age involves a tradeoff between inequality and delay. The older the predetermined age, the more equitable will be the distribution, but the longer the older beneficiaries may have to wait for that distribution.

6. If we assume that Cassie's residence state has an antilapse statute similar to the one in the text, and if we assume that John is Cassie's relative, then John's surviving issue will receive the securities. Alternatively, if no antilapse statute applies, or if John is not a relative, then Mary, as residuary beneficiary, will receive the securities.

7. You will probably have to wait until the beneficiary actually receives the asset distributions before you can legally act to seize them, unless your state has a statutory exception permitting you to require the trustee to turn over trust assets directly to you, as would be the case in some states for revocable living trusts and divorce situations.

8. A. Simple will: Regardless of the plan, Kris's estate will incur an estate tax of $335,250 on a $1,500,000 taxable estate. With simple wills Pat will inherit $1,164,750, after the tax is paid. Pat's taxable estate will total $1,464,750, on which an estate tax of $194,843 will be paid. The net amount of $1,169,907 will presumably pass to Pat's relatives. The total combined estate tax will be $530,093.

   B. AB Trust plan, Trust B pays all taxes: Trust B receives $675,000, less the $335,250 estate tax, leaving $339,750 that will eventually go to the remaindermen chosen by Kris. Pat receives $825,000, free of tax. Pat's estate will total $1,125,000, which will generate a tax of $51,250. The net amount going to Pat's relatives will be $1,073,750. The total combined estate tax will be $386,500.

   C. AB Trust, taxes paid proportionately: Again, Trust B receives $675,000, but it pays only $150,863 of the taxes ($335,250 * $675,000/1,500,000) leaving $524,138 to eventually go to relatives of Kris. Pat will receive $875,000, less taxes of $184,388 ($335,250 * $825,000/$1,500,000) for a net of $640,613. Pat's estate will total $940,613, which will be less than the exclusion amount, hence no additional tax, and the entire estate will go to Pat's relatives. The total combined taxes will be just the $335,200 paid on Kris's estate.

   D. AsuperB Trust: This time Trust B receives all of Kris's estate net of the estate tax, i.e., $1,500,000 - $335,200 = $1,164,750. This will eventually go to the remaindermen selected by Kris. Pat's estate will be just $300,000, and no tax will be due. Again, the total combined tax will be just that paid when Kris died.

   E. If Pat survived Kris by less than ten years, Pat's estate could take the *credit for tax on prior transfers* (PTC), if it exceeds the exclusion amount. The credit would be based on the fact that some property bequeathed by Kris to Pat was previously taxed in Kris's estate. This would be true even if some of the property was held in a trust, so long as the trust gave Pat a live estate. The PTC value of the property "passing" to Pat would depend on how much passed out right and much was based upon a life estate in Trust B (or superB).

   F. *Simple will/joint tenancy*: If both Kris and Pat wish to ultimately leave their own property to their own relatives, simple wills and joint tenancy arrangements will not work since the one who lives longest controls the final distribution. Only the AsuperB plan completely accomplishes the goal. Although, one of the other trust plans might be acceptable, but only if they both considered their property as belonging to both of them, even though legally such was not the case.

G. Due to the unavailability of the marital deduction, any attempt to equalize estates would require use of the annual exclusion since there is no point in using up Kris's unified credit by making larger gifts. Thus, large outright *lifetime* gifts from Kris to Pat would not save much estate tax and would not be consistent with their objectives.

9. Alternative in property planning for incapacity:

   a. Conservatorship: Advantage: Substantial court supervision.
       Conservatorship: Disadvantages: (1) Relatively expensive; (2) inflexible; and (3) public.

   b. Trust: Advantages: (1) Private; (2) flexible; and (3) potentially less expensive.
       Trust: Disadvantage: Not court supervised

   c. Durable Power of Attorney for property: Advantages: (1) Private; (2) flexible; and (3) potentially less expensive.
       Durable Power Disadvantage: Not court supervised

   NOTE: The trust and the durable power of attorney for property need not be considered alternatives; they can both be used by the same person.

10. Planning is still possible for an aging mentally competent person who refuses to immediately transfer assets to anyone. She may execute a *"springing" durable power of attorney*, one that takes effect at her incapacity. She could also create a *living trust*, naming herself as trustee, with a successor trustee appointed when a private determination of incapacity is made by several physicians. The point is that planning for incapacity can and should begin when the person is still mentally competent.

11. -   *Living trust:* A trust taking effect during the lifetime of the trustor. Also called an inter vivos trust.

-   *Pour over will:* A will that distributes, at the testator's death, probate assets to a trust that had been created during the testator's lifetime.

-   *Durable power of attorney for property:* A durable power of attorney granting to the attorney-in-fact the power to make decisions concerning the property of the principal.

-   *Durable power of attorney for health care (DPOAHC):* A durable power of attorney granting to the attorney-in-fact the power to make medical decisions on behalf of the principal.

12. a.   She is talking about the durable power of attorney for property and either the durable power of attorney for health care or the living will.

b.   There is some truth to her cynicism. In a few cases, attorneys have reported that attorneys in fact, usually children, have "misappropriated" the principal's property, and others likely have ended the principal's life somewhat prematurely, against what they knew to be the principal's expressed wishes. Of course, these are exceptional cases, but people should be calmly apprized of these possibilities, particularly when the attorney-in-fact is someone other than a loving spouse.

13. a.   Marriage:
-to include new spouse in will/trust document
-to undertake marital deduction planning
-to change life insurance and pension beneficiary designations
-to acquire life and disability insurance

b.   Birth of a child:
-to prevent omitted child intestacy problems
-to provide for parental guardianship and trustee property management at death of surviving spouse
-to acquire more life and disability insurance
-to execute durable powers of attorney

c. Divorce:
-to ensure that the document will be recognized (in some states, divorce revokes an entire will, not just those provisions pertaining to the spouse)
-to remove ex-spouse's name from any and all beneficiary, or trustee, or attorney-in-fact designations

d. Remarriage:
-to include new spouse in documents
-to undertake marital deduction (QTIP) planning
-to provide for all of the person's children of all marriages
-to consider a premarital agreement

e. Death, separation or divorce of any child: to review all documents for names of all beneficiary, or trustee, or attorney-in-fact designations

f. Family estate becomes medium sized: to undertake gift and estate tax planning

g. Retirement:
-if moving to a different state, to write new will/trust documents that conform to laws of the new state
-to execute durable powers of attorney
-to drop life and disability insurance coverages
-to discuss nursing home plans with children

h. Death of spouse:
-to encourage the person not to make any drastic changes (e.g. sell home) for several months
-to revise will/trust
-to undertake post-mortem tax planning
-to remove spouse's name from all beneficiary, or trustee, or attorney-in-fact designations

    i.   Death of parent:
        -to revise will/trust, based on changed wealth due to bequests from parent
        -to revise other documents, deleting parent's name from planning

    j.   Changes in tax laws:
        -to revise all tax related documents, including wills, revocable trusts, durable powers, and property agreements.
        -to consider gifting in light of changed tax laws

    k.   A change in the value of the person's business:
        -to adopt a business buyout agreement
        -to consider revising the overall estate plan, in view of potential change in estate tax

    l.   A change in the person's state of residency: to consider revising all documents and planning strategies, in the light of changed local law

14. The answer, in two words: not much. Successful estate planning should involve an ongoing process of plan revision to reflect changed circumstances, in connection with both the individual and the laws.

17A: Florida Designation of Health Care Surrogate*

17B: Florida Living Will*

* Reprinted by permission of Choice in Dying, 1035 30th Street, NW, Washington, DC 20007. Telephone 1-800-989-9455. Choice in Dying strongly advises using documents specific to the state in which one lives.

APPENDIX 17A

INSTRUCTIONS	**FLORIDA DESIGNATION OF HEALTH CARE SURROGATE**

INSTRUCTIONS

PRINT YOUR NAME

Name:_____
    (Last)   *(First)*   *(Middle Initial)*

In the event that I have been determined to be incapacitated to provide informed consent for medical treatment and surgical and diagnostic procedures, I wish to designate as my surrogate for health care decisions:

PRINT THE NAME, HOME ADDRESS AND TELEPHONE NUMBER OF YOUR SURROGATE

Name:_____

Address: _____

_____ Zip Code: _____

Phone: _____

If my surrogate is unwilling or unable to perform his or her duties, I wish to designate as my alternate surrogate:

PRINT THE NAME, HOME ADDRESS AND TELEPHONE NUMBER OF YOUR ALTERNATE SURROGATE

Name: _____

Address: _____

_____ Zip Code: _____

Phone: _____

I fully understand that this designation will permit my designee to make health care decisions and to provide, withhold, or withdraw consent on my behalf; to apply for public benefits to defray the cost of health care; and to authorize my admission to or transfer from a health care facility.

ADD PERSONAL INSTRUCTIONS (IF ANY)

Additional instructions (optional):

© 1998
CHOICE IN DYING, INC.

SAMPLE

APPENDIX 17A *(concluded)*

I further affirm that this designation is not being made as a condition of treatment or admission to a health care facility. I will notify and send a copy of this document to the following persons other than my surrogate, so they may know who my surrogate is:

PRINT THE NAMES AND ADDRESSES OF THOSE WHO YOU WANT TO KEEP COPIES OF THIS DOCUMENT

Name: _____

Address: _____

Name: _____

Address: _____

SIGN AND DATE THE DOCUMENT

Signed: _____

Date: _____

WITNESSING PROCEDURE

TWO WITNESSES MUST SIGN AND PRINT THEIR ADDRESSES

Witness 1:

    Signed: _____

    Address: _____

Witness 2:

    Signed: _____

    Address: _____

Courtesy of **Choice In Dying, Inc.**   5/98
1035 30th Street, NW Washington, DC 20007 800-989-9455

© 1998
CHOICE IN DYING, INC.

APPENDIX 17B

FLORIDA LIVING WILL

Declaration made this _____ day of _____, 19_____.

I, _____, willfully and voluntarily make known my desire that my dying not be artificially prolonged under the circumstances set forth below, and I do hereby declare:

If at any time I have a terminal condition and if my attending or treating physician and another consulting physician have determined that there is no medical probability of my recovery from such condition, I direct that life-prolonging procedures be withheld or withdrawn when the application of such procedures would serve only to prolong artificially the process of dying, and that I be permitted to die naturally with only the administration of medication or the performance of any medical procedure deemed necessary to provide me with comfort care or to alleviate pain.

It is my intention that this declaration be honored by my family and physician as the final expression of my legal right to refuse medical or surgical treatment and to accept the consequences for such refusal.

In the event that I have been determined to be unable to provide express and informed consent regarding the withholding, withdrawal, or continuation of life-prolonging procedures, I wish to designate, as my surrogate to carry out the provisions of this declaration:

Name: _____

Address: _____

_____ Zip Code: _____

Phone: _____

APPENDIX 17B *(concluded)*

FLORIDA LIVING WILL — PAGE 2 OF 2

PRINT NAME, HOME ADDRESS AND TELEPHONE NUMBER OF YOUR ALTERNATE SURROGATE

I wish to designate the following person as my alternate surrogate, to carry out the provisions of this declaration should my surrogate be unwilling or unable to act on my behalf:

Name: _____

Address: _____

_____ Zip Code: _____

Phone: _____

ADD PERSONAL INSTRUCTIONS (IF ANY)

Additional instructions (optional):

I understand the full import of this declaration, and I am emotionally and mentally competent to make this declaration.

SIGN THE DOCUMENT

Signed: _____

WITNESSING PROCEDURE

Witness 1:

Signed: _____

Address: _____

TWO WITNESSES MUST SIGN AND PRINT THEIR ADDRESSES

Witness 2:

Signed: _____

Address: _____

© 1998
CHOICE IN DYING, INC.

Courtesy of **Choice In Dying, Inc.** 5/98 1035 30th Street, NW Washington, DC 20007 800-989-9455

ENDNOTES

1. California Probate Code §15642(b)(6)(B)

2. §2206.

3. §2207.

4. §2207A.

5. §2207B.

6. UPC §2-603.

7. *Pollock v. Phillips* 41 S.E. 2d 242 (W. Va., 1991).

8. In *Marsman v. Nasca* 573 N.E. 2d 1025 (Mass. App. 1991), the court exonerated an attorney-trustee's "abuse of discretion," where a trust clause exculpated the trustee from liability except for "willful neglect or fraud." For a contrary holding see, *First Alabama Bank of Huntsville v. Spraquins* 515 S. 2d 962 (Ala. 1987).

9. "How much sharper than a serpent's tooth it is to have a thankless child." *King Lear*, Act 1, Scene V.

10. For example, see California Probate Code §2590-95.

11. Rev. Rul. 8623004

12. Modified version of the sample form contained in Charles M. Hamann. "Durable Powers of Attorney," *Trusts and Estates*, February 1983, pp. 30-31.

13. *Estate of Casey v. Commissioner*, 948 F2d. 895 (1991). Also see LR 9231003.

14. *J. Ridenour Estate*, 46 TCM 1850 (1992).

15. California Civil Code §2480.5.

16. 42 USC §1396. The Omnibus Budget Reconciliation Act of 1993, besides increasing the period from thirty months, made several other restrictive changes, reflecting Congressional interest in discouraging spend down planning.

17. Wall Street Journal articles on December 3 and 4, 1992. Both on page A1.

18. 110 S.Ct. 2841 (1990)

19. *Lancet*, Sept. 11, 1993, p. 645.

CHAPTER 18

Postmortem Tax Planning

OVERVIEW

The estate planning process does not end at the client's death. Assets must still be marshaled, preserved, and distributed by the decedent's representatives, a group that includes executors, trustees, accountants, attorneys, and survivors. In the transmission process, tax law often enables these aides to recommend and make choices. This chapter focuses on the tax elections available to them as parties dealing in the decedent's property. The technical detail in this chapter is testimony to the claim that estate administration after the client's death can involve complex tax issues requiring the expert advice of an estate planning attorney, not one conducting a general law practice.

The chapter will begin with an overview of the principles of postmortem tax compliance, better known as the preparation of tax returns. Next, it will survey those planning devices primarily designed to reduce income taxes, including estate expense elections, choice of tax year, and distribution-planning strategies. Finally, the chapter will present those planning devices primarily designed to save death taxes, including the alternate valuation date, the use of disclaimers, and the decision to make the QTIP election.

TAX RETURNS AFTER DEATH

We already know that the death of an individual may trigger estate and inheritance taxes. But can the transfer of a decedent's property be done free of income tax? Will the death of an income-earning individual terminate the obligation to pay taxes on all income received thereafter? Of course, the answer to both questions is no, because income ordinarily subject to taxation will be received by survivors, estates, and trusts. If income ordinarily subject to taxation is being received, you can be sure that the Internal Revenue Code imposes a tax on that income in the year that a recipient receives it.

Since death can create or continue the obligation to pay transfer and income taxes, we must first study the nature of these tax obligations and their effects on the survivors. Several transfer tax and income tax returns will usually be filed after the client's death. This section will introduce principles of postmortem federal tax *compliance*, that is, the completion of federal tax returns and the payment of federal taxes on income and on property in connection with the death of a decedent.

Transfer Taxes

With regard to transfer taxes, the decedent's representatives may be required to file a state estate or inheritance tax return, and a Form 706, federal estate tax return, which is due within nine months after date of death. As mentioned in Chapter 6, a federal estate tax return must be filed for decedents dying with a total gross estate plus adjusted taxable gifts equaling or exceeding the exclusion amount for the year of death (e.g., equal to, or over, $850,000 in 2004). For example, the estate of a decedent who dies in the year 2004, having a gross estate of $775,000 and adjusted taxable gifts of $100,000 must file a return because their sum exceeds the exclusion amount by $25,000. Filing is required even though no estate tax will be due, as in the case where the entire estate is left to a surviving spouse.

Income Taxes

For many estates, the personal representatives will be required to at least two sets of state and federal income tax returns. First, the *decedent's final income tax return* will be reported on Federal Form 1040 and on the comparable state income tax form (unless the state of domicile was one of the few that has no state income tax). These returns will cover all income for the last tax year up to, and including, the date of death. Second, if the decedent leaves a probate estate or a living trust, an *estate fiduciary income tax return*, Form 1041 and its state counterpart, will be filed for each tax year of the estate's existence. The fiduciary return for the first year will report all income starting with the day after the decedent's date of death to the end of the first tax year. When the estate is terminated, usually by final distribution, the last estate income tax return will be filed for a "short" year, from the beginning of the tax year to the date of distribution. After the estate terminates, the beneficiaries will report the income from distributed estate property on their own tax returns.

The following example summarizes these federal income tax rules and assumes that all taxpayers report taxes on a *calendar year* basis; that is, their tax year begins January 1 and ends December 31. Actually, an estate need not use a calendar year. Planning with the use of a fiscal rather than calendar year will be discussed later in the chapter.

> EXAMPLE 18 - 1. Farley, a widower, died on May 12, 2000. In his will, Farley left 100 shares of XYZ stock outright to his son Jordan, and the residue of his estate in trust for the benefit of his granddaughter Sheila. The date of final estate distribution to Jordan and to the trust was February 25, 2002. The following post-death tax returns were filed. All income earned by the decedent from January 1 through May 12, 2000, was reported by the executor on the decedent's final income tax return, Form 1040. All income earned by the estate between May 13 and December 31, 2000, was reported by the executor on the first estate income tax return, Form 1041. The executor filed a second Form 1041 return for all estate income for the entire year 2001, and a third for income earned during the period from January 1 to February 25, 2002. Jordan reported on his Form 1040 all income received on the stock after February 25, 2002. Trust property income, or DNI, earned after that date will either be reported by the trust on Form 1041 or by Sheila on her Form 1040, to the extent the income is actually distributed to her.

All capital gains income on trust property will be reported by the trust except in the trust's last year, when these gains will be "carried out" and reported by the beneficiaries. All non-grantor trusts must use a calendar tax year.

A *joint return* may be filed for a decedent and the surviving spouse for the year of death, covering income of the decedent to the date of death and income of the spouse for the entire year.[1] Alternatively, returns may be filed for each spouse separately. In most situations, filing jointly will save total taxes in the same way it does when both spouses are alive. The greater the difference between the two spousal incomes, the greater the tax usually saved by filing jointly. The surviving spouse will also be permitted to enjoy the lower rates applicable to joint returns for *two years after the decedent's death*, provided that he or she (*a*) has not remarried and (*b*) maintains a home for one or more dependent children.[2]

Next, we turn to postmortem income tax planning ideas.

PLANNING DEVICES TO SAVE INCOME TAXES

Some postmortem planning strategies are primarily undertaken to reduce the income tax bite. They include various expense elections, selection of probate estate tax year, and distribution planning. Before examining these techniques, let us survey three tax principles on which most of them will be based.

First, income tax is reduced when taxable income can be spread among taxpaying entities. Proper pre-death planning can result in the creation of *additional taxpaying entities* after the client's death. These tax entities can include the estate, several trusts (with at least one trust for each beneficiary), and the beneficiaries themselves. After death, proper timing of distributions among these entities can often save significant tax dollars, as we shall see.

A second tax principle on which postmortem income tax planning is based is the notion of the *conduit*. The conduit principle prevents double taxation of estate or trust income. It is derived from the concept of distributable net income, or DNI, which is roughly equal to the estate or trust's fiduciary accounting income. DNI constitutes the maximum amount of income taxable to the beneficiaries, as well as the maximum amount deductible by the estate or trust. The amount taxable to an estate or trust roughly equals its total income, including capital gains and losses, reduced by the distribution deduction, which roughly equals the lesser of the amount distributed or its DNI. Thus, a trust or estate that distributes all of its income will be taxed only on its capital gains. Consequently, under the conduit principle, DNI earned by an estate or trust which is distributed to the beneficiaries in the year earned will be taxed to the beneficiaries and not to the estate or trust, which simply acts as a conduit for delivering income from the source to the beneficiaries. Conversely, any DNI retained by the estate or trust will not be offset by a distribution deduction, which will make that DNI taxable to the trust or estate rather than to the beneficiaries.

A third tax principle on which postmortem income tax planning is based is that in the year in which an estate or trust makes its final distribution, all income, including capital gains, will be *carried out* to and *taxed* to the beneficiaries. Thus in its *termination year,* a trust or estate will have no taxable income.

These tax principles represent only the briefest summary of the principles of income taxation of estates and trusts detailed in Chapter 8. The reader is strongly urged to review that more comprehensive section before continuing.

Expense Elections Available to the Executor

During administration, the executor is able to make several informal elections with regard to estate expenses. We will refer to the executor's ability to make elections because the executor is the person having that legal authority. Of course, most executors rely on their attorney or accountant to apprize them of the tax alternatives. These elections include the medical expense election, the administration expense and losses election, and the election to waive the executor's commission. They are covered next.

Medical expense election. Any of the decedent's unreimbursed medical expenses which are unpaid at death may be deducted either on the decedent's final income tax return or on the federal estate tax return, but not on both.[3] The choice of where to deduct unpaid medical expenses will depend on which alternative will yield the greater tax savings. The amount of tax saved is a function of the marginal tax rates which are influenced by the size of the estate tax base and the amount of the decedent's income.

Smaller estates may be unable to benefit from a deduction on either return. If deducted on the *income tax return*, only the excess of the medical expense amount over 7.5% of adjusted gross income is deductible. Any nondeductible amount may not be deducted on the estate tax return. With regard to the *estate tax return*, no estate tax may be due for smaller estates, either because no estate tax return need be filed or because other deductions, particularly the marital deduction, may reduce the taxable estate to zero.

Administration expense and losses election. Expenses in administering the decedent's estate, including executor's commission, attorney's fees, and casualty losses, are deductible either on the federal estate tax return or on the estate income tax return, or partly on each.[4] However, double deductions are not allowed.

Again, the choice of where to deduct these items will usually turn on which return will produce the greater tax savings. And again, smaller estates may be unable to enjoy a deduction on either return. Casualty losses are deductible against income only to the extent that they exceed 10% of adjusted gross income. And there may be no estate tax to save in the case of a small estate, or any size estate for that matter, if the estate simply passes to the surviving spouse. Larger estates not incorporating a 100% marital deduction often will be able to choose because they can save taxes on either return. Generally, f an amount is deductible on another return, it is imprudent to deduct it on any estate tax return that can already shelter all taxable estate property with the unified credit or with the marital deduction.

Election to waive executor's commission. The executor's commission, as a deductible administration expense, is taxable as income to the executor. However, the executor may elect to waive (i.e., refuse) that commission. Waiver of the commission may be worthwhile if the executor is a residuary beneficiary of the estate and if his or her personal marginal income tax rate exceeds the marginal tax rate for both the estate tax and the estate income tax. If the executor is not a residuary beneficiary of the estate, a waiver of the commission will mean a complete forfeit of that amount. Thus, the non-residuary executor will usually prefer to receive the commission, regardless of the tax cost.

EXAMPLE 18 - 2. An estate has been left entirely to the decedent's *daughter*, who is the executor. The executor's commission will be $10,000. The estate's marginal estate tax rate is 41% and its marginal income tax rate is 28%. The daughter's marginal income tax rate is 31%. *Not waiving* the commission will lower the estate tax by $4,100 and raise daughter's income tax by $3,100, for a net tax saving of $1,000.

EXAMPLE 18 - 3. Facts similar to the last example, except that the decedent left his entire estate to his *spouse*, who is executor. Due to the unlimited marital deduction, the effective marginal estate tax rate is 0%. Regarding income tax rates, assuming that the spouse's effective marginal rate is 31%, and the estate's marginal rate is 28%, *waiving* the commission will raise the estate income tax by $2,800 and lower the spouse's income tax by $3,100, for a net tax saving of $300.

EXAMPLE 18 - 4. Facts similar to the prior example, except that the entire estate has been left outright *to the decedent's children* by a former marriage. Waiving the executor's commission would mean totally forfeiting the receipt of that amount. As executor, the spouse, not wishing to forfeit all cash flow from the estate, elects take the commission. Instead of receiving nothing, the spouse will receive $6,900, after tax, from the estate.

Selection of Estate Taxable Year

The executor of a probate estate has considerable flexibility in choosing the estate's income tax year. Although all income tax years except the first and the last must be 12 months long, the executor can choose the estate's tax year to end on the last day of any month. If it ends on December 31, the estate is said to be on a *calendar year* with the first tax year running from date of death to December 31. All other tax years will then run from January 1 to December 31, except for the year of final distribution of the estate assets, which will run for a "short year" from January 1 to date of distribution. Alternatively, if the estate's elected tax year ends on the last day of any month other than December, it is said to be on a *fiscal year*.

Whether an estate is on a calendar year or fiscal year, two basic income tax benefits are available to it. First, the estate is a separate taxpaying entity, capable of *splitting income* with the other tax entities involved in the estate distribution process. By increasing tax rates and by radically compressing bracket amounts for estates, tax reform since 1986 has reduced the tax saving benefit of splitting income.

Second, tax saving can be realized in the first and last tax years of an estate's life, since both years are usually shorter than 12 months. The first tax year is shorter because date of death does not usually coincide with the last day of the tax year. The last tax year is shorter than 12 months because the date of final distribution seldom coincides with the last day of the tax year. A *short tax year* produces income tax savings because proportionately less income is ordinarily taxed in those years.

In contrast to the tax benefits available to all estates, some benefits are available only to estates having a carefully selected fiscal year. Regardless of when income is actually distributed to a beneficiary, it will be treated for tax purposes as though it was distributed on the last day of the estate's tax year. In each of the next two examples, assume that the decedent died on March 10, 2000.

> EXAMPLE 18 - 5. The estate of a decedent is planning the distribution of income to its beneficiary, the surviving spouse. It elects a fiscal year ending January 31. If the estate distributes income earned on March 15, 2001, to the spouse during the month of November, 2001, it will be treated as though she received it on January 31, 2002, and the spouse will not have to report the income until April 15, 2003, more than two full years after the income was initially received by the estate.

If the executor of an estate expects an unusually large income receipt shortly after the period of administration begins, he or she may wish to elect a year end which would give it a rather short first year, so that other taxable income received later will be taxed during the following year rather than lumped with the large receipt and taxed at a higher rate.

> EXAMPLE 18 - 6. Decedent Malley was an accountant who died on May 19 owning, among other things, account receivables amounting to $50,000. The estate elects a fiscal year ending July 31 to include most of this income in the first tax year, while causing most other income to be taxed in the second and later years.

On the other hand, a relatively long first tax year would be desirable if a large deduction is expected within 6 to 12 months from the date of death.

> EXAMPLE 18 - 7. Combined with a large amount of early income, as in example 18 - 8, the estate expects to make a large distribution to the beneficiaries in April of the following year. The estate instead elects a fiscal year closing on April 30, so that the deduction can be used to reduce estate taxable income.

Distribution Planning

Although federal tax reform since 1986 reduced income tax rates substantially for all tax entities, an estate or trust may be able to save some income tax for its beneficiaries by properly planning the amount and timing of beneficiary distributions. Much of distribution planning hinges on the existence of differentials in marginal tax rates, and thus one of the planner's tasks is to compare the tax rates of the various entities and allocate taxable income to those in lower brackets. In this section, we will consider situations where the beneficiaries are, alternatively, in a higher bracket and in a lower bracket in comparison with the distributing estate or trust. This section will also examine the income tax advantage of prolonging the estate's life.

Estate or trust in lower bracket than beneficiaries. When the estate or trust is in a lower income tax bracket than its beneficiaries, consideration should be given to distribution arrangements that will generate a greater taxable income to itself and a correspondingly lesser taxable income to its beneficiaries.

Accumulation of income. The most common device used accumulates income by reducing and delaying distributions of DNI. However, with the very compressed marginal rates for estates and trusts, the amount of tax savings is minimal.

> EXAMPLE 18 - 8. Jonathan died earlier this year, leaving his entire estate to his wife, Kathleen. The estate has earned some income this year but elects *not to distribute* it to Kathleen until next year. This year, Kathleen, who has earned considerable income herself, is also recipient of a large lump-sum pension distribution from Jonathan's employer. Consequently, she is in the 31% marginal tax bracket. The estate, on the other hand, is subject to a 15% marginal tax rate, partly because the executor has elected a fiscal year that will give the estate a very short first taxable year.

Realization of a gain. Another way to benefit from the estate or trust having a lower tax rate than the beneficiaries is through the realization of a gain. If an estate asset has appreciated after death and is expected to be sold soon after its receipt by the designated beneficiary, the executor of a lower-bracket estate should give consideration to *selling the asset* prior to distribution so that the estate can recognize the gain. The after-tax proceeds can be distributed to the beneficiary tax free, assuming all DNI has already been distributed. However, to be taxed to the estate, the sale will have to be made before its last taxable year so that the gain is not automatically "carried out" to the beneficiary.

Despite having a lower marginal tax rate, the executor of an estate may wish to distribute rather than sell the asset if the beneficiary has a *realized loss* that is presently unusable for lack of any offsetting gains. The beneficiary, who could sell the asset, then would not have to carry over an unused loss to future years.

Estate or trust in higher marginal tax bracket than beneficiaries. In cases where an estate or trust is subject to a higher marginal income tax rate than one or more of its beneficiaries, the executor or trustee may prefer to *distribute income* to them in the year the income is received, so that it is taxed at the beneficiaries lower rate. In addition, when the estate or trust's tax year overlaps those of the beneficiaries, the executor or trustee can time the distribution so that it is made in one of two years in which the beneficiaries' tax rate is lower.

> EXAMPLE 18 - 9. In the month of November Arleen, the sole beneficiary of her dad's estate, lost her job as a law firm associate where she had been making pretty good money. She was contemplating either opening her own office or going to business school for a year. To help her out, the executor elected a fiscal year end of February 28 and distributed $50,000 (out of income) to her in early December. It was to help Arleen get through the Holidays. Since the estate's fiscal year ends February 28, the distribution is treated as having been made on that date, hence Arleen will report the income in a year in which she expects to be in a low tax bracket, even though she received it in a year in which she was in a high tax bracket.

Unduly prolonging the estate life. By now, the reader is aware of several potential income tax advantages to having a probate estate remain open. This will encourage some executors to delay closing their estates. Since termination of an estate by final distribution cuts off the tax benefits available to this separate taxpayer, tax planning would suggest undertaking this ploy by delaying the estate's date of final distribution. However, the IRS has authority to treat an estate as *terminated* for tax purposes if it concludes that the estate's life had been "unduly" prolonged.[5]

How long can an estate usually be kept open without generating IRS disapproval? Some authorities believe that a reasonable life is about 3 to 4 years for an ordinary estate, and as long as 15 years for an estate which elects to defer payment of taxes under Section 6166. However, the income tax benefit from prolonging an estate's life has been significantly curtailed in recent years due to tax reform's compression of income tax rates.

PLANNING DEVICES TO SAVE DEATH TAXES

We turn now to an examination of several postmortem tax planning strategies which have their greatest impact on death taxes. They include the alternate valuation date election, disclaimers, the QTIP election, and several other miscellaneous techniques discussed briefly in earlier chapters.

Alternate Valuation Date Election

The size of the estate tax for an estate is a direct function of the value of the interests includible in the gross estate. An intelligent executor or estate adviser will try to keep valuation as low as possible. Often, conflicts with the IRS arise regarding the correct valuation of particular estate assets and deductions. While such conflicts make the entire subject of estate valuation seem quite subjective, there is one specific rule in this field that offers some objective certainty. The Code allows the executor the option to value estate assets and deductions at one of two different points in time.

Under Section 2032, the value of the assets included in the gross estate (and corresponding liabilities) may be determined as of the date of death, *or* they may be determined as of the alternate valuation date (AVD), which is *six months after the date of death*. This section was enacted after the Great Depression to limit the adverse tax and liquidity effects that radical changes in market values could have on an estate. For example, consider a hypothetical decedent who died in mid- to late 1929 owning a considerable amount of stock, which had to be included in the gross estate at high, pre-crash date-of-death values. By the time the taxes were due, the value of the estate might be less than the taxes owed.

Under AVD rules, the executor may not pick and choose which assets to value at which of the two dates. If the election is made, *all* assets (and deductions) must be valued at the AVD. However, any assets sold or distributed after death and before the AVD must be valued as of that sale or distribution date.

Prior to 1984, the AVD election was permitted in situations where it *increased* the gross estate, thereby resulting in greater step-up in basis for assets owned at death. For income tax purposes, this strategy was attractive for estates completely sheltered by the unified credit and/or marital deduction. §2032(c) now permits the AVD election only if it reduces both the value of the gross estate and the estate tax (and GSTT, if any).

Of course making the AVD election has income tax ramifications, with a smaller step-up (or greater step-down), a lower estate tax value will save estate tax but it might also result in additional income taxes when assets are sold. Since the minimum marginal estate tax rate is 37% while, for most sales the maximum capital gains tax rate is 20%, the AVD election should lower net taxes by at least 17 cents for every dollar of reduced valuation. In addition, if the inherited asset is not sold, the AVD advantage increases to at least 37 cents per dollar. Finally, even if the heir chooses to sell the asset, a time value of money savings will result to the extent that the income tax is paid later than the estate tax.

Effective Disclaimers

A disclaimer is an unqualified refusal to accept a gift. We have already studied disclaimers in two earlier chapters. First, in Chapter 7, covering the federal gift tax, we examined the transfer tax aspects of disclaimers, including the requirements for a valid disclaimer. Second, in Chapter 12, surveying marital deduction and bypass planning, we saw how a disclaimer provision could be included in a bypass arrangement to add postmortem flexibility to the client's estate plan. That discussion also mentioned several disadvantages of the use of disclaimers. The purpose of the present discussion is to add additional detail to disclaimer planning, in the context of general postmortem planning.

Because of the requirement that the disclaiming donor cannot have accepted any interest in the benefits, the client's survivors must be told as soon as possible not to accept the decedent's property or income if a disclaimer is anticipated. The following material describes three general situations where disclaimers can be effectively utilized. They include spousal disclaimers to reduce the marital deduction, disclaimers by a nonspouse to increase the size of the marital deduction, and disclaimers to correct defective or inefficient dispositive documents.

Spousal disclaimer to reduce the marital deduction. We have seen how a spousal disclaimer of a marital deduction bequest can add postmortem flexibility by enabling the surviving spouse to choose the amount of the marital bequest to disclaim to the bypass share, thereby self-determining the amount of estate tax to defer to the second death. That section was described as Option 4, "100% marital deduction with disclaimer into bypass," in which the surviving spouse was bequeathed the entire amount of the decedent spouse's estate, subject to S2's ability to disclaim all or part of it in the event that a bypass eventually became desirable.

The marital deduction disclaimer can be used for any size estate but is probably most needed for certain rapidly appreciating *smaller estates*. For example, a plan for an estate that is currently too small to justify the use of a bypass could include a disclaimer provision, available in the event that the estate grew large enough to warrant a bypass distribution.

On the other hand, the disclaimer can also work well in *larger estates* in which S1 has under-utilized the million dollar GSTT exemption. The surviving spouse, at S1's death, may be able to disclaim assets being received outright *into* a GSTT-exempt credit shelter bypass trust or QTIP trust.

Factors that may help the surviving spouse decide whether and how much to disclaim include S2's needs and his or her income tax bracket. First, the greater S2's perceived *need* for S1's assets to live comfortably, the less S2 will probably be willing to disclaim. This, in turn, will depend on the size of S2's estate. Of course, by disclaiming, S2 would not ordinarily be relinquishing all interests in the property, since the typical recipient bypass or QTIP trust provides for some invasion powers and for most or all income to be paid to S2. However, many S2s are still likely to react emotionally that, by disclaiming, they are in reality making a complete relinquishment.

Second, S2's willingness to disclaim will also depend on his or her marginal *income tax rate*. If S2's rate is high, a disclaimer is desirable because it has the effect of redirecting taxable income to other beneficiaries.

For further discussion of the benefits and drawbacks of providing for a spousal disclaimer into a bypass, see Chapter 12.

Disclaimer by a nonspouse to increase the marital deduction. A disclaimer can be used to raise a marital deduction that is subsequently found to be inadequate. For example, a client may have died with an estate plan that neither included a bypass nor took full use of the unlimited marital deduction. This can occur when a person dies intestate or dies owning a considerable amount of property in *joint tenancy* with someone other than a spouse. The nonspouse beneficiary may be encouraged to disclaim the interest so that it may qualify for the marital deduction by passing to the surviving spouse. However, problems in implementation may arise. First, only a *donee* of property held in joint tenancy may disclaim.[6] Thus, such a disclaimer will work only if the decedent was the original donor of the property. Second, courts may be unwilling to allow the guardian of a minor child (or unborn child) to disclaim rights to property, reasoning that full relinquishment of property is not in the child's best interest. However, since a disclaimer cannot be made by a person until he or she reaches age 21, a disclaimer that is delayed until the disclaimant reaches majority might be effective.

Third, until recently, the IRS had been taking the position that the disclaimer had to be made within nine months of the date the joint tenancy was *created*, rather than the date of death. After losing in the courts, the Service acquiesced with regard to joint tenancies where state law gives the joint tenant the right to sever the joint tenancy or cause the property to be partitioned.[7] In other words, disclaimers of joint interests may not be valid in some states. For example, a qualified disclaimer is not permitted for *tenancy by the entirety property* because it cannot be partitioned by one spouse without the permission of the other.[8]

Disclaimers to correct defective and inefficient dispositive documents. Occasionally, wills and trusts are drafted erroneously. One always hopes that these mistakes will be discovered during the client's lifetime. If not, they can still often be corrected by disclaimer. For example, a disclaimer may also be used to refuse an undesirable bequest of a general power of appointment.

> EXAMPLE 18 - 10. Barbara died seven months ago leaving a will that provides for a bypass trust for the benefit of her husband, Jake. The will gives Jake the right to invade the trust for reasons of "health or happiness." Since courts have consistently held that the term *happiness* does not constitute an ascertainable standard, Jake will be deemed to be the holder of a general power of appointment over the entire trust corpus, which will be includible in Jake's gross estate at his later death. Jake may be able to prevent this unfortunate result by properly disclaiming his power over the corpus.

A disclaimer can also be used to overcome an inefficient disposition, thereby increasing the size of a charitable contribution.

> EXAMPLE 18 - 11. Sally, a widow, was 90 years old when she died six months ago. She left one surviving relative, her son Abbott, who is 73 and in failing health. Sally's will, paraphrased somewhat, reads, "All to Abbott, but if he does not survive me by 30 days, then all to the Girl Scouts of America." Abbott, who should be able to live for 30 days but is not likely to live more than six months, has no issue and

would not mind leaving all of the property inherited from his mother to the Girl Scouts. To avoid taxation of the property in Sally's estate, Abbott could disclaim all interest in Sally's bequest. Consequently, the property would pass to the Girl Scouts without being subject to taxation in Sally's estate.

A disclaimer may be made with respect to an undivided *portion* of an interest, which the IRS defines as a fraction or percentage of each and every substantial interest owned by the disclaimant extending over the entire term of the disclaimant's interest.[9]

EXAMPLE 18 - 12. Lynn survived her husband, who bequeathed her 100 shares of stock outright and a life estate in trust property producing $10,000 in annual income. Lynn may disclaim fewer than 100 shares of the stock, and she may disclaim a life estate in less than $10,000 annually of the trust property. But she may not disclaim only a remainder interest in the stock, or only a term for years portion of her life estate, such as for the first five years of the income.

These examples are merely illustrative of the many situations where post-mortem disclaimers can be used to alter estate dispositions to obtain more desirable results.[10] Disclaimers are generally considered to be an extremely powerful estate planning tool. It should be noted that since the stakes can be quite high in this technical area of the law, the client is encouraged to seek competent counsel prior to attempting to make a qualified disclaimer.

QTIP Election Planning

Overview. As mentioned in Chapter 6, property normally can qualify for the marital deduction only if it "passes" to the spouse. In other words, the spouse cannot ordinarily receive an interest that might terminate; the interest cannot be terminable. Over the years, however, the Code has carved out several exceptions to this rule. Up to 1982, the most commonly used marital trust designed to take advantage of an exception was the power of appointment trust, i.e., the one giving the spouse a life estate in the income and a general power of appointment over the corpus.[11] Since then, the QTIP trust, based on the QTIP election exception, has become far more popular. It is found in §2056(b)(7) and provides that property subject to a terminable interest can qualify for the marital deduction if it meets the following two requirements for "qualified terminable interest property:"

1. The surviving spouse must be entitled to receive all income from the property for life, payable at least annually.
2. No person may have the power to appoint the property to anyone other than the surviving spouse.

Why might a person wish to bequeath only a terminable interest to his or her spouse? Why might a person prefer not to give marital deduction property to the spouse outright, or in trust with the spouse receiving a general power of appointment over the property? Why restrict a spouse's ability to control disposition of the property? There are several possible reasons, including the desire to protect the estate from the consequences of S2's immaturity or senility and the goal of protecting assets from the surviving spouse's creditors. But perhaps the most common reason is a desire by S1 to absolutely *guarantee the ultimate disposition* to an intended remainder beneficiary. The typical S1 choosing a QTIP arrangement has children of a former marriage and wishes to provide for the surviving spouse's income needs during lifetime, yet still absolutely ensure that his or her own children will eventually receive the property after the surviving spouse's death. Only a QTIP-type arrangement will do all this and still qualify the property for the marital deduction.

Some planners also recommend the QTIP plan for clients still married to their first spouse to eliminate the risk that their surviving spouse might remarry and leave substantial property to the new spouse rather than the children. Others disagree, pointing out that most S2's either do not remarry or act prudently when they do.

From the above, it should be clear that a QTIP marital trust inherently conflicts with the goal of maximum *dispositive* flexibility through the use of surrogate decision makers. More specifically, this approach is in direct contrast with the less popular power of appointment trust, discussed in Chapter 11, that grants to S2 a general power of appointment over the trust property. A QTIP plan, on the other hand, usually allows no discretionary distributions by S2 to others, relying instead on the "dead hand" control and directives of the immutable S1 will or trust instrument. Commentators strongly recommend that the QTIP trusts of more trusting clients grant the surviving spouse a limited power of appointment to distribute, at death, principal to permissible appointees named in the instrument. This power will add additional flexibility, for example, by allowing a surrogate decision maker to take greater advantage of GSTT exemptions under changing circumstances. Thus, while the effect of federal legislation was once to foster dispositive flexibility by requiring, as a condition for qualifying for the marital deduction, that the surviving spouse be granted a general power of appointment, its effect now is to discourage it by allowing a marital deduction for property over which the surviving spouse may have little or no control. However, in contrast to dispositive inflexibility, the QTIP plan can offer some additional *estate tax planning* flexibility by means of the actual QTIP election. This will be shown in the next three examples, presented shortly.

Making the election. "QTIP'able" property need not be included in the S1 marital deduction; to include it, an election must be made at S1's death.

Uniqueness of QTIP election. In contrast with the decision as to who will ultimately *receive* the property outright, the final decision whether to make that election to *include* QTIP property in the S1 marital deduction will not be up to the S1-transferor. And in contrast with the spousal disclaimer, that decision will not be up to S2. Instead, *S1's executor* will be required to make the choice on S1's estate tax return.

Deferral versus equalization revisited. If the election is made, the QTIP property can qualify for the S1 marital deduction, and S1's taxable estate and estate tax will be reduced. However, at S2's death, the S2 date of-death value of the qualifying property *must* be taxed as though it were includible in S2's gross estate.[12] The estate of S2 will receive reimbursement from the QTIP trust for the tax incurred by it.[13]

Thus, in considering the QTIP election, the S1 executor must choose one of the following two tax consequences: (1) making the election will defer the estate tax by reducing the S1 taxable estate and increasing the S2 taxable estate; or, alternatively, (2) not making the election will accelerate the estate tax by producing a larger S1 taxable estate, but can result in a smaller S2 taxable estate, via bypass. The choice whether or not to make the election essentially boils down to a tax issue: whether to *defer or to equalize spousal* estate tax. The reader is directed back to Chapter 12 for an extended discussion of the factors influencing this decision.

As you study and review the present section, you might keep in mind that the S1 executor's QTIP election has nothing to do with determining who will receive the property; the trust terms decide that and, except for the possibility of disclaimer by a beneficiary, it is no longer subject to change by anyone.

EXAMPLE 18 - 13. Kenneth died three months ago. He is survived by his ex-wife, his second wife (S2), and D, E, and F, three adult children of the first marriage. There are no children from the second marriage. At his death, Kenneth owned $2 million in property. S2 owns $1 million in property, and she intends to leave it to X and Y, the children of *her* first marriage. Kenneth's will creates two trusts, trust B and trust A. Trust B is a bypass trust and will receive an amount equal to the exemption equivalent of the unified credit. Trust A will receive the residue of Kenneth's estate. The trustees of both trusts are required to pay all income monthly to S2 for her life. At S2's death, the amount of each corpus will pass outright in equal shares to Kenneth's three children. S2 is given a power to invade the corpus of trust B, subject to an ascertainable standard. S2 is given no power over the corpus of trust A. The property in trust A, which includes the decedent's residence, meets the requirements for qualified terminable interest property. As executor of Kenneth's estate, S2 *decides to elect* to include the value of this property in the S1 marital deduction. By so electing, S2 has made it certain that this QTIP property will be included in her gross estate at her death. During his lifetime, Kenneth created a plan which both ensures that the children of his first marriage will eventually receive all of his property, and preserves the marital deduction for his estate. Trust A is called the QTIP trust.

EXAMPLE 18 - 14. Modifying the facts in the preceding example a bit, assume that S2, as executor of the S1 estate, *does not elect* to include the A trust property in the S1 marital deduction. The property will still pass to the children upon S2's death, but will neither be deductible from S1's gross estate nor be includible in S2's gross estate. By not electing, S2 has chosen not to defer the estate tax. *Both trusts*, not just the B trust, will *bypass* S2's estate. Both are called bypass trusts.

EXAMPLE 18 - 15. Again modifying the facts in Example 18- 15 a bit, assume that S2, as executor of Kenneth's estate, makes a QTIP election as to only five fourteenths, or $500,000 of the trust A property. A partial bypass of the A trust property will result.

Tax law permits *partial QTIP elections* with regard to fractional asset shares.

EXAMPLE 18 - 16. In all three examples above, Kenneth's three children, as named remainder beneficiaries, will be certain to receive the entire corpus of each trust at S2's death. Making or not making the QTIP election will not alter this result. However, it can influence the size of each remainder distribution to the extent that it influences the size of the total estate tax.

Disclaimers and QTIP elections can partially raise the marital deduction for an S2 in spite of the forced application of the pre-1982 marital deduction rules for certain wills and trusts executed before September 12, 1981.

Thus, as an alternative to the power of appointment marital trust described in Chapter 12, the QTIP election, while offering less dispositive flexibility to S2, does give S2 some greater flexibility in marital deduction and bypass planning, while enabling S1 to retain total dispositive control over the property.

QTIP election versus disclaimer. The astute reader will observe that the disclaimer and the QTIP election are *both* strategies that can enable a surrogate decision maker to decide on behalf of the deceased client whether or not to defer the estate tax. One advantage of the QTIP alternative over the disclaimer is the ability to delay the decision an additional six months. While a disclaimer must usually be made within 9 months after date of death, a QTIP election is made on the federal estate tax return which, when including a 6-month extension to file, allows up to 15 months after the date of death before a decision must be made.

Perhaps the most fundamental difference between the disclaimer and the QTIP arrangement concerns the amount of control S2 is given over the assets involved. Often, it is the single deciding factor in making the choice. Thus, if the client wishes the spouse to have complete control, an outright transfer anticipating the possibility of a disclaimer will be preferred. If, on the other hand, minimal S2 control is desired, a transfer to a QTIP trust will be the better choice.

Additional Postmortem Tax-Saving Devices

Three other postmortem tax elections often available to the estates of business owners include the §6166 election to pay the estate tax in installments, the §303 redemption of stock, and the §2032A special-use valuation election. These elections were covered in some detail earlier in the text and are mentioned here just as a reminder that the elections are not made until after the business owner dies.

This chapter has focused on postmortem planning techniques designed to reduce income and death taxes. They have been the subject of this last chapter because they represent, conceptually, the final phase of planning undertaken on behalf of an individual.

QUESTIONS AND PROBLEMS

1. List the federal tax returns that may have to be filed during a period of administration of a decedent's property.

2. Maxie, a widower, died recently, leaving his $2 million gross estate to his brother Morey. Maxie spent the last six months in a hospital, paying $50,000 of the $80,000 hospital bill before he died. Marginal tax rates for the taxpaying entities are as follows: Maxie's final Form 1040, 31%; the Form 1041, 28%; the Form 706, 41%. Determine much tax Maxie's estate will save if the allowable expense is deducted, alternatively, on: (a) Form 706; (b) Form 1040; and (c) Form 1041.

3. Moose died recently, leaving his entire $2 million gross estate to his wife, Trixie, who is named executor. Assume that the only estate expense is the executor's commission of $100,000. Marginal tax rates for the taxpaying entities are: Trixie's Form 1040, 31%; the final Form 1040, 15%; the Form 1041, 28%; the Form 706, 41%.

    a. Should Trixie accept or waive the commission? Why?
    b. Where, if at all, should the estate deduct the commission? Why?
    c. Would your answers to parts "a" and "b" change if Moose's net estate was $200,000?
    d. Would your answers to parts "a" and "b" probably change if Trixie, the executor, was Moose's cousin to whom Moose left nothing by will or otherwise? Assume a $2 million taxable estate.

4. Describe the income tax advantages available to all estates and those advantages available only to estates having a carefully chosen fiscal year.

5. How can the executor of an estate or the trustee of a trust reduce income taxes by planning the distributions to beneficiaries if the beneficiaries marginal tax rates are: (a) Higher than that of the estate or trust? (b) Lower than that of the estate or trust?

6. What is the benefit of prolonging an estate's life, and what is the tax consequence if it is "unduly" prolonged?

7. What two conditions must be met before an estate can make the alternate valuation date election? What is the tax advantage? When are assets valued?

8. Give two specific examples where a disclaimer can reduce the estate tax.

9. Describe the unique contribution of a QTIP arrangement to estate planning.

10. Is it clearly erroneous for an executor to fail to take the marital deduction on QTIP property when doing so would eliminate taxes on S1's estate?

11. (a) Can a QTIP arrangement and a disclaimer provision be alternative methods of achieving a common objective? Why or why not? (b) Which places greater property rights in the hands of S2? Why?

12. Brunk owned three assets at his death. Their description and appraised values at date of death, six months after death and nine months after death, respectively, are as follows: Home and furnishings, $300,000, $320,000, $340,000; securities, $800,000, $700,000, $600,000; and an interest in a closely held business, $500,000, $400,000, $300,000. Brunk bequeathed all assets to his son, who, as executor, sold the home for $310,000 four months after Brunk died, and sold the business for $320,000 eight months after Brunk died. Assuming no deductions, calculate Brunk's taxable estate.

13. With regard to the QTIP election:

    a. Who makes it?
    b. If the election is made, will it influence either the ultimate disposition of the property, or taxation of the qualifying property, or both?
    c. If the election is not made, how will the tax result change?

ANSWERS TO THE QUESTIONS AND PROBLEMS

1. Federal tax returns:

    a. Estate tax: Form 706, due nine months after date of death.
    b. Income tax:

        1. Form 1040: Decedent's final income tax return, for all income for the last year up to the date of death.
        2. Form 1041: Estate income tax return (if there is a probate estate), for each tax year of the estate's existence.
        3. Form 1041: Trust income tax return for each tax year of any trust created by the decedent.

2. Taxes saved = amount deducted times the tax rate. $50,000 of the total must be deducted on the final 1040. The other $30,000 can be deducted on the 706 or the final 1040. To save the most taxes, the $30,000 should be deducted on the 706.

    a. 706: 41% * ($30,000 + $9,300) = $15,183 saved. Remember, the additional income tax due to not claiming these medical expenses on the 1040 is a debt that is deductible on the 706.
    b. Final 1040: 31% * $30,000 = $9,300 saved.
    c. Estate's 1041: Not deductible.

3. a. If Trixie accepts the $100,000 commission, that amount will be taxable income to her, resulting in an income tax outlay of 31 % * ($100,000) = $31,000. If the expense is deducted on the 706, estate tax will not be reduced, because the entire estate is already sheltered by the marital deduction and the exemption equivalent of the unified credit.

        If, alternatively, the expense is deducted on the estate's 1041, there will be an estate income tax saving of ($100,000) * 28% = $28,000. Thus, Trixie should *waive* the commission because it will result in a net increase in her after-tax proceeds of $31,000 - $28,000 = $3,000.
    b. The estate should not pay or deduct the commission, for the reasons mentioned above.

c. The results would change. Trixie would be indifferent between waiving and accepting the commission. At equal marginal tax rates, the tax saved on the form 1041 would just equal the higher tax on Trixie's 1040. However, cutting the hypothetical gross estate to $200,000 would not in itself alter the results. For any size estate, a 100% marital deduction would prevent additional tax savings with other deductions. Thus, the effective marginal estate tax rate would still be 0%.

d. The answers would very likely change. Trixie would probably rather accept the commission. Her after-tax proceeds would be $69,000, which is far better than receiving nothing.

4. a. Income tax advantages available to all estates:

1. Estate can be a separate taxpaying entity, thereby splitting income and enjoying the benefit of deduction elections for administrative expenses and losses.
2. Estate can take advantage of short tax years, which are the first and the last years of the estate's existence.

b. Income tax advantages available only to estates having a carefully chosen fiscal year:

1. Timing of distributions to delay the reporting of taxable income to beneficiaries.
2. Selecting a fiscal year to spread income out over as many tax years as possible.

5. Tax planning for distributions to beneficiaries:

a. When the estate or trust is in a lower bracket than the beneficiaries, it should consider accumulating income, realizing gains, and, if it is an estate, prolonging its life.
b. When the estate is in a higher bracket, it should use the conduit principle to distribute income in the year received.

6. The benefit of prolonging an estate's life is subjecting estate income to a lower tax rate. The tax consequence of "unduly" prolonging it is that the IRS will treat the estate as terminated, taxing the income to the beneficiaries as if they received it.

7. The alternate valuation date election can reduce the value of assets in the gross estate (or raise deductions), and therefore the estate tax, if their total value 6 months after date of death is lower (higher) than the date of death value.

8. Disclaimers to reduce the estate tax:

   a. Disclaimer into a bypass trust,
   b. Disclaimer by a non-spouse to increase the marital deduction,
   c. Disclaimer by a non-spouse to increase the charitable deduction,
   d. Disclaimer of a taxable power of appointment.

9. The unique contribution of a QTIP arrangement to estate planning is to enable property (remainder interest) which will not at all pass to S2 to qualify for the marital deduction.

10. a. Yes, if the executor for S1's estate chooses not to make the QTIP election and, thereby, does not claim the marital deduction.
    b. The QTIP arrangement cannot be considered a bust if the decision was knowingly made. Taxes may be save by not making the election because the end result may be to have a more effective use of the lower marginal rates and to obtain for S2's estate a prior transfer credit.

11. a. Yes, a QTIP arrangement and a disclaimer provision can be alternative methods of achieving the same objective, which is estate tax minimization. Both typically enable S2 to decide whether or not to qualify certain property for the marital deduction and, consequently, to determine the size of the bypass share.

b. The disclaimer provision will place greater property rights in the hands of S2 because, if S2 does not disclaim, her or she will receive it. On the other hand, the QTIP election only influences estate taxation, not property disposition; disposition of the property is in complete control of S1.

12. Calculation of Brunk's taxable estate:

Estate assets	DOD Value	AVD Value
Home & furnishings	$300,000	$310,000
Securities	$800,000	$700,000
Business	$500,000	$400,000
Total	$1,100,000	$1,010,000

AVD values are determined 6 months after death; the nine month values, included as a 'red herring,' are inapplicable. For purposes of AVD values, all estate assets sold prior to the AVD are valued at selling price and assets distributed are valued as of date of distribution.

13. a. The executor of the estate of S1 makes the election, since S1 is the decedent whose document qualifies for the QTIP election.

   b. If the QTIP election is made, it will influence taxation of the qualifying property, but not its disposition. Except for adjustments for payment of estate tax, all named beneficiaries will still receive their designated shares. Tax wise, the property will be deductible from S1's gross estate and included in S2's gross estate at his or her later death.

   c. If the QTIP election is not made, the qualifying property will be included in S1's taxable estate and not included (via bypass) in S2's estate. Thus, a greater bypass may increase S1 estate tax (but only if, under simple assumptions, the bypass becomes greater than the exclusion amount.

ENDNOTES

1. §6013(a)(2).

2. §1(a)(2), §2(a)(1).

3. §213; §2053

4. Reg. 1.642 (g)-2.

5. Reg. §1.641(b)-3(a).

6. Reg 25.2518-2(c)(4)(I).

7. LR 9106016; TAM 9208003.

8. LR 9208003.

9. Reg. 25.2518-3(b).

10. For an example of an unsuccessful disclaimer to correct a defect in a trust intended to achieve QTIP treatment, see *Estate of Bennett*, 100 TC No. 5 (1993).

11. §2056(b)(5).

12. §2044.

13. §2207(a).

CHAPTER 19

Estate Planning Study Aids

OVERVIEW

This chapter features three study aids. The first two are hypothetical case studies, included for two primary reasons. First, estate planning is an intensely fact oriented and client oriented subject, and the more analysis of family situations studied, the better. Second, some readers may be preparing to take a final exam or a certification examination in estate planning, estate and gift tax, or financial planning. These questions should help in that preparation. Students interested in becoming licensed as Certified Financial Planners and using the CFP marks might wish to visit the Certified Financial Planner Board of Standards, Inc., (the Board or the CFP Board) Website at *http://www.cfp-board.org/index.html*.

The first case is one used in at least one CFP Certification Examination.[1] It was released in 1994, so the reader should be aware that the answers may not be current. Indeed, none of the 1997 and 1998 changes would be present. It is offered as sample of the format of the case portion of the exams. At the Board's Website one can download 77 multiple-choice questions and a case scenario released in 1999. The reader will notice from the samples that the exam questions test other financial planning subjects besides estate planning, which is the subject matter of less than one third of the seventeen questions. The Board has indicated that it will continue to use cases that test a financial planner's ability to integrate various aspects of financial planning, hence expect a wide range of financial planning topic areas to be covered.

The second case, written for this book, is estate planning oriented, and can be used to better test one's knowledge of numerous technical issues in estate planning.

The third part of the chapter includes that portion of the CFP Board of Standards' topic list that relates directly to estate planning. The topic list came from the Board's most recent "Job Analysis" study.

ONE: CFP CERTIFICATION EXAM CASE

Case Scenario And Multiple-Choice Questions

The following case scenario with multiple-choice questions appeared on a CFP certification examination. The answers are located on a separate page at the end of the case. The case has been approved for publication by the CFP Board of Examiners.

Instructions: Read the information provided about William and Marilyn Mathews and choose the best answer to the multiple choice questions that follow.

WILLIAM AND MARILYN MATHEWS

Your clients, Bill and Marilyn Mathews, have asked you to help them with a number of issues facing them as Bill prepares to sell his business and formally retire. Marilyn will also retire, having worked as the company bookkeeper for twenty years. Negotiations for the sale of Bill's business, Calculator City, are almost concluded, pending resolution of a number of questions Bill raised regarding installment payments for the business as well as a request from the proposed owner that Bill continue to provide consulting services.

Personal Information

	Age	Health	Occupation
William Mathews	65	Excellent	Business Owner
Marilyn Mathews	63		Bookkeeper
John Mathews (son)	32	Excellent	Engineer
James Mathews (son)	30	Excellent	CPA
Grandchildren	3,4,5, & 7	Excellent	

Neither son has any intention of becoming involved in the business. The Mathews file a joint tax return. Client and spouse have simple wills leaving all to each other.

Economic Environment : The current economic environment exhibits low real short-term rates, high real long-term rates, little economic growth, and high unemployment.

Client Objectives:

1. Maintain current lifestyle, including frequent travel.
2. Revise estate plan to minimize taxes, take advantage of opportunities in various elections available in the Internal Revenue Code, and maximize amounts passing to children and grandchildren.
3. Review investment portfolio and make changes as necessary to reflect different priorities and risk tolerance levels during retirement. Initial indications are that the clients are willing to take normal investment risks, desirous of adequate current income, reasonable safety of principal, inflation protection, tax advantage, and some modest long term appreciation, in that order of priority.
4. Review and revise total risk management and insurance situation as necessary to provide adequate protection, and eliminate gaps and overlaps.
5. Determine the most advantageous method of taking distributions from the 401(k) accounts.

WILLIAM AND MARILYN MATHEWS
Statement of Financial Position as of 12/31/92

Assets		Liabilities	
Invested Assets			
Cash/Cash Equivalents	$8,000	Auto Loan	$6,000
Marketable Securities[1]	1,580,000	Mortgage[2]	12,000
Business Interest[3]	1,500,000	Mortgage[4]	74,000
Life Ins Cash Value[5]	$60,000		$92,000
Annuity	120,000		
	$3,268,000		
Use Assets			
Primary Residence	$188,000		
Summer Home	126,000		
Personal Property	60,000		
Automobiles	26,000		
	$400,000		
Retirement Plan Assets[6]			
IRA (H)	$27,000		
IRA (W)	28,000		
401(k) (H)	280,000		
401(k) (W)	40,000		
	$375,000	Net Worth	$3,951,000
		Total Liabilities	
Total Assets	$4,043,000	& Net Worth	$4,043,000

---

[1] See separate Investment Portfolio Supplement

[2] Principal residence; originally, 30 years @ 7%

[3] Business is to be sold for $1.5 million. Purchase price was $700,000 in 1982. Terms of sale include $300,000 down payment on July 1, 1993, with the balance to be paid over 120 months starting August 1, 1993, at 10% interest.

[4] Summer home; originally, 15 years @9%

[5] Face Amount: $200,000; Bill is insured, Marilyn is beneficiary.

[6] Spouse is beneficiary for IRA and 401(k). The IRAs are invested in a common stock growth mutual fund. The 401(k) plans are invested in 3-year Treasury notes.

WILLIAM AND MARILYN MATHEWS
Projected Monthly Cash Flow Statement - (Incomplete)
1/1/93 through 12/31/93

*Cash Inflows

Social Security (H)	$820
Social Security (W)	$410
Installment Payments (120 pmts @ 10%)	?
Interest Income (tax-exempt)	$600
Dividend Income	$540
Interest Income (taxable)	?
Other Investment Income	?

Outflows

Savings and Investment	?
Mortgage (residence: PITI)	$600
Mortgage (summer home: PITI)	$1,100
Food	$300
Utilities	$400
Transportation (gas, oil, maintenance)	$200
Car Payment	$600
Clothing	$250
Entertainment	$450
Travel	$1,680
Family Gifts	$1,666
Charitable Gifts	$500
Life Insurance	$300
Hospitalization (Medigap/Medicare)	$100
Automobile Insurance	$150
Miscellaneous	?
Federal income Tax	$5,800
State Income Tax	$900
Other	?

WILLIAM AND MARILYN MATHEWS
INSURANCE AND ANNUITY INFORMATION

Whole Life Policy
Person Insured/Owner	Bill
Face Amount	$200,000
Dividend Option	Paid-Up Additions
Issue Date	2/13/77
Beneficiary	Marilyn
Current Cash Value	$60,000
Premium	$300 per month

Single Premium Deferred Annuity
Person Insured/Owner	Bill
Fixed or Variable	Fixed
Current Value	$120,000
Current Interest Rate	6.5%
Issue Date	1/1/81
Purchase Price	$40,000

Homeowners Policy
Type	HO-3
Amount on Dwelling	$175,000
Personal Property Coverage	$ 87,500
Personal Liability	$100,000

Automobile Policy
Type	Personal Auto policy
Bodily Injury/Property	$300,000 Combined Single Limit
Collision	$250 Deductible
Comprehensive	Full, with $100 Deductible
Uninsured Motorist	$300,000 Single Limit

WILLIAM AND MARILYN MATHEWS
INVESTMENT PORTFOLIO SUPPLEMENT

Common Stocks	Fair Market Value
AT&T	$30,000
Bell South	10,000
Bell Atlantic	9,000
Ameritech	8,500
NYNEX	7,000
Pacific Telesis	8,000
Southwestern Bell	8,000
US West	7,000
Canon	22,000
Comerica Bank	29,000
Danko	7,000
de Beers	8,000
du Pont	29,000
Disney	12,000
Dow Chemical	9,000
Detroit Edison	24,000
General Motors	8,000
GME	10,500
D&T, Inc.*	25,000
Common stock mutual fund (IRAs)	55,000
Municipal Bonds	
Franklin Intermediate Tax Exempt Fund	$100,000
Annuities and Insurance	
Cash value life insurance	$60,000
Single Premium Deferred Annuity	120,000
Bonds	
Treasury notes (401(k))	$320,000
US EE Savings Bonds	75,000
Cash and Equivalents	
Cash	$8,000
Cash equivalents, incl. Money Markets	134,000
Treasury Securities (T-Bills)	1,000,000
TOTAL	$2,143,000

*Small Business Corp. (§ 1244 stock) solely owned by Bill and originally purchased for $76,000 in 1/1/87.

QUESTIONS

1. The tax treatment of the down payment made to Bill for the sale of his business is:

    a. not taxable as a return of basis.
    b. fully taxable as a capital gain.
    c. partially a return of basis and partially taxable as ordinary income.
    d. partially a return of basis, partially a capital gain, and partially ordinary income.
    e. partially a return of capital and partially a capital gain.

2. How much will Bill receive from the monthly installment payments during 1993 (rounded to the nearest dollar)?

    a. $79,290   b. $95,149   c. $190,297   d. $379,290   e. $395,149

3. The amount of interest income from the installment sale for the year ending 12/31/93 is approximately:

    a. $49,000   b. $59,000   c. $60,000   d. $72,000   e. $120,000

4. How will Bill's receipt of installment payments for the sale of his business affect his Social Security benefits?

    a. His Social Security benefits will be reduced because of his installment payments.
    b. His Social Security benefits will not be taxable because installment payments are not wages.
    c. Receipt of installment payments will increase the amount of Modified Adjusted Gross Income, causing some of the Social Security benefits to be taxable.
    d. Because Bill is 65, his Social Security benefits will be subject to the excess earnings test applied to the installment payments. Benefits will be reduced $1 for every $2 earned over the base amount.

e. Because Bill is 65, his Social Security benefits will be subject to the excess earnings test applied to the Installment payments. Benefits will be reduced $1 for every $3 earned over the base amount.

5. Bill and Marilyn both have account balances in the 401(k) Plan, and they want to determine what options they can pursue. Which of the following statements describe options available for Bill and Marilyn?

    (1) Bill can make an IRA Rollover with his account; Marilyn can elect 10-Year Special Averaging for hers.
    (2) Both Bill and Marilyn can make IRA Rollovers.
    (3) Bill can elect a partial rollover and use 5-Year Special Averaging on the balance; Marilyn can roll over her entire amount.
    (4) Both Bill and Marilyn can elect either 5-Year or 10-Year Special Averaging for their respective distributions.

    a. (1), (2) & (4) only   b. (1) & (3) only   c. (2) only

        d. (2) & (3) only   e. (1), (2), (3) & (4)

6. The Mathews family is considering the purchase of a survivorship life insurance policy, payable on the second death of either Bill or Marilyn, for the primary purpose of providing liquidity for the payment of the federal estate tax. The ownership and beneficiary arrangements are being studied for the best overall result. Which of the following options for ownership and beneficiary arrangements are viable?

    (1) Bill and Marilyn can purchase the policy and retain ownership; the proceeds will not be includible in either estate because of the unlimited marital deduction.
    (2) Bill and Marilyn can purchase the policy, then transfer ownership to one or both of their sons, so that the proceeds avoid inclusion in either Bill's or Marilyn's estate no matter when death occurs because they do not have any incidents of ownership.
    (3) Ownership can be vested immediately in an irrevocable life insurance trust, with appropriate "Crummey" provisions, to avoid inclusion of the proceeds in either estate.

(4) The Mathews family Revocable Living Trust can be the initial owner and beneficiary, in order to avoid estate taxes in either estate, because life insurance death proceeds retain their tax-free character in the trust.

   a. (1), (3) & (4) only   b. (2) & (4) only   c. (2) only

      d. (3) only   e. (1) & (4) only

7. If Bill decides to make a partial withdrawal from his Single Premium Deferred Annuity, what income tax result will ensue?

   a. The withdrawal will be taxed as long-term capital gain, subject to a maximum rate of 28%.
   b. The withdrawal will be subject to ordinary income tax, since there is no preference for long-term capital gain.
   c. The withdrawal will be taxed according to the annuity rules, so that a portion will be taxable as ordinary income and the balance will be a tax-free recovery of capital.
   d. The withdrawal will be tax-free up to Bill's cost basis, since FIFO treatment applies to this annuity.
   e. The withdrawal will be taxable on a LIFO basis to the extent of earnings in the contract.

8. Bill is contemplating selling his D&T, Inc. stock for the fair market value. Assuming he sold D&T on 12/31/92, the tax impact would be:

   a. a fully deductible capital loss of $51,000.
   b. a capital loss limited to $3,000 assuming no other investment transactions; carryover $48,000 long-term capital loss.
   c. an ordinary loss of $50,000 with a $1,000 loss carryover.
   d. an ordinary loss of $51,000.
   e. a short-term capital loss of $51,000 because of Section 1244 status.

9. In view of the combined estate values for Bill and Marilyn, which of the following estate planning techniques may be appropriate?

(1) placing life insurance in an irrevocable trust

(2) making use of annual gift tax exclusion

(3) establishing a revocable living trust, using the unlimited marital deduction and the full unified credit.

(4) arranging for a preferred stock recapitalization for Bill's business interest

a. (2) & (3) only   b. (1), (2) & (3) only   c. (1), (3) & (4) only

d. (1), (2) & (4) only   e. (1), (2), (3) & (4)

10. The Mathews currently own a number of tax-advantaged financial instruments. Which of the following statements is/are true with respect to these various instruments?

(1) Interest income and capital appreciation from the municipal bond fund is federally tax exempt.

(2) An initial partial withdrawal from the single premium deferred annuity is fully taxable.

(3) When redeemed, the return on the savings bonds is <u>not</u> subject to state income taxes.

(4) The Treasury bills are federally taxed only upon maturity.

a. (1), (2) & (3) only   b. (2) & (4) only   c. (3) only

d. (3) & (4) only   e. (1), (2), (3) & (4)

11. If Bill and Marilyn wish to limit the growth of their combined estate, which techniques may be advisable?

(1) use of the annual gift tax exclusion and split gift election

(2) current use of both unified credits

(3) payment of tuition for grandchildren

(4) payment of direct medical expenses for children and grandchildren

a. (1) & (2) only   d. (1), (2) & (3) only
b. (2), (3) & (4) only   e. (1), (2), (3) & (4)
c. (1) only

12. Assume Bill provides consulting services for the new owner and is properly classified as an independent contractor. Which statements properly describe Bill's ability to shelter current taxable income?

    (1) Bill may take a non-deductible IRA for $2,000
    (2) Bill may set up a profit-sharing Keogh
    (3) Bill can set up a money purchase plan.
    (4) Bill can set up a combined money purchase and profit-sharing plan, but his contributions will be limited to 20% of Schedule C income.

    a. (2) & (3) only   d. (1), (2), (3) & (4)
    b. (1), (2) & (3) only   e. (1) & (3) only
    c. (2), (3) & (4) only

13. In reviewing Bill and Marilyn's cash-flow projections as well as the investment portfolio supplement, you question the appropriateness of some of the holdings. Which combination of portfolio weaknesses best summarizes a valid critique of their investments?

    a. excessive liquidity, inadequate tax advantage, marginal equity diversification
    b. inadequate tax advantage, excessive growth orientation, marginal equity diversification
    c. excessive liquidity, excessive growth orientation, inadequate tax advantage
    d. excessive reliance on Treasury Bills, insufficient growth opportunities, inadequate current income
    e. insufficient growth opportunities, inadequate liquidity, excessive tax advantage

14. Assuming that Bill reaches agreement with the new owner as to the installment payments for the business interest, what are the estate tax ramifications if Bill dies at the end of the third year of the ten-year payout schedule?

a. The remaining value of the installments is <u>not</u> includible in Bill's estate, because the payments continuing to Marilyn qualify for the marital deduction.

b. Seventy percent of the original cash purchase price upon which the installments were based is includible in Bill's estate but qualifies for the marital deduction because payments will continue to Marilyn.

c. The present value of the future income stream to Marilyn in included in Bill's estate, but the continuing payments qualify for the marital deduction.

d. The present value of the future income stream to Marilyn is included in Bill's estate, but the continuing income payments do <u>not</u> qualify for the marital deduction because it is a terminable interest.

e. Nothing is included in the estate because the installment payments are <u>not</u> guaranteed.

15. The inadequacies in their estate planning can be summarized as follows:
    (1) failure to take full advantage of each unified credit.
    (2) failure to avoid probate.
    (3) lack of proper documents to address the potential problem of incapacity.
    (4) failure to coordinate titling of assets with documentation.

    a. (1) & (2) only   d. (2) & (4) only
    b. (2) & (3) only   e. (1), (2), & (3)
    c. (1) & (3) only

Regarding question 16 and given the current economic conditions, you recommend allocating the Mathews' investment funds into three asset categories: equity, debt, and cash.

16. In order to meet their goals, the Matthews should:
    (1) reduce cash level, expand fixed income securities,
    (2) expand fixed income securities.
    (3) increase cash level, decrease equities.
    (4) expand fixed income securities, decrease equities.

a. (1) only
b. (1) & (4) only
c. (2) & (3) only

d. (2), (3) & (4)
e. none of the above

17. You are considering liquidating the individual equity holdings and moving this amount into equity mutual funds. The following alternative allocations have been proposed:

Choice A		Choice B	
Market index fund	40%	Growth fund	33%
Growth fund	20%	International equity fund	33%
Value-oriented fund	20%	Value-oriented fund	34%
International equity fund	20%		
Choice C		Choice D	
Market index fund	30%	Small company fund	25%
Gold stock fund	50%	Aggressive growth fund	45%
Equity-income fund	20%	Growth fund	30%

a. Choice A is preferred because it includes multiple management styles and market diversification.
b. Choice B is preferred because it employs both active and passive funds.
c. Choice C is preferred because it best meets the Mathews' goals.
d. Choice D is preferred because it maximizes growth while meeting the Mathews' goal.
e. Do not liquidate the current portfolio.

Answers to Mathews Case Questions

1.	E	6.	C	11.	E	16.	E
2.	A	7.	D	12.	C	17.	A
3.	A	8.	D	13.	A		
4.	C	9.	B	14.	C		
5.	A	10.	D	15.	E		

Since the release of the Mathews case, the CFP Board of Examiners has responded to candidates' questions regarding some of the exam items. Those responses, as they appear in the CFP Information Bulletin, are as follows:

Item #

2. This is based on a sale price of $1.5 million with a down payment of $300,000, leaving a balance of $1.2 million. Payments are for 120 months at an interest rate of 0.83% per month (10% divided by 12). By the end of 1993, Bill will have received five payments. The answer to the question can be arrived through normal annuity calculations. I would agree that it probably should be calculated as an annuity due, in which case, the answer would have been slightly different, the amount of $78,635. Even if calculated this way, clearly the closest and best answer would be A.

7. See IRS Publication 575 which is on point.

TWO: ESTATE PLANNING CASE: Sheila and Jerry Briggs

The Briggs case focuses on estate planning. This sets it apart from CFP exam cases, which are designed to cover several different financial planning areas. However, many of the concepts covered in the Briggs case (calculation of gross estate, the calculation of the estate tax, choice of trust type, etc) could be tested in a more general examination case. The answers to the questions appear just before the chapter endnotes.

"I knew I should have talked with you first, I just knew it"..., exclaimed Jerry Briggs one day in June of 1997. "...but our family attorney sounded so convincing..." Jerry had just finished showing you a copy of the wills that the attorney had just prepared for him and his wife, Sheila. You, of course, know them to be standard 'simple wills,' each document simply leaving everything outright to the spouse, if surviving, otherwise outright in equal shares to the children of their current marriage. After examining the wills, you pointed out some planning omissions and mistakes, and recommended that Jerry and Sheila set up an appointment for next week to discuss and develop an overall financial plan, with the assistance of an attorney specializing in estate planning. They agreed, and before they left filled out a questionnaire about their financial situation and objectives.

Jerry and Sheila Briggs, age 67 and 62 respectively, have been happily married for nearly 38 years. They have two children, Bob, 36 and Gail, 34. Jerry also has a son, Steve, 46, from a former marriage. While Sheila is in excellent health, the stress of Jerry's business has taken its toll. Jerry suffers from a heart condition, having experienced a mild attack three years ago.

Figure 1 depicts Jerry and Sheila Briggs' financial statement. Jerry is a 50 percent stockholder in Gardens Unlimited, a rapidly growing mail order garden supply distributor. The sole co-owner is Craig Toft, an old college buddy. Sales last year were $23 million, making the firm's common stock worth approximately $1,800,000. The firm has a defined contribution profit sharing plan, and Jerry's account is currently worth $200,000. Sheila is named surviving beneficiary in this plan. Jerry thrives in his business environment, but because of his bad heart, realizes that he must slow down. Sheila entered the job market about 12 years ago, after Bob and Gail graduated college, and is presently enjoying work as a senior citizen's supervisor for the local recreation district.

This year, Jerry will pay himself a salary of $90,000, and Sheila will earn $28,000. Their son Bob, a personal injury attorney for a large firm, has a wife, Mary, and two children, Chris and Cass. Bob has always been regarded by his parents as relatively mature and responsible. On the other hand, Gail, who is not married, has been a bit of a problem for her parents. She never finished college, and may now have a drug problem; for the past year she has acted confused at times, and has frequently asked Jerry for money. To date, Gail has received nearly $6,000 "to help pay the rent and other odds and ends".

The Briggs are living quite comfortably, but, considering their sizable income, have been strikingly unable to save much money. And currently, their monthly cash inflows just equal their outflows, with fixed outflows of $82,000 and variable outflows of $42,000.

As indicated in the accompanying financial statement for 1996, their principal asset is Jerry's interest in his company's stock. The profit sharing plan invests primarily in commercial real estate. Three years ago, just before he died, Sheila's father gave her one sixth of his interest in his closely held Uniform Company, which is a thriving industrial uniform supply distributor. Her dad's basis in this interest was $175,000 and its FMV at date of gift was $160,000. Sheila would have difficulty selling this stock, as there is no secondary market. At his death, Sheila's dad left her his 30 year high yield bond issued by Trigger Co.

Jerry has always handled the financial affairs for the family, and Sheila admits, quite frankly, to being terrified of being placed in the position of undertaking this role. The Briggs live in a common law, non-community property state, having a "pickup" tax equal to the amount of the federal credit for state death taxes. In your analysis, you have decided to make several simplifying assumptions. First, there will be no funeral or administrative expenses incurred at either Jerry's or Sheila's death. Second, there will be no future appreciation in asset values, unless otherwise specified. Third, in estimating estate taxes we will assume the first death is in 1997 before the unified credit started moving up again, and that the second death will occur in 2007 when it will have settled down again. Four, assume that the annual exclusion is still $10,000 in at the time of any gifts even though we know that it has been indexed for inflation.

Sheila and Jerry's objectives include the following:

- To plan for Jerry's complete withdrawal from the firm by age 70.
- To provide for adequate income during retirement.

- To incur no death taxes at the death of the first spouse.
- To minimize death taxes at the death of the second spouse.
- To ensure adequate liquidity at all times.
- To dispose of the Briggs family assets in the following manner:
  - At the death of the first spouse, everything to the surviving spouse.
- At the death of the surviving spouse:
  - Sheila - all of her property to go equally to Bob and Gail.
  - Jerry - approximately one-half of his property to go to Steve and one quarter to Bob and Gail each.

JERRY AND SHEILA BRIGGS
Statement of Financial Condition (1996)

ASSETS[1]		LIABILITIES AND NET WORTH	
Cash/Cash Equivalents		Liabilities[2]	
Checking account (JT)[3]	$10,000	Credit card balance	$5,000
Money market account (JT)	100,000	Auto note balance	13,000
Total Cash/Cash Equivalents	$110,000	Home mortgage bal.	32,000
Invested Assets		Total Liabilities	$50,000
Uniform Co. Common Stock (W)	$150,000		
Trigger Co. Bond (W)[4]	50,000		
Gardens Unlimited			
Com Stk (basis $50,000)(H)	900,000		
Profit sharing			
Plan benefits (H)	200,000		
Total Invested assets	1,300,000		
Use Assets			
Personal residence (JT)	$280,000		
Personal Property (JT)	100,000		
Automobiles (JT)	60,000		
Total Use Assets	$440,000	Net Worth	$1,800,000
		TOTAL LIABILITIES	
TOTAL ASSETS	$1,850,000	& NET WORTH	$1,850,000

1. Presented at fair market   3. Joint tenancy with right of survivorship.
2. Principal only.   4. "W" means Sheila owns it & "H" that Jerry does.

QUESTIONS

1. If Jerry were to predecease Sheila and die today, without further planning, what would be the size of his federal gross estate, for estate tax purposes?

    a. zero   b. $1,175,000   c. $1,375,000   d. $1,800,000
    e. none of the above

2. If Jerry were to predecease Sheila and die today, without further planning, how much of his gross estate would pass under his present will?

    a. zero (none)   b. $900,000   c. $1,100,000   d. $1,175,000
    e. all of his gross estate

3. If when Jerry died the Uniform Company common stock was worth $168,000 and a year later Sheila sold it for $170,000, what would be her realized gain or loss? Negative number means a loss.

    a. ($2,000)   b. ($7,000)   c. no gain or loss   d. $8,000
    e. none of the above are correct

   For all further questions, assume that Jerry and Sheila each presently own one additional asset that is not shown on the financial statement: each was given a gift of a valuable painting from Jerry's dad. The gifts bring the net value of Jerry's estate to $1,600,000 and the net value of Sheila's estate to $500,000.

4. If Jerry were to die this year (1997) without further planning, what would be the federal estate tax due on behalf of Jerry's estate?

    a. zero   b. $396,750   c. $408,000   d. $589,550
    e. $600,800

5. If Jerry died in 1997 and Sheila died, still unmarried, in 2007, without further planning, how much of the Briggs' family assets would the children receive in total, after payment of death taxes? Assume no further savings or asset appreciation, no gifting or consumption of presently owned assets, and that all $50,000 of debts were paid off over time entirely with disposable income, not principal, prior to her death.

a. more than $1,000,000 but no more than $1,400,000
b. more than $1,400,000 but no more than $1,500,000
c. more than $1,500,000 but no more than $1,600,000
d. more than $1,600,000 but no more than $1,700,000
e. more than $1,700,000

6. How much of the Briggs family estate would the children receive, after payment of estate taxes, if Jerry were to die today with an AB Trust plan?

a. more than $1,000,000 but no more than $1,700,000
b. more than $1,700,000 but no more than $1,800,000
c. more than $1,800,000 but no more than $1,900,000
d. more than $1,900,000 but no more than $2,000,000
e. more than $2,000,000

7. In considering the amount of property passing to the bypass at the death of the first spouse, you are trying to determine the federal estate tax consequences of recommending a bypass of an amount <u>not</u> equal to the exemption equivalent of the unified credit. Assuming that the surviving spouse does not remarry and does not consume or make gifts of principal, which statement below is the most correct appraisal, in light of the Briggs' situation?

a. When compared with a credit shelter bypass, a bypass of an amount smaller than the exemption equivalent would probably reduce the federal estate tax for the estate of the first spouse to die.
b. When compared with a credit shelter bypass, a bypass of an amount smaller than the exemption equivalent would probably increase federal estate tax for the estate of the second spouse to die.
c. When compared with a credit shelter bypass, a bypass of an amount smaller than the exemption equivalent would probably increase federal estate tax for the estates of both spouses.
d. When compared with a credit shelter bypass, a bypass of an amount larger than the exemption equivalent would probably reduce federal estate tax for the estate of the first spouse to die.

e. When compared with a credit shelter bypass, a bypass of an amount larger than the exemption equivalent would probably increase federal estate tax for the estate of the second spouse to die.

8. In planning for the initial funding of the marital and bypass shares with specific assets, efficient estate tax planning for the Briggs would recommend funding Trust A (marital trust) with assets that are _____ likely to appreciate, and funding Trust B (exclusion amount trust) with assets that are _____ likely to appreciate.

    a. more, less   b. more, more   c. less, more   d. less, less
    e. None of the above are true, relative appreciation has little bearing on trust funding.

9. In recommending a bypass for Jerry's plan, you are considering how to structure the marital deduction portion. Based on the facts, select the best disposition arrangement for Jerry, with regard to assets that qualify for the marital deduction.

    a. An outright bequest, partly because it is simple and tax effective.
    b. A power of appointment trust, partly because the limited power of appointment given to Sheila will ensure the preservation of trust assets for other beneficiaries.
    c. A bypass trust, partly to qualify bypass assets for the marital deduction.
    d. A QTIP trust, partly because of Steve.
    e. A charitable remainder unitrust (CRUT), partly because Jerry has a charitable motive and has been a member of the Uniform Denominational Church for many years.

10. For this question, assume that you recommend to the Briggs that Jerry's estate plan 1) contain a bypass, and 2) incorporate two trusts, a bypass trust and a QTIP trust. What type of control over these trusts would you want the instrument to grant to Sheila, as surviving spouse?

   a. A power of appointment over the principal of the bypass trust to invade for her benefit, subject to an ascertainable standard.
   b. A power of appointment over the principal of the bypass trust to invade for her benefit, not subject to an ascertainable standard.
   c. A power of appointment over the principal of the QTIP trust to invade for her benefit, not subject to an ascertainable standard.
   d. A power of appointment over the principal of the QTIP trust to invade for her benefit or her children's benefit, subject to an ascertainable standard.
   e. A power of appointment over the principal of the QTIP trust, with only Sheila and the children as permissible appointees.

11. Regarding planning for the federal generation-skipping transfer tax (GST), which of the following best describes the Briggs' situation?

   a. The Briggs do not need any planning for the GST since no GST, as we presently know it, could possibly be incurred, whether or not the Briggs do any further death tax planning.
   b. The present arrangement will likely result in a GST at Sheila's death, if she survives Jerry.
   c. No planning for the Briggs can prevent an inevitable GST from being incurred.
   d. Based on the $1 million exemption, the Brigg's family assets are vulnerable to the GSTT on amounts in excess of $1 million, even with the most careful planning.
   e. None of the above are true.

12. In recommending a bypass estate plan for the Briggs, you intend to suggest that their estate planning attorney include certain clauses in the final principal dispositive instrument, whether it turns out to be a will or a living trust. Which clause would you <u>not</u> want to recommend?

    a.   A perpetuities saving clause, to prevent a contingent gift from being ruled invalid because it vests too long after the decedent's death.

    b.   A residuary clause.

    c.   A survival clause, because of the danger of lapsation.

    d.   A clause allocating death taxes, because the alternative, state and federal law (by default), may be inefficient and undesirable.

    e.   You would recommend all of the above clauses for the Briggs.

13. In this question only, assume that five years have gone by, and that Jerry died of a second heart attack ten months ago. Sheila has not remarried. The Briggs never returned to your lawyer-associate's office to sign any documents, which means that no additional planning has been implemented. In administering the affairs of Jerry's estate, Sheila has permitted Steve to drive Jerry's sports car, which is currently worth $18,000. Sheila intends to let Steve have the car, in accordance with Jerry's deathbed statements. If Sheila writes a letter today "irrevocably and unqualifiedly" refusing to accept the bequest of the car, and transfers title of the car to Steve in two weeks,

    a.   Steve will be legally entitled to at least part ownership in the car. Sheila will not have been considered to have made a "gross" or "taxable" gift to Steve because she will never have owned the car.

    b.   Steve will be legally entitled to full ownership in the car. Sheila will have made a "gross" gift, but will not have been considered to have made a "taxable" gift to Steve because of the benefit of the annual exclusion and the unified credit.

    c.   Steve will be legally entitled to full ownership in the car. Sheila will have been considered to have made a "taxable" gift because she will have owned the car.

d. Steve will be legally entitled to full ownership in the car. Sheila will have been considered to have made a taxable gift because she will have owned the car and the gift is one of a future interest.

e. Steve will not be legally entitled to any ownership interest in the car.

14. You are now attempting to decide whether to recommend that Jerry dispose of his assets with a will or with a living trust document. If you recommend a will, you intend to make sure that title to all assets in joint tenancy between Jerry and Sheila will be converted to equal tenants in common. The costs for the will alternative are: drafting and changing title to assets will cost $1,000 and probate administration costs will be $20,000. The costs for the trust alternative are: drafting the trust will cost $3,800 and non-probate administration costs at death will be $4,000. Assuming no other relevant costs, a discount rate of 10 percent, that any drafting costs will be incurred today, and that all administration costs in connection with Jerry's death will be incurred exactly 10 years from today, which answer below comes the closest to summarizing (within a few hundred dollars) a present value cost analysis taking into account the time value of money? The net advantage of -
- the living trust over a will is roughly: a. $1,500;   b. $3,500
- the will over the living trust is roughly: c. $1,500.;   d. $3,500
- the will versus the living trust is: e. pretty much the same, i.e., less than a $500 difference.

15. While in your office, Jerry and Sheila mentioned that their family attorney had made several questionable assertions regarding the selection of either joint tenancies (WROS), the will, or the living trust as the overall best type of dispositive instrument for them. Which of that attorney's comments, all listed below, is correct?

a. He said taking title to all assets in joint tenancy will prevent a step-up in tax basis of some or all property at the first spouse's death, thereby making joint tenancies distinctly disadvantageous in comparison with the other instruments of transfer.

b. He said that proper planning with a living trust makes having a will unnecessary.

ESTATE PLANNING STUDY AIDS ■ 871

c.   He said that a will is capable of disposing of all of the Briggs' present assets, except those held currently in joint tenancy form.

d.   He said that if the Briggs execute a will, at either of their deaths the posting of notice to creditors in a legal newspaper will effectively insulate the decedent's estate from all known creditors who delay in filing claims beyond the creditor's period.

e.   None of the above statements are true.

16. Jerry and Sheila (who have never made taxable gifts) are considering giving the Gardens unlimited stock to their children. If they arrange a split gift of stock worth 300,000 in the year 1999, with each child receiving shares worth $100,000, how much of Jerry's unified credit will be used up?

    a. $84,400   b. $77,600   c. $38,800   d. $35,800
    e. $29,800

17. What planning recommendations would be appropriate in connection with Gail's situation?

1. In the event of both spouse's premature death, give an independent trustee of any trust created the discretionary power to sprinkle income and principal among beneficiaries.

2. Provide for outright distribution of assets immediately at the death of the surviving spouse.

3. Name Gail to be a surrogate decision maker during the remaining lifetime of the surviving spouse.

4. Include a restriction against assignment in all trust documents.

    a. 1 only   d. 3 and 4 only
    b. 1 and 4 only   e. 1, 2, 3 and 4
    c. 2 and 3 only

18. You next turn to liquidity and life insurance planning for the Briggs. Based on the family situation, and assuming that the final plan will include a credit shelter bypass plan, which statement below represents the best analysis and recommendation for the Briggs?

   a. The Briggs should consider an irrevocable life insurance trust having the following characteristics: trustee is owner and beneficiary of policy.

   b. The Briggs should consider a irrevocable life insurance trust having the following characteristics: trustee is owner of policy and Bob and Gail are co-beneficiaries.

   c. The Briggs should consider a irrevocable life insurance trust having the following characteristics: Jerry and Sheila are owners of policy and trustee is beneficiary.

   d. The Briggs should consider a revocable life insurance trust having the following characteristics: trustee is owner and beneficiary of policy.

   e. No liquidity problems can be reasonably anticipated in the future, since all expected future debts can be easily paid with available assets.

19. Continuing your planning for liquidity, you estimate that if Jerry were to die today, Sheila would need, among other funds, a cash lump sum of $122,000 exactly one year from today and an annual cash inflow of $43,000 per year for 25 years with the first inflow arriving in exactly six years. Ignoring other cash needs and other sources of liquidity, how much life insurance (give or take a few thousand dollars) should the Briggs own to fund these two needs? Assume a discount rate of 8%.

   a. $325,000   b. $375,000   c. $425,000   d. $450,000
   e. $475,000

20. In planning for Jerry's business interests, which of the following represents a preferred recommendation and correct analysis, given the facts?

  a. While still alive, Jerry's selling his entire interest in Gardens Unlimited sometime in the next two years for $900,000 would be attractive from the point of view of both income tax and the overall objectives of the family.
  b. An entity business buyout arrangement between Jerry and Craig funded with life insurance would be preferable to a cross purchase arrangement because it would mean fewer policies would be needed and because the surviving owner would incur less income tax if and when he finally sells the firm.
  c. Jerry should bequeath the stock to Sheila, either outright or in trust, to be able to obtain a step-up in basis.
  d. If Jerry and Craig immediately sell the business to a ABC Corp., a large mail order firm, in exchange for ABC stock, they will incur no immediate income tax liability and will be able to diversify their holdings free of income tax consequences.
  e. None of the above statements represents preferred recommendations or correct analysis.

21. In recommending planning for the Briggs' incapacity, which statement below is correct?

  a. A living trust can explicitly provide for expert management of Jerry's property in the event of his incapacity.
  b. A living trust can explicitly provide for Jerry's personal care in the event of his incapacity.
  c. A will can explicitly provide for expert management of Jerry's property in the event of his incapacity.
  d. A will can explicitly provide for Jerry's personal care in the event of his incapacity.
  e. More than one of the answers above is correct.

THREE: ESTATE PLANNING TOPICS

In the process of developing appropriate examination questions for the CFP comprehensive exams, the Board of Standards and Practices for the Certified Financial Planner commissioned an extensive survey of practicing CFP licensees to determine the "job knowledge" requirements for persons wishing to practice personal financial planning. The following outline is just the estate planning section from the job knowledge topics list found in the CFP Board of Standards' General Information Booklet.[2] The Booklet is a manual that describes the certification requirements for the CFP license.[3]

The numbers in parentheses refer to ratings made by the panel. The first number describes relative importance: 1 = important, 2 = more important. The second number describes the target cognitive level: 1 = knowledge of facts/terms, 2 = comprehension/application, 3 = analysis/synthesis, 4 = evaluation.

Job Knowledge Requirements of The Certified Financial Planner: Topics, Relative Importance And Target Cognitive Level

The following topics become effective for certification examinations administered by the CFP Board of Standards after December 31, 1996

Estate Planning Benefits and Strategies

77. Estate planning overview (4)
   A. The meaning of "estate planning"
   B. Situations in which individuals need estate planning and consequences of integrated planning
   C. Steps in estate planning process
   D. The financial planner's role on the estate planning team

78. Estate planning pitfalls and weaknesses (4)
   A. Weaknesses in a client's existing estate plan
   B. Common pitfalls to avoid during estate planning

79. Methods for property transfer at death (4)
   A. The probate process (wills and intestate succession)
   B. Title (operation of law)
   C. Trusts
   D. Contracts (insurance/pensions)

80. Estate planning documents (4)
    A. Wills
    B. Trusts
    C. Personal care documents
    D. Marital agreements
    E. Durable power of attorney for property
    F. Business agreements

81. Overview of the federal unified tax system (4)
    A. Unified transfer tax system
    B. Generation-skipping transfer tax

82. Federal gift taxation (4)
    A. Basic concepts
    B. Techniques for managing gift tax liability
    C. Analysis and calculation of federal gift tax liability

83. Federal gross estate (4)
    A. Inclusions in a decedent's gross estate
    B. Exclusions from a decedent's gross estate

84. Valuation techniques and the federal gross estate (4)
    A. Valuation of specific property interests
    B. Valuation techniques

85. Federal estate tax deductions (4)
    A. Defining the gross estate
    B. Deductions (debts and expenses)
    C. Adjusted gross estate
    D. Deductions (marital/charitable)
    E. Taxable estate
    F. Adjusted taxable gifts
    G. Tax base

86. Calculation of federal estate tax liability (4)
    A. Steps to calculate the estate tax
    B. Various credits affecting the estate tax calculation (unified credit, state death tax, prior transfer, etc.)

87. Characteristics and tax aspects of property interests (4)
    A. Title forms
    B. Other interests
    C. Advantages and disadvantages of forms of property interests
    D. Taxation aspects

      E.   Recommendation and justification of the most appropriate form of property interests

88.   Probate (4)
      A.   Probate process
      B.   Advantages and disadvantages of probate
      C.   Techniques of avoiding probate
      D.   Recommendation and justification of the most appropriate probate avoidance techniques

89.   Liquidity planning (4)
      A.   Sale of assets
      B.   Life insurance
      C.   Special techniques for closely-held business owners (e.g., §§ 6166, 303, 2032A and buy-sell agreements)

90.   Powers of appointment (4)
      A.   Use and purpose in estate planning
      B.   General and special (limited)
      C.   "5 & 5" power (§ 2041(b)(2))
      D.   Federal gift and estate tax implications

91.   Features of trusts (4)
      A.   Classification of trusts
      B.   Characteristics of selected trust provisions
      C.   Rule against perpetuities

92.   Taxation of trusts and estates (4)
      A.   Income tax implications of trusts
            1)   Exemptions
            2)   Simple and complex trusts
            3)   Distributable net income
      B.   Federal gift tax implications of trusts
      C.   Federal estate tax implications of trusts
      D.   Income tax implications of estates
      E.   Recommendation and justification of the most appropriate trust
      F.   Excise tax on retirement plans at death

93.   Estate freeze issues
      A.   Limitations on corporate and partnership freezes (§ 2701)
      B.   Trust freezes (§ 2702 including qualified personal residence trusts)

94. Life insurance for estate planning (4)
    A. Advantages and disadvantages of specific life insurance techniques in estate planning
    B. Life insurance trusts
    C. Ownership, beneficiary designation and settlement options
    D. Gift and estate taxation of life insurance
    E. Recommendation and justification of the most appropriate life insurance technique

95. Gifts (4)
    A. Suitability of gifts for client and recipient
    B. Techniques for gift-giving

96. Taxation of gifts (4)
    A. Income taxation of lifetime transfers
    B. Federal gift taxation of lifetime transfers
    C. Circumstances causing inclusion of gifts in gross estate
    D. Calculation and analysis of the effect of a lifetime gift program

97. Recommendation and justification of the most appropriate property to give as a gift (4)
    A. Selection of the most appropriate property to give as a gift
    B. The most appropriate lifetime gift-giving techniques
    C. Justification of the lifetime gift-giving techniques selected for the client's situation

98. Marital deduction and bypass planning (4)
    A. Characteristics of the marital deduction
    B. Recommendation and justification of property interests that qualify for the marital deduction
    C. QTIP planning and the prior transfer credit
    D. Special planning for non-U.S. spouse

99. Federal estate tax implications of the marital deduction and bypass planning (4)
    A. Federal estate tax implications of using the marital deduction
    B. Calculation of increased wealth transfer generated from modifying a client's estate plan

100. Recommendation of the most appropriate marital or non-marital transfer (4)
    A. Factors to consider in selecting the optimum mix of marital and non-marital transfers
    B. Selection of the most appropriate single or combination of marital and/or non-marital transfers for a client's situation
    C. Justification of the marital and non-marital transfer techniques selected for the client's situation

101. Estate planning for nontraditional relationships (4)
    A.   Children of another relationship
    B.   Cohabitation
    C.   Adoptions
    D.   Same sex relationships
    E.   Communal relationships

102. Charitable contributions and transfers (4)
    A.   Considerations for contributions and transfers
    B.   Requirements for a gift to qualify for a charitable deduction
        1)   Charitable remainder trusts
        2)   Charitable lead trusts
    C.   Tax and non-tax characteristics of specific forms of charitable transfers including alternative minimum tax considerations
    D.   Charitable income tax deduction limitations
    E.   Calculation of the maximum total and/or maximum current year income tax deduction for a client's situation
    F.   Recommendation and justification of the most appropriate property and form of charitable transfer

103. Intra-family business and property transfers (4)
    A.   Characteristics of intra-family transfers
    B.   Federal income, gift and estate tax implications of intra-family transfers
    C.   Recommendation and justification of the most appropriate intra-family business and property transfer technique

104. Postmortem planning techniques (4)
    A.   Characteristics of postmortem estate planning techniques
    B.   Determination of whether a client qualifies for special tax treatment
    C.   Recommendation and justification of the most appropriate postmortem planning technique

105. Planning for incapacity (4)
    A.   Definition of incapacity
    B.   Care of client's dependents
    C.   Personal care of incapacitated client
    D.   Care of incapacitated client's property

106. Special topics in estate planning (4)
    A.   Divorce/remarriage
    B.   Selection of fiduciaries and guardians

Answers for the Briggs Case:

1. Answer "c"

Cash/MM/2 =	$55,000
Stock, Gardens Unlimited	$900,000
Pensions	$200,000
Residence/2	$140,000
Personal Property/2	$50,000
Autos/2	$30,000
Gross Estate	$1,375,000

2. Answer "b" Only Jerry's $900,000 Gardens Unlimited stock would pass by will. All joint tenancy assets pass by operation of law (the right of survivorship) and the profit sharing account would pass to the beneficiary designation according to the contract.

3. Answer "c" Sheila owns this stock so Jerry's will does not control. Since it was a gift from her father that had a higher basis that its FMV when he gave it to her the special rule for calculating her gain or loss applies. Since she sold it for more than the date of gift value but less than the carry over basis there is no gain or loss.

4. Answer "a" They have simple wills, therefore everything to the surviving spouse. With the 100% marital deduction the taxable estate would be zero, therefore no tax.

5. Answer "d" When Sheila dies she would own all of the property, $1,600,000 from Jerry and $500,000 of her own property for a total of $2,100,000. Debts and expenses assumed to be zero:

Taxable estate	$2,100,000
Tentative tax	$829,800
Unified Credit	($345,800)
Death taxes	$484,000
Net to the children	
Sheila's estate	$2,100,000
less death taxes	($484,000)
Net to the children	$1,616,000

6. Answer "c" Utilize a bypass to use Jerry's unified credit

Jerry's estate

Gross estate	$1,600,000
Marital deduction	($1,000,000)
Taxable estate	$600,000
Tentative tax	$192,800
Unified Credit	($192,800)
Death taxes	$0

Sheila's estate

Taxable estate	$1,500,000
Tentative tax	$555,800
Unified Credit	($345,800)
Death taxes	$210,000

Net to the children

From Sheila	$1,500,000
less taxes	($210,000)
Plus Trust B amount	$600,000
Net amount	$1,890,000

7. Answer "b" because a smaller bypass will increase the marital share at the first death, and thereby probably "load up" the estate of the second spouse to die. The other answers are wrong because:

   a. a credit shelter bypass plan already zeros out the tax; it cannot be reduced any more.
   c. a smaller bypass will increase the marital share and therefore could not possibly increase the tax on the first estate.
   d. a larger bypass will leave unsheltered some property at the first death, thereby probably increasing the tax.
   e. a larger bypass will reduce the marital share, thereby probably reducing the surviving spouse's estate and estate tax.

8. Answer "c" Funding the marital share with assets less likely to appreciate will avoid loading up the surviving spouse's estate. Funding the bypass share with assets more likely to appreciate will enable a greater amount of property to avoid (i.e., to bypass) taxation at the surviving souse's death.

9. Answer "d" The QTIP trust will enable Jerry to retain control over the eventual disposition of the corpus such that Steve will receive his full share. The other answers are incorrect because:
   a. Jerry does not want Sheila to have fee simple control over the property.
   b. A general power would cause this property to be included in Sheila's estate and she would control it.
   c. a bypass trust would not qualify for the marital deduction.
   e. A CRUT would not leave property to their children.

10. Answer "a" Sheila can invade based upon ascertainable standards, thus a limited power, the property is not included in her estate. The other answers are incorrect because:

    b. There would be no bypass & the property would be in Sheila's estate.
    c, d, & e: No one, other than S2, can have any right to corpus so long as S2 is alive if the QTIP election is desired.

11. Answer "e" The other answers are incorrect because:

    a. A GSTT may be incurred if, due to any of their children predeceasing her, property then goes to grandchildren.
    b. Neither Sheila nor the children are skip persons.
    c. Gifts may keep the Briggs' assets below $2 million which can be sheltered by their GSTT exemptions.
    d. Each spouse has a $1 million dollar exemption that can shelter $2 million.

12. Answer "e" All of the clauses are standard estate planning provisions commonly included in estate planning documents.

13. Answer "c" Jerry's deathbed statements do not constitute a valid testamentary transfer. Thus, under the Briggs' simple will, Sheila was bequeathed the car. Because Sheila did not disclaim it within 9 months of his death, she will have made a gift of it to Steve. Thus, her transfer of title to Steve is a taxable gift to the extent the value of the car exceeded the annual exclusion amount.

14. Answer "b" PV factor @ 10% for 10 years is .385543.

    With a will: $1,000 + $20,000*.385543 = $8,711.
    Living trust: $3,800 + $4,000*.385543 = $5,342
    Advantage of trust: $8,711 - $5,342 = $3,368 (closest to $3,500)

15. Answer "e" The other answers are incorrect because:

    a. a step-up as to one half of the value of the assets will occur whether in joint tenancy or will or living trust.
    b. need a pourover will.
    c. certain assets are not probate assets, such as the pension plan benefits.
    d. Tulsa requires actual notice to known creditors.

16. Answer "e"

Jerry's gift tax return	
Gross gifts	$150,000
Annual exclusion	$30,000
Current taxable gifts	$120,000
Tentative tax	$29,800
Unified credit used	$29,800
Gift tax	$0

    a. Assumes $300,000 gross gifts and a $10,000 total annual exclusion.
    b. Assumes $300,000 gross gifts and $30,000 total annual exclusions.
    c. Assumes $150,000 gross gifts and a $10,000 total annual exclusion.
    d. Assumes $150,000 gross gifts and no annual exclusion.

17. Answer "b"

1. Correct, an independent trustee can have a limited power of appointment, and based upon Gail's health can determine the appropriate distributions.
2. incorrect Gail might receive too much money which she could use to support her drug habit.
3. incorrect, Gail may not be capable of handling that task.
4. correct because Gail cannot pledge trust assets to support a drug habit.

18. Answer "a" Only by naming the trustee of an irrevocable trust to be both owner and beneficiary of the policy will the Briggs be able to both avoid probate and federal estate tax on the proceeds.

19. Answer "c" Using a rate of 8%:

Present value of $122,000 in one year = $122,000 * .925926 = $112,963.

Present value of $43,000 annually for 25 years: $43,000 * 10.6748 = $459,016 Discount that for 5 years (remember the valuation tables assume that all payments, including the annuity, start at the end of each year): $459,016 * .680583 = 312,399.

Add the two values together: $112,963 + $312,399 = $425,362 This closest to "c" a choice of $425,000.

20. Answer "e" The other answers are incorrect because:

a. An income tax on the $850,000 would be immediately incurred.
b. The same number of policies (two) will have to be purchased under either plan.
c. Sheila will have difficulty selling the business for a reasonable value.
d. The only way to diversify is by selling the AVC stock, in the process incurring a capital gains tax.

21. Answer "a" because a successor trustee can be authorized to take over at the onset of Jerry's incapacity. The other answers are incorrect because:

    b. The trust authorizes property management not health care.
    c. A will becomes a controlling document only after the testator is dead.
    d. A will becomes a controlling document only after the testator is dead.
    e. Only "a" is correct.

ENDNOTES

1.   Reprinted with permission of the Certified Financial Planner Board of Standards, Inc., all rights reserved.

2.   Reprinted with permission of the Certified Financial Planner Board of Standards., Inc., all rights reserved.

3.   The General Information Booklet, revised annually, is available free from the CFP Board. Its address is 1700 Broadway, suite 2100, Denver CO 80290-2101. Telephone (303) 830-7500. FAX (303) 860-7388.

Tax and Valuation Tables

TABLE 1 Federal Unified Transfer-Tax Rates - Since 1/1/77

If the Amount is:		Tentative Tax:		
Over	But Not Over	Base Amount +	Percent	On Excess
For all years after 1976 the marginal rates are the same up to a $2,500,000 taxable				
$0	$10,000	$0	18%	$0
$10,000	$20,000	$1,800	20%	$10,000
$20,000	$40,000	$3,800	22%	$20,000
$40,000	$60,000	$8,200	24%	$40,000
$60,000	$80,000	$13,000	26%	$60,000
$80,000	$100,000	$18,200	28%	$80,000
$100,000	$150,000	$23,800	30%	$100,000
$150,000	$250,000	$38,800	32%	$150,000
$250,000	$500,000	$70,800	34%	$250,000
$500,000	$750,000	$155,800	37%	$500,000
$750,000	$1,000,000	$248,300	39%	$750,000
$1,000,000	$1,250,000	$345,800	41%	$1,000,000
$1,250,000	$1,500,000	$448,300	43%	$1,250,000
$1,500,000	$2,000,000	$555,800	45%	$1,500,000
$2,000,000	$2,500,000	$780,800	49%	$2,000,000
$2,500,000	$3,000,000	$1,025,800	53%	$2,500,000
1977 through 1981				
$3,000,000	$3,500,000	$1,290,800	57%	$3,000,000
$3,500,000	$4,000,000	$1,575,800	61%	$3,500,000
$4,000,000	$4,500,000	$1,880,800	65%	$4,000,000
$4,500,000	$5,000,000	$2,205,800	69%	$4,500,000
$5,000,000		$2,550,800	70%	$5,000,000
1982				
$3,000,000	$3,500,000	$1,290,800	57%	$3,000,000
$3,500,000	$4,000,000	$1,575,800	61%	$3,500,000
$4,000,000		$1,880,800	65%	$4,000,000
1983				
$3,000,000	$3,500,000	$1,290,800	57%	$3,000,000
$3,500,000		$1,575,800	60%	$3,500,000
1984 and after				
$3,000,000	$10,000,000	$1,290,800	55%	$3,000,000
$10,000,000		$5,140,800	60%	$10,000,000
*At the end of the "bubble" the rate drops back to 55%			55%	See Table 2.

* For post-1987 transfers above $10,000,000 there is a 5% surcharge that is imposed until the benefit of the unified credit and of lower marginal rates has been taken back.

TABLE 2 Federal Unified Credits, Exclusion Amounts, and the End of the Bubble by Year Since 1977

Year	Unified Credit	Exclusion Amount	End of the Bubble
1977	$30,000	$120,667	
1978	$34,000	$134,000	
1979	$38,000	$147,333	
1980	$42,500	$161,563	
1981	$47,000	$175,625	
1982	$62,800	$225,000	
1983	$79,300	$275,000	*The 5% surcharge started in 1988.*
1984	$96,300	$325,000	
1985	$121,800	$400,000	
1986	$155,800	$500,000	
1987 - 1997	$192,800	$600,000	$21,040,000
1998	$202,050	$625,000	$21,225,000
1999	$211,300	$650,000	$21,410,000
2000	$220,550	$675,000	$21,595,000
2001	$220,550	$675,000	$21,595,000
2002	$229,800	$700,000	$21,780,000
2003	$229,800	$700,000	$21,780,000
2004	$287,300	$850,000	$22,930,000
2005	$326,300	$950,000	$23,710,000
2006 & after	$345,800	$1,000,000	$24,100,000

TABLE 3 Maximum Credit against Federal Estate Tax for State Death Taxes

Adjusted taxable		Maximum Credit		
At Least	But Not Over	Base Amount	Plus Percent	On Excess Over
$40,000	$90,000	$0	0.8%	$40,000
$90,000	$140,000	$400	1.6%	$90,000
$140,000	$240,000	$1,200	2.4%	$140,000
$240,000	$440,000	$3,600	3.2%	$240,000
$440,000	$640,000	$10,000	4.0%	$440,000
$640,000	$840,000	$18,000	4.8%	$640,000
$840,000	$1,040,000	$27,600	5.6%	$840,000
$1,040,000	$1,540,000	$38,800	6.4%	$1,040,000
$1,540,000	$2,040,000	$70,800	7.2%	$1,540,000
$2,040,000	$2,540,000	$106,800	8.0%	$2,040,000
$2,540,000	$3,040,000	$146,800	8.8%	$2,540,000
$3,040,000	$3,540,000	$190,800	9.6%	$3,040,000
$3,540,000	$4,040,000	$238,800	10.4%	$3,540,000
$4,040,000	$5,040,000	$290,800	11.2%	$4,040,000
$5,040,000	$6,040,000	$402,800	12.0%	$5,040,000
$6,040,000	$7,040,000	$522,800	12.8%	$6,040,000
$7,040,000	$8,040,000	$650,800	13.6%	$7,040,000
$8,040,000	$9,040,000	$786,800	14.4%	$8,040,000
$9,040,000	$10,040,000	$930,800	15.2%	$9,040,000
$10,040,000		$1,082,800	16.0%	$10,040,000

* Adjusted taxable estate is taxable estate less $60,000.

TABLE 4 Federal Gift Tax Rates prior to January 1, 1977

| Taxable Gift* | | Gift Tax | | |
At Least	But Not Over	Base Amount	Plus Percent	On Excess Over
$0	$5,000	$0	2.25%	$0
$5,000	$10,000	$113	5.25%	$5,000
$10,000	$20,000	$375	8.25%	$10,000
$20,000	$30,000	$1,200	10.50%	$20,000
$30,000	$40,000	$2,250	13.50%	$30,000
$40,000	$50,000	$3,600	16.50%	$40,000
$50,000	$60,000	$5,250	18.75%	$50,000
$60,000	$100,000	$7,125	21.00%	$60,000
$100,000	$250,000	$15,525	22.50%	$100,000
$250,000	$500,000	$49,275	24.00%	$250,000
$500,000	$750,000	$109,275	26.25%	$500,000
$750,000	$1,000,000	$174,900	27.75%	$750,000
$1,000,000	$1,250,000	$244,275	29.25%	$1,000,000
$1,250,000	$1,500,000	$317,400	31.50%	$1,250,000
$1,500,000	$2,000,000	$396,150	33.75%	$1,500,000
$2,000,000	$2,500,000	$564,900	36.75%	$2,000,000
$2,500,000	$3,000,000	$748,650	39.75%	$2,500,000
$3,000,000	$3,500,000	$947,400	42.00%	$3,000,000
$3,500,000	$4,000,000	$1,157,400	44.50%	$3,500,000
$4,000,000	$5,000,000	$1,378,650	47.25%	$4,000,000
$5,000,000	$6,000,000	$1,851,150	50.25%	$5,000,000
$6,000,000	$7,000,000	$2,353,650	52.50%	$6,000,000
$7,000,000	$8,000,000	$2,878,650	54.75%	$7,000,000
$8,000,000	$10,000,000	$3,426,150	57.00%	$8,000,000
$10,000,000		$4,566,150	57.75%	$10,000,000

* Taxable amount after the annual exclusion and the gift exemption.

WARNING:

THESE ARE **PRE-1977 GIFT** TAX RATES

TABLE 5 Federal Estate Rates prior to January 1, 1977

Taxable Estate*		Estate Tax		
At Least	But Not Over	Base Amount	Plus Percent	On Excess Over
$0	$5,000	$0	3.0%	$0
$5,000	$10,000	$150	7.0%	$5,000
$10,000	$20,000	$500	11.0%	$10,000
$20,000	$30,000	$1,600	14.0%	$20,000
$30,000	$40,000	$3,000	18.0%	$30,000
$40,000	$50,000	$4,800	22.0%	$40,000
$50,000	$60,000	$7,000	25.0%	$50,000
$60,000	$100,000	$9,500	28.0%	$60,000
$100,000	$250,000	$20,700	30.0%	$100,000
$250,000	$500,000	$65,700	32.0%	$250,000
$500,000	$750,000	$145,700	35.0%	$500,000
$750,000	$1,000,000	$233,200	37.0%	$750,000
$1,000,000	$1,250,000	$325,700	39.0%	$1,000,000
$1,250,000	$1,500,000	$423,200	42.0%	$1,250,000
$1,500,000	$2,000,000	$528,200	45.0%	$1,500,000
$2,000,000	$2,500,000	$753,200	49.0%	$2,000,000
$2,500,000	$3,000,000	$998,200	53.0%	$2,500,000
$3,000,000	$3,500,000	$1,263,200	56.0%	$3,000,000
$3,500,000	$4,000,000	$1,543,200	59.0%	$3,500,000
$4,000,000	$5,000,000	$1,838,200	63.0%	$4,000,000
$5,000,000	$6,000,000	$2,468,200	67.0%	$5,000,000
$6,000,000	$7,000,000	$3,138,200	70.0%	$6,000,000
$7,000,000	$8,000,000	$3,838,200	73.0%	$7,000,000
$8,000,000	$10,000,000	$4,568,200	76.0%	$8,000,000
$10,000,000		$6,088,200	77.0%	$10,000,000

* Taxable amount after the estate exemption.

WARNING:

THESE ARE **PRE-1977 ESTATE** TAX RATES

TABLE 6   Federal Income Tax Rates: Estates and Trusts - 1999

Taxable Income

Over	But not over	Base amount	+ percent	On excess over
$0	$1,750	$0.00	15.0%	$0
$1,750	$4,050	$262.50	28.0%	$1,750
$4,050	$6,200	$906.50	31.0%	$4,050
$6,200	$8,450	$1,573.00	36.0%	$6,200
$8,450	....	$2,383.00	39.6%	$8,450

Table 7   Estate Planning Indexed Values

Year	Annual Exclusion Regular	Annual Exclusion Non-US Spouse	GSTT Exemption	6601j 2% portion on 6166 payments	2032A	"Kiddie Tax" Threshold
1987						**$1,000**
1997	**$10,000**	**$100,000**	**$1,000,000**	**$1,000,000**	**$750,000**	$1,300
1998	$10,000	$100,000	$1,000,000	$1,000,000	$750,000	$1,400
1999	$10,000	$101,000	$1,010,000	$1,010,000	$760,000	$1,400
2000						
2001						
2002						
2003						

Numbers in bold indicate the base amount and the base year. Shown are only those years in which a change occurred for at least one of the items.

ACTUARIAL VALUE TABLES

Note: Tables that follow are taken from Department of the Treasury's *Internal Revenue Service Publication 1457* (8-89), *Actuarial Values Alpha Volume*. We will use the designation for each table as is used by the Treasury, i.e., Tables K, S, B, and 80CNSMT. The Mortality Table (80CNSMT) is drawn from the 1980 census. We can expect Table S and Table 80CNSMT to be updated once the 1990 census information is digested by the U.S. Department of Health and Human Services, Public Health Service, National Center for Health Statistics.

Table K

Adjustment Factors for Annuities Payable at the End of Each Interval

Interest Rate	Annually	Semi-Annually	Quarterly	Monthly	Weekly
6%	1.0000	1.0148	1.0222	1.0272	1.0291
8%	1.0000	1.0196	1.0295	1.0362	1.0387
10%	1.0000	1.0244	1.0368	1.0450	1.0482
12%	1.0000	1.0292	1.0439	1.0539	1.0577

The factors in Table K are used to adjust the values for life estates, remainders, annuities, and interests for a term of years when the payments are made other than annually.

TABLE B -Term Certain

PV of Annuity (A), Income Interest (Inc. Int.), & Remainder Interests

	(6%) Six Percent				(8%) Eight Percent		
Year	A	Inc.Int.	REM	Year	A	Inc.Int.	REM
1	.09434	.05660	.943396	1	0.9259	.074074	.925926
2	1.8334	.11000	.889996	2	1.7833	.142661	.857339
3	2.6730	.16038	.839619	3	2.5771	.206168	.793832
4	3.4651	.20790	.792094	4	3.3121	.264970	.735030
5	4.2124	.25274	.747258	5	3.9927	.319417	.680583
6	4.9173	.29503	.704961	6	4.6229	.369830	.630170
7	5.5824	.33494	.665057	7	5.2064	.416510	.583490
8	6.2098	.37258	.627412	8	5.7466	.459731	.540269
9	6.8017	.40810	.591898	9	6.2469	.499751	.500249
10	7.3601	.44160	.558395	10	6.7101	.536807	.463193
15	9.7122	.58273	.417265	15	8.5595	.684758	.315242
20	11.4699	.68819	.311805	20	9.8181	.785452	.214548
25	12.7834	.76700	.232999	25	10.674	.853982	.146018
30	13.7648	.82589	.174110	30	11.257	.900623	.099377
35	14.4982	.86989	.130105	35	11.654	.932365	.067635
40	15.0463	.90277	.097222	40	11.924	.953969	.046031
45	15.4558	.92735	.072650	45	12.108	.968672	.031328
50	15.7619	.94571	.054288	50	12.233	.978679	.021321
55	15.9905	.95943	.040567	55	12.318	.985489	.014511
60	16.1614	.96968	.030314	60	12.376	.990124	.009876

TABLE B -Term Certain

PV of Annuity (A), Income Interest (Inc.Int.), & Remainder Interests

	(10%) Ten Percent				(12%) Twelve Percent		
Year	A	Inc.Int.	REM	Year	A	Inc.Int.	REM
1	0.9091	.090909	.909091	1	0.8929	.107143	.892857
2	1.7355	.173554	.826446	2	1.6901	.202806	.797194
3	2.4869	.248685	.751315	3	2.4018	.288220	.711780
4	3.1699	.316987	.683013	4	3.0373	.364482	.635518
5	3.7908	.379079	.620921	5	3.6048	.432573	.567427
6	4.3553	.435526	.564474	6	4.1114	.493369	.506631
7	4.8684	.486842	.513158	7	4.5638	.547651	.452349
8	5.3349	.533493	.466507	8	4.9676	.596117	.403883
9	5.7590	.575902	.424098	9	5.3282	.639390	.360610
10	6.1446	.614457	.385543	10	5.6502	.678027	.321973
15	7.6061	.760608	.239392	15	6.8109	.817304	.182696
20	8.5136	.851356	.148644	20	7.4694	.896333	.103667
25	9.0770	.907704	.092296	25	7.8431	.941177	.058823
30	9.4269	.942691	.057309	30	8.0552	.966622	.033378
35	9.6442	.964416	.035584	35	8.1755	.981060	.018940
40	9.7791	.977905	.022095	40	8.2438	.989253	.010747
45	9.8628	.986281	.013719	45	8.2825	.993902	.006098
50	9.9148	.991481	.008519	50	8.3045	.996540	.003460
55	9.9471	.994711	.005289	55	8.3170	.998037	.001963
60	9.9672	.996716	.003284	60	8.3240	.998886	.001114

TABLE S - Single Life

PV of Annuity (A), Life Estate (LE), & Remainder Interests (REM)

	(6%) Six Percent				(8%) Eight Percent		
Age	A	LE	REM	Age	A	LE	REM
0	16.0427	.96256	.03744	0	12.1984	.97587	.02413
5	16.1438	.96863	.03137	5	12.3137	.98510	.01490
10	15.9954	.95973	.04027	10	12.2492	.97994	.02006
15	15.7958	.94775	.05225	15	12.1534	.97227	.02773
20	15.5847	.93508	.06492	20	12.0581	.96465	.03535
25	15.3348	.92009	.07991	25	11.9452	.95562	.04438
30	14.9997	.89998	.10002	30	11.7796	.94237	.05763
35	14.5550	.87330	.12670	35	11.5402	.92321	.07679
40	13.9928	.83957	.16043	40	11.2168	.89734	.10266
45	13.3093	.79856	.20144	45	10.8011	.86409	.13591
50	12.5056	.75034	.24966	50	10.2879	.82303	.17697
55	11.5878	.69527	.30473	55	9.6749	.77399	.22601
60	10.5543	.63326	.36674	60	8.9526	.71621	.28379
65	9.4331	.56599	.43401	65	8.1360	.65088	.34912
70	8.2265	.49359	.50641	70	7.2190	.57752	.42248
75	6.9766	.41860	.58140	75	6.2305	.49844	.50156
80	5.6919	.34151	.65849	80	5.1710	.41368	.58632
85	4.5120	.27072	.72928	85	4.1633	.33307	.66693
90	3.5239	.21143	.78857	90	3.2953	.26362	.73638
95	2.7526	.16516	.83484	95	2.6006	.20805	.79195
100	2.2788	.13673	.86327	100	2.1694	.17356	.82644
105	1.8323	.10994	.89006	105	1.7638	.14110	.85890
109	0.4717	.02830	.97170	109	0.4630	.03704	.96296

TABLE S - Single Life

PV of Annuity (A), Life Estate (LE), & Remainder Interests (REM)

	(10%) Ten Percent				(12%) Twelve Percent		
Age	A	LE	REM	Age	A	LE	REM
0	9.8078	.98078	.01922	0	8.1918	.98302	.01698
5	9.9138	.99138	.00862	5	8.2852	.99422	.00578
10	9.8806	.98806	.01194	10	8.2657	.99188	.00812
15	9.8262	.98262	.01738	15	8.2301	.98762	.01238
20	9.7771	.97771	.02229	20	8.2015	.98418	.01582
25	9.7216	.97216	.02784	25	8.1720	.98064	.01936
30	9.6329	.96329	.03671	30	8.1208	.97450	.02550
35	9.4937	.94937	.05063	35	8.0341	.96409	.03591
40	9.2945	.92945	.07055	40	7.9037	.94845	.05155
45	9.0264	.90264	.09736	45	7.7214	.92657	.07343
50	8.6818	.86818	.13182	50	7.4794	.89753	.10247
55	8.2550	.82550	.17450	55	7.1710	.86052	.13948
60	7.7326	.77326	.22674	60	6.7814	.81376	.18624
65	7.1213	.71213	.28787	65	6.3122	.75746	.24254
70	6.4093	.64093	.35907	70	5.7482	.68979	.31021
75	5.6144	.56144	.43856	75	5.0993	.61191	.38809
80	4.7295	.47295	.52705	80	4.3517	.52221	.47779
85	3.8608	.38608	.61392	85	3.5962	.43155	.56845
90	3.0929	.30929	.69071	90	2.9126	.34951	.65049
95	2.4638	.24638	.75362	95	2.3401	.28081	.71919
100	2.0696	.20696	.79304	100	1.9781	.23737	.76263
105	1.6997	.16997	.83003	105	1.6398	.19678	.80322
109	0.4545	.04545	.95455	109	0.4464	.05357	.94643

TABLE 80CNSMT - Mortality Table

Age x	L(x)	Age x	L(x)	Age x	L(x)	Age x	L(x)
0	100,000						
1	98,740	31	96,350	61	82,581	91	11,908
2	98,648	32	96,220	62	81,348	92	9,863
3	98,584	33	96,088	63	80,024	93	8,032
4	98,535	34	95,951	64	78,609	94	6,424
5	98,495	35	95,808	65	77,107	95	5,043
6	98,459	36	95,655	66	75,520	96	3,884
7	98,426	37	95,492	67	73,846	97	2,939
8	98,396	38	95,317	68	72,082	98	2,185
9	98,370	39	95,129	69	70,218	99	1,598
10	98,347	40	94,926	70	68,248	100	1,150
11	98,328	41	94,706	71	66,165	101	815
12	98,309	42	94,465	72	63,972	102	570
13	98,285	43	94,201	73	61,673	103	393
14	98,248	44	93,913	74	59,279	104	267
15	98,196	45	93,599	75	56,799	105	179
16	98,129	46	93,256	76	54,239	106	149
17	98,047	47	92,882	77	51,599	107	78
18	97,953	48	92,472	78	48,878	108	51
19	97,851	49	92,021	79	46,071	109	33
20	97,741	50	91,526	80	43,180	110	0
21	97,623	51	90,986	81	40,208		
22	97,499	52	90,402	82	37,172		
23	97,370	53	89,771	83	34,095		
24	97,240	54	89,087	84	31,012		
25	97,110	55	88,348	85	27,960		
26	96,982	56	87,551	86	24,961		
27	96,865	57	86,695	87	22,038		
28	96,730	58	85,776	88	19,235		
29	96,604	59	84,789	89	16,598		
30	96,477	60	83,726	90	14,154		

Internal Revenue Code: Selected Edited Sections[*]

---

[*]Note: Omitted passages are marked with five asterisks (*****).

CHAPTER 1 - NORMAL TAXES AND SURTAXES
Subchapter J. Estates, Trusts, Beneficiaries, and Decedents
Subpart D - Income Tax Grantor Trust Rules

SEC. 671. TRUST INCOME, DEDUCTIONS, AND CREDITS ATTRIBUTABLE TO GRANTORS AND OTHERS AS SUBSTANTIAL OWNERS

Where it is specified in this subpart that the grantor or another person shall be treated as the owner of any portion of a trust, there shall then be included in computing the taxable income and credits of the grantor or the other person those items of income, deductions, and credits against tax of the trust which are attributable to that portion of the trust to the extent that such items would be taken into account under this chapter in computing taxable income or credits against the tax of an individual. Any remaining portion of the trust shall be subject to subparts A through D. *****

SEC. 672. DEFINITIONS AND RULES

(a) ADVERSE PARTY.-For purposes of this subpart, the term "adverse party" means any person having a substantial beneficial interest in the trust which would be adversely affected by the exercise or nonexercise of the power which he possesses respecting the trust. A person having a general power of appointment over the trust property shall be deemed to have a beneficial interest in the trust.

(b) NONADVERSE PARTY.-For purposes of this subpart, the term "nonadverse party" means any person who is not an adverse party.

(c) RELATED OR SUBORDINATE PARTY.-For purposes of this subpart, the term "related or subordinate party" means any nonadverse party who is-

> (1) the grantor's spouse if living with the grantor;
> (2) any one of the following: The grantor's father, mother, issue, brother or sister, an employee of the grantor, a corporation or any employee of a corporation in which the stock holdings of the grantor and the trust are significant from the viewpoint of voting control; a subordinate employee of a corporation in which the grantor is an executive.

For purposes of sections 674 and 675, a related or subordinate party shall be presumed to be subservient to the grantor in respect of the exercise or nonexercise of the powers conferred on him unless such party is shown not to be subservient by a preponderance of the evidence.

(d) RULE WHERE POWER IS SUBJECT TO CONDITION PRECEDENT.- A person shall be considered to have a power described in this subpart even though the exercise of the power is subject to a precedent giving of notice or takes effect only on the expiration of a certain period after the exercise of the power.

(e) GRANTOR TREATED AS HOLDING ANY POWER OR INTEREST OF GRANTOR'S SPOUSE.-For purposes of this subpart. if a grantor's spouse is living with the grantor at the time of the creation of any power or interest held by such spouse. the grantor shall be treated as holding such power or interest.

SEC. 673. REVERSIONARY INTERESTS

(a) GENERAL RULE.-The grantor shall be treated as the owner of any portion of a trust in which he has a reversionary interest in either the corpus or the income therefrom, if, as of the inception of that portion of the trust, the value of such interest exceeds 5 percent of the value of such portion.

(b) REVERSIONARY INTEREST TAKING EFFECT AT DEATH OF MINOR LINEAL DESCENDANT BENEFICIARY.-In the case of any beneficiary who-

> (1) is a lineal descendant of the grantor, and
> (2) holds all of the present interests in any portion of a trust, the grantor shall not be treated under subsection (a) as the owner of such portion solely by reason of a reversionary interest

in such portion which takes effect upon the death of such beneficiary before such beneficiary attains age 21.

SEC. 674. POWER TO CONTROL BENEFICIAL ENJOYMENT

(a) GENERAL RULE.-The grantor shall be treated as the owner of any portion of a trust in respect of which the beneficial enjoyment of the corpus or the income therefrom is subject to a power of disposition, exercisable by the grantor or a nonadverse party, or both, without the approval or consent of any adverse party.

(b) EXCEPTIONS FOR CERTAIN POWERS.-Subsection (a) shall not apply to the following powers regardless of by whom held:

(1) POWER TO APPLY INCOME TO SUPPORT OF A DEPENDENT.-A power described in section 677(b) to the extent that the grantor would not be subject to tax under that section.

(2) POWER AFFECTING BENEFICIAL ENJOYMENT ONLY AFTER OCCURRENCE OF EVENT.-A power, the exercise of which can only affect the beneficial enjoyment of the income for a period commencing after the occurrence of an event such that a grantor would not be treated as the owner under section 673 if the power were a reversionary interest, but the grantor may be treated as the owner after the occurrence of the event unless the power is relinquished.

(3) POWER EXERCISABLE ONLY BY WILL.-A power exercisable only by will, other than a power in the grantor to appoint by will the income of the trust where the income is accumulated for such disposition by the grantor or may be so accumulated in the discretion of the grantor or a nonadverse party, or both, without the approval or consent of any adverse party.

(4) POWER TO ALLOCATE AMONG CHARITABLE BENEFICIARIES.-A power to determine the beneficial enjoyment of the corpus or the income therefrom if the corpus or income is irrevocably payable for a purpose specified in section 170(c) (relating to definition of charitable contributions).

(5) POWER TO DISTRIBUTE CORPUS.-A power to distribute corpus either-

(A) to or for a beneficiary or beneficiaries or to or for a class of beneficiaries (whether or not income beneficiaries) provided that the power is limited by a reasonably definite standard which is set forth in the trust instrument; or

(B) to or for any current income beneficiary, provided that the distribution of corpus must be chargeable against the proportionate share of corpus held in trust for the payment of income to the beneficiary as if the corpus constituted a separate trust.

A power does not fall within the powers described in this paragraph if any person has a power to add to the beneficiary or beneficiaries or to a class of beneficiaries designated to receive the income or corpus, except where such action is to provide for after-born or after-adopted children.

(6) POWER TO WITHHOLD INCOME TEMPORARILY.-A power to distribute or apply income to or for any current income beneficiary or to accumulate the income for him, provided that any accumulated income must ultimately be payable-

(A) to the beneficiary from whom distribution or application is withheld, to his estate, or to his appointees (or persons named as alternate takers in default of appointment) provided that such beneficiary possesses a power of appointment which does not exclude from the class of possible appointees any person other than the beneficiary, his estate, his creditors, or the creditors of his estate, or

(B) on termination of the trust, or in conjunction with a distribution of corpus which is augmented by such accumulated income, to the current income beneficiaries in shares which have been irrevocably specified in the trust instrument.

Accumulated income shall be considered so payable although it is provided that if any beneficiary does not survive a date of distribution which could reasonably have been expected to occur within the beneficiary's lifetime, the share of the deceased beneficiary is to be paid to his appointees or to one or more designated alternate takers (other than the grantor or the grantor's estate) whose shares have been irrevocably specified. A power does not fall within the powers described in this paragraph if any person has a power to add to the beneficiary or beneficiaries or to a class of beneficiaries designated to receive the income or corpus except where such action is to provide for after-born or after-adopted children.

(7) POWER TO WITHHOLD INCOME DURING DISABILITY OF A BENEFICIARY.-A power exercisable only during-

(A) the existence of a legal disability of any current income beneficiary, or

(B) the period during which any income beneficiary shall be under the age of 21 years, to distribute or apply income to or for such beneficiary or to accumulate and add the income to corpus. A power does not fall within the powers described in this paragraph if any person has a power to add to the beneficiary or beneficiaries or to a class of beneficiaries designated to receive the income or corpus, except where such action is to provide for after-born or after-adopted children.

(8) POWER TO ALLOCATE BETWEEN CORPUS AND INCOME.-A power to allocate receipts and disbursements as between corpus and income. even though expressed in broad language.

(c) EXCEPTION FOR CERTAIN POWERS OF INDEPENDENT TRUSTEES.- Subsection (a) shall not apply to a power solely exercisable (without the approval or consent of any other person) by a trustee or trustees, none of whom is the grantor. and no more than half of whom are related or subordinate parties who are subservient to the wishes of the grantor-

(1) to distribute, apportion, or accumulate income to or for a beneficiary or beneficiaries, or to, for, or within a class of beneficiaries; or

(2) to pay out corpus to or for a beneficiary or beneficiaries or to or for a class of beneficiaries (whether or not income beneficiaries).

A power does not fall within the powers described in this subsection if any person has a power to add to the beneficiary or beneficiaries or to a class of beneficiaries designated to receive the income or corpus, except where such action is to provide for after-born or after-adopted children.

(d) POWER TO ALLOCATE INCOME IF LIMITED BY A STANDARD. Subsection (a) shall not apply to a power solely exercisable (without the approval or consent of any other person) by a trustee or trustees, none of whom is the grantor or spouse living with the grantor, to distribute, apportion, or accumulate income to or for a beneficiary or beneficiaries, or to, for, or within a class of beneficiaries, whether or not the conditions of paragraph (6) or (7) of subsection (b) are satisfied, if such power is limited by a reasonably definite external standard which is set forth in the trust instrument. A power does not fall within the powers described in this subsection if any person has a power to add to the beneficiary or beneficiaries or to a class of beneficiaries designated to receive the income or corpus except where such action is to provide for after-born or after-adopted children.

SEC. 675. ADMINISTRATIVE POWERS

The grantor shall be treated as the owner of any portion of a trust in respect of which-

(1) POWER TO DEAL FOR LESS THAN ADEQUATE AND FULL CONSIDERATION.- A power exercisable by the grantor or a nonadverse party, or both, without the approval or consent of any adverse party enables the grantor or any person to purchase, exchange, or otherwise deal with or dispose of the corpus or the income therefrom for less than an adequate consideration in money or money's worth.

(2) POWER TO BORROW WITHOUT ADEQUATE INTEREST OR SECURITY.-A power exercisable by the grantor or a nonadverse party, or both, enables the grantor to borrow the corpus or income, directly or indirectly, without adequate interest or without adequate security

except where a trustee (other than the grantor) is authorized under a general lending power to make loans to any person without regard to interest or security.

(3) BORROWING OF THE TRUST FUNDS.-The grantor has directly or indirectly borrowed the corpus or income and has not completely repaid the loan, including any interest, before the beginning of the taxable year. The preceding sentence shall not apply to a loan which provides for adequate interest and adequate security, if such loan is made by a trustee other than the grantor and other than a related or subordinate trustee subservient to the grantor.

(4) GENERAL POWERS OF ADMINISTRATION.-A power of administration is exercisable in a nonfiduciary capacity by any person without the approval or consent of any person in a fiduciary capacity. For purposes of this paragraph, the term "power of administration" means any one or more of the following powers: (A) a power to vote or direct the voting of stock or other securities of a corporation in which the holdings of the grantor and the trust are significant from the viewpoint of voting control; (B) a power to control the investment of the trust funds either by directing investments or reinvestments, or by vetoing proposed investments or reinvestments, to the extent that the trust funds consist of stocks or securities of corporations in which the holdings of the grantor and the trust are significant from the viewpoint of voting control; or (C) a power to reacquire the trust corpus by substituting other property of an equivalent value.

SEC. 676. POWER TO REVOKE

(a) GENERAL RULE.-The grantor shall be treated as the owner of any portion of a trust, whether or not he is treated as such owner under any other provision of this part, where at any time the power to revest in the grantor title to such portion is exercisable by the grantor or a non-adverse party or both.

(b) POWER AFFECTING BENEFICIAL ENJOYMENT ONLY AFTER OCCURRENCE OF EVENT. Subsection (a) shall not apply to a power the exercise of which can only affect the beneficial enjoyment of the income for a period commencing after the occurrence of an event such that a grantor would not be treated as the owner under section 673 if the power were a reversionary interest. But the grantor may be treated as the owner after the occurrence of such event unless the power is relinquished.

SEC. 677. INCOME FOR BENEFIT OF GRANTOR

(a) GENERAL RULE.-The grantor shall be treated as the owner of any portion of a trust, whether or not he is treated as such owner under section 674, whose income without the approval or consent of any adverse party is, or, in the discretion of the grantor or a nonadverse party, or both, may be-

(1) distributed to the grantor or the grantor's spouse;

(2) held or accumulated for future distribution to the grantor or the grantor's spouse; or

(3) applied to the payment of premiums on policies of insurance on the life of the grantor or the grantor's spouse (except policies of insurance irrevocably payable for a purpose specified in section 170(c) (relating to definition of charitable contributions)).

This subsection shall not apply to a power the exercise of which can only affect the beneficial enjoyment of the income for a period commencing after *the occurrence of an event* such that the grantor would not be treated as the owner under section 673 if the power were a reversionary interest; but the grantor may be treated as the owner after *the occurrence of the event* unless the power is relinquished.

(b) OBLIGATIONS OF SUPPORT.-Income of a trust shall not be considered taxable to the grantor under subsection (a) or any other provision of this chapter merely because such income in the discretion of another person, the trustee, or the grantor acting as trustee or co-trustee, may be applied or distributed for the support or maintenance of a beneficiary (other than the grantor's spouse) whom the grantor is legally obligated to support or maintain, except to the extent that such income is so applied or distributed. In cases where the amounts so applied or distributed are paid out of corpus or out of other than income for the taxable year, such amounts shall be considered to be an amount paid or credited within the meaning of paragraph (2) of section 661(a) and shall be taxed to the grantor under section 662.

SEC. 678. PERSON OTHER THAN GRANTOR TREATED AS SUBSTANTIAL OWNER

(a) GENERAL RULE.-A person other than the grantor shall be treated as the owner of any portion of a trust with respect to which:

(1) such person has a power exercisable solely by himself to vest the corpus or the income therefrom in himself, or

(2) such person has previously partially released or otherwise modified such a power and after the release or modification retains such control as would, within the principles of sections 671 to 677, inclusive, subject a grantor of a trust to treatment as the owner thereof.

(b) EXCEPTION WHERE GRANTOR IS TAXABLE.-Subsection (a) shall not apply with respect to a power over income, as originally granted or thereafter modified, if the grantor of the trust or a transferor (to whom section 679 applies) is otherwise treated as the owner under the provisions of this subpart other than this section.

(c) OBLIGATIONS OF SUPPORT. Subsection (a) shall not apply to a power which enables such person, in the capacity of trustee or co-trustee, merely to apply the income of the trust to the support or maintenance of a person whom the holder of the power is obligated to support or maintain except to the extent that such income is so applied. In cases where the amounts so applied or distributed are paid out of corpus or out of other than income of the taxable year, such amounts shall be considered to be an amount paid or credited within the meaning of paragraph (2) of section 661(a) and shall be taxed to the holder of the power under section 662.

(d) EFFECT OF RENUNCIATION OR DISCLAIMER.-Subsection (a) shall not apply with respect to a power which has been renounced or disclaimed within a reasonable time after the holder of the power first became aware of its existence.   *****

CHAPTER 11 - ESTATE TAX
Subchapter A. Estates of Citizens or Residents
Part I - Tax Imposed

SEC. 2001. IMPOSITION AND RATE OF TAX

(a) IMPOSITION.-A tax is hereby imposed on the transfer of the taxable estate of every decedent who is a citizen or resident of the United States.

(b) COMPUTATION OF TAX.-The tax imposed by this section shall be the amount equal to the excess (if any) of-

(1) a tentative tax computed in accordance with the rate schedule set forth in subsection (c) on the sum of-

(A) the amount of the taxable estate, and

(B) the amount of the adjusted taxable gifts, over

(2) the aggregate amount of tax which would have been payable under chapter 12 with respect to gifts made by the decedent after December 31, 1976, if the rate schedule set forth in subsection (c) (as in effect at the decedent's death) had been applicable at the time of such gifts.

For purposes of paragraph (1)(b), the term "adjusted taxable gifts" means the total amount of the taxable gifts (within the meaning of section 2503) made by the decedent after December 31, 1976, other than gifts which are includible in the gross estate of the decedent.

(c) RATE SCHEDULE

(1) ***** [Author's note: Transfer tax rates will be found inside the back cover.]
(2) PHASEOUT OF GRADUATED RATES AND UNIFIED CREDIT.--The tentative tax determined under paragraph (1) shall be increased by an amount equal to 5 percent of so much of the amount (with respect to which the tentative tax is to be computed) as exceeds $10,000,000 but does not exceed $21,040,000.
(d) ADJUSTMENT FOR GIFT TAX PAID BY SPOUSE. *****
(e) COORDINATION OF SECTIONS 2513 AND 2035. *****

SEC. 2002. LIABILITY FOR PAYMENT
Except as provided in section 2210, the tax imposed by this chapter shall be paid by the executor.

Part II - Credits Against Tax

SEC. 2010. UNIFIED CREDIT AGAINST ESTATE TAX
(a) GENERAL RULE A credit of the applicable credit amount shall be allowed to the estate of every decedent against the tax imposed by section 2001.
(b) ADJUSTMENT TO CREDIT FOR CERTAIN GIFTS MADE BEFORE 1977 The amount of the credit allowable under subsection (a) shall be reduced by an amount equal to 20 percent of the aggregate amount allowed as a specific exemption under section 2521 (as in effect before its repeal by the Tax Reform Act of 1976) with respect to gifts made by the decedent after September 8, 1976.
(c) APPLICABLE CREDIT AMOUNT For purposes of this section, the applicable credit amount is the amount of the tentative tax which would be determined under the rate schedule set forth in section 2001(c) if the amount with respect to which such tentative tax is to be computed were the applicable exclusion amount determined in accordance with the following table:

In the case of estates of decedents dying,: and gifts made, during	The applicable exclusion amount is:
1998	$625,000
1999	$650,000
2000 and 2001	$675,000
2002 and 2003	$700,000
2004	$850,000
2005	$950,000
2006 or thereafter	$1,000,000

(d) LIMITATION BASED ON AMOUNT OF TAX The amount of the credit allowed by subsection (a) shall not exceed the amount of the tax imposed by section 2001.

SECTION 2011. CREDIT FOR STATE DEATH TAXES
(a) IN GENERAL - The tax imposed by section 2001 shall be credited with the amount of any estate, inheritance, legacy, or succession taxes actually paid to any State or the District of Columbia, in respect of any property included in the gross estate (not including any such taxes paid with respect to the estate of a person other than the decedent).
(b) AMOUNT OF CREDIT - The credit allowed by this section shall not exceed the appropriate amount stated in the following table: ***** [See Table 3 *State Death Tax Credit* in Appendix A]

(f) LIMITATION BASED ON AMOUNT OF TAX - The credit provided by this section shall not exceed the amount of the tax imposed by section 2001, reduced by the amount of the unified credit provided by section 2010.

SECTION 2013. CREDIT FOR TAX ON PRIOR TRANSFERS

(a) GENERAL RULE - The tax imposed by section 2001 shall be credited with all or a part of the amount of the Federal estate tax paid with respect to the transfer of property (including property passing as a result of the exercise or non-exercise of a power of appointment) to the decedent by or from a person (herein designated as a "transferor") who died within 10 years before, or within 2 years after, the decedent's death. If the transferor died within 2 years of the death of the decedent, the credit shall be the amount determined under subsections (b) and (c). If the transferor predeceased the decedent by more than 2 years, the credit shall be the following percentage of the amount so determined--

 (1) 80 percent, if within the third or fourth years preceding the decedent's death;

 (2) 60 percent, if within the fifth or sixth years preceding the decedent's death;

 (3) 40 percent, if within the seventh or eighth years preceding the decedent's death; and

 (4) 20 percent, if within the ninth or tenth years preceding the decedent's death.

(b) COMPUTATION OF CREDIT - Subject to the limitation prescribed in subsection (c), the credit provided by this section shall be an amount which bears the same ratio to the estate tax paid (adjusted as indicated hereinafter) with respect to the estate of the transferor as the value of the property transferred bears to the taxable estate of the transferor (determined for purposes of the estate tax) decreased by any death taxes paid with respect to such estate. For purposes of the preceding sentence, the estate tax paid shall be the Federal estate tax paid increased by any credits allowed against such estate tax under section 2012, or corresponding provisions of prior laws, on account of gift tax, and for any credits allowed against such estate tax under this section on account of prior transfers where the transferor acquired property from a person who died within 10 years before the death of the decedent.

(c) LIMITATION ON CREDIT

 (1) IN GENERAL -The credit provided in this section shall not exceed the amount by which--

  (A) the estate tax imposed by section 2001 or section 2101 (after deducting the credits provided for in sections 2010, 2011, 2012, and 2014) computed without regard to this section, exceeds

  (B) such tax computed by excluding from the decedent's gross estate the value of such property transferred and, if applicable, by making the adjustment hereinafter indicated. If any deduction is otherwise allowable under section 2055 or section 2106(a)(2) (relating to charitable deduction) then, for the purpose of the computation indicated in subparagraph (B), the amount of such deduction shall be reduced by that part of such deduction which the value of such property transferred bears to the decedent's entire gross estate reduced by the deductions allowed under sections 2053 and 2054, or section 2106(a)(1) (relating to deduction for expenses, losses, etc.). For purposes of this section, the value of such property transferred shall be the value as provided for in subsection (d) of this section.

 (2) TWO OR MORE TRANSFERORS- If the credit provided in this section relates to property received from 2 or more transferors, the limitation provided in paragraph (1) of this subsection shall be computed by aggregating the value of the property so transferred to the decedent. The aggregate limitation so determined shall be apportioned in accordance with the value of the property transferred to the decedent by each transferor.

(d) VALUATION OF PROPERTY TRANSFERRED - The value of property transferred to the decedent shall be the value used for the purpose of determining the Federal estate tax liability of the estate of the transferor but--

(1) there shall be taken into account the effect of the tax imposed by section 2001 or 2101, or any estate, succession, legacy, or inheritance tax, on the net value to the decedent of such property;

(2) where such property is encumbered in any manner, or where the decedent incurs any obligation imposed by the transferor with respect to such property, such encumbrance or obligation shall be taken into account in the same manner as if the amount of a gift to the decedent of such property was being determined; and

(3) if the decedent was the spouse of the transferor at the time of the transferor's death, the net value of the property transferred to the decedent shall be reduced by the amount allowed under section 2056 (relating to marital deductions), as a deduction from the gross estate of the transferor.

(e) PROPERTY DEFINED - For purposes of this section, the term "property" includes any beneficial interest in property, including a general power of appointment (as defined in section 2041).

(f) TREATMENT OF ADDITIONAL TAX IMPOSED UNDER SECTION 2032A - If section 2032A applies to any property included in the gross estate of the transferor and an additional tax is imposed with respect to such property under section 2032A(c) before the date which is 2 years after the date of the decedent's death, for purposes of this section--

(1) the additional tax imposed by section 2032A(c) shall be treated as a Federal estate tax payable with respect to the estate of the transferor; and

(2) the value of such property and the amount of the taxable estate of the transferor shall be determined as if section 2032A did not apply with respect to such property.

SEC. 2014. CREDIT FOR FOREIGN DEATH TAXES

(a) IN GENERAL - The tax imposed by section 2001 shall be credited with the amount of any estate, inheritance, legacy, or succession taxes actually paid to any foreign country in respect of any property situated within such foreign country and included in the gross estate (not including any such taxes paid with respect to the estate of a person other than the decedent). The determination of the country within which property is situated shall be made in accordance with the rules applicable under subchapter B (sec. 2101 and following) in determining whether property is situated within or without the United States.

(b) LIMITATIONS ON CREDIT - The credit provided in this section with respect to such taxes paid to any foreign country--

(1) shall not, with respect to any such tax, exceed an amount which bears the same ratio to the amount of such tax actually paid to such foreign country as the value of property which is--

(A) situated within such foreign country,

(B) subjected to such tax, and

(C) included in the gross estate bears to the value of all property subjected to such tax; and

(2) shall not, with respect to all such taxes, exceed an amount which bears the same ratio to the tax imposed by section 2001 (after deducting from such tax the credits provided by sections 2010, 2011, and 2012) as the value of property which is--

(A) situated within such foreign country,

(B) subjected to the taxes of such foreign country, and

(C) included in the gross estate bears to the value of the entire gross estate reduced by the aggregate amount of the deductions allowed under sections 2055 and 2056.

(c) VALUATION OF PROPERTY

(1) The values referred to in the ratio stated in subsection (b)(1) are the values determined for purposes of the tax imposed by such foreign country.

(2) The values referred to in the ratio stated in subsection (b)(2) are the values determined under this chapter; but, in applying such ratio, the value of any property described in subparagraphs (A), (B), and (C) thereof shall be reduced by such amount as will properly reflect, in accordance with regulations prescribed by the Secretary, the deductions allowed in respect of such property under sections 2055 and 2056 (relating to charitable and marital deductions).

(d) PROOF OF CREDIT - The credit provided in this section shall be allowed only if the taxpayer establishes to the satisfaction of the Secretary--

(1) the amount of taxes actually paid to the foreign country,

(2) the amount and date of each payment thereof,

(3) the description and value of the property in respect of which such taxes are imposed, and

(4) all other information necessary for the verification and computation of the credit.

(e) PERIOD OF LIMITATION - The credit provided in this section shall be allowed only for such taxes as were actually paid and credit therefor claimed within 4 years after the filing of the return required by section 6018, except that--

(1) If a petition for redetermination of a deficiency has been filed with the Tax Court within the time prescribed in section 6213(a), then within such 4-year period or before the expiration of 60 days after the decision of the Tax Court becomes final.

(2) If, under section 6161, an extension of time has been granted for payment of the tax shown on the return, or of a deficiency, then within such 4-year period or before the date of the expiration of the period of the extension.

Refund based on such credit may (despite the provisions of sections 6511 and 6512) be made if claim therefor is filed within the period above provided. Any such refund shall be made without interest.

(f) ADDITIONAL LIMITATION IN CASES INVOLVING A DEDUCTION UNDER SECTION 2053(d) - In any case where a deduction is allowed under section 2053(d) for an estate, succession, legacy, or inheritance tax imposed by and actually paid to any foreign country upon a transfer by the decedent for public, charitable, or religious uses described in section 2055, the property described in subparagraphs (A), (B), and (C) of paragraphs (1) and (2) of subsection (b) of this section shall not include any property in respect of which such deduction is allowed under section 2053(d).

(g) POSSESSION OF UNITED STATES DEEMED A FOREIGN COUNTRY - For purposes of the credits authorized by this section, each possession of the United States shall be deemed to be a foreign country.

(h) SIMILAR CREDIT REQUIRED FOR CERTAIN ALIEN RESIDENTS - Whenever the President finds that--

(1) a foreign country, in imposing estate, inheritance, legacy, or succession taxes, does not allow to citizens of the United States resident in such foreign country at the time of death a credit similar to the credit allowed under subsection (a),

(2) such foreign country, when requested by the United States to do so has not acted to provide such a similar credit in the case of citizens of the United States resident in such foreign country at the time of death, and

(3) it is in the public interest to allow the credit under subsection (a) in the case of citizens or subjects of such foreign country only if it allows such a similar credit in the case of citizens of the United States resident in such foreign country at the time of death,

the President shall proclaim that, in the case of citizens or subjects of such foreign country dying while the proclamation remains in effect, the credit under subsection (a) shall be allowed only if such foreign country allows such a similar credit in the case of citizens of the United States resident in such foreign country at the time of death.

Part III - Gross Estate

SEC. 2031. DEFINITION OF GROSS ESTATE

(a) GENERAL.-The value of the gross estate of the decedent shall be determined by including to the extent provided for in this part, the value at the time of his death of all property, real or personal, tangible or intangible, wherever situated.

(b) VALUATION OF UNLISTED STOCK AND SECURITIES.-In the case of stock and securities of a corporation the value of which, by reason of their not being listed on an exchange and by reason of the absence of sales thereof, cannot be determined with reference to bid and asked prices or with reference to sales prices, the value thereof shall be determined by taking into consideration, in addition to all other factors, the value of stock or securities of corporations engaged in the same or similar line of business which are listed on an exchange.

(c) ESTATE TAX WITH RESPECT TO LAND SUBJECT TO A QUALIFIED CONSERVATION EASEMENT

(1) IN GENERAL - If the executor makes the election described in paragraph (6), then, except as otherwise provided in this subsection, there shall be excluded from the gross estate the lesser of--

(A) the applicable percentage of the value of land subject to a qualified conservation easement, reduced by the amount of any deduction under section 2055(f) with respect to such land, or

(B) the exclusion limitation.

(2) APPLICABLE PERCENTAGE - For purposes of paragraph (1), the term "applicable percentage" means 40 percent reduced (but not below zero) by 2 percentage points for each percentage point (or fraction thereof) by which the value of the qualified conservation easement is less than 30 percent of the value of the land (determined without regard to the value of such easement and reduced by the value of any retained development right (as defined in paragraph (5)).

(3) EXCLUSION LIMITATION - For purposes of paragraph (1), the exclusion limitation is the limitation determined in accordance with the following table:

In the case of estates of decedents dying during:	The exclusion limitation is:
1998	$100,000
1999	$200,000
2000	$300,000
2001	$400,000
2002 or thereafter	$500,000

(4) TREATMENT OF CERTAIN INDEBTEDNESS

A) IN GENERAL - The exclusion provided in paragraph (1) shall not apply to the extent that the land is debt-financed property.

(B) DEFINITIONS - For purposes of this paragraph--

(i) DEBT-FINANCED PROPERTY

The term "debt-financed property" means any property with respect to which there is an acquisition indebtedness (as defined in clause (ii)) on the date of the decedent's death.

(ii) ACQUISITION INDEBTEDNESS - The term "acquisition indebtedness" means, with respect to debt-financed property, the unpaid amount of--

(I) the indebtedness incurred by the donor in acquiring such property,

(II) the indebtedness incurred before the acquisition of such property if such indebtedness would not have been incurred but for such acquisition,

(III) the indebtedness incurred after the acquisition of such property if such indebtedness would not have been incurred but for such acquisition and the incurrence of such indebtedness was reasonably foreseeable at the time of such acquisition, and

(IV) the extension, renewal, or refinancing of an acquisition indebtedness.

(5) TREATMENT OF RETAINED DEVELOPMENT RIGHT

(A) IN GENERAL - Paragraph (1) shall not apply to the value of any development right retained by the donor in the conveyance of a qualified conservation easement.

(B) TERMINATION OF RETAINED DEVELOPMENT RIGHT - If every person in being who has an interest (whether or not in possession) in the land executes an agreement to extinguish permanently some or all of any development rights (as defined in subparagraph (D)) retained by the donor on or before the date for filing the return of the tax imposed by section 2001, then any tax imposed by section 2001 shall be reduced accordingly. Such agreement shall be filed with the return of the tax imposed by section 2001. The agreement shall be in such form as the Secretary shall prescribe.

(C) ADDITIONAL TAX - Any failure to implement the agreement described in subparagraph (B) not later than the earlier of--

(i) the date which is 2 years after the date of the decedent's death, or

(ii) the date of the sale of such land subject to the qualified conservation easement, shall result in the imposition of an additional tax in the amount of the tax which would have been due on the retained development rights subject to such agreement. Such additional tax shall be due and payable on the last day of the 6th month following such date.

(D) DEVELOPMENT RIGHT DEFINED - For purposes of this paragraph, the term "development right" means any right to use the land subject to the qualified conservation easement in which such right is retained for any commercial purpose which is not subordinate to and directly supportive of the use of such land as a farm for farming purposes (within the meaning of section 2032A(e)(5)).

(6) ELECTION - The election under this subsection shall be made on the return of the tax imposed by section 2001. Such an election, once made, shall be irrevocable.

(7) CALCULATION OF ESTATE TAX DUE - An executor making the election described in paragraph (6) shall, for purposes of calculating the amount of tax imposed by section 2001, include the value of any development right (as defined in paragraph (5)) retained by the donor in the conveyance of such qualified conservation easement. The computation of tax on any retained development right prescribed in this paragraph shall be done in such manner and on such forms as the Secretary shall prescribe.

(8) DEFINITIONS - For purposes of this subsection--

(A) LAND SUBJECT TO A QUALIFIED CONSERVATION EASEMENT

The term "land subject to a qualified conservation easement" means land--

(i) which is located--

(I) in or within 25 miles of an area which, on the date of the decedent's death, is a metropolitan area (as defined by the Office of Management and Budget),

(II) in or within 25 miles of an area which, on the date of the decedent's death, is a national park or wilderness area designated as part of the National Wilderness Preservation System (unless it is determined by the Secretary that land in or within 25 miles of such a park or wilderness area is not under significant development pressure), or

(III) in or within 10 miles of an area which, on the date of the decedent's death, is an Urban National Forest (as designated by the Forest Service),

(ii) which was owned by the decedent or a member of the decedent's family at all times during the 3-year period ending on the date of the decedent's death, and

(iii) with respect to which a qualified conservation easement has been made by an individual described in subparagraph (C), as of the date of the election described in paragraph (6).

(B) QUALIFIED CONSERVATION EASEMENT - The term "qualified conservation easement" means a qualified conservation contribution (as defined in section 170(h)(1)) of a qualified real property interest (as defined in section 170(h)(2)(C)), except that clause (iv) of section 170(h)(4)(A) shall not apply, and the restriction on the use of such interest described in section 170(h)(2)(C) shall include a prohibition on more than a de minimus use for a commercial recreational activity.

(C) INDIVIDUAL DESCRIBED - An individual is described in this subparagraph if such individual is-

(i) the decedent,

(ii) a member of the decedent's family,

(iii) the executor of the decedent's estate, or

(iv) the trustee of a trust the corpus of which includes the land to be subject to the qualified conservation easement.

(D) MEMBER OF FAMILY - The term "member of the decedent's family" means any member of the family (as defined in section 2032A(e)(2)) of the decedent.

(9) APPLICATION OF THIS SECTION TO INTERESTS IN PARTNERSHIPS, CORPORATIONS, AND TRUSTS - This section shall apply to an interest in a partnership, corporation, or trust if at least 30 percent of the entity is owned (directly or indirectly) by the decedent, as determined under the rules described in section 2033A(e)(3).

(d) CROSS REFERENCE FOR EXECUTOR'S RIGHT TO BE FURNISHED ON REQUEST A STATEMENT REGARDING ANY VALUATION MADE BY THE SECRETARY WITHIN THE GROSS ESTATE, SEE SECTION 7517.

SEC. 2032. ALTERNATE VALUATION

(a) GENERAL.-The value of the gross estate may be determined, if the executor so elects, by valuing all the property included in the gross estate as follows:

(1) In the case of property distributed, sold, exchanged, or otherwise disposed of, within six months after the decedent's death such property shall be valued as of the date of distribution, sale, exchange, or other disposition.

(2) In the case of property not distributed, sold, exchanged, or otherwise disposed of, within six months after the decedent's death such property shall be valued as of the date six months after the decedent's death.

(3) Any interest or estate which is affected by mere lapse of time shall be included as its value as of the time of death (instead of the later date) with adjustment for any difference in its value as of the later date not due to mere lapse of time.

(b) SPECIAL RULES. *****

(c) ELECTION MUST DECREASE GROSS ESTATE AND ESTATE TAX.- No election may be made under this section with respect to an estate unless such election shall decrease-

(1) the value of the gross estate. and

(2) the amount of the tax imposed by this chapter (reduced by credits allowable against such tax).

(d) ELECTION.

(1) In General.-The election provided for in this section shall be made by the executor on the return of the tax imposed by this chapter. Such election, once made, shall be irrevocable.

(2) Exception.-No election may be made under this section if such return is filed more than 1 year after the time prescribed by law (including extensions) for filing such return.

SEC. 2032A. VALUATION OF CERTAIN FARM, ETC., REAL PROPERTY

(a) VALUE BASED ON USE UNDER WHICH PROPERTY QUALIFIES

(1) GENERAL RULE - If--

(A) the decedent was (at the time of his death) a citizen or resident of the United States, and

(B) the executor elects the application of this section and files the agreement referred to in subsection (d)(2), then, for purposes of this chapter, the value of qualified real property shall be its value for the use under which it qualifies, under subsection (b), as qualified real property.

(2) LIMITATION ON AGGREGATE REDUCTION IN FAIR MARKET VALUE - The aggregate decrease in the value of qualified real property taken into account for purposes of this chapter which results from the application of paragraph (1) with respect to any decedent shall not exceed $750,000.

(3) INFLATION ADJUSTMENT - In the case of estates of decedents dying in a calendar year after 1998, the $750,000 amount contained in paragraph (2) shall be increased by an amount equal to

(A) $750,000, multiplied by

(B) the cost-of-living adjustment determined under section 1(f)(3) for such calendar year by substituting "calendar year 1997" for "calendar year 1992" in subparagraph (B) thereof.

If any amount as adjusted under the preceding sentence is not a multiple of $10,000, such amount shall be rounded to the next lowest multiple of $10,000.

(b) QUALIFIED REAL PROPERTY

(1) IN GENERAL - For purposes of this section, the term "qualified real property" means real property located in the United States which was acquired from or passed from the decedent to a qualified heir of the decedent and which, on the date of the decedent's death, was being used for a qualified use by the decedent or a member of the decedent's family, but only if--

(A) 50 percent or more of the adjusted value of the gross estate consists of the adjusted value of real or personal property which--

(i) on the date of the decedent's death, was being used for a qualified use by the decedent or a member of the decedent's family, and

(ii) was acquired from or passed from the decedent to a qualified heir of the decedent.

(B) 25 percent or more of the adjusted value of the gross estate consists of the adjusted value of real property which meets the requirements of subparagraphs (A)(ii) and (C),

(C) during the 8-year period ending on the date of the decedent's death there have been periods aggregating 5 years or more during which--

(i) such real property was owned by the decedent or a member of the decedent's family and used for a qualified use by the decedent or a member of the decedent's family, and

(ii) there was material participation by the decedent or a member of the decedent's family in the operation of the farm or other business, and

(D) such real property is designated in the agreement referred to in subsection (d)(2).

(2) QUALIFIED USE - For purposes of this section, the term "qualified use" means the devotion of the property to any of the following:

    (A) use as a farm for farming purposes, or

    (B) use in a trade or business other than the trade or business of farming.

(3) ADJUSTED VALUE - For purposes of paragraph (1), the term "adjusted value" means-

    (A) in the case of the gross estate, the value of the gross estate for purposes of this chapter (determined without regard to this section), reduced by any amounts allowable as a deduction under paragraph (4) of section 2053(a), or

    (B) in the case of any real or personal property, the value of such property for purposes of this chapter (determined without regard to this section), reduced by any amounts allowable as a deduction in respect of such property under paragraph (4) of section 2053(a).

*****

(c) TAX TREATMENT OF DISPOSITIONS AND FAILURES TO USE FOR QUALIFIED USE

(1) IMPOSITION OF ADDITIONAL ESTATE TAX - If, within 10 years after the decedent's death and before the death of the qualified heir--

    (A) the qualified heir disposes of any interest in qualified real property (other than by a disposition to a member of his family), or

    (B) the qualified heir ceases to use for the qualified use the qualified real property which was acquired (or passed) from the decedent, then, there is hereby imposed an additional estate tax.

(2) AMOUNT OF ADDITIONAL TAX

    (A) IN GENERAL - The amount of the additional tax imposed by paragraph (1) with respect to any interest shall be the amount equal to the lesser of--

        (i) the adjusted tax difference attributable to such interest, or

        (ii) the excess of the amount realized with respect to the interest (or, in any case other than a sale or exchange at arm's length, the fair market value of the interest) over the value of the interest determined under subsection (a).

    (B) ADJUSTED TAX DIFFERENCE ATTRIBUTABLE TO INTEREST - For purposes of subparagraph (A), the adjusted tax difference attributable to an interest is the amount which bears the same ratio to the adjusted tax difference with respect to the estate (determined under subparagraph (C)) as--

        (i) the excess of the value of such interest for purposes of this chapter (determined without regard to subsection (a)) over the value of such interest determined under subsection (a), bears to

        (ii) a similar excess determined for all qualified real property.

    (C) ADJUSTED TAX DIFFERENCE WITH RESPECT TO THE ESTATE - For purposes of subparagraph (B), the term "adjusted tax difference with respect to the estate" means the excess of what would have been the estate tax liability but for subsection (a) over the estate tax liability. For purposes of this subparagraph, the term "estate tax liability" means the tax imposed by section 2001 reduced by the credits allowable against such tax.

    (D) PARTIAL DISPOSITIONS *****

(4) DUE DATE - The additional tax imposed by this subsection shall become due and payable on the day which is 6 months after the date of the disposition or cessation referred to in paragraph (1).

(5) LIABILITY FOR TAX; FURNISHING OF BOND - The qualified heir shall be personally liable for the additional tax imposed by this subsection with respect to his interest unless the heir has furnished bond which meets the requirements of subsection (e)(11).

(6) CESSATION OF QUALIFIED USE - For purposes of paragraph (1)(B), real property shall cease to be used for the qualified use if--

(A) such property ceases to be used for the qualified use set forth in subparagraph (A) or (B) of subsection (b)(2) under which the property qualified under subsection (b), or

(B) during any period of 8 years ending after the date of the decedent's death and before the date of the death of the qualified heir, there had been periods aggregating more than 3 years during which--

(i) in the case of periods during which the property was held by the decedent, there was no material participation by the decedent or any member of his family in the operation of the farm or other business, and

(ii) in the case of periods during which the property was held by any qualified heir, there was no material participation by such qualified heir or any member of his family in the operation of the farm or other business.

(7) SPECIAL RULES *****

(C) ELIGIBLE QUALIFIED HEIR - For purposes of this paragraph, the term "eligible qualified heir" means a qualified heir who--

(i) is the surviving spouse of the decedent,

(ii) has not attained the age of 21,

(iii) is disabled (within the meaning of subsection (b)(4)(B)), or

(iv) is a student.

(D) STUDENT *****

(d) ELECTION; AGREEMENT

(1) ELECTION - The election under this section shall be made on the return of the tax imposed by section 2001. Such election shall be made in such manner as the Secretary shall by regulations prescribe. Such an election, once made, shall be irrevocable.

(2) AGREEMENT - The agreement referred to in this paragraph is a written agreement signed by each person in being who has an interest (whether or not in possession) in any property designated in such agreement consenting to the application of subsection (c) with respect to such property.

(3) MODIFICATION OF ELECTION AND AGREEMENT TO BE PERMITTED *****

(e) DEFINITIONS; SPECIAL RULES

For purposes of this section--

(1) QUALIFIED HEIR - The term "qualified heir" means, with respect to any property, a member of the decedent's family who acquired such property (or to whom such property passed) from the decedent. If a qualified heir disposes of any interest in qualified real property to any member of his family, such member shall thereafter be treated as the qualified heir with respect to such interest.

(2) MEMBER OF FAMILY - The term "member of the family" means, with respect to any individual, only--

(A) an ancestor of such individual,

(B) the spouse of such individual,

(C) a lineal descendant of such individual, of such individual's spouse, or of a parent of such individual, or

(D) the spouse of any lineal descendant described in subparagraph (C).

For purposes of the preceding sentence, a legally adopted child of an individual shall be treated as the child of such individual by blood.

(3) CERTAIN REAL PROPERTY INCLUDED - In the case of real property which meets the requirements of subparagraph (C) of subsection (b)(1), residential buildings and related improvements on such real property occupied on a regular basis by the owner or lessee of such real property or by persons employed by such owner or lessee for the purpose of

operating or maintaining such real property, and roads, buildings, and other structures and improvements functionally related to the qualified use shall be treated as real property devoted to the qualified use.

(4) FARM - The term "farm" includes stock, dairy, poultry, fruit, furbearing animal, and truck farms, plantations, ranches, nurseries, ranges, greenhouses or other similar structures used primarily for the raising of agricultural or horticultural commodities, and orchards and woodlands.

(5) FARMING PURPOSES *****

(6) MATERIAL PARTICIPATION *****

(12) ACTIVE MANAGEMENT - The term "active management" means the making of the management decisions of a business (other than the daily operating decisions). *****

    (D) ELECTION - An election under subparagraph (A) shall be made on the return of the tax imposed by section 2001. Such election shall be made in such manner as the Secretary shall by regulations prescribe. Such an election, once made, shall be irrevocable. *****

(14) TREATMENT OF REPLACEMENT PROPERTY ACQUIRED IN SECTION 1031 OR 1033 TRANSACTIONS *****

(f) STATUTE OF LIMITATIONS - If qualified real property is disposed of or ceases to be used for a qualified use, then--

(1) the statutory period for the assessment of any additional tax under subsection (c) attributable to such disposition or cessation shall not expire before the expiration of 3 years from the date the Secretary is notified (in such manner as the Secretary may by regulations prescribe) of such disposition or cessation (or if later in the case of an involuntary conversion or exchange to which subsection (h) or (i) applies, 3 years from the date the Secretary is notified of the replacement of the converted property or of an intention not to replace or of the exchange of property), and

(2) such additional tax may be assessed before the expiration of such 3-year period notwithstanding the provisions of any other law or rule of law which would otherwise prevent such assessment. *****

(h) SPECIAL RULES FOR INVOLUNTARY CONVERSIONS OF QUALIFIED REAL PROPERTY *****

SEC. 2033. PROPERTY IN WHICH THE DECEDENT HAD AN INTEREST
The value of the gross estate shall include the value of all property to the extent of the interest therein of the decedent at the time of his death.

SEC. 2034. DOWER OR CURTESY INTERESTS
The value of the gross estate shall include the value of all property to the extent of any interest therein of the surviving spouse, existing at the time of the decedent's death as dower or curtesy, or by virtue of a statute creating an estate in lieu of dower or curtesy.

SEC. 2035. ADJUSTMENTS FOR GIFTS MADE WITHIN 3 YEARS OF DECEDENT'S DEATH
(a) INCLUSION OF CERTAIN PROPERTY IN GROSS ESTATE - If--

(1) the decedent made a transfer (by trust or otherwise) of an interest in any property, or relinquished a power with respect to any property, during the 3-year period ending on the date of the decedent's death, and

(2) the value of such property (or an interest therein) would have been included in the decedent's gross estate under section 2036, 2037, 2038, or 2042 if such transferred interest or relinquished power had been retained by the decedent on the date of his death, the value

of the gross estate shall include the value of any property (or interest therein) which would have been so included.

(b) INCLUSION OF GIFT TAX ON GIFTS MADE DURING 3 YEARS BEFORE DECEDENT's DEATH

The amount of the gross estate (determined without regard to this subsection) shall be increased by the amount of any tax paid under chapter 12 by the decedent or his estate on any gift made by the decedent or his spouse during the 3-year period ending on the date of the decedent's death.

(c) OTHER RULES RELATING TO TRANSFERS WITHIN 3 YEARS OF DEATH

    (1) IN GENERAL - For purposes of--

        (A) section 303(b) (relating to distributions in redemption of stock to pay death taxes),

        (B) section 2032A (relating to special valuation of certain farms, etc., real property), and

        (C) subchapter C of chapter 64 (relating to lien for taxes), the value of the gross estate shall include the value of all property to the extent of any interest therein of which the decedent has at any time made a transfer, by trust or otherwise, during the 3-year period ending on the date of the decedent's death.

    (2) COORDINATION WITH SECTION 6166 - An estate shall be treated as meeting the 35 percent of adjusted gross estate requirement of section 6166(a)(1) only if the estate meets such requirement both with and without the application of paragraph (1).

    (3) MARITAL AND SMALL TRANSFERS - Paragraph (1) shall not apply to any transfer (other than a transfer with respect to a life insurance policy) made during a calendar year to any donee if the decedent was not required by section 6019 (other than by reason of section 6019(2)) to file any gift tax return for such year with respect to transfers to such donee.

(d) EXCEPTION - Subsection (a) shall not apply to any bona fide sale for an adequate and full consideration in money or money's worth.

(e) TREATMENT OF CERTAIN TRANSFERS FROM REVOCABLE TRUSTS - For purposes of this section and section 2038, any transfer from any portion of a trust during any period that such portion was treated under section 676 as owned by the decedent by reason of a power in the grantor (determined without regard to section 672(e)) shall be treated as a transfer made directly by the decedent.

SEC. 2036. TRANSFERS WITH RETAINED LIFE ESTATE

(a) GENERAL RULE.-The value of the gross estate shall include the value of all property to the extent of any interest therein of which the decedent has at any time made a transfer (except in case of a bona fide sale for an adequate and full consideration in money or money's worth), by trust or otherwise, under which he has retained for his life or for any period not ascertainable without reference to his death or for any period which does not in fact end before his death-

    (1) the possession or enjoyment of, or the right to the income from, the property, or

    (2) the right, either alone or in conjunction with any person, to designate the persons who shall possess or enjoy the property or the income therefrom.

(b) VOTING RIGHTS

    (1) IN GENERAL, For purposes of subsection (a)(l), the retention of the right to vote (directly or indirectly) shares of stock of a controlled corporation shall be considered to be a retention of the enjoyment of transferred property.

    (2) CONTROLLED CORPORATION. *****

    (3) COORDINATION WITH SECTION 2035. *****

(c) LIMITATION ON APPLICATION OF GENERAL RULE. [Author's note: In 1990, the anti-freeze provisions of old §2036(c) were repealed retroactive to inception, and old §2036(d) was relabeled new §2036(c).] *****

SEC. 2037. TRANSFERS TAKING EFFECT AT DEATH

(a) GENERAL RULE.-The value of the gross estate shall include the value of all property to the extent of any interest therein of which the decedent has at any time after September 7, 1916, made a transfer (except in case of a bona fide sale for an adequate and full consideration in money or money's worth), by trust or otherwise, if-

(1) possession or enjoyment of the property can, through ownership of such interest, be obtained only by surviving the decedent, and

(2) the decedent has retained a reversionary interest in the property (but in the case of a transfer made before October 8, 1949, only if such reversionary interest arose by the express terms of the instrument of transfer), and the value of such reversionary interest immediately before the death of the decedent exceeds 5 percent of the value of such property.

(b) SPECIAL RULES. *****

SEC. 2038. REVOCABLE TRANSFERS

(a) IN GENERAL.-The value of the gross estate shall include the value of all property-

(1) Transfers after June 22, 1936- To the extent of any interest therein of which the decedent has at any time made a transfer (except in case of a bona fide sale for an adequate and full consideration in money or money's worth), by trust or otherwise, where the enjoyment thereof was subject at the date of his death to any change through the exercise of a power (in whatever capacity exercisable) by the decedent alone or by the decedent in conjunction with any other person (without regard to when or from what source the decedent acquired such power), to alter, amend, revoke, or terminate, or where such power is relinquished during the three-year period ending on the date of the decedent's death.

(2) TRANSFERS ON OR BEFORE JUNE 22, 1936. *****

SEC. 2039. ANNUITIES

(a) GENERAL.-The gross estate shall include the value of an annuity or other payment receivable by any beneficiary by reason of surviving the decedent under any form of contract or agreement entered into after March 3, 1931 (other than as insurance under policies on the life of the decedent), if, under such contract or agreement, an annuity or other payment was payable to the decedent, or the decedent possessed the right to receive such annuity or payment, either alone or in conjunction with another for his life or for any period not ascertainable without reference to his death or for any period which does not in fact end before his death.

(b) AMOUNT INCLUDIBLE. *****

SEC. 2040. JOINT INTERESTS

(a) GENERAL RULE.-The value of the gross estate shall include the value of all property to the extent of the interest therein held as joint tenants with right of survivorship by the decedent and any other person, or as tenants by the entirety by the decedent and spouse, or deposited, with any person carrying on the banking business, in their joint names and payable to either or the survivor, except such part thereof as may be shown to have originally belonged to such other person and never to have been received or acquired by the latter from the decedent for less than an adequate or full consideration in money or money's worth: *Provided*, That where such property or any part thereof, or part of the consideration with which such property was acquired, is shown to have been at any time acquired by such other person from the decedent for less than an adequate and full consideration in money or money's worth, there shall be excepted only such part of the value of such property as is proportionate to the consideration furnished by such other person: *Provided further*, that where any property has been acquired by gift, bequest, devise, or inheritance, as a tenancy by the entirety by the decedent and spouse, then to the extent of one half of the value thereof, or, where so acquired by the decedent and any other person as joint tenants with right of survivorship and their interests are not otherwise specified or fixed by law, then to the extent of the value of a fractional part to be determined by dividing the value of the property by the number of joint tenants with right of survivorship.

(b) CERTAIN JOINT INTERESTS OF HUSBAND AND WIFE.-

(1) INTERESTS OF SPOUSE EXCLUDED FROM GROSS ESTATE,-Notwithstanding subsection (a), in the case of any qualified joint interest, the value included in the gross estate with respect to such interest by reason of this section is one half of the value of such qualified joint interest,

(2) QUALIFIED JOINT INTEREST DEFINED.-For purposes of paragraph (1), the term "qualified joint interest" means any interest in property held by the decedent and the decedent's spouse as-

(A) tenants by the entirety, or

(B) joint tenants with right of survivorship, but only if the decedent and the spouse of the decedent are the only joint tenants.

SECTION 2041. POWERS OF APPOINTMENT

(a) IN GENERAL.-The value of the gross estate shall include the value of all property.

(1) POWERS OF APPOINTMENT CREATED ON OR BEFORE OCTOBER 21, 1942. *****

(2) POWERS CREATED AFTER OCTOBER 21, 1942.-To the extent of any property with respect to which the decedent has at the time of his death a general power of appointment created after October 21, 1942, or with respect to which the decedent has at any time exercised or released such a power of appointment by a disposition which is of such a nature that if it were a transfer of property owned by the decedent, such property would be includible in the decedent's gross estate under section 2035 to 2038, inclusive. For purposes of this paragraph (2), the power of appointment shall be considered to exist on the date of the decedent's death even though the exercise of the power is subject to a precedent giving of notice or even though the exercise of the power takes effect only on the expiration of a stated period after its exercise, whether or not on or before the date of the decedent's death notice has been given or the power has been exercised.

(3) CREATION OF ANOTHER POWER IN CERTAIN CASES. *****

(b) DEFINITIONS.-For purposes of subsection (a)-

(1) GENERAL POWER OF APPOINTMENT-The term "general power of appointment" means a power which is exercisable in favor of the decedent, his estate, his creditors, or the creditors of his estate; except that-

(A) A power to consume, invade, or appropriate property for the benefit of the decedent which is limited to an ascertainable standard relating to the health, education, support, or maintenance of the decedent shall not be deemed a general power of appointment.

(B) A power of appointment created on or before October 21, 1942, which is exercisable by the decedent only in conjunction with another person shall not be deemed a general power of appointment.

(C) In the case of a power of appointment created after October 21, 1942, which is exercisable by the decedent only in conjunction with another person-

(i) If the power is not exercisable by the decedent except in conjunction with the creator of the power-such power shall not be deemed a general power of appointment.

(ii) If the power is not exercisable by the decedent except in conjunction with a person having a substantial interest in the property, subject to the power, which is adverse to the exercise of the power in favor of the decedent-such power shall not be deemed a general power of appointment.

*****

(2) LAPSE OF POWER-The lapse of a power of appointment created after October 21, 1942, during the life of the individual possessing the power shall be considered a release of such power. The preceding sentence shall apply with respect to the lapse of powers during any calendar year only to the extent that the property, which could have been appointed by exercise of such lapsed powers, exceeded in value, at the time of such lapse, the greater of the following amounts:

    (A) $5,000, or

    (B) 5 percent of the aggregate value, at the time of such lapse, of the assets out of which, or the proceeds of which, the exercise of the lapsed powers could have been satisfied.

    *****

SEC. 2042. PROCEEDS OF LIFE INSURANCE

The value of the gross estate shall include the value of all property-

    (1) RECEIVABLE BY THE EXECUTOR.-To the extent of the amount receivable by the executor as insurance under policies on the life of the decedent.

    (2) RECEIVABLE BY OTHER BENEFICIARIES.-To the extent of the amount receivable by all other beneficiaries as insurance under policies on the life of the decedent with respect to which the decedent possessed at his death any of the incidents of ownership, exercisable either alone or in conjunction with any other person. *****

SEC. 2043. TRANSFERS FOR INSUFFICIENT CONSIDERATION

(a) IN GENERAL.-If any one of the transfers, trusts, interests, rights, or powers enumerated and described in sections 2035 to 2038, inclusive, and section 2041 is made, created, exercised, or relinquished for a consideration in money or money's worth, but is not a bona fide sale for an adequate and full consideration in money or money's worth, there shall be included in the gross estate only the excess of the fair market value at the time of death of the property otherwise to be included on account of such transaction, over the value of the consideration received therefore by the decedent.

(b) MARITAL RIGHTS NOT TREATED AS CONSIDERATION

    (1) IN GENERAL - For purposes of this chapter, a relinquishment or promised relinquishment of dower or curtesy, or of a statutory estate created in lieu of dower or curtesy, or of other marital rights in the decedent's property or estate, shall not be considered to any extent a consideration "in money or money's worth".

    (2) EXCEPTION - For purposes of section 2053 (relating to expenses, indebtedness, and taxes), a transfer of property which satisfies the requirements of paragraph (1) of section 2516 (relating to certain property settlements) shall be considered to be made for an adequate and full consideration in money or money's worth.

SEC. 2044. CERTAIN PROPERTY FOR WHICH MARITAL DEDUCTION WAS PREVIOUSLY ALLOWED.

(a) GENERAL RULE.--The value of the gross estate shall include the value of any property to which this section applies in which the decedent had a qualifying income interest for life.

(b) PROPERTY TO WHICH THIS SECTION APPLIES.-- This section applies to any property if-

    (1) a deduction was allowed with respect of the transfer of such property to the decedent--

        (A) under section 2056 by reason of subsection (b)(7) thereof, or

        (B) under section 2523 by reason of subsection (f) thereof, and

    (2) section 2519 (relating to dispositions of certain life estates) did not apply with respect to a disposition by the decedent of part or all such properties.

(c) PROPERTY TREATED AS HAVING PASSED FROM DECEDENT For purposes of this chapter and chapter 13, property includible of the gross estate of the decedent under subsection (a) shall be treated as property passing from the decedent.

SEC. 2045. PRIOR INTERESTS
Except as otherwise specifically provided by law, sections 2034 to 2042, inclusive, shall apply to the transfers, trusts, estates, interests, rights, powers, and relinquishment of powers, as severally enumerated and described therein, whenever made, created, arising, existing, exercised, or relinquished.

SEC. 2046. DISCLAIMERS
For provisions relating to the effect of a qualified disclaimer for purposes of this Chapter, see Section 2518.

Part IV - Taxable Estate

SEC. 2051. DEFINITION OF TAXABLE ESTATE
For purposes of the tax imposed by section 2001, the value of the taxable estate shall be determined by deducting from the value of the gross estate the deductions provided for in this part.

SEC. 2053. EXPENSES, INDEBTEDNESS, AND TAXES
(a) GENERAL RULE.-- For purposes of the tax imposed by section 2001, the value of the taxable estate shall be determined by deducting from the value of the gross estate such amounts--
> (1) for funeral expenses
> (2) for administration expenses,
> (3) for claims against the estate, and
> (4) for unpaid mortgages on, or any indebtedness in respect of, property where the value of the decedent's interest therein, undiminished by such mortgage or indebtedness, is included in the value of the gross estate, as are allowed by the laws of jurisdiction, whether within or without the United States, under which the estate is being administered.

(b) OTHER ADMINISTRATION EXPENSES.--Subject to the limitations in paragraph (1) of subsection (c), there shall be deducted in determining the taxable estate amounts representing expenses incurred in administering property not subject to claims which is included in the gross estate to the same extent such amounts would be allowable as a deduction under subsection (a) if such property were subject to claims, and such amounts are paid before the expiration of the period of limitation for assessment provided in section 6501.

(c) LIMITATIONS.--
> (1) LIMITATIONS APPLICABLE TO SUBSECTIONS (a) AND (b).--
>> (A) CONSIDERATION FOR CLAIMS.--The deduction allowed by this section in the case of claims against the estate, unpaid mortgages, or any indebtedness shall, when founded on a promise or an agreement, be limited to the extent that they were contracted bona fide and for an adequate and full consideration in money or money's worth; except that in any case in which any such claim is founded on a promise or agreement of the decedent to make a contribution or gift to or for the use of any donee described in section 2055 for the purposes specified therein, the deduction for such claims shall not be so limited, but shall be limited to the extent that it would be allowable as a deduction under section 2055 if such promise or agreement constituted a bequest.
>> (B) CERTAIN TAXES.--Any income taxes on income received after the death of the decedent, or property taxes not accrued before his death, or any estate, succession,

legacy, or inheritances taxes, shall not be deductible under this section. This subparagraph shall not apply to any increase in the tax imposed by this chapter by reason of section 4980A(d).

(C) CERTAIN CLAIMS BY REMAINDERMEN.--No deduction shall be allowed under this section for a claim against the estate by a remainderman relating to any property described in section 2044.

(2) LIMITATIONS APPLICABLE ONLY TO SUBSECTION (a).--In the case of the amounts described in subsection (a), there shall be disallowed the amount by which the deductions specified exceed the value, at the time of the decedent's death, of property subject to claims, except to the extent that such deductions represent amounts paid before the date prescribed for the filing of the estate tax return. For purposes of this section, the term "property subject to claims" means property includible in the gross estate of the decedent which, or the avails of which, would under the applicable law, bear the burden of the payment of such deductions in the final adjustment and settlement of the estate, except that the value of the property shall be reduced by the amount of the deduction under section 2054 attributable to such property.

(d) CERTAIN STATE AND FOREIGN DEATH TAXES *****

SEC. 2054. LOSSES

For purposes of the tax imposed by section 2001, the value of the taxable estate shall be determined by deducting from the value of the gross estate losses incurred during the settlement of estates arising from fires, storms, shipwrecks, or other casualties, or from theft, when such losses are not compensated for by insurance or otherwise.

SEC. 2055. TRANSFERS FOR PUBLIC, CHARITABLE, AND RELIGIOUS USES

(a) IN GENERAL.-- For purposes of the tax imposed by section 2001, the value of the taxable estate shall be determined by deducting from the value of the gross estate the amount of all bequests, legacies, devises, or transfers--

(1) to or for the use of the United States, any state, any political subdivision thereof, or the District of Columbia, for exclusively public purposes;

(2) to or for the use of any corporation organized and operated exclusively for religious, charitable, scientific, literary, or educational purposes, including the encouragement of art, or to foster national or international amateur sports competition (but only if no part of its activities involve the provision of athletic facilities or equipment), and prevention of cruelty to children or animals, no part of the net earnings of which inures to the benefit of any private stockholder or individual, which is not disqualified for tax exemption under section 501 (c)(3) by reason of attempting to influence legislation, and which does not participate in, or intervene in (including the publishing or distributing of statements), any political campaign on behalf of(or in opposition to) any candidate for public office;

(3) to a trustee or trustees, or a fraternal society, order or association operating under the lodge system, but only if such contributions or gifts are to be used by such trustee or trustees, or by such fraternal society, order, or association, exclusively for religious, charitable, scientific, literary, or educational purposes, or for the prevention of cruelty to children or animals, such trust, fraternal society, order, or association would not be disqualified for tax exemption under section 501(c)(3) by reason of attempting to influence legislation, and such trustee or trustees, or such fraternal society, order or association, does not participate in, or intervene in (including the publishing or distributing of statements), any political campaign on behalf of (or in opposition to) any candidate for public office; or

(4) to or for the use of any veterans' organization incorporated by Act of Congress, or of its departments or local chapters or posts, no part of the net earnings of which inures to the benefit of any private shareholder or individual.

For purposes of this subsection, the complete termination before the date prescribed for the filing of the estate tax return of a power to consume, invade, or appropriate property for the benefit of an individual before such power has been exercised by reason of the death of such individual or for any other reason shall be considered and deemed to be a qualified disclaimer with the same full force and effect as though he had filed such qualified disclaimer. Rules similar to the rules of section 501(j) shall apply for purposes of paragraph (2). *****

SEC. 2056. BEQUESTS, ETC., TO SURVIVING SPOUSE

(a) ALLOWANCE OF MARITAL DEDUCTION.-For purposes of the tax imposed by section 2001, the value of the taxable estate shall, except as limited by subsection (b), be determined by deducting from the value of the gross estate an amount equal to the value of any interest in property which passes or has passed from the decedent to his surviving spouse, but only to the extent that such interest is included in determining the value of the gross estate.

(b) LIMITATION IN THE CASE OF LIFE ESTATE OR OTHER TERMINABLE INTEREST-

(1) GENERAL RULE.-Where, on the lapse of time, on the occurrence of an event or contingency, or on the failure of an event or contingency to occur, an interest passing to the surviving spouse will terminate or fail, no deduction shall be allowed under this section with respect to such interest-

(A) if an interest in such property passes or has passed (for less than an adequate and full consideration in money or money's worth) from the decedent to any person other than such surviving spouse (or the estate of such spouse); and

(B) if by reason of such passing such person (or his heirs or assigns) may possess or enjoy any part of such property after such termination or failure of the interest so passing to the surviving spouse; and no deduction shall be allowed with respect to such interest [even if such deduction is not disallowed under subparagraphs (A) and (B)]-

(C) if such interest is to be acquired for the surviving spouse, pursuant to directions of the decedent, by his executor or by the trustee of a trust. *****

(2) INTEREST IN UNIDENTIFIED ASSETS. *****

(3) INTEREST OF SPOUSE CONDITIONAL ON SURVIVAL FOR LIMITED PERIOD-For purposes of this subsection, an interest passing to the surviving spouse shall not be considered as an interest which will terminate or fail on the death of such spouse if-

(A) such death will cause a termination or failure of such interest only if it occurs within a period not exceeding six months after the decedent's death, or only if it occurs as a result of a common disaster resulting in the death of the decedent and the surviving spouse, or only if it occurs in the case of either such event; and

(B) such termination or failure does not in fact occur.

(4) VALUATION OF INTEREST PASSING TO SURVIVING SPOUSE. *****

(5) LIFE ESTATE WITH POWER OF APPOINTMENT IN SURVIVING SPOUSE-In the case of an interest in property passing from the decedent, if his surviving spouse is entitled for life to all the income from the entire interest, or all the income from a specific portion thereof, payable annually or at more frequent intervals, with power in the surviving spouse to appoint the entire interest, or such specific portion (exercisable in favor of such surviving spouse, or of the estate of such surviving spouse, or in favor of either, whether or not in each case the power is exercisable in favor of others), and with no power in any other person to appoint any part of the interest, or such specific portion, to any person other than the surviving spouse-

(A) the interest or such portion thereof so passing shall, for purposes of subsection (a), be considered as passing to the surviving spouse, and

(B) no part of the interest so passing shall, for purposes of paragraph (1)(A), be considered as passing to any person other than the surviving spouse.

This paragraph shall apply only if such power in the surviving spouse to appoint the entire interest, or such specific portion thereof, whether exercisable by will or during life, is exercisable by such spouse alone and in all events.

(6) LIFE INSURANCE OR ANNUITY PAYMENTS WITH POWER OF APPOINTMENT IN SURVIVING SPOUSE. *****

(7) ELECTION WITH RESPECT TO LIFE ESTATE FOR SURVIVING SPOUSE-

(A) IN GENERAL.-In the case of qualified terminable interest property-

(i) for purposes of subsection (a), such property shall be treated as passing to the surviving spouse, and

(ii) for purposes of paragraph (1)(A), no part of such property shall be treated as passing to any person other than the surviving spouse.

(B) QUALIFIED TERMINABLE INTEREST PROPERTY DEFINED.-For purposes of this paragraph-

(i) IN GENERAL.-The term "qualified terminable interest property" means property-

(I) which passes from the decedent,

(II) in which the surviving spouse has a qualifying income interest for life, and

(III) to which an election under this paragraph applies.

(ii) Qualifying Income Interest For Life- The surviving spouse has a qualifying income interest for life if-

(I) the surviving spouse is entitled to all the income from the property, payable annually or at more frequent intervals, or has a usifruct interest for life in the property, and

(II) no person has a power to appoint any part of the property to any person other than the surviving spouse.

Subclause (II) shall not apply to a power exercisable only at or after the death of the surviving spouse. To the extent provided in regulations, an annuity shall be treated in a manner similar to an income interest in property (regardless of whether the property from which the annuity is payable can be separately identified).

(iii) PROPERTY INCLUDES INTEREST THEREIN.- The term "property" includes an interest in property.

(iv) SPECIFIC PORTION TREATED AS SEPARATE PROPERTY.- A specific portion of property shall be treated as separate property.

(v) ELECTION.-An election under this paragraph with respect to any property shall be made by the executor on the return of tax imposed by section 2001. Such an election, once made, shall be irrevocable.

(8) SPECIAL RULE FOR CHARITABLE REMAINDER TRUSTS. *****

(9) DENIAL OF DOUBLE DEDUCTION. *****

SEC. 2056A. QUALIFIED DOMESTIC TRUST

(a) QUALIFIED DOMESTIC TRUST DEFINED - For purposes of this section and section 2056(d), the term "qualified domestic trust" means, with respect to any decedent, any trust if--

(1) the trust instrument--

(A) except as provided in regulations prescribed by the Secretary, requires that at least 1 trustee of the trust be an individual citizen of the United States or a domestic corporation, and

(B) provides that no distribution (other than a distribution of income) may be made from the trust unless a trustee who is an individual citizen of the United States or a domestic corporation has the right to withhold from such distribution the tax imposed by this section on such distribution,

(2) such trust meets such requirements as the Secretary may by regulations prescribe to ensure the collection of any tax imposed by subsection (b), and

(3) an election under this section by the executor of the decedent applies to such trust.

(b) TAX TREATMENT OF TRUST

(1) IMPOSITION OF ESTATE TAX

There is hereby imposed an estate tax on--

(A) any distribution before the date of the death of the surviving spouse from a qualified domestic trust, and

(B) the value of the property remaining in a qualified domestic trust on the date of the death of the surviving spouse.

(2) AMOUNT OF TAX

(A) IN GENERAL - In the case of any taxable event, the amount of the estate tax imposed by paragraph (1) shall be the amount equal to--

(i) the tax which would have been imposed under section 2001 on the estate of the decedent if the taxable estate of the decedent had been increased by the sum of--

(I) the amount involved in such taxable event, plus

(II) the aggregate amount involved in previous taxable events with respect to qualified domestic trusts of such decedent, reduced by

(ii) the tax which would have been imposed under section 2001 on the estate of the decedent if the taxable estate of the decedent had been increased by the amount referred to in clause (i)(II).

(B) TENTATIVE TAX WHERE TAX OF DECEDENT NOT FINALLY DETERMINED

(i) IN GENERAL - If the tax imposed on the estate of the decedent under section 2001 is not finally determined before the taxable event, the amount of the tax imposed by paragraph (1) on such event shall be determined by using the highest rate of tax in effect under section 2001 as of the date of the decedent's death.

(ii) REFUND OF EXCESS WHEN TAX FINALLY DETERMINED - If--

(I) the amount of the tax determined under clause (i), exceeds

(II) the tax determined under subparagraph (A) on the basis of the final determination of the tax imposed by section 2001 on the estate of the decedent, such excess shall be allowed as a credit or refund (with interest) if claim therefor is filed not later than 1 year after the date of such final determination.

(C) SPECIAL RULE WHERE DECEDENT HAS MORE THAN 1 QUALIFIED DOMESTIC TRUST - If there is more than 1 qualified domestic trust with respect to any decedent, the amount of the tax imposed by paragraph (1) with respect to such trusts shall be determined by using the highest rate of tax in effect under section 2001 as of the date of the decedent's death (and the provisions of paragraph (3)(B) shall not apply) unless, pursuant to a designation made by the decedent's executor, there is 1 person--

(i) who is an individual citizen of the United States or a domestic corporation and is responsible for filing all returns of tax imposed under paragraph (1) with respect to such trusts and for paying all tax so imposed, and

(ii) who meets such requirements as the Secretary may by regulations prescribe.

(3) CERTAIN LIFETIME DISTRIBUTIONS EXEMPT FROM TAX

(A) INCOME DISTRIBUTIONS - No tax shall be imposed by paragraph (1)(A) on any distribution of income to the surviving spouse.

(B) HARDSHIP EXEMPTION - No tax shall be imposed by paragraph (1)(A) on any distribution to the surviving spouse on account of hardship.

(4) TAX WHERE TRUST CEASES TO QUALIFY - If any qualified domestic trust ceases to meet the requirements of paragraphs (1) and (2) of subsection (a), the tax imposed by paragraph (1) shall apply as if the surviving spouse died on the date of such cessation.

(5) DUE DATE

(A) TAX ON DISTRIBUTIONS - The estate tax imposed by paragraph (1)(A) shall be due and payable on the 15th day of the 4th month following the calendar year in which the taxable event occurs; except that the estate tax imposed by paragraph (1)(A) on distributions during the calendar year in which the surviving spouse dies shall be due and payable not later than the date on which the estate tax imposed by paragraph (1)(B) is due and payable.

(B) TAX AT DEATH OF SPOUSE - The estate tax imposed by paragraph (1)(B) shall be due and payable on the date 9 months after the date of such death.

(6) LIABILITY FOR TAX - Each trustee shall be personally liable for the amount of the tax imposed by paragraph (1). Rules similar to the rules of section 2204 shall apply for purposes of the preceding sentence.

(7) TREATMENT OF TAX - For purposes of section 2056(d), any tax paid under paragraph (1) shall be treated as a tax paid under section 2001 with respect to the estate of the decedent.

(8) LIEN FOR TAX - For purposes of section 6324, any tax imposed by paragraph (1) shall be treated as an estate tax imposed under this chapter with respect to a decedent dying on the date of the taxable event (and the property involved shall be treated as the gross estate of such decedent).

(9) TAXABLE EVENT - The term "taxable event" means the event resulting in tax being imposed under paragraph (1).

(10) CERTAIN BENEFITS ALLOWED

(A) IN GENERAL - If any property remaining in the qualified domestic trust on the date of the death of the surviving spouse is includible in the gross estate of such spouse for purposes of this chapter (or would be includible if such spouse were a citizen or resident of the United States), any benefit which is allowable (or would be allowable if such spouse were a citizen or resident of the United States) with respect to such property to the estate of such spouse under section 2011, 2014, 2032, 2032A, 2055, 2056, or 6166 shall be allowed for purposes of the tax imposed by paragraph (1)(B).

(B) SECTION 303 - If the estate of the surviving spouse meets the requirements of section 303 with respect to any property described in subparagraph (A), for purposes of section 303, the tax imposed by paragraph (1)(B) with respect to such property shall be treated as a Federal estate tax payable with respect to the estate of the surviving spouse.

(C) SECTION 6161(a)(2) - The provisions of section 6161(a)(2) shall apply with respect to the tax imposed by paragraph (1)(B), and the reference in such section to the executor shall be treated as a reference to the trustees of the trust.

(11) SPECIAL RULE WHERE DISTRIBUTION TAX PAID OUT OF TRUST - For purposes of this subsection, if any portion of the tax imposed by paragraph (1)(A) with respect to any distribution is paid out of the trust, an amount equal to the portion so paid shall be treated as a distribution described in paragraph (1)(A).

(12) SPECIAL RULE WHERE SPOUSE BECOMES CITIZEN - If the surviving spouse of the decedent becomes a citizen of the United States and if--

(A) such spouse was a resident of the United States at all times after the date of the death of the decedent and before such spouse becomes a citizen of the United States,

(B) no tax was imposed by paragraph (1)(A) with respect to any distribution before such spouse becomes such a citizen, or

(C) such spouse elects--

(i) to treat any distribution on which tax was imposed by paragraph (1)(A) as a taxable gift made by such spouse for purposes of--

(I) section 2001, and

(II) determining the amount of the tax imposed by section 2501 on actual taxable gifts made by such spouse during the year in which the spouse becomes a citizen or any subsequent year, and

(ii) to treat any reduction in the tax imposed by paragraph (1)(A) by reason of the credit allowable under section 2010 with respect to the decedent as a credit allowable to such surviving spouse under section 2505 for purposes of determining the amount of the credit allowable under section 2505 with respect to taxable gifts made by the surviving spouse during the year in which the spouse becomes a citizen or any subsequent year,

paragraph (1)(A) shall not apply to any distributions after such spouse becomes such a citizen (and paragraph (1)(B) shall not apply).

(13) COORDINATION WITH SECTION 1015 - For purposes of section 1015, any distribution on which tax is imposed by paragraph (1)(A) shall be treated as a transfer by gift, and any tax paid under paragraph (1)(A) shall be treated as a gift tax.

(14) COORDINATION WITH TERMINABLE INTEREST RULES - Any interest in a qualified domestic trust shall not be treated as failing to meet the requirements of paragraph (5) or (7) of section 2056(b) merely by reason of any provision of the trust instrument permitting the withholding from any distribution of an amount to pay the tax imposed by paragraph (1) on such distribution.

(15) NO TAX ON CERTAIN DISTRIBUTIONS - No tax shall be imposed by paragraph (1) on any distribution to the surviving spouse to the extent such distribution is to reimburse such surviving spouse for any tax imposed by subtitle A on any item of income of the trust to which such surviving spouse is not entitled under the terms of the trust.

(c) DEFINITIONS - For purposes of this section--

(1) PROPERTY INCLUDES INTEREST THEREIN The term "property" includes an interest in property.

(2) INCOME - Except as provided in regulations, the term "income" has the meaning given to such term by section 643(b).

(3) TRUST - To the extent provided in regulations prescribed by the Secretary, the term "trust" includes other arrangements which have substantially the same effect as a trust.

(d) ELECTION - An election under this section with respect to any trust shall be made by the executor on the return of the tax imposed by section 2001. Such an election, once made, shall be irrevocable. No election may be made under this section on any return if such return is filed more than one year after the time prescribed by law (including extensions) for filing such return.

(e) REGULATIONS - The Secretary shall prescribe such regulations as may be necessary or appropriate to carry out the purposes of this section, including regulations under which there may be treated as a qualified domestic trust any annuity or other payment which is includible in the decedent's gross estate and is by its terms payable for life or a term of years.

SEC. 2057. FAMILY-OWNED BUSINESS INTERESTS.

(a) GENERAL RULE

(1) ALLOWANCE OF DEDUCTION For purposes of the tax imposed by section 2001, in the case of an estate of a decedent to which this section applies, the value of the taxable estate shall be determined by deducting from the value of the gross estate the adjusted value of the qualified family-owned business interests of the decedent which are described in subsection (b)(2).

(2) MAXIMUM DEDUCTION- The deduction allowed by this section shall not exceed $675,000.

(3) COORDINATION WITH UNIFIED CREDIT

(A) In general--Except as provided in subparagraph (B), if this section applies to an estate, the applicable exclusion amount under section 2010 shall be $625,000.

(B) Increase in unified credit if deduction is less than $675,000--

If the deduction allowed by this section is less than $675,000, the amount of the applicable exclusion amount under section 2010 shall be increased (but not above the amount which would apply to the estate without regard to this section) by the excess of $675,000 over the amount of the deduction allowed.

(b) ESTATES TO WHICH SECTION APPLIES

(1) IN GENERAL- This section shall apply to an estate if--

(A) the decedent was (at the date of the decedent's death) a citizen or resident of the United States,

(B) the executor elects the application of this section and files the agreement referred to in subsection (h),

(C) the sum of--

(i) the adjusted value of the qualified family-owned business interests described in paragraph (2), plus

(ii) the amount of the gifts of such interests determined under paragraph (3), exceeds 50 percent of the adjusted gross estate, and

(D) during the 8-year period ending on the date of the decedent's death there have been periods aggregating 5 years or more during which--

(i) such interests were owned by the decedent or a member of the decedent's family, and

(ii) there was material participation (within the meaning of section 2032A(e)(6)) by the decedent or a member of the decedent's family in the operation of the business to which such interests relate.

(2) INCLUDIBLE QUALIFIED FAMILY-OWNED BUSINESS INTERESTS- The qualified family-owned business interests described in this paragraph are the interests which-

(A) are included in determining the value of the gross estate, and

(B) are acquired by any qualified heir from, or passed to any qualified heir from, the decedent (within the meaning of section 2032A(e)(9)).

(3) INCLUDIBLE GIFTS OF INTERESTS- The amount of the gifts of qualified family-owned business interests determined under this paragraph is the sum of--

(A) the amount of such gifts from the decedent to members of the decedent's family taken into account under section 2001(b)(1)(B), plus

(B) the amount of such gifts otherwise excluded under section 2503(b), to the extent such interests are continuously held by members of such family (other than the decedent's spouse) between the date of the gift and the date of the decedent's death.

(c) ADJUSTED GROSS ESTATE- For purposes of this section, the term "adjusted gross estate" means the value of the gross estate--

(1) reduced by any amount deductible under paragraph (3) or (4) of section 2053(a), and

(2) increased by the excess of--

(A) the sum of--

(i) the amount of gifts determined under subsection (b)(3), plus

(ii) the amount (if more than de minimus) of other transfers from the decedent to the decedent's spouse (at the time of the transfer) within 10 years of the date of the decedent's death, plus

(iii) the amount of other gifts (not included under clause (i) or (ii)) from the decedent within 3 years of such date, other than gifts to members of the decedent's family otherwise excluded under section 2503(b), over

(B) the sum of the amounts described in clauses (i), (ii), and (iii) of subparagraph (A) which are otherwise includible in the gross estate.

For purposes of the preceding sentence, the Secretary may provide that de minimus gifts to persons other than members of the decedent's family shall not be taken into account.

(d) ADJUSTED VALUE OF THE QUALIFIED FAMILY-OWNED BUSINESS INTERESTS- For purposes of this section, the adjusted value of any qualified family-owned business interest is the value of such interest for purposes of this chapter (determined without regard to this section), reduced by the excess of--

(1) any amount deductible under paragraph (3) or (4) of section 2053(a), over

(2) the sum of--

(A) any indebtedness on any qualified residence of the decedent the interest on which is deductible under section 163(h)(3), plus

(B) any indebtedness to the extent the taxpayer establishes that the proceeds of such indebtedness were used for the payment of educational and medical expenses of the decedent, the decedent's spouse, or the decedent's dependents (within the meaning of section 152), plus

(C) any indebtedness not described in subparagraph (A) or (B), to the extent such indebtedness does not exceed $10,000.

(e) QUALIFIED FAMILY-OWNED BUSINESS INTEREST

(1) IN GENERAL- For purposes of this section, the term "qualified family-owned business interest" means--

(A) an interest as a proprietor in a trade or business carried on as a proprietorship, or

(B) an interest in an entity carrying on a trade or business, if--

(i) at least--

(I) 50 percent of such entity is owned (directly or indirectly) by the decedent and members of the decedent's family,

(II) 70 percent of such entity is so owned by members of 2 families, or

(III) 90 percent of such entity is so owned by members of 3 families, and (ii) for purposes of subclause (II) or (III) of clause (i), at least 30 percent of such entity is so owned by the decedent and members of the decedent's family.

For purposes of the preceding sentence, a decedent shall be treated as engaged in a trade or business if any member of the decedent's family is engaged in such trade or business.

(2) LIMITATION- Such term shall not include--

(A) any interest in a trade or business the principal place of business of which is not located in the United States,

(B) any interest in an entity, if the stock or debt of such entity or a controlled group (as defined in section 267(f)(1)) of which such entity was a member was readily tradable on an established securities market or secondary market (as defined by the Secretary) at any time within 3 years of the date of the decedent's death,

(C) any interest in a trade or business not described in section 542(c)(2), if more than 35 percent of the adjusted ordinary gross income of such trade or business for the taxable year which includes the date of the decedent's death would qualify as personal holding company income (as defined in section 543(a) without regard to paragraph (2)(B) thereof) if such trade or business were a corporation,

(D) that portion of an interest in a trade or business that is attributable to--

(i) cash or marketable securities, or both, in excess of the reasonably expected day-to-day working capital needs of such trade or business, and

(ii) any other assets of the trade or business (other than assets used in the active conduct of a trade or business described in section 542(c)(2)), which produce, or are held for the production of, personal holding company income (as defined in subparagraph (c)) or income described in section 954(c)(1) (determined without regard to subparagraph (A) thereof and by substituting "trade or business" for "controlled foreign corporation").

In the case of a lease of property on a net cash basis by the decedent to a member of the decedent's family, income from such lease shall not be treated as personal holding company income for purposes of subparagraph (C), and such property shall not be treated as an asset described in subparagraph (D)(ii), if such income and property would not be so treated if the lessor had engaged directly in the activities engaged in by the lessee with respect to such property.

(3) RULES REGARDING OWNERSHIP--

    (A) OWNERSHIP OF ENTITIES- For purposes of paragraph (1)(B)--

        (i) CORPORATIONS- Ownership of a corporation shall be determined by the holding of stock possessing the appropriate percentage of the total combined voting power of all classes of stock entitled to vote and the appropriate percentage of the total value of shares of all classes of stock.

        (ii) PARTNERSHIPS- Ownership of a partnership shall be determined by the owning of the appropriate percentage of the capital interest in such partnership.

    (B) OWNERSHIP OF TIERED ENTITIES- For purposes of this section, if by reason of holding an interest in a trade or business, a decedent, any member of the decedent's family, any qualified heir, or any member of any qualified heir's family is treated as holding an interest in any other trade or business--

        (i) such ownership interest in the other trade or business shall be disregarded in determining if the ownership interest in the first trade or business is a qualified family-owned business interest, and

        (ii) this section shall be applied separately in determining if such interest in any other trade or business is a qualified family-owned business interest.

    (C) INDIVIDUAL OWNERSHIP RULES- For purposes of this section, an interest owned, directly or indirectly, by or for an entity described in paragraph (1)(B) shall be considered as being owned proportionately by or for the entity's shareholders, partners, or beneficiaries. A person shall be treated as a beneficiary of any trust only if such person has a present interest in such trust.

(f) TAX TREATMENT OF FAILURE TO MATERIALLY PARTICIPATE IN BUSINESS OR DISPOSITIONS OF INTERESTS

    (1) IN GENERAL- There is imposed an additional estate tax if, within 10 years after the date of the decedent's death and before the date of the qualified heir's death--

        (A) the material participation requirements described in section 2032A(c)(6)(B) are not met with respect to the qualified family-owned business interest which was acquired (or passed) from the decedent,

        (B) the qualified heir disposes of any portion of a qualified family-owned business interest (other than by a disposition to a member of the qualified heir's family or through a qualified conservation contribution under section 170(h)),

        (C) the qualified heir loses United States citizenship (within the meaning of section 877) or with respect to whom an event described in subparagraph (A) or (B) of section 877(e)(1) occurs, and such heir does not comply with the requirements of subsection (g), or

        (D) the principal place of business of a trade or business of the qualified family-owned business interest ceases to be located in the United States.

(2) ADDITIONAL ESTATE TAX

(A) IN GENERAL- The amount of the additional estate tax imposed by paragraph (1) shall be equal to-

(i) the applicable percentage of the adjusted tax difference attributable to the qualified family-owned business interest, plus

(ii) interest on the amount determined under clause (i) at the underpayment rate established under section 6621 for the period beginning on the date the estate tax liability was due under this chapter and ending on the date such additional estate tax is due.

(B) APPLICABLE PERCENTAGE- For purposes of this paragraph, the applicable percentage shall be determined under the following table–

If the event described in paragraph (1) occurs in the following year of material participation:	The applicable percentage is:
1 through 6	100
7	80
8	60
9	40
10	20

(C) ADJUSTED TAX DIFFERENCE- For purposes of subparagraph (A)--

(i) In general-- The adjusted tax difference attributable to a qualified family-owned business interest is the amount which bears the same ratio to the adjusted tax difference with respect to the estate (determined under clause (ii)) as the value of such interest bears to the value of all qualified family- owned business interests described in subsection (b)(2).

(ii) Adjusted tax difference with respect to the estate: For purposes of clause (i), the term `adjusted tax difference with respect to the estate' means the excess of what would have been the estate tax liability but for the election under this section over the estate tax liability. For purposes of this clause, the term `estate tax liability' means the tax imposed by section 2001 reduced by the credits allowable against such tax.

(3) USE IN TRADE OR BUSINESS BY FAMILY MEMBERS- A qualified heir shall not be treated as disposing of an interest described in subsection (e)(1)(A) by reason of ceasing to be engaged in a trade or business so long as the property to which such interest relates is used in a trade or business by any member of such individual's family.

(g) SECURITY REQUIREMENTS FOR NONCITIZEN QUALIFIED HEIRS

(1) IN GENERAL- Except upon the application of subparagraph (F) of subsection (i)(3), if a qualified heir is not a citizen of the United States, any interest under this section passing to or acquired by such heir (including any interest held by such heir at a time described in subsection (f)(1)(C)) shall be treated as a qualified family-owned business interest only if the interest passes or is acquired (or is held) in a qualified trust.

(2) QUALIFIED TRUST- The term "qualified trust" means a trust--

(A) which is organized under, and governed by, the laws of the United States or a State, and

(B) except as otherwise provided in regulations, with respect to which the trust instrument requires that at least 1 trustee of the trust be an individual citizen of the United States or a domestic corporation.

(h) AGREEMENT-The agreement referred to in this subsection is a written agreement signed by each person in being who has an interest (whether or not in possession) in any property designated in such agreement consenting to the application of subsection (f) with respect to such property.

(i) OTHER DEFINITIONS AND APPLICABLE RULES- For purposes of this section--

   (1) QUALIFIED HEIR- The term "qualified heir"--

      (A) has the meaning given to such term by section 2032A(e)(1), and

      (B) includes any active employee of the trade or business to which the qualified family-owned business interest relates if such employee has been employed by such trade or business for a period of at least 10 years before the date of the decedent's death.

   (2) MEMBER OF THE FAMILY- The term "member of the family" has the meaning given to such term by section 2032A(e)(2).

   (3) APPLICABLE RULES- Rules similar to the following rules shall apply:

      (A) Section 2032A(b)(4) (relating to decedents who are retired or disabled).

      (B) Section 2032A(b)(5) (relating to special rules for surviving spouses).

      (C) Section 2032A(c)(2)(D) (relating to partial dispositions).

      (D) Section 2032A(c)(3) (relating to only 1 additional tax imposed with respect to any 1 portion).

      (E) Section 2032A(c)(4) (relating to due date).

      (F) Section 2032A(c)(5) (relating to liability for tax; furnishing of bond).

      (G) Section 2032A(c)(7) (relating to no tax if use begins within 2 years; active management by eligible qualified heir treated as material participation).

      (H) Paragraphs (1) and (3) of section 2032A(d) (relating to election; agreement).

      (I) Section 2032A(e)(10) (relating to community property).

      (J) Section 2032A(e)(14) (relating to treatment of replacement property acquired in section 1031 or 1033 transactions).

      (K) Section 2032A(f) (relating to statute of limitations).

      (L) Section 2032A(g) (relating to application to interests in partnerships, corporations, and trusts).

      (M) Subsections (h) and (i) of section 2032A.

      (N) Section 6166(b)(3) (relating to farmhouses and certain other structures taken into account).

      (O) Subparagraphs (B), (C), and (D) of section 6166(g)(1) (relating to acceleration of payment).

      (P) Section 6324B (relating to special lien for additional estate tax).

Subchapter B. Nonresidents Not Citizens

SEC. 2101. TAX IMPOSED

(a) IMPOSITION.--Except as provided in section 2107, a tax is hereby imposed on the transfer of the taxable estate(determined as provided in section 2106) of every decedent nonresident not a citizen of the United States.

(b) COMPUTATION OF TAX.-- The tax imposed by this section shall be the amount equal to the excess (if any) of--

   (1) a tentative tax computed under section 2001 (c) on the sum of--

      A) amount of the taxable estate, and

B) the amount of the taxable gifts, over

(2) a tentative tax computed under section 2001 (c) on the amount of adjusted taxable gifts. For purposes of the preceding sentence, there shall be appropriate adjustments in the application of section 2001 (c)(2) to reflect the difference between the amount of credit provided under section 2012(c) and the amount of credit provided under section 2010.

(c) ADJUSTMENTS FOR TAXABLE GIFTS.--

1) ADJUSTED TAXABLE GIFTS DEFINED.--For purposes of this section, the term "adjustable taxable gifts" means the total amount of the taxable gifts (within the meaning of section 2503 as modified by section 2511) made by the decedent after December 31, 1976, other than gifts which are includible in the gross estate of the decedent.

2) ADJUSTMENT FOR CERTAIN GIFT TAX.-- For purposes of this section, the rules of section 2001 (d) shall apply.

SEC. 2102. CREDITS AGAINST TAX

(a) IN GENERAL - The tax imposed by section 2101 shall be credited with the amounts determined in accordance with sections 2011 to 2013, inclusive (relating to State death taxes, gift tax, and tax on prior transfers), subject to the special limitation provided in subsection (b).

(b) SPECIAL LIMITATION - The maximum credit allowed under section 2011 against the tax imposed by section 2101 for State death taxes paid shall be an amount which bears the same ratio to the credit computed as provided in section 2011(b) as the value of the property, as determined for purposes of this chapter, upon which State death taxes were paid and which is included in the gross estate under section 2103 bears to the value of the total gross estate under section 2103. For purposes of this subsection, the term "State death taxes" means the taxes described in section 2011(a).

(c) UNIFIED CREDIT

(1) IN GENERAL - A credit of $13,000 shall be allowed against the tax imposed by section 2101.

(2) RESIDENTS OF POSSESSIONS OF THE UNITED STATES - In the case of a decedent who is considered to be a "nonresident not a citizen of the United States" under section 2209, the credit under this subsection shall be the greater of--

(A) $13,000, or

(B) that proportion of $46,800 which the value of that part of the decedent's gross estate which at the time of his death is situated in the United States bears to the value of his entire gross estate wherever situated.

(3) SPECIAL RULES

(A) COORDINATION WITH TREATIES - To the extent required under any treaty obligation of the United States, the credit allowed under this subsection shall be equal to the amount which bears the same ratio to the applicable credit amount in effect under section 2010(c) for the calendar year which includes the date of death as the value of the part of the decedent's gross estate which at the time of his death is situated in the United States bears to the value of his entire gross estate wherever situated. For purposes of the preceding sentence, property shall not be treated as situated in the United States if such property is exempt from the tax imposed by this subchapter under any treaty obligation of the United States.

(B) COORDINATION WITH GIFT TAX UNIFIED CREDIT - If a credit has been allowed under section 2505 with respect to any gift made by the decedent, each dollar amount contained in paragraph (1) or (2) or subparagraph (A) of this paragraph (whichever applies) shall be reduced by the amount so allowed.

(4) LIMITATION BASED ON AMOUNT OF TAX - The credit allowed under this subsection shall not exceed the amount of the tax imposed by section 2101.

(5) APPLICATION OF OTHER CREDITS - For purposes of subsection (a), sections 2011 to 2013, inclusive, shall be applied as if the credit allowed under this subsection were allowed under section 2010.

SEC. 2103. DEFINITION OF GROSS ESTATE
For the purpose of the tax imposed by section 2101, the value of the gross estate of every decedent nonresident not a citizen of the United States shall be that part of his gross estate (determined as provided in section 2031) which at the time of his death is situated in the United States.

SEC. 2106. TAXABLE ESTATE
(a) DEFINITION OF TAXABLE ESTATE - For purposes of the tax imposed by section 2101, the value of the taxable estate of every decedent nonresident not a citizen of the United States shall be determined by deducting from the value of that part of his gross estate which at the time of his death is situated in the United States--

(1) EXPENSES, LOSSES, INDEBTEDNESS, AND TAXES - That proportion of the deductions specified in sections 2053 and 2054 (other than the deductions described in the following sentence) which the value of such part bears to the value of his entire gross estate, wherever situated. Any deduction allowable under section 2053 in the case of a claim against the estate which was founded on a promise or agreement but was not contracted for an adequate and full consideration in money or money's worth shall be allowable under this paragraph to the extent that it would be allowable as a deduction under paragraph (2) if such promise or agreement constituted a bequest.

(2) TRANSFERS FOR PUBLIC, CHARITABLE, AND RELIGIOUS USES

(A) IN GENERAL - The amount of all bequests, legacies, devises, or transfers (including the interest which falls into any such bequest, legacy, devise, or transfer as a result of an irrevocable disclaimer of a bequest, legacy, devise, transfer, or power, if the disclaimer is made before the date prescribed for the filing of the estate tax return)--

(i) to or for the use of the United States, any State, any political subdivision thereof, or the District of Columbia, for exclusively public purposes;

(ii) to or for the use of any domestic corporation organized and operated exclusively for religious, charitable, scientific, literary, or educational purposes, including the encouragement of art and the prevention of cruelty to children or animals, no part of the net earnings of which inures to the benefit of any private stockholder or individual, which is not disqualified for tax exemption under section 501(c)(3) by reason of attempting to influence legislation, and which does not participate in, or intervene in (including the publishing or distributing of statements), any political campaign on behalf of (or in opposition to) any candidate for public office; or

(iii) to a trustee or trustees, or a fraternal society, order, or association operating under the lodge system, but only if such contributions or gifts are to be used within the United States by such trustee or trustees, or by such fraternal society, order, or association, exclusively for religious, charitable, scientific, literary, or educational purposes, or for the prevention of cruelty to children or animals, such trust, fraternal society, order, or association would not be disqualified for tax exemption under section 501(c)(3) by reason of attempting to influence legislation, and such trustee or trustees, or such fraternal society, order, or association, does not participate in, or intervene in (including the publishing or distributing of statements), any political campaign on behalf of (or in opposition to) any candidate for public office;

(B) POWERS OF APPOINTMENT - Property includible in the decedent's gross estate under section 2041 (relating to powers of appointment) received by a donee described in this paragraph shall, for purposes of this paragraph, be considered a bequest of such decedent.

(C) DEATH TAXES PAYABLE OUT OF BEQUESTS - If the tax imposed by section 2101, or any estate, succession, legacy, or inheritance taxes, are, either by the terms of the will, by the law of the jurisdiction under which the estate is administered, or by the law of the jurisdiction imposing the particular tax, payable in whole or in part out of the bequests, legacies, or devises otherwise deductible under this paragraph, then the amount deductible under this paragraph shall be the amount of such bequests, legacies, or devises reduced by the amount of such taxes.

(D) LIMITATION ON DEDUCTION - The amount of the deduction under this paragraph for any transfer shall not exceed the value of the transferred property required to be included in the gross estate.

(E) DISALLOWANCE OF DEDUCTIONS IN CERTAIN CASES - The provisions of section 2055(e) shall be applied in the determination of the amount allowable as a deduction under this paragraph.

(F) CROSS REFERENCES ****

(3) MARITAL DEDUCTION - The amount which would be deductible with respect to property situated in the United States at the time of the decedent's death under the principles of section 2056.

(b) CONDITION OF ALLOWANCE OF DEDUCTIONS - No deduction shall be allowed under paragraphs (1) and (2) of subsection (a) in the case of a nonresident not a citizen of the United States unless the executor includes in the return required to be filed under section 6018 the value at the time of his death of that part of the gross estate of such nonresident not situated in the United States.

SEC. 2107. EXPATRIATION TO AVOID TAX

(a) TREATMENT OF EXPATRIATES.--

(1) RATE OF TAX.-- - A tax computed in accordance with the table contained in section 2001 is hereby imposed on the transfer of the taxable estates determined as provided in section 2106, of every decedent nonresident not a citizen of the United States if, within the 10-year period ending with the date of death, such decedent lost United States citizenship, unless such loss did not have for one of its principal purposes the avoidance of taxes under this subtitle or subtitle A.

(2) CERTAIN INDIVIDUALS TREATED AS HAVING TAX AVOIDANCE PURPOSE.

(A) IN GENERAL.-- - For purposes of paragraph (1), an individual shall be treated as having a principal purpose to avoid such taxes if such individual is so treated under section 877(a)(2).

(B) EXCEPTION.-- - Subparagraph (A) shall not apply to a decedent meeting the requirements of section 877(c)(1).

(b) GROSS ESTATE - For purposes of the tax imposed by subsection (a), the value of the gross estate of every decedent to whom subsection (a) applies shall be determined as provided in section 2103, except that--

(1) if such decedent owned (within the meaning of section 958(a)) at the time of his death 10 percent or more of the total combined voting power of all classes of stock entitled to vote of a foreign corporation, and

(2) if such decedent owned (within the meaning of section 958(a)), or is considered to have owned (by applying the ownership rules of section 958(b)), at the time of his death, more than 50 percent of-

(A) the total combined voting power of all classes of stock entitled to vote of such corporation, or

        (B) the total value of the stock of such corporation,

then that proportion of the fair market value of the stock of such foreign corporation owned (within the meaning of section 958(a)) by such decedent at the time of his death, which the fair market value of any assets owned by such foreign corporation and situated in the United States, at the time of his death, bears to the total fair market value of all assets owned by such foreign corporation at the time of his death, shall be included in the gross estate of such decedent. For purposes of the preceding sentence, a decedent shall be treated as owning stock of a foreign corporation at the time of his death if, at the time of a transfer, by trust or otherwise, within the meaning of sections 2035 to 2038, inclusive, he owned such stock.

(c) CREDITS

    (1) UNIFIED CREDIT

        (A) IN GENERAL - A credit of $13,000 shall be allowed against the tax imposed by subsection (a).

        (B) LIMITATION BASED ON AMOUNT OF TAX - The credit allowed under this paragraph shall not exceed the amount of the tax imposed by subsection (a).

    (2) CREDIT FOR FOREIGN DEATH TAXES.--

        (A) IN GENERAL.-- - The tax imposed by subsection (a) shall be credited with the amount of any estate, inheritance, legacy, or succession taxes actually paid to any foreign country in respect of any property which is included in the gross estate solely by reason of subsection (b).

        (B) LIMITATION ON CREDIT.-- - The credit allowed by subparagraph (A) for such taxes paid to a foreign country shall not exceed the lesser of--

            (i) the amount which bears the same ratio to the amount of such taxes actually paid to such foreign country as the value of the property subjected to such taxes by such foreign country and included in the gross estate solely by reason of subsection (b) bears to the value of all property subjected to such taxes by such foreign country, or

            (ii) such property's proportionate share of the excess of--

                (I) the tax imposed by subsection (a), over

                (II) the tax which would be imposed by section 2101 but for this section.

        (C) PROPORTIONATE SHARE - In the case of property which is included in the gross estate solely by reason of subsection (b), such property's proportionate share is the percentage which the value of such property bears to the total value of all property included in the gross estate solely by reason of subsection (b).

    (3) OTHER CREDITS - The tax imposed by subsection (a) shall be credited with the amounts determined in accordance with subsections (a) and (b) of section 2102. For purposes of subsection (a) of section 2102, sections 2011 to 2013, inclusive, shall be applied as if the credit allowed under paragraph (1) were allowed under section 2010.

(d) BURDEN OF PROOF - If the Secretary establishes that it is reasonable to believe that an individual's loss of United States citizenship would, but for this section, result in a substantial reduction in the estate, inheritance, legacy, and succession taxes in respect of the transfer of his estate, the burden of proving that such loss of citizenship did not have for one of its principal purposes the avoidance of taxes under this subtitle or subtitle A shall be on the executor of such individual's estate.

(e) CROSS REFERENCE.-- - For comparable treatment of long-term lawful permanent residents who ceased to be taxed as residents, see section 877(e).

Subchapter C. Miscellaneous

SEC. 2201. Members of the Armed Forces Dying in Combat Zone or by Reason of Combat-zone-incurred Wounds, Etc.
The additional estate tax as defined in section 2011(d) shall not apply to the transfer of the taxable estate of a citizen or resident of the United States dying while in active service as a member of the Armed Forces of the United States, if such decedent--

(1) was killed in action while serving in a combat zone, as determined under section 112(c); or

(2) died as a result of wounds, disease, or injury suffered, while serving in a combat zone (as determined under section 112(c)), and while in line of duty, by reason of a hazard to which he was subjected as an incident of such service.

SEC. 2203. DEFINITION OF EXECUTOR
The term "executor" wherever it is used in this title in connection with the estate tax imposed by this chapter means the executor or administrator of the decedent, or, if there is no executor or administrator appointed, qualified, and acting within the United States, then any person in actual or constructive possession of any property of the decedent.

SEC. 2204. DISCHARGE OF FIDUCIARY FROM PERSONAL LIABILITY
(a) GENERAL RULE - If the executor makes written application to the Secretary for determination of the amount of the tax and discharge from personal liability therefor, the Secretary (as soon as possible, and in any event within 9 months after the making of such application, or, if the application is made before the return is filed, then within 9 months after the return is filed, but not after the expiration of the period prescribed for the assessment of the tax in section 6501) shall notify the executor of the amount of the tax. The executor, on payment of the amount of which he is notified (other than any amount the time for payment of which is extended under sections 6161, 6163, or 6166), and on furnishing any bond which may be required for any amount for which the time for payment is extended, shall be discharged from personal liability for any deficiency in tax thereafter found to be due and shall be entitled to a receipt or writing showing such discharge.
(b) FIDUCIARY OTHER THAN THE EXECUTOR - If a fiduciary (not including a fiduciary in respect of the estate of a nonresident decedent) other than the executor makes written application to the Secretary for determination of the amount of any estate tax for which the fiduciary may be personally liable, and for discharge from personal liability therefor, the Secretary upon the discharge of the executor from personal liability under subsection (a), or upon the expiration of 6 months after the making of such application by the fiduciary, if later, shall notify the fiduciary (1) of the amount of such tax for which it has been determined the fiduciary is liable, or (2) that it has been determined that the fiduciary is not liable for any such tax. Such application shall be accompanied by a copy of the instrument, if any, under which such fiduciary is acting, a description of the property held by the fiduciary, and such other information for purposes of carrying out the provisions of this section as the Secretary may require by regulations. On payment of the amount of such tax for which it has been determined the fiduciary is liable (other than any amount the time for payment of which has been extended under section 6161, 6163, or 6166), and on furnishing any bond which may be required for any amount for which the time for payment has been extended, or on receipt by him of notification of a determination that he is not liable for any such tax, the fiduciary shall be discharged from personal liability for any deficiency in such tax thereafter found to be due and shall be entitled to a receipt or writing evidencing such discharge.
(c) SPECIAL LIEN UNDER SECTION 6324A - For purposes of the second sentence of

subsection (a) and the last sentence of subsection (b), an agreement which meets the requirements of section 6324A (relating to special lien for estate tax deferred under section 6166) shall be treated as the furnishing of bond with respect to the amount for which the time for payment has been extended under section 6166.

(d) GOOD FAITH RELIANCE ON GIFT TAX RETURNS - If the executor in good faith relies on gift tax returns furnished under section 6103(e)(3) for determining the decedent's adjusted taxable gifts, the executor shall be discharged from personal liability with respect to any deficiency of the tax imposed by this chapter which is attributable to adjusted taxable gifts which--

   (1) are made more than 3 years before the date of the decedent's death, and

   (2) are not shown on such returns.

SEC. 2205. REIMBURSEMENT OUT OF ESTATE

If the tax or any part thereof is paid by, or collected out of, that part of the estate passing to or in the possession of any person other than the executor in his capacity as such, such person shall be entitled to reimbursement out of any part of the estate still undistributed or by a just and equitable contribution by the persons whose interest in the estate of the decedent would have been reduced if the tax had been paid before the distribution of the estate or whose interest is subject to equal or prior liability for the payment of taxes, debts, or other charges against the estate, it being the purpose and intent of this chapter that so far as is practicable and unless otherwise directed by the will of the decedent the tax shall be paid out of the estate before its distribution.

SEC. 2206. LIABILITY OF LIFE INSURANCE BENEFICIARIES

Unless the decedent directs otherwise in his will, if any part of the gross estate on which tax has been paid consists of proceeds of policies of insurance on the life of the decedent receivable by a beneficiary other than the executor, the executor shall be entitled to recover from such beneficiary such portion of the total tax paid as the proceeds of such policies bear to the taxable estate. If there is more than one such beneficiary, the executor shall be entitled to recover from such beneficiaries in the same ratio. In the case of such proceeds receivable by the surviving spouse of the decedent for which a deduction is allowed under section 2056 (relating to marital deduction), this section shall not apply to such proceeds except as to the amount thereof in excess of the aggregate amount of the marital deductions allowed under such section.

SEC. 2207. LIABILITY OF RECIPIENT OF PROPERTY OVER WHICH DECEDENT HAD POWER OF APPOINTMENT

Unless the decedent directs otherwise in his will, if any part of the gross estate on which the tax has been paid consists of the value of property included in the gross estate under section 2041, the executor shall be entitled to recover from the person receiving such property by reason of the exercise, nonexercise, or release of a power of appointment such portion of the total tax paid as the value of such property bears to the taxable estate. If there is more than one such person, the executor shall be entitled to recover from such persons in the same ratio. In the case of such property received by the surviving spouse of the decedent for which a deduction is allowed under section 2056 (relating to marital deduction), this section shall not apply to such property except as to the value thereof reduced by an amount equal to the excess of the aggregate amount of the marital deductions allowed under section 2056 over the amount of proceeds of insurance upon the life of the decedent receivable by the surviving spouse for which proceeds a marital deduction is allowed under such section.

SEC. 2207A. RIGHT OF RECOVERY IN THE CASE OF CERTAIN MARITAL DEDUCTION PROPERTY

(a) RECOVERY WITH RESPECT TO ESTATE TAX

(1) IN GENERAL - If any part of the gross estate consists of property the value of which is includible in the gross estate by reason of section 2044 (relating to certain property for which marital deduction was previously allowed), the decedent's estate shall be entitled to recover from the person receiving the property the amount by which--

(A) the total tax under this chapter which has been paid, exceeds

(B) the total tax under this chapter which would have been payable if the value of such property had not been included in the gross estate.

(2) DECEDENT MAY OTHERWISE DIRECT - Paragraph (1) shall not apply with respect to any property to the extent that the decedent in his will (or a revocable trust) specifically indicates an intent to waive any right of recovery under this subchapter with respect to such property.

(b) RECOVERY WITH RESPECT TO GIFT TAX - If for any calendar year tax is paid under chapter 12 with respect to any person by reason of property treated as transferred by such person under section 2519, such person shall be entitled to recover from the person receiving the property the amount by which--

(1) the total tax for such year under chapter 12, exceeds

(2) the total tax which would have been payable under such chapter for such year if the value of such property had not been taken into account for purposes of chapter 12.

(c) MORE THAN ONE RECIPIENT OF PROPERTY - For purposes of this section, if there is more than one person receiving the property, the right of recovery shall be against each such person.

(d) TAXES AND INTEREST - In the case of penalties and interest attributable to additional taxes described in subsections (a) and (b), rules similar to subsections (a), (b), and (c) shall apply.

SEC. 2207B. RIGHT OF RECOVERY WHERE DECEDENT RETAINED INTEREST

(a) ESTATE TAX

(1) IN GENERAL - If any part of the gross estate on which tax has been paid consists of the value of property included in the gross estate by reason of section 2036 (relating to transfers with retained life estate), the decedent's estate shall be entitled to recover from the person receiving the property the amount which bears the same ratio to the total tax under this chapter which has been paid as--

(A) the value of such property, bears to

(B) the taxable estate.

(2) DECEDENT MAY OTHERWISE DIRECT - Paragraph (1) shall not apply with respect to any property to the extent that the decedent in his will (or a revocable trust) specifically indicates an intent to waive any right of recovery under this subchapter with respect to such property.

(b) MORE THAN ONE RECIPIENT - For purposes of this section, if there is more than 1 person receiving the property, the right of recovery shall be against each such person.

(c) PENALTIES AND INTEREST - In the case of penalties and interest attributable to the additional taxes described in subsection (a), rules similar to the rules of subsections (a) and (b) shall apply.

(d) NO RIGHT OF RECOVERY AGAINST CHARITABLE REMAINDER TRUSTS - No person shall be entitled to recover any amount by reason of this section from a trust to which section 664 applies (determined without regard to this section).

CHAPTER 12 - GIFT TAX
Subchapter A. Determination of Tax Liability

SEC. 2501. IMPOSITION OF TAX
(a) TAXABLE TRANSFERS.--
    (1) GENERAL RULE.-- A tax, computed as provided in section 2502, is hereby imposed for each calendar year on the transfer of property by gift during such calendar year by any individual, resident or nonresident.
    (2) TRANSFERS OF INTANGIBLE PROPERTY.-- Except as provided in paragraph (3), paragraph (1) shall not apply to the transfer of intangible property by a nonresident not a citizen of the United States.
    (3) EXCEPTIONS--Paragraph (2) shall not apply in the case of a donor who at any time after March 8, 1965, and within the 10-year period ending with the date of transfer lost United States citizenship unless--
        (A) such donor's loss of United States citizenship resulted from the application of section 301(b), 350, or 355 of the Immigration and Nationality Act, as amended (8 U. S. C. 1401 (b), 1482, or 1487), or
        (B) such loss did not have for one of its principal purposes the avoidance of taxes under this subtitle or subtitle A.
    (4) BURDEN OF PROOF.-- If the Secretary establishes that it is reasonable to believe that an individual's loss of United States citizenship would, but for paragraph (3), result in the substantial reduction for the calendar year in the taxes on the transfer of property by gift, the burden of proving that such loss of citizenship did not have for one of its principal purposes the avoidance of taxes under this subtitle A shall be on such individual.
    (5) TRANSFERS TO POLITICAL ORGANIZATIONS.--Paragraph (1) shall not apply to the transfer of money or other property to a political organization (within the meaning of section 527(e)(1)) for the use of such organization.
(b) CERTAIN RESIDENTS OF POSSESSIONS CONSIDERED CITIZENS OF THE UNITED STATES.--A donor who is a citizen of the United States and a resident of a possession thereof shall, for the purposes of the taxes imposed by this chapter, be considered a "citizen" of the United States within the meaning of the term wherever used in this title unless he acquired his United States citizenship solely by reason of, 1) his being a citizen of such possession of the United States, or 2) his birth or residence within such possession of the United States.
(c) CERTAIN RESIDENTS OF POSSESSIONS CONSIDERED NONRESIDENTS NOT CITIZENS OF THE UNITED STATES.--A donor who is a citizen of the United States and a resident of a possession thereof shall, for purposes of the tax imposed by this chapter, be considered a "nonresident not a citizen of the United States" within the meaning of the term wherever used in this title, but only if such donor acquired his United States citizenship solely by reason of (1) his being a citizen of such possession of the United States, or (2) his birth or residence within such possession of the United States.
(d) CROSS REFERENCES.--
    (1) For increase in basis of property acquired by gift for gift tax paid, see section 1015(d).
    (2) For exclusion of transfers of property outside the United States

SEC. 2502. RATE OF TAX
(a) COMPUTATION OF TAX - The tax imposed by section 2501 for each calendar year shall be an amount equal to the excess of--
    (1) a tentative tax, computed under section 2001(c), on the aggregate sum of the taxable gifts for such calendar year and for each of the preceding calendar periods, over

(2) a tentative tax, computed under such section, on the aggregate sum of the taxable gifts for each of the preceding calendar periods.

(b) PRECEDING CALENDAR PERIOD - Whenever used in this title in connection with the gift tax imposed by this chapter, the term "preceding calendar period" means--

(1) calendar years 1932 and 1970 and all calendar years intervening between calendar year 1932 and calendar year 1970,

(2) the first calendar quarter of calendar year 1971 and all calendar quarters intervening between such calendar quarter and the first calendar quarter of calendar year 1982, and

(3) all calendar years after 1981 and before the calendar year for which the tax is being computed.

For purposes of paragraph (1), the term "calendar year 1932" includes only that portion of such year after June 6, 1932.

(c) TAX TO BE PAID BY DONOR - The tax imposed by section 2501 shall be paid by the donor.

SEC. 2503. TAXABLE GIFTS

(a) GENERAL DEFINITION.-The term "taxable gifts" means the total amount of gifts made during the calendar year, less the deductions provided in subchapter C (section 2522 and following).

(b) EXCLUSIONS FROM GIFTS.-In the case of gifts (other than gifts of future interests in property) made to any person by the donor during the calendar year, the first $10,000 of such gifts to such person shall not, for purposes of subsection (a), be included in the total amount of gifts made during such year. Where there has been a transfer to any person of a present interest in property, the possibility that such interest may be diminished by the exercise of a power shall be disregarded in applying this subsection, if no part of such interest will at any time pass to any other person.

(c) TRANSFER FOR THE BENEFIT OF A MINOR.-No part of a gift to an individual who has not attained the age of 21 years on the date of such transfer shall be considered a gift of a future interest in property for purposes of subsection (b) if the property and the income therefrom-

(1) may be expended by, or for the benefit of, the donee before his attaining the age of 21 years, and

(2) will to the extent not so expended-

(A) pass to the donee on his attaining the age of 21 years, and

(B) in the event that the donee dies before attaining the age of 21 years, be payable to the estate of the donee or as he may appoint under a general power of appointment as defined in section 2514(c).

(d) Repealed.

(e) EXCLUSION FOR CERTAIN TRANSFERS FOR EDUCATIONAL EXPENSES OR MEDICAL EXPENSES.-

(1) IN GENERAL-Any qualified transfer shall not be treated as a transfer of property by gift for purposes of this chapter.

(2) QUALIFIED TRANSFER.-For purposes of this subsection, the term "qualified transfer" means any amount paid on behalf of an individual-

(A) as tuition to an educational organization described in section 170(b)(I)(A)(ii) for the education or training of such individual, or

(B) to any person who provides medical care [as defined in section 213(e)] with respect to such individual as payment for such medical care.

(f) WAIVER OF CERTAIN PENSION RIGHTS.- If any individual waives, before the death of a participant, any survivor benefit, or right to such benefit, under section 401(a)(11) or 417, such waiver shall not be treated as a transfer of property by gift for purposes of this chapter.

(g) TREATMENT OF CERTAIN LOANS OF ARTWORKS

(1) IN GENERAL- For purposes of this subtitle, any loan of a qualified work of art shall not be treated as a transfer (and the value of such qualified work of art shall be determined as if such loan had not been made) if--

(A) such loan is to an organization described in section 501(c)(3) and exempt from tax under section 501(c) (other than a private foundation), and

(B) the use of such work by such organization is related to the purpose or function constituting the basis for its exemption under section 501.

(2) DEFINITIONS- For purposes of this section--

(A) QUALIFIED WORK OF ART.-The term "qualified work of art" means any archaeological, historic, or creative tangible personal property.

(B) PRIVATE FOUNDATION.- The term "private foundation" has the meaning given such term by section 509, except that such term shall not include any private operating foundation (as defined in section 4942(j)(3)).

SEC. 2505. UNIFIED CREDIT AGAINST GIFT TAX

(a) GENERAL RULE - In the case of a citizen or resident of the United States, there shall be allowed as a credit against the tax imposed by section 2501 for each calendar year an amount equal to--

(1) the applicable credit amount in effect under section 2010(c) for such calendar year, reduced by

(2) the sum of the amounts allowable as a credit to the individual under this section for all preceding calendar periods.

(b) ADJUSTMENT TO CREDIT FOR CERTAIN GIFTS MADE BEFORE 1977 - The amount allowable under subsection (a) shall be reduced by an amount equal to 20 percent of the aggregate amount allowed as a specific exemption under section 2521 (as in effect before its repeal by the Tax Reform Act of 1976) with respect to gifts made by the individual after September 8, 1976.

(c) LIMITATION BASED ON AMOUNT OF TAX - The amount of the credit allowed under subsection (a) for any calendar year shall not exceed the amount of the tax imposed by section 2501 for such calendar year.

Subchapter B. Transfers

SEC. 2511. TRANSFERS IN GENERAL

(a) SCOPE - Subject to the limitations contained in this chapter, the tax imposed by section 2501 shall apply whether the transfer is in trust or otherwise, whether the gift is direct or indirect, and whether the property is real or personal, tangible or intangible; but in the case of a nonresident not a citizen of the United States, shall apply to a transfer only if the property is situated within the United States.

(b) INTANGIBLE PROPERTY - For purposes of this chapter, in the case of a nonresident not a citizen of the United States who is excepted from the application of section 2501(a)(2)--

(1) shares of stock issued by a domestic corporation, and

(2) debt obligations of--

(A) a United States person, or

(B) the United States, a State or any political subdivision thereof, or the District of Columbia,

which are owned and held by such nonresident shall be deemed to be property situated within the United States.

SEC. 2512. VALUATION OF GIFTS

(a) If the gift is made in property, the value thereof at the date of the gift shall be considered the amount of the gift.

(b) Where property is transferred for less than an adequate and full consideration in money or money's worth, then the amount by which the value of the property exceeded the value of the consideration shall be deemed a gift, and shall be included in computing the amount of gifts made during the calendar year.

(c) CROSS REFERENCE - For individual's right to be furnished on request a statement regarding any valuation made by the secretary of a gift by that individual, see Section 7517.

SEC. 2513. GIFT BY HUSBAND OR WIFE TO THIRD PARTY

(a) CONSIDERED AS MADE ONE-HALF BY EACH.--

(1) IN GENERAL.--A gift made by one spouse to any person other than his spouse shall, for the purpose of this chapter, be considered made one-half by him and one-half by his spouse, but only if at the time of the gift each spouse is a citizen or resident of the United States. This paragraph shall not apply with respect to a gift of an interest in property if he creates in his spouse a general power of appointment, as defined in section 2514 (c), over such interest. For purposes of this section, an individual shall be considered as a spouse of another individual only if he is married to such individual at the time of the gift and does not remarry during the remainder of the calendar year.

(2) CONSENT OF BOTH SPOUSES.--Paragraph (1) shall apply only if both spouses have signified (under the regulations provided for its subsection(b)) their consent to the application of paragraph (1) in the case of all such gifts made during the calendar year by either while married to the other.

(b) MANNER AND TIME OF SIGNIFYING CONSENT.--

(1) MANNER.--A consent under this section shall be signified in such manner as is provided under regulations prescribed by the secretary.

(2) TIME.--Such consent may be so signified after the close of the calendar year in which the gift was made, subject to the following limitations--

(A) The consent may not be signified after the 15th of April following the close of such year, unless before the 15th day no return has been filed for such year by either spouse, in which case the consent may not be signified after a return for such year is filed by either spouse.

(B) The consent may not be signified after a note of deficiency with respect to the tax for such year has been set to either spouse in accordance with section 6212(a).

(c) REVOCATION OF CONSENT.--Revocation of consent previously signified shall be made in such manner as is provided under regulations prescribed by the secretary, but the right to revoke a consent previously signified with respect to a calendar year-

(1) shall not exist after the 15th day of April following the close of such year if the consent was signified on or before such 15th day; and

(2) shall not exist if the consent was not signified until after such 15th day.

(d) JOINT AND SEVERAL LIABILITY FOR TAX.--If the consent required by subsection (a)(2) is signified with respect to a gift made in the calendar year, the liability with respect to the entire tax imposed by this chapter of each spouse for such year shall be joint and several.

SEC. 2514. POWERS OF APPOINTMENT

(a) POWERS CREATED ON OR BEFORE OCTOBER 21, 1942.-- An exercise of general power of appointment created on or before October 21, 1942, shall be deemed a transfer of property by the individual possessing such power; but the failure to exercise such a power or the complete release of such a power shall not be deemed an exercise thereof. If a general power of appointment created on or before October 21, 1942, has been partially released so that it is no longer a general power of appointment, the subsequent exercise of such power shall not be deemed to be the exercise of a general power of appointment if--

(1) such partial release occurred before November 1, 1951, or

(2) the donee of such power was under a legal disability to release such power on October 21, 1942, and such partial release occurred not later than six months after the termination of such legal disability.

(b) POWERS CREATED AFTER OCTOBER 21, 1942.-- The exercise or release of a general power of appointment created after October 21, 1942, shall be deemed a transfer of property by the individual possessing such power.

(c) DEFINITION OF GENERAL POWER OF APPOINTMENT.--For purposes of this section, the term "general power of appointment" means a power which is exercisable in favor of the individual possessing the power (hereafter in this subsection referred to as the "possessor"), his estate, his creditors, or the creditors of his estate; except that--

(1) A power to consume, invade, or appropriate property for the benefit of the possessor which is limited by an ascertainable standard relating to health, education, support, or maintenance of the possessor shall not be deemed a general power of appointment.

(2) A power of appointment created on or before October 21, 1942, which is exercisable by the possessor only in conjunction with another person shall not be deemed a general power of appointment.

(3) In the case of a power appointment created on or before October 21, 1942, which is exercisable by the possessor only in conjunction with another person--

(A) if the power is not exercisable by the possessor in conjunction with the creator of the power--such power shall not be deemed a general power of appointment;

(B) if the power is not exercisable by the possessor except in conjunction with a person having a substantial interest in the property subject to the power, which is adverse to exercise of the power in favor of the possessor-- property subject to the power, which is adverse to exercise of the power in favor of the possessor-- such power shall not be deemed a general power of appointment. For the purposes of this subparagraph a person who, after the death of the possessor, may be possessed of a power of appointment(with respect to the property subject to the possessors power) which he may exercise in his own favor shall be deemed as having interest in the property and such interest shall be deemed adverse to such exercise of the possessor's power;

(C) if (after the application of subparagraphs(A) and (B) the power is a general power of appointment and is exercisable in favor of such other person--such power shall be deemed a general power of appointment only in respect of a fractional part of the property subject to such power, such part to be determined by dividing the value of such property by the number of such persons(including the possessor) in favor of whom such power is exercisable.

For purposes of subparagraphs (B) and (C), a power shall be deemed to be exercisable in favor of a person if it is exercisable in favor of such person, his estate, his creditors, or the creditors of his estate.

(d) CREATION OF ANOTHER POWER IN CERTAIN CASES.-- If a power of appointment created after October 21, 1942, is exercised by creating another power of appointment which, under the applicable local law, can be validly exercised so as to postpone the vesting of any estate or interest in the property which was subject to the first power, or suspend the absolute ownership or power of alienation of such property, for a period ascertainable without regard to the date of the creation of this first power, such exercise of the first power shall, to the extent of the property subject to the second power, be deemed a transfer of property by the individual possessing such power.

(e) LAPSE OF POWER.--The lapse of a power of appointment created after October 21, 1942, during the life of the individual possessing the power shall be considered a release of such power. The rule of the preceding sentence shall apply with respect to the lapse of powers during any calendar year only to the extent that the property which could have been appointed by exercise of such lapsed powers exceeds in value the greater of the following amounts:

(1) $5,000, or

(2) 5 percent of the aggregate value of the assets out of which, or the proceeds of which, the exercise of the lapsed powers could be satisfied.

(f) DATE OF CREATION OF POWER.--For purposes of this section a power of appointment created by a will executed on or before October 21, 1942, shall be considered a power on or before such date if the person executing the will dies before July 1, 1949, without having republished such will, by codicil or otherwise, after October 21, 1942.

SEC. 2515. TREATMENT OF GENERATION-SKIPPING TRANSFER TAX

In the case of any taxable gift which is a direct skip (within the meaning of chapter 13), the amount of such gift shall be increased by the amount of any tax imposed on the transferor under chapter 13 with respect to such gift.

SEC. 2516. CERTAIN PROPERTY SETTLEMENTS

Where a husband and wife enter into a written agreement relative to their marital and property rights and divorce occurs within the 3-year period beginning on the date 1 year before such agreement is entered into (whether or not such agreement is approved by the divorce decree), any transfers of property or interests in property made pursuant to such agreement--

(1) to either spouse in settlement of his or her marital or property rights, or

(2) to provide a reasonable allowance for the support of issue of the marriage during minority,

shall be deemed to be transfers made for a full and adequate consideration in money or money's worth.

SEC. 2518. DISCLAIMERS

(a) GENERAL RULE.-- For purposes of this subtitle, if a person makes a qualified disclaimer with respect to any interest in property, this subtitle shall apply with respect to such interest as if the interest had never been transferred to such person.

(b) QUALIFIED DISCLAIMER DEFINED.-- For purposes of subsection (a), the term "qualified disclaimer" means an irrevocable and unqualified refusal by a person to accept an interest in property but only if--

(1) such refusal is in writing

(2) such writing is received by the transferor of the interest, his legal representative, or the holder of the legal title to which the interest relates not later than the date which is nine months after the later of--

(A) the date on which the transfer in such person is made, or

(B) the day on which such person attains age 21,

(3) such person has not accepted the interest or any benefits, and

(4) as a result of such refusal, the interest passes without any direction on the part of the person making the disclaimer and passes either--

(A) to the spouse of the decedent, or

(B) to a person other than the person making the disclaimer.

(c) OTHER RULES.--For purposes of subsection (a)--

(1) DISCLAIMER OF UNDIVIDED PORTION OF INTEREST.-- A disclaimer with respect to an undivided portion of an interest which meets the requirements of the preceding sentence shall be treated as a qualified disclaimer of such portion of the interest.

(2) POWERS.-- A power with respect to property shall be treated as an interest in such property.

(3) CERTAIN TRANSFERS TREATED AS DISCLAIMERS.--A written transfer of the transferor's [*sic*] entire interest in the property--

   (A) which meets requirements similar to the requirements of paragraphs (2) and (3) of subsection(b), and

   (B) which is to a person or persons who would have received the property had the transferor [*sic*] made a qualified disclaimer (within the meaning of subsection (b)), shall be treated as a qualified disclaimer.

SEC. 2519. DISPOSITIONS OF CERTAIN LIFE ESTATES

(a) GENERAL RULE - For purposes of this chapter and chapter 11, any disposition of all or part of a qualifying income interest for life in any property to which this section applies shall be treated as a transfer of all interests in such property other than the qualifying income interest.

(b) PROPERTY TO WHICH THIS SUBSECTION APPLIES - This section applies to any property if a deduction was allowed with respect to the transfer of such property to the donor--

   (1) under section 2056 by reason of subsection (b)(7) thereof, or

   (2) under section 2523 by reason of subsection (f) thereof.

(c) CROSS REFERENCE - For right of recovery for gift tax in the case of property treated as transferred under this Section, see Section 2207a(b).

CHAPTER 13 - TAX ON GENERATION-SKIPPING TRANSFERS
Subchapter A. Tax Imposed

SEC. 2601. TAX IMPOSED

A tax is hereby imposed on every generation-skipping transfer (within the meaning of subchapter B).

SEC. 2602. AMOUNT OF TAX

The amount of the tax imposed by section 2601 is--

   (1) the taxable amount (determined under subchapter C), multiplied by

   (2) the applicable rate (determined under subsection E).

SEC. 2603. LIABILITY FOR TAX

(a) PERSONAL LIABILITY.--

   (1) TAXABLE DISTRIBUTIONS.--In the case of a taxable distribution, the tax imposed by section 2601 shall be paid by the transferee.

   (2) TAXABLE TERMINATION.-- In the case of a taxable termination or a direct skip from a trust, the tax shall be paid by the trustee.

   (3) DIRECT SKIP.-- In the case of a direct skip (other than a direct skip from trust), the tax shall be paid by the transferor.

(b) SOURCE OF TAX.--Unless otherwise directed pursuant to the governing instrument by specific reference to the tax imposed by this chapter, the tax imposed by this chapter on a generation- skipping transfer shall be charged to the property constituting such transfer.

(c) CROSS REFERENCE.-- For provisions making estate and gift tax provisions with respect to transferee liability, liens, and related matters applicable to the tax imposed by section 2601, see section 2661.

SEC. 2604. CREDIT FOR CERTAIN STATE TAXES

(a) GENERAL RULE - If a generation-skipping transfer (other than a direct skip) occurs at the same time as and as a result of the death of an individual, a credit against the tax imposed by section 2601 shall be allowed in an amount equal to the generation-skipping transfer tax actually paid to any State in respect to any property included in the generation-skipping transfer.

(b) LIMITATION - The aggregate amount allowed as a credit under this section with respect to any transfer shall not exceed 5 percent of the amount of the tax imposed by section 2601 on such transfer.

Subchapter B. Generation-Skipping Transfers

SEC. 2611. GENERATION-SKIPPING TRANSFER DEFINED

(a) IN GENERAL.--For purposes of this chapter, the term "generation-skipping transfer," means-

    (1) a taxable distribution,

    (2) a taxable termination, and

    (3) a direct skip.

(b) CERTAIN TRANSFERS EXCLUDED.-- The term "generation-skipping transfer" does not include--

    (1) any transfer which, if made inter vivos by an individual, would not be treated as a taxable gift by reason of section 2503 (e) (relating to exclusion of certain transfers for educational or medical expenses), and

    (2) any transfer to the extent--

        (A) the property transferred was subject to a prior tax imposed under this chapter,

        (B) the transferee in the prior transfer was assigned to the same generation as (or a lower generation than) the generation assignment of the transferee in this transfer, and

        (C) such transfers do not have the effect of avoiding tax under this chapter with respect to any transfer.

SEC. 2612. TAXABLE TERMINATION; TAXABLE DISTRIBUTION; DIRECT SKIP

(a) TAXABLE TERMINATION.--

    (1) GENERAL RULE.--For purposes of this chapter, the term "taxable termination" means the termination (by death, lapse of time, release of power, or otherwise) of an interest in property held in a trust unless--

        (A) immediately after such termination, a non-skip person has an interest in such property, or

        (B) at no time after such termination may a distribution (including distributions on termination) be made from such trust to a skip person.

    (2) CERTAIN PARTIAL TERMINATIONS TREATED AS TAXABLE.-- If, upon the termination of an interest in property held in trust by reason of the death of a lineal descendant of the transferor, a specified portion of the trust's assets are distributed to 1 or more skip persons (or 1 or more trusts for the exclusive benefit of such persons), such termination shall constitute a taxable termination with respect to such portion of the trust property.

(b) TAXABLE DISTRIBUTION.-- For purposes of this chapter the term "taxable distribution" means any distribution from a trust to a skip person (other than taxable termination or direct skip).

(c) DIRECT SKIP.-For purposes of this chapter--

    (1) IN GENERAL.--The term "direct skip" means a transfer subject to a tax imposed by chapter 11 or 12 of an interest in property to a skip person.

(2) SPECIAL RULE FOR TRANSFERS TO GRANDCHILDREN.-- For purposes of determining whether any transfer is a direct skip, if--

(A) an individual is a grandchild of the transferor or the transferor's spouse or former spouse) and

(B) as of the time of the transfer, the parent of such individual who is a lineal descendant of the transferor (or the transferor's spouse or former spouse) is dead, such individual shall be treated as if such individual were a child of the transferor and all of that grandchild's children shall be treated as if they were grandchildren of the transferor. In the case of lineal decedents below a grandchild, the preceding sentence may be reapplied. If any transfer of property to a trust would be a direct skip but for this paragraph, any generation assignment under this paragraph shall apply also for purposes of applying this chapter to transfers from the portion of the trust attributable to such property.

(3) LOOK-THRU RULES NOT TO APPLY.--Solely for the purposes of determining whether any transfer to a trust is a direct skip, the rules of section 2651 (e)(2) shall not apply.

SEC. 2613. SKIP PERSON AND NON-SKIP PERSON DEFINED

(a) SKIP PERSON.-- For purposes of this chapter, the term "skip person" means--

(1) a natural person assigned to a generation which is 2 or more generations below the generation assignment of the transferor, or

(2) a trust--

(A) if all intents in such trust are held by skip persons, or

(B) if--

(i) there is no holding an interest in such trust, and

(ii) at no such time after the transfer may a distribution (including distributions on termination) be made from such trust to a non-skip person.

(b) NON-SKIP PERSON.--For purposes of this chapter, the term "non-skip person" means any person who is not a skip person.

Subchapter C. Taxable Amount

SEC. 2621. TAXABLE AMOUNT IN CASE OF TAXABLE DISTRIBUTION

(a) IN GENERAL - For purposes of this chapter, the taxable amount in the case of any taxable distribution shall be--

(1) the value of the property received by the transferee, reduced by

(2) any expense incurred by the transferee in connection with the determination, collection, or refund of the tax imposed by this chapter with respect to such distribution.

(b) PAYMENT OF GST TAX TREATED AS TAXABLE DISTRIBUTION - For purposes of this chapter, if any of the tax imposed by this chapter with respect to any taxable distribution is paid out of the trust, an amount equal to the portion so paid shall be treated as a taxable distribution.

SEC. 2622. TAXABLE AMOUNT IN CASE OF TAXABLE TERMINATION

(a) IN GENERAL - For purposes of this chapter, the taxable amount in the case of a taxable termination shall be--

(1) the value of all property with respect to which the taxable termination has occurred, reduced by

(2) any deduction allowed under subsection (b).

(b) DEDUCTION FOR CERTAIN EXPENSES - For purposes of subsection (a), there shall be allowed a deduction similar to the deduction allowed by section 2053 (relating to expenses, indebtedness, and taxes) for amounts attributable to the property with respect to which the taxable termination has occurred.

SEC. 2623. TAXABLE AMOUNT IN CASE OF DIRECT SKIP
For purposes of this chapter, the taxable amount in the case of a direct skip shall be the value of the property received by the transferee.

SEC. 2624. VALUATION
(a) GENERAL RULE - Except as otherwise provided in this chapter, property shall be valued as of the time of the generation-skipping transfer.
(b) ALTERNATE VALUATION AND SPECIAL USE VALUATION ELECTIONS APPLY TO CERTAIN DIRECT SKIPS - In the case of any direct skip of property which is included in the transferor's gross estate, the value of such property for purposes of this chapter shall be the same as its value for purposes of chapter 11 (determined with regard to sections 2032 and 2032A).
(c) ALTERNATE VALUATION ELECTION PERMITTED IN THE CASE OF TAXABLE TERMINATIONS OCCURRING AT DEATH - If 1 or more taxable terminations with respect to the same trust occur at the same time as and as a result of the death of an individual, an election may be made to value all of the property included in such terminations in accordance with section 2032.
(d) REDUCTION FOR CONSIDERATION PROVIDED BY TRANSFEREE - For purposes of this chapter, the value of the property transferred shall be reduced by the amount of any consideration provided by the transferee.

Subchapter D. GST Exemption

SEC. 2631. GST EXEMPTION
(a) GENERAL RULE.--For purposes of determining the inclusion ratio, every individual shall be allowed a GST exemption of $1,000,000 which may be allocated by such individual (or his executor) to any property with respect to which such individual is the transferor.
(b) ALLOCATIONS IRREVOCABLE.--Any allocation under subsection (a), once made, shall be irrevocable.

SEC. 2632. SPECIAL RULES FOR ALLOCATION OF GST EXEMPTION
(a) TIME AND MANNER OF ALLOCATION
(1) TIME - Any allocation by an individual of his GST exemption under section 2631(a) may be made at any time on or before the date prescribed for filing the estate tax return for such individual's estate (determined with regard to extensions), regardless of whether such a return is required to be filed.
(2) MANNER - The Secretary shall prescribe by forms or regulations the manner in which any allocation referred to in paragraph (1) is to be made.
(b) DEEMED ALLOCATION TO CERTAIN LIFETIME DIRECT SKIPS
(1) IN GENERAL - If any individual makes a direct skip during his lifetime, any unused portion of such individual's GST exemption shall be allocated to the property transferred to the extent necessary to make the inclusion ratio for such property zero. If the amount of the direct skip exceeds such unused portion, the entire unused portion shall be allocated to the property transferred.

(2) UNUSED PORTION - For purposes of paragraph (1), the unused portion of an individual's GST exemption is that portion of such exemption which has not previously been allocated by such individual (or treated as allocated under paragraph (1) with respect to a prior direct skip).

(3) SUBSECTION NOT TO APPLY IN CERTAIN CASES - An individual may elect to have this subsection not apply to a transfer.

(c) ALLOCATION OF UNUSED GST EXEMPTION

(1) IN GENERAL - Any portion of an individual's GST exemption which has not been allocated within the time prescribed by subsection (a) shall be deemed to be allocated as follows--

(A) first, to property which is the subject of a direct skip occurring at such individual's death, and

(B) second, to trusts with respect to which such individual is the transferor and from which a taxable distribution or a taxable termination might occur at or after such individual's death.

(2) ALLOCATION WITHIN CATEGORIES

(A) IN GENERAL - The allocation under paragraph (1) shall be made among the properties described in subparagraph (A) thereof and the trusts described in subparagraph (B) thereof, as the case may be, in proportion to the respective amounts (at the time of allocation) of the nonexempt portions of such properties or trusts.

(B) NONEXEMPT PORTION - For purposes of subparagraph (A), the term "nonexempt portion" means the value (at the time of allocation) of the property or trust, multiplied by the inclusion ratio with respect to such property or trust.

Subchapter E. Applicable Rate; Inclusion Ratio

SEC. 2641. APPLICABLE RATE

(a) GENERAL RULE.--For purposes of this chapter, the term "applicable rate" means, with respect to any generation-skipping transfer, the product of--

(1) the maximum Federal estate tax rate, and

(2) the inclusion ratio to the transfer.

(b) MAXIMUM FEDERAL ESTATE TAX RATE.--For purposes of subsection (a), the term "maximum Federal estate tax rate" means the maximum rate imposed by section 2001 on the estates decedents dying at the time of the taxable distribution, taxable termination, or direct skip, as the case may be.

SEC. 2642. INCLUSION RATIO

(a) INCLUSION RATIO DEFINED.--For purposes of this chapter--

(1) IN GENERAL.--Except as provided in this section, the inclusion ratio with respect to any property transferred in a generation-skipping transfer shall be excess (if any) of 1 over--

(A) except as provided in subparagraph (b), the applicable fraction determined for the trust from which such transfer is made, or

(B) in the case of a direct skip, the applicable fraction determined for such skip.

(2) APPLICABLE FRACTION.--For purposes of paragraph (1), the applicable fraction is a fraction--

(A) the numerator of which is the amount of the GST exemption allocated to the trust (or in the case of a direct skip, allocated to the property transferred in such skip), and

(B) the denominator of which is--

(i) the value of the property transferred to the trust (or involved in the direct skip), reduced by

(ii) the sum of-

(I) any Federal tax or State death tax actually recovered from the trust attributable such property, and

(II) any charitable deduction allowed under section 2055 or 2522 with respect to such property.

(b) VALUATION RULES, ETC. *****

(c) TREATMENT OF CERTAIN DIRECT SKIPS WHICH ARE NONTAXABLE GIFTS.

(1) IN GENERAL. In the case of a direct skip which is a nontaxable gift, the inclusion ratio shall be zero.

(2) EXCEPTION FOR CERTAIN TRANSFERS IN TRUST. Paragraph (1) shall not apply to any transfer to a trust for the benefit of an individual unless--

(A) during the life of such individual, no portion of the corpus or income of the trust may be distributed to (or for the benefit of) any person other than such individual, and

(B) if the trust does not terminate before the individual dies, the assets of such trust will be includible in the gross estate of such individual.

Rules similar to the rules of section 2652(c)(3) shall apply for purposes of subparagraph (A).

(3) NONTAXABLE GIFT. For purposes of this subsection, the term "nontaxable gift" means any transfer of property to the extent such transfer is not treated as a taxable gift by reason of--

(A) section 2503(b) (taking into account the application of section 2513), or

(B) section 2503(e)

(d) SPECIAL RULES WHERE MORE THAN ONE TRANSFER MADE TO TRUST.-- *****

(e) SPECIAL RULES FOR CHARITABLE LEAD ANNUITY TRUSTS.-- *****

(f) SPECIAL RULES FOR CERTAIN INTER VIVOS TRANSFERS.-- Except as provided in regulations--

(1) IN GENERAL. For purposes of determining the inclusion ratio, if--

(A) an individual makes an inter vivos transfer of property, and

(B) the value of such property would be includible in the gross estate of such individual under chapter 11 if such individual died immediately after making such transfer (other than by reason of section 2035), any allocation of GST exemption to such property shall not be made before the close of the estate tax inclusion period (and the value of such property shall be determined under paragraph (2)). If such transfer is a direct skip, such skip shall be treated as occurring as of the close of the estate tax inclusion period.

(2) VALUATION. In the case of any property to which paragraph (1) applies, the value of such property shall be--

(A) if such property is includible in the gross estate of the transferor (other than by reason of section 2035), its value for purposes of chapter 11, or

(B) if subparagraph (A) does not apply, its value as of the close of the estate tax inclusion period (or, if any allocation of GST exemption to such property is not made on a timely filed gift tax return for the calendar year in which such period ends, its value as of the time such allocation is filed with the Secretary).

(3) ESTATE TAX INCLUSION PERIOD. For purposes of this subsection, the term "estate tax inclusion period" means any period after the transfer described in paragraph (1) during which the value of the property involved in such transfer would be includible in the gross estate of the transferor under chapter 11 if he died. Such period shall in no event extend beyond the earlier of--

(A) the date on which there is a generation-skipping transfer with respect to such property, or

(B) the date of the death of the transferor.

(4) TREATMENT OF SPOUSE. Except as provided in regulations, any reference in this subsection to an individual or transferor shall be treated as including a reference to the spouse of such individual or transferor.

(5) COORDINATION WITH SUBSECTION (d). Under regulations, appropriate adjustments shall be made in the application of subsection (d) to take into account the provisions of this subsection.

Subchapter F. Other Definitions and Special Rules

SEC. 2651. GENERATION ASSIGNMENT

(a) IN GENERAL - For purposes of this chapter, the generation to which any person (other than the transferor) belongs shall be determined in accordance with the rules set forth in this section.

(b) LINEAL DESCENDANTS

(1) IN GENERAL - An individual who is a lineal descendant of a grandparent of the transferor shall be assigned to that generation which results from comparing the number of generations between the grandparent and such individual with the number of generations between the grandparent and the transferor.

(2) ON SPOUSE'S SIDE - An individual who is a lineal descendant of a grandparent of a spouse (or former spouse) of the transferor (other than such spouse) shall be assigned to that generation which results from comparing the number of generations between such grandparent and such individual with the number of generations between such grandparent and such spouse.

(3) TREATMENT OF LEGAL ADOPTIONS, ETC. - For purposes of this subsection--

(A) LEGAL ADOPTIONS - A relationship by legal adoption shall be treated as a relationship by blood.

(B) RELATIONSHIPS BY HALF-BLOOD - A relationship by the half-blood shall be treated as a relationship of the whole-blood.

(c) MARITAL RELATIONSHIP

(1) MARRIAGE TO TRANSFEROR - An individual who has been married at any time to the transferor shall be assigned to the transferor's generation.

(2) MARRIAGE TO OTHER LINEAL DESCENDANTS - An individual who has been married at any time to an individual described in subsection (b) shall be assigned to the generation of the individual so described.

(d) PERSONS WHO ARE NOT LINEAL DESCENDANTS - An individual who is not assigned to a generation by reason of the foregoing provisions of this section shall be assigned to a generation on the basis of the date of such individual's birth with--

(1) an individual born not more than 12 ½ years after the date of the birth of the transferor assigned to the transferor's generation,

(2) an individual born more than 12 ½ years but not more than 37 ½ years after the date of the birth of the transferor assigned to the first generation younger than the transferor, and

(3) similar rules for a new generation every 25 years.

(e) SPECIAL RULE FOR PERSONS WITH A DECEASED PARENT

(1) IN GENERAL - For purposes of determining whether any transfer is a generation-skipping transfer, if-

(A) an individual is a descendant of a parent of the transferor (or the transferor's spouse or former spouse), and

(B) such individual's parent who is a lineal descendant of the parent of the transferor (or the transferor's spouse or former spouse) is dead at the time the transfer (from which an interest of such individual is established or derived) is subject to a tax imposed by chapter 11 or 12 upon the transferor (and if there shall be more than 1 such time, then at the earliest such time), such individual shall be treated as if such individual were a member of the generation which is 1 generation below the lower of the transferor's generation or the generation assignment of the youngest living ancestor of such individual who is also a descendant of the parent of the transferor (or the transferor's spouse or former spouse), and the generation assignment of any descendant of such individual shall be adjusted accordingly.

(2) LIMITED APPLICATION OF SUBSECTION TO COLLATERAL HEIRS - This subsection shall not apply with respect to a transfer to any individual who is not a lineal descendant of the transferor (or the transferor's spouse or former spouse) if, at the time of the transfer, such transferor has any living lineal descendant.

(f) OTHER SPECIAL RULES

(1) INDIVIDUALS ASSIGNED TO MORE THAN 1 GENERATION - Except as provided in regulations, an individual who, but for this subsection, would be assigned to more than 1 generation shall be assigned to the youngest such generation.

(2) INTERESTS THROUGH ENTITIES - Except as provided in paragraph (3), if an estate, trust, partnership, corporation, or other entity has an interest in property, each individual having a beneficial interest in such entity shall be treated as having an interest in such property and shall be assigned to a generation under the foregoing provisions of this subsection.

(3) TREATMENT OF CERTAIN CHARITABLE ORGANIZATIONS AND GOVERNMENTAL ENTITIES - Any--

(A) organization described in section 511(a)(2),

(B) charitable trust described in section 511(b)(2), and

(C) governmental entity,

shall be assigned to the transferor's generation.

SEC. 2652. OTHER DEFINITIONS

(a) TRANSFEROR - For purposes of this chapter--

(1) IN GENERAL - Except as provided in this subsection or section 2653(a), the term "transferor" means--

(A) in the case of any property subject to the tax imposed by chapter 11, the decedent, and

(B) in the case of any property subject to the tax imposed by chapter 12, the donor.

An individual shall be treated as transferring any property with respect to which such individual is the transferor.

(2) GIFT-SPLITTING BY MARRIED COUPLES - If, under section 2513, one-half of a gift is treated as made by an individual and one-half of such gift is treated as made by the spouse of such individual, such gift shall be so treated for purposes of this chapter.

(3) SPECIAL ELECTION FOR QUALIFIED TERMINABLE INTEREST PROPERTY - In the case of--

(A) any trust with respect to which a deduction is allowed to the decedent under section 2056 by reason of subsection (b)(7) thereof, and

(B) any trust with respect to which a deduction to the donor spouse is allowed under section 2523 by reason of subsection (f) thereof, the estate of the decedent or the donor spouse, as the case may be, may elect to treat all of the property in such trust for purposes of this chapter as if the election to be treated as qualified terminable interest property had not been made.

(b) TRUST AND TRUSTEE (1) TRUST - The term "trust" includes any arrangement (other than an estate) which, although not a trust, has substantially the same effect as a trust.

(2) TRUSTEE - In the case of an arrangement which is not a trust but which is treated as a trust under this subsection, the term "trustee" shall mean the person in actual or constructive possession of the property subject to such arrangement.

(3) EXAMPLES - Arrangements to which this subsection applies include arrangements involving life estates and remainders, estates for years, and insurance and annuity contracts.

(c) INTEREST

(1) IN GENERAL - A person has an interest in property held in trust if (at the time the determination is made) such person--

(A) has a right (other than a future right) to receive income or corpus from the trust,

(B) is a permissible current recipient of income or corpus from the trust and is not described in section 2055(a), or

(C) is described in section 2055(a) and the trust is--

(i) a charitable remainder annuity trust,

(ii) a charitable remainder unitrust within the meaning of section 664, or

(iii) a pooled income fund within the meaning of section 642(c)(5).

(2) CERTAIN INTERESTS DISREGARDED - For purposes of paragraph (1), an interest which is used primarily to postpone or avoid any tax imposed by this chapter shall be disregarded.

(3) CERTAIN SUPPORT OBLIGATIONS DISREGARDED - The fact that income or corpus of the trust may be used to satisfy an obligation of support arising under State law shall be disregarded in determining whether a person has an interest in the trust, if--

(A) such use is discretionary, or

(B) such use is pursuant to the provisions of any State law substantially equivalent to the Uniform Gifts to Minors Act.

(d) EXECUTOR - For purposes of this chapter, the term "executor" has the meaning given such term by section 2203.

SEC. 2653. TAXATION OF MULTIPLE SKIPS

(a) GENERAL RULE - For purposes of this chapter, if--

(1) there is a generation-skipping transfer of any property, and

(2) immediately after such transfer such property is held in trust,

for purposes of applying this chapter (other than section 2651) to subsequent transfers from the portion of such trust attributable to such property, the trust will be treated as if the transferor of such property were assigned to the first generation above the highest generation of any person who has an interest in such trust immediately after the transfer.

(b) TRUST RETAINS INCLUSION RATIO

(1) IN GENERAL - Except as provided in paragraph (2), the provisions of subsection (a) shall not affect the inclusion ratio determined with respect to any trust. Under regulations prescribed by the Secretary, notwithstanding the preceding sentence, proper adjustment shall be made to the inclusion ratio with respect to such trust to take into account any tax under this chapter borne by such trust which is imposed by this chapter on the transfer described in subsection (a).

(2) SPECIAL RULE FOR POUR-OVER TRUST

(A) IN GENERAL - If the generation-skipping transfer referred to in subsection (a) involves the transfer of property from 1 trust to another trust (hereinafter in this paragraph referred to as the "pour-over trust"), the inclusion ratio for the pour-over trust shall be determined by treating the nontax portion of such distribution as if it were a part of a GST exemption allocated to such trust.

(B) NONTAX PORTION - For purposes of subparagraph (A), the nontax portion of any distribution is the amount of such distribution multiplied by the applicable fraction which applies to such distribution.

SEC. 2654. SPECIAL RULES

(a) BASIS ADJUSTMENT

(1) IN GENERAL - Except as provided in paragraph (2), if property is transferred in a generation-skipping transfer, the basis of such property shall be increased (but not above the fair market value of such property) by an amount equal to that portion of the tax imposed by section 2601 (computed without regard to section 2604) with respect to the transfer which is attributable to the excess of the fair market value of such property over its adjusted basis immediately before the transfer.

(2) CERTAIN TRANSFERS AT DEATH - If property is transferred in a taxable termination which occurs at the same time as and as a result of the death of an individual, the basis of such property shall be adjusted in a manner similar to the manner provided under section 1014(a); except that, if the inclusion ratio with respect to such property is less than 1, any increase or decrease in basis shall be limited by multiplying such increase or decrease (as the case may be) by the inclusion ratio.

(b) CERTAIN TRUSTS TREATED AS SEPARATE TRUSTS - For purposes of this chapter--

(1) the portions of a trust attributable to transfers from different transferors shall be treated as separate trusts, and

(2) substantially separate and independent shares of different beneficiaries in a trust shall be treated as separate trusts.

Except as provided in the preceding sentence, nothing in this chapter shall be construed as authorizing a single trust to be treated as 2 or more trusts. For purposes of this subsection, a trust shall be treated as part of an estate during any period that the trust is so treated under section 645.

(c) DISCLAIMERS - FOR PROVISIONS RELATING TO THE EFFECT OF A QUALIFIED DISCLAIMER FOR PURPOSES OF THIS CHAPTER, SEE SECTION 2518.

(d) LIMITATION ON PERSONAL LIABILITY OF TRUSTEE - A trustee shall not be personally liable for any increase in the tax imposed by section 2601 which is attributable to the fact that--

(1) section 2642(c) (relating to exemption of certain nontaxable gifts) does not apply to a transfer to the trust which was made during the life of the transferor and for which a gift tax return was not filed, or

(2) the inclusion ratio with respect to the trust is greater than the amount of such ratio as computed on the basis of the return on which was made (or was deemed made) an allocation of the GST exemption to property transferred to such trust.

The preceding sentence shall not apply if the trustee has knowledge of facts sufficient reasonably to conclude that a gift tax return was required to be filed or that the inclusion ratio was erroneous.

CHAPTER 14 - SPECIAL VALUATION RULES

SEC. 2701. SPECIAL VALUATION RULES IN CASE OF CERTAIN INTERESTS IN CORPORATIONS OR PARTNERSHIPS.

(a) Valuation Rules.

(1) IN GENERAL.--Solely for purposes of determining whether a transfer of an interest in a corporation or partnership to (or for the benefit of) a member of the transferor's family is a gift (and the value of such transfer), the value of any right--

(A) which is described in subparagraph (A) or (B) of subsection (b)(1), and

(B) which is with respect to any applicable retained interest that is held by the transferor or an applicable family member immediately after the transfer, shall be determined under paragraph (3). This paragraph shall not apply to the transfer of any interest for which market quotations are readily available (as of the date of transfer) on an established securities market.

(2) EXCEPTIONS FOR MARKETABLE RETAINED INTERESTS, ETC.-- Paragraph (1) shall not apply to any right with respect to an applicable retained interest if--

(A) market quotations are readily available (as of the date of the transfer) for such interest on an established securities market,

(B) such interest is of the same class as the transferred interest, or

(C) such interest is proportionally the same as the transferred interest, without regard to nonlapsing differences in voting power (or, for a partnership, nonlapsing differences with respect to management and limitations on liability).

Subparagraph (C) shall not apply to any interest in a partnership if the transferor or an applicable family member has the right to alter the liability of the transferee of the transferred property. Except as provided by the secretary, any difference described in subparagraph (C) which lapses by reason of any Federal or State law shall be treated as a nonlapsing difference for purposes of such subparagraph.

(3) VALUATION OF RIGHTS TO WHICH PARAGRAPH (1) APPLIES.--

(A) IN GENERAL.--The value of any right described in paragraph (1), other than a distribution right which consists of a right to receive a qualified payment, shall be treated as being zero.

(B) VALUATION OF QUALIFIED PAYMENTS.--If--

(i) any applicable retained interest confers a distribution right which consists of the right to a qualified payment, and

(ii) there are 1 or more liquidation, put, call, or conversion rights with respect to such interest, the value of all such rights shall be determined as if each liquidation, put, call, or conversion right were exercised in the manner resulting in the lowest value being determined for all such rights.

(4) MINIMUM VALUATION OF JUNIOR EQUITY.--

(A) IN GENERAL.--In the case of a transfer described in paragraph (1) of a junior equity interest in a corporation or partnership, such interest shall in no event be valued at an amount less than the value which would be determined if the total value of all the junior equity interests in the entity were equal to 10 percent of the sum of--

(i) the total value of all of the equity interests in such entity, plus

(ii) the total amount of indebtedness of such entity to the transferor (or an applicable family member).

(B) DEFINITIONS.--For purposes of this paragraph--

(i) JUNIOR EQUITY INTEREST.--The term "junior equity interest" means common stock or, in the case of a partnership, any partnership interest under which the rights as to income and capital are junior to the rights of all other classes of equity interests.

(ii) EQUITY INTEREST.--The term "equity interest" means stock or any interest as a partner, as the case may be.

(b) APPLICABLE RETAINED INTERESTS.--For purposes of this section--

(1) IN GENERAL.--The term "applicable retained interest" means any interest in an entity with respect to which there is--

(A) a distribution right, but only if, immediately before the transfer described in subsection (a)(1), the transferor and applicable family members hold (after application of subsection (e)(3)) control of the entity, or

(B) a liquidation, put, call, or conversion right.

(2) CONTROL.--For purposes of paragraph (1)--

(A) CORPORATIONS.--In the case of a corporation, the term "control" means the holding of at least 50 percent (by vote or value) of the stock of the corporation.

(B) PARTNERSHIPS.--In the case of a partnership, the term "control" means--

(i) the holding of at least 50 percent of the capital or profits interests in the partnership, or

(ii) in the case of a limited partnership, the holding of any interest as a general partner.

(c) DISTRIBUTION AND OTHER RIGHTS; QUALIFIED PAYMENTS.--

For purposes of this section--

(1) DISTRIBUTION RIGHT.--

(A) IN GENERAL.--The term "distribution right" means--

(i) a right to distributions from a corporation with respect to its stock, and

(ii) a right to distributions from a partnership with respect to a partner's interest in the partnership.

(B) EXCEPTIONS.--The term "distribution right" does not include--

(i) a right to distributions with respect to any junior equity interest (as defined in subsection (a) (4)(B)(i));

(ii) any liquidation, put, call, or conversion right, or

(iii) any right to receive any guaranteed payment described in section 707(c) of a fixed amount.

(2) LIQUIDATION, ETC. RIGHTS.--

(A) IN GENERAL.--The term "liquidation, put, call, or conversion right" means any liquidation, put, call, or conversion right, or any similar right, the exercise or nonexercise of which affects the value of the transferred interest.

(B) EXCEPTION FOR FIXED RIGHTS.--

(i) IN GENERAL.--The term "liquidation, put call, or conversion right" does not include any right which must be exercised at a specific time and at a specific amount.

(ii) TREATMENT OF CERTAIN RIGHTS.--If a right is assumed to be exercised in a particular manner under subsection (a)(3)(B), such right shall be treated as so exercised for purposes of clause (i).

(C) EXCEPTION FOR CERTAIN RIGHTS TO CONVERT.--The term "liquidation, put, call, or conversion right" does not include any right which--

(i) is a right to convert into a fixed number (or a fixed percentage) of shares of the same class of stock in a corporation as the transferred stock in such corporation under subsection (a)(1) (or stock which would be of the same class but for nonlapsing differences in voting power),

(ii) is nonlapsing,

(iii) is subject to proportionate adjustments for splits, combinations, reclassification, and similar changes in the capital stock, and

(iv) is subject to adjustments similar to the adjustments under subsection (d) for accumulated but unpaid distributions.

A rule similar to the rule of the preceding sentence shall apply for partnerships.

(3) QUALIFIED PAYMENT.--

(A) IN GENERAL.-- Except as otherwise provided in this paragraph, the term "qualified payment" means any dividend payable on a periodic basis under any cumulative preferred stock (or a comparable payment under any partnership interest) to the extent that such dividend (or comparable payment) is determined at a fixed rate.

(B) TREATMENT OF VARIABLE RATE PAYMENTS.--For purposes of subparagraph (A), a payment shall be treated as fixed as to rate if such payment is determined at a rate which bears a fixed relationship to a specified market interest rate.

(C) ELECTIONS.--

(i) WAIVER OF QUALIFIED PAYMENT TREATMENT.--A transferor or applicable family member may elect with respect to payments under any interest specified in such election to treat such payments as payments which are not qualified payments.

(ii) ELECTION TO HAVE INTEREST TREATED AS QUALIFIED PAYMENT.--A transferor or any applicable family member may elect to treat any distribution right as a qualified payment, to be paid in the amounts and at the times specified in such election. The preceding sentence shall apply only to the extent that the amounts and times so specified are not inconsistent with the underlying legal instrument giving rise to such right.

(iii) ELECTIONS IRREVOCABLE.--Any election under this subparagraph with respect to an interest shall, once made, be irrevocable.

(d) TRANSFER TAX TREATMENT OF CUMULATIVE BUT UNPAID DISTRIBUTIONS.--

(1) IN GENERAL.--If a taxable event occurs with respect to any distribution right to which subsection (a)(3)(B) applied; the following shall be increased by the amount determined under paragraph (2):

(A) the taxable estate of the transferor in the case of a taxable event described in paragraph (3)(A)(i).

(B) The taxable gifts of the transferor for the calendar year in which the taxable event occurs in the case of a taxable event described in paragraph (3)(A)(ii) or (iii).

(2) AMOUNT OF INCREASE.--

(A) IN GENERAL.--The amount of the increase determined under this paragraph shall be the excess (if any) of--

(i) the value of the qualified payments payable during the period beginning on the date of the transfer under subsection (a)(1) and ending on the taxable event determined as if--

(I) all such payments were paid on the date payment was due, and

(II) all such payments were reinvested by the transferor as of the date of payment at a yield equal to the discount rate used in determining the value of the applicable retained interest described in subsection (a)(1), over

(ii) the value of such payments paid during such period computed under clause (i) on the basis of the time when such payments were actually paid.

(B) LIMITATIONS ON AMOUNT OF INCREASE.--

(i) IN GENERAL.--The amount of the increase under subparagraph (A) shall not exceed the applicable percentage of the excess (if any) of--

(I) the value (determined as of the date of the taxable event) of all equity interests in the entity which are junior to the applicable retained interest, over
(II) the value of such interests (determined as of the date of the transfer to which subsection (a)(1) applied).
(ii) APPLICABLE PERCENTAGE.--For purposes of clause (i), the applicable percentage is the percentage determined by dividing--
(I) the number of shares in the corporation held (as of the date of the taxable event) by the transferor which are applicable retained interests of the same class, by
(II) the total number of shares in such corporation (as of such date) which are of the same class as the class described in subclause (I).
A similar percentage shall be determined in the case of interests in a partnership.
(iii) DEFINITION.--For purposes of this subparagraph, the term "equity interest" has the meaning given such term by subsection (a)(4)(B).
(C) GRACE PERIOD.--For purposes of subparagraph (A), any payment of any distribution during the 4-year period beginning on its due date shall be treated as having been made on such due date.
(3) TAXABLE EVENTS.--For purposes of this subsection--
(A) IN GENERAL.--The term "taxable event" means any of the following:
(i) The death of the transferor if the applicable retained interest conferring the distribution right is includible in the estate of the transferor.
(ii) The transfer of such applicable retained interest.
(iii) At the election of the taxpayer, the payment of any qualified payment after the period described in paragraph (2)(C), but only with respect to the period ending on the date of such payment.
(B) EXCEPTION WHERE SPOUSE IS TRANSFEREE.--
(i) DEATHTIME TRANSFERS.--Subparagraph (A)(i) shall not apply to any interest includible in the gross estate of the transferor if a deduction with respect to such interest is allowable under section 2056 or 2106(a)(3).
(ii) LIFETIME TRANSFERS.--A transfer to the spouse of the transferor shall not be treated as a taxable event under subparagraph (A)(ii) if such transfer does not result in a taxable gift by reason of–
(I) any deduction allowed under section 2523, or
(II) consideration for the transfer provided by the spouse.
(iii) SPOUSE SUCCEEDS TO TREATMENT OF TRANSFEROR.--If an event is not treated as a taxable event by reason of this subparagraph, the transferee spouse or surviving spouse (as the case may be) shall be treated in the same manner as the transferor in applying this subsection with respect to the interest involved.
(4) SPECIAL RULES FOR APPLICABLE FAMILY MEMBERS.--
(A) FAMILY MEMBER TREATED IN SAME MANNER AS TRANSFEROR.--For purposes of this subsection, an applicable family member shall be treated in the same manner as the transferor with respect to any distribution right retained by such family member to which subsection (a)(3)(B) applied.
(B) TRANSFER TO APPLICABLE FAMILY MEMBER.--In the case of a taxable event described in paragraph (3)(A)(ii) involving the transfer of an applicable retained interest to an applicable family member (other than the spouse of the transferor), the applicable family member shall be treated in the same manner as the transferor in applying this subsection to distributions accumulating with respect to such interest after such taxable event.

(5) TRANSFER TO INCLUDE TERMINATION.--For purposes of this subsection, any termination of an interest shall be treated as a transfer.

(e) OTHER DEFINITIONS AND RULES.--For purposes of this section--

(1) MEMBER OF THE FAMILY.--The term "member of the family" means, with respect to any transferor--

(A) the transferor's spouse,

(B) a lineal descendant of the transferor or the transferor's spouse, and

(C) the spouse of any such descendant.

(2) APPLICABLE FAMILY MEMBER.--The term "applicable family member" means, with respect to any transferor--

(A) the transferor's spouse,

(B) an ancestor of the transferor or the transferor's spouse, and

(C) the spouse of any such ancestor.

(3) ATTRIBUTION RULES.--

(A) INDIRECT HOLDINGS AND TRANSFERS.--An individual shall be treated as holding any interest to the extent such interest is held indirectly by such individual through a corporation, partnership, trust, or other entity. If any individual is treated as holding any interest by reason of the preceding sentence, any transfer which results in such interest being treated as no longer held by such individual shall be treated as a transfer of such interest.

(B) CONTROL.--For purposes of subsections (b)(1), an individual shall be treated as holding any interest held by the individual's brothers, sisters, or lineal descendants.

(4) EFFECT OF ADOPTION.--A relationship by legal adoption shall be treated as a relationship by blood.

(5) CERTAIN CHANGES TREATED AS TRANSFERS.--Except as provided in regulations, a contribution to capital or a redemption, recapitalization, or other change in the capital structure of a corporation or partnership shall be treated as a transfer of an interest in such entity to which this section applies if the taxpayer or an applicable family member--

(A) receives an applicable retained interest in such entity pursuant to such contribution to capital or such redemption, recapitalization, or other change, or

(B) under regulations otherwise holds, immediately after the transfer, an applicable retained interest in such entity.

This paragraph shall not apply to any transaction (other than a contribution to capital) if the interests in the entity held by the transferor, applicable family members, and members of the transferor's family before and after the transaction are substantially identical.

(6) ADJUSTMENTS.--Under regulations prescribed by the Secretary, if there is any subsequent transfer, or inclusion in the gross estate, of any applicable retained interest which was valued under the rules of subsection (a), appropriate adjustments shall be made for purposes of chapter 11, 12, or 13 to reflect the increase in the amount of any prior taxable gift made by the transferor or decedent by reason of such valuation.

(7) TREATMENT AS SEPARATE INTERESTS.--The Secretary may by regulation provide that any applicable retained interest shall be treated as 2 or more separate interests for purposes of this section.

SEC. 2702. SPECIAL VALUATION RULES IN CASE OF TRANSFERS OF INTERESTS IN TRUSTS

(a) VALUATION RULES.-

(1) IN GENERAL.- Solely for purposes of determining- whether a transfer of an interest in trust to (or for the benefit of) a member of the transferor's family is a gift (and the value of such transfer), the value of any interest in such trust retained by the transferor or any

applicable family member (as defined in section 2701(e)(2)) shall be determined as provided in paragraph (2).

(2) VALUATION OF RETAINED INTERESTS.-

(A) IN GENERAL.- The value of any retained interest which is not a qualified interest shall be treated as being zero.

(B) VALUATION OF QUALIFIED INTEREST.- The value of any retained interest which is a qualified interest shall be determined under section 7520.

(3) EXCEPTIONS

(A) IN GENERAL.- This subsection shall not apply to any transfer-

(i) to the extent that such transfer is an incomplete transfer, or

(ii) if such transfer involves the transfer of an interest in trust all the property in which consists of a residence to be used as a personal residence by persons holding term interests in such trust.

(B) INCOMPLETE TRANSFER.- For purposes of subparagraph (A), the term "incomplete transfer" means any transfer which would not be treated as a gift whether of not consideration was received for such transfer.

(b) QUALIFIED INTEREST.- For purposes of this section, the term "qualified interest" means-

(1) any interest which consists of the right to receive fixed amounts payable not less frequently than annually,

(2) any interest which consists of the right to receive fixed amounts which are payable not less frequently than annually and are a fixed percentage of the fair market value of the property in the trust (determined annually), and

(3) any noncontingent remainder interest if all of the other interests in the trust consists of interests described in paragraph (1) or (2).

(c) CERTAIN PROPERTY TREATED AS HELD IN TRUST.- For purposes of this section-

(1) IN GENERAL.- The transfer of an interest in property with respect to which there is 1 or more term interests shall be treated as a transfer of an interest in a trust.

(2) JOINT PURCHASES.- If 2 or more members of the same family acquire interests in any property described in paragraph (1) in the same transaction (or a series of related transactions), the person (or persons) acquiring the term interests in such property shall be treated as having acquired the entire property and then transferred to the other persons the interests acquired by such other persons in the transaction (or series of transactions). Such transfer shall be treated as made in exchange for the consideration (if any) provided by such other persons for the acquisition of their interests in such property.

(3) TERM INTEREST.- The term "term interest" means-

(A) a life interest in property, or

(B) an interest in property for a term of years.

(4) VALUATION RULE FOR CERTAIN TERM INTERESTS.- If the nonexcercise of rights under a term interest in tangible property would not have a substantial effect on the valuation of the remainder interest in such property-

(A) subparagraph (A) of subsection (a)(2) shall not apply to such term interest, and

(B) the value of such term interest for purposes of applying subsection (a)(1) shall be the amount which the holder of a term interest establishes as the amount for which such interest could be sold to an unrelated third party.

(d) TREATMENT OF TRANSFERS OF INTEREST IN PORTION OF TRUST.- In the case of a transfer of an income or remainder interest with respect to a specified portion of the property in a trust, only such portion shall be taken into account in applying this section to such transfer.

(e) MEMBER OF THE FAMILY.- For purposes of this section, the term "member of the family" shall have the meaning given such term by section 2704(c)(2).

SEC. 2703 CERTAIN RIGHTS AND RESTRICTIONS DISREGARDED

(a) GENERAL RULE.- For purposes of this subtitle, the value of any property shall be determined without regard to-

(1) any option, agreement, or other right to acquire or use the property at a price less than the fair market value of the property (without regard to such option, agreement, or right), or

(2) any restriction on the right to sell or use such property.

(b) EXCEPTIONS.- Subsection (a) shall not apply to any option, agreement, right or restriction which meets each of the following requirements:

(1) It is a bona fide business arrangement.

(2) It is not a device to transfer such property to members of the decedent's family for less than full and adequate consideration in money or money's worth.

(3) Its terms are comparable to similar arrangements entered into by persons in an arm's length transaction.

SEC. 2704. TREATMENT OF CERTAIN LAPSING RIGHTS AND RESTRICTIONS

(a) TREATMENT OF LAPSED VOTING OR LIQUIDATION RIGHTS.--

(1) IN GENERAL.--For purposes of this subtitle, if--

(A) there is a lapse of any voting or liquidation right in a corporation or partnership, and

(B) the individual holding such right immediately before the lapse and members of such individual's family hold, both before and after the lapse, control of the entity, such lapse shall be treated as a transfer by such individual by gift, or a transfer which is includible in the gross estate of the decedent, whichever is applicable, in the amount determined under paragraph (2).

(2) AMOUNT OF TRANSFER.-- For purposes of paragraph (1), the amount determined under this paragraph is the excess (if any) of--

(A) the value of all interests in the entity held by the individual described in paragraph (1) immediately before the lapse (determined as if the voting and liquidation rights were nonlapsing), over

(B) the value of such interests immediately after the lapse.

(3) SIMILAR RIGHTS.--The Secretary may by regulations apply this subsection to rights similar to voting and liquidation rights.

(b) CERTAIN RESTRICTIONS ON LIQUIDATION DISREGARDED.--

(1) IN GENERAL.--For purposes of this subtitle, if--

(A) there is a transfer of an interest in a corporation or partnership to (or for the benefit of) a member of the transferor's family, and

(B) the transferor and members of the transferor's family hold, immediately before the transfer, control of the entity, any applicable restriction shall be disregarded in determining the value of the transferred interest.

(2) APPLICABLE RESTRICTION.--For purposes of this subsection, the term "applicable restriction" means any restriction--

(A) which effectively limits the ability of the corporation or partnership to liquidate, and

(B) with respect to which either of the following applies:

(i) The restriction lapses, in whole or in part, after the transfer referred t to in paragraph (1).

(ii) The transferor or any member of the transferor's family, either alone of collectively, has the right after such transfer to remove, in whole or in part, the restriction.

(3) EXCEPTIONS.--The term "applicable restriction" shall not include--

(A) any commercially reasonable restriction which arises as part of any financing by the corporation or partnership with a person who is not related to the transferor or transferee, or a member of the family of either, or

(B) any restriction imposed, or required to be imposed, by any Federal or State law.

(4) OTHER RESTRICTIONS.--The secretary may by regulations provide that other restrictions shall be disregarded in determining the value of the transfer of any interest in a corporation or partnership to a member of the transferor's family if such restriction has the effect of reducing the value of the transferred interest for purposes of this subtitle but does not ultimately reduce the value of such interest to the transferee

CHAPTER 62 - TIME AND PLACE FOR PAYING TAX
Subchapter B. Extensions of Time for Payment

SEC. 6161. EXTENSION OF TIME FOR PAYING TAX
(a) AMOUNT DETERMINED BY TAXPAYER ON RETURN

(1) GENERAL RULE - The Secretary, except as otherwise provided in this title, may extend the time for payment of the amount of the tax shown, or required to be shown, on any return or declaration required under authority of this title (or any installment thereof), for a reasonable period not to exceed 6 months (12 months in the case of estate tax) from the date fixed for payment thereof. Such extension may exceed 6 months in the case of a taxpayer who is abroad.

(2) ESTATE TAX - The Secretary may, for reasonable cause, extend the time for payment of--

(A) any part of the amount determined by the executor as the tax imposed by chapter 11, or

(B) any part of any installment under section 6166 (including any part of a deficiency prorated to any installment under such section). for a reasonable period not in excess of 10 years from the date prescribed by section 6151(a) for payment of the tax (or, in the case of an amount referred to in subparagraph (B), if later, not beyond the date which is 12 months after the due date for the last installment).

(b) AMOUNT DETERMINED AS DEFICIENCY

(1) INCOME, GIFT, AND CERTAIN OTHER TAXES *****

(2) ESTATE TAX - Under regulations prescribed by the Secretary, the Secretary may, for reasonable cause, extend the time for the payment of any deficiency of a tax imposed by chapter 11 for a reasonable period not to exceed 4 years from the date otherwise fixed for the payment of the deficiency.

(3) NO EXTENSION FOR CERTAIN DEFICIENCIES - No extension shall be granted under this subsection for any deficiency if the deficiency is due to negligence, to intentional disregard of rules and regulations, or to fraud with intent to evade tax.

(c) CLAIMS IN CASES UNDER TITLE 11 OF THE UNITED STATES CODE OR IN RECEIVERSHIP PROCEEDINGS - Extensions of time for payment of any portion of a claim for tax under chapter 1 or chapter 12, allowed in cases under title 11 of the United States Code or in receivership proceedings, which is unpaid, may be had in the same manner and subject to the same provisions and limitations as provided in subsection (b) in respect of a deficiency in such tax.

(d) CROSS REFERENCES

(1) PERIOD OF LIMITATION - For extension of the period of limitation in case of an extension under subsection (a)(2) or subsection (b)(2), see Section 6503(d).

(2) SECURITY - For authority of the Secretary to require security in case of an extension under subsection (A)(2) or subsection (B), see Section 6165.

SEC. 6163. EXTENSION OF TIME FOR PAYMENT OF ESTATE TAX ON VALUE OF REVERSIONARY OR REMAINDER INTEREST IN PROPERTY

(a) EXTENSION PERMITTED - If the value of a reversionary or remainder interest in property is included under chapter 11 in the value of the gross estate, the payment of the part of the tax under chapter 11 attributable to such interest may, at the election of the executor, be postponed until 6 months after the termination of the precedent interest or interests in the property, under such regulations as the Secretary may prescribe.

(b) EXTENSION FOR REASONABLE CAUSE - At the expiration of the period of postponement provided for in subsection (a), the Secretary may, for reasonable cause, extend the time for payment for a reasonable period or periods not in excess of 3 years from the expiration of the period of postponement provided in subsection (a).

(c) CROSS REFERENCE - For authority of the Secretary to require security in the case of an extension under this Section, see Section 6165.

SEC. 6165. BONDS WHERE TIME TO PAY TAX OR DEFICIENCY HAS BEEN EXTENDED

In the event the Secretary grants any extension of time within which to pay any tax or any deficiency therein, the Secretary may require the taxpayer to furnish a bond in such amount (not exceeding double the amount with respect to which the extension is granted) conditioned upon the payment of the amount extended in accordance with the terms of such extension.

SEC. 6166. EXTENSION OF TIME FOR PAYMENT OF ESTATE TAX WHERE ESTATE CONSISTS LARGELY OF INTEREST IN CLOSELY HELD BUSINESS

(a) 5-YEAR DEFERRAL; 10-YEAR INSTALLMENT PAYMENT

(1) IN GENERAL - If the value of an interest in a closely held business which is included in determining the gross estate of a decedent who was (at the date of his death) a citizen or resident of the United States exceeds 35 percent of the adjusted gross estate, the executor may elect to pay part or all of the tax imposed by section 2001 in 2 or more (but not exceeding 10) equal installments.

(2) LIMITATION - The maximum amount of tax which may be paid in installments under this subsection shall be an amount which bears the same ratio to the tax imposed by section 2001 (reduced by the credits against such tax) as--

(A) the closely held business amount, bears to

(B) the amount of the adjusted gross estate.

(3) DATE FOR PAYMENT OF INSTALLMENTS - If an election is made under paragraph (1), the first installment shall be paid on or before the date selected by the executor which is not more than 5 years after the date prescribed by section 6151(a) for payment of the tax, and each succeeding installment shall be paid on or before the date which is 1 year after the date prescribed by this paragraph for payment of the preceding installment.

(b) DEFINITIONS AND SPECIAL RULES

(1) INTEREST IN CLOSELY HELD BUSINESS - For purposes of this section, the term "interest in a closely held business" means--

(A) an interest as a proprietor in a trade or business carried on as a proprietorship;

(B) an interest as a partner in a partnership carrying on a trade or business, if--

(i) 20 percent or more of the total capital interest in such partnership is included in determining the gross estate of the decedent, or (ii) such partnership had 15 or fewer partners; or

(C) stock in a corporation carrying on a trade or business if--

(i) 20 percent or more in value of the voting stock of such corporation is included in determining the gross estate of the decedent, or

(ii) such corporation had 15 or fewer shareholders.

(2) RULES FOR APPLYING PARAGRAPH (1) - For purposes of paragraph (1)--

(A) TIME FOR TESTING - Determinations shall be made as of the time immediately before the decedent's death.

(B) CERTAIN INTERESTS HELD BY HUSBAND AND WIFE - Stock or a partnership interest which--

(i) is community property of a husband and wife (or the income from which is community income) under the applicable community property law of a State, or

(ii) is held by a husband and wife as joint tenants, tenants by the entirety, or tenants in common,

shall be treated as owned by one shareholder or one partner, as the case may be.

(C) INDIRECT OWNERSHIP - Property owned, directly or indirectly, by or for a corporation, partnership, estate, or trust shall be considered as being owned proportionately by or for its shareholders, partners, or beneficiaries. For purposes of the preceding sentence, a person shall be treated as a beneficiary of any trust only if such person has a present interest in the trust.

(D) CERTAIN INTERESTS HELD BY MEMBERS OF DECEDENT'S FAMILY - All stock and all partnership interests held by the decedent or by any member of his family (within the meaning of section 267(c)(4)) shall be treated as owned by the decedent.

(3) FARMHOUSES AND CERTAIN OTHER STRUCTURES TAKEN INTO ACCOUNT - For purposes of the 35-percent requirement of subsection (a)(1), an interest in a closely held business which is the business of farming includes an interest in residential buildings and related improvements on the farm which are occupied on a regular basis by the owner or lessee of the farm or by persons employed by such owner or lessee for purposes of operating or maintaining the farm.

(4) VALUE - For purposes of this section, value shall be value determined for purposes of chapter 11 (relating to estate tax).

(5) CLOSELY HELD BUSINESS AMOUNT - For purposes of this section, the term "closely held business amount" means the value of the interest in a closely held business which qualifies under subsection (a)(1).

(6) ADJUSTED GROSS ESTATE - For purposes of this section, the term, "adjusted gross estate" means the value of the gross estate reduced by the sum of the amounts allowable as a deduction under section 2053 or 2054. Such sum shall be determined on the basis of the facts and circumstances in existence on the date (including extensions) for filing the return of tax imposed by section 2001 (or, if earlier, the date on which such return is filed).

(7) PARTNERSHIP INTERESTS AND STOCK WHICH IS NOT READILY TRADABLE

(A) IN GENERAL - If the executor elects the benefits of this paragraph (at such time and in such manner as the Secretary shall by regulations prescribe), then--

(i) for purposes of paragraph (1)(B)(i) or (1)(C)(i) (whichever is appropriate) and for purposes of subsection (c), any capital interest in a partnership and any non-readily-tradable stock which (after the application of paragraph (2)) is treated as owned by the decedent shall be treated as included in determining the value of the decedent's gross estate,

(ii) the executor shall be treated as having selected under subsection (a)(3) the date prescribed by section 6151(a), and

(iii) for purposes of applying section 6601(j), the 2- percent portion (as defined in such section) shall be treated as being zero.

(B) NON-READILY-TRADABLE STOCK DEFINED - For purposes of this paragraph, the term "non-readily-tradable stock" means stock for which, at the time of the decedent's death, there was no market on a stock exchange or in an over-the-counter market.

(8) STOCK IN HOLDING COMPANY TREATED AS BUSINESS COMPANY STOCK IN CERTAIN CASES

    (A) IN GENERAL - If the executor elects the benefits of this paragraph, then--

        (i) HOLDING COMPANY STOCK TREATED AS BUSINESS COMPANY STOCK - For purposes of this section, the portion of the stock of any holding company which represents direct ownership (or indirect ownership through 1 or more other holding companies) by such company in a business company shall be deemed to be stock in such business company.

        (ii) 5-YEAR DEFERRAL FOR PRINCIPAL NOT TO APPLY - The executor shall be treated as having selected under subsection (a)(3) the date prescribed by section 6151(a).

        (iii) 2-PERCENT INTEREST RATE NOT TO APPLY - For purposes of applying section 6601(j), the 2-percent portion (as defined in such section) shall be treated as being zero.

    (B) ALL STOCK MUST BE NON-READILY-TRADABLE STOCK - No stock shall be taken into account for purposes of applying this paragraph unless it is non-readily-tradable stock (within the meaning of paragraph (7)(B)).

    (C) APPLICATION OF VOTING STOCK REQUIREMENT OF PARAGRAPH (1)(C)(i) - For purposes of clause (i) of paragraph (1)(C), the deemed stock resulting from the application of subparagraph (A) shall be treated as voting stock to the extent that voting stock in the holding company owns directly (or through the voting stock of 1 or more other holding companies) voting stock in the business company.

    (D) DEFINITIONS - For purposes of this paragraph--

        (i) HOLDING COMPANY - The term "holding company" means any corporation holding stock in another corporation.

        (ii) BUSINESS COMPANY - The term "business company" means any corporation carrying on a trade or business.

(9) DEFERRAL NOT AVAILABLE FOR PASSIVE ASSETS

    (A) IN GENERAL - For purposes of subsection (a)(1) and determining the closely held business amount (but not for purposes of subsection (g)), the value of any interest in a closely held business shall not include the value of that portion of such interest which is attributable to passive assets held by the business.

    (B) PASSIVE ASSET DEFINED - For purposes of this paragraph--

        (i) IN GENERAL - The term "passive asset" means any asset other than an asset used in carrying on a trade or business.

        (ii) STOCK TREATED AS PASSIVE ASSET - The term "passive asset" includes any stock in another corporation unless--

            (I) such stock is treated as held by the decedent by reason of an election under paragraph (8), and

            (II) such stock qualified under subsection (a)(1).

        (iii) EXCEPTION FOR ACTIVE CORPORATIONS - If--

            (I) a corporation owns 20 percent or more in value of the voting stock of another corporation, or such other corporation has 15 or fewer shareholders, and

            (II) 80 percent or more of the value of the assets of each such corporation is attributable to assets used in carrying on a trade or business,

        then such corporations shall be treated as 1 corporation for purposes of clause (ii). For purposes of applying subclause (II) to the corporation holding the stock of the other corporation, such stock shall not be taken into account.

(c) SPECIAL RULE FOR INTEREST IN 2 OR MORE CLOSELY HELD BUSINESSES - For purposes of this section, interest in 2 or more closely held businesses, with respect to each of which there is included in determining the value of the decedent's gross estate 20 percent or more of the total value of each such business, shall be treated as an interest in a single closely held business. For purposes of the 20-percent requirement of the preceding sentence, an interest in a closely held business which represents the surviving spouse's interest in property held by the decedent and the surviving spouse as community property or as joint tenants, tenants by the entirety, or tenants in common shall be treated as having been included in determining the value of the decedent's gross estate.

(d) ELECTION - Any election under subsection (a) shall be made not later than the time prescribed by section 6075(a) for filing the return of tax imposed by section 2001 (including extensions thereof), and shall be made in such manner as the Secretary shall by regulations prescribe. If an election under subsection (a) is made, the provisions of this subtitle shall apply as though the Secretary were extending the time for payment of the tax.

(e) PRORATION OF DEFICIENCY TO INSTALLMENTS - If an election is made under subsection (a) to pay any part of the tax imposed by section 2001 in installments and a deficiency has been assessed, the deficiency shall (subject to the limitation provided by subsection (a)(2)) be prorated to the installments payable under subsection (a). The part of the deficiency so prorated to any installment the date for payment of which has not arrived shall be collected at the same time as, and as a part of, such installment. The part of the deficiency so prorated to any installment the date for payment of which has arrived shall be paid upon notice and demand from the Secretary. This subsection shall not apply if the deficiency is due to negligence, to intentional disregard of rules and regulations, or to fraud with intent to evade tax.

(f) TIME FOR PAYMENT OF INTEREST - If the time for payment of any amount of tax has been extended under this section--

(1) INTEREST FOR FIRST 5 YEARS - Interest payable under section 6601 of any unpaid portion of such amount attributable to the first 5 years after the date prescribed by section 6151(a) for payment of the tax shall be paid annually.

(2) INTEREST FOR PERIODS AFTER FIRST 5 YEARS - Interest payable under section 6601 on any unpaid portion of such amount attributable to any period after the 5-year period referred to in paragraph (1) shall be paid annually at the same time as, and as a part of, each installment payment of the tax.

(3) INTEREST IN THE CASE OF CERTAIN DEFICIENCIES - In the case of a deficiency to which subsection (e) applies which is assessed after the close of the 5-year period referred to in paragraph (1), interest attributable to such 5-year period, and interest assigned under paragraph (2) to any installment the date for payment of which has arrived on or before the date of the assessment of the deficiency, shall be paid upon notice and demand from the Secretary.

(4) SELECTION OF SHORTER PERIOD - If the executor has selected a period shorter than 5 years under subsection (a)(3), such shorter period shall be substituted for 5 years in paragraphs (1), (2), and (3) of this subsection.

(g) ACCELERATION OF PAYMENT

(1) DISPOSITION OF INTEREST; WITHDRAWAL OF FUNDS FROM BUSINESS

(A) If--

(i) (I) any portion of an interest in a closely held business which qualifies under subsection (a)(1) is distributed, sold, exchanged, or otherwise disposed of, or (II) money and other property attributable to such an interest is withdrawn from such trade or business, and

(ii) the aggregate of such distributions, sales, exchanges, or other dispositions and withdrawals equals or exceeds 50 percent of the value of such interest,

then the extension of time for payment of tax provided in subsection (a) shall cease to apply, and the unpaid portion of the tax payable in installments shall be paid upon notice and demand from the Secretary.

(B) In the case of a distribution in redemption of stock to which section 303 (or so much of section 304 as relates to section 303) applies--

(i) the redemption of such stock, and the withdrawal of money and other property distributed in such redemption, shall not be treated as a distribution or withdrawal for purposes of subparagraph (A), and

(ii) for purposes of subparagraph (A), the value of the interest in the closely held business shall be considered to be such value reduced by the value of the stock redeemed.

This subparagraph shall apply only if, on or before the date prescribed by subsection (a)(3) for the payment of the first installment which becomes due after the date of the distribution (or, if earlier, on or before the day which is 1 year after the date of the distribution), there is paid an amount of the tax imposed by section 2001 not less than the amount of money and other property distributed.

(C) Subparagraph (A)(i) does not apply to an exchange of stock pursuant to a plan of reorganization described in subparagraph (D), (E), or (F) of section 368(a)(1) nor to an exchange to which section 355 (or so much of section 356 as relates to section 355) applies; but any stock received in such an exchange shall be treated for purposes of subparagraph (A)(i) as an interest qualifying under subsection (a)(1).

(D) Subparagraph (A)(i) does not apply to a transfer of property of the decedent to a person entitled by reason of the decedent's death to receive such property under the decedent's will, the applicable law of descent and distribution, or a trust created by the decedent. A similar rule shall apply in the case of a series of subsequent transfers of the property by reason of death so long as each transfer is to a member of the family (within the meaning of section 267(c)(4)) of the transferor in such transfer.

(E) CHANGES IN INTEREST IN HOLDING COMPANY - If any stock in a holding company is treated as stock in a business company by reason of subsection (b)(8)(A)--

(i) any disposition of any interest in such stock in such holding company which was included in determining the gross estate of the decedent, or

(ii) any withdrawal of any money or other property from such holding company attributable to any interest included in determining the gross estate of the decedent,

shall be treated for purposes of subparagraph (A) as a disposition of (or a withdrawal with respect to) the stock qualifying under subsection (a)(1).

(F) CHANGES IN INTEREST IN BUSINESS COMPANY - If any stock in a holding company is treated as stock in a business company by reason of subsection (b)(8)(A)--

(i) any disposition of any interest in such stock in the business company by such holding company, or

(ii) any withdrawal of any money or other property from such business company attributable to such stock by such holding company owning such stock,

shall be treated for purposes of subparagraph (A) as a disposition of (or a withdrawal with respect to) the stock qualifying under subsection (a)(1).

(2) UNDISTRIBUTED INCOME OF ESTATE

(A) If an election is made under this section and the estate has undistributed net income for any taxable year ending on or after the due date for the first installment, the executor shall, on or before the date prescribed by law for filing the income tax return for such taxable year (including extensions thereof), pay an amount equal to such undistributed net income in liquidation of the unpaid portion of the tax payable in installments.

(B) For purposes of subparagraph (A), the undistributed net income of the estate for any taxable year is the amount by which the distributable net income of the estate for such taxable year (as defined in section 643) exceeds the sum of--

(i) the amounts for such taxable year specified in paragraphs (1) and (2) of section 661(a) (relating to deductions for distributions, etc.);

(ii) the amount of tax imposed for the taxable year on the estate under chapter 1; and

(iii) the amount of the tax imposed by section 2001 (including interest) paid by the executor during the taxable year (other than any amount paid pursuant to this paragraph).

(C) For purposes of this paragraph, if any stock in a corporation is treated as stock in another corporation by reason of subsection (b)(8)(A), any dividends paid by such other corporation to the corporation shall be treated as paid to the estate of the decedent to the extent attributable to the stock qualifying under subsection (a)(1).

(3) FAILURE TO MAKE PAYMENT OF PRINCIPAL OR INTEREST

(A) IN GENERAL - Except as provided in subparagraph (B), if any payment of principal or interest under this section is not paid on or before the date fixed for its payment by this section (including any extension of time), the unpaid portion of the tax payable in installments shall be paid upon notice and demand from the Secretary.

(B) PAYMENT WITHIN 6 MONTHS - If any payment of principal or interest under this section is not paid on or before the date determined under subparagraph (A) but is paid within 6 months of such date--

(i) the provisions of subparagraph (A) shall not apply with respect to such payment,

(ii) the provisions of section 6601(j) shall not apply with respect to the determination of interest on such payment, and

(iii) there is imposed a penalty in an amount equal to the product of--

(I) 5 percent of the amount of such payment, multiplied by

(II) the number of months (or fractions thereof) after such date and before payment is made.

The penalty imposed under clause (iii) shall be treated in the same manner as a penalty imposed under subchapter B of chapter 68.

(h) ELECTION IN CASE OF CERTAIN DEFICIENCIES

(1) IN GENERAL - If--

(A) a deficiency in the tax imposed by section 2001 is assessed,

(B) the estate qualifies under subsection (a)(1), and

(C) the executor has not made an election under subsection (a),

the executor may elect to pay the deficiency in installments. This subsection shall not apply if the deficiency is due to negligence, to intentional disregard of rules and regulations, or to fraud with intent to evade tax.

(2) TIME OF ELECTION - An election under this subsection shall be made not later than 60 days after issuance of notice and demand by the Secretary for the payment of the deficiency, and shall be made in such manner as the Secretary shall by regulations prescribe.

(3) EFFECT OF ELECTION ON PAYMENT - If an election is made under this subsection, the deficiency shall (subject to the limitation provided by subsection (a)(2)) be prorated to the installments which would have been due if an election had been timely made under subsection (a) at the time the estate tax return was filed. The part of the deficiency so prorated to any installment the date for payment of which would have arrived shall be paid at the time of the making of the election under this subsection. The portion of the deficiency so prorated to installments the date for payment of which would not have so arrived shall be paid at the time such installments would have been due if such an election had been made.

(i) SPECIAL RULE FOR CERTAIN DIRECT SKIPS - To the extent that an interest in a closely held business is the subject of a direct skip (within the meaning of section 2612(c)) occurring at the same time as and as a result of the decedent's death, then for purposes of this section any tax imposed by section 2601 on the transfer of such interest shall be treated as if it were additional tax imposed by section 2001.

(j) REGULATIONS - The Secretary shall prescribe such regulations as may be necessary to the application of this section.
(k) CROSS REFERENCES ****

CHAPTER 67 - INTEREST
Subchapter A. Interest on Underpayments

SEC. 6601. INTEREST ON UNDERPAYMENT, NONPAYMENT, OR EXTENSIONS OF TIME FOR PAYMENT, OF TAX

(a) GENERAL RULE - If any amount of tax imposed by this title (whether required to be shown on a return, or to be paid by stamp or by some other method) is not paid on or before the last date prescribed for payment, interest on such amount at the underpayment rate established under section 6621 shall be paid for the period from such last date to the date paid. *****

(c) SUSPENSION OF INTEREST IN CERTAIN INCOME, ESTATE, GIFT, AND CERTAIN EXCISE TAX CASES - In the case of a deficiency as defined in section 6211 (relating to income, estate, gift, and certain excise taxes), if a waiver of restrictions under section 6213(d) on the assessment of such deficiency has been filed, and if notice and demand by the Secretary for payment of such deficiency is not made within 30 days after the filing of such waiver, interest shall not be imposed on such deficiency for the period beginning immediately after such 30th day and ending with the date of notice and demand and interest shall not be imposed during such period on any interest with respect to such deficiency for any prior period. In the case of a settlement under section 6224(c) which results in the conversion of partnership items to nonpartnership items pursuant to section 6231(b)(1)(C), the preceding sentence shall apply to a computational adjustment resulting from such settlement in the same manner as if such adjustment were a deficiency and such settlement were a waiver referred to in the preceding sentence. *****

(e) APPLICABLE RULES - Except as otherwise provided in this title--

(1) INTEREST TREATED AS TAX - Interest prescribed under this section on any tax shall be paid upon notice and demand, and shall be assessed, collected, and paid in the same manner as taxes. Any reference to this title (except subchapter B of chapter 63, relating to deficiency procedures) to any tax imposed by this title shall be deemed also to refer to interest imposed by this section on such tax.

(2) INTEREST ON PENALTIES, ADDITIONAL AMOUNTS, OR ADDITIONS TO THE TAX

(A) IN GENERAL - Interest shall be imposed under subsection (a) in respect of any assessable penalty, additional amount, or addition to the tax (other than an addition to tax imposed under section 6651(a)(1) or 6653 or under part II of subchapter A of chapter 68) only if such assessable penalty, additional amount, or addition to the tax is not paid within 21 calendar days from the date of notice and demand therefor (10 business days if the amount for which such notice and demand is made equals or exceeds $100,000), and in such case interest shall be imposed only for the period from the date of the notice and demand to the date of payment.

(B) INTEREST ON CERTAIN ADDITIONS TO TAX - Interest shall be imposed under this section with respect to any addition to tax imposed by section 6651(a)(1) or 6653 or under part II of subchapter A of chapter 68 for the period which--

(i) begins on the date on which the return of the tax with respect to which such addition to tax is imposed is required to be filed (including any extensions), and

(ii) ends on the date of payment of such addition to tax.

(3) PAYMENTS MADE WITHIN SPECIFIED PERIOD AFTER NOTICE AND DEMAND. - If notice and demand is made for payment of any amount and if such amount is paid within 21 calendar days (10 business days if the amount for which such notice and

demand is made equals or exceeds $100,000) after the date of such notice and demand, interest under this section on the amount so paid shall not be imposed for the period after the date of such notice and demand.

(f) SATISFACTION BY CREDITS - If any portion of a tax is satisfied by credit of an overpayment, then no interest shall be imposed under this section on the portion of the tax so satisfied for any period during which, if the credit had not been made, interest would have been allowable with respect to such overpayment. The preceding sentence shall not apply to the extent that section 6621(d) applies.

(g) LIMITATION ON ASSESSMENT AND COLLECTION - Interest prescribed under this section on any tax may be assessed and collected at any time during the period within which the tax to which such interest relates may be collected.

(h) EXCEPTION AS TO ESTIMATED TAX - ****

(j) 2-PERCENT RATE ON CERTAIN PORTION OF ESTATE TAX EXTENDED UNDER SECTION 6166

(1) IN GENERAL - If the time for payment of an amount of tax imposed by chapter 11 is extended as provided in section 6166, then in lieu of the annual rate provided by subsection (a)--

(A) interest on the 2-percent portion of such amount shall be paid at the rate of 2 percent, and

(B) interest on so much of such amount as exceeds the 2-percent portion shall be paid at a rate equal to 45 percent of the annual rate provided by subsection (a).

For purposes of this subsection, the amount of any deficiency which is prorated to installments payable under section 6166 shall be treated as an amount of tax payable in installments under such section.

(2) 2-PERCENT PORTION - For purposes of this subsection, the term "2-percent portion" means the lesser of-

(A) --

(i) the amount of the tentative tax which would be determined under the rate schedule set forth in section 2001(c) if the amount with respect to which such tentative tax is to be computed were the sum of $1,000,000 and the applicable exclusion amount in effect under section 2010(c), reduced by

(ii) the applicable credit amount in effect under section 2010(c), or

(B) the amount of the tax imposed by chapter 11 which is extended as provided in section 6166.

(3) INFLATION ADJUSTMENT - In the case of estates of decedents dying in a calendar year after 1998, the $1,000,000 amount contained in paragraph (2)(A) shall be increased by an amount equal to-

(A) $1,000,000, multiplied by

(B) the cost-of-living adjustment determined under section 1(f)(3) for such calendar year by substituting "calendar year 1997" for "calendar year 1992" in subparagraph (B) thereof.

If any amount as adjusted under the preceding sentence is not a multiple of $10,000, such amount shall be rounded to the next lowest multiple of $10,000.

(4) TREATMENT OF PAYMENTS - If the amount of tax imposed by chapter 11 which is extended as provided in section 6166 exceeds the 2-percent portion, any payment of a portion of such amount shall, for purposes of computing interest for periods after such payment, be treated as reducing the 2-percent portion by an amount which bears the same ratio to the amount of such payment as the amount of the 2-percent portion (determined without regard to this paragraph) bears to the amount of the tax which is extended as provided in section 6166.

(k) NO INTEREST ON CERTAIN ADJUSTMENTS ****

CHAPTER 77 - MISCELLANEOUS PROVISIONS

SEC. 7502. TIMELY MAILING TREATED AS TIMELY FILING AND PAYING
(a) GENERAL RULE

(1) DATE OF DELIVERY - If any return, claim, statement, or other document required to be filed, or any payment required to be made, within a prescribed period or on or before a prescribed date under authority of any provision of the internal revenue laws is, after such period or such date, delivered by United States mail to the agency, officer, or office with which such return, claim, statement, or other document is required to be filed, or to which such payment is required to be made, the date of the United States postmark stamped on the cover in which such return, claim, statement, or other document, or payment, is mailed shall be deemed to be the date of delivery or the date of payment, as the case may be.

(2) MAILING REQUIREMENTS - This subsection shall apply only if--

(A) the postmark date falls within the prescribed period or on or before the prescribed date--

(i) for the filing (including any extension granted for such filing) of the return, claim, statement, or other document, or

(ii) for making the payment (including any extension granted for making such payment), and

(B) the return, claim, statement, or other document, or payment was, within the time prescribed in subparagraph (A), deposited in the mail in the United States in an envelope or other appropriate wrapper, postage prepaid, properly addressed to the agency, officer, or office with which the return, claim, statement, or other document is required to be filed, or to which such payment is required to be made.

(b) POSTMARKS - This section shall apply in the case of postmarks not made by the United States Postal Service only if and to the extent provided by regulations prescribed by the Secretary

(c) REGISTERED AND CERTIFIED MAILING; ELECTRONIC FILING--

(1) Registered mail-- - For purposes of this section, if any return, claim, statement, or other document, or payment, is sent by United States registered mail--

(A) such registration shall be prima facie evidence that the return, claim, statement, or other document was delivered to the agency, officer, or office to which addressed, and

(B) the date of registration shall be deemed the postmark date.

(2) Certified mail; electronic filing-- - The Secretary is authorized to provide by regulations the extent to which the provisions of paragraph (1) with respect to prima facie evidence of delivery and the postmark date shall apply to certified mail and electronic filing.

(d) EXCEPTIONS - This section shall not apply with respect to--

(1) the filing of a document in, or the making of a payment to, any court other than the Tax Court,

(2) currency or other medium of payment unless actually received and accounted for, or

(3) returns, claims, statements, or other documents, or payments, which are required under any provision of the internal revenue laws or the regulations thereunder to be delivered by any method other than by mailing.

(e) MAILING OF DEPOSITS   *****

(f) TREATMENT OF PRIVATE DELIVERY SERVICES.

(1) IN GENERAL. - Any reference in this section to the United States mail shall be treated as including a reference to any designated delivery service, and any reference in this section to a postmark by the United States Postal Service shall be treated as including a reference to any date recorded or marked as described in paragraph (2)(C) by any designated delivery service.

(2) DESIGNATED DELIVERY SERVICE. - For purposes of this subsection, the term "designated delivery service" means any delivery service provided by a trade or business if

such service is designated by the Secretary for purposes of this section. The Secretary may designate a delivery service under the preceding sentence only if the Secretary determines that such service--

(A) is available to the general public,

(B) is at least as timely and reliable on a regular basis as the United States mail,

(C) records electronically to its data base, kept in the regular course of its business, or marks on the cover in which any item referred to in this section is to be delivered, the date on which such item was given to such trade or business for delivery, and

(D) meets such other criteria as the Secretary may prescribe.

(3) EQUIVALENTS OF REGISTERED AND CERTIFIED MAIL. - The Secretary may provide a rule similar to the rule of paragraph (1) with respect to any service provided by a designated delivery service which is substantially equivalent to United States registered or certified mail.

SEC. 7520. VALUATION TABLES

(a) GENERAL RULE.- For purposes of this title, the value of any annuity, any interest for life or a term of years, or any remainder or reversionary interest shall be determined-

(1) under tables prescribed by the Secretary, and

(2) by using an interest rate (rounded to the nearest 2/10ths of 1 percent) equal to 120 percent of the Federal midterm rate in effect under section 1274(d)(1) for the month in which the valuation date falls.

If an income, estate, or gift tax charitable contribution is allowable for any part of the property transferred, the taxpayer may elect to use such Federal midterm rate for either of the two months preceding the month in which the valuation date falls for purposes of paragraph (2). In the case of transfers of more than 1 interest in the same property with respect to which the taxpayer may use the same rate under paragraph (2), the taxpayer shall use the same rate with respect to each such interest.   *****

Federal Estate Tax Return (Form 706)

Form **706**	United States Estate (and Generation-Skipping Transfer)		
(Rev. July 1998)	**Tax Return**		OMB No. 1545-0015
Department of the Treasury Internal Revenue Service	Estate of a citizen or resident of the United States (see separate instructions). To be filed for decedents dying after December 31, 1997, and before January 1, 1999. For Paperwork Reduction Act Notice, see page 1 of the separate instructions.		

Part 1.—Decedent and Executor

1a Decedent's first name and middle initial (and maiden name, if any)	1b Decedent's last name	2 Decedent's social security no.
3a Legal residence (domicile) at time of death (county, state, and ZIP code, or foreign country)	3b Year domicile established	4 Date of birth	5 Date of death
6a Name of executor (see page 2 of the instructions)	6b Executor's address (number and street including apartment or suite no. or rural route; city, town, or post office; state; and ZIP code)
6c Executor's social security number (see page 2 of the instructions)	
7a Name and location of court where will was probated or estate administered	7b Case number

8 If decedent died testate, check here ▶ ☐ and attach a certified copy of the will. | 9 If Form 4768 is attached, check here ▶ ☐

10 If Schedule R-1 is attached, check here ▶ ☐

Part 2.—Tax Computation

1	Total gross estate less exclusion (from Part 5, Recapitulation, page 3, item 12)	**1**		
2	Total allowable deductions (from Part 5, Recapitulation, page 3, item 23)	**2**		
3	Taxable estate (subtract line 2 from line 1)	**3**		
4	Adjusted taxable gifts (total taxable gifts (within the meaning of section 2503) made by the decedent after December 31, 1976, other than gifts that are includible in decedent's gross estate (section 2001(b)))	**4**		
5	Add lines 3 and 4	**5**		
6	Tentative tax on the amount on line 5 from Table A on page 10 of the instructions	**6**		
7a	If line 5 exceeds $10,000,000, enter the lesser of line 5 or $17,184,000. If line 5 is $10,000,000 or less, skip lines 7a and 7b and enter -0- on line 7c . **7a**			
b	Subtract $10,000,000 from line 7a **7b**			
c	Enter 5% (.05) of line 7b	**7c**		
8	Total tentative tax (add lines 6 and 7c)	**8**		
9	Total gift tax payable with respect to gifts made by the decedent after December 31, 1976. Include gift taxes by the decedent's spouse for such spouse's share of split gifts (section 2513) only if the decedent was the donor of these gifts and they are includible in the decedent's gross estate (see instructions)	**9**		
10	Gross estate tax (subtract line 9 from line 8)	**10**		
11	Maximum unified credit against estate tax **11**	202,050	00	
12	Adjustment to unified credit. (This adjustment may not exceed $6,000. See page 7 of the instructions.) **12**			
13	Allowable unified credit (subtract line 12 from line 11)	**13**		
14	Subtract line 13 from line 10 (but do not enter less than zero)	**14**		
15	Credit for state death taxes. Do not enter more than line 14. Figure the credit by using the amount on line 3 less $60,000. See Table B in the instructions and **attach credit evidence** (see instructions) .	**15**		
16	Subtract line 15 from line 14	**16**		
17	Credit for Federal gift taxes on pre-1977 gifts (section 2012) (attach computation) **17**			
18	Credit for foreign death taxes (from Schedule P). (Attach Form(s) 706-CE.) **18**			
19	Credit for tax on prior transfers (from Schedule Q) **19**			
20	Total (add lines 17, 18, and 19)	**20**		
21	Net estate tax (subtract line 20 from line 16)	**21**		
22	Generation-skipping transfer taxes (from Schedule R, Part 2, line 10)	**22**		
23	Total transfer taxes (add lines 21 and 22)	**23**		
24	Prior payments. Explain in an attached statement **24**			
25	United States Treasury bonds redeemed in payment of estate tax . **25**			
26	Total (add lines 24 and 25)	**26**		
27	Balance due (or overpayment) (subtract line 26 from line 23)	**27**		

Under penalties of perjury, I declare that I have examined this return, including accompanying schedules and statements, and to the best of my knowledge and belief, it is true, correct, and complete. Declaration of preparer other than the executor is based on all information of which preparer has any knowledge.

Signature(s) of executor(s)   Date

Signature of preparer other than executor   Address (and ZIP code)   Date

Cat. No. 20548R

Form 706 (Rev. 7-98)

Estate of:

Part 3.—Elections by the Executor

Please check the "Yes" or "No" box for each question. (See instructions beginning on page 3.)

		Yes	No
1	Do you elect alternate valuation?		
2	Do you elect special use valuation? If "Yes," you must complete and attach Schedule A–1.	███	███
3	Do you elect to pay the taxes in installments as described in section 6166? . . . . If "Yes," you must attach the additional information described on page 5 of the instructions.	███	███
4	Do you elect to postpone the part of the taxes attributable to a reversionary or remainder interest as described in section 6163?		

Part 4.—General Information (Note: *Please attach the necessary supplemental documents.* **You must attach the death certificate.**)
(See instructions beginning on page 6.)

Authorization to receive confidential tax information under Regulations section 601.504(b)(2)(i), to act as the estate's representative before the Internal Revenue Service, and to make written or oral presentations on behalf of the estate if return prepared by an attorney, accountant, or enrolled agent for the executor:

Name of representative (print or type)	State	Address (number, street, and room or suite no., city, state, and ZIP code)

I declare that I am the ☐ attorney/ ☐ certified public accountant/ ☐ enrolled agent (you must check the applicable box) for the executor and prepared this return for the executor. I am not under suspension or disbarment from practice before the Internal Revenue Service and am qualified to practice in the state shown above.

Signature	CAF number	Date	Telephone number

1   Death certificate number and issuing authority (attach a copy of the death certificate to this return).

2   Decedent's business or occupation. If retired, check here ▶ ☐ and state decedent's former business or occupation.

3   Marital status of the decedent at time of death:
   ☐ Married
   ☐ Widow or widower—Name, SSN, and date of death of deceased spouse ▶ _____

   ☐ Single
   ☐ Legally separated
   ☐ Divorced—Date divorce decree became final ▶

4a Surviving spouse's name	4b Social security number	4c Amount received (see page 6 of the instructions)

5   Individuals (other than the surviving spouse), trusts, or other estates who receive benefits from the estate (do not include charitable beneficiaries shown in Schedule O) (see instructions). For Privacy Act Notice (applicable to individual beneficiaries only), see the Instructions for Form 1040.

Name of individual, trust, or estate receiving $5,000 or more	Identifying number	Relationship to decedent	Amount (see instructions)

All unascertainable beneficiaries and those who receive less than $5,000 . . . . ▶

Total . . . .

Please check the "Yes" or "No" box for each question.

		Yes	No
6	Does the gross estate contain any section 2044 property (qualified terminable interest property (QTIP)) from a prior gift or estate) (see page 6 of the instructions)?		

Page 2

(continued on next page)

Form 706 (Rev. 7-98)

Part 4.—General Information (continued)

Please check the "Yes" or "No" box for each question.

		Yes	No
7a	Have Federal gift tax returns ever been filed? . . . . If "Yes," please attach copies of the returns, if available, and furnish the following information:		
7b	Period(s) covered	7c	Internal Revenue office(s) where filed		

If you answer "Yes" to any of questions 8–16, you must attach additional information as described in the instructions.

8a	Was there any insurance on the decedent's life that is not included on the return as part of the gross estate?		
b	Did the decedent own any insurance on the life of another that is not included in the gross estate?		
9	Did the decedent at the time of death own any property as a joint tenant with right of survivorship in which **(a)** one or more of the other joint tenants was someone other than the decedent's spouse, and **(b)** less than the full value of the property is included on the return as part of the gross estate? If "Yes," you must complete and attach Schedule E		
10	Did the decedent, at the time of death, own any interest in a partnership or unincorporated business or any stock in an inactive or closely held corporation?		
11	Did the decedent make any transfer described in section 2035, 2036, 2037, or 2038 (see the instructions for Schedule G beginning on page 9 of the separate instructions)? If "Yes," you must complete and attach Schedule G		
12	Were there in existence at the time of the decedent's death:		
a	Any trusts created by the decedent during his or her lifetime?		
b	Any trusts not created by the decedent under which the decedent possessed any power, beneficial interest, or trusteeship?		
13	Did the decedent ever possess, exercise, or release any general power of appointment? If "Yes," you must complete and attach Schedule H		
14	Was the marital deduction computed under the transitional rule of Public Law 97-34, section 403(e)(3) (Economic Recovery Tax Act of 1981)? If "Yes," attach a separate computation of the marital deduction, enter the amount on item 20 of the Recapitulation, and note on item 20 "computation attached."		
15	Was the decedent, immediately before death, receiving an annuity described in the "General" paragraph of the instructions for Schedule I? If "Yes," you must complete and attach Schedule I		
16	Was the decedent ever the beneficiary of a trust for which a deduction was claimed by the estate of a pre-deceased spouse under section 2056(b)(7) and which is not reported on this return? If "Yes," attach an explanation		

Part 5.—Recapitulation

Item number	Gross estate	Alternate value	Value at date of death
1	Schedule A—Real Estate		
2	Schedule B—Stocks and Bonds		
3	Schedule C—Mortgages, Notes, and Cash		
4	Schedule D—Insurance on the Decedent's Life (attach Form(s) 712)		
5	Schedule E—Jointly Owned Property (attach Form(s) 712 for life insurance) . . .		
6	Schedule F—Other Miscellaneous Property (attach Form(s) 712 for life insurance) .		
7	Schedule G—Transfers During Decedent's Life (attach Form(s) 712 for life insurance)		
8	Schedule H—Powers of Appointment		
9	Schedule I—Annuities		
10	Total gross estate (add items 1 through 9).		
11	Schedule U—Qualified Conservation Easement Exclusion		
12	Total gross estate less exclusion (subtract item 11 from item 10). Enter here and on line 1 of the Tax Computation		

Item number	Deductions	Amount
13	Schedule J—Funeral Expenses and Expenses Incurred in Administering Property Subject to Claims	
14	Schedule K—Debts of the Decedent	
15	Schedule K—Mortgages and Liens	
16	Total of items 13 through 15	
17	Allowable amount of deductions from item 16 (see the instructions for item 17 of the Recapitulation)	
18	Schedule L—Net Losses During Administration	
19	Schedule L—Expenses Incurred in Administering Property Not Subject to Claims	
20	Schedule M—Bequests, etc., to Surviving Spouse	
21	Schedule O—Charitable, Public, and Similar Gifts and Bequests	
22	Schedule T—Qualified Family-Owned Business Interest Deduction	
23	Total allowable deductions (add items 17 through 22). Enter here and on line 2 of the Tax Computation . .	

Page 3

Form 706 (Rev. 7-98)

Estate of:

SCHEDULE A—Real Estate

- *For jointly owned property that must be disclosed on Schedule E, see the instructions on the reverse side of Schedule E.*
- *Real estate that is part of a sole proprietorship should be shown on Schedule F.*
- *Real estate that is included in the gross estate under section 2035, 2036, 2037, or 2038 should be shown on Schedule G.*
- *Real estate that is included in the gross estate under section 2041 should be shown on Schedule H.*
- *If you elect section 2032A valuation, you must complete Schedule A and Schedule A-1.*

Item number	Description	Alternate valuation date	Alternate value	Value at date of death
1				
	Total from continuation schedules or additional sheets attached to this schedule . . .			
	TOTAL. (Also enter on Part 5, Recapitulation, page 3, at item 1.)			

(If more space is needed, attach the continuation schedule from the end of this package or additional sheets of the same size.)

(See the instructions on the reverse side.)

Schedule A— Page 4

Form 706 (Rev. 7-98)

Instructions for Schedule A—Real Estate

If the total gross estate contains any real estate, you must complete Schedule A and file it with the return. On Schedule A list real estate the decedent owned or had contracted to purchase. Number each parcel in the left-hand column.

Describe the real estate in enough detail so that the IRS can easily locate it for inspection and valuation. For each parcel of real estate, report the area and, if the parcel is improved, describe the improvements. For city or town property, report the street and number, ward, subdivision, block and lot, etc. For rural property, report the township, range, landmarks, etc.

If any item of real estate is subject to a mortgage for which the decedent's estate is liable, that is, if the indebtedness may be charged against other property of the estate that is not subject to that mortgage, or if the decedent was personally liable for that mortgage, you must report the full value of the property in the value column.

Enter the amount of the mortgage under "Description" on this schedule. The unpaid amount of the mortgage may be deducted on Schedule K. If the decedent's estate is NOT liable for the amount of the mortgage, report only the value of the equity of redemption (or value of the property less the indebtedness) in the value column as part of the gross estate. Do not enter any amount less than zero. Do not deduct the amount of indebtedness on Schedule K.

Also list on Schedule A real property the decedent contracted to purchase. Report the full value of the property and not the equity in the value column. Deduct the unpaid part of the purchase price on Schedule K.

Report the value of real estate without reducing it for homestead or other exemption, or the value of dower, curtesy, or a statutory estate created instead of dower or curtesy.

Explain how the reported values were determined and attach copies of any appraisals.

Schedule A Examples

In this example, alternate valuation is not adopted; the date of death is January 1, 1998.

Item number	Description	Alternate valuation date	Alternate value	Value at date of death
1	House and lot, 1921 William Street NW, Washington, DC (lot 6, square 481). Rent of $2,700 due at end of each quarter, February 1, May 1, August 1, and November 1. Value based on appraisal, copy of which is attached			108,000
	Rent due on item 1 for quarter ending November 1, 1997, but not collected at date of death			2,700
	Rent accrued on item 1 for November and December 1997			1,800
2	House and lot, 304 Jefferson Street, Alexandria, VA (lot 18, square 40). Rent of $600 payable monthly. Value based on appraisal, copy of which is attached			96,000
	Rent due on item 2 for December 1997, but not collected at date of death . . .			600

In this example, alternate valuation is adopted; the date of death is January 1, 1998.

Item number	Description	Alternate valuation date	Alternate value	Value at date of death
1	House and lot, 1921 William Street NW, Washington, DC (lot 6, square 481). Rent of $2,700 due at end of each quarter, February 1, May 1, August 1, and November 1. Value based on appraisal, copy of which is attached. Not disposed of within 6 months following death	7/1/98	90,000	108,000
	Rent due on item 1 for quarter ending November 1, 1997, but not collected until February 1, 1998	2/1/98	2,700	2,700
	Rent accrued on item 1 for November and December 1997, collected on February 1, 1998	2/1/98	1,800	1,800
2	House and lot, 304 Jefferson Street, Alexandria, VA (lot 18, square 40). Rent of $600 payable monthly. Value based on appraisal, copy of which is attached. Property exchanged for farm on May 1, 1998	5/1/98	90,000	96,000
	Rent due on item 2 for December 1997, but not collected until February 1, 1998 .	2/1/98	600	600

Schedule A— Page 5

Form 706 (Rev. 7-98)

Instructions for Schedule A-1.—Section 2032A Valuation

The election to value certain farm and closely held business property at its special use value is made by checking "Yes" to line 2 of Part 3, Elections by the Executor, Form 706. Schedule A-1 is used to report the additional information that must be submitted to support this election. In order to make a valid election, you must complete Schedule A-1 and attach all of the required statements and appraisals.

For definitions and additional information concerning special use valuation, see section 2032A and the related regulations.

Part 1.—Type of Election

Estate and GST Tax Elections.—If you elect special use valuation for the estate tax, you must also elect special use valuation for the GST tax and vice versa.

You must value each specific property interest at the same value for GST tax purposes that you value it at for estate tax purposes.

Protective Election.—To make the protective election described in the separate instructions for line 2 of Part 3, Elections by the Executor, you must check this box, enter the decedent's name and social security number in the spaces provided at the top of Schedule A-1, and complete line 1 and column A of lines 3 and 4 of Part 2. For purposes of the protective election, list on line 3 all of the real property that passes to the qualified heirs even though some of the property will be shown on line 2 when the additional notice of election is subsequently filed. You need not complete columns B–D of lines 3 and 4. You need not complete any other line entries on Schedule A-1. Completing Schedule A-1 as described above constitutes a Notice of Protective Election as described in Regulations section 20.2032A-8(b).

Part 2.—Notice of Election

Line 10.—Because the special use valuation election creates a potential tax liability for the recapture tax of section 2032A(c), you must list each person who receives an interest in the specially valued property on Schedule A-1. If there are more than eight persons who receive interests, use an additional sheet that follows the format of line 10. In the columns "Fair market value" and "Special use value," you should enter the total respective values of all the specially valued property interests received by each person.

GST Tax Savings

To compute the additional GST tax due upon disposition (or cessation of qualified use) of the property, each "skip person" (as defined in the instructions to Schedule R) who receives an interest in the specially valued property must know the total GST tax savings on all of the interests in specially valued property received. This GST tax savings is the difference between the total GST tax that was imposed on all of the interests in specially valued property received by the skip person valued at their special use value and the total GST tax that would have been imposed on the same interests received by the skip person had they been valued at their fair market value.

Because the GST tax depends on the executor's allocation of the GST exemption and the grandchild exclusion, the skip person who receives the interests is unable to compute this GST tax savings. Therefore, for each skip person who receives an interest in specially valued property, you must attach worksheets showing the total GST tax savings attributable to all of that person's interests in specially valued property.

How To Compute the GST Tax Savings.—Before computing each skip person's GST tax savings, you must complete Schedules R and R-1 for the entire estate (using the special use values).

For each skip person, you must complete two Schedules R (Parts 2 and 3 only) as worksheets, one showing the interests in specially valued property received by the skip person at their special use value and one showing the same interests at their fair market value.

If the skip person received interests in specially valued property that were shown on Schedule R-1, show these interests on the Schedule R, Parts 2 and 3 worksheets, as appropriate. Do not use Schedule R-1 as a worksheet.

Completing the Special Use Value Worksheets.—On lines 2–4 and 6, enter -0-.

Completing the Fair Market Value Worksheets.—*Lines 2 and 3, fixed taxes and other charges.*—If valuing the interests at their fair market value (instead of special use value) causes any of these taxes and charges to increase, enter the increased amount (only) on these lines and attach an explanation of the increase. Otherwise, enter -0-.

Line 6—GST exemption.—If you completed line 10 of Schedule R, Part 1, enter on line 6 the amount shown for the skip person on the *line 10 special use allocation schedule* you attached to Schedule R. If you did not complete line 10 of Schedule R, Part 1, enter -0- on line 6.

Total GST Tax Savings.—For each skip person, subtract the tax amount on line 10, Part 2 of the special use value worksheet from the tax amount on line 10, Part 2 of the fair market value worksheet. This difference is the skip person's total GST tax savings.

Part 3.—Agreement to Special Valuation Under Section 2032A

The agreement to special valuation by persons with an interest in property is required under section 2032A(a)(1)(B) and (d)(2) and must be signed by all parties who have any interest in the property being valued based on its qualified use as of the date of the decedent's death.

An interest in property is an interest that, as of the date of the decedent's death, can be asserted under applicable local law so as to affect the disposition of the specially valued property by the estate. Any person who at the decedent's death has any such interest in the property, whether present or future, or vested or contingent, must enter into the agreement. Included are owners of remainder and executory interests; the holders of general or special powers of appointment; beneficiaries of a gift over in default of exercise of any such power; joint tenants and holders of similar undivided interests when the decedent held only a joint or undivided interest in the property or when only an undivided interest is specially valued; and trustees of trusts and representatives of other entities holding title to, or holding any interests in the property. An heir who has the power under local law to caveat (challenge) a will and thereby affect disposition of the property is not, however, considered to be a person with an interest in property under section 2032A solely by reason of that right. Likewise, creditors of an estate are not such persons solely by reason of their status as creditors.

If any person required to enter into the agreement either desires that an agent act for him or her or cannot legally bind himself or herself due to infancy or other incompetency, or due to death before the election under section 2032A is timely exercised, a representative authorized by local law to bind the person in an agreement of this nature may sign the agreement on his or her behalf.

The Internal Revenue Service will contact the agent designated in the agreement on all matters relating to continued qualification under section 2032A of the specially valued real property and on all matters relating to the special lien arising under section 6324B. It is the duty of the agent as attorney-in-fact for the parties with interests in the specially valued property to furnish the IRS with any requested information and to notify the IRS of any disposition or cessation of qualified use of any part of the property.

Schedule A-1— Page 6

Form 706 (Rev. 7-98)

Checklist for Section 2032A Election.—*If you are going to make the special use valuation election on Schedule A-1, please use this checklist to ensure that you are providing everything necessary to make a valid election.*

To have a valid special use valuation election under section 2032A, you must file, in addition to the Federal estate tax return, **(a)** a notice of election (Schedule A-1, Part 2), and **(b)** a fully executed agreement (Schedule A-1, Part 3). You must include certain information in the notice of election. To ensure that the notice of election includes all of the information required for a valid election, use the following checklist. The checklist is for your use only. Do not file it with the return.

1. Does the notice of election include the decedent's name and social security number as they appear on the estate tax return?

2. Does the notice of election include the relevant qualified use of the property to be specially valued?

3. Does the notice of election describe the items of real property shown on the estate tax return that are to be specially valued and identify the property by the Form 706 schedule and item number?

4. Does the notice of election include the fair market value of the real property to be specially valued and also include its value based on the qualified use (determined without the adjustments provided in section 2032A(b)(3)(B))?

5. Does the notice of election include the adjusted value (as defined in section 2032A(b)(3)(B)) of **(a)** all real property that both passes from the decedent and is used in a qualified use, without regard to whether it is to be specially valued, and **(b)** all real property to be specially valued?

6. Does the notice of election include **(a)** the items of personal property shown on the estate tax return that pass from the decedent to a qualified heir and that are used in qualified use and **(b)** the total value of such personal property adjusted under section 2032A(b)(3)(B)?

7. Does the notice of election include the adjusted value of the gross estate? (See section 2032A(b)(3)(A).)

8. Does the notice of election include the method used to determine the special use value?

9. Does the notice of election include copies of written appraisals of the fair market value of the real property?

10. Does the notice of election include a statement that the decedent and/or a member of his or her family has owned all of the specially valued property for at least 5 years of the 8 years immediately preceding the date of the decedent's death?

11. Does the notice of election include a statement as to whether there were any periods during the 8-year period preceding the decedent's date of death during which the decedent or a member of his or her family **(a)** did not own the property to be specially valued, **(b)** use it in a qualified use, or **(c)** materially participate in the operation of the farm or other business? (See section 2032A(e)(6).)

12. Does the notice of election include, for each item of specially valued property, the name of every person taking an interest in that item of specially valued property and the following information about each such person: **(a)** the person's address, **(b)** the person's taxpayer identification number, **(c)** the person's relationship to the decedent, and **(d)** the value of the property interest passing to that person based on both fair market value and qualified use?

13. Does the notice of election include affidavits describing the activities constituting material participation and the identity of the material participants?

14. Does the notice of election include a legal description of each item of specially valued property?

(In the case of an election made for qualified woodlands, the information included in the notice of election must include the reason for entitlement to the woodlands election.)

Any election made under section 2032A will not be valid unless a properly executed agreement (Schedule A-1, Part 3) is filed with the estate tax return. To ensure that the agreement satisfies the requirements for a valid election, use the following checklist.

1. Has the agreement been signed by each and every qualified heir having an interest in the property being specially valued?

2. Has every qualified heir expressed consent to personal liability under section 2032A(c) in the event of an early disposition or early cessation of qualified use?

3. Is the agreement that is actually signed by the qualified heirs in a form that is binding on all of the qualified heirs having an interest in the specially valued property?

4. Does the agreement designate an agent to act for the parties to the agreement in all dealings with the IRS on matters arising under section 2032A?

5. Has the agreement been signed by the designated agent and does it give the address of the agent?

Form 706 (Rev. 7-98)

Estate of:	Decedent's Social Security Number

SCHEDULE A-1—Section 2032A Valuation

Part 1.—Type of Election (Before making an election, see the checklist on page 7.):

☐ **Protective election (Regulations section 20.2032A-8(b)).**—Complete Part 2, line 1, and column A of lines 3 and 4. (See instructions.)
☐ **Regular election.**—Complete all of Part 2 (including line 11, if applicable) and Part 3. (See instructions.)

Before completing Schedule A-1, see the checklist on page 7 for the information and documents that must be included to make a valid election.

The election is not valid unless the agreement (i.e., Part 3—Agreement to Special Valuation Under Section 2032A)—
● Is signed by each and every qualified heir with an interest in the specially valued property, and
● Is attached to this return when it is filed.

Part 2.—Notice of Election (Regulations section 20.2032A-8(a)(3))
Note: *All real property entered on lines 2 and 3 must also be entered on Schedules A, E, F, G, or H, as applicable.*

1 Qualified use—check one ► ☐ Farm used for farming, or
  ► ☐ Trade or business other than farming
2 Real property used in a qualified use, passing to qualified heirs, and to be specially valued on this Form 706.

A Schedule and item number from Form 706	B Full value (without section 2032A(b)(3)(B) adjustment)	C Adjusted value (with section 2032A(b)(3)(B) adjustment)	D Value based on qualified use (without section 2032A(b)(3)(B) adjustment)
Totals			

Attach a legal description of all property listed on line 2.
Attach copies of appraisals showing the column B values for all property listed on line 2.

3 Real property used in a qualified use, passing to qualified heirs, but not specially valued on this Form 706.

A Schedule and item number from Form 706	B Full value (without section 2032A(b)(3)(B) adjustment)	C Adjusted value (with section 2032A(b)(3)(B) adjustment)	D Value based on qualified use (without section 2032A(b)(3)(B) adjustment)
Totals			

If you checked "Regular election," you must attach copies of appraisals showing the column B values for all property listed on line 3.

(continued on next page) **Schedule A-1— Page 8**

Form 706 (Rev. 7-98)

4 Personal property used in a qualified use and passing to qualified heirs.

A Schedule and item number from Form 706	B Adjusted value (with section 2032A(b)(3)(B) adjustment)	A (continued) Schedule and item number from Form 706	B (continued) Adjusted value (with section 2032A(b)(3)(B) adjustment)
		"Subtotal" from Col. B, below left	

Subtotal . . . .   Total adjusted value . . .

5 Enter the value of the total gross estate as adjusted under section 2032A(b)(3)(A). ▶

6 Attach a description of the method used to determine the special value based on qualified use.

7 Did the decedent and/or a member of his or her family own all property listed on line 2 for at least 5 of the 8 years immediately preceding the date of the decedent's death? . . . . ☐ Yes ☐ No

8 Were there any periods during the 8-year period preceding the date of the decedent's death during which the decedent or a member of his or her family:

Yes | No

a Did not own the property listed on line 2 above? . . . .

b Did not use the property listed on line 2 above in a qualified use? . . . .

c Did not materially participate in the operation of the farm or other business within the meaning of section 2032A(e)(6)?. . . . .

If "Yes" to any of the above, you must attach a statement listing the periods. If applicable, describe whether the exceptions of sections 2032A(b)(4) or (5) are met.

9 Attach affidavits describing the activities constituting material participation and the identity and relationship to the decedent of the material participants.

10 Persons holding interests. Enter the requested information for each party who received any interest in the specially valued property. (Each of the qualified heirs receiving an interest in the property must sign the agreement, and the agreement must be filed with this return.)

	Name	Address
A		
B		
C		
D		
E		
F		
G		
H		

	Identifying number	Relationship to decedent	Fair market value	Special use value
A				
B				
C				
D				
E				
F				
G				
H				

You must attach a computation of the GST tax savings attributable to direct skips for each person listed above who is a skip person. (See instructions.)

11 **Woodlands election.**—Check here ▶ ☐ if you wish to make a woodlands election as described in section 2032A(e)(13). Enter the Schedule and item numbers from Form 706 of the property for which you are making this election ▶

You must attach a statement explaining why you are entitled to make this election. The IRS may issue regulations that require more information to substantiate this election. You will be notified by the IRS if you must supply further information.

Schedule A-1— Page 9

Form 706 (Rev. 7-98)

Part 3.—Agreement to Special Valuation Under Section 2032A

Estate of:	Date of Death	Decedent's Social Security Number

There cannot be a valid election unless:

● The agreement is executed by each and every one of the qualified heirs, and

● The agreement is included with the estate tax return when the estate tax return is filed.

We (list all qualified heirs and other persons having an interest in the property required to sign this agreement)

_____

_____ ,

being all the qualified heirs and _____

_____ ,

being all other parties having interests in the property which is qualified real property and which is valued under section 2032A of the Internal Revenue Code, do hereby approve of the election made by _____ ,

Executor/Administrator of the estate of _____ ,

pursuant to section 2032A to value said property on the basis of the qualified use to which the property is devoted and do hereby enter into this agreement pursuant to section 2032A(d).

The undersigned agree and consent to the application of subsection (c) of section 2032A of the Code with respect to all the property described on line 2 of Part 2 of Schedule A-1 of Form 706, attached to this agreement. More specifically, the undersigned heirs expressly agree and consent to personal liability under subsection (c) of 2032A for the additional estate and GST taxes imposed by that subsection with respect to their respective interests in the above-described property in the event of certain early dispositions of the property or early cessation of the qualified use of the property. It is understood that if a qualified heir disposes of any interest in qualified real property to any member of his or her family, such member may thereafter be treated as the qualified heir with respect to such interest upon filing a Form 706-A and a new agreement.

The undersigned interested parties who are not qualified heirs consent to the collection of any additional estate and GST taxes imposed under section 2032A(c) of the Code from the specially valued property.

If there is a disposition of any interest which passes or has passed to him or her or if there is a cessation of the qualified use of any specially valued property which passes or passed to him or her, each of the undersigned heirs agrees to file a **Form 706-A**, United States Additional Estate Tax Return, and pay any additional estate and GST taxes due within 6 months of the disposition or cessation.

It is understood by all interested parties that this agreement is a condition precedent to the election of special use valuation under section 2032A of the Code and must be executed by every interested party even though that person may not have received the estate (or GST) tax benefits or be in possession of such property.

Each of the undersigned understands that by making this election, a lien will be created and recorded pursuant to section 6324B of the Code on the property referred to in this agreement for the adjusted tax differences with respect to the estate as defined in section 2032A(c)(2)(C).

As the interested parties, the undersigned designate the following individual as their agent for all dealings with the Internal Revenue Service concerning the continued qualification of the specially valued property under section 2032A of the Code and on all issues regarding the special lien under section 6324B. The agent is authorized to act for the parties with respect to all dealings with the Service on matters affecting the qualified real property described earlier. This authority includes the following:

● To receive confidential information on all matters relating to continued qualification under section 2032A of the specially valued real property and on all matters relating to the special lien arising under section 6324B.

● To furnish the Service with any requested information concerning the property.

● To notify the Service of any disposition or cessation of qualified use of any part of the property.

● To receive, but not to endorse and collect, checks in payment of any refund of Internal Revenue taxes, penalties, or interest.

● To execute waivers (including offers of waivers) of restrictions on assessment or collection of deficiencies in tax and waivers of notice of disallowance of a claim for credit or refund.

● To execute closing agreements under section 7121.

(continued on next page)

Schedule A-1— Page 10

Form 706 (Rev. 7-98)

Part 3.—Agreement to Special Valuation Under Section 2032A *(Continued)*

Estate of:	Date of Death	Decedent's Social Security Number

● Other acts (specify) ▶ _____

By signing this agreement, the agent agrees to provide the Service with any requested information concerning this property and to notify the Service of any disposition or cessation of the qualified use of any part of this property.

Name of Agent	Signature	Address

The property to which this agreement relates is listed in Form 706, United States Estate (and Generation-Skipping Transfer) Tax Return, and in the Notice of Election, along with its fair market value according to section 2031 of the Code and its special use value according to section 2032A. The name, address, social security number, and interest (including the value) of each of the undersigned in this property are as set forth in the attached Notice of Election.

IN WITNESS WHEREOF, the undersigned have hereunto set their hands at _____ .

this _____ day of _____ .

SIGNATURES OF EACH OF THE QUALIFIED HEIRS:

Signature of qualified heir	Signature of qualified heir
Signature of qualified heir	Signature of qualified heir
Signature of qualified heir	Signature of qualified heir
Signature of qualified heir	Signature of qualified heir
Signature of qualified heir	Signature of qualified heir
Signature of qualified heir	Signature of qualified heir

Signatures of other interested parties

Signatures of other interested parties

Schedule A-1— Page 11

Form 706 (Rev. 7-98)

Estate of:

SCHEDULE B—Stocks and Bonds

(For jointly owned property that must be disclosed on Schedule E, see the instructions for Schedule E.)

Item number	Description including face amount of bonds or number of shares and par value where needed for identification. Give 9-digit CUSIP number.	Unit value	Alternate valuation date	Alternate value	Value at date of death
	CUSIP number				
1					
	Total from continuation schedules (or additional sheets) attached to this schedule . . .				
	TOTAL. (Also enter on Part 5, Recapitulation, page 3, at item 2.)				

(If more space is needed, attach the continuation schedule from the end of this package or additional sheets of the same size.)

(The instructions to Schedule B are in the separate instructions.)

Schedule B— Page 12

Form 706 (Rev. 7-98)

Estate of:

SCHEDULE C—Mortgages, Notes, and Cash

(For jointly owned property that must be disclosed on Schedule E, see the instructions for Schedule E.)

Item number	Description	Alternate valuation date	Alternate value	Value at date of death
1				

Total from continuation schedules (or additional sheets) attached to this schedule . .

TOTAL. (Also enter on Part 5, Recapitulation, page 3, at item 3.). . . . . . .

(If more space is needed, attach the continuation schedule from the end of this package or additional sheets of the same size.)
(See the instructions on the reverse side.)

Schedule C— Page 13

Form 706 (Rev. 7-98)

Instructions for Schedule C.— Mortgages, Notes, and Cash

Complete Schedule C and file it with your return if the total gross estate contains any:

- mortgages,
- notes, or
- cash.

List on Schedule C:

- Mortgages and notes payable **to the decedent** at the time of death.
- Cash the decedent had at the date of death.

Do not list on Schedule C:

- Mortgages and notes payable **by the decedent.** (If these are deductible, list them on Schedule K.)

List the items on Schedule C in the following order:

- mortgages,
- promissory notes,
- contracts by decedent to sell land,
- cash in possession, and
- cash in banks, savings and loan associations, and other types of financial organizations.

What to enter in the "Description" column:

For mortgages, list:

- face value,
- unpaid balance,
- date of mortgage,
- date of maturity,
- name of maker,
- property mortgaged,
- interest dates, and
- interest rate.

Example to enter in "Description" column:

"Bond and mortgage of $50,000, unpaid balance: $24,000; dated: January 1, 1980; John Doe to Richard Roe; premises: 22 Clinton Street, Newark, NJ; due: January 1, 1998; interest payable at 10% a year--January 1 and July 1."

For promissory notes, list:

- in the same way as mortgages.

For contracts by the decedent to sell land, list:

- name of purchaser,
- contract date,
- property description,
- sale price,
- initial payment,
- amounts of installment payment,
- unpaid balance of principal, and
- interest rate.

For cash in possession, list:

- such cash separately from bank deposits.

For cash in banks, savings and loan associations, and other types of financial organizations, list:

- name and address of each financial organization,
- amount in each account,
- serial or account number,
- nature of account--checking, savings, time deposit, etc., and
- unpaid interest accrued from date of last interest payment to the date of death.

Important: If you obtain statements from the financial organizations, keep them for IRS inspection.

Form 706 (Rev. 7-98)

Estate of:

SCHEDULE D—Insurance on the Decedent's Life

You must list **all** policies on the life of the decedent and attach a Form 712 for each policy.

Item number	Description	Alternate valuation date	Alternate value	Value at date of death
1				

Total from continuation schedules (or additional sheets) attached to this schedule . .

TOTAL. (Also enter on Part 5, Recapitulation, page 3, at item 4.) . . . .

(If more space is needed, attach the continuation schedule from the end of this package or additional sheets of the same size.)

(See the instructions on the reverse side.)

Schedule D— Page 15

Form 706 (Rev. 7-98)

Instructions for Schedule D.—Insurance on the Decedent's Life

If you are required to file Form 706 and there was any insurance on the decedent's life, whether or not included in the gross estate, you must complete Schedule D and file it with the return.

Insurance you must include on Schedule D.—Under section 2042 you must include in the gross estate:

- Insurance on the decedent's life receivable by or for the benefit of the estate; and
- Insurance on the decedent's life receivable by beneficiaries other than the estate, as described below.

The term "insurance" refers to life insurance of every description, including death benefits paid by fraternal beneficiary societies operating under the lodge system, and death benefits paid under no-fault automobile insurance policies if the no-fault insurer was unconditionally bound to pay the benefit in the event of the insured's death.

Insurance in favor of the estate.—Include on Schedule D the full amount of the proceeds of insurance on the life of the decedent receivable by the executor or otherwise payable to or for the benefit of the estate. Insurance in favor of the estate includes insurance used to pay the estate tax, and any other taxes, debts, or charges that are enforceable against the estate. The manner in which the policy is drawn is immaterial as long as there is an obligation, legally binding on the beneficiary, to use the proceeds to pay taxes, debts, or charges. You must include the full amount even though the premiums or other consideration may have been paid by a person other than the decedent.

Insurance receivable by beneficiaries other than the estate.—Include on Schedule D the proceeds of all insurance on the life of the decedent not receivable by or for the benefit of the decedent's estate if the decedent possessed at death any of the incidents of ownership, exercisable either alone or in conjunction with any person.

Incidents of ownership in a policy include:

- The right of the insured or estate to its economic benefits;
- The power to change the beneficiary;
- The power to surrender or cancel the policy;
- The power to assign the policy or to revoke an assignment;
- The power to pledge the policy for a loan;
- The power to obtain from the insurer a loan against the surrender value of the policy;
- A reversionary interest if the value of the reversionary interest was more than 5% of the value of the policy immediately before the decedent died. (An interest in an insurance policy is considered a reversionary interest if, for example, the proceeds become payable to the insured's estate or payable as the insured directs if the beneficiary dies before the insured.)

Life insurance not includible in the gross estate under section 2042 may be includible under some other section of the Code. For example, a life insurance policy could be transferred by the decedent in such a way that it would be includible in the gross estate under section 2036, 2037, or 2038. (See the instructions to Schedule G for a description of these sections.)

Completing the Schedule

You must list every policy of insurance on the life of the decedent, whether or not it is included in the gross estate.

Under "Description" list:

- Name of the insurance company and
- Number of the policy.

For every policy of life insurance listed on the schedule, you must request a statement on **Form 712,** Life Insurance Statement, from the company that issued the policy. Attach the Form 712 to the back of Schedule D.

If the policy proceeds are paid in one sum, enter the net proceeds received (from Form 712, line 24) in the value (and alternate value) columns of Schedule D. If the policy proceeds are not paid in one sum, enter the value of the proceeds as of the date of the decedent's death (from Form 712, line 25).

If part or all of the policy proceeds are not included in the gross estate, you must explain why they were not included.

Form 706 (Rev. 7-98)

Estate of:

SCHEDULE E—Jointly Owned Property

(If you elect section 2032A valuation, you must complete Schedule E and Schedule A-1.)

PART 1.—Qualified Joint Interests—Interests Held by the Decedent and His or Her Spouse as the Only Joint Tenants (Section 2040(b)(2))

Item number	Description For securities, give CUSIP number.	Alternate valuation date	Alternate value	Value at date of death
Total from continuation schedules (or additional sheets) attached to this schedule				
1a Totals				
1b Amounts included in gross estate (one-half of line 1a)				

PART 2.—All Other Joint Interests

2a State the name and address of each surviving co-tenant. If there are more than three surviving co-tenants, list the additional co-tenants on an attached sheet.

Name	Address (number and street, city, state, and ZIP code)
A.	
B.	
C.	

Item number	Enter letter for co-tenant	Description (including alternate valuation date if any) For securities, give CUSIP number.	Percentage includible	Includible alternate value	Includible value at date of death
	Total from continuation schedules (or additional sheets) attached to this schedule				
2b	Total other joint interests				
3	**Total includible joint interests** (add lines 1b and 2b). Also enter on Part 5, Recapitulation, page 3, at item 5				

(If more space is needed, attach the continuation schedule from the end of this package or additional sheets of the same size.)
(See the instructions on the reverse side.) **Schedule E— Page 17**

Form 706 (Rev. 7-98)

Instructions for Schedule E.—Jointly Owned Property

If you are required to file Form 706, you must complete Schedule E and file it with the return if the decedent owned any joint property at the time of death, whether or not the decedent's interest is includible in the gross estate.

Enter on this schedule all property of whatever kind or character, whether real estate, personal property, or bank accounts, in which the decedent held at the time of death an interest either as a joint tenant with right to survivorship or as a tenant by the entirety.

Do not list on this schedule property that the decedent held as a tenant in common, but report the value of the interest on Schedule A if real estate, or on the appropriate schedule if personal property. Similarly, community property held by the decedent and spouse should be reported on the appropriate Schedules A through I. The decedent's interest in a partnership should not be entered on this schedule unless the partnership interest itself is jointly owned. Solely owned partnership interests should be reported on Schedule F, "Other Miscellaneous Property."

Part 1—Qualified joint interests held by decedent and spouse.—Under section 2040(b)(2), a joint interest is a qualified joint interest if the decedent and the surviving spouse held the interest as:

● Tenants by the entirety, or

● Joint tenants with right of survivorship if the decedent and the decedent's spouse are the only joint tenants.

Interests that meet either of the two requirements above should be entered in Part 1. Joint interests that do not meet either of the two requirements above should be entered in Part 2.

Under "Description," describe the property as required in the instructions for Schedules A, B, C, and F for the type of property involved. For example, jointly held stocks and bonds should be described using the rules given in the instructions to Schedule B.

Under "Alternate value" and "Value at date of death," enter the full value of the property.

Note: *You cannot claim the special treatment under section 2040(b) for property held jointly by a decedent and a surviving spouse who is not a U.S. citizen. You must report these joint interests on Part 2 of Schedule E, not Part 1.*

Part 2—Other joint interests.—All joint interests that were not entered in Part 1 must be entered in Part 2.

For each item of property, enter the appropriate letter A, B, C, etc., from line 2a to indicate the name and address of the surviving co-tenant.

Under "Description," describe the property as required in the instructions for Schedules A, B, C, and F for the type of property involved.

In the "Percentage includible" column, enter the percentage of the total value of the property that you intend to include in the gross estate.

Generally, you must include the full value of the jointly owned property in the gross estate. However, the full value should not be included if you can show that a part of the property originally belonged to the other tenant or tenants and was never received or acquired by the other tenant or tenants from the decedent for less than adequate and full consideration in money or money's worth, or unless you can show that any part of the property was acquired with consideration originally belonging to the surviving joint tenant or tenants. In this case, you may exclude from the value of the property an amount proportionate to the consideration furnished by the other tenant or tenants. Relinquishing or promising to relinquish dower, curtesy, or statutory estate created instead of dower or curtesy, or other marital rights in the decedent's property or estate is not consideration in money or money's worth. See the Schedule A instructions for the value to show for real property that is subject to a mortgage.

If the property was acquired by the decedent and another person or persons by gift, bequest, devise, or inheritance as joint tenants, and their interests are not otherwise specified by law, include only that part of the value of the property that is figured by dividing the full value of the property by the number of joint tenants.

If you believe that less than the full value of the entire property is includible in the gross estate for tax purposes, you must establish the right to include the smaller value by attaching proof of the extent, origin, and nature of the decedent's interest and the interest(s) of the decedent's co-tenant or co-tenants.

In the "Includible alternate value" and "Includible value at date of death" columns, you should enter only the values that you believe are includible in the gross estate.

Form 706 (Rev. 7-98)

Estate of:

SCHEDULE F—Other Miscellaneous Property Not Reportable Under Any Other Schedule
(For jointly owned property that must be disclosed on Schedule E, see the instructions for Schedule E.)
(If you elect section 2032A valuation, you must complete Schedule F and Schedule A-1.)

		Yes	No
1	Did the decedent at the time of death own any articles of artistic or collectible value in excess of $3,000 or any collections whose artistic or collectible value combined at date of death exceeded $10,000? . . . . If "Yes," submit full details on this schedule and attach appraisals.		
2	Has the decedent's estate, spouse, or any other person, received (or will receive) any bonus or award as a result of the decedent's employment or death? . . . . If "Yes," submit full details on this schedule.		
3	Did the decedent at the time of death have, or have access to, a safe deposit box? . . . . If "Yes," state location, and if held in joint names of decedent and another, state name and relationship of joint depositor.		

If any of the contents of the safe deposit box are omitted from the schedules in this return, explain fully why omitted.

Item number	Description For securities, give CUSIP number.	Alternate valuation date	Alternate value	Value at date of death
1				

Total from continuation schedules (or additional sheets) attached to this schedule . .

TOTAL. (Also enter on Part 5, Recapitulation, page 3, at item 6.) . . . .

(If more space is needed, attach the continuation schedule from the end of this package or additional sheets of the same size.)
(See the instructions on the reverse side.)

Schedule F— Page 19

Form 706 (Rev. 7-98)

Instructions for Schedule F.—Other Miscellaneous Property

You must complete Schedule F and file it with the return.

On Schedule F list all items that must be included in the gross estate that are not reported on any other schedule, including:

- Debts due the decedent (other than notes and mortgages included on Schedule C)
- Interests in business
- Insurance on the life of another (obtain and attach **Form 712,** Life Insurance Statement, for each policy)

Note for single premium or paid-up policies: *In certain situations, for example where the surrender value of the policy exceeds its replacement cost, the true economic value of the policy will be greater than the amount shown on line 56 of Form 712. In these situations, you should report the full economic value of the policy on Schedule F. See Rev. Rul. 78-137, 1978-1 C.B. 280 for details.*

- Section 2044 property (see **Decedent Who Was a Surviving Spouse** below)
- Claims (including the value of the decedent's interest in a claim for refund of income taxes or the amount of the refund actually received)
- Rights
- Royalties
- Leaseholds
- Judgments
- Reversionary or remainder interests
- Shares in trust funds (attach a copy of the trust instrument)
- Household goods and personal effects, including wearing apparel
- Farm products and growing crops
- Livestock
- Farm machinery
- Automobiles

If the decedent owned any interest in a partnership or unincorporated business, attach a statement of assets and liabilities for the valuation date and for the 5 years before the valuation date. Also attach

statements of the net earnings for the same 5 years. You must account for goodwill in the valuation. In general, furnish the same information and follow the methods used to value close corporations. See the instructions for Schedule B.

All partnership interests should be reported on Schedule F unless the partnership interest, itself, is jointly owned. Jointly owned partnership interests should be reported on Schedule E.

If real estate is owned by the sole proprietorship, it should be reported on Schedule F and not on Schedule A. Describe the real estate with the same detail required for Schedule A.

Line 1.—If the decedent owned at the date of death articles with artistic or intrinsic value (e.g., jewelry, furs, silverware, books, statuary, vases, oriental rugs, coin or stamp collections), check the "Yes" box on line 1 and provide full details. If any one article is valued at more than $3,000, or any collection of similar articles is valued at more than $10,000, attach an appraisal by an expert under oath and the required statement regarding the appraiser's qualifications (see Regulations section 20.2031-6(b)).

Decedent Who Was a Surviving Spouse

If the decedent was a surviving spouse, he or she may have received qualified terminable interest property (QTIP) from the predeceased spouse for which the marital deduction was elected either on the predeceased spouse's estate tax return or on a gift tax return, Form 709. The election was available for gifts made and decedents dying after December 31, 1981. List such property on Schedule F.

If this election was made and the surviving spouse retained his or her interest in the QTIP property at death, the full value of the QTIP property is includible in his or her estate, even though the qualifying income interest terminated at death. It is valued as of the date of the surviving spouse's death, or alternate valuation date, if applicable. Do not reduce the value by any annual exclusion that may have applied to the transfer creating the interest.

The value of such property included in the surviving spouse's gross estate is treated as passing from the surviving spouse. It therefore qualifies for the charitable and marital deductions on the surviving spouse's estate tax return if it meets the other requirements for those deductions.

For additional details, see Regulations section 20.2044-1.

Form 706 (Rev. 7-98)

Estate of:

SCHEDULE G—Transfers During Decedent's Life
(If you elect section 2032A valuation, you must complete Schedule G and Schedule A-1.)

Item number	Description For securities, give CUSIP number.	Alternate valuation date	Alternate value	Value at date of death
A.	Gift tax paid by the decedent or the estate for all gifts made by the decedent or his or her spouse within 3 years before the decedent's death (section 2035(b))	X X X X X		
B.	Transfers includible under section 2035(a), 2036, 2037, or 2038:			
1				
	Total from continuation schedules (or additional sheets) attached to this schedule . .			
	TOTAL. (Also enter on Part 5, Recapitulation, page 3, at item 7.)			

SCHEDULE H—Powers of Appointment
(Include "5 and 5 lapsing" powers (section 2041(b)(2)) held by the decedent.)
(If you elect section 2032A valuation, you must complete Schedule H and Schedule A-1.)

Item number	Description	Alternate valuation date	Alternate value	Value at date of death
1				
	Total from continuation schedules (or additional sheets) attached to this schedule . .			
	TOTAL. (Also enter on Part 5, Recapitulation, page 3, at item 8.)			

(If more space is needed, attach the continuation schedule from the end of this package or additional sheets of the same size.)
(The instructions to Schedules G and H are in the separate instructions.)

Schedules G and H— Page 21

Form 706 (Rev. 7-98)

Estate of:

SCHEDULE I—Annuities

Note: *Generally, no exclusion is allowed for the estates of decedents dying after December 31, 1984 (see page 13 of the instructions).*

A Are you excluding from the decedent's gross estate the value of a lump-sum distribution described in section 2039(f)(2)? . . . .

			Yes	No

If "Yes," you must attach the information required by the instructions.

Item number	Description Show the entire value of the annuity before any exclusions.	Alternate valuation date	Includible alternate value	Includible value at date of death
1				
	Total from continuation schedules (or additional sheets) attached to this schedule . .			
	TOTAL. (Also enter on Part 5, Recapitulation, page 3, at item 9.)			

(If more space is needed, attach the continuation schedule from the end of this package or additional sheets of the same size.)

(The instructions to Schedule I are in the separate instructions.)

Schedule I— Page 22

Form 706 (Rev. 7-98)

Estate of:

SCHEDULE J—Funeral Expenses and Expenses Incurred in Administering Property Subject to Claims

Note: *Do not list on this schedule expenses of administering property not subject to claims. For those expenses, see the instructions for Schedule L.*

If executors' commissions, attorney fees, etc., are claimed and allowed as a deduction for estate tax purposes, they are not allowable as a deduction in computing the taxable income of the estate for Federal income tax purposes. They are allowable as an income tax deduction on Form 1041 if a waiver is filed to waive the deduction on Form 706 (see the Form 1041 instructions).

Item number	Description	Expense amount	Total amount
1	**A. Funeral expenses:**		
	Total funeral expenses		
	B. Administration expenses:		
1	Executors' commissions—amount estimated/agreed upon/paid. (Strike out the words that do not apply.)		
2	Attorney fees—amount estimated/agreed upon/paid. (Strike out the words that do not apply.) . . .		
3	Accountant fees—amount estimated/agreed upon/paid. (Strike out the words that do not apply.) . .		
4	Miscellaneous expenses:	Expense amount	
	Total miscellaneous expenses from continuation schedules (or additional sheets) attached to this schedule		
	Total miscellaneous expenses		
	TOTAL. (Also enter on Part 5, Recapitulation, page 3, at item 13.)		

(If more space is needed, attach the continuation schedule from the end of this package or additional sheets of the same size.)
(See the instructions on the reverse side.)

Schedule J— Page 23

Instructions for Schedule J.—
Funeral Expenses and Expenses Incurred in Administering Property Subject to Claims

General.—You must complete and file Schedule J if you claim a deduction on item 13 of Part 5, Recapitulation.

On Schedule J, itemize funeral expenses and expenses incurred in administering property subject to claims. List the names and addresses of persons to whom the expenses are payable and describe the nature of the expense. **Do not list expenses incurred in administering property not subject to claims on this schedule. List them on Schedule L instead.**

The deduction is limited to the amount paid for these expenses that is allowable under local law but may not exceed:

1. The value of property subject to claims included in the gross estate, plus

2. The amount paid out of property included in the gross estate but not subject to claims. This amount must actually be paid by the due date of the estate tax return.

The applicable local law under which the estate is being administered determines which property is and is not subject to claims. If under local law a particular property interest included in the gross estate would bear the burden for the payment of the expenses, then the property is considered property subject to claims.

Unlike certain claims against the estate for debts of the decedent (see the instructions for Schedule K in the separate instructions), you cannot deduct expenses incurred in administering property subject to claims on both the estate tax return and the estate's income tax return. If you choose to deduct them on the estate tax return, you cannot deduct them on a Form 1041 filed for the estate. Funeral expenses are only deductible on the estate tax return.

Funeral Expenses.—Itemize funeral expenses on line A. Deduct from the expenses any amounts that were reimbursed, such as death benefits payable by the Social Security Administration and the Veterans Administration.

Executors' Commissions.—When you file the return, you may deduct commissions that have actually been paid to you or that you expect will be paid. You may not deduct commissions if none will be collected. If the amount of the commissions has not been fixed by decree of the proper court, the deduction will be allowed on the final examination of the return, provided that:

● The District Director is reasonably satisfied that the commissions claimed will be paid;

● The amount entered as a deduction is within the amount allowable by the laws of the jurisdiction where the estate is being administered;

● It is in accordance with the usually accepted practice in that jurisdiction for estates of similar size and character.

If you have not been paid the commissions claimed at the time of the final examination of the return, you must support the amount you deducted with an affidavit or statement signed under the penalties of perjury that the amount has been agreed upon and will be paid.

Schedule J— Page 24

You may not deduct a bequest or devise made to you instead of commissions. If, however, the decedent fixed by will the compensation payable to you for services to be rendered in the administration of the estate, you may deduct this amount to the extent it is not more than the compensation allowable by the local law or practice.

Do not deduct on this schedule amounts paid as trustees' commissions whether received by you acting in the capacity of a trustee or by a separate trustee. If such amounts were paid in administering property not subject to claims, deduct them on Schedule L.

Note: *Executors' commissions are taxable income to the executors. Therefore, be sure to include them as income on your individual income tax return.*

Attorney Fees.—Enter the amount of attorney fees that have actually been paid or that you reasonably expect to be paid. If on the final examination of the return the fees claimed have not been awarded by the proper court and paid, the deduction will be allowed provided the District Director is reasonably satisfied that the amount claimed will be paid and that it does not exceed a reasonable payment for the services performed, taking into account the size and character of the estate and the local law and practice. If the fees claimed have not been paid at the time of final examination of the return, the amount deducted must be supported by an affidavit, or statement signed under the penalties of perjury, by the executor or the attorney stating that the amount has been agreed upon and will be paid.

Do not deduct attorney fees incidental to litigation incurred by the beneficiaries. These expenses are charged against the beneficiaries personally and are not administration expenses authorized by the Code.

Interest Expense.—Interest expenses incurred after the decedent's death are generally allowed as a deduction if they are reasonable, necessary to the administration of the estate, and allowable under local law.

Interest incurred as the result of a Federal estate tax deficiency is a deductible administrative expense. Penalties are not deductible even if they are allowable under local law.

Note: *Beginning with the estates of decedents dying in 1998, if you elect to pay the tax in installments under section 6166, you may* **not** *deduct the interest payable on the installments.*

Miscellaneous Expenses.—Miscellaneous administration expenses necessarily incurred in preserving and distributing the estate are deductible. These expenses include appraiser's and accountant's fees, certain court costs, and costs of storing or maintaining assets of the estate.

The expenses of selling assets are deductible only if the sale is necessary to pay the decedent's debts, the expenses of administration, or taxes, or to preserve the estate or carry out distribution.

Form 706 (Rev. 7-98)

Estate of:

SCHEDULE K—Debts of the Decedent, and Mortgages and Liens

Item number	Debts of the Decedent—Creditor and nature of claim, and allowable death taxes	Amount unpaid to date	Amount in contest	Amount claimed as a deduction
1				

Total from continuation schedules (or additional sheets) attached to this schedule . . . .

TOTAL. (Also enter on Part 5, Recapitulation, page 3, at item 14.) . . . .

Item number	Mortgages and Liens—Description	Amount
1		

Total from continuation schedules (or additional sheets) attached to this schedule . . . .

TOTAL. (Also enter on Part 5, Recapitulation, page 3, at item 15.) . . . .

(If more space is needed, attach the continuation schedule from the end of this package or additional sheets of the same size.)
(The instructions to Schedule K are in the separate instructions.)

Schedule K— Page 25

Form 706 (Rev. 7-98)

Estate of:

SCHEDULE L—Net Losses During Administration and Expenses Incurred in Administering Property Not Subject to Claims

Item number	Net losses during administration (**Note:** Do not deduct losses claimed on a Federal income tax return.)	Amount
1		
	Total from continuation schedules (or additional sheets) attached to this schedule	
	TOTAL. (Also enter on Part 5, Recapitulation, page 3, at item 18.)	

Item number	Expenses incurred in administering property not subject to claims (Indicate whether estimated, agreed upon, or paid.)	Amount
1		
	Total from continuation schedules (or additional sheets) attached to this schedule	
	TOTAL. (Also enter on Part 5, Recapitulation, page 3, at item 19.)	

(If more space is needed, attach the continuation schedule from the end of this package or additional sheets of the same size.)

Schedule L— Page 26   (The instructions to Schedule L are in the separate instructions.)

Form 706 (Rev. 7-98)

Estate of:

SCHEDULE M—Bequests, etc., to Surviving Spouse

Election To Deduct Qualified Terminable Interest Property Under Section 2056(b)(7).—If a trust (or other property) meets the requirements of qualified terminable interest property under section 2056(b)(7), and

    a. The trust or other property is listed on Schedule M, and

    b. The value of the trust (or other property) is entered in whole or in part as a deduction on Schedule M,

then unless the executor specifically identifies the trust (all or a fractional portion or percentage) or other property to be excluded from the election, the executor shall be deemed to have made an election to have such trust (or other property) treated as qualified terminable interest property under section 2056(b)(7).

    If less than the entire value of the trust (or other property) that the executor has included in the gross estate is entered as a deduction on Schedule M, the executor shall be considered to have made an election only as to a fraction of the trust (or other property). The numerator of this fraction is equal to the amount of the trust (or other property) deducted on Schedule M. The denominator is equal to the total value of the trust (or other property).

Election To Deduct Qualified Domestic Trust Property Under Section 2056A.—If a trust meets the requirements of a qualified domestic trust under section 2056A(a) and this return is filed no later than 1 year after the time prescribed by law (including extensions) for filing the return, and

    a. The entire value of a trust or trust property is listed on Schedule M, and

    b. The entire value of the trust or trust property is entered as a deduction on Schedule M,

then unless the executor specifically identifies the trust to be excluded from the election, the executor shall be deemed to have made an election to have the entire trust treated as qualified domestic trust property.

		Yes	No
1	Did any property pass to the surviving spouse as a result of a qualified disclaimer?		
	If "Yes," attach a copy of the written disclaimer required by section 2518(b).		
2a	In what country was the surviving spouse born? _____		
b	What is the surviving spouse's date of birth? _____		
c	Is the surviving spouse a U.S. citizen?		
d	If the surviving spouse is a naturalized citizen, when did the surviving spouse acquire citizenship?_____		
e	If the surviving spouse is not a U.S. citizen, of what country is the surviving spouse a citizen? _____		
3	**Election Out of QTIP Treatment of Annuities.**—Do you elect under section 2056(b)(7)(C)(ii) **not** to treat as qualified terminable interest property any joint and survivor annuities that are included in the gross estate and would otherwise be treated as qualified terminable interest property under section 2056(b)(7)(C)? (see instructions)		

Item number	Description of property interests passing to surviving spouse	Amount
1		
	Total from continuation schedules (or additional sheets) attached to this schedule	
4	**Total** amount of property interests listed on Schedule M	**4**

5a	Federal estate taxes payable out of property interests listed on Schedule M . .	**5a**	
b	Other death taxes payable out of property interests listed on Schedule M . . .	**5b**	
c	Federal and state GST taxes payable out of property interests listed on Schedule M	**5c**	
d	Add items a, b, and c		**5d**
6	Net amount of property interests listed on Schedule M (subtract 5d from 4). Also enter on Part 5, Recapitulation, page 3, at item 20		**6**

(If more space is needed, attach the continuation schedule from the end of this package or additional sheets of the same size.)
(See the instructions on the reverse side.)

Schedule M— Page 27

Form 706 (Rev. 7-98)

Examples of Listing of Property Interests on Schedule M

Item number	Description of property interests passing to surviving spouse	Amount
1	One-half the value of a house and lot, 256 South West Street, held by decedent and surviving spouse as joint tenants with right of survivorship under deed dated July 15, 1957 (Schedule E, Part I, item 1)	$132,500
2	Proceeds of Gibraltar Life Insurance Company policy No. 104729, payable in one sum to surviving spouse (Schedule D, item 3)	200,000
3	Cash bequest under Paragraph Six of will	100,000

Instructions for Schedule M.—Bequests, etc., to Surviving Spouse (Marital Deduction)

General

You must complete Schedule M and file it with the return if you claim a deduction on item 20 of Part 5, Recapitulation.

The marital deduction is authorized by section 2056 for certain property interests that pass from the decedent to the surviving spouse. You may claim the deduction only for property interests that are included in the decedent's gross estate (Schedules A through I).

Note: *The marital deduction is generally not allowed if the surviving spouse is **not** a U.S. citizen. The marital deduction is allowed for property passing to such a surviving spouse in a "qualified domestic trust" or if such property is transferred or irrevocably assigned to such a trust before the estate tax return is filed. The executor must elect qualified domestic trust status on this return. See the instructions on pages 29–30 for details on the election.*

Property Interests That You May List on Schedule M

Generally, you may list on Schedule M all property interests that pass from the decedent to the surviving spouse and are included in the gross estate. However, you should not list any "Nondeductible terminable interests" (described below) on Schedule M unless you are making a QTIP election. The property for which you make this election must be included on Schedule M. See "Qualified Terminable Interest Property" on the following page.

For the rules on common disaster and survival for a limited period, see section 2056(b)(3).

You may list on Schedule M only those interests that the surviving spouse takes:

1. As the decedent's legatee, devisee, heir, or donee;

2. As the decedent's surviving tenant by the entirety or joint tenant;

3. As an appointee under the decedent's exercise of a power or as a taker in default at the decedent's nonexercise of a power;

4. As a beneficiary of insurance on the decedent's life;

5. As the surviving spouse taking under dower or curtesy (or similar statutory interest); and

6. As a transferee of a transfer made by the decedent at any time.

Property Interests That You May Not List on Schedule M

You should not list on Schedule M:

1. The value of any property that does not pass from the decedent to the surviving spouse;

2. Property interests that are not included in the decedent's gross estate;

3. The full value of a property interest for which a deduction was claimed on Schedules J through L. The value of the property interest should be reduced by the deductions claimed with respect to it;

4. The full value of a property interest that passes to the surviving spouse subject to a mortgage or other encumbrance or an obligation of the surviving spouse. Include on Schedule M only the net value of the interest after reducing it by the amount of the mortgage or other debt;

5. Nondeductible terminable interests (described below);

6. Any property interest disclaimed by the surviving spouse.

Terminable Interests

Certain interests in property passing from a decedent to a surviving spouse are referred to as *terminable interests.* These are interests that will terminate or fail after the passage of time, or on the occurrence or nonoccurrence of some contingency. Examples are: life estates, annuities, estates for terms of years, and patents.

The ownership of a bond, note, or other contractual obligation, which when discharged would not have the effect of an annuity for life or for a term, is not considered a terminable interest.

Nondeductible terminable interests.— A terminable interest is *nondeductible,* and should not be entered on Schedule M (unless you are making a QTIP election) if:

1. Another interest in the same property passed from the decedent to some other person for less than adequate and full consideration in money or money's worth; and

2. By reason of its passing, the other person or that person's heirs may enjoy part of the property after the termination of the surviving spouse's interest.

This rule applies even though the interest that passes from the decedent to a person other than the surviving spouse is not included in the gross estate, and regardless of when the interest passes. The rule also applies regardless of whether the surviving spouse's interest and the other person's interest pass from the decedent at the same time.

Property interests that are considered to pass to a person other than the surviving spouse are any property interest that: **(a)** passes under a decedent's will or intestacy; **(b)** was transferred by a decedent during life; or **(c)** is held by or passed on to any person as a decedent's joint tenant, as appointee under a decedent's exercise of a power, as taker in default at a decedent's release or nonexercise of a power, or as a beneficiary of insurance on the decedent's life.

For example, a decedent devised real property to his wife for life, with remainder to his children. The life interest that passed to the wife does not qualify for the marital deduction because it will terminate at her death and the children will thereafter possess or enjoy the property.

However, if the decedent purchased a joint and survivor annuity for himself and his wife who survived him, the value of the survivor's annuity, to the extent that it is included in the gross estate, qualifies for the marital deduction because even though the interest will terminate on the wife's death, no one else will possess or enjoy any part of the property.

The marital deduction is not allowed for an interest that the decedent directed the executor or a trustee to convert, after death, into a terminable interest for the surviving spouse. The marital deduction is not allowed for such an interest even if there was no interest

Page 28

Form 706 (Rev. 7-98)

in the property passing to another person and even if the terminable interest would otherwise have been deductible under the exceptions described below for life estate and life insurance and annuity payments with powers of appointment. For more information, see Regulations sections 20.2056(b)-1(f) and 20.2056(b)-1(g), Example (7).

If any property interest passing from the decedent to the surviving spouse may be paid or otherwise satisfied out of any of a group of assets, the value of the property interest is, for the entry on Schedule M, reduced by the value of any asset or assets that, if passing from the decedent to the surviving spouse, would be nondeductible terminable interests. Examples of property interests that may be paid or otherwise satisfied out of any of a group of assets are a bequest of the residue of the decedent's estate, or of a share of the residue, and a cash legacy payable out of the general estate.

Example: A decedent bequeathed $100,000 to the surviving spouse. The general estate includes a term for years (valued at $10,000 in determining the value of the gross estate) in an office building, which interest was retained by the decedent under a deed of the building by gift to a son. Accordingly, the value of the specific bequest entered on Schedule M is $90,000.

Life Estate With Power of Appointment in the Surviving Spouse.—A property interest, whether or not in trust, will be treated as passing to the surviving spouse, and will not be treated as a nondeductible terminable interest if: **(a)** the surviving spouse is entitled for life to all of the income from the entire interest; **(b)** the income is payable annually or at more frequent intervals; **(c)** the surviving spouse has the power, exercisable in favor of the surviving spouse or the estate of the surviving spouse, to appoint the entire interest; **(d)** the power is exercisable by the surviving spouse alone and (whether exercisable by will or during life) is exercisable by the surviving spouse in all events; and **(e)** no part of the entire interest is subject to a power in any other person to appoint any part to any person other than the surviving spouse (or the surviving spouse's legal representative or relative if the surviving spouse is disabled. See Rev. Rul. 85-35, 1985-1 C.B. 328). If these five conditions are satisfied only for a specific portion of the entire interest, see the section 2056(b) regulations to determine the amount of the marital deduction.

Life Insurance, Endowment, or Annuity Payments, With Power of Appointment in Surviving Spouse.—A property interest consisting of the entire proceeds under a life insurance, endowment, or annuity contract is treated as passing from the decedent to the surviving spouse, and will not be treated as a nondeductible terminable interest if: **(a)** the surviving spouse is entitled to receive the proceeds in installments, or is entitled to interest on them, with all amounts payable during the life of the spouse, payable only to the surviving spouse; **(b)** the installment or interest payments are payable annually, or more frequently, beginning not later than 13 months after the decedent's death; **(c)** the surviving spouse has the power, exercisable in favor of the surviving spouse or of the estate of the surviving spouse, to appoint all amounts payable under the contract; **(d)** the power is exercisable by the surviving spouse alone and (whether exercisable by will or during life) is exercisable by the surviving spouse in all events; and **(e)** no part of the amount payable under the contract is subject to a power in any other person to appoint any part to any person other than the surviving spouse. If these five conditions are satisfied only for a specific portion of the proceeds, see the section 2056(b) regulations to determine the amount of the marital deduction.

Charitable Remainder Trusts.—An interest in a charitable remainder trust will **not** be treated as a nondeductible terminable interest if:

1. The interest in the trust passes from the decedent to the surviving spouse; and

2. The surviving spouse is the only beneficiary of the trust other than charitable organizations described in section 170(c).

A "charitable remainder trust" is either a charitable remainder annuity trust or a charitable remainder unitrust. (See section 664 for descriptions of these trusts.)

Election To Deduct Qualified Terminable Interests (QTIP)

You may elect to claim a marital deduction for qualified terminable interest property or property interests. You make the QTIP election simply by listing the qualified terminable interest property on Schedule M and deducting its value. You are presumed to have made the QTIP election if you list the property and deduct its value on Schedule M. If you make this election, the surviving spouse's gross estate will include the value of the "qualified terminable interest property." See the instructions for line 6 of General Information for more details. **The election is irrevocable.**

If you file a Form 706 in which you do not make this election, you may not file an amended return to make the election

unless you file the amended return on or before the due date for filing the original Form 706.

The effect of the election is that the property (interest) will be treated as passing to the surviving spouse and will not be treated as a nondeductible terminable interest. All of the other marital deduction requirements must still be satisfied before you may make this election. For example, you may not make this election for property or property interests that are not included in the decedent's gross estate.

Qualified terminable interest property is property **(a)** that passes from the decedent, and **(b)** in which the surviving spouse has a qualifying income interest for life.

The surviving spouse has a *qualifying income interest for life* if the surviving spouse is entitled to all of the income from the property payable annually or at more frequent intervals, or has a usufruct interest for life in the property, and during the surviving spouse's lifetime no person has a power to appoint any part of the property to any person other than the surviving spouse. An annuity is treated as an income interest regardless of whether the property from which the annuity is payable can be separately identified.

The QTIP election may be made for all or any part of a qualified terminable interest property. A partial election must relate to a fractional or percentile share of the property so that the elective part will reflect its proportionate share of the increase or decline in the whole of the property when applying sections 2044 or 2519. Thus, if the interest of the surviving spouse in a trust (or other property in which the spouse has a qualified life estate) is qualified terminable interest property, you may make an election for a part of the trust (or other property) only if the election relates to a defined fraction or percentage of the entire trust (or other property). The fraction or percentage may be defined by means of a formula.

Qualified Domestic Trust Election (QDOT)

The marital deduction is allowed for transfers to a surviving spouse who is not a U.S. citizen only if the property passes to the surviving spouse in a "qualified domestic trust" (QDOT) or if such property is transferred or irrevocably assigned to a QDOT before the decedent's estate tax return is filed.

A QDOT is any trust:

1. That requires at least one trustee to be either an individual who is a citizen of the United States or a domestic corporation;

FEDERAL ESTATE TAX RETURN (FORM 706) ■ 1007

Form 706 (Rev. 7-98)

2. That requires that no distribution of corpus from the trust can be made unless such a trustee has the right to withhold from the distribution the tax imposed on the QDOT;

3. That meets the requirements of any applicable regulations; and

4. For which the executor has made an election on the estate tax return of the decedent.

Note: *For trusts created by an instrument executed before November 5, 1990, paragraphs 1 and 2 above will be treated as met if the trust instrument requires that all trustees be individuals who are citizens of the United States or domestic corporations.*

You make the QDOT election simply by listing the qualified domestic trust or the **entire value** of the trust property on Schedule M and deducting its value. You are presumed to have made the QDOT election if you list the trust or trust property and deduct its value on Schedule M. **Once made, the election is irrevocable.**

If an election is made to deduct qualified domestic trust property under section 2056A(d), the following information should be provided for each qualified domestic trust on an attachment to this schedule:

1. The name and address of every trustee;

2. A description of each transfer passing from the decedent that is the source of the property to be placed in trust; and

3. The employer identification number for the trust.

The election must be made for an entire QDOT trust. In listing a trust for which you are making a QDOT election, unless you specifically identify the trust as not subject to the election, the election will be considered made for the entire trust.

The determination of whether a trust qualifies as a QDOT will be made as of the date the decedent's Form 706 is filed. If, however, judicial proceedings are brought before the Form 706's due date (including extensions) to have the trust revised to meet the QDOT requirements, then the determination will not be made until the court-ordered changes to the trust are made.

Line 1

If property passes to the surviving spouse as the result of a qualified disclaimer, check "Yes" and attach a copy of the written disclaimer required by section 2518(b).

Line 3

Section 2056(b)(7) creates an automatic QTIP election for certain joint and survivor annuities that are includible in the estate under section 2039. To qualify, only the surviving spouse can have the right to receive payments before the death of the surviving spouse.

The executor can elect out of QTIP treatment, however, by checking the "Yes" box on line 3. Once made, the election is irrevocable. If there is more than one such joint and survivor annuity, you are not required to make the election for all of them.

If you make the election out of QTIP treatment by checking "Yes" on line 3, you cannot deduct the amount of the annuity on Schedule M. If you do not make the election out, you must list the joint and survivor annuities on Schedule M.

Listing Property Interests on Schedule M

List each property interest included in the gross estate that passes from the decedent to the surviving spouse and for which a marital deduction is claimed. This includes otherwise nondeductible terminable interest property for which you are making a QTIP election. Number each item in sequence and describe each item in detail. Describe the instrument (including any clause or paragraph number) or provision of law under which each item passed to the surviving spouse. If possible, show where each item appears (number and schedule) on Schedules A through I.

In listing otherwise nondeductible property for which you are making a QTIP election, unless you specifically identify a fractional portion of the trust or other property as not subject to the election, the election will be considered made for all of the trust or other property.

Enter the value of each interest before taking into account the Federal estate tax or any other death tax. The valuation dates used in determining the value of the gross estate apply also on Schedule M.

If Schedule M includes a bequest of the residue or a part of the residue of the decedent's estate, attach a copy of the computation showing how the value of the residue was determined. Include a statement showing:

● The value of all property that is included in the decedent's gross estate (Schedules A through I) but is not a part of the decedent's probate estate, such as lifetime transfers, jointly owned property that passed to the survivor on decedent's death, and the insurance payable to specific beneficiaries.

● The values of all specific and general legacies or devises, with reference to the applicable clause or paragraph of the decedent's will or codicil. (If legacies are made to each member of a class, for example, $1,000 to each of decedent's employees, only the number in each class and the total value of property received by them need be furnished.)

● The date of birth of all persons, the length of whose lives may affect the value of the residuary interest passing to the surviving spouse.

● Any other important information such as that relating to any claim to any part of the estate not arising under the will.

Lines 5a, b, and c.—The total of the values listed on Schedule M must be reduced by the amount of the Federal estate tax, the Federal GST tax, and the amount of state or other death and GST taxes paid out of the property interest involved. If you enter an amount for state or other death or GST taxes on lines 5b or 5c, identify the taxes and attach your computation of them.

Attachments.—If you list property interests passing by the decedent's will on Schedule M, attach a certified copy of the order admitting the will to probate. If, when you file the return, the court of probate jurisdiction has entered any decree interpreting the will or any of its provisions affecting any of the interests listed on Schedule M, or has entered any order of distribution, attach a copy of the decree or order. In addition, the District Director may request other evidence to support the marital deduction claimed.

Page 30

Form 706 (Rev. 7-98)

Estate of:

SCHEDULE O—Charitable, Public, and Similar Gifts and Bequests

	Yes	No
1a If the transfer was made by will, has any action been instituted to have interpreted or to contest the will or any of its provisions affecting the charitable deductions claimed in this schedule? . . . . If "Yes," full details must be submitted with this schedule.		
b According to the information and belief of the person or persons filing this return, is any such action planned? If "Yes," full details must be submitted with this schedule.		
2 Did any property pass to charity as the result of a qualified disclaimer? . . . . If "Yes," attach a copy of the written disclaimer required by section 2518(b).		

Item number	Name and address of beneficiary	Character of institution	Amount
1			

Total from continuation schedules (or additional sheets) attached to this schedule . . . .

3 Total	**3**	
4a Federal estate tax payable out of property interests listed above	**4a**	
b Other death taxes payable out of property interests listed above	**4b**	
c Federal and state GST taxes payable out of property interests listed above	**4c**	
d Add items a, b, and c	**4d**	
5 Net value of property interests listed above (subtract 4d from 3). Also enter on Part 5, Recapitulation, page 3, at item 21.	**5**	

(If more space is needed, attach the continuation schedule from the end of this package or additional sheets of the same size.)
(The instructions to Schedule O are in the separate instructions.)

Schedule O— Page 31

Form 706 (Rev. 7-98)

Estate of:

SCHEDULE P—Credit for Foreign Death Taxes

List all foreign countries to which death taxes have been paid and for which a credit is claimed on this return.

If a credit is claimed for death taxes paid to more than one foreign country, compute the credit for taxes paid to one country on this sheet and attach a separate copy of Schedule P for each of the other countries.

The credit computed on this sheet is for the _____
(Name of death tax or taxes)

_____ imposed in _____
(Name of country)

Credit is computed under the _____
(Insert title of treaty or "statute")

Citizenship (nationality) of decedent at time of death _____

(All amounts and values must be entered in United States money.)

1 Total of estate, inheritance, legacy, and succession taxes imposed in the country named above attributable to property situated in that country, subjected to these taxes, and included in the gross estate (as defined by statute)	
2 Value of the gross estate (adjusted, if necessary, according to the instructions for item 2)	
3 Value of property situated in that country, subjected to death taxes imposed in that country, and included in the gross estate (adjusted, if necessary, according to the instructions for item 3)	
4 Tax imposed by section 2001 reduced by the total credits claimed under sections 2010, 2011, and 2012 (see instructions)	
5 Amount of Federal estate tax attributable to property specified at item 3. (Divide item 3 by item 2 and multiply the result by item 4.)	
6 Credit for death taxes imposed in the country named above (the smaller of item 1 or item 5). Also enter on line 18 of Part 2, Tax Computation	

SCHEDULE Q—Credit for Tax on Prior Transfers

Part 1.—Transferor Information

	Name of transferor	Social security number	IRS office where estate tax return was filed	Date of death
A				
B				
C				

Check here ▶ ☐ if section 2013(f) (special valuation of farm, etc., real property) adjustments to the computation of the credit were made (see page 16 of the instructions).

Part 2.—Computation of Credit (see instructions beginning on page 16)

Item	Transferor			Total A, B, & C
	A	B	C	
1 Transferee's tax as apportioned (from worksheet, (line 7 ÷ line 8) × line 35 for each column) . .				
2 Transferor's tax (from each column of worksheet, line 20)				
3 Maximum amount before percentage requirement (for each column, enter amount from line 1 or 2, whichever is smaller)				
4 Percentage allowed (each column) (see instructions)	%	%	%	
5 Credit allowable (line 3 × line 4 for each column)				
6 TOTAL credit allowable (add columns A, B, and C of line 5). Enter here and on line 19 of Part 2, Tax Computation				

Schedules P and Q— Page 32   (The instructions to Schedules P and Q are in the separate instructions.)

Form 706 (Rev. 7-98)

SCHEDULE R—Generation-Skipping Transfer Tax

Note: *To avoid application of the deemed allocation rules, Form 706 and Schedule R should be filed to allocate the GST exemption to trusts that may later have taxable terminations or distributions under section 2612 even if the form is not required to be filed to report estate or GST tax.*

The GST tax is imposed on taxable transfers of interests in property located **outside the United States** *as well as property located inside the United States.*

See instructions beginning on page 17.

Part 1.—GST Exemption Reconciliation (Section 2631) and Section 2652(a)(3) (Special QTIP) Election

You no longer need to check a box to make a section 2652(a)(3) (special QTIP) election. If you list qualifying property in Part 1, line 9, below, you will be considered to have made this election. See page 19 of the separate instructions for details.

1 Maximum allowable GST exemption	1	$1,000,000
2 Total GST exemption allocated by the decedent against decedent's lifetime transfers	2	
3 Total GST exemption allocated by the executor, using Form 709, against decedent's lifetime transfers	3	
4 GST exemption allocated on line 6 of Schedule R, Part 2	4	
5 GST exemption allocated on line 6 of Schedule R, Part 3	5	
6 Total GST exemption allocated on line 4 of Schedule(s) R-1	6	
7 Total GST exemption allocated to intervivos transfers and direct skips (add lines 2–6)	7	
8 GST exemption available to allocate to trusts and section 2032A interests (subtract line 7 from line 1)	8	

9 Allocation of GST exemption to trusts (as defined for GST tax purposes):

A Name of trust	B Trust's EIN (if any)	C GST exemption allocated on lines 2–6, above (see instructions)	D Additional GST exemption allocated (see instructions)	E Trust's inclusion ratio (optional—see instructions)

9D Total. May not exceed line 8, above	**9D**			

10 GST exemption available to allocate to section 2032A interests received by individual beneficiaries (subtract line 9D from line 8). You must attach special use allocation schedule (see instructions) | **10** |

(The instructions to Schedule R are in the separate instructions.)

Schedule R— Page 33

Form 706 (Rev. 7-98)

Estate of:

Part 2.—Direct Skips Where the Property Interests Transferred Bear the GST Tax on the Direct Skips

Name of skip person	Description of property interest transferred	Estate tax value

1 Total estate tax values of all property interests listed above **1**

2 Estate taxes, state death taxes, and other charges borne by the property interests listed above . **2**

3 GST taxes borne by the property interests listed above but imposed on direct skips other than those shown on this Part 2 (see instructions) **3**

4 Total fixed taxes and other charges (add lines 2 and 3). **4**

5 Total tentative maximum direct skips (subtract line 4 from line 1) **5**

6 GST exemption allocated **6**

7 Subtract line 6 from line 5 . . . . **7**

8 GST tax due (divide line 7 by 2.818182). **8**

9 Enter the amount from line 8 of Schedule R, Part 3 . . . . **9**

10 **Total GST taxes payable by the estate** (add lines 8 and 9). Enter here and on line 22 of the Tax Computation on page 1 . . . . **10**

Schedule R— Page 34

Form 706 (Rev. 7-98)

Estate of:

Part 3.—Direct Skips Where the Property Interests Transferred Do Not Bear the GST Tax on the Direct Skips

Name of skip person	Description of property interest transferred	Estate tax value

1 Total estate tax values of all property interests listed above	1	
2 Estate taxes, state death taxes, and other charges borne by the property interests listed above .	2	
3 GST taxes borne by the property interests listed above but imposed on direct skips other than those shown on this Part 3 (see instructions)	3	
4 Total fixed taxes and other charges (add lines 2 and 3).	4	
5 Total tentative maximum direct skips (subtract line 4 from line 1)	5	
6 GST exemption allocated	6	
7 Subtract line 6 from line 5	7	
8 GST tax due (multiply line 7 by .55). Enter here and on Schedule R, Part 2, line 9	8	

Schedule R— Page 35

SCHEDULE R-1 (Form 706) (Rev. July 1998) Department of the Treasury Internal Revenue Service	**Generation-Skipping Transfer Tax** Direct Skips From a Trust Payment Voucher	OMB No. 1545-0015

Executor: File one copy with Form 706 and send two copies to the fiduciary. Do not pay the tax shown. See the separate instructions.
Fiduciary: See instructions on the following page. Pay the tax shown on line 6.

Name of trust	Trust's EIN

Name and title of fiduciary	Name of decedent

Address of fiduciary (number and street)	Decedent's SSN	Service Center where Form 706 was filed

City, state, and ZIP code	Name of executor

Address of executor (number and street)	City, state, and ZIP code

Date of decedent's death	Filing due date of Schedule R, Form 706 (with extensions)

Part 1.—Computation of the GST Tax on the Direct Skip

Description of property interests subject to the direct skip	Estate tax value

1 Total estate tax value of all property interests listed above	**1**	
2 Estate taxes, state death taxes, and other charges borne by the property interests listed above .	**2**	
3 Tentative maximum direct skip from trust (subtract line 2 from line 1)	**3**	
4 GST exemption allocated	**4**	
5 Subtract line 4 from line 3	**5**	
6 **GST tax due from fiduciary** (divide line 5 by 2.818182) **(See instructions if property will not bear the GST tax.)**	**6**	

Under penalties of perjury, I declare that I have examined this return, including accompanying schedules and statements, and to the best of my knowledge and belief, it is true, correct, and complete.

	Date
Signature(s) of executor(s)	

	Date

	Date
Signature of fiduciary or officer representing fiduciary	

Schedule R-1 (Form 706)— Page 36

Form 706 (Rev. 7-98)

Instructions for the Trustee

Introduction	Schedule R-1 (Form 706) serves as a payment voucher for the Generation-Skipping Transfer (GST) tax imposed on a direct skip from a trust, which you, the trustee of the trust, must pay. The executor completes the Schedule R-1 (Form 706) and gives you 2 copies. File one copy and keep one for your records.
How to pay	You can pay by check or money order. • Make it payable to the "Internal Revenue Service." (DO NOT abbreviate Internal Revenue Service.) • Make the check or money order for the amount on line 6 of Schedule R-1. • Write "GST Tax" and the trust's EIN on the check or money order.
Signature	You must sign the Schedule R-1 in the space provided.
What to mail	Mail your check or money order and the copy of Schedule R-1 that you signed.
Where to mail	Mail to the Service Center shown on Schedule R-1.
When to pay	The GST tax is due and payable 9 months after the decedent's date of death (shown on the Schedule R-1). You will owe interest on any GST tax not paid by that date.
Automatic extension	You have an automatic extension of time to file Schedule R-1 and pay the GST tax. The automatic extension allows you to file and pay by 2 months after the due date (with extensions) for filing the decedent's Schedule R (shown on the Schedule R-1). If you pay the GST tax under the automatic extension, you will be charged interest (but no penalties).
Additional information	For more information, see Code section 2603(a)(2) and the instructions for Form 706, United States Estate (and Generation-Skipping Transfer) Tax Return.

Schedule R-1 (Form 706)— Page 37

Form 706 (Rev. 7-98)

Estate of:

SCHEDULE T.—Qualified Family-Owned Business Interest Deduction

For details on the deduction, including trades and businesses that do not qualify, see page 20 of the separate Instructions for Form 706.

Part 1.—Election

Note: *The executor is deemed to have made the election under section 2057 if he or she files Schedule T and deducts any qualifying business interests from the gross estate.*

Part 2.—General Qualifications

		Yes	No
1	Did the decedent and/or a member of the decedent's family own the business interests listed on line 5 of this schedule for at least 5 of the 8 years immediately preceding the date of the decedent's death? .	☐ Yes	☐ No

2 Were there any periods during the 8-year period preceding the date of the decedent's death during which the decedent or a member of his or her family:

		Yes	No
a	Did not own the business interests listed on this schedule?		
b	Did not materially participate, within the meaning of section 2032A(e)(6), in the operation of the business to which such interests relate?.		

If "Yes" to either of the above, you must attach a statement listing the periods. If applicable, describe whether the exceptions of sections 2032A(b)(4) or (5) are met.

Attach affidavits describing the activities constituting material participation and the identity and relationship to the decedent of the material participants.

3 Check the applicable box(es). The qualified family-owned business interest(s) is:

☐ An interest as a proprietor in a trade or business carried on as a proprietorship.

☐ An interest in an entity, at least 50% of which is owned (directly or indirectly) by the decedent and members of the decedent's family.

☐ An interest in an entity, at least 70% of which is owned (directly or indirectly) by members of 2 families and at least 30% of which is owned (directly or indirectly) by the decedent and members of the decedent's family.

☐ An interest in an entity, at least 90% of which is owned (directly or indirectly) by members of 3 families and at least 30% of which is owned (directly or indirectly) by the decedent and members of the decedent's family.

4 Persons holding interests. Enter the requested information for each party who received any interest in the family-owned business. If any qualified heir is not a U.S. citizen, see the line 4 instructions beginning on page 20 of the separate instructions.

(Each of the qualified heirs receiving an interest in the business must sign the agreement that begins on page 40, and the agreement must be filed with this return.)

	Name	Address
A		
B		
C		
D		
E		
F		
G		
H		

	Identifying number	Relationship to decedent	Value of interest
A			
B			
C			
D			
E			
F			
G			
H			

Schedule T (Form 706)—Page 38

Form 706 (Rev. 7-98)

Part 3.—Adjusted Value of Qualified Family-Owned Business Interests

5 Qualified family-owned business interests reported on this return.
Note: *All property listed on line 5 must also be entered on Schedules A, B, C, E, F, G, or H, as applicable.*

A Schedule and item number from Form 706	B Description of business interest and principal place of business	C Reported value

6 **Total** reported value	**6**	
7 Amount of claims or mortgages deductible under section 2053(a)(3) or (4) (see separate instructions).	**7**	
8a Enter the amount of any indebtedness on qualified residence of the decedent (see separate instructions)	**8a**	
b Enter the amount of any indebtedness used for educational or medical expenses (see separate instructions)	**8b**	
c Enter the amount of any indebtedness other than that listed on line 8a or 8b, but do not enter more than $10,000 (see separate instructions)	**8c**	
d Total (add lines 8a through 8c).	**8d**	
9 Subtract line 8d from line 7	**9**	
10 Adjusted value of qualified family-owned business interests (subtract line 9 from line 6)	**10**	

Part 4.—Qualifying Estate

11 Includible gifts of qualified family-owned business interests (see separate instructions):

a Amount of gifts taken into account under section 2001(b)(1)(B)	**11a**	
b Amount of such gifts excluded under section 2503(b)	**11b**	
c Add lines 11a and 11b	**11c**	
12 Add lines 10 and 11c	**12**	

13 Adjusted gross estate (see separate instructions):

a Amount of gross estate	**13a**	
b Enter the amount from line 7	**13b**	
c Subtract line 13b from line 13a	**13c**	
d Enter the amount from line 11c	**13d**	
e Enter the amount of transfers, if any, to the decedent's spouse	**13e**	
f Enter the amount of other gifts	**13f**	
g Add the amounts on lines 13d, 13e, and 13f	**13g**	
h Enter any amounts from line 13g that are otherwise includible in the gross estate	**13h**	
i Subtract line 13h from line 13g	**13i**	
j Adjusted gross estate (add lines 13c and 13i).	**13j**	
14 Enter one-half of the amount on line 13j	**14**	

Note: *If line 12 does not exceed line 14, stop here; the estate does not qualify for the deduction. Otherwise, complete line 15.*

15 Net value of qualified family-owned business interests you elect to deduct (line 10 reduced by any marital or other deductions)—**DO NOT** enter more than $675,000—(see instructions) (attach schedule)—enter here and on Part 5, Recapitulation, page 3, at item 22 ..... **15**

Schedule T—Page 39

Form 706 (Rev. 7-98)

Part 5.—Agreement to Family-Owned Business Interest Deduction Under Section 2057

Estate of:	Date of Death	Decedent's Social Security Number

There cannot be a valid election unless:
- The agreement is executed by each and every one of the qualified heirs, and
- The agreement is included with the estate tax return when the estate tax return is filed.

We (list all qualified heirs and other persons having an interest in the business required to sign this agreement)

_____ ,

being all the qualified heirs and _____

_____ ,

being all other parties having interests in the business(es) which are deducted under section 2057 of the Internal Revenue Code, do hereby approve of the election made by _____ ,

Executor/Administrator of the estate of _____

pursuant to section 2057 to deduct said interests from the gross estate and do hereby enter into this agreement pursuant to section 2057(h).

The undersigned agree and consent to the application of subsection (f) of section 2057 of the Code with respect to all the qualified family-owned business interests deducted on Schedule T of Form 706, attached to this agreement. More specifically, the undersigned heirs expressly agree and consent to personal liability under subsection (c) of 2032A (as made applicable by section 2057(i)(3)(F) of the Code) for the additional estate tax imposed by that subsection with respect to their respective interests in the above-described business interests in the event of certain early dispositions of the interests or the occurrence of any of the disqualifying acts described in section 2057(f)(1) of the Code. It is understood that if a qualified heir disposes of any deducted interest to any member of his or her family, such member may thereafter be treated as the qualified heir with respect to such interest upon filing a new agreement and any other form required by the Internal Revenue Service.

The undersigned interested parties who are not qualified heirs consent to the collection of any additional estate tax imposed under section 2057(f) of the Code from the deducted interests.

If there is a disposition of any interest which passes or has passed to him or her, each of the undersigned heirs agrees to file the appropriate form and pay any additional estate tax due within 6 months of the disposition or other disqualifying act.

It is understood by all interested parties that this agreement is a condition precedent to the election of the qualified family-owned business deduction under section 2057 of the Code and must be executed by every interested party even though that person may not have received the estate tax benefits or be in possession of such property.

Each of the undersigned understands that by making this election, a lien will be created and recorded pursuant to section 6324B of the Code on the interests referred to in this agreement for the applicable percentage of the adjusted tax differences with respect to the estate as defined in section 2057(f)(2)(C).

As the interested parties, the undersigned designate the following individual as their agent for all dealings with the Internal Revenue Service concerning the continued qualification of the deducted property under section 2057 of the Code and on all issues regarding the special lien under section 6324B. The agent is authorized to act for all the parties with respect to all dealings with the Service on matters affecting the qualified interests described earlier. This authority includes the following:

- To receive confidential information on all matters relating to continued qualification under section 2057 of the deducted interests and on all matters relating to the special lien arising under section 6324B.

- To furnish the Service with any requested information concerning the interests.

- To notify the Service of any disposition or other disqualifying events specified in section 2057(f)(1) of the Code.

- To receive, but not to endorse and collect, checks in payment of any refund of Internal Revenue taxes, penalties, or interest.

- To execute waivers (including offers of waivers) of restrictions on assessment or collection of deficiencies in tax and waivers of notice of disallowance of a claim for credit or refund.

- To execute closing agreements under section 7121.

(continued on next page)

Form 706 (Rev. 7-98)

Part 5.—Agreement to Family-Owned Business Interest Deduction Under Section 2057 (continued)

Estate of:	Date of Death	Decedent's Social Security Number

● Other acts (specify) ▶ _____

By signing this agreement, the agent agrees to provide the Service with any requested information concerning the qualified business interests and to notify the Service of any disposition or other disqualifying events with regard to said interests.

Name of Agent	Signature	Address

The interests to which this agreement relates are listed in Form 706, United States Estate (and Generation-Skipping Transfer) Tax Return, along with their fair market value according to section 2031 (or, if applicable, section 2032A) of the Code. The name, address, social security number, and interest (including the value) of each of the undersigned in this business(es) are as set forth in the attached Schedule T.

IN WITNESS WHEREOF, the undersigned have hereunto set their hands at _____,

this _____ day of _____ .

SIGNATURES OF EACH OF THE QUALIFIED HEIRS:

Signature of qualified heir	Signature of qualified heir
Signature of qualified heir	Signature of qualified heir
Signature of qualified heir	Signature of qualified heir
Signature of qualified heir	Signature of qualified heir
Signature of qualified heir	Signature of qualified heir
Signature of qualified heir	Signature of qualified heir

Signature(s) of other interested parties

Signature(s) of other interested parties

Schedule T Part 5—Page 41

Form 706 (Rev. 7-98)

Estate of:

SCHEDULE U.—Qualified Conservation Easement Exclusion

Part 1.—Election

Note: *The executor is deemed to have made the election under section 2031(c)(6) if he or she files Schedule U and excludes any qualifying conservation easements from the gross estate.*

Part 2.—General Qualifications

1 Describe the land subject to the qualified conservation easement (see separate instructions) _____

2 Did the decedent or a member of the decedent's family own the land described above during the 3-year period ending on the date of the decedent's death? . . . . ☐ Yes ☐ No

3 The land described above is located (check whichever applies) (see separate instructions):
   ☐ In or within 25 miles of an area which, on the date of the decedent's death, is a metropolitan area.
   ☐ In or within 25 miles of an area which, on the date of the decedent's death, is a national park or wilderness area.
   ☐ In or within 10 miles of an area which, on the date of the decedent's death, is an Urban National Forest.

4 Describe the conservation easement with regard to which the exclusion is being claimed (see separate instructions).

Part 3.—Computation of Exclusion

5 Estate tax value of the land subject to the qualified conservation easement (see separate instructions)	5	
6 Date of death value of any easements granted prior to decedent's death and included on line 11 below (see instructions)	6	
7 Add lines 5 and 6	7	
8 Value of retained development rights on the land (see instructions)	8	
9 Subtract line 8 from line 7	9	
10 Multiply line 9 by 30% (.30).	10	
11 Value of qualified conservation easement for which the exclusion is being claimed (see instructions) . . . . **Note:** *If line 11 is less than line 10, continue with line 12. If line 11 is equal to or more than line 10, skip lines 12 through 14, enter ".40" on line 15, and complete the schedule.*	11	
12 Divide line 11 by line 9. Figure to 3 decimal places (e.g., .123) . . *If line 12 is equal to or less than .100, stop here; the estate does not qualify for the conservation easement exclusion.*	12	
13 Subtract line 12 from .300. Enter the answer in hundredths by rounding any thousandths up to the next higher hundredth (i.e., .030 = .03; but .031 = .04).	13	
14 Multiply line 13 by 2	14	
15 Subtract line 14 from .40	15	
16 Deduction under section 2055(f) for the conservation easement (see separate instructions)	16	
17 Amount of indebtedness on the land (see separate instructions)	17	
18 Total reductions in value (add lines 8, 16, and 17)	18	
19 Net value of land (subtract line 18 from line 5)	19	
20 Multiply line 19 by line 15	20	
21 Enter the smaller of line 20 or $100,000. Also enter this amount on item 11, Part 5, Recapitulation, Page 3	21	

Schedule U—Page 42

Form 706 (Rev. 7-98)   (Make copies of this schedule before completing it if you will need more than one schedule.)

Estate of:

CONTINUATION SCHEDULE

Continuation of Schedule _____
(Enter letter of schedule you are continuing.)

Item number	Description For securities, give CUSIP number.	Unit value (Sch. B, E, or G only)	Alternate valuation date	Alternate value	Value at date of death or amount deductible
	TOTAL. (Carry forward to main schedule.)				

See the instructions on the reverse side.

Continuation Schedule— Page 43

Form 706 (Rev. 7-98)

Instructions for Continuation Schedule

When you need to list more assets or deductions than you have room for on one of the main schedules, use the Continuation Schedule on page 43. It provides a uniform format for listing additional assets from Schedules A through I and additional deductions from Schedules J, K, L, M, and O.

Please keep the following points in mind:

● Use a separate Continuation Schedule for each main schedule you are continuing. Do not combine assets or deductions from different schedules on one Continuation Schedule.

● Make copies of the blank schedule before completing it if you expect to need more than one.

● Use as many Continuation Schedules as needed to list all the assets or deductions.

● Enter the letter of the schedule you are continuing in the space at the top of the Continuation Schedule.

● Use the *Unit value* column <u>only</u> if continuing Schedule B, E, or G. For all other schedules, use this space to continue the description.

● Carry the total from the Continuation Schedules forward to the appropriate line on the main schedule.

If continuing	Report	Where on Continuation Schedule
Schedule E, Pt. 2	*Percentage includible*	*Alternate valuation date*
Schedule K	*Amount unpaid to date*	*Alternate valuation date*
Schedule K	*Amount in contest*	*Alternate value*
Schedules J, L, M	*Description of deduction continuation*	*Alternate valuation date* **and** *Alternate value*
Schedule O	*Character of institution*	*Alternate valuation date* **and** *Alternate value*
Schedule O	*Amount of each deduction*	*Amount deductible*

Federal Gift Tax Return
(Form 709)

Form **709**

Department of the Treasury
Internal Revenue Service

United States Gift (and Generation-Skipping Transfer) Tax Return

(Section 6019 of the Internal Revenue Code) (For gifts made after December 31, 1997)

▶ **See separate instructions. For Privacy Act Notice, see the Instructions for Form 1040.**

OMB No. 1545-0020

1998

Part 1—General Information

1 Donor's first name and middle initial	2 Donor's last name	3 Donor's social security number
4 Address (number, street, and apartment number)		5 Legal residence (domicile) (county and state)
6 City, state, and ZIP code		7 Citizenship

		Yes	No
8	If the donor died during the year, check here ▶ ☐ and enter date of death _____ , _____ .		
9	If you received an extension of time to file this Form 709, check here ▶ ☐ and attach the Form 4868, 2688, 2350, or extension letter		
10	Enter the total number of separate donees listed on Schedule A—count each person only once. ▶		
11a	Have you (the donor) previously filed a Form 709 (or 709-A) for any other year? If the answer is "No," do not complete line 11b .		
11b	If the answer to line 11a is "Yes," has your address changed since you last filed Form 709 (or 709-A)?		
12	Gifts by husband or wife to third parties.—Do you consent to have the gifts (including generation-skipping transfers) made by you and by your spouse to third parties during the calendar year considered as made one-half by each of you? (See instructions.) (If the answer is "Yes," the following information must be furnished and your spouse must sign the consent shown below. **If the answer is "No," skip lines 13–18 and go to Schedule A.**)		
13	Name of consenting spouse	14 SSN	
15	Were you married to one another during the entire calendar year? (see instructions)		
16	If the answer to 15 is "No," check whether ☐ married ☐ divorced or ☐ widowed, and give date (see instructions) ▶		
17	Will a gift tax return for this calendar year be filed by your spouse?		
18	**Consent of Spouse**—I consent to have the gifts (and generation-skipping transfers) made by me and by my spouse to third parties during the calendar year considered as made one-half by each of us. We are both aware of the joint and several liability for tax created by the execution of this consent.		

Consenting spouse's signature ▶   Date ▶

Part 2—Tax Computation

1	Enter the amount from Schedule A, Part 3, line 15	1		
2	Enter the amount from Schedule B, line 3	2		
3	Total taxable gifts (add lines 1 and 2)	3		
4	Tax computed on amount on line 3 (see Table for Computing Tax in separate instructions) . . .	4		
5	Tax computed on amount on line 2 (see Table for Computing Tax in separate instructions) . . .	5		
6	Balance (subtract line 5 from line 4)	6		
7	Maximum unified credit (nonresident aliens, see instructions)	7	202,050	00
8	Enter the unified credit against tax allowable for all prior periods (from Sch. B, line 1, col. C) . .	8		
9	Balance (subtract line 8 from line 7)	9		
10	Enter 20% (.20) of the amount allowed as a specific exemption for gifts made after September 8, 1976, and before January 1, 1977 (see instructions)	10		
11	Balance (subtract line 10 from line 9)	11		
12	Unified credit (enter the smaller of line 6 or line 11)	12		
13	Credit for foreign gift taxes (see instructions)	13		
14	Total credits (add lines 12 and 13)	14		
15	Balance (subtract line 14 from line 6) (do not enter less than zero)	15		
16	Generation-skipping transfer taxes (from Schedule C, Part 3, col. H, Total)	16		
17	Total tax (add lines 15 and 16)	17		
18	Gift and generation-skipping transfer taxes prepaid with extension of time to file	18		
19	If line 18 is less than line 17, enter BALANCE DUE (see instructions)	19		
20	If line 18 is greater than line 17, enter AMOUNT TO BE REFUNDED	20		

Under penalties of perjury, I declare that I have examined this return, including any accompanying schedules and statements, and to the best of my knowledge and belief it is true, correct, and complete. Declaration of preparer (other than donor) is based on all information of which preparer has any knowledge.

Donor's signature ▶   Date ▶

Preparer's signature
(other than donor) ▶   Date ▶

Preparer's address
(other than donor) ▶

Attach check or money order here.

For Paperwork Reduction Act Notice, see page 8 of the separate instructions for this form.   Cat. No. 16783M   Form **709** (1998)

Form 709 (1998)　　　　　　　　　　　　　　　　　　　　　　　　　　　　　　　　　Page **2**

SCHEDULE A　　Computation of Taxable Gifts

A　Does the value of any item listed on Schedule A reflect any valuation discount? If the answer is "Yes," see instructions　.　. Yes ☐　No ☐

B　☐　◄ Check here if you elect under section 529(c)(2)(B) to treat any transfers made this year to a qualified state tuition program as made ratably over a 5-year period beginning this year. See instructions. Attach explanation.

Part 1—Gifts Subject Only to Gift Tax. *Gifts less political organization, medical, and educational exclusions—see instructions*

A Item number	B <ul><li>Donee's name and address</li><li>Relationship to donor (if any)</li><li>Description of gift</li><li>If the gift was made by means of a trust, enter trust's identifying number and attach a copy of the trust instrument</li><li>If the gift was of securities, give CUSIP number</li></ul>	C Donor's adjusted basis of gift	D Date of gift	E Value at date of gift
1				

Total of Part 1 (add amounts from Part 1, column E)　.　.　.　.　.　.　.　.　.　.　.　►

Part 2—Gifts That are Direct Skips and are Subject to Both Gift Tax and Generation-Skipping Transfer Tax. You must list the gifts in chronological order. *Gifts less political organization, medical, and educational exclusions—see instructions. (Also list here direct skips that are subject only to the GST tax at this time as the result of the termination of an "estate tax inclusion period." See instructions.)*

A Item number	B <ul><li>Donee's name and address</li><li>Relationship to donor (if any)</li><li>Description of gift</li><li>If the gift was made by means of a trust, enter trust's identifying number and attach a copy of the trust instrument</li><li>If the gift was of securities, give CUSIP number</li></ul>	C Donor's adjusted basis of gift	D Date of gift	E Value at date of gift
1				

Total of Part 2 (add amounts from Part 2, column E)　.　.　.　.　.　.　.　.　.　.　.　.　►

Part 3—Taxable Gift Reconciliation

1	Total value of gifts of donor (add totals from column E of Parts 1 and 2)　.　.　.　.　.　.　.　.	1	
2	One-half of items _____attributable to spouse (see instructions)	2	
3	Balance (subtract line 2 from line 1)　.　.　.　.　.　.　.　.　.　.　.　.　.　.	3	
4	Gifts of spouse to be included (from Schedule A, Part 3, line 2 of spouse's return—see instructions) . .	4	
	If any of the gifts included on this line are also subject to the generation-skipping transfer tax, check here ► ☐　and enter those gifts also on Schedule C, Part 1.		
5	Total gifts (add lines 3 and 4)　.　.　.　.　.　.　.　.　.　.　.　.　.　.　.	5	
6	Total annual exclusions for gifts listed on Schedule A (including line 4, above) (see instructions)　.　.　.	6	
7	Total included amount of gifts (subtract line 6 from line 5)　.　.　.　.　.　.　.　.　.	7	

Deductions (see instructions)

8	Gifts of interests to spouse for which a marital deduction will be claimed, based on items _____ of Schedule A　.　.　.　.　.　.	8		
9	Exclusions attributable to gifts on line 8　.　.　.　.　.　.　.　.　.　.	9		
10	Marital deduction—subtract line 9 from line 8　.　.　.　.　.　.　.　.　.	10		
11	Charitable deduction, based on items _____less exclusions　.　.	11		
12	Total deductions—add lines 10 and 11　.　.　.　.　.　.　.　.　.　.　.　.		12	
13	Subtract line 12 from line 7　.　.　.　.　.　.　.　.　.　.　.　.　.　.　.		13	
14	Generation-skipping transfer taxes payable with this Form 709 (from Schedule C, Part 3, col. H, Total)		14	
15	Taxable gifts (add lines 13 and 14). Enter here and on line 1 of the Tax Computation on page 1　.　.　.		15	

(If more space is needed, attach additional sheets of same size.)

SCHEDULE A   **Computation of Taxable Gifts** *(continued)*

16 Terminable Interest (QTIP) Marital Deduction. (See instructions for line 8 of Schedule A.)

If a trust (or other property) meets the requirements of qualified terminable interest property under section 2523(f), and

 a. The trust (or other property) is listed on Schedule A, and

 b. The value of the trust (or other property) is entered in whole or in part as a deduction on line 8, Part 3 of Schedule A,

then the donor shall be deemed to have made an election to have such trust (or other property) treated as qualified terminable interest property under section 2523(f).

 If less than the entire value of the trust (or other property) that the donor has included in Part 1 of Schedule A is entered as a deduction on line 8, the donor shall be considered to have made an election only as to a fraction of the trust (or other property). The numerator of this fraction is equal to the amount of the trust (or other property) deducted on line 10 of Part 3, Schedule A. The denominator is equal to the total value of the trust (or other property) listed in Part 1 of Schedule A.

 If you make the QTIP election (see instructions for line 8 of Schedule A), the terminable interest property involved will be included in your spouse's gross estate upon his or her death (section 2044). If your spouse disposes (by gift or otherwise) of all or part of the qualifying life income interest, he or she will be considered to have made a transfer of the entire property that is subject to the gift tax (see Transfer of Certain Life Estates on page 3 of the instructions).

17 Election Out of QTIP Treatment of Annuities

☐ ◀ Check here if you elect under section 2523(f)(6) **NOT** to treat as qualified terminable interest property any joint and survivor annuities that are reported on Schedule A and would otherwise be treated as qualified terminable interest property under section 2523(f). (See instructions.) Enter the item numbers (from Schedule A) for the annuities for which you are making this election ▶

SCHEDULE B   **Gifts From Prior Periods**

If you answered "Yes" on line 11a of page 1, Part 1, see the instructions for completing Schedule B. If you answered "No," skip to the Tax Computation on page 1 (or Schedule C, if applicable).

A Calendar year or calendar quarter (see instructions)	B Internal Revenue office where prior return was filed	C Amount of unified credit against gift tax for periods after December 31, 1976	D Amount of specific exemption for prior periods ending before January 1, 1977	E Amount of taxable gifts

1 Totals for prior periods (without adjustment for reduced specific exemption) **1**			
2 Amount, if any, by which total specific exemption, line 1, column D, is more than $30,000 . . . . . **2**			
3 Total amount of taxable gifts for prior periods (add amount, column E, line 1, and amount, if any, on line 2). (Enter here and on line 2 of the Tax Computation on page 1.) **3**			

(If more space is needed, attach additional sheets of same size.)

Form 709 (1998)

SCHEDULE C | **Computation of Generation-Skipping Transfer Tax**

Note: Inter vivos direct skips that are completely excluded by the GST exemption must still be fully reported (including value and exemptions claimed) on Schedule C.

Part 1—Generation-Skipping Transfers

A Item No. (from Schedule A, Part 2, col. A)	B Value (from Schedule A, Part 2, col. E)	C Split Gifts (enter ½ of col. B) (see instructions)	D Subtract col. C from col. B	E Nontaxable portion of transfer	F Net Transfer (subtract col. E from col. D)
1					
2					
3					
4					
5					
6					

If you elected gift splitting and your spouse was required to file a separate Form 709 (see the instructions for "Split Gifts"), you must enter all of the gifts shown on Schedule A, Part 2, of your spouse's Form 709 here. In column C, enter the item number of each gift in the order it appears in column A of your spouse's Schedule A, Part 2. We have preprinted the prefix "S-" to distinguish your spouse's item numbers from your own when you complete column A of Schedule C, Part 3. In column D, for each gift, enter the amount reported in column C, Schedule C, Part 1, of your spouse's Form 709.	Split gifts from spouse's Form 709 (enter item number)	Value included from spouse's Form 709	Nontaxable portion of transfer	Net transfer (subtract col. E from col. D)
	S-			
	S-			
	S-			
	S-			
	S-			
	S-			
	S-			
	S-			

Part 2—GST Exemption Reconciliation (Section 2631) and Section 2652(a)(3) Election

Check box ► ☐ if you are making a section 2652(a)(3) (special QTIP) election (see instructions)

Enter the item numbers (from Schedule A) of the gifts for which you are making this election ► _____

1	Maximum allowable exemption	**1**	$1,000,000
2	Total exemption used for periods before filing this return	**2**	
3	Exemption available for this return (subtract line 2 from line 1)	**3**	
4	Exemption claimed on this return (from Part 3, col. C total, below)	**4**	
5	Exemption allocated to transfers not shown on Part 3, below. **You must attach a Notice of Allocation. (See instructions.)**	**5**	
6	Add lines 4 and 5	**6**	
7	Exemption available for future transfers (subtract line 6 from line 3)	**7**	

Part 3—Tax Computation

A Item No. (from Schedule C, Part 1)	B Net transfer (from Schedule C, Part 1, col. F)	C GST Exemption Allocated	D Divide col. C by col. B	E Inclusion Ratio (subtract col. D from 1.000)	F Maximum Estate Tax Rate	G Applicable Rate (multiply col. E by col. F)	H Generation-Skipping Transfer Tax (multiply col. B by col. G)
1					55% (.55)		
2					55% (.55)		
3					55% (.55)		
4					55% (.55)		
5					55% (.55)		
6					55% (.55)		
					55% (.55)		
					55% (.55)		
					55% (.55)		
					55% (.55)		

Total exemption claimed. Enter here and on line 4, Part 2, above. May not exceed line 3, Part 2, above . . . . . .

Total generation-skipping transfer tax. Enter here, on line 14 of Schedule A, Part 3, and on line 16 of the Tax Computation on page 1 . . . .

(If more space is needed, attach additional sheets of same size.) ✪

Federal Fiduciary Income Tax Return

(Form 1041)

Form **1041**

Department of the Treasury—Internal Revenue Service

U.S. Income Tax Return for Estates and Trusts

1998

For calendar year 1998 or fiscal year beginning _____ , 1998, and ending _____ , 19 ___

OMB No. 1545-0092

A Type of entity:	Name of estate or trust (If a grantor type trust, see page 8 of the instructions.)	**C** Employer identification number
☐ Decedent's estate		
☐ Simple trust		**D** Date entity created
☐ Complex trust		
☐ Grantor type trust	Name and title of fiduciary	**E** Nonexempt charitable and split-interest trusts, check applicable boxes (see page 10 of the instructions):
☐ Bankruptcy estate–Ch. 7		
☐ Bankruptcy estate–Ch. 11	Number, street, and room or suite no. (If a P.O. box, see page 8 of the instructions.)	
☐ Pooled income fund		☐ Described in section 4947(a)(1)
B Number of Schedules K-1 attached (see instructions) ▶	City or town, state, and ZIP code	☐ Not a private foundation
		☐ Described in section 4947(a)(2)

F Check applicable boxes: ☐ Initial return ☐ Final return ☐ Amended return ☐ Change in fiduciary's name ☐ Change in fiduciary's address

G Pooled mortgage account (see page 10 of the instructions): ☐ Bought ☐ Sold Date: _____

Income

1	Interest income	1
2	Ordinary dividends	2
3	Business income or (loss) (attach Schedule C or C-EZ (Form 1040))	3
4	Capital gain or (loss) (attach Schedule D (Form 1041))	4
5	Rents, royalties, partnerships, other estates and trusts, etc. (attach Schedule E (Form 1040))	5
6	Farm income or (loss) (attach Schedule F (Form 1040))	6
7	Ordinary gain or (loss) (attach Form 4797)	7
8	Other income. List type and amount _____	8
9	**Total income.** Combine lines 1 through 8 ▶	9

Deductions

10	Interest. Check if Form 4952 is attached ▶ ☐	10
11	Taxes	11
12	Fiduciary fees	12
13	Charitable deduction (from Schedule A, line 7)	13
14	Attorney, accountant, and return preparer fees	14
15a	Other deductions NOT subject to the 2% floor (attach schedule)	15a
b	Allowable miscellaneous itemized deductions subject to the 2% floor	15b
16	**Total.** Add lines 10 through 15b	16
17	Adjusted total income or (loss). Subtract line 16 from line 9. Enter here and on Schedule B, line 1 ▶	17
18	Income distribution deduction (from Schedule B, line 15) (attach Schedules K-1 (Form 1041))	18
19	Estate tax deduction (including certain generation-skipping taxes) (attach computation)	19
20	Exemption	20
21	**Total deductions.** Add lines 18 through 20 ▶	21

Tax and Payments

22	Taxable income. Subtract line 21 from line 17. If a loss, see page 14 of the instructions	22
23	**Total tax** (from Schedule G, line 8)	23
24	**Payments: a** 1998 estimated tax payments and amount applied from 1997 return	24a
b	Estimated tax payments allocated to beneficiaries (from Form 1041-T)	24b
c	Subtract line 24b from line 24a	24c
d	Tax paid with extension of time to file: ☐ Form 2758 ☐ Form 8736 ☐ Form 8800	24d
e	Federal income tax withheld. If any is from Form(s) 1099, check ▶ ☐	24e
	Other payments: **f** Form 2439 _____ ; **g** Form 4136 _____ ; Total ▶	24h
25	**Total payments.** Add lines 24c through 24e, and 24h ▶	25
26	Estimated tax penalty (see page 15 of the instructions)	26
27	**Tax due.** If line 25 is smaller than the total of lines 23 and 26, enter amount owed	27
28	**Overpayment.** If line 25 is larger than the total of lines 23 and 26, enter amount overpaid	28
29	Amount of line 28 to be: **a** Credited to 1999 estimated tax ▶ _____ ; **b** Refunded ▶	29

Please Sign Here

Under penalties of perjury, I declare that I have examined this return, including accompanying schedules and statements, and to the best of my knowledge and belief, it is true, correct, and complete. Declaration of preparer (other than fiduciary) is based on all information of which preparer has any knowledge.

▶ _____ Signature of fiduciary or officer representing fiduciary   Date

EIN of fiduciary if a financial institution (see page 5 of the instructions)

Paid Preparer's Use Only

Preparer's signature ▶	Date	Check if self-employed ▶ ☐	Preparer's social security no.
Firm's name (or yours if self-employed) and address ▶		EIN ▶	
		ZIP code ▶	

For Paperwork Reduction Act Notice, see the separate instructions.

Cat. No. 11370H

Form **1041** (1998)

FEDERAL FIDUCIARY INCOME TAX RETURN (FORM 1041) ■ 1031

Form 1041 (1998)   Page **2**

Schedule A   **Charitable Deduction.** Do not complete for a simple trust or a pooled income fund.

1	Amounts paid or permanently set aside for charitable purposes from gross income (see page 15)	1
2	Tax-exempt income allocable to charitable contributions (see page 16 of the instructions) . .	2
3	Subtract line 2 from line 1	3
4	Capital gains for the tax year allocated to corpus and paid or permanently set aside for charitable purposes	4
5	Add lines 3 and 4	5
6	Section 1202 exclusion allocable to capital gains paid or permanently set aside for charitable purposes (see page 16 of the instructions)	6
7	**Charitable deduction.** Subtract line 6 from 5. Enter here and on page 1, line 13	7

Schedule B   **Income Distribution Deduction**

1	Adjusted total income (from page 1, line 17) (see page 16 of the instructions)	1
2	Adjusted tax-exempt interest	2
3	Total net gain from Schedule D (Form 1041), line 16, column (1) (see page 16 of the instructions)	3
4	Enter amount from Schedule A, line 4 (reduced by any allocable section 1202 exclusion) . .	4
5	Capital gains for the tax year included on Schedule A, line 1 (see page 16 of the instructions)	5
6	Enter any gain from page 1, line 4, as a negative number. If page 1, line 4, is a loss, enter the loss as a positive number	6
7	**Distributable net income (DNI).** Combine lines 1 through 6. If zero or less, enter -0-. . . .	7
8	If a complex trust, enter accounting income for the tax year as determined under the governing instrument and applicable local law 8	
9	Income required to be distributed currently	9
10	Other amounts paid, credited, or otherwise required to be distributed	10
11	Total distributions. Add lines 9 and 10. If greater than line 8, see page 17 of the instructions	11
12	Enter the amount of tax-exempt income included on line 11	12
13	Tentative income distribution deduction. Subtract line 12 from line 11	13
14	Tentative income distribution deduction. Subtract line 2 from line 7. If zero or less, enter -0-	14
15	**Income distribution deduction.** Enter the smaller of line 13 or line 14 here and on page 1, line 18	15

Schedule G   **Tax Computation** (see page 17 of the instructions)

1	**Tax: a** ☐ Tax rate schedule or ☐ Schedule D (Form 1041) . . 1a	
	b Tax on lump-sum distributions (attach Form 4972). . . . 1b	
	c Total. Add lines 1a and 1b. . . . . ▶ 1c	
2a	Foreign tax credit (attach Form 1116) 2a	
b	Check: ☐ Nonconventional source fuel credit ☐ Form 8834 . . . 2b	
c	General business credit. Enter here and check which forms are attached: ☐ Form 3800 or ☐ Forms (specify) ▶ _____ 2c	
d	Credit for prior year minimum tax (attach Form 8801) 2d	
3	**Total credits.** Add lines 2a through 2d . . . . ▶	3
4	Subtract line 3 from line 1c	4
5	Recapture taxes. Check if from: ☐ Form 4255 ☐ Form 8611.	5
6	Alternative minimum tax (from Schedule I, line 39).	6
7	Household employment taxes. Attach Schedule H (Form 1040)	7
8	**Total tax.** Add lines 4 through 7. Enter here and on page 1, line 23 . . . . ▶	8

Other Information   **Yes** | **No**

1   Did the estate or trust receive tax-exempt income? If "Yes," attach a computation of the allocation of expenses. Enter the amount of tax-exempt interest income and exempt-interest dividends ▶ $ _____

2   Did the estate or trust receive all or any part of the earnings (salary, wages, and other compensation) of any individual by reason of a contract assignment or similar arrangement? . . . .

3   At any time during calendar year 1998, did the estate or trust have an interest in or a signature or other authority over a bank, securities, or other financial account in a foreign country? See page 19 of the instructions for exceptions and filing requirements for Form TD F 90-22.1. If "Yes," enter the name of the foreign country
▶ _____

4   During the tax year, did the estate or trust receive a distribution from, or was it the grantor of, or transferor to, a foreign trust? If "Yes," the estate or trust may have to file Form 3520. See page 19 of the instructions . . . .

5   Did the estate or trust receive, or pay, any seller-financed mortgage interest? If "Yes," see page 19 for required attachment

6   If this is an estate or a complex trust making the section 663(b) election, check here (see page 19). . ▶ ☐

7   To make a section 643(e)(3) election, attach Schedule D (Form 1041), and check here (see page 19). ▶ ☐

8   If the decedent's estate has been open for more than 2 years, attach an explanation for the delay in closing the estate, and check here ▶ ☐

9   Are any present or future trust beneficiaries skip persons? See page 19 of the instructions . . . .

Form 1041 (1998)   Page **3**

Schedule I	Alternative Minimum Tax (see pages 19 through 24 of the instructions)

Part I—Estate's or Trust's Share of Alternative Minimum Taxable Income

1	Adjusted total income or (loss) (from page 1, line 17)	1	
2	Net operating loss deduction. Enter as a positive amount	2	
3	Add lines 1 and 2	3	
4	**Adjustments and tax preference items:**		
a	Interest	4a	
b	Taxes	4b	
c	Miscellaneous itemized deductions (from page 1, line 15b) . . .	4c	
d	Refund of taxes	4d ( )	
e	Depreciation of property placed in service after 1986	4e	
f	Circulation and research and experimental expenditures	4f	
g	Mining exploration and development costs	4g	
h	Long-term contracts entered into after February 28, 1986 . . .	4h	
i	Amortization of pollution control facilities	4i	
j	Installment sales of certain property	4j	
k	Adjusted gain or loss (including incentive stock options) . . .	4k	
l	Certain loss limitations	4l	
m	Tax shelter farm activities	4m	
n	Passive activities	4n	
o	Beneficiaries of other trusts or decedent's estates	4o	
p	Tax-exempt interest from specified private activity bonds . . .	4p	
q	Depletion	4q	
r	Accelerated depreciation of real property placed in service before 1987	4r	
s	Accelerated depreciation of leased personal property placed in service before 1987	4s	
t	Intangible drilling costs	4t	
u	Other adjustments	4u	
5	Combine lines 4a through 4u	5	
6	Add lines 3 and 5	6	
7	Alternative tax net operating loss deduction (see page 23 of the instructions for limitations) .	7	
8	Adjusted alternative minimum taxable income. Subtract line 7 from line 6. Enter here and on line 13	8	
	Note: *Complete Part II below before going to line 9.*		
9	Income distribution deduction from line 27 below	9	
10	Estate tax deduction (from page 1, line 19)	10	
11	Add lines 9 and 10	11	
12	Estate's or trust's share of alternative minimum taxable income. Subtract line 11 from line 8	12	
	If line 12 is:		

- $22,500 or less, stop here and enter -0- on Schedule G, line 6. The estate or trust is not liable for the alternative minimum tax.
- Over $22,500, but less than $165,000, go to line 28.
- $165,000 or more, enter the amount from line 12 on line 34 and go to line 35.

Part II—Income Distribution Deduction on a Minimum Tax Basis

13	Adjusted alternative minimum taxable income (from line 8)	13	
14	Adjusted tax-exempt interest (other than amounts included on line 4p)	14	
15	Total net gain from Schedule D (Form 1041), line 16, column (1). If a loss, enter -0- . . .	15	
16	Capital gains for the tax year allocated to corpus and paid or permanently set aside for charitable purposes (from Schedule A, line 4) .	16	
17	Capital gains paid or permanently set aside for charitable purposes from gross income (see page 23 of the instructions) .	17	
18	Capital gains computed on a minimum tax basis included on line 8	18 ( )	
19	Capital losses computed on a minimum tax basis included on line 8. Enter as a positive amount	19	
20	Distributable net alternative minimum taxable income (DNAMTI). Combine lines 13 through 19. If zero or less, enter -0-	20	
21	Income required to be distributed currently (from Schedule B, line 9)	21	
22	Other amounts paid, credited, or otherwise required to be distributed (from Schedule B, line 10)	22	
23	Total distributions. Add lines 21 and 22	23	
24	Tax-exempt income included on line 23 (other than amounts included on line 4p)	24	
25	Tentative income distribution deduction on a minimum tax basis. Subtract line 24 from line 23 .	25	
26	Tentative income distribution deduction on a minimum tax basis. Subtract line 14 from line 20. If zero or less, enter -0-	26	
27	**Income distribution deduction on a minimum tax basis.** Enter the smaller of line 25 or line 26. Enter here and on line 9	27	

FEDERAL FIDUCIARY INCOME TAX RETURN (FORM 1041) ■ 1033

Part III—Alternative Minimum Tax

28	Exemption amount			**28**	$22,500
29	Enter the amount from line 12	**29**			
30	Phase-out of exemption amount	**30**	$75,000		
31	Subtract line 30 from line 29. If zero or less, enter -0-	**31**			
32	Multiply line 31 by 25% (.25)			**32**	
33	Subtract line 32 from line 28. If zero or less, enter -0-			**33**	
34	Subtract line 33 from line 29			**34**	
35	If the estate or trust completed Schedule D (Form 1041) and has an amount on line 24 or 26 (or would have had an amount on either line if Part V had been completed) (as refigured for the AMT, if necessary), go to Part IV below to figure line 35. **All others:** If line 34 is— • $175,000 or less, multiply line 34 by 26% (.26). • Over $175,000, multiply line 34 by 28% (.28) and subtract $3,500 from the result			**35**	
36	Alternative minimum foreign tax credit (see page 23 of instructions)			**36**	
37	Tentative minimum tax. Subtract line 36 from line 35			**37**	
38	Enter the tax from Schedule G, line 1a (minus any foreign tax credit from Schedule G, line 2a)			**38**	
39	**Alternative minimum tax.** Subtract line 38 from line 37. If zero or less, enter -0-. Enter here and on Schedule G, line 6			**39**	

Part IV—Line 35 Computation Using Maximum Capital Gains Rates

Caution: *If the estate or trust did not complete Part V of Schedule D (Form 1041), complete lines 19 through 26 of Schedule D (as refigured for the AMT, if necessary) before completing this part.*

40	Enter the amount from line 34			**40**	
41	Enter the amount from Schedule D (Form 1041), line 26 (as refigured for AMT, if necessary)	**41**			
42	Enter the amount from Schedule D (Form 1041), line 24 (as refigured for AMT, if necessary)	**42**			
43	Add lines 41 and 42. If zero or less, enter -0-	**43**			
44	Enter the amount from Schedule D (Form 1041), line 21 (as refigured for AMT, if necessary)	**44**			
45	Enter the **smaller** of line 43 or line 44			**45**	
46	Subtract line 45 from line 40. If zero or less, enter -0-			**46**	
47	If line 46 is $175,000 or less, multiply line 46 by 26% (.26). Otherwise, multiply line 46 by 28% (.28) and subtract $3,500 from the result ▶			**47**	
48	Enter the amount from Schedule D (Form 1041), line 35 (as figured for the regular tax)			**48**	
49	Enter the **smallest** of line 40, line 41, or line 48			**49**	
50	Multiply line 49 by 10% (.10) ▶			**50**	
51	Enter the **smaller** of line 40 or line 41			**51**	
52	Enter the amount from line 49			**52**	
53	Subtract line 52 from line 51. If zero or less, enter -0-			**53**	
54	Multiply line 53 by 20% (.20) ▶			**54**	
55	Enter the amount from line 40			**55**	
56	Add lines 46, 49, and 53			**56**	
57	Subtract line 56 from line 55			**57**	
58	Multiply line 57 by 25% (.25) ▶			**58**	
59	Add lines 47, 50, 54, and 58			**59**	
60	If line 40 is $175,000 or less, multiply line 40 by 26% (.26). Otherwise, multiply line 40 by 28% (.28) and subtract $3,500 from the result			**60**	
61	Enter the **smaller** of line 59 or line 60 here and on line 35 ▶			**61**	

SCHEDULE D (Form 1041)	Capital Gains and Losses	OMB No. 1545-0092
Department of the Treasury Internal Revenue Service	▶ Attach to Form 1041 (or Form 5227). See the separate instructions for Form 1041 (or Form 5227).	1998

Name of estate or trust	Employer identification number

Note: *Form 5227 filers need to complete ONLY Parts I and II.*

Part I — Short-Term Capital Gains and Losses—Assets Held One Year or Less

(a) Description of property (Example, 100 shares 7% preferred of "Z" Co.)	(b) Date acquired (mo., day, yr.)	(c) Date sold (mo., day, yr.)	(d) Sales price	(e) Cost or other basis (see page 26)	(f) GAIN or (LOSS) (col. (d) less col. (e))	
1						

2 Short-term capital gain or (loss) from Forms 4684, 6252, 6781, and 8824	**2**		
3 Net short-term gain or (loss) from partnerships, S corporations, and other estates or trusts	**3**		
4 Short-term capital loss carryover. Enter the amount, if any, from line 9 of the 1997 Capital Loss Carryover Worksheet	**4** (	)	
5 **Net short-term gain or (loss).** Combine lines 1 through 4 in column (f). Enter here and on line 14 below ▶	**5**		

Part II — Long-Term Capital Gains and Losses—Assets Held More Than One Year

(a) Description of property (Example, 100 shares 7% preferred of "Z" Co.)	(b) Date acquired (mo., day, yr.)	(c) Date sold (mo., day, yr.)	(d) Sales price	(e) Cost or other basis (see page 26)	(f) GAIN or (LOSS) (col. (d) less col. (e))	(g) 28% RATE GAIN or (LOSS) *(see instr. below)
6						

7 Long-term capital gain or (loss) from Forms 2439, 4684, 6252, 6781, and 8824	**7**			
8 Net long-term gain or (loss) from partnerships, S corporations, and other estates or trusts	**8**			
9 Capital gain distributions	**9**			
10 Gain from Form 4797, Part I	**10**			
11 Long-term capital loss carryover. Enter in both columns (f) and (g) the amount, if any, from line 14, of the 1997 Capital Loss Carryover Worksheet	**11** (	) (	)
12 Combine lines 6 through 11 in column (g)	**12**			
13 **Net long-term gain or (loss).** Combine lines 6 through 11 in column (f). Enter here and on line 15 below ▶	**13**			

*28% Rate Gain or (Loss) includes **all** "collectibles gains and losses" (as defined on page 27 of the instructions) and up to 50% of the eligible gain on qualified small business stock (see page 25 of the instructions).

Part III — Summary of Parts I and II

		(1) Beneficiaries' (see page 27)	(2) Estate's or trust's	(3) Total
14 **Net short-term gain or (loss)** (from line 5 above)	**14**			
15 **Net long-term gain or (loss):**				
a 28% rate gain or (loss) (from line 12 above)	**15a**			
b Unrecaptured section 1250 gain (see worksheet on page 26)	**15b**			
c Total for year (from line 13 above)	**15c**			
16 **Total net gain or (loss).** Combine lines 14 and 15c ▶	**16**			

Note: *If line 16, column (3), is a net gain, enter the gain on Form 1041, line 4. If lines 15c and 16, column (2) are net gains, go to Part V, and DO NOT complete Part IV. If line 16, column (3), is a net loss, complete Part IV and the **Capital Loss Carryover Worksheet**, as necessary.*

For Paperwork Reduction Act Notice, see the Instructions for Form 1041.   Cat. No. 11376V   **Schedule D (Form 1041) 1998**

Part IV **Capital Loss Limitation**

17 Enter here and enter as a (loss) on Form 1041, line 4, the **smaller** of:
  a The loss on line 16, column (3); **or**
  b $3,000 . . . . **17** (   )
If the loss on line 16, column (3) is more than $3,000, OR if Form 1041, page 1, line 22, is a loss, complete the **Capital Loss Carryover Worksheet** on page 27 of the instructions to determine your capital loss carryover.

Part V **Tax Computation Using Maximum Capital Gains Rates** (Complete this part **only** if both lines 15c and 16 in column (2) are gains, and Form 1041, line 22 is more than zero.)

18	Enter taxable income from Form 1041, line 22	**18**
19	Enter the **smaller** of line 15c or 16 in column (2) **19**	
20	If you are filing Form 4952, enter the amount from Form 4952, line 4e . **20**	
21	Subtract line 20 from line 19. If zero or less, enter -0- **21**	
22	Combine lines 14 and 15a, column (2). If zero or less, enter -0- . . . **22**	
23	Enter the **smaller** of line 15a, column (2), or line 22, but not less than zero **23**	
24	Enter the amount from line 15b, column (2). **24**	
25	Add lines 23 and 24 . . . . **25**	
26	Subtract line 25 from line 21. If zero or less, enter -0-	**26**
27	Subtract line 26 from line 18. If zero or less, enter -0-	**27**
28	Enter the **smaller** of line 18 or $1,700	**28**
29	Enter the **smaller** of line 27 or line 28	**29**
30	Subtract line 21 from line 18. If zero or less, enter -0-	**30**
31	Enter the **larger** of line 29 or line 30	**31**
32	Tax on amount on line 31 from the 1998 Tax Rate Schedule . . . . . ▶	**32**
33	Enter the amount from line 28	**33**
34	Enter the amount from line 27	**34**
35	Subtract line 34 from line 33. If zero or less, enter -0-	**35**
36	Multiply line 35 by 10% (.10) . . . . ▶	**36**
37	Enter the **smaller** of line 18 or line 26	**37**
38	Enter the amount from line 35	**38**
39	Subtract line 38 from line 37. If zero or less, enter -0-	**39**
40	Multiply line 39 by 20% (.20) . . . . ▶	**40**
41	Enter the **smaller** of line 21 or line 24	**41**
42	Add lines 21 and 31 . . . . **42**	
43	Enter the amount from line 18 . . . . . . **43**	
44	Subtract line 43 from line 42. If zero or less, enter -0-	**44**
45	Subtract line 44 from line 41. If zero or less, enter -0-	**45**
46	Multiply line 45 by 25% (.25) . . . . ▶	**46**
47	Enter the amount from line 18	**47**
48	Add lines 31, 35, 39, and 45	**48**
49	Subtract line 48 from line 47	**49**
50	Multiply line 49 by 28% (.28) . . . . ▶	**50**
51	Add lines 32, 36, 40, 46, and 50	**51**
52	Tax on the amount on line 18 from the 1998 Tax Rate Schedule	**52**
53	**Tax on taxable income (including capital gains).** Enter the **smaller** of line 51 or line 52 here and on line 1a of Schedule G, Form 1041 . . . . ▶	**53**

⊕

SCHEDULE J (Form 1041)	**Accumulation Distribution for Certain Complex Trusts**	OMB No. 1545-0092
Department of the Treasury Internal Revenue Service	▶ **Attach to Form 1041.** ▶ **See the Instructions for Form 1041.**	**1998**

Name of trust	Employer identification number

Part I   Accumulation Distribution in 1998

Note: *See the Form 4970 instructions for certain income that minors may exclude and special rules for multiple trusts.*

1	Other amounts paid, credited, or otherwise required to be distributed for 1998 (from Schedule B of Form 1041, line 10)	**1**
2	Distributable net income for 1998 (from Schedule B of Form 1041, line 7) . . .	**2**
3	Income required to be distributed currently for 1998 (from Schedule B of Form 1041, line 9)	**3**
4	Subtract line 3 from line 2. If zero or less, enter -0-	**4**
5	Accumulation distribution for 1998. Subtract line 4 from line 1	**5**

Part II   Ordinary Income Accumulation Distribution (Enter the applicable throwback years below.)

Note: *If the distribution is thrown back to more than five years (starting with the earliest applicable tax year beginning after 1968), attach additional schedules. (If the trust was a simple trust, see Regulations section 1.665(e)-1A(b).)*		Throwback year ending 19 ____	Throwback year ending 19 ____	Throwback year ending 19 ____	Throwback year ending 19 ____	Throwback year ending 19 ____
6 Distributable net income (see page 28 of the instructions) .	**6**					
7 Distributions (see page 28 of the instructions)	**7**					
8 Subtract line 7 from line 6 .	**8**					
9 Enter amount from page 2, line 25 or line 31, as applicable	**9**					
10 Undistributed net income Subtract line 9 from line 8 .	**10**					
11 Enter amount of prior accumulation distributions thrown back to any of these years	**11**					
12 Subtract line 11 from line 10	**12**					
13 Allocate the amount on line 5 to the earliest applicable year first. Do not allocate an amount greater than line 12 for the same year (see page 28 of the instructions) . . .	**13**					
14 Divide line 13 by line 10 and multiply result by amount on line 9	**14**					
15 Add lines 13 and 14 . . .	**15**					
16 Tax-exempt interest included on line 13 (see page 29 of the instructions)	**16**					
17 Subtract line 16 from line 15	**17**					

For Paperwork Reduction Act Notice, see page 1 of the Instructions for Form 1041.   Cat. No. 11382Z   **Schedule J (Form 1041) 1998**

Schedule J (Form 1041) 1998   Page **2**

Part III   **Taxes Imposed on Undistributed Net Income**   (Enter the applicable throwback years below.) (see page 29 of the instructions)
Note: *If more than five throwback years are involved, attach additional schedules. If the trust received an accumulation distribution from another trust, see Regulations section 1.665(d)-1A.*

If the trust elected the alternative tax on capital gains (repealed for tax years beginning after 1978), **SKIP** lines 18 through 25 and **COMPLETE** lines 26 through 31.		Throwback year ending 19 ____	Throwback year ending 19 ____	Throwback year ending 19 ____	Throwback year ending 19 ____	Throwback year ending 19 ____
18 Regular tax	**18**					
19 Trust's share of net short-term gain	**19**					
20 Trust's share of net long-term gain	**20**					
21 Add lines 19 and 20	**21**					
22 Taxable income	**22**					
23 Enter percent. Divide line 21 by line 22, but do not enter more than 100%	**23**	%	%	%	%	%
24 Multiply line 18 by the percentage on line 23 . . .	**24**					
25 Tax on undistributed net income. Subtract line 24 from line 18. Enter here and on page 1, line 9	**25**					
Do not complete lines 26 through 31 unless the trust elected the alternative tax on long-term capital gain.		██████	██████	██████	██████	██████
26 Tax on income other than long-term capital gain . .	**26**					
27 Trust's share of net short-term gain	**27**					
28 Trust's share of taxable income less section 1202 deduction	**28**					
29 Enter percent. Divide line 27 by line 28, but do not enter more than 100%	**29**	%	%	%	%	%
30 Multiply line 26 by the percentage on line 29 . . .	**30**					
31 Tax on undistributed net income. Subtract line 30 from line 26. Enter here and on page 1, line 9	**31**					

Part IV   **Allocation to Beneficiary**

Note: *Be sure to complete* **Form 4970,** *Tax on Accumulation Distribution of Trusts.*

Beneficiary's name				Identifying number	

Beneficiary's address (number and street including apartment number or P.O. box)		(a) This beneficiary's share of line 13	(b) This beneficiary's share of line 14	(c) This beneficiary's share of line 16
City, state, and ZIP code				
32 Throwback year 19 ____	**32**			
33 Throwback year 19 ____	**33**			
34 Throwback year 19 ____	**34**			
35 Throwback year 19 ____	**35**			
36 Throwback year 19 ____	**36**			
37 Total. Add lines 32 through 36. Enter here and on the appropriate lines of Form 4970	**37**			

�帯

SCHEDULE K-1 (Form 1041)	Beneficiary's Share of Income, Deductions, Credits, etc.		OMB No. 1545-0092

Department of the Treasury
Internal Revenue Service

for the calendar year 1998, or fiscal year
beginning _____ , 1998, ending _____ , 19 _____
► Complete a separate Schedule K-1 for each beneficiary.

1998

Name of trust or decedent's estate

☐ Amended K-1
☐ Final K-1

Beneficiary's identifying number ►

Estate's or trust's EIN ►

Beneficiary's name, address, and ZIP code

Fiduciary's name, address, and ZIP code

(a) Allocable share item		(b) Amount	(c) Calendar year 1998 Form 1040 filers enter the amounts in column (b) on:
1	Interest.	1	Schedule B, Part I, line 1
2	Ordinary dividends	2	Schedule B, Part II, line 5
3	Net short-term capital gain	3	Schedule D, line 5
4	Net long-term capital gain: **a** 28% rate gain	4a	Schedule D, line 12, column (g)
b	Unrecaptured section 1250 gain	4b	Line 11 of the worksheet for Schedule D, line 25
c	Total for year	4c	Schedule D, line 12, column (f)
5a	Annuities, royalties, and other nonpassive income before directly apportioned deductions	5a	Schedule E, Part III, column (f)
b	Depreciation	5b	
c	Depletion	5c	Include on the applicable line of the appropriate tax form
d	Amortization	5d	
6a	Trade or business, rental real estate, and other rental income before directly apportioned deductions (see instructions)	6a	Schedule E, Part III
b	Depreciation	6b	
c	Depletion	6c	Include on the applicable line of the appropriate tax form
d	Amortization	6d	
7	Income for minimum tax purposes	7	
8	Income for regular tax purposes (add lines 1, 2, 3, 4c, 5a, and 6a)	8	
9	Adjustment for minimum tax purposes (subtract line 8 from line 7)	9	Form 6251, line 12
10	Estate tax deduction (including certain generation-skipping transfer taxes)	10	Schedule A, line 27
11	Foreign taxes	11	Form 1116 or Schedule A (Form 1040), line 8
12	Adjustments and tax preference items (itemize):		
a	Accelerated depreciation	12a	
b	Depletion	12b	Include on the applicable line of Form 6251
c	Amortization	12c	
d	Exclusion items	12d	1999 Form 8801
13	Deductions in the final year of trust or decedent's estate:		
a	Excess deductions on termination (see instructions)	13a	Schedule A, line 22
b	Short-term capital loss carryover	13b ( )	Schedule D, line 5
c	Long-term capital loss carryover	13c ( )	Schedule D, line 12, columns (f) and (g)
d	Net operating loss (NOL) carryover for regular tax purposes	13d ( )	Form 1040, line 21
e	NOL carryover for minimum tax purposes	13e	See the instructions for Form 6251, line 20
f		13f	Include on the applicable line
g		13g	of the appropriate tax form
14	Other (itemize):		
a	Payments of estimated taxes credited to you	14a	Form 1040, line 58
b	Tax-exempt interest	14b	Form 1040, line 8b
c		14c	
d		14d	
e		14e	Include on the applicable line
f		14f	of the appropriate tax form
g		14g	
h		14h	

For Paperwork Reduction Act Notice, see the Instructions for Form 1041.   Cat. No. 11380D   **Schedule K-1 (Form 1041) 1998**

GLOSSARY

Abatement The legal process of reducing or eliminating the bequests of a decedent-testator who died owning insufficient assets to pay all bequests, debts and administration expenses.

Ademption The failure to fulfill a specific bequest in a will because the property bequeathed was sold, given away or lost before the testator's death.

Adjusted basis The dollar amount subtracted from the amount realized to calculate gain or loss on the sale or exchange of property. It is generally thought of as the price paid for property, but an owner's basis is generally determined by how the person acquired the property, e.g., by purchase, by gift, or by inheritance. It is also increased by capital improvements and decreased by depreciation.

Adjusted taxable gifts In federal estate tax, the sum of post-1976 taxable gifts, other than those included in the gross estate. It is added to the taxable estate on the federal estate tax return to arrive at the estate tax base.

Administrator A personal representative of a decedent's estate who was not nominated in the decedent's will.

Administrator with will annexed. A personal representative of an estate where the decedent's will is admitted to probate but the personal representative was not nominated in the will as the executor.

Adverse party In the Internal Revenue Code, a person having a substantial interest in property that is subject to a power of appointment, where that person's interest would be diminished if the holder of the power exercised it.

After-born child A child who was born after the execution of his or her parent's will.

Alternate valuation date Under Federal estate tax law assets are usually valued as of the date of death, but the personal representative may elect to value them as of six months after the date of death if doing so will reduce the value of the gross estate and reduce the estate tax.

Annual exclusion Under the federal gift tax, a deduction up to $10,000 (indexed after 1997) from gross gifts for gifts by any donor to any donee in a given calender year.

Annual exclusion gift A gift of property worth no more than the annual gift tax exclusion.

Antilapse statute A state statutory provision that specifies, in the absence of a provision in the will, to whom a lapsed testamentary bequest will pass.

Appointee (of a power of appointment) The party or parties whom the holder of a power of appointment actually appoints property.

Apportionment statute See Equitable apportionment statute.

Ascertainable standard Wording in a will or trust intentionally limiting the freedom of a holder of a power of appointment over property to assure that the property subject to the power will not be included in the holder's gross estate. The most common words of limitation (derived from Section 2041) are that the holder can withdraw property from a trust for his or her benefit if such is needed for "health, education, support, or maintenance."

Assignment Any transfer a claim, right, or interest in property.

Assignment of income doctrine Under income tax law, a doctrine holding that earnings from services performed will always be taxed to the person performing those services.

Bargain sale Part-gift, part-sale of an asset for some amount that the parties know is less than what would be regarded as full and adequate consideration. The difference between the consideration received by the seller-donor and the value of the asset transferred constitutes a gift, for tax purposes.

Basis See adjusted basis.

Beneficial interest An interest in property that carries an economic benefit. Examples of beneficial interests in property include the temporary or permanent right to possess, consume, and pledge the property.

Beneficiary A person who is receiving or will receive a gift of a beneficial interest in property. See Donee.

Bequest A gift, by will, of personal property. Also called a legacy.

Blockage discount A valuation discount given to a large quantity of a stock listed on an exchange, or certain other property, if its sale all at one time could have a temporarily depressing effect on the market price.

Bond In probate, an agreement under which an insurance company guarantees that the personal representative will faithfully perform required probate duties.

Business buyout agreement An agreement between one or more owners of a closely held business and one or more other persons that obligates one or more of the parties to purchase the interest of one of the others upon the occurrence of specific future events, such as the latter's death and, often, the onset of his or her permanent disability.

Buyout agreement See Business buyout agreement.

Buy-sell agreement See Business buyout agreement.

Bypass An arrangement under which property owned by a decedent and intended for the lifetime benefit of the surviving spouse does not actually pass to the surviving spouse, thereby avoiding inclusion in the latter's gross estate.

Bypass trust A trust designed to contain property that bypasses the surviving spouse's estate. See Bypass.

By right of representation The distribution of a decedent's estate whereby the children of the decedent share equally, with the share of a deceased child who left issue going to his or her children in equal shares, again with the share of a deceased child who left issue passing in like manner to his or her issue. See per stirpes.

Cash value life insurance policy A policy that accumulates economic value because the insurer charges a constant premium that is considerably higher than mortality costs requires during the earlier years. Part of this overpayment accumulates as a cash surrender value which, prior to the death of the insured, can be enjoyed by the owner, basically in one of two ways. First, at any time the owner can surrender the policy and receive this value in cash. Second, the owner can make a policy loan and borrow up to the amount of this value.

Charitable lead trust A trust under which the settlor donates an asset's income interest to a charity for a period of time, at the end of which the remainder interest passes to a private party, typically children or grandchildren for a specified term of years. The settlor (or the settlor's estate) will receive an income tax deduction for the value of the income interest.

Charitable remainder annuity trust (CRAT) A trust into which the settlor transfers assets in exchange for a fixed annuity income of at least 5 percent of the original value of the assets transferred into trust, payable at least annually, usually for life. The value of the remainder is deductible on the income tax return.

Charitable remainder unitrust (CRUT) A trust that is much like the charitable remainder annuity trust, except that the annual income depends on a fixed percentage of the current fair market value of the assets in the trust, determined annually.

Chose in action A claim or debt recoverable in a lawsuit.

Closely held business A firm privately owned by no more than a few individuals or families.

Codicil A written document that amends or revokes a will.

Collateral A relative who shares a common ancestor with a person but who is neither a descendant nor an ascendant of that person, e.g., a cousin. Contrast with issue.

Community property In the eight states recognizing it, all property that has been acquired by the efforts of either spouse during their marriage while living in a community property state, except property acquired by only one of the spouses by gift, devise, bequest or inheritance, or, in most of the community property states, by the income therefrom. The eight states are: Arizona, California, Idaho, Louisiana, Nevada, New Mexico, Texas, and Washington. In addition, Wisconsin has recently adopted a form of community property known as "marital partnership property."

Completed gift A gift in which the donor has so parted with dominion and control over an interest in property that the donor has no power to change its disposition, whether for his or her own benefit or for the benefit of another.

Complex trust A nongrantor trust which, in a given year, either (a) accumulates some fiduciary accounting income (FAI) (i.e., does not pay out all of that year's FAI to the beneficiaries) or (b) distributes principal.

Conduit principle In the income taxation of estates and trusts, the rule that fiduciary accounting income distributed to beneficiaries will be taxed to them, rather than to the estate or trust.

Consanguinity Degree of blood relationship between one person and another.

Conservator A court-appointed fiduciary responsible for the protection of the person and/or the person's property after the court has determined that the person is mentally incapable of handling such matters on his or her own.

Consideration furnished test Under the federal estate tax, the proposition that includes in a decedent's gross estate the entire value of property held by the decedent in joint tenancy, reduced only by an amount attributable to that portion of the consideration in money or money's worth which can clearly be shown to have been furnished by the survivors.

Contingent interest A future interest that is not vested; that is, an interest whose possession and enjoyment are dependent on the happening of some future event, not on just the passage of time.

Corpus The property in a trust. Also called principal or the *res* (Latin for a thing or object).

Creator The person, also called grantor, settlor, or trustor, who creates a trust and transfers property into it (technically transfers it to the trustee).

Credit shelter bypass Property equal in value to the exclusion amount that is taxed when the owner of the property dies, but the unified credit matches the tentative tax, so no tax is actually paid. The property may be held intrust, benefitting certain individuals for a period of time, before eventually being transferred, without being taxed again, to someone else.

Crummey provision A general power clause found in some trusts that give one or more beneficiaries the right to withdraw, for a limited period of time each year, the lesser of the amount of the annual exclusion or the value of the gift property transferred into the trust. Allows the donor to claim an annual exclusion. Often found in trusts for minors and in irrevocable life insurance trusts.

Cumulative gift doctrine The requirement that all lifetime gifts be accumulated; that is, that prior taxable gifts be added to current taxable transfers to determine the estate or gift tax base.

Curtesy A surviving husband's life interest in a portion of the real property owned by his deceased wife.

Custodial gift A gift to a custodian for the benefit of a child, under the Uniform Gifts to Minors Act or the Uniform Transfers to Minors Act.

Death tax A tax levied on certain property owned or transferred by the decedent at death. Either an estate tax or an inheritance tax.

Decedent In estate planning nomenclature, the person who has died.

Descendant *See* issue.

Devise A gift, by will, of real property.

Devisee A beneficiary, under a will, of a devise, i.e., a gift of real property.

Direct skip Under federal generation-skipping tax law, a transfer to a skip person that is subject to the gift tax or the estate tax.

Disclaimant One who disclaims an interest in property.

Disclaimer An unqualified refusal to accept a gift, bequest, or the right to exercise a power of appointment. In estate planning, a tax-effective disclaimer must meet the requirements of both local law and IRC Section 2518. Tax-effective means that the disclaimant will not be treated as having made a gift.

Dispositive provisions Parts of a will or trust that set forth how property is to be distributed.

Distributable net income (DNI) An amount more or less equal to fiduciary accounting income (FAI) that acts as the measuring rod for estate and trust income taxation.

Distribution deduction In the income taxation of estates and trusts, an amount equal to the lesser of distributable net income or the amount actually distributed to beneficiaries.

Distribution planning Planning the amount and timing of beneficiary distributions from an estate or irrevocable trust, usually with the objective of reducing income tax.

DNI See Distributable net income.

Donee A person who receives a gift of a beneficial interest in property. See Beneficiary.

Donor A person who make a gift.

Dower A surviving wife's interest in a portion of the real property owned by her deceased husband. Usually, the interest was a life estate.

Durable power of attorney A written agency agreement that continues to have validity even during the principal's incapacity. At common law an agent's authority ceased as soon as the principal was mentally incapacitated.

Durable power of attorney for health care (DPOAHC) A written power of attorney granting to the agent (sometimes called the attorney-in-fact) the authority to make medical decisions on behalf of the principal during such times as the principal is unable to make such decisions.

Durable power of attorney for property A durable power of attorney granting to the attorney-in-fact the power to make decisions concerning the property of the principal.

Equalization A term used in this text to mean a plan of property disposition by the spouses so that the taxable estates (or estate tax bases) of the two are more or less equal as of the first death.

Equitable apportionment statute A state statute that spreads the death tax burden in direct proportion to each beneficiaries share of the taxable estate.

Escheat The transfer of an intestate decedent's property to the state, because either the decedent left no next of kin, or all surviving relatives are considered under state law to be too remote for purposes of inheritance.

Estate A quantity of wealth or property. See also Net estate, Gross estate, and Probate estate.

Estate tax A federal or state tax on the decedent's right to transfer property.

Estate planning The study of the principles of planning for the use, conservation, and efficient transfer of an individual's wealth.

Estate tax base On the federal estate tax return, it is the sum of the taxable estate plus adjusted taxable gifts. It is the amount used to calculate the tentative estate tax.

Estate trust One type of marital trust, rarely if ever used, under which the corpus (and any accumulated income) is made payable to the estate of the surviving spouse at his or her death. Its unique feature is that it qualifies for the marital deduction even though the surviving spouse may not receive all of the income during his or her lifetime. However, income cannot be payable to anyone else.

Exclusion Amount The maximum value of property that, when transferred by gift or bequest, generates a tentative tax exactly equal to the unified credit available for the year of the transfer. See IRC 2010. Prior to the TRA of 1997, this was commonly referred to as the unified credit equivalent amount or the credit shelter amount.

Execute To complete a document (i.e., to do what is necessary to render it valid).

Executor A personal representative of a decedent's estate who was nominated in the will.

Exercise a power of appointment To invoke the power by appointing a permissible appointee.

FAI See Fiduciary accounting income.

Family limited partnership A limited partnership meeting the requirements of §704(e) for the benefit of family members, generally with parents as the general partners and children as the limited partners. Used to take advantage of lack of control discounts and lack of marketability discounts as the parents transfer limited partnership units to the children.

Family-owned business interest deduction The estate tax deduction that combines with the exclusion amount to shelter property worth up to $1,300,000 from federal estate taxes. IRC §2057 makes the deduction available for estates that meet certain requirements, such as that the value of the family owned business interest equals or exceeds 50% of the decedent's adjusted gross estate.

Family pot trust See Pot trust.

Fee simple interest The greatest ownership interest that a person can have over property, corresponding to the layperson's usual notion of complete ownership.

Fiduciary A person in a position of trust and confidence; one who has a legal duty to act for the benefit of another. Examples include executor, trustee, agent, custodian, and attorney.

Fiduciary accounting income (FAI) In the income taxation of estates and trusts, most sources of federal gross income, including cash dividends, interest, and rent (reduced by certain expenses) but not including stock dividends and capital gains.

Fiscal year An income tax year that ends on the last day of any month except December.

Flower bonds Certain long-term U.S. Treasury bonds (no longer in circulation) which, if owned by the decedent at death, were redeemable at par value to pay the federal estate tax.

Fractional interest discount A valuation discount for a partial interest in real property (e.g., a 25% interest as a tenant in common) because it is neither easily partitioned nor readily marketable.

Freezing the estate tax value Using estate planning transfer techniques to effectively ensure that the future value of certain appreciating property includible in the estate tax base will not be significantly higher than its current value.

Future interest A beneficial interest in property in which the right to possess or enjoy the property is delayed, either by a specific period of time or until the happening of a future event.

General bequest A gift payable out of the general assets of the estate, but not one that specifies one or more particular items.

General power of appointment The holder of a power has the right to use the property that is subject to the power for his or her own benefit or for the benefit of his or her estate. The property subject to the power at the holder's death will be included in the holder's gross estate even if the power is unexercised.

General power of attorney A document executed by one person called the principal, authorizing another person called the attorney-in-fact, to perform designated acts on behalf of the principal.

Generation-skipping transfer tax (GSTT) A federal or state tax on certain property transfers to a skip person, that is, someone who is two generations or more younger than the donor.

Gift A completed lifetime or deathtime transfer of property by an individual in exchange for any amount that is less than full consideration.

Gift tax A tax on a completed lifetime transfer of property for less than full consideration.

Grantor A person who creates a trust and whose property is transferred into it. Also called creator, settlor, or trustor.

Grantor retained annuity trust (GRAT) A grantor retained trust that pays the grantor a fixed income for a specified period and meets all other requirements of IRC §2702.

Grantor retained trust (GRIT) An irrevocable trust into which the settlor transfers appreciating property in exchange for the right to receive income for a period of years. Under most GRITs, distribution of corpus at the end of the period depends upon whether or not the settlor survived the period, and if not, the corpus likely reverts to the settlor's estate; if the settlor does survive the period, the corpus likely passes to younger-generation beneficiaries.

Grantor retained unitrust (GRUT) A grantor retained trust that pays the grantor a fixed percentage of the trust's principal, revalued each year, for a specified period and meets all other requirements of IRC §2702.

Grantor trust A trust in which the settlor has retained sufficient interest to make the income received by the trust taxable to the grantor, not to the trust or its other beneficiaries.

Grantor trust rules The federal income tax rules concerning grantor trusts located in Internal Revenue Code §§671-78.

Gross estate An estate tax term meaning all property in which the decedent had an interest at the time of his or her death, any property transferred by the decedent under which the decedent retained an interest or control, and any life insurance transferred, or any retained interests released, within three years of death.

Grossing up Inclusion in the gross estate of gift taxes paid on any gifts made within three years of death. See IRC §2035(b).

GSTT See Generation-skipping transfer tax.

Guardian A court-appointed fiduciary responsible for the person or property of a minor or, in some cases, an incompetent adult, or both. In some states, a guardian is called a committee, in others, a guardian for an incompetent adult is called a conservator.

Heir A person who inherits; or one who would inherit if another person died intestate.

Holder (of a power of appointment) A person who has received a power of appointment, i.e., the one who has the right to appoint designated property to a permissible appointee. Also called the donee of the power.

Holding period In income tax law, the length of time that property is held. It determines whether a gain is short term or long term. The current threshold is one year for long term capital gains, however, property received from a decedent is automatically long term.

Holographic will A will, recognized as valid in most states even though it is not witnessed. The state law is likely to require that at least the dispositive portions of the will be the testator's handwriting.

Incidents of ownership Powers and interests over an insurance policy on decedent's life that would subject the proceeds to inclusion in the decedent's gross estate under Section 2042.

Income beneficiary The beneficiary of a trust who has a life estate or estate for years in the trust income.

Income shifting See Shifting income.

Income tax A tax levied on income earned by a taxpayer during a given year.

Incomplete In conjunction with transfers, it means a gift made without total relinquishment of dominion and control. i.e., it is rescindable or amendable.

Inherit To receive property by intestate succession or by a bequest.

Inheritance tax A state tax on the right of a beneficiary to receive property from a decedent.

Installment sale The sale of an asset in exchange for an installment note, in which the buyer agrees to make periodic payments of principal and interest, based on a fair market rate of interest.

Intangible personal property Personal property that is not in itself valuable, but derives its value from that which it represents.

Intentionally defective grantor trust A funded irrevocable trust that is complete for estate tax purposes and incomplete for income tax. The purpose of this arrangement is to give have the grantor pay the income tax rather than having it paid by the trustee or by the beneficiary.

Inter vivos transfer A transfer made while the transferor is alive.

Inter vivos trust A trust funded during the life of the trustor. Also called a living trust.

Interest by the entirety An interest in property similar to a joint interest; however, it can be created only between husband and wife. Unlike joint tenancy, neither spouse may transfer or encumber the property without the consent of the other.

Interest for years A property interest for a fixed period of time.

Interest-free loan A loan, having no interest charge, usually to a family member in a lower income tax bracket. TRA 1986 limited its use by requiring lenders to impute interest income for many of these low-interest, no-interest family loan arrangements.

Interest in common An interest in property held by two or more persons, each having an undivided right to possess property. Unlike a joint interest, however, an interest in common may be owned in unequal percentages, and when one owner dies the remaining owners do not automatically succeed in ownership. Instead, the decedent's interest passes through his or her estate, by will, by some other document, or by the laws of intestate distribution.

Intestate Having died leaving probate property not disposed of by a valid will.

Instrument Any legal document.

Inventory and appraisement A probate document that delineates all probate assets at their fair market value as of the date of death.

Irrevocable Subject to no right to rescind or amend (the terms of a transfer of one or more interests in property).

Issue A person's direct offspring, including children, grandchildren, great-grandchildren, and the like. Also called descendants or lineal descendants. Contrast with Collateral relatives.

Itemized deductions In federal income tax law, deductions from adjusted gross income that are specifically listed, and taken in lieu of the standard deduction.

Joint tenancy A form of equal, undivided ownership in property that, upon death of one owner, automatically passes to the surviving owner(s). All interests must be equal, therefore, there cannot be a joint tenancy held 25% by one person and 75% by another.

Kiddie tax The term given to the federal income tax law that requires the unearned income of a child under the age of 13 be taxed at the parent's top marginal rate.

Lack of marketability discount A valuation discount given stock in a closely held business arising from the lack of an established market making the stock more difficult to sell.

Lapse The result when a beneficiary named in a will fails to survive the testator. Also, a power of appointment is said to lapse if the holder does not exercise it within the permitted period.

Leasehold An interest in property entitling the lessee to possess and use the property for a specified time, usually in exchange for a series of payments.

Legacy A gift, by will, of personal property. Also called a bequest.

Legatee A beneficiary, under a will, of a gift of personal property.

Letters testamentary A formal court document used as evidence of the probate court's authorization of the estate's personal representative to act on behalf of a decedent's estate.

Leveraging The process by which a given amount of exclusion, exemption, or credit can shelter more than that amount from future transfer taxation.

Life estate An interest in property that ceases upon someone's death.

Life insurance policy A contract in which the insurance company agrees to pay a cash lump-sum amount (the face value or policy proceeds) to the person named in the policy to receive it (the beneficiary) upon the death of the subject of the insurance (the insured).

Limited liability companies A business organization in which the owners, called members, do not have personal liability for the contracts or the torts of the business, yet the organization is taxed like a partnership.

Limited power of appointment The holder of a power cannot use it to transfer the property that is subject to the power for his or her own benefit or for the benefit of his or her estate. It is not considered a gift if the holder exercises the power and the property subject to the power is not included in the holder's gross estate when the holder dies.

Living trust A trust funded during the lifetime of the trustor. Also called an inter vivos trust.

Living will A document detailing those health care interventions that a person does or does not want to be subjected to in situations when he or she is no longer capable of making those decisions.

Marital deduction In federal gift and estate taxation, the deduction for certain transfers to a spouse.

Marital trust A trust structured to receive property that will qualify for the marital deduction.

Minority discount A valuation discount allowed for an interest in a business because the interest is not a controlling interest.

Net estate The net worth of a person; i.e., total assets minus total liabilities.

Omitted child See Omitted heir.

Omitted heir Any living spouse, child, or issue of any deceased child who is not provided for in a will.

Omitted spouse See Omitted heir.

Opportunity shifting The transfer of a rapidly appreciating wealth- or of an income-producing opportunity to another family member.

Outright transfer A transfer in which the transferee receives both legal interests and all beneficial interests, subject to no restrictions or conditions.

Partnership capital freeze Like a recapitalization, the reorganization of a partnership for the purpose of freezing the estate value of a partner's partnership interest. Severely restricted by the Revenue Reconciliation Act of 1990.

Permissible appointee (of a power of appointment) A party whom the holder may appoint by exercising the power.

Per capita A scheme of distribution from a will or trust requiring that issue of a decedent of all degrees share equally.

Perfect unification When applied to the estate and gift tax laws, a set of conditions in which an individual would be indifferent, from a total transfer tax planning point of view, between making lifetime and deathtime gifts. It helps identify the factors that make the current system imperfect, which serves as the basis for some transfer tax planning.

Per stirpes A scheme of distribution from a will or trust requiring that certain issue of a decedent, as a group, inherit the share of an estate that their immediate ancestor would have inherited if he or she had been living. Also called right of representation.

Perpetuities saving clause A clause in a will or trust that prevents interests from being ruled invalid under the rule against perpetuities.

Personal exemption In federal income tax law, amounts deductible on behalf of the taxpayer, the spouse, and each dependent, in calculating taxable income.

Personal property All property except fee simple and life estates in land and its improvements.

Personal representative The person appointed by the probate court to represent and manage the estate. If nominated in the will, called an executor.

Pickup tax A state death tax set as exactly equal to the federal credit for state death taxes.

Pooled income fund An investment fund created and maintained by the target charity, which "pools" property from many similar contributors. This arrangement ordinarily provides that the charity will pay to the grantor an income for life and, if desired, for the life of the grantor's spouse, based on the rate of return actually earned by the fund as a whole. At their death, the property passes to the charity.

Pot trust A trust established at the death of parents for the benefit of their minor children. Typically, the trust corpus remains undivided until the youngest child reaches an age specified in the trust, e.g., age 18 or 21. At that time, the assets are divided into equal separate shares, one for each child. The assets are distributed outright, or they are held for distribution at some older age. Also called a Family Pot Trust.

Pour-over will A will that distributes, at the testator's death, probate assets to a trust that had been created during the testator's lifetime.

Power of appointment A power to name someone to receive a beneficial interest in property.

Power of appointment trust A marital trust that gives to the surviving spouse the right to receive all income from the property for life, payable at least annually. It also gives him or her a general power of appointment over the principal, exercisable alone and in all events, at death or during life.

Power of attorney A document executed by one person, called the principal, authorizing another person, called the attorney-in-fact, to perform designated acts on behalf of the principal.

Precatory language Language in a will that does not direct or command, but merely expresses a wish, hope or desire. Precatory language is not given recognition by the courts in probate.

Present interest An immediate right to possess or enjoy property.

Pretermitted heir See omitted heir.

Principal The property in a trust. Also called corpus.

Private annuity A transfer of property under which the seller receives an unsecured promise of a life annuity.

Probate The legal process of administering the estate of a decedent. It focuses on the probate estate, that is, property which will be disposed of by, and only by, either the decedent's will or by the state laws of intestate succession. More narrowly and less commonly, probate is used to mean certifying or proving the validity of the will after the death of the testator.

Probate estate All of the decedent's property passing to others by means of the probate process. This includes all property owned by the decedent except joint tenancy interests. The probate estate does not include property transferred by the decedent before death to a trustee, life insurance proceeds on the decedent's life when paid directly to a beneficiary, nor the decedent's interest in pension and profit sharing plans.

QTIP election An election by the executor of the estate of the first spouse to die to treat certain property as QTIP property, thereby qualifying it for the marital deduction.

QTIP trust A marital trust for which a federal estate tax election can be made so as to qualify the trust property for the marital deduction. It must provide that the surviving spouse is entitled to all of the income from the trust property, payable at least annually. In addition, the trust cannot give anyone a power to appoint any of the property to anyone other than to the surviving spouse so long as he or she is alive. Its uniqueness lies in the fact that it qualifies for the marital deduction even though its property neither passes to nor is controlled by the surviving spouse.

Real property Interests in land and any improvements attached to land.

Recapitalization A reorganization of a closely held corporation for the purpose of freezing the value of a primary owner's interest in the company. Severely restricted by enactment of Revenue Reconciliation Act of 1990.

Reciprocal wills Wills for two people (usually a married couple) that are virtually identical; each leaves all (or substantially all) property to the other if the latter survives, otherwise to third persons. Sometimes called mirror wills. Reciprocal wills are usually simple wills; more complex wills are more likely to have unique features.

Remainder In the context of trusts, the future interest right to the remaining trust assets at the termination of all other interests. More technically, the right to use, possess and enjoy property after a prior owner's interest ends, in a situation where both interests were created at the same time and in the same document.

Remainderman The beneficiary of a trust who will receive the trust corpus (i.e., that which remainders) at the termination of all other interests.

Residuary bequest A gift by will of that part of the testator's estate that remains after taking care of all specific and pecuniary bequests.

Reversion A future interest in property that is retained by the transferor; it will become a present interest (revert back to the transferor) when all other interests created at the time of the transfer have ended. Usually used in connection with trusts established for a very limited duration.

Revocable Subject to the right to rescind or amend (the terms of a transfer of one or more interests in property).

Rule against perpetuities A common law principle invalidating a dispositive clause in a will or a trust if the contingent interest transferred might vest in a transferee too long after the settlor's death.

S1 Shorthand nomenclature for the first spouse to die.

S2 Shorthand nomenclature for the second spouse to die.

Sale A transfer of property under which each transferor exchanges consideration that the parties regard as equivalent in value.

Self-canceling installment note (SCIN) An installment note which provides that no further payments will be made after the seller's death.

Self-proved will A will containing a formal affidavit by witnesses stating that all formalities have been complied with. It eliminates the need for the witnesses to verify the correctness of the execution of the document after the testator dies.

Separate property In community property states, all property that is not community property. That is, all property acquired by a person prior to marriage, and all property acquired during a marriage by gift, devise, bequest or inheritance, or, in most community property states, income earned on property so acquired. Community property may be converted to separate property by the written agreement of the couple.

Settlor The person who creates the trust and whose property is transferred to it. Also called creator, grantor, or trustor.

Shifting income In estate planning, saving income tax by enabling income otherwise taxable to a high income tax individual to be taxed to a lower tax bracket family member.

Short-term trust An irrevocable trust that reverts to the grantor sometime after 10 years or after the life of the income beneficiary. The income was taxed to the beneficiary, not to the settlor. TRA 86, in subjecting this trust to the grantor trust rules, virtually eliminated its further use.

Simple will A will prepared for a family having a small estate, one for whom death tax planning is not a significant concern, with the typical pattern being "everything to my spouse, if she survives, and if she does not, then to my children per stirpes."

Skip person In federal generation-skipping transfer tax law, a beneficiary who is at least two generations younger than the transferor.

Soak-up tax See sponge tax.

Special use valuation A provision in federal estate tax law (Section 2032A) that permits qualifying estates to value farmland or business use real estate at its "qualified-use value" rather than at its "highest and best use" value. The maximum decrease is $750,000 (indexed after 1997).

Specific bequest A gift of a particular item of property which is capable of being identified and distinguished from all other property. Contrasted with general bequest and residuary bequest.

Spendthrift clause A clause in a trust that restricts the beneficiary from transferring any of his or her future interest in the corpus or income. For example, a typical spendthrift clause would not permit the beneficiary to pledge the interest as collateral against a loan.

Splitting a gift Treating a gift of the property owned by one spouse, on the federal gift tax return, as if it were made one-half by each spouse.

Sponge tax Where a state's inheritance tax produces total death taxes for a decedent's estate that are less than that estate's allowable federal credit for state death taxes, the state collects the difference between the total and the allowable credit. Because the federal credit is a dollar for dollar credit, this sponge tax does not increase the overall taxes for a decedent's estate.

Spousal remainder trust An irrevocable trust providing for income for a period to a lower-income tax bracket family member, then remainder to the trustor's spouse. Use of this trust was virtually eliminated by TRA 86, which subjected it to the grantor trust rules.

Springing durable power of attorney A durable power of attorney that becomes effective at the onset of the principal's mental incapacity.

Standard deduction In federal income tax law, a fixed amount that may be deducted from adjusted gross income. It may be used instead of specifically subtracting actual "itemized" deductions.

Standby trust An unfunded living trust whose principal financial management and control provisions do not come into effect until the grantor dies or is determined to be incapacitated. At that point, the trust is usually funded by the probate process or, if the grantor is still alive but incapacitated, by the grantor's attorney-in-fact.

Step-up in basis Shorthand for the change in basis that occurs when the owner of property dies. Technically, it will only be a "step-up" in basis if, at the owner's death, the property has a fair market value that is higher than the basis was immediately before his or her death.

Surrogate decision makers Individuals capable of making decisions regarding a person's property and family at times when the person is unable, either due to incapacity or death. Examples include attorney-in-fact, trustee, and executor.

Survival clause A disposition provision in a will or trust naming an alternate taker of certain property if the donee fails to survive the donor for some period of time.

Takers in default Persons who receive property subject to a power of appointment if the holder permits the power to lapse unexercised.

Tangible personal property Personal property which has value because of its physical characteristics.

Taxable estate In federal estate tax law, the gross estate reduced by all allowable deductions.

Taxable distribution In federal generation-skipping transfer tax law, any distribution of property out of a trust to a skip person (other than a taxable termination or a direct skip).

Taxable gift In federal gift tax law, for a given year, total gross gifts reduced by all allowable deductions, exemptions, and exclusions.

Taxable termination In federal generation-skipping transfer tax law, the termination of all the interests of one generation in the income or principal of a trust, with the result that the interest shift to another lower generation of skip persons.

Tax clause A provision in a will specifying which property bears the burden of paying taxes.

Tenancy by the entirety *See* interest by the entirety.

Terminable interest An interest which might terminate or fail on the lapse of time, on the occurrence of an event or contingency, or on the failure of an event or contingency to occur. Property otherwise qualifying for the marital deduction will not qualify if the interest passing to the spouse is terminable, unless there is an exception such exists for QTIP property.

Terminal value Used to indicate the value of a cash value life insurance policy that is currently in force. Formally called the policy's interpolated terminal reserve value, its amount is nearly equal to its cash surrender value.

Term life insurance A type of life insurance policy that has no value prior to the death of the insured because the premium charged, which increases over time with increasing risk of death, just covers the risk of death for that period. Term insurance simply buys pure protection: if the insured dies during the policy term, the company will pay the face value; otherwise, it will pay nothing.

Testamentary capacity The mental ability required of a testator to validly execute a will.

Testamentary transfer A transfer at death by will.

Testamentary trust A trust established by a will. The funding mechanism is the probate process.

Testate Dying with a valid will.

Testator The person who executes a will.

Throwback rules In the income taxation of trusts, rules that, prior to being repealed by TRA '97, subjected income accumulated by a trust in one year and distributed to a beneficiary in another year to possible additional taxation to the beneficiary.

Totten trust A pay on death bank account. The owner of the account specifies that, if the owner dies while the account is still open, it should be transferred (without probate) to a named beneficiary.

TOD account A bank account or brokerage account that is set up to follow the requirements of the Uniform Transfer on Death Act, such that upon the owners death the account is transferred to a named beneficiary without probate. See Totten trust.

TRA '86 Tax Reform Act of 1986.

TRA '97 Taxpayer Relief Act of 1997.

Transfer Any type of passing of property in which the transferor gives up some kind of interest to the transferee. Sometimes called an assignment.

Trust A legal arrangement between trustor and trustee that divides legal and beneficial interests in property among two or more people. In estate planning the trust agreement is likely to be many pages long, and to spell out in detail the trustees obligations concerning the management and distribution of the trust income and corpus.

Trust beneficiary A person who is named to enjoy a beneficial interest in the trust.

Trust-will See Testamentary trust.

Trustor The person who creates a trust and whose property is transferred to the trustee. Also called creator, grantor, or settlor.

Undue influence Influence by a confidante which has the effect of impeding the testator's free will. A will can be denied probate (or at least certain clauses will be disregarded) if it can be established that the testator, at execution, was subject to undue influence. To be undue, the influence must be wrongful in some way.

Unification of gift and estate taxes Partially successful efforts by Congress in 1976 to tax lifetime and deathtime transfers equally, so that an individual would be indifferent, from a total transfer tax planning point of view, between making lifetime and deathtime gifts.

Unified credit The credit allowed against the tentative tax that results in sheltering modest taxable gifts and modest taxable estates from the transfer tax.

Uniform Gifts to Minors Act Like the Uniform Transfers to Minors Act, a statute in many states permitting custodial gifts for the benefit of a minor.

Uniform Probate Code (UPC) A complete set of probate laws originally promulgated by legal scholars and practitioners and currently adopted in whole or in part by about two fifths of the states.

Uniform Simultaneous Death Act (USDA) A statute providing that when transfer of title to property depends on the order of deaths, and that when no sufficient evidence exists that two people died other than simultaneously, the property of each is disposed of as if each had survived the other.

Uniform Transfer on Death Act A uniform law adopted by many states that allows accounts at financial institutions (e.g., banks, savings and loans, thrifts, credit unions) and at brokerages to have a designation that allows the account to be transferred to a named beneficiary, without passing through probate, if the account is still open when the owner dies.

Uniform Transfers to Minors Act Like the older Uniform Gifts to Minors Act, this provides a means of transferring property to young people through the use of a custodian.

Vested interest A nonforfeitable future interest whose possession and enjoyment are delayed only by time and not dependent on the happening of any future event.

Wait-and-see statute A provision in some state statutes that can overcome the effect of the rule against perpetuities by finding an interest void only if its turns out, in fact, not to vest within the required period.

Will A written document disposing of a person's probate property at death.

Witnessed will A written will, recognized in all states, that must be signed by two or more witnesses who acknowledge, among other things, that the testator asked them to witness the will, that they in fact did witness the testator's signing, and that the testator is mentally competent to execute a will (in accordance with state law).

Index